THE ENCYCLOPAEDIA OF SPORTS & GAMES

THE ENCYCLOPAEDIA OF SPORTS & GAMES

(In Two Volumes)

Volume 1

Edited by
YOGRAJ THANI

Compiled by
LOKESH THANI

GYAN

The Encyclopaedia of Sports and Games

ISBN: 81-212-0407-0 Set
ISBN: 81-212-0410-0 (Vol. 1)

Reprinted in 2013 in India by
Gyan Publishing House
23, Main Ansari Road, Daryaganj,
New Delhi - 110002
Phone : 23282060, 23261060
Fax : (011) 23285914
E-mail : books@gyanbooks.com
Website: gyanbooks.com

Printed at: G. Print Process, Delhi

FOREWORD

The history of Indian sports in encyclopaedic form by Mr. Lokesh is yet another landmark in the ever growing field of Indian sports literature. It comes on the heels of his *Encyclopaedia of Cricket* which was well received.

Mr. Lokesh has codified 41 sports disciplines in well defind pattern listing each game's history, skills, rules, cup and trophies and award winners in that order. A final chapter on terminology is added to explain to the reader the nuances of sports language.

The disciplines had been listed in alphabetical order beginning with the game of American Football and covers even non-conventional Indian games such as Kabaddi and Kho-kho. The range also extends to baseball, billiards, carrom, motor racing and riding.

The inclusion, in brief of rules of each game should make the anthology a really useful publication for particularly the young reader who is ever in search of information and knowledge.

Mr. Lokesh draws most of its inspiration from Mr. Yog Raj Thani who has been dominating the Indian sports journalism scene for more than three decades now. He has established quite a place for himself in Indian language sports journalism and his column/stories today publish in more than 30 publications all over India. He is also a well-known personality over the radio and his inimitable style of writing has no peers.

The latest anthology should go well with the Indian sports reading public and I am happy to lend my name to this work of great industry and imagination.

Gopesh Mehra

CONTENTS

AMERICAN FOOTBALL

American football is an exciting sport played by two teams of 11 players, although up to 40 men can play for each team during a single match. The tactics of the game can be very complicated, but the object is simple - to score points by crossing the opponents' goal-line with the ball (a "touchdown") or by kicking the ball between their goalposts. The game is therefore based around the teams' attempts to gain ground up the field. It was first played in the field. It was first played in the American colleges in the late 19th century and is, without doubt, the team sport with the greatest amount of physical contact. The helmets and huge shoulder pads worn by the players help make this one of the most spectacular of all sports. Canadian football has slightly different rules.

RULES OF THE GAMES

The field The area between the end lines and sidelines is the field of play. The field is divided between the goal lines by parallel yardlines, 5yd apart. These are intersected by short inbound lines 70ft 9in from each sideline. Between the inbound lines there are marks at 1 yd intervals. All measurements are made from the inside edges of the lines. Sidelines and end lines are out of bounds; goal lines are in the end zones. No benches or rigid fixtures are allowed within 5yd of the sidelines.

Teams Each team fields 11 players, one of whom is the captain. No team is allowed more than 40 players in uniform.

Playing the ball Players may kick, carry, and throw the ball (1,2,3,) Subject to certain restrictions, such as the number of forward passes allowed.

They may not bat or punch : a loose ball toward the opponents' goal line; a loose ball in an end zone; the ball when a player has posession.

A pass in flight may be batted in any direction by the defending side; but the offensive side may only bat such a ball to prevent the other team intercepting the ball.

If the player with the ball touches he ground with any part of his body except his hands or feet, the ball is dead (4).

A team in possession is allowed 30 seconds to put the ball into play.

A down is a period of action starting from the moment the ball is put into play and ending when the ball becomes dead (goes out of play).

Scoring Touchdown (6 points) occurs when a player carries the ball to the opponents' end zone and touches the goal line with the ball, or recovers a loose ball on or behind the opponents' goal line. It may be awarded if prevented by a foul.

CUP & TROPHIES

AFC Championship Games

1970 Baltimore 27 Oakland 17
1971 Miami 21 Baltimore 0
1972 Miami 21 Pitsburgh 17
1973 Miami 27 Oakland 10
1974 Pittsburgh 24 Oakland 13
1975 Pittsburgh 16 Oakland 10
1976 Oakland 24 Pittsburgh 7
1977 Denver 20 Oakland 17
1978 Pittsburgh 34 Houston 5
1979 Pittsburgh 27 Houston 13
1980 Oakland 34 San Diego 27
1981 Cincinnati 27 San Diego 7
1982 Miami 14 New York Jets 0
1983 Los Angeless 30 Seattle 14
1984 Miami 45 Pittsburgh 28

Tackling

Blocking

1985 New England 31 Miami 14
1986 Denver 23 Cleveland 20
1987 Denver 38 Cleveland 33
1988 Cincinnati 21 Buffalo 10
1989 Denver 37 Cleveland 21

NFC Championship Games

1970 Dallas 17 San Francisco 10
1971 Dallas 14 San Francisco 3
1972 Washington 26 Dallas 3
1973 Minnesota 27 Dallas 10
1974 Minnesota 14 Los Angeles 10
1975 Dallas 37 Los Angeles 7
1976 Minnesota 24 Los Angeles 13
1977 Dallas 23 Minnesota 6
1978 Dallas 28 Los Angeles 0
1979 Los Angeles 9 Tampa Bay 0
1980 Philadelphia 20 Dallas 7
1981 San Francisco 28 Dallas 27
1982 Washington 31 Dallas 17
1983 Washington 24 San Francisco 21
1984 San Francisco 23 Chicago 0
1985 Chicago 24 LA Rams 0
1986 New York 17 Washington 0
1987 Washington 17 Minnesota 10
1988 San Francisco 28 Chicago 3
1989 San Francisco 30 LA Rams 3

Super Bowl

1967 Green Bay Packers 35
1968 Green Bay Packers 33
1969 New York Jets 16
1970 Kansas City Chiefs 23
1971 Baltimore Colts 16
1972 Dallas Cowboys 24
1973 Miami Dolphins 14
1974 Miami Dolphins 24
1975 Pittsburgh Steelers 16
1976 Pittsburgh Steelers 21
1977 Oakland Raiders 32
1978 Dallas Cowboys 27
1979 Pittsburgh Steelers 35
1980 Pittsburgh Steelers 31
1981 Oakland Raiders 27
1982 San Francisco 49ers 26
1983 Washington Redskins 27
1984 Los Angeles Raiders 38
1985 San Francisco 49ers 38
1986 Chicago Bears 46
1987 New York Giants 39
1988 Washington Redskins 42
1989 San Francisco 49ers 20

Super Bowl MVPs

1967 Bart Starr (QB), Green Bay Packers
1968 Bart Starr (QB), Green Bay Packers
1969 Joe Namath (QB), New York Jets
1970 Len Dawson (QB), Kansas City
1971 Chuck Howley (LB), Dallas Cowboys
1972 Roger Staubach (QB), Dallas Cowboys
1973 Jake Scott (S), Miami Dolphins
1974 Larry Csonka (RB), Miami Dolphins
1975 Franco Harris (RB), Pittsburgh Steelers
1976 Lynn Swann (WR), Pittsburgh Steelers
1977 Fred Biletnikoff (WR), Oakland Raiders
1978 Randy White (DT) & Harvey Martin (DE), Dallas
1979 Terry Bradshaw (QB), Pitsburgh Steelers
1980 Terry Bradshaw (QB), Pittsburgh Steelers
1981 Jim Plunkett (QB), Oakland Raiders
1982 Joe Montana (QB), San Francisco 49ers
1983 Joe Riggins (RB), Washington Redskins
1984 Marcus Allen (RB), Los Angeles Raiders
1985 Joe Montana (QB), San Francisco 49ers
1986 Richard Dent (DE), Chicago Bears
1987 Phil Simms (QB), New York Giants
1988 Doug Williams (QB), Washington Redskins
1989 Jerry Rice (WR), San Francisco 49ers

National College Football Champions

1936 Minnesota
1937 Pittsburgh
1938 Texas Christian
1939 Texas A & M
1940 Minnesota
1941 Minnesota
1942 Ohio State
1943 Notre Dame
1944 Army
1945 Army
1946 Notre Dame
1947 Notre Dame
1948 Michigan
1949 Notre Dame

1950	Oklahoma
1951	Tennessee
1952	Michigan State
1953	Maryland
1954	Ohio State & UCLA
1955	Oklahoma
1956	Oklahoma
1957	Auburn & Ohio State
1958	Louisiana State
1959	Syracuse
1960	Minnesota
1961	Alabama
1962	South Carolina
1963	Texas
1964	Alabama
1965	Alabama & Michigan State
1966	Notre Dame
1967	South Carolina
1968	Ohio State
1969	Texas
1970	Texas & Nebraska
1971	Nebraska
1972	South Carolina
1973	Notre Dame
1974	Oklahoma & South Carolina
1975	Oklahoma
1976	Pitsburgh
1977	Notre Dame
1978	Alabama & South Carolina
1979	Alabama
1980	Georgia
1981	Clemson
1982	Penn State
1983	Miami (Florida)
1984	Brigham Young
1985	Oklahoma
1986	Penn State
1987	Miami (Florida)
1988	Notre Dame
1989	Miami (Florida)

ARCHERY

The practice of Archery can be traced back to very ancient times, though authorities differ as to when the use of the bow first became common in England. The many statutes for the encouragement and directing of the practice of Archery, the provisions made by them that practically every one should be skilled in the use of the bow, are sufficient evidence of the value which our ancestors placed upon it before "villanous saltpete" ousted it from the proud position of our national weapon. After fire-arms had taken the place of the bow in war, the practice of archery appears in a great measure to have died out, though it still existed in the north of England, and up to about 1760 in the Finsbury fields.

The revival of Archery as a pastime can be traced to 1780, when Mr. Waring, the Secretary or Manager of the Museum belonging to Sir Ashton Lever at Leicester House, took it up. Finding that it improved his health, he persuaded Sir Ashton Lever to try it. He did so, and, fascinated by it, with the assistance of his friends founded in 1781 the Royal Toxophilite Society which, from that time to the present day, has maintained its position as the head of the sport. Patronised and practised by the Prince of Wales and other Royal Dukes, archery at once sprang into popularity and numerous Societies were founded, which flourished till the stern reality of war gave people little time to practise the peaceable sport of the bow. On the conclusion of peace, it was again warmly taken up, old Societies were revived, new ones were started all over the country and in 1844, the first Grand National Archery Meeting took place at York. At present, there are numerous Societies all over England, and the five public meetings held annually show the popularity of the sport.

Of the pleasures of archery and the facilities which it affords to both ladies and gentlemen for physical and graceful exercise there can be no doubt, and its fascination is well known to all who shoot. Unfortunately, it has the drawback of being difficult and without regular practice and knowledge of how to do it, it is not easy to excel, this however, in the eyes of its votaries being one of its principal charms.

Equipment

Arrow: The arrow should be one inch longer than where your fingers reach.

Bow: On the average, a man's first bow should be about thirty pounds and a lady's about twenty four pounds.

Tab : Tab is specially shaped piece of leather which fits over the finger.

1. Arrows
2. Bow
3. Bracher
4. Armguard
5. Quiver with a belt to go round the waist
6. A ground quiver
7. Tassle for wiping off earth

SKILLS OF THE GAME

Holding the Anchor

With your right hand take an arrow from your quiver by the nock, bring it over the bow and lay it across the bow on the arrow-rest. You will see that one of the three feathers is of different colour to the other two, and turn the arrow until this one, the 'cock-feather', is uppermost, away from the bow. Now push the arrow on the nocking-point correctly. The arrow will stay there.

The string is pulled back with the first three fingers of the right hand, so place your forefinger on the string above the arrow and the second and third fingers together on the string below the arrow. The

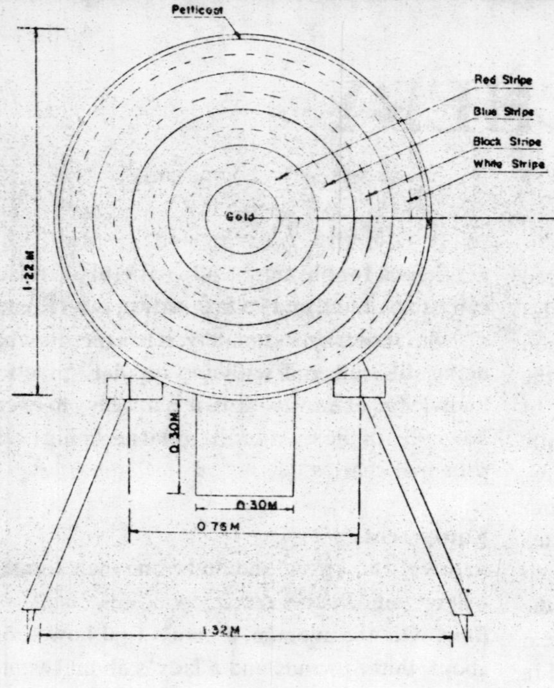
Petticoat
Red Stripe
Blue Stripe
Black Stripe
White Stripe
Gold
1·22 M
0.30M
0.30M
0.75M
1.32M

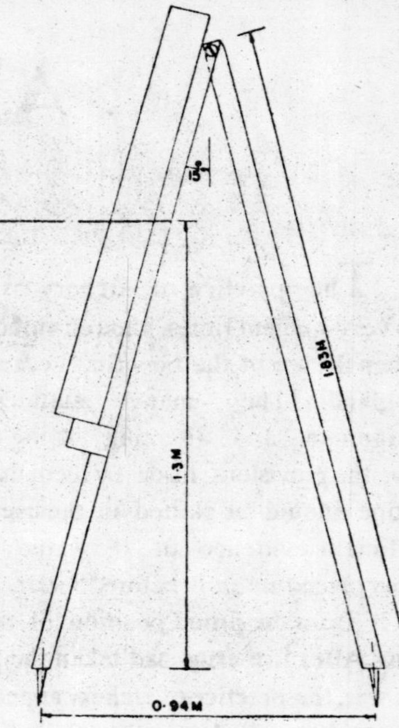
15°
1.83M
1.3M
0·94M

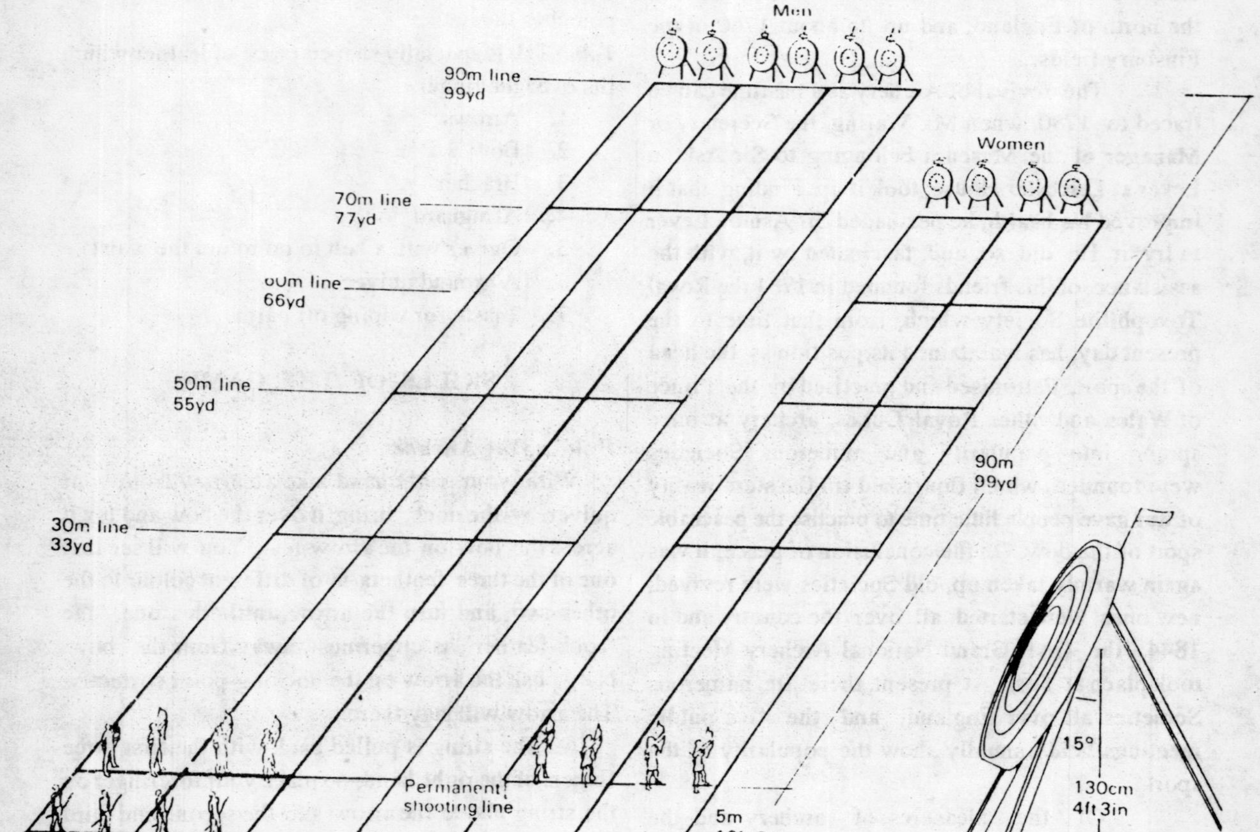
Men
90m line
99yd
Women
70m line
77yd
60m line
66yd
50m line
55yd
90m
99yd
30m line
33yd
15°
130cm
4ft 3in
Permanent
shooting line
Waiting line
5m
16ft 3in
5m
16ft 3in

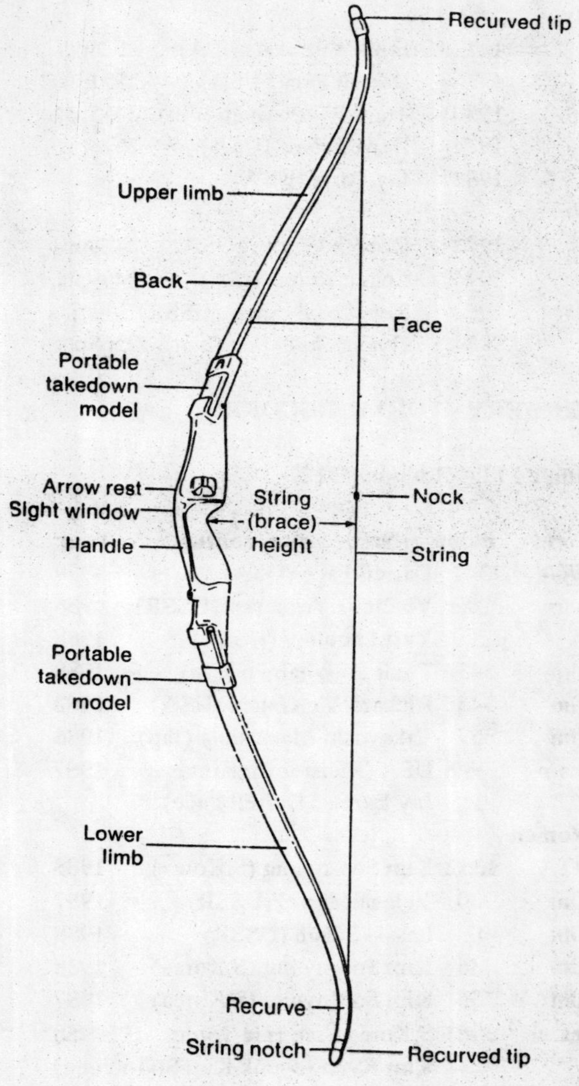

tab will be between the fingers and the string and the slot in the tab will allow the nock to lie between the first two fingers. Take the string in the first crease of the fingers and make sure that the third finger is well on, for this one tends to be a lazy one. The middle finger should not touch the arrow; there should be a gap of an eighth of an inch between them,but no more. Roll back the string for an inch or two, and see that the back of the hand, the wrist and the forearm are all in a straight line.

RULES OF THE GAME

1. Any bow except a crossbow may be used for competition.
2. Arrows should have a distinctive crest in order to distinguish each archer's arrow.
3. After the signal to shoot, arrows should be nocked.
4. Arrows that fall from the bow and cannot be reached with the bow from the shooting line, are considered to be shot.
5. Only six arrows may be shot at the designated target; if more than six are shot, only the lowest six scores are counted, and any arrow(s) shot at any other target shall not be scored.
6. An archer should shoot from the longest distance first, the second longest distance next, and so forth.
7. Scores are recorded from the highest score to the lowest score.
8. Arrows should be retrived only after the signal is given.

CUP & TROPHIES

Gold In Olympics

1900 Au cordon dore 50m
Henri Herouin (Fra)
Au cordon dore 33m
Hubert van Innis (Bel)
Au chapelet 50m
Eugene Mougin (Fra)
Au chapelet 33m
Hubert van Innis (Bel)
Sur la perche a la herse
Emmanuel Foulon (Fra)

1904 **Men**
Doble York Round
Philip Bryant (USA)
Double American Round
Philip Bryant (USA)
Team Round
Potamac Archers (USA)

Women

Double National Round
Lida Howell (USA)
Double Columbia Round
Lida Howell (USA)
Team Round
Cincinatti Archery Club (USA)

1908 Men

York Round
William Dod (UK)
Continental Style
E.G.Grisot (Fra)

Women

National Round
Queenie Newall (UK)

1920 Fixed bird target-small birds-individual
Edmond van Moer (Bel)
Fixed bird target-small birds-team
Belgium
Fixed bird target-large birds-individual
Edouard Cloetens (Bel)
Fixed bird target-large birds-team
Belgium
Moving bird target-28m-individual
Hubert van Innis (Bel)
Moving bird target-28m-team
Netherlands
Moving bird target-33m-individual
Hubert van Innis (Bel)
Moving bird target-33m-team
Belgium
Moving bird target-50m-individual
Julien Brule (Fra)
Moving bird target-50m-team
Belgium

Double Fita Round

Men

1972	John Williams (USA)	2528pts
1976	Darrell Pace (USA)	2571pts
1980	Tomi Poikloainen (Fin)	2455pts
1984	Darrell Pace (USA)	2616pts
1988	Jay Barrs (USA)	

Women

1972	Doreen Wilber (USA)	2424pts
1976	Luann Ryon (USA)	2499pts
1980	Keto Losaberidze (USSR)	2491pts
1984	Hyang-Soon Seo (Kor)	2568pts

ARCHERY WORLD RECORDS

Single FITA Rounds (MEN)

Event	Points	Name and Country	Year
FITA	1341	Darrell Pace (USA)	1979
90m	329	Vladimir Yesheyev (USSR)	1988
	329	Yuri Leontiev (USSR)	1988
70m	343	Tomi Poikolainen (Fin)	1988
50m	345	Richard McKinney (USA)	1982
30m	357	Takayoshi Matsushita (Jap)	1986
Team	3948	USA (Richard McKinney, Jay Barrs, ; Darrell Pace)	1987
Women			
FITA	1352	Kim Soo-nyung (S.Korea)	1988
70m	330	Yelena Marfel (USSR)	1987
60m	342	Lessia Schah (USSR)	1988
50m	336	Kim Soo-nyung (S.Korea)	1988
30m	356	Kim Soo-nyung (S.Korea)	1987
Team	3981	S.Korea (Lee Hae-young, Kim Kyung-wook,Kim Soo-nyung)	1988

ATHLETICS

Men have run, jumped and thrown things in competition with one another for thousands of years. The Lugnasad or Tailteann Games in Ireland are thought to have been founded as far back as 1829 B.C., some four and a half centuries before the Olympic Games are believed to have been started in Greece.

The first Olympic champion whose name we know is 'Coroebas, the winner of the stade (202 yds.) foot race in the Games of 776 B.C. Thirty Olympiads later, in 656 B.C., a Spartan athlete called Chionis long jumped 23 ft. 1(½) in. the earliest measured performance known to posterity.

Following the abolition of the Olympic Games in A.D.393 athletics plunged into the Dark Ages. There are vague reports of spasmodic athletic activity in medieval England but it was not until the 19th century that the sport became popular.

Mention should be made, though, of the sport of pedestrianism, which began in 17th century in England, in which men of menas waged on the road running ability of their footmen.

Details of performances prior to last century are hard to come by, but Horace Walpole wrote in 1787 of a mile run in 4(½) minutes. That sounds reasonable, which is more than can be said of such reports as "a butcher of Croydon on December 1st, 1653, ran twenty miles, from St. Albans to London, in less than an hour and a half, and the last four miles so gently that he seemed to meditate."

A glimpse of the standards achieved 150 years ago is provided by Donald Walker in his book, *Walker's Manly Exercises (1834).*

A quarter of a mile in a minute is good running. The mile was perhaps never run in four minutes, but it has been done in four and a half minutes. The mile in five minutes is good running. Two miles in ten minutes is more often failed than accomplished. Four miles in twenty minutes is said to puzzle the cleverest. Fifteen miles in one and a half hours has never perhaps been done. Forty miles in four and three quarters hours, it is said was done by one individual.

A good high-leaper will clear 5 (½) feet, and an extraordinary one 6 feet. On level ground 20 feet long jump is a first rate leap, 21 feet is extraordinary and 22 feet is rarely accomplished. A good walker did do 6 miles an hour for one hour on a good road, 12 miles in two hours.

The world's first athletic club, the Necton Guild, was established in Norfolk in 1817. By then regular competitions were already being held at the Royal Military Academy at Sandhurst.

TRACK EVENTS

The most important games in athletics are races. These are the following types of races:

1. Short Distance Race
2. Middle Distance Race
3. Steeplechase
4. Long Distance Race
5. Hurdle Race
6. Relay Race

THE SPRINTS

Whether it be in the 100 metres, where power and short-term energy are all-important, or the 400 metres, where sustained energy is needed to avoid the burn-out over the final 200 metres the technique in sprints is very much in the hands of the coaches.

These races are timed accurately up to one hundredth of a second by electronc timing device.

The athlete is expected to have an explosive start, great acceleration from start up to around 30m (pick-up stage), a sustained speed for the middle portion, and then a slight deceleration for the remainder of the race. The athlete has to strive for maximum stride length and leg speed. The start is the main deciding factor of the sprint. Two styles of starts are the crouch start and the standing start. Depending on one's experience, one can develop any type of start.

At the start, the feet of the athlete must be in contact with the ground, fingers behind the start line. When all athletes are steady on the start mark, the starter gives the command 'set' and 1.5 to 3.0 sec. after that he fires the gun. The first step should be accompanied by powerful drive from the lead legs with vigorous arm actions. If any athlete has two false starts, he is disqualified. The official finish is the finishing line, where photo-finish cameras determine first, second and third positions. The athlete should continue the sprint in full speed even when the finish line is drawn across the track at right angles to the inner edge and a tape is held right above this line. The competitors have to break the tape by torso. The competitors try to do so by inclining their body forward.

The lists of the world record holders and Olympic medallists at the sprints are dominated by athletes from U.S.A.

100 Metres World Record at Ten-Yearly Intervals :

Year	*Sec.*	*Name*	*Country*
1905	10.8	Luther Cary	USA
1915	10.5	Richard Rau	Ger
1925	10.2	Charles Paddock	USA
1935	10.2	Charles Paddock	USA
1945	10.2	Jesse Owens	USA
1955	10.1	Lloyd La Beach	Pan
1965	10.0	Armin Hary	GFR
1975	9.8	Steve Williams	USA
1985	9.93	Calvin Smith	USA

200 Metres

The 200 metres race is run on a curve in lanes with a staggered start, with the blocks set on the outside of the bend. The runner has thus to run the bend with just the right body angle to maintain speed.

200 metres race consists of four important phases :

(i) The start and the straight line acceleration to the point where this straight line forms a tangent to the inside of his lane and is very similar to the 100 metres start.

(ii) The run for the 200 metres runner presents technical difficulties, since he must continue accelerating and hope to reach to top speed while running through the part of a circle. In order to run in a circle close to the inside line of his lane he must lean into the centre to maintain balance. The right leg has to swing across the body to hold it in to the curve in the left leg support phase. An unbalanced runner or one who tends to carry weight on the right leg will have trouble while running a bend well. Runners with strong lateral movements, such as the short stocky 'power' type runners, will find this style as not effective in the 200 metres bend since the feet need to drive under the body in the line of movement. The smooth flowing stylists are often the 200 metre specialists. On the bend, then, the outside leg and arm must work hard to maintain the lean-in. There is some coasting period in this part of the 200 metres and stamina is needed to ensure that the athlete comes out of the bend with top sprinting speed.

(iii) Coming out of the turn into the straight requires a change of posture again, so that a central balance is achieved. This is a crucial stage of the race because the style of running has to change. The turn requires a fast cadence, but as the athlete enters the straight the emphasis is on a stronger leg action.

(iv) The straight part of the 200 draws on the mental and endurance reserves of the runner, for he must maintain his form and try to lose as little speed as possible as he nears the finish. The danger is in 'tying up' with tense muscles as fatigue sets in.

The 200 metres runner, like the 100 metres athlete, must train for greater speed through high-quality sprinting, paying special attention to particular points of technique during repetition runs. In addition he must train at high speed bend running, and he must work for stamina with full and over distance repetitions.

200 Metres World Record for 220 yds (Straight Track) at Ten-Yearly Intervals

1905	21.2	Bernie Wefers (USA)
1915	20.8	Albert Robinson(USA)
1925	20.8	Charles Paddock(USA)
1935	20.3	Jesse Owens(USA)
1945	20.3	Jesse Owens (USA)
1955	20.2	Mel Patton (USA)
1965	20.0	Dave Sime (USA)
	20.0	Frank Budd (USA)
1975	19.5	Tommie Smith (USA)
1985	19.72	Pietro Mennea (Ita)

World Record for 200 Metres Around a Turn at Ten-Yearly Intervals

1905	21.4	(for 220y)James Maybury(USA)
1915	21.2	(for220y) William Applegarth(UK)
1925	21.2	(for 220y)H.T.Evans(USA)
	21.2	Charles Paddock(USA)
1935	20.6	(for 220y) James Carlton(Aus)
1945	20.6	James Carlton (Aus)
1955	20.6	(for 220y) Andy Stanfield (USA)
	20.81	Andy Stanfield (USA)
1965	20.2	(for 220 y) HenryCarr (USA)
1975	19.83	Tommie Smith (USA)
1985	19.72	Pietro Mennea (Ita)

400 Metres

This is a sprint for the well-trained athlete. The distribution of energy has to be carefully controlled because very few can maintain an all-out sprint over the entire distance. It is very important for the 400 metre runner to judge pace and to be able to assess his own ability in relation to the competitors. An evenly paced race will be more economical and effective; for example, it is better to run each 200 metres in 25 seconds and 27 seconds than in 23 seconds and 30 seconds. It is the total time that counts, and even if that last example ended with 29 seconds, the rapidly slowing athlete would act as incentive for other competitors to chase and overtake him. The first 200 metres is generally run faster than the second because of the fatigue in the second, but an even faster time will not necessarily cancel out the slower time recorded in the second half. A common pattern is to try for a good start and on the first bent, a comfortable fast stride down the back straight, and a big effort on the last bend while trying to maintain relaxation and speed to the finish. The good 400 metre runner often has a buoyant, (relaxed style with a long stride, keeping mainly on the ball of the foot).

400 Metres World Record at Ten-Yearly Intervals

Women

1925	60.8	Eileen Edwards	UK
1935	56.8	Nellie Halstead	UK
1945	56.8	Nellie Halstead	UK
1955	53.9	Maria Itkina	USSR
1965	51.2	Shin Keum Dan	NKo
1975	49.9	Irena Szewinska	Pol
1985	47.6	Marita Koch	GDR

MIDDLE DISTANCE RACE

The province of middle distance running may, for the purposes of this sction, be said to stretch from 800m. (875 yds.) to 2 miles. Olympic and European championships are staged at 800 m. and 1500 m. (1200 yds. less than a mile); world records are officially recognised at 800 m., 880 yds., 1000 m. (1,093 yds.), 1500m., mile, 2000m. (1mile 427yds.), 3000m. (1 mile 1,521 yds.) and 2 miles.

800 Metres

The first of the "modern" half milers is generally acknowledged to be Mel Sheppard (USA), winner of the 1908 Olympic 800 m. in a world record of 1 min. 52.8 sec. after covering the first 400 m. in a sparkling 53.0 sec. He was succeeded by James Ted Meredith, another American, who not only won the 1912 gold medal in the world record time of 1 min. 51.9 sec. but carried on for another five yards to complete 880 yds. in 1 min. 52.5 sec., another record.

800 Metres World Record At Ten-Yearly Intervals

1905	1:53.4	Charles Kilpatrick	(USA)
1915	1:51.9	Ted Meredith	(USA)
1925	1:52.2	Ted Meredith	(USA)
1935	1:49.8	Ben Eastman	(USA)
	1:49.70	Tom Hampson	(UK)
1945	1:46.6	Rudolf Harbig	(Ger)
1955	1:45.7	Roger Moens	(Bel)
1965	1:44.3	Peter Snell	(NZ)
1975	I:44.1	Rick Wohlhuter	(USA)
1985	1:41.73	Sebastian Coe	(UK)

1000 Metres Record At Ten-Yearly Intervals

1905	2:35.8	Henri Deloge	(Fra)
1915	2:32.3	George Mickler	(Ger)
1925	2:28.5	Sven Lundgen	(Swe)
1935	2:23.6	Jules Ladoumegue	(Fra)
1945	2:21.5	Rudolf Harbig	(Ger)
1955	2:19.0	Aden Boysen	(Nor)
	2:19.0	Istvan Rozsaolgyi	(Hun)
1965	2:16.2	Jurgen May	(GDR)
1975	2:13.9	Rick Wohhuter	(USA)
1985	2:12.18	Sebastian Coe	(UK)

1500 Metres World Record

3.55.8	Abel Kiwiat (USA), Cambridge, 8-6-12
3.54.7	John Zander(SWE), Stockholm, 5-8-17
3.52.6	Paavo Nurmi(Fin), Helsinki, 19-6-24
3.51.0	Orro Peltzer (GER), Berlin, 11-9-26
3:49.2	Jules Ladoumegue(FRA), Paris, 5-10-30
3:49.2	Luigi Beccali(ITA), Turin, 9-9-33
3:49.0	Luigi Beccali(ITA), Milan, 17-9-33
3:48.8	Bill Bonthron(USA) , Milwaukee, 30-6-34
3:47.8	Jack Lovelock(NZL), Berlin, 10-8-41
3:47.6	Gunder Haegg(SWE),Stockholm, 10-8-41
3:45.8	Gunder Haegg(SWE), Stockholm,17-7-42
3:45.0	Arne Andersson(SWE),Gottenburg,17-8-43
3:43.0	Gunder Haegg (SWE), Gottenburg, 7-7-44
3:43.0	Lennart Strand (SWE), Malmo, 15-7-47
3:43.0	Werner Lueg (GER), Berlin, 29-6-52
3:42.8	Wes Santee (USA), Compton, 4-6-54
3:41.8	John Landy (AUS), Turku, 21-6-54
3:40.8	Sandor Iharos (HUN), Helsinki, 28-7-55
3:40.8	LasloTabori (HUN), Oslo, 6-9-55
3:40.8	Gunnar Nielsen (DEN), Oslo, 6-9-55
3:40.6	Istvan Rozsavolgyi(HUN), Tata, 3-8-56

3:40.2 Olavi Salsola (FIN), Turku, 11-7-57
3:38.I Stanislav Jungwirth(TCH), Stara Boleslaw, 12-7-57
3:36.0 Herb Elliott (AUS), Gothenburg, 28-8-58
3:35.6 Herb Elliott (AUS), Rome, 6-9-60
3:33.1 Jim Ryun(USA), Los Angeles, 8-7-67
3:32.2 Filbert Bayi (TAN), Christchurch, 2-2-74
3:32.I Sebastian Coe(GBR), Zurich, 15-8-79
3:32.I Steve Ovett (GBR), Oslo, I5-7-80
3:31.6 Steve Ovett(GBR), Koblenz, 27-8-80
3:31.24 Sydney Maree(USA), Cologne, 28-2-83
3:30.77 Steve Ovett (GBR), Rieti, 4-9-83
3:29.67 Steve Cram (GBR), Nice, 16-7-85
3:29.46 Said Aouita (MOR), Oslo, 23-8-85.

STEEPLECHASE

The standard steeplechasing distance is 3000 m. which is approximately 239 yards less than 2 miles. The race comprises of 28 hurdles and seven water jumps. All the obstacles are three feet in height. Unlike those used in conventional hurdle races the steeplechase barriers are solid and weigh between 176 (½) and 220 (½) lb. The width of the top of the hurdle is five inches, which enables an athlete to step on and off if he chooses. The waterjump is 12 feet in length and width, the water being 2 ft. 6 in. deep immediately in front of the hurdle. The trough slopes to ground level at the further end.

The first steeplechase to be traced was held over open country near Oxford in 1850, the 2 miles course including 24 obstacles. The event was introduced into the Oxford University sports in 1860 for a few years and two races (2500 and 4000m.) were held at the 1900 Olympics.

The distance was internationally standardised at 3000 m. with Percy Hodge (GB) in 1920 winning the first Olympic title over that length course. An official's error at the 1932 Olympics resulted in the runners covering one lap (460 m.) too many ! The winner, Volmari Iso-Hollo (Finland) successfully defended his title in 1936 and is regarded as the father of modern steeplechasing .

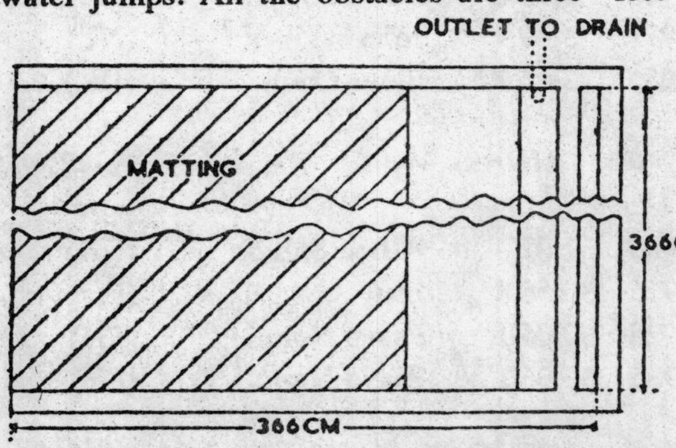

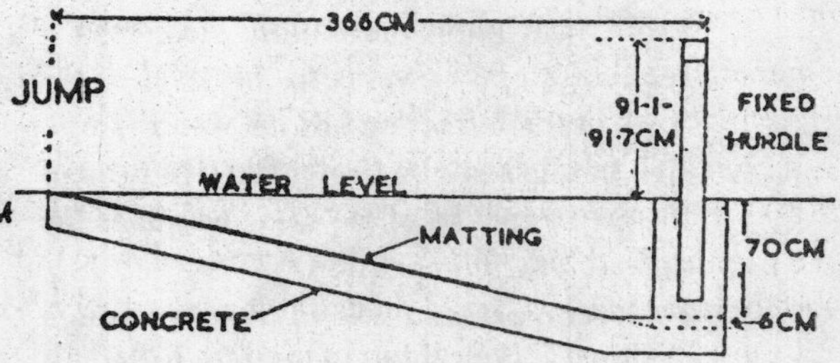

Rules of Steeplechase

1. The standard distances shall be: 2000 metres and 3000 metres.
2. There shall be 28 hurdle jumps and 7 water jumps included in the 3000 metres event, and 18 hurdle jumps and 5 water jumps in the 2000 metres event.
3. For both races the water jumps shall be the fourth jump in each lap. If necessary, the finish line shall be moved to another part of the track.
   It is recommended that, in the 2000 metres, the water jump be the second jump of the first lap, and thereafter the fourth jump.
4. In the 3000 metres steeplechase, the distance from the start to the beginning of the first lap shall not include any jumps, the hurdles being removed until the competitors have entered the first lap.
5. The hurdles shall be 0.914 metres high (3 ft.) with a tolerance of 3 millimetres above or below this height and shall be at least 3.96 metres (13 ft.) in width. The section of the top bar of the hurdles, and the hurdle at the water jump, shall be 127 millimetres (5 in.) square.
   The weight of each hurdle shall be between 80 kilograms and 100 kilograms. Each hurdle shall have on either side a base between 1.20 metres and 1.40 metres.
   The hurdle shall be placed on the track so that 0.30 metres of the top bar, measured from the inside edge of the track, will be inside the field.
6. The water jump, including the hurdle, shall be 3.66 metres in length and width.
   The water shall be in level with the track surface and at the hurdle end shall be 0.70 metres deep for a space of about 0.3 metres. From this point the bottom shall have a regular slope upwards to the level of the track at the farther end of the water jump.
   The hurdle shall be firmly fixed in front of the water and be of the same height as the others in the competition.
7. Each competitor must go over or through the water and anyone who steps to the one side or other of the jump or trails his foot or leg alongside any hurdle shall be disqualified. He may jump or vault over each hurdle, or place a foot on each hurdle and on the hurdle at the water jump.

World Record At Ten-Yearly Intervals

1945	8:59.6	Erik Elmsater	Swe
1955	8:40.3	Jerzy Chromik	Pol
1965	8:26.4	Gaston Roelants	Bel
1975	8:09.7	Anders Garderud	Swe
1985	8:05.4	Henry Rono	Ken

LONG DISTANCE RACE

Opinions vary as to where middle distance running leaves off and long distance takes over. For the purpose of this section, long-distance comprises events from 3 miles upwards.

The following track events in this category are included in the IAAF's schedule of world records: 3 miles, 5000 m. (3 miles 188 yds), 6 miles, 10,000 m. (6 miles 376 yds), 10 miles, 20,000 m. (12 miles 753 yds), 1 hour run, 15 miles, 25,000 m. (15 miles 941 yds) and 30,000 m. (18 miles 1,129 yds). Two of these events, the 5000 and 10,000 m. feature in the Olympic programme. AAA championships are contested at 3,6 and 10 miles.

One Mile World Record At Ten-Yearly Intervals

1905	4:12 3/4	Walter George	(UK)
1915	4:12.6	Nurman Taber	(USA)
1925	4:10.4	Paavo Nurmi	(Fin)
1935	4:06.7	Glenn Cunningham	(USA)
1945	4:01.3	Gunder Hagg	(Swe)
1955	3:57.9	John Landy	(Aus)
1965	3:53.6	MichelJazy	(Fra)
1975	3:49.4	John Walker	(NZ)
1985	3:46.32	Steve Cram	(UK)

10,000 Metres World Record At Ten-Yearly Intervals

1905	31:02.4	Alfred Shrubb	(UK)
1915	30:58.8	Jean Bouin	(Fra)
1925	30:06.1	Paavo Nurmi	(Fin)
1935	30:06.1	Paavo Nurmi	(Fin)

1945	29:35.4	Viljo Heino	(Fin)
1955	28:54.2	Emil Zatopek	(Cs)
1965	27.39.4	Ron Clarke	(Aus)
1975	27:30.80	David Bedford	(UK)
1985	27:13.81	Fernando Mamede	(Por)

3000 Metres

Who can halt the Soviet bloc? Rumania's Maricica Puica claimed the Olympic 3,000m title, profiting perhaps from Decker's controversial exit. But Puica is now into her mid thirties. With Decker dedicating 1986 to motherhood, the expectations fall on the slender shoulders of Zola Budd, innocent party in Decker's Olympic debacle, and rapidly maturing into a distance runner of the highest possible class.

3000 Metres World Record (Women)

8:53.0	Lyudmilla Bragina (URS), 12.8.72, Moscow
8:52.8	Lyudmilla Bragina (URS), 6.7.74 , Durham
8:26.78	Syvetiana Ulmasova (URS), 25.7.82, Kiev
8:22.62	Tatyana Kazankina(URS),26.8.84, Leningrad

3000 Metres World Record At Ten-Yearly Intervals

Men

1905	9:02.4	Louis de Flemrac	(Fra)
1915	8:36.9	Hanes Kolehmainen	(Fin)
1925	8:27.5	Edvin Wide	(Swe)
1935	8:18.3	Henry Nielsen	(Den)
1945	8:01.2	Gunder Haegg	(Swe)
1955	7:55.6	Sandor Iharos	(Hun)
1965	7:39.5	Kipchoge Keino	(Ken)
1975	7:35.2	Brendan Foster	(UK)
1985	7.32.1	Henry Rono	(Ken)

2000m World Record At Ten-Yearly Intervals

1905	5:37.0	Alfred Shrubb	(UK)
1915	5:37.0	Alfred Shrubb	(UK)
1925	5:25.9	Edvin Wide	(Swe)
1935	5:21.8	Jules Ladoumegue	(Fra)
1945	5:11.8	Gunder Haegg	(Swe)
1955	5:02.2	Istvan Rozsavolgyi	(Hun)
1965	5:01.2	Josef Odlozil	(Cs)
1975	4:56.2	Michel Jazy	(Fra)
1985	4:51.39	Steve Cram	(UK)

HURDLES

100 -110 Metres Hurdle Race

The 110 metres and 100 metres hurdles are perhaps the most demanding of all the athletics events on the physical attributes of the athlete,because the spacings between the hurdles are such that stride patterns have to be very nearly the same for all competitors.Certainly one sees very few short men at the starting lines of top-class 110 metres hurdles events. The rigidity of the stride and the demands of clearing the high hurdles ensure that this is not an event for the casual athlete.Indeed Marlow considers that the true champion 110 metres hurdler is the athlete with all the necessary speed,skill etc.but he is also fortunate enough to have a leg length and natural stride that exactly matches the height and spacing of the hurdles. The athletes will not need to'shuffle' or overstride.It also means that it is not easy for the beginner, who must spend a long preparatory period learning the skill over lower hurdles.

Short athletes and beginners are at less of disadvantage relative to all,experienced 400 metres hurdlers as there is more flexibility in their stride requirements, but high-level competition tends to be dominated by those with taller physiques.

The 110-metre hurdles specifications for this race are the most demanding on the athlete's skill.

As we saw in the case of sprinting in the 110 metres hurdles race the first hurdle comes so near the start,the more upright running becomes relevant sooner.Byson recommends a medium black spacing with the front block about 38-46 on behind the starting line, and about 40-50 on between the blocks,though he recognizes that there may be individual variations.Most hurdlers use an eight-stride run to the first hurdle,but some of the longer athletes stride in only seven.Ewen is of the opinion that, at the highest level 110 metres hurdling requires a 'shuffle step' for the three strides between the barriers, and that it is not logical to stretch out seven strides only to have to change to a shuffle for the next 27.He considers that the eight stride approach leads to a smoother transition from start to rhythm between the barriers.

The foot that the hurdler has on his front block will be his take-off front for the hurdle if he takes eight strides.Similarly the foot that the hurdler has on his rear block will be his take-off foot for the hurdle if he takes seven strides.An athlete who finds he is the 'wrong way round' and cannot change stride patterns will have to learn to start with the other foot forward.

400 Metres Hurdler Specifications

The 400 metres hurdler is less rigidly bound by the specifications in his stride pattern and hurdle technique than the high hurdler. The hurdles are 15.2 cm lower and more than three time further apart, so some scope exists for different stride patterns. On the other hand,the athlete has to negotiate some hurdles while running the two bends, and is subject to considerable fatigue in the second part of the race, when his anaerobic capacity is put severely to the test.

Although beginners may be better off with a standing start, the serious 400 metres hurdler should learn the crouch start from blocks, preferably setting them like a 200 metres sprinter and coming out fast on the gun to run a straight line on the tangent to the bend. World-class athletes run anything; take off foot for the first hurdle will be the one that is placed in the front block when the number of strides is even.

400 Metres Hurdles World Records At Ten-Yearly Intervals

1915	54.6	William Meanix	(USA)
1925	52.1	Ivan Riley	(USA)
1935	50.6	Glenn Hardin	(USA)
1945	50.6	Glenn Hardin	(USA)
1955	50.4	Yurjy Lifuyev	(USSR)

1965	49.1	Rex Cawley	(USA)
	49.3	Gert Potgieter	(SAF)
1975	47.82	John AkilBua	(Uga)
1985	47.02	Edwin Moses	(USA)

RELAY RACES

These are the only true team events in athletics, usually placed at the end of the competition programme to provide an exciting finish to a match.There are world records listed for 4x100 metres, 4x200 metres,4x400 metres,and 4x800 metres,for men and women,and 4x1500 metres for men only but the relays generally incorporated in most athletics competition are those of 4x100 metres and 4x400 metres.

In all relay races the baton (a smooth hollow tube 280-330mm long with a circumference of 120-130mm) must be passed within the 20 metres take-over zone.In the 4x100 metres the runners,other than the first,may start running not more than 10 metres before the beginning of the take-over zone.The first lap and that part of the second lap up to the exit from the first bend in the 4x400 metres are run in lanes, after which the competitors are free to take up any position on the track.

The logic of which hand each runner uses to receive and carry the baton and the line of run he adopts is based on the principle that the shortest distance around a bend is the inside limit of that bend.

It is therefore most important that the first and the third runners, who are required because of the track layout to run the bends,do so on the inside of their lane, whereas the second and fourth runners, who run the straights, can keep on a line along the outside of their lane without running any significant extra distance. This means that the maximum efficiency in baton changing the first runner should hug the bend and carry the baton in his right hand so that he can pass it to the second runner's left hand.The second runner keeps to the outside of his lane and passes the baton into the right hand of the third runner, and so on.

The outgoing runner at each of the take-over must be able to judge when to sart running so that he reaches the maximum speed just as the incoming runner comes to within comfortable baton-passing distance.In other words, the out-going runner accelerates as the incoming runner closes the distance between them and the pass is made at top sprinting speed without either of them having to slow down.

A modified crouch start is preferable to the less predictable standing start,but the runner must be able to look back comfortably to the check mark and the incoming runner.The decision when to start running is critical and the outgoing runner must be able to guarantee a consistent start and acceleration every time if training change-overs are to have any meaning in competition.This means that baton-changing practices must be made at full competitive speed so that check marks can be accurately worked out.Any glancing sideways or downwards by the receiver must be resisted.

Rules of Relay Races

1. Lines 50mm wide shall be drawn across the track to mark the distances of the stages and to denote the scratch line.
2. Lines 50 mm wide also shall be drawn 10 metres before and after the scratch line to denote the take-over zone, within which lines the baton must be passed. These lines are to be included in the zonal measurements. In races up to 4 x 200 metres, members of a team other than the first runner may commence running not more than 10 metres outside the takeover zone. A distinctive mark shall be made in each lane to denote this extended limit.
   In races up to 4 x 200 metres relay, the first two stages, as well as that part of the third stage up to the exit from the first bend, will be run entirely in lanes.
   In 4 x 400 metres relay races, the first lap, as well as that part of the second lap up to the exit from the first bend, will be run entirely in lanes.
   The competitors are free to take over any position on the track at the entrance to the following straight, which shall be marked with a flag set on a post at least 1.50 metres high on each side of the track, and with a line 50 millimetres wide across the track.
3. Check Marks:- When a relay race is being run in lanes, a competitor may make a check mark on the track within his own lane, e.g.by scratching with his shoe, but may not place marking objects on or alongside the track. Where the track is of a material which will not permit scratching with a shoe, some material supplied by the organisers may be used, at the discretion of the judge.
4. *The Baton* :- The baton must be carried in the hand throughout the race. If dropped, it must be recovered by the athlete who dropped it.
   In all relay races, the baton must be passed within the take over zone. The passing of the baton is completed at the moment it is in the hand of the receiving runner only. Within the take-over zone, it is only the position of the baton which is decisive, and not the position of the body or limbs of the competitors.
   Construction :- The baton shall be a smooth hollow tube circular in section, made of wood or metal or any other rigid material in one piece, the length of which shall not be more than 300 mm and not less than 280 mm. The circumference shall be 120 mm to 130 mm and it shall not weigh less than 50 grams.
5. The position of the teams at the start of the race shall be drawn and shall be retained at each take-over zone. After lanes cease to be used, waiting runners can move to an inner position on the track as incoming team-mates arrive, provided this can be done without fouling.
6. In events where the first part of the race is run in lanes, competitors, after completing this part, are free to take up any position on the track.
7. Competitors, after handing over the baton should remain in their lanes or zones until the course is clear, to avoid obstruction to other competitors. Should any competitor wilfully impede a member of another team by running out of position or lane at the finish of the stage, he is liable to cause the disqualification of his own team.
8. Assistance by pushing-off or by any other method will cause disqualification.
9. Once a relay team has started in a competition, only two additional athletes may be used as substitutes in the composition of the team for subsequent rounds.
   Substitutions may only be made from the list of athletes already entered for the meeting whether for that event or any other event.
   The exact composition of the teams and the order of the teams for the relay must be

officially declared before the start of each round of the compeition.

Relay Records

4 x 100m Relay (Men)

World record	37.83	USA on 11th August, 1984
Olympic record	37.83	USA on 11th August, 1984
European record	38.02	SU on 6th Sep., 1987
Commonwealth record	38.39	Jam on 19th October, 1968
African record	38.73	IvC on 13th Sep., 1979
Asian record	39.05	Chn on 5th Sep., 1987

4 x 400m Relay (Men)

World record	2:56.16	USA on 20th October, 1968
Olympic record	2:56.16	USA on 20th October, 1968
European record	2:58.86	UK on 6th Sep., 1987
African record	2:59.32	Nig on 11th August, 1984
Asian record	3:02.33	Jap on 5th October, 1986

4 x 100m Relay (Women)

World record	41.37	GDR on 6th October, 1985
Olympic record	41.60	GDR on 1st August, 1980
Commonwealth record	42.43	UK on 1st August, 1980
African record	43.44	Nig on 9th August, 1987
Asian record	44.61	Chn on 25th November, 1987
European record	41.37	GDR on 6th October, 1985

4 x 400m Relay (Women)

World record	3:15.92	GDR on 3rd January, 1984
Olympic record	3:18.29	USA on 11th August, 1984
Commonwealth record	3:21.21	Can on 11th August, 1984
African record	3:27.08	Nig on 12th August, 1987
Asian record	3:31.55	Ind on 5th Sep., 1987

FIELD EVENTS

Throwing and jumping is an inborn art in every human being which needs planned and programmed development at an early stage of life so as to become a good athlete. The above traits have been found in human beings from times immemorial. They are a part of his struggle for survival. As a sport, jumping and throwing were introduced in ancient Greece in Pan-Hellenic games. In 1864 jumping and throwing events were for the first time included in modern world competitions between Oxford and Cambridge in U.K.

Track and field events have developed into highly technical competitions requiring regular coaching, training and practice. It is essential to start the training at as early a stage as possible. Although a small school boy cannot develop sufficient competence in these events, he can certainly learn the fundamentals of these events, understand the techniques and make efforts to develop his skills and art and groom himself into a star performer in due course.

Major field events are :

1. Long Jump and Hop-step Jump
2. High Jump
3. Pole Vault
4. Triple Jump
5. Shot Put
6. Discus Throw
7. Javelin Throw
8. Hammer Throw

LONG JUMP

Long jump is a popular field event. This is an exciting item and requires a competitor to have speed,bounce as well as proper coordination of distance, strides and spring action of body at take-off stage. Normally, strong sprinters take part in this events, because of the advantage of speed. However, this is not essential. In fact, the event does not require any particular body type.

Rules of Long Jump and Triple Jump

(i) Each competitor may be allowed 3 to 6 trials as agreed upon by judges.

(ii) The best of all the 3 or 6 trials will be considered for credit.

(iii) The take-off shall be from a board, the edge nearest to the landing area shall be called the 'scratch line'.

(iv) If a competitor takes off before reaching the scratch line, it shall not be counted as a failure but the competitor will be at a disadvantage for the distance.

(v) The distance of run though recommended as 35-40 metres, is unlimited.

(vi) If any competitor touches the ground beyond the scratch line or scratch line extended, with any part of his body, the jump is considered as a failure.

(vii) The measurements of his jumps shall be made at right angles from the nearest break in the ground in the landing area made by any part of the competitor's body on the scratch line.

(viii) The use of any additional weights or grips is not permitted.

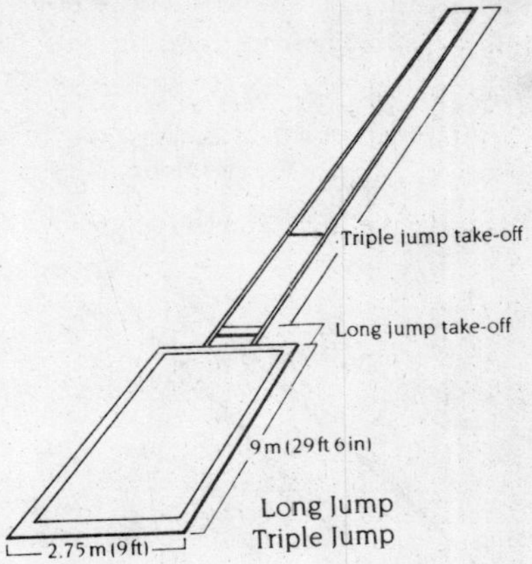

World Record at Ten-yearly Intervals

1905	7.61m	Peter O'Connor	(Ire)
1915	7.61m	Peter O'Connor	(Ire)
1925	7.89m	William Hubbard	(U.S.A.)
1935	8.13m	Jesse Owens	(U.S.A.)
1945	8.13m	Jesse Owens	(U.S.A.)
1955	8.13m	Jesse Owens	(U.S.A.)
1965	8.35m	Ralph Boston	(U.S.A.)
1975	8.90m	Bob Beamon	(U.S.A.)
1985	8.90m	Bob Beamon	(U.S.A.)

HIGH JUMP

High jump is an important and popular field event. To be a successful high jumper one must have proper leg spring off the bounce. Moreover, he should have light build and light weight . In other words, a well coordinated man of average height and weight can develop himself to be a good high jumper.

Style of High Jump: Although the most popular,natural and easy style of jump is the "scissors style" but it is not much encouraged.

Rules of High Jump

(a) The uprights or posts shall not be moved during the competition unless the Judges consider the take-off or landing ground has become unsuitable. Such a change shall be made only after a round is completed.

(b) Unless such details are specified on the programme, the Judges shall decide the height at which the competition shall start, and the different heights to which the bar will be raised at the end of each round. The competitors shall be informed of the details before the competition begins.

(c) A competitor may commence jumping at any height above the minimum height and may jump at his own discretion at any subsequent height. Three consecutive failures, regardless of the height at which any of them occurs, disqualifies from further jumping.

N.B. The effect of this Rule is that a competitor may for go his second and third jumps or vaults at a particular height (after failing one or twice) and still jump at a subsequent height.

(d) Even after all the other competitors have failed, a competitor is entitled to continue jumping until he has forfeited his right to compete further and his best jump shall be recorded as the winning height.

(e) A competitor may place marks to assist him in his run up and take-off and a handkerchief on the cross-bar for sighting purposes. The distance of the run is unlimited.

(f) All measurements shall be made perpendicularly from the ground to the upperside of the cross-bar where it is lowest. A steel or fibre-glass measure should be used. Any measurements of a new height should be made before competitors attempt that height. In the case of records the officials must check the measurement after the height has been cleared. The height shall be recorded to the nearest 1 cm below the height measured; *i.e.* fractions less than 1 cm must be ignored.

(g) A competitor fails if he : (i) in the course of a jump dislodges the bar so that it falls from the pegs; or (ii) touches the ground or landing area beyond the plane of the uprights without clearing the bar (if a jumper when he jumps touches the landing area and in the opinion of the judges no advantage is gained, the jump should not for that reason be considered a failure); or (iii) takes off from both feet.

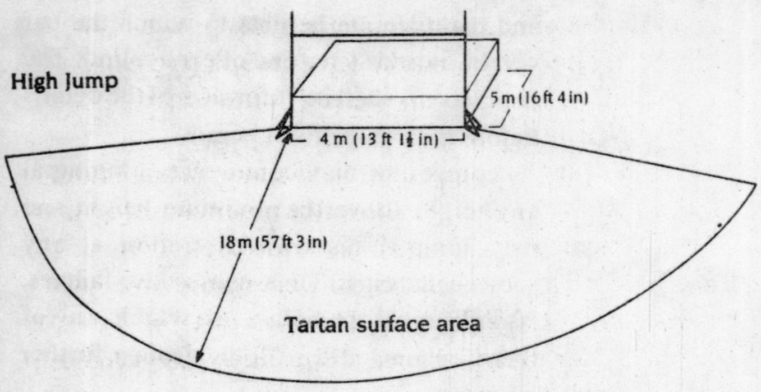

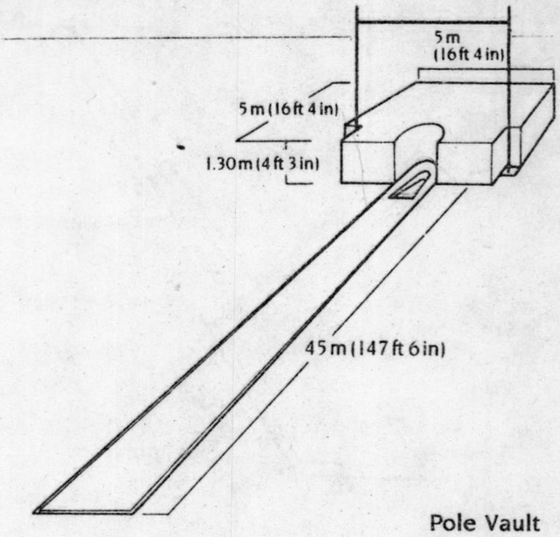

Pole Vault

High Jump World Record at Ten-Yearly Intervals

1905	1.97m	Michael Sweeney	(USA)
1915	2.01m	Edward Beeson	(USA)
1935	2.07m	Walter Marty	(USA)
1945	2.11m	Lester Steers	(USA)
1955	2.12m	Walt Davis	(USA)
1965	2.28m	Valeriy Brumel	(USSR)
1975	2.30m	Dwight Stones	(USA)
1985	2.41m	Igor Paklin	(USSR)

POLE VAULT

Pole vault is an excellent field event enjoyed equally by the competitors as well as the spectators. The event involves speed of a sprinter and agility and strength of a gymnast. It is essential that a vaulter has exceptional neuro muscular coordination together with leg speed and arm and shoulder strength. It is observed that tall men with long arms make good vaulters.

Specification for Pole Vault

(a) Landing Area
Length: 5 meters
Width: 5 meters.

(b) Distance between Uprights
Minimum 3.66meters
Maximum 4.32 meters.

(c) Length of Cross Bar
Minimum 3.86 meters
Maximum 4.52 meters.

(d) Weight of Cross Bar
Maximum 2.26 Kilogrammes.

(e) Support for Cross Bar extension
75 milimeters

(f) Planting box
Length: 1 meter

Width at Front end: 600 milimeters
Thickness Metal Sheet: 2.5 milimeters.

Length of the sheet from the front of the box towards stop board 800 milimeters.

Rules of Pole Vault

1. Any competitor may have the uprights moved in either direction, but they must not be moved more than 2 feet from the prolongation of the inside edge of the top of the stop board.
2. The judges should make a re-measurement to ensure that there is no variation in height.
3. The take-off for the pole shall be from a wooden or metal box as per the specifications given earlier. The front edge of the box must be in level with the run up and finally fixed to the ground.
4. The pole may be of any material and any length or diameter, but the basic surface of the metal must be smooth.
5. An athlete fails in the competition if :

(a) in the course of a vault he dislodges the bar so that it falls from the pegs;

(b) Without first having cleared the bar, he touches any part of his body,or the pole, or the ground beyond the veritical plane of the upper part of the stop board;

(c) he makes three runs without completing the vault;

(d) he leaves the ground to make a vault and fails to clear the bar;

(e) he clears the bar himself but lets the pole go off and allows it pass under;

(f) while he is making the vault or after leaving the ground places his lower hand above the upper one or moves the upper hand higher up on the pole.

World Record at Ten-Yearly Intervals

1905	3.74m	Fernand Gonder	(Fra)
1915	4.02m	Marcus Wright	(U.S.A.)
1925	4.25m	Charles Hoff	(Nor)
1935	4.39m	Keith Brown	(U.S.A.)
1945	4.77m	Cornelius Warmerdam	(U.S.A.)
1955	4.77m	Cornelius Warmerdam	(U.S.A.)
1965	5.28m	Fred Hanson	(U.S.A.)
1975	5.65m	Dave Roberts	(U.S.A.)
1985	6.00m	Sergei Bubka	(U.S.S.R.)

TRIPLE JUMP

In addition to the training done as a sprinter the triple jumper must devote much of his training time to ploymetrics-the explosive type, eccentric muscle contraction work of depth jumping. A few examples of this training method are:

1. Jumping from the top of a box (typically 1 metre length on to one leg, followed by a hop, step and Jumps.
2. Jumping from the top of a box to the floor, immediately rebounding from one or both feet to another box, to the floor, to a box etc.
3. Hopping, or double foot bounding, over low hurdles placed about 2 metres apart.
4. Vertical jumps in rapid sequence while holding dumb bells.

This type of training ensures that the muscles concerned are attempting to contract while they are being streched by the much larger force of the landing. The tensions in the muscle and tendons are very much greater in this so-called eccentric contraction than in normal concentric contraction at the appropriate joints. In addition,the movement is of an intense, short-duration in which the muscles are called upon to exert a very large force in a short time, which is exactly what is required of them in the triple jump take-off.

In triple jump the hop is made first so that the competitor lands first upon the same foot as that from which he has taken off. In the next step he lands on the other foot, from which subsequently the jump is performed.

The rules allow an unlimited length of run way (minimum 40 metres). In addition to the rules defining failures, which include those for the long jump, they also specify that : If a competitor while jumping touches the ground with the "sleeping" leg it shall be considered a failure". Simple sounding rules, but then simple rules quite often define highly technical events-as is the case with the triple jump. Because the objectives is to triple jump as far as possible, one may think that an enormous hop is the best way to start the movement of the take-off board. However, even the strongest triple jumpers have to keep this phase under control.

World Record at Ten-Yearly Intervals

1915	15.52m	Daniel Ahearne	(USA)
1925	15.52m	Daniel Ahearne	(USA)
1935	15.78m	Jack Metcalfe	(Aus)
1945	16.00m	Naoto Tajima	(Jap)

1955	16.56m	Adhemar Ferreira	(Bra)
1965	17.03m	Jozef Schmidt	(Pol)
1975	17.89m	Joao Carlos de Oliveira	(Bra)
1985	17.97m	Willie Banks	(USA)

SHOT PUT

The shot is a heavy, cannonball-like ball. It is held in one hand against the side of the chin and propelled by pubshing it away from the body-actually throwing it, is against the rules. As for all throwing events, different weights are used for men and women and for different age groups.

Rules of the putting the shot

1. In making his puts the competitor may rest his feet against but not on top of the stop board.
2. The shot shall be put from the shoulder with one hand only.
3. At the time the competitor takes his stance in the ring, the shot shall not be dropped below this position during the act of putting. The shot must not be brought behind the line of the shoulders.
4. For a valid put the shot must fall so that the point from which measurement is to be made is within the inner edges of lines marking a sector of about 65 degree set out on the ground so that the radii lines touch, with their edges, the extremities of the stop board and cross at the centre of the circle.
5. Immediately after each put the measurements should be made.

World Record at Ten-Yearly Intervals (Women)

1925	10.68m	Violette Morris	(Fra)
1935	14.38m	Gisela Mauermayer	(Ger)
1945	14.89m	Tatyana Sevryukova	(USSR)
1955	16.67m	Galina Zybina	(USSR)
1965	18.59m	Tamara Press	(USSR)
1975	21.60m	Marianne Adam	(GDR)
1985	22.53m	Natalya Lisovskaya	(USSR)

DISCUS THROW

Introduced by Greeks in ancient Olympics the modern Discus Throw has undergone a lot of changes in the rules of the event, its arena and even in the technique. The event requires a well-developed body,large, strong hands, long arms and perfect agility. Like other field events it requires proper neuro-muscular coordination of a very high order to be good discus thrower.

Rules of Discus Throw

(i) All discus throws shall be made from an enclosure or cage.

(ii) For a valid throw the discus must fall so that the point from which measurement is to be made is within the inner edges of lines marking a sector of 40 degree set out on the ground so that the radai lines cross at the centre of the circle.

(iii) Immediately after the throw all measurements should be made.

(iv) The competitor may adopt any position of throw as per his convenience.

Discus World Record at Ten -Yearly Intervals

1905 49.66m Martin Sheridan (USA)

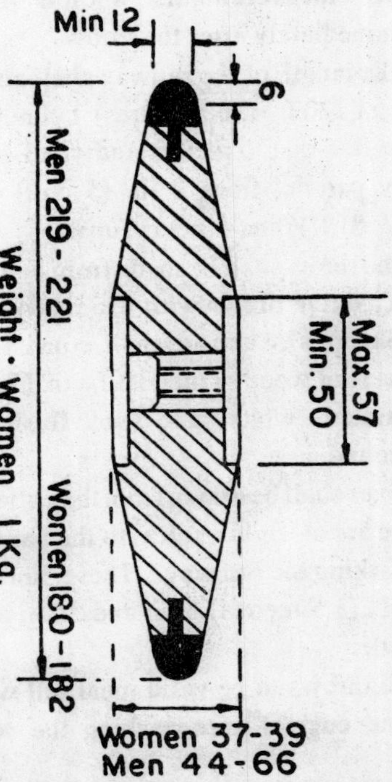

1915 48.27m Unofficial- Armas Taipale (Fin)
47.58m Oficial- James Duncan (U.S.A.)
1925 47.89m Official Glenn Hartranft (U.S.A.)
1935 53.79m Unofficial Gordon Dunn(USA)
53.10m Official Wilhelm Schroder (GFR)
1945 53.34m Official Adolfo Cosolini(Ita)
1955 59.28m Fortune Gordien (U.S.A.)
1965 65.22m Ludvik Danek(Cs)
1975 69.08m John Powell (U.S.A.)
1985 71.86m Yuriy Dumchev (U.S.S.R.)

HAMMER THROW

It is believed that in order to show his powers, Henry VIII used to throw the blacksmith's heavy hammer after rotating it over his head and then would challenge his courtiers to beat him in the throw. Subsequently the game found its way in sports events but it is not exactly known when and how the head of the hammer was changed into a ball and handle into a chain to give it the present form.

It essentially being a sport event to display one's strength, men with long strong arms, exceptionally well-developed physique together with a perfect neuro-muscular coordination can be successful Hammer throwers.

Rules of Hammer Throw

1. The competitor may choose any position for initial stance.
2. For a valid throw, the hammer must fall so that the point from which measurement is to be made is within the inner edges of lines marking a sector of approximately 65 degree set out on the ground so that the radii lines touch, with the edges, the extremities of the stop board and cross at centre of the circle.
3. Immediately after the throw all measurements should be made.
4. All hammer throws shall be made from an enclosure or cage.

Hammer Throw World Record at Ten-Yearly Intervals

1905	52.71m	John Flanagan	(USA)
1915	57.77m	Pat Ryan	(USA)
1925	57.77m	Pat Ryan	(USA)

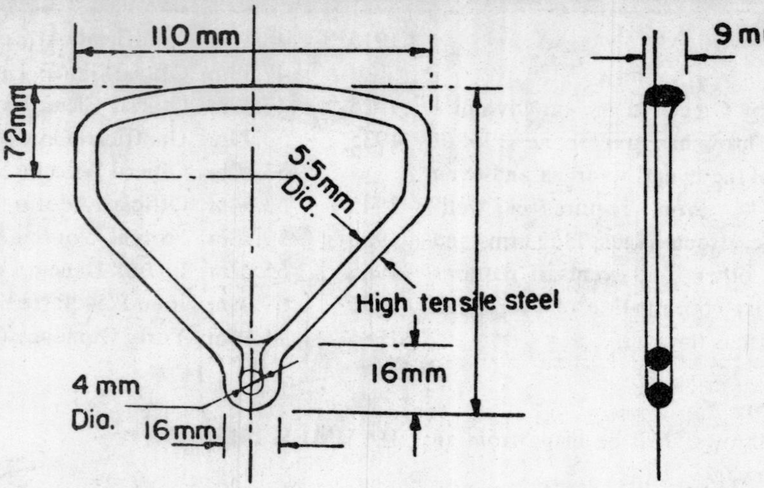

1935	57.77m	Pat Ryan	(USA)
1945	59.00m	Erwin Blask	(Ger)
1955	62.52m	Mikhail Krivonosov	(USSR)
1965	73.74m	Gyula Zsivotzky	(Hun)
1975	79.30m	Walter Schmidt	(GFR)
1985	86.34m	Yuriy Sedykh	(USSR)

JAVELIN

Throwing of spear to kill the hunt and also in the ancient warfare was a very popular and common weapon from the time immemorial. In Scandanvia and Finland the skill was given a modern shape among the athletic events in 1910's. Like other throw events, a strong tall man with a strong arm and well-developed neuro-muscular coordination will make a successful Javelin thrower.

Rules of Javelin Throw

1. The competitor may adopt any position to suit his convenience.
2. The Javelin must be held with one hand only, and at the grip, so that the little finger is nearest to the point. The Javelin shall be thrown over the shoulder or upper part of the throwing arm, and must not be slung or hurled.
3. The throw shall not be measured if the point of the Javelin does not strike the ground before any part of the shaft or if the competitor crosses the scratch line or its extension. The competitor must not place his foot or feet upon the scratch line or board.
4. For a valid throw, the Javelin must fall so that the point from which the measurement is to be made is within the inner edges of lines marking a sector of approximately 65 degree set out on the ground and so that the radii line touch, with their edges, the extremities of the stop board and cross at the centre of the circle.
5. All measurements should be made immediately after the throw.
6. The length of the runway shall not be more than 120 ft. (36.5 metres) but not less than 98 ft. 6 in. (30 metres)and shall be marked by parallel lines 2 in. (5 cm.) wide and 13 ft. 1(½)in.(4 metres) apart.
7. The throw shall be made from behind an arc of a circle drawn with a radius of 26 ft. 3in. (8 metres). Such arc shall consist of a strip made of wood or metal 2(3/4)in. (7cm.) wide painted white and sunk flush with the ground.
8. Lines shall be drawn from the extremities of the arc at right angles to the parallel lines marking the run way. These lines shall be 5 ft. (1.5 metres) long and 2(3/4) in. (7cm.) wide.
9. All throws to be valid must fall within the inner edge of lines marking the sector set

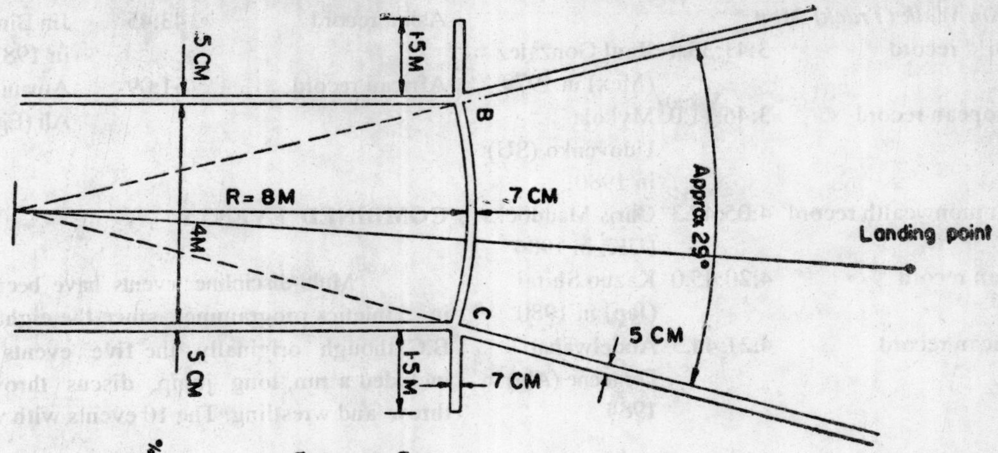

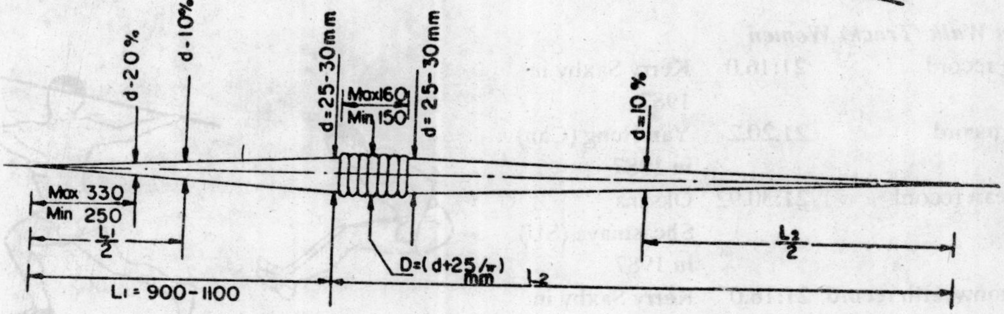

out on the ground by extending for a distance of 95 yards of the lines from the centre of the circle, of which the arc is a part,through the points at which the arc joins the lines marking the run way. The outer ends of sector lines should be marked with flags.

10. A competitor's throw must not be marked and measured if he steps on the arc or extended scratch lines or if he crosses the scratch line on the ground marked N at any time, before a fair throw has been indicated by the judge at the throwing end. He is allowed to run on or outside the run-up lines provided that at the moment of throwing he is behind the arc and between the run up lines.

WALKING

Race walking may appear to be the natural link between ordinary walking and running, and in some respects this is true-with increase in speed, the force-time decreases. However, the horizontal forces at right-angles to the direction of movement do not reveal this tidy progression, because although ordinary walking and running produce only small wasted forces in this direction, race walking shows much the largest peaks which represent a significance of energy.

50 Km Walk (Road) Men

World record	3:38:17	Ronald Weigel (GDR) in 1986
Commonwealth record	3:46:34	Willi Sawall (Aus) in 1980
Asian record	3:52:51	Li Baojin (Chn) in 1987
African record	4:14:30	Eddie Michaels (RSA) in 1967
European record	3:38:17	Ronald Weigel (GDR) in 1986
Olympic record	3:47:26	Raul Gonzalez (Mex) in 1984

50Km Walk (Track) Men

World record	3:41:38.4	Raul Gonzalez (Mex) in 1979
European record	3:46:11.0	Mykola Udovenko (SU) in 1980
Commonwealth record	4:05:47.3	Chris Maddocks (UK) in 1984
Asian record	4:20:45.0	Kazuo Shirai (Jap) in 1980
African record	4:21:44.5	Abdelwahab Ferguene (Alg) in 1984

5000m Walk (Track) Women

World record	21:16.0	Kerry Saxby in 1987
Asian record	21.20.2	Yan Hong (Chn) in 1987
European record	21:30.92	Oksana Shcastnaya (SU) in 1987
Commonwealth record	21:16.0	Kerry Saxby in 1987
African record	24:51.7	Sabeha Mansouri (Alg) in 1987

10,000m Walk (Track) Women

World record	43.52.1	Chen Yaoling (Chn) in 1987
Asian record	43.52.1	Chen Yaoling (Chn) in 1987
European record	44:32.50	Yelena Kuznetsova (SU) in 1986
Commonwealth record	45:08.13	Kerry Saxby (Aus) in 1986
African record	54:18.6	Sabeha Mansouri (Alg) in 1987

10km Walk (Road) Women

World record	42:52	Kerry Saxby (Aus) in 1987
Commonwealth record	42:52	Kerry Saxby (Aus) in 1987
European record	43:22	Olga Krishtop (SU) in 1987
Asian record	43:45	Jin Bingjie (Chn) in 1987
African record	61:09	Amani Mohamed Ali (Egy) in 1987

COMBINED EVENTS

Multi-discipline events have been included in athletics programmes since the eighth century B.C.,though originally the five events for men included a run, long jump, discus throw, javelin throw and wrestling. The 10 events with which we

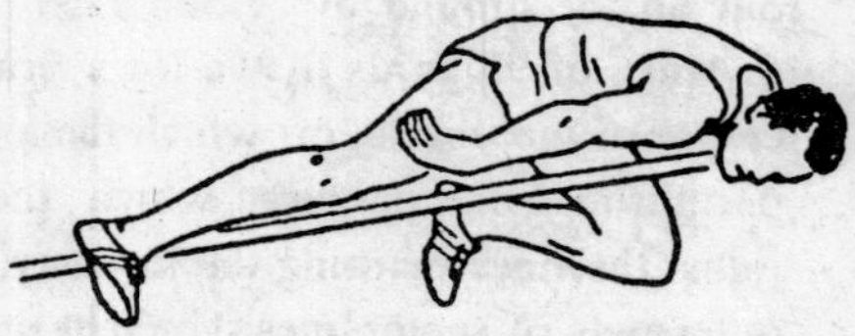

are familiar today were practised first in Scandinavia, and the event is now developed in importance for the genuine all-rounders who may not be supreme in any one event but who can maintain a high overall standard. In the early days good sprinter-jumpers tended to be elite, compensating for their weaker events by expertise in the stronger events. Today it is an event for the decathlon or heptathlon specialist who prepares for it and competes in the event as a whole rather than in series of separate competitions.

The decathlete or heptathlete needs to be a balanced personality with well-rounded physical development to cope with:

1. *Decathlon (Men)* Day 1: 100 metres, long jump,shot, high jump, 400 metres.
   Day 2: 110 metres hurdles, discus, pole vault, javelin, 1,500 metres.

2. ***Heptathlon*** Day 1: 100 metres hurdles, shot,high jump, 200 metres (Women).
   Day 2: Long jump, javelin, 800 metres.

Decathlon World Record Performances at Ten-Yearly Intervals

1915 Jim Thorpe (USA)
1925 Jim Thorpe (USA)
1935 Hans-Heinrich Sievert (Ger)
1945 Glenn Morris (USA)
1955 Rafer Johnson (USA)
1965 Yang Chuang-kwang(Tai)
Phil Mulkey (USA)
1975 Bruce Jenner (USA)
1985 Daley Thompson (UK)
Jurgen Hingsen (GFR)

MARATHON HISTORICAL HIGHLIGHTS

25 November1892

Baron Pierre de Coubertin made a statement at the Sorbonne in Paris regarding the revival of the ancient Olympic Games.

Michel Breal wrote to de Coubertin suggesting that the Olympic programme include a distance race in 1894.

Two runners left Athens at 8am to run to Marathon.G Grigoriou finished in 3:45:00,ten minutes after J.Vanoulis who had taken a lift in a cart for 5km during the run on February 1896.

The first official marathon to be held over the Marathon to Athens route, and the first national championship race on 10 March 1896.

The second authenticated marathon to be held as part of the Pan-Hellenic sports celebrations,acting as an Olympic trial on 24 March 1896.

The first women , Stamatis Rovithi, to run the distance on

March 1896.

The first modern Olympic Games marathon took place with one runner each from Australia, France, Hungary and the United States, as well as those representing Greece on 10 April 1896.

The first marathon to be held outside Greece from Paris to Conflans,France.The winner received 2000 French Francs, plus another 2000 Francs on 19 July 1896.

The first marathon to be staged in the Western Hemisphere from Stamford,CT to the Columbia Oval, New York, over 25 miles on 20 September 1896.

The first Boston marathon from Ashland to Exter Street on 19 April 1897.

First Olympic marathon to be held outside Europe at St. Louis on 30 August 1904.

First Yonkers,NY marathon on 28 November 1907.

First marathon in Great Britain at Conventry over 25 miles on 9 May 1908.

Olympic Games marathon from Windsor to the White City over a distance of 26 miles 385 yd for the first time on 24 July 1908.

First professional marathon in Great Britain over the Olympic Course on 10 October 1908.

First professional marathon in the United States at Madison Square Garden on 25 November 1908.

First marathon in the Australian continent held at Sydney on 12 April 1909.

First Polytechnic Harriers' marathon for sporting life trophy from Windsor to Stamford Bridge on 26 May 1909.

First indoor marathon in Great Britain held at the Royal Albert Hall on 18 December 1909.

First professional marathon to be held in South America at Buenos Aires on 24 May 1910.

First Open marathon in Asia over 24 miles as the Japanese Olympic trial on 19 November 1911.

Formation of the International Amateur Athletic Federation on 17 July 1912.

The fourth I.A.A.F. Congress meeting at Geneva,by which time the World Records Committee had proposed that the standard distance for the Olympic marathon be 26 miles 385 yd. on 27 May 1921.

First Kosice marathon.International from 1925 in 28 October 1924.

First A.A.U. marathon championship at Boston on 19 April 1925.

First A.A.A. championship marathon from Windsor to Stamford Bridge on 30 May 1925.

First British Empire Games' marathon at Hamilton on 21 August 1930.

First European Championship marathon at Turin on 9 September 1934.

First Mainichi marathon at Osaka on 10 February 1946.

First Enschede marathon on 12 July 1947.

First Asahi marathon on 7 December 1947.

First Asian Games marathon at New Delhi.

First Olympic Games marathon to be held in Australasia (Melbourne) on 1 December 1956.

First Olympic marathon to be held at high altitude, at Mexico City on 20 October 1968.

First marathon to be held at the African Games at Lagos.

First London marathon on 29 March 1981.

First World Championship marathons on 14 August 1983.

World Best at Ten-Yearly Intervals

1915	2:36:06.6	Alexis Ahlgren (Swe)
1925	2:29:10.8	Al Michelsen (U.S.A.)
1935	2:26:42.1	Sohn Kee Chung (Kor)
1945	2:26:42.1	Sohn Kee Chung (Kor)
1955	2:17:39.4	Jim Peters (U.K.)
1965	2:12:00.0	Morio Shigematsu (Jap)
1975	2:08:33.6	Derek Clayton (Aus)
1985	2:07:11.6	Carlos Lopes (Por)

RULES OF THE GAME

1. Athletes should wear clean clothes, not subject to any objection.
2. An athlete can participate in a game bare-footed or with footwear on one foot or both. The foot wear should be such as does not give them additional help for play.
3 A competitor who obstructs the play of others or retards their progress may be disqualified.
4 Each athlete shall bear marks distinctly on his chest and back. He will not be able to run without number.
5. In lanes races, a competitor shall confine himself to his lane from the beginning to the end of a play.
6. An athlete knowingly, running out of his lane may be disqualified. If in the opinion of the referee he has not done it knowingly, the referee may or may not disqualify him.
7. A player leaving his track of his own will not be allowed to continue his race.
8. A judge can order an athlete to take part in a different way if track and field events start simultaneously.
9. A point shall be scored against an athlete who makes an unnecessary delay in field events and he shall not be permitted to participate in trial. If he persists in it, he shall not be permitted to participate in one more trial, but his first performance shall be reckoned. Normally two minutes are given for field events and three minutes for pole vault.
10 Use of intoxicants and such other drugs is forbidden for an athlete. He cannot even keep them with him during the event. The competitor keeping such drugs is liable to be disqualified.
11. Upto 800 metres race, the starter shall say in his own language" On your marks".........." set " and when all athletes are ready ,pistol shot shall be fired and the athletes start the race. For races above 800m only these words shall be said, "On your marks", and when the players get ready, the pistol shot shall be fired.
12 A competitor shall not touch the floor in front of him or start line with his hands or feet when he is in a position 'On his marks'
13 If an athlete crosses the start line before the pistol shot, his start shall be a foul. He shall be given a warning for it. If he persists in it he shall be disqualified in Pentathlon and Decathlon.
14. The position of the competitors is decided on the finish line first with toes is considered to have reached across first.
15. A competitor in hurdle race shall be disqualified if
(i) he obstructs other player by extending his hand and feet.
(ii) he covers the hurdle of others lane
(iii) in the opinion of a refree he fells the hurdle knowingly.
16. A competitor shall not be disqualified due to some reason other than the above mentioned rules.

A.A.A. (AMATEUR ATHLETIC ASSOCIATION)

Amateur Athletic Association was founded on 24 April 1880 at Oxford.It controls the sports section of men in England and Wales.The 400m hurdles champion of 1928 Olympic was the President known as Lord Burghley. The annual AAA Chamnpionships were first held in I980 now traditionally held at Crystal Palace in South London. Now AAA has its offices at Francis House,London.

THE MANAGER

The Manager shall be responsible for the correct conduct of the Meeting. He shall check that all officials have reported for duty, appoint substitutes when necessary and in cooperation with the appointed Marshal, arrange that only authorised persons are allowed in the centre of the arena.

UMPIRES (TRACK EVENTS)

Umpires are assistants to the Referee without authority to make final decision.

The Umpire shall be placed by the Referee in such a position that he may observe the competition closely and in the case of a foul or violation of the rules by a competitor or other person, make an immediate written report of the incident to the Referee.

Any such breach of the rules should be indicated by the raising of a red flag.

A sufficient number of Umpires should also be appointed to supervise the take over zones in relay races.

THE RECORDER

The recorder shall collect the full results of each event, details of which shall be provided by the Referee, the Chief Timekeeper or Chief Photo Finish Judge and the Wind Gauge Operator. He shall immediately relay these details to the Announcer, note the time this is done,record the results and hand the result sheet to the Manager of the meeting.

THE ANNOUNCER

The Announcer shall inform the public of the names and numbers of the competitors taking part in each event and all relevant information such as the composition of the heats, lanes or stations drawn and intermediate times. The result of each event should be announced at the earliest possible moment after receipt of the information from the Recorder.

THE INDOOR STADIUM

The stadium shall be completely enclosed and covered. Lighting, heating and ventilation shall be provided to give satisfactory conditions for competition.

The arena should include an oval track; a straight track for sprints and hurdles; runways and landing areas for high jump, pole vault and long jump or triple jump. In addition, a circle and landing sector for shot put should be provided, either permanently or temporarily.

All the tracks, runways or take-off surface areas shall be covered with a synthetic material or have a wooden surface. The former should preferably be able to accept 6mm spikes in running shoes.

REGISTRATION

Anyone competing in any open athletic competition in England or Wales promoted by a Club, Association or Managing Body which is not in possession of a permit for that particular competition, shall thereby disqualify himself from competing under A.A.A. Laws.

The following do not require registration:events promoted by and confined to H.M. Services;events confined to eomployees of a County or Local Authority; events open to pre-Service Organisations, combinations of Schools, Boy Scouts, Youth Clubs and other Juvenile Organisation.

Open Cross Country Races and Tug-of-War competitions may be held only by organisations holding permits from those sports associations.

ENTRIES

Every entry shall be made to the Secretary of the promoting body, who has the right to refuse an entry without giving a reason.

No entry either for individual or team events may be made except upon the form of entry issued or approved by the A.A.A.,which must be dated and completed with all the particulars required.

Every entry must be made in the real name of the competitor, which shall appear on the programme.

Every individual entry shall be signed by the intending competitor himself, who shall be responsible for all statements there in.

Every entry for a Colts, Boys, Youths, Juniors or Veterans race shall state the date of birth and present age in years and months of the intending competitor.

PRIZES

Money, saving certificates, bonds, stamps or cheques must not be offered as prizes; nor may vouchers or orders on tradesmen, except for book or record tokens and athletic clothing or equipment.

Every objection by a competitor to the value of a prize shall be made within 14 days.

DRESSING ACCOMMODATION

Every promoting body shall provide sufficient and convenient accommodation for the competitors.

Where a competition for colts or boys is included, separate dressing accommodation shall whenever possible be provided.

CLOTHING AND FOOTWEAR

In all events competitors must wear at least a vest and shorts which are clean and so designed and worn as not to be objectionable.

Competitors may compete in bare feet or with shoes on one or both feet. The purpose of shoes is to give protection and stability to the feet and a firm grip of the ground; they must not be constructed so as to give the competitor any additional assistance.

DIET

The good news is that most runners have a healthy appetite and stay trim. The bad news is that a poor diet can adversely affect performance. In this context poor meals lacking in nutrients rather than quantity, even if ample quantities are consumed, will be of only limited help unless they are properly balanced. It would be possible to fill several volumes on the subject of diet, but as most people in the West already enjoy a diet which is adequate to sustain a moderate amount of training, guidelines only are offered here.

Some athletes see diet as a possible short cut to improve performance,and many exaggerated claims have been made for particular foods. Even in the so called lands of plenty, there is considerable confusion and ignorance about this basic, fundamental fact of our existence and with the increasingly hectic pace of life and advent of convenient foods, many people are not getting the best out of the food stuffs available. On the other hand there are others who perhaps put too great a store on their plates and not enough in their training.

NUMBERS

Every competitor shall be supplied with and wear during competition a distinctive number corresponding with his number in the programme.

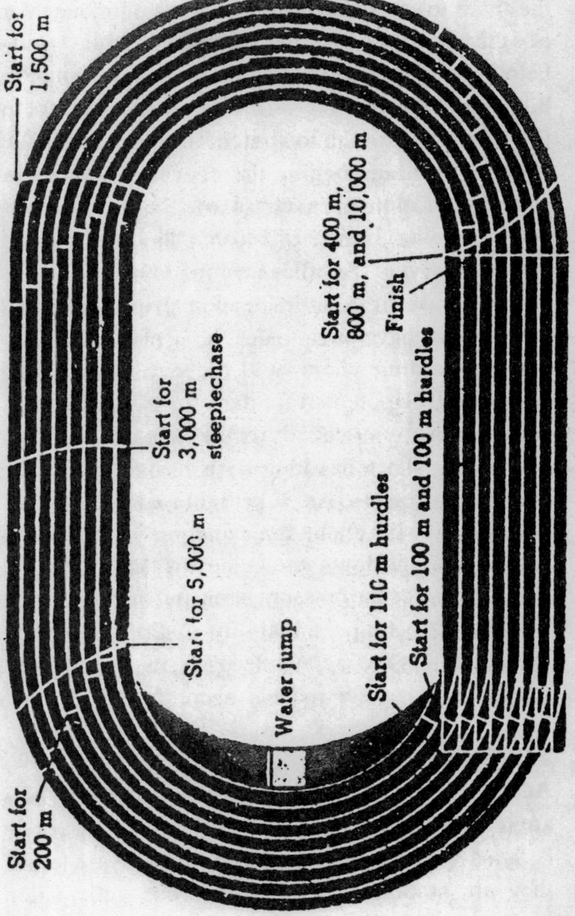

TRACK AND MEASUREMENTS

The inner edge of all tracks must be distinctly marked, cinder and other permanent tracks preferably by a raised border of concrete or other suitable material 2in (5cm) high otherwise by a chalk line or white tape.

Races upto 110m must be run on a straight course, in lanes, so as to alow a separate course for each competitor. The width between the lanes must be not less than 1.22m.

ATHLETICS INJURIES

ACHILLES TENDON

The Achilles tendon, which connects the calf to the heel bone, is frequently the site of pain among distance runners.Temporary insertion of heel pads in the shoes to slightly reduce the range of movement of the tendons, is the most effective self-help.Sudden change in training, such as a switch to hill running or wearing spiked shoes after months in flat shoes , is enough to stretch the tendon a little further. Training, jogging the recover in spikes can actually put more of a strain on the tendons than actual running. Exercises before and after training can help prevent Achilles tendon strain.

In case of Achilles tendon pain by training shoes which have worn under the heels,nothing less than discarding them will prevent the problem recurring. The potential for damage to the Achilles being caused by so-called Achilles tendon protectors on running shoes has long been recognised by the medical profession. As a precaution,the cutting of two vertical slits,about three quarters of an inch in length, straight down each side of the offending tabs,can reduce the pressure being put on the tendon without affecting the stability of the shoe. Shoe manufacturers are acknowledging this design and adapting their new models accordingly.

ADRENALINE

Adrenaline and Noradrenaline are hormones which are released by the adrenal glands when the body is faced with a stressful situation. In athletic terms, they are associated with the nervous anticipation of a competition,or a strenuous challenge like a marathon, and the heart rate and blood pressure are involuntarily increased in readiness for hard physical effort. If the anticipation of this sporting equivalent of fight or light is insufficient to set off this chain reaction, the athlete may complain of feeling flat, and subsequently perform below his normal level. But there is little doubt that to a reasonable degree such nervousness will actually heighten the ability of the body to perform well through the release of these hormones into the bloodstream.

Other physical signs of nervousness are yawning before a race and an increased need to visit the toilets. In normal pre-race circumstances, neither is a cause for concern.

AEROBIC RUNNING

Running at a pace at which the athletes can inhale sufficient oxygen to replenish that being burned up by the muscles. Conversely, an aerobic running involves a rate of activity that burns up oxygen faster than the athlete can replenish it, as in sprint races.

ARCH PROBLEMS

If you have trouble with the arch of your foot, such that it is too painful to run on, you should try to get a shoe with ample arch support or see a podiatrist about orthotics. In addition, you can strengthen your arches by rolling a towel in your toes or standing and rising on your toes while turning them inward.

BLISTERS

These skin injuries, caused by the heat of friction, can be prevented by wearing correctly fitting shoes and two pairs of socks, and keeping your feet dry by sprinkling powder in your shoes . If you get a blister, you should puncture it with a sterile needle, drain the fluid, and try to put some sort of protection around the blistered area, such as a foam donut or gauze and tape.

CALF

The calf is formed by two muscles. The gastrocnemius is the wide,dual muscle extending from the rear of the knee to midway down the lower leg, while the soleus lies beneath it but more towards the outer side of the leg.These muscles, known jointly as the triceps, merge into the Achilles tendon halfway down the leg and when the triceps is contracted the heel is pulled back and up by the Achilles tendon which is also known as the heel cord.

CALLISTHENICS

Stretching and suppling exercises used by sprinters, hurdlers, jumpers and throwers as part of the warm up routine to improve mobility for competition.

CALLUSES

Calluses large rough, thick areas of dead skin on the foot and are usually irritating to run on. An experienced person can shave them down with a razor blade, but caution is essential to avoid cutting live skin. You can also smooth a callus with a pumice stone, but the best ounce of prevention is a good pair of running shoes.

CHECK-UPS

The doctor's surgery is not the most exciting starting line for a sporting career, but for some it is an advisable port of call. If you have any doubts at all about your health you should go for a check up first, and if your own doctor is not prepared to do it, there are lots of other fitness testing centres that will. Even if you feel sure you are ready to run but if you fall into any of the following categories then a check up is a must.

- a are seriously overweight.
- b are over forty years of age
- c smoke or drink heavily
- d have not exercised for ten years
- e already have a medical condition
- f huff and puff after climbing the stairs
- g have high blood pressure
- h have a high pulse rate

It is, after all, only a minor inconvenience and a small price to pay for an all clear that can launch a new lifestyle.

COMMON COLD

Common cold is more of a problem for runners because they experience frequent changes in temperature and weather and are often in between being wet and dry. They also run down their reserves, so more care should be taken in showering and changing quickly, with an intake of vitamin C as an added insurance. Once you have got a cold, the best policy is to rest and certainly not to run. It could turn to something much worse. Running should never be considered if you have a temperature. On the other hand, asthma and hay fever should not stop you getting out, but ensure you always have your inhaler with you.

CRAMP

Cramp is one of the most common, usually in the calf muscles, which occurs when you are overtired or have lost a lot of minerals in your sweat. You can treat it by grabbing hold of your leg and gradually stretching it in the opposite direction of the contraction. Cramp can be prevented by taking in adequate amounts of electrolytes before and during your run.

HAMSTRING INJURY

Common athletics injury, especially in sprinters and hurdlers, in which the tendon located behind the knee is wrenched or even torn, usually when the athlete is running at full speed.

INJURY

Vast majority of distance runners experienced injuries caused through constant repetition of an exercise(running). Other sport injuries are direct, involving physical contact, such as in a crushing soccer tackle. Indirect injury is caused by a violent force involving physical contact such as twisting an ankle by stepping in a hole.

The human body is designed to work in symmetry, but if one small aspect of the machine goes wrong, the whole work is thrown out of synchronization.

KNEE

The knee is one of the three great stabilizers for the runner, along with the ankle and hip. Knee pain can take frustrating form of injury, because of the inaccessibility of its complex working. The knee is the joint where the lower end of the thigh bone meets the upper end of the shinbone to form what is basically a hinge, but with some limited rotational movement.

Within the knee are two semilunar shaped cartilages, or menisci, which act as cushioning. It is this type of cartilage, rather than the normal connective tissue on joint surfaces, which may be surgically removed if damaged. The growing use of arthroscopy in knee surgery has meant that the joint is not quite the stubborn challenge to the medical world it used to be, but it is still the area in which specific expertise is most needed for diagnosis of injury.

LEGS AND LUNGS

Distance running has little to do with style or skill. Look at any group of distance runners doing their laps. You will see many kinds of styles and different stride lengths. There are tall and short runners, well built and skinny ones. But they all run in a relaxed manner. To do this at good speed, lap after lap requires a lot of training. Training, or conditioning, develops the legs and lungs, and helps the heart adjust to the strain.

LOWER BACK PAIN

Sometimes lower-back pain stems from foot problems; the feet and legs adjust to the problems, but the runner's gait changes, altering the centre of gravity in the lower back and causing strain. Adequate stretching can prevent foot problems and thus, lower back problems.

Lower-back pain may also come from having weak abdominal muscles, which is why a cornerstone exercise for all athletes is the bent-knee sit-up.A regular regimen of bent-knee sit-ups, along with other conditioning exercises, is an excellent means to keep both abdominal and back muscles in proper shape.

LUNGS

The lungs are the organs which provide the facility for fresh oxygen to be absorbed into the blood and the unwanted carbon dioxide, created by energy production, to exhale. When breathing the lungs expand to their maximum volume as air is taken in through the nose and mouth and down windpipe. There are 300 million alveoli in an adult pair of lungs and each is covered with a network of blood capillaries which come from the pulmonary artery, then return to the pulmonary vein, taking back blood cells which have been replenished with fresh oxygen. The maximum volume of the lungs known as the vital capacity, can be measured on a special device known as a spirometer, into which the subject exhales as completely as possible after taking one very deep breath. When running, the breathing rate increases quite considerably, usually upto fifty times a minute, as the need for oxygen in the muscles becomes much greater. Particularly in middle distance events this efficiency can be crucial, as the value of training sessions which stimulate this situation and thus help the body adapt to it in preparation for a race can be realized.

ORTHOTICS

Where foot or leg imbalance occurs or there are other joint problems, it is now possible to construct custom-made shoe inserts, which are built up in specific areas, in order to correct imbalances during the running action. Many athletes have found that orthotics have cured long-standing injury problems.

RUNNERS KNEE

Runner's or jumper's knee is a catch all name for an irritating injury that can be tendinitis, tenosynovitis or torn cartilage. Depending on the extent of the condition, many trainers have found that you can still practice and compete with runner's or jumper's knee so long as you warm it up with heat before practice and treat it with ice after practice. It also helps if you take a slow,long warmup and jog before competition.

SIDE STITCHES

Side stitches, which can occur during a run, are severe pains below the rib cage in the abdominal area and you feel as if a knife is sticking into your body. They occur when the diaphragm is deprived of oxygen. They will disappear if you slow your pace and use more stomach muscles to inhale and exhale more deeply. You can also squeeze your side as you run, which may relieve the pain.

STAMINA

Sprinters need stamina to keep them going once they have reached their maximum speed. Distance runners need stamina to keep running lap after lap. Building up stamina is a matter of conditioning your legs and your breathing. This means running regularly and gradually building up your training programme. It is possible to run too much in training or do things that may do more harm than good. Any one who thinks seriously of taking up running as a sport should seek the advice of a coach.There are certainly several theories. Finding the method that suits you best might involve much trial and error. But you have to have confidence in your training programme.

WHO'S WHO IN ATHLETICS

ABADA, PATRICK

France (born 20th March,1954)- The veteran Abada made a great comeback after missing 1980/81 season. In World Cup 1979 he won silver and in European Cup 1983 captured gold. He was rated number three in the World in 1983.

ABASCAL, JOSE
Spain (born 17th March,1958) - In 1982, when Sebastian Coe and Steve Ovett were missing he got a European bronze in Athens. In 1983, he was fifth in 1500m World Championships.

ABRAHAMS, H.M.
U.K. (born 15th December, 1899). Distinguished himself in athletics in five fields-performer, administrator, writer, broadcaster and statistician. Won the 1924 Olympic 100m title.

ABRAMOV, VALERIY
U.S.S.R. (born 22nd Aug,1956) - He was eleventh in 5000m of World Championships 1983 and sixth in European Championships 1982 of 5000m.

ACKERMANN, ROSEMARIE
East Germany (born 1952) - In high jump Rosi Ackermann made history in West Berlin on 26 August 1977, when she became the first woman to clear 2 metres. It was, however, her last major success, as she struggled to overcome a succession of injuries and flight off the challenge of her main rival, Italy's Sara Simeoni. She was East German national champion six times.

AKABUSI, KRISS
U.K. (born 28th November,1958) Has been an invaluable member of 4x400m relay teams and consistently sub 46 seconds. Turned to 400m hurdling in 1987 and improved in his first three meetings. Made a great breakthrough with 48.64 sec and 48.74 sec at the World Championships.

AKII-BUA,JOHN
Uganda (born 1949) - Olympic 400m hurdles champion in 1972, Akii-Bua started his athletics career as an unsuccessful high hurdler, failing to qualify for the 1968 Olympic Games in Mexico. He topped the world rankings in 1973 with 48.5, but did not compete in the Commonwealth Games 1974.

ALDER, J.N.C.
U.K. (born 10th June, 1940) - Won 1960 Commonwealth marathon title in Tokyo in 2 hr. 22 min. 07.8 sec. Captured the world record of 30,000m during two hour track race at Walton.

AMBROZENE, ANNA
U.S.S.R. (born 14th August,1955) - Ambrozene's world record did not help her in Helsinki when she was beaten in Helsinki by her team mate. She earned silver in 400m 1983 World Championships. She also won a silver in European Cup 1981 and 1983, in 400m hurdles.

AOUITA, SAID
Morocco (born 2nd November,1960) - The middle distance sensation of 1983, he took third place in World Championships in Helsinki.He won the Gold Medal in 1500m in 1981. In African Championship he won silver in 1982.

APPLEGARTH, W.R.
U.K. (1890-1958)- He did marvellously well in furlong. In this event he owned or shared the world record for all of 17 year.

ARKHIPENKO, VASILIY
U.S.S.R. (born 28th January,1957) - One of Europe's most consistent performers in 400m. hurdles. He holds the Soviet record with 48.34 sec. In 1980 Olympic games he won silver in 400m hurdle. He was lucky to win silver in Moscow with the Americans boycott of the game.

ASHFORD, EVELYN
U.S.A. (born 15th April,1957). In the World Cups 1979 and 1981 she won gold in 100m and 200m sprints. She has an unorthodox heelflicking style, which she has refused to modify.

ATKINS, KEVIN
U.S.A. (born 27th January,1960) - At the age of 22 he won American Championship in shot put and won a gold in 1982.He could not get it in Helsinki and was a sensational non-qualifier.

AUDAIN, ANNE
New Zealand (born 1st November,1955) - Has had considerable success in recent years on the US road running circuit. Ran the then fastest debut marathon for fourth at Chicago in 1983.

AYRTON, ZENIA
India (born 16th March,1972) A University student

from Bombay, has represented the country in 100m and won a Bronze medal in the Asian Junior Championships in 1990 in Beijing.

BALAS, I.
Romania (born 12th December, 1936). 6ft. 0 1/4 in. tall. She has completely dominated the women high jumping ever since 1958. Won Olympic golds in 1960 and 1964, the European titles in 1958 and 1962. And she has cleared 6 ft. or higher in more than 50 competitions since 1958.

BALCHA, KEBEDE
Ethiopia (born 9th September,1951) - He won the Montreal marathon three times, and was fourth in the London Marathon in 1983 and also won silver in World Championships marathon.

BANKS, WILLIE
U.S.A. (born 11th March,1956) - Willie Banks has turned one of the track and field's more esoteric disciplines into a fun event with his bubbling personality. In World Championships 1983 he won silver in triple jump and bronze in 1981 World Cup.

BANNISTER, ROGER
U.K. (born 23rd March, 1929) - Although he only won one CG medal, it was in one of the Games'with classic confrontations. In the 1954 with mile he was matched against Australian John Landy the only two men in the world to have bettered four minutes and it was the Englishman who came out the winner as he ran his second and last sub-4minute mile. In his only Olympics he finished 4th in the 1500 metres in 1952. He won 1954 European 1500 metres and as everyone knows,ran the first 4 minute mile at Oxford in 1954. He was knighted in 1975.

BARBOSA, JOSE LUIS
Brazil (born 27th May, 1961) - A very consistent 800m runner. He won silver in Pan American Games 1987, and gold in 1987 World Indoor Championships.

BARRIOS, ARTURO
Mexico (born 12th December,1963) - Had an outstanding season on the 1986 US road running circuit, when he set a world 10km road best for a loop course of 27:41 at Phoenix and also had important 15km wins at Jacksonville and Portland. First major win was in 1980 Pan American Junior 5000m

BARRY, STEVE
U.K. (born 25th October, 1950) - The first British walker to approach true world class in almost a decade, he captured the Commonwealth Games 30 km title, ahead of a strong international field, in a fast time of 2h. 10min. 16sec. in 1982. He also set UK track records at 20 km and 10 km in 1981 and 1982, respectively. A super fast 20 km road walk of 1:22:51 early in 1983 suggested great things at the World Championships but injury eventually ruled him out of the reckoning.

BAUTISTA, DANIEL
Mexico (born 1952) - He won the I.A.A.F.Race Walking World Cup (the Lugano Trophy) twice, in 1977 and 1979, setting his world best 20 km mark at the latter event in Eschborn,West Germany. He retired soon after the 1980 Olympic Games.

BAYI, FILBERT
Tanzania (born 23 June,1953) - Bayi 1500 Commonwealth Games metres win in 1974 was one of the all time great races, Bayi leading from start to finish in a new world record time of 3:32.2 to beat John Walker. He set second world record the following year when he lowered the mile record to 3:51.0. He lost his Commonwealth Games 1500 metres title to Dave Moorcroft in 1978 after coming back from a serious injury, though he led for almost of the race. In 1980 he again lost in the last few strides in the Olympic steeplechase final to Poland's Bronislaw Manilowski.

BEAMON, BOB
U.S.A. (born 29th August,1946) -His claim to fame was an incredible leap of 8.90 metres during the 1968 Olympics in Mexico- 29ft 2(1/2)in when the rest of the world were struggling to clear 27ft. It is a record that has only come under threat with the appearance of Carl Lewis. It was a leap that astonished everyone, including Britain's Lynn Davies who had won the gold medal four years earlier in Tokyo. It made nonsense of the previous

30 years record, in which the gap had been increased by the nearest of decimals. It also became a one off, for never again did Beamon get near his achievement. According to the record books, he never got past 8.20 metres after Mexico. In fairness, he did suffer serious hamstring injuries to his right leg, and finally turned professional in 1973.

BEARDSLEY, DICK

U.S.A. (born 21st March,1956) - He was the joint winner of the London Marathon in 1981, but a leg injury put stop to his world championship hopes.

BECKER, U.W.E.

West Germany (born 10th December,1955) - He like everybody else in the 800 and 1500 metres,has suffered because of the excellence of Coe and Ovett. He was 11th in 1983 World Championships and 6th in European Championships.

BENOIT, JOAN

U.S.A. (born 16th March, 1957) - Already the third fastest woman marathoner at the end of 1982. she produced an astonishing run in the 1983 Boston race smashing the previous women's world best by 2 min. 47 sec. with 2:22:43, which would have won the gold medal in the men's marathon at the 1956 Olympic Games.

BENNETT, TODD

U.K. (born 6th July,1962) - A precacious talent as a teenager, he won the European Junior Championships 400 metres title in 1981. He picked up gold and silver medals in the 4x400 metres relays in Brisbane and at the European Championships the same year.

BEYER, OLAF

East Germany (born 4th August,1957) - His victory in the 1978 European Championships was one of the biggest shock of the decade.After that he won bronze in 800m European Cup 1981.

BEYER, UDO

East Germany (born 9th August,1955) - In Olympic Games 1976 and 1980, in shot put he won gold and bronze respectively. He captured gold in European Championships. In the World Cup 1977,1979, and 1981 he won gold in shot put. Still a sports student at the age of 28, has ruled world shot putting since he won a surprise gold in Montreal.

BIKILA, ABEBE

Ethopia (1932-1973) -As a virtual unknown and running barefoot, Abebe Bikila won the 1960 Olympic marathon in 2hr 15min 16.2sec, a world's best time. In 1964 he became the first man to win the Olympic marathon twice, recording another world's best with 2hr 12min 11.2 sec. in Tokyo. In 1968 a serious leg injury forced his retirement from the Olympics. A year later he received severe injuries in a car crash, which left him paralysed and led to his death in 1973.

BLACK, ROGER

U.K. (born 31st March, 1966) - Made a brilliant start to his international career with six gold medals both 400m and 4x400m relay, in three international championships in 1985-86.

BLANKERS-KOEN, F.E.

The Netherlands (born 26th April, 1918) - She won four gold medals at the 1948 Olympic Games in London in 100m, 200m and 800m hurdles and enabled the Dutch 4x100m relay team to victory. Between 1938 and 1951, she set official world records in no fewer than seven individual events.

BLAZER, K.

East Germany (born 5th June, 1938) - Twice hurdles champion in the European Championships.

BOARD, LILLIAN

South Africa (1948-1970) - She was born in South Africa, her family came to Britain in 1950, and, on moving to London, Lillian was soon running well for her club, London Olympiades. She first started placing at high level in 1966, coming fourth in the W.A.A.A. Championships 440 yards (in a very respectable 54.6), and fifth in the Commonwealth Games final at the same distance.

BOIT, MOKE

Kenya (born 1st January,1949) - In 1981, he twice chased Sebastian Coe home in his two world mile record races and in 1982 was still able to lift a medal in the Commonwealth 1500 metres. He won silver in 1979 World Cup 800 metres championship.

BOLOTNIKOV, P.

U.S.S.R. (born 8th March, 1930) - In 1957, won the Soviet 10,000m. championship. In 1960, he won the Olympic title and lowered the world record to 28 min. 18.8 sec. In 1962, he won the European title and improved his record to 28 min. 18.2 sec.

BOSTON, R. H.

U.S.A. (born 9th May, 1939) - Won the Olympic Championship in long jump in 1960 breaking Jesse Owens' world record after 25 years, no doubt a most outstanding achievement and became the first to leap over 27 ft. In 1964, he improved his mark to 27ft. 5in. He was an all-rounder of high order.

BOXER, CHRISTINA

U.K. (born 25th March, 1953) - In 1979, she set a UK mile record of 4:30.2 and became the first British woman to break 2 minutes for 800 metres. She had to wait until 1982 to win her first major international title, winning the 1500 metres at the Commonwealth Games. She also reached the 1980 Olympic 800 metres semi-finals and the 1500 metres final at the 1983 World Championships.

BRASHER, C.W.

U.K. (born 21st August, 1928). Won the 1960 Olympic race at Melbourne in record time of 8 min. 41.2 sec.He cut his mile time to 4 min. 09.0 sec. He was later known as Roger Bannister' pacemaker and training companion.

BRIGHTWELL, R.I.

U.K. (born 27th October, 1939) - He won the AAA junior title in 220 yds. in 1957. At the 1960 Olympics he just failed to reach the 400 m. final after twice breaking the UK record in the preliminary rounds.

BRILL, DEBBIE

Canada (born 10th March,1953) - A twelve year gap separated Brill's two Commonwealth Games triumphs and proved that even at twenty nine, and a mother, she can take on the best in the world.She won gold in high-jump in Commonwealth Games 1970 and 1982,silver in 1978. She won another gold in World Cup 1979.

BROWN, A.G.K.

U.K. (born 21st February, 1915) - In 1936 Olympic 400 m. final in Britain, he lowered the European record to 46.7 sec. only to lose by a mere two-hundredths of a second to the world record holder Archie Williams. He anchored the British team to an easy victory in the 4x400 m relay. In his finest run just after the games, he was timed at 45.9 sec. for a 440 yd. relay leg and snatched a win for his Commonwealth team. In 1938,he won the European 400 m title.

BRUMEL, V.

U.S.S.R. (born 14th April, 1942) - In 1960, at the age of 18, he set a European record of 7 ft. 2 (½) in. in high jump and won the silver medal in the Olympic games. He shared the Olympic record of 7 ft. 1 in. He shared the 1964 Olympic title with John Thomas at 7ft. 1 (½) in. He is the highest jumper of all-time both in terms of elevation {7 ft. 5 (½ in} and the number of inches he has leapt above his own head.

BRYGGARE, ARTO

Finland (born 26th May,1958) - He became the first Finnish to win a medal in the 1983 110m hurdles World Championships. He also won bronze in 1978 and 1982 European Championships.

BUBKA, SURGEY

U.S.S.R. (born 4th December,1963) - World champion in 1983 has gone on to dominate the world of Pole Vaulting, and has not been beaten in championships since then. Has the speed and strength to manage a very high hold on the pole.

BUDD, ZOLA

South Africa (born 26th May, 1966) - Zola Budd was a marvellous bare foot runner. She made a series of unofficial world junior records at the age of 17, plus a 5000m time of 15;O1.83 which was nearly seven seconds inside Mary Decker's world record. Because of being a South African and due to apartheid policy, she was banned from the Olympics and from international competitions. She, however, acquired British citizenship as her grandfather was a Londoner after great botheration. Physically protected and facing heavy opposition, she made her mark in many events. Her first Olympics in Los Angles were to end in highly charged controversy.Watched by hundreds of millions on television, the do-or-die just between Zola and American number one runner Mary Decker in the 3000 metres final climaxed in Decker's crashing fall, tears. and tension in the most debated debacle in modern Olympics. After humiliation, she decided to settle in South Africa permanently but changed her mind and came again to England. Again she ran in the face of great opposition and heavy odds. In the European Cup final in Moscow, she led all the way in the 3000 m to record Britain's first European Cup final women's track win for eighteen years. Her time of 8:35.32 was a Commonwealth record and she reduced it to 8:28.83 in Rome, as well as becoming the first female UK runner to break four minutes for 1500m (with 3.59 in Brussels), had set a Commonwealth mile record of 4:17.57 in Zurich and broken the world 5000m record.

BUGAR, IMRICH

Czechoslovakia (born 14th April,1955) -The ability of this country to produce world class discus throwers continued with Bugar, who took over from the great Ludvik Danek, holder of silver in discus at 1980 Olympics. He too had gold in 1983 World Championships. Again in European Championships 1978 and 1982 he captured gold and bronze.

BURKI, CORNELIA

Switzerland (born 3rd October,1953) - Her two daughters were born in 1972, before she began her running career. Very consistent in major events, she achieved her best ever placings in Rome 1987.

BURGHLEY, LORD

U.K. (born 5th February,1905) - Olympic 400 m hurdles winner in 1928 and fourth (in his fastest time) in 1932, silver medallist in the 1932 Olympic 4 x 400 m. relay, triple gold medallist at the 1930 Commonwealth Games - 120 yds. hurdles, 440 yds. hurdles and 4 x 440 yds. relay. He has been president of the AAA since 1936 and of the International Amateur Athletic Federation since 1946.

BUTLER, G.M.

U.K. (Born -25th August, 1899). For 40 years Guy Butler remained Britain's most bemedalled Olympian with one gold, one silver and two bronze awards to his name. In 1920 Olympics, he won silver in 400 m and brought the British team to victory in the 4 x 400 m relay. In 1924, he was third in the Olympic 400 m. Another bronze, he gained in the relay. He also worked as coach, writer and cine photographer.

BYKOVA, TAMARA

U.S.S.R. (born 21st December,1958) - A fascinating racial mixture, half Greek/half Russian, the statuesque blonde won the gold in high jump in 1983 World Championships. Earned a silver in 1982 European Championships and another silver in European Cup 1983. In World Student Games she earned gold in 1983.

CAETANO DA SILVA, ROBSON

Brazil (born 4th September, 1964) - In 1987 World Championships he was placed fourth in 200m and won gold in 1985 World Cup.

CALHOUN, L.Q.

U.S.A. (born 23rd February, 1933) - He won the Olympics 110m hurdles twice in 1956 and 1960. He is co-holder of the world records for 110 m and 120 yd hurdles at 13.2 sec. in 1960 and is considered one of the finest hurdling exponent of all -time.

CAMERON, BERT

Jamaica (born 16th November,1959) - In 1982 he won his third NCAAA 400 metres title in 44.62, which was the fastest in the world that year. He won gold in 400m in World Championships and Commonwealth Games.

CAMPBELL, TONIE

U.S.A. (born 14th June, 1960) - He is reckoned by statisticians to be the best athlete who did not go to the World Championships. In 1981 World's

Students games he claimed 4th position in 110 metres hurdles.

CANTO, ERNESTO

Mexico (born 18th October,1959) - Continuing Mexico's fine tradition in race walking, he captured the 20 km title at the 1983 World Championships at the age of 23 and quickly followed that with a second win, over the same distance, at the Pan American Games. One of the first walkers to clock sub 1h 20min. for 20 km, he won his first major event,the Lugano Trophy.

CARISTAN, STEPHANE

France (born 31st May, 1964) - In 1986, European Championships he won gold in 110m hurdle. Two European 110m hurdle records in 1986. Operation on right knee in March held back his 1987 season.

CARR, H.

U.S.A. (born 27th November,1942) - He established himself as the greatest furlong athlete the world had yet seen. He won over 400 m in 45.4 sec in the 1963 West Germany vs. USA match and over 440 yd. in 46.0 sec. in Australia shortly after the 1964 Olympics. He won two gold medals in 1964 Olympic in 200 m in 20.3 sec and anchoring USA in the 4x400 m relay.

CASTELLA, ROBERT DE

Australia (born 1957) - He became one of the world's most consistent marathon runners after he made his debut at the distance in 1979. He has since completed 16 marathons, six under 2:10 and all under 2:15 and has won eight of them. The only one he failed to finish was in Rome in 1987 at the I.A.A.F.World Championships, where he was strongly fancied to win.

CASTRO,DOMINGOS

Portugal (born 22nd November,1963) - Broke into top class in 1986 and continued the progress in 1987 when he was a surprise silver medalist at 5000m in Rome.

CAWLEY, W.J.

U.S.A. (born 6th July, 1940) - When 18, he made history by becoming the only athlete ever to place in the first six of all three hurdles finals at the American AAU Championships. He set a new world's 400 m hurdles record of 49.1 sec in the final of US Olympic Trials and powered to victory in the Olympics (49.6 sec) in 1964.

CHATAWAY, C.J.

U.K. (born 31st January, 1931) - Few athletes have enjoyed such widespread popularity as Chri Chataway. It was Chataway who pulled Roger Bannister to the first four minute mile and pushed John Landy to the second, and thereafter himself broke the barrier in 1955.

CIERPINSKI, WALDEMAR

East Germany (borh 3rd August,1950) - He managed fastest of 2:12.20 when finished 4th in the Prague Europeans marathon, but he emulated Bikila's feat of retaining the Olympic title with 2:11.03, the second fastest time of his life.

He won marathon gold in 1976 and 1980 Olympic Games.

CLARK, DARREN

Australia (born 6th September, 1965) - At 17 won 400m AAA title in 1983. Ran a 43.86 relay leg in 1984 Olympics. Three Australian 400m records in 1985-1986 and two Commonwealth 300m bests in 1985-86.

CLARKE, DAVE

U.K. (born 1st January, 1958) - One of the best and outstanding British cross country runners in recent years. Finished second in 1981 and 1983. He is also an accomplished track runner.

CLARKE, R.W.

Australia (born 21st February, 1937) - He was setter of world records for seven events simultaneously - 3 miles, 500m, 6miles, 10,000m, 10 miles, 20,000m.

In 1964, he won the Olympic 10,000 m and in 1966 he won two silver medals in addition to the one he obtained in the 3 mi four years earlier.

Altogether he won three silver medals at the Commonwealth Games from 1962 to 1966 and finally bowed out with yet another silver at the Commonwealth Games in the 10,000 metres in 1970.

CLAYTON, DEREK

Australia (born 1942) - One of only three men to have set two world bests in the marathon (the other two are Jim Peters of Great Britain and Abebe Bikila of Ethiopia). At the Olympics in 1968 he could only finish seventh,having been plagued by cartilage trouble earlier in the year. He went into the Olympics as only the ninth fastest man that year, with a 1968 best of 2:14:47.8.

COOK, KATHY

U.K. (born 3rd.May,1960) - She won silver in 1982 European Championships in 400m sprints. She again won a silver in Comonwealth Games in the same year. She married to Garry Cook,one of the Britain's top 800 metres men.

COE, SEBASTIAN

U.K. (born 29 Sep., 1956) - When Sebastian Coe became the first man ever to retain the Olympic 1500m title in 1984 at Los Angeles it helped to reduce the painful memories in the intervening four years since he had first won the title at Moscow.

After Coe's decade in the top strata of international middle distance running,with a host of world records and big victories, it is still surprising to realize that upto the end of 1986 his tally of gold medals in major championships was just three. His rivalry with Steve Ovett, constantly if unconvincingly denied, helped to promote public awareness of the sports in the U.K. London born Coe joined the Sheffield Club,Hallamshire Harriers at the age of 12. His father studied books and magazines and attended coaching courses, to learn all he could to devise a training schedule suitable for his son. At the age of 14 he was Yorkshire schools junior cross country champion. Far from becoming a 1500/ 3000m specialist, Sebastian decided with his father that his competitive career should be moving down in distance rather than up. His further training,which now included a great deal of sprinting and mobility work was clearly paying off and by 1978 it was certain that Coe would be a force at that year's European Championship in Prague especially when he improved his own UK record. Coe and Ovett met in the final at Prague. Coe stormed through the first lap in under 50 seconds with Ovett right on his shoulder. It was disappointing for both of them as the East German's Olaf Beyer passed them to snatch the gold. They finally met for only the second time on the track at the 1980 Moscow Olympics where both ran the 800m and 1500m, despite not having raced each other during the selection process. Yet on the eve of the games, in Oslo, both had set world records within an hour.But six days later in the 1500m final, the tables were turned . Coe, desperate to make amends for his disappointment in the 800m,turned in a last lap. Ovett, unable to mount a real challenge , was third.

As early as 10 June 1981, Coe produced a phenomenal world 800m record in Florence, and was so dominant on the stop-watch that the average of his five fastest 800m races at that moment (1:43.27) was faster than any other rumner had achieved even once. Ovett, contented with his Olympic gold medal at the 800m,left the shorter distance records to Coe. The 1982 season offered chances of gold medals to both the Champions, but for Coe it was to prove a dismal year. Following a stress fracture in his foot he pulled out of the Commonwealth Games due to glandular fever. By the time of the European Championships Coe had recovered, and in a glorious moment for British Athletics, he, Cram, and the young Scot Tom Mckean battled out the 800m medals down the home straight. This time at last,Coe was the winner in 1:44.50, but a few days later, attempting the double, he had to give best to the determined Cram in the 1500m, losing in a furious last 800m run in 1:46.0. Coe was ready to explore a new chapter of his career, while combining his running with a part-time post as Vice Chairman of the Sports Council.

COGHLAN, EAMONN

Ireland (born 21st November,1952) - Eamonn's delight at winning gold in Helsinki was understandable; he finished Ist in the major championships. He finished 4th in 5000m and 1500m in Olympic Games 1976 and 1980 respectively. He claimed gold medal in 1983 World Championships and World Cup.

CONSOLINI, A.

Italy (born 5th January, 1917) - He had a consistent

long career in the top flight as discus thrower. He broke the world record three times - in 1941 (175ft. 0in.), 1946 (177ft. 11in.) and 1948 (181ft. 6(1/2)in.). However, his throw (186ft. 11(1/2)in) in 1955 was his best. He was Olympic Champion in 1948 and silver medallist in 1952. In 1946, 1950 and 1954 he was European Champion.

CONNOR, KEITH

West Indies (born 16th September,1957) - Connor went into the World Championships as favourite but he came out as a non qualifier. He was fourth in Olympic Games 1980 triple jump. In European Games he won a gold in 1982.

COOPER, J.H.

U.K. (born 18th December, 1940). He was the sole holder of the U.K. 400m hurdle record in 1963 when he won against the Russian Federation Republic in Volgograd in 50.5 sec. In 1964 Olympic he won 400m hurdle in 50.5 sec. and semi-final in 50.4 sec. and in the final he got Olympic silver medal with yet another U.K. record 50.1 sec. Later in the Games with his official personal best 440 yds. time of 47.9 sec., he stormed through his 400m in 45.6 sec., making Britain take second place.

COOPER, BRAD

Bahamas (born 30th June,1957) - An immense man, Cooper shows the difference in throwing event standards between the Commonwealth, the USA and Eastern bloc. He won gold in Commonwealth Games 1982 and silver in 1978 for discus throw.

COVA, ALBERTO

Italy (born 1st December,1958) - He will be a favourite for the 5000m and 10,000m. He won the gold in 1983 World Championships and 1982 European Championships in 10,000m. He also won silver in 1983 European Cup.

CRAM, STEVE

U.K. (born 14 October,1960)- It seemed unlikely, at a time around 1980, when British athletics was still marvelling at its good fortune in simultaneously having two such brilliant 1500m runners as Steve Ovett and Sebastian Coe, that a third runner of similar stature could emerge.

He followed both his countrymen as a holder of the world record but to reach that position, he passed through a number of obstacles which could have side tracked him. His attention became focused more on running and encouraged by Jimmy Hedley, coach.

Some encouraging performances in 1975, notably in the English Schools Junior Championships,where he was third in the cross country and fourth in the 1500m, helped reassure Cram that he had made the right choice of sport, and guided by Hedley he soon made his mark as one of Britain's leading young middle distance pospects. In May 1977, Cram surprised the athletics world by running a UK age 16 best of 3:47.7 for 1500m at Gateshead. During the Durham School Championships in June ,passing 400m in 58 seconds during a self-made run in a race which he won by over 15 seconds. His time was 2.2 seconds faster than the UK best set by Steve Ovett. A month later with the Commonwealth Games approaching,the Scottish selectors did not send Williamson and Cram was picked for England and although he did not get through his heat, it was the start of an international apprenticeship which was to continue for some years, but then pay valuable dividends. At the UK Championships in June ,the main trial, disaster struck Cram, who tripped and fell just after the bell, and jogged home a dejected last, while Williamson finished second to Dave Moorcroft. But with Moorcroft opting for the 5000m in Moscow instead and Cram a few days later in Norway running the fastest time by a British athlete in 1980 with a 3:37.3 to ease his frustration the selectors asked Williamson and Cram to race again during a Dream Mile in Oslo in July. Cram finished second. In 1981, he continued to be rather overshadowed by the Big Two (Seb. Coe & Steve Ovett), but he was getting closer. But if,in 1982, he was able to step out of the shadow a little, he still did not feel he was fully accepted although he won both the titles that year as Coe was ill. A year later,at the inaugural World Championships in Helsinki, he added another gold medal to his collection as Coe was again absent and Ovett had run an uncharacteristically poor tactical race.

Most memorable race for British fans that

season came in the IAC Coca Cola Floodlit event at Crystal Palace on 9th September. Ovett announced that he,too, would run the mile. He wanted another crack at Cram before the end of the year. Ovett had lost the World title, but he wanted to even the score,especially as his world 1500m record had shown him he was in terrific form. Cram made the first move from 350m out, and Ovett chased him all the way to the finish, just a stride behind. In the home straight, he could not get on terms and Cram remained just infront, to win. Meanwhile, Cram was being treated for an injury to his right calf, which had seriously interrupted his Los Angeles preparation. He finished second to Coe in Los Angeles. He set his first world record for 1500m narrowly beating Olympic 5000m Champion Said Aouita of Morocco in July 1985 and take revenge on Sebastian Coe by beating him in Oslo and taking his world mile record away on 27th July. He even narrowly missed setting a world 1000m record in poor weather conditions at his native Gateshead on 9 August,and while he was still getting faster in training, beat Olympic 800m Champion Joaquim Cruz in Zurich in his fastest ever 800m time of 1:42.88. But a hamstring injury, frustratingly, ended his phenomenal season.Cram turned the tables again on Coe, outsprinting him on the final lap of the 1500m final, to end the championship season on a high note, with at least three of his four gold medals.

In some ways, not winning the 1984 Olympic title may have been a godsend to Cram. Trying to win the one 1500m title to have eluded him keeps him motivated. "I have got to try to win it in Seoul, otherwise when I am 50 people will still come up to me and say you weren't as good as Coe because you never won the Olympics."

CRAWFORD, HASELY

Trinidad (born 1950) - He was the winner of the 100m title in Montreal in 1976. Facing an impressive field, including defending champion Valeriy Borzov of the Soviet Union, Don Quarrie of Jamaica, and Havey Glance of the USA, his winning time of 10.06 seconds placed him sixth on the all time list.

CRUZ, JOAQUIM

Brazil (born 12th March,1963) - He was world junior record holder in 1981. He won bronze in the World Championships of 800m. 1983. Missed 1986 season due to Achilles Tendinitis and had surgery, although he came back in 1987, also had to miss World Championships.

CUSMIR, ANISOARA

Romania (born 28th June,1962) - She won silver in 1983 World Championships of long jump event. In 1982, she got silver in European Championships and a gold in 1983 in World Students Games.

CUTHBERT, B.

Australia (born 20th April, 1938) - In the 1956 Olympic games in Melbourne, she won three gold medals - 100 m., 200 m. and 4x100 m. relay. In the 1962 Commonwealth Games, she got victory for the Australian relay team. At the 1964 Olympics, she won the 400 m. in 52.0 sec.

DAMILANO, MAURIZIO

Italy (born 6th April,1957) -He won 20km walk gold in 1980 Olympic Games and was seventh in 20 km walk World Championships. His twin brother Giorgio, coached like Maurizio by brother Sandro, was eleventh in Moscow.

DANEK, L.

Czechoslovakia (born 29th September, 1927) - A brilliant discus thrower. He was world record holder with 211ft. 9 ½in. He finished second , 19in. behind in 1964 Olympics. In 1965, he raised his world record to 213 ft. 11 ½in. He exceeded 60 m. in more than 80 different meetings, no other thrower reached even 30.

DIAZ, CRUZ MARIA

Spain (born 24th October,1969) - Was the youngest ever Spanish internatonal at the age of 13 in 1983 World Race Walking Cup and the youngest ever individual European Champion in 1986.

DA SILVA, A.F.

Brazil (born 29th September, 1927) - He won every major triple jump he participated. He was Olympic Champion in 1952 and 1956, Pan-American Champion in 1951, 1955 and 1959. He held the world record from 1950 to 1953 and from 1955 to 1958. His best was 54ft. 4in. in 1950.

DAUTE, HEIKE

East Germany (born 16th December,1964) - Two gold medals, at the age of only eighteen, including a shock first place in World Championship 1983 in long jump.

DAVIS, G.A.

U.S.A. (born 12th July, 1932) - He set many world records in hurdles - 440yd. flat (45.7 sec.), 400m. hurdles (49.2 sec.), 440 yd. hurdles (49.9 ,sec.), equalled the world record of 225 sec. for 200m. hurdles(turn) and anchored the USA team to win the 4x400m. relay in the world record of 3 min. 02.2 sec. Both in 1956 and 1960 Olympics he won gold medals in 400m. hurdles.

DAVIES, L.

U.K. (born 20th May, 1942) - In 1964 Olympics in Tokyo he won championship in long jump - 26ft. 10in. In 1966, he won gold medals in both the Commonwealth (26ft. 2 3/4in.) and European (26ft. 2 1/4in.) competitions.

DAVIS, O.C.

U.S.A. (born 12th July, 1932) - In the 1960 Olympics, he shared the world record time on 44.9 sec. in 400 m with Germany's Carl Kanfmann. He anchored the USA to victory in 4x400m relay in a world record of 3 min. 02.2 sec.

DE CASTELLA, ROBERT

Australia (born 27th May,1957) - De Castella has proved himself to be the hardest and toughest event competitor on Los Angeles marathon with the second fastest time in history of 2h 08:18. He won marathon gold in 1983 World Championships and Commonwealth Games 1982.

DE LA HUNTY, SHIRLEY

Australia (born 18th July,1925) - Collected seven gold medals. It was in the London Olympics of 1948 that she appeared to have finished third in the 200m. only to be given fourth place. She was third in the 180m. hurdles in the 1948 Games but became champion in 1952 and retained the title in Melbourne. She was also bronze medallist in the 100m. in 1948 and 1952 and collected a silver for the sprint relay. She earned a gold in the same squad. In addition, she won two gold and two silver medals at the Commonwealth Games.

DELEZE, PIERRE

Switzerland (born 25th September,1958) - Moved upto 5000 metres and ran fast times, although only seventh in Stuttgart. Progressed to fourth in Rome in 1987.

DECKER, MARY

U.S.A. (born 4th August,1958) - At the age of 14 she pigtailed with a race on her teeth, delighted the whole of the USA by beating Soviet Olympic silver medal list Niele Sabaite . In World Championships of 1500m and 3000m 1983 she won gold.

DELIS, LUIS

Cuba (born 6th December,1957) - In discus he won bronze in 1980 Olympic Games, silver in discus World Championships 1983 and bronze in 1979 World Cup and again a gold in World Student Games 1983.

DESRUELLES, RONALD

Belgium (born 14th February, 1955) - After winning 1980 European Indoor title he was disqualified on a positive drugs test. Now concentrates on sprints rather than long jump. His brother Patrick is Belgian pole vault record holder.

DICKERSON, MARIANE

U.S.A. (born 14th November,1960) - She ran only marathon in June 1982. Her career best was World Championships 1983 when she picked up a silver. She is a Master's Degree holder from University of Michigan.

DIDRIKSON, MILDRED

U.S.A. (1914-1956) - One of the most remarkable female athletes of all times. Won the American Women's team championships in 1932 single handed. Restricted to three events at the 1932 Olympics, she won golds in the hurdles and javelin and was relegated to second place in the high jump by a dubious judging decision. She took up golf, and as Mrs. Zaharias she became the best woman golfer in the world, winning tournament after tournament in the 1940s and early 1950s. She died of cancer in 1956.

DILLARD, HARRISON

U.S.A. (born 8 July, 1923) - Inspired to become an athlete with the sight of Jesse Owens being paraded through the streets of his home town after the 1936 Olympics, Dillard achieved his first world record in the 220 yards in 1946. Between May 1947 and June 1948, he won 82 successive sprint and hurdle races,yet he fell in the US Olympic trials that year and failed to make the hurdles squad.

But his third place qualified him for Wembley at 100 metres and he equalled Owens' Olympic record of 10.3sec and four years later won the hurdles title in Helsinki.

DINSUMO, BELAYNETH

Ethiopia (born 1965) - He won Ist major Ethiopian marathon race in 1986. Second in Tokyo and Rotterdam marathons and won at the Goodwill Games, Rotterdam and African Games 1987.

DIXON, ROD

New Zealand (born 7th July,1950) - After running a 2:11 marathon in 1982 in Christchurch, he realized he can yet chase Olympic glory. He followed it with a 2h 09mi victory in New York. He was first in New York Marathon.

DOMBROWSKI, LUTZ

East Germany (born 25th June,1959) - He is a long jumper, who wants to be a triple jumper but is not as good as it. He won a gold in 1980 Olympic Games in long jump. He again captured a gold in European Championships 1982 long jump event. He broke his leg in a car accident and missed World Championships 1983.

DONKOVA, YORDANKA

Bulgaria (born 28th September, 1961) - Displayed the finest ever sprint hurdling by a woman in 1986, with very sharp speed and technique, running ten sub 12.50 sec. She ran a further four such times in 1987. She lost three fingers on her right hand in an accident on her fifth birthday.

DORIO, GABRIELLA

Italy (born 27th June,1957) - The fastest 1500m runner in free Europe, she won silver in 1500m in 1981 World Cup. She is also among the prettiest 1500m. runners.

DRUPPERS, ROB

The Netherlands (born 29th April,1962) - He was fifth in Athens European Championships of 800m. In 1983 World Championships of 800m he claimed silver.

DRUT, GUY

France (born 1950) - He became the first Frenchman in 56 years to win an Olympic gold medal on the track when he won the 110m in Montreal in 1976. He readily accepted that he was the favourite to win the gold medal in Montreal.

DUMAS, C.E.

U.S.A. (born 12th February, 1937) - In 1956, at the age of 19, he made world record by jumping 7ft. He also won Olympic Championship in that year. For five successive years (1955-59) he won US Championship He also won Pan-American Championship in 1959. He was also a useful high hurdler with a best time of 14.1 sec. for 120 yds.

DUMBADZE, N.

U.S.S.R. (born 23rd January, 1919) - In discus throw, she was European Champion in 1946 and 1950. She made a world record at 174ft. 8 1/2in. and later raised it to 187ft 1 1/4in. Surprisingly, it exceeded the previous world record by 11ft. 3in. Her new record remained unchallenged for eight years.

EASTMAN, B.B.

U.S.A. (born 9th July, 1911) - The world record of 440 yds. in 47.4 sec. set up by Ted Meredith (USA) in 1916 remained unbeaten for 15 years though it was equalled by three athletes but in March 1932, Eastman broke the record by running 440 yds. in 46.4 sec. A few months later he created world record of 880yd. in 1 min. 58sec.

ELLIOTT, PETER

U.K. (born 9th October,1962) - In 1982 he won the AAA 800m title.He deservedly won a place in the Helsinki team and finished a gutsy fourth. In 800m 1983 World Championships he stood fourth and claimed bronze in European Cup in 800m in the same year.

ELLIOT, H.J.

Australia (born 25th February, 1938) - Continuously for nine years (1954 to 1962) Herb Elliott never lost a mile or 1500 m race. In the three major championships he contested, he won 880 yds and mile at the 1958 Commonwealth Games and 1500m. in the 1960 Olympics.

EL HASSAN, KHASHIEF

Sudan (born 26th March,1956) - He stood 7th in the 400m. World Cup of 1979 and claimed gold medal.

EMMELMANN, FRANK

East Germany (born 15th September,1961) - His best event was 200 sprints, when he claimed fifth place in World Championships 1983.

FELL, GRAEME

U.K. (born 19th March,1959) - In 1982 and 1983 he claimed silver in the Steaplechase of European Championships and Commonwealth Games.

FESEKO, EKATERINA

U.S.S.R. (born 10th March,1956) - She won 400m hurdles gold in 1983 World Championships, and won a gold of World Students Games also.She says, "I didn't think I would win, but my performance was technically perfect."

FIBINGEROVA, HELENA

Czechoslovakia (born 13th July,1949) - Fibingerora's exuberant delight in winning the first world title in World Championships 1983 was not surprising. She won silver in 1981 World Cup and in 1983 she earned gold in European Cup.

FINLAY, D.O.

U.K. (born 27th May, 1909) - In 1932 Olympics, he was third in the 110m hurdles. In 1936 Olympics, he came second. In the European championship in 1938 he was at the top with his best time of 14.3 sec. He also won the Commonwealth title.

FIXX, JAMES

U.S.A. (1932-1984)- James was the son of a New York magazine editor and adopted the same career. In 1964, at the age of 32, he started playing tennis to remove his stress. He suffered a tennis injury in 1967 and became interested in running and entering races. He ran 60-80 miles a week. He completed eight Boston Marathons, with a best time of 3 hours 12 minutes. It was an irony of fate that he collapsed and died while on a ten mile run in Northern Vermon at the age of 52.

His contribution to the game as a writer is notable. He created hundreds of runners by his writings. He wrote about his enthusiasm in running in his classic ' *The Complete Book of Running* ' It sold around 1 million copies and had sixteen foreign editions. Other books followed and these further added to his laurels.

FLANAGAN, J.J.

Ireland/U.S.A. (1873-1938) - A marvellous hammer thrower. He held seven American titles. In 1900,1904 and 1908 Olympics, he won gold medals. He raised the world record 14 times ending up with 184ft.

FOSBURY, DICK

U.K. (born 6th March, 1947) - With famous flop style of jumping that won him the 1968 Olympics title it has now become the accepted style for the event. He began the experiments that were to win him the gold, as a 16 year old and by the time he had left school he was clearing two metres and recorded 7ft as a 20 year old.

In 1968, he cleared 2.24 metres to win the title, a height that is still only one centimetre below the current British record, but he was lost to the sport five years later when he turned professional.

FOSTER, GREG

U.S.A. (born 14th August,1958) - His first big win came in the 1981 World Cup but two years later he reached the pinnacle in his event taking the 110m hurdles gold medal in a time of 13.42 at the World

Championships in 1979 he figured in a unique indoor world best dead heat with Nehemiah for 60 yards hurdles.

GARDERUD, ANDERS

Sweden (born 1946) - He won the European Junior 1500m steeplechase title in 1964, it was assumed, in Sweden at least, that he would go on one day to win an Olympic gold medal.He finally made it with his last attempt at the age of 30, after one of the most thrilling Olympic steeplechase finals of all time. In the meantime he repeatedly had to overcome being branded a failure after poor performances at major championships.

GARDNER, M.A.

U.K. (born 12th November, 1928) - In 1948 Olympics Gardner made the 80m hurdle in the Olympic record time 11.2 sec. Koen of Holland, who was declared first but she lost to Fanny Blankers. She was again runner up to Fanny in the European hurdles final in 1951.

GASSER, SANDRA

Switzerland (born 27 July,1962) - Made superb breakthrough to top world class in 1987, but suspended for drugs abuse in Rome, and thus lost her bronze medal and in the Grand Prix, third overall and the mile first place. She is however vigorously protesting against this ban.

GEORGE, W.G.

U.K. (1858-1943) - He made world records in 1884 for the mile (4min.18.4sec), 2 miles (9min.17.4sec), 3 miles (14min.39.0 sec), 6mi(30 min.21.5sec.), 10mi (51min.20.0sec) and one hour (11mi.932 yds.) In 1886, he made a mile in 4min 12 ¼ sec. a record unbeaten until 1915.

GAUDER, HARTWIG

East Germany (born 10th November, 1954) - He won gold in 50 km walk in 1980 Olympic Games and 1987 World Cup. The feat of winning European junior and senior, Olympic and World titles is matched only by Daley Thompson.

GERSCHLER, WOLDEMAR

Germany (born 1904) - A famous German coach and physiologist who innovated the unique interval training method, which is presently being used by most of the middle and long-distance runners. Born in 1904, he graduated from Leipzig University and qualified as a school teacher. He was offered the job of chief coach to Dresdner, one of Germany's top sports clubs before War. He coached the German Rudolf Harbig to a world 800m record of 1:46.6 in 1939 which survived until 1955. He was at the zenith of his career when under his training Josy Barthel won the 1952 Olympics 1500m title. Gerschler made tough demands on the athletes. On the basis of physiological research he carried out while in charge of the Freiburg University Institute of Education, he proved that athletes could undergo a great deal more training if it was rightly monitored.

GIVENS, RANDY

U.S.A. (born 27th March 1962) - She finished 4th in the 1983 American Championships. She also won gold in 200 sprints of World Students Games 1983 and a silver.

GOATER, JULIAN

U.K. (born 12th January,1953) - He finished 2nd in the European Cup 10,000m and at the end of the 1976 season became the second fastest British 5000m runner of all time with 13:15.59. He won the bronze in Commonwealth Games 10,000m.

GOHR, MARLIES

East Germany (born 21st March,1958) - She cracked 11 seconds for the 100m. at the East Germany Championships in 1977. In the World Cup 1977 she won a gold for 100m sprints. She was beaten in the 1980 Olympics final, but she fought back to win Helsinki title.

GORCHAKOVA, Y.

U.S.S.R. (born 17th May, 1933) - She came third in the 1952 Olympic javelin encounter. In 1963,she won the U.S.S.R. title at 182ft 5 ½ in. In the qualifying round at the Tokyo Olympics, she reached the world record distance of 204ft.8 ½ in. In the

Olympics final due to an injury, she finished third with 187ft.2 (½) inches.

GRATTON, MIKE

U.K. (born 28th November,1954) - He won the marathon London Race in 1983. He had to drop out of the World Championships marathon because of the back trouble. In Commonwealth Games he took bronze in 1982.

GUAN,PING

China (born 1st. February,1966) - World best 5000m and 10000m walk records in 1986. She won gold in 1986 Asian Games. Placed 2nd in 10km walk 1985 World Cup.

GUNTHOR, WERNER

Switzerland (born 1 June, 1961) - Had a brilliant season 1986, with European titles both indoors and outdoors. In the latter he added 56cm to his Swiss record. Carried this form over to 1987, when he was defeated only once outdoors.

HAGG, G.

Sweden (born 13th December1918) -Hagg set 15 world records in different distances. In 1945 ,he made a mile in 4 min.01.3sec. breaking the previous record by 3.3 sec.

HALBERG, M.G.

New Zealand (born 7th July,1933) - In racing he gained title in the 1958 and 1962 Commonwealth Games and in the 1960 Olympiics 5000m.

HANSEN, F.M.

U.S.A.(born 29th December,1940) - He was the first Olympic Pole Vault Champion to utilise fibre glass at the 1964 Games. He cleared 16ft.8 3/4 in. at his final attempt for victory. In 1963 he cleared 17ft.1in. and 17ft.2in. for a pair of world records in June and 17ft.4in. for another global mark in July's USA vs USSR match.

HERB, ELLIOTT

Australia (born 25th February,1938) - Between 1954-1962 he never lost a race over one mile or 1500 metres, with 44 consecutive wins and a host of records and admirers. He contested just three major events, and won the 880 yards and mile at the 1958 Commenwealth Games and the 1960 Olympics 1500 metres. He broke the world 1500 metres record twice, in 1958 and at the Olympics of 1960 and the world mile record in Dublin in 1958. His was the perfect record.

HARBIG, R.

Germany (born 8th November,1913) - Rudolf Harbig made record for 800m in 1min.46.6sec. in1939. It was broken only after a long period of 16 years. He broke another world record in 1939 i.e. 400m in 46.0 sec. In 1941 he broke a Rudo metre record for 2min.21.5sec. He won a bronze medal in Berlin Olympics and in 1938 he captured the European 800m title as well assisted Germany to victory in the relay. He won 55 consecutive races at all distances from 50 to 1000m between August 1938 to September 1940.

HARDIN, G.F.

U.S.A. (born 1st July,1910) - His world record of 50.6 sec. for 400m hurdles remained unbroken for 10 years from 1934 to 1953. He was the second fastest in 46.8 sec. and tied the 220 yds. hurdles (straight) record of 22.7. In the 1936 Olympics final he equalled the world record of 52.0sec. He won the Olympic title at the second attempt in 1936.

HARY, A.

West Germany (born 22nd March,1937) - In 1960 Olympics he won the title in 100m. He won another gold medal in the 4x100m relay to bring his total to 4 since he scored in the same event at the 1958 European Championships.

HAYER, R.L.

U.S.A. (born 20th December, 1942) - In 1959, he was only a tenth of a second outside the straight 220 yds. record of 20.0sec. Next year he matched the world record of 9.2 sec. of Frank Budd and in 1963 he made his own world record of 100 yds. in 9.1 sec. Earlier in the season, he had tied the world records for 200m and 220 yds.(turn) of 20.5 sec. In 1964 Olympics he won 4x100m relay for the USA in world record time in 10.10sec.

HEATLEY, B.B.B.

U.K. (born 25th December,1933) - He won the English Cross Country title in 1960,1961 and 1963, the international championship in 1961 and in 1960 and 1961 SSS 10,000m track breaking world record of 48m.120sec. by 25 sec. in 1964 Olympics, he won the marathon in a world's best time of 2hr.13min.55sec. He gained the silver medal in 2hr.16min.19sec.

HEINO, VILJO

Finland (born 1914) - He was the leading finnish distance runner of the 1940s, following in the footsteps of the great Paavo Nurmi. Double world record holder at six miles and holder of eight world records at distances from six-miles to 20,000m. He is credited as being the first amateur to break 50 minutes for ten miles, recording 49:41.6 in Turku, Finland on 30th September, 1945. He retired from racing in 1951.

HERRIOTT, M.

U.K. (born 8th October,1939) - He won the AAA Junior titles in 1957 and 1958. He became the first under 19 in the world to break 9 minutes for the 3000m steeplechase. In 1959, he began his sequence of AAA Championship victories. On four occasions, he lowered British record. Even not keeping in good health, he was fourth in the 1966 Commonwealth Games and eighth in the European Championships.

HEWSON B.S.

U.K. (born 4th April,1933) - In 1958 Commonwealth Games, Hewson was selected to run for the 1500m instead of 800m. No doubt a disturbing shift, but Hewson won the title. In both the Commonwealth Games in 1954 and 1958, he was runner up. On 26 occasions he beat 1min.50sec. for 800m and for five years he held the European 880 yds. record.

HILL, A.G.

U.K. (born 24th March,1889) - He won both the 800m and 1500m at the 1920 Olympic Games.He ran a total of four races winning 800m in 1min.53.4sec. and 1500m in 4 min.01.8sec.

HILL, R.

U.K. (born 25th September,1938) - He is one of the most versatile of the world's distance runners. He broke world record of 15 mile and 25,000m and won a number of National titles. He has yet to do himself justice in a major Championship. He was nineteanth in the 1964 Olympic marathon, eighteenth in the 10,000m and fifth in the 1966 Commonwealth Games .

HINES, JIM

Dumas (born 10th September,1946) - He ran 9.9sec at the AAU Championships in Sacramento in 1968, he staked his claim to a place in the history of the sport, for he was the first man to break the 10sec. barrier with a legal time after earlier running a wind assisted 9.8sec. He won the Olympics title in Mexico the same year with 9.95sec.

HITOMI, KINUE

Japan (1908-1931) - He was perhaps the greatest female all-rounder. In the Women's World Games, organized by the Federation Sportive Feminine Internationale at four yearly intervals from 1922 to 1934, she won eight medals, more than any other woman. In 1926, she was first in the long jump and the standing long jump, second in the discus and third in the 100 yards. In 1930 she won the long jump, came third in the 60m and the javelin.

HOGGAN, J.J.

U.K. (born 28th May, 1933) - In his most distinguished Cross Country career, he was the winner of many English titles in 1938 and 1939 and the International Championship in 1933, 1934,1935 and 1939. In track running he won four AAA titles to his credit.

HOFFMAN, ZDZISLAW

Poland (born 27th August,1959) - He was one of several surprise field events winners. In 1983 World Championships in triple jump he won gold and silver in European Cup 1983.

HOLDOF, W.

West Germany (born 17th February,1940) - A brilliant all rounder. In Tokyo Olympics in 1964, he set personal record in three events and finished with a best score of 7,887 points. He was co-holder of unofficial European holder of 60yds. best of 60sec. He took part in racing, hurdles, high jump, long jump, pole vault, shotput, discuss. A talented all rounder

HOLTOM, MARK
U.K. (born 6th February,1958) - He was a favourite for the Commonwealth Games in 1982. He won gold in 1981 European Cup 110m hurdles.

HONEY, GARY
Australia (born 26th July,1959) - A great competitor, Honey's best may be only 8:13, but in major events he seems to be able to beat rivals. Won gold in long jump in 1982 Commonwealth Games. Before that he had earned silver in 1979 World Cup.

HOPKINS, T.E.
U.K. (born 16th March,1936) - In 1952 Olympics, while only 16, she finished fourth. In 1952 she won the Commonwealth and European titles and in 1956 she tied for the silver medal at the Olympics. In high jump she broke the world record at 5ft.8 (1/2). In 1954 she was runner up in 1954 Commonwealth long jump, won WAAA titles at 100m. hurdles as well as in the jumps and is a best holder of the British Pentathlon record hurdles.

IBBOTSON, G.D.
U.K. (born 17th June,1932) - He won the bronze medal in 1956 Olympics in 5000m. However, in a mile he equalled Roger Bannister's British record of 3 min.

IHAROS, S.
Hungary (born 10th March,1930) - He is one of the all time great on a stop watch basis. During 1955 and 1956 he bròke world records at not less than seven distances, from 5,000 to 10,000m.

IKANGAA, JUMA
Tanzania (born 19th July, 1957) - First African to better 2hrs. 10min. for marathon, when second to de Castella in epic Commonwealth duel in 1982. Improved his African best when second at Fukuoka in 1983. Has won 7 of his 19 marathons including Melbourne 1983-84, Tokyo 1984 and 1986, Fukuoka 1986, Beijing 1987.

ILG, PATRIZ
West Germany (born 5 December, 1957) - The former World and European steeplechase champion missed most of the 1979 and 1984 seasons through injuries. A great finisher who did run all out for fast times. He is the only steeplechaser to win medals at three European Championships.

ISO-HOLLO,VOLMARI
Finland (1907-1969) - A long-distance runner with an equal liking for the flat and the steeplechase. Between Los Angeles and the 1936 Berlin Games he ran the second fastest 3000m race ever, finishing in 9:03.8, an Olympic record that was not beaten until 1952. In the 10,000m he finished third in 30:2.2 in a race where the Finns took a clean sweep o the medals.

JACKSON, M.
Australia (born 13th September,1931) - In Commonwealth Games in 1950 she won in 100m breaking world record . Again in 1952 Olympics she was champion in 100m and 200m race breaking world record.

JAHN, BETTINE
East Germany (born 3rd August,1958) - She excelled at the 1983 World Championships winning the 100 metres hurdles gold medal in a wind assisted 12.35, faster than the world record. Amazingly, this was her first major success, although she had missed the bronze medal at the 1982 European Championships by only 0.01 sec. and finished 7th in the 1980 Olympic final.

JARVINEN, M.H.
Finland (born 18th February,1909) - He raised the world record in Javelin ten times from 234ft 9 1/2 in to 253ft.4(1/2)in. during 1930 to 1936. He won the Olympic title in 1932 and the European titles in 1934 and 1938. He was also a brilliant all rounder.

JAZY, M.
France (born 13th June,1936) - He set nine world middle distance records (including two relays) during an International career of ten years. He was a runner up in the 1960 Olympic 1500m. In 1962, he won the European Championship. In 1964 Olympics 5000m he finished fourth. In 1966, he won the European Championship in 5000m.

JENNER, BRUCE

U.S.A. (born 28th October,1949) - Jenner was considered the greatest all rounder until Daley Thompson appeared on the scene. He won the decathlon title at the 1976 Olympics with a world record score adding more than 160 points to the total which had brought the title in Munich. He is said to be one of the athletes who have moved into millionaire status.

JERMORE, H. W.

Canada (born 30th September,1940) - At the Tokyo Olympics, he gained bronze medal in 100m and finished fourth in the 200m. In 1966, at the Commonwealth Games he won the title in 100 yds.

JIAN-HUA, ZHU

China (born 29th May.,1963) - In 1983 high jumping, he became the first male athlete from the People's Republic of China to set official athletics world records. His major high jump victories prior to 1983 came at the 1981 Asian Championships and 1982 Asian Games where he cleared the second highest jump in the world that year. He gained only country medal at the 1983 World Championships.

JOHNSON, D.I.N.

U.K. (born 5th January,1933) - He won the half mile championship in the 1954 Commonwealth Games. In the 1956 Olympics, he won silver medal in the 800m final. In 1957 he returned the then UK 800m record of 1m.46.6 sec. In 1959, he displayed his potential as a miler by topping the British 1500m list with a 3m.42.9sec.

JOHNSON, R.L.

U.S.A. (born 18th August,1934) - He was a marvellous all rounder. In 1955, he set world record in decathlon at 7985 points. He was second at the 1956 Olympic decathlon and was first in the 1960 Olympic decathlon. His best score was 8683 points. Of the eleven decathlons he competed, he won nine.

JOHNSTON, T.F.K.

U.K. (born 11th March, 1941) - He won his first international in 1963. In 1965 he beat the world record for 30000m. by 1/4min. He covered 18 miles 1128 yds. distance in 1hr. 32min.34.6sec. in a record time.

JONES, H.W.

U.S.A. (born 4th August,1938) - At the 1960 Olympic hurdles he secured a bronze medal and in the 1964 a gold at hurdles. His best time of 13.4 sec. at hurdles has been shattered by only a few athletes so far. He was unbeaten in not less than 55 indoor meetings during four years between 1960 and 1964. His most brilliant record was 6.8 sec. for 60 yds. He was also a world class sprinter. He was a member of the USA team that set a world record of 39.1sec. in the 4x100m. relay in 1961.

JONES, HUGH

U.K. (born 1st November,1955) - He won the AAA title in Rugby in 1981, finishing fifth in the European Cup and then third in New York.He also won the London marathon in 2:09.24, his fastest till date.

JONES, STEVE

U.K. (born 4th August, 1955) - World marathon best 1984 and a further Commonwealth record in 1985. UK half marathon best 1986.

JORDAN, J.W.

U.K. (born 15th November,1935) - Her performance in half mile has been brilliant. She won the WAAA 880 yds. for five years between 1958-62 and won 11 of her 14 international races for Britain securing 63 out of a possible 70 points. She broke the world record in 880 yds. in 1954 at 2min.09.0sec. Again she held the world record with 2min.06.1sec in 1960.

JUANTORENA, ALBERTO

Cuba (born 11th November,1950) - In Olympic Games 1976,1980 he won the gold for 800m and 400m. He was the winner of gold medals in the same event (800m and 400m) of World Cup of 1977. A severe Achilles tendon injury stopped him defending both Olympic titles in Moscow, but he attempted the 400m and although not fully fit nearly got a medal.

KALEK, LUCYNA

Poland (born 9th January,1956) - She has one of the finest competitive records. Reaching world class in 1979 with a 100 metres hurdles victory at the World Students Games in a fast 12.62, she went on to take the sprint hurdles bronze medal at the 1980 Olympic Games. Two years later she crowned her career with a resounding 100 metres hurdles win at the European Championships in one of the fastest recorded time of 12.45.

KAZANKINA, TATYANA

U.S.S.R. (born 17th December,1951) - The greatest middle distance runner that the Soviet Union has yet produced, she won the 800, 1500 metres double at the 1976 Olympic Games and retained the latter title four years later in Moscow. Of her four world records at 800, 1500 metres her last mark of 3:52.4 at the longer distance represents one of the finest performances in athletics history.

KEDIR, MOHAMMED

Ethiopia (born 6th September,1953) - He dutifully set up Yifter's victories in the Moscow 5000 and 10,000 metres, but was a disappointment in the next World Cross Country Championships at Gateshead.

KEINO, K.

Kenya (born January,1940) - In the 1962 Commonwealth Games in Australia, he finished 11th in the 3 miles. in 13min. 50.0 sec. and set a national record of 4min. 07.0sec. in the mile heats. In the 1964 Tokyo Olympic he returned 13min. 49.6sec. in his 5000m heat(a 23 sec. improvement) 3in.45.8sec.in his 1500m heat, 13min.50.4 sec for 5th in the 5000 m final and a sub-four mile (3min. 41.9 sec). In 1965 in 3000m. he set a phenomenal world record of 7min.39.6sec. He won the 1500m and 5000m at the first African Games. In New Zealand he beat 5000m world record with 13min 24.2 sec. In the 1966 Commonwealth Games he returned with 12min. 57.4 sec. in 5000 m. and secured fastest mile in history (3min.53.4 sec.).

KHALIFA, OMER

Sudan (born 18th December, 1956) - As the torch bearer in the Sport Aid run 1986, he set out from a relief camp in the Sudan to reach the United Nations via 12 European cities in eight days.

KHARLOV, ALEXANDER

U.S.S.R. (born 18th March,1958) - In 400m hurdles he won bronze of the World Championships held during 1983. He was sixth in 400m European Championships of 1982. He claimed gold medal of World Students Games in 1983 of 400m hurdles.

KILBY, B.L.

U.K. (born 26th February,1938) - He was a distinguished marathon runner. In 1962 he captured both the European and Commonwealth titles. He finished fourth in the Tokyo Olympics.

KINCH, B.E.V.

U.K. (born 14th January,1964) - Bev Kinch became the girl at last to beat Mary Rand's nineteen year old British long jump record. She won the only gold in World Student's games of 100m. long jump.

KIPKOECH, PAUL

Kenya (born 1963) - He is becoming known more through his road and cross-country running than for his massive talent over 10,000m on the track. His talent encompasses many distances. He was fifth in the 1984 Olympic 5000m final behind Said Aouita, and has a best 1500m time of 3:41.41. Three times he has finished runner-up in the World Cross-Country Championships, once to Lopes of Portugal in 1985 and twice, in 1987 and 1988, to Ngugi.

KISELEYO, VLADIMIR

U.S.S.R. (born 1st January,1957) - He won gold in 1980 Olympic Games shot event and finished seventh in 1982 European Championships.

KLIM, R.

U.S.S.R. (born 25th May,1933) - He won gold medal in hammer throw in 1964 Olympics. In 1966, European Championships, he was European record holder.

KLOBUKOWSKA, E.

Poland (born 1st October,1946) - In 1964 Olympics she equalled the European 100m. record of 11.3 sec. and gained bronze (100m) and gold (4x100 relay)medals. Next season she achieved a world record of 11.1 sec.for 100m and cut her fastest 200m from 24.5sec. to 23.0 sec. In the 1966 championship she won the 100m and came second in the 200m. She secured victory in relay for her country.

KOCEMBOVA, TATYANA

Czechoslovakia (born 2nd May,1962) - In 1983 became the world's third fastest female 400metres runner with her 48.59 in second place in the World Championships final, before earning another silver medal with the Czech 4x400 metres relay team.

KOCH, MARITA

East Germany (born 22nd February,1957) - Perhaps the most celebrated female athlete of the last decade, Marita Koch first emerged as a threat to Irena Szewinska's domination of women's 400m running in 1977 when, at the age of 20, she won the European indoor crown and triumphed in the European Cup final. She then fought a terrific duel with Szewinska in the 1977 World Cup final in Dusseldorf, losing to the "Polish princess" by less than a quarter of a second. However, she made amends in the 1978 European Championships final with a world record of 48.94sec.

But only another twelve months elapsed before she eclipsed Szewinska. After twice breaking the world 400m record and setting new figures for 200m, she set her fourth world record of the year in the European Championships to take the gold medal in 48.94 seconds and thus became the first woman to break the 49sec.and barrier. In 1979 she emulated the record-smashing feats of Sebastian Coe by twice breaking her world 200m record (22.02 secs. and 21.71 secs) and doing likewise in the one lap event before winning the Olympic title in Moscow in 1980.

KODAMA, TAISUKE

Japan (born 26th July, 1958) - Has run 11 marathons, winning Beppu and Beijing in 1986.

KONCHELLAH, BILLY

Kenya (born 20th October, 1961) - The Masai man made a great impact as a Junior in 1979-80, then little until his Olympic fourth place in 1984. In 1985, he contacted tuberculosis, but came back as the world's number one 800m runner in 1987.

KONDRATYEVA, LYUDMILA

U.S.S.R. (born 11th April,1958) - She was a shock winner of the Moscow Olympics 100m, when she beat the overwhelming favourite and then world record holder Marlies Gohr of East Germany. She had been best known as a 200m runner winning the Prague European title. She earned silver in 100m of European Cup in 1979.

KOSTADINOVA, STEFKA

Bulgaria (born 25th March,1965) - Won 34 successive high jump competitions 1984-6, her one loss in 1986 followed by 19 further wins. Lost three times in 1987, but showed brilliant form to set world record in Rome. Has jumped 2 metres in 46 competitions.

KOZAKIEWICZ

Poland (born 12th December,1953) - There can be few more satisfying moments for a Pole than to win Olympic gold medals in pole vault 1976 and 1980. In World Cup 1977 he won a silver.

KRAENZLEIN, A.C.

U.S.A. (1928 - 1976) - In Olympics, he won gold medals in four events 60 m, 110 m hurdles, 200 m. hurdles and long jump. His world record is for 120 yds (15.2 sec.) and 220 yds.

KPALEMAIINEN, H.

Finland (born 23 February,1891) - He won three Olympic gold medals in 1912, in 5000m, 10,000m and cross country. In 5000m he created world record with finish in 14 min. 36.6 sec. which lasted for 10 years. In 1920 Olympics, he won marathon and held world records at numerous events from 3000 to 30,000 m.

KRATOCHVILOVA, JARMILA

Czechoslovakia (born in 1953) -This powerfully built Czech girl became the sensation of the first World Championships in Helsinki in 1983, by winning the semi-final of the 400metres and then less than 30 minutes later, returning to the track to win the 800m gold medal.

By a series of injuries her arrival on the world scene was delayed until she was 25 and it was not until 1978 that her name began to appear regularly.

The major medals eluded her again in 1980 at the Moscow Olympics when she was well beaten in the 400 metres by Marita Koch. In 1981, at the age of 30 she gained her revenge over Koch, by beating her in both the European and World Cup finals.

KRISTIANESEN, INGRID

Norway (born 21st March,1956) - Won Houston marathon just five months after giving birth to son. Has won 11/20 marathons and all five track 10km races. She is the only athlete to hold world records at 5,000m, 10,000m and marathon.

KRZESINSKA, ELZBIETA

Poland (born 1934) - She is the only woman to have won two medals in Olympic long jump competition, winning the gold in 1956 with world record 6.35m and coming second eight years later in 1964. She was ranked number one in the world in 1956, and set one other world record of 6.35m several months before the Olympics prior to equalling that mark in the final. In the 1960 Olympics in Rome she lost by ten centimetres to Vera Krepkina (URS),6.27m to 6.37m.

KULA, DANIUS

U.S.S.R. (born 28th April,1959) - A javelin gold in 1980 Olympic Games, bronze in World Championships 1983, again a gold in World Cup 1981. He was fortunate to win in Moscow. His third round throw landed in the opinion of most experts,flat as a pancake. But the officials, who were ludicrously accused of opening the Lenin stadium doors to create a favourable draught, ruled his throw was valid.

KUTS, V.

U.S.S.R. (born 7th February,1927) - In 1953, he ran 5000m in 13 min 31 .4 sec., a second faster than the world record. In 1954 in the European 5000m championship he won in the world record time of 13m in 56.6 sec. Again in London he won 5000m race in 13 min. 51.2 sec. Just before the 1956 Melbourne Olympics, he set world records of 28 min 30.4 sec for 10,000m and 13 min 35.0 sec for 5000m. In the Olymics he won the 5000m and 10000 m.Next year he made 5000m. in world record time of 13 min 35.0 sec. which remained unbeaten for seven years.

KUTTY, ROSA

India (born 3rd January,1964) She is employed in Southern Railway. Has represented the country in the Asian Track & Field Meet in 1989. Best performance 2:05.7 sec in 800m and 4:20.56 sec. in 1500m.

LANDY, J.M.

Australia (born 4th April, 1930) - Landy made hectic efforts to become the first four minute miler but failed. In 1952 he ran a mile in 4 m. 02.1 sec. In May 1954, when Roger Bannister made that achievement, he made a mile in 3 min. 57.9 sec. taking 1 ½ seconds more than Bannister. He created a world record of 3 min. 41.8 sec. for 1500m. In the Commonwealth Games 1954 he was second and in the 1956 Olympics he won a bronze medal in 1500 m.

LARRABEE, M.D.

U.S.A. (born 2nd December, 1930) - He won the first national title - 400m, 45.4 sec. in Europe and equalled the world record of 44.9 sec.in the US Olympic Trials. He won two gold medals in the 1960 Olympics - 400m in 45.1 sec. and anchored USA relay team to world record victory.

LATTANY, MEL

U.S.A. (born 10th August,1959) - In 1981, he won both 100m and 200m World Students Games and World Cup 200 metres titles. He hit the top form in 1983 to lose a shoe during the vital 200 metres trial race for American World Championships team. He underlined what he might have achieved in Helsinki by smashing the world figures for 300 metres.

LAUER, K.M.

Germany (born 2nd January, 1937) - In 1956 Olympics high hurdle finals he came fourth. In 1958, he won 110m hurdles in European Championships. In 1959, he set world record of 13.2 sec. for 110 m. high hurdles and 22.5 sec for 200m low hurdles (turn). He anchored Germany in 4x100m relay victory and won a gold medal. In 1959 in decathlon he got 7,955 points, fourth best score ever made at that time.

LEATHER, D.S.

U.K. (born 7th January, 1933) - In 1954, she became

the first female five minute mile runner (4 min 59.6 sec). Next year she reduced her timing to 4 min 45.0 sec. In 880 yd. she broke world record in 2 min 09.0 sec in 1954. In 1957, she secured W.A.A.A. titles in 880 yds and mile.

LEITAO, ANTONIO

Portugal (born 22nd July, 1960) - Had posted several fast times but little of major success until the Olympics, when he ensured that the pace was fast in the final, and reaped his reward with a bronze medal.

LERWILL, S.

U.K. (born 16th August, 1928) - In high jumping she won the European title in 1950 and broke the women's record in the event at 5 ft. 7 ½ in. The record remained unbeaten from 1951 to 1954. In 1952 Olympics she got silver medal. She won the W.A.A.A. title four times.

LEWIS, CARL

U.S.A. (born Ist July,1961).At the age of 19 Carl Lewis clocked the fastest ever 100m time. In 1983, Lewis began his magnificent season by achieving three individual wins at the US championships.Lewis went on to complete another famous hat trick at the inaugural World Championships in Helsinki. He became the star of the strongest ever athletics championship by winning gold medals in 100m and long jump. He won gold in long jump of World Cup 1981. Lewis, set to become one of the millionaires of athletics, has brought the day closer when it may be possible that someone will break the long jump record that Bob Beamon set in Mexico in 1968. Lewis has cleared the 28 ft. mark on numerous occasions and his 28ft. 10 in. in 1983 in Indianapolis at the US Championships, is the best ever at sea level. Earlier in the same meet he had recorded 19.75 sec, again the fastest 200 metres at sea level. He went to Helsinki for the World Championships with all the flare of a superstar and he proved he was . He outran Calvin Smith, the world 100 metres record holder, in the final with Olympic champion Allan Wells in fourth. In the long jump he killed off all the opposition with his first effort of 8.55 metres and then produced another of 8.42 metres which would also have won him the gold, just for good measure. Then with Emmit King, Willie Gault and Calvin Smith, produced 37.86 sec against the world relay record of 38.03 sec. It is likely that he could have won the 200 metres as well. He took four gold medals in Los Angeles 1986 and equalled the 1936 record of his childhood hero Jesse Owens.

LIDDELL, E.H.

U.K. (1902-1945)- Liddell won a gold medal in the 400m in 47.6 seconds and a bronze medal in the 200 m in the 1924 Olympic. His 100 yds. in 9.7 sec in 1923 remained unbeaten as the U.K. record for 35 years. In China in 1925 he made 400m in 49.0 sec.

LILLAK, TINA

Finland (born 15th April,1961) - She won the only gold in 1983 in javelin 1983 World Championships. The javelin soared beyond the 70m mark and the title was her's. The crowd went wild and Tina danced around the track in a premature lap of honour. She was fourth in 1983 European Championships.

LISOVSKAYA, NATALYA

U.S.S.R. (born 16th July, 1962) - Undefeated in 1987, when she won the world titles indoors and outdoors and made up for her disappointing showing in Stuttgart the previous year.

LITVINOV, SERGEY

U.S.S.R. (born 23rd January,1958) - In World Championships 1983 his first throw was 82.68 and no one could get any where near that he won the gold in that Hammer throw,beating the Russian. In 1980 he got silver. In European Cup 1979 he had to satisfy with silver.

LONG, D.C.

U.S.A. (born 13th June, 1940) - In 1960 he raised the world record twice in the shot. He won the bronze medal in Rome Olympic. In 1962 he raised the world record by half an inch with a put of 65ft 10 ½in. In 1963 he was in the best performers list. In 1964 he made a put of 67ft. 10in. and in the Olympic that year won the gold medal.

LOPES, CARLOS
Portugal (born 18th February,1947) - In 1982, at the Athens Europeans he finished fourth. He took second place in the World Cross Country Championships in Gateshead. He won silver in 1976 Olympic Games marathon.

LOSCH, CLAUDIA
West Germany (born 10th January, 1960) - A superb competitor, who has made a habit of winning important competitions. Since his first major success when he won the 1979 European Cup Final high jump at the age of 17 in 1987 he was below par through injury, but cleared season's best in Rome. 52 competitions at 2.30m or more.

LOVELOCK, J.E.
New Zealand (born 28th December, 1949)- In 1932, he set a British mile record of 4m. 12.0 sec and was seventh in the Olympic 1500m final. In 1933, he made a world record of 4m in 07.6 sec and in 1934 won the Commonwealth mile. In 1936 Olympic 1500m , Lovelock won victory in record time of 3 min 47.8 sec.

LOWE, D.G.A.
U.K. (born 7th August, 1902) - In 1924 Olympics 800m he won gold medal and in 1928 Olympics he again won gold medal lowering the Olympic record to 1 min 51.8 sec. In Berlin after the Olympics he scored the fastest 800m in 1 min 51.2 sec.

MACHURA, REMIGIUS
Czechoslovakia (born 3rd July,1960) - Disqualified for 18 months on a positive drugs test when second at the 1985 European Cup final, she won gold in 1985 World Indoor Championships. Her brother Martin is the decathlon record holder.

MALINOWSKI, BRONISLAW
Poland (1951-1981) - A tragic car accident brought to an end the career of possibly the greatest steeplechaser the world is ever likely to see. A popular figure in Britain, Malinowski who boasted of a Scottish mother and said at one time he would like to run for that country. He went on to win the European senior 3,000 metres title in 1974 and 1978 but had to wait for three Olympics before finally winning the gold as he did in Moscow, coming back from over 30 metres behind to win in 8 min 9.7sec. He had a best of 1min 49.8 sec for the 800 metres and 28min 25.2 sec for the 10,000 metres.

MAMINSKI, BOGUSLAW
Poland (born 18th December,1955) - In 1980 Olympic Games he was placed seventh in 3000 metres steeplechase. He won silver in 1983 World Cup and again in European Championships he claimed silver.In 1981 World Cup of 3000 metres steeplechase he fetched gold. He has stoutly defended the memory of his father who died in a car crash in 1982.

MANOLIU, LIA
Bulgaria (born 1932) - She won the gold medal for throwing the discus in her fifth Olympics. In 1956 she came ninth, before winning two bronze medals in 1960 and 1964.

MARTI, DEBBIE
U.K. (born 14th May,1968) - An exciting new British female high jumping talent, she jumped 1.88m in 1983 at the age of 15 to exceed anything previously achieved by a British teenager. Competing against girls two and three years her senior at the European Championships that year she performed brilliantly, filling the bronze medal position with her second 1.88m clearance of the season.

MARTIN, LISA
Australia (born 12th May, 1960) - Started as a hurdler, switching to distance running in 1981. Has won six out of twelve marathons to Osaka 1988, 2nd New York 1985-6. Ran Commonwealth half marathon best of 1:09:45 to win Great North Run 1986.

MARSH, HENRY
U.S.A. (born 15th March,1954) - The unluckiest athlete in his event, he finished first in the 1981 World Cup steeplechase but was disqualified for running around a barrier and in 1983 at the World Championships, he looked certain for the silver medal before falling over the final barrier. He won

the 1979 Pan American Games and ran the fastest times in the world in both 1982 and 1983.

MARIN, JOSE

Spain (born 21st January,1950) - He made his name in 1982 becoming the European 20km champion and 50km silver medallist within three days. Again displaying superb form at the World Championships the following year, he was placed second in the 50 km event and narrowly failed to take the bronze medal in the 20km.

MARKOV, KHRISTO

Bulgaria (born 27th January,1965) - World Junior record 1984 and five European Junior record 1983-4. Ten Bulgarian triple jump records 1983-7, the last four also European records. Equalled European indoor long jump best 1985.

MATHIAS, R.B.

U.S.A. (born 17th November, 1930) - Mathias was the youngest of all the athletes to have won gold medal in decathlon in 1948 Olympics at Wembley. He was on by 17 ½ . He broke world record three times and maintained his position till 1952. He won all the ten of the competitions he contested from 1948 to 1956.

MATSON, J.R.

U.S.A. (born 5th March, 1945) - In 1963, Matson, a school student of 18 years , crashed the formidable 60 ft. barrier, created in a period of 45 years. He bettered his titles to 62 ft., 63ft., 64ft., and 65 ft. At the 1964 Olympics he won silver.

MATTHEWS, K.J.

U.K. (21st June,1934) - He participated in five major international 20 kilometers walk test.Of these he won four, the European title in 1962,the Lugano Trophy finals in 1961 and 1963 and Olympic gold medal in 1964.

MC COY, MARK

Guyana (born 10th December,1961) - He was the surprise of Brisbane Commonwealth Games. He bettered 14 seconds with a time 13.97 in high hurdles in 1982. In 110m hurdle of World Championships he stood fourth during 1983. He won gold also in 1982 in the same event.

McDERMOTT, KIRSTY

U.K. (born 6th August,1962) - A poor fourth place in the WAAA Championships 800 metres final in 1982 didn't augur well for her medal chances at that year's Commonwealth Games, but a Welsh 800 metres record of 2:00.56 just before the games seemed to point to something special in Brisbane.Sure enough, she won the 800 metres to become Wales first female representative to win a Commonwealth Games athletics gold medal.

MC GUIRE, E.M.

U.S.A. (born 3rd June,1944) - In 1963, at the Pan-American games she won the 100m. in 11.5sec. She also won a gold medal in the 200m. (23.0sec) and silver medals in the 100m and relay at the 1964 Olympic Games.

MCKEAN, TOM

U.K. (born 27th October,1963) - Made a great debut in international athletics in 1985, when, in the absence of other top UK 800m runners, he had a string of successes culminating in his win in the European Cup final. He earlier completed a remarkable 34 successive win at 800m.Won medals in both his major races in 1986.

MENNEA, PIETRO

Italy (born 28th June,1952) - The most bemedalled of all the world's top sprinters, his greatest achievements include his Olympic 200 metres victory in 1980 and his European Championships wins at 200 (1974 and 1978) and 100 metres (1978). Following a brief period of retirement he captured the 1983 World Championships 200 metres bronze medal, clocking 20.51.

MEKONNEN, ABEBE

Ethiopia (born 5th January,1963) - Of his 17 marathons has won five - Rotterdam, Addis Ababa and Montreal 1986, Paris 1987, Tokyo 1988. Nephew of double Olympic champion Abebe Bikila.

MENNEA, PIETRO
Italy (born 28th July,1952) - He retired after winning the Moscow Olympic title in sprinting. Not only did he hold the world record set at altitude for the 200m,but his time of 19.96sec. at sea level was considered to be the best performance ever.He edged Wells out of a second Olympic gold in the 200 metres by 2/100th of a second. He claimed gold in 200 sprints of European Cup during 1975.

MERLENE, OTTEY
Jamaica (born 10th May, 1969) - She won bronze in 200m sprints of 1980 Olympic Games. Won silver in World Championships, 1983. Her marriage deflected her attention from the Olympics and the baby stopped her competing again at top level.

MEYFARTH, ULRIKE
West Germany (born 4th May,1956) - Meyfarth was only sixteen when she became darling of West Germany by winning the Olympic title in 1972 high jump event. She got silver in 1983 World Championships. In European Championships she earned gold in 1982.

MICHEL, DETLEF
East Germany (born 13th October,1955) - The 28 year old gas engineer took advantage by capturing gold in World Championships 1983 in javelin throw. In European Championships and World Cup 1981, 1983 he won bronze and silver.

MINEYEVA, OLGA
U.S.S.R. (born 1st October,1952) - Overshadowed by her record breaking countrywoman Nadezhda Olizarenko in the 1980 Olympic Women's 800 m. final, in which she was placed second in a faster time than the previous world record, Mineyeva made no mistake at the European Championships in Athens two years later. There she won the 800 metres in convincing style clocking a fast 1:55.41. Nowadays, with the quick turnover of world class female middle distance runners, it is rare for a girl to win medals at more than one major championships.

MORLEY, SUE
U. K. (born 6th January,1960) - She just missed out a medal in the women's 400 metres hurdles at the 1982 Commonwealth Games but began to realize her obvious potential in 1983. Breaking 57 seconds for the first time early that year, she reached the World Championships final finishing 7th with a U.K. record of 56.04. Shortly after that she achieved an excellent third place in the women's European Cup final 400 metres hurdles behind two World Championships medallists.

MOORCROFT, DAVE
U.K. (born 10th April,1953) - One of the most underrated of all world class distance runners, he finally gained just recognition, at the age of 29 when he smashed the 5000 metres world record by a huge 5.79 seconds margin to achieve one of the most remarkable performances ever.Surprisingly, he finished only third in the European Championships 5000 metres that year but won the gold medal in the same event at the Commonwealth Games some weeks later. He was placed third in the European Championships 1500 metres in the same season.

MOIUTAWAKIL, EL NAWAL
Morocco (born 15th April,1962) - First Moroccan and first African woman, apart from South Africans, to win an Olympic gold medal Second smallest ever Olympic champion. Won six gold medals at the Pan Arab Games in 1985 and four at the 1987 Arab Championships.

MOLLER, LORRAINE
New Zealand (born 1st June, 1955) - Won her first eight marathons, before second to Joyce Smith at London in 1982. Of 19 marathons she has now won 12, including Avon 1980, 1982 and 1984; Boston 1982,1984; Osaka 1986-7.

MOTA, ROSA
Portugal (born 29th June, 1958) - Has won eight of her eleven marathons, including the European gold in her first marathon in 1982, and again in 1986. She improved her best in each of her first seven marathons and won the first ever Olympic medal by a Portuguese woman.

MILES, W.M.
U.S.A. (born 30th June,1938) - Before the Tokyo Olympics, he raced 10,000m. on five occasions, winning once. In the Olympic 10,000m he won gold medal in 28min.24.4sec.

MOGENBURG, DIETMAR
West Germany (born 15th August,1961) - The tall architectural student had more reason than most to be angry at the West German boycott of the 1980 Olympics. He was unquestionably the best high jumper in the world. He won gold in European Championships 1982 for high jump and silver and bronze in 1979,1983 European Cup.

MOORCROFT, DAVID
U.K. (born 10th April,1953) - In 1982 he produced a shattering performance. He slashed six second off Henry Rono's World best of 5000 metres. He won bronze in 1500m. in 1978. In European Cup he claimed gold during 1981 of 5000m. After his world record he went to Athens as favourite, but had to settle for the third place.

MORROW, B.J.
U.S.A. (born 15th October,1935) - Between 1955 and 1958 he lost only one sprint competition. In the 1956 Olympics he secured three gold medals by winning the 100m and 200m and contributing to the United States relay victory.

MOSES, E.D.
U.S.A. (born 31st August,1955) Moses is unquestionably an event for the greatest athlete the world has ever seen in terms of dominance over his peers.He won gold in 400m. hurdles at Olympic Games in 1976, and another gold in 1983 in World Championships for the same event.

MUNKELT, THOMAS
East Germany (born 3rd August,1952) - Europe's leading 110 metres hurdler for several years he has compiled an enviable competitive record without ever seriously challenging Frenchman Guy Drut's 1975 European Sprint hurdles record of 13.28. He won three European Cup final wins 1977/79/83 and a World Cup victory in 1977, his greatest successes include European Championships hurdles titles in 1978 and 1982, in between which he became Olympic Champion.

MYERS, I.E
U.S.A. (born 16th February,1858) - He broke three world records for 100yds. 440yds. and 880yds. from 1880 to 1888. This has been a marvellous feat. In 1880, he succeeded in winning eight national titles in a week, first the American and then Canadian Championships at 100,200, 440 and 880 yds.

NEDI, DEREJE
Ethiopia (born 10th October,1955) - Started athletics in 1974. Won Frankfurt and Moscow marathons in1984.

NEHEMIAN, RENALDO
U.S.A. (born 24th March 1959) - Renaldo or 'skeets' as he is known, ran the heart out of the European hurdlers in 1980 but because of the American ban was not allowed to chase what he wanted most, the Olympic title in Moscow with the 12.93 sec. set in 110m. Zurich in 1981. Nehemian made his mark at high school, breaking record after record and it was in 1979 that he eliminated the name of Alejandro Casanas of Cuba from the record books when he recorded 13.16sec, only to run even faster, 13 sec flat, when he won the Pan American games and the Word Cup. He is a useful long jumper as well as a flat 100 and 200 metres runner.

NEUBERT, RAMONA
East Germany (born 26th July,1958) - Totally dominant in the heptathlon, she had broken the world record four times upto the end of 1983. Her highest is 6836 points. Having finished just out of the medals in the Pentathlon at the 1980 Olympic Games, she immediately took to the new event, comfortably winning the European and world heptathlon titles in 1982 and 1983. Her strongest event is long jump.

NEVALA, P.L.
Finland (born 30th November,1940) - In 1963, he secured second position with 283ft.2(1/2)in. and in the world all time list in javelin throw. In 1964 Olympic he won the championship winning 13 (1/2)

with 271ft. 2 (½) in. He came fourth in the 1966 European Championship.

NIHILL, V.P.

U.K. (born 5th Sep., 1939) - In 1962, he won the first national title (the Irish mile) in walking. He won silver in 1964 Olympics 50 km. in 4 hr. 11 min. 31.2 sec. He displayed his exceptional versatility in 1965 by winning national titles.

NORMAN, DECIMA

Australia (born 1915) - Decima holds the record for winning most gold medals by one athlete at a single Commonwealth Games celebration. She won five in 1938 in the 100yards, 660 yards relay, 440 yards relay and long jump. She did not enjoy the Olympic glory, mainly because her best events, the 220 yards and long jump, were not included in the women's programme before the war. She live with her memories at Albany in the remote south of Western Australia.

NURMI, P.J.

Finland (1897-1973) - He won nine gold medals in seven individual and two team events in three Olympiads and a score of world records over distances ranging from 1500m to 20,000m. He also won a silver medal in 5,000m in 1928. He won silver medals in the 5000m and 3000m steeplechase. By his achievements he nearly became an idol in athletics.

NYLANDER, SVEN

Sweden (born 1 January,1962) - Has a remarkable record of making all major championships finals 1982-7, setting national records in 1982, 1986 and 1987 in these races.

NIKULIN, IGOR

U.S.S.R. (born 14th August,1960) - He became the youngest ever 80m hammer thrower in 1980. His father Yuriy was fourth in the 1964 Olympic hammer.

OAKES, GARY

U.K. (born 21st September,1958) - One of the smallest international 400 metres hurdlers at 1.77m he excelled in placing third in the 1980 Olympic final clocking a lifetime best of 49.11, the fourth fastest time by a U.K. hurdler.

O'BRIEN, W.P.

U.S.A. (born 28th January, 1932) - He revolutionised shot putting and he introduced techniques which bear his name. In 1951 he terminated Jim Fuch's long supremacy by defeating him for the USA title. In 1952, he won Olympic title and between 1952 and 1956 he won 116 consecutive competitions. In 1953, he broke Fuch's record of 58 ft. 10 (¼) in. and subsequently carried the record to 59,60,61,62 and 63 ft. He again won the Olympic title in 1956 and also won the Pan-American title in 1955 and 1959 . He has records too of 63 ft 2 (½) in. 63 ft. 4 in. and 64 ft. 7 (½) in.

OERTER, A.A.

U.S.A. (born 19th September, 1936) - In discus throwing he won gold medals thrice in 1954, 1960 and 1964 Olympics. He was the first man to exceed 200 feet. He further improved his record to 235 ft. 5 (½) in.

OLIZAREKO, NADYEZHDA

U.S.S.R. (born 28th November, 1953) - In 800m she won a gold at Moscow Olympic 1980 and obliterated the world and Olympic records. She earned silver in 1979 World Cup 800m. A year before she won a silver in European Championships again for 800m.

OPITZ, MARTINA

East Germany (born 12th December,1960)-A sociology student who improved nearly 6m. in 1983. She should dominate the event for years to come. In discus she earned a gold in 1983 World Championships. In the same year she won another gold in European Cup.

OTKALENKO, N.

U.S.S.R. (born 23rd May, 1928)-In 1951 she won the Soviet 800 m. title in a record time of 2 min. 12.0 sec. In 1954 she again won the European Championship. Her final season of major competition was 1961 when she clocked a respectable 2 min. 08.6 sec.

OTTEY, MERLENE

Jamaica (born 10th May,1969) - One of the most accomplished of Commonwealth born female sprinters ever, she entered real world class in 1980, placing third in that year's Olympic 200 metres final in 22.20, before going on to capture the 1982 Commonwealth 200 metres title and a silver in the 100m. Her finest performance to date came when placing second in the 200 metres at the inaugural World Championships in which she also gained 4x100 metres relay bronze medal.

OTTLEY, DAVE

U.K. (born 5th August, 1955) - He broke the UK javelin record in 1980 throwing 85.52 m. His major championship results since 1977 have on the whole, been disappointing but he did well to place 4th in his event at both the 1979 and 1983 European Cup finals.

OVETT, STEVE

U.K. (born 9th October,1955) - Fourth place in the 1500m final at the 1983 World Championships brought an end to his reign as the world's leading mile/1500m competitor. In 1980 Olympics bronze and gold in 1981 World Cup for 1500m were just the tips of his achievements. His reputation as one of the world's greatest tactical middle distance runners was well and truly shattered three years later in the inaugural World Championships when he allowed himself to become hopelessly boxed in at the bell and could not claw his way back to Steve Cram, Steve Scott and Said Aouita on the last lap. His latest triumph came at Reiti in Italy in September,1983 when he gained world record 1500m from Sydney Maree with a time of 3 min. 30.78sec. Now established as a television star.

OWENS, J.C.

U.S.A. (born 12th Sep.1913) - He was the supreme physical genius of his age is less an opinion than a statement of fact. His sparkling career culminated in his quadruple success at the 1936 Olympics. In 1936 Olympics he won gold medals in the 100 m.,200m. long jump and 4 x 100m relay. In the Berlin Olympics he pulled a magnificent leap of 25 ft. 9 (½) in. His best marks in long jump was 26 ft. 8 (½) in. He began his career at an early age with some of his school figures still the envy of modern day athletes, including a 7.61 metres long jump. After his success in Berlin, Owens turned professional and in 1948 he was still long jumping at around 7.90 metres. In 1955, at the age of 41, he ran the 100 metres in 9.8 sec. It was a tribute that both Harrison Dillard and later Carl Lewis based their early training on him.

PADDOCK, C.W.

U.S.A. (1900- 1943) - In 1920 Olympics, he won two gold medals in 100m. and one silver medal in 200m . In 1924 Olympics he won a silver medal in 200m . During 1921 and 1924 he equalled the 100 yds. record of 96 sec. five times. In 1926, he broke the record at 95 sec. . The record he made in 110 yds. in 10.2 sec remained unbeaten for 29 years.

PAMICH, A.

Italy (born 3rd Oct, 1933) - He has been the walker of the highest class. He made world tracking records at 30km. (4 hr. o4min 56.8 sec.) and 50 Km. (4 hr. 14min. 02.4 sec.). He was 7th in 1954 European, 4th in 1956 Olympics, 2nd in 1958 European, 3rd in 1960 Olympics, 1st in 1962 European Championship, 1st in 1964 Olympics and 1st in 1966 European Championship. He won three gold medals, a silver and a bronze.

PARSONS, GEOFF

U.K. (born 14th August,1964) - The tallest ever UK internatonal, he achieved the unique feat, in 1983, of setting a UK senior record when winning an English Schools title.

PEACOCK, TYKE

U.S.A. (born 24th February,1961) - Peacock ranked number one in the World in 1981 World Cup in high jump. He also captured silver in World Championships 1983.

PEDERSEN, T.O.

Norway (born 9th February, 1943) - In 1960 Olympics, he was the youngest at 17 to reach a final in javelin throwing. In 1964, he broke the world record with 285 ft. 10in. Later the same year he broke his own record with 300 ft. 11 in.

PENES, M.

Romania (born 22nd July,1947) - In 1964 Olympics in Tokyo, she was the champion in javelin throwing 198ft. 7 (½)in. She was the youngest athletic champion of all times - only 17 years and 2 months old. In 1966 European Championships she finished second.

PENNEL, J.T.

U.S.A. (born 25th July, 1940) - In 1963, he established seven world records in pole vault highest being 17 ft. ¼ in. He established another record in 1966 at 17 ft. 6 (¼) in.

PETERS, J.H.

U.K. (born 24th October, 1918) - In 1946 marathon he won the AAA 6 mi. In 1947 he won the 10 miles title. In 1948, his timing was 30 min. 07.0 sec. for 6 miles and came ninth in the Olympic 10,000m. In 1951, he ran from Windsor to Chiswick in the British record time of 2 h. 29m. 24 sec. In 1952, he created his first world record of 2 hr. 20 m. 42.2 sec. Again he created world record and his timing was 2 hr. 17 min. 39.4 sec. for 10 miles.

PETER, JORG

East Germany (born 23rd October,1955) - Has won four of his 13 marathons during 1980-8, including at Kosice 1987. Third at Tokyo 1988 in national record.

PETERS, MARY

Ireland (born 6th July, 1939) - After 17 years in the Pentathlon Mary received her just reward when she beat Heidi Rosendahl by 10 points to win the 1972 Olympics title with a new world record. Northern Ireland's finest athlete, her first Commonwealth Games medal was a silver in the shot in 1966 and in 1970 she was a double gold medallist in the shot and pentathlon. She retained the pentathlon title at 1974 Commonwealth Games. A superb ambassador for the sports.

PIRIE, D.A.G.

U.K. (born 10th February, 1931) - In 1951. he won his first AAA 6 miles title in the English record time of 29 min. 32.0 sec. In 1952, he broke more national records . In 1953, he captured three English cross country titles. In 1956, he created a record in 5000 m. with a time of 13 min. 36.8 sec. The remarkable achievement he tied the 3000m. world record of 7 min. 55.6 sec. and won over 1500m. in 3 min. 43.7 sec. against Klaus Richtzenhain, the German who was destined to win the Olympic silver medal later in the year.

POLLOCK, J.F.

Australia (born 25th June,1940)- In 1962, she ran 440 yds. in 54.2 sec. She won a bronze medal at the Tokyo Olympics. In 1965, she set a world record of 52.4 sec. for 440 yds. In 1966 she won the Commonwealth title.

PONOMARYEVA, N.

U.S.S.R. (born 27th April, 1929) - She was one of the most distinguished discus thrower. In 1952, Olympics she won the gold, in 1956 the bronze and in 1960 again a gold . She was a world record holder. In 1954, she was European Champion.

POTGIETER, G.C.

South Africa (born 16th April , 1937) - In 1956, he beat the world record for 440 yds. hurdle with 50.7 sec. In 1958, he created a new world record with 49.7 sec. in winning at the Commonwealth Games. In 1960, he set a fresh record of 49.3 sec. In 1966, he won the South African decathlon title with 6,534 points.

PRESS, I.

U.S.S.R. (born 10th March, 1939) - In 1959 she set the pentathlon, world record at 4,880 points. In 1960 Olympics she won the 80 m. hurdles with a world record of 10.3 sec. In 1964 Olympics she won the pentathlon with a world record of 5,246 points.

PRESS, T.

U.S.S.R. (born 10th May, 1937) - In European Competitions , she won gold medal in discus and bronze medal in shot in 1958, gold medal in shot and silver medal in discus in 1960 and gold medals both in discus and shot in 1964. In 1965 she made world records both in shot 61 ft. in and discus 195 ft. 10 (½) in.

QUARRIE, DON

Jamaica (born 25th. February,1951) - He took both sprints in 1970 and 1974 Commonwealth Games. He was selected as a 17 year old for the Mexico Olympics but was injured in training in Mexico City. He had to miss out on the 1983 World Championships when he collided with an official while warming up for his semi-final.

QUINTON, C.L.

U.K. (born 11th July, 1936) - In 1958 she won silver, medals in hurdles in the Commonwealth Games and relay in the European Championships. Again in 1960 Olympics she won silver medal in hurdles.

QUOW, ELLIOT

U.S.A. (born 3rd March, 1962) - He was the American Champion over 200m., and won silver in 1983 World Championships.

RADFORD, P.F.

U.K. (born 20th Sep., 1939) - He won a gold medal in relay and got fourth position in 100 yd. at the Commonwealth Games and 3rd in the European 100 m. in 1958. He improved his 100 yd. time to 9.4 sec. in 1959 and repeated that in 1960. He created a world record in 220 yds. in 20.5 sec. In 1960 Olympics he helped the British relay team to win a bronze medal. In indoor 50m ; he was equal to the world's best 5.5 sec.

RAND, M.D.

U.K. (born 10th February, 1940) - In 1957 she set her first national record in the pentathlon (4,046pts.). In 1958 Commonwealth Games she won a silver medal in long jump and remained fourth in hurdles in 1960 Olympics. In 1962 she earned a bronze medal in the European long jump, and shared the world relay record in 1963.

REITZ, COLIN

U.K. (born 5th April,1960) - He got one of Helsinki's luckiest medals, one which had him launching the last 30m to the line. He won bronze in 3000 steeplechase of 1983 World Championships and again silver in European Cup.

RHEIM, HEINZ KARL

West Germany (born 31st March,1951) - Rheim a lover of classical music, is rated as the best hammer thrower never to win an olympic medal. He won bronze at European Championships in 1978. In European Cup he won gold in 1975,1977 and 1979.

RICHARDS, R.E

U.S.A. (born 20th February,1926) - In both in 1952 and 1956 Olympics he was Olympic champion in pole vaulting. In 1951 and 1955 he was Pan-American champion. Between 1948 and 1957, he was American Champion indoors and outdoors. He was three times American Champion in decathlon.

RITCHIE, MEG

U.K. (born 6th July,1952) - The first British women's discus thrower of real world class, she set a Commonwealth discus record of 67.48m in 1981. She won her first major title in 1982 at the Commonwealth Games with a throw of 62.98m, her longest in major competition. She also set women's shot record in 1983.

ROBINSON, JAMES

U.S.A. (born 27th August,1954) - One of the most durable 800m. runners. He won silver in the World Cup during 1979 and 1981. He was still good enough at almost 29 to take fifth place in Helsinki.

ROELANTS, G.

Belgium (born 5th February,1937) - He came fourth in 1960 steeplechase. In 1962 he won European title . He scored another great victory at the 1964 Olympics. He was world record holder for the 3000m steeplechase. In 1966 he slashed over a minute off the Australian's figures for 20,000m and carried on to add over a quarter of a mile to his one hour record. He is also holder of the European 10,000m record.

RONO, HENRY

Kenya (born 12th February,1952) - Rono's small collection of gold medals does not do justice to his enormous talent. In 1978 he won two Commonwealth golds, two African Games golds and created four world records.

ROSE, NICK

U.K. (born 30th December,1951) - An outstanding track and cross country runner with a 1977 European Cup final 5000 metres win and a third place in the 1980 World Cross Country Championships. In 1979 he clocked 46 min.37sec. for 10 miles. His 10 km time of 27.43 in a New York road race in 1981 was thought to be a world best, but the course was later found to be short.

RONO, KIP

Kenya (born 4th January,1958) - The little front running Kenyan is always game to inject an exciting surge of pace, but he has yet to develop the necessary sprint finish that wins the major Games titles. He won gold in 1979 World Cup and bronze in 1978 Commonwealth Games.

ROWE, A.

U.K. (born 17th August,1936) - In shot putting in 1956 he attained 51ft. 7in and 55ft. 7in (British record). He triumphed at both the Commonwealth Games and European Championships in 1958 and 1959. He carried the European record out to 61ft.0in. In 1961, he raised the European and British records to 64ft.2in.

RUDOLPH, W.G.

U.S.A. (born 23rd June,1940) - At the Melbourne Olympics, she won a bronze medal as a member of the United States sprint relay team. She developed into the finest female runner. In 1960 Olympics at Melbourne she won three gold medals. She was world record holder for 200m (22.9sec). She won both individual sprint with some three yards to spare her time for the 100m being a phenomenal 11.0sec.

RYUN, J.R.

U.S.A. (29th April 1947) - He captured the world record of 1 min 44.9sec. for 880yds. and a share in the American 2 miles. record of 8min. 25.2sec. as well as being the second fastest 1500m performer (3min. 36.1sec.) of all time. He has already levelled 1 mile time twelve times- his latest 3mi.51.3sec. in 1966.

SALAZAR, ALBERTO

U.S.A. (born 7th August,1958) - In 1981, he ran the Big Apple race again and this time did a world's best. Salazar was lucky to be running at all for in the Falmouth seven mile road race in 1978 he collapsed and was given the last rites. Fortunately, he recovered.

SALMON, GRAHAM

U.K. (born 5th Sep.,1952) - Graham holds the British Blind record for high jump and 100 metres, European and World Blind records for 400 metres and has broken the World Blind 400 metres record 5 times. Before taking up running in 1977, Graham tried cross-country skiing and represented Great Britain in the 1976 Disabled Winter Olympics.

SAMOLENKO, TATYANA

U.S.S.R. (born 12th August,1961) - The European silver medal was her only loss at 1500m in 1986. Added three gold medals and a silver at World Championships in 1987. Fast finisher, who also stepped down in distance to win European Cup 800m.

SAMUELSON, JOAN

U.S.A. (born 16th May, 1957) - Has won eight of her thirteen marathons, climaxed by her sensational Olympic victory, made possible by winning the US Trials race just 17 days after undergoing arthroscopic surgery on her right knee. Won 1985 Chicago marathon.

SANDERSON, TESSA

Jamaica (born 14th March,1956) - She earned a silver in javelin 1978 European Championships. Won a gold in Commonwealth Games and silver in European Cup 1981.

SANEYEV, VIKTOR

U.S.S.R. (born 3rd October,1945) - Russian triple jumper Saneyev was a supreme competitor, winning three Olympic golds and narrowly failing to equal Certer's unique fourtimer at Moscow in 1980 when at 34 he was beaten by fellow countryman Jaak Uudmae. His first success, in 1968, came in that memorable competition in which the world record was surpassed five times, twice by Saneyev himself, who went on to notch his third world record with 17.44 metres in 1972.

SARUL, EDWARD
Poland (born 16th November,1958) - One of the biggest shock,when Sarul won the gold in the shot at 1983 World Championships. His best of 20.64 did not even put him in the all time 50 tops.Yet he beat all the big names and showed his victory was no fluke by winning the European Cup final in 1983 with a gold.

SCARTEZZINI, MARIANO
Italy (born 7th November,1954) - His best time of 8:12.5 would have got him a silver in Moscow, but he did it a month later,not having competed in the Moscow Olympics. He won gold in 1981 and 1979 European Cup steeplechase.

SCHMIDT, J.
Poland (born 28th March,1935) -As a jumper he won European Championship in 1958 and 1962 and gold medals in 1960 and 1964 Olympics. In 1960, he achieved world record of 55ft.10 (½) in.

SCHUL,R.K.
U.S.A. (born 28th September,1937) - He achieved world record of 8min 26.4sec for 2mi. and won gold medal in 5000m in 1964 Olympic.

SCHILDAUER, WARNER
East Germany (born 5th June,1959) - He won silver in 10,000m and 5000m during World Championships 1983. Again he repeated the same in European Championships. He also won gold in 1981 World Cup in 10,000m.

SCHMID, HARALD
West Germany (born 29th September,1957) - He won 1983 World Championships in 400m hurdles with a silver. He again captured gold in European Championships 1978,1982. In European Cup of 1979 1981 and 1983 he won gold in 400m hurdles.

SCUTT, MICHELLE
U.K. (born 17th June,1960) - Good enough to reach the 400 metres semi-finals and share in the British quartet's third place in the 4x400 metres relay final at the 1980 Olympic Games, she had an even better year in 1982. That year she set a Commonwealth and UK 400 metres record of 50.63 and went on to take the 400 metres silver medal at the Commonwealth Games at Brisbane.

SCOTT, STEVE
U.S.A. (born 5th May,1956) - Scott has been the U.S. 1500 metres champion every year since 1977, except in 1981 when he was beaten. Californian was always second best. Even when he set his best time for a mile in 1982, he won silver in 1500m. world Championships of 1983.

SEDYKH, YURIY
U.S.S.R. (born 11th July,1955) - Unquestionably the greatest hammer thrower and competitor of modern times, Sedykh has mastered the art of peaking for the major occasion. Gold in Olympic Games 1976,1980, silver in World Championships 1983, gold in European Championships 1978,1982, another gold in World Cup 1981, and still another gold in European Cup 1981. He is the technical innovator in his event,but may be past his best now.

SEKO, TOSHI
Japan (born 15th July,1956) - The fastest Japanese marathoner of all time when he recorded 2hr 8:38 to win the 1982 Tokyo marathon. He confirmed his world class in 1984 by finishing Ist in the Fukioka marathon in 2hr 08:52.

SHAHANGA, GIDAMIS
Tanzania (born 4th September,1957) - Shahanga's victory in the Edmonton Commonwealth Games was achieved, according to him, when he was only 17. He after his 10,000 metres victory he was of 21 and stating that contrary to common belief his Christian name is spelt Gidamis not Gidimas.

SHCHELKANOVA, T.
U.S.S.R. (born 18th April,1937) - In 1961, she broke the world record in shot put at 21ft.3in improving it further every year until 1964 when she reached 21ft. 11(3/4) in. In 1965, she became the second woman to surpass 22ft. and in 1966 she covered 22ft.10in.

SHARP, CAMERON

U.K. (born 3rd June,1958) - Emerging from Alan Wells' shadow in 1982 sharp was selected for the European Championships and against all odds took the 200 metres silver medal, clocking 20.47 behind the winner. At the Commonwealth Games later in the year he won three bronze medals, in the individual 100 and 200 metres and the 4x100 metres relay.

SHRUBB, A.

U.K. (1897-1964) - He has been one of the most outstanding runners. His eminence can be judged considering the number of records he made and the period for which these remained unbeaten. He held nearly every British record from 1(½) miles to one hour, many of them surviving for over 30 years and the last for 49 years. He held world record of 10 miles in 50min.40.6sec for 24 years, 9 miles. in 9min 09.6sec for 22 years, 3 miles in 14min. 17.2sec for 18 years, 11mi, 1,137yd. hour run for 9 years, 6miles in 29min 59.4 sec. and 10,000 miles. in 31min 02.4sec. for7 years.

SIMPSON, A.

U.K. (born 22nd May, 1940) - He has been Britain's faster mile and most prolific sub-four minute performer. He was the holder of world indoor 5000m best. He was fourth in the 1964 Olympics 1500m and 2nd in the 1966 Commonwealth Games mile.

SIMEONI, SARA

Italy (born 11th April,1953) - Tall, graceful Simeoni earned gold in 1980 Olympics high jump event. She also earned gold in 1978 European Championships and silver in 1979 European Cup.

SINGH, BHADUR

India (born 8th February,1946) He is employed in TISCO, Jamshedpur. A veteran athlete, has represented the country in the Olympic Games, Asian Games, Commonwealth Games. An 'Arjuna Award' winner. Best performance in Shot Put 18.53m.

SINKIM, DAN

North Korea (born 3rd July,1938) - She established herself as the fastest female quarter miler. In 1959, she established a world record of 2min.04.3sec. for 800m. and in 1961 reduced it to 2min 01.2sec. In 1964, she completed 800m. in 1min.58.0sec and 400m. in 51.2sec.

SKOGLUND, LOUISE ANN

Sweden (born 28th Jun.,1962) - Has met peak form at the European Championships. She won in 1982 with a Swedish record which she improved in 1986 when she was fourth. Missed 1987 season after operation on injury.

SLANEY, RICHARD

U.K. (born 16th May,1956) - The top UK discuss thrower in 1982 and 1983, by exceeding UK record by 32 cm, but the performance was never ratified as a new national mark. He narrowly failed to win his first major championship medal at the 1982 Commonwealth Games by throwing just 20cm short of the bronze medal winning mark.

SLUPIANEK, BRIESENICK LLONA

East Germany (born 24th September,1956) - Her hand injury undoubtedly cost her the first World Championship gold, but whenever she competes she seems to upset some people.She was suspended, and then reinstated, after being found guilty of taking anabolic steroids. This blots her record as the finest shot putter of modern times.She earned gold in shot of 1980 Olympic Games, European Championships 1978,1982 and in 1977,1979 and 1981 of European Cup.

SMITH, T.C.

U.S.A. (born 12th January,1944) - He was a furlong-cum-quarter mile runner of high order. In 1966, he set four world records-200m. and 220yds straight and turn.

SMITH, CALVIN

U.S.A. (born 8th January,1961) - He is the fastest man of all time. He won gold and silver in 200 and 100 sprints of 1983 World Championships. There was little in his career to suggest that the quietly spoken boy from the deep south would become one of the all time greats.

SMITH, JOYCE

U.K. (born 26th October,1937) - An international track athlete since 1956, with a 1974 European Championships 3000 metres bronze medal to her credit, she finaly turned to the marathon in 1979. She set six British women's marathon bests in all, her finest performances coming in the 1981 and 1982 London marathons, in the first of which she achieved her first sub 2(½) hours clocking (2:29:57)(1982).

SNELL, P.G.

New Zealand (born 17th December,1938) - He won the titles in the 1960 Olympics 800m, 1962 Commonwealth 880 yds and mile and 1964 Olympics 800m and 1500m. In 1962, he established mile world record of 3min. 54.5sec. and also established world record at 800m (1min. 44.3sec) and 880yds. (1 min. 45.1sec)

SOLEBERG TRINE

Norway (born 18th April,1966) - She was the top goal scorer in Norwegian second division handball in 1984, and but for her interest in the javelin would have been a candidate for the national team.

STEPHENS, H.H.

U.S.A. (born 3rd February, 1918) - She won nearly 100 races. In 1935, she set world records of 10.8sec for 100 yds. and 11.6sec. (twice) for 100yds. In 1936 Olympics she won gold medals in the 100m in 11.5 sec. and the 4x100m relay.

STONES, DWIGHT

U.S.A. (born 6th December,1953) - Stones returned to the amateur ranks after a period as a professional, but although he regained his place in the United States team he found Europe's young lions too hard to beat. Won bronze in 1976 Olympics in high jump. Captured silver in 1977 World Cup.

STRONG , SHIRLEY

U.K. (born 18th November,1958) - Most talented British female sprint hurdler for many years, she finally broke into real world class in 1983. Three times she broke the UK 100 metres hurdles record. Her earlier career highlights include a second and first in the Commonwealth Games 100 metres hurdles finals and 1978 and 1982,respectively.

SZEWINSKA, IRENA

Poland (born 24th May, 1946) - She enjoyed the title of European queen of athletics for many years. Beginning as an 18 year old at the Tokyo Olympics she won the silver medal for the long jump gained another in the 200 metres in a European record time and then helped Poland win the 4x400 metres in a world record. She set world records for both sprints in 1965 and then won the 200 metres and the long jump at the European Championships a year later, as well as helping Poland win the sprint relay.

In 1968, in Mexico, she won the Olympics 200 metres gold with a world record of 22.58 sec and also picked up a bronze in the 100 metres.

More bronze medals followed in the European Games and the Olympics of 1972 before she started serious 400 metres running in 1973, setting world record leading up to the breaking of the 50 sec barrier.

She emphasised her tremendous ability by winning the 400 metres in the 1976 Montreal Olympics in a world record 49.28sec. She even competed in the Moscow Olympics her fifth but at 34 her career came to an end with a leg injury and she was eliminated in the semi-final stage.

TAYLOR, ANGELLA

Canada (born 28th September, 1958) - One of the new breed of Canadian runners from the West Indies. Canada is benefiting from the Carribean, just like Britain.

THOMPSON, D.J.

U.K. (born 20th January,1933) - In 1955, he won the race from London to Brighton (25 mi)for the first of eight successive years. He also established his first natural 50,000m title. On the track he set UK records at 20min. 30mi. and 50,000m. In 1960 Olympics in Rome he won the 50,000m road walk in record time of 4hr.25min. 30sec.

THOMAS, SHIRLEY

U.K. (born 15th June,1963) - A bright sprint prospect for the future, she took the 100 metres silver medal at the 1981 European Junior Championships, clocking 11.43, and added European and World Championship sprint relay silver medals to her collection in 1982 and 1983, respectively. She also showed promise in reaching the World Championships individual 100 metres semi-finals in the later year.

THORPE, J.H.

U.S.A. (1888 - 1953) - He won two gold medals in Pentathlon and decathlon at the Olympics but was stripped off them because of his having turned professional. But there is no doubt that he was the outstanding athlete of his times.

After his imposed professionalism, Thorpe went on to play not only baseball but football and he received the consolaton of being voted the greatest footballer in America.

TOOMEY, W.

U.S.A. (10th January,1939) - In 1959, he won his first AAA 3miles title and set his first British record in 1960. In 1901, he set a European 3 miles record of 13min. 12.0sec. In 1962, he made mile in four minutes, made U.K. 2mi. record and won European 5000m. championship. In 1966, he set a European 6mi. record.

TYLER, D.J.B.

U.K. (born 14th March,1920) - In 1936 and 1948 Olympics she cleared the height of the winner but in accordance with the rules then in force, she was declared second in both. She won the Commonwealth titles both in 1938 and 1950. In 1939 she set a world record of 5ft.5 (½) in. She was second in both the 1950 European and 1954 Commonwealth Games competitions. In 1952 and 1956 Olympics she was 7th and 12th respectively.

TYSON, CÀROL

U.K. (born 15th December,1957) - One of the more recent pioneers of women's race walking, she set world marks on the track at 3km and 5km in 1979 whilst only 21. In addition to several WAAA titles at 5 and 10km she also holds the unofficial UK record for the mile walk, which she set during a 3km race back in 1977 when still only 19.

TYUS, W.

U.S.A. (born 29th August,1945) - In 1964, she got the first position in the 70yds (7.5sec). In the Olympics at Tokyo she won the gold medal to equal world record in 100m in 11.2sec. She also equalled the world record in both 110yds (10.3sec) and 100m (11.1 sec) in the following season.

ULMASOVA, SVETLANA

U.S.S.R. (born 4th February,1953) - The world's leading women's 3000 metres runner for several years,she finally broke the 6 year old world record in 1982 recording 8:26.78. In addition to a World Cup 3000 metres win in 1979, she became the first woman to retain a European Championships 3000 metres title with her second win in Athens in 1982. She finished fourth in 1983 World Championships

USHA, P.T.

India (born 20th May,1964) - Her phenomenal starting from birth and childhood in a remote, miniscule village in Kerala, she has been blazing the trail of Indian athletic scene ever since she was 13 years of age by breaking one record after another. Her spirited performance at the 1984 Los Angeles Olympics, where she narrowly lost a medal by one-hundredth of a second. Her subsequent feast of 6 medals at Jakarta and 5 medals at Seoul 1986 Asian Games have won her much acclaimed.

VALENT, GEJZA

Czechoslovakia (born 3rd October,1953) - Leapt into world class in the 1980s after a decade of little progress. His father,Gejza, had a personal best discus mark of 53.84m in 1956, which ranked him 16th in the world.

VAINIO, MARTTI

Finland (born 30th December,1950) - He burst into the limelight in 1978 at the European Championships, when his long prancing style took him to the 10,000 metres title. Vainio made a supreme effort in the 5000 metres, throwing himself over the line for a medal.

VEROULI, ANNA

U.K. (born 13th November,1956) - Verouli sent the Athens crowd into ecstasy when she won the European Championships 1982 javelin gold. In World Championships 1983 she earned bronze.

VAN DIJCK, WILLIAM
Belgium (born 24th January,1961) - Won the 1986 Grand Prix at 3000m steeplechase, with a series of fine wins, although he disappointed with fifth place at Stuttgart.

VIGNERON,THIERRY
France (born 9th March,1960) - The first man to pole vault 19 feet, he is a prolific record breaker in this event yet has continually failed to perform well under major competition pressure. In 1979, he set a world junior pole vault record which still stood at the end of 1983, in 1980 he twice vaulted a world record 5.75 m but placed only 7th at the Olympics. In 1983, he placed only 8th at the World Championships and then set another record of 5.83 m.

VOLKOV, KONSTANTIN
U.S.S.R. (born 28th February,1960) - The world's leading vaulter of 1981, he placed first in the world Students Games, European Cup and World Cup competitions and achieved a vault of 5.84m at an unofficial meeting to exceed the then world record by 3cm. His finest performances include silver medal winning vaults at both the 1980 Olympic Games and 1983 World Championships and he has remained a tremendously consistent vaulter over several seasons in one of athletics' most difficult events.

VIGNERON, THIERRY
France (born 9th March,1960) - A prolific vaulter, who has set many records and who in recent years also has the championship results to match. His last world record lasted just ten minutes for it came in his epic duel with Sergey Bubka in Rome in 1984.

VIREN, LASSE
Finland (born 22nd July 1949) - Viren became the hero of Finland when he followed in the traditions of Finnish greats by completing the double of 5,000 and 10,000 metres gold medals at the Munich Olympics, the latter at which he set a world record of 27min 38.4sec, despite falling during the race.

Four years later, despite looking on also-ran in the in between years , he went to Montreal and retained both his titles and then ran into 5th place in the marathon only 24 hours after winning the 5,000m. gold.

After another four years of mediocre performances dotted by injuries and illness, Viren attempted to do the impossible at Moscow and when he took the lead in the 10,000 metres with 1200 metres to go, he appeared to have achieved it, only to be beaten on the final lap and eventually finished in fifth place.

His first notice on the athletic scene had been posted when he set a world two mile record shortly before Munich and then added a 5,000 metres best later that year.

His only other medal of note,however, came in the 1974 European Championships when he gained the bronze in the 5,000 metres.

VOLKOV, KONSTANTIN
U.S.S.R. (born 28th February,1960) - Volkov has threatened to win a major title ever since he burst into limelight in 1979. He won silver in pole vault 1980 Olympic Games, silver in World Championships 1983 and gold in 1981 European Cup.

VOSS, TORSTEN
East Germany (born 24th March,1963) - Added 121 points to his personal best to win the 1987 world title, when he set no individual event personal bests, but performed consistently close to them.

WAITZ, GRETE
Oslo (born 1st October,1953) - Waitz is the greatest woman long distance runner of all time. When she won the World Championships marathon in Helsinki in 1983, there was never a more popular and fitting winner. Slimly built and blond, she first came to the forefront in 1974 by winning the bronze medal at 1500 metres at the European Championships, as Greta Andersen. It was 12 months later that she decided to increase her distance and shattered the world 3,000m record with 8min 46.6sec and then lowered it by almost a second in 1976, the year of the Olympics.

With a longer distance than 1500m. for women still a way off, Waitz failed to make the final- and lost her world record shortly. In 1978, she moved into marathon running. In New York she lowered the existing world record by over two minutes with a time of 2hr.32min 30sec. She has dominated cross country at which she has won five out of the six world titles- and in 1979 set world record for the 10,000m., the 10 miles and again the marathon in New York. In 1980, she set a new world record for the 15km, the 10,000m., the indoors 3,000m. and astonishingly, the marathon record in New York for the third successive time.

WAKIIHURI, DOUGLAS

Kenya (born 26th September,1963) - Went to Japan in 1983 to train under the late Kiyoshi. Made his marathon debut in 1986, and then to win the world title in 2:11:48.

WALASIEWICZ, S.

Poland (born 11th April,1911) - In 1932 and 1936 Olympics in 100m she won gold and silver medals respectively. In 1938, in European 100 and 200m she won the titles and in the long jump silver medals. In the 1930 women's World Games she was first in 60m. and second both in 100m and 200m running.

WALKER, JOHN

New Zealand (born 12th January,1952) - The first man ever to duck under 3:50 for a mile, Walker suffered a serious Achilles tendon injury in the late 1970. Walker's greatest achievement was winning the 1976 Olympic 1500 metres title in Montreal but it was as a world record breaker that he achieved his fame, especially on the European circuit. In 1974, Walker first came to notice in a race that he lost. The occasion was the 1974 Commonwealth Games in Christchurch when Filbert Bayi smashed the 1500 metres world record of Jim Ryun, a time that Walker also got inside in second place, a defeat he made up for in Helsinki later in the year. He came to Europe a year later and was the first man in racing history to break 3 min 50 sec for the mile, he ran 3 min 49.4sec. He broke the 2,000m world record of Michel Jazy shortly before the 1976 Olympics with 4 min 51.4 sec, a time that stands today, despite the attempts of Wessinghage, Coe and Ovett. A great competitor, Walker not often outspoken, upset officialdom in 1983 by warning them of the increasing dangers of drugs that he claimed were in widespread use at the World Championships in Helsinki 1500 metres.

He won gold in 1500m Olympic Games 1976.He also won silver in 1981 World Cup.

WARMERDAM, C.A.

U.S.A. (born 22nd June,1915) - In 1940, he created a world record with his fifteen foot pole vault. He improved upon his world record by 15ft.7 (1/2) in outdoors in 1942 and 15ft. 8in indoors in 1943. He leapt 15ft. or over on 43 occasions. That no other athlete could manage to scale 15ft. till 1951, speaks of his supremacy in the game.

WATSON, LESLIE

U.K. (born 4th February,1948) - A prolific marathon and ultra distance runner, she competed in as many as 20 marathons during 1981, in which year she also set a world best mark of 6h. 02 min. 37 sec. for 50 miles on the road. Smashed the 50 mile track world record with 6h. 20 min. 42 sec.

WEIGEL, RONALD

East Germany (born 8th August,1950) - A relatively undistinguished career, since his second place in the 1977 European Junior Championships 10km and a world best indoor 20km in 1980, was dramatically transformed at the 1983 World Championships when he achieved a decisive victory in the 50km event.

WEIR, ROBERT

U.K. (born 4th January,1961) - He achieved his first major success at the 1982 Commonwealth Games, taking the gold medal with a new UK hammer record of 75.08 m. He is also a top international class discus thrower and placed a very respectable fifth in that event at the European Cup finals of 1981 and 1983.

WEBER, HARTMUT

West Germany (born 17th October,1960) -The bespectacled Weber, champion in Athens in 1982 could well turn to the 400m hurdles in the future. In European Cup 1981 he won a gold, and repeated again in European championship 1982.

WELLS, ALLAN

Scotland (born 3rd May,1952) - In 1978, Allan Wells was on his way to becoming one of the world's leading sprinters, taking gold and silver in the Edmonton Commonwealth Games.He won gold in 100m sprints of Commonwealth Games and yet another gold in 200m sprints. In World Cup 1981 he won gold and silver in 100m and 200m sprints. It was thought that the IAAF ruling that all sprinters' must use blocks, which Wells had scorned, would affect him, but he adapted magnificently to achieve success in Moscow where the absence of the US team took some glory off his achievement. He won the Commonwealth Games 100m again in 1982, but then had to settle for a dead heat in the 200 metres with Mike McFarlane.

WESSIG, GERD

East Germany (born 16th July,1959) - The only high point of his remarkable career came in Moscow with a gold in Olympic Games 1980.He managed more than 8000 in the 10 discipline event last year but did not jump in any of the international meetings.

WESSINGHAGE, TOMAS

West Germany (born 22nd February,1952) - He won gold in 5000m of European Championships and bronze in 1974. Again in 1975 he won yet another gold in 1500m.

WHITBREAD, FATIMA

U.K. (born 3rd March, 1961) - World silver javelin medallist in 1983 Fatima is unequalled in British javelin throwing history. In 1979, she became the only British woman ever to win the Junior European title and her World silver in 1983 was the first major throwing medal for Britain in 59 years.

WHITFIELD, M.G

U.S.A. (born 11th October,1924) - In both 1948 and 1952 Olympics 800m he won gold medals, both the times taking 1min. 49.2sec. In 1948 Olympics he also got another gold in 4x400m relay. In 1952, in addition to gold he won silver medal in relay. In 1948 Olympics he got a bronze medal in 400m.

WHITLOCK, H.H

U.K. (born 16th December,1903) - In 1931, he was second in the RWA 50,000m. Championship. In 1933, he won his first title. In 1936, he won the Olympic race and in 1938 he won the European title. He won the RWA Championship in 1936 in his fastest time for 50km. in 4hr.30min. 38sec.

WILEY, CLIFF

U.S.A. (born 21,May, 1955) - He claimed the American title, winning against the Soviets and also triumphed at the World University Games. He won gold in 400m. world cup 1981.

WINCH, MIKE

U.K. (born 20th July,1948) - Ranked second only to shot put record holder Geoff Capes among British throwers during his career, he has thrown further than any other Briton bar Capes having reached his best ever distance of 20.43 m. His outstanding international achievements include silver medal winning efforts at both the 1974 and 1982 Commonwealth Games.

WOCKEL, BARBEL

East Germany (born 21st March,1955) - Although not the fastest female over 200 metres she has certainly been the most competitive, winning every major 200 metres title that she has contested, including both the 1976 and 1980 Olympic titles, the 1982 European title and the European Junior title in 1973. She was placed second in the 1982 European Championships 100 metres.

WOODERSON, S.C.

U.K. (born 30th August,1914) - In 1937, he made a world record of 4min.06.4sec.for mile. In 1938, he made world record of 1min. 48.4sec. for 800m and 1min. 49.2sec. for 880yd.in the European Championships. In European Championships in 1946 he won the 5000m in 14min. 08.6sec.

WOODRUFF, J.Y.

U.S.A. (born 5th July,1915) - In 1936 Olympics won a gold medal in 800m. clocked in 50.3sec. He won another gold in reducing the time to 1min. 47.7sec in 1940.

WSZOLA, JACEK

Poland (born 30th December,1956) - When he was only seventeen he was fifth in the Rome European Championships. Two years later and still a teenager, he shocked Dwight Stones and won the Olympic title in High Jump in 1976 and silver in 1980. In 1979 World Cup he won silver and bronze in 1977.The Poles had a contract with Adidas that Wszola would wear Tiger shoes and he refused to change them. So he was pulled out.

WULBECK, WILLI

West Germany (born 18th December,1954) - Wulbeck has been a leading world performer since before the Montreal Olympics, when he finished fourth behind Alberto Juantorena. He won gold in 800m. of 1983 World Championships, and again repeated the same feat in European Cup.

YIFTER, MIRUTS

Ethiopia (born 15th May,1944) - He won gold in 5000m of Olympic Games 1980 and bronze in 10,000m. In World Cup 1979 he won another gold in 5000m. His Olympic record is 13:21.00 in 5000m of 1980 Olympics.

ZATOPEK, E.

Czechoslovakia (born 12th September,1922) - Her achievements have been great. In 1952 Olympics she won three gold medals each in 5000m in 14min.06.6sec, 10,000 in 29min. 17.0sec. and marathon in 2hr. 23min. 03.2sec. each in Olympic record time.

ZSIVOTZKY, G.

Hungary (born 25th February,1937) - In 1960 and 1964 Olympics he won silver medals in hammer throwing. In 1962, he won the European title. In 1965, he created world record with a throw of 241ft.11in. He also put the shot 52ft. 2in. and has thrown discus 166ft.8in.

ZYBINA, G.

U.S.S.R. (born 22nd January,1931) - In shot putting in the Olympics in 1952 she won a gold medal, in 1956 a silver medal, in 1964 a bronze medal and in 1960 she was seventh. In the European Championships, she won a gold medal in 1954, a bronze in 1962 and was fourth in 1966.Between 1952 and 1956 she created world record around dozen times. In javelin she was third in 1950 European Championships and fourth in 1954 Olympics. In discus she was third in 1954 European Championships.

ATHLETICS : CUP & TROPHY

AFRICAN GAMES

The first African Games, were contested in Brazzaville, Congo on 18-25 July, 1965. Subsequent Games were staged at Lagos, Nigeria in 1973 and Algiers in 1978. Games scheduled for Kenya in 1982 were cancelled. African Championships, for athletics only, were first held at Dakar, Senegal in 1979, and have subsequently been held at Cairo, Egypt in 1982, Rabat, Morocco in 1984 and Cairo in 1985.

African Players Record (Men)

	hr:min:Sec		
100m	10.00	Chidi Imoh (Nig)	1986
200m	20.31	Tsahakile Nzimande(Rsa)	1987
400m	44.17	Innocent Egbunike (Nig)	1987
800m	1:42.28	Sammy Koskei (Ken)	1984
1500m	3:29.46	Said Aouita (Mor)	1985
1 Mile	3:46.76	Said Aouita (Mor)	1987
3000m	7:32.23	Said Aouita (Mor)	1986
5000m	12:58.39	Said Aouita (Mor)	1987
10000m	27:22.47	Henry Rono (Ken)	1978
110mh	13.69	Fatwel Kimaiyo (Ken)	1974
	13.69	Godwin Obasogie (Nig)	1976
400mh	47.82	John Akii-Bua (Uga)	1972
	metres		
High jump	2.28	Othmane Belfaa (Alg)	1983
Pole vault	5.34	Lakhdar Rahal (Alg)	1979
Long jump	8.25	Paul Emordi (Nig)	1987
Triple jump	17.26	Ajayi Agbebaku (Nig)	1983
Shot put	20.71	Nagui Asaad (Egy)	1972
Discus	68.48	John Van Reenen (Rsa)	1984
Hammer	73.86	Adam Barnard (Rsa)	1976
Javelin	82.06	Chris De Beer (Rsa)	1987
Decathlon	7934m	Ahmed Mahour (Alg)	1985

Marathon	2:08.08	Djama Robleh (Dji)	1985
20km walk	1:26.17	Abdelwahab Ferguene (Alg)	1987
50km walk	4:14.30	Eddie Michaels (Rsa)	1967

Women

	hr:min:Sec		
100m	11.22	Evette Armstrong (Rsa)	1986
200m	22.42	Evette Armstrong (Rsa)	1986
400m	50.12	Myrtle Bothma (Rsa)	1986
800m	1:59.39	Ilze Venter (Rsa)	1983
1500m	4:01.81	Zola Budd (Rsa)	1984
1 Mile	4:28.40	Sarina Cronje (Rsa)	1980
3000m	8:37.50	Zola Budd (Rsa)	1984
5000m	15:01.83	Zola Budd (Rsa)	1984
10000m	32:50.25	Esther Kiplagat (Ken)	1984
110mh	13.09	Ina Van Rensburg (Rsa)	1986
400mh	53.74	Myrtle Bothma (Rsa)	1986
	metres		
High jump	2.01	Desiree Du Plessis (Rsa)	1986
Long jump	6.80	Maryna Van Niekerk(Rsa)	1986
Shot put	17.32	Mariette Heerden (Rsa)	1980
Discus	58.80	Nanette Der Walt (Rsa)	1986
Javelin	62.34	Susan Lion Cachet (Rsa)	1987
Marathon	2:35.43	Sonja Laxton (Rsa)	1986

Asian Players Best Performancs (Men)

	hr:min:Sec	
100m	10.26	Li Tao (Chn) in 1986
200m	20.41	Chang Jee Keun (Sko) in 1985
400m	45.00	Susumu Takano (Jap) in 1986
800m	1:45.77	Sri Ram Singh (Ind) in 1976
1500m	3:38.24	Takashi Ishil (Jap) in 1977
1 Mile	3:59.70	Takashi Ishil (Jap) in 1977
3000m	7:54.00	Takao Nakamura (Jap) in 1979
5000m	13:24.29	Toshihiko Seko (Jap) in 1986
10000m	27:35.33	Takeyuki Nakayama (Jap) in 1987
110mh	13.72	Yu Zhicheng (Chn) in 1987
400mh	49.20	Ryoichi Yoshida (Jap) in 1987
	metres	
High jump	2.39	Zhu Jianhua (Chn) in 1984
Pole Vault	5.57	Liang Xueren (Chn) in 1987
Long jump	8.23	Chen Zunrong (Chn) in 1986
Triple jump	17.34	Zou Zhenxian (Chn) in 1981
Shot put	19.09	Ma Youngfeng (Chn) in 1980
Discus	61.06	Djalal-Ali Keshmiri (Irn) in 1974
Hammer	75.94	Shigenobu Murofushi (Jap) in 1984
Marathon	2:07.35	Taishuke Kodama (Jap) in 1986
20km walk	1:21.39	Liu Jianli (Chn) in 1985
50km walk	3:52.51	Li Baojin (Chn) in 1987

Women

	hr : min : Sec	
100m	11.22	Chi Cheng (Tai) in 1970
200m	22.62	Chi Cheng (Tai) in 1970
400m	51.61	P.T.Usha (Ind) in 1985
800m	1:58.00	Shin Keum Dan (NKo) in 1964
1500m	4:12.80	Zheng Lijuan (Chn) in 1987
3000m	8:50.68	Wang Xiuting (Chn) in 1987
5000m	15.27.44	Wang Xiuting (Chn) in 1987
10000m	31:27.00	Wang Xiuting (Chn) in 1987
110mh	12.89	Liu Huajin (Chn) in 1987
400mh	55.42	P.T.Usha (Ind) in 1984
	metres	
High jump	1.96	Yung Wenqin (Chn) in 1985
Long jump	6.70	Huang Zhihui (Chn) in 1987
Shot put	20.95	Li Meisu (Chn) in 1987
Discus	66.76	Yu Houruen (Chn) in 1987
Javelin	65.50	Li Baolian (Chn) in 1987
Marathon	2:30.30	Akemi Masuda (Jap) in 1983
50km walk	21.20.20	Yan Hong (Chn) in 1987

ASIAN TRACK & FIELD MEETINGS

The first Asian Track & Field Meetings were held at Marakina, near Manila, Philippines in 1973.

Venues

1973	Marakina
1975	Seoul
1977	not held
1979	Tokyo
1981	Tokyo
1983	Kuwait
1985	Djakarta
1987	Seoul
1989	N.Delhi

ASIAN GAMES (ASIAD)

Asian Games, as we know them today, were born largely as a result of the efforts of an inspired Indian, Prof. Guru Dutt Sondhi. To Sondhi, sports were a passion.

The first Asian Games were held at New Delhi, India on 8-11 March 1951, when ten nations took part. These multi-sport Games have since 1954 been held at four-yearly intervals, and a record number of (over 30) nations competed in 1986.

Venues:-

1951	New Delhi
1954	Manila
1958	Tokyo
1962	Djakarta
1966	Bangkok
1970	Bangkok
1974	Teheran
1978	Bangkok
1982	New Delhi
1986	Seoul
1990	Beijing

Asian Games Best Performances

Men

	hr:min:Sec	
100m	10.26	Lee Tao China in 1986
200m	20.41	Chang Jee Keun (Kor) in 1982
400m	45.00	Susumu Takano (Jap) in 1986
800m	1:46.81	Charles Boromeo (Ind) in 1982
1500m	3:43.49	Faleh Naji Jarallah (Iraq) in 1982
5000m	13:24.29	Toshihiko Seko (Jap) in 1986
10000m	29:37.56	Zhang Guo wei (Chn) in 1982
Marathon	2:15:29.7	Minetaku Sakamoto (Jap) in 1978
110mh	14.09	Yoshifumi Fujimori (Jap) in 1978
400mh	50.60	Takashi Nagao (Jap) in 1982
	metres	
High jump	2.33	Zhu Jian hua (Chn) in 1982
Pole vault	5.30	Tomomi Takahashi (Jap) in 1982
Long jump	8.07	T.C.Yohanan (Ind) in 1974
Triple jump	16.80	Zou Zhen xian (Chn) in 1982
Shortput	18.53	Bahadur Singh (Ind) in 1982
Discus	58.50	Li Wei nan (Chn) in 1982
Hammer	71.14	Shigenobu Morofushi (Jap) in 1982
Javelin	79.24	Shen Mao Mao (Chn) in 1978

Women

	hr:min:Sec	
100m	11.76	Lydia de Vega (Phi) in 1982
200m	23.79	P.T. Usha (Ind.) in 1986
400m	54.11	P.T. Usha (Ind.) in 1986
800m	2:05.69	Chang Jong (N.Ko) in 1982
1500m	4:18.40	Chang Jong (N.Ko) in 1982
3000m	9:24.70	Kim Ok (N.Ko) in 1978
100mh	13.31	Esther Rot (Isr) in 1974
400mh	57.23	P.T.Usha (Ind) in 1986
	metres	
High jump	1.89	Zheng Da zhen (Chn) in 1982
Long jump	6.41	Liao When feng (Chn) in 1986
Shotput	17.17	Li Mei su (Chn) in 1982
Discus	57.24	Li Xiao hui (Chn) in 1982
Javelin	60.52	Emi Matsui (Jap) in 1982

COMMONWEALTH GAMES

The first British Commonwealth Games were played at Hamilton, Canada in 1930. In the second Commonwealth Games in London in 1934, women's events were introduced. The games are held in various Commonwealth countries every four year.

The centrepiece of the Games,where the Olympic greats and world-record holders mingle with emerging world-class competitors. Africa, West Indies, Canada, Australia and New Zealand usually play a prominent part, and with Steve Cram, Seb Coe, Steve Ovett and Daley Thompson to call on, England will be favourites to win a crop of gold medals. But this is where unknown Africans descend from altitude to upset the dedicated long-distance runners from lowland countries. Commonwealth Games athletics provides a platform for a host of world-class athletes to display their talents at the very highest level, whilst giving stage to those who, if only for a fleeting moment, capture the attention of millions.

Commonwealth Players Records (Men)

	hr:min:Sec	
100m	9.83	Ben Johnson (Can) in 1987
200m	19.86	Donald Quarrie (Jam) in 1971
400m	44.17	Innocent Egbunike (Nig) in 1987
800m	1:41.73	Sebastian Coe (UK) in 1981
1500m	3:29.67	Steve Cram (UK) in 1985
1 Mile	3:46.32	Steve Cram (UK) in 1985
3000m	7:32.10	Henry Rono (Ken) in 1978
5000m	13.00.41	Dave Moorcroft (UK) in 1982
10000m	27.22.47	Henry Rono (Ken) in 1978
110mh	13.23	Mark Mckoy (Can) in 1987
400mh	47.82	John Akii-Bua in 1972

	metres	
High jump	2.33	Milt Ottey (Can) in 1986
Pole vault	5.65	Keith Stock (UK) in 1981
Long jump	8.27	Gary Honey (Aus) in 1984
Triple jump	17.57	Keith Connor (UK) in 1982
Shot put	21.68	Geoff Capes (UK) in 1980
Discus	67.32	Rob Gray (Can) in 1984
Hammer	77.54	Martin Girvan (NI) in 1984
Javelin	85.24	Mick Hill (UK) in 1987
Marathon	2:07.13	Steve Jones (Wal) in 1985
20km walk	1:19.22	Dave Smith (Aus) in 1987
50km walk	3:46.34	Willi Sawall (Aus) in 1980

Women

	hr:min:Sec	
100m	10.87	Merlene Ottey (Jam) in 1987
200m	21.93	Merlene Ottey (Jam) in 1985
400m	49.43	Kathy Cook (UK) in 1984
800m	1:57.42	Kirsty McDermott (Wal)in 1985
1500m	3:59.96	Zola Budd (UK) in 1985
1Mile	4:17.57	Zola Budd (UK) in 1985
3000m	8:28.83	Zola Budd (UK) in 1985
5000m	14.48.07	Zola Budd (UK) in 1985
10000m	31:19.82	Liz Lynch (Sco) in 1987
110mh	12.87	Shirley Strong (UK) in 1983
400mh	53.76	Debbie Flintoff (Aus) in 1986
	metres	
High jump	1.99	Debbie Brill (Can) in 1982
Long jump	6.90	Beverley Kinch (UK) in 1983
Shot put	19.74	Gael Martin (Aus) in 1984
Discus	67.48	Meg Ritchie (Sco) in 1981
Javelin	77.44	Fatima Whitbread (U.K.) in 1986
Marathon	2:26.06	Lisa Martin (NZ) in 1986
5000m walk	21:16.0	Kerry Saxby (Aus) in 1987

CROSS-COUNTRY RUNNING

What exactly constitutes 'cross country' has been interpreted differently over the years. Even the IAAF conceded in its rules that owing to the extremely varying circumstances in which cross-country running in regard to different seasons, climatic condition and distances, it is not possible to lay down any rigid legislation for internal standardization of this sport. For championship and international events, it is ,however, laid down that the race shall be run over a course confined, as far as possible, to open country, fields, heathland, commons and grassland. A limited amount of ploughed land may be included. If the course passes through woodland without any clearly defined path or track, it must be clearly marked for the .runners. The traversing of roads of any description should be limited to the minimum.

It is much more difficult to measure distances as accurately as on road. Further, the exact distances even on the same course may vary year to year , according to the laces where the flags are placed. Time is slower because of mud, uneven ground, and long grass. Spiked or studded shoes are necessary to retain some grip. It is actually a game of stamina and strength.

The first English Cross-country Championship as such was staged in Epping Forest in 1876, but all thirty-two competitors went off course and the race was declared void. The 1988 race, held over eleven and a quarter miles at Roechampton was won by Percy Stenning. The English Cross-country Union (ECCU) was founded in 1883, it grew steadily and in 1973 it came under the wing of the world'governing body ,the International Amateur Athletic Federation, which has subsequently helped expand it into a more representative annual World Championship. In 1986 runners from sixty-one countries took part.The Junior Men's race in these championships was first held in 1961.

France held a Women's National Championship in 1923 and England held its first Women 's National Championship in 1927.The first international women's match was held at Douai, in France, in 1931. But it was not until 1967, that their matches were held regularly. From 1973 they became a part of IAAF World Cross-country Championship.

World Cross Country Championships

Year	*Winner*	*Nationality*
1903	Alf Shrubb	England(Glasgow)
1904	Alf Shrubb	England(St Helen)
1905	Albert Aldridge	England(Dublin)
1906	Charles Straw	England(Caerleon)
1907	Alfred Underwood	England(Glasgow)
1908	Arthur Robertson	England(Paris)
1909	Edward Wood	England(Derby)

1980	Grete Waitz (Nor)	U.S.S.R. (Paris)
1981	Grete Waitz (Nor)	U.S.S.R. (Madrid)
1982	Maricica Puica (Rum)	U.S.S.R. (Rome)
1983	Grete Waitz (Nor)	U.S.A. (Gateshead)
1984	Maricica Puica (Rum)	U.S.A. (New York)
1985	Zola Budd (Eng)	U.S.A. (Lisbon)
1986	Zola Budd (Eng)	England(Neuchatel)
1987	Annette Sergent(Fra)	U.S.A. (Warsaw)

EUROPEAN CHAMPIONSHIPS

First held in 1934 (men) and 1938 (women). The European Championships are now contested over a full range of events every four years.

Venues

1934	Turin
1938	Paris
1946	Oslo
1950	Brussels
1954	Berne
1958	Stockholm
1962	Belgrade
1966	Budapest
1969	Athens
1971	Helsinki
1974	Rome
1978	Prague
1982	Athens
1986	Stuttgart

European Players Best Performances

	hr:min:Sec	
100m	10.00	Marian Woronin (Pol) in 1984
200m	19.72	Pietro Mennea (Ita) in 1979
400m	44.33	Thomas Schonlebe (Ger) in 1987
800m	1:41.73	Sabastian Coe (UK) in 1981
1500m	3:29.67	Steve Cram (UK) in 1985
1Mile	3:46.32	Steve Cram (UK) in 1985
3000m	7:32.79	Dave Moorcroft (UK) in 1982
5000m	13:00.41	Dave Moorcroft (UK) in 1982
10000m	27:13.81	Pernando Mamede (Por) in 1984
110mh	13.20	Stephane Caristan (Fra) in 1986
400mh	47.48	Harald Schmid (FRG) in 1982
	metres	
High jump	2.42	Patrik Sjoberg (Swe) in 1987
Pole vault	6.03	Sergeiy Bubka (SU) in 1987
Long jump	8.86	Robert Emmiyan (SU) in 1987
Triple jump	17.92	Khristo Markov (Bul) in 1987
Shot put	22.91	Alessandro Andrei (Ita) in 1987
Discus	74.08	Jiirgen Schult (GDR) in 1986
Hammer	86.74	Yuriy Sedykh (SU) in 1986
Marathon	2:07.12	Carlos Lopes (Por) in 1985
20km walk	1:19.12	Axel Noack (GDR) in 1987
50km walk	3:38.17	Ronald Weigel (GDR) in 1986

Women

	hr:min:Sec	
100m	10.81	Marlies Gohr (GDR) in 1983
200m	21.71	Marita Koch (GDR) in 1979 Heike Drechsler (GDR) in 1986
400m	47.60	Marita Koch (GDR) in 1985
800m	1:53.28	Jarmila Kratochvilova in 1983
1500m	3:52.47	Tatyana Kazankina (SU) in 1980
1 Mile	4:15.80	Natalya Artyomova (SU) in 1984
3000m	8:22.62	Tatyana Kazankina (SU) in 1984
5000m	14:37.33	Ingrid Kristiansen (Nor) in 1986
10000m	30:13.74	Ingrid Kristiansen (Nor) in 1986
110mh	12.25	Ginka Zagorcheva (Bul) in 1987
400mh	52.94	Marina Stepanova (SU) in 1986
	metres	
High jump	2.09	Stefka Kostadinova (Bul) in 1987
Long jump	7.45	Heike Drechsler (GDR) in 1986
Shot put	22.63	Natalya Lisovskaya (SU) in 1987
Discus	74.56	Zdenka Silhava (CS) in 1984
Javelin	78.90	Petra Felke (GDR) in 1987
Marathon	2:21.06	Ingrid Kristiansen (Nor)in 1985
5000m walk	21.30.92	Oksana Shchastnaya (SU) in 1987

EUROPA CUP

A European Cup, featuring qualifying semi-finals and one athlete per nation per event, was conceived by Bruo Zauli, a former president of the IAAF's European Committee. During that period they failed to win only one of the fourteen trophies contested. They narrowly lost the women's competition to the Soviet Union in 1973.

Venues

1965	Stuttgart (men) Kassel (women)
1967	Kiev
1970	Stockholm (men) Budapest (women)
1973	Edinburgh
1975	Nice

1977	Helsinki
1979	Turin
1981	Zagreb
1983	London
1985	Moscow

EUROPEAN INDOOR CHAMPIONSHIPS

This is a major winter event for non-distance athletes in Europe. These championships have been held annually-usually in February or March since 1966. They acted as a springboard to international stardom for Valery Borzov, the powerful Russian sprinter who has been the championships' most successful competitor. Borzov, who became the first European to land the coveted Olympic spring double when he won the 100m and 200m at the 1972 Games. He took the European indoor 50m or 60m title seven times between 1970 and 1977.

EUROPEAN JUNIOR CHAMPIONSHIPS

European Junior Championships recognized as official by the European AA were staged in 1966 and 1968 as European Junior Games and since 1970 competitions have been the European Championships for Juniors. Junior men must not reach 20 and junior wcmen 19 during the year of competition.

Venues

1966	Odessa
1968	Leipzig
1970	Paris
1973	Duisberg
1975	Athens
1977	Donyetsk
1979	Bydgoszcz
1981	Utrecht
1983	Schwechat
1985	Cottbus

IAAF WORLD CUP MARATHON

This event was first staged at Hiroshima,Japan on 13-14th April, 1985. With three team members to score, 41 men's teams and 17 women's teams completed the course. The men's race was of exceptionally high standard, with the first three running times in the world's fastest six of all times.

IAAF WOMEN'S WORLD ROAD RACE

This annual event was first held at 10km at San Diego, California on 4th December, 1983. The 1984 venue was Madrid and in 1985 Gateshead, when the distance was increased to 15km.

IAAF WORLD JUNIOR CHAMPIONSHIPS

The inaugural championships was held at Athens on 16 to 20 July 1986.

IAAF WORLD VETERANS CHAMPIONSHIPS

The first major veterans championships were the US Masters in 1968, although the Veterans Athletic Championships had been formed in London back in 1931. In recent years veterans athletics has flourished, the World Veterans Championships in Rome in 1985 attracting over 4000 athletes from 50 countries. This event was the sixth such championships- the first, then entitled World Masters, was held in Toronto in 1975. The other venues have been: 1977 Goteborg, 1979 Hanover, 1981 Christchurch, 1983 Puerto Rico. Veterans compete in five year age bands, from the minimum ages of 40 (men) and 35(women)

IAAF WORLD RACE WALKING CUP

This competition is held biennially for the Lugano Trophy (Men) and the Eschborn Cup (Women). Lugano, Switzerland was the first venue for this competition, which was then for men's European teams, the first team from the rest of the world to take part was the USA in 1967. From 1977 the event has been officially recognized by the IAAF with the above name. The finalists are nations from each continent, with additional European nations qualifying for the final from three qualifying matches.

INDOOR ATHLETICS

The Amateur Athletic Union of the United States instituted natural indoor championships in 1906. English Championships were organised by the AAA at Wembley from 1935 to 1939 and were revised in 1962. An inaugural European Indoor Game was held in Dortmund in 1966. Two types of surfaces are used for major indoor competitions. Wood where the track is usually banked around the bends, and dirt, clay or cinders. The size of the track varies from eight to twelve laps to the mile.

In 1985 they were contested by representatives of 70 nations, each of whom had been allocated by the IAAF a number of places based on their athletics strengths.

World Indoor Games Record

Men		*hr:min:Sec*
60m	Ben Johnson (Can)	6.62
200m	Aleksandr Yevgenyev (USSR)	20.95
400m	Thomas Schonlebe (GDR)	45.60
800m	Coloman Trabado (Spa)	1:47.42
1500m	Mike Hillardt (Aus)	3:40.27
3000m	Joao Campos (Por)	7:57.63
60mh	Stephane Caristan (Fra)	7.67
		metres
High Jump	Patrik Sjoberg (Swe)	2.32
Polevault	Sergey Bubka (USSR)	5.75
Long Jump	Jan Leitner (CS)	7.96
Tripple Jump	Khristo Markov (Bul)	i7.22
Shotput	Remigius Machura (CS)	21.22
50kmW	Gerard Lelievre (Fra)	19:06.22

Women		*hr:min:Sec*
60m	Silke Gladisch(GDR)	7.20
200m	Marita Koch(GDR)	23.09
400m	Diane Dixon (USA)	53.35
800m	Cristina Cojocaru(Rom)	2:04.22
1500m	Elly Van Hulst (Hol)	4:11.41
3000m	Debbie Scott (Can)	9:04.99
60mh	Xenia kSiska (Hun)	8.03
		metres
High Jump	Stefka Kostadinova (Bul)	1.97
Long Jump	Helga Radtke (GDR)	6.86
Shortput	Natalya Lisovskaya (USSR)	20.07
30kmW	Giuliana Salce (Ita)	12:53.42

OLYMPIC GAMES

The Olympics are held every four years, and include a great variety of different sports, as well as athletics. The Olympic symbol of five interlocking circles represents the five continents of the world.

The track and field events have been the centre-piece of every Olympic Games since 1896

Venues

1896	Athens
1900	Paris
1904	St Louis
1908	London
1912	Stockholm
1920	Antwerp
1924	Paris
1928	Amsterdam
1932	Los Angeles
1936	Berlin
1948	London
1952	Helsinki
1956	Melbourne
1960	Rome
1964	Tokyo
1968	Mexico City
1972	Munich
1976	Montreal
1980	Moscow
1984	Los Angeles
1988	Seoul

Olympic Games Gold Medallist (1896-1988)

Men

100 Metres

GOLD

1896	Thomas Burke (USA)	12.0
1900	Frank Jarvis (USA)	11.0
1904	Archie Hahn (USA)	11.0
1906	Archie Hahn (USA)	11.0
1908	Reginald Walker (SAF)	10.8
1912	Ralph Craig (USA)	10.8
1920	Charles Paddock (USA)	10.8
1924	Harold Abrahams (UK)	10.6
1928	Percy Williams (CAN)	10.8
1932	Eddie Tolan (USA)	10.3
1936	Jesse Owens (USA)	10.3
1948	Harrison Dillard (USA)	10.3
1952	Lindy Remigino (USA)	10.4
1956	Bobby Joe Morow (USA)	10.54
1960	Armin Hary (GER)	10.2
1964	Bob Hayes (USA)	10.0
1968	James Hines (USA)	9.9
1972	Valeriy Borzov (URS)	10.14
1976	Hasely Crawford (TRI)	10.06
1980	Allan Wells (UK)	10.25
1984	Carl Lewis (USA)	9.99
1988	Carl Lewis (USA)	9.92

SILVER

1896	Hofmann (GER)	12.2
1900	Tewksbury (USA)	11.1
1904	Cartmell (USA)	11.2
1908	Rector (USA)	10.9
1912	Meyer (USA)	10.9
1920	Kirksey (USA)	10.8
1924	Scholz (USA)	10.7
1928	London (UK)	10.9
1932	Metcalfe (USA)	10.3
1936	Metcalfe (USA)	10.4
1948	Ewell (USA)	10.4
1952	Mckenley (JAM)	10.4
1956	Baker (USA)	10.5
1960	Sime (USA)	10.2
1964	Figuerola (CUB)	10.2
1968	Miller (JAM)	10.0
1972	Taylor (USA)	10.24
1976	Quarrie (JAM)	10.07
1980	Leonard (CUB)	10.25
1984	Graddy (USA)	10.19
1988	Christie (UK)	9.97

BRONZE

1896	Szokolyi (HUN)	12.6
1900	Rowley (AUS)	11.2
1904	Hogenson (USA)	11.2
1908	Kerr (CAN)	11.0
1912	Lippincott (USA)	10.9
1920	Edward (UK)	9.97
1924	Porritt (NZL)	10.8
1928	Lammers (GER)	10.9
1932	Jonath (GER)	10.4
1936	Osendarp (HOL)	10.5
1948	LaBeach (PAN)	10.4
1952	McD.Bailey (UK)	10.4
1956	Hogan (AUS)	10.6
1960	Radford (UK)	10.3
1964	Jeromel (CAN)	10.2
1968	Greene (USA)	10.0
1972	Miller (JAM)	10.33
1976	Borzov (URS)	10.14
1980	Petrov (BUL)	10.39
1984	Johnson (CAN)	10.22
1988	C.Smith (USA)	9.99

200 Metres

GOLD

1900	Walter Tewksbury (USA)	22.2
1904	Archie Hahn (USA)	21.6
1908	Robert Kerr (CAN)	22.6
1912	Ralph Craig (USA)	21.7
1920	Allen Woodring (USA)	22.0
1924	Jackson Scholz (USA)	21.6
1928	Percy Williams (CAN)	21.8
1932	Eddie Tolan (USA)	21.2
1936	Jesse Owens (USA)	20.7
1948	Mel Patton (USA)	21.1
1952	Andrew Stanfield (USA)	20.7
1956	Bobby Joe Morrow (USA)	20.6
1960	Livio Berutti (ITA)	20.5
1964	Henry Carr (USA)	20.3
1968	Tommie Smith (USA)	19.8
1972	Valeriy Borzov (URS)	20.00
1976	Don Quarrie (JAM)	20.23
1980	Pietro Mennea (ITA)	20.19
1984	Carl Lewis (USA)	19.80
1988	Deloach (USA)	19.75

SILVER

1900	Pitchard (IND)	22.8
1904	Cartmell (USA)	21.9
1908	Cloughen (USA)	22.6
1912	Lippincott (USA)	21.8
1920	Paddock (USA)	22.1
1924	Paddock (USA)	22.7
1928	Rangeley (UK)	21.9
1932	Simpson (USA)	21.4
1936	Robinson (USA)	21.1
1948	Ewell (USA)	21.1
1952	Baker (USA)	20.8
1956	Stanfield (USA)	20.7
1960	Carney (USA)	20.6
1964	Drayton (USA)	20.5
1968	Norman (AUS)	20.0
1972	Black (USA)	20.19
1976	Hampton (USA)	20.29
1980	Wells (UK)	20.21
1984	Baptiste (USA)	19.79
1988	Carl Lewis (USA)	19.79

BRONZE

1900	Rowley (AUS)	22.9

1904	Hogenson (USA)	22.8
1908	Cartmell (USA)	22.7
1912	Applegarth (UK)	22.0
1920	Edward (UK)	22.2
1924	Liddell (UK)	21.9
1928	Kornig (GER)	21.9
1932	Matcalfe (USA)	21.5
1936	Osendarp (HOL)	21.3
1948	LaBeach (PAN)	21.2
1952	Gathers (USA)	20.8
1956	Baker (USA)	20.9
1960	Şeye (FRA)	20.7
1964	Roberts (TRI)	20.6
1968	Carlos (USA)	20.0
1972	Mennea (ITA)	20.30
1976	Evans (USA)	20.43
1980	Quarrie (JAM)	20.29
1984	Jefferson (USA)	20.26
1988	DA Silva (BRA)	20.04

400 Metres

GOLD

1896	Thomas Burke (USA)	54.2
1900	Maxwell Long (USA)	49.4
1904	Harry Hillman (USA)	49.2
1906	Paul Pilgrrim (USA)	53.2
1908	Wyndham Halswelle (UK)	50.0
1912	Charles Reidpath (USA)	48.2
1920	Bevil Rudd (SAF)	49.6
1924	Eric Liddell (GBR)	47.6
1928	Ray Barbuti (USA)	47.8
1932	William Carr (USA)	46.2
1936	Archie Williams (USA)	46.5
1948	Arthur Wint (JAM)	46.2
1952	George Rhoden (JAM)	45.9
1956	Charles Jenkins (USA)	46.7
1960	Otis Davis (USA)	44.9
1964	Mike Larrabee (USA)	45.1
1968	Lee Evans (USA)	43.8
1972	Vince Mathews (USA)	44.66
1976	Alberto Juantorena (CUB)	44.26
1980	Viktor Markin (URS)	44.60
1984	Alonzo Babers (USA)	44.27
1988	Carl Lewis (USA)	43.87

SILVER

1896	Jamison (USA)	54.5
1900	Holland (USA)	49.6
1904	Waller (USA)	49.9
1908	Halswelle only finalist	
1912	Braun (GER)	48.3
1920	Butler (UK)	49.9
1924	Fitch (USA)	48.4
1928	Ball (CAN)	48.0
1932	Eastman (USA)	46.4
1936	Brown (UK)	46.7
1948	McKenley (JAM)	46.4
1952	McKenley (JAM)	45.9
1956	Haas (FRG)	46.8
1960	Kaufmann (FRG)	44.9
1964	Mottley (TRI)	45.2
1968	James (USA)	43.9
1972	Collett (USA)	44.80
1976	Newhouse (USA)	44.40
1980	Mitchell (AUS)	44.84
1984	Tiacoh (CIV)	44.45
1988	Reynolds (USA)	43.93

BRONZE

1896	Hofmann (GER)	56.0
1900	Schulz (DEN)	50.1
1904	Groman (USA)	50.0
1908	Halswelle only finalist	—
1912	Lindberg (USA)	48.4
1920	Engdahl (SWE)	49.9
1924	Butler (UK)	48.6
1928	Biichner (GER)	48.2
1932	Wilson (CAN)	47.7
1936	LuValle (USA)	46.8
1948	Whitfield (USA)	46.9
1952	Matson (USA)	46.8
1956	Hellsten (FIN)	47.0
	Ignatyev (URS)	47.0
1960	Spence (SA)	45.5
1964	Badenski (POL)	45.6
1968	Freeman (USA)	44.4
1972	Sang (KEN)	44.92
1976	Frazier (USA)	44.95
1980	Schaffer (GDR)	44.87
1984	Mckay (USA)	44.71
1988	Everett (USA)	—

800 metres

GOLD

1896	Edwin Flack (AUS)	2:11.0
1900	Alfred Tyson (UK)	2:01.2
1904	James Lightbody (USA)	1:56.0
1906	Paul Pilgrim (USA)	2:01.5
1908	Mel Sheppard (USA)	1:52.8
1912	James Meredith (USA)	1:51.9
1920	Albert Hill (UK)	1:53.4
1924	Doughlas Lowe (UK)	1:52.4
1928	Doughlas Lowe (UK)	1:51.8
1932	Thomas Hampson (UK)	1:49.7
1936	John Woodruff (USA)	1:52.9
1948	Mal Whitfield (USA)	1:49.2
1952	Mal Whitfield (USA)	1:49.2
1956	Tom Courtney (USA)	1:47.7
1960	Peter Snell (NZL)	1:46.3
1964	Peter Snell (NZL)	1:45.1
1968	Ralph Doubell (AUS)	1:44.3
1972	DaveWottle (USA)	1:45.9
1976	Alberto Juantorena (CUB)	1:43.5
1980	Steve Ovett (UK)	1:45.4
1984	Joaquim Cruz (BRA)	1:43.00
1988	Ereng (KEN)	1:43.45

SILVER

1896	Dani (HUN)	2:11.8
1900	Cregan (USA)	2:03.0
1904	Valentine (USA)	1:56.3
1908	Lunghi (ITA)	1:54.2
1912	Sheppard (USA)	1:52.0
1920	Eby (USA)	1:53.6
1924	P.Martin (SWZ)	1:52.6
1928	Bylehn (SWE)	1:52.8
1932	Wilson (CAN)	1:49.9
1936	Lanzi (ITA)	1:53.3
1948	Wint (JAM)	1:49.5
1952	Wint (JAM)	1:49.4
1956	Johnson (UK)	1:47.8
1960	Moens (BEL)	1:46.5
1964	Crothers (CAN)	1:45.6
1968	Kiprugut (KEN)	1:44.5
1972	Arzhanov (SU)	1:45.9
1976	Van Damme (BEL)	1:43.9
1980	Coe (UK)	1:45.9
1984	Coe (UK)	1:43.64
1988	Cruz (BRA)	1:43.90

BRONZE

1896	Golemis (GER)	2:11.9
1900	Hall (USA)	2:03.08
1904	Breitkreutz (USA)	1:56.4
1908	Braun (GER)	1:55.2
1912	Davenport (USA)	1:52.0
1920	Rudd (SA)	1:54.0
1924	Enck (USA)	1:53.0
1928	Engelhard (GER)	1:53.2
1932	Edwards (CAN)	1:51.5
1936	Edwards (CAN)	1:53.6
1948	Hansenne (FRA)	1:49.7
1952	Ulzheimer (FRG)	1:49.7
1956	Boysen (NOR)	1:48.1
1960	Kerrr (JAM)	1:47.1
1964	Kiprugut (KEN)	1:45.9
1968	Farrell (USA)	1:45.4
1972	Boit (KEN)	1:46.0
1976	Wohlhuter (USA)	1:44.1
1980	Kirov (URS)	1:46.0
1984	Jones (USA)	1:43.83
1988	Aouita (MOR)	1:44.6

1500 Metres

GOLD

1896	Edwin Flack (AUS)	4:33.2
1900	Charles Bennett (UK)	4:06.2
1904	James Lightbody (USA)	4:05.4
1906	James Lightbody (USA)	4:12.06
1908	Mel Sheppard (USA)	4:03.4
1912	Arnold Jackson (UK)	3:56.8
1920	Albert Hill (UK)	4:01.8
1924	Paavo Nurmi (FIN)	3:53.6
1928	Harri Larva (FIN)	3:53.2
1932	Luigi Beccali (ITA)	3:51.2
1936	Jack Lovelock (NZL)	3:47.8
1948	Henry Eriksson (SWE)	3:49.8
1952	Josef Barthel (LUX)	3:45.1
1956	Ron Delany (IRL)	3:41.2
1960	Herb Elliott (AUS)	3:35.6
1964	Peter Snell (NZL)	3:38.1
1968	Kipchoge Keino (KEN)	3:34.9
1972	Pekka Vasala (FIN)	3:36.3
1976	John Walker (NZL)	3:39.2
1980	Sebastian Coe (UK)	3:38.4
1984	Sebastian Coe (UK)	3:32.53
1988	Rono (KEN)	3:35.96

SILVER

1896	Blake (USA)	4:34.0
1900	Deloge (FRA)	4:06.6
1904	Verner (USA)	4:06.8
1908	Wilson (UK)	4:03.6
1912	Kiviat (USA)	3:56.9
1920	Baker (UK)	4:02.4
1924	Scharer (SUI)	3:55.0
1928	Ladoumegue (FRA)	3:53.8
1932	Cornes (UK)	3:52.6
1936	Cunningham (USA)	3:48.4
1948	Strand (SWE)	3:50.4
1952	McMillen (USA)	3:45.2
1956	Richtzenhain (UK)	3:42.0
1960	Jazy (FRA)	3:38.4
1964	Odlozil (TCH)	3:39.6
1968	Ryun (USA)	3:37.8
1972	Keino (KEN)	3:36.8
1976	Van Damme (BEL)	3:39.3
1980	Straub (GDR)	3:38.8
1984	Cram (UK)	3:33.40
1988	Elliott (UK)	3:36.15

BRONZE

1896	Lermusiaux (FRA)	4:36.0
1900	Bray (USA)	4:07.2
1904	Hearn (USA)	4:06.1
1908	Hallows (UK)	4:04.0
1912	Taber (USA)	3:56.9
1920	Shields (USA)	4:03.1
1924	Stallard (UK)	3:55.6
1928	Purje (FIN)	3:56.4
1932	Edwards (CAN)	3:52.8
1936	Beccali (ITA)	3:49.2
1948	Slykhuis (HOL)	3:50.4
1952	Lueg (FRG)	3:45.4
1956	Landy (AUS)	3:42.0
1960	Rozsavolgyi (HUN)	3:39.2
1964	Davies (NZL)	3:39.6
1968	Tummler (FRG)	3:39.0
1972	Dixon (NZL)	3:37.5
1976	Wellmann (FRG)	3:39.3
1980	Ovett (UK)	3:39.0
1984	Abascal (ESP)	3:34.0
1988	Herold (GDR)	3:36.21

5000 Metres

GOLD

1912	Hannes Kolehmainen (FIN)	14:36.6
1920	Joseph Guillemot (FRA)	14:55.6
1924	Paavo Nurmi (FIN)	14:31.2
1928	Ville Ritola (FIN)	14:38.0
1932	Lauri Lehtinen (FIN)	14:30.0
1936	Gunnar Hockert (FIN)	14:22.2
1948	Gaston Rieff (BEL)	14:17.6
1952	Emil Zatopek (TCH)	14:06.6
1956	Vladimir Kuts (URS)	13:39.6
1960	Murray Halberg (NZL)	13:43.4
1964	Bob Schul (USA)	13:48.8
1968	Mohamed Gammoudi (TUN)	14:05.0
1972	Lasse Viren (FIN)	13:26.4
1976	Lasse Viren (FIN)	13:24.8
1980	Miruts Yifter (ETH)	13:21.0
1984	Said Aouita (MAR)	13:05.59
1988	Ngugi(KEN)	13:11.70

SILVER

1912	Bouin (FRA)	14:36.7
1920	Nurmi (FIN)	15:00.0
1924	Ritola (FIN)	14:31.4
1928	Nurmi (FIN)	14.40.0
1932	Hill (USA)	14:30.0
1936	Lehtinen (FIN)	14:25.8
1948	Zatopek (TCH)	14:17.8
1952	Mimoun (FRA)	14:07.4
1956	Pirie (UK)	13:50.6
1960	Grodotzki (UK)	13:44.6
1964	Norpoth (FRG)	13:49.6
1968	Keino (KEN)	14:05.2
1972	Gammoudi (TUN)	13:27.4
1976	Quaz (NZL)	13:25.2
1980	Nyambui (TAN)	13:21.6
1984	Ryffel (SUI)	13:07.4
1988	Baumann (FRG)	13:15.52

BRONZE

1912	Hutson (UK)	15:07.6
1920	Backman (SWE)	15:13.0
1924	Wide (SWE)	15:01.8
1928	Wide (SWE)	14:41.2
1932	Virtanen (FIN)	14.44.0
1936	Jonsson (SWE)	14:29.0
1948	Slykhuis (HOL)	14:26.8

1952	Schade (FRG)	14:08.6
1956	Ibbotson (UK)	13:54.4
1960	Zimny (POL)	13:44.8
1964	Dellinger (USA)	13:49.8
1968	Temu (KEN)	14:06.4
1972	I.Stewart (UK)	13:27.6
1976	Hidenbrand (FRG)	13:25.4
1980	Maaninka (FIN)	13:22.0
1984	Leitao (POR)	13:09.2
1988	Kunze (GDR)	13:15.73

10 000 Metres

GOLD

1912	Kolehmainen (FIN)	31:20.8
1920	Nurmi (FIN)	31:45.8
1924	Ritola (FIN)	30:23.2
1928	Nurmi (FIN)	30:18.8
1932	Kusocinski (POL)	30:11.4
1936	Salminen (FIN)	30:15.4
1948	Zatopek (TCH)	29:59.6
1952	Zatopek (TCH)	29:17.0
1956	Kuts (URS)	28:45.6
1960	Bolotnikov (URS)	28:32.2
1964	Mills (USA)	28:24.4
1968	Temu (KEN)	29:27.4
1972	Viren (FIN)	27:38.2
1976	Viren (FIN)	27:45.2
1980	Yifter (ETH)	27:42.7
1984	Cova (ITA)	27:47.5
1988	Boutaib (MAR)	27:21.46

SILVER

1912	Tewanima (USA)	32:06.6
1920	Guillemot (FRA)	31:47.2
1924	Wide (SWE)	30:55.2
1928	Ritola (FIN)	30:19.4
1932	Isohollo (FIN)	30:12.6
1936	Askola (FIN)	30.12.6
1948	Mimoun (FRA)	30:47.4
1952	Mimoun (FRA)	29:32.8
1956	Kovacs (HUN)	28:52.2
1960	Grodotzki (GDR)	28:37.0
1964	Gammoudi (TUN)	28:24.8
1968	Wolde (ETH)	29:28.0
1972	Puttemans (BEL)	27:39.6
1976	Lopes (POR)	27:45.2
1980	Maaninka (FIN)	27:44.3
1984	Mcleod (UK)	28:06.2
1988	Antibo (ITA)	27:23.55

BRONZE

1912	Stenroos (FIN)	32:21.8
1920	Wilson (UK)	31:50.8
1924	Berg (FIN)	31:43.0
1928	Wide (SWE)	31:00.8
1932	Virtanen (FIN)	30:35.0
1936	Isohollo (FIN)	30:20.2
1948	Albertsson (SWE)	30:53.6
1952	Anufriyev (URS)	29:48.2
1956	Lawrence (AUS)	28:53.6
1960	Power (AUS)	28:38.2
1964	Clarke (AUS)	28:38.2
1968	Gammoudi (TUN)	29:34.2
1972	Yifter (ETH)	27:41.0
1976	Foster (UK)	27:54.9
1980	Kedir (ETH)	27:44.7
1984	Mysocki (KEN)	28:06.46
1988	Kimeli (KN)	27:25.16

Marathon

GOLD

1896	Spyridon Louis (GRE)	2h 58:50
1900	Michel Theato (FRA)	2h 59:45
1904	Thomas Hicks (USA)	3h 28:35
1906	William Sherring (CAN)	2h 51:23.6
1908	John Hayes (USA)	2h 55:18.4
1912	Kenneth McArthur (SAF)	2h 36:50.8
1920	Hannes Kolehmainen (FIN)	2h 41:22.6
1924	Albin Stenroos (FIN)	2h 41:22.6
1928	Mohammed El Quafi (FRA)	2h 32:57
1932	Juan Carlos Zabala (ARG)	2h 31:36
1936	Kitei Son (JPN)	2h 29:19.2
1948	Delfo Carera (ARG)	2h 34:51.6
1952	Emil Zatopek (TCH)	2h 23:03.2
1956	Alain Mimoun (FRA)	2h 25:00
1960	Abebe Bikila (ETH)	2h 15:16.2
1964	Abebe Bikila (ETH)	2h 12:11.2
1968	Mamo Wolde (ETH)	2h 20:26.4
1972	Frank Shorter (USA)	2h 12:19.8
1976	Waldemar Cierpinski (GDR)	2h 09:55.0
1980	Waldemar Cierpinski (GDR)	2h 11:03
1984	Carlos Lopes (POR)	2h 09:21
1988	Bordin (ITA)	2h 10:32

SILVER

1896	Vasilakos (GER)	3h 06:3
1900	Champion (FRA)	3h 04:17
1904	Corey (USA)	3h 34:52
1908	Hefferon (SA)	2h 56:06
1912	Gitsham (SA)	2h 37:52
1920	Lossman (EST)	2h 32:49
1924	Bertini (ITA)	2h 47:20
1928	Plaza (CHI)	2h 33:23
1932	Ferris (UK)	2h 31:55
1936	Harper (UK)	2h 31:24
1948	Richards (UK)	2h 35:08
1952	Gorno (ARG)	2h 25:35
1956	Mihalic (YUG)	2h 26:32
1960	Rhadi (MOR)	2h 15:42
1964	Heatley (UK)	2h 16:20
1968	Kimihara (JAP)	2h 23:31
1972	Lismont (BEL)	2h 14:32
1976	Shorter (USA)	2h 10:46
1980	Nijboer (HOL)	2h 11:20
1984	Treacy (IRL)	2h 09:56
1988	Wakihuru (KEN)	2h 10:47

BRONZE

1896	Kellner (HUN)	3h 06:35
1900	Fast (SWE)	3h 37:14
1904	Newton (USA)	3h 47:33
1908	Foshaw (USA)	2h 57:11
1912	Strobino (USA)	2h 38:43
1920	Arri (ITA)	2h 36:33
1924	DeMar (USA)	2h 48:14
1928	Marttelin (FIN)	2h 35:02
1932	Toivonen (FIN)	2h 32:12
1936	Nan (JAP)	2h 31:42
1948	Gailly (BEL)	2h 35:34
1952	Jansson (SWE)	2h 26:07
1956	Karvonen (FIN)	2h 27:47
1960	Magee (NZL)	2h 17:19
1964	Tsuburaya (JAP)	2h 16:23
1968	Ryan (NZL)	2h 23:45
1972	Wolde (ETH)	2h 15:09
1976	Lismont (BEL)	2h 15:09
1980	Dzhumanazarov (URS)	2h 11:35
1984	Spedding (UK)	2h 09:58
1988	Saleh (DJI)	2h 10:59

3000 Metres Steeplechase

GOLD

1900	George Orton (CAN)	7:34.4
1902	John Rimmer (UK)	12:58.4
1904	James Lightbody (USA)	7:39.6
1908	Arthur Russell (UK)	10:47.8
1912	Not contested	
1920	Percy Hodge (UK)	10:00.4
1924	Ville Ritola (FIN)	9:33.6
1928	Toivo Loukola (FIN)	9:21.8
1932	Volmari Iso Hollo (FIN)	10:33.4
1936	Volmari Iso Hollo (FIN)	9:03.8
1948	Tore Sjostrand (SWE)	9:04.6
1952	Horace Ashenfelter (USA)	8:45.4
1956	Chris Brasher (UK)	8:41.2
1960	Zdzislaw Krzyszkowiak (POL)	8:34.2
1964	Gaston Roelants (BEL)	8:30.8
1968	Amos Biwott (KEN)	8:51.0
1972	Kipchoge Keino (KEN)	8:23.6
1976	Anders Garderud (SWE)	8:08.0
1980	Bronislaw Malinowski (POL)	8:09.7
1984	Julius Korir (KEN)	8:11.80

SILVER

1900	Robinson (UK)	7:38.0
1904	Daly (UK)	7:40.6
1908	Robertson (UK)	10:48.4
1912	Not contested	
1920	Flynn (USA)	10:05.4
1924	Katz (FIN)	9:44.0
1928	Nurmi (FIN)	9:31.2
1932	Evenson (UK)	10:46.0
1936	Tuominen (FIN)	9:06.8
1948	Elmsater (SWE)	9:08.2
1952	Kazantsev (URS)	8:36.4
1956	Rozsnyoi (HUN)	8:43.6
1960	Sokolov (URS)	8:36.4
1964	Herriott (UK)	8:32.4
1968	Kogo (KEN)	8:51.6
1972	Jipcho (KEN)	8:24.6
1976	Malinowski (POL)	8:09.2
1980	Bayi (TAN)	8:12.5
1984	Mahmoud (FRA)	8:13.31
1988	Koech (KEN)	8:06.79

BRONZE

1900	Chastaniee (FRA)	—

1904	Newton (USA)	—
1908	Eisele (USA)	—
1912	Not contested	—
1920	Ambrosini (ITA)	—
1924	Bontemps (FRA)	9:45.2
1928	Andersen (FIN)	9:35.6
1932	McCluskey (USA)	10:46.2
1936	Dompert (UK)	9:07.2
1948	Hagstron (SWE)	9:11.8
1952	Disley (UK)	8:51.8
1956	Larsen (NOR)	8:44.0
1960	Rzhishchin (URS)	8:42.2
1964	Belyayev (URS)	8:33.8
1968	Young (USA)	8:51.8
1972	Kantanen (FIN)	8:24.8
1976	Baumgartl (GDR)	8:10.4
1980	Tura (ETH)	8:13.6
1984	Diemer (USA)	8:14.0
1988	Rowland (UK)	8:07.96

110 Metres Hurdles

GOLD

1896	Thomas Curtis (USA)	17.6
1900	Alvin Kraenziein (USA)	15.4
1904	Frederick Schule (USA)	16.0
1906	Robert Leavitt (USA)	16.2
1908	Forrest Smithson (USA)	15.0
1912	Frederick Kelly (USA)	15.1
1920	Earl Thomson (CAN)	14.8
1924	Daniel Kinsey (USA)	15.0
1928	Sydney Atkinson (SAF)	14.8
1932	George Saling (USA)	14.6
1936	Forest Towns (USA)	14.2
1948	William Porter (USA)	13.9
1952	Harrison Dilard (USA)	13.7
1956	Lee Calhoun (USA)	13.5
1960	Lee Calhoun (USA)	13.8
1964	Hayes Jones (USA)	13.6
1968	Willie Davenport (USA)	13.3
1972	Rod Milburn (USA)	13.24
1976	Guy Drutn(FRA)	13.30
1980	Thomas Munkelt (GDR)	13.39
1984	Roger Kingdom (USA)	13.20
1988	Roger Kingdom (USA)	12.98

SILVER

1896	Goulding (UK)	17.7
1900	McLean (USA)	15.5
1904	Schideler (USA)	16.3
1908	Garrels (USA)	15.7
1912	Wendell (USA)	15.2
1920	Barron (USA)	15.1
1924	Atkinson (SA)	15.0
1928	Anderson (USA)	14.8
1932	Beard (USA)	14.7
1936	Finlay (UK)	14.4
1948	Scott (USA)	14.1
1952	J.Davis (USA)	13.7
1956	J. Davis (USA)	13.5
1960	May (USA)	13.8
1964	Lindgren (USA)	13.7
1968	Hall (USA)	13.4
1972	Drut (FRA)	13.34
1976	Casanas (CUB)	13.33
1980	Casanas (CUB)	13.40
1984	Foster (USA)	13.23
1988	Jackson (UK)	13.28

BRONZE

1896	—	—
1900	Moloney (USA)	—
1904	Ashburner (USA)	16.4
1908	Shaw (USA)	—
1912	Hawkins (USA)	15.3
1920	Murray (USA)	15.2
1924	Pettersson (SWE)	15.4
1928	Collier (USA)	14.9
1932	Finlay (UK)	14.8
1936	Pollard (USA)	14.4
1948	Dixon (USA)	14.1
1952	Barnard (USA)	14.1
1956	Shankle (USA)	14.1
1960	H.Jones (USA)	14.0
1964	Mikhailov (URS)	13.7
1968	Ottoz (ITA)	13.4
1972	Hill (USA)	13.48
1976	Davenport (USA)	13.38
1980	Puchkov (URS)	13.44
1984	Bryggare (FIN)	13.40
1988	Campbell (USA)	13.38

400 Metres Hurdles

GOLD

1900	Walter Tewksbury (USA)	57.6
1904	Harry Hillman (USA)	53.0
1908	Charles Bacon (USA)	55.0
1912	Not contested	
1920	Frank Loomis (USA)	54.0
1924	Morgan Taylor (USA)	52.6
1928	Lord Burghley (UK)	53.4
1932	Bob Tisdall (IRL)	51.7
1936	Glenn Hardin (USA)	52.4
1948	Roy Cochran (USA)	51.1
1952	Charlie Moore (USA)	50.8
1956	Glenn Davis (USA)	50.1
1960	Glenn Davis (USA)	49.3
1964	Rex Cawley (USA)	49.6
1968	David Hemery (UK)	48.1
1972	John Akii Bua (UGA)	47.82
1976	Edwin Moses (USA)	47.64
1980	Volker Beck (GDR)	48.70
1984	Edwin Moses (USA)	47.75
1988	Phillips (USA)	47.19

SILVER

1900	Tauzin (FRA)	58.3
1904	Waller (USA)	53.2
1908	Hillman (USA)	55.3
1912	Not contested	
1920	Norton (USA)	55.3
1924	Vilen (FIN)	53.8
1928	Cuhel (USA)	53.6
1932	Hardin (USA)	51.9
1936	Loaring (CAN)	52.7
1948	White (CEY)	51.8
1952	Lituyev (URS)	51.3
1956	Southern (USA)	50.8
1960	Cushman (USA)	49.6
1964	Coopr (UK)	50.1
1968	Hennige (FRG)	49.0
1972	Mann (USA)	48.51
1976	Shine (USA)	48.69
1980	Arkhipyenko (URS)	48.86
1984	Harris (USA)	48.13
1988	Dia Ba (SEN)	47.23

BRONZE

1900	Orton (CAN)	—
1904	Poage (USA)	—
1908	Tremeer (UK)	57.0
1912	Not contested	
1920	Desch (USA)	54.5
1924	Riley (USA)	54.2
1928	Taylor (USA)	53.6
1932	Taylor (USA)	52.0
1936	White (PHI)	52.8
1948	R.Larsson (SWE)	52.2
1952	Holland (NZL)	52.2
1956	Culbreath (USA)	51.6
1960	Howard (USA)	49.7
1964	Morale (ITA)	50.1
1968	Sherwood (UK)	49.0
1972	Hemery (UK)	48.52
1976	Gavrilyenko (URS)	49.45
1980	Oakes (UK)	49.11
1984	Schmid (FRG)	48.19
1988	Moses (USA)	47.56

4 x 100 Metres Relay

GOLD

1912	Great Britain	42.4
1920	United States	42.2
1924	United States	41.0
1928	United States	41.0
1932	United States	40.0
1936	United States	39.8
1948	United States	40.6
1952	United States	40.1
1956	United States	39.5
1960	Germany	39.5
1964	United States	39.0
1968	United States	38.2
1972	United States	38.19
1976	United States	38.33
1980	Soviet Union	38.26
1984	United States	37.83
1988	Soviet Union	38.19

SILVER

1912	Sweden	42.6
1920	France	42.6
1924	UK	41.2
1928	Germany	41.2
1932	Germany	40.9

1936	Italy	41.1
1948	UK	41.3
1952	USSR	40.3
1956	USSR	39.8
1960	USSR	40.1
1964	Poland	38.3
1968	Cuba	38.3
1972	USSR	38.50
1976	Germany	36.66
1980	Poland	38.33
1984	Jamaica	38.62
1988	UK	38.28

BRONZE

1912	—	—
1920	Sweden	42.9
1924	Holland	41.8
1928	UK	41.8
1932	Italy	41.2
1936	Germany	41.2
1948	Italy	41.5
1952	Hungary	40.5
1956	Germany	40.3
1960	UK	40.2
1964	France	39.3
1968	France	38.4
1972	FRG	38.79
1976	USSR	38.78
1980	France	38.53
1984	Canada	38.70
1988	France	38.40

4 x400 Metres Relay

GOLD

1908	United States	3:29.4
1912	United States	3:16.6
1920	Great Britain	3:22.2
1924	United States	3:16.0
1928	United States	3:14.2
1932	United States	3:08.2
1936	Great Britain	3:09.0
1948	United States	3:10.4
1952	Jamaica	3:03.9
1956	United States	3:04.8
1960	United States	3:02.2
1964	United States	3:00.7
1968	United States	2:56.1
1972	Kenya	2:59.83
1976	United States	2:58.65
1980	Soviet Union	3:01.08
1984	United States	2:57.91
1988	United States	2:56.16

SILVER

1908	GER	- -
1912	FRA	3:20.7
1920	SA	3:24.2
1924	SWE	3:17.0
1928	GER	3:14.8
1932	UK	3:11.2
1936	USA	3:11.0
1948	FRA	3:14.8
1952	USA	3:04.0
1956	AUS	3:06.2
1960	FRG	3:02.7
1964	UK	3:01.6
1968	KEN	2:59.6
1972	UK	3:00.5
1976	POL	3:01.4
1980	GDR	3:01.3
1984	UK	2:59.13
1988	JAM	3:00.30

BRONZE

1908	HUN	- -
1912	UK	3:23.2
1920	FRA	3:24.8
1924	UK	3:17.4
1928	CAN	3:15.4
1932	CAN	3:12.8
1936	GER	3:11.8
1948	SWE	3:16.0
1952	GER	3:06.6
1956	UK	3:07.1
1960	W.INDIES	3:04.0
1964	TRI	3:01.7
1968	TRI	3:00.5
1972	FRA	3:00.7
1976	FRG	3:02.0
1980	ITA	3:04.3
1984	NGR	2:59.32
1988	FRG	3:00.56

20 000 Metres Road Walk

GOLD

1956	Leonid Spirin (URS)	1h 31:27.4
1960	Vladimir Golubnichiy (URS)	1h 34:07.2
1964	Ken Matthews (UK)	1h 29:34.0
1968	Vladimir Golubnichiy (URS)	1h 33:58.4
1972	Peter Frenkel (GDR)	1h 26:42.4
1976	Daniel Bautista (MEX)	1h 24:40.6
1980	Maurizio Damilano (ITA)	1h 23:35.5
1984	Ernesto Canto (MEX)	1h 23:13
1988	Pribilenic (TCH)	1h 19:57

SILVER

1956	Mikenas (URS)	1h 32:03
1960	Freeman (AUS)	1h 34:17
1964	Lindner (GDR)	1h 31:14
1968	Pedraza (MEX)	1h 34:00
1972	Golubnichiy (URS)	1h 26:56
1976	Reimann (GDR)	1h 25:14
1980	Pochinchuk (URS)	1h 24:46
1984	Gonzalez (MEX)	1h 23:20
1988	Weigel (GDR)	1h 19:60

BRONZE

1956	Junk (URS)	1h 32:12
1960	Vickers (UK)	1h 32:12
1964	Golubnichiy (URS)	1h 32:00
1968	Smaga (URS)	1h 34:04
1972	Reimann (GDR)	1h 27:17
1976	Frenkel (GDR)	1h 25:30
1980	Wieser (GDR)	1h 25:59
1984	Damilano (ITA)	1h 23:26
1988	Damilano (I TA)	1h 20:14

50 000 Metres Road Walk

GOLD

1932	Thomas Green (UK)	4h 50:10
1936	Harold Whitlock (UK)	4h 30:41.1
1948	John Ljunggren (SWE)	4h 41:52
1952	Giuseppe Dordoni (ITA)	4h 28:07.8
1956	Norman Read (NZL)	4h 30:42.8
1960	Don Thompson (UK)	4h 25:30.0
1964	Abdon Pamich (ITA)	4h 11:12.4
1968	Christoph Hohne (GDR)	4h 20:13.6
1972	Bernd Kannenberg (FRG)	3h 56:11.6
1976	Not contested	
1980	Hertwig Gauder (GDR)	3h 49:24
1984	Raul Gonzalez (MEX)	3h 47:26
1988	Ivanenko (URS)	3h 28:29

SILVER

1932	Dalins (LAT)	4h 57:20
1936	Schwab (SUI)	4h 32:10
1948	Godel (SUI)	4h 48:17
1952	Dolezal (TCH)	4H 30:18
1956	Maskinskov (URS)	4h 32:57
1960	Ljunggren (SWE)	4h 25:47
1964	Nihill (UK)	4h 11:32
1968	Kiss (HUN)	4h 30:17
1972	Soldatyenko (URS)	3h 58:24
1976	Not contested	
1980	Llopart (ESP)	3h 51:25
1984	Gustafsson (SWE)	3h 53:19
1988	Weigel (GDR)	3h 38:56

BRONZE

1932	Frigerio	4h 59:06
1936	Bubenko (LAT)	4h 32:43
1948	Lloyd-Johnson (UK)	4h 48:31
1952	Roka (HUN)	4h 31:28
1956	Ljunggren (SWE)	4h 35:02
1960	Pamich (ITA)	4h 27:56
1964	Pettersson (SWE)	4h 14:18
1968	Young (USA)	4h 31:56
1972	Young (USA)	4h 00:46
1976	Not contested	
1980	Ivchenko (URS)	3h 56:32
1984	Bellucci (ITA)	3h 53:45
1988	Gauder (GDR)	3h 39:45

High Jump

GOLD

1896	Ellery Clark (USA)	1.81m
1900	Irving Baxter (USA)	1.90m
1904	Samuel Jones (USA)	1.80m
1906	Con Leahy (UK)	1.77m
1908	Harry Porter (USA)	1.95m
1912	Alma Richards (USA)	1.93m
1920	Richmond Landon (USA)	1.94m
1924	Harold Osborn (USA)	1.98m
1928	Robert King(USA)	1.94m
1932	Duncan McNaughton (CAN)	1.97m

1936	Cornelius Johnson (USA)	2.03m
1948	John Winter (AUS)	1.98m
1952	Walt Davis (USA)	2.04m
1956	Charlie Dumas (USA)	2.12m
1960	Robert Shavlakadze (URS)	2.16m
1964	Valeriy Brumel (URS)	2.18m
1968	Dick Fosbury (USA)	2.24m
1972	Yuriy Tarmak (URS)	2.23m
1976	Jacek Wszola (POL)	2.25m
1980	Gerd Wessig (GDR)	2.36m
1984	Dietmar Mogenburg (FRG)	2.35m
1988	Avdeyenko (URS)	2.38m

SILVER

1896	Connolly (USA)	1.65m
1900	P.Leahy (UK)	1.78m
1904	Serviss (USA)	1.77m
1908	C.Leahy (UK)	1.88m
	Somody (HUN)	1.88m
	G. Andre (FRA)	1.88m
1912	Liesche (GER)	1.91m
1920	Muller (USA)	1.90m
1924	Brown (USA)	1.95m
1928	Hedges (USA)	1.91m
1932	Van Osdel (USA)	1.97m
1936	Albritton (USA)	2.00m
1948	Paulson (USA)	1.95m
1952	Wiesner (USA)	2.01m
1956	Porter (AUS)	2.10m
1960	Brumel (URS)	2.16m
1964	Thomas (USA)	2.18m
1968	Caruthers (USA)	2.22m
1972	Junge (GDR)	2.21m
1976	Joy (CAN)	2.23m
1980	Wszola (POL)	2.31m
1984	Sjoberg (SWE)	2.33m
1988	Conway (USA)	2.36m

BRONZE

1896	Garrett (USA)	1.65m
1900	Gonczy (HUN)	1.75m
1904	Weinstein (GER)	1.77m
1908	—	—
1912	Horine (USA)	1.89m
1920	Ekelund (SWE)	1.90m
1924	Lewden (FRA)	1.92m
1928	Menard (FRA)	1.91m
1932	Toribio (PHI)	1.97m
1936	Thurber (USA)	2.00m
1948	Stanich (USA)	1.95m
1952	Conceicao (BRA)	1:98m
1956	Kashkarov (URS)	2.08m
1960	Thomas (USA)	2.14m
1964	Rambo (USA)	2.16m
1968	Gavrilov (URS)	2.20m
1972	Stones (USA)	2.21m
1976	Stones (USA)	2.21m
1980	Freimuth (GDR)	2.31m
1984	Zhu (CHN)	2.31m
1988	Povarnitsyn (URS)	2.36m
	Sjoberg (SWE)	2.36m

Pole Vault

GOLD

1896	William Hoyt (USA)	3.30m
1900	Irving Baxter (USA)	3.30m
1904	Charles Dvorak (USA)	3.50m
1906	Fernand Gonder (FRA)	3.40m
1908	Edward Cooke (USA)	3.70m
	Alfred Gilbert (USA)	3.70m
1912	Frank Foss (USA)	4.09m
1920	Frank Foss (USA)	4.09m
1924	Lee Barnes (USA)	3.95m
1928	Sabin Carr (USA)	4.20m
1932	William Miller (USA)	4.31m
1936	Earle Meadows (USA)	4.35m
1948	Guinn Smith (USA)	4.30m
1952	Bob Richard (USA)	4.55m
1956	Bob Richards (USA)	4.56m
1960	Don Bragg (USA)	4.70m
1964	Fred Hansen(USA)	5.10m
1968	Bob Seagren (USA)	5.40m
1972	Wolfgang Nordwig (GDR)	5.50m
1976	Tadeusz Slusarski (POL)	5.50m
1980	Wladislaw Kozakiewicz (POL)	5.78m
1984	Pierre Quinon (FRA)	5.75m
1988	Bubka (URS)	5.90m

SILVER

1896	Tyler (USA)	3.25m
1900	Colkett (USA)	3.25m
1904	Damse (USA)	3.43m
1908	—	

1912	Nelson (USA)	3.85m
	Wright (USA)	3.85m
1920	Petersen (DEN)	3.70m
1924	Graham (USA)	3.95m
1928	Droegemuller (USA)	4.10m
1932	Nishida (JAP)	4.30m
1936	Nishida (JAP)	4.25m
1948	Kataja (FIN)	4.20m
1952	Las (USA)	4.50m
1956	Gutowski (USA)	4.53m
1960	Morris (USA)	4.60m
1964	Reinhardt (FRG)	5.05m
1968	Schiprowski (FRG)	5.40m
1972	Seagren (USA)	5.40m
1976	Kallimoaki (FIN)	5.50m
1980	Volkov (URS)	5.65m
	Slusarski (POL)	5.65m
1984	Tully (USA)	5.65m
1988	Gataulline (URS)	5.85m

BRONZE

1896	Damaskos (GER)	2.85m
1900	Andersen (NOR)	3.20m
1904	Wilkins (USA)	3.43m
1908	Jacobs (USA)	3.58m
	Archibald (CAN)	3.58m
	Soderstrom (SWE)	3.58m
1912	—	—
1920	Mysers (USA)	3.60m
1924	Brooker (USA)	3.90m
1928	McGinnis (USA)	3.95m
1932	Jefferson(USA)	4.20m
1936	Oe(JAP)	4.25m
1948	Richards (USA)	4.20m
1952	Lundberg (SWE)	4.40m
1956	Roubanis (GRE)	4.50m
1960	Landstrom(FIN)	4.55m
1964	Lehnertz(FRG)	5.00m
1968	Nordwig(GDR)	5.40m
1972	J.Johnson (USA)	5.35m
1976	Roberts (USA)	5.50m
1980	—	—
1984	Bell (USA)	5.60m
	Vigneron (FRA)	5.60m
1988	Yegorov (URS)	5.80m

Long Jump

GOLD

1896	Ellery Clark (USA)	6.35m
1900	Alvin Kraenzlein (USA)	7.18m
1904	Myer Prinstein (USA)	7.34m
1906	Myer Prinstein (USA)	7.20m
1908	Francis Irons (USA)	7.48m
1912	Albert Gutterson (USA)	7.60m
1920	William Pettersson (SWE)	7.15m
1924	William DeHart Hubbard (USA)	7.44m
1928	Edward Hamm (USA)	7.73m
1932	Ed Gordon (USA)	7.63m
1936	Jesse Owens (USA)	8.06m
1948	Willie Steele (USA)	7.82m
1952	Jerome Biffle (USA)	7.57m
1956	Greg Bell (USA)	7.83m
1960	Ralph Boston (USA)	8.12m
1964	Lynn Davies (UK)	8.07m
1968	Bob Beamon (USA)	8.90m
1972	Randy Williams (USA)	8.24m
1976	Arnie Robinson (USA)	8.35m
1980	Lutz Dombrowski (GDR)	8.54m
1984	Carl Lewis (USA)	8.54m
1988	Carl Lewis (USA)	8.72m

SILVER

1896	Garrett (USA)	6.18m
1900	Prinstein (USA)	7.17m
1904	Frank (USA)	6.89m
1908	Kelly (USA)	7.09m
1912	Bricker (CAN)	7.21m
1920	Johnson (USA)	7.09m
1924	Ed Gourdin(USA)	7.27m
1928	Cator (HAI)	7.58m
1932	Redd (USA)	7.60m
1936	Long (GER)	7.87m
1948	Bruce (AUS)	7.55m
1952	Meredith Gourdine (USA)	7.53m
1956	Bennett (USA)	7.68m
1960	Robertson (USA)	8.11m
1964	Boston (USA)	8.03m
1968	Beer (GDR)	8.19m
1972	Baumgartner (FRG)	8.18m
1976	R.Williams (USA)	8.11m
1980	Paschek (GDR)	8.21m
1984	Honey (AUS)	8.24m
1988	Powell (USA)	8.49m

BRONZE

1896	Connolly (USA)	6.11m
1900	P. Leahy (UK)	6.95m
1904	Stangland (USA)	6.88m
1908	Bricker (CAN)	7.08m
1912	Aberg (SWE)	7.18m
1920	Abrahamsson (SWE)	7.08m
1924	Hansen (NOR)	7.26m
1928	Bates (USA)	7.40m
1932	Nambu (JAP)	7.45m
1936	Tajima (JAP)	7.74m
1948	Douglas (USA)	7.54m
1952	Foldessy (HUN)	7.30m
1956	Valkama (FIN)	7.48m
1960	Ter-Ovanesyan (URS)	8.04m
1964	Ter-Ovanesyan (URS)	7.99m
1968	Boston (USA)	8.16m
1972	Robinson (USA)	8.03m
1976	Wartenberg(GDR)	8.02m
1980	Podluzhniy (URS)	8.18m
1984	Evangelisti (ITA)	8.24m
1988	Myricks (USA)	8.27m

Triple Jump

GOLD

1896	James Connolly (USA)	13.71m
1900	Myer Prinstein (USA)	14.47m
1904	Myer Prinstein (USA)	14.35m
1906	Peter O'Conor (UK)	14.07m
1908	Tim Ahearne (UK)	14.91m
1912	Gustaf Lindblom (SWE)	14.76m
1920	Vilho Tuulos (FIN)	14.50m
1924	Anthony Winter (AUS)	15.52m
1928	Mikio Oda (JPN)	15.21m
1932	Chuhei Nambu (JPN)	15.72m
1936	Naoto Tajima (JPN)	16.00m
1948	Arne Ahman(SWE)	15.40m
1952	Adhemar Ferreira da Silva (BRA)	16.22m
1956	Adhemar Ferreira da Silva (BRA)	16.35m
1960	Jozef Schmidt (POL)	16.81m
1964	Jozef Schmidt (POL)	16.85m
1968	Viktor Saneyev (URS)	17.39m
1972	Viktor Saneyev (URS)	17.29m
1976	Viktor Saneyev (URS)	17.35m
1980	Jaak Uudmae (URS)	17.35m
1984	Al Joyner (USA)	17.26m
1988	Markov (BUL)	17.61m

SILVER

1896	Tuffefre (FRA)	12.70
1900	Connolly (USA)	13.97
1904	Englehardt (USA)	13.90
1908	MacDonald (CAN)	14.76
1912	Aberg (SWE)	14.51
1920	Jansson (SWE)	14.48
1924	Brunetto (ARG)	15.42
1928	Casey (USA)	15.17
1932	Svensson (SWE)	15.32
1936	Harada (JAP)	15.66
1948	Avery (AUS)	15.36
1952	Shcheerbakov(URS)	15.98
1956	Einarsson (ICE)	16.26
1960	Goryayev (URS)	16.63
1964	Fedosyeyev (URS)	16.58
1968	Prudençio (BRA)	17.27
1972	Drehmel (GDR)	17.31
1976	Butts (USA)	17.18
1980	sanyeyev (USA)	17.18
1984	Conley (USA)	17.18
1988	Lapchine (URS	17.52

BRONZE

1896	Persakis (GRE)	12.52
1900	Sheldon (USA)	13.64
1904	Stangland (USA)	13.36
1908	Larsen (NOR)	14.39
1912	Almlof (SWE)	14.17
1920	Almlof (SWE)	14.27
1924	Tuulos (FIN)	15.37
1928	Tuulos (FIN)	15.11
1932	Oshima (JAP)	15.12
1936	Metcalfe (AIS)	15.50
1948	Seerialp (TUR)	15.02
1952	Devonish (VEN)	15.52
1956	Kreyer (URS)	16.02
1960	Kreyer (URS)	16.43
1964	Kravchenko (URS)	16.57
1968	Gentile (ITA)	17.22
1972	Predencio (BRA)	17.05
1976	de Oliveria (BRA)	16.90
1980	de Oliveria (BRA)	17.22

1984	Conner (UK)	16.87
1988	Kovalenko (URS)	17.42

Shot Put

GOLD

1896	Robert Garrett (USA)	11.22m
1900	Richard Sheldon (USA)	14.10m
1904	Ralph Rose (USA)	14.80m
1906	Martin Sheridan (USA)	12.32m
1908	Ralph Rose (USA)	14.80m
1912	Patrick McDonald (USA)	15.34m
1920	Ville Porhola (FIN)	14.81m
1924	Clarence Houser (USA)	14.99m
1928	John Kuck (USA)	15.87m
1932	Leo Sexton (USA)	16.00m
1936	Hans Woellke (GDR)	16.20m
1948	Wilbur Thompson(USA)	17.12m
1952	Parry O'Brien (USA)	17.41m
1956	Parry O'Brien (USA)	18.57m
1960	Bill Nieder (USA)	19.68m
1964	Dallas Long (USA)	20.33m
1968	Randy Matson (USA)	20.54m
1972	Wladyslaw Komar (POL)	21.18m
1976	Udo Beyer (GDR)	21.05m
1980	Vladimir Kiselyev (URS)	21.35m
1984	Alessandro Andrei (ITA)	21.26m
1988	Timmermann (GDR)	22.47m

SILVER

1896	Gouskos (GRE)	11.20
1900	Mc Cracken (USA)	12.85
1904	Coe (USA)	14.40
1908	Horgan (GBR)	13.62
1912	Rose (USA)	15.25
1920	Niklander (FIN)	14.15
1924	Hartranft (USA)	14.89
1928	Brix (USA)	15.75
1932	Rothert (USA)	15.67
1936	Barlund (FIN)	16.12
1948	Delaney (USA)	16.68
1952	Hooper (USA)	17.39
1956	Nieder (USA)	18.18
1960	O'Brien (USA)	19.11
1964	Matson (USA)	20.20
1968	Woods (USA)	20.12
1972	Woods (USA)	21.17
1976	Mironov (URS)	21.03
1980	Barishnikov (URS)	21.08
1984	Carter (USA)	21.09
1988	Barnes (USA)	22.39

BRONZE

1896	Papasideris (GRE)	10.36
1900	Garrett (USA)	12.37
1904	L. Feuerbach (USA)	13.18
1908	Garrels (USA)	13.18
1912	Whitney (USA)	13.93
1920	Liversedge (USA)	14.15
1924	Hills (USA)	14.64
1928	Hirschfeld (GER)	15.66
1932	Douda (TCH)	15.61
1936	Stock (GER)	15.66
1948	Fuchs (USA)	16.42
1952	Fuchs (USA)	17.06
1956	Skobla (TCH)	17.65
1960	Long (USA)	19.01
1964	Varju (HUN)	19.39
1968	Gushchin (URS)	20.09
1972	Briesenick (GDR)	21.14
1976	Barishnikov (URS)	21.00
1980	Beyer (GDR)	21.06
1984	Laut (USA)	20.97
1988	Guenthoer (SUI)	21.99

Discus

GOLD

1896	Robert Garrett (USA)	29.15m
1900	Rudolf Bauer (HUN)	36.04m
1904	Martin Sheridan (USA)	39.28m
1906	Martin Sheridan (USA)	41.46m
1908	Martin Sheridan (USA)	40.89m
1912	Armas Taipale (FIN)	45.21m
1920	Elmer Niklander (FIN)	44.68m
1924	Clarence Houser (USA)	46.15m
1928	Clarence Houser (USA)	47.32m
1932	John Anderson (USA)	49.49m
1936	Ken Carpenter (USA)	50.48m
1948	Adolfo Consolini (ITA)	52.78m
1952	Sim Iness (USA)	55.03m
1956	Al Oerter (USA)	56.36m
1960	Al Oerter (USA)	59.18m
1964	Al Oerter (USA)	61.00m

1968	Al Oerter (USA)	64.78m
11972	Ludvik Danes (TCH)	64.40m
1976	Mac Wilkins (USA)	67.50m
1980	Viktor Rashchupkin (URS)	66.64m
1984	Rolf Danneberg (FRG)	66.60m
1988	Schult (GDR)	68.82

SILVER

1896	Paraskevopoulos (GRE)	28.95
1900	Janda-Suk (BOH)	35.25
1904	Rose (USA)	39.28
1908	Giffin (USA)	40.70
1912	Byrd (USA)	42.32
1920	Taipale (FIN)	44.19
1924	Nittymaa (FIN)	44.95
1928	Kivi (FIN)	47.23
1932	Laborde (USA)	48.47
1936	Dunn (USA)	49.36
1948	Tosi (ITA)	51.78
1952	Consolini (ITA)	53.78
1956	Gordien (USA)	54.81
1960	Babka (USA)	58.02
1964	Danek (TCH)	60.52
1968	Milde (GDR)	63.08
1972	Silvester (USA)	63.50
1976	Schmidt (GDR)	66.22
1980	Bugar (TCH)	66.38
1984	Wikins (USA)	66.30
1988	Ubarts (URS)	67.48

BRONZE

1896	Versis (GRE)	28.78
1900	Sheldon (USA)	34.60
1904	Georgantas (GRE)	37.68
1908	H. Jorr (USA)	39.44
1912	Duncan (USA)	42.28
1920	Pope (USA)	42.13
1924	Lieb (USA)	44.83
1928	Corson (USA)	47.10
1932	Winter (FRA)	47.85
1936	Oberweger (ITA)	49.23
1948	Gordien (USA)	50.77
1952	Dillion (USA)	53.28
1956	Koch (USA)	54.40
1960	Cochran (USA)	57.16
1964	Weill (USA)	59.49
1968	Danek (TCH)	62.92

1972	Bruch (WE)	63.40
1976	Powell (USA)	65.70
1980	Delis (CUB)	66.32
1984	Powell (USA)	65.46
1988	Danneberg (FRG)	67.38

Hammer

GOLD

1900	John Flanagan (USA)	49.73m
1904	John Flanagan (USA)	51.23m
1908	John Flanagan (USA)	51.92m
1912	Matt McGrath (USA)	54.74m
1920	Patrick Ryan (USA)	52.87m
1924	Fred Tootell (USA)	53.29m
1928	Patrick O'Callaghan (IRL)	51.39m
1932	Patrick O'Callaghan(IRL)	53.92m
1936	Karl Hein (GER)	56.49m
1948	Imre Nemeth (HUN)	56.07m
1952	Jozsef Csermak (HUN)	60.34m
1956	Harold Connolly (USA)	63.19m
1960	Vasiliy Rudenkov (URS)	67.10m
1964	Romuald Klim (URS)	69.74m
1968	Gyula Zsivotzky (HUN)	73.36m
1972	Anatoliy Bondarchuk (URS)	75.50m
1976	Yuriy Sedykh (URS)	77.52m
1980	Yuriy Sedykh (URS)	81.80m
1984	Juha Tiainen (FIN)	78.08m
1988	Litvinov (URS)	84.80m

SILVER

1896Not contested

1900	Hare (USA)	49.13
1904	De Witt (USA)	50.26
1908	Mc Grath (USA)	51.18
1912	Gillis (CAN)	48.39
1920	Lind (SWE)	48.43
1924	Mc Grath (USA)	50.84
1928	Skiold (SWE)	51.29
1932	Porhola (FIN)	52.27
1936	Blask (GER)	55.04
1948	Gubijan (YUG)	54.27
1952	Storch (GER)	58.86
1956	Krivonosov (URS)	63.03
1960	Zsivotzky (HUN)	65.79
1964	Zsivotzky (HUN)	69.09
1968	Klim (URS)	73.28

1972	Sachse (GDR)	74.96
1976	Spiridonov (URS)	76.08
1980	Litvinov (URS)	80.64
1984	Riehm (FRG)	77.98
1988	Sedykh (URS)	83.76

BRONZE

1896 Not contested

1900	Mc Cracken (USA)	42.46
1904	Rose (USA)	45.73
1908	Walsh (USA)	48.50
1912	Childs (USA)	48.17
1920	Bennet (USA)	48.25
1924	Nokes (UK)	48.87
1928	Black (USA)	49.03
1932	Zaremba (USA)	50.33
1936	Warngard (SWE)	54.83
1948	R. Bennett (USA)	53.73
1952	I. Nemeth (HUN)	57.74
1956	Samotsvyetov (URS)	62.56
1960	Rut (POL)	65.64
1964	Uwe Beyer (FRG)	68.09
1968	Lovasz (HUN)	69.78
1972	Khmyelesvkiy (URS)	74.04
1976	Bondarchuk (URS)	75.48
1980	Tamm (URS)	78.96
1984	Ploghaus (FRG)	76.68
1988	Tamm (URS)	81.16

Javelin

GOLD

1904	Erik Lemming (SWE)	53.90m
1908	Erik Lemming (SWE)	54.82m
1912	Erik Lemming (SWE)	60.64m
1920	Jonni Myyra (FIN)	65.78m
1924	Jonni Myyra (FIN)	62.96m
1928	Erik Lundkvist (SWE)	66.60m
1932	Matti Jarvinen (FIN)	72.71m
1936	Gerhard Stock (GER)	71.84m
1948	Tapio Rautavara (FIN)	69.77m
1952	CyrusYoung (USA)	73.78m
1956	Egil Danielsen (NOR)	85.71m
1960	Viktor Tsibulenko (URS)	84.64m
1964	Pauli Nevala (FIN)	82.66m
1968	Janis Lusis (URS)	90.10m
1972	Klaus Wolfermann (FRG)	90.48m
1976	Miklos Nemeth (HUN)	94.58m
1980	Dainis Kula (URS)	91.20m
1984	Arto Harkonen (FIN)	86.76m
1988	Korjus (FIN)	84.28

SILVER

1904	—	—
1908	Halse (NOR)	50.57
1912	Saristo (FIN)	58.66
1920	Peltonen (FIN)	64.50
1924	Lindstrom (SWE)	60.92
1928	Szepes (HUN)	65.26
1932	Sippala (FIN)	69.80
1936	Nikkanen (FIN)	70.77
1948	Seymour (USA)	67.56
1952	Miller (USA)	72.46
1956	Sidlo (POL)	79.98
1960	Kruger (GDR)	79.36
1964	Kulcsar (HUN)	82.32
1968	Kinnunen (FIN)	88.58
1972	Lusis (URS)	90.46
1976	Siitonen (FIN)	87.92
1980	Makarov (URS)	89.64
1984	Ottley (UK)	85.74
1988	Zelezny (TCH)	84.12

BRONZE

1908	Nilsson (SWE)	47.10
1912	Koczan (HUN)	5.50
1920	Johansson (FIN)	63.09
1924	Oberst (USA)	58.35
1928	Sunde (NOR)	63.97
1932	Penttila (FIN)	68.70
1936	Toivonen (FIN)	70.72
1948	Varszegi (HUN)	67.03
1952	Hyytiainen (FIN)	71.89
1956	Tsibulenko (URS)	79.50
1960	Kulcsafr (HUN)	78.57
1964	Lusis (URS)	80.57
1968	Kulcsar (HUN)	87.06
1972	Schmidt (USA)	84.42
1976	Megelea (ROM)	87.16
1980	Hanisch (GDR)	86.72
1984	Eldebrink (SWE)	83.72
1988	Raty (FIN)	83.26

Decathlon

GOLD

1904	Thomas Kiely (UK)	6036pts.
1912	Hugo Wieslander (SWE)	6162pts.
1920	Helge Lovland (NOR)	5970pts.
1924	Harold Osborn (USA)	6668pts.
1928	Paavo Yrjola (FIN)	6774pts.
1932	Jim Bausch (USA)	6986pts.
1936	Glenn Morris (USA)	7421pts.
1948	Bob Mathias (USA)	6826pts.
1952	Bob Mathias (USA)	7731pts.
1956	Milt Campbell (USA)	7708pts.
1960	Rafer Johnson (USA)	8001pts.
1964	Willi Holdorf (GER)	7887pts.
1968	Bill Toomey(USA)	8193pts.
1972	Nikolai Avilov (URS)	8454pts.
1976	Bruce Jenner (USA)	8617pts.
1980	Daley Thompson (UK)	8495pts.
1984	Daley Thompson (UK)	8798pts.
1988	Schenk (GDR)	2448pts.

SILVER

1912	Wieslander(SWE)	7724/6161
1920	Hamilton (USA)	6770/5912
1924	Norton (USA)	7350/6340
1928	Jarvinen(FIN)	7931/6815
1932	Javinen (FIN)	8292/7038
1936	Clark (USA)	7601/7226
1948	Heinrich (FRA)	6974/6740
1952	Campbell (USA)	6975/7132
1956	Johnson (USA)	7587/7568
1960	Yang (TPE)	8334/7930
1964	Aun (URS)	7842
1968	Walde (FRG)	8111
1972	Litvinyenko (URS)	8035
1976	Kratschmer(FRG)	8411
1980	Kustsenko(URS)	8331
1984	Hingsen (FRG)	8673
1988	Voss (GDR)	8399

BRONZE

1912	Lomberg (SWE)	7413/5943
1920	Olsson (SWE)	6579/5825
1924	Klumberg (EST)	7329/6260
1928	Doherty (USA)	7706/6593
1932	Eberle (GER)	8030/6830
1936	Parker (USA)	7275/6918
1948	Simmons (USA)	6950/6711
1952	Simmons (USA)	6788/7069
1956	Kuznyetsov (URS)	7465/7461
1960	Kuznyetsov (URS)	7809/7624
1964	Walde (FRG)	7809
1968	Bendlin (FRG)	8064
1972	Katus (POL)	7984
1976	Avilov (URS)	8369
1980	Zhelanov (URS)	8135
1984	Wentz (FRG)	8412
1988	Steen (CAN)	8328

TRACK AND FIELD (Women)

100 Metres

GOLD

1928	Elizabeth Robinson (USA)	12.2
1932	Stanislawa Walasiewics (POL)	11.9
1936	Helen Stephens (USA)	11.5
1948	Fanny Blankers Koen (HOL)	11.9
1952	Marjorie Jackson (AUS)	11.5
1956	Betty Cuthbert (AUS)	11.5
1960	Wilma Rudolph (USA)	11.0
1964	Wyomia Tyus (USA)	11.4
1968	Wyomia Tyus (USA)	11.0
1972	Renate Stecher (GDR)	11.07
1976	Annegret Richter (FRG)	11.08
1980	Ludmila Kondratyeva (URS)	11.06
1984	Evelyn Ashford (USA)	10.97
1988	Joyner (USA)	10.54

SILVER

1928	Rosenfeld (CAN)	12.3
1932	Strike (CAN)	11.9
1936	Walasiewicz (POL)	11.7
1948	Manley (GBR)	12.2
1952	Hasenjager (SA)	11.8
1956	Stubnick (GDR)	11.7
1960	Hyman (GBR)	11.3
1964	Mc Guire (USA)	11.6
1968	Ferrell (USA)	11.11
1972	Boyle (AUS)	11.23
1976	Stecher (GDR)	11.13
1980	Gohr (GDR)	11.07
1984	Brown (USA)	11.13
1988	Ashford (USA)	10.83

BRONZE

1928	E. Smith (CAN)	12.3
1932	Von Bremen (USA)	12.0
1936	Krauss (GER)	11.9
1948	Strickland (AUS)	12.2
1952	Strickland (AUS)	11.9
1956	Matthews (AUS)	11.7
1960	Leone (ITA)	11.31
1964	Klobukowska (POL)	11.6
1968	Szewinska (POL)	11.1
1972	Chivas (CUB)	11.24
1976	Helten (FRG)	11.17
1980	Auerswald (GDR)	11.14
1984	Ottey-Page (JAM)	11.16
1988	Drechsler (GDR)	10.85

200 Metres

GOLD

1948	Fanny Blankers Koen (HOL)	24.4
1952	Marjorie Jackson (AUS)	23.7
1956	Betty Cuthbert (AUS)	23.4
1960	Wilma Rudolph (USA)	24.0
1964	Edith Maguire (USA)	23.0
1968	Irena Szewinska (POL)	22.5
1972	Renate Stecher (GDR)	22.40
1976	Barbel Eckert (GDR)	22.37
1980	Barbel Wockel (GDR)	22.03
1984	Valerie Brisco-Hooks (USA)	21.81
1988	Joyner (USA)	21.34

SILVER

1948	Williamson (UK)	25.1
1952	Brouwer (HOL)	24.2
1956	Stibnick (GDR)	23.7
1960	Heine (GER)	24.2
1964	Szewinska (POL)	23.1
1968	Boyle (AUS)	22.7
1972	Boyle (AUS)	22.45
1976	Richter (FRG)	22.39
1980	Bochina (URS)	22.19
1984	Griffith (USA)	22.04
1988	Jackson (JAM)	21.72

BRONZE

1948	Petterson (USA)	25.2
1952	Khnikina (URS)	24.2
1956	Matthews (AUS)	23.8
1960	Hyman (UK)	24.7
1964	Black (AUS)	23.1
1968	Lamy (AUS)	22.8
1972	Szewinska (POL)	22.74
1976	Stecher (GDR)	22.47
1980	Ottey (JAM)	22.20
1984	Ottey (JAM)	22.09
1988	Drechsler (GDR)	21.95

400 Metres

GOLD

1964	Betty Cuthbert (AUS)	52.0
1968	Colette Besson (FRA)	52.0
1972	Monika Zehrt (GDR)	51.08
1976	Irena Szewinska (POL)	49.29
1980	Marita Koch (GDR)	48.88
1984	Valerie Brisco-Hooks (USA)	48.83
1988	Bryzgina (URS)	48.65

SILVER

1964	Packer (UK)	52.2
1968	Board (UK)	52.1
1972	Wilden (FRG)	51.21
1976	Brehmer (GDR)	50.51
1980	Kratochvilova (TCH)	49.46
1984	Cheeseborough (USA)	49.05
1988	Mueller (GDR)	4945

BRONZE

1964	Amoore (AUS)	53.4
1968	Pechenkina (URS)	52.2
1972	Hammond (USA)	51.64
1976	Streidt (GDR)	50.55
1980	Lathan (GDR)	49.66
1984	Cook (GBR)	49.42
1988	Nazarova (URS)	49.90

800 Metres

GOLD

1928	Lina Radke (GER)	2:16.8

1932Not contested
1936 Not contested
1948Not contested
1952Not contested

1958 Not contested		
1960	Ludmila Shevtsova (URS)	2:04.3
1964	Ann Packer (GBR)	2:01.1
1968	Madeline Manning (USA)	2:00.0
1972	Hildegard Falck (FRG)	1:58.6
1976	Tatyana Kazankina (URS)	1:54.9
1980	Nadyezda Olizarenko (URS)	1:53.5
1984	Doina Melinte (ROM)	1:57.6
1988	Wodars (GDR)	1:56.10

SILVER

1928	Hitomi (JAP)	2:17.6
1932 Not contested		
1936 Not contested		
1948 Not contested		
1952 Not contested		
1956 Not contested		
1960	Jones (AUS)	2:04.4
1964	Dupureur (FRA)	2:01.9
1968	Sailai (ROM)	2:02.5
1972	Sbaite (URS)	1:58.7
1976	Shtereva (BUL)	1:55.4
1980	Mineyeva (URS)	1:54.9
1984	Gallagher (USA)	1:58.6
1988	Wachtel (GDR)	1:56.64

BRONZE

1928	Gentzel (SWE)	2:17.8
1932 Not contested		
1936 Not contested		
1948 Not contested		
1952 Not contested		
1956 Not contested		
1960	Donath (GDR)	2:05.6
1964	Chamberlain (NZL)	2:02.8
1968	Gommers (HOL)	2:02.6
1972	Hoffmeister (GDR)	1:59.2
1976	Zinn (GDR)	1:55.6
1980	Providokhina (URS)	1:55.5
1984	Lovin (ROM)	1:58.8
1988	Gallagher (USA)	1:56.91

1500 Metres

GOLD

1972	Ludmila Bragina (URS)	4:01.4
1976	Tatyana Kazankina (URS)	4:05.6
1980	Tatyana Kazankina (URS)	1:54.9
1984	Gabriella Doria (ITA)	4:03.25
1988	Ivan (ROM)	3:53.96

SILVER

1972	Hoffmeister (GDR)	4:02.8
1976	Hoffmeister (GDR)	4:06.0
1980	Wartenberg (GDR)	3:57.8
1984	Melinte (ROM)	4:03.7
1988	Baikauskaite (URS)	4:00.24

BRONZE

1972	Pigni- Cacchi (ITA)	4:02.9
1976	Klapezynski (GDR)	4:06.1
1980	Olizaryenko (URS)	3:59.6
1984	Maricica Puica (ROM)	4:04.1
1988	Samolenko (URS)	4:00.30

3000 Metres

GOLD

1984	Maricica Puica (ROM)	8:35.96
1988	Samolenko (URS)	8:26.53

SILVER

1984	Wendy Sly(UK)	8:39.47
1988	Ivan (Rom)	8:27.15

BRONZE

1984	Lynn Williams (CAN)	8:42.17
1988	Murray (UK)	8:29.2

Marathon

GOLD

1984	Joan Benoit (USA)	2h 24:52
1988	Mota (POR)	2h 25:40

SILVER

1984	Waitz (NOR)	2h 26:18
1988	Martin (AUS)	2h 25:53

BRONZE

1984	Mota (POR)	2h 26:57
1988	Doere (GDR)	2h 25:53

100 Metres Hurdles

GOLD

Year	Name	Time
1932	Mildred Didrikson (USA)	11.7
1936	Trebisonda Valla (ITA)	11.7
1948	Fanny Blankers Koen (HOL)	11.2
1952	Shirley de la Hunty (AUS)	10.9
1956	Shirley de la Hunty (AUS)	10.7
1960	Irina Press (URS)	10.8
1964	Karin Balzer (GER)	10.5
1968	Maureen Caird (AUS)	10.3
1972	Annelie Ehrhardt (GDR)	12.59
1976	Johanna Schaller (GDR)	12.77
1980	Vera Komisova (URS)	12.56
1984	Benita Fitzgerald Brown (USA)	12.84
1988	Donkova (BUL)	12.38

SILVER

Year	Name	Time
1932	Hall (USA)	11.7
1936	Steuer (GER)	11.7
1948	Gardner (UK)	11.2
1952	Golubnichaya (URS)	11.1
1956	Birkemeyer (GDR)	10.9
1960	Quinton (UK)	10.9
1964	Ciepla (POL)	10.5
1968	Ryan-Kilborn (AUS)	10.4
1972	Bufanu (ROM)	12.84
1976	Anisimova (URS)	12.78
1980	Klier-Schaller (GDR)	12.63
1984	Strong (UK)	12.88
1988	Siebert (GDR)	12.61

BRONZE

Year	Name	Time
1932	Clark (SA)	11.8
1936	Taylor (CAN)	11.7
	Testoni (ITA)	11.7
1948	Strickland (AUS)	11.4
1952	Sander (GER)	11.1
1956	Thrower (AIS)	11.0
1960	Birkemeyer (GDR)	11.0
1964	Ryan (AUS)	10.5
1968	Chi Cheng (TPE)	10.4
1972	Balzer (GDR)	12.90
1976	Lebedyeva (URS)	12.80
1980	Langer(POL)	12.65
1984	Turner (USA)	13.06
1988	Zackiewicz (FRG)	12.75

400 Metres Hurdles

GOLD

Year	Name	Time
1984	Nawal El Moutawakel (MAR)	54.61
1988	Flintoff-King (AUS)	53.17

SILVER

Year	Name	Time
1984	Brown (USA)	55.20
1988	Ledovskaia (URS)	53.18

BRONZE

Year	Name	Time
1984	Cojocaru (ROM)	55.41
1988	Fiedler (GDR)	53.63

4 x100 Metres Relay

GOLD

Year	Team	Time
1928	Canada	48.4
1932	USA	47.0
1936	USA	46.9
1948	The Netherlands	47.5
1952	USA	45.9
1956	Australia	44.5
1960	USA	44.5
1964	Poland	43.6
1968	USA	42.8
1972	FRG	42.81
1976	GDR	42.55
1980	GDR	41.60
1984	USA	41.65
1988	USA	41.98

SILVER

Year	Team	Time
1928	USA	48.8
1932	CAN	47.0
1936	UK	47.6
1948	AUS	47.6
1952	GER	45.9
1956	UK	44.7
1960	FRG	44.8
1964	USA	43.9
1968	CUB	43.3
1972	GDR	42.95
1976	FRG	42.95
1980	URS	42.10
1984	CAN	42.77
1988	GDR	42.09

BRONZE

1928	GER	49.0
1932	UK	47.6
1936	CAN	47.8
1948	CAN	47.8
1952	UK	46.2
1956	USA	44.9
1960	POL	45.0
1964	UK	44.0
1968	URS	43.4
1972	CUB	43.36
1976	URS	43.09
1980	UK	42.43
1984	UK	43.11
1988	URS	42.75

4x400 Metres Relay

GOLD

1972	GDR	3:22.95
1976	GDR	3:19.23
1980	SRS	3:20.12
1984	USA	3:18.29
1988	URS	3:15.18

SILVER

1972	USA	3:25.2
1976	USA	3:22.8
1980	GDR	3:20.4
1984	CAN	3:21.21
1988	USA	3:15.51

BRONZE

1972	FRG	3:26.6
1976	URS	3:24.2
1980	GBR	3:27.5
1984	FRG	3:22.9
1988	GDR	3:18.29

High Jump

GOLD

1928	Ethel Catherwood (CAN)	1.59m
1932	Jean Shiley (USA)	1.65m
1936	Ibolya Csak (HUN)	1.60m
1948	Alice Coachman (USA)	1.68m
1952	Esther Brand (SAF)	1.67m
1956	Mildred McDaniel (USA)	1.76m
1960	Iolanda Balas (ROM)	1.85m
1964	Iolanda Balas (ROM)	1.90m
1968	Miloslava Rezkova (TCH)	1.82m
1972	Ulrike Meyfarth (FRG)	1.92m
1976	Rosemarie Ackermann (GDR)	1.93m
1980	Sara Simeoni (ITA)	1.97m
1984	Anisoara Stanciu (ROM)	6.96m
1988	Ritter (USA)	2.03m

SILVER

1928	Gisølf (HOL)	1.56
1932	Didrikson (USA)	1.65
1936	Dorothy Odam (UK)	1.60
1948	Dorothy Tyler (UK)	1.68
1952	Lerwill (UK)	1.65
1956	Pisaryeva (URS)	1.67
	Hopkins (UK)	1.67
1960	Jozwiakowska (POL)	1.71
	Shirley (UK)	1.71
1964	Brown (AUS)	1.80
1968	Okorokova (URS)	1.80
1972	Blagoyeva (BUL)	1.88
1976	Simeoni (ITA)	1.91
1980	Kielan (POL)	1.94
1984	Simeoni (FRG)	2.07
1988	Kosadinova (BUL)	2.01

BRONZE

1928	Wiley (USA)	1.56
1932	Dawes (CAN)	1.60
1936	Kaun (GER)	1.60
1948	Ostermeyer (FRA)	1.61
1952	Chudina (URS)	1.63
1956	- -	
1960	- -	
1964	Chenchik (URS)	1.78
1968	Kozir (URS)	1.80
1972	Gusenbauer (AUT)	1.88
1976	Blagoyeva (BUL)	1.91
1980	Kirst (GDR)	1.94
1984	Huntely (USA)	2.00
1988	Bykova(URS)	1.99

Shot Put

GOLD

1948	Micheline Ostermeyer (FRA)	13.75m
1952	Galina Zybina (URS)	15.28m
1956	Tamara Tyshkevich (URS)	16.59m
1960	Tamara Press (URS)	17.32m
1964	Tamara Press (URS)	18.14m
1968	Margitta Gummel (GDR)	19.61m
1972	Nadyezda Chizhova (URS)	21.03m
1976	Ivanka Khristova (BUL)	21.16m
1980	Ilona Sľupianek(GDR)	22.41m
1984	Claudia Losch (FRG)	22.48m
1988	Lisovskaya (URS)	22.24m

SILVER

1948	Piccinini (ITA)	13.09
1952	Werner (GER)	14.57
1956	Zibina (URS)	16.53
1960	Luttge (GDR)	16.61
1964	Garisch (GDR)	17.61
1968	Lange (GDR)	18.78
1972	Gummel (GDR)	20.22
1976	Chizhova (URS)	20.96
1980	Krachevskaya (URS)	21.42
1984	Loghin (ROM)	20.47
1988	Neimke (GDR)	21.07

BRONZE

1948	Schafer (AUT)	13.08
1952	Tochonova (URS)	14.50
1956	Werner (GER)	15.61
1960	Brown (USA)	16.42
1964	Zibina (URS)	17.45
1968	Chizhova (URS)	18.19
1972	Khristova (BUL)	19.35
1976	Fibingerova (TCH)	20.67
1980	Pufe (GDR)	21.20
1984	Martin (AUS)	19.19
1988	Meisu (PRC)	21.06

Discus

GOLD

1928	Helena Konopacka (POL)	39.62m
1932	Lillian Copeland (USA)	40.58m
1936	Gisela Mauermayer (GER)	47.63m
1948	Micheline Ostermeyer (FRA)	41.92m
1952	Nina Romashkova (URS)	51.42m
1956	Olga Fikotova (TCH)	53.69m
1960	Nina Ponomaryeva (URS)	55.10m
1964	Tamara Press (URS)	57.27m
1968	Lia Manoliu (ROM)	58.28m
1972	Faina Melnik (URS)	66.62m
1976	Evelin Schlaak(GDR)	69.00m
1980	Evelin Jahl (GDR)	69.96m
1984	Ria Stalman (HOL)	65.36m
1988	Hellman (GDR)	72.30m

SILVER

1928	Copeland (USA)	37.08
1932	Osborn (USA)	40.12
1936	Wajsowna (POL)	46.22
1948	Gentile (ITA)	41.17
1952	Bagryantseva (URS)	47.08
1956	Beglvakova (URS)	52.54
1960	T. Press (URS)	52.59
1964	Lotz (GDR)	57.21
1968	Westermann (FRG)	57.76
1972	Menis (ROM)	65.06
1976	Vergova (BUL)	67.30
1980	Vergova-Perkova (BUL)	67.90
1984	Deniz (USA)	64.86
1988	Gansky (GDR)	71.88

BRONZE

1928	Svedberg (SWE)	35.92
1932	Wajsowna (POL)	38.74
1936	Mollenhauer (GER)	39.80
1948	Mezeas (FRA)	40.47
1952	Dumbadze (URS)	46.29
1956	Romashkova (URS)	52.02
1960	Manoliu (ROM)	52.36
1964	Manoliu (ROM)	56.87
1968	Kleiber (HUN)	54.90
1972	Stoeva (BUL)	64.34
1976	Hinzmann GDR)	66.84
1980	Lyesovaya (URS)	67.40
1984	Craciunescu (ROM)	63.64
1988	Kristova (BUL)	69.74

Javelin

GOLD

1932	Mildred Didrikson (USA)	43.68m

1936	Tilly Fleischer (GER)	45.18m
1948	Herma Bauma (AUT)	45.57m
1952	Dana Zatopkova (TCH)	50.47m
1956	Ines Jaunzeme (URS)	53.86m
1960	Elvira Ozolina (URS)	55.98m
1964	Mihaela Penes (ROM)	60.64m
1968	Angela Nemeth (HUN)	60.36m
1972	Ruth Fuchs (GDR)	63.88m
1976	Ruth Fuchs (GDR)	65.94m
1980	Maria Colon (CUB)	68.40m
1984	Tessa Sanderson(UK)	69.56m
1988	Felke (GDR)	74.68m

SILVER

1932	Braumuller (GER)	43.49
1936	Kruger (GER)	43.29
1948	Parviainen (FIN)	43.79
1952	Chudina (URS)	50.01
1956	Ahrens (CHI	50.38
1960	Zatopkova (TCH)	53.78
1964	Rudas (HUN)	58.27
1968	Penes (ROM)	59.92
1972	Todten (GDR)	62.54
1976	M. Becker (FRG)	64.70
1980	Gunba (URS)	67.76
1984	Lillak (FIN)	69.00
1988	Whitbread (UK)	70.32

BRONZE

1932	Fleischer (GER)	43.00
1936	Kwasniewska (POL)	41.80
1948	Çarlstedt (DEN)	42.08
1952	Gorchakova (URS)	49.76
1956	Konyayeva (URS)	50.28
1960	Kalediene (URS)	53.45
1964	Gorchaova (URS)	57.06
1968	Janko (AUT)	58.04
1972	Schmidt USA)	59.94
1976	Schmidt (USA)	63.96
1980	Hommola (GDR)	66.56
1984	Whitbread (UK)	67.14
1988	Koch (GDR)	67.30

Pentathlon

GOLD

1964	Irina Press (URS)	5246pts.
1968	Ingrid Becker (FRG)	5098pts.
1972	Mary Peters (UK)	4801pts
1976	Siegrun Siegl (GDR)	4745pts
1980	Nadyezda Tkachenko (URS)	5083pts

Heptathlon

(Replaced Pentathlon in 1984)

1984	Glynis Nunn (Aus)	6390 pts.
1988	Joyner (USA)	7291 pts.

SILVER

1964	Rand (UK)	5035 pts.
1968	Prokop (AUT)	4966 pts.
1972	Rosendahl (FRG)	4791 pts.
1976	Laser (GDR)	4745 pts.
1980	Rukavishnikova (URS)	4937 pts.
1984	Joyner (USA)	6385 pts.
1988	John (GDR)	6897 pts.

BRONZE

1964	Bistrova (URS)	4956 pts.
1968	Toth (HUN)	4959 pts.
1972	Pollak (GDR)	4768 pts.
1976	Pollak (GDR)	4740 pts.
1980	Kuragina (URS)	4875 pts.
1984	Everts (FRG)	6363 pts.
1988	Behmer (GDR)	6858 pts.

Track and Field Medals (including Tug-of-war)

	Men(Gold)	Women(Gold)
United States	235	26
Soviet Union	29	25
Great Britain (UK)	42	4
Germany (FRG)	11	12
Finland	46	-
Sweden	19	-
GDR	11	21
Australia	6	10
France	7	3
Canada	9	2
Italy	12	3
Poland	9	6
Hungary	6	3
Greece	3	-
Romania	-	8
Czechoslovakia	5	3
Jamaica	4	-

New Zealand	7	1
Kenya	6	-
South Africa	4	1
The Netherlands	-	5
Japan	4	-
Norway	3	-
Cuba	2	1
Belgium	2	-
Ethiopia	5	-
Bulgaria	-	1
Brazil	3	-
Ireland	4	-
Mexico	3	-
Argentina	2	-
Austria	-	1
Trinidad	1	-
Tunisia	1	-
Denmark	1	-
Portugal	1	-
Morocco	1	1
Luxemburg	1	-
Uganda	1	-

PAN-AMERICAN GAMES

The Pan-American Games were instituted in 1951, the first being held in Buenos Aires. Subsequent venues have been Mexico City 1955, Chicago 1959, Sao Paulo 1963, Winnipeg 1967, Cali 1971, Mexico City 1975, San Juan 1979, Caracas 1983 and Indianapolis 1987.

TUG OF WAR

This sport was part of the athletics programme 1900-1920. Three men won a record two golds and one silver from 1908 to 1920. John Shepherd, Frederick Humphreys and Edwin Mills, all from Great Britain.

Gold	
1900	Sweden/Denmark
1904	USA
1906	Germany
1908	Great Britain
1912	Sweden
1920	Great Britain

UNOFFICIAL OLYMPICS

An unofficial Olympic celebration was staged in Athens in 1906. For the record, the winners were as follows:

100m	A Hahn (USA)	11.2 sec.
400m	P.H.Pilgrim (USA)	53.2 sec.
800m	P.H.Pilgrim (USA)	2 min. 11.2sec.
1500m	J.D.Lighbody (USA)	4 min. 12.0sec.
Marathon	W.J.Sherring (Canada)	2 hr. 51min. 23.6sec.
110mh	R.G. Leavitt (USA)	16.2 sec.
		metres
High jump	C.Leahy (Ireland)	5ft. 9 in.
Pole vault	F. Gonder(France)	11 ft. 6 in.
Long jump	M.Prinstein (USA)	23 ft. 7(½)in.
Triple jump	P.J.O'Connor (Ireland)	46ft. 2 in.
Shot	M.J.Sheridan (USA)	40 ft. 5 in.
Discus	M.J.Sheridan (USA)	136ft. ¼in.
Javelin	E. Lemming (Sweden)	175 ft. 6 in.

WORLD CHAMPIONSHIPS

From parochial British origins, the World Cross Country Championships have developed into the main athletics event of the winter. The first international was staged between the four home countries in 1903 and the competition was dominated by England until it came under the jurisdiction of the IAAF in 1973, when it was renamed the IAAF World Cross country Championships. Since then, only one British runner Ian Stewart, of Scotland has won the men's individual title.

WORLD CUP

The IAAF's inaugural World cup competition, held in Dusseldorf in 1977, was a resounding success both as a major world athletics event and as a source of finance for the federation to divert towards the development of athletics in the Third World. The format of the world's strongest individual nations competing against continental teams proved immensely popular with the world's leading athletes battling not only for their own honour, but for the pride of their nation or continent. Although the second World cup in Montreal in 1979 was much less spectacular, the 1981 event in Rome was another great success. The competition was temporarily suspended in 1983 because of the IAAF's decision to hold it once every four years instead of bi-annually in order to fit their World Championships into the athletics diary.

BEST WORLD CUP PERFORMANCES

Men

	min:sec		
100m	10.00	Ben Johnson (Can)	1985
200m	20.17	Clancy Edwards (USA)	1977
400m	44.47	Mike Franks (USA)	1985
800m	1:44.04	Alberto Juantorena (Cub)	1977
1500m	3:34.45	Steve Ovett(UK)	1977
5000m	13:13.82	Miruts Yifter (Eth)	1977
10000m	27:38.43	Werner Schildhauer(GDR)	1981
3000m st	8:19.89	Boguslaw Marminski(Pol)	1981
110mh	13.32	Greg Foster (USA)	1981
400mn	47.31	Edwin Moses (USA)	1981
4x100mr	38.03	USA	1977
4x400mr	2:59.12	USA	1981
	metres		
High jump	2.31	Petrik Sjoberg (Swe)	1985
Pole vault	5.85	Sergey Bubka(USSR)	1985
Long jump	8.52	Larry Myricks (USA)	1979
Triple jump	17.58	Willie Banks (USA)	1985
Shotput	22.00	Ulf Timmermann(GDR)	1985
Discus	69.08	Gennadiy Kolnootchenko(USSR)	1985
Hammer	82.12	Juri Tamm (USSR)	1985
Javelin	96.96	Uwe Hohn (GDR)	1985

Women

	min.sec.		
100m	11.02	Evelyn Ashford (USA)	1981
200m	21.83	Evelyn Ashford (USA)	1979
400m	47.60	Marita Koch (GDR)	1985
800m	1:57.48	Lyudmila Veselkova (USSR)	1981
1500m	4:03.33	Tamaa Sorokina (USSR)	1981
3000m	8:36.32	Svyetlana Ulmasova (USSR)	1979
10000m	32:07.50	Aurora Cunha (Por)	1985
100mh	12.67	Grazyna Rabsztyn (Pol)	1979
400mn	54.45	Sabine Busch (GDR)	1985
4x100mR	41.37	GDR	1985
4x400mR	3:19.50	GDR	1985
	metres		
High jump	2.00	Stefka Kostadinova (Bul)	1985
Long Jump	7.27	Heike Drechsler (GDR)	1985
Shot	20.98	Ilona Slupianek (GDR)	1979
Discus	69.78	Martina Opitz (GDR)	1985
Javelin	70.08	Antoaneta Todorova (Bul)	1981

WORLD STUDENTS GAMES

The Universiade or World Students Games organized by the Federation Internatonale du Sport Universitaire is well established as one of the world's most important meetings.

Championship Best Performances

Men

	Hr.min.sec		
100m	10.07	Lee McRace (USA)	1987
	9.97	Andres Simon(Cub)(heat)	1985
200m	19.72	Pietro Mennea (Ita)	1979
400m	44.98	Harald Shmid (GFR)	1979
800m	1:43.44	Alberto Juantorena(Cub)	1977
1500m	3:38.43	Said Aouita (Mor)	1981
5000m	13:41.25	Mikhail Zhelobovskiy (USSR)	1973
10000m	28.48.90	Dane Korica (Yug)	1973
Marathon	2:17:10	Osvaldo Faustini (Ita)	1983
3000m. St	8:21.26	John Gregorek (USA)	1981
110mh	13.21	Alejandro Casanas (Cub)	1977
400mh	48.44	Harry Schulting (Hol)	1979
4x100mR	3:00.98	Italy	1979
4x400mR	1:24:03	Guillaume Le Blanc(Can)	1983
	metres		
High jump	2.41	James Lott (USA)	1987
Pole Vault	5.75	Konstantin Volkov (USSR)	1981
	5.75	Rodion Gataullin (USSR)	1985
Long jump	8.21	Yussuf Allil (Nig)	1983
	8.23	Laszlo Szalma (Hun)	1981
Triple jump	17.86	Charlie Simpkins (USA)	1985
Shotput	21.13	Remigius Machura (Cs)	1985
	20.85	Alessandro Andrei (Ita)	1985
Discus	69.46	Luis Delis (Cub)	1983
Hammer	77.74	Klaus Ploghaus (GFR)	1981
Javelin	89.52	Dainis Kula (USSR)	1981
Decathlon	8194 pts	Josef Zeilbauer (Aut)	1979

Women

	Min:sec		
100m	11.00	Marlies Gohr (GDR)	1979
200m	21.91	Marita Koch (GDR)	1979
400m	50.35	Maria Pinigina (USSR)	1979
800m	1:57.81	Doina Melinte (Rom)	1981
1500m	4:05.35	Gabriella Dorio (Ita)	1981
3000m	8:53.78	Breda Pergar (Yug)	1981

Event	Record	Athlete	Year
10000m	32:58.45	Marina Rodchenkova (USSR)	1985
100mh	12.62	Lucyna Langer (Pol)	1979
400mh	54.97	Yekaterina Fesenko (USSR)	1983
4x100mR	42.82	USA	1983
4x400mR	3:24.97	USSR	1983
5km walk	22:21.10	Aleksandra Grigoryeva(USSR)	1985
	metres		
High jump	2.01	Silvia Costa (Cub)	1985
Long Jump	7.04	Irina Valyukevich (USSR)	1985
	7.06	Anisoara Cusmir (Rom)	1983
Shot	20.82	Nadyezhda Chizhoiva(USR)	1973
Discus	67.48	Florenta Craciunescu(Rom)	1981
Javelin	71.82	Ivonne Leal (Cub)	1985
Heptathlon	6616pts	Malgorzata Nowak (Pol)	1985

NATIONAL RECORDS (INDIA)

Men

Event	Record	Athlete	Venue	Year
100m	10.3	K.Natarajan	Manila	1973
200m	20.7	Milkha Singh	Lahore	1960
400m	45.6	Milkha Singh	Rome	1960
110mh	14.0	Gurbachan Singh	Tokyo	1964
400mh	51.6	K.S.Balasubramaniam	Bangalore	1981
800m	1:45.7	Sriram Singh	Montreal	1976
1500m	3:43.7	Edward Sequeira	New Delhi	1966
3000m	8:06.4	Bahadur Singh	England	1989
5000m	13:46.4	Rajkumar	Brisbane	1982
10000m	28:48.72	Hari Chand	Montreal	1976
3000mSt.	8:30.88	Gopal Saini	Tokyo	1981
Marathon	2:12.48	Shivnath Singh	Jalandhar	1978
20km Wk	1:27:19.5	Chand Ram	Jakarta	1985
50km Wk	4:19:48.0	Krishan Singh	Cuttack	1970
4 x 100 relay	40.41	Indian Team	Tokyo	1979
4 x 400 relay	3:08.2	Indian Team	Seoul	1975
	metres			
High Jump	2.16	Nallusamy Annavi	Calcutta	1987
Long Jump	8.07	T.C.Yohannan	Teheran	1974
Triple Jump	16.79	Mohinder Singh	Fresno	1971
Pole Vault	5.10	Vijay Pal	Trivandrum	1987
Shot Put	18.71	Iqbal Singh	New Delhi	1988
Discus	57.70	Shakti Singh	Madras	1989
Hammer	65.76	Praveen Kumar	Ajmer	1969
Javelin	70.40	Shyamdar Mishra	Madras	1989
Decathlon	7,380pts.	Suresh Babu	Quilon	1978

Women

Event	Record	Athlete	Venue	Year
100m	11.39	P.T.Usha	Jakarta	1985
200m	23.44	P.T.Usha	Seoul	1986
400m	51.61	P.T.Usha	Canberra	1985
110mh	13.9	M.Valsamma	Trivandrum	1985
400mh	55.42	P.T.Usha	Los Angeles	1984
800m	2:03.16	Shiny Abraham	Jakarta	1985
1500m	4:19.33	Geeta Zutshi	New Delhi	1982
3000m	9:14.70	Suman Rawat	Seoul	1986
5000m	17:53.9	Nanda Jadhav	Bombay	1988
10000m	35:29.65	Suman Rawat	Calcutta	1987
Marathon	2:43:27.0	Asha Aggarwal	HongKong	1986
4 x 100m	45.22	Indian Team	Jakarta	1985
4 x 400m	3:31.55	Indian Team	Rome	1987
	metres			
Long jump	6.26	Mercy Kuttan	New Delhi	1982
High jump	1.72	Angela Lincy	Trivandrum	1987
Shot Put	14.58	Bhaktawar Khambatta	Patiala	1982
Discus	48.92	Vijayamala Bhanot	New Delhi	1987
Javelin	51.88	Shiny Varghese	New Delhi	1988
Heptathlon	5244 pts	Angel Mary Joseph	New Delhi	1982

ARJUNA AWARD WINNERS

1961	Gurbachan Singh Randhava
1962	Tarlok Singh
1963	Stephie D'Souza
1964	Makhan Singh
1965	K.L. Powell
1966	Ajmere Singh
	B.S. Barua
1967	Parveen Kumar
	Bhim Singh
1968	Joginder Singh
	Manjit Walia
1969	Harnek Singh
1970	Mohinder Singh Gill
1971	Edward Sequeira
1972	Vijay Singh Chauhan

1973	Ram Singh
1974	T.Yohannam
	Shivnath Singh Rajpoot
1975	Hari Chand
	V.Anusuya Bai
1976	Bahadur Singh
	Geeta Zutshi
1978-79	Suresh Babu
	Angel Mary Joseph
1979-80	Ramaswamy Gnanasekaran
1980-81	Gopal Saini
1982	Charles Borromeo
	Chand Ram
	M.D.Valsamma
1983	Suresh Yadav
	P.T. Usha
1984	Raj Kumar
	Shiny K. Abraham
1985	R.S. Bal
	Asha Aggarwal
	Adille Jehangir Sumariwalla
1986	Adil Jehangir
	Sumariwalla
	Suman Rawat
1987	Balwinder Singh
	Vandana Rao
	Bagicha Singh
	Vandana Shanbagh
1988	Ashwini Nachappa

BADMINTON

Badminton, at first played only at Bath, Cheltenham, and other places where retired Indians congregate, is now widely known. Clubs are formed all over the country. The game has stood the test of time, is more popular than ever, and will doubtless by continue to flourish.

Webster's Encyclopaedia tells us that the word Badminton denotes "a residence of the Dukes of Beaufort. An outdoor game, similar to lawn tennis, but played with shuttlecocks and light rackets with a high net dividing the court."

Badminton is a game of science and strength. The quickest and most active player is almost sure to win, but he must also possess that instinct which enables him in the heat of a rally to decide in a moment where to place the shuttlecock so as to be in the most difficult position for the adversary to reach it.

It is believed that the game of Badminton, originated in India a long time back and was known as 'Poone'. Subsequently, the English saw this game being played by Indians and took it to England. In 1873, it is said that the Duke of Beaufort introduced this game at a party given by him at his residence called Badminton in Gloucestershire. Thereafter gradually the game itself came to be known as Badminton. In 1895, the Badminton Association of England formulated official rules of the game. The first National Doubles championship was held in 1899 to be followed by 'Singles championship' in the next year.

SKILLS OF THE GAME

The game of Badminton is played in a Court forty-four feet long by twenty feet wide. The net. which ought to be as light as possible and made with a small mesh, should be stretched for twenty feet across the centre of the court, and should not be less than eighteen inches deep. Its lower edge should be five feet from the ground and as taut as possible.

THE GRIP

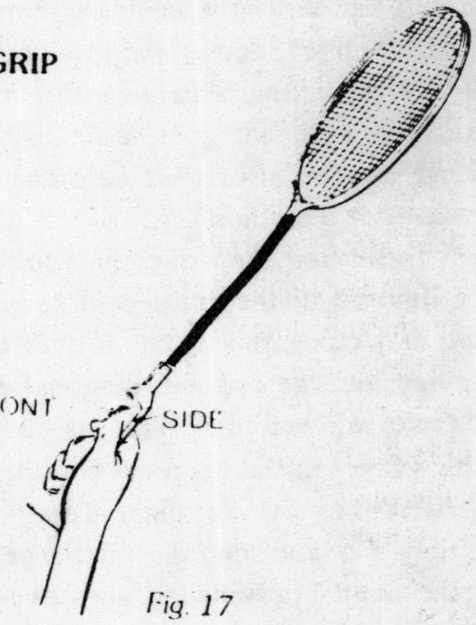

Fig. 17

Forehand

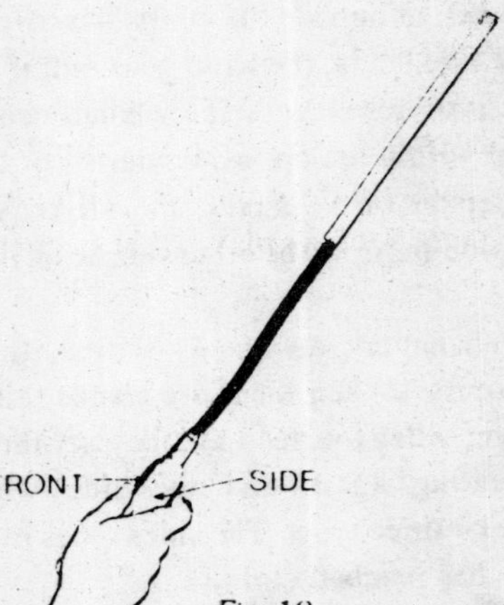

Fig. 18

Backhand

Badminton is best played in a well-lighted room or hall, where the wind cannot affect the flight of the shuttlecock. It can be played very well with the larger shuttlecock in the open air on a calm day. The game is often played with three or four players on a side. This is not, however, the scientific game; for with more than two on a side the players in front cannot help getting in the way of their partners behind.

The Service lines are drawn across the court parallel with the net and six and a half feet on each side of it. A line down the centre, joining the service lines and baselines, forms the four courts.

In beginning, a game with two players on each side, the side that goes in first is only allowed one hand in, but after the first round the partners go in one after the other.

In Serving, the striker must stand behind the service line and hit the shuttlecock so as to give it an upward trajectory and send it over the opposite service line into the opposite diagonal court. There are no faults allowed in serving as in lawn-tennis. Only the player in the diagonal court can take the serve. After the serve, the players can go as near the net as they like and send the shuttlecock anywhere within the courts, provided it goes over the net and between the poles. If the shuttlecock touches the net in going over, it does not invalidate the stroke, but the striker must not touch the net with his racket.

If the striker sends the shuttlecock into or under the net, or outside the courts, it scores against him. If his side be in, the hand goes out; if the other side be in, it scores an ace. If the shuttlecock touch the ground within the opposite courts, or touch the dress or person of a player, the striker scores an ace if his side be in if the other side be in, their hand goes out.

Whenever an ace is scored, the server changes courts. When the score stands thirteen all, they set five; when fourteen all, they set three. They begin counting again and the side which first scores five or three wins. The sides cross over when their score has reached eight.

Badminton is a quicker game than lawn tennis. The courts being smaller, there is not so much running about, but there is more hard hitting and the exercise to the arm is greater.

It is a great advantage to put the server out at the first stroke, to prevent his side scoring. The policy of the server is to send the shuttlecock high, so that it may drop as perpendicularly as possible into the farthest corner of the diagonal court, and thus make it difficult for the adversary to cut it down and kill it. It is generally a good play to keep sending the shuttlecock high at the back of the adversary's court until an opportunity comes to cut it down and kill it. In cutting down the striker should try not to send it within the reach of the adversary. When the shuttlecock is being driven hard backward and forward, an ace is often secured by suddenly altering the pace and dropping the shuttlecock just over the net.

In the doubles game the first server stands in his right-hand service court and hits the shuttle when it is below waist level, both feet stationary on the ground, into his opponent's right-hand service court. If the shuttle touches the net and falls short of the court a fault is called. If the server gains the point he then serves from the left-hand court and so on from each court in turn to each opponent in turn until he serves a fault, commits one in play, or his side loses a rally by letting the shuttle fall in court on their side of the net, by hitting it out or into the net. (After the service, players receive the shuttle anywhere on their side of the net).

During the normal course of a game his partner would then serve, but after the opening service of a match the right passes to the server's opponents. The opponent in the right-hand court serves first; when he fails his partner serves. When both hands are 'out' the right to serve passes across the net once more, and so on.

Only the serving side scores, and the game is normally one of fifteen points. At thirteen-all, the side first reaching thirteen may set to five points, at fourteen-all, to three points.

Equipment

COURT

The badminton court for singles is 670 cms long on each side and 518 cms wide with back gallery 76 cms wide and short service line at 198 cms from the net line. In the doubles, in addition to the above a side gallery of 46 cms is added to the single court.

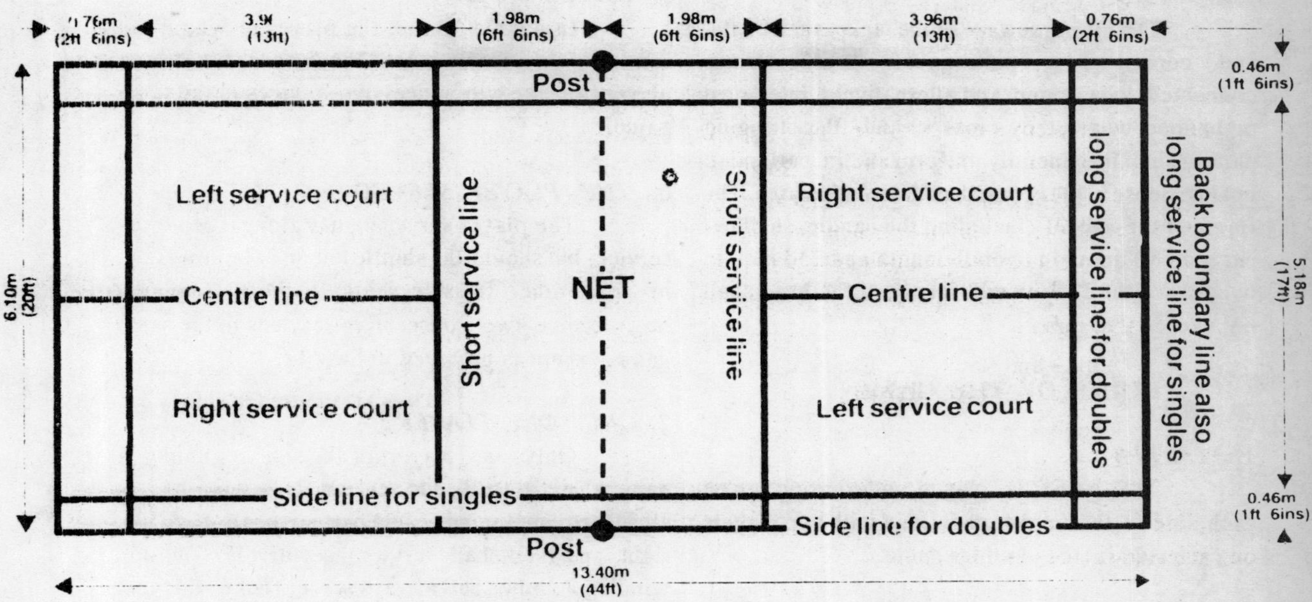

POSTS

The net is made of fine tanned cord of 3/4 inch to 5/8 inch diameter and is tied to the posts at a height five feet from the floor. The width of the net is 2 feet 6 inches with a 3 inch white edge at the top.

The posts are at leat 5 feet 1 inch in height from the floor, and strong enough to keep the net in stretched position and at right angles to the net cord.

NET

The net shall be made of natural cord or artificial fiber of a dark colour and an even thickness not less than 15 mm. (5/8 inch) and not more than 20 mm. (3/4 inch) mesh. It shall be firmly stretched from post to post, and shall be 760 mm. (2feet 6 inches) in depth. The top of the net shall be 1.524 metres (5 feet) in height from the floor at the centre, and 1.55 metres (5 feet 1 inch) at the posts, and shall be edged with a 75 mm. (3 inches) white tape doubled and supported by a cord or cable run through the tape and strained over and flush with the top of the posts.

THE SHUTTLE

The shuttle should weigh 37-85 grains and consists of 14 to 16 feathers fixed in a cork of 1 inch to 1(½) inch diameter. The feathers should be 2(½) to 2(3/4) inches in length with a spread of 2(1/8) to 2(½) inches at the top.

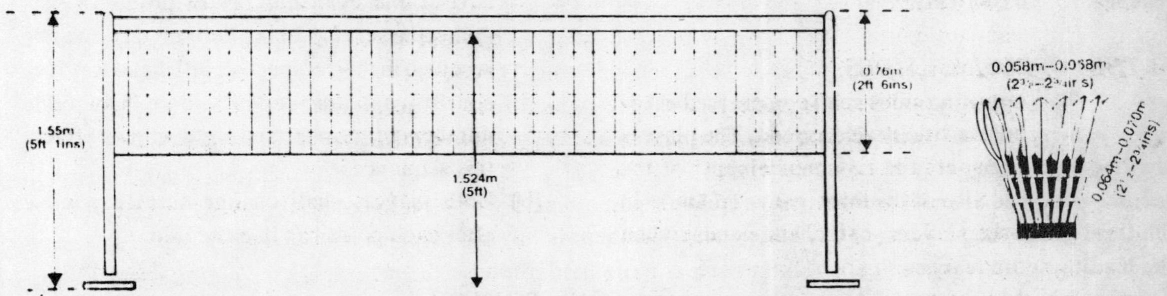

THE RACKET

The hitting surface of the racket shall be flat and consist of a pattern of crossed strings connected to a frame and alternatively interlaced or bonded where they cross - and the stringing pattern shall be generally uniform and in particular, not less dense in the centre than in any other area. The frame of the racket, including the handle, shall not exceed 680 mm. in overall length and 230 mm. in overall width. The overall length of the head shall not exceed 290 mm.

RULES OF THE GAME

1. *PLAYERS*

The game is played with one player on each side in the singles game and with two players on each side in the doubles game.

2. *THE TOSS*

The two sides shall toss before starting the game. The side winning the toss shall have the option of either sarving first or for choosing ends.

3. *SCORING*

The doubles and men's singles game consists of 15 points provided that,when the score is 13-all, the side which first reached 13 has the option of "setting" the game of 5, and that when the score is 14-all, the side which first reached 14 has the option of setting the game to 3. After a game has been `set' the score is called `love all' and the side which first scores 5 or 3 points, according as the game has been `set' at 13 or 14 all, wins the game. In either case the claim to `set' the game must be made before the next service is delivered after the score has reached 13 all or 14 all.

4. *THE OPPOSING SIDES*

The opposing sides shall contest the best of three games, unless other-wise agreed. The players shall change ends at the commencement of the second game and also of the third game (if any). In the third game the players shall change ends when the leading score reaches:-

(a) 8 in a game of 15 points;
(b) 6 in a game of 11 points;

5. *DOUBLES PLAY*

In doubles game, the player to whom the service is directed may take the service. Besides,no player can take two successive services in the same game.

6. *THE PLAYER SERVED*

The player served to may alone receive the service, but should the shuttle touch, or be struck by, his partner the "In" side scores a point. No player may receive two consecutive services in the same game, except as provided in Law 12.

7. *ONLY ONE PLAYER*

Only one player of the side beginning a game shall be entitled to serve in its first innings. In all subsequent innings each partner shall have the right and they shall serve consecutively. The side winning a game shall always serve first in the next game but either of the winners may serve and either of the losers may receive the service.

8. *PLAYER SERVES*

If a player serves out of turn, or from the wrong service court (owing to a mistake as to the service court from which service is at the time being in order) and his side wins the rally, it shall be a "Let" be claimed and allowed, or ordered by the umpire, before the next succeeding service is delivered.

9. *SINGLES PLAY*

In singles forth coming three laws hold good except that:-

(a) The players shall serve from and receive service in their respective right-hand service courts only when the server's score is 0 or and even number of points in the game, the service being delivered from and received in their respective left-hand service courts when the server's score is an odd number of points. Setting does not affect this sequence.
(b) Both players shall change service courts after each point has been scored.

10. *FAULTS*

While attempting to serve, if a player

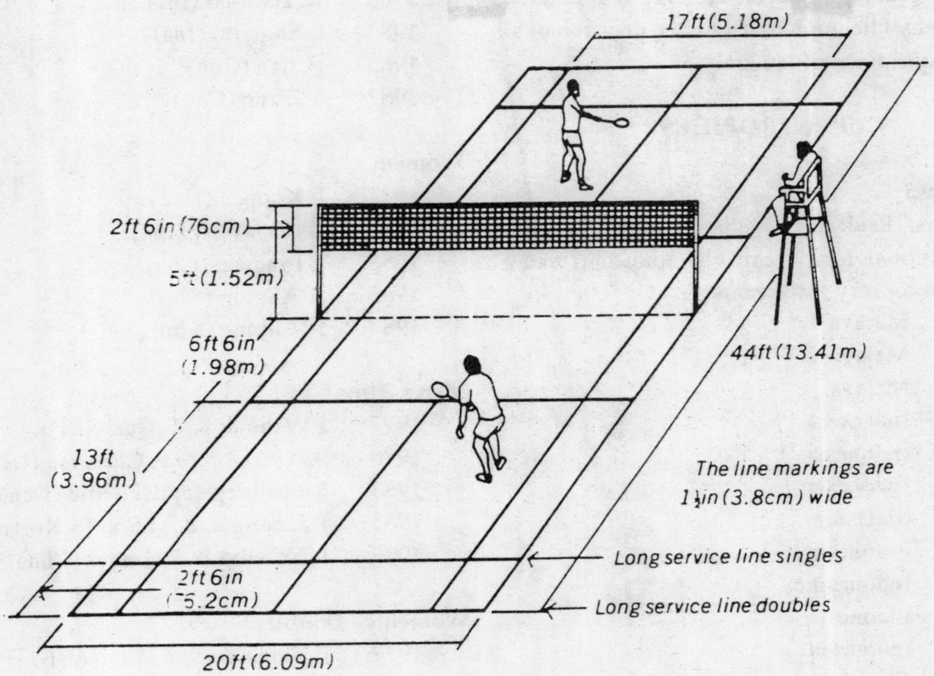

misses the shuttle altogether, it is not counted as a fault.

11. *GENERAL*

The server may not serve till his opponent is ready, but the opponent shall be deemed to be ready if a return of the service be attempted.

12. *THE SERVER*

The server and the player served to must stand within the limits of their respective service courts (as bounded by the short and long service, the centre, and side lines), and some part of both feet of these players must remain in contact with the surface of the court in a stationary position until the service is delivered. A foot on or touching a line in the case of either the server or the receiver shall be held to be outside his service court. The respective partners may take up any position, provided they do not unsight or otherwise obstruct an opponent.

If the server, in attempting to serve, misses the shuttle, it is not a fault; but if the shuttle be touched by the racket, a service is there by delivered.

13. *WHEN IN PLAY*

If, when in play, the shuttle strikes the net and remains suspended there, or strikes the net and falls towards the surface of the court on the striker's side of the net, or hits the surface outside the court and an opponent then touches the net or shuttle with his racket or person, there is no penalty, as the shuttle is not then in play.

If a player has a chance of striking the shuttle in a downward direction when quite near the net, his opponent must not put up his racket near the net on the chance of the shuttle rebounding from it. This is obstruction within the meaning of Law 14.

14. *DUTY OF THE UMPIRE*

It shall be the duty of the umpire to call "fault" or "let" should either occur, without appeal being made by the players and to give his decision on any appeal regarding a point in dispute, if made before the next service; and also to appoint linesmen and service judge at his discretion. The umpire's decision shall be final, but he shall uphold the decision of a linesman or service judge. This shall not preclude the umpire also from faulting the serve or receiver. Where, however, a referee is appointed, an appeal shall lie to him from the decision of an umpire on questions of law only.

CUP & TROPHIES

Thomas Cup

First held in 1949, the Thomas Cup is the international men's team championship, and is contested every three years.

1949 Malaya
1952 Malaya
1955 Malaya
1958 Indonesia
1961 Indonesia
1964 Indonesia
1967 Malaysia
1970 Indonesia
1973 Indonesia
1976 Indonesia
1979 Indonesia
1982 China
1984 Indonesia
1986 China

Uber Cup

First held in 1957, the Uber Cup is the international women's team championship, and is held every three years.

1957 United States
1960 United States
1963 United States
1966 Japan
1969 Japan
1972 Japan
1975 Indonesia
1978 Japan
1981 Japan
1984 China
1986 China

World Championships

The first-ever world championships were held in 1977 and are to be held every three years.

Men

1977 F. Delfs (Den)
1980 R. Hartono (Ina)
1983 I. Sugiarto (Ina)
1985 H.Jian (Chn)
1987 Y.Yang (Chn)

Women

1977 L.Koppen (Den)
1980 W.Verawaty (Ina)
1983 L.Lingwei (Chn)
1985 H.Aliping (Chn)
1987 H.Aliping (Chn)

Men's Doubles

1977 J.Wahjudi & T.Tjun (Ina)
1980 A. Chandra & H.Christian (Ina)
1983 S.Fladberg & J.Helledie (Den)
1985 P.J.Bong & K.M.Soo (S.Korea)
1987 L.Yongbo & T.Hingyi (Chn)

Women's Doubles

1977 E.Tuganoo & E. Vero (Jap)
1980 N.Perry & J.Webster (UK)
1983 L.Ying& W. Dixi (Chn)
1985 H.Aliping & L.Lingwei (Chn)
1987 L.Yin & G.Weizhen (Chn)

Mixed Doubles

1977 S.Stovgaard & L.Koppen (Den)
1980 H.Christian & I.Wigoeno (Jap)
1983 T.Kihlstrom (Swe) & N.Perry (UK)
1985 P.J.Bong & S.Hee (S.Korea)
1987 W.Pengrin & S. Fanglin (Chn)

All England Championship

First held in 1899 and until the advent of the world championships, it was the premier tournament in the world.

Men's Singles

1900 S.Smith (Eng)
1901 H.Davies (Eng)
1902 R.Watling (Eng)
1903 R.Watling (Eng)
1904 H.Marrett (Eng)
1905 H.Marrett (Eng)

1906	N.Wood (Eng)
1907	N.Wood (Eng)
1908	H.Marrett (Eng)
1909	F.Chesterton (Eng)
1910	F.Chesterton (Eng)
1911	G.Sautter (Eng)
1912	F.Chesterton (Eng)
1913	G.Sautter (Eng)
1914	S.Sautter (Eng)
1915	Not held
1916	Not held
1917	Not held
1918	Not held
1919	Not held
1920	G.Thomas (Eng)
1921	G.Thomas (Eng)
1922	G.Thomas (Eng)
1923	G.Thomas (Eng)
1924	G.Mack (Ire)
1925	F.Devlin (Ire)
1926	F.Devlin (Ire)
1927	F.Devlin (Ire)
1928	F.Devlin (Ire)
1929	F.Devlin (Ire)
1930	D.Hulme (Eng)
1931	F.Devlin (Ire)
1932	R.Nichols (Eng)
1933	R.White (Eng)
1934	R.Nichols (Eng)
1935	R.White (Eng)
1936	R.Nichols (Eng)
1937	R.Nichols (Eng)
1938	R.Nichols (Eng)
1939	T.Madsen (Den)
1940	Not held
1941	Not held
1942	Not held
1943	Not held
1944	Not held
1945	Not held
1946	Not held
1947	C.Jepsen (Swe)
1948	J.Skaarup (Den)
1949	D.Freeman (USA)
1950	W.P.Soon (Mal)
1951	W.P.Soon (Mal)
1952	W.P.Soon (Mal)
1953	E.Choong (Mal)
1954	E.Choong (Mal)
1955	W.P.Soon (Mal)
1956	E.Choong (Mal)
1957	E.Choong (Mal)
1958	E.Kops (Den)
1959	T.J.Hok (Ina)
1960	E.Kops (Den)
1961	E.Kops (Den)
1962	E.Kops (Den)
1963	E.Kops (Den)
1964	K.Nielsen (Den)
1965	E.Kops (Den)
1966	T.A.Huang (Mal)
1967	E.Kops (Den)
1968	R.Hartono (Ina)
1969	R.Hartono (Ina)
1970	R.Hartono (Ina)
1971	R.Hartono (Ina)
1972	R.Hartono (Ina)
1973	R.Hartono (Ina)
1974	R.Hartono (Ina)
1975	S.Puri (Den)
1976	R.Hartono (Ina)
1977	F.Delfs (Den)
1978	L.S.King (Ina)
1979	L.S.King (Ina)
1980	P.Padukone (Ind)
1981	L.S.King (Ina)
1982	M.Frost (Den)
1983	L.Jin (Chn)
1984	M.Frost (Den)
1985	Z.Jinhua (Chn)
1986	M.Frost (Den)
1987	M.Frost (Den)

Women's Singles

1900	E.Thomson (Eng)
1901	E.Thomson (Eng)
1902	M.Lucas (Eng)
1903	E.Thomson (Eng)
1904	E.Thomson (Eng)
1905	M.Lucas (Eng)
1906	E.Thomson (Eng)
1907	M.Lucas (Eng)
1908	M.Lucas (Eng)
1909	M.Lucas (Eng)
1910	M.Lucas (Eng)
1911	M.Larminie (Eng)

1912	M.Larminie - Tragett (Eng)
1913	L.Radeglia (Eng)
1914	L.Radeglia (Eng)
1915	Not held
1916	Not held
1917	Not held
1918	Not held
1919	Not held
1920	K.Mckane (Eng)
1921	K.Mckane (Eng)
1922	K.Kckane (Eng)
1923	L.Radeglia (Eng)
1924	K.McKane (Eng)
1925	M.Stocks (Eng)
1926	M.Barrett (Eng)
1927	M.Barrett (Eng)
1928	M.Larminie-Tragett (Eng)
1929	M.Barrett (Eng)
1930	M.Barrett (Eng)
1931	M.Barrett (Eng)
1932	L.Kingsbury (Eng)
1933	A Woodroffe (Eng)
1934	L.Kingsbury (Eng)
1935	B.Uber (Eng)
1936	T.Kingsbury (Eng)
1937	T.Kingsbury (Eng)
1938	D.Young (Eng)
1939	D.Walton (Can)
1940	Not held
1941	Not held
1942	Not held
1943	Not held
1944	Not held
1945	Not held
1946	Not held
1947	M.Ussing (Den)
1948	K.Thorndahl (Den)
1949	A.Jacobsen (Den)
1950	T.Olsen-Ahm (Den)
1951	A.Jacobsen (Den)
1952	T.Olsen-Ahm (Den)
1953	M.Ussing (Den)
1954	J.Devlin (USA)
1955	M.Varner (USA)
1956	M.Varnber (USA)
1957	J. Devlin (USA)
1958	J. Devlin (USA)
1959	H.Ward (Eng)
1960	J.Devlin (USA)
1961	J.Devlin-Hashman (USA)
1962	J.Devlin-Hashman (USA)
1963	J.Devlin-Hashman (USA)
1964	J.Devlin-Hashman (USA)
1965	U.Smith (Eng)
1966	J.Devlin-Hashman (USA)
1967	J.Devlin-Hashman (USA)
1968	E.Twedberg (Swe)
1969	H.Yuki (Jap)
1970	E.Takenaka (Jap)
1971	E.Twedberg (Swe)
1972	N.Nakayama (Jap)
1973	M.Beck (Eng)
1974	H.Yuki (Jap)
1975	H.Yuki (Jap)
1976	G.Gilks (Eng)
1977	H.Yuki (Jap)
1978	G.Gilks (Eng)
1979	L.Koppen (Den)
1980	L.Loppen (Den)
1981	S. A. Hwang (S.Korea)
1982	Z.Ailing (Chn)
1983	Z.Ailing (Chn)
1984	L. Lingwei (Chn)
1985	H.Aliping (Chn)
1986	K.Yun-Ja (S.Korea)
1987	K. Larsen (Den)

PADMA SHRI AWARD WINNER

1-	Meena Shah
2-	Prakash Paduknone

ARJUNA AWARD WINNERS

1961	Nandu M. Natekar
1962	Meena Shah
1965	Dinesh Khanna
1967	Suresh Goel
1969	Dipu Ghosh
1970	Damayanti V. Tambay
1971	Shobha Moorthy
1972	Prakash Padukone
1974	Raman Ghosh
1975	Davinder Ahuja
1976	Ami Ghia
1977-78	Kanwal Thakur Singh
1980-81	Syed Modi
1982	Partho Ganguli
	Madhumita Goswami

BASEBALL

It is a truism that baseball, as America's national pastime, has become part of the warp and woof of the country's social fabric, but what is perhaps less widely appreciated is how quickly baseball began to spin off into the general culture. The first authenticated game between two organized teams had barely been played in Hoboken, New Jersey, on 19 June 1846, when Currier & Ives was selling coloured lithographs depicting it. Even something as seemingly modern as commercial endoresements by ballplayers was beginning by the turn of the century.

Before that the origin is vague. Credit has been given to the Egyptians and every succeeding culture. It was in America that the English game of "rounders" finally evolved into baseball.

Although Cartwright's conception of the game as it was then played has changed somewhat, it served as the foundation on which organized amateur teams throughout the country were built. The amateurs flourished for twenty-three years before a group of Cincinnatians decided that their city needed a winnner.

It was 1896, the territory of Wyoming was organized and woman suffrage was proudly proclaimed. Dimitri Mendeleev devised the periodic table of elements. A financial panic on Wall Street shook the economy of the country and the headline "Black Friday" became etched on the pages of American history.

Cincinnati also made news, although it affected fewer people at the time. Two years earlier a barnstorming team, the Washington Nationals, trounced the local favorites. For citizens of that Midwestern community it was an act of humiliation. They were determined to have a winning team even if it meant paying the players. And they did.

MAJOR CHANGES IN PLAYING RULES

1877 Time at bat not charged to the batter on a base on balls.

1880 Base on balls on eight balls instead of nine.
Runner out if hit by a batted ball.
Catcher must catch ball on a fly to retire the batter on a strike-out.

1881 Pitcher's box located 50 feet from home plate instead of 45 feet.

1882 Base on balls on seven balls.

1883 Error charged to the pitcher for a base on balls, wild pitch, hit batter, and balk.
Error charged to the catcher for a passed ball.
Fould ball caught on the first bounce is no longer an out.

Baseball Rules

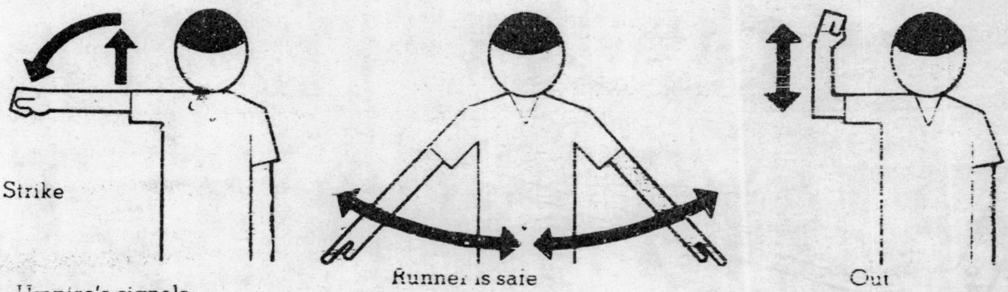

Umpire's signals

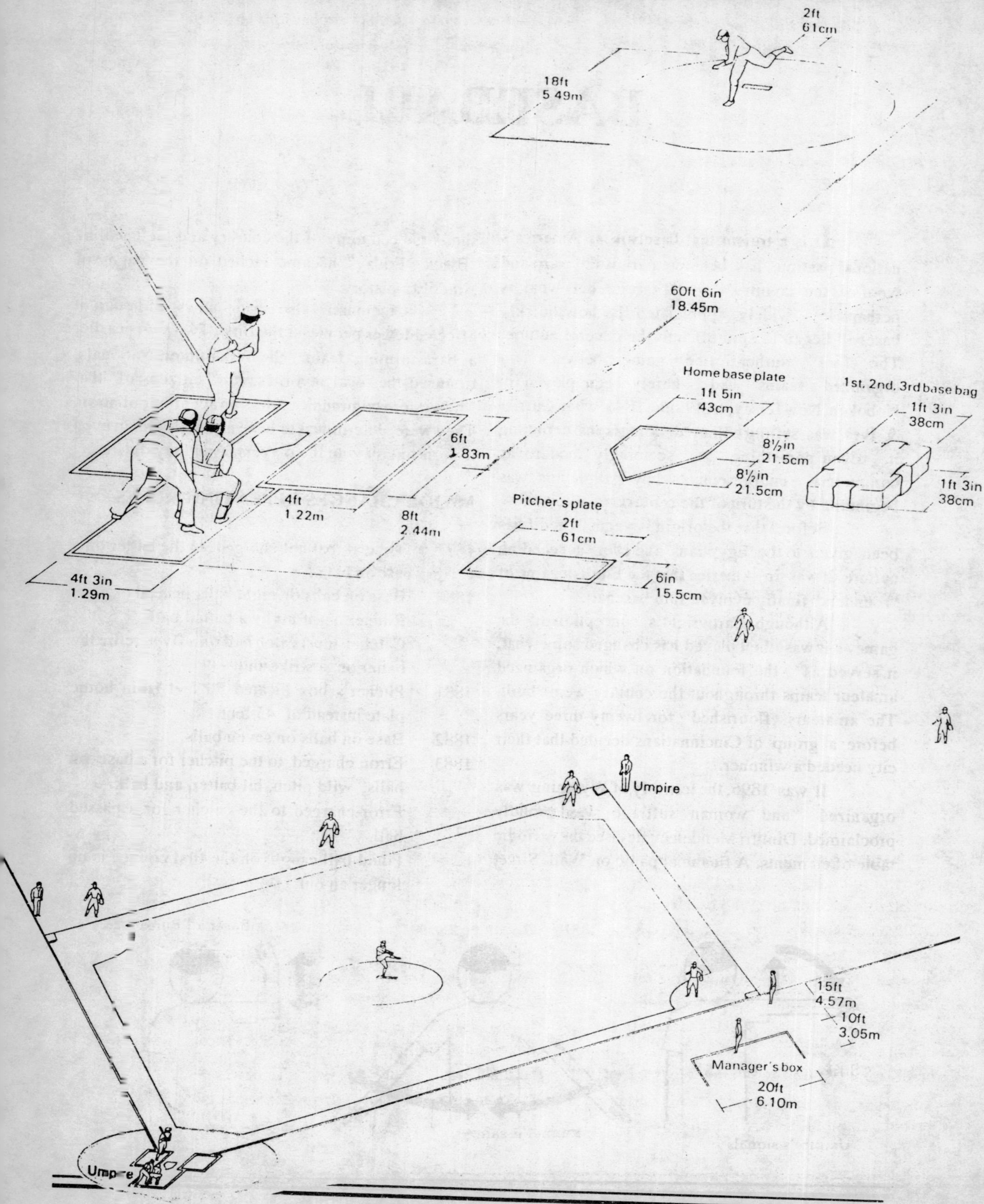
2ft
61cm
18ft
5.49m
60ft 6in
18.45m
Home base plate
1ft 5in
43cm
1st, 2nd, 3rd base bag
1ft 3in
38cm
6ft
1.83m
8½in
21.5cm
8½in
21.5cm
1ft 3in
38cm
4ft
1.22m
8ft
2.44m
Pitcher's plate
2ft
61cm
6in
15.5cm
4ft 3in
1.29m
Umpire
15ft
4.57m
10ft
3.05m
Manager's box
20ft
6.10m
Umpire

1884 Pitcher's motion limited to a shoulder-high delivery, instead of a delivery where his hand must pass below his hip.
Base on balls on six ball.

1885 Official averages to include performances in all tie games of five or more innings.
A Portion of one side of the bat may be flat instead of round.
Pitcher credited with an assist on batter's strike-out.

1886 Pitcher's box changed to 4 x 7 feet, instead of 6 x 6 feet.
Base on balls on seven balls.
Stolen base credited to the runner for each base advanced by his own volition.

1887 Batter no longer allowed to call for a high or low pitch.
Strike zone defined as the area between the top of the shoulder and the bottom of the knee.
Pitcher's box changed to 4 x 5(½) feet.
Batter hit by pitched ball entitled to first base and not charged with the time at bat.
Base on balls on five balls.
Batter's base on balls credited as a hit, and charged as a time at bat.
No error charged to the catcher on a passed ball.
No error charged to the pitcher for a base on balls, wild pitch, hit batter and balk.
Strike-out on four strikes instead of three strikes, where the first called third strike did not count.

1888 Batter's base on balls not a hit or a time at bat.
Error charged to the pitcher for a base on balls, wild pitch,hit batter, and balk.
Batter credited with a hit if the base runner is struck by a batted ball.
Strike-out on three strikes.
Ground rule double instead of a home run if the ball is batted over the fence in fair territory where the fence is less than 210 feet from home plate.
Error charged to the catcher on a passed ball.

1889 No error charged to the catcher on a passed ball.
No error charged to the pitcher for a base on balls, wild pitch, hit batter, and balk.
Sacrifice bunt recognized, but the batter charged with a time at bat.
Bases on balls on four balls.
Pitcher not credited with an assist for batter's strike-out.

1891 Any player may be substituted during a game, but the player substituted for may not re-enter the game.

1892 Ground rule double if the ball is hit over the fence in fair territory where the fence is less than 235 feet from home plate.

1893 Pitching distance lengthened 60 feet 6 inches, and marked by a rubber slab 12 inches long and 4 inches wide.

1894 When a bunt results in advancing a base runner and the batter is put out, or could have been put out, the batter is credited with a sacrifice hit and not charged with a time at bat.

1895 Pitcher's rubber enlarged to 24 x 6 inches.
Maximum diameter of the bat increased to 2(3/4) inches from 2(½) inches.

1897 Earned run is a run scored by the aid of hits only.

1898 Stolen base credited to the base runner whenever he reaches a base he attempted to steal without the aid of battery or fielding errors or a hit by the batter.
Error not charged to the infielder attempting to complete a double play unless the throw is so wild it gives the runner an additional base.
Error not charged against the catcher attempting to prevent a stolen base uless the throw is so wild it gives the runner an additional base.

1900 A pitcher must win at least 15 games to qualify as the league leader in Winning Percentage, instead of appearing in at least 25 games.
Home plate changed from a 12-inch square to a 5-sided figure 17 inches wide.

1901 Infield fly rule changed to be in effect when there are no outs, as well as when there is one out.

Any fould ball not caught on a fly is a strike unless the batter has two strikes on him.

1903 Pitcher's mound must not be higher than 15 inches above the base lines and home plate. Any fould ball not caught on a fly is a strike unless the batter has two strikes on him.

1907 All appearances by a player in an official game count as a game played (American League). Before this, pinch hitters, pinch runners, and defensive substitutes often were not credited with a game played.

1908 Batter credited with a sacrifice fly and not charged with a time at bat if he hits a fly ball which is caught, but a runner scores on the catch.

1909 Pitcher or catcher charged with an error if a wild pitch or passed ball on the third strike allows the batter to reach first base.

Stolen base not credited to any runner on an attempted double steal if either runner is thrown out.

Bunt on third strike is a strike-out and the catcher is credited with the put out.

1917 Earned runs also include runs scored by the aid of stolen base.

1959 Professional fields constructed after June 1, 1958,must have a minimum distance of 325 feet on both the first and third base fould lines to the out-field fence, and a minimum of 400 feet to the center field fence.

1963 Strike zone to include the area from the top of the shoulder to the bottom of the knee.

1967 A player must have a total of at least 3.1 plate appeaances for every scheduled game to qualify as the league leader in Batting Average or Slugging Average. However, if there is any player with fewer than the required number of plate appearances whose average would be the highest if he were charged with this required number of plate appearances, then the player shall be recognized as the league leader in Batting Average or Slugging Average.

1969 Strike zone to include only the area from the armpit to the top of the knee.

Earned runs for a relief pitcher entering a game in the middle of an inning are determined by treating the pitcher as if he entered the game at the beginning of an inning.

Pitcher's mound lowered to 10 inches above the base lines and home plate.

1971 The Official Major League Scoring Committee, at the behest of the Baseball Writers' Association of America, changed the qualifications for a rookie. In order to qualify for a rookie, a player must have not more than 130 at bats or 50 innings pitched in the major leagues during a previous season or seasons, nor more than 45 days on a major league roster during the 25-player limit from the start of the season to August 31,1971.

CUP & TROPHIES

World Series

1903	Boston Red Sox (AL)
1904	Not held
1905	New York Giants (NL)
1906	Chicago White Sox (AL)
1907	Chicago Cubs (NL)
1908	Chicago Cubs (NL)
1909	Pittsburgh Pirates (NL)
1910	Philadelphia Athletics (AL)
1911	Philadelphia Athletics (AL)
1912	Boston Red Sox (AL)
1913	Philadelphia Athletics (AL)
1914	Boston Braves (NL)
1915	Boston Red Sox (AL)
1916	Boston Red Sox (AL)
1917	Chicago White Sox (AL)
1918	Boston Red Sox (AL)
1919	Cincinnati Reds (NL)
1920	Cleveland Indians (AL)
1921	New York Giants (NL)
1922	New York Giants (NL)
1923	New York Yankees (AL)
1924	Washington Senators (AL)
1925	Pittsburgh Pirates (NL)
1926	St.Louis Cardinals (NL)
1927	New York Yankees (AL)
1928	New York Yankees (AL)
1929	Philadelphia Athletics (AL)

1930 Philadelphia Athletics (AL)
1931 St. Louis Cardinals (NL)
1932 New York Yankees (AL)
1933 New York Yankees (AL)
1934 St.Louis Cardinals (NL)
1935 Detroit Tigers (AL)
1936 New York Yankees (AL)
1937 New York Yankees (AL)
1938 New York Yankees (AL)
1939 New York Yankees (AL)
1940 Cincinnati Reds (NL)
1941 New York Yankees (AL)
1942 St.Louis Cardinals (NL)
1943 New York Yankees (AL)
1944 St.Louis Cardinals (NL)
1945 Detroit Tigers (AL)
1946 St.Louis Cardinals (NL)
1947 New York Yankees (AL)
1948 Cleveland Indians (AL)
1949 New York Yankees (AL)
1950 New York Yankees (AL)
1951 New York Yankees (AL)
1952 New York Yankees (AL)
1953 New York Yankees (AL)
1954 New York Giants (NL)
1955 Brooklyn Dodgers (NL)
1956 New York Yankees (AL)
1957 Milwaukee Braves (NL)
1958 New York Yankees (AL)
1959 Los Angeles Dodgers (NL)
1960 Pittsburgh Pirates (NL)
1961 New York Yankees (AL)
1962 New York Yankees (AL)
1963 Los Angeles Dodgers (NL)
1964 St.Louis Cardinals (NL)
1965 Los Angeles Dodgers (NL)
1966 Baltimore Orioles (AL)
1967 St.Louis Cardinals (NL)
1968 Detroit Tigers (AL)
1969 New York Mets (NL)
1970 Baltimore Orioles (AL)
1971 Pittsburgh Pirates (NL)
1972 Oakland 'A' (AL)
1973 Oakland 'A' (AL)
1974 Oakland 'A'(AL)
1975 Cincinnati Reds (NL)
1976 Cincinnati Reds (NL)
1977 New York Yankees (AL)
1978 New York Yankees (AL)
1979 Pittsburgh Pirates (NL)
1980 Philadelphia Phillies (NL)
1981 Los Angeles Dodgers (NL)
1982 St.Louis Cardinals (NL)
1983 Baltimore Orioles (AL)
1984 Detriot Tigers (AL)
1985 Kansas City Royals (AL)
1986 New York Mets (NL)

BASKETBALL

Basketball as we know it today, was born in the United States in 1891 as a recreational activity and quickly spread, culminating in its debut at the Olympic Games in 1936 as a men's sport. The final game was played outside in the rain on tennis courts when the USA defeated Canada by 19-8. The USA continued their Olympic dominance until 1972 when in a dramatic and still controversial finish the USSR stole the game in the last three seconds. The USA reclaimed the Olympic title in 1976 defeating Yugoslavia, another very strong nation which triumphed in Moscow in 1980 in the absence of the USA and Canada.

Basketball has been called the international sport of the 1980s. There is hardly a corner of the earth where people of all ages and both sexes have not been attracted by this game of fast movement, amazing accuracy and thrilling, sometimes extraordinary, finishes. The game is supported by over 160 national federations from the developing countries of Africa to the sophisticated and intensively presented competitions of North America and Europe. In China there are estimated to be around 100 million players - roughly equal to the combined populations of Great Britain and France-playing on dust courts and in palatial arenas.

Basketball skills should be developed in the early elementary grades through various games involving running, jumping, dodging, quick starting and stopping, ball handling and guarding.

The game itself probably should not be introduced as such before the last year in junior high school. It should be regarded as a game of some complexity, and reserved until that age for better understanding and, therefore, greater enjoyment.

SKILLS OF THE GAME

Coaching of girls' basketball teams should be done by women rather than men. It is only natural that men may be influenced by men's rules and techniques suitable for those rules. The modified rules that have been developed for girls and women attempt to reduce personal contact to a minimum and to eliminate injuries. Women coaches and officials should be better trained to interpret the spirit of the rules and to meet with sympathy and understanding the problems presented in the training of girls' team.

The game is played between two teams of five players each, made up of one center, two forwards, and two guards. To win points the ball must be thrown into an elevated goal that resembles an open-end basket. The playing area (indoors or outdoors) is a rectangular hard surface court with minimum dimensions of 74 feet long by 42 feet wide and maximum dimensions of 94 feet by 50 feet wide. The players may pass, throw, bat, or dribble the ball, that is, bounce it but they may not run with it. They are not allowed to hold, push, charge, trip, or impede the progress of an opponent by extending an arm, shoulder, hip, or knee. If they are guilty of transgressing any of these rules they are charged with a personal foul and the player they have offended is permitted, depending on the circumstances, to throw one or more free throws to win points for his team. One point is allowed for each successful free throw; two points are allowed for any goal scored from the field.

The ball may be passed, thrown, batted, rolled or dribbled but may not be held by two players at once, nor fisted or kicked. A dribble consists of

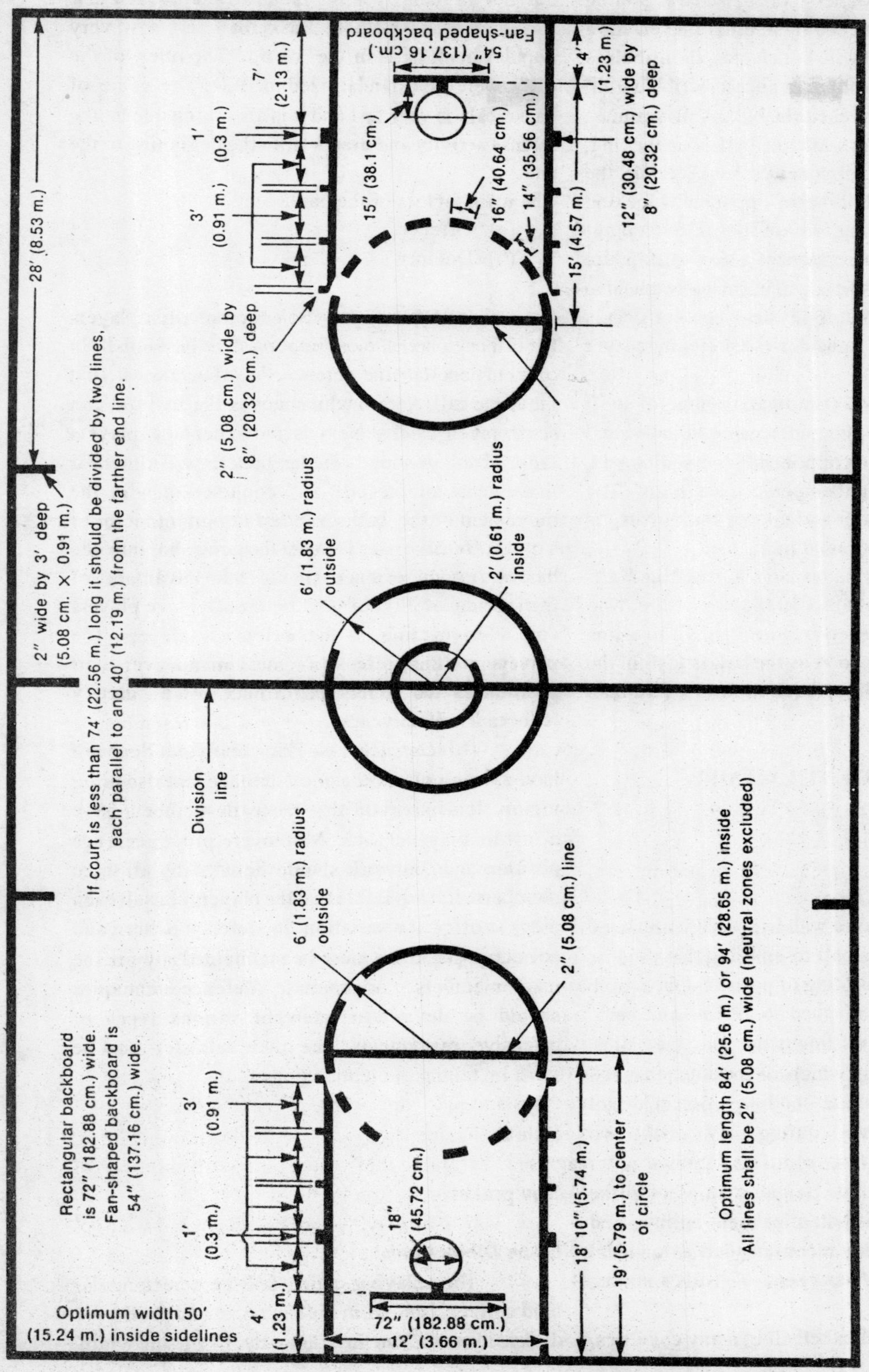

Fig. 5-1. Basketball court for men and women—official through 1981-1982 school year. Left end shows large backboard for college games; right end shows small backboard for high school games. For the brokenline semicircle in the free throw lane, it is recommended that there be eight marks 16 inches (40.64 cm.) long and seven spaces 14 inches (35.56 cm.) long. There should be a minimum of 3 feet (0.91 m.), and preferably 10 feet (3.05 m.) of unobstructed space outside the court. If this is impossible, a narrow broken 1-inch (2.54-cm.) line should be marked inside the court parallel with and 3 feet (0.91 m.) inside the boundary. (Reprinted by permission of the National Collegiate Athletic Association.)

throwing, batting or bouncing the ball and regaining control before it is touched by another player. If a player touches the ball with both hands, the dribble is at an end and he can't begin another dribble until another player has touched the ball. A player must not touch is own basket while the ball is on the ring, or touch the ball or his opponent's basket while the ball is in the basket. Holding an opponent, blocking him,charging or pushing him are illegal. Screening-that is, standing in an opponent's way to stop him reaching a desired position, without actually touching him is not forbidden but if physical contact occurs the referee is likely to consider the screening player responsible.

Basketball is a combination game of swift passing and position play, not a game of individual rush and rampage. If an opponent is screening you, pass low; if you are unhampered pass high. The bounce pass, on the floor and up to a team-mate, is useful when you're hemmed in.

Attack play is usually a combined all-player movement or a concentration on centre, who waits as shooter to receive passes. Five-in-a-line defence means that as soon as the ball is lost in the front court the team drops back to form a five-man barrier.

RULES OF THE GAME

Rule No.1

The Game

Basketball is played with five aside, substitutes being permitted, with a ball resembling that used in Football and goals consisting of posts that have iron rings and short nets attached to them and back boards. It is purely a handling game and the ball is advanced by dribbling, which means bouncing and by passing . Deliberate bodily contact is not allowed. Goals thrown during play count two points and goals thrown from free throws after infringements one point. Height is an asset in the game, which demands stamina and agility and which has been highly recommended as an ideal training activity by coaches of other sports, particularly athletics.

Girls also play Basketball in many countries, but not in India where the nearest approach to it for women is Netball. Basketball is now very popular in all parts of the world. The rules of the game were first standardized in 1934. The game of basketball is very fast and it is absorbing due to the intense activity and drama from the beginning to the end.

The main factors of the game are :

(a) Offence
(b) Defence

(a) *Offence* : — Selection of right players for offence play is most important in basketball. In order to penetrate the defence, the offence must first move the ball. A team which moves the ball fast can score much easily. Next is movement of players themselves. A sound offence pattern will allow for movement of players in conjunction with the movement of the ball. Another important factor of a good offensive play is to get the good shot into the basket. A good offence should take advantage of the scoring ability of the better offensive players and overpowering the defensive players. The players in the offensive must manoeuver their position as the stereotype offence often greatly reduces its effectiveness.

(b) *Defence* : — For a team that does not have a strong offence, a good defence can also bring victory. It is important that the team members have desire to play defence. Moreover, proper defence position and footwork should be used by all team members. It is advisable that the players consult each other to offer the variation in defence pattern and correct positioning must be maintained by all the team members. Appropriate defence techniques should be devised to intercept various types of offensive movements. The pivot defender must be swift in taking the reboundings.

Rule 2

Equipment

Court Dimensions

The playing court shall be a rectangular hard surface free from obstructions and shall have dimensions of 26m in length by 14 m in width, measured from the inside edge of the boundary lines.

The following variations in the dimensions are permitted: plus or minus 2m on the length and plus or minus 1 m on the width, the variations being proportional to each other.

The height of the ceiling should be at least 7 m. The playing surface should be uniformly and adequately lighted. The light units should be placed where they will not hinder the vision of players.

Boundary lines

The playing court shall be marked by well defined lines, which shall be at every point at least 12 m from any obstruction. The lines of the long sides of the court shall be termed the Side Lines, those of the short sides, the End Lines. The distance between these lines and the spectators should be at least 2 m.The lines mentioned in this article and in the following must be drawn so as to be perfectly visible and be 5 cm in width.

Centre Circle

The centre circle shall have a radius of 1.80 m and it shall be marked in the centre of the court. The radius shall be measured to the outer edge of the circumference.

Centre Line - Front Court, Back Court

A Centre Line shall be drawn,parallel to the end lines, from the mid points of the side lines and shall extend 15 cm beyond each side line.

A team's Front Court is that part of the court between the end line behind the opponent's basket and the nearer edge of the Centre Line. The other part of the court,including the Centre Line, is the team's Back Court.

Free Throw Lines

A free throw line shall be drawn parallel to each line. It shall have its further edge 5.80 m from the inner edge of the end line, and it shall be 3.60 m long and its mid point shall lie on the line joining the mid points of the two end lines.

Restricted Areas and Free Throw Lanes

The restricted areas shall be spaces marked in the court which are limited by the end lines, the free throw lines and by lines which originate at the end lines, their outer edges being 3 m from the mid points of the end lines, and terminate at the ends of the free throw lines.

The free throw lanes are the restricted areas extended in the playing court by semi -circles with a radius of 1.80m, their centres at the mid points of the free throw lines. Similar semi circles shall be drawn with a broken line within the restricted areas.

Spaces along the free throw lanes, to be used by players during free throws, shall be marked as follows:

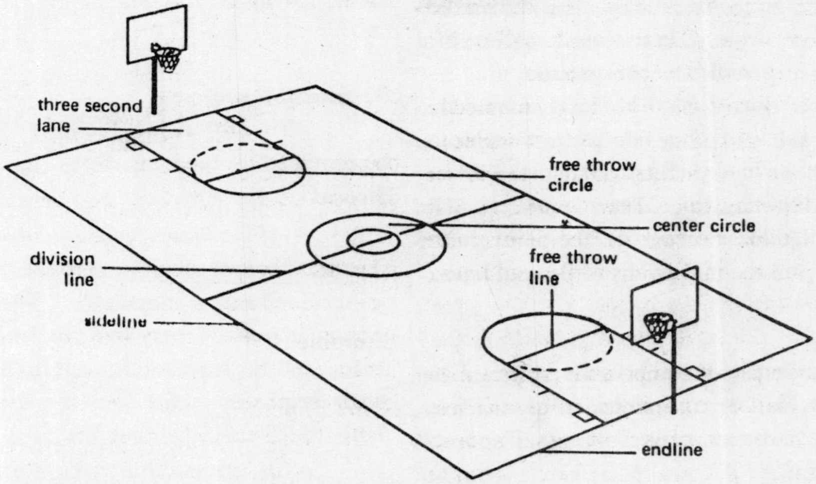

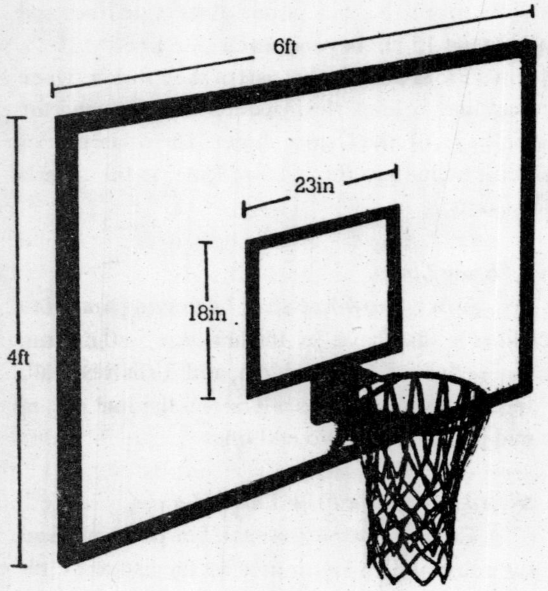

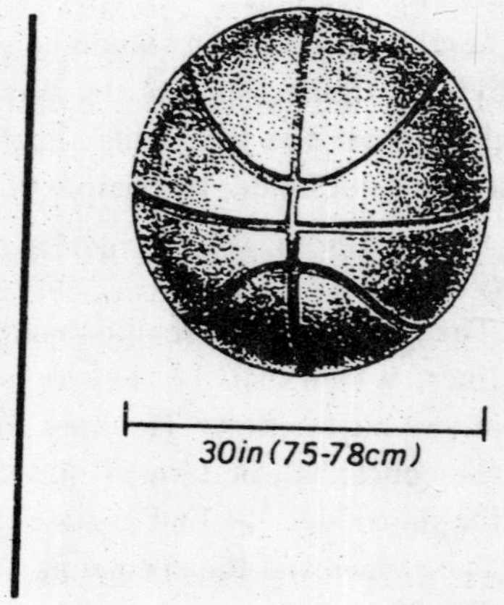

The first space shall be situated 1.80 m from the inside edge of the end line, measured along the line at the side of the free throw lane, and shall be 85 cm in width.

Backboards size, Material and Position

Each of the two backboards shall be made of hard wood, 3cm; thick, or of a suitable transparent material and their dimensions shall be 1.80 m horizontally and 1.20 m vertically.

Borders of the backboards shall be marked with a line, 5 cm wide. These lines shall be of a colour contrasting with the background.

The backboards shall be rigidly mounted in a position at each end of the court at right angles to the floor, parallel to the end lines and with their lower edges 2.75 m above the floor. Their centres shall lie in the perpendiculars erected at the points in the court 1.20 m from the mid points of the end lines.

Baskets

The basket shall comprise the rings and the nets. The rings shall be constructed from solid iron, 45 cm in inside diameter, painted orange. The metal of the rings shall be 20 mm in diameter, with the possible addition of small gauge loops on the under edge or similar device for attaching the nets. The nets shall be 40 cm in length.

Ball-Material, Size and Weight

The ball shall be spherical; it shall be made with an outer surface of leather, rubber or synthetic material; it shall be not less than 75 cm nor more than 78 cm in circumference; it shall weigh not less than 600 gm nor more than 650 gm; and it shall be inflated to an air pressure such that when it is dropped on to a solid wooden floor or the playing surface from a height of about 1.80 m measured to the top of the all,of not less than about 1.20 m nor more than about 1.40 m.

Technical Equipment

The following Technical Equipment shall be provided by the home team. Land shall be at the disposal of the Officials and their assistants:

(a) The Game Clock and the time out watch. The time keeper shall be provided with at least a game clock and a stopwatch. The clock, used for timing periods of play and the intervals between them, and the stop watch, used for timing time-outs shall be placed so that they may be clearly seen by both the Timekeeper and the Scorer.

(b) A suitable device, visible to players and spectators, shall be provided for the administration of the 30 seconds Rule and shall be operated by the 30 seconds Operator.

(c) The official Score Sheet shall be the one approved by the International Amateur Basketball Federation.

(d) There shall be a equipment for all signals provided under rules, including a Score Board visible to players, spectators and the Scorer's Table.

(e) The Markers numbered 1 to 5 shall be at the disposal of the Scorer.

(f) The Scorer shall be provided with two Team Foul Markers. These shall be in red, constructed in such a way that when positioned on the Scorer's Table they are easily visible to players,coaches and officials.

Rule 3

Players, Substitutes and Coaches

Teams

Each team shall consist of not more than ten players one of whom shall be the Captain. Where a team has to play more than 5 games the number of players in each team may be increased to twelve. Shirts of each player shall be numbered on the front and at the back in solid colour with 2 cm in width.

Player Leaving Court

A player may not leave the playing court to gain an unfair advantage.

Captain - Duties and Powers

The Captain shall be the representative of his team and shall control its play. Before leaving the playing court for any valid reason, he shall inform the Referee regarding the player who will replace him.

Coaches

Twenty minutes before the game the Coaches shall furnish the Scorer with number and name of the players as well as the names of the Captain. At least 10 minutes before the game the Coaches will confirm their agreement with the names and numbers of their players and Coaches inscribed by signing the scoresheet and the same time to name the five players who are to start the game.

Rule 4

Officials and their Assistants

The Officials shall be a Referee and an Umpire, who shall be assisted by a Timekeeper, a Scorer and a 30 seconds Operator.

Duties and Power of Referee

The Referee shall inspect and approve all equipment, including all the signals used by the Officials and Assistants. He shall not permit any player to wear objects which in his judgment are dangerous to other players. He shall have power to forfeit a game when conditions warrant. He shall decide matters upon which the Timekeeper and the Scorer disagree. He shall carefully examine the Scoresheet, approve the score and confirm the time of extra period of each half. He shall have power to make decisions on any point not specifically covered in the Rules.

Duties of Officials - Referee and Umpire

Before the beginning of the game, the officials shall agree upon a division of the playing court, to be covered by each of them.

The officials shall blow their whistles and simultaneously give the signals, to stop the clock, followed by all the signals.

The officials shall not whistle after a goal from the field or resulting from a free throw, but shall clearly indicate that a goal has been scored by using signal 1 or 3.

Time and Place for Decisions

The official shall have powers to make decisions for infractions of the rules committed either within or outside the boundary lines; these powers shall start when they arrive on the court, which shall be 20 minutes before.

If during the period between the end of playing time and the signing of the Score Sheet there is any unsports man like behaviour by players, Coaches, Asstt. Coaches or team followers, the Referee must record it on the Score Sheet that an incident has occurred and submit to the responsible authority which shall deal with the matter with appropriate severity.

Calling of Fouls

When a personal foul has been committed the Official shall blow his whistle and simultaneously give the signal to stop the clock. He shall then indicate to the offender of the foul. The player is required to acknowledge this by raising his hand in the air. If there is a flagrant case of such conduct, the official shall penalise it by disqualifying the offender from the game banishing any offending substitute.

Duties of Scorer

The scorer shall keep a chronological running summary of the points scored, he shall record the field goals and free throws made or missed. He shall record the personal and technical fouls called on each player and shall notify the Referee immediately when the fifth foul is called on any player. Scorer shall keep a record of the names and numbers of players who are to start the game and of all substitutes who enter the game. He should be careful to sound his signal only when the ball is dead and the game watch is stopped, and before the ball is again in play.

Duties of Timekeeper

The Timekeeper shall note when each half is to start and shall notify the Referee more than three minutes before this time so that he may notify the teams. For a charged time-out the Timekeeper shall start a time out watch and shall direct the scorer to signal the Referee when it is time to resume play.

The Timekeeper shall indicate with a gong, pistol or bell the expiration of playing time in each half or extra period.

Rule 5

Playing Regulations

Playing Time

The game shall consist of two halves of 20 minutes each, with normally an interval of 10 minutes between halves.

Beginning of Game

The game shall be started by a jump ball in the Centre circle. The Referee shall make the toss between any two opponents. The game cannot begin if one of the teams is not on the court with five players.

Jump-Ball

A jump-ball takes place when the Official tosses the ball between two opposing players. The Official shall toss the ball upward between the jumpers, to a height greater than either of them can reach by jumping and so that it will drop between them. Neither jumper shall tap the ball before it reaches its highest point, nor leave their positions until the ball has been tapped.

When a jump-ball takes place, the eight non-jumpers shall remain outside the circle until the ball has been tapped. During a jump-ball the official shall see that the other players are in such positions that they do not interfere with the jumpers.

Violation during Jump-Ball

A player shall not violate provisions governing jump-ball. If, before the ball is tapped, a jumper leaves the jumping position or if a non jumper enters the circle, it is a violation which shall be called immediately by one of the Officials. If the Official make a bad toss, the jump-ball shall be re-taken.

Goal - When Made and its Value

A goal is made when a live ball enters the basket from above and remains in or passes through. If the ball accidentally enters the basket from below, it shall become dead and play shall be resumed by a jump-ball at the nearest free throw line.

If, however, a player deliberateiy causes the ball to enter the basket from below, it is a violation and play shall be resumed by an opponent throwing the ball in from the side line out of bounds at the point nearest to where the violation occurred.

Interfere with Ball in Offence

An offensive player may not touch the ball when it is in line with its downward flight above the level of the ring and is directly above the restricted area. This restriction applies only until the ball touches the ring.

An offensive player shall not touch his

opponent's basket or backboard while the ball is on the ring during a shot for goal.

Interfere with Ball in Defence

A defensive player shall not touch the ball after it has started its downward flight during an opponent's shot for goal and while the ball is above the level of the ring.

The ball becomes dead when violation occurs. The shooter is awarded the point if during a free throw if a shot for goal from the field according to the place from where the shot for goal was attempted.

Throw in after Field Goal or Successful Last Free Throw

After a field goal or successful last free throw, any opponent of the team credited with the score shall be entitled to throw the ball in from any point out of bounds at the end of the court where the goal was made. The official should not handle the ball unless by so doing the game can be resumed more quickly, but if a player delays the game by interfering with the ball, it is a technical foul.

Decision of Game

A game shall be decided by the scoring of the greater number of points in the playing time.

Game to be forfeited

A team shall forfeit the game if it refuses to play after being instructed to do so by the Referee. If the team to which the game is forfeited is ahead, the score at the time of forfeiture shall stand.

Tied Score and Extra Periods

If the score is a tie at the expiration of the second half, the game shall be continued for an extra period of five minutes or as many such periods of five minutes as may be necessary to break the tie. An interval of two minutes shall be allowed before each extra period. At the beginning of each extra period, the game shall be re-started with a jump ball at the centre circle.

When Game is Terminated

The game shall terminate at the sounding of the Timekeeper's signal indicating the end of playing time. When a foul is committed simultaneously with or just previous to the Timekeeper's signal ending a half or an extra period, time shall be allowed for the free throw or throws if any are involved in the Penalty.

Rule 6

Timing Regulations

Game Clock Operations

The game clock shall be stopped at the end of each half and extra period and when an official blows his whistle for various reasons or when a goal is scored against the team of a coach who had requested a charged time out.

Ball Goes into Play

The ball goes into play when the Official enters the circle to administer a jump ball or the official enters the free throw lane to administer a free throw. Thirdly, when an out of bounds situation the ball is at the disposal of the player who is at the point of the throw-in.

Ball Becomes Alive

(a) after having reached its highest point in a jump-ball it is tapped by the first player, or
(b) when the official places it at the disposal of a free throw shooter.

Dead Ball

The ball becomes dead when

(a) Any goal is made
(b) Any violation occurs
(c) A foul occurs while the ball is alive or in play
(d) Held ball occurs or ball lodges on the basket support.
(e) It is apparent that the ball will not go into the basket; on a free throw for a technical foul by Coach, Assistant Coach, or a free throw.
(f) Official's whistle is blown while the ball is alive or in play.
(g) The 30 seconds Operator's signal is sounded while the ball is alive.
(h) Time expires for a half or extra period.

Time Out

(a) A violation
(b) A foul
(c) A held ball
(d) Unusual delay in the game being resumed.
(e) Suspension of play
(f) Suspension or removal of a player.
(g) When the 30 seconds signal is sounded; or
(h) When a basket is scored against the team of a coach who has requested a charged time out.
(i) Time out in case of injury.

Rule 7

Player's Regulations

Substitutions

A substitute before going on the court shall report to the Scorer and must be ready to play immediately. The Scorer shall sound his signal immediately if the ball is dead and the Game Clock stopped, or as soon as the ball becomes dead and the Game Clock is stopped, but before the ball is again in play as the one of the following situation:

(a) a held ball has been called
(b) a foul has been called
(c) a charged time out has been granted, or
(d) game has been stopped, to attend an injured player.

The substitute shall remain outside the boundary line until an official beckons him on whereupon he shall enter the court immediately. If in the opinion of the official, there is an unreasonable delay,a time out shall be charged against the offending team. A player involved in a jump ball may not be substituted by another player. A substitution is not permitted from the moment that the ball is in play for the first or only free throw until the ball becomes dead after being alive against after the free throw or throws.

Location of Player and Official

The location of a player is determined by where he is touching the floor.

The location of an official is determined in the same manner as that of a player. When the ball touches an official it is the same as touching the floor at the Official's location.

Control of the Ball

A player is in control when he is holding or dribbling a live ball or in an out of bounds situation when the ball is at his disposal for a throw in. Team control continues until an opponent secures control or the ball becomes dead or on a shot for goal when the ball is no longer in contact with the hand of the shooter.

How Ball Goes out of Bounds

The ball is caused to go out of bounds by the last player to touch it before it goes out, even in the event of the ball going out of bounds by touching something other than a player.

An Official shall clearly indicate the team which shall take the throw in from out of bounds. Out of bound decisions are clearly signalled by the Officials.

Dribbling

A dribble is made when a player, having gained control of the ball, gives impetus to it by throwing, tapping or rolling it and touches it again before it touches another player.

After giving impetus to the ball as described in the foregoing, the player completes his dribble the instant he touches the ball simultaneously with both hands, or permits the ball to come to rest in one or both hands. A player shall not dribble a second time after his first dribble has ended, unless it is after he has lost control.

Held Ball

A held ball shall be declared when two or more players of opposing teams have one or both hands firmly on the ball. Officials should not declare held ball too quickly, thereby interrupting the continuity of the game, and unjustly taking the ball from the player who gained or is about to gain possession. A held ball decision is not warranted merely on the grounds that the defensive player gets his hands on the ball. When held ball is called, the ball shall be tossed up between the two contending players at the nearest circle. If there are more than

Pass received. Ball under control. Check defense.

Step in the direction of hook shot take-off. Watch defense.

The take-off. Right leg pulls high to get full body action into the shot.

There she goes! Notice the arch and backspin on the ball. Practice hooks with both hands—all court positions.

two players involved, the ball shall be tossed up between two contending players of approximately the same height.

Player in the Act of Shooting

A Player is in the act of shooting when in the judgment of an Official he starts an attempt to score by throwing, dunking, or tapping the ball and it continues until the ball has left the player's hand.

Fouls

A foul is an infraction of the Rules involving personal contact with an opponent or unsportsman like conduct, charged against the offender and consequently penalised according to the provisions contained in the relevant article of these Rules.

Procedure when a Violation is Called

When a violation is called the ball becomes dead. The ball is awarded to a nearby opponent for a throw in from the side line at the point nearest that where the violation occurred. If the ball goes into a basket during the dead ball which follows such a violation, no point can be scored.

Throw in from out of Bounds

The player who is to throw the ball in from out of bounds shall stand out of bounds at the side line at a spot nearest the point where the ball left the court or the violation or foul was committed.

Whenever the ball is awarded to a team for a throw in from out of bounds at the side line in its back court, the Official, if there is confusion as to the decision, shall hand the ball to the thrower in at the side line closest to the violation.

Player to Attempt Free Throw

When a personal foul is called, and a free throw penalty is awarded, the player upon whom the foul was committed shall be designated by the Official to attempt the free throws. Should a player, by mistake, execute a free throw into his own basket, the free throw shall be annulled, whether, successful or not, and a new try shall be granted at the other basket.

When a technical foul is called, the free throw or throws may be attempted by any player of the opposing team.

Ball in Play if Free Throw is Unsuccessful

If the free throw is unsuccessful,play shall continue after the last free throw following a player foul. If the ball misses the ring it is a violation and the game shall be resumed by a throw in from the side line at the point opposite the free throw line by the opposing team .

Rule 9

Rules of Conduct

Definition

The proper conduct of the Game demands the full and loyal cooperation of members of both teams, including Coaches and substitutes, with the officials and their assistants.

Personal Foul

A personal foul is a player foul which involves contact with an opponent whether the ball is in play, alive or dead. Illegal use of hands occurs when a player contacts an opponent with his hand(s) unless such contact is only with the opponent's hand while it is on the ball and is incidental to an attempt to play the ball.

Intentional Foul

An intentional foul is a personal foul which in the opinion of the Official was committed deliberately by a player.

CUP & TROPHIES

Medal In Olympics

First held in 1936 for men and 1976 for women.

Men

	Gold	*Silver*	*Bronze*
1936	USA	Canada	Maxico
1948	USA	France	Brazil
1952	USA	USSR	Uruguay
1956	USA	USSR	Uruguay
1960	USA	USSR	Brazil
1964	USA	USSR	Brazil
1968	USA	Yugoslavia	USSR
1972	USSR	USA	Cuba

1976	USA	Yugoslavia	USSR
1980	Yug.	Italy	USSR
1984	USA	Spain	Yugoslavia
1988	USSR	USA	

Women

1978	USSR	USA	Bulgaria
1980	USSR	Bulgaria	Yugoslavia
1984	USA	Korea	China
1988	USA		

World Champions

First held in 1950, the World Championships for men are held between Olympic Games. Contested by amateur teams.

Men

1950	Argentina
1954	United States
1959	Brazil
1963	Brazil
1967	USSR
1970	Yugoslavia
1974	USSR
1978	Yugoslavia
1982	USSR
1986	United States

Women

Women's World Championships were first held in 1953.

1953	United States
1957	United States
1959	USSR
1964	USSR
1967	USSR
1971	USSR
1975	USSR
1979	United States
1983	USSR

ARJUNA AWARD WINNERS

1961	Sarabjit Singh
1967	Khushi Ram
1968	Subedar Gurdial
1969	Hari Dutt
1970	Abbas Moontasir
1971	Officer Man Mohan Singh
1973	Surinder Kumar Kataria
1974	Anil Kumar Punj
1975	Hanuman Singh
1977-78	T. Vijayaraghawan
1979-80	Om Prakash
1983	Radhey Shyam
	Suman Sharma

BILLIARDS

The billiards originated mysteriously in the sixteenth century in India and the snooker in the colonial India of the nineteenth.

The first public billiards room was opened during the nineteenth century; the Billiards Association was formed in 1885 and a code of rules copyrighted. In 1908, the Billiards Control Club started in opposition to the Billiards Association when the professionals seceded from the B.A., and the game was played under two different sets of rules. These bodies were amalgamated in 1919. Amateurs and professionals now play under the rules of the Billards Association and Control Council.

Equipment

Billards consists, to put it crudely, in poling balls about a smooth table to score by sending them into small pockets, or by striking two balls with a third. The bed of a full-sized billiards table is 12 ft. by 6 ft. 1(1/2)in., and consists of green cloth over slate. Cushions surround the table and there are six small netting pockets, one at each corner and one halfway down each side. The bulk is the space behind a line drawn across the table parallel to the bottom cushion and 29 in. from it. There is a half-circle or D, its centre coinciding with that of the baulk-line. The billiard sport is marked 12(3/4) in. from the centre of the top cushion,the centre spot is precisely between the two middle pockets, and the pyramid sport halfway between the centre spot and the face of the top cushion.

SKILLS OF THE GAME

The game is played with three balls red, white and spot-white. One player takes white, the other spot-white as his own. Red is always an object ball (that is, 'making a cannon'), or sending one two or all three balls into pockets in order to score.

At the opening of a game, red is placed on the billiard spot and is replaced after being pocketed or forced off the table. If it is pocketed from the spot twice in succession during one break, it is placed on the centre spot, or if that is occupied, on the pyramid spot; and if it is pocketed again it is replaced on the billiard spot.

Two points are scored for pocketing the opponent's ball by hitting it with your own; pocketing your own ball off the opponent's; making a cannon. Three points are scored for pocketing the red ball by hitting it with your own; pocketing your own ball off red. All other scores are combinations of the two points for a cannon and 'in off' white or spotwhite and the three points for pocketing red or going in off red. When a cannon is combined with pocketing, the pocketed ball is considered 'in off' the first ball struck.

Cannon

When the player's ball strikes against the other two ball in succession, it is called a 'cannon'.

Potting

When a player's ball hits anyone of the object balls and the object a ball (whether red or white) goes into any pocket, it is called potting the ball.

Loser

When a striker manages to pocket his own ball after touching it with any one of the object balls, it is called a 'loser'and points are scored in favour of the striker. 3 points are scored if the loser is off the red ball and 2 points if the loser is off the white ball. In common parlance it is also called 'in-off'.

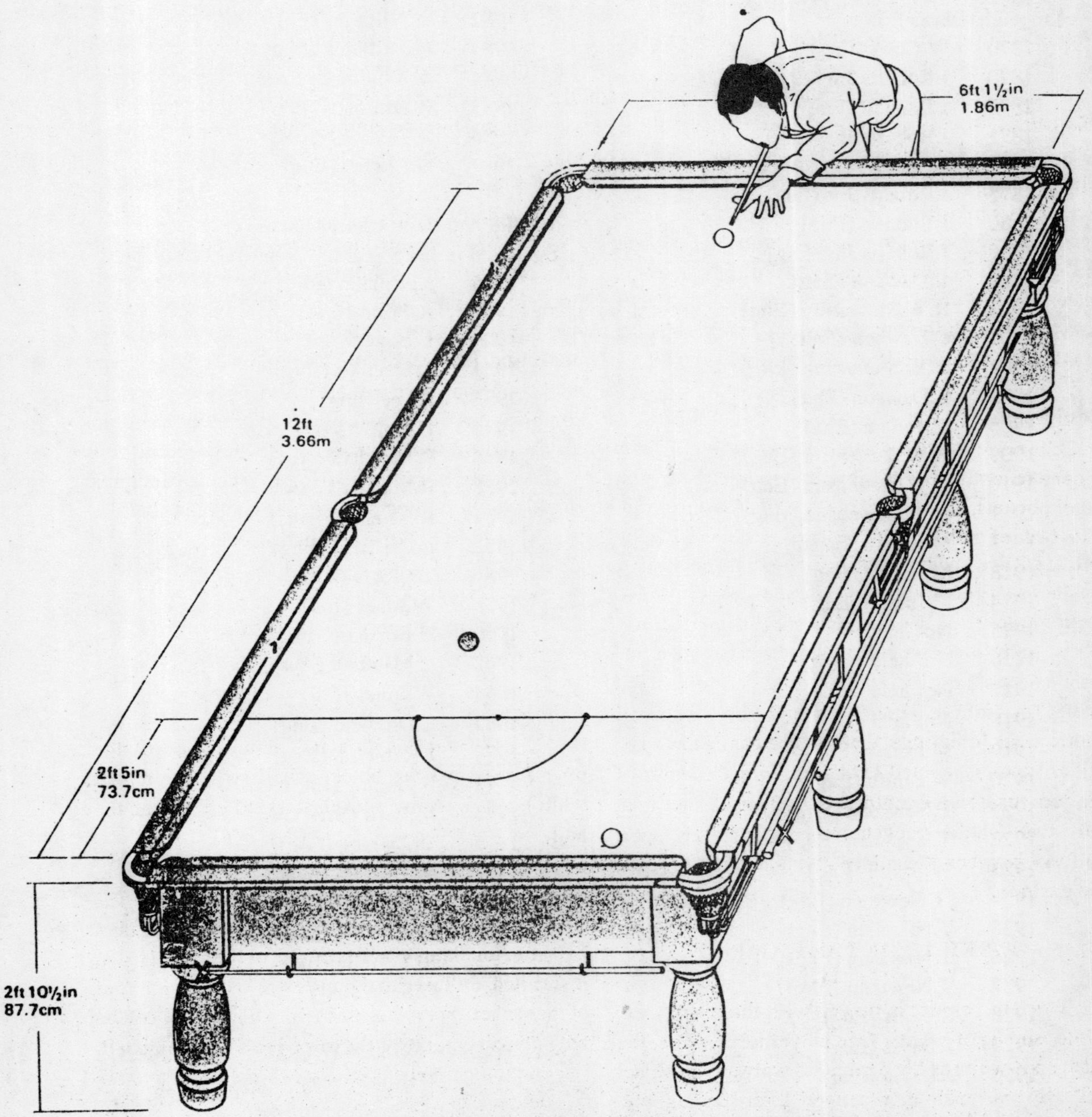
6ft 1½in
1.86m
12ft
3.66m
2ft 5in
73.7cm
2ft 10½in
87.7cm

Break

The total number of points which a player scores during one visit to the table, is known as a 'break'.

CUP & TROPHIES

World Professional Championship

The first world champion to be recognised was William Cook in 1870. The championship has changed hands as follows:

1870	W.Cook (Eng)
1870	J.Roberts,Jnr (Eng)
1870	J.Bennett (Eng)
1871	J.Roberts,Jnr (Eng)
1871	W.Cook (Eng)
1875	J.Roberts,Jnr (Eng)
1880	J.Bennett (Eng)
1885	J.Roberts Jnr (Eng)
1889	C.Dawson (Eng)
1901	H.W.Stevenson (Eng)
1901	C.Dawson (Eng)
1901	H.W.Stevenson (Eng)
1903	C.Dawson (Eng)
1908	M.Inman (Eng)
1909	H.W.Stevenson (Eng)
1910	H.W.Stevenson (Eng)
1911	H.W.Stevenson (Eng)
1912	M.Inman (Eng)
1913	M.Inman (Eng)
1914	M.Inman (Eng)
1915	Not held
1916	Not held
1917	Not held
1918	Not held
1919	M.Inman (Eng)
1920	W.Smith (Eng)
1921	T.Newman (Eng)
1922	T.Newman (Eng)
1923	W.Smith (Eng)
1924	T.Newman (Eng)
1925	T.Newman (Eng)
1926	T.Newman (Eng)
1927	T.Newman (Eng)
1928	J.Davis (Eng)
1929	J.Davis (Eng)
1930	J.Davis (Eng)
1931	Not held
1932	J.Davis (Eng)
1933	W.Lindrum (Aus)
1934	W.Lindrum (Aus)
1951	C.McConachy (NZ)
1968	R.Williams (Eng)
1971	L.Drifield (Eng)
1971	R.Williams (Eng)
1980	F.Davis (Eng)
1981	Not held
1982	R.Williams (Eng)
1983	R.Williams (Eng)
1984	M.Wildman (Eng)
1985	R.Edmonds (Eng)
1986	R.Foldvari (Aus)
1987	N.Dagley (Eng)

World Amateur Championship

First held in 1926 and now contested biennially.

1926	J.Earlham (Eng)
1927	A.Prior (S.Af)
1929	L.Hayes (Aus)
1931	L.Steeples (Eng)
1933	S.Lee (Eng)
1935	H.Coles (Wal)
1936	R.Marshall (Aus)
1938	R.Marshall (Aus)
1951	R.Marshall (Aus)
1952	L.Driffield (Eng)
1954	T.Cleary (Aus)
1958	W.Jones (Ind)
1960	H.Beetham (Eng)
1962	R.Marshall (Aus)
1964	W.Jones (Ind)
1967	L.Driffield (Eng)
1979	J.Karnehm (Eng)
1971	N.Dagley (Eng)
1973	M.Lafir (Sri)
1975	N.Dagley (Eng)
1977	M.Ferreira (Ind)
1979	P.Mifsud (Mal)
1981	M.Ferreira (Ind)
1983	M.Ferreira (Ind)
1985	G.Sethi (Ind)

PADMA SHRI AWARD	WINNER
1-	Wilson Jones

2-	O.B. Agarwal
3-	Geet Sethi

ARJUNA AWARD WINNERS

1962	Wilson Jones
1970	Michael Ferreira
1972	Satish Kumar Mohan
1973	Shyam Shroff
1978-79	Arvind Savur
1983	Subhash B. Agrawal
1984	Om B. Agrawal
1985	Geet S. Sethi

BOWLING

Bowls is a game for everyone. Indeed, most of the new stars are young people. This is an out-and out game of skill, and although the sexes will be in separate competitions here, there is a considerable lobbying for mixed events in future. After all, the sport demands accuracy, timing and subtlety rather than physical strength. The sport or game of bowling involves two or more players competing at the same time. Their object is simple: to send a large, heavy, hard-surface ball down a long lane of polished wood towards ten tenpins, and to cause as many of these pins to fall down as possible. When two or more people bowl a game, they keep a record of their performance by frame on a score sheet. A strike is worth ten points plus the number of pins knocked down by the player's next two rolls. A spare counts for ten points plus the number of pins felled by the next roll. If the player fails either to achieve a strike or to convert the spare, his score for the frame is simply the total number of pins picked off by his two rolls.

RULES OF THE GAME

(i) A game of American Tenpins shall consist of ten frames. Each player shall bowl two balls in each of the first nine frames except when he shall make a strike. A player who scores a strike or spare in the tenth frame shall deliver three balls.

(ii) A strike is recorded when the player completes a legal delivery and bowls down the full setup of ten pins with the first ball. The count in each frame where a strike is bowled shall be left open until the player has completed two more deliveries. The maximum count on the one strike when followed by a spare is 20.

(iii) When a player bowls two strikes in succession legally delivered, he shall have scored double. The count in the frame where the first strike was bowled shall be left open until the player has completed his next delivery. When all pins are down twice in succession the count for the first strike is 20 plus the number of pins knocked down with the first ball of the third frame following. The maximum count on a double figuring a nine pin count on the first ball following the second strike is 29.

(iv) In scoring three successive strikes, the player shall be credited with 30 pins in the frame in which the first strike was bowled. Thus, in a game of ten full frames, a player must bowl 12 strikes in

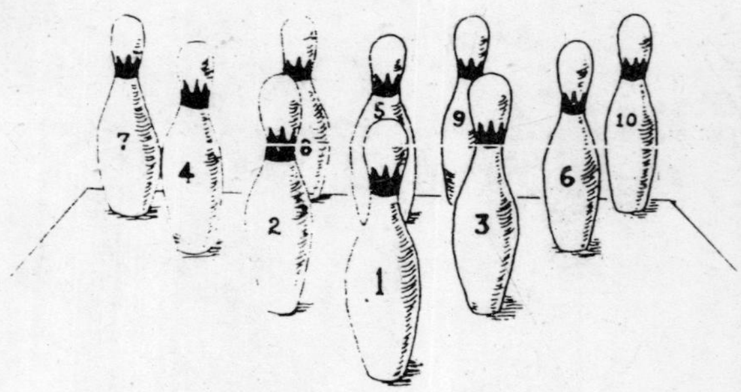

The pindeck.

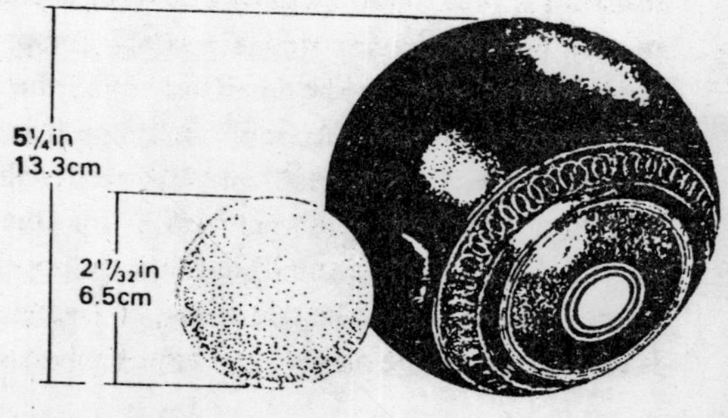

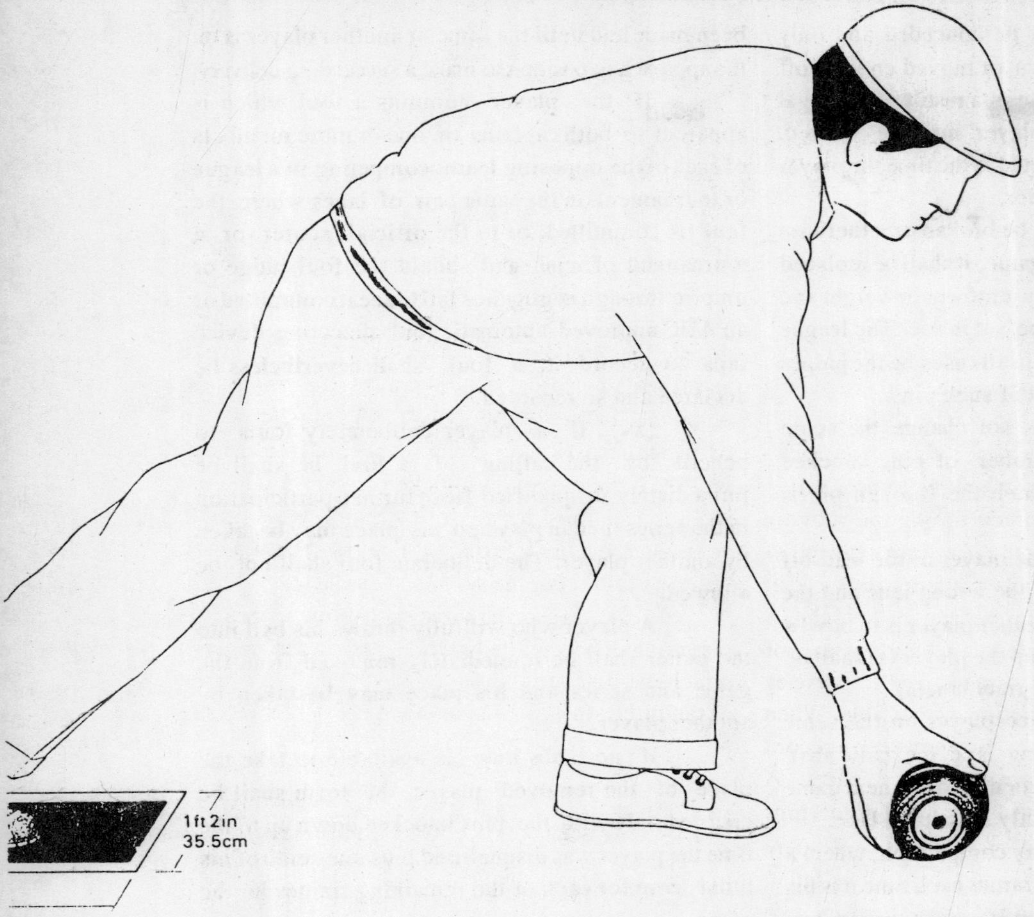

succession in order to bowl a game of 300.

(v) Any player who bowls down the remaining pins with a legally delivered second ball in any frame has scored a spare. A spare is designated by a (/) in the small square in the upper right-hand corner of the frame in which it is made. The number of pins knocked down after the first delivery before the player bowls for the spare should be marked by a small figure in the upper right corner of the frame. The count in such frame proper is left open until the player shall have bowled his first ball in the next frame following, when the number of pins knocked down by the first ball shall be added to the ten pins represented by his spare, and the total shall be credited therein. When a spare is scored in the tenth frame, a third ball shall be bowled in that frame.

(vi) A playershall have made an error when he fails to bowl down all ten pins after having completed twodeliveryin a given frame provided the pins left standing after the first ball is bowled do not constitute a split. An error is designated by a (-) in the small square in the upper right-hand corner of the frame in which the error is made. The number of pins knocked down after the first delivery, before the player bowls the remaining pins, should be marked in the upper right corner of the frame. The count in every frame where an error is committed shall be recorded immediately following the player's second delivery.

(vii) Every ball delivered by the playershall count, unless declared a dead ball. Pins must then be respotted after the cause for declaring such dead ball has been removed.

(viii) When any of the following incidents occur the ball counts as a ball rolled, but pins knocked down shall not count:

(ix) A ball shall be declared dead if any of the following occur in which case such ball shall not count. The pins must be respotted after the cause for declaring such dead ball has been removed and player shall be required to rebowl.

(x) No pins may be conceded and only those actually knocked down or moved entirely off the playing surface of the lane as a result of the legal delivery of the ball by the player may be counted. Every frame must be completed at the time the player is bowling in his regular order.

(xi) Should a pin be broken or otherwise badly damaged during the game, it shall be replaced at once by another as nearly uniform in weight and condition as possible with the set in use. The league or tournament officials shall in all cases be the judges in the matter of replacement of such pins.

A broken pin does not change the score made by a bowler. The number of pins knocked down are counted, after which the broken pin is replaced.

(xii) When only one player or the lead-off men on both teams bowl on the wrong lane and the error is discovered before another player is to bowl a dead ball shall be declared and the player (s) shall be required to rebowl on the correct lane(s).

When more than one player on the same team has bowled on the wrong lane, the game shall be completed without adjustment and the next game shall be started on the correctly scheduled lane.

In singles match play competition, where a player normally bowls two frames each time it is his turn to bowl, and a player bowls on the wrong lane for these two frames, a dead ball shall be declared providing the error is discovered prior to the time the opposing player hasmade a legal delivery. If the error is not discovered until the opposing player has bowled, the score shall count and the player shall be required to bowl his subsequent frames on the correct lanes.

(xiii) Bowling balls used in the game and marked by their owners are considered private and other participants in the game are prohibited from using the same, unless the owner consents to such use.

(xiv) A foul is committed with no pinfall being credited to the player although the ball counts as a ball rolled, when a part of the bowler's person encroaches upon or goes beyond the foul line and touches any part of the lane, equipment or building during or after executing a legal delivery. A ball is in play and a foul may be called after legal delivery has been made and until the same or another player is on the approach in position to make a succeeding delivery.

If the player commits a foul which is apparent to both captains or one or more members of each of the opposing teams competing in a league or tournament on the same pair of lanes where the foul is committed, or to the official scorer or a tournament official, and should the foul judge or umpire through negligence fail to see it committed or an ABC approved automatic foul detecting device fails to record it, a foul shall nevertheless be declared and so recorded.

(xv) If a player deliberately fouls to benefit by the calling of a foul, he shall be immediately disqualified from further participation in the series then in play and his place may be taken by another player. The deliberate foul shall not be allowed.

A player who willfully throws his ball into the gutter shall be immediately removed from the game and series and his place may be taken by another player.

If no substitute is available to take the place of the removed player, his team shall be credited only with the pins knocked down up to the time the player was disqualified plus one-tenth of his blind score for each of the remaining frames in the game.

(xvi) A foul ball shall be recorded as a ball bowled by the player, but any pins bowled down when a foul if committed shall not count. When the player fouls upon delivering the first ball of a frame, all pins knocked down must be respotted, and only those pins knocked down by the second ball may be counted. If he bowls down all the pins with his second ball after fouling with the first, it shall be scored as a spare. When less than ten pins are bowled down on the second ball after fouling on the first, it shall be scored as an error. A player who fouls when delivering his second ball of a frame shall be credited with only those pins bowled down with his first ball provided no foul was committed when the first ball was delivered. When a bowler fouls during the delivery of his first ball in the tenth frame and bowls down all ten pins with his second ball (making a spare) he bowls a third ball and is credited with a spare plus the pins bowled down ball

in the tenth frame, only those pins bowled down in delivering his first two balls shall be counted.

(x vii) Wherever it is deemed necessary to determine fouls, the officials of any local association, upon authorization by their Board of Directors, may require that a foul line be plainly painted on the walls, posts division boards, or any other structure in a bowling establishment at any point on a line with the regular foul line.

(xviii) When a protest involving a foul or the legality of pinfall is entered and it cannot immediately be resolved between the two team captains, a provisional ball or frame shall be bowled by the contestant.

It the protest occurs on the first delivery in a frame, the player shall complete his frame and then bowl another complete frame immediately, unless it involves a question of whether a bowler should receive credit for a strike or a lesser number of pins on his first delivery. In such event, the pin or pins which were protested as constituting illegal pinfall shall be respotted and the player required to bowl another ball.

When the protest occurs on the second delivery, the player shall bowl a provisional ball against the same setup of pins which were standing at the time except when the protest involves a foul in which case no provisional ball shall be necessary.

A record of both scores for the frame in which the provisional delivery was made shall be maintained and the protest referred to the league's Board of Directors or the tournament's managing committee for decision. If unable to reach a decision, the local association or the Congress can be asked for

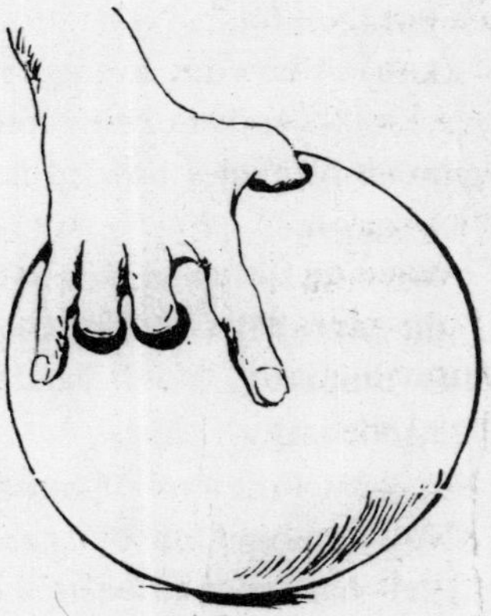

a. Full conventional grip.

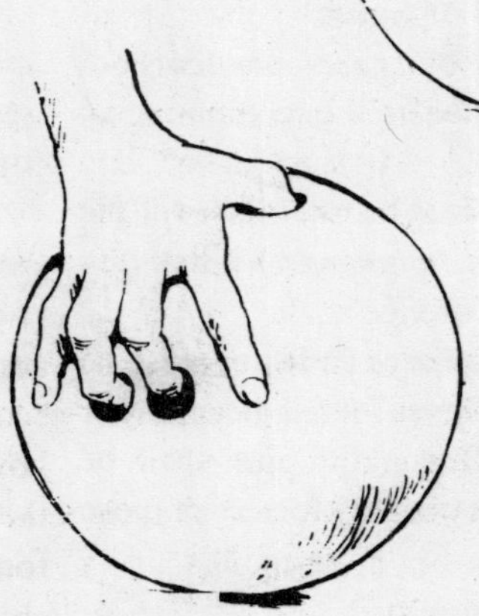

b. Full fingertip grip

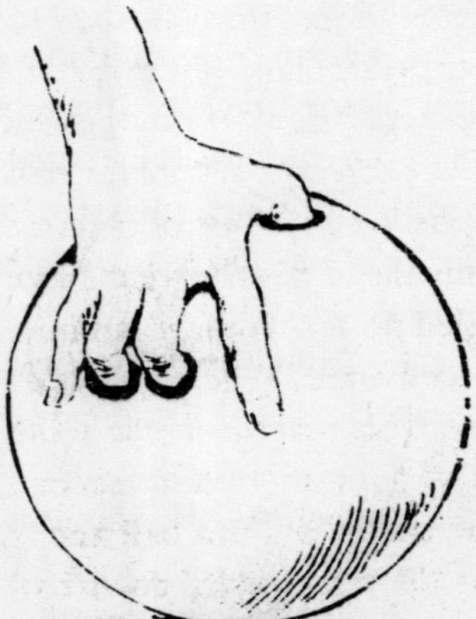

c. Semi-fingertip grip

a decision upon submission of all the facts relating to the protest.

(xix) The league or tournament officials shall allow no unreasonable delay in the progress of any game. Should any member or team participating in a league or tournament refuse to proceed with the game after being directed to do so by the proper authorities, such game or series shall be declared forfeited.

(xx) League and tournament officials may adopt and use any ABC- approved automatic foul detecting device and where none is available a foul judge must be stationed so he has an unobstructed view of the foul line.

(xxi) No appeal shall be allowed when a foul is indicated by an approved automatic foul detecting device or is called by a foul judge except when it is proved that the device is not operating properly, or there is a preponderance of evidence that the bowler did not foul.

(xxii) A bowling average is determined by dividing the total number of pins credited to a bowler by the number of games bowled in one sanctioned league in a season.

When establishing an average in league play, a right-handed bowler must bowl right-handed at all times. Similarly, a left-handed bowler must bowl left-handed at all times.

Penalty, forfeiture of game.

No combination of scores bowled both right-and left-handed shall be used in computing an average.

A new average must be established if the bowler finds it necessary to change his delivery from right-to left-handed or vice versa.

In all cases, extra pins or fractions must be disregarded when using averages for handicapping or classification purposes. The extra pins shall be reduced to a percentage of a pin only for the purpose of deciding individual position standings in a league.

(xxiii) When a sanctioned tournament is sponsored by the management of a bowling center and the scheduled games are bowled solely in that establishment, the owner or employees of the center shall be ineligible to receive individual or all events prizes unless the tournament rules specifically provide otherwise. This shall not apply in annual championships tournaments of local and state associations.

All other tournaments and leagues may, by rule, restrict the owner of the bowling establishment or his employees from qualifying for individual or all events prizes when the games of the league or tournament are bowled solely in the establishments with which they are associated.

(xxiv) Any member of the American Bowling Congress violating the provisions of this rule as outlined below shall be liable for the penalties indicated, and anyone who is not a member of the Congress but who violates the provisions of this rule shall be refused membership in the Congress until the Board of Directors of the Congress approves his application.

(xxv) A bowler whose sanctioned high league average is under 190 shall submit himself for rerating and shall be rerated before entering a sanctioned classified for handicap tournament.

(xxvi) A bowler who libels or utters slanderous accusations against an official or officials, member or members of an associations, league or team affiliated with the American Bowling Congress, which cannot be substantiated by sworn facts in the case, shall be deemed unworthy of retaining membership in the ABC.

(xxvii) No person shall bowl under an assumed name or bowl under the name of another person scheduled to bowl in any sanctioned league or tournament.

(xxviii) When a bowler is suspended from or denied membership in ABC he shall be ineligible to bowl or pace in any sanctioned league or tournament until reinstated by ABC.

(xxix) When an officer of a sanctioned league, ABC or American Junior Bowling Congress, chartered local or state association embezzles, defalcates or absconds with any funds entrusted to him, he shall be liable for indefinite suspension from membership in the Congress.

(xxx) When the Executive Secretary-Treasurer of the American Bowling Congress is advised, after appropriate investigation, that a member who is covered under the ABC bonding program has been guilty of acts within the meaning of Sections Rule 30, he shall cause action to be instituted

(xxxi) Protests involving eligibility scoring or general playing rules in sanctioned leagues and tournaments shall be governed a follows:

(xxxii) No bowling proprietor shall allow on his premises handbooks, pools or any schemes of gambling nature to be made or handled involving the outcome of bowling games whether the bowling game be sanctioned league or tournament play. Failure to terminate such gambling practices in his establishments , or any part thereof, when such practices are within his knowledge, or when he shall have been notified of same shall be cause for such violations being called to the attention of the local association officers.

(xxxiii) Members of the American Bowling Congress may not participate in or operate any pool, lottery or any gambling scheme or arrangement where the scores bowled in sanctioned league or tournament play, partially or otherwise, are used to determine the prize winners. In addition, no member of the ABC shall pay a supplemental league or tournament score or scores to qualify for prizes outside the specific league or tournament in which the score was bowled except as provided in this rule for charity purposes.

The penalty for a violaion of this rule both for the participants and promoters shall be suspension form ABC membership.

(xxxiv) No one shall mark on or shall introduce on any part of the approach or lane any substance which will have a tendency to injure, disfigure the place for approach or lane in such condition as to detract from the possibility of other bowlers being able to take aristol, talcum powder, pumice, resin, etc., on shoes; the use of soft rubber soles and heels the rub off, and in any manner alter the normal condition of the approach, are strictly prohibited.

(xxxv) An automatic scoring device which has been approved by the ABC Board of Directors may be used in sanctioned league and tournament play.

This device shall provide a printed recorded of the score which can be audited frame by frame and otherwise comply with the scoring and playing rules of the game.

(xxxvi) When a member(s) of the American Bowling Congress files charges against another member(s) and fails to appear without sufficient cause to testify at a hearing on the case conducted by an association or a special ABC Investigations Committee, such ABC member(s) shall be liable for suspension from ABC membership.

(xxxvii) When charges of misappropriation or mishandling of funds or a bond claim has been filed against an association or league officer,the association and/or league shall temporarily suspend the officer from all offices held until the matter has been considered by the ABC Legal Committee. In the interim, another officer shall be appointed to perform the duties of the officer who is under temporary suspension.

This procedure shall apply in all such cases except where an appeal is made to the ABC Executive Secretary-Treasurer who may at his discreation authorize the officer to resume his duties pending before Legal Committee action.

CUP & TROPHIES

World Outdoor Championships

The first world championships for lawn bowls were held in 1966 in Sydney, Australia and have subsequently been held in 1972, 1976,1980 and 1984.

Men (Singles)

1966	G.Bryant (Eng)
1972	M.Evans (Wal)
1976	D.Watson (S.Af)
1980	D.Bryant (Eng)
1984	P.Belliss (NZ)

Pairs

1966	Australia
1972	Hong Kong
1976	South Africa
1980	Australia
1984	United States

Triples

1966	Australia

1972 United States
1976 South Africa
1980 England
1984 Ireland

Fours

1966 New Zealand
1972 England
1976 South Africa
1980 Hong Kong
1984 England

Leonard Trophy

(Presented to the winning team)

1966 Australia
1972 Scotland
1976 South Africa
1980 England
1984 Scotland

Women (Singles)

1969 G.Doyle (Eng)
1973 E.Wilke (NZ)
1977 E.Wilke (NZ)
1981 N.Shaw (Eng)
1985 M.Richardson (Aus)

Pairs

1969 South Africa
1973 Australia
1977 Hong Kong
1981 Ireland
1985 Australia

Triples

1969 South Africa
1973 New Zealand
1977 Wales
1981 Hong Kong
1985 Australia

Fours

1969 South Africa
1973 New Zealand
1977 Australia
1981 England
1985 Scotland

Team Title

1969 South Africa
1973 New Zealand
1977 Australia
1981 England

World Indoor Championship

The Embassy World Indoor Championships began in 1979 at the Coatbridge IBC near Glasgow. Now one of the most prestigious events in the bowling calendar, this tournament evolved from a one-day International Invitation event jointly organized by the Coatbridge Club and the Monklands District Council in 1976.

1979 D.Bryant (Eng)
1980 D.Bryant (Eng)
1981 D.Bryant (Eng)
1982 J.Watson (Sco)
1983 B.Sutherland (Sco)
1984 J.Baker (Ire)
1985 T.Sullivan (Wal)
1986 T.Allcock (Eng)
1987 T.Allcock (Eng)

Commonwealth Games

Men (Singles)

1930 R.Colquhoun (Eng)
1934 R.Sprot (Sco)
1938 H.Harvey (S.Af)
1950 J.Pirret (NZ)
1954 R.Hodges (Srh)
1958 P.Danilowitz (S.Af)
1962 D.Bryant (Eng)
1970 D.Bryant (Eng)
1974 D.Bryant (Eng)
1978 D.Bryant (Eng)
1982 W.Wood (Sco)
1986 I.Dickison (NZ)

Pairs

1930 England
1934 England
1938 New Zealand
1950 New Zealand
1954 N.Ireland
1958 New Zealand

1962	New Zealand
1970	England
1974	Scotland
1978	Hong Kong
1982	Scotland
1986	Scotland

Fours

1930	England
1934	England
1938	New Zealand
1950	South Africa
1954	South Africa
1958	England
1962	England
1970	Hong Kong
1974	New Zealand
1978	Hong Kong
1982	Australia
1986	Wales

BOXING

Boxing, sometimes called " The Noble Art of Self-Defence", though actually aggression is its keynote and defence an incidental, is a modern continuation of the old sport of prize fighting which, though always illegal, was popular from the time of Regency until it was succeeded by the present-day glove fighting at the end of the nineteenth century.

In prize fighting bare sets were used and wrestling holds were allowed. Rounds ended when a fighter went down and fights continued until following a knock-down, a man failed to come up to the scratch line in 30 seconds. In modern times boxing gloves are worn and no wrestling is allowed. Rounds last for a fixed time, generally 3 minutes with 1 minute between rounds and fights last only for a fixed number of rounds never more than fifteen. A knock-down does not end a round, the man who is down has 10 seconds in which to rise. If he fails to do so, his opponent wins by a knock-out. If a man fails to come up at the beginning of a round or if the fight is stopped to save a man from further injury, the victory is by a technical knock-out. If however,both man are still at their feet at the end of the stipulated number of rounds, a decision is given on points . Boxing is thus technically a contest of skill for points, and as such, far removed from prize fights to a finish.

Fights are controlled by a referee and in professional boxing,the referee is solely responsible for any points decision. In amateur boxing the decision is given by several judges, who sit apart from each other. The difference between a good professional and a good amateur is probably more marked in boxing than in any other sport.

Boxing is an exciting sport and requires a great deal of courage and strength. The quick reaction and active reflexes are the secret of the fight. Learning Boxing besides a challange of wits is ideal teacher technique for self-defence against attack from enemy, thieves or hooligans.

In amateur boxing where boxers compete not for enemy, stakes, bet or in any way professional, the cox of the boxes decides the category of the boxer. The Amateur Boxing Association Championship classified boxers into following categories :

Light - Flyweight	- 48 kg.
Fly-Weight	- 51 kg.
Bantam-Weight	- 54 kg.
Feather-Weight	- 57 kg.
Light-Weight	- 60 kg.
Light Welter	- 63.5 kg.
Welter-Weight	- 67 kg.
Light-Middle	- 71 kg.
Middle Weight	- 75 kg.
Light-Heavy	- 81 kg.
Heavy-Weight	- 91 kg.
Super Heavy weight	- 91 +

RULES OF THE GAME

(1) The ring shall not be less than 12 feet or more than 20 feet square. The height from ring floor level to the top rope shall be not less than four feet, not more than five feet.

(2) Competitors shall box in a vest completely covering chest and back, shorts being of resonable length reaching to mid-thigh position and light boots or shoes.

(3) The gloves should be of the standard weight of eight ounces each.

(4) Competitors to weigh -in on the day of competition may be stripped or in boxing costume, as they may prefer.

(5) The number and duration of rounds for senior competitions and contest shall be as follows:

(a) Novices- 3 round of 2 minutes each.

(b) Intermediate - 2 rounds of 2 minutes each and a third round of 3 minutes.

(c) Open - 3 rounds of 3 minutes each.

(6) (a) Between open class boxers-4 rounds of 3 minute each.

(b) Between an open class boxer and an intermediate class boxer - 3 rounds of 3 minutes each.

(c) Between intermediate class boxers - 3 rounds of 3 minutes each or 4 rounds of 2 minutes each.

(d) Between an intermediate class boxer and a novice class boxer - 3 rounds of 2 minutes each.

(e) Between novice class boxers - rounds of 2 minutes each.

There will be an interval of one minute between the rounds.

(7) Each competitor shall be attended by one second, and no adviser coaching shall be given to a competitor by his second during the progress of a round.

(8) Boxers shall be required to shake hands twice only - at the commencement of the contest and at the end of it.

(9) The boxer who strikes his opponent the greater number of scoring blows shall be awarded 20 points at the end of each round. The other boxer shall receive a lesser number of points in proportion to the number of scoring blows he has struck.

(10) Scoring blows are struck with the knuckle part of the closed glove of either hand on the front or sides of the head or body above the belt. There must be force behind the blow.

(11) An attack is, striking first or attempting to strike first. One additional point is awarded to the boxer who has attacked the most.

(12) For a match, one referee, judges, time keepers and clears for scales are appointed.

(13) The decision of judges or referee shall be final and without appeal.

(14) Following fouls can lead to the disqualification of a boxer:

(a) Hitting with the elbow
(b) Using the Kidney Punch
(c) Deliberate blows on the back of neck or head
(d) Lying on the head or body
(e) Roughing
(f) Persistently covering up
(g) Holding
(h) Hitting below the belt
(i) Hitting with the open glove
(j) Butting
(k) Unfair use of the ropes
(l) Shouldering
(m) Hitting with inside or butt of hand
(n) Intentionally falling without receiving a blow
(o) Wrestling
(p) Striking a competitor when he is down
(q) Ducking below the belt
(r) Using the pivot blow

CUP & TROPHIES

World Championships

There are now two governing bodies that recognise world champions, the World Boxing Council (WBC) and the World Boxing Association (WBA). In the lists that follow, all Heavyweight world champions are shown and for the other weights the longest reign as titleholder (for those weights which have been contested for many years) and winners since 1970 are detailed, with WBC (World Boxing Council) or WBA (World Boxing Association) were the champion is recognised by one of these bodies only.

Heavy Weight Boxing Champions Through The Years

1882	John L. Sullivan (USA)
1892	James J. Corbett(USA)
1897	Bob Fitzsimmons (UK)
1899	James J. Jeffries (USA)
1905	Marvin Hart (USA)
1906	Tommy Burns (Can)
1908	Jack Johnson (USA)
1915	Jess Willard (USA0
1919	Jack Dempsey (USA)
1926	Gene Tunney (USA)
1930	Max Schmeling (Ger)
1932	Max Baer (USA)
1933	Primo Carnera (Ita)
1934	Max Baer (USA)
1935	James J. Braddock (USA)
1937	Joe Louis (USA)
1949	Ezzard Charles (USA)
1951	Jersey Joe Walcott (USA)
1952	Rocky Mariano (USA)
1956	Floyd Patterson (USA)
1959	Ingemar Johansson (Swe)
1960	Floyd Patterson (USA)
1962	Sonny Liston (USA)
1964	Cassius Clay /Muhammad Ali (USA)
1965	Ernie Terrell (USA)
1968	Joe Frazier (USA)
	Jimmy Ellis (USA)

1970 Joe Frazier (USA)
1973 George Foreman (USA)
1974 Muhammad Ali (USA)
1978 Leon Spinks (USA)
Muhammad Ali (USA)
Ken Norton (USA)
Larry Holmes (USA)
1979 John Tate (USA)
1980 Mike Weaver (USA)
1982 Mike Dokes (USA)
1983 Gerry Coetzee (S.Africa)
1984 Tim Witherspoon (USA)
Pinklon Thomas (USA)
Greg Page (USA)
1985 Tony Tubbs (USA)
Michael Spinks (USA)
1986 Trevor Berbick (Canada)
Tim Witherspoon (USA)
Mike Tyson (USA)
James Smith (USA)
1987 Mike Tyson (USA)
Tony Tucker (USA)

Cruiser-weight

1979 Marvin Camel (USA)
1980 Carlos de Leon (PR)
1982 Ossie Osasio (PR)
S.T.Gordon (USA)
1983 Carlos de Leon (PR)
1984 Piet Crous (S.Af)
1985 Alfonso Ratliff (USA)
Dwight Muhammad Qawi (USA)
Bernard Benton (USA)
1986 Carlos de Leon (PR)
Evander Holyfield (USA)
1987 Francesco Damiani (Ita)

Light- Heavy-weight

1903 Jack Root (Aut)
George Gardner (Ire)
Bob Fitzsimmons (UK)
1905 Jack O'Brien (USA)
1912 Jack Dillon (USA)
1916 Battling Levinsky (USA)
1920 Georges Carpentier (Fra)
1922 Battling Siki (Sen)
1923 Mike McTigue (Ire)
1925 Paul Berlenbach (USA)
1926 Jack Delaney (Can)
1927 Jim Slattery (USA)
Tommy Loughran (USA)
1930 Maxie Rosenbloom (USA)
Jim Slattery (USA)
1934 Bob Olin (USA)
1935 John Henry Lewis (USA)
1939 Melio Bettina (USA)
Billy Conn (USA)
1941 Anton Christoforidis (Ger)
Gus Lesnevich (USA)
1948 Freddie Mills (UK)
1950 Joey Maxim (USA)
1952 Archie Moore (USA)
1962 Harold Johnson (USA)
1963 Willie Pastrano (USA)
1965 Jose Torres (PR)
1966 Dick Tiger (Nig)
1968 Bob Foster (USA)
1971 Vicente Rondon (Ven)
1974 John Conteh (UK)
Victor Galindez (Arg)
1977 Miguel Cuello (Arg)
1978 Mate Parlov (Yug)
Mike Rossman (USA)
Marvin Johnson (USA)
1979 Victor Galindez (Arg)
Matthew Saad Muhammad (USA)
Marvin Johnson (USA)
1980 Eddie Mustaffa Muhammad (USA)
1981 Dwight Muhammad
1983 Michael Spinks (USA)
1985 J.B.Williamson (USA)
1986 Marvin Johnson (USA)
Dennis Andries (UK)
1987 Thomas Hearnes (USA)
Leslie Stewart (Jam)

Middle-weight

1891 Nonpareil Jack Dempsey (Ire)
1891 Bob Fitzsimmons (UK)
1897 Kid McCoy (USA)
1898 Tommy Ryan (USA)
1908 Stanley Ketchel (USA)
Billy Papke (USA)
Stanley Ketchel (USA)

1910 Billy Papke (USA)
1911 Cyclone Thompson (USA)
Billy Papke (USA)
1912 Frank Mantell (USA)
Billy Papke (USA)
1913 Frank Klaus (USA)
George Chip (USA)
1914 Al McCoy (USA)
1917 Mike O'Dowd (USA)
1920 Johnny Wilson (USA)
1923 Harry Greb (USA)
1926 Tiger Flowers (USA)
Mickey Walker (USA)
1931 Gorilla Jones (USA)
1932 Marcel Thil (Fra)
1937 Fred Apostoli (USA)
1939 Ceferino Garcia (Phi)
1940 Ken Overlin (USA)
1941 Billy Soose (USA)
Tony Zale (USA)
1947 Rocky Graziano (USA)
1948 Tony Zale (USA)
Marcel Cerdan (Alg)
1949 Jake la Motta (USA)
1951 Sugar Ray Robinson (USA)
Randolph Turpin (UK)
Sugar Ray Robinson (USA)
1953 Carl Bobo Olson (Haw)
1955 Sugar Ray Robinsn (USA)
1957 Gene Fullmer (USA)
Sugar Ray Robinson (USA)
Carmen Basilio (USA)
1958 Sugar Ray Robinson (USA)
1960 Paul Pender (USA)
1961 Terry Downes (UK)
1962 Paul Pender (USA)
Dick Tiger (Nig)
1963 Joey Giardello (USA)
1965 Dick Tiger (Nig)
1966 Emile Griffith (Vi)
1968 Nino Benvenuti (Ita)
1970 Carlos Monzon (Arg)
1974 Rodrigo Valdez (Col)
1976 Carlos Monzon (Arg)
1977 Rodrigo Valdez (Col)
1978 Hugo Corro (Arg)
1979 Vito Antuofermo (Ita)
1980 Alan Minter (UK)
Marvin Hagler (USA)
1987 Sugar Ray Leonard (USA)

Light-Middle-weight

1962 Denny Moyer (USA)
1963 Ralph Dupas (USA)
1963 Sandro Mazzinghi (Ita)
1965 Nino Benvenuti (Ita)
1966 Ki-Soo Kim (Kor)
1968 Sandro Mazzinghi (Ita)
1969 Freddie Little (USA)
1970 Carmelo Bossi (Ita)
1971 Koichi Wajima (Jap)
1974 Oscar Albarado (USA)
1975 Koichi Wajima (Jap)
1975 Miguel de Oliviera (Bra)
1975 Jae-Do Yuh (Sko)
1975 Elisha Obed (Bah)
1976 Koichi Wajima (Jap)
1976 Jose Duran (Spa)
1976 Eckhard Dagge (Frg)
1976 Angel Cstellini (Arg)
1977 Eddie Gazo (Nic)
1977 Rocky Mattioli (Ita)
1978 Masashi Kudo (Jap)
1979 Maurice Hope (UK)
1979 Ayube Kalule (Uga)
1981 Wilfred Benitez (USA)
1981 Sugar Ray Leonard (USA)
1981 Tadashi Mihara (Jap)
1982 Davey Moore (USA)
1982 Thomas Hearns (USA)
1983 Roberto Duran (Pan)
1984 Mike McCallum (Jam)
1986 Duane Thomas (USA)

Welter - weight

1892 Billy Smith (USA)
1894 Tommy Ryan (USA)
1898 Billy Smith (USA)
1900 Rube Ferns (USA)
1900 Matty Matthews (USA)
1901 Rube Ferns (USA)
1901 Joe Walcott (Bar)
1904 Dixie Kid (USA)
1905 Joe Walcott (Bar)

1906 Honey Mellody (USA)
1907 Mike Sullivan (USA)
1908 Harry Lewis (USA)
1914 Waldemar Holberg (Den)
1915 Mike Glover (USA)
1915 Jack Britton (USA)
1915 Ted Kid Lewis (UK)
1916 Jack Britton (USA)
1917 Ted Kid Lewis (UK)
1919 Jack Britton (USA)
1922 Mickey Walker (USA)
1926 Pete Latzo (USA)
1927 Joe Dundee (Ita)
1928 Jack Thompson (USA)
1929 Jackie Fields (USA)
1930 Jack Thompson (USA)
1931 Jack Thompson (USA)
1931 Lou Brouillard (Can)
1932 Jackie Fields (USA)
1933 Young Corbett III (Ita)
1933 Jimmy McLarnin (Ire)
1934 Barney Ross (USA)
1934 Jimmy McLarnin (Ire)
1935 Barney Ross (USA)
1938 Henry Armstrong (USA)
1940 Fritzie Zivic (USA)
1941 Red Cochrane (USA)
1946 Marty Servo (USA)
1946 Sugar Ray Robinson (USA)
1951 Johnny Bratton (USA)
1951 Kid Gavilan (Cub)
1954 Johnny Saxton (USA)
1955 Tony de Marco (USA)
1955 Carmen Basilio (USA)
1956 Johnny Saxton (USA)
1956 Carmen Basilio (USA)
1958 Virgil Atkins (USA)
1958 Don Jordon (Dom)
1960 Benny Kid Paret (Cub)
1961 Emile Griffith (Vir)
1961 Benny Kid Paret (Cub)
1962 Emile Griffith (Vir)
1963 Luis Rodriguez (Cub)
1966 Curtis Cokes (USA)
1969 Jose Napoles (Cub)
1970 Billy Backus (USA)
1971 Jose Napoles (Cub)
1975 Angel Espada (Pr)
1976 Carlos Palomino (Mex)
1976 Pipino Cuevas (Mex)
1979 Sugar Ray Leonard (USA)
1980 Roberto Duran (Pan)
1980 Thomas Hearns (USA)
1980 Sugar Ray Leonard (USA)
1981 Sugar Ray Leonard (USA)
1983 Don Curry (USA)
1983 Milton McCrory (USA)
1985 Don Curry (USA)
1986 Lloyd Honeyghan (UK)
1987 Lloyd Honeyghan (UK)
1987 Mark Breland (USA)

Junior-Welter-weight

1922 Pinky Mitchell (USA)
1926 Mushy Callahan (USA)
1930 Jackie Kid Berg (UK)
1931 Tony Canzoneri (USA)
1932 Johnny Jaddick (USA)
1933 Battling Shaw (Max)
1933 Tony Canzoneri (USA)
1933 Barney Ross (USA)
1946 Tippy Larkin (USA)
1959 Carlos Ortiz (Pr)
1960 Duilio Loi (Ita)
1962 Eddie Perkins (USA)
1962 Duilio Loi (Ita)
1963 Roberto Cruz (Phi)
1963 Eddie Perkins (USA)
1965 Carlos Hernandez (Ven)
1966 Sandro Lopopolo (Ita)
1967 Paul Fuji (Haw)
1968 Nicolino Loche (Arg)
1968 Pedro Adigue (Phi)
1970 Bruno Arcari (Ita)
1972 Alfonso Frazer (Pan)
1972 Antonio Cervantes (Col)
1974 Perico Fernandez (Spa)
1975 Saensak Muangsurin (Tha)
1976 Wilfred Benitez (USA)
1976 Miguel Velasquez (Spa)
1976 Saensak Muangsurin (Tha)
1977 Antonio Cervantes (Col)
1978 Sang-Hyum Kim (Kor)
1980 Saoul Mamby (USA)

1980 Aaron Pryor (USA)
1982 Leroy Haley (USA)
1983 Bruce Curry (USA)
1984 Johnny Bumphus (USA)
1984 Billy Costello (USA)
1984 Gene Hatcher (USA)
1985 Lonnie Smith (USA)
1985 Ubaldo Sacco (Arg)
1986 Patrizio Oliva (Ita)
1986 Rene Arredondo (Mex)
1986 Tsuyoshi Hamada (Jap)

Light - weight

1896 George Lavigne (USA)
1899 Frank Erne (Swi)
1902 Joe Gans (USA)
1908 Battling Nelson (Den)
1910 Ad Wolgast (USA)
1912 Willie Ritchie (USA)
1914 Freddie Welsh (UK)
1917 Benny Leonard (USA)
1925 Jimmy Goodrich (USA)
1925 Rocky Kansas (USA)
1926 Sammy Mandell (USA)
1930 Al Singer (USA)
1930 Tony Canzeroni (USA)
1933 Barney Ross (USA)
1935 Tony Canzeroni (USA)
1936 Lou Ambers (USA)
1938 Henry Armstrong (USA)
1939 Lou Ambers (USA)
1940 Lew Jenkins (USA)
1941 Sammy Angott (USA)
1942 Beau Jack (USA)
1943 Bob Montgomery (USA)
1943 Sammy Angott (USA)
1944 Juan Zurita (Mex)
1945 Ike Williams (USA)
1951 Jimmy Carter (USA)
1952 Lauro Salas (Mex)
1954 Jimmy Carter (USA)
1955 Wallace Bud Smith (USA)
1956 Joe Brown (USA)
1962 Carlos Ortiz (Pr)
1965 Ismael Laguna (Pan)
1965 Carlos Ortiz (Pr)
1968 Carlos Teo Cruz (Dom)
1969 Mando Ramos (USA)
1970 Ismael Laguna (Pan)
1970 Ken Buchanan (UK)
1971 Perdo Carrasco (Spa)
1972 Mando Ramos (USA)
1972 Roberto Duran (Pan)
1972 Chango Carmona (Mex)
1972 Rodolfo Gonzalez (Mex)
1974 Guts Ishimastu (Jap)
1976 Esteban de Jesus (Pr)
1978 Roberto Duran (Pan)
1979 Jim Watt (UK)
1979 Ernesto Espana (Ven)
1979 Ernesto Espana (Ven)
1980 Hilmer Kenty (USA)
1981 Sean O'Grady (USA)
1981 Alexis Arguello (Nic)
1981 Claude Noel (Tri)
1981 Arturo Frias (USA)
1982 Rany Mancini (USA)
1983 Edwin Rosario (Pr)
1984 Livingstone Bramble (USA)
1984 Jose Luis Ramirez (Mex)
1985 Hector Camacho (Pr)
1986 Edwin Rosario (Pr)

Junior-Light-weight

1921 Johnny Dundee (Ita)
1923 Jack Bernstein (USA)
1923 Johnny Dundee (Ita)
1924 Kid Sullivan (USA)
1925 Mike Balerino (USA)
1925 Tod Morgan (USA)
1929 Benny Bass (USSR)
1931 Kid Chocolate (Cub)
1933 Frankie Klick (USA)
1959 Harold Gomes (USA)
1960 Flash Elorde (Phi)
1967 Yoshiaki Numata (Jap)
1967 Hiroshi Kobayashi (Jap)
1969 Rene Barrientos (Phi)
1970 Yoshiaki Numata (Jap)
1971 Alfredo Macano (Ven)
1971 Ricardo Arredondo (Mex)
1972 Ben Villaflor (Phi)
1973 Kuniaki Shibata (Jap)
1973 Ben Villaflor (Phi)

1974 Kuniaki Shibata (Jap)
1975 Alfredo Escalera (Pr)
1976 Sam Serrano (Pr)
1978 Alexis Arguello (Nic)
1980 Yasutsune Uehara (Jap)
1980 Rafael Limon (Mex)
1981 Cornelius Boza Edwards (Uga)
1981 Sam Serrano (Pr)
1981 Rolando Navrette (Phi)
1982 Rafael Limon (Mex)
1982 Bobby Chacon (USA)
1983 Roger Mayweather (USA)
1983 Hector Camacho (Pr)
1984 Rocky Lockridge (USA)
1984 Julio Cesar Chavez (Mex)
1985 Wilfredo Gomez (Pr)
1986 Alfrdo Layne (Pan)
1986 Brian Mitchell (S.Af)
1987 Julio Cesar Chavez (Mex)

Feather - weight

1891 Young Griffo (Aus)
1892 George Dixon (Can)
1897 Solly Smith (USA)
1898 Dave Sullivan (Ire)
1900 Terry McGovern (USA)
1901 Young Corbett II (USA)
1904 Jimmy Britt (USA)
1904 Brooklyn Tommy Sullivan (USA)
1906 Abe Attell (USA)
1912 Johnny Kilbane (USA)
1923 Eugene Criqui (Fra)
1925 Kid Kaplan (USSR)
1927 Benny Bass (USSR)
1928 Tony Canzoneri (USA)
1929 Battling Battalino (USA)
1932 Kid Chocolate (Cub)
1933 Freddie Miller (USA)
1936 Peter Sarron (USA)
1937 Henry Armstrong (USA)
1938 Joey Armstrong (USA)
1940 Harry Jeffra (USA)
1941 Joey Archibald (USA)
1941 Chalky Wright (Max)
1942 Willie Pep (USA)
1948 Sandy Saddler (USA)
1949 Willie Pep (USA)
1950 Sandy Saddler (USA)
1957 Hogan Kid Bassey (Nig)
1959 Davey Moore (USA)
1963 Sugar Ramos (Cub)
1964 Vicente Saldivar (Mex)
1968 Howard Winstone (UK)
1968 Raul Rojas (USA)
1968 Jose Legra (Cub)
1968 Shozo Saiyo (Jap)
1969 Johnny Famechon (Fra)
1970 Vicente Saldivar (Mex)
1971 Antonio Gomez (Ven)
1972 Clemente Sanchez (Mex)
1972 Jose Legra (Cub)
1973 Eder Jofre (Bra)
1974 Ruben Olivares (Mex)
1974 Bobby Chacon (USA)
1974 Alexis Arguello (Nic)
1975 Ruben Olivares (Mex)
1975 David Kotey (Gha)
1976 Danny Lopez (USA)
1977 Rafael Ortega (Pan)
1977 Cecilio Lastra (Spa)
1978 Eusebio Pedroza (Pan)
1980 Salvador Sanchez (Mex)
1982 Juan Laporte (Pr)
1984 Wilfrdo Gomez (Pr)
1985 Barry McGuigan (Ire)
1986 Steve Cruz (USA)
1987 Antonio Esparragoza (Ven)

Junior-Feather-weight

1922 Jack Kid Wolfe (USA)
1923 Carl Duane (USA)
1976 Rigoberto Riasco (Pan)
1976 Royal Kobayashi (Jap)
1976 Dong-Kyun Yum (S.Korea)
1977 Wilfredo Gomez (Pr)
1977 Soo-Hwan Hong (S.Korea)
1978 Ricardo Cardona (Col)
1980 Leo Randolph (USA)
1980 Sergio Palma (Arg)
1982 Leo Cruz (Dom)
1983 Jaime Garza (USA)
1984 Loris Stecca (Ita)
1984 Juan Meza (Mex)
1985 Lupe Pintor (Mex)

1986 Samart Payakarun (Tha)
1987 Louis Espinozaa (USA)
1987 Jeff Fenech (Aus)

Bantam-weight

1891 George Dixon (Can)
1892 Billy Plimmer (UK)
1895 Pedlar Palmer (UK)
1899 Terry McGovern (USA)
1901 Harry Forbes (USA)
1903 Frankie Neil (USA)
1904 Joe Bowker (UK)
1905 Jimmy Walsh (USA)
1907 Owen Moran (UK)
1908 Johnny Coulon (Can)
1914 Kid Williams (Den)
1917 Pete Herman (USA)
1920 Joe Lynch (USA)
1921 Pete Herman (USA)
1921 Johnny Buff (USA)
1922 Joe Lynch (USA)
1924 Abe Goldstein (USA)
1924 Eddie Martin (USA)
1925 Charlie Rosenberg (USA)
1927 Bud Taylor (USA)
1928 Bushy Graham (Ita)
1929 Al Brown (Pan)
1935 Baltazar Sangchilli (Spa)
1936 Tony Marino (USA)
1936 Sixto Escobar (Spa)
1937 Harry Jeffra (USA)
1938 Sixto Escobar (Spa)
1940 Lou Salica (USA)
1942 Manuel Ortiz (USA)
1947 Harold Dade (USA)
1947 Manuel Ortiz (USA)
1950 Vic Toweel (S.Af)
1952 Jimmy Carruthers (Aus)
1954 Robert Cohen (Alg)
1956 Mario D'Agata (Ita)
1957 Alphonse Halimi (Alg)
1959 Joe Becerra (Mex)
1960 Eder Jofre (Bra)
1965 Fighting Harada (Jap)
1968 Lionel Rose (Aus)
1969 Ruben Olivares (Mex)
1970 Chucho Castillo (Mex)
1971 Ruben Olivares (Mex)
1972 Rafael Herrera (Mex)
1972 Enrique Pinder (Pan)
1973 Romeo Anaya (Mex)
1973 Rafael Herrera (Mex)
1973 Arnold Taylor (S.Af)
1974 Soo-Hwan Hong (S.Korea)
1974 Rodolfo Martinez (Mex)
1975 Alfonso Zamora (Mex)
1976 Carlos Zarate (Mex)
1977 Jorge Lujan (Pan)
1979 Lupe Pintor (Mex)
1980 Julian Solis (Pr)
1980 Jeff Chandler (USA)
1983 Alberto Davila (USA)
1984 Richard Sandoval (USA)
1985 Daniel Zaragoza (Mex)
1985 Miguel Lora (Col)
1986 Gaby Canizales (USA)
1986 Bernardo Pinango (Ven)
1987 Miguel Lora (Col)
1987 Park Chan-Young (S.Korea)

Super-Fly-weight

1980 Rafael Orono (Ven)
1981 Chul-Ho Kim (S.Korea)
1981 Gustavo Ballas (Arg)
1981 Rafael Pedroza (Pan)
1982 Jiro Watanabe (Jap)
1982 Rafael Orono (Ven)
1983 Payao Poontarat (Tha)
1984 Jiro Watanabe (Jap)
1984 Kaosai Galaxy (Tha)
1986 Kaosai Glaxy (Tha)
1987 Santos Laciar (Arg)

Fly-weight

1913 Sid Smith (UK)
1913 Bill Ladbury (UK)
1914 Percy Jones (UK)
1915 Joe Symonds (UK)
1916 Jimmy Wilde (UK)
1923 Pancho Villa (Phi)
1925 Fidel la Barba (USA)
1928 Frankie Genaro (USA)
1929 Frankie Genaro (USA)
1931 Young Perez (Tun)

1932 Jackie Brown (Eng)
1935 Binny Lynch (UK)
1938 Peter Kane (UK)
1943 Jackie Paterson (UK)
1948 Rinty MOnaghan (UK)
1950 Terry Allen (UK)
1950 Dado Marino (Haw)
1952 Yoshio Shirai (Jap)
1954 Pascual Perez (Arg)
1960 Pone Kingpetch (Tha)
1962 Fighting Harada (Jap)
1963 Pone Kingpetch (Tha)
1963 Hiroyuki Ebihara (Jap)
1964 Pone Kingpetch (Tha)
1965 Salvatore Burruni (Ita)
1966 Walter McGowan (UK)
1966 Horacio Accavallo (Arg)
1966 Chartchai Chionoi (Tha)
1969 Hiroyuki Ebihara (Jap)
1969 Efren Torres (Mex)
1969 Bernabe Villacampo (Phi)
1970 Chartchai Chionoi (Tha)
1970 Berkrerk Chartvanchai (Tha)
1970 Masao Ohba (Jap)
1970 Erbito Salavarria (Phi)
1972 Venica Borkorsor (Tha)
1973 Chartchai Chionoi (Tha)
1973 Betulio Gonzalez (Ven)
1974 Shoji Oguma (Jap)
1974 Susuma Hanagata (Jap)
1975 Miguel Canto (Mex)
1975 Erbito Salavarria (Phi)
1976 Alfonso Lopez (Pan)
1976 Guty Espadas (Mex)
1978 Betulio Gonzalez (Ven)
1979 Chan-Hee Park (S.Korea)
1979 Luis Ibarra (Pan)
1980 Tae-Shik Kim (S.Korea)
1980 Shoji Oguma (Jap)
1981 Santos Laciar (Arg)
1981 Antonio Avelar (Mex)
1981 Luis Ibarra (Pan)
1981 Juan Herera (Mex)
1982 Prudencio Cardona (Col)
1982 Freddie Castillo (Mex)
1982 Eleoncio Mercedes (Dom)
1983 Charlie Magri (UK)
1983 Frank Cedeno (Phi)
1984 Koji KOboyashi (Jap)
1984 Gabriel Bernal (Mex)
1984 Sot Chitalada (Tha)
1985 Hilario Zapata (Pan)
1987 Fidel Bassa (Col)

GOLD IN OLYMPICS

Boxing has been included at each Olympic Games since 1904.

Light-Fly-weight

1968 Francisco Rodriguez (Ven)
1972 Gyorgy Gedo (Hun)
1976 Jorge Hernandez (Cub)
1980 Shamil Sabirov (URS)
1984 Paul Gonzales (USA)
1988 Ivalio Khristov (Bul)

Fly-weight

1904 George Finnegan (USA)
1920 Frank De Genaro (USA)
1924 Fidel LaBarba (USA)
1928 Antal Kocsis (Hun)
1932 Istvan Enekes (Hun)
1936 Willi Kaiser (Ger)
1948 Pascual Peez (Arg)
1952 Nathan Brooks (USA)
1956 Terence Spinks (UK)
1960 Gyula Torok (Hun)
1964 Fernando Atzori (Ita)
1968 Ricardo Delgado (Mex)
1972 Gheorghi Kostadinov (Bul)
1976 Leo Randolph (USA)
1980 Peter Lessov (Bul)
1984 Steve McCrory (USA)
1988 Kim Kwang-Sum (S.Kor)

Bantam-weight

1904 Oliver Kirk (USA)
1908 Henry Thomas (UK)
1920 Clarence Walker (S.Af)
1924 Willam Smith (S.Af)
1928 Vittorio Tamagnini (Ita)
1932 Horace Gwynne (Can)
1936 Ulderico Sergo (Ita)

1948 Tibor Csik (Hun)
1952 Pentti Hamalainen (Fin)
1956 Woifgang Behrendt (Ger)
1960 Oleg Grigaryer (URS)
1964 Takao Sakurai (Jap)
1968 Valriy Sokolov (URS)
1972 Orlando Martinez (Cub)
1976 Yong Jo Gu (PRK)
1980 Juan Hernandez (Cub)
1984 Maurizio Stecca (Ita)
1988 Kennedy McKinney (USA)

Feather-weight

1904 Oliver Kirk (USA)
1908 Richard Gunn (UK)
1920 Paul Fritsch (FRA)
1924 John Fields (USA)
1928 Lambertuz van Klaveren (Hol)
1932 Carmelo Robledo (Arg)
1936 Oscar Casanovas (Arg)
1948 Ernesto Formenti (Ita)
1952 Jan Zachara (Tch)
1956 Vladimir Safronov (URS)
1960 Francesco Musso (Ita)
1964 Stanislav Stepashkin (URS)
1968 Antonio Roldan (Mex)
1972 Boris Kuznestsov (URS)
1976 Angel Herrera (Cub)
1980 Rudi Fink (GDR)
1984 Meldrick Taylor (USA)
1988 Giovanni Parisi (Ita)

Light-weight

1904 Harry Spanger (USA)
1908 Frederick Grace (UK)
1920 Samuel Mosberg (USA)
1924 Hans Nielsen (Den)
1928 Carlo Orlandi (Ita)
1932 Lawerence Stevens (S.Af)
1936 Imer Harangi (Hun)
1948 Gerald Dreyer (S.Af)
1952 Aureliano Bolognesi (Ita)
1956 Richard McTaggart (UK)
1960 Kazimierz Pazdzior (Pol)
1964 Jozef Grudzien (Pol)
1968 Ronald Harris (USA)
1972 Jan Szczepanski (Pol)
1976 Howard Davis (USA)
1980 Angel Herrena (Cub)
1984 Pernell Whitaker (USA)
1988 Andreas Zuelow (E.Ger)

Light-Welter-weight

1952 Charies Adkins (USA)
1956 Vladimir Yengibaryan (URS)
1960 Bohumil Nemecek (Tch)
1964 Jerzy Kulej (Pol)
1968 Jerzy Kulej (Pol)
1972 Ray Seales (USA)
1976 Ray Leonard (USA)
1980 Patrizio Oliva (Ita)
1984 Jerry Page (USA)
1988 Vyatcheșlav Yanovskiy (URS)

Welter-weight

1904 Albert Young (USA)
1920 Albert Schneider (Can)
1924 Jean Delarge (Bel)
1928 Edward Morgan (Nzl)
1932 Edward Flynn (USA)
1936 Sten Suvio (Fin)
1948 Julius Torma (Tch)
1952 Zygmunt Chychia (Pol)
1956 Nicholae Lince (Rom)
1960 Giovanni Benvenuti (Ita)
1964 Marian Kasprzyk (Pol)
1968 Manfred Wolke (GDR)
1972 Enukui Correa (Cub)
1976 Jochean Bachfeld (GDR)
1980 Andres Aldama (Cub)
1984 Mark Breland (USA)
1988 Robert Wanglia (Ken)

Light-Middle-weight

1952 Laszio Papp (Hun)
1956 Laszio Papp (Hun)
1960 Wilbert McClure (USA)
1964 Boris Lagutin (URS)
1968 Boris Lagutin (URS)
1972 Dieter Kottysch (Ger)
1976 Jerrzy Rybicki (Pol)
1980 Armando Martinez (Cub)
1984 Frank Tate (USA)
1988 Park Si-Hun (S.Korea)

Middle-weight

1904	Charles Mayer (USA)
1908	John Douglas (UK)
1920	Harry Mallin (UK)
1924	Harry Mallin (UK)
1928	Piero Toscani (Ita)
1932	Carmen Barth (USA)
1936	Jean Despeaux (Fra)
1948	Laszlo Papp (Hun)
1952	Floyd Patterson (USA)
1956	Gennadiy Schatkov (URS)
1960	Edward Crook (USA)
1964	Valeriy Popentschenko (URS)
1968	Christopher Finnegan (UK)
1972	Vyatcheslav Lemechev (URS)
1976	Michael Spinks (USA)
1980	Jose Gomez (Cub)
1984	Joon-Sup Shin (Kor)
1988	Henry Maske (E.Ger)

Light-Heavy-weight

1920	Edward Eagan (USA)
1924	Harry Mitchell (UK)
1928	Victor Avendano (Arg)
1932	David Carstens (S.Af)
1936	Roger Michelot (Fra)
1948	George Hunter (S.Af)
1952	Norvel Lee (USA)
1956	James Boyd (USA)
1960	Cassius Clay (USA)
1964	Cosimo Pinto (Ita)
1968	Dan Poznyak (URS)
1972	Mate Parlov (Yug)
1976	Leon Spinks (USA)
1980	Slobodan Kacar (Yug)
1984	Anton Josipovic (Yug)
1988	Andrew Maynard (USA)

Heavy-weight

1904	Samuel Berger (USA)
1908	A.L. Oldham (UK)
1920	Ronald Rawson (UK)
1924	Otto von Porat (Nor)
1928	Arturo Rodriguez Jurado (Arg)
1932	Santiago Lovell (Arg)
1936	Herbert Runge (Ger)
1948	Rafael Iglesias (Agr)
1952	Hayes Edward Sanders (USA)
1956	Peter Rademacher (USA)
1960	Franco de Piccoli (Ita)
1964	Joe Frazier (USA)
1968	George Foreman (USA)
1972	Teofilo Stevenson (Cub)
1976	Teofilo Stevenson (Cub)
1980	Teofilo Stevenson (Cub)
1984	Henry Tillman (USA)
1988	Ray Mercer (USA)

Super-Heavy-weight

1984	Tyrell Biggs (USA)
1988	Lennox Lewis (Can)

PADMA SHRI AWARD WINNER

Kaur Singh

ARJUNA AWARD WINNERS

1961	L. 'Buddy' D'Souza
1962	Padam Bahadur Mal
1966	Hawa Singh
1968	Dennis Swamy
1971	Muniswamy Venu
1972	Chandrayanarayanan
1973	Mehtab Singh
1977-78	Birender Singh Thapa
1978-79	C.C.Machaiah
1979-80	Bakhshish Singh
1980-81	Isaac Amaldas
1981	G. Monoharan
1982	Kaur Singh
1983	Jas Lal Pradhan
1986	Jaipal Singh
1987	Seera Jayaram

CARROM

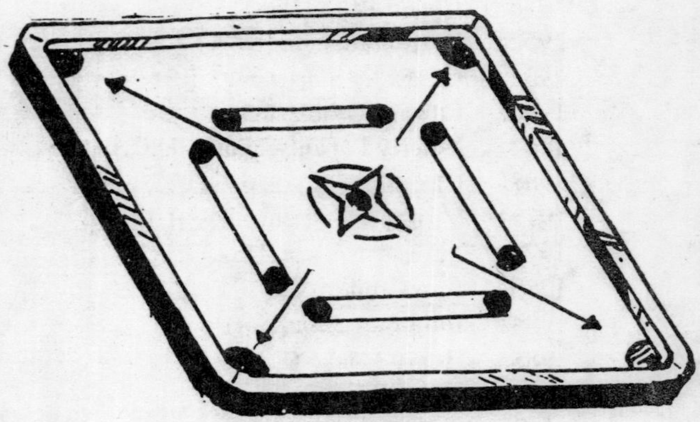

Carrom is an interesting indoor game. This game is for all–children, youngmen and elderly persons. The main feature of this game is that it can be played silently.

Carrom can be enjoyed in a room or in open place of home. There is no need to acquire more place for it. Players sit round the carrom board to play. Thumb and fingers are used in this game. The movement of eyes with draughts is necessary.

This game gives us the benefit of many small exercises. To strike the draughts with fingers, we have to use the force of all veins of arm. To drop the draught with the movement of eyes is just like learning how to aim. We have to keep our brain very cautious during this game.

RULES OF THE GAME

Before describing the laws of the game. It is necessary to tell that these laws are both for single and double game.

1. Striker should touch the both striker lines. If the striker touches only one line, it will be considered as a foul. At the foul, a chance is to be missed as a penalty and other player plays the draughts.
2. On pushing the striker, finger or any part of hand should not touch the surface of the board. If so, the player can miss the chance.
3. While pushing the striker, any part of finger or hand should not be out of the arrow signs which are marked at the corners of striker lines. Otherwise the player has to miss the chance.
4. If the hand slips while pushing the striker and striker moves from its place the play is accepted not dropping any draught, the player misses the chance.
5. While pushing the striker, if striker also drops in the pocket with the draught, it is called Double drop. For this penalty, the player has to place two draughts inside the circle on the board. These draughts are picked from the pocket, which has been dropped by the player on playing.
6. If double due occurs when the player has pocketed only one draught and two draughts are not available to place then that player places the draughts when he pockets the draughts in his next chance.

   When he places two draughts, then the other player who gets the use of penalty, should place the draughts immediately otherwise he has no right to take the penalty of Double due. So the opponent after the chance must place the draughts in the centre immediately.
7. If there is one white and one black draught left at the end of the play, then it is essential to take the Queen. Only then he can play

his draught has to be placed in the Centre because the last draught is properly the cover of the Queen. The player must drop his draught as the cover of Queen.

8. At many places, it is also a law that if Queen is with last black and white draught then first draught is dropped and Queen can be dropped after that. It is an argument that no cover for the Queen is left then it is not compulsory to have a cover for the Queen.
9. Here is an other argument,suppose if a player needs only one point then what will he do? He has to drop draught first and the Queen afterwards. He will not get the points of Queen because he has dropped the Queen after playing a cover.
10. It is meant of unbalancing the points, suppose a player has obtained 18 points. If he makes cover after taking Queen, then he gets 6 points and he makes 24 points. After 24 points, the player can not get the points of Queen. Then for 5 points,if he gets one or two points in a turn, he has to take 3 or 4 turns. In this period the opponent can go forward in his points and he can win the game.

    So, in this position, the player shall like to take one point leaving the greediness of 6 points, so that he may get the benefit of 5 points of Queen when he has obtained 19 points.

    If, in the end, the same position arises, that there is balance of one white one black and Queen on the board, then what should be done to make a point. he will not do so because if he does not get point, he may take risk of 6 points to opponent and unbalance his game.
11. Any player, who obtains 24 points, he can not take the benefit of 5 points of the Queen. If he wins the board by taking Queen but he will get the points of balance draughts of the opponent.
12. During the play, if any draught is touched by hand or finger, the umpire places the draught in the centre of board as penalty. If the player is playing, he misses the chance.
13. If both the players get 27 points each, the game becomes of 31 points.
14. At double due or any foul, at which the player has the right to place the draught, he can place that behind his any draught by which his draught may drop easily in the pocket at the aim.

CHESS

Chess, a game of skill for two players, is the world's most popular game. Nearly a hundred nations compete in the biannual Olympiads, but Chess is equally a family game, to be played for amusement and five year olds are not too young to learn.

The game originated in India and is perhaps 14 centuries old, sharing a common ancestry with Shogi and Xiangqi. It was brought to Europe by the Moors but it was not until the fifteenth century that Chess as we know it today was played. It has flourished ever since, though it is only in recent times that the game has been popularized. In the last few decades it has enjoyed a remarkable expansion and is now dominated by youth.

THE PAWNS

These humble foot soldiers have no less than five ways of aiding their general on the battlefield of the chessboard.

The ordinary movement of the pawn is one square straight forward along the file on which it stands. When a pawn stands on its starting square, a player may move it forward two squares on its first move instead of one. Thus the white pawns at b2 and g2 can be moved to b4 and g4 respectively. This privilege is, however, optional, and a player may advance his pawn only one square on its first move if he so wishes.

The white pawn at c7 will reach c8 with its next move. When it does so it is immediately removed from the board and replaced (on c8) by any white piece other than a king. When a player promotes a pawn by attaining the 8th rank he almost invariably promotes it to a queen, which is the strongest piece. It is this possibility of promotion which makes a one-pawn advantage a frequently decisive factor in games between strong players.

The fourth type of move a pawn may make is a capture. The pawn can only capture on square diagonally forward; thus the white pawn at d4 can capture the black pawn at e5, and the black pawn at e5 can capture the white pawn at d4.

THE ROOKS

The rook move is a simple one-rooks travel as far as they like along any unobstructed rank or file. The rook is a powerful, fast moving piece, but it requires open lines to exploit its strength. At the beginning of the game, the rooks will be obstructed by friendly men for some time, but later, after some pawns have been exchanged, they will do staunch work.'

THE BISHOPS

Bishops move diagonally. Thus the bishop, like the rook, is a long-ranking piece, requiring open lines to conduct its operations.

The bishop can be a handy attacking piece but it has a serious limitation; since it moves diagonally, it is on fined to squares of the colour on which it started. Thus any one bishop can only cover half the squares on the board.

THE KNIGHTS

A knight makes an L-shaped move, two squares up and one along, it any direction. This is represented schematically by the arrows drawn from the knight at h 1 to the squares f2 and g3.

It will help you to think of the knight's

move in this way because it explains why it can apparently jump over pieces of either colour on the way to its destination. The knight passes between the squares, as it were, and it is therefore the only piece that can be developed before a pawn is moved in the initial position.

A knight functions more effectively than a bishop or rook in positions without open lines due to its jumping process. Also, a knight can reach any square on the board, unlike the colour-bound bishop, though it is slower moving and clumsy beside a rook or bishop on a board with few obstructions.

A white queen
usually indicated by the symbol: ♕
Two white rooks
usually indicated by the symbol: ♖
Two white bishops
usually indicated by the symbol: ♗
Two white knights
usually indicated by the symbol: ♘
Eight white pawns
usually indicated by the symbol: ♙
A black king
usually indicated by the symbol: ♚
A black queen
usually indicated by the symbol: ♛
Two black rooks
usually indicated by the symbol: ♜
Two black bishops
usually indicated by the symbol: ♝
Two black knights
usually indicated by the symbol: ♞
Eight black pawns
usually indicated by the symbol: ♟

The initial position of the pieces on the chess-board is as follows:

THE QUEEN

The queen is a very powerful piece. She combines the moves of a rook and a bishop, and moves as far as she likes along any unobstructed line. The queen moves only like a rook or like a bishop in any one turn though.

From a central square, the queen controls as many as twenty-seven squares on an open board; from the corner, twenty-one squares.

The strength of a queen is sometimes a weakness. Because she is so powerful, she must always flee and attack of an opposing rook, bishop, or knight, as to allow the exchange of a queen for one of these pieces would be a very poor bargain.

THE KING

The king can move only one square at a time, but in any direction. Thus it is quite strong at close quarters, but is a slow-moving piece. Like the knight it controls more squares from a central post than from the edge of the board, and can travel more quickly to any square from the former position.

There is a special privilege available to the king known as castling. Once, and only once, during a game, a player may move his previously unmoved king two squares towards a previously unmoved rook, and place the rook on the square which the king has crossed. This is the sole occasion when a player can move two pieces at the same time.

LAW OF THE GAME

Introduction

The game of chess is played by two opposing players by moving pieces on a square board called a "chessboard".

LAW 1

The Chess-Board

1. The chessboard is made up of 64 equal squares in colour alternatively light and dark.
   (" white and black" squares respectively).

2. The chessboard is placed between the players in such a way that the square in the corner to the right of each player is white.
3. The eight rows of squares running from one player to the other are called "files".
4. The eight rows of squares running at right angles to the files are called "ranks".
5. The rows of squares of the same colour touching at corners are called "diagonals". The initial position of the pieces on the chessboard is as follows :

LAW 2

The Pieces

At the beginning of the game one player has 16 light coloured pieces (the"White"pieces),the other has 16 dark coloured pieces(the "Black" pieces).

These pieces on each side are as follows : a King, a Queen, two Rooks, two Bishops, two Knights and eight Pawns.

LAW 3

The Right to Move

1. The two players shall play alternatively and make one move at a time. The player with the White pieces commences the game.
2. A player whose turn it is to play is said "to have the move".

LAW 4

The General Definition of the Move

1. With the exception of castling (Article 6) a move is the transfer of a piece from one square to another which is either unoccupied or occupied by an opponent's piece.
2. No piece, except the Rook when castling or the Knight (Article 6), can cross a square occupied by another piece.
3. When a piece is played to a square occupied by an opponent's piece, the opponent's piece is said to have been "captured" and it is immediately removed from the chess-board by the player who has made the capture. See Article 6 (b) for taking "en passant".

LAW 5

The Moves of the Individual Pieces

The King-except when castling, the King moves to an adjacent square that is not attacked by an opponent's piece. Castling is a move of the King and a Rook, counting as a single move (of the King) carried out in the following manner: The King is transferred from its original square to either of the two squares of the same colour nearest in the same rank, then the Rook towards which the King has been moved is transferred over the King to the square which the King has just crossed.

Castling is permanently impossible (a) if the King has already been moved, or (b) with a Rook that has already been moved.

Castling is prevented for the time being: (a) if the original square of the King or the squares which the King must cross or that which it is to occupy is attacked by an opponent's piece, or (b) if there is any piece between the Rook involved in the move and the King.

The Queen : — The Queen moves to any square on the rank, file, or either of the diagonals on which it stands.

The Rook : — The Rook moves to any square on the rank or file on which it stands.

The Knight :-- The Knight's move is made up to two different steps. It takes one step of a single square along the file or rank, and then, still moving away from the square it left, takes one step along a diagonal. (Note: Another simple way of remembering the Knight's move is to consider it as moving the diagonal of a rectangle of 3x2 squares).

The Pawn - The pawn can only move forward.

(a) Except when making a capture, it advances from its original square either one or two vacant squares along the file on which it stands, and on subsequent moves it advances on vacant square along the file. When making a capture it advances one square along either of the diagonals on which it stands.

(b)、 A Pawn attacking a square crossed by an opponent's Pawn which has been advanced two squares on the previous move can capture the opponent's Pawn as though the latter had only been moved one Square. This can only be made on the move immediately following such advance and is known as taking "en passant".

(c) On reaching the eighth rank the pawn must immediately as part of the same move be exchanged for a Queen, a Rook, A Bishop or a Knight at the player's choice without taking into account the other pieces still remaining on the chessboard. This exchanging of a pawn is called "promotion". The promoted piece must be of the same colour as the Pawn and its action is immediate.

LAW 6

The Completion of the Move

A move is completed:

(a) In the case of the transfer of a piece to a vacant square, when the player's hand has quieted the piece; or

(b) In the case of a capture,when the captured piece has been removed from the chess board and when the player, having placed the piece on its new square, has quitted the piece with his hand; or

(c) In the case of castling, when the player's hand has quitted the Rook on the square crossed by the King; when the player's hand has quitted the King the move is still incomplete but the player has no longer the right to make any other move except castling; or

(d) In the case of promotion of a Pawn, the Pawn has been removed from the chessboard and the player's hand has quitted the new piece after placing it on the promotion square; if the player's hand has quitted the Pawn that has reached the promotion square the move is still incomplete but the player no longer has the right to move the Pawn to another square.

LAW 7

The Touched Piece

Provide that he first warns his opponent. The player whose turn it is to move may adjust one or move pieces on their squares.

Apart from the above case,if the player whose turn it is to move touches one by moving or taking the piece first touched which can be moved or taken.

The touching of a piece or pieces entails no obligation if a breach of this rule is not pointed out by the opponent before he touches a piece, or if none of the moves indicated above can be carried out in accordance with the rules.

LAW 8

Illegal Positions

1. If, during the game, it is found out that an illegal move has been made, then the position shall be reconstructed as it was immediately before the illegal move was played. The game shall then continue in accordance with the rules given in Article 8 as regards the move replacing the illegal move.

   If it proves impossible to reconstruct the position, then the game shall be annulled and a fresh game played.
2. If during a game, one or more pieces have been accidentally displaced and are not correctly replaced, the position shall be set up as it was immediately before the mistake and the game continued.

   If it proves impossible to set up the position again, the game shall be annulled and a fresh game started.
3. If, after an adjournment,the position is

incorrectly put up, then the position as it was on adjournment shall be set up again and the game continued.

4. If,during a game, it is found that the initial position of the pieces was incorrect, then the game shall be annulled and a fresh game played.

   (F.I.D.E.Interpretation- This has been extended to apply to the case where the players have started with the wrong colours.)

5. If,during a game it is found that the position of the chessboard is incorrect,then the position reached shall be transferred to a chessboard correctly placed and the game continued.

   (F. I. D. E. Interpretations-All irregularities cited in Article 9 are ignored if discovered after a game has in fact ended. But, within a reasonable time after the agreed "end" of the game, it may be proved that it had in fact ended earlier,e.g., by an unnoticed mate or stalemate or by a valid but incorrectly disallowed claim of a draw or an exceeding of the time limit. (Article 17). Any moves or agreements that occurred after the game did in fact end, are null and void. The F.I.D.E. has also ruled that an unfinished game subject to adjudication is not finished until adjudicated).

LAW 9

Check

1. The King is in check when the square it occupies is attacked by an opponent's piece; the latter is said to be "checking the King".
2. The check must be warded off on the move immediately following. If the check cannot be avoided then it is "mate" (See Article 11:1).
3. A piece that intercepts a check to its King can itself give check to the opponent's King.

LAW 10

The Completed Game

1. The game is won for the player who has mated the opponent's King.
2. The game is considered won for the player whose opponent declares he resigns.

Drawn Game

1. When the King or the player whose turn it is to move is not in check, and the player cannot make a legal move, situation is called "stalemate".
2. By agreement between the players. (see Article 17 A).
3. On demand by one of the players when the same position appears three times, the same player having the move each time. The position is considered the same if pieces of the same kind and colour occupy the same squares and the possible moves of all pieces are unchanged.

   This right of claiming the draw belongs only to the player:

   (a) Who is in a position to play a move leading to such repetition of the position, if he indicates this move and claims the draw before making it; or

   (b) Who is due to reply to a move by which such repeated position has been produced, provided he does not move before claiming.

   If a player's claim of a draw under clause (a) proves incorrect (Article 17 A) and the game continues, that player is still bound to play the move he indicated.

   If a player makes a move without having claimed a draw in the manner prescribed in (a) or (b) he then loses his right to claim a draw; this right is, however, restored to him if the same position appears again with the same player having the move, and with the possible moves of all pieces unchanged.

4. When the player whose turn it is to move proves that at least fifty moves have been played by each side without a capture of a piece and without a Pawn-move having been made.

   This number of fifty moves can be increased for certain positions provided the number is clearly laid down before the start of the game.

LAW 11

The Recording of Games

1. During the play, each player is required to record the game (moves of his own and his opponent's), move by move, as clearly and legibly as possible, on the score-sheet provided for the contest.
2. If,acutely pressed for time, a player is clearly unable to comply with the Section 1 above, he shall nevertheless do his best to indicate on his score-sheet the number of moves made. As soon as his time trouble is over he shall immediately complete his record of the game by writing down the comitted moves. But he shall not have the right to claim a draw under Article 12: Section 3 if the moves in question were not recorded in conformity with Section 1 above.

F.I.D.E.Interpretation - (a) The word "acutely pressed for time" is open for the referee's decision at the spot taking into account the time on the clock, number of moves to be made and the nature of the position at the moment. The referee may decide that a player is not "acutely pressed for time" and require the player to record the moves in conformity with Section1. If the player refuses, the referee may rule that the player loses the game under Article 17:Section 4.

(b) If, on the referee's instruction to write down the moves, a player declares that he cannot fill the missing moves without consulting his opponent's score-sheet, the request for the sheet shall be made to the referee, who will judge whether the player's form can be completed before the time control without embarrassing the opponent. The later shall not refuses his scoresheet, for two reasons: The record belongs to the organisers of the contest, and the player who is to complete his record shall do so in his own time.

(c) In all other cases, the score-sheets can be completed only after the time control. There are then two possibilities: One player alone has not completed his record, in which case he shall do so in his own playing time; both players have not completed records, in which case both clocks shall be stopped until the two records are completed, if necessary with the help of a chessboard under the control of the referee, who shall, beforehand, have recorded the position existing at the moment of the interruption. If in the first possibility the referee sees that the player's score-sheet, although filled in, will not help in reconstituting the game, he shall act as in the second possibility.

LAW 12

The Chess Clock

1. Each player has to complete a certain number of moves within a certain time, these two factors having been laid down in advance.**
2. The time control for each player is effected by means of a clock provided with a special apparatus usually a "flag".
3. The clock of the player who has White is set in motion at the time fixed for the commencement of the game. After that, each player,having made his move, stops his clock and starts that of his opponent.

   (F.I.D.E.Interpretation - The first sentence of Section 3 applies even if both players are late.)
4. When considering whether the prescribed

number of moves has been made in the given time the last move is not considered as made until after the player has stopped his clock.

(F.I.D.E Interpretation - Section 4 of Article 14 does not apply if the last move ends the game, e.g. by mate, stalemate, or, draw under Article 12; Section 3, clause (a). This is consistent with F.I.D.E. Interpretation of Article 9.)

5. All indications given by a clock or its apparatus are considered as conclusive in the absence of evident defects. The player who claims that there is such a defect is bound to do so as soon as he becomes aware of it.

F.I.D.E. Interpretation -The second sentence of Section 5 does not imply that the harm suffered by a player through an evident defect must be rectified, retrospectively. For example, if a player shows that his opponent's clock has ceased to function, he is entitled to be provided with a sound clock but not to have the clock times changed.

** *Note* : Generally the following time limits are observed:

(a) for a five hour session-each player to complete 40 moves in the first 2(1/2) hours (on his clock) and 16 moves per hour thereafter.

(b) for a four hour session-36 moves in the first two hours and 18 moves an hour thereafter.

(c) for a three hour session - 32 moves in the first one and a half hour and 20 moves an hour thereafter.

6. If the game has been interrupted for some reason for which neither player is responsible the clock shall be stopped until the point concerned has been dealt with. This shall be done, for example, in the case of an illegal position necessitating correction, or in that of a defective clock that must be changed, or if a piece for pawn promotion is not immediately at hand.

7. In cases arising out of Article 9, clauses 1 and 2, when it proves impossible to determine the time taken by each player upto the moment when the illegality occurred, each player shall be allotted up to this moment a time proportional to that indicated on the clock at the moment when the illegality was found out.

LAW 13

The Adjournment of the Game

1. If, after the lapse of the time laid down for play, the game is not finished, the player whose turn it is to move shall write down his move in unambiguous notation on his score-sheet, put this score-sheet as well as of his opponent in an envelope, close the envelope and then stop his clock. This move is called the "sealed move". Should the player make his move on the chessboard he shall Seal the same move on his scoresheet.

2. On the envelope shall be stated:

   (a) the name of the players.

   (b) the position immediately before the sealed move.

   (c) the time taken by each player.

   (d) the name of the player who has sealed his move and the number of this move.

3. The envelope shall be put in safe custody.

LAW 14

The Resumption of the Adjourned Game

1. When the game is to be resumed, position immediately before the sealed move shall be set up and the time taken by each of the players when the game was adjourned shall be indicated on the clocks.

2. The envelope shall not be opened until the player whose turn it is move (i.e. the one who is to reply to the sealed move) is

present. The clock of this player shall be started when the sealed move has been made on the chessboard.

3. If the player whose turn it is to move is absent, then his clock shall be started, but the envelope shall be opened only when he arrives.
4. When the player who has sealed the move is absent, then the player whose turn it is to move need not make his reply to the sealed move on the chessboard. He has the right to write down his move in reply on his score sheet, put this move in an envelope, stop his clock and start his opponent's clock. The envelope shall then be put into safe custody and opened on the opponent's arrival.
5. If the envelope containing the sealed move has disappeared without it being possible to re-establish, with the agreement of the two players, the position and the times used for the adjourned game, or if for any other reason the said position and the said times cannot be re-established, the game is annulled and a fresh game shall be played instead of the adjourned game.

   If the envelope enclosing the move sealed according to Sub Article 4 has disappeared then the game shall be resumed as from the position at the time of the adjournment and with the clock time used at the same time.
6. If, at the resumption of play, either clock has been incorrectly set, and if either player points this out before making his first move, then the error shall be corrected. If the error is not so pointed out the game continues without correction.

LAW 15

Loss of the Game

A game is lost by a player:

1. Who has not played the prescribed number moves in the given time;
2. Who arrives at the chessboard more than one hour late, either at the commencement or the resumption;
3. Who has sealed a move the real significance of which is impossible to establish.

   (F.I.D.E. Interpretation-If the game has already been ended by an agreement or otherwise before the sealed move is opened, the sealed move is null and void.)
4. Who during the game refuses to comply with the Laws of Chess.

   If both players arrive at the chessboard more than one hour late, or if both refuse to comply with the Laws of Chess, the game shall be declared lost by both.

Drawn Game

A proposal of a draw may be made by a player only at the moment when he has made a move. On proposing a draw he starts his opponent's clock. The opponent may accept or, either orally or by making a move, reject the proposal. In the interval, the player who has made the proposal cannot withdraw it.

CUP & TROPHIES

World Champions

The first officially recognised match was won by Wilhelm Steinitz in 1886.

World Championship Totals

	Matches	*Games*	*W*	*D*	*L*	*%*
Lasker	7	102	45	42	15	64.7
Fischer	1	21	7	11	3	59.5
Alekhine	5	140	43	73	24	56.8
Reshevsky	1	20	6	9	5	52.8
Keres	1	20	8	5	7	52.5
Karpov	4	122	20	87	15	52.5
Smyslov	4	89	24	44	21	51.7
Petrosyan	3	69	13	45	11	51.4

Botvinnik	8	177	46	90	41	51.4
Capablanca	2	48	7	35	6	51.0
Bronstein	1	24	5	14	5	50.0
Kasparov	2	72	8	56	8	50.0
Schlechter	1	10	1	8	1	50.0
Steinitz	6	115	43	29	43	50.0
Tal	2	40	11	17	12	48.8
Spassky	3	68	12	41	15	47.8
Korchnoi	2	50	7	31	12	45.0
Gunsberg	1	19	4	9	6	44.7

World Junior Championship

1951	Coventry/Birmingham	Ivkov (Yugoslavia)
1953	Copenhagen	Panno (Argentina)
1955	Antwerp	Spassky (USSR)
1957	Toronto	Lombardy(USA)
1959	Munchenstein	Bielicki (Argentina)
1961	The Hague	Parma (Yugoslavia)
1963	Vrnjącka Banja	Gheorghiu (Romania)
1965	Barcelona	Kurajica (Yugoslavia)
1967	Jerusalem	Kaplan (Puerto Rico)
1969	Stockholm	Karpov (USSR)
1971	Athens	Hug (Switzerland)
1973	Teesside	Belyavsky (USSR)
1974	Manila	Miles (England)
1975	Tjentiste	Chekhov (USSR)
1976	Groningen	Diesen (USA)
1977	Innsbruck	Yusupov (USSR)
1978	Graz	Dolmatov (USSR)
1979	Skien	Seirawan (USA)
1980	Dortmund	Kasparov (USSR)
1981	Mexico City	Cvitan (Yugoslavia)
1982	Copenhagen	Sokolov (USSR)
1983	Belfort	Georgiev (Bulgaria)
1984	Kiljava	Hansen (Denmark)
1985	Sharjah	Dlugy (USA)

World Championship (Under 16)

1974	Pont St Maxence	Mestel (England)
1975	Creil	Goodman (England)
1976	Wattignies	Grinberg (Israel)
1977	Cagnes sur Mer	Arnason (Iceland)
1978	Sas van Gent	Motwani (Scotland)
1979	Belfort	Tempone (Argentina)
1980	Le Havre	Salov (USSR)
1981	Embulse	Conquest (England)
1982	Guayaquil	Bareyev (USSR)
1983	Bucaramanga	Dreyev (USSR)
1984	Paris	Dreyev (USSR)
1985	Petach Tikua	Rojas (Chile)

World Youth Team Championship

1954	Oslo	Czechoslovakia
1955	Lyons	USSR
1956	Uppsala	USSR
1957	Reykjavik	USSR
1958	Varna	USSR
1959	Budapest	Bulgaria
1960	Leningrad	USA
1961	Helsinki	USSR
1962	Marianske Lazne	USSR
1963	Budva	Czechoslovakia
1964	Cracow	USSR
1965	Sinaia	USSR
1966	Orebro	USSR
1967	Harrachov	USSR
1968	Vienna	USSR
1969	Dresden	USSR
1970	Haifa	USA
1971	Mayaguez	USSR
1972	Graz	USSR
1973	Not held	
1974	Teeside	USSR
1975	Not held	
1976	Caracas	USSR
1977	Mexico City	USSR
1978	Mexico City	England
1979	Not held	
1980	Mexico City	USSR
1981	Graz	USSR
1982	Not held	
1983	Chicago	USSR
1984	Not held	
1985	Mendoza	USSR

Olympiads

First held in 1927, and now held every two years.

1952	Hungary

1955	Czechoslovakia
1961	USSR
1964	USSR
1968	Czechoslovakia
1972	USSR
1976	USSR
1982	USSR

World Chess Oscar

1967	Larsen
1968	Spassky
1969	Spassky
1970	Fischer
1971	Fischer
1972	Fischer
1973	Karpov
1974	Karpov
1975	Karpov
1976	Karpov
1977	Karpov
1978	Korchnoi
1979	Karpov
1980	Karpov
1981	Karpov
1982	Kasparov
1983	Kasparov
1984	Karpov
1985	Kasparov

Nordic Championship

1897	Stockholm	Svensson,S.
1899	Copenhagen	Moller,J.
1901	Goteborg	Moller,J.
1903	Christiana	Giersing
1905	Stockholm	Pettersson,A.H.
1907	Copenhagen	Leonhardt
1909	Goteborg	Vidmar
1912	Mexico City	USSR
1916	Copenhagen	Johner,P.
1917	Christiana	Nyholm,G.
1919	Goteborg	Spielmann & Olson
1924	Copenhagen	Nimzowitsch
1928	Oslo	Berndtsson
1929	Goteborg	Stahlberg
1930	Stockholm	Andersen, E.
1934	Copenhagen	Nimzowitsch
1936	Helsinki	Lundin
1938	Orebro	Stahlberg
1939	Oslo	Stahlberg & Lundin
1946	Copenhagen	Kaila
1947	Helsinki	Book & Stoltz
1948	Orebro	Moller,B.
1950	Reykjavik	Moller,B.
1953	Esbjerg	Olafsson
1955	Oslo	Larsen
1957	Helsinki	Sterner
1959	Orebro	Johanessen,S.
1961	Reykjavik	Johanessen,I.
1963	Odense	Brinck-Claussen
1965	Oslo	Thorbergsson
1967	Hango	Hoen
1969	Lidkoping	Jakobsen,O.
1971	Reykjavik	Olafsson
1973	Grena	Larsen
1975	Sandefjord	Holm
1977	Rajamaki	Pettersson,L.E.
1979	Sundsvall	Niklasson
1981	Reykjavik	Helmers
1983	Esbjerg	Hansen
1985	Gjovik	Agdestein

European Cup

1976	Burevestnik (USSR)
1979	Burevestnik (USSR)
1982	Spartacus (Hungary)
1984	Trud (USSR)

European Team Championship

1957	Vienna	USSR
1961	Oberhausen	USSR
1965	Hamburg	USSR
1970	Kapfenberg	USSR
1973	Bath	USSR
1977	Moscow	USSR
1980	Skara	USSR
1983	Plovdiv	USSR

European Junior Championship

1962	Zuidema (Netherlands)

1963 Solth (Denkark)& Hartoch (Netherlands)
1964 Hubner (W.Germany) & Ree (Netherlands)
1965 Ree (Netherlands) & Whiteley (England)
1966 Steinberg (USSR)
1967 Karpov (USSR)
1968 Maeder (W.Germany),Ribli (Hungary) & Vaganyan (USSR)
1969 Adorjan (Hungary)
1970 Ribli (Hungary)
1971 Sax (Hungary)
1972 Romanishin (USSR)
1973 Makarychev (USSR)
1974 Nunn (England)
1975 Kochyev (USSR)
1976 Ftachik (Czechoslovakia)
1977 Taulbut (England)
1978 Van der Wiel (Netherlands)
1979 Chernin (USSR)
1980 Akesson (Sweden)
1981 Curt Hansen (Denmark)
1982 Ehlvest (USSR)
1983 Salov (USSR)
1984 Hellers (Sweden)
1985 Khalifman (USSR)

European Junior Women's Championships

1977	Novi Sad	Sikora (Poland) & Kas (Hungary)
1978	Kikinda	Ioseliani(USSR)
1979	Kula	Ioseliani (USSR)
1980	Backa Topola	Brustman (Poland)
1981	Panonija	Stupina (USSR)
1984	Katowice	Madl (Hungary)

Asian Team Championships

1974 Philippines
1977 Philippines
1979 Philippines
1981 Philippines
1983 China
1984 China

Commonwealth Championships

1950	Oxford	Fairhurst (Scotland)
1983	Melbourne	Rogers, Hjorth (Both Australia)'
1984	Hong Kong	Spraggett (Canada) & Chandler (England)
1985	London	Thipsay (India) & Spraggett (Canada)

PADMA SHRI AWARD WINNERS

1- Abhyankar
2- Bhagyashri Vasantrao Sathe
3- Viswanathan Anand

ARJUNA AWARD WINNERS

1961	Manuel Aaron
1980-81	Rohini Khadilkar
1983	Dibyendu Barua
1984	Praveen Mahadeo Thipsey
1985	Viswanathan Anand
1987	D.V. Prasad
	Bhagyashree Sathe

CRICKET

Gillette first breached the game's independence on a large scale with the introduction of their knockout cup in 1963. Since then, Benson and Hedges, John Player, Schweppes, Prudential, Cornhill, Net West Bank and many other companies have given financial support on varying scales.

Cricket took healthy root in England and grew in popularity largely through the support it received from gamblers and sponsorship-in the form of patronage by some of the more wealthy families in the country-when the game was adopted as a leisure-time pursuit by members of the more privileged classes during the early 18th century.

When the Australians heard about the tour to Canada and America they quickly arranged for a side to visit 'down under. A Melbourne firm of caterers, Spiers and Pond, provided the financial backing-another early form of sponsorship-and in 1861-62 a touring side went out. Visits to South Africa, West Indies and New Zealand were made before the end of the century and teams from Australia and South Africa made reciprocal trips to England.

Although tours were becoming quite fashionable after that first visit to Australia in 1861 the Test series between England and Australia did not really get under way, until the 1876-77 tour, the first Test between the two countries being staged at Melbourne in the March of 1877. Australia winning by 45 runs. England won the second Test, also at Melbourne by four wickets, to level the series. The first Test in England was not until 1880 when England won the only game played at the Oval.

In 1888-89 the first England side had gone to South Africa and played a test series, although the strength of the South Africans was poor. For some time this series and the three following tours by England sides were not counted in the first-class figures and it was not until the 1905-06 visit by a touring side to South Africa that real Tests are considered to have started between the two countries. Nevertheless the previous tours remain in the official statistics. The first Test series against the West Indies was not until 1928 in England. The series against New Zealand began in 1929-30 and against India in 1932. The latest countries to gain Test status were Pakistan, following partition, and Sri Lanka, in 1981.

As a result of the South African apartheid policy there has never been a full Test-playing programme. South Africa have not met West Indies,Pakistan,India or Sri Lanka at Test level. These were interrupted in 1968 when the South African Government found the presence of Basil D'Oliveira.

DRESS

Cream is a preferable colour to white for shirt, trousers, sweater and socks. Clothes should be clean and well-pressed.

A cricketer's shirt is not a beach shirt. It should be of flannel or of wool and cotton, heavy enough to absorb perspiration. Sleeves should be of full length and rolled carefully to the elbows or a little lower unless under a sweater. Then they should be buttoned at the wrist. Caps and sweaters should be uniform and in the case of bowlers they should be handed to the umpire before going into action. Nothing is more uncricket-like-and it should never happen-than a player throwing his cap on the ground, or having it protruding from his hip

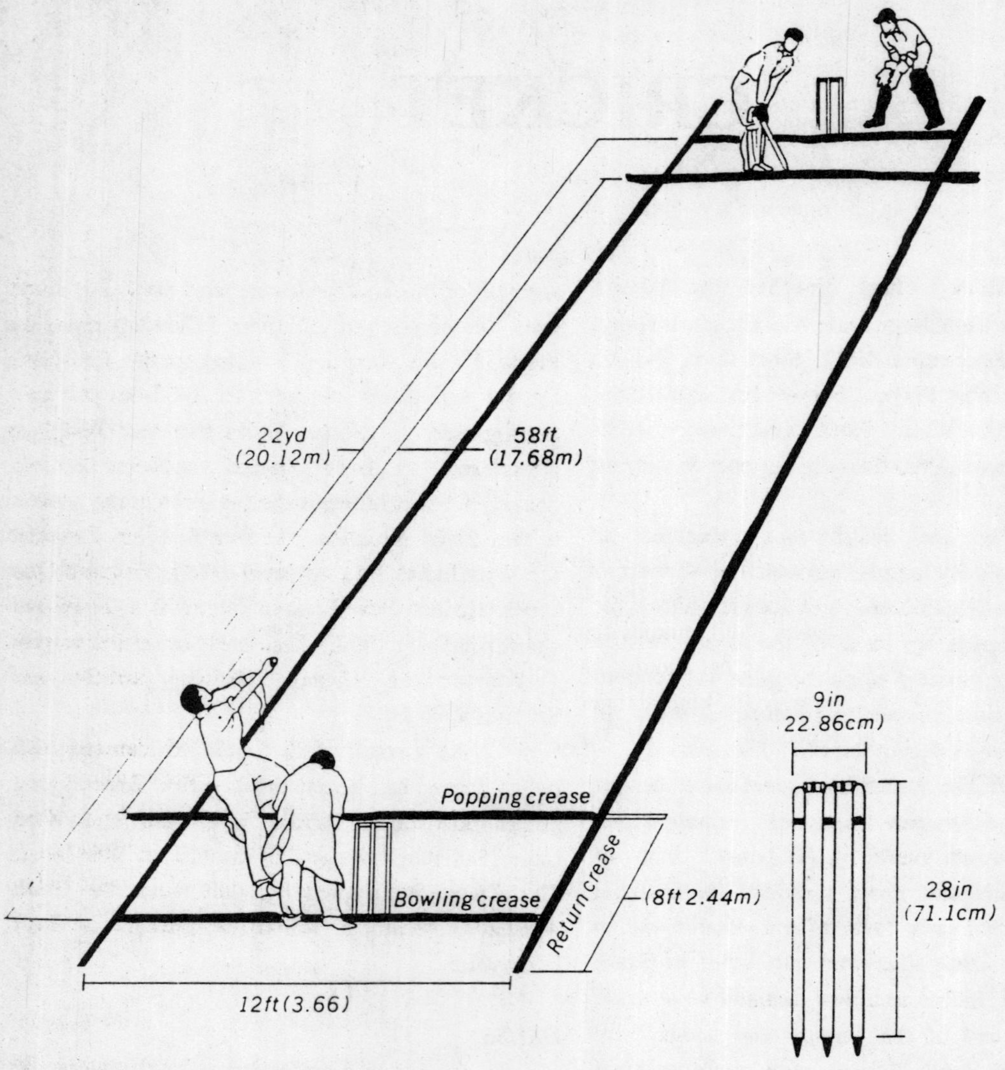

BATTING

pocket. A cricketer's boots are most important part of his equipment. Too often batsmen have been run out through wearing faulty-sprigged boots. A box of hammer in studs should be one of the first things packed into a cricket-bag. Boots must fit comfortably, but not loosely, and must be well sprigged. It is most helpful to wear two pairs of reasonably heavy socks (or at least one heavy hand-knitted pair) as a precaution against soreness caused by friction.

When the bowler runs to the wicket and delivers the ball, there are four things the batsman has to do. He must watch the ball, decide which shot to play and then make the shot. Watching the ball is not easy; it takes a lot of concentration although some batsmen appear to find it much easier than others. To decide correctly which stroke to play is a natural instinct which may be improved by practice, up to a certain standard. Making the shot correctly is the least difficult thing to do.

The Right Bat

But before going into bat, it is very important to get a bat that suits you. It is often seen that a younger player chooses a bat which is too larger or too heavy for him, and this a great handicap. It is said that the lighter the bat the less tired a batsman will be after a long innings. The selection of a suitable bat depends on a number of things- the grip, the height, and the strength of the batsman. So at first you choose your bat according to above mentioned description.

A Straight Bat

You will never develop your game unless you learn to play a straight bat. Your left hand is rudder, the guiding hand. Your right hand is one that gives power to the stroke.

As soon as the ball leaves the bowler's hand you should lift your bat. It is this back-lift that is perhaps the most common fault among the beginners. For as it is lifted, the bat should be almost if not perfectly straight. The chief danger is the right hand; can be depended upon to lift the bat straight.

Grip

The grip of the bat is of great importance and must be comfortable. No method can be specified as the only correct grip. It varies according to a particular batsman's "style" or "method" of stroke play, but certain fundamentals should be observed. The hands must almost be together with the lower hand on the handle about a couple of inches from the shoulder of the bat. The left hand should remain in its original position firmly holding the handle. To allow better control in playing some strokes behind the wicket and also for some defensive strokes, the right hand may move slightly down the handle towards the blade of the bat. In the case of left-handed batsmen, reverse the position of the hands.

Stance

It is a fault to stand too erect or to crouch too much; somewhere between two such extremes is best. Stand naturally and comfortably, with the knees bent very slightly and relaxed with the weight of the body distributed evenly on both feet. The heels of both feet should be approximately in line with each other, and to avoid the danger of a l.b.w. decision, care must be taken to have the toes of both feet just slightly outside the line of the leg-stump. The knees should be slightly relaxed-not rigid-to allow quick movement. The head should be as still as possible, upright and turned to look directly towards the bowler. Both eyes must be focussed fully on the on-coming ball.

Back Lift

Keeping eyes on the ball in the bowler's hands, your first movement is to pick the bat up as the bowler's arm is coming over to deliver the ball. Now you keep your head and body stiff, and push the bat straight back in line with the middle stump by the left arm bending at the elbow, and keep the right hand fairly close to the side. The face of your bat will open towards point. Don't pick the bat up too high until you are sure of the short which you have to play. This technique will also provide you enough time to judge the ball. If it is a bad ball you will have then time to pick the bat up a little higher. Perfectness will come out with enough practice, and you find that the bat will be picked up according to the ball to be

back lift

speed of the bowler. First movement for the batsman concerns the feet. The left leg should be placed as near the line of flight as possible, leaving enough space for the bat to come alongside the leg. With the left hand in control of the bat, the ball, if edged, will not carry to the slips or short-legs.

The back defensive short is made from a ball just short of good length, and is made by drawing the right foot back six to nine inches, and bringing the

played.You have to be very careful in picking the bat up. You should not get into the habit of picking the bat up too high, as it is very vulnerable to the fast ball.

A very good method of practicing the pick-up is to take your stance as close as possible and then pick the bat up without the bat touching the wall.

Helmets

A strong, protective headgear worn by batsman as a protection against fast bowling. Sometimes also worn by fielders in close catching positions. Helmets are usually made of plastic, have webbing of foam padding inside to serve as a cushion, and generally protect the head and ears of the players.

Guard

The position adopted by the batsman in which the bat is held upright in front of the wicket. Batsman take guard after arriving at the crease so that when he take up stance and place his bat in the position indicated by the umpire.

Defence

When playing a defensive shot, the bat should be near the body and the left hand should always have control over the bat.

The forward defensive stroke is played to a ball of perfect length, varying of course with the

left foot to the right, keeping the bat perfectly straight. This shot, after years of practice, can be made into a great scoring stroke, especially on an easy-paced wicket.

The most beautiful strokes in cricket are those played to the off-drives, whether straight past mid-off or wider through the covers and cuts, especially the late cut which is so rarely seen in modern cricket. The young batsman should do everything he can to learn these strokes as soon as possible, for unless he acquires them early he will find them difficult to learn later on.

Defensive Shots

For most players, straight,good length balls require defensive shots, especially at the start of an innings. The artworks below show the forward defence and the back defence.

Forward defence :— (i) The head and front shoulder lead with the front leg moving towards and bending into the pitch of the ball. (ii) The head is in the line of the ball, which is pitching just outside off stump. The bat and pad are close together. The top hand controls the stroke and holds the bat at a slight angle to direct the ball down.

Back defence :— A good sideways position for the back defence, with the weight on the back foot. The top hand is in control, as for the forward defensive, and the bottom hand is relaxed.

Hook

A cross-batted stroke but differing from the cut in that it is designed to hit the ball to the legside. Also, it is probably the most belligerent shot in the book and, in consequence, one of the most risky. At its most effective, the one that will bring you most sixes, or caught on the boundary dismissals. The hook is employed against the short-pitched ball coming at some speed - in other words the infamous bouncer - and rising to some height. With not much time to decide, the choice is to duck or to go for the hook. And speedy footwork is of the essence. The right foot goes all the way back and to the off stump so that it is outside the line of flight, whereas head and shoulders are in line and facing the bowler. Lift the bat outwards in the direction of third man and then sweep across the chest.

Avoiding Action

Against short pitched bowling you have four choice: a defensive shot, a hook, ducking and swaying. Whichever you choose, try to keep your eye on the ball.

(i) A good ducking position with the batsman still looking at the ball and keeping his bat out of ball's way.

(ii) Swaying to the leg side to allow a high, rising ball to pass harmlessly over the stumps. The bat is lowered.

Leg Glance

In batting, to deflect the ball off the angled face of the bat away behind square leg.

Forward Leg Glance

Play the leg glance to balls that are missing the leg stump.

(i) The leading shoulder dips slightly as the front foot lands in line with the ball.

(ii) The ball is met in front of the pads. The wrists turn the blade of the bat on impact.

(iii) The head and trunk are kept ahead of the front pad. The aim is square and there is no falling away of the body to the off side.

Backward Leg Glance

(i) The top hand controls the bat, bringing it down close to the body.

(ii) The balance is forward as the rising ball is pushed away.

THE HOOK

The hook can be played to a short, fast delivery that rises to shoulder height. Before an innings a batsman should know how he intends to react to such deliveries.

The finish of the hook – the body pivots with the batsman looking to hook down.

Back Foot Drive

This shot is played to a ball that is short of a length and too straight to cut. It is often favoured by taller players. Shorter players tend to be more adept at cutting.

(i) The backlift is high. As the body turns the back foot is back and across to allow space for the stroke.

(ii) A good high finish, with the bat pointing in the direction of the hit and the batsman coming onto his toes to use his height as he strike the ball.

Slash

To flay with a half cross-bat motion at a ball outside the off stump sending the ball flying high over the off-side field, usually behind point.

Square Drive

An attacking stroke off the front foot aimed at scoring through the point-cover point region. Two players famous for this stroke are the West Indies Learie Constantine and the Englishman Walter Hammond.

Late Cut

The only stroke on the off-side of the wicket now remaining for us to consider is the late cut. The stroke is usually attempted and considered safe against medium and fast medium bowling, when the ball is pitched a little short of a good length, is well wide of the off- stump, and coming straight through or moving away to the off-side and bouncing no higher than the stumps. It should never be attempted when the ball is coming in towards the stumps from the off-side. It is a particularly dangerous stroke to play against fast bowling and balls rising abnormally high. The margin for error is so small and the reward rarely exceeds one run as the fieldsman at deep third man is generally situated close to the boundary. It is a splendid tactical stroke off a slow bowler who attacks the off and middle stumps and spins the ball away to slips. Often a batsman who is strong at driving this type of bowling, is thwarted by the opposing captain placing an outer circle of defence.

Square Cut

The square cut is played with a cross-bat and can be made off the front foot or off the back foot, depending on how short the ball is pitched and the height it rises.

Square cut off the front foot :—

(i) The bat has been brought straight back by the left hand: the left foot moves well forward but only slightly across of the off.

(ii) The ball is pitched short of a good length

and wide of the stumps: weight of the body is being transferred to the left foot. The bat has been lifted upwards and backwards and points towards fine-leg.

(iii) As the stroke is played with a "cross bat" the left hand brings down the bat to a horizontal position. The ball is hit at the top of its rise.

(iv) The weight of the body has been transferred to the front foot: wrists and arms move the bat at full stretch across the body.

(v) The ball has been hit past point with great power: at the moment of impact the wrists were rolled to keep the face of the bat downward to avoid lofting the ball.

Square cut off the back foot

(i) The bat is lifted back mainly by the right hand so that the right elbow is free and away from the body.

(ii) The weight of the body is moved to the right foot which points in the direction of the stroke. At the top of the back lift the back of the bat faces usually towards mid-wicket.

(iii) Arms and wrists bring the bat outwards and downwards: at the moment of impact the hands are just forward of the right knee.

(iv) The right hand rolls the face of the bat over the completion of the stroke: impact of bat with ball was made well behind the batting crease line.

(v) The stroke must be made smoothly and with power: keep the head as steady as possible and eyes focussed on the ball.

Forward - Cut

A batting stroke in which the front foot is brought forward and somewhat across towards the off and the ball, typically a short-pitched delivery well outside the off stump, is struck with a horizontal bat into the area between point and cover.

Chop

A form of cut, usually played to a ball that keeps unexpectedly low, in which the bat is held horizontally and brought sharply down on the ball just after it has passed the batsman.

Cover Drive

Cover drive is played for a delivery which bounces within reach or arrives on the full toss wide of the stumps on the off side. The first movements of the cover drive are identical to those of the front-foot drive, but the movement of the front foot, head and eyes and the front shoulder, elbow and knee will be more towards the cover position and the ball will be struck far squarer, towards cover. The toe of your front foot should point towards cover point. This shot can be risky since the direction of the stroke is across the line of the ball in an off-side direction.

Drive

A stroke made with the left foot (for a right-handed batsman) brought forward and the bat swinging downward,sending the ball back towards the bowler (a straight drive), to mid-off (an off-drive) on mid-on (an on drive), towards cover (a cover drive) or sometime towards point (square drive).

Front Foot Off/ On Drives

Batsmen play front foot drives to balls that are bowled to a full length. The illustration show the off or cover drive and the finish of the on-drive.

(i) The backlift is high. The head and front shoulder lean on to the line of the ball.
(ii) Contact, the ball is struck with the full face of the bat. The weight is on the front foot-there is no pivot on the back foot.
(iii) A full follow through with good balance.
(iv) A short stride helps the batsman maintain his balance for the finish of the on-drive.

Half-Volley

A delivery that bounces so close to the batsman that he can hit it just as it leaves the ground without having to stride forward.

Harrow Drive

The batsman deflects the ball off the inside edge of the bat, either through the slips or down towards long leg, when attempting to play a normal off drive, he fails to get properly in line of the ball.

OFF/ON DRIVES

The backlift is high. The head and front shoulder lead on to the line of the ball.

Contact! The ball is struck with the full face of the bat. The weight is on the front foot there is no pivot on the back foot.

Pad Play

Thrushing the padded leg it the line of the ball, rather than letting the ball go or offering a stroke. The practice of pad-play was so prevalent among English batsmen when trying to cope with spin bowling that the laws were altered recently to enable a batsman to be given out leg-before-wicket when struck on the pad outside the line of the off stump.

Pull

Cross-bat stroke offered at a short-pitched delivery on a line from about middle stump to outside the off stump, the attempt being to hit the ball away for runs on the on side in front of square leg.

(i) The backlift is high. The back foot is taken back and across, but the balance of the body is forward.

(ii) The left foot is brought away to the leg side to open up the chest in the direction of the oncoming ball. The ball is struck at arms length, in line with the head.

(iii) At the completion of the stroke the weight has been transferred to the left leg. The head is kept still.

Pull Out

Colloquial term for declaring an innings closed. Also, for a batsman getting into a position to play a stroke and then changing his mind and stoppng the shot.

Full Toss

To hit the full toss there are two methods. If the ball is fairly low-that is, just below knee height-it is better to play it with a straight bat and hit in the normal manner. Remember that the full toss may swing in the air and you are taking an unnecessary risk if you hit across the line.

THE PULL

The pull is played against a short ball or long hop, which is too close to the body for the batsman to cut. Don Bradman, when glimpsed on film, always seems to be pulling.

Below left The backlift is high. The back foot is taken back and across, but the balance of the body is forward.

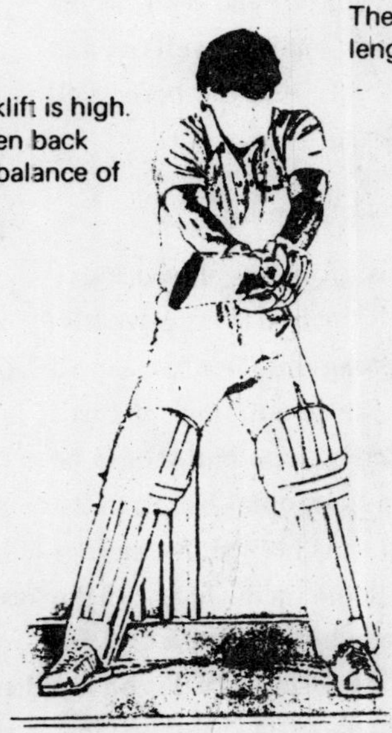

Below left The left foot is brought away to the leg side to open up the chest in the direction of the oncoming ball. The ball is struck at arms length, in line with the head.

THE SWEEP

The sweep is usually played to a ball of good length pitching outside leg stump (unless you're Alan Knott).

The head and shoulder lead to bring the pad onto the line of the ball.

The knee of the back leg bends. The arms are at full stretch as they bring the bat down.

A good finish, with the head over the front knee and not turning away too early.

Anything above knee high and up to almost the head, and providing it is fairly in line with the leg side, can be played with a cross bat. The left leg should move well out and over to the line of the ball and the body move well out and over to the line of the ball and the body well forward over a bent left knee.

Sweep Shot

The sweep to leg is probably played today more than it has ever been. If the ball is hit correctly, there is little chance of it going into the air, but so often, particularly by boys, it is not, and the ball often goes up towards square leg. The ball should be hit on the half-volley with a horizontal bat and the wrists turned over at impact. It is played in a similar manner as the shot to the full toss on the leg, with the left leg well forward, and reaching with the arm out to the pitch. So often a boy sees that a ball is on the leg side and, without thought as to its length, he just hoicks at it round the corner.

(i) The head and shoulder lead to bring the pad onto the line of the ball.

(ii) The knee of the back leg bends. The arms are at full stretch as they bring the bat down.

(iii) A good finish, with the head over the front knee and not turning away too early.

BOWLING

The main purpose of the run-up is to bring you to the crease properly balanced, and with the momentum needed for your normal delivery. You can only determine the length of your run through practise, but, once you have done so, you must keep to it whenever and wherever you bowl. It should build up gradually and smoothly, and your muscles should never be tensed but relaxed. The balance of your body should be slightly forward, your head kept as steady as possible, and your eyes looking at the spot where you want to drop the ball.

BOWLING BASICS

These diagrams demonstrate the basic action which any beginner should seek to emulate. The grip shown is for a seam bowler.

Don't worry if you don't fulfil all the criteria – Procter, Garner, Willis and Thomson didn't either.

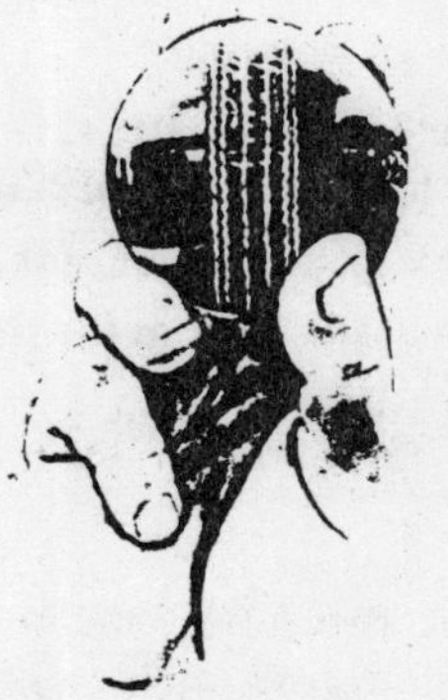

Left The ball is held between the first two fingers and the thumb. The fingers are placed either side of the seam, which is upright, while the thumb and third finger support the ball.

Right The body is turning sideways. The front shoulder will point down the pitch. The bowler's landing foot (right) is also turning to land parallel to the crease

The front leg is straightening as the ball is released from a high front arm.

The head is looking along the leading shoulder. The stride length is important for establishing a firm base.

Only through a basic action, in which the body plays a vital part, can a bowler ensure control of length and direction line of the pitch. This is applicable for all bowlers whatever their type. In this action the body, with the arm as an extension, winds up like a spring in its approach and is released in the delivering and follow-through.

A good-length ball is one which bounces in such a position on the pitch that it presents the batsman with the problem of whether to go forward to play it as it pitches, or to go back. This may seem quite a straightforward explanation but, in fact, to define it satisfactorily it is not easy. Length depends on so many things : the speed of the bowler, the pace of the pitch, how much the ball is turning and to some extent, the height of the batsman. The good-length ball lies between a full-pitch and a long-hop. The fast bowler on a hard pitch will have a margin of error of about six feet. This means that the bowler can pitch the ball from about six feet from the batsman up to twelve feet away and the batsman will be forced to defend either forward or back. In the case of a slow bowler spinning the ball a lot on a slow pitch, the margin of error is much less, possibly as little as two feet: that is four feet to six feet from the batsman. The more the ball turns, the farther up it must be pitched to be of good length.

Fast

To a fast bowler, all that has been said about the easy rhythmical delivery is of the first importance, for a fast bowler's worst enemy is fatigue and one does not want to develop a tiring, unrhythmical action which is only effective for three or four overs. A fast bowler must make his run exact and automatic. A fast bowler's usual methods of getting a batsman out are:

1. Hitting the wicket. This is usually done by an off-cutter by a yorker or by sheer speed.
2. Making the batsman touch the ball into the hands of the wicket-keeper, silps or gully. This kind of ball is an out-swinger, pitching on or near the off-stump so as to make the batsman reach out to play it and then swinging away towards the off.
3. By bowling 'leg theroy'. This means bowling at the leg stump and pitching an occasional ball.

Grip of the Ball

Obviously the grip of the ball differs according to the type of delivery the bowler desires. For example, it may be a leg-break or an off-break, or one of the many varieties you will find explained in the following pages on Bowling.

The illustration shows a basic or standard grip for most types of bowling and will demonstrate to the beginner the elementary, but fundamental essential that the ball must be held in the fingers and not in the palm of the hand.

Seam

The stitching that holds together the two halves of the outer covering of a cricket ball. It offers the bowlers something to grip when delivering the ball, and it helps the bowler make the ball spin or swing. Also, it determines the deviation of the ball to the left or right after it has landed on its seam. Both the bowler (who can achieve this movement off the wicket) and the type of delivery are known as 'seamers'.

Outswinger

When bowling to a right-handed batsman, the outstanding bowler should be pitching the ball on the length in line with the off-stump or just outside, attempting to bring the batsman forward.

The ball is held so that the seam is vertical and pointing towards first slip. The first and second fingers are placed either side of the seam with the edge of the thumb on the seam.This action can cause a slow backward rotation of the ball that helps steady the seam for maximum swing towards the slips.

Inswinger

A delivery from a bowler of any pace, usually from medium to fast, that deviates through the air from off to leg to the batsman. The ball is

The grip

Grip for the leg cutter

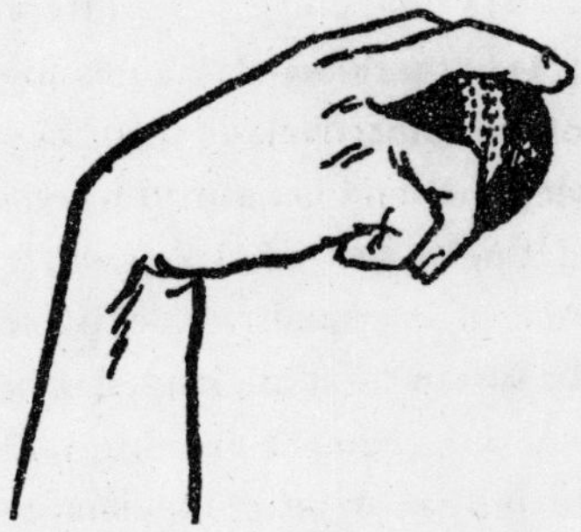

Grip for the leg break

Grip for the off-break

Grip for the away

Grip for the in-swerve

held for inswing when the vertical seam points towards fine leg. The first and second fingers are close together on either side of the vertical seam. The ball on the thumb is flat against the underside of the seam.

Leg-Cutter

Similar to the inswinger, but with the second finger wedged alongside the seam which points in the same direction as the inswinger. Everything must be just right at the instant of delivery when the second finger pulls the seam down in an anticlockwise direction. The thumb helps by twisting the ball as it is released. Like the inswinger, the bowler has the feeling of pushing the ball down the legside. In fact, the bowler should look to pitch the legcutter on or just outside the off-stump.

Leg Break

A delivery from a pace bowler that deviates from leg to off upon landing on the wickets.

Off Cutter

A pace bowler's delivery that deviates from the off to the leg after hitting the pitch.

Intimidation

The use of the fast, short-pitched delivery in an attempt to intimidate the batsman. The hope is that it will claim a wicket by having the batsman caught while fending the ball off his body, while trying to play the hook shot, or by dismissing him in some other way within a few deliveries as a result of the unsettling effect of the intimidation. Umpires are now empowered to take action against intimidating tactic by bowlers. This is a contentius issue pherhaps exacerbated by the recent tactic of loading teams with up to four fast bowlers.

Inner

A delivery from a bowler of any pace, usually from medium to fast, that deviates through the air from off to leg to the batsman. Also, a soft, close-fitting glove worn by a wicket-keeper inside his main glove.

Short-Pitched

A delivery that hits the pitch well short of a good length. Usually related to fast bowling and often to intimidatory bowling.

Spinner

A slow bowler whose main weapon is his ability to make the ball turn when it hits the wicket. He also uses flight and drift (or curve) through the air and obtains his wicket either out of the front of the hand (in the case of the 'finger spinner') or the back of the hand (as with the 'wrist spinner').

Finger-Spin

A ball after pitching from leg (a leg break), or from the off (an off break), or it may make haste off the pitch (a top-spinner). Broadly speaking, there are two ways of producing these breaks. One is by means of the fingers, clicking them as we sometimes do in order to attract the attention of a dog; this is known as 'finger spin'. The other way is by changing the position of the hand as the ball leaves it, thus rolling the ball out and making it spin in a certain direction; this is called 'rolled spin'. On the whole, finger spin is used by slow bowlers and rolled spin by medium-paced and fast bowlers.

The way in which a bowler grips the ball is particularly important for spin. First and foremost, a bowler does not hold the ball in his hand. It is all fingers and the principle is to get as much friction between the fingers and the ball as possible, so as to start it spinning at the same time as it is being propelled forward.

Flight

To bowl a ball in such a way as to cause it to drop suddenly or to carry a little beyond the point at which the batsman expects it to bounce.

Flipper

It is typically produced slow ball mainly with the tips of the first and third fingers and squeezing or 'flipping' it out so that it emerges from the back or side of the hand with an extra helping of top spin on it. If successfully executed it will hurry through without deviation, gaining pace as it pitches and keeping low. The flipper has been described as 'the most arcane and esoteric ball in cricket'.

Googly

A ball which is bowled by a right-handed bowler and released with the same wrist action as a leg-break but which spins like an off-break upon striking the ground.

Leg-Spin

For leg spin/break the seam is at right angles to the comfortably spaced first and second fingers. The top joint of the third finger lies along the seam. The ball is spun off the inside of the top joint of the third finger. You should cock forward, and keep the leverage same as in turning a door knob from right to left. The palm of your hand must be kept facing the batsman as long as possible, if turned over too soon, top spin or googly and not leg spin will result. There can be more valuable variants to leg spin. In bowling leg spin, you keep your arm as straight as you can. A bent arm makes accuracy of length and direction much more difficult.

Off-Spin

The delivery that pitches and turns from the off to the leg, when bowled to a right-handed batsman. Grip for spin:- For off-spin the seam is at right angles to the widely spaced first and second fingers. The top joints of the fingers are on the seam.

No Ball

A delivery which in the judgment of either umpire is unfair or not legal because the ball was thrown or because the bowler did not have one foot behind the bowling crease at the time the ball was released. A no-ball cannot take a wicket, and it does not count as one of the six good deliveries of an over: the batting team automatically credited with a run unless the batsman are able to score more by running. A no-ball is not dead, and the batsman may run on a bye or a wide or the batsman may hit the ball without being out if it is caught. When playing the ball, the batsman will be out on a no-ball if he hits the balls twice, either batsman, when running, can be run out or be out by handling the ball or obstructing the field. Any runs gained as a result of hitting the ball are credited to the batsman's total; runs scored without hitting the ball are extras.

FIELDING

Fielders fall into two categories - the close catcher and the outfielder, and it should become quickly apparent which is the most suitable category for you.

Close catchers comprise the slip fielders, gully, point, short leg, silly mid-on and silly mid-off.

Field

A generally oval or rectangular field with no specific dimensions. A representative British cricket field may be 200 yards long and 120 yards wide. Near the centre of the field is a firm closely-cut strip 22 yards long and 10 feet wide (the pitch) at each end of which is erected a wicket. On the ground through each wicket is an 8-foot-8-inch line (the bowling crease) and 4 feet in front of and parallel to each bowling crease is a popping crease of unlimited length but usually marked no longer than 10 feet. All 4 lines are parallel. Extending back at right angles from the ends of each bowling crease is a return crease. The return creases and the bowling crease mark the area in which the bowler must have his rear foot when delivering the ball; the popping crease marks the forward edge of the batsman's ground.

Ground Fielding

Ground fielding is the most important department of cricket, and every player ought to make a close study of this branch of the game. Whether in the deep or in close the fielder must be ready to make the fastest possible move to any ball that comes his way. For those fielding deep at cover, mid-off and mid-on, the main task is to stop ground

FIELDING POSITION

Field placements

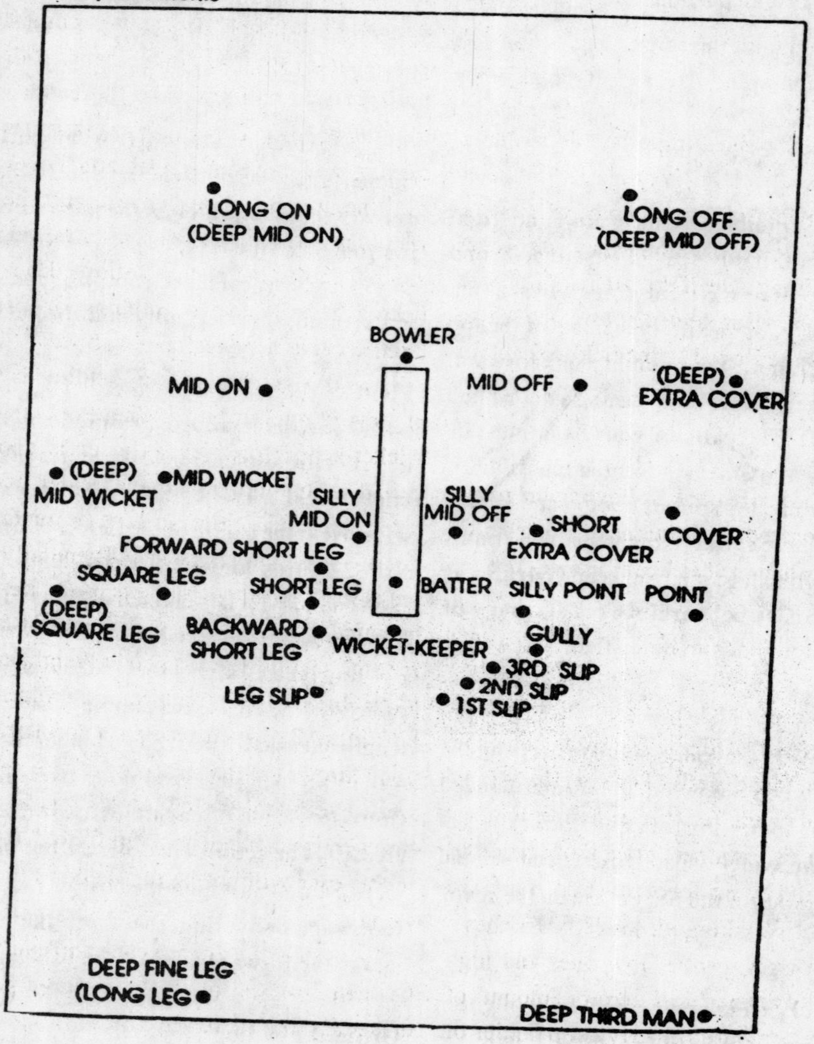

shots and save runs and if they are already moving as the ball is bowled, they will be all the better equipped to do so. One can easily tell the trained fielder by noting whether he is walking in as the bowler runs. Close fielders, of course, crouch motionless, ready for a ball coming head-high or at their toes. They should also be on their toes, too, with weight evenly divided so that they can move either way.

Defensive Field

Fielding is the most important department of cricket. Defensive fielding is primarily intended to prevent the batsmen from scoring runs rather than to get them out. A defensive field may either be forced upon the fielding side, if the batsman are able to dominate the bowling and disperse the close fielder, or it may be deployed by the fielding captain for good tactical reasons.

C & B

Used in the score book, following the name of a batsman and preceding the name of a bowler, to indicate that the batsman has been dismissed by a catch taken by the bowler of the ball.

Catch

Catches win matches - the phrase explains the most vital part of fielding. The catch comes in two categories: the close catch taken near the bat and the lengthy judged catch.

Catching is another branch of fielding and is almost entirely a matter of practice. If you are a beginner, practice taking all kinds of catches - snicks, slow high ones, gentle low ones and high drives. Later on, you can do a certain amount of specializing by becoming primarily a slip fielder or a deep fielder.

Whenever possible, take a catch with the hands about four to five inches away from the chest, allowing the ball to come down, passing your eyes. Keep your eyes all the time on the ball, judge its flight correctly and as the ball meets the hands, the fingers must be closed round it to hold it tight and at the same time the hands should be allowed to sink down on the body so as to receive the ball gently. Care should be taken not to push the hands upwards. If the ball is skied and going too far beyond the position you have occupied, then keep your eyes on the ball and without looking on the ground, turn quickly, simultaneously following straight towards the travelling ball and run as fast as you can, watching the ball throughout. As the ball comes down near your reach stretch your hands fully outwards towards the ball and take the catch in the same running action. The important thing is that while turning and running you should never look down on the ground. Your eyes must be constantly watching the ball. Besides, after turning never take zig-zag course but always follow dead straight the line of the ball. Avoid grabbing or snapping at the ball. Receive it, as explained above.

A golden rule in fielding is to back up at every opportunity. Whenever a bowler or a wicket-keeper or even a fielder is about to stop a ball, it is imperative that the fielder nearby should try to get behind him, in case he misfields the ball.

One very sad mistake generally noticed is to put a man in the wrong position, *i.e.* , in a place to which he is not accustomed or suited. Good fielding requires speed, good eyesight and quick use of the brain. These requirements vary in different positions. It is useless to put a sprinter as well as a good thrower in the slips, conversely, a person with weak eyes who is slow on his feet and not a good thrower, is not much good for the out field. The fault in this case will not be the fielder's but that of the captain.

It is the duty of each and every cricketer to be able to field in all the required positions with efficiency but there are always some fielders who excel in certain positions.

The slip fielders must bend down properly with the legs comfortably kept apart so that they can get up quickly till it has been played by the batsman. The slips must take positions according to the type of bowlers and the situation of the wicket where the lowest possible catch can be easily taken. Besides,

Wicket-keeper's stance

Wicket-keeper balanced, taking a rising ball

the distance between two slip fielders should be such that they may not clash with each other while taking a catch nor should they allow a ball to pass between them. The other close fielders should also bend down comfortably keeping their eyes on the batsman's bat and expect that each and every ball is coming towards them. They must be so accustomed to the job that they can be able to judge from the batsman's movement of the bat as to the angle as well as the direction the ball is likely to take.

Caught

A mode of dismissal in which a batsman is given out if the ball touches his bat or if it touches below the wrist his hand or glove holding the bat, and is subsequently held by a fieldsman before it touches the ground. The catcher must be within the field of play with no part of his body grounded over the boundary line-throughout the act of making the catch. The dismissal is credited to the bowler and is entered in the scorebook as caught. A batsman cannot be out caught off a no-ball. See also CATCH.

WICKETKEEPING

The most industrious member of a fielding side is the wicketkeeper for, unlike anyone else, he is actively involved with every ball of the innings, crouching behind the stumps prepared to take every ball bowled, alert for catches and stumping, ready to run to the legside to stop snap singles, capable of taking cleanly everything thrown to him from the fielders and is also able to advise a bowler on some technical point from his perfect position of vision.

Important points to watch in wicket-keeping are:

1- Watch the ball from the time the bowler starts his run.
2- Make sure you get a good view of the delivery of the ball.
3- Be balanced on both feet so that you can move either way very quickly.
4- Get your body well behind the ball, except when you think you have a chance of stumping off a wide ball.
5- Do not 'snatch' at the ball; let it sink into the gloves and try to 'give' with it.

1-Equipment

It is essential that the wicket-keeping gauntelts and the inner gloves are of good quality. They should have as much protection as possible without being too stiff and awkward, and should feel very comfortable.

2-Stance

The basic stance is a comfortable squatting position with the weight on the balls of the feet. The eyes are in level and looking directly ahead. The hands are together with the palms facing outwards, towards the bowler and the backs of the gloves touching the ground.

3-Movement of the Feet

Drive your legs sideways when standing back and take the ball on the side of your body closer to the stumps. When standing up, work in a semicircle around the stumps. Drive your legs up to the stumps to take fielders' returns.

4-The Hands,Head and Eyes

Fingers sideways or downwards, soft hands rise with the ball.Never take your eyes off the ball while it is in play.

5-Stumping

When a batsman, having received a delivery other than a no-ball, leaves his ground in an attempt to play a stroke and the wicket is broken by the wicket-keeper, the batsman has been stumped. The wicket-keeper is the only member of the fielding side who may effect a stumpings and in doing so, he may not take the ball in front of the stumps unless it has touched the bat or the striker's person.

However, once the batsman has left his ground in an attempt to run and the wicket keeper breaks the wicket the batsman is out, run out.

CAPTAIN

Cricket is a game to be enjoyed both by players and spectators. It should be played according to the highest standards and within the laws and traditions of the game. A sound knowledge of the general principles of effective captaincy makes for better team work, more effective use of the ability of players, better out-cricket, more enjoyment to players and better entertainment for spectators.

A captain should know the batting strength of the opposition against the bowling team attack. In most cases the captain should decide to bat, to put runs on the board and thus create a psychological hurdle for the side batting second.

It is true that the captain's decision is final, but to keep up the team spirit and faith of the senior players he should consult his colleagues.

A captain is the image of his team. Thus at the time of crisis he should keep his teams' spirit and in between he should praise the player giving good performance.

As a tactician, the captain's first decision is whether to bat or bowl upon winning the toss. For this he should have thorough knowledge of the wicket. If the opposition team bats first and puts on huge total, then too the captain will be blamed. Thus a good captain is he, who keeps his nerves cool and capable of executing a flexible, well-planned policy aimed at winning a match in an ethical manner.

The captain's task is not easy. Specific instructions must be given to individual. A great part of the captain's responsibility on the field lies in consultation with the bowler and at times with other players, such as the wicket keeper, before placing the field. It is very important for the captain to place his top batsmen and or bowlers while fielding in such a position that they do not have to run too much, or get exhausted.

The captain must be aware of the psychological make-up of the team: who will best stand up to crisis and pressures? Bowlers who are tired must be given rest .

The captain of the side must know when certain types of bowlers are ineffective - under certain conditions and against certain types of batsmen - and change them accordingly. A good skipper appreciates when to take the new ball, when to attack for quick runs, when to pressurise a batsman newly arrived at the crease, and when to slow down the opposition's scoring rate. Judgement is needed to know when to enforce the follow-on and when to instruct to consolidate the team's position.

It may become obvious that the opposition is attacking in a certain way, and that his tactics has to be countered. A restrictive opposition bowling and fielding policy, with a declaration approaching, may call for adventurousness on the part of the batsmen. Aggression from the opposition batsmen or an inclination to go for quick singles demands a knowledge of sensible field changes to increase the batting risks and prevent the flow of runs.

LAWS OF CRICKET

LAW 1. THE PLAYERS

(i) Number of Players and Captain

A match is played between eleven players on each of the two sides. One of the players on each side shall be captain. In the event of the captain not being available at any time, a deputy shall act in his place.

(ii) Nomination of Players

Before the toss for innings, players shall be nominated by the captain. They may not be changed thereafter without the consent of the opposing captain.

LAW 2. SUBSTITUTES AND RUNNERS: BATSMAN OR FIELDSMAN LEAVING THE FIELD: BATSMAN RETIRING: BATSMAN COMMENCING INNINGS

(i) Substitutes

Substitutes shall be allowed to the field for any player who, is, incapacitated by illness or injury during the match. The consent of the opposing captain is to be obtained for the use of such substitute if any player is prevented from fielding for any other reason.

(ii) Objection to Substitutes

The opposing captain has no right of objection to any player acting as substitute in the field, nor as to where he is to field, although he can object to the substitute acting as a wicket-keeper.

(iii) Substitute not to Bat or Bowl

A substitute shall not be allowed to bat or bowl.

(iv) A Player for whom a Substitute has Acted

A player is entitled to bat, bowl or field even though a substitute has acted for him.

(v) Runner

A runner is allowed for a batsman who, during the match, is incapacitated by injury or illness. The player acting as runner shall be a member of the batting team and shall, if possible, have already batted in that innings.

(vi) Runner's Equipment

The acting runner for an injured batsman shall wear batting gloves and pads if the injured batsman is so equipped.

(vii) Transgression of the Laws by an Injured Batsman or Runner

The injured batsman (when not a striker) shall stand where he does not interfere the play. Should he bring himself into the game, then he shall suffer the penalties that any transgression of the Law demands.

(viii) Fieldsman Leaving the Field

Without the consent of the umpire, no fieldsman shall leave the field or return during a session of play. If a substitute is required for a fieldsman, the consent of umpire is also required, when his side returns to the field after an interval. If a member of a fielding side leaves the field or fails to return after an interval and is absent from the field for over fifteen minutes, he shall not be permitted to bowl after his return until he has been on the field for atleast the length of time for which he was absent.

(ix) Batsman Leaving the Field or Retiring

Having previously notified the umpire at the bowler's end, a batsman may leave the field or retire at any time owing to illness, injury or other unavoidable cause. He can resume his innings at the fall of a wicket, which for the purposes of this Law shall include the retirement of another batsman.

If he leaves the field or retires for any other reason, he may resume his innings with the consent of the opposing captain.

When a batsman leaving the field is unable to return owing to illness, injury or other unavoidable cause, his innings to be recorded as 'retired, not out'. Otherwise is to be recored as 'retired, out'.

(x) Commencement of a Batsman's Innings

A batsman shall be considered to have commenced his innings once he has stepped on to the field of play.

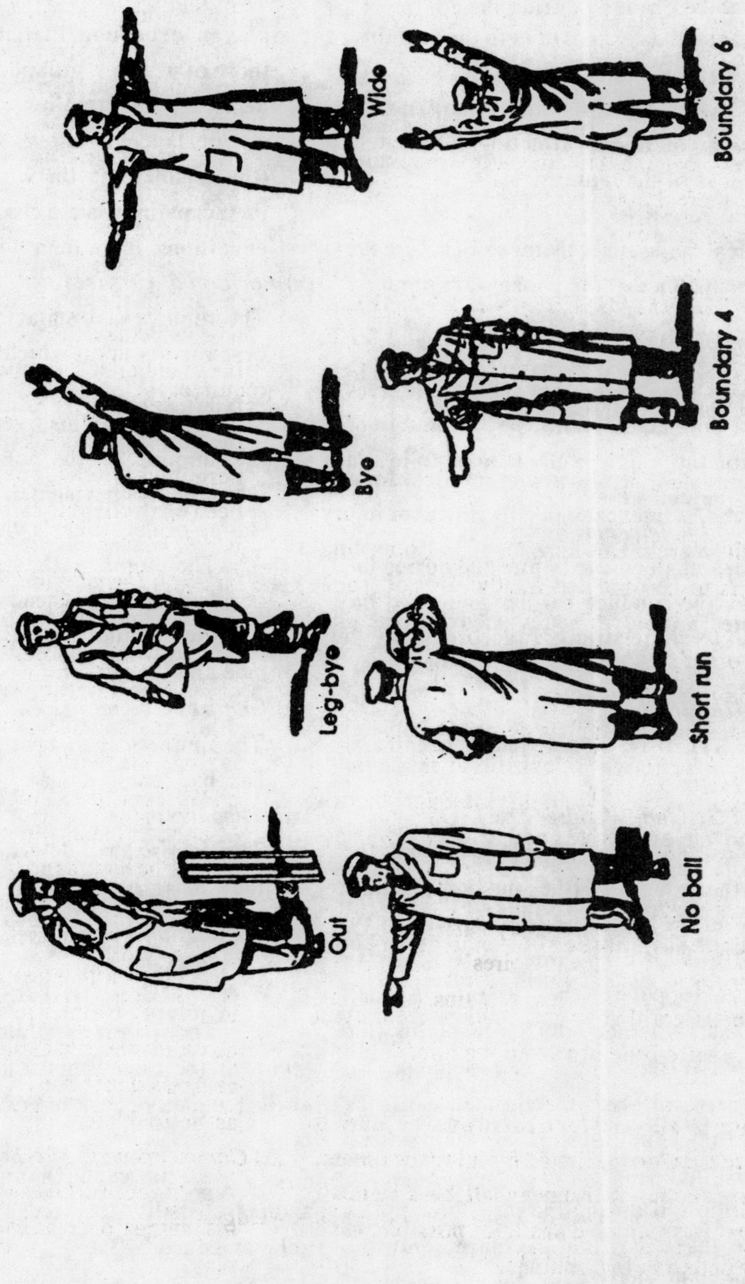
Out
No ball
Leg-bye
Short run
Bye
Boundary 4
Wide
Boundary 6

LAW 3. THE UMPIRES

(i) Appointment

Before the toss of the, innings, two umpires shall be appointed, one for each end, to control the game with absolute impartiality as deemed by the Laws.

(ii) Change of Umpires

No umpire can be changed during the course of a match without the consent of both the captains.

(iii) Special Condition

The umpires shall agree with both the captains on any special conditions affecting the match, before the toss of the innings.

(iv) The Wickets

The umpires shall satisfy themselves before the start of the match that the wickets are properly pitched.

(v) Clock or Watch

The umpires shall agree between themselves and inform both the captains before the start of the match on the watch or clock to be followed during the match.

(vi) Conduct and Implements

The umpires shall ensure before and during the match that the conduct of the game and the implements used are strictly in accordance with the Laws.

(vii) Fair and Unfair Play

The umpires shall be the sole judges of fair and unfair play.

(viii) Fitness of Ground, Weather and Light

The umpires shall be the sole judges of the fitness of the ground, weather and light for play.

(a) However, before deciding to suspend play, or not to start or resume play after an interval/stoppage, the umpires shall establish whether both the captains (the batsmen at the wicket may deputise for their captain) wish to commence in the prevailing conditions: if so, their wishes shall be met.

(b) In addition, if during the play the umpires decide that the light is unfit, only the batting side shall have the option of continuing play. After agreeing to continue in unfit light, the captain of the batting side (or a batsman at the wicket) may appeal against the light for their opinion if the light has deteriorated since the agreement to continue was made.

(ix) Exceptional Circumstances

The umpires may decide to suspend or abandon play in exceptional circumstances, other than those of weather, ground, or light. Before such decision, the umpires shall establish, if the circumstances allow, whether both captains (the batsmen at the wicket may deputise for their captain) wish to continue in the prevailing conditions. If so, their wishes shall be met.

(x) Position of Umpires

The umpires shall stand from where they can see best any act upon which their decision may be required.

Subject to this over-riding consideration, the umpire at the bolower's end shall stand where he does not interfere with either the bowler's run-up or the striker's view.

The umpire at the striker's end may elect to stand on the off instead of leg side of the pitch, provided he informs the captain of the fielding side and the striker.

(xi) Umpires Changing Ends

The umpires shall change ends after each side has had one innings.

(xii) Disputes

The umpire shall determine all disputes, and if they disagree the actual state of things shall continue.

LAW 4. THE SCORERS

The scorers appointed for the purpose shall record all the runs. Where there are two scorers they shall frequently check to ensure that the score sheet tally.

All instructions and signals given to the scorers shall be accepted and immediately acknowledged by them.

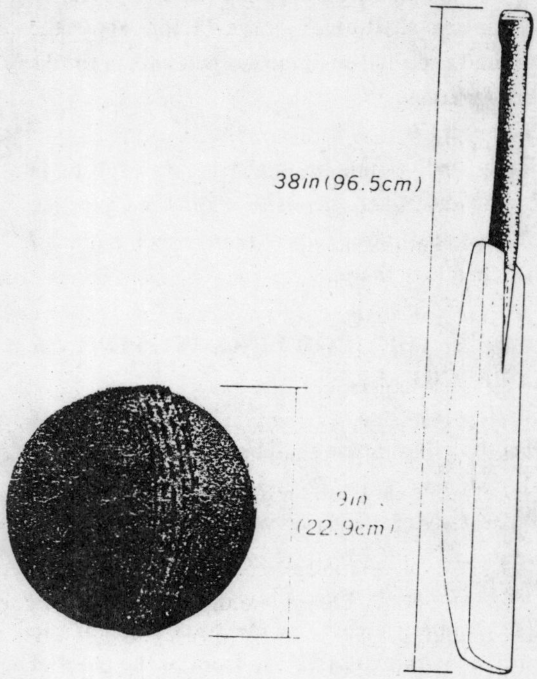

LAW 5. THE BALL

(i) Weight and Size

The ball shall weigh not less than 5(½) ounces / 155.9g and not more than 5(3/4) ounces/163g. It shall measure not less than 8(13/16) inches / 22.4 cm and not more than 9 inches/22.9cm in circumference.

(ii) Approval of Balls

All balls shall be approved by the umpires and the captains before the start of the match.

(iii) New Ball

Either captain may demand a new ball at the start of each innings, subject to agreement to the contrary having been made before the toss.

(iv) New Ball in Match of Three or More Days' Duration

The captain of the fielding side may demand a new ball after the prescribed number of overs has been bowled with the old one, in a match of three or more days'duration. The governing body of the cricket in the country concerned shall be not less than 75 six-ball overs (55 eight-ball overs).

(v) Ball Lost

In the event of a ball during the course of play being lost or in the opinion of the umpires, becoming unfit for play, the umpires shall allow it to be replaced by one that in their opinion has had a similar amount of wear. If a ball is to be replaced,the umpires shall inform the batsman.

LAW 6. THE BAT

The overall bat shall not be more than 38 inches / 96.5cm in length; the blade of the bat shall be made of wood and shall not exceed 4(¼)inches/10.8cm at the widest part.

LAW 7. THE PITCH

(i) Area of Pitch

The pitch is the area between bowling creases. It shall measure 5ft/1.52m in width on either

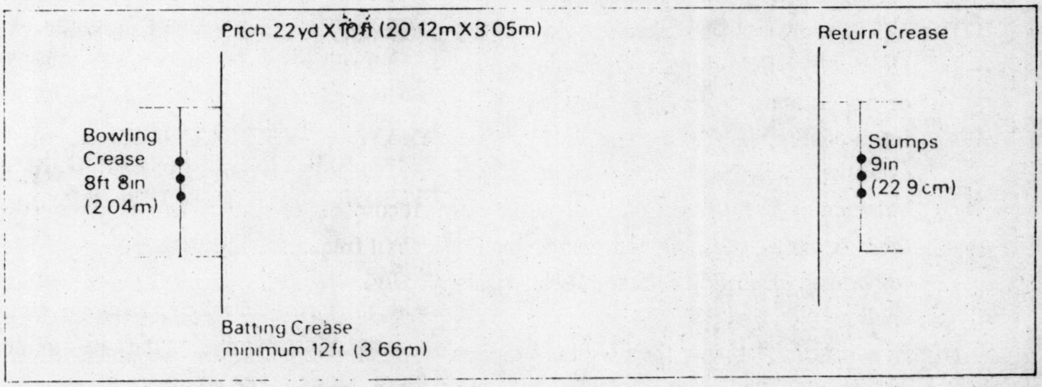

The Pitch

side of a line joining the centre of the middle stumps of the wickets - see Law 8 (The Wickets).

(ii) Selection and Preparation

Before the toss for innings, the executive of the ground shall be responsible for the selection and preparation of the pitch; thereafter the umpires shall control its use and maintenance.

(iii) Changing Pitch

The pitch shall not be changed during a match unless it becomes unfit for play, and that too with the consent of both captains.

(iv) Non-Turf Pitches

The following shall apply in the event of non-turf pitch:

(a) *Length*: That of the playing surface to a minimum of 58ft/17.68m.

(b) *Width*: That of the playing surface to a minimum of 6ft/1.83m.

See Law 10 (Rolling, Mowing, Watering the Pitch & Re-marking of Creases).

LAW 8. THE WICKETS

(i) Width and Pitching

The sets of wickets, of 9 inches/22.86cm wide each, and consisting of three wooden stumps with two wooden bails on the top, shall be pitched opposite & parallel to each other at a distance of 22 yards/20.12m. between the centres of the two middle stumps.

(ii) Size of Stumps

The distance between the stumps shall be sufficient to prevent the ball from passing between them. Their tops shall be 28 inches/71.1cm above the ground, and shall be dome shaped except for the bail grooves.

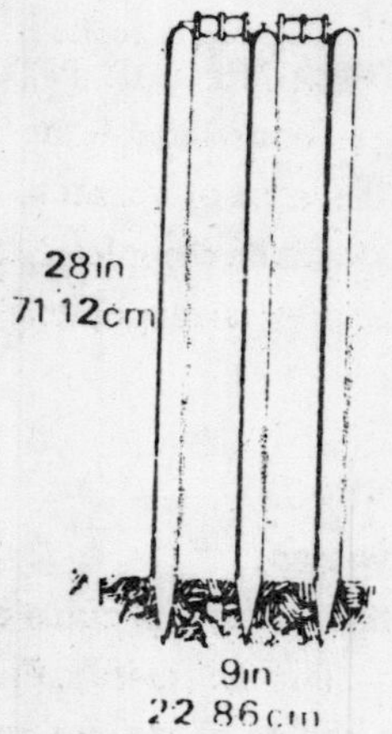

(iii) Size of Bails

Each bail shall be 4(3/8) inches/11.1cm in length and when in position on the top of the stumps shall not project more than 1/2inch / 1.3cm above them.

LAW 9. THE BOWLING, POPPING & RETURN CREASES

(i) The Bowling Crease

The bowling crease shall be marked in line with the stumps at each end and shall be 8 feet 8 inches/2.64m in length, with the stumps in the centre.

(ii) The Popping Crease

The popping crease, i.e.the back edge of the crease marking, shall be in front of the parallel with the bowling crease. It shall have the back edge of the crease marking of 4 feet/1.22m from the centre of the stumps and shall extend to a minimum of 6 feet/1.83m on either side of the line of the wicket. The popping crease shall be considered to be unlimited in length.

(iii) The Return Crease

The return crease marking of which the inside edge is the crease shall be at each end of the bowling crease and at right angles to it. The return crease shall be marked to a minimum of 4 feet/1.22m behind the wicket and shall be considered to be unlimited in length. A forward extension shall be marked to the popping crease.

LAW10. ROLLING, SWEEPING, MOWING, WATERING THE PITCH & RE-MARKING OF CREASE

(i) Rolling

The pitch may be rolled during the match at the request of the captain of the batting side, for not more than seven minutes before the start of each innings, other than the first innings of the match, and before the start of each day's play. If the start is delayed after the toss and before the first innings of the match, the captain of the batting side shall have the right to have the pitch rolled for not more than seven minutes.

The pitch shall not otherwise be rolled during match. The seven minutes' rolling permitted before the start of a day's play shall take place not earlier than half an hour before the start of play. The captain of the batting side may delay such rolling until ten minutes before the start of play, should he so desire.

If an innings is declared closed by a captain in less than fifteen minutes of resumption of play, and the other captain is thereby prevented from exercising his option of seven minutes' rolling or if he is so prevented for any other reason, the time for rolling shall be taken out of the normal playing time.

(ii) Sweeping

The necessary sweeping of the pitch during the match shall be done so that the seven minutes allowed for rolling the pitch, provided for in above, is not affected.

(iii) Mowing

(a) *Responsibilities of Ground Authority & of Umpires* - All mowings which are carried out before the toss for innings shall be the responsibility of the ground authority. Thereafter, they shall be carried out under the supervision of the umpires. See Law 7 (Selection & Preparation).

(b) *Initial Mowing* - The pitch shall be mown before play begins on the day the match is scheduled to start,or in the case of a delayed start on the day the match is expected to start.See iii (a) above (Responsibilities of Ground Authority & of Umpires)- (c) *Subsequent Mowing in a Match of Two or More Days* - In a match of two or more day's duration, the pitch shall be mown daily before play begins. Should this mowing not take place because of weather conditions, rest day or other reasons the pitch shall be mown on the first day on which the match is resumed.

(d) *Mowing of the Outfields in Match of Two or More Days* - In order to ensure that the conditions are as similar as possible for both sides, the outfield shall normally be mown before the commencement of play on each day of the match, if ground and weather conditions allow. See Note (b) to this Law.

(iv) Watering

The pitch shall not be watered during a match. Whenever possible, the creases shall be re-marked.

(v) Maintence of Foot-holes

In wet weather, the umpires shall ensure that the holes made by the bowlers and batsmen are cleaned out and dried whenever necessary to facilitate play. In matches of two or more days' duration, the umpires shall allow, if necessary, the returfing of foot-holes made by the bowler in his delivery stride, or the use of quick setting fillings for the same purpose, before the start of each day's play.

(vi) Securing of Footholds and Maintenance of Pitch

During the play, the umpires shall allow the batsman to beat the pitch with bat and to the fielders to secure footholds by using sawdust, provided no damage is caused to the pitch and Law 42 (unfair play) is not contravened.

LAW 11. COVERING THE PITCH

Complete covering of the pitch shall be allowed before the start of a match.

Pitch shall not be completely covered during a match unless prior arrangement or regulations provide this.

LAW 12. INNINGS

(i) Number of Innings

Not later than fifteen minutes before the time schedule to start the match, the captains shall toss for the choice of innings on the field of play. Or before the time agreed upon for play to start.

(ii) The Toss

The toss winner shall notify his decision to bat or field not later than ten minutes before the time schedule. The decision shall not thereafter be altered.

Each side shall take their innings alternatively in a two innings match except in the case provided in Law 13.

According to an agreement reached before the start of play, a match shall be of one or two innings.

LAW 13. THE FOLLOW-ON

In case no play takes place on the first day of a match of two or more days', below shall apply in accordance with the number of days' play remaining from the actual start of the match.

In a two innings match the side which leads by 200 runs and bats first in a match of five days or more, by 150 runs in a three day or four day match, by 100 runs in a two day match or by 75 runs in a one day match, shall have the option of requiring the other side to follow their innings.

LAW 14. DECLARATIONS

Second innings may be forefeited by a captain, provided the decision to do so is notified to the opposing captain and umpires in sufficient time to allow seven minutes rolling of the pitch.

Irrespective of its duration, the captain of the batting side may declare an innings closed at any time during a match.

LAW 15. START OF PLAY

There shall not be any practice on the pitch at no time on any day of the match.

The umpire at the bowler's end shall call "play" at the start of each innings and of each day's play, and on the resumption of play after any interval or interruption.

After play has resumed no bowler shall have a trial run-up, except at the fall of a wicket when an umpire may allow such a trial run-up if he is satisfied that it will not cause any waste of time.

LAW 16. INTERVALS

(i) Luncheon Interval

If an innings ends or there is a stoppage caused by weather or bad light within ten minutes of the agreed time for the lunch on interval, the interval shall be taken immediately.

The time remaining in the session of play shall be added to the agreed length of the interval but no extra allowance shall be made for the ten minute interval between innings.

(ii) Tea Interval

If an innings is stopped due to weather or bad light within thirty minutes of the agreed time for the tea interval, the interval shall be taken immediately.

The interval shall be of an agreed length and, if possible, shall include the ten minute interval between innings.

The umpires shall allow such intervals as have been agreed upon for meals, and ten minutes between each innings.

If at the agreed time for the tea interval, nine wickets are down, play shall continue for a period not exceeding thirty minutes or until the innings is concluded.

LAW 17. CESSATION OF PLAY

(i) Call of Time

The umpire at the bowler's end shall call "time" on the cessation of play before any interval or interruption of play, at the end of each day's play, and at the conclusion of the match.

(ii) Removal of Bails

After the call of "time", the umpires shall remove the bails from both the wickets.

(iii) Starting a Last Over

The last over before an interval or the close of play shall be started, provided the umpire after walking at his normal pace, has arrived at the position behind the stumps at the bowler's end before time as been reached.

(iv) Completion of the Last Over of a Session

Last over before an interval or at the close of play shall be completed unless a batsman is out or retires during that over within two minutes of the interval or the close of play or unless the players have occasion to leave the field.

(v) Completion of the Last Over of a Match

At the close of play, an over in progress on the final day of a match shall be completed at the request of either captain, even if a wicket falls after time has been reached.

(vi) Last Hour of Match

If, during the last over, the players have occasion to leave the field, the umpires shall call "time" and there shall be no resumption of play and the match shall be at an end.

According to the agreed hours of play the umpires shall indicate when one hour of play time of the match remains. The next over after that shall be the first of a minimum of 20 six ball overs, provided a result is not reached earlier or there is no interval or interruption of play.

If, at the commencement of the last hour of the match, there is an interval or interruption of play or if during the last hour,there is an interval between innings or an interruption of play, the minimum number of overs to be bowled on the resumption of play shall be reduced in proportion to the duration within the last hour of the match of any such interval or interruption.

LAW 18. SCORING

(i)Striker Caught

If the striker is caught, no run shall be scored.

(ii)Batsman Run Out

If a batsman is run out, the run which was being attempted shall not be scored. If however, an injured striker himself is run out, no runs shall be scored.

(iii)A Run

The score shall be reconed by runs. A run is scored:

(a) So often as the batsmen, after a hit or at any time while the ball is in play, shall have crossed ground and made good their from end to end.

(b) When a boundary is scored.

(c) When penalty runs are awarded.

(iv)Batsman Obstructing the Field

When a batsman is out obstructing a field, any run completed before the obstruction occur shall be scored unless such obstruction prevents a catch being made, in which case no runs shall be scored.

(v)Batsman Returning to Wicket he has Left

If the ball is in play and the batsmen have crossed in running neither shall return to the wicket he has left, even though a short run has been called or no run has been scored as in the case of a catch. Batsmen, however, shall return to the wickets they originally left in the cases of a boundary and of any disallowance of runs and of an injured batsman being himself, runout.

Under Law 20 (Lost Ball), 24 (No ball),25 (Wide ball), 41.1 (Fielding the Ball) and for boundary allowances under Law 19 (Boundaries), runs shall be scored for penalties.

LAW 19. BOUNDARIES

(i) The Boundary of the Playing Area

The umpires shall agree with both captains on the boundary of the playing area before the toss of innings. The boundary shall be marked by a white line, a rope laid on the ground, or a fence. If flags or posts only are used to mark a boundary, the imaginary line joining such points shall be regarded as the boundary.

(ii) A Boundary

A boundary shall be scored and signalled by the umpire at the bowler's end whenever, in his opinion:

(a) A ball in play touches or crosses the boundary marked.

(b) A fieldsman with ball in hand touches or grounds any part of his person on or over a boundary line.

(iii) Overthrows

An overthrow resulting in a boundary or from the wilful act of the fieldsman,any runs already completed and the allowance shall be added to the score. The run in progress shall count provided that the batsman has crossed at the instant of the throw or act.

LAW 20. LOST BALL

If in a play a ball cannot be found or recovered, any fieldsman may call "lost ball" when 6 runs shall be added to the score; but if more than six have been run before"lost ball" is called, as many runs as have been completed shall be scored. The run in progress shall count provided that the batsmen have crossed at the instant of the call of "lost ball".

The runs shall be added to the score of the striker if the ball has been struck, but otherwise to the score of byes, leg-byes, no balls or wides as the case may be.

LAW 21. THE RESULT

(i)A Win-One-innings Matches

One innings matches, unless played out as below, shall be decided on the first innings.

If the captains agree to continue the play after completion of one innings of each side in accordance with Law 12 and a result is not achieved on the second, the first innings result shall stand.

(ii) A Win-Two-innings Matches

A side which has scored a total of runs in excess of that scored by the opposing side in its two completed innings shall be the winner.

(iii) A Tie

When the scores are equal at the conclusion of play, but only if the side batting last has completed its innings, the result of a match shall be a 'tie'.

(iv)A Draw

A match not determined in any of the ways as in i, ii and iii above shall count as a draw.

LAW 22. THE OVER

(i) Call of "Over"

When agreed numbers of balls have been bowled, and as the ball becomes dead or when it becomes clear to the umpire at the bowlers' end that both the fielding side and the batsmen at the wicket have ceased to regard the ball as in play, the umpire shall call "over" before leaving the wicket.

(ii) Number of Balls

According to agreement before the match, the ball shall be bowled from each wicket alternately in overs of either six or eight balls.

(iii) No Ball

Neither a no-ball nor a wide ball shall be reckoned as one of over.

(iv) Umpire Miscounting

Miscounting the number of balls by umpire the over as counted by the umpire shall stand.

(v) Bowler Changing Ends

A bowler shall be allowed to change ends as often as desired, provided only that he does not bowl two overs consecutively in an innings.

(vi) Position of Non-striker

The batsman at the bowler's end shall normally stand on the opposite side of the wicket to that from which the ball is being delivered, unless request to do otherwise is granted by the umpire.

LAW 23. DEAD BALL

(i) The Ball Becomes Dead

When

(a) It is finally settled in the hands of the wicket-keeper or the bowler.

(b) It reaches or pitches over the boundary.

(c) A batsman is out.

(d) Whether played or not, it lodges in the clothing or equipment of a batsman or the clothing of an umpire.

(e) A ball lodges in a protective helmet worn by a member of the fielding side.

(f) A penalty is awarded under Law 20 or Law 41.

(g) The umpire calls "over" or "time".

(ii) Either Umpire Shall Call and Signal "Dead Ball" ***When:***

(a) A serious injury to a player or umpire occurs.
(b) He intervenes in a case of unfair play.
(c) The bowler drops the ball accidently before the delivery or the ball does not leave his hand.
(d) For an adequate reason, the striker is not ready to receive the ball and makes no attempt to play it.
(e) He leaves his normal position for consultation.
(f) Before the delivery, one or both bails fall from the striker's wicket.

(iii)The Ball Ceases to be Dead

A ball ceases to be dead when the bowler starts his run-up or bowling action.

LAW 24. NO-BALL

(i)Fair Delivery - The Feet

The umpire shall indicate "no-ball"if he is not satisfied that in the delivery stride:

(a) Some part of the front foot whether grounded or raised was behind the popping crease.
(b) The bowler's back foot has landed within and not touching the return crease or its forward extension.

(ii)Fair Delivery - The Arm

For a delivery to be fair the ball must be bowled and not thrown (see not 'a'above). If either umpire is not entirely satisfied about fairness of a delivery in this respect, he shall call and signal "no ball".

(iii)Mode of Delivery

The bowler's intention to bowl round the wicket or over the wicket shall be indicated to the striker by the umpire.

Failure on the part of the bowler to indicate in advance a change in his mode of delivery is unfair and the umpire shall call and signal "no ball".

(iv) Infringement of Laws by a Wicket-keeper or a Fieldsman

The Umpire shall call and signal "no ball", if the bowler, before delivering the ball,throws it at the striker's end in an attempt to run him out.

(v)Bowler Attempting to Run Out Non-striker before Delivery

If a bowler before delivering the ball, throws it at the striker's end in an attempt to run him out.

(vi)Runs from a No-ball

A no ball may be hit by a striker and runs resulting shall be added to his score. Runs made otherwise from a no-ball shall be scored no-balls.

(vii)Revoking a Call

If the ball does not leave the bowler's hand for any reason the umpire shall revoke the call "no-ball".

(viii)Penalty

In case of a no-ball, a penalty of 1 run shall be scored if no runs are made otherwise.

LAW 25. WIDE-BALL

(i) Judging a Wide

If the bowler bowls the ball so wide of the wicket or so high over that in the opinion of the umpire,it passes out of the reach of the striker.

The umpire shall not adjudge a ball as being wide if :

(a) The striker moves and thus brings the ball within his reach.
(b) By moving from his guard position, causes the ball to pass out of his reach.

(ii) Ball Coming to Rest in Front of the Striker

If in the opinion of the umpire, a ball delivered comes to rest in front of the line of the striker's wicket, "wide" shall not be called. Without interference from the fielding side, a striker has the right to make one attempt to hit the ball. If the fielding side interfere, the umpire shall replace the ball where it came to rest and shall order the fieldsmen to resume the places they occupied in the field before the ball was delivered. The umpire shall call and signal "dead ball" as soon as it is clear that the striker does not intend to hit the ball, or after the striker has made an unsuccessful attempt to hit the ball.

(iii)Batsman Given Out off a Wide

If a batsman be given out off a wide, the penalty for bowling it shall stand unless runs are otherwise made.

(iv)Runs Resulting from a Wide

All runs resulting from a wide ball which is not a no ball shall be considered as wide balls, or if no runs are made 1 run shall be scored.

(v) If Law 35 (Hit wicket), or Law 39 (Stumped) are surpassed, the striker shall be out from a wide ball. Either batsman shall be run out if he breaks Law 33 (Handled the ball) or Law 37 (Obstructing the Field).

(vi)Out from a Wide

The umpire shall revoke the call if the striker hits a ball which has been called "wide".

(vii)Runs Resulting from a Wide

A penalty of 1 run for a wide shall be scored if no runs are made otherwise.

LAW 26. BYE AND LEG BYE

(i) Leg-byes

If a ball not called "wide" or "no ball", is unintentionally deflected by the striker's dress or person, except a hand holding the bat, and any runs are obtained, the umpire shall signal "leg-bye" and the run or runs so scored shall be credited as such to the batting side.

Such leg-byes shall be scored only if the striker has :

(a) Attempted to play the ball with his bat.

(b) Tried to avoid being hit by the ball.

(ii)Byes

If a ball that has not been called "wide" or "no ball" passes the striker without touching his bat or person, and any runs are scored, the umpire shall signal"bye" and the run or runs shall be credited as such to the batting side.

(iii) Disallowance of Leg-byes

If a deflection by the striker's person results, other than in

(a) above & (b) above, the umpire shall call and signal "dead ball" as soon as 1 run has been completed or when it is clear that a run is not being attempted, or the ball has reached the boundary. On the call and signal of "dead ball" the batsmen shall return to their original ends and no runs shall be allowed.

LAW 27. APPEALS

(i) Time of Appeals

Unless appealed by the other side which shall be done prior to the bowler beginning his run-up or bowling action to deliver the next ball, the umpires shall not give a batsman out.

Under Law 23(e) the ball is dead on "over" being called; this does not, however, invalidate an appeal made prior to the first ball of the following over provided "time" has not been called - see Law 17 (Call of Time).

The umpire's decision is final. He may alter his decision, provided that such alteration is made promptly.

(ii)Batsman Leaving his Wicket under a Misapprehension

The umpire shall intervene if satisfied that a batsman has left his wicket under a misapprehension that he has been dismissed but having not been given out.

(iii)Withdrawal of an Appeal

The captain of the fielding side shall seek permission (in exceptional cases) of the umpire to withdraw an appeal provided the outgoing batsman has not left the playing area. If this is allowed, the umpire shall cancel his decision.

(iv)Consultation by Umpires

An umpire may consult another umpire on a point of fact which the later may have been in a better position to judge and shall then give his decision. If, after consultation there is still doubt remaining the decision shall be in favour of the batsman.

LAW 28. THE WICKET IS DOWN

(i) Dispensing with Bails

If it has been agreed to dispense with the bails in accordance with Law 8 (a). Dispensing with

Bails, owing to the strength of the wind, the decision as to when the wicket is down is one for the umpire to decide on the facts before them. In such circumstances and if the umpires so decide, the wicket shall be held to be down even though a stump has not been struck out of the ground.

(ii) One Bail Off

It shall be sufficient for the purpose of putting the wicket down to remove the remaining bail, if one bail is off, or to strike or pull any of the three stumps out of the ground in many of the ways.

(iii) All the Stumps Out of the Ground

If all stumps are out of the ground, the fielding side shall be allowed to put back one or more stumps in order to have an opportunity to putting the wicket down.

LAW 29. BATSMAN OUT OF HIS GROUND

Unless some part of his bat in his hand or of his person is grounded behind the line of the popping crease the batsman shall be considered to be out of his ground.

LAW 30. BOWLED

The striker shall be out Bowled if:

(a) He breaks his wicket by hitting or kicking the ball on to it before the completion of a stroke, or as a result of attempting to guard his wicket.

(b) His wicket is bowled down, even if the ball first touches his bat or person.

LAW 31. TIMED OUT

If a batsman wilfully takes more than two minutes to come in, he shall be out 'Time out'- the two minutes being timed from the moment a wicket falls until the new batsman steps on the field of play.

The time taken by the umpires to investigate the cause of the delay shall be added at the normal close of play.

LAW 32. CAUGHT

The striker shall be caught out if the ball touches his bat or if it touches below the wrist of his hand or glove, holding the bat, and is subsequently held by a fieldsman before it touches the ground.

LAW 33. HANDLED THE BALL

Either of the batsman shall be out 'Handled the Ball'on appeal, if he wilfully touches the ball while in play with the hand not holding the bat unless he does so with the consent of the opposite side.

LAW 34. HIT THE BALL TWICE

If, after the ball is struck or is stopped by any part of his person, he wilfully strikes it again with his bat or person except for the sole purpose of guarding his wicket, the striker on appeal, shall be out ' Hit the Ball Twice'.This he may do with his bat or any part of his person other than his hands, but see Law 37. For the purpose of this law, a hand holding the bat shall be regarded as part of the bat.

No runs except those resulting from an overthrow or penalty-(see Law 41) shall be scored from a ball lawfully struck twice.

Under this law the striker shall be out if, without the consent of the opposite side, he uses his bat or person to return the ball to any of the fielding side.

LAW 35. HIT WICKET

The striker shall be out "Hit Wicket" if,

(a) He hits down his wicket lawfully making a second stroke for the purpose of guarding his wicket within the provisions of Law 34 (Out Hit the Ball Twice).

(b) With any part of his person, dress, or equipment as a result of any action taken by him in preparing to receive a delivery, or in setting off for his first run, immediately after playing, or playing at the ball, his wicket is broken.

LAW 36. LEG BEFORE WICKET

The striker shall be out LBW in the circumstances set below:

(a) *Striker attempting to Play the Ball.*

The striker shall be out LBW if he first intercepts with any part of his person, dress or equipment, a fair ball which would have hit the wicket and which has not previously touched his bat or a hand holding the bat, provided :

(i) The point of impact is in a straight line between wicket and wicket, even if above the level of bails.

(ii) The ball pitched in a straight line between wicket and wicket or on the off side of the striker's wicket, or in the case of a ball intercepted full pitch would have pitched in a straight line between wicket and wicket.

(b) *Striker Making No Attempt to play the Ball.*

The striker shall be given out LBW if the ball is intercepted outside the line of the off stump if, in the opinion of the umpire, he has made no genuine attempt to play the ball with his bat, but has intercepted the ball and if the circumstances set out in (a) above apply.

LAW 37. RUN OUT

On appeal, either batsman shall be given out obstructing the field if he wilfully obstructs the opposite side by work or action.

On appeal, the striker shall be given out should he wilfully obstructs a fielder and prevent a catch being made.

This shall apply even though the striker causes the obstruction in lawfully guarding his wicket under the provisions of Law 34. See Law 34 (Out Hit the Ball Twice).

LAW 38. RUN OUT

Either batsman shall be given out "Run Out" if during running of at any time while the ball is in play-except in the case of Law 39 (Stumped)- he is out of his ground and his wicket is put down by the opposite side. If, however, a batsman in running to make good his ground he shall not be run out if he

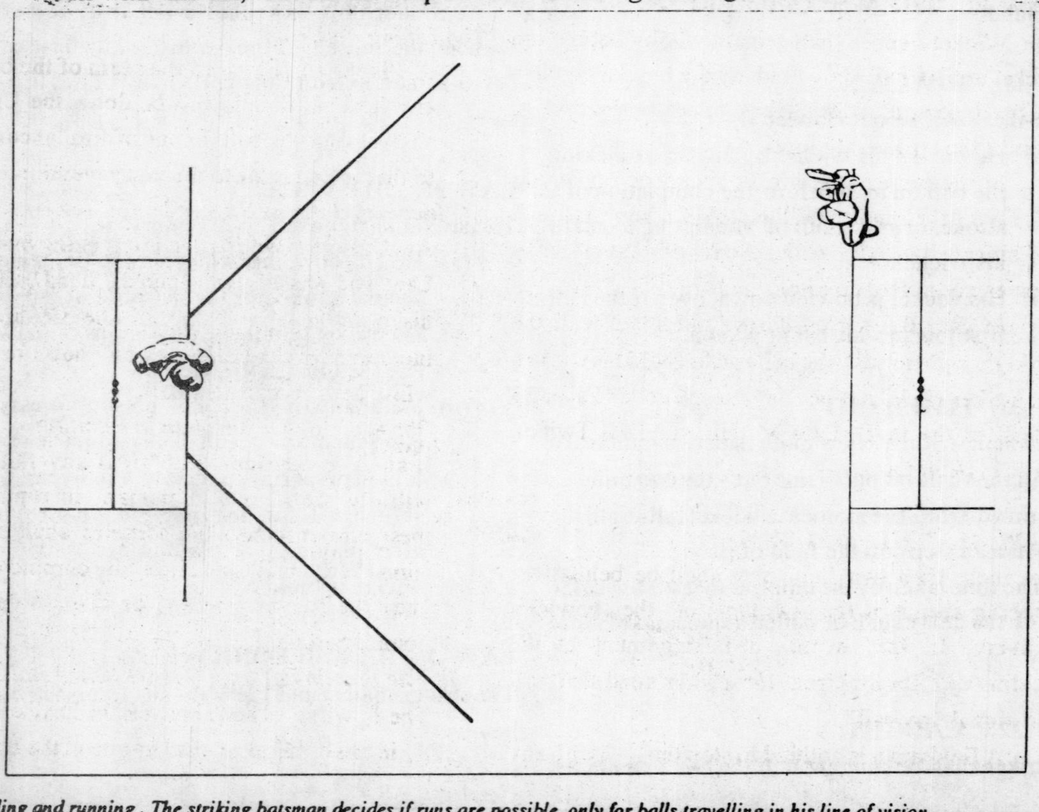

Calling and running. The striking batsman decides if runs are possible only for balls travelling in his line of vision.

subsequently leaves his ground, in order to avoid injury, and the wicket is put down.

In the event of a batsman being run out only that run which is being attempted shall not be scored. However, if an injured striker himself is run out, no runs shall be scored. See Law 27 (Transgression of the Laws by an Injured Batsman or Runner).

He who runs for the wicket which is put down shall be out, if the batsmen have crossed in running. If they have not crossed, he who has left the wicket which is put down shall be out. If a batsman remains in his ground or returns to his ground and the other batsman joins him there, the later shall be out if his wicket is put down.

LAW 39. STUMPED

If in receiving the ball, not being a no-ball, he is out of his ground otherwise than in attempting a run and the wicket is put down by the wicket-keeper without the intervention of another fieldsman the striker shall be out Stumped.

LAW 40. THE WICKET-KEEPER

The Wicket-keeper shall remain wholly behind the wicket until a ball delivered by the bowler touches the bat or person of the striker, or passes the wicket, or until the striker attempts a run.

In the event of the wicket-keeper contravening this Law, the umpire at the striker's end shall call and signal "no-ball" at the instant of delivery or as soon as possible thereafter.

In case the wicket-keeper interferes with the striker's right to play the ball and to guard his wicket, the striker shall not be out except under Laws 33 (Handled the Ball), Law 34 (Hit the Ball Twice), Law 37 (Run Out).

LAW 41. THE FIELDSMAN

Not more than two fieldsmen shall be behind the popping crease at the instant of the bowler's delivery. In the event of infringement by the fielding side, the umpire at the striker's end shall call and signal "no ball".

A fieldsman is entitled to stop the ball with any part of his person, but if he intentionally stops it otherwise, 5 runs will be added to the run or runs already scored. If no runs have been scored, 5 penalty runs shall be awarded. The run in progress shall count provided that the batsmen have crossed at the act. If the ball has been struck, the penalty shall be added to the score of the striker, else to the score of byes, leg-byes, no-balls or wides as the case may be.

LAW 42. UNFAIR PLAY

(i) Responsibility of Captains

The captains are responsible at all times for ensuring that play is conducted within the spirit of the game as well as within the Laws.

(ii) Responsibility of Umpires

The umpires are the sole judges of fair and unfair play.

(iii) Intervention by the Umpire

The Umpires shall intervene without appeal by calling and signalling "dead ball" in the case of unfair play, but should not otherwise interfere with the progress of the game except as required to do so by the laws.

(iv) Lifting the Seam

A Player shall not lift the seam of the ball for any reason. Should this be done, the Umpires shall change the ball for one of similar condition to that in use prior to the contravention.

(v) Incommoding the Striker

An Umpire is justified in intervening under this Law and shall call and signal "dead ball" if, in his opinion, any Player of the fielding side incommodes the Striker by any noise or action while he is receiving a ball.

(vi) Obstruction of a Batsman in Running

It shall be considered unfair if any fieldsman wilfully obstructs a Batsman in running. In these circumstances the Umpire shall call and signal "dead ball" and allow any completed runs and the run in progress or alternatively any boundary scored.

(vii) The Bowling of Fast Short Pitched Balls

The bowling of fast short-pitched balls is unfair if, in the opinion of the Umpire at the Bowler's end, it constitutes an attempt to intimidate the Striker.

Umpires shall consider intimidation to be the deliberate bowling of fast short-pitched balls which by their length, height and direction are intended or likely to inflict physical injury on the Striker. The relative skill of the Striker shall also be taken into consideration.

(viii) The Bowling of Fast High Full Pitches

The bowling of fast high full pitches is unfair. In the event of such unfair bowling the Umpire at the bowler's end shall adopt the procedures of caution, final warning, action against the Bowler and reporting as set out in (vii), above.

WHO'S WHO IN CRICKET

A'BECKETT, EDWARD LAMBERT

Australia (born 1907) - A right-handed batsman and medium-fast bowler. He played for Victoria. Test Record - 4 Tests, 143 runs (Av. 20.42), 3 wickets (Av. 105.66) and 4 catches.

ABDUL KADIR

Pakistan (born 1944) - A wicket-keeper and sound right-handed batsman. He played for Karachi. Test Record - 4 Tests, 272 runs (Av. 34.00) and 1 stumping.

ABDUL QADIR

Pakistan (born 1955) - A stocky leg-spin and googly bowler. A useful right-handed batsman. He plays for Lahore and Habib Bank. Test Record - 59 Tests, 967 runs (Av. 15.59) 224 wickets (Av. 31.74) and 15 catches.

ABEL, ROBERT

England (1857-1936) - Mastered all types of attack. Test Record - 13 Tests, 744 runs (Av. 37.20) including 2 centuries, 13 catches.

ABID ALI, SYED

India (born 1941) - A right-handed batsman and right-arm medium-fast bowler. He played for Hyderabad. Test Record - 29 Tests, 1,018 runs (Av. 20.36), 47 wickets (Av. 42.12) and 33 catches.

ACHONG, ELLIS EDGAR

West Indies (born 1904) - A slow left-arm bowler of immaculate length. He played for Trinidad. Test Record - 6 Tests, 81 runs (Av. 8.10), 8 wickets (Av. 47.25) and 6 catches.

ADCOCK, NEIL AMWIN TREHARNE

South Africa (born 1931) - He is a right-arm medium-fast bowler with a smooth, rhythmic run. He played for Transvaal and Natal. Test Record - 26 Tests, 146 runs (Av. 5.40), 104 wickets (Av. 21.10) and 4 catches.

ADHIKARI, HEMCHANDRA RAMCHANDRA

India (born 1919) - A right-handed batsman and right-arm leg-break bowler. Test Record - 21 Tests, 872 runs (Av. 31.12), 3 wickets (Av.27.33) and 8 catches.

AFAQ HUSSAIN

Pakistan (born 1939) - A useful right-arm off-break bowler. He played for Karachi. Test Record - 2 Tests, 64 runs and 2 catches.

AFTAB BALOCH

Pakistan (born 1953) - A very sound right-handed batsman and occasional off-break bowler. He played for Karachi and Sind. Test Record - 2 Tests, 97 runs (Av. 48.50).

AFTAB GUL

Pakistan (born 1946) - A stocky, right-handed opening batsman. He played for Lahore. Test Record - 6 Tests, 182 runs (Av. 22.75) 3 catches.

AGNEW, JONATHAN PHILIP

England (born 1960) - A right-arm fast bowler and tail-end right-handed batsman. He played for Leicestershire. Test Record - 3 Tests, 10 runs (Av. 10.00) and 4 wickets (Av. 93.25).

AHANGAMA, FRANKLYN SALIYA
Sri Lanka (born 1959) - A right-arm medium-pace bowler and left-handed tail-end batsman. He played for Sinhalese. Test Record - 3 Tests, 11 runs (Av. 5.50) and 18 wickets (Av. 19.33).

ALCOTT, CYRIL FRANCIS WALTER
New Zealand (1896-1973) - A very good all-rounder, a left-handed batsman and left-arm orthodox slow bowler. He played for Auckland. Test Record - 6 Tests, 113 runs (Av. 22.60) 6 Wickets (Av. 90.16) and 3 catches.

ALDERMAN, TERENCE MICHAEL
Australia (born 1956) - A right-arm medium-fast bowler with fine control of swing and cut. He plays for Western Australia. Test Record - 24 Tests, 125 runs (Av.5.95), 86 wickets (Av. 32.16) and 18 catches.

ALEXANDER, FRANZ COPELAND MURRAY
West Indies (born 1928) - An aggressive right-handed batsman and sound, sometimes brilliant, wicket-keeper. He played for Cambridge University and Jamaica. Test Record - 25 Tests, 961 runs (Av. 30.03) including 1 century, and 90 dismissals (85ct, 5st).

ALEXANDER, GEORGE
Australia (1851-1930) - A hard-hitting right-handed batsman, a useful medium-fast change bowler.He played for Victoria. Test Record - 2 Tests, 52 runs (13.00), 2 wickets (Av. 46.50) and 2 catches.

ALI, INSHAN
West Indies (bron 1949) - A small, left-hand back-of-the-hand spinner. He played for Trinidad. Test Record - 12 Tests, 172 runs (Av. 10.75), 34 Wickets (Av. 47.67) and 7 catches.

ALIMUDDIN
Pakistan (born 1930) - A stocky right-handed opening batsman and a magnificent fielder. He played for Karachi. Test Record - 25 Tests, 1,091 runs (Av. 25.37) including 2 centuries and 8 catches.

ALLAN, DAVID WALTER
West Indies (born 1937) - He visited England as a first-string wicket-keeper in 1963. He played for Barbados. Test Record - 5 Tests, 75 runs (Av. 12.50) and 18 dismissals (15ct, 3st).

ALLEN, DAVID ARTHUR
England (born 1935) - He could bowl accurately for long spells, turning his off-spinner substantially. He played for Gloucestershire. Test Record - 39 Tests, 918 runs (Av. 25.50), 122 wickets (Av. 30.96) and 10 catches.

ALLEN, SIR GEORGE OSWALD BROWNING
England (born 1902) - He was born in Australia and had an uncle, R.C.Allen, who played for Australia. He played for Cambridge University and Middlesex. Test Record - 25 Tests, 750 runs (Av.24.19), including 1 century, 81 wickets (Av. 29.37) and 20 catches.

ALLOM, MAURICE JAMES CARRICK
England (born 1906) - He was a medium-fast right-arm bowler. He played for Cambridge University and Surrey. Test Record - 5 Tests, 14 runs (Av. 14.00) and 14 wickets (Av. 18.92).

ALLOTT, PAUL JOHN WALTER
England (born 1956) - A useful right- handed batsman and right-arm fast-medium bowler. He played for Cheshire and Lancashire. Test Record - 13 Tests, 213 runs (Av.14.20) and 26 wickets (Av. 41.69).

AMAR SINGH, LADHA
India (1910-40) - A right-handed batsman and right-arm medium-fast bowler. He played for Western India and Nawanagar. Test Record - 7 Tests, 292 runs (Av. 22.46), 28 wickets (Av. 30.64) and 3 catches.

AMARNATH, LALA
India (born 1911) - A right-handed batsman and right-arm medium-pace bowler. Test Record - 24 Tests, 878 runs (Av. 24.38), 45 wickets (Av. 32.91) and 13 catches.

AMARNATH, MOHINDER
India (born 1950)- A right-handed batsman and right-arm medium-pace bowler. Test Record - 69 Tests, 4,377 runs (Av. 42.49) including 11 centuries, 32 wickets (Av.55.68) and 47 catches.

AMARNATH, SURINDER
India (born 1948) - A left-handed batsman and right-arm off-break bowler. Test Record - 10 Tests, 550 runs (Av. 30.55) including 1 century and 1 wicket.

AMERSINGHE, MUDALIGE JAYANTHA GAMINI
SriLanka (born 1954) - A leg-spinner who came into Test cricket at the age of thirty. He plays for Bloomfield. Test Record - 2 Tests, 54 runs (Av. 18.00), 3 wickets (Av. 50.00) and 3 catches.

AMES, LESLIE ETHELBERT GEORGE
England (born 1905)- He was a fine, strongly built, all-round wicket-keeper. He played for Kent. Test Record - 47 Tests, 2,434 runs (Av.40.56) including 8 centuries, and 97 dismissals (74ct, 23st).

AMIR ELAHI
India (1908-80) - A right-handed batsman and right-arm leg-break googly bowler. He played for Northern India. Test Record - For India - 1 Test, 17 runs (Av.8.50)

For Pakistan - 5 Tests, 65 runs (Av.10.83) and 7 wickets.

AMISS, DENNIS LESLIE
England (born 1943) - The image of Dennis Amiss was one of a loyal and dedicated professional cricketer. He played for Warwickshire. Test Record - 50 Tests, 3612 runs (Av. 46.30) including 11 centuries, and 24 catches.

ANDERSON, ROBERT WICKHAM
New Zealand (born 1948) - A right-handed opening batsman and athletic fielder. He played for Canterbury. Test Record - 12 Tests, 381 runs (Av. 31.75).

ANDREW, KEITH VINCENT
England (born 1929) - Played only twice for England. He played for Northamptonshire.

Test Record - 2 Tests, 29 runs (Av. 9.66) and 1 dismissal (1ct).

ANDREWS, BRYAN
New Zealand (born 1945) - A very useful right arm meadium-pace bowler. He played for Canterbury. Test Record - 2 Tests, 22 runs (Av. 22.00) and 2 Wickets (Av. 77.00).

ANDREWS, THOMAS JAMES EDWIN
Australia (1890-1970) - A right-handed with powerful wrists and a straight bat with a wide range of strokes. He played for New South Wales. Test Record - 16 Tests, 592 runs (Av. 26.90) and 12 catches.

ANIL DALPAT
Pakistan (born 1963) - A right-handed batsman and a neat and agile wicket-keeper. He played for Karachi. Test Record - 9 Tests, 167 runs (Av. 15.18) and 25 dismissals (22ct, 3st).

ANURASIRI, SANGARANGE DON
Sri Lanka (born 1966) - A left-arm spinner, and a right-handed tail-ender batsman. He plays for Panadura. Test Record - 4 Tests, 13 runs (Av.4.33).

ANWAR HUSSIAN
Pakistan (born 1920) - A sound right-handed batsman and fast-medium seam bowler. He played for Karachi. Test Record - 4 Tests, 42 runs(Av. 7.00), 1 wicket.

APTE, ARVIND LAXMANRAO
India (born 1934)- A right-handed opening batsman. He played for Bombay. Test Record - 1 Test, 15 runs (Av. 7.50).

APTE, MADHAV LAXMANRAO
India (born 1932) - A right-handed opening batsman and right-arm leg-spin bowler. He played for Bombay. Test Record - 7 Tests, 542 runs (Av. 49.27) including 1 century and 2 catches.

ARCHER, KENNETH ALLAN
Australia (born 1928) - A right-handed opening batsman and a good stroke player. He played for Queensland. Test Record - 5 Tests, 234 runs, (Av. 26.00).

ARCHER, RONALD GRAHAM
Australia (born 1933) - A vigorous all-rounder of fine physique. He played for the Queensland. Test Record - 19 Tests, 713 runs, (Av.24.58) including 1 century, 48 wickets (Av. 27.45) and 20 catches.

ARIF BUTT
Pakistan (born 1944) - A right-arm fast-medium bowler and useful tail-end batsman. He played for Lahore. Test Record - 3 Tests, 59 runs (Av. 11.80) and 14 wickets (Av. 20.57).

ARMITAGE, THOMAS
England (1848-1922) - He was a useful right-handed batsman and a round-arm, medium-pace or slow-lob bowler. He played for Yorkshire. Test Record - 2 Tests, 33 runs (Av. 11.00),no wicket.

ARMSTRONG, WARWICK WINDRIDGE
Australia (1879-1947) - A right-handed batsman. He played for Victoria. Test Record - 50 Tests, 2,863 runs (Av. 38.68) including 6 centuries, 87 wickets (Av. 33.59) and 44 catches.

ARNOLD, EDWARD GEORGE
England (1876-1942)- A long, loose-limbed all-rounder. He played for Devon and Worcestershire. Test Record - 10 Tests, 160 runs (13.33), 31 wickets (25.41) and 8 catches.

ARNOLD, GEOFFREY GRAHAM
England (born 1944)- He was an outstanding all-round player. He played for Surrey. Test Record - 34 Tests, 421 runs (Av. 12.02), 115 wickets (Av. 28.29) and 9 catches.

ARUN LAL
India (1955) - A right-handed opener and good close fielder. Test Record - 16 Tests, 729 runs (Av. 26.03) 13 catches.

ASGAR ALI, NYRON
West Indies (bron 1922) - A sound right-handed opening batsman . He played for Trinidad. Test Record - 2 Tests, 62 runs (Av. 15.50).

ASHRAF ALI
Pakistan (born 1958) - A right-handed batsman with considerable flair. He played for Lahore. Test Record - 5 Tests, 206 runs (Av. 103.00) and 11 dismissals (9ct, 2st).

ASIF IQBAL RAZVI
Pakistan (born 1943) - An exciting stroke-playing right-handed batsman. He played for Karachi. Test Record - 52 Tests, 3,308 runs (Av. 39.85) including 11 centuries, 51 wickets (Av. 28.03) and 32 catches.

ASIF MASOOD
Pakistan (born 1946) - He was a right-arm fast-medium bowler. He played for Lahore. Test Record - 16 Tests, 93 runs (Av. 10.33) 38 wickets (Av. 41.26) and 5 catches.

ASTILL, WILLIAM EWART
England (1888-1948)- He was an orthodox right-handed batsman and off-spin bowler. He played for Leicestershire. Test Record - 9 Tests, 190 runs (Av. 12.66), 25 wickets (34.24) and 7 catches.

ATHEY, CHARLES WILLIAN JEFFREY
England (born 1957)- A right-handed batsman and useful medium-paced bowler. He plays for Yorkshire. Test Record - 17 Tests,722 runs (Av.24.89) and 10 catches.

ATKINSON, DENIS ST EVAL
West Indies (born 1926) - A sound right-handed batsman and medium-pace bowler. He played for Barbados and Trinidad. Test Record - 22 Tests, 922 runs (Av. 31.79) including 1 century and 47 wickets (Av. 35.04).

ATKINSON, ERIC ST EVAL
West Indies (bron 1925) - A right-handed batsman and medium-fast bowler. He played for Barbados. Test Record - 8 Tests, 126 runs (Av. 15.75) 25 Wickets (Av. 23.56) and 2 catches.

ATTEWELL, WILLIAM
England (1861-1927) - A right-arm medium pace bowler. He played for Nottinghamshire. Test Record - 10 Tests, 150 runs (Av. 16.66), 27 wickets (Av. 23.18) and 9 catches.

AUSTIN, RICHARD ARKWRIGHT
West Indies (born 1954) - A sound right-handed batsman and medium-pace bowler. He played for Jamaica. Test Record - 2 Tests, 22 runs (Av. 11.00).

AYUB, ARSHAD
India (born 1958) - A right-arm off spinner and right-handed batsman. Test Record - 11 Tests, 246 runs (Av.18.92), 41 wickets (Av.27.75) and 2 catches.

AZAD, KIRTI
India (born 1959) - A right-handed batsman and right-arm off-break bowler. He plays for Delhi. Test Record - 7 Tests, 135 runs (Av. 11.25), 3 wickets (Av. 124.33) and 3 catches.

AZHARUDDIN, MOHAMMED
India (born 1963) - A right-handed batsman and medium-pace bowler. He plays for Hyderabad. Test Record - 30 Tests, 1,912 runs (Av. 46.53) including 6 centuries, 24 catches.

BAICHAN, LEONARD
West Indies (born 1946) - A left-handed opening batsman. He played for Guyana. Test Record - 3 Tests, 184 runs (Av. 46.00) including 1 century.

BAIG, ABBAS ALI
India (born 1939) - A right-handed batsman and right-arm leg-spin bowler. He played for Hyderabad. Test Record - 10 Test, 428 runs (Av. 23.77) including 1 century and 6 catches.

BAILEY, TREVOR EDWARD
England (born 1923) - A right-arm, medium-fast bowler, brilliant fielder and a sound batsman. He played for Nottinghamshire. Test Record - 61 Tests, 2,290 runs (Av. 29.74) including 1 century, 132 wickets (Av. 29.21) and 32 catches.

BAKEAWLL, ALFRED HARRY
England (1908-1983) - A right-handed batsman and a useful fielder. He played for Northamptonshire. Test Record - 6 Tests, 409 runs (Av. 45.44) and 3 catches.

BALASKAS, XENOPHON CONSTANTINE
South Africa (born 1910) - A right-arm slow leg-spin bowler and a very useful lower-order batsman. He played for Border. Test Record - 9 Tests, 174 runs (Av. 14.50) including 1 century, and 22 wickets (Av. 36.63).

BANERJEE, SAROBINDU NATH SHUTE
India (1913-1980) - A right-handed batsman and right-arm medium-fast bowler. He played for Bengal and Bihar. Test Record - 1 Test, 13 runs (Av. 6.50) and 5 wickets (Av. 25.49).

BANERJEE, SUDANGSU ABINASH MONTU
India (born 1919) - A right-handed batsman and right-arm medium pace bowler. Test Record - 1 Test, 0 run and 5 wickets (Av. 36.20).

BANNERMAN, ALEXANDER CHALMERS
Australia (1854-1924) - He made many large scores and was invaluable as a partner for bigger

hitters. Test Record - 28 Tests, 1,108 runs (Av. 23.08), 4 wickets (Av. 40.75) and 21 catches.

BANNERMAN, CHARLES

Australia (1851-1930) - He was fine, upstanding and polished batsman. He played for New South Wales. Test Record - 3 Tests, 239 runs (Av. 59.75) including 1 century.

BAPTISTE, ELDINE ASHWORTH ELDERFIELD

West Indies (born 1960) - A relatively slimly built right-handed batsman. He played for Leeward Islands and Kent. Test Record - 9 Tests, 224 runs (Av. 24.88), 15 wickets (Av. 32.40), and 2 catches.

BAQA, JILANI MOHAMMAD

India (1911-1941) - A right-handed batsman and right-arm medium-fast bowler. He played for Northern India. Test Record - 1 Test, 16 runs.

BARBER, ROBERT WILLIAM

England (born 1935) - A left-handed opening batsman, talented leg-break bowler. He played for Lancashire and Warwickshire. Test Record - 28 Tests, 1,495 runs (Av. 35.59) including 1 century, 42 wickets (Av. 43.00) and 21 catches.

BARBER, WILFRED

England (1901-1968) - He was a text-book right-handed batsman and was a first-rate outfielder. He played for Yorkshire. Test Record - 2 Tests, 83 runs (Av. 20.75).

BARDSLEY, WARREN

Australia (1882-1954) - A stylish left-handed opening batsman . He played for New South Wales. Test Record - 41 Tests, 2,469 runs (Av. 40.47) including 6 centuries, and 12 catches.

BARLOW, EDGAR JOHN

South Africa (born 1940) - A right-handed opening batsman.He played for Transvaal and Derbyshire. Test Record - 30 Tests, 2,516 runs (Av. 45.74) including 6 centuries, 40 wickets (Av. 34.05) and 35 catches.

BARLOW, GRAHAM DEREK

England (born 1950) - A right-handed batsman. He played for Middlesex. In his first class career he made, 12,387 runs including 26 centuries, took 3 wickets and 136 catches.
Test Record - 3 Tests, 17 runs (Av. 4.25).

BARLOW, RICHARD GORTON

England (1851-1919) - A right-handed batsman and was also a left-arm, medium-pace bowler. He played for Lancashire. Test Record - 17 Tests, 591 runs (Av. 22.73), 34 wickets (Av. 22.55) and 14 catches.

BARNES, SIDNEY GEORGE

Australia (1916-1973) - A right-handed batsman. He played for New South Wales. Test Record - 13 Tests, 1,072 runs (Av. 63.05) including 3 centuries, 4 wickets (Av. 54.50) and 14 catches.

BARNES, SYDNEY FRANCIS

England (1873-1967) - He was a right-arm, medium-fast bowler. He played for Warwickshire and Lancashire. Test Record - 27 Tests, 242 runs (Av. 8.06), 189 wickets (Av. 16.43) and 12 catches.

BARNES, WILLIAM

England (1851-1899) - A right-handed batsman and a medium-pace bowler. He played for Nottinghamshire. Test Record - 21 Tests, 725 runs (Av. 23.38) including 1 century, 51 wickets (Av. 15.54) and 19 catches.

BARNETT, BENJAMIN ARTHUR

Australia (1908-1979) - He was a wicket-keeper and steady left-handed batsman. He played for Victoria and Buckinghamshire. Test Record - 4 Tests, 195 runs (Av. 27.85) and 5 dismissals (3ct, 2st).

BARNETT, CHARLES JOHN

England (born 1910) - An opening right-handed batsman. He played for Gloucestershire. Test

Record - 20 Tests, 1,098 runs (Av. 35.41) including 2 centuries and 14 catches.

BARRATT, FREDERICK

England (1894-1947) -A right-arm fast bowler. He played for Nottinghamshire. Test Record - 5 Tests, 28 runs (Av. 9.33) and 5 wickets (Av. 47.00) and 2 catches.

BARRETT, ARTHUR GEORGE

West Indies (born 1944) - A right-arm leg-break bowler. He played for Jamaica. Test Record - 6 Tests, 40 runs (Av. 6.66) and 13 wickets (Av. 46.38).

BARRETT, DR. JOHN EDWARD

Australia (1866-1916) - A patient left-handed batsman and useful medium-paced change-bowler. He played for Victoria. Test Record - 2 Tests, 80 runs (Av. 26.66) and 1 catch.

BARRINGTON, KENNETH FRANK

England (1930-1981) - He was a useful but underused leg-break and googly bowler. He played for Berkshire and Surrey. Test Record - 82 Tests, 6,806 runs (Av. 58.67) including 20 centuries, and 29 wickets (Av. 44.82) and 58 catches.

BARTLETT, EDWARD LAWSON

West Indies, (1906-1976) - A slightly built right-handed batsman. He played for Barbados. Test Record - 5 Tests, 131 runs (Av. 18.71) and 2 catches.

BARTLETT, GARY ALEXANDER

New Zealand (born 1941) - A right-arm medium-fast bowler and useful batsman. He played for Central Districts and Canterbury. Test Record - 10 Tests, 263 runs (Av. 15.47), 24 wickets (Av. 33.00) and 8 catches.

BARTON, PAUL THOMAS

New Zealand (born 1935) - A composed, correct and polished right-handed batsman. He played for Wellington. Test Record - 7 Tests, 285 runs (Av. 20.35) including 1 century.

BATES, WILLIAM

England (1855-1900) - A right-handed batsman and a first-rate slow, round-arm bowler. He played for Yorkshire. Test Record - 15 Tests, 656 runs (Av. 27.33), 50 wickets (Av. 16.42) and 9 catches.

BEAN, GEORGE

England (1864-1923) - He was a fast-scoring right-handed batsman and also a useful medium-pace bowler. He played for Nottinghamshire. Test Record - 3 Tests, 92 runs (Av. 18.40).

BEARD, DONALD DEREK

New Zealand (1920-1982) - A right-arm medium-pace bowler and a flambuoyant hitter. He played for Wellington. Test Record - 4 Tests, 101 runs (Av. 20.20), 9 wickets (Av. 33.55).

BEDI, BISHEN SINGH GIAN SINGH

India (born 1946) - A left-arm slow spin bowler and right-handed batsman. He played for Delhi. Test Record - 67 Tests, 656 runs (Av. 8.98), 266 wickets (Av. 28.71) and 26 catches.

BEDSER, ALEC VICTOR

England (born 1918) - He was a talented county all-rounder. He played for Surrey. Test Record - 51 Tests, 714 runs (Av. 12.75), 236 wicket (Av. 24.89) and 26 catches.

BEGBIE, DENIS WARBURTON

South Africa (born 1914) - A quick-scoring but rather inconsistent batsman and change-bowler. He played for Transvaal. Test Record - 5 Tests, 138 runs (Av. 19.71) and 2 catches.

BELL, ALEXANDER JOHN

South Africa (1906-1985) - A right-arm medium-fast bowler. He played for Western Province and Rhodesia. Test Record - 16 Tests, 69 runs (Av. 6.27), 48 wickets (Av. 32.64) and 6 catches.

BELL, WILLIAM

New Zealand (born 1931) - A right-arm and leg-break bowler. He played for Canterbury. Test Record - 2 Tests, 21 runs and 2 wickets (Av. 117.50).

BENAUD, JOHN
Australia (born 1944) - A right-handed batsman. He played for New South Wales. Test Record - 3 Tests, 223 runs (Av. 44.60) including 1 century.

BENAUD, RICHARD
Australia (born 1930) - A forcing right-handed batsman. He played for New South Wales. Test Record - 63 Tests, 2,201 runs (Av. 24.45) including 3 centuries, 248 wickets (Av. 27.03) and 65 catches.

BENNETT, MURRAY JOHN
Australia (born 1956) - A bespectacled slow left-arm bowler and useful lower-order right-handed batsman. He played for New South Wales. Test Record - 3 Tests, 71 runs (Av. 23.66), 6 wickets (Av. 54.16) and 5 catches.

BENSON, RICHARD MARK
England (born 1958) - A solidly left-handed opening batsman of a little under medium height. He played for Kent. Test Record - 1 Test, 51 runs (Av. 25.50).

BERRY, ROBERT
England (born 1926) - A left-arm, spin bowler. He played for Lancashire and Worcestershire. Test Record - 2 Tests, 6 runs (Av. 3.00), 9 wickets (Av. 25.33) and 2 catches.

BEST, CARLISLE ALONZA
West Indies (born 1959) - A right-hander who sometimes opens and a useful occasional off-spin bowler. He played for Barbados. Test Record - 3 Tests, 78 runs (Av. 26.00) and 4 catches.

BHANDARI, PARKASH
India (born 1935) - A right-handed batsman and right-arm off-break bowler. Test Record - 3 Tests, 77 runs (Av. 19.25) and 1 catch.

BILBY, GRAHAME PAUL
New Zealand (born 1941) - A competent right-handed opening batsman. He played for Wellington. Test Record - 2 Tests, 55 runs (Av. 13.75) and 3 catches.

BINKS, JAMES GRAHAM
England (born 1935) - He was a highly skilled but often underrated wicket-keeper. He played for Yorkshire and Lincolnshire. Test Record - 2 Tests, 91 runs (Av. 22.75) and 8 catches.

BINNS, ALFRED PHILLIP
West Indies (born 1929) - A right-handed batsman and wicket-keeper. He played for Jamaica. Test Record - 5 Tests, 64 runs (Av. 9.14) and 17 dismissals (14ct, 3st).

BINNY, ROGER
India (born 1955) - A right-handed batsman and right-arm medium-fast bowler. He played for Karnataka. Test Record - 27 Tests, 830 runs (Av. 23.05), 47 wickets (Av. 32.63) and 11 catches.

BIRD, MORICE CARLOS
England (1888-1933) - He was a fine, forcing, right-handed batsman, and a good medium-pace bowler. He played for Lancashire and Surrey. Test Record - 10 Tests, 280 runs (Av. 18.66), 8 wickets (Av. 15.00) and 5 catches.

BIRKENSHAW, JACK
England (born 1940) - An orthodox, right-arm, slow, off-break bowler. He played for Yorkshire. Test Record - 5 Tests, 148 runs (Av. 21.14) 13 wickets (Av. 36.07) and 3 catches.

BIRKETT, LIONEL SYDNEY
West Indies (born 1905) - A right-handed batsman and a useful medium-pace change-bowler. He played for Barbados. Test Record - 4 Tests, 136 runs (Av. 17.00) and 4 catches.

BLACKHAM, JOHN MCCARTHY

Australia (1854-1932) - He was very useful right-handed batsman and wicket-keeper. He played for Victoria. Test Record - 35 Tests, 800 runs (Av. 15.68) and 60 dismissals (36ct, 24st).

BLAIR, ROBERT WILLIAM

New Zealand (born 1932) - A right-arm medium-fast bowler and occasionally useful late-order batsman. He played for Wellington. Test Record - 19 Tests, 189 runs (Av. 6.75), 43 wickets (Av. 35.23) and 5 catches.

BLANCKENBERG, JAMES MANUEL

South Africa (born 1893 presumed dead) - He was a right-arm medium-pace bowler. He played for Natal and Western Province. Test Record - 18 Tests, 455 runs (Av. 19.78), 60 wickets (Av. 30.28) and 9 catches.

BLAND, KENNETH COLIN

South Africa (born 1938) - A right-handed forcing batsman. He played for Rhodesia and Eastern Province. Test Record - 21 Tests, 1,669 runs (Av. 49.08) including 3 centuries, 2 wickets (Av. 62.50) and 10 catches.

BLIGH,HON. IVO FRANCIS WALTER

England (1859-1927) - A right-handed batsman. He played for Cambridge University and Kent. Test Record - 4 Tests, 62 runs (Av. 10.33) and 7 catches.

BLUNT, ROGER CHARLES

New Zealand (1900-1966) - He was a very useful right-arm leg-break bowler. He played for Canterbury. Test Record - 9 Tests, 330 runs (Av. 27.50), 12 wickets (Av. 39.33) and 5 catches.

BLYTHE, COLIN

England (1879-1917) - A slow left-arm bowler . He played for kent. Test Record - 19 Tests, 183 runs (Av. 9.63), 100 wickets (Av. 18.63) and 6 catches.

BOARD, JOHN HENRY

England (1867-1924) - A fearless and untiring wicket-keeper. He played for Hawkes Bay and Gloucestershire. Test Record - 6 Tests, 108 runs (Av. 10.80) and 11 dismissals (8ct, 3st).

BOLUS, JOHN BRAIN

England (born 1934) - He was an occasional left-arm medium-pace bowler. He played for Yorkshire. Test Record - 7 Tests, 496 runs (Av. 41.33) and 2 catches.

BONNOR, GEORGE JOHN

Australia (1855-1912) - He was a hitter with extraordinary power. He played for Victoria. Test Record - 17 Tests, 512 runs (Av. 17.06) including 1 century, 2 wickets (Av. 42.00) and 16 catches.

BOOCK, STEPHEN LEWIS

New Zealand (born 1951) - He was a slow left-arm orthodox spin bowler. He played for Otago. Test Record - 26 Tests, 192 runs (Av. 6.62), 65 wickets (Av. 32.33) and 13 catches.

BOON, DAVID CLARENCE

Australia (born 1960) - A right-hand opening batsman. He plays for Tasmania. Test Record - 42 Tests, 2,852 runs (Av.40.74) including 7 centuries.

BOOTH, BRAIN CHARLES

Australia (born 1933) - A very slim right-handed batsman . He played for New South Wales. Test Record - 29 Tests, 1,773 runs (Av. 42.21) including 5 centuries, 3 wickets (Av. 48.66) and 17 catches.

BOOTH; MAJOR WILLIAM

England (1886-1916) - A right-handed batsman and fast-medium bowler. He played for Yorkshire. Test Record - 2 Tests, 46 runs (Av. 23.00) and 7 wickets (Av. 18.57).

BORDE, CHANDERKANT GULABRAO

India (born 1934) - A right-handed batsman and

right-arm leg-break bowler. He played for Maharashtra and Baroda. Test Record - 55 Tests, runs 3,061 (Av. 35.59) including 5 centuries, 52 wickets (Av. 46.48) and 37 catches.

BORDER, ALLAN ROBERT

Australia (born 1955) - A stocky left-handed batsman, specialist slip fielder and steady slow left-arm orthodox spin bowler. He plays for New South Wales. Test Record - 102 Tests, 7,831 runs (Av. 52.55) including 23 centuries and 113 catches.

BOSANQUET, BERNARD JAMES TINDAL

England (1877-1936) - A right-handed batsman, and also a medium-fast bowler. He played for Oxford University. Test Record - 7 Tests, 147 runs (Av. 13.36), 25 wickets (Av. 24.16) and 9 catches.

BOTHAM, IAN TERENCE

England (born 1955) - Ian Botham is the most exciting all-rounder. He played for Somerset. Test Record - 94 Tests, 5,057 runs (Av. 34.87) 373 wickets (Av. 27.86) and 109 catches.

BOWDEN, MONTAGUE PARKER

England (1865-1892) - He was a right-handed batsman and wicket-keeper. He played for Surrey. Test Record - 2 Tests, 25 runs (Av. 12.50) and 1 catch.

BOWES, WILLIAM ERIC

England (born 1908) - A right-hand batman and right-arm fast bowler.He played for Yorkshire. Test Record - 15 Tests, 28 runs (Av. 4.66), 68 wickets (Av. 22.33) and 2 catches.

BOWLEY, EDWARD HENRY

England (1890-1974) - A right-handed batsman. He played for Auckland and Sussex. Test Record - 5 Tests, 252 runs (Av. 36.00) including 1 century and 2 catches.

BOYCE, KEITH DAVID

West Indies (born 1943) - He was an exciting all-rounder. He played for Barbados and Essex. Test Record - 21 Tests, 657 runs (Av. 24.33), 60 wickets (Av. 30.01) and 5 catches.

BOYCOTT, GEOFFREY

England (born. 1940) - A right-handed batsman and medium-pace bowler. He played for Yorkshire. Test Record - 108 Tests, 8,114 runs (Av. 47.72),including 22 centuries,7 wickets (Av. 54.57) and 33 catches.

BOYLE, HENRY FREDERICK

Australia (1847-1907) - A right-handed overarm bowler. He played for Victoria. Test Record - 12 Tests, 153 runs (Av. 12.75), 32 wickets (Av. 20.03) and 10 catches.

BRACEWELL, BRENDON PAUL

New Zealand (born 1959) - A right-arm fast bowler. He played for Otago. Test Record - 6 Tests, 24 runs (Av. 2.40), 14 wickets (Av. 41.78) and one catch.

BRACEWELL, JOHN GARRY

New Zealand (born 1958) - A off-break bowler and right-handed batsman. He played for Otago and Auckland. Test Record - 20 Tests, 441 runs (Av. 20.04), 58 wickets (Av. 29.86) and 16 catches.

BRADBURN, WYNNE PENNELL

New Zealand (born 1939) - A sound right-handed batsman and slow-medium change bowler. He played for Northern Districts. Test Record - 2 Tests, 62 runs, (Av. 15.50).

BRADLEY, WALTER MORRIS

England (1875-1944) - A right-arm bowler and right-handed batsman. He played for Kent. Test Record - 2 Tests, 23 runs (Av. 23.00) and 6 wickets (Av. 38.83).

BRADMAN, SIR DONALD GEORGE

Australia (born 1908) - Bradman remains the only great batsman in history who was never really out of form. He played for New South Wales. Test

Record - 52 Tests, 6,996 runs (Av.99.94) including 29 centuries, 2 wickets (Av. 36.00) and 32 catches.

BRANN, WILLIAM HENRY
South Africa (1899-1953) - A right-handed batsman. He played for Eastern Province. Test Record - 3 Tests, 71 runs (Av. 14.20) and 2 catches.

BRAUND, LEONARD CHARLES
England (1875-1955) - He was one of the greatest all-rounder. He played for Surrey. Test Record - 23 Tests, 987 runs (Av. 25.97) including 3 centuries, 47 wickets (Av. 38.51) and 39 catches.

BREARLEY, JOHN MICHAEL
England (born 1942) - A solid right-handed opening batsman. He played for Cambridge University and Middlesex. Test Record - 39 Tests, 1,442 runs (Av.22.88) and 52 catches.

BREARLEY, WALTER
England (1876-1937) - A right-arm fast bowler. He played for Lancashire. Test Record - 4 Tests, 21 runs (Av.7.00) and 17 wickets (Av. 21.11).

BRENNAN, DONALD VINCENT
England (1920-1985) - A wicket-keeper and right-handed batsman. He played for Yorkshire. Test Record - 2 Tests, 16 runs (Av. 8.00) and 1 stumping.

BRIGGS, JOHN
England (1862-1902) - He was an aggressive right-handed batsman and left-arm slow bowler. He played for Lancashire. Test Record - 33 Tests, 815 runs (Av. 18.11), 118 wickets (Av. 17.74) and 12 catches.

BRIGHT, RAYMOND JAMES
Australia (born 1954) - Left-arm spin bowler. Test Record - 22 Tests, 407 runs (Av. 14.13), 45 wickets (Av. 41.97) and 11 catches.

BRISCOE, ARTHUR WELLESLEY
South Africa (1911-1941) - A right-handed batsman. He played for Transvaal. Test Record - 2 Tests, 33 runs (Av.11.00) and 1 catch.

BROAD, BRAIN CHRISTOPHER
England (born 1957) - A left-handed opening batsman and occasional right-arm medium-paced bowler. He played for Gloucestershire, Nottinghamshire and Orange Free State. Test Record - 23 Tests, 1,579 runs, (Av.41.55) and 8 catches.

BROCKWELL, WILLIAM
England (1865-1935) - A brilliant right-handed batsman and useful medium-paced bowler. He played for Surrey. Test Record - 7 Tests, 202 runs (Av. 16.83), 5 wickets (Av. 61.80) and 6 catches.

BROMFIELD, HENRY DUDLEY
South Africa (born 1932) - A competent right-arm off-spin bowler. He played for Western Province. Test Record - 9 Tests, 59 runs (Av.11.80), 17 wickets (Av. 35.23) and 13 catches.

BROMLEY, DAVENPORT HUGH RICHARD
England (1870-1954) - He was a medium-fast left-arm bowler and a useful batsman. He played for Cambridge University. Test Record - 4 Tests, 128 runs, (Av. 21.33) and 4 wickets (Av. 24.50).

BROMLEY, ERNEST HARVEY
Australia (1912-1967) - A left-handed batsman and superb fielder. He played for Victoria. Test Record - 2 Tests, 38 runs (Av. 9.50) and 2 catches.

BROWN, DAVID JOHN
England (born 1942) - A right-arm medium-fast bowler. He played for Warwickshire. Test Record - 26 Tests, 342 runs (Av. 11.79), 79 wickets (Av. 28.31) and 7 catches.

BROWN, FREDERICK RICHARD
England (born 1910) - He was a hard-hitting right-handed batsman and leg-spin googly bowler. He played for Cambridge University, Surrey and

Northamptonshire. Test Record - 22 Tests, 734 runs (Av. 25.31), 45 wickets (Av. 31.06) and 22 catches.

BROWN, WILLIAM ALFRED
Australia (born 1912) - A right-handed opening batsman and an excellent fielder. He played for Queensland. Test Record - 22 Tests, 1,592 runs (Av. 46.82) including 4 centuries and 14 catches.

BROWNE, CYRIL RUGHERFORD
West Indies (1890-1964) - A right-handed hard-hitting batsman and medium-pace leg-break bowler. He played for Barbados and British Guiana. Test Record - 4 Tests, 176 runs (Av. 25.14), 6 wickets (Av. 48.00) and 1 catch.

BRUCE, WILLIAM
Australia (born 1864-1925) - A left-arm,medium-paced bowler and left-handed opening batsman. He played for Victoria. Test Record - 14 Tests, 702 runs (Av. 29.25), 12 wickets (Av. 36.66) and 12 catches.

BUCKENHAM, CLAUDE PERCIVCAL
England (1876-1937) - He bowled very fast with a good high delivery and a hard-hitting batsman. He played for Essex. Test Record - 4 Tests, 43 runs (Av.6.14), 21 wickets (Av. 28.23) and 2 catches.

BURGE, PETER JOHN PARNELL
Australia (born 1932) - An attractive right-handed batsman. He played for Queensland. Test Record - 42 Tests, 2,290 runs (Av. 38.16) including 4 centuries and 23 catches.

BURGESS, MARK GORDON
New Zealand (born 1944) - A right-handed batsman. He played for Auckland. Test Record - 50 Tests, 2,684 runs (Av.31.20) including 5 centuries and 34 catches.

BURKE, JAMES WALLACE
Australia (1930-1979) - He was a right-handed batsman. He played for New South Wales. Test Record - 24 Tests, 1,280 runs (Av. 34.59) including 3 centuries and 8 wickets (Av. 28.75).

BURKE, SYDNEY FRANK
South Africa (born 1934) - A right-arm medium-fast bowler. He played for Orange Free State. Test Record - 2 Tests, 42 runs (Av. 14.00) and 11 wickets (Av. 23.36).

BURN, EDWIN JAMES KENNETH
Australia (1862-1956) - An attractive right-handed batsman. He played for Wellington and Tasmania. Test Record - 2 Tests, 41 runs (Av. 10.25).

BURTT, THOMAS BROWNING
New Zealand (born 1915) - A left-arm slow bowler and a left-handed batsman. He played for Canterbury. Test Record - 10 Tests, 252 runs (Av.21.00), 33 wickets (Av. 35.45) and 2 catches.

BUTCHER, ROLAND ORLANDO
England (born 1953) - A very sound right-hand batsman. He played with modest success for Barbados in the 1974-75. Test Record - 3 Tests, 71 runs (Av. 14.20) and 3 catches.

BUTT, HARRY RIGDEN
England (1965-1928) - A right-handed batsman and wicket-keeper. He played for Sussex. Test Record - 3 Tests, 22 runs (Av. 7.33) and 2 dismissals (1 ct, 1 st).

BYNOE, MICHAEL ROBIN
West Indies (born 1941)- A stylish right-handed opening batsman and left-arm medium-pace bowler. He played for Barbados. Test Record - 4 Tests, 111 runs (Av. 18.50) and 4 catches.

CAIRNS, BERNARD LANCE
New Zealand (born 1949) - A right-arm medium-pace bowler. He played for Central Districts. Test Record - 43 Tests, 928 runs (Av. 16.28), 130 wickets (Av. 32.91) and 30 catches.

CALLAWAY, SYDNEY THOMAS
Australia (1868-1923) - A splendid batsman when in form and a medium-fast bowler. He played for New South Wales. Test Record - 3 Tests, 87 runs (Av. 17.40) and 6 wickets (Av. 23.66).

CALTHORPE, HON. FREDERICK SOMEREST GOUCH
England (1892-1935) - He was an attractive right-handed batsman and a medium-pace bowler. He played for Cambridge University and Sussex. Test Record - 4 Tests, 129 runs (Av. 18.42), 1 wicket (Av. 91.00) and 2 catches.

CAMACHO, GEORGE STEPHEN
West Indies (born 1945) - A very sound right-handed opening batsman. He played for Guyana. Test Record - 11 Tests, 640 runs (Av. 29.09) and 4 catches.

CAMERON, FRANCIS JAMES
West Indies (born 1923) - A right-handed batsman and off-break bowler. He played for Jamaica. Test Record - 5 Tests, 151 runs (Av. 25.16) and 3 wickets (Av. 92.66).

CAMERON, FRANCIS JAMES
New Zealand (born 1932) - A wily right-arm medium-fast bowler. He played for Otago. Test Record - 19 Tests, 116 runs (Av. 11.60) and 61 wickets (Av. 30.31).

CAMERON, HORACE BRAKENRIDGE
South Africa (1905-1935) - A high ranking wicket-keeper and batsman. He played for Transvaal. Test Record - 26 Tests, 1,239 runs (Av. 30.21) and 51 dismissals (39ct, 12st).

CAMERON, JOHN HENSLEY
West Indies (born 1914) - A right-handed batsman, reliable fielder and off-break bowler. He played for Cambridge University and Jamaica. Test Record - 2 Tests, 6 runs (Av. 2.00) and 3 wickets (Av. 29.33).

CAMPBELL, THOMAS
South Africa (1882-1924) - A competent wicket-keeper. He played for Transvaal. Test Record - 5 Tests, 90 runs (Av. 15.00) and 8 dismissals (7ct, 1st).

CAREW, GEORGE MCDONALD
West Indies (1910-1974) - A right - handed batsman. He played for Barbados. Test Record - 4 Tests, 170 runs (Av. 28.33) including 1 century and 1 catch.

CAREW, MICHAEL CONRAD
West Indies (born 1937) - A left-handed opening batsman and a useful right-arm leg-break bowler. He played for Trinidad. Test Record - 19 Tests, 1,127 runs (Av. 34.15) including 1 century, 8 wickets (Av. 54.62) and 13 catches.

CARKEEK, WILLIAM
Australia (1878-1937) - A left-handed batsman and a useful wicket-keeper. He played for Victoria. Test Record - 6 Tests, 16 runs (Av. 5.33) and 6 dismissals (6ct).

CARLSON, PHILIP HENRY
Australia (born 1951) - A useful medium-pace bowler, swing bowler and gifted batsman. He played for Queensland. Test Record - 2 Tests, 23 runs (Av. 5.75), 2 wickets (Av. 49.50) and 2 catches.

CARLSTEIN, PETER RUDOLPH
South Africa (born 1938) - A fine fielder, right-handed batsman. He played for Orange Free State. Test Record - 8 Tests, 190 runs (Av. 14.61) and 3 catches.

CARR, ARTHUR WILLIAM
England (1893-1963) - A fine right-handed attacking batsman. He played for Nottinghamshire. Test Record - 11 Tests, 237 runs (Av. 19.75) and 3 catches.

CARR, DONALD BRYCE
England (born 1926) - A right-handed batsman and

a very good slow left-arm bowler. He played for Oxford University and Derbyshire. Test Record - 2 Tests, 135 runs (Av. 33.75) and 2 wickets (Av. 70.00).

CARTER, CLAUDE PAGET

South Africa (1881-1952) - He was a left-arm slow bowler and also a hard-hitting batsman. He played for Natal. Test Record - 10 Tests, 181 runs (Av. 18.10), 28 wickets (Av. 24.78) and 2 catches.

CARTER, HANSON

Australia (1878-1948) - He was one of the best wicket-keepers and also a useful batsman. He played for New South Wales. Test Record - 28 Tests, 873 runs (Av. 22.97) and 65 dismissals (44ct, 21st).

CARTWRIGHT, THOMAS WILLIAM

England (born 1935) - He was a medium-pace bowler and also an effective batsman. He played for Warwickshire. Test Record - 5 Tests, 26 runs (Av. 5.20), 15 wickets (Av. 36.26) and 2 catches.

CATTERALL, ROBERT HECTOR

South Africa (1900-1961) - He was a right-handed batsman. He played for Natal. Test Record - 24 Tests, 1,555 runs (Av. 37.92) including 3 centuries 7 wickets (Av, 23.14) and 12 catches.

CAVE, HENRY BUTLER

New Zealand (born 1922) - He was an economical right-arm medium- pace bowler. He played for Wellington. Test Record - 19 Tests, 229 runs (Av. 8.80), 34 wickets (Av. 43.12) and 8 catches.

CHALLENOR, GEORGE

West Indies (1888-1947) - He was an opening batsman and off-side player of perfect timing. He played for Barbados. Test Record - 3 Tests, 101 runs (Av. 16.83).

CHANDRASEKHAR, BHAGWAT SUBRAHMANYA

India (born 1945) - A right-handed batsman and right-arm googly bowler. He played for Mysore. Test Record- 58 Tests, 167 runs, 242 wickets (Av.29.74) and 25 catches.

CHAPMAN, ARTHUR PERCY FRANK

England (1900-1961) - He was a left-handed batsman. He played for Cambridge University and Kent. Test Record - 26 Tests, 925 runs (Av. 28.90) including 1 century and 32 catches.

CHAPPELL, GREGORY STEPHEN

Australia (born 1948) - A right-handed batsman and right-arm medium-pace bowler. He played for South Australia and Somerest. Test Record - 87 Tests, 7,110 runs (Av. 53.86) including 24 centuries, 47 wickets (Av. 40.70) and 122 catches.

CHAPPELL, IAN MICHAEL

Australia (born 1943) - A right-handed batsman and useful leg-spin bowler. He played for South Australia. Test Record - 75 Tests, 5,345 runs (Av. 42.42) including 14 centuries, 20 wickets (Av. 65.80) and 105 catches.

CHAPPELL, TREVOR MARTIN

Australia (born 1952)- A right-handed batsman and right-arm medium-paced bowler. He played for South Australia. Test Record - 3 Tests, 79 runs (Av. 15.80) and 2 catches.

CHAPPLE, MURRAY ERNEST

New Zealand ((born 1930) - A steady, stroke making right-handed batsman and a left-arm change slow bowler. He played for Canterbury. Test Record - 14 Tests, 497 runs (Av. 19.11).

CHARLTON, DR PERCIE CHATOR

Australia (1867-1954) - He was a batsman and fast-medium bowler. He played for New South Wales. Test REcord - 2 Tests, 29 runs (Av. 7.25) and 3 Wickets (Av. 8.00).

CHARLWOOD, HENRY RUPERT JAMES

England (1846-1888) - He was the most useful and

the most dashing batsman. He played for Sussex. Test Record - 2 Tests, 63 runs (Av. 15.75).

CHATFIELD, EWEN JOHN
New Zealand (born 1951)- A right-arm medium-fast bowler. He plays for Wellington. Test Record - 43 Test, 180 runs (Av. 8.57), 123 wickets (Av. 32.15) and 16 catches.

CHAUHAN, CHETANDRA PRATAP SINGH
India (born 1947) - A right-handed opening batsman and right-arm off-break bowler. He played for Delhi and Maharashtra. Test Record - 40 Tests, 2,084 runs (Av. 31.57), 2 wickets (Av. 53.00) and 38 catches.

CHEETHAM, JOHN ERSKINE
South Africa (1920-1980) - A captain and very capable batsman. He played for Western Province. Test Record - 24 Tests, 883 runs (Av. 23.86) and 13 catches.

CHIPPERFIELD, ARTHUR GORDON
Australia (Born 1905) - He was a solid batsman and spin bowler. He played for New South Wales. Test Record - 14 Tests, 552 runs (Av. 32.47) including 1 century, 5 wicket (Av. 87.40) and 15 catches.

CHOWDHURY, NIRODE RANJAN
India (1923-1979) - A right-handed batsman and right-arm medium-fast and off-break bowler. Test Record - 2 Test, 3 runs (Av. 3.00).

CHRISTIANI, ROBERT JULLIAN
West Indies (born 1920) - A right-handed batsman and off-break bowler. He played for British Guiana. Test Record - 22 Tests, 896 runs (Av. 26.35) including 1 century, 3 wickets (Av. 36.00), 21 dismissals (19ct, 2st).

CHRISTY, JAMES ALEXANDER JOSEPH
South Africa (1904-1971) - A powerful right-handed batsman and fast bowler. He played for Transvaal and Queensland. Test Record - 10 Tests, 618 runs (Av. 34.33) including 1 century, 2 wickets (Av. 46.00) and 3 catches.

CHUBB, GEOFFREY WALTER ASHTON
South Africa (1911-1982) - A right-arm medium-pace bowler. He played for Border. Test Record - 5 Tests, 63 runs (Av. 10.50) and 21 wickets (Av. 27.47).

CLARK, EDWARD WINCHESTER
England (1902-1982) - He was left-arm fast bowler and right-handed batsman. He played for Northamptonshire and Cambridgeshire. Test Record - 8 Tests, 36 runs (Av. 9.00) and 32 Wickets (Av. 28.09).

CLARK, WAYNE MAXWELL
Australia (born 1953) - A strong medium-fast right-arm swing bowler. He played for Western Australia. Test Record - 10 Tests, 98 runs (Av. 5.76) 43 wickets (Av. 28.75) and 6 catches.

CLARKE, DR. CARLOS BERTRAM
West Indies (born 1918) - He was a right-arm slow leg-break bowler. He played for Barbados. Test Record - 3 Tests, 3 runs (Av. 1.00) and 6 Wickets (Av. 43.50).

CLARKE, SYLVESTER THEOPHILUS
West Indies (born 1954) - A former carpenter and a genuinely fast bowler. Test Record - 11 Tests, 172 runs (Av. 15.63), 42 wickets (Av. 27.88) and 2 catches.

CLOSE, DENNIS BRIAN
England (born 1931) - He was a gifted left-handed bat, and right-arm medium-pace bowler. He played for Yorkshire and Somerset. Test Record - 22 Tests, 887 runs (Av. 25.34), 18 wickets (Av. 29.55) and 24 catches.

COEN, STANLEY KEPPEL
South Africa (1902-1967) - He was a right-handed batsman. He played for Transvaal and Border. Test Record - 2 Tests, 101 runs (Av. 50.50).

COLAH, SORABJI HORMASJI M.
India (1902-1950) - A right-handed batsman and right-arm medium pace bowler. He played for Western India. Test Record - 2 Tests, 69 runs (Av. 17.25) and 2 catches.

COLDWELL, LEONARD JOHN
England (born 1933) - A medium-fast, right-arm inswing bowler. He played for Devon and Worcestershire. Test Record - 7 Tests, 9 runs (Av. 4.50) and 22 wickets (Av. 27.72).

COLLEY, DAVID JOHN
Australia (born 1947) - A right-arm fast-medium bowler and late order batsman. He played for New South Wales. Test Record - 3 Tests, 84 runs (Av. 21.00), 6 wickets (Av. 52.00) and 1 catch.

COLLINGE, RICHARD OWEN
New Zealand (born 1946) - A left-arm medium-fast bowler and a right-handed batsman. He played for Central Districts and Wellington. Test Record - 35 Tests, 533 runs (Av. 14.40), 116 wickets (Av. 29.25) and 10 catches.

COLLINS, HERBERT LESLIE
Australia (1889-1959) - He was a right-handed batsman and a slow left-arm bowler. He played for New South Wales. Test Record - 19 Tests, 1,352 runs (Av. 45.06) including 4 centuries, 4 wickets (Av. 63.00) and 13 catches.

COMMAILLE, JOHN MCILLWAIN MOORE
South Africa (1883-1956) - He was a right-handed opening batsman. He played for Western Province. Test Record - 12 Tests, 355 runs (Av. 16.90) and 1 catch.

COMPTON, DENIS CHARLES SCOTT
England (born 1918) - He was a dazzling right-handed batsman, left-arm unorthodox spin bowler. He played for Middlesex. Test Record - 78 Tests, 5,807 runs (Av. 50.06) including 17 centuries, 25 wickets (Av. 56.40) and 49 catches.

CONEY, JEREMY VERNON
New Zealand (born 1952) - A right-handed batsman and medium-pace bowler. He played for Wellington. Test Record - 52 Tests, 2,668 runs (Av. 37.57) including 3 centuries, 27 wickets (Av. 35.77) and 64 catches.

CONNOLLY, ALAN NORMAN
Australia (born 1939) - A right-arm fast-medium bowler. Test Record - 29 Tests, 260 runs (Av. 10.40), 102 wickets (Av. 29.22) and 17 catches.

CONSTANTINE, SIR LEARIE NICHOLAS
West Indies (1902-1971) - He was great all-rounder, right-handed hitter with powerful drives. He played for Trinidad and Barbados. Test Record - 18 Tests, 635 runs (Av. 19.24) 58 wickets (Av. 30.10) and 28 catches.

CONTRACTOR, NARIMAN JAMSHEDJI
India (born 1934) - A left-handed opening batsman and right-arm medium-pace bowler. He played for Gujarat and Railways. Test Record - 31 Tests, 1,611 runs (Av.31.58) including 1 century and 18 catches.

COOK, GEOFFREY
England (born 1951) - A right-handed batsman and slow left-arm bowler. He played for Northamptonshire. Test Record - 7 Tests, 203 runs (Av. 15.61).

COOK, NICHOLAS
England (born 1956) - An accurate slow left-arm spin bowler. He played for Leicestershire. Test Record - 9 Tests, 101 runs (Av. 7.21), 40 wickets (Av. 30.30) and 5 catches.

COOPER, WILLIAM HENRY
Australia (1849-1939) - He was a right-arm, slow, leg break bowler. He played for Victoria. Test Record - 2 Tests, 13 runs (Av. 6.50), 9 wickets (Av. 25.11) and 1 catch.

COPE, GEOFFREY ALAN
England (born 1947) - He was off-spin bowler,

determined tail-end batsman. He played for Yorkshire and Leicestershire. Test Record- 3 Tests, 40 runs (Av. 13.33), 8 wickets (Av. 34.62) and 1 catch.

CORLING, GRAHAME EDWARD

Australia (born 1941) - An opening right-arm fast-medium bowler. He played for New South Wales. Test Record - 5 Tests, 5 runs (Av. 1.66) and 12 wickets (Av. 37.25).

CORNFORD, WALTER LATTER

England (1900-1964) - He was one of the best wicket-keepers. He played for Sussex.
Test Record - 4 Tests, 36 runs (Av. 9.00) and 8 dismissals (5ct, 3st).

COSIER, GARY JOHN

Australia (born 1953)- A right-handed batsman and also a very useful slow-medium bowler. He played for Victoria. Test Record - 18 Tests, 897 runs (Av. 28.93) including 2 centuries, 5 wickets (Av. 68.20) and 14 catches.

COTTAM, ROBERT MICHAEL HENRY

England (born 1944) - A tall, right-arm medium-fast bower. He played for Hampshire and Northamptonshire. Test Record - 4 Tests, 27 runs (Av. 6.75), 14 wickets (Av. 23.35) and 2 catches.

COTTER, ALBERT

Australia (1883-1917) - He was a right-handed batsman and medium-fast bowler. He played for New South Wales. Test Record - 21 Tests, 457 runs (Av. 13.05), 89 wickets (Av. 28.64) and 8 catches.

COWANS, NORMAN GEORGE

England (born 1961) - He was a right-arm medium-fast bowler. He played for Middlesex.
Test Record - 19 Tests, 175 runs (Av. 7.95) and 51 wickets (Av. 39.27).

COWDREY, CHRISTOPHER STUART

England (born 1957) - A useful medium-pace bowler. He played for Kent. Test Record - 6 Tests, 101 runs (Av. 14.42), 4 wickets (Av. 77.25) and 5 catches.

COWDREY, MICHAEL COLIN

England (born 1932) - He was an attacking batsman and leg-spin bowler. He played for Oxford University and Kent. Test Record - 114 Tests, 7,624 runs (Av. 44.06) including 22 centuries and 120 catches.

COWIE, JOHN

New Zealand (born 1912) - A well-built right-arm fast bowler. He played for Auckland. Test Record - 9 Tests, 90 runs (Av. 10.00), 45 Wickets (Av. 21.53) and 3 catches.

COWPER, ROBERT MASKEW

Australia (born 1940) - He was a well-built left-handed batsman and a useful off-spin bowler. He played for Victoria and Western Australia. Test Record - 27 Tests, 2,061 runs (Av. 46.84) including 5 centuries, 36 wickets (Av. 31.63) and 21 catches.

COX, JOSEPH LOVELL

South Africa (1886-1971) - He was a right-arm fast-medium pace bowler. He played for Natal. Test Record - 3 Tests, 17 runs (Av. 3.40) and 4 wickets (Av. 61.25).

CRANSTON, KENNETH

England (born 1917) - A forcing right-handed batsman and fast-medium bowler. He played for Lancashire. Test Record - 8 Tests, 209 runs (Av. 14.92), 18 wickets (Av. 25.61) and 3 catches.

CRAPP, JOHN FREDERICK

England (1912 - 1981) - He was an extremely sound left-handed batsman. He played for Gloucestershire. Test Record - 7 Tests, 319 runs (Av. 29.00) and 7 catches.

CRAWFORD, JOHN NEVILLE

England (1986 - 1963) - A right-handed batsman and a medium-pace bowler. He played for Surrey. Test Record - 12 Tests, 469 runs (Av. 22.33), 39 wickets (Av. 29.48) and 13 catches.

CRAWFORD, WILLIAM PATRICK ANTHONY

Australia (born 1933) - A right-arm medium-fast bowler and right-handed batsman. He played for New South Wales. Test Record - 4 Tests, 53 runs (Av. 17.66), 7 wickets (Av. 15.28) and 1 catch.

CRISP, ROBERT JAMES

South Africa (born 1911) - A right-arm medium pace bowler and right-handed batsman. He played for Rhodesia and Western Province. Test Record - 9 Tests, 123 runs (Av. 10.25) and 20 wickets (Av. 37.25).

CROFT, COLIN EVERTON HUNTE

West Indies (born 1953) - A right-arm medium-fast bowler. He played for Guyana and Lancashire. Test Record - 27 Tests, 158 runs (Av. 10.53), 125 wickets (Av 23.30) and 8 catches.

CROMB, IAN BURNS

New Zealand (1905-1984) - He was a right-arm fast-medium bowler and a late-order batsman. He played for Canterbury. Test Record - 5 Tests, 123 runs (Av. 20.50), 8 wickets (Av. 55.25) and 1 catch.

CROWE, JEFFREY JOHN

New Zealand (born 1958) - A right-handed batsman. He played for Auckland. Test Record - 37 Tests, 1,536 runs (Av. 26.48), including 3 centuries and 40 catches.

CROWE, MARTIN DAVID

New Zealand (born 1962) - A right-handed sound batsman. He plays for Auckland. Test Record - 44 Tests, 3,035 runs (Av. 45.29) including 10 centuries, 13 wickets (Av. 46.69) and 46 catches.

CUNIS, ROBERT SMITH

New Zealand (born 1941) - A right-arm fast-medium bowler and right-handed batsman. He played for Auckland. Test Record - 20 Tests, 295 runs (Av. 12.82), 51 wickets (Av. 37.00) and 1 catch.

CURNOW, SYDNEY HARRY

South Africa (1907-1986) - A right-handed impressive batsman. He played for Transvaal. Test Record - 7 Tests, 168 runs (Av. 12.00) and 5 catches.

D'ARCY, JOHN WILLIAM

New Zealand (born 1936) - He was a right-handed opening batsman . He played for Wellington and Otago. Test Record - 5 Tests, 136 runs (Av. 13.60).

D'OLIVEIRA, BASIL LEWIS

England (born 1931) - He was a right-handed batsman and medium- pace bowler. Test Record - 44 Tests, 2,484 runs (Av. 40.06) including 5 centuries, 47 wickets (Av. 39.55) and 29 catches.

D'SOUZA,ANTAO

Pakistan (born 1939) - A very useful right-handed medium-fast bowler sometimes bowled slower off-break and a tail-end batsman. He played for Karachi. Test Record - 6 Tests, 76 runs (Av. 38.00), 17 wickets (Av. 43.82) and 3 catches.

DA, COSTA OSCAR C.

West Indies (1907-1936) - A very talented all-rounder and a reliable right-handed batsman, useful medium pace bowler and versatile fielder. He played for Jamaica. Test Record - 5 Tests, 153 runs (Av. 19.12) and 3 wickets (Av. 58.33) and 3 catches.

DALTON, ERIC LONDESBROUGH

South Africa (1906-1981) - He was a determined and hard-hitting right-handed batsman and useful change bowler. He played for Natal. Test Record - 15 Tests, 698 runs (Av. 31.72) including 2 centuries, 12 wickets (Av. 40.83) and 5 catches.

DANIEL, WAYNE WENDELL

West Indies (born 1956) - He was a right-handed strong fast bowler. He played for Barbados and Middlesex. Test Record - 10 Tests, 46 runs (Av. 6.57), 36 wickets (Av. 25.27) and 4 catches.

DARLING, HON. JOSEPH
Australia (1870-1946) - He was a great left-handed batsman. He played for South Australia. Test Record - 34 Tests, 1,657 runs (Av. 28.56) including 3 centuries and 27 catches.

DARLING, LEONARD STUART
Australia (born 1909) - He was a left-handed batsman. He played for Victoria. Test Record - 12 Tests, 474 runs (Av. 27.88) and 8 catches.

DARLING, WARRICK MAXWELL
Australia (born 1957) - A right-handed opening batsman and brilliant cover fielder and also a brilliant hooker and cover driver. He played for South Australia. Test Record - 14 Tests, 697 runs (Av. 26.80) and 5 catches.

DAVIDSON, ALAN KEITH
Australia (Born 1929) - He was a left-handed batsman and left left-handed fast bowler. He played for New South Wales. Test Record - 44 Test, 1,328 runs (Av. 24.59), 186 wickets (Av. 20.53) and 42 catches.

DAVIES, ERIC QUAIL
South Africa (1909-1976) - A right-arm out-swinger fast bowler. He played for Eastern Province, Transvaal and North-Eastern Transvaal. Test Record - 5 Tests, 9 runs (Av. 1.80) and 7 Wickets (Av. 68.71).

DAVIS, BRYAN ALAN
West Indies (born 1940) - A sound right-handed batsman opened the batting, an occasional leg-break bowler and an excellent close-in fielder. He played for Trinidad and Glamorgan. Test Record - 4 Tests, 245 runs (Av. 30.62) and 1 catch.

DAVIS, CHARLES ALAN
West Indies (born 1944) - A sound slow right-handed batsman and useful medium-pace bowler. He played for Trinidad. Test Record - 15 Tests, 1,301 runs (Av. 54.20) including 4 centuries, 2 wickets (Av. 165.00) and 4 catches.

DAVIS, IAN CHARLES
Australia (Born 1953) - He was right-handed opening or middle-order batsman. He played for New South Wales and Queensland. Test Record - 15 Tests, 692 runs (Av. 26.61) including 1 century and 9 catches.

DAVIS, WINSTON WALTER
West Indies (born 1958) - He was a right-arm fast bowler. He plays for Windward Islands, Glamorgan and Tasmania. Test Record - 11 Tests, 157 runs (Av. 19.62) 32 wickets (Av. 33.81) and 7 catches.

DAWSON, EDWARD WILLIAM
England (1904-1979) - A very sound right-handed batsman. He played for Cambridge University and Leicestershire. Test Record - 5 Tests, 175 runs (Av. 19.44).

DAWSON, OSCAR CHARLES
South Africa (born 1919) - He was a right-handed batsman and also a medium-pace, out-swing bowler. He played for Natal and Border. Test Record - 9 Tests, 293 runs (Av. 20.92) 10 wickets (Av. 57.80) and 10 catches.

DE, MEL ASANTHA LAKDASA FRANCIS
Sri Lanka (born 1959) - A right-handed medium-fast bowler and a good out-swinger. He plays for Sinhalese. Test Record - 17 Tests, 326 runs (Av. 14.17), 59 wickets (Av. 36.94) and 9 catches.

DE SILVA, ELLEWELAKANKANANGE ASOKA RANJIT
Sri Lanka (born 1956) - A left-handed tail-ender leg-spin bowler. He played for Colombo. Test Record - 5 Tests, 72 runs (Av. 14.40) and 2 wickets. (206.50).

DE SILVA, GINIGALGODANGE RAMBA AJITH
Sri Lanka (born 1952) - He was a very steady, orthodox slow left-arm bowler and useful late-order left-handed batsman. He played for Bloomfield. Test Record - 4 Tests, 41 runs (Av. 8.20) and 7 wickets (Av. 55.00).

DE SILVA, PINNADUWAGE ARAVINDA

Sri Lanka (born 1965) - A tall right-handed batsman and loves cut and hook strokes. He plays or Nondescripts. Test Record - 15 Tests, 660 runs (Av. 25.38) including 2 centuries and 8 catches.

DEANE, HUBERT GOUVAINE

South Africa (1895-1939) - He was an attractiv fast-scoring right-handed batsman. He played for Natal and Transvaal. Test Record - 17 Tests, 628 runs (Av. 25.12) and 8 catches.

DEMPSTER, CHARLES STEWART

New Zealand (1903-1974) - As an opening batsman Dempster was one of the finest New Zealand ever produced, and a brilliant fielder. He played for Leicestershire and Wellington. Test Record - 10 Tests, 723 runs (Av. 65.72) including 2 centuries and 2 catches.

DENNESS, MICHAEL HENRY

England (born 1940) - A right-handed attacking batsman. He played for Scotland, Kent and Essex. Test Record - 28 Tests, 1,669 runs (Av. 39.69) including 4 centuries and 28 catches.

DENTON, DAVID

England (1874-1950) - He was a right-handed batsman. He played for Yorkshire. Test Record - 11 Tests, 424 runs (Av. 20.19) including 1 century and 8 catches.

DESAI, RAMAKANT BHIKAJI

India (born 1939) - A right-handed batsman and a right-arm medium-fast bowler. He played for Bombay. Test Record - 28 Tests, 418 runs (Av. 13.48), 74 wickets (Av. 37.31) and 9 catches.

DESILVA, DANDENIYAGE SOMACHANDRA

Sri Lanka (born 1944) - He was a right-arm leg-spin bowler and a useful right-handed batsman. He plays for Moratuwa, Lincolnshire and Shorpshire. Test Record - 12 Tests, 406 runs (Av. 21.36), 37 wickets (Av. 36.40) and 5 catches.

DEWDNEY, DAVID THOMAS

West Indies (born 1933) - A tall well-developed right-arm fast bowler. He played for Jamaica. Test Record - 9 Tests, 17 runs (Av. 2.42) and 21 wickets (Av. 38.42).

DEWES, JOHN GORDON

England (born 1926) - A left-handed batsman and a fine outfielder. He played for Cambridge University and Middlesex. Test Record - 5 Tests, 121 runs (Av. 12.10).

DEXTER, EDWARD RALPH

England (born 1935) - A right-handed batsman and useful medium-pace bowler. He played for Cambridge University. Test Record - 62 Tests, 4,502 uns (Av. 47.89) including 9 centuries, 66 wickets Av. 34.93) and 29 catches.

IAS, ROY LUKE

S Lanka (born 1952) - A right-handed batsman a right-arm medium-paced bowler. He played for Shalese. Test Record - 20 Tests, 1,285 runs (Av. 3(1) including 3 centuries, and 6 catches.

DIK, ARTHUR EDWARD

NeZealand (born 1936) - An outstanding wicket-keer and right-handed batsman. He played for Ota and Wellington. Test Record - 17 Tests, 370 runsAv. 14.23) and 51 dismissals (47ct, 4st).

DILVAR, HUSSAIN DR.

India 907-1967) - A right-handed batsman and wickeeeper. He played for Central India. Test Recor 3 Tests, 254 runs (Av. 42.33) and 7 dismiss (6ct, 1st).

DIVE(A, RAMES VITHALDAO

India rn 1923) - A right-handed batsman and a righ m medium-fast bowler. He played for BombaTest Record - 5 Tests, 60 runs (Av. 12.00), 11 wic (Av. 32.81) and 5 catches.

DOLLERY, HORACE EDGAR

England (born 1914) - A right-handed batsman and useful deputy wicket-keeper. He played for Berkshire and Warwickshire. Test Record - 4 Tests, 72 runs (Av. 10.28) and 1 catch.

DOSHI, DILIP RAZAKLAL

India (born 1947) - A left-arm slow spin bowler and left-handed batsman. He played for Bengal. Test record - 33 Tests, 129 runs (Av. 4.60), 114 wickets (Av. 30.71) and 10 catches.

DOUGLAS, JOHN WILLIAM HENRY TYLER

England (1882-1930) - He was a right-handed batsman and left-arm bowler. He played for Essex. Test Record - 23 Tests, 962 runs (Av. 29.15) including 1 century,45 wickets (Av. 33.02) and 9 catches.

DOWLING, GRAHAM THORNE

New Zealand (born 1937) - A lean athletic, righ handed batsman. He played for Canterbury. Tt Record - 39 Tests, 2,306 runs (Av. 31.16) includg 3 centuries and 23 catches.

DOWNTON, PAUL

England (born 1957) - A wicket-keeper and ht-handed batsman. He plays for Kent and Middlex. Test Record - 27 Tests, 701 runs (Av. 19.47) a 66 dismissals (61ct, 5st).

DRAPER, RONALD GEORGE

South Africa (1926) - A wicket-keeper but prarily a fast-scoring right-handed opening batsn. He played for Eastern Province and Griqualand West. Test Record - 2 Tests, 25 runs (Av. 8.33).

DUCKWORTH, GEORGE

England (1901-1966) - A wicket-keeper a right-handed batsman. He played for Lancash. Test Record - 24 Tests, 234 runs (Av. 14.62nd 60 dismissals (45ct, 15st).

DUFF, REGINALD ALEXANDER

Autralia (1878-1911) - A right-handed batsman. Heplayed for New South Wales. Test Record - 22 Tsts, 1,317 runs (Av. 35.59) including 2 centuries 4 vickets (Av. 21.25) and 14 catches.

IUJON, PETER JEFFREY

Vest Indies (born 1956) - A right-handed batsman nd wicket-keeper. He plays for Jamaica. Test Record 64 Tests, 2,885 runs (Av. 36.06) including 5 centuries and 208 dismissals (203ct, 5st).

DULEEPSINHJI, KUMAR SHRI

England (1905-1959) - A right-handed batsman and leg-break bowler. He played for Cambridge University. Test Record - 12 Tests, 995 runs (Av. 58.52) including 3 centuries and 10 catches.

DURRANI, SALIM AZIZ

India (born 1934) - A left- handed batsman and left-arm slow spin bowler. He played for Gujarat and Rajasthan. Test record - 29 Tests, 1,202 runs (Av. 25.04) including 1 century, 75 wickets (Av.35.42) and 14 catches.

DYER, DENNIS VICTOR

England (born 1914) - A right-handed opening batsman. He played for Natal. Test Record - 3 Tests, 96 runs (Av. 16.00).

DYMOCK, GEOFFREY

Australia (born 1945) - A medium-fast left-arm opening bowler. He played for Queensland. Test Record - 21 Tests, 236 runs (Av. 9.44) 78 wickets (Av. 27.18) and 1 catch.

DYSON, JOHN

Australia (born 1954) - A right-handed opening batsman. He played for New South Wales. Test Record - 30 Tests, 1,359 runs (Av. 26.64) including 2 centuries and 10 catches.

EDGAR, BRUCE ADRIAN

New Zealand (born 1956) - A left-handed batsman. He played for Wellington. Test Record - 39 Tests, 1,958 runs (Av. 30.59) including 3 centuries and 14 catches.

EDMONDS, PHILIPPE HENRI

England (born 1951) - An orthodox slow left-arm spinner, hard-hitting middle-order batsman. He played for Cambridge University and Middlesex. Test Record - 41 Tests, 765 runs (Av. 17.79) 106 wickets (Av. 33.16) and 37 catches.

EDRICH, JOHN HUGH

England (born 1937) - He was a left-handed batsman. He played for Surrey. Test Record - 77 Tests, 5,138 runs (Av. 43.54) and 43 catches.

EDRICH, WILLIAM JOHN

England (1916-1986) - He was a right-handed batsman. He played for Norfolk and Middlesex. Test Record - 39 Tests, 2,440 runs (Av. 40.00) including 6 centuries, 41 wickets (Av. 41.29) and 39 catches.

EDWARDS, GRAHAM NEIL

New Zealand (born 1955) - A short heavily built wicket-keeper, very hard-hitting right-handed batsman. He played for Central Districts. Test Record - 8 Tests, 377 runs (Av. 25.13) and 7 dismissals (7ct).

EDWARDS, RICHARD MARTIN

West Indies (born 1940) - A right-arm fast-medium bowler. He played for Barbados. Test Record - 5 Tests, 65 runs (Av. 9.28) and 18 wickets (Av. 34.77).

EDWARDS, ROSS

Australia (born 1942) - A right-handed batsman and a superb cover fielder. He played for Western Australia and New South Wales. Test Record - 20 Tests, 1,171 runs (Av. 40.37) including 2 centuries and 7 catches.

EDWARDS, WALTER JOHN

Australia (born 1950) - He was an attractive left-handed opening batsman. He played for Western Australia. Test Record - 3 Tests, 68 runs (Av. 11.33).

ELLISON, RICHARD MARK

England (born 1959) - A right-arm swing bowler and a left-handed middle-order batsman. He played for Kent and Tasmania. Test Record - 11 Tests, 202 runs (Av. 13.46), 35 wickets (Av. 29.94) and 2 catches.

EMBUREY, JOHN ERNEST

England (born 1952) - A tall off-spiner. He played for Middlesex and Western Province. Test Record - 57 Tests, 1,409 runs (Av. 21.89), 130 wickets (Av. 30.61) and 33 catches.

ENDEAN, WILLIAM RUSSELL

South Africa (born 1924) - A fine batsman and all-round fielder . He played for Transvaal. Test Record - 28 Tests, 1,630 runs (Av. 33.95) including 3 centuries and 41 catches.

ENGINEER, FAROKH MANEKSHA

India (born 1938)- A right-handed batsman and wicket-keeper. Test Record - 46 Tests, 2,611 runs (Av.31.08) including 2 centuries and 82 dismissals (66ct, 16st).

EVANS, THOMAS GODFREY

England (born 1920) - A right-handed batsman and wicket-keeper. He played for Kent. Test Record - 91 Tests, 2,439 runs (Av. 20.49) including 2 centuries and 219 dismissals (173ct, 46st).

FANE, FREDERICK LUTHER

England (1875-1960) - A fine attractive right-handed, batsman . He played for Oxford University. Test Record - 14 Tests, 682 runs (Av. 26.33) including 1 century, and 6 catches.

FAULKENER, MAJOR GEORGE AUBREY

South Africa (1881-1930) - A right-handed batsman.

He played for Transvaal. Test Record - 25 Tests, 1,754 runs (Av. 40.79) including 4 centuries, 82 wickets (Av. 26.58) and 20 catches.

FAVELL, LESLIE ERNEST
Australia (born 1929) - A stocky hard-hitting right-handed batsman. He played for South Australia. Test Record - 19 Tests, 757 runs (Av. 27.03) including 1 century and 9 catches.

FAZAL, MAHMOOD
Pakistan (born 1927) - A right-arm fast-medium pace bowler and a very good fielder. He played for Lahore. Test Record - 34 Tests, 620 runs (Av. 14.09), 139 wickets (Av. 24.70) and 11 catches.

FENDER, PERCY GEORGE HERBERT
England (1892-1985) - A right-handed batsman and slow leg-break bowler. He played for Sussex and Surrey. Test Record - 13 Tests, 380 runs (Av. 19.00), 29 wickets (Av. 40.86) and 14 catches.

FINDLAY, THADDEUS MICHAEL
West Indies (born 1943) - A wicket-keeper and right-handed batsman. He played for Windward Island. Test Record - 10 Tests, 212 runs (Av. 16.30) and 21 dismissals (19ct, 2st).

FINGLETON, JOHN HENRY WEBB
Australia (1908-1981) - A right-handed opening batsman. He played for New South Wales. Test Record - 18 Tests, 1,189 runs (Av. 42.46) including 5 centuries and 13 catches.

FLEETWOOD-SMITH, LESLIE O'BRIEN
Australia (1910-1971) - A left-arm back-of-the-hand spin bowler. He played for Victoria. Test Record - 10 Tests, 54 runs (Av. 9.00) and 42 wickets (Av. 37.38).

FLETCHER, KEITH WILLIAM ROBERT
England (born 1944) - He was a right-handed batsman and leg-spinner. He played for Essex. Test Record - 59 Tests, 3,272 runs (Av. 39.90) including 7 centuries, 2 wickets (Av. 96.50) and 54 catches.

FOSTER, FRANK ROWBOTHAM
England (1889-1958) - A right-handed batsman and also a left-arm medium-fast bowler. He played for Warwickshire. Test Record - 11 Tests, 330 runs (Av. 23.57) 45 wickets (Av. 20.57) and 11 catches.

FOSTER, MAURICE LINTON CHURCHILL
West Indies (born 1943) - A right-handed batsman and a useful off-break bowler. He played for Jamaica. Test Record - 14 Tests, 580 runs (Av. 30.52) including 1 century, 9 wickets (Av. 66.66) and 3 catches.

FOSTER, NEIL ALAN
England (born 1962) - A right-arm fast-medium pace bowler. He plays for Essex. Test Record - 25 Tests, 342 runs (Av. 10.68), 76 wickets (Av. 31.26) and 6 catches.

FOSTER, REGINALD ERSKINE
England (1878-1914) - He was a right-handed batsman. He played for Oxford University and Worcestershire. Test Record - 8 Tests, 602 runs (Av. 46.30) including 1 century and 13 catches.

FOWLER, GRAEME
England (born 1957) - A left-handed opening batsman and very useful wicket-keeper. Test Record - 21 Tests, 1,307 runs (Av. 35.52) including 3 centuries and 10 catches.

FRANCIS, BRUCE COLLIN
Australia (born 1948) - A right-handed opening batsman. He played for New South Wales. Test Record - 3 Tests, 52 runs (Av. 10.40) and 1 catch.

FRANCIS, GEORGE NATHANIEL
West Indies (1897-1942) - He was right-handed fast bowler. He played for Barbados. Test Record - 10 Tests, 81 runs (Av. 5.78) and 23 wickets (Av. 33.17).

FRANCOIS, CYRIL MATTHEW

South Africa (1897-1944) - A hard-hitting right-handed batsman and fast-medium pace bowler. He played for Griqualand West . Test Record - 5 Tests, 252 runs (Av. 31.50) 6 wickets (Av. 37.50) and 5 catches.

FRANKLIN, TREVOR JOHN

New Zealand (born 1962) - An exceptionally tall right-handed batsman of sound techniques. He plays for Auckland. Test Record - 8 Tests, 220 runs (Av.15.00) and 4 catches.

FREDERICKS, ROY CLINTON

West Indies (born 1942) - He was a tough left-handed opening batsman. He played for Guyana and Glamorgan. Test Record - 59 Tests, 4,334 runs (Av. 42.49) incluing 8 centuries, 7 wickets (Av. 78.28) and 62 catches.

FREEMAN, ALFRED PERCY

England (1888-1965) - He was a right-arm googly and a top spinner. He played for Kent. Test Record - 12 Tests, 154 runs (Av. 14.00), 66 wickets (Av. 25.86) and 4 catches.

FRY, CHARLES BURGESS

England (1872-1956) -A right-handed batsman. He played for Oxford University. Test Record - 26 Tests, 1,223 runs (Av. 32.18) including 2 centuries and 17 catches.

FUNSTON, KENNETH JAMES

South Africa (1925) - A right-handed batsman. He played for North-Eastern Province, Transvaal, and Orange Free State. Test Record - 18 Tests, 824 runs (Av. 25.75) and 7 catches.

GADKARI, CHANDRASEKHAR VAMAN

India (born 1928) - A right-handed batsman and right-arm medium pace bowler. He played for Maharashtra. Test Record - 6 Tests, 129 runs (Av. 21.50) and 6 catches.

GAEKWAD, ANSHUMAN DATTAJIRAO

India (born 1952) - A right-handed batsman and right-arm off break bowler. Test Record - 40 Tests, 1,985 runs (Av. 30.07) including 2 centuries and 15 catches.

GAEKWAD, DATTAJIRAO KRISHNARAO

India (born 1928) - A right-handed batsman and right-arm leg-break bowler. He played for Baroda. Test Record - 11 Tests, 350 runs (Av. 18.42) and 5 catches.

GAMSY, DENNIS

South Africa (born 1940) - An outstanding wicket-keeper. He played for Natal. Test Record - 2 Tests, 39 runs (Av. 19.50) and 5 catches.

GANDOTRA, ASHOK

India (born 1948) - A left-handed batsman and left-arm slow spin bowler. He played for Delhi. Test Record - 2 Tests, 54 runs (Av. 13.50) and 1 catch.

GANNON, JOHN BRIAN

Australia (born 1947) - A fast-medium paced left-arm bowler and athletic fielder. He played for Western Australia. Test Record - 3 Tests, 3 runs (Av. 3.00), 11 wickets (Av. 32.82) and 3 catches.

GARNER, JOEL

West Indies (born 1952) - A strongly built as well as very tall, right-handed fast-medium bowler. He plays for Barbados. Test Record - 58 Tests, 672 runs (Av. 12.44), 259 wickets (Av. 20.97) and 42 catches.

GARRETT, THOMAS WILLIAM

Australia (1858-1943) - A good right-arm medium-pace fast bowler. Test Record - 19 Tests, 339 runs (Av. 12.55), 36 wickets (Av. 26.94) and 7 catches.

GATTING, MICHAEL WILLIAM

England (born 1957) - A right-handed batsman,useful medium-pace bowler and a good all-round fielder. He plays for Middlesex. Test Record - 67 Test, 3,848 runs (Av. 38.09) including 9 centuries, 4 wickets (Av. 79.25) and 51 catches.

GAUNT, RONALD ARTHUR

Australia (born 1934) - A right-arm fast-medium pace bowler, and a useful left-handed batsman. He played for Western Australia and Victoria. Test Record - 3 Tests, 6 runs (Av. 3.00), 7 wickets (Av. 44.28) and 1 catch.

GAVASKAR, SUNIL MANOHAR

India (born 1949) - A right-handed opening batsman and right-arm medium-pace and leg-break bowler. He played for Bombay and Somerset. In his first class career he made 25,834 runs including 81 centuries, took 22 wickets and 293 catches. Test Record - 125 Tests, 10,122 runs (Av. 51.12) including 34 centuries, 1 wicket and 108 catches.

GEARY, GEORGE

England (1893-1981) - He was a right-arm, fast-medium pace bowler. He played for Leicestershire. Test Record - 14 Tests, 249 runs (Av. 15.56), 46 wickets (Av. 29.41) and 13 catches.

GHAVRI, KARSAN DEVJIBHAI

India (born 1951)- A left-handed batsman and left-arm fast medium and slow spin bowler. He played for Saurashtra. Test Record - 39 Tests, 913 runs (Av. 21.23), 109 wickets (Av. 33.54) and 16 catches.

GHAZALI, MOHAMMED EBRAHIM ZAINUDDIN

Pakistan (born 1924) - A forcing right-handed batsman, useful leg-break bowler and an excellent fielder. He played for Services. Test Record - 2 Tests, 32 runs (Av. 8.00).

GHORPADE, JAYASINGHRAO MANSINGHRAO

India (1930-1978) - A right-handed batsman and right-arm leg-break bowler. He played for Baroda and Maharashtra. Test Record - 8 Tests, 229 runs (Av. 15.26) and 4 catches.

GIBB, PAUL ANTHONY

England (1913-1977) - He was a right-handed batsman and also a very useful wicket-keeper. He played for Cambridge University. Test Record - 8 Tests, 581 runs (Av. 44.69) including 2 centuries, 4 dismissals (3ct, 1st).

GIBBS, LANCELOT RICHARD

West Indies (born 1934) - A right-arm off-spinner. He played for Guyana, South Australia and Warwickshire. Test Record - 79 Tests, 488 runs (Av. 6.97), 309 wickets (Av. 29.09) and 52 catches.

GIFFEN, GEORGE

Australia (1859-1927) -A right-handed batsman and slow-medium pace bowler. He played for South Australia. Test Record - 31 Tests, 1,238 runs (Av. 23.25) including 1 century, 103 wickets (Av. 27.09) and 24 catches.

GIFFORD, NORMAN

England (born 1940) - He was a beautiful leg-arm spin bowler. He played for Worcestershire and Warwickshire. Test Record - 15 Tests, 179 runs (Av. 16.27), 33 wickets (Av. 31.09) and 8 catches.

GILBERT, DAVID ROBERT

Australia (born 1960) - A well-built right-arm fast bowler. He played for New South Wales. Test Record - 7 Tests, 56 runs (Av. 8.00) and 15 wickets (Av. 48.26).

GILCHRIST, ROY

West Indies (born 1934) - He was a fast-medium pace bowler. He played for Jamaica. Test Record - 13 Tests, 60 runs (Av. 5.45), 57 wickets (Av. 26.68) and 4 catches.

GILMOUR, GARY JOHN

Australia (born 1951) - He was a left-handed all-rounder and a fast-medium over-the-wicket bowler. He played for New South Wales. Test Record - 15 Tests, 483 runs (Av. 23.00) including 1 century, 54 wickets (Av. 26.03) and 8 catches.

GLEESON, JOHN WILLIAM

Australia (born 1938) - A right-arm spin bowler. He played for New South Wales. Test Record - 29 Tests, 395 runs (Av. 10.39), 93 wickets (Av. 36.20) and 17 catches.

GODDARD, JOHN DOUGLAS CLAUDE

West Indies (born 1919) - A left-handed batsman and a right-arm medium-pace bowler. He played for Barbodos. Test Record - 27 Tests, 859 (Av. 30.67) 33 wickets (Av. 31.81) and 22 catches.

GODDARD, THOMAS WILLIAM JOHN

England (1900-1966) - He was a right-arm fast bowler. He played for Gloucetershire. Test Record - 8 Tests, 13 runs (Av. 6.50) 22 wickets (Av. 26.72) and 3 catches.

GODDARD, TREVOR LESLIE

South Africa (born 1931) - A left-handed opening batsman and bowler. He played for Natal and Northern-Eastern Transvaal. Test Record - 41 Tests, 2,516 runs (Av. 34.46) including 1 century, 123 wickets (Av. 26.22) and 48 catches.

GOMES, HILARY ANGELO

West Indies (born 1953) - A left-handed batsman, a good fielder and a useful right-arm bowler. He played for Trinidad and Middlesex. Test Record - 54 Tests, 3,032 runs (Av. 42.70) including 9 centuries, 13 wickets (Av. 66.69) and 17 catches.

GOMEZ, GERALD ETHRIDGE

West Indies (born 1919) - A right-handed batsman, and fast-medium swing bowler. He played for Trinidad. Test Record - 29 Tests, 1,243 runs (Av. 30.31) including 1 century, 58 wickets (Av. 27.41) and 18 catches.

GOOCH, GRAHAM ALAN

England (born 1953) - A right-handed opening batsman and a useful medium-pace seam bowler. He played for Essex and Western Province. Test Record - 68 Tests, 4,541 runs (Av. 38.15) including 8 centuries, 13 wickets (Av. 42.30) and 69 catches.

GOWER, DAVID IVON

England (born 1957) - A left-handed batsman. He played for Leicestershire. Test Record - 100 Tests, 7,000 runs (Av. 44.02) including 14 centuries and 68 catches.

GRACE, DR WILLIAM GILBERT

England (1848-1915) - A right-handed batsman. He played for London County. Test Record - 22 Tests, 1,098 runs (Av. 32.39) including 2 centuries, 9 wickets (Av. 26.22) and 39 catches.

GRANT, GEORGE COPELAND

West Indies (1907-1978) - A good right-handed batsman. He played for Cambridge University. Test Record - 12 Tests, 413 runs (Av. 25.81) and 10 catches.

GRANT, ROLPH STEWART

West Indies (1909-1977) - A right-handed batsman. He played for Cambridge University. Test Record - 7 Tests, 220 runs (Av. 22.00), 11 wickets (Av. 32.09) and 13 catches.

GRAVENEY, THOMAS WILLIAM

England (born 1927) - A right-handed batsman and useful leg-break bowler. He played for Gloucestershire. Test Record - 79 Tests, 4,882 runs (Av. 44.38) including 11 centuries and 80 catches.

GRAY, EVAN JOHN

New Zealand (born 1954) - A left-arm slow bowler and right-handed batsman. He played for Wellington. Test Record - 8 Tests, 208 runs (Av. 17.33), 14 wickets (Av. 44.07) and 4 catches.

GREENHOUGH, THOMAS

England (born 1931) - A right-handed leg-break bowler. He played for Lancashire. Test Record - 4 Tests, 4 runs (Av. 1.33), 16 wickets (Av. 22.31) and 1 catch.

GREENIDGE, ALVIN TALBERT
West Indies (born 1956) - A right-handed batsman. He played for Barbados. Test Record - 6 Tests, 222 runs (Av. 22.00) and 5 catches.

GREENIDGE, CUTHBERT GORDON
West Indies (born 1951) - A right-handed opening batsman. He plays for Barbados and Hampshire. Test Record - 96 Tests, 6,826 runs (Av. 46.12) including 17 centuries and 90 catches.

GREENIDGE, GEOFFREY ALAN
West Indies (born 1948) - A right-handed opening batsman and leg-break bowler. He played for Barbados and Sussex. Test Record - 5 Tests, 209 runs (Av. 29.85), and 3 catches.

GREGORY, JOHN MORRISON
Australia (1895-1973) - A left-handed batsman and a useful right-arm fast bowler. He played for New South Wales. Test Record - 24 Tests, 1,146 runs (Av. 36.96) including 2 centuries, 85 wickets (Av. 31.15) and 37 catches.

GREGORY, ROSS GERALD
Australia (1916-1942) - A very quick-footed right-handed batsman. He played for Victoria. Test Record - 2 Tests, 153 (Av. 51.00) and 1 catch.

GREGORY, SYDNEY EDWARD
Australia (1870-1929) - A right-handed batsman. He played for New South Wales. Test Record - 58 Tests, 2,282 runs (Av. 24.53) including 4 centuries and 25 catches.

GREIG, ANTHONY WILLIAM
England (born 1946) - He was a right-handed batsman. He played for Eastern Province and Sussex: Test Record - 58 Tests, 3,599 runs (Av. 40.43) including 8 centuries, 141 wickets (Av. 32.20) and 87 catches.

GREIG, IAN ALEXANDER
England (born 1955) - A right-handed batsman and a medium-fast bowler. He played for Cambridge University, Sussex, Border, and Griqualand West. Test Record - 2 Tests, 26 runs (Av. 6.50) and 4 wickets (Av. 28.50).

GRIEVESON, RONALD EUSTACE
South Africa (born 1909) - A splendid wicket-keeper and batsman. He played for Transvaal. Test Record - 2 Tests, 114 runs (57.00) and 10 dismissals (7 ct, 3 st).

GRIFFIN, GEOFFREY MERTON
South Africa (born 1939) - A fast bowler. He played for Natal and Rhodesia. Test Record - 2 Tests, 25 runs (Av. 6.25) and 8 wickets (Av. 24.00).

GRIFFITH, CHARLES CHRISTOPHER
West Indies (born 1938) - He was a right-arm spinner. He played for Barbados. Test Record - 28 Tests, 530 runs (Av. 16.56), 94 wickets (Av 28.54) and 16 catches.

GRIFFITH, HERMAN CLARENCE
West Indies (1893-1980) - He was a fast bowler. He played for Barbados. Test Record - 13 Tests, 91 runs (Av. 5.05), 44 wickets (Av. 28.25) and 4 catches.

GRIFFITH, STEWART CATHIE
England (born 1914) - A wicket-keeper and right-handed opening batsman. Test Record - 3 Tests, 157 runs (Av. 31.40) including 1 century and 5 dismissals (5ct).

GRIMMETT, CLARENCE VICTOR
Australia (1891-1980) - He was a leg-break bowler. He played for Victoria, South Australia and Wellington. Test Record - 37 Tests, 557 runs (Av. 13.92) and 216 wickets (Av. 24.21) and and 17 catches.

GROUT, ARTHUR THEODORE WALLACE
Australia (1927-1968) - A right-handed batsman and wicket-keeper. He played for Queensland. Test Record - 51 Tests, 890 runs (Av. 15.08), and 187 dismissals (163ct, 24st).

GUARD, GHULAM MUSTAFA

India (1925-1978)- A left-handed batsman and left-arm medium fast bowler. He played for Bombay and Gujarat. Test Record - 2 Tests, 11 runs (Av. 5.50), 3 wickets (Av. 60.66) and 2 catches.

GUHA, SUBROTO

India (born 1946) - A right-handed batsman and right-arm medium- fast bowler. He played for Bengal. Test Record - 4 Tests, 17 runs (Av. 3.40), 3 wickets (Av. 103.00) and 2 catches.

GUILLENSIMPSON, CHAIRMONTE

West Indies (born 1924) - A wicket-keeper and a right-handed batsman. He played for Trinidad and Canterbury. Test Record - (*West Indies* - 5) - 104 runs (Av. 26.00) and 11 dismissals (9ct, 2st). (*New Zealand* - 3) - 98 runs (Av. 16.33) and 5 dismissals (4ct, 1st).

GUL MAHOMED

India (born 1921)- A left-handed batsman and left-arm bowler. He played for Baroda, Hyderabad and Punjab. Test Record - (India) - 8 Tests, 166 runs (Av. 11.06), 2 wickets and 3 catches. (Pakistan) - 1 Test, 39 runs (Av. 39.00).

GUNN, JOHN RICHMOND

England (1876-1963) - A left-handed batsman and a slow medium pace bowler. He played for Nottinghamshire. Test Record - 6 Tests, 85 runs (Av. 10.62), 18 wickets (Av. 21.50) and 3 catches.

GUNN, WILLIAM

England (1858-1921) - A right-handed batsman and a useful slow, round arm bowler. He played for Nottinghamshire. Test Record - 11 Tests, 392 runs (Av. 21.77) including 1 century.

GUPTE, BALKRISHNA PANDHARINATH

India (born 1934) - A right-handed batsman and right-arm leg-break bowler. He played for Bombay. Test Record - 3 Tests, 28 runs (Av. 28.00) and 3 wickets.

GUPTE, SUBHAS PANDHARINATH

India (born 1929)- A right-handed batsman and right-arm leg-break bowler. Test Record - 36 Tests, 183 runs (Av. 6.31), 149 wickets (Av. 29.55) and 14 catches.

GURUSINHA, ASANKA PRADEEP

Sri Lanka (born 1966) - A left-handed batsman and wicket-keeper. He plays for Sinhalese. Test Record - 7 Tests, 351 runs (Av. 35.10) including 1 century and 3 catch.

GUY, JOHN WILLIAM

New Zealand (born 1934) - A left-handed batsman. He played for Central Districts. Test Record - 12 Tests, 440 runs (Av. 20.95) including 1 century and 2 catches.

HADLEE, DAYLE ROBERT

New Zealand (born 1948) - He was a right-arm fast-medium pace bowler.He played for Canterbury. Test Record - 26 Tests, 530 runs (Av. 14.32), 71 wickets (Av. 33.64) and 8 catches.

HADLEE, RICHARD JOHN

New Zealand (born 1951) - A fast-bowler, all-rounder famous for his supreb bowling. A hard-hitting, left-handed batsman. He plays for Canterbury. Test Record - 79 Tests, 2,884 runs (Av. 26.70) including 2 centuries, 396 wickets (Av. 22.22) and 37 catches.

HADLEE, WALTER ARNOLD

New Zealand (born 1915) - A right-handed batsman. He played for Canterbury and Otago. Test Record - 11 Tests, 543 runs (Av. 30.16) including 1 century and 6 catches.

HALL, WESLEY WINFIELD

West Indies (born 1937) - A right-arm fast bowler. He played for Barbados, Trinidad and Queensland. Test Record - 48 Tests, 818 runs (Av. 15.73), 192 wickets (Av. 26.38) and 11 catches.

HAMMOND, WALTER REGINALD
England (1903-1965) - A brilliant right-handed batsman and off stroke-player. He played for Gloucestershire. Test Record - 85 Tests, 7,249 runs (Av. 58.45) including 22 centuries, 85 wickets (Av. 37.80) and 110 catches.

HANIF MOHAMMAD
Pakistan (born 1934) -A right-handed opening batsman and useful right-arm bowler. He played for Bahawalpur and Pakistan International Airlines (PIA). Test Record - 55 Tests, 3,915 runs (Av. 43.98) including 12 centuries, and 40 catches.

HANUMANT SINGH
India (born 1939) - A right-handed batsman and leg-break bowler. He played for Madhya Pradesh and Rajasthan. Test Record - 14 Tests, 686 runs (Av. 31.18) including 1 century and 11 catches.

HARDIKAR, MANOHAR SHANKAR
India (born 1936) - A right-handed batsman and right-arm off-break bowler. He played for Bombay. Test Record - 2 Tests, 56 runs (Av. 18.66), and 3 catches.

HARDSTAFF, JOSEPH JUNIOR
England (born 1911) - A right-handed attacking batsman. He played for Nottinghamshire and Auckland. Test Record - 23 Tests, 1,636 runs (Av. 46.74) including 4 centuries, and 9 catches.

HARDSTAFF, JOSEPH SENIOR
England (1882-1947) - A right-handed batsman. He played for Nottinghamshire. Test Record - 5 Tests, 311 runs (Av. 31.10) and 1 catch.

HAROON RASHID
Pakistan (born 1953) - A right-handed batsman. He played for Karachi, Sind, National Bank, Pakistan International Airways and United Bank. Test Record - 23 Tests, 1,217 runs (Av. 34.77) including 3 centuries and 16 catches.

HARPER, ROGER ANDREW
West Indies (born 1963) - A right-arm off-spin bowler.He plays for Guyana and Northamptonshire. Test Record - 24 Tests, 532 runs (Av. 19.00), 45 wickets (Av. 27.82) and 35 catches.

HARVEY, ROBERT NEIL
Australia (born 1928) - A left-handed batsman. He played for Victoria and New South Wales. Test Record - 79 Tests, 6,149 runs (Av. 48.42) including 21 centuries, 3 wickets (40.00) and 64 catches.

HASEEB AHSAN
Pakistan (born 1939) - A right-arm off-break bowler. He played for Peshawar and Karachi. Test Record - 12 Tests, 61 runs (Av. 6.77), 27 wickets (Av. 49.25) and 1 catch.

HASSETT, ARTHUR LINDSAY
Australia (born 1913) - He was a right-handed attacking batsman. He played for Victoria. Test Record - 43 Tests, 3,073 runs (Av. 46.56) including 10 centuries and 30 catches.

HASTINGS, BRIAN FREDERICK
New Zealand(born 1940) - A right-handed batsman, a clip medium-fast bowler. He played for Wellington, Central Districts and Canterbury. Test Record - 31 Tests, 1,510 runs (Av. 30.20) including 4 centuries and 23 catches.

HAWKE, NEIL JAMES NAPIER
Australia (born 1939) - A right-arm fast-medium bowler and a useful late-order batsman. He played for Western Australia, South Australia and Tasmamia. Test Record - 27 Tests, 365 runs (Av. 16.59), 91 wickets (Av. 29.41) and 9 catches.

HAYES, ERNEST GEORGE
England (1876-1953) - A right-handed bastman and a useful leg-break bowler. He played for Surrey and Leicestershire. Test Record - 5 Tests, 86 runs (Av. 10.75) and 2 catches.

HAYES, FRANK CLARLES
England (born 1946) - He was a right-handed batsman. He played for Lancashire. Test Record - 9 Tests, 244 runs (Av. 15.25) including 1 century and 7 catches.

HAYES, JOHN ARTHUR
New Zealand (born 1927) - A right-arm fast bowler. He played for Auckland and Canterbury.
Test Record - 15 Tests, 73 runs (Av. 4.86), 30 wickets (Av. 40.56) and 3 catches.

HAYNES, DESMOND LEO
West Indies (born 1956) - A right-handed opening batsman. He plays for Barbados. Test Record - 85 Tests, 5,340 runs (Av. 41.39) including 12 centuries, 1 wicket (Av. 8.00) and 55 catches.

HAYWARD, THOMAS WALTER
England (1871-1939) - He was a right-handed batsman and medium-pace off-break bowler. He played for Cambridgeshire and Surrey. Test Record - 35 Tests, 1,999 runs (Av. 34.46) including 3 centuries and 14 wickets (Av. 36.71) and 19 catches.

HAZARE, VIJAY SAMUEL
India (born 1915) - He was a right-handed batsman and right-arm medium -fast bowler.He played for Maharashtra and Baroda. Test Record - 30 Tests, 2,192 runs (Av. 47.65) including 7 centuries, 20 wickets (Av. 61.00) and 11 catches.

HEARNE, JOHN THOMAS
England (1867-1944) - He was a right-arm medium pace bowler. He played for Middlesex. Test Record - 12 Tests, 126 runs (Av. 9.00), 49 wickets (Av. 22.08) and 4 catches.

HEARNE, JOHN WILLIAM
England (1891-1965) - A right-handed batsman and a useful leg-break and googly bowler. He played for Middlesex. Test Record - 24 Tests, 806 runs (Av. 26.00) including 1 century, 30 wickets (Av. 48.73) and 13 catches.

HENDREN, ELIAS HENRY
England (1889-1962) - He was a right-handed batsman. He played for Middlesex. Test Record - 51 Tests, 3,525 runs (Av. 47.63) including 7 centuries and 33 catches.

HENDRICK, MICHAEL
England (born 1948) - He was one of the fast-medium bowlers.He played for Derbyshire and Nottinghamshire. Test Record - 30 Tests, 128 runs (Av. 6.40), 87 wickets (Av. 25.83) and 25 catches.

HENDRIKS, JOHN LESLIE
West Indies (born 1933) - A tall wicket-keeper, slow bowler and a useful right-handed batsman. He played for Jamaica. Test Record - 20 Tests, 447 runs (Av. 18.62) and 47 dismissals (42ct, 5st).

HENDRY, HUNTER SCOTT THOMAS LAURIE
Australia (born 1895) - He was a right-handed batsman and a fast-medium change-bowler and a fine slip fielder. He played for New South Wales and Victoria.Test Record - 11 Tests, 335 runs (Av. 20.93) including 1 century, 16 wickets (Av. 40.00) and 10 catches.

HILL, CLEMENT
Australia (1877-1945) - He was a left-handed batsman. He played for South Australia. Test Record - 49 Tests, 3,412 runs (Av. 39.21) including 7 centuries and 33 catches.

HILL, JOHN CHARLES
Australia (1923-1974) - An inelegant right-arm leg-break bowler. He played for Victoria. Test Record - 3 Tests, 21 runs (Av. 7.00), 8 wickets (Av. 34.12) and 2 catches.

HIRST, GEORGE HERBERT
England (1871-1954) - He was a left-arm bowler and a useful right-handed batsman. He played for Yorkshire. Test Record - 24 Tests, 790 runs (Av. 22.57), 59 wickets (Av. 30.00) and 18 catches.

HIRWANI, NARENDRA
India (born 1968) - A right-arm leg-spinner. Test Record - 7 Tests, 26 runs (Av. 5.20), 42 wickets (Av. 20.71) and 4 catches.

HOBBS, SIR JOHN BERRY
England (1882-1963) - He was a right-handed batsman and an occasional bowler. He played for Cambridgeshire and Surrey. Test Record - 61 Tests, 5,410 runs (Av. 56.94) including 15 centuries and 17 catches.

HODGES, JOHN HENRY
Australia (1856-1933) - A left-arm fast-medium bowler. He played for Victoria. Test Record - 2 Tests, 10 runs (Av. 3.33) and 6 wickets (Av. 14.00).

HOGG, RODNEY MALCOLM
Australia (born 1951) - He was a right-arm fast-medium bowler.He played for Victoria and South Australia. Test Record - 38 Tests, 439 runs (Av. 9.75), 123 wickets (Av. 28.47) and 7 catches.

HOLDER, VANBURN ALONZA
West Indies (born 1945) - A tall, fast-medium bowler.He played for Barbados, Worcestershire and Oranage Free State. Test Record - 40 Tests, 682 runs (Av. 14.21), 109 wickets (Av. 33.28) and 16 catches.

HOLDING, MICHAEL ANTHONY
West Indies (born 1954) - A right-arm fast bowler. He plays for Jamaica, Lancashire, Derbyshire and Tasmania. Test Record - 60 Tests, 910 runs (Av. 13.78), 249 wickets (Av. 23.68) and 22 catches.

HOLE, GRAEME BLAKE
Australia (born 1931) - A tall right-handed middle-order batsman. He played for New South Wales and South Austrlia. Test Record - 18 Tests, 789 runs (Av. 25.45), 3 wickets (Av. 42.00) and 21 catches.

HOLFORD, DAVID ANTHONY JEROME
West Indies (born 1940) - A tall, silm right-arm leg-break bowler. He played for Barbados. Test Record - 24 Tests, 768 runs (Av. 22.58), including 1 century, 51 wickets (Av. 39.39) and 18 catches.

HOLLAND, ROBERT GEORGE
Australia (born 1946) - A leg-spin bowler. He played for New South Wales. Test Record - 11 Tests, 35 runs (Av. 3.18), 34 wickets (Av. 39.76) and 5 catches.

HOLLIES, WILLIAM ERIC
England (1912-1981) - A right-arm, leg-break bowler. He played for Warwickshire and Staffordshire.Test Record - 13 Tests, 37 runs (Av. 5.28), 44 wickets (Av. 30.27) and 2 catches.

HOLMES, ERROL REGINALD THOROLD
England (1905-1960) - A right-handed batsman and medium-fast bowler. He played for Oxford University and Surrey. Test Record - 5 Tests, 114 runs (Av. 16.28), 2 wickets (Av. 38.00)and 4 catches.

HOLMES, PERCY
England (1886-1971) - An attacking right-handed batsman and a good fielder. He played for Yorkshire. Test Record - 7 Tests, 357 runs (Av. 27.46) and 3 catches.

HOLT, JOHN KENNETH JUNIOR
West Indies (born 1923) - A right-handed batsman with strokes all round the wickets. He played for Jamaica. Test Record - 17 Tests, 1,006 runs (Av. 36.75) including 2 centuries and 8 catches.

HOOKES, DAVID WILLIAM
Australia (born 1955) - A left-handed batsman. He played for South Australia. Test Record - 23 Tests, 1,306 runs (Av. 34.36) including 1 century and 12 catches.

HOPKINS, ALBERT JOHN YOUNG
Australia (1876-1931) - A right-arm slow-medium bowler. He played for New South Wales. Test Record - 20 Tests, 509 runs (Av. 16.42), 26 wickets (Av. 26.76) and 11 catches.

HOPWOOD, JOHN LEONARD

England (1903-1985) - He was a right-handed batmsan and a left-arm medium-pace bowler. He played for Lancashire.Test Record - 2 Tests, 12 runs (Av. 6.00).

HORAN, THOMAS PATRICK

Australia (1854-1916) - A medium-pace change-bowler. He played for Victoria. Test Record - 15 Tests, 471 runs (Av. 18.84), including 1 century, 11 wickets (Av. 13.00) and 6 catches.

HORDERN, DR HERBERT VIVIAN

Australia (1884-1938) - A googly bowler and useful batsman. He played for New South Wales and Philadelphia. Test Record - 7 Tests, 254 runs (Av. 23.09), 46 wickets (Av. 23.36) and 6 catches.

HOWARTH, GEOFFREY PHILIP

New Zealand (born 1951) - A neat right-handed batsman and useful off-spin bowler. He played for Northern Districts, Auckland and Surrey. Test Record - 47 Tests, 2,531 runs (Av. 32.44) including 6 centuries, 3 wickets (Av. 90.33) and 29 catches.

HOWARTH, HEDLEY JOHN

New Zealand (born 1943) - A orthodox left-arm spinner.He played for Auckland. Test Record - 30 Tests, 291 runs (Av. 12.12), 86 wickets (Av. 36.95) and 33 catches.

HOWELL, HENRY

England (1890-1932) - A right-arm bowler.He played for Warwickshire. Test Record - 5 Tests, 15 runs, (Av. 7.50) and 7 wickets (Av. 79.85).

HOWELL, WILLIAM PETER

Australia (1869-1940) - A medium pace bowler and also a left-handed batsman. He played for New South Wales. Test Record - 18 Tests, 158 runs (Av. 7.52), 49 wickets (Av. 28.71) and 12 catches.

HOWORTH, RICHARD

England (1909-1980) - A left-handed batsman and slow-left-arm bowler.He played for Worcestershire. Test Record - 5 Tests, 145 runs (Av. 18.12), 19 wickets (Av. 33.42) and 2 catches.

HUGHES, KIMBERLEY JOHN

Australia (born 1954) - A fine all-round right-handed batsman . He played for Western Australia. In his first class career he made, 11,395 runs including 25 centuries and 135 catches.Test Record - 70 Tests, 4,415 runs (Av. 37.41) including 9 centuries and 50 catches.

HUMPHRIES, JOSEPH

England (1876-1946) - A wicket-keeper.He played for Derbyshire. Test Record - 3 Tests, 44 runs (Av. 8.80) and 7 dismissals (7ct).

HUNTE, CONRAD CLEOPHAS

West Indies (born 1932) - A right-handed opening batsman and slow-medium cutter. He played for Barbados. Test Record - 44 Tests, 3,245 runs (Av. 45.06) including 8 centuries, 2 wickets (Av. 55.00) and 16 catches.

HUTTON, SIR LEONARD

England (born 1916) - He was right-handed stockey batsman, a good useful leg-break bowler. He played for Yorkshire. Test Record - 79 Tests, 6,971 runs (Av. 56.67) including 19 centuries, 3 wickets (Av. 77.33) and 57 catches.

IBRAHIM, KHANMOHAMMED CASSUMBHOY

India (born 1919) - A right-handed opening batsman. He played for Bombay. Test Record - 4 Tests, 169 runs (Av. 21.12).

IJAZ AHMED

Pakistan (born 1968) - Bats right-hand but a handy left-arm slow bowler too. He plays for Pakistan club team PACO.Test Record - 13 Tests, 457 runs (Av. 28.56) and 13 catches.

IJAZ BUTT

Pakistan (born 1938) - A sound right-handed batsman and wicket-keeper. He played for Rawalpindi. Test Record - 8 Tests, 279 runs (Av. 19.92) and 5 catches.

IJAZ FAQIH

Pakistan (born 1956) - A skilful all-rounder, a right-handed batsman and an off-break bowler. He played for Karachi and Muslim Commercial Bank. Test Record - 2 Tests, 63 runs (Av. 15.75) and 1 wickets (Av. 85.00).

IKIN, JOHN THOMAS

England (1918-1984) - A left-handed batsman and also a right-arm leg-break and googly bowler. A brilliant and daring fielder. He played for Lancashire. Test Record - 18 Tests, 606 runs (Av. 20.89), 3 wickets (Av. 118.00) and 31 catches.

ILLINGWORTH, RAYMOND

England (born 1932) - An all-rounder and he was a right-arm bowler. He played for Yorkshire and Leicestershire. Test Record - 61 Tests, 1,836 runs (Av. 23.24) including 2 centuries, 122 wickets (Av. 31.20) and 45 catches.

IMRAN KHAN

Pakistan (born 1952) - An all-rounder. A right-handed batsman and right-arm fast-medium bowler.He played for Lahore, Pakistan International Airways, Oxford University, Sussex and New South Wales. Test Record - 74 Tests, 3000 runs (Av.33.70) including 4 centuries,341 wickets (Av.22.04) and 25 catches.

IMTIAZ AHAMED

Pakistan (born 1928) - A right-handed batsman and one of the best fast bowlers. He played for Northern ndia and Services. Test Record - 41 Tests, 2,079 runs (Av. 29.28) including 3 centuries and 93 dismissals (77ct, 16st).

INTIKHAB ALAM

Pakistan (born 1941) - A leg-spin and googly bowler and hard-hitting right-handed batsman. He played for Karachi and Surrey. Test Record - 47 Tests, 1,493 runs (Av. 22.28) including 1 century, 125 wickets (Av. 35.93) and 20 catches.

IQBAL QASIM MOHAMMAD

Pakistan (born 1953) - A left-arm spin bowler and a fine close fielder. He played for Karachi, Sind and National Bank. Test Record - 50 Tests, 551 runs (Av. 13.11), 171 wickets (Av. 28.10) and 41 catches.

IREDALE, FRANCIS ADAMS

Australia (1867-1926) - A right-handed batsman. He played for New South Wales.Test Record - 14 Tests, 807 runs (Av. 36.68) including 2 centuries and 16 catches.

IRONMORGER, HERBERT

Australia (1881-1971) - A slow left-arm medium-pace bowler. He played for Victoria. Test Record - 14 Tests, 42 runs (Av. 2.62), 74 wickets (Av. 17.97) and 3 catches.

IRONSIDE, DAVID ERNEST JAMES

South Africa (born 1925) - A medium-pace bowler. Test Record - 3 Tests, 37 runs (Av. 18.50), 15 wickets (Av. 18.33) and 1 catch.

JACKMAN, ROBIN DAVID

England (born 1945) - A medium-fast bowler. He played for Surrey, Western Province and Rhodesia. Test Record - 4 Tests, 42 runs (Av. 7.00) and 14 Wickets (Av. 31.78).

JACKSON, SIR FRANCIS STANLEY

England (1870-1947) - A right-handed batsman and a medium-pace bowler. He played for Cambridge University and Yorkshire. Test Record - 20 Tests, 1,415 runs (Av. 48.79) including 5 centuries, 24 wickets (Av. 33.29) and 10 catches.

JAHANGIR KHAN, DR MOHAMMED

India (1910 - 1968) - A right-handed batsman and right-arm fast medium bowler.He played for Northern India and Cambridge University. Test Record - 4 Tests, 39 runs (Av. 5.57), 4 wickets (Av. 63.75) and 4 catches.

JAISIMHA, MOTGANHALLI LAKSHMINARSU

India (born 1939)- A right-handed batsman and a right-arm off-break bowler. He played for Hyderabad. Test Record - 39 Tests, 2,056 runs (Av.30.68) including 3 centuries and 17 catches.

JARDINE, DOUGLAS ROBERT

England (1900-1958) - A right-handed batsman. He played for Oxford University and Surrey. Test Record - 22 Tests, 1,296 runs (Av. 48.00) including 1 century and 26 catches.

JARMAN, BARRINGTON NOEL

Australia (born 1936) - He was a good wicket-keeper and a good right-handed batsman. He played for South Australia. Test Record - 19 Tests, 400 runs (Av. 14.81) and 54 dismissals (50ct, 4st).

JARVIS, ARTHUR HARWOOD

Australia (1860-1933) - A useful wicket-keeper. He played for South Australia. Test Record - 11 Tests, 303 runs (Av. 16.83) and 18 dismissals (9 ct, 9 st).

JARVIS, TERRENCE WAYNE

New Zealand (born 1944) - A right-handed opening batsman and a fine fielder. He played for Auckland and Canterbury. Test Record - 13 Tests, 625 runs (Av. 29.76) including 1 century and 3 catches.

JAVED BURKI

Pakistan (born 1938) - A right-handed middle-order batsman and an medium-pace bowler. He played for Oxford University and Karachi. Test Record - 25 Tests, 1,341 runs (Av. 30.47) including 3 centuries and 7 catches.

JAVED MIANDAD KHAN

Pakistan (born 1957) - A right-handed batsman also a right-arm leg-spin bowler. He played for Karachi, Sind, Habib Bank, Sussex and Glamorgan. Test Record - 97 Tests, 7,422 runs (Av. 57.09) including 21 centuries, 17 wickets (Av. 40.11), 84 catches and 1 stumping.

JESSOP, GILBERT LAIRD

England (1874-1955) - He was a right-handed batsman. He played for Gloucestershire. Test Record - 18 Tests, 569 runs (Av. 21.88) including 1 century, 10 wickets (Av. 35.40) and 11 catches.

JOHNSON, IAN WILLIAM

Australia (Born 1918) - A very slow-off-spinner. He played for Victoria. Test Record - 45 Tests, 1,000 runs (Av. 18.51), 109 wickets (Av. 29.19) and 30 catches.

JOHNSTON, WILLIAM ARRAS

Australia (born 1922) - A left-arm fast-medium bowler. He played for Victoria. Test Record - 40 Tests, 273 runs (Av. 11.37), 160 wickets (Av. 23.91) and 16 catches.

JONES, ARTHUR OWEN

England (1872-1914) - He was a leg-break bowler. He played for Cambridge University, and Nottinghamshire. Test Record - 12 Tests, 291 runs (Av. 13.85), 3 wickets (Av. 44.33) and 15 catches.

JONES, DEAN MERVYN

Australia (born 1961) - A right-handed batsman. He plays for Victoria. Test Record - 21 Tests, 1,546 runs (Av.45.47) and 11 catch.

JONES, ERNEST

Australia (1869-1943) - A right-arm fast bowler. He played for South Australia. Test Record - 19 Tests, 126 runs (Av. 5.04), 64 wickets (Av. 29.01) and 21 catches.

JONES, SAMUEL PERCY
Australia (1861-1951) - A right-handed batsman and a useful change bowler. He played for New South Wales. Test Record - 12 Tests, 432 runs (Av. 21.60), 6 wickets (Av. 18.66) and 12 catches.

JOSHI, PADMANABH GOVIND
India (born 1926)- A right-handed batsman and wicket-keeper. He played for Maharashtra. Test Record - 12 Tests, 207 runs (Av. 10.89) and 27 dismissals (18ct, 9 st).

JULIEN, BERNARD DENIS
West Indies (born 1950) - A left-arm seam bowler and also bowled slow orthodox or unorthodox spin. He played for Trinidad and Kent. Test Record - 24 Tests, 866 runs (Av. 30.92) including 2 centuries, 50 wickets (Av. 37.36) and 14 catches.

JUMADEEN, RAPHICK RASIF
West Indies (born 1948) - A left-arm orthodox bowler. He played for Trinidad. Test Record - 12 Tests, 84 runs (Av. 21.00), 29 wickets (Av. 39.34) and 4 catches.

KELLEWAY, CHARLES
Australia (1889-1944) - A very sound right-handed batsman and also a medium-fast bowler. He played for New South Wales. Test Record - 26 Tests, 1,422 runs (Av. 37.42) including 3 centuries, 52 wickets (Av. 32.36) and 24 catches.

KENYON, DONALD
England (born 1924) - A right-handed opening batsman. He played for Worcestershire. Test Record - 8 Tests, 192 runs (Av. 12.80) and 5 catches.

KNIGHT, BARRY ROLFE
England (born 1938) - A right-arm medium-fast bowler, right-handed batsman. He played for Essex and Leicestershire. Test Record - 29 Tests, 812 runs (Av. 26.19) including 2 centuries, 70 wickets (Av. 31.75) and 14 catches.

KALLICHARRAN, ALVIN ISAAC
West Indies (born 1949) - A brilliant left-handed batsman. He played for Guyana, Warwickshire, Queensland, Transvaal and Orange Free State. Test Record - 66 Tests, 4,399 runs (Av. 44.43) including 12 centuries, 4 wickets (Av. 39.50) and 51 catches.

KANHAI, ROHAN BABULAL
West Indies (born 1935) - A small, right-handed batsman. He played for Guyana, Trinidad, Warwickshire, Western Australia and Tasmania. Test Record - 79 Tests, 6,227 runs (Av. 47.53) including 15 centuries and 50 catches.

KANITKAR, HEMANT SHAMSUNDER
India (born 1942)- A right-handed batsman and wicket-keeper. Test Record- 2 Tests, 111 runs (Av. 27.75)

KAPIL DEV NIKHANJ
India (born 1959) -A right-handed batsman and right-arm fast medium bowler. He plays for Haryana. Test Record - 99 Tests, 4,087 runs (Av. 31.19) including 6 centuries, 347 wickets (Av. 29.02) and 53 catches.

KARDAR, ABDUL HAFEEZ
India (born 1925)- A left-handed batsman. He played for Northern India, Oxford University and Warwickshire. Test Record - India - 3 Tests, 80 runs (Av. 16.00) and 1 catch. Pakistan -23 Tests, 847 runs (Av. 24.91) and 21 wickets.

KELLY, JAMES JOSEPH
Australia (1867-1938) - An outstanding wicket-keeper and a right-handed batsman. He played for New South Wales. Test Record - 36 Tests, 664 runs (Av. 17.02) and 63 dismissals (43ct, 20st).

KENDALL, THOMAS
Australia (1851-1924) - A left-arm slow bowler, he bowled left-arm spin. He played for Victoria and Tasmania.Test Record - 2 Tests, 39 runs (Av. 13.00), 14 wickets (15.35) and 2 catches.

KENNEDY, ALEXANDER STUART

England (1891-1959) - He was a right-handed batsman and right-arm medium-fast bowler. He played for Hampshire. Test Record - 5 Tests, 93 runs (Av. 15.50), 31 wickets (Av. 19.32) and 5 catches.

KENNY, RAMNATH BHAURA

India (1930 - 1985) A right-handed batsman. He played for Bombay. Test Record - 5 Tests, 245 runs (Av. 27.22) and 1 catch.

KING, FRANK MC DONALD

West Indies (born 1926) - A right-arm fast bowler. He played for Barbados. Test Record - 14 Tests, 116 runs (Av. 8.28), 29 wickets (Av. 39.96) and 5 catches.

KING, LESTER ANTHONY

West Indies (born 1939) - A right-arm medium-fast bowler. He played for Jamaica and Bengal. Test Record - 2 Tests, 41 runs (Av. 10.25), 9 wickets (Av. 17.11) and 2 catches.

KIPPAX, ALAN FALCONER

Australia (1897-1972) - He was a right-handed batsman. He played for New South Wales. Test Record - 22 Tests, 1,192 runs (Av. 36.12) including 2 centuries and 13 catches.

KIRMANI, SYED MUJTABA HUSSAIN

India (born 1949)- A right-handed batsman and wicket-keeper. He played for Mysore (Karnataka). Test Record - 88 Tests, 2,759 runs (Av. 27.04) including 2 centuries and 198 dismissals.

KISCHENCHAND, GOGUMAL

India (born 1925)- A right-handed batsman. He played for Delhi, Sind, Gujarat, and Baroda. Test Record - 5 Tests, 89 runs (Av. 8.90) and 1 catch.

KLINE, LINDSAY FRANCIS

Australia (born 1934) - A left-arm off-break and googly bowler and a tail-end batsman. He played for Victoria. Test Record - 13 Tests, 58 runs (Av. 8.28), 34 wickets (Av. 22.82) and 9 catches.

KNIGHT, ALBERT ERNEST

England (1872-1946) - He was a very good hard-wicket player, right-handed batsman. He played for Leicestershire. Test Record - 3 Tests, 81 runs (Av. 16.20) and 1 catch.

KNOTT, ALAN PHILIP ERIC

England (born 1946) - A brilliant wicket-keeper, a right-handed batsman. He played for Kent. Test Record - 95 Tests, 4,389 runs (Av. 32.75) including 5 centuries and 269 dismissals (250ct, 19st).

KRIPAL SINGH AMRITSAR GOVINDSINGH

India (born 1933)- A right-handed batsman and right-arm off-break bowler.He played for Madras. Test Record - 14 Tests, 422 runs (Av. 28.13) including 1 century, 10 wickets (Av. 58.40) and 4 catches.

KRISHNAMURTHY , POLLAMANI

India (born 1947) - A right-handed batsman and wicket keeper. He played for Hyderabad. Test Record - 5 Tests, 33 runs (Av. 5.50) and 8 dismissals.

KULKARNI, UMESH NARAYAN

India (born 1942) - A left-handed batsman and left-arm medium fast bowler.He played for Bombay. Test Record - 4 Tests, 13 runs (Av. 4.33) and 5 wickets.

KUMAR, VAMAN VISHWANATH

India (born 1935)- A right-handed batsman and right-arm leg-break and googly bowler. He played for Madras. Test Record - 2 Tests, 6 runs (Av. 3.00) and 7 wickets (Av. 20.05).

KUNDERAN, BUDHISAGAR KRISHNAPPA

India (born 1939)-A right- handed batsman and wicket-keeper. He played for Mysore. Test Record - 18 Tests, 981 runs (Av. 32.70) including 2 centuries and 30 dismissals.

LAIRD, BRUCE MALCOLM

Australia (born 1950) - A right-handed opening

batsman. He played for Western Australia. Test Record - 21 Tests, 1,341 runs (Av. 35.28) and 16 catches.

LAKER, JAMES CHARLES

England (1922-1986) - He was the best of all off-spinners. He played for Surrey and Essex. Test Record - 46 Tests, 676 runs (Av. 14.08), 193 wickets (Av. 21.24) and 12 catches.

LALL SINGH

India (born 1909)- A right-handed batsman and right-arm bowler. He played for Punjab. Test Record - 1 Test , 44 runs (Av. 22.00) and 1 catch.

LAMB, ALLAN JOSEPH

England (born 1954) - A right-handed batsman.He played for Western Province and Northamptonshire. Test Record.- 56 Tests, 2,969 runs (Av. 33.35) including 8 centuries, 1 wicket (Av. 23.00) and 53 catches.

LANCE, HERBERT ROY

South Africa (born 1940) - He was a right-handed batsman and a useful change medium-fast bowler. He played for North-Eastern Transvaal and Transvaal. Test Record - 13 Tests, 591 runs (Av. 28.14), 12 wickets (Av. 39.91) and 7 catches.

LANGLEY, GILBERT ROCHE ANDREWS

Australia (born 1919) - He was one of the best wicket-keepers and a right-handed batsman. He played for South Australia. Test Record - 26 Tests, 374 runs (Av. 14.96) and 98 dismissals (83 ct, 15 st).

LANGRIDGE, JAMES

England (1906-1966) - He was a left-arm bowler. He played for Sussex and Auckland. Test Record - 8 Tests, 242 runs (Av. 26.88), 19 wickets (Av. 21.73) and 6 catches.

LANGTON, ARTHUR BEAUMONT CHUDLEIGH

South Africa (1912-1942) - He was a left-arm medium-pace bowler. He played for Transvaal. Test Record - 15 Tests, 298 runs (Av. 15.68), 40 wickets (Av. 45.67) and 8 catches.

LARWOOD, HAROLD

England (born 1904) - A right-arm medium-fast bowler and a useful hard-hitting batsman. He played for Nottinghamshire.

Test Record - 21 Tests, 485 runs (Av. 19.40), 78 wickets (Av. 28.35) and 15 catches.

LASHLEY, PATRICK DOUGLAS

West Indies (born 1937) - A left-handed batsman, an occasional medium-pace bowler. He played for Barbados. Test Record - 4 Tests, 159 runs (Av. 22.71), and 4 catches.

LAVER, FRANK

Australia (1869-1919) - A medium-pace bowler. He played for Victoria. Test Record - 15 Tests, 196 runs (Av. 11.52), 37 wickets (Av. 26.05) and 8 catches.

LAWRENCE, GODFREY BERNARD

South Africa (born 1932) - A right-arm opening medium-fast bowler and also a useful batsman. He played for Natal and Rhodesia. Test Record - 5 Tests, 141 runs (Av. 17.62), 28 wickets (Av. 18.28) and 2 catches.

LAWSON, GEOFFREY FRANCIS

Australia (born 1957) - A tall, silm, right-arm medium-fast bowler and hard-hitting batsman. He played for New South Wales.Test Record - 38 Tests, 756 runs (Av. 15.12), 148 wickets (Av. 30.52) and 8 catches.

LEADBERATER, EDRIC

England (born 1927) - A right-arm leg-break bowler and also a very useful batsman. He played for Yorkshire and Warwickshire.Test Record - 2 Tests, 40 runs (Av. 20.00), 2 wickets (Av. 109.00) and 3 catches.

LEE, PHILIP KEITH

Australia (1904-1980) - He was a right-arm off-spin bowler. He played for South Australia.Test Record - 2 Tests, 57 runs (Av. 19.00), 5 wickets (Av. 42.40) and 1 catch.

LEES, WALTER SCOTT

England (1875-1924) - He was right-arm medium-pace bowler and also a useful batsman. He played for Surrey.Test Record - 5 Tests, 66 runs (Av. 11.00), 26 wickets (Av. 17.96) and 2 catches.

LEES, WARREN KENNETH

New Zealand (born 1952) - He was a wicket-keeper and a right-handed batsman. He played for Otago.Test Reocrd - 21 Tests, 778 runs (Av. 23.57) including 1 century, and 59 dismissals (52ct, 7st).

LEGALL, RALPH ARCHIBALD

West Indies (born 1926) - A competent wicket-keeper and a right-handed batsman. He played for Barbados and Trinidad.Test Record - 4 Tests, 50 runs (Av. 10.00) and 9 dismissals (8ct, 1st).

LEGGAT, JOHN GORDON

New Zealand (1926-1973) - A right-handed opening batsman. He played for Canterbury.Test Record - 9 Tests, 351 runs (Av. 21.93).

LEGGE, GEOFFREY BEVINGTON

England (1903-1940) - He was a right-handed batsman. He played for Oxford University and Kent.Test Record - 5 Tests, 299 runs (Av. 49.83) including 1 century and 1 catch.

LESLIE, CHARLES FREDERICK HENRY

England (1861-1921) - A right-handed batsman and an all-rounder. He played for Oxford University, Middlesex and Shropshire.Test Record - 4 Tests, 106 runs (Av. 15.14), 4 wickets (Av. 11.00) and 1 catch.

LEVER, JOHN KENNETH

England (born 1949) - A fast-medium left-arm bowler, brilliant outfielder. He played for Essex and Natal.Test Record - 21 Tests, 306 runs (Av.11.76), 73 wickets (Av.62.73) and 11 catches.

LEVER, PETER

England (born 1940) - A right-arm medium-fast bowler and a right-handed batsman. He played for Lancashire and Tasmania.Test Record - 17 Tests, 350 runs (Av. 21.87), 41 wickets (Av. 36.80) and 11 catches.

LEVESON, GOWER

England (1873-1954) - He was a right-handed batsman and revelled in the cut and as a slow-medium-pace bowler.Test Record - 3 Tests, 95 runs (Av. 23.75) and 1 catch.

LEWIS, ANTHONY ROBERT

England (born 1938) - He was a right-handed batsman and an occasional leg-break bowler. He played for Cambridge University and Glamorgan. Test Record - 9 Tests, 457 runs (Av. 32.64) including 1 century.

LEWIS, DESMOND MICHAEL

West Indies (born 1946) - A right-handed batsman and wicket-keeper of high potential. He played for Jamaica.Test Record - 3 Tests, 259 runs (Av. 86.33) and 8 dismissals (8ct).

LEYLAND, MORRIS

England (1900-1967) - He was a left-handed batsman and also a right-arm spin bowler. He played for Yorkshire.Test Record - 41 Tests, 2,764 runs (Av. 46.06) including 9 centuries, 6 wickets (Av. 97.50) and 13 catches.

LIAQAT ALI KHAN

Pakistan (born 1955) - A left-arm medium-paced seam bowler. He played for Karachi, Habib Bank and Sind.Test Record - 5 Tests, 28 runs (Av. 7.00), 6 wickets (Av. 59.83) and 1 catch.

LILLEE, DENNIS KEITH

Australia (born 1949) - A glorious action was at the heart of his success. He was a right-arm medium-fast bowler and a useful tailend right-handed batsman who played very straight.Test Record - 70 Tests, 905 runs (Av. 13.71), 355 wickets (Av. 23.92) and 23 catches.

LILLEY, ARTHUR FREDERICK AUGUSTUS

England (1866-1929) - He was a wicket-keeper and a right-handed batsman. He played for Warwickshire. Test Record - 35 Tests, 903 runs (Av. 20.52) and 92 dismissals (70ct, 22st).

LILLYWHITE, JAMES JUNIOR

England (1842-1929) - A left-arm slow bowler with a high and exceptionally accurate delivery. He was also a left-handed batsman. He played for Sussex.Test Record - 2 Tests, 16 runs (Av. 8.00), 8 wickets (Av. 15.75) and 1 catch.

LINDSAY, DENIS THOMSON

South Africa (born 1939) - A brilliant wicket-keeper and a right-handed attacking stroke-player. He played for North-Eastern Transvaal and Transvaal.Test Record - 19 Tests, 1,130 runs (Av. 37.66) including 3 centuries, and 59 dismissals (57ct, 2st).

LINDSAY, JOHN DIXON

South Africa (born 1909) - A brilliant wicket-keeper. He played for North-Eastern Transvaal and Transvaal.Test Record - 3 Test, 21 runs (Av. 7.00), and 5 dismissals (4ct, 1st).

LINDWALL, RAYMOND RUSSELL

Australia (born 1921) - He was a right-arm swing bowler.Test Record - 61 Tests, 1,502 runs (Av. 21.15) including 2 centuries, 228 wickets (Av. 23.03) and 26 catches.

LING, WILLIAM VICTOR STONE

South Africa (1891-1960) - A right-arm googly bowler and a very useful batsman. He played for Griqualand West.Test Record - 6 Tests, 168 runs (Av. 16.80) and 1 catch.

LISSETTE, ALAN FISHER

New Zealand (1919-1973) - He was a left-arm slow bowler. He played for Waikato, Auckland and Northern Districts.Test Record - 2 Tests, 2 runs (Av. 1.00), 3 wickets (Av. 41.33) and 1 catch.

LLEWELLYN, CHARLES BENNETT

South Africa (1876-1964) - He was a left-handed forcing batsman, a left-arm slow to medium-paced bowler and a fine fielder. He played for Natal and Hampshire.Test Record - 15 Tests, 544 runs (Av. 20.14), 48 wickets (Av. 29.60) and 7 catches.

LLOYD, CLIVE HUBERT

West Indies (born 1944) - A tall and commanding left-handed batsman and useful right-arm medium-paced bowler. He played for Guyana and Lancashire.Test Record - 110 Tests, 7,515 runs (Av. 46.67) including 19 centuries, 10 wickets (Av. 62.20) and 90 catches.

LLOYD, DAVID

England (born 1947) - He was an under-used, slow, left-arm orthodox spinner, a brilliant close fielder and a left-handed batsman. He played for Lancashire and Cumberland. Test Record - 9 Tests, 552 runs (Av. 42.46) including 1 century and 11 catches.

LOCK, GRAHAM ANTHONY RICHARD

England (born 1929) - He was an orthodox slow left-arm spinner. He played for Surrey, Leicestershire and Western Australia.Test Record - 49 Tests, 742 runs (Av. 13.74), 174 wickets (Av. 25.58) and 59 catches.

LOCKWOOD, WILLIAM HENRY

England (1868-1932) - A right-handed batsman and a great bowler. He played for Nottinghamshire and Surrey.Test Record - 12 Tests, 231 runs (Av. 17.76), 43 wickets (Av. 20.55) and 4 catches.

LOGIE, AUGUSTINE LAWRENCE
West Indies (born 1960) - A right-handed batsman. He played for Trinidad.Test Record - 37 Tests, 1,707 runs (Av. 34.14) including 2 centuries and 41 catches.

LOHMANN, GEORGE ALFRED
England (1865-1901) - He was a right-handed quick-footed, match winning batsman, a useful fielder and a graceful medium pace bowler. He played for Surrey and Western Province.Test Record - 18 Tests, 213 runs (Av. 8.87), 112 wickets (Av. 10.75) and 28 catches.

LOXTON, SAMUEL JOHN EVERETT
Australia (born 1921) - He was a right-handed batsman and a useful right-arm medium-fast bowler. He played for Victoria.Test Record - 12 Tests, 554 runs (Av. 36.93) including 1 century, 8 wickets (Av. 43.62) and 7 catches.

LUCAS, ALFRED PERRY
England (1857-1923) - A classic and defensive batsman. He played for Cambridge University and Middlesex.Test Record - 5 Tests, 157 runs (Av. 19.62) and 1 catch.

LUCKHURST, BRIAN WILLIAM
England (born 1939) - He was a right-handed opening batsman. He played for Kent.Test Record - 21 Tests, 1,298 runs (Av. 36.05) including 4 centuries and 14 catches.

LYONS, JOHN JAMES
Australia (1863-1927) - He was a hard-hitting right-handed opening batsman and also right-arm spin bowler. He played for South Australia.Test Record - 14 Tests, 731 runs (Av. 27.07) including 1 century, 6 wickets (Av. 24.83) and 3 catches.

LYTTELTON, RT HON. ALFRED
England (1857-1913) - A right-handed batsman, front-foot batsman in the classical mould and a useful wicket-keeper. He played for Cambridge University and Middlesex.Test Record - 4 Tests, 94 runs (Av. 15.66), 4 wickets (Av. 4.75) and 2 dismissals (2ct).

MACARTNEY, CHARLES GEORGE
Australia (1886-1958) - A great right-handed batsman. He played for New South Wales and Otago. Test Record - 35 Tests, 2,131 runs (Av. 41.78) including 7 centuries, 45 wickets (Av. 27.55) and 17 catches.

MACAULAY, GEORGE GINBSON
England (1897-1940) - A right-arm bowler. He played for Yorkshire. Test Record - 8 Tests, 112 runs (Av. 18.66), 24 wickets (Av. 27.58) and 5 catches.

MACGIBBON, ANTHONY ROY
New Zealand (born 1924) - A right-arm medium-fast bowler. He played for Canterbury. Test Record - 26 Tests, 814 runs (Av. 19.85), 70 wickets (Av. 30.85) and 13 catches.

MACGREGOR, GREGOR
England (1869-1919) - A useful wicket-keeper. He played for Cambridge University and Middlesex. Test Record - 8 Tests, 96 runs (Av. 12.00) and 17 dismissals (14ct, 3st).

MACKAY, KENNETH DONALD
Australia (1925-1982) - A left-handed batsman and also right-arm medium-pace bowler. He played for Queensland. Test Record - 37 Tests, 1,507 runs (Av. 33.48), 50 wickets (Av. 34.42) and 16 catches.

MACLAREN, ARCHIBALD CAMPBELL
England (1871-1944) - A right-handed batsman. He played for Lancashire. Test Record - 35 Tests, 1,931 runs (Av. 33.87) including 5 centuries, and 29 catches.

MACLEAN, JOHN ALEXANDER
Australia (born 1946) - A right-handed batsman and a wicket-keeper. He played for Queensland. Test Record - 4 Tests, 79 runs (Av. 11.28) and 18 dismissals (18ct).

MADAN LAL UDHOURAM SHARMA

India (born 1951) - A right-handed batsman and a right-arm medium-fast bowler. He played for Delhi and Punjab. Test Record - 39 Tests, 1,042 runs (Av. 22.65), 71 wickets (Av. 40.08) and 15 catches.

MADDOCKS, LEONARD VICTOR

Australia (born 1926) - A very useful right-handed batsman and a wicket-keeper. He played for Victoria and Tasmania. Test Record - 7 Tests, 177 runs (Av. 17.70) and 19 dismissals (18ct, 1st).

MADRAY, IVAN SAMUEL

West Indies (born 1934) - A right-handed batsman and a leg-break bowler. He played for British Guiana. Test Record - 2 Tests, 3 runs (Av. 1.00) and 2 catches.

MADUGALLE, RANJAN SENERATH

Sri Lanka (born 1959) - An effective leg-spin bowler and a right-handed batsman. He played for Nondescripts. Test Record - 21 Tests, 1,029 runs (Av. 29.40) including 1 century and 9 catches.

MAGUIRE, JOHN NORMAN

Australia (born 1956) - A tall, right-arm medium-fast pace bowler. He played for Queensland. Test Record - 3 Tests, 28 runs (Av. 7.00), 10 wickets (Av. 32.30) and 2 catches.

MAHANAMA, ROSHAN SIRIWARDENE

Sri Lanka (born 1966) - A tiny right-handed opening batsman. He played for Bloomfield. Test Record - 3 Tests, 79 runs (Av. 15.80) and 1 catch.

MAHMOOD HUSSAIN

Pakistan (born 1932) - A medium-fast in-swing bowler. He played for Karachi Whites. Test Record - 27 Tests, 336 runs (Av. 10.18), 68 wickets (Av. 38.64) and 5 catches.

MAILEY, ARTHUR ALFRED

Australia (1886-1967) - A right-arm leg-break and googly bowler. He played for New South Wales. Test Record - 21 Tests, 222 runs (Av. 11.10), 99 wickets (Av. 33.91) and 14 catches.

MAJID, JAHANGIR KHAN

Pakistan (born 1946) - A good all-rounder. He was a brilliant attacking right-handed batsman. He played for Lahore, Pakistan International Airways and Cambridge University. Test Record - 63 Tests, 3,931 runs (Av. 38.92) including 8 centuries, 27 wickets (Av. 53.92) and 70 catches.

MAKA, EBRAHIM SULEMAN

India (born 1922)- A right-handed batsman and a wicket-keeper. He played for Bombay. Test Record - 2 Tests, 2 runs and 3 dismissals (2ct, 1st).

MAKEPEACE, JOSEPH WILLIAM HENRY

England (1882-1952) - A right-handed opening batsman. He played for Lancashire. Test Record - 4 Tests, 279 runs (Av. 34.87) including 1 century.

MALHOTRA, ASHOK OMPRAKASH

India (born 1957) - A right-handed batsman. He played for Haryana and Bengal. Test Record - 7 Tests, 226 runs (Av. 25.11) and 2 catches.

MALLETT, ASHLEY ALEXANDER

Australia (born 1945) - A right-handed batsman right-arm off-break bowler. He played for South Australia. Test Record - 38 Tests, 430 runs (Av. 11.62), 132 wickets (Av. 29.85) and 30 catches.

MANINDER SINGH HARBANSINGH BILLA

India (born 1956) - A tall, athletic left-arm orthodox spin bowler. He plays for Delhi. Test Record - 31 Tests, 88 runs (Av.3.82), 79 wickets (Av. 36.43) and 9 catches.

MANJREKAR, VIJAY LAXMAN

India (1931-1983) - A right-handed batsman, right-arm off-break bowler.He played for Bombay, Bengal and Rajasthan. Test Record - 55 Tests, 3,208 runs (Av. 39.12) including 7 centuries, 19 catches and 2 stumpings.

MANKAD, ASHOK VINOO
India (born 1946) - A right-handed batsman and a right-arm off-break bowler. He played for Bombay. Test Record - 22 Tests, 991 runs (Av. 25.41) and 12 catches.

MANKAD, BULVANTRAI HIMATLAL
India (1917-1978) - A right-handed batsman and a left-arm slow spin bowler. He played for Western India and Rajasthan. Test Record - 44 Tests, 2,109 runs (Av. 31.47) including 5 centuries, 162 wickets (Av. 32.32) and 33 catches.

MANN, ANTHONY LONGFORD
Australia (born 1945) - A slow, right-arm leg-break bowler, a useful left-handed batsman. He played for Western Australia. Test Record - 4 Tests, 189 runs (Av. 23.62) including 1 century, 4 wickets (Av. 79.00) and 2 catches.

MANN, FRANCIS GEORGE
England (born 1917) - A right-handed attacking batsman. He played for Cambridge University and Middlesex. Test Record - 7 Tests, 376 runs (Av. 37.60) including 1 century and 3 catches.

MANN, FRANCIS THOMAS
England (1884-1964) - A powerful right-handed batsman. He played for Cambridge University and Middlesex. Test Record - 5 Tests, 281 runs (Av. 35.12) and 4 catches.

MANN, NORMAN BERTRAM FLEETWOOD
South Africa (1920-1955) - A right-arm bowler. He played for Natal and Eastern Province. Test Record - 19 Tests, 400 runs (Av. 13.33), 58 wickets (Av. 33.10) and 3 catches.

MANSELL, PERCY NEVILLE FRANK
South Africa (born 1920) - A right-handed batsman and leg-break bowler. He played for Rhodesia. Test Record - 13 Tests, 355 runs (Av. 17.75), 11 wickets (Av. 66.90) and 15 catches.

MANSOOR AKHTAR
Pakistan (born 1956) - A right-handed batsman. He played for Karachi and United Bank. Test Record - 18 Tests, 636 runs (Av. 26.50) including 1 century and 7 catches.

MANZOOR ELAHI
Pakistan (born 1963) - A right-arm medium-pace bowler and right-handed batsman. He played for Multan and Pakistan Railways. Test Record - 4 Tests, 109 runs (Av. 21.80), 2 wickets (Av.42.00) and 5 catches.

MAQSOOD AHMED
Pakistan (born 1925) - A right-handed batsman and medium-pace bowler. He played for Bahawalpur. Test Record - 16 Tests, 507 runs (Av. 19.50), 3 wickets (Av. 63.66) and 13 catches.

MARKS, VICTOR JAMES
England (born 1955) - A middle-order batsman and a useful off-break bowler. He played for Oxford University and Somerset. Test Record - 6 Tests, 249 runs (Av. 27.66) and 11 wickets (Av. 44.00).

MARSH, GEOFFREY ROBERT
Australia (born 1958) - A stocky, correct and determined right-handed batsman. He played for Western Australia. Test Record - 27 Tests, 1,669 runs (Av. 34.77) including 3 centuries and 19 catches.

MARSH, RODNEY WILLIAM
Australia (born 1947) - One of the best wicket-keepers and a very useful left-handed batsman. He played for Western Australia. Test Record - 96 Tests, 3,633 runs (Av. 26.51) including 3 centuries, 355 dismissals (343ct, 12st).

MARSHALL, ROY EDWIN
West Indies (born 1930) - An attacking and forceful right-handed opening batsman. He played for Barbados. Test Record - 4 Tests, 143 runs (Av. 20.42) and 1 catch.

MARSHALLL, MALCOLM DENZIL
West Indies (born 1958) - A lithe, whipping bowler with electric speed and useful right-handed batsman. He played for Barbados and Hampshire. Test Record - 66 Tests,1438 runs (Av. 18.92),326 wickets (Av. 20.54) and 25 catches.

MARTIN, JOHN WESLEY
Australia (born 1931) - A left-arm off-break and googly bowler, a right-handed batsman and a good fielder. He played for South Australia and New South Wales. Test Record - 8 Tests, 214 runs (Av. 17.83), 17 wickets (Av. 48.94) and 5 catches.

MARX, WALDEMAR FREDERICK ERIC
South Africa (1895-1974) - A useful right-arm medium-pace change bowler. He played for Transvaal. Test Record - 3 Test, 125 runs (Av. 20.83) and 4 wickets (Av. 36.00).

MATHIAS, WALLIS
Pakistan (born 1935) - A right-handed batsman and medium-pace bowler. He played for Karachi. Test Record - 21 Tests, 783 runs (Av. 23.72) and 22 catches.

MATTHEWS, GREGORY RICHARD JOHN
Australia (born 1959) - A right-arm off-spinner and left-handed batsman. He played for New South Wales. Test Record - 21 Tests,1,031 runs (Av. 30.82) including 3 centuries, 39 wickets (Av. 43.76) and 13 catches.

MATTHEWS, THOMAS JAMES
Australia (1884-1943) - A right-arm leg-break bowler and a useful right-handed batsman. He played for Victoria. Test Record - 8 Tests, 153 runs (Av. 17.00), 16 wickets (Av. 26.18) and 7 catches.

MAY, PETER BARKER HOWARD
England (born 1929) - A right-handed batsman. He played for Cambridge University. Test Record - 66 Tests, 4,537 runs (Av. 46.77) including 13 centuries and 42 catches.

MAYNE, LAURENCE CHARLES
Australia (born 1942) - A right-arm fast-medium pace bowler. He played for Western Australia. Test Record - 6 Tests, 76 runs (Av. 9.50), 19 wickets (Av. 33.05) and 3 catches.

McCABE, STANLEY JOSEPH
Australia (1910-1968) - A right-handed batsman and fast-medium bowler. He played for New South Wales. Test Reocrd - 39 Tests, 2,748 runs (Av. 48.21) including 6 centuries and 36 wickets (Av. 42.86) and 41 catches.

McCONNON, JAMES EDWARD
England (born 1922) - A tall right-arm off-spinner. He played for Glamorgan. Test Record - 2 Tests, 18 runs (Av. 9.00), 4 wickets (Av. 18.50) and 4 catches.

McCOOL, COLIN LESLIE
Australia (1915-1986) - A right-handed stroke-playing batsman, a leg-break bowler. He played for New South Wales and Somerset. Test Record - 14 Tests, 459 runs (Av. 35.30) including 1 century, 36 wickets (Av. 26.61) and 14 catches.

McCORMICK, ERNEST LESLIE
Australia (born 1906) - He was tall and slim. He played for Victoria. Test Record - 12 Tests, 54 runs (Av. 6.00), 36 wickets (Av. 29.97) and 8 catches.

McCOSKER, RICHARD BEDE
Australia (born 1946) - A right-handed opening batsman. He played for New South Wales. Test Record - 25 Tests, 1,622 runs (Av. 39.56) including 4 centuries and 21 catches.

McDERMOTT, CRAIG JOHN
Australia (born 1965) - A right-arm fast bowler and a right-handed lower-order batsman. He played for Queensland. Test Record - 24 Tests, 339 runs (Av.11.30), 80 wickets (Av. 34.18) and 6 catches.

McDONALD, COLIN CAMPBELL
Australia (born 1928) - A most able right-handed

opening batsman. He played for Victoria. Test Record - 47 Tests, 3,107 runs (Av. 39.32) including 5 centuries and 14 catches.

McDONALD, EDGAR ARTHUR
Australia (1892-1937) - A right-arm fast-medium bowler. He played for Tasmania, Victoria and Lancashire. Test Record - 11 Tests, 116 runs (Av. 16.57), 43 wickets (Av. 33.27) and 3 catches.

MCGLEW, DERRICK JOHN
South Africa (born 1929) - A right-handed opening batsman. He played for Natal. Test Record - 34 Tests, 2,440 runs (Av. 42.06) including 7 centuries and 18 catches.

MCGREGOR, SPENCER NOEL
New Zealand (born 1931) - A right-handed batsman. He played for Otago. Test Record - 25 Tests, 892 runs (Av. 19.82) including 1 century, and 9 catches.

MCINTYRE, ARTHUR JOHN WILLIAM
England (born 1918) - A sound right-handed batsman and wicket-keeper. He was orginally a leg-spinner. He played for Surrey. Test Record - 3 Tests, 19 runs (Av. 3.16) and 8 dismissals (8ct).

McKENZIE, GRAHAM DOUGLAS
Australia (born 1941) - A fast-medium bowler and a right-handed batsman. He played for Western Australia and Leicestershire. Test Record - 60 Tests, 945 runs (Av. 12.27), 246 wickets (Av. 29.78) and 34 catches.

MCLEAN, ROY ALASTAIR
South Africa (born 1930) - A right-handed batsman. He played for Natal. Test Record - 40 Tests, 2,120 runs (Av. 30.28) including 5 centuries and 23 catches.

MCLEOD, CHARLES EDWARD
Australia (1869-1918) - A right-handed batsman and medium-pace bowler. He played for Victroia. Test Record - 17 Tests, 573 runs (Av. 23.87) including 1 century, 33 wickets (Av. 40.15) and 9 catches.

McLEOD, ROBERT WILLIAM
Australia (1868-1907) - A left-handed batsman and right-arm medium-pace bowler. He played for Victoria. Test Record - 6 Tests, 146 runs (Av. 13.27), 12 wickets (Av. 32.00) and 3 catches.

MCMAHON, TREVOR GEORGE
New Zealand (born 1929) - A useful wicket-keeper. He played for Wellington. Test Record - 5 Tests, 7 runs (Av. 2.33) and 8 dismissals (7ct, 1st).

MCMILLAN, QUINTIN
South Africa (1904-1948) - A right-arm slow leg-spin and googly bowler . He played for Transvaal. Test Record - 13 Tests, 306 runs (Av. 18.00), 36 wickets (Av. 34.52) and 8 catches.

MCMORRIS, EASTON DUDLEY EASTON DUDLEY ASHTON ST JOHN
West Indies (born 1935) - A right-handed opening batsman. He played for Jamaica. Test Record - 13 Tests, 564 runs (Av. 26.85) including 1 century and 5 catches.

MEHRA, VIJAY LAXMAN
India (born 1938) - A right-handed batsman and right-arm leg-spin bowler. He played for Western India and Bombay. Test Record - 8 Tests, 329 runs (Av. 25.30) and 1 catch.

MEINTJES, DOUGLAS JAMES
South Africa (1890-1979) - A very good all-rounder from a powerful province. He played for Transvaal. Test Record - 2 Tests, 43 runs (Av. 14.33), 6 wickets (Av. 19.16) and 3 catches.

MELLE, MICHAEL GEORGE
South Africa (born 1930) - A fast right-arm bowler. He played for Transvaal and Western Province. Test Record - 7 Tests, 68 runs (Av. 8.50), 26 wickets (Av. 32.73) and 4 catches.

MELVILLE, ALAN
South Africa (1910-1983) - A graceful right-handed batsman with a classical upright method. He played for Oxford University, Sussex, Natal and Transvaal. Test Record - 11 Tests, 894 runs (Av. 52.58) including 4 centuries, and 8 catches.

MENDIS, LOUIS ROHAN DULEEP
Sri Lanka (born 1952) - A right-handed batsman and a right-arm medium pace bowler. He played for Sinhalese. Test Record - 24 Tests, 1,329 runs (Av. 31.64) including 4 centuries and 9 catches.

MENDONCA, IVOR LEON
West Indies (born 1934) - A wicket-keeper and right-handed batsman. He played for British Guiana. Test Record - 2 Tests, 81 runs (Av. 40.50) and 10 dismissals (8 ct, 2 st).

MERCHANT, THACKERSEY VIJAY MADHAVJI
India (born 1911) - A right-handed opening batsman and a right-arm medium-fast as well as off-break bowler. He played for Bombay. Test Record - 10 Tests, 859 runs (Av. 47.72) including 3 centuries and 7 catches.

MILBURN, COLIN
England (born 1941) - A right-handed batsman, sound and straight. He was medium-pace bowler and a reliable forward short-leg field. He played for Durham, Northamptonshire and Western Province. Test Record - 9 Tests, 654 runs (Av. 46.71) including 2 centuries and 7 catches.

MILKHA SINGH AMRITSAR GOVINDSINGH
India (born 1941) - A left-handed batsman. He played for Madras.' Test Record - 4 Tests, 92 runs (Av. 15.33), and 2 catches.

MILLER, GEOFFREY
England (born 1952) - He was a right-arm off-spin bowler, a right-handed batsman. He played for Derbyshire and Essex. Test Record - 34 Tests, 1,213 runs (Av. 25.80), 60 wickets (Av. 30.98) and 17 catches.

MILLER, KEITH ROSS
Australia (born 1919) - A right-handed batsman. He played for Victoria, New South Wales and Nottinghamshire. Test Record - 55 Tests, 2,958 runs (Av. 36.97) including 7 centuries, 170 wickets (Av. 22.97) and 38 catches.

MILLER, LAWRENCE SOMERVILLE MARTIN
New Zealand (born 1923) - A tall and likeable left-handed opening batsman. He played for Central Districts and Wellington. Test Record - 13 Tests, 346 runs (Av. 13.84) and 1 catch.

MILLIGAN, FRANK WILLIAM
England (1870-1900) - He was a right-arm fast bowler. He played for Yorkshire. Test Record - 2 Tests, 58 runs (Av. 14.50) and 1 catch.

MILLMAN, GEOFFREY
England (born 1934) - An accomplished wicket-keeper and a useful batsman. He played for Bedfordshire and Nottinghamshire. Test Record - 6 Tests, 60 runs (Av. 12.00) and 15 dismissals (13ct, 2 st).

MILLS, JOHN ERNEST
New Zealand (1905-1972) - A left-handed opening batsman. He played for Auckland. Test Record - 7 Tests, 241 runs (Av. 26.77) including 1 century and 1 catch.

MILTON, CLEMENT ARTHUR
England (born 1928) - A right-handed opening batsman and a useful medium-pace bowler. He played for Gloucestershire. Test Record - 6 Tests, 204 runs (Av. 25.50) including 1 century and 5 catches.

MITCHELL, BRUCE
South Africa (born 1909) - A right-handed opening

batsman. He played for Transvaal. Test Record - 42 Tests, 3,471 runs (Av. 48.88) including 8 centuries, 27 wickets (Av. 51.11) and 56 catches.

MITCHELL, THOMAS BIGNELL

England (born 1902) - A right-arm leg-break and googly bowler. He played for Derbyshire. Test Record - 5 Tests, 20 runs (Av. 5.00), 8 wickets (Av. 62.25) and 1 catch.

MODI, RUSI SHERIYAR

India (born 1924) - A right-handed batsman and right-arm medium-pace bowler. He played for Bombay. Test Record - 10 Tests, 736 runs (Av. 46.00) including 1 century and 3 catches.

MOHAMMAD FAROOQ

Pakistan (born 1938) - A right-arm medium-fast bowler. He played for Karachi. Test Record - 7 Tests, 85 runs (Av. 17.00), 21 wickets (Av. 32.47).

MOHAMMAD ILYAS

Pakistan (born 1946) - An attacking right-handed opening batsman and a leg-break googly bowler. He played for Pakistan International Airlines. Test Record - 10 Tests, 441 runs (Av. 23.21) including 1 century and 6 catches.

MOHAMMAD MUNAF

Pakistan (born 1935) - A right-arm medium-fast bowler and a useful late-order batsman. He played for Karachi. Test Record - 4 Tests, 63 runs (Av. 12.60) and 11 wickets (Av. 31.00).

MOHAMMAD NAZIR JUNIOR

Pakistan (born 1946) - A right-arm off-spinner. He played for Pakistan Railways. Test Record - 14 Tests, 144 runs (Av. 18.00), 34 wickets (Av. 33.02) and 4 catches.

MOHSIN HASAN KHAN

Pakistan (born 1955) - A right-handed batsman. He played for Pakistan Railways. Test Record - 48 Tests, 2,709 runs (Av. 37.10) including 7 centuries and 34 catches.

MOHSIN KAMAL

Pakistan (born 1963) - A fast-medium bowler with smooth run-up and fine action. He played for Lahore. Test Record - 7 Tests, 31 runs (15.50) 17 wickets (Av. 35.11) and 2 catches.

MOIR, ALEXANDER MCKENZIE

New Zealand (born 1919) - A right-arm leg-break and googly bowler and a useful late-order batsman. He played for Otago. Test Record - 17 Tests, 327 runs (Av. 14.86), 28 wickets (Av. 50.64) and 2 catches.

MOLD, ARTHUR WEBB

England (1863-1921) - A great right-arm medium-fast bowler. He played for Northamptonshire and Lancashire. Test Record - 3 Tests, 0 runs, 7 wickets (Av. 33.42) and 1 catch.

MOLONEY, DENIS ANDREW ROBERT

New Zealand (1910-1942) - A right-handed batsman and a useful medium-pace change-bowler. He played for Wellington, Otago and Canterbury. Test Record - 3 Tests, 156 runs (Av. 26.00), and 3 catches.

MOON, LEONARD JAMES

England (1878-1916) - A right-handed batsman. He played for Cambridge University and Middlesex. Test Record - 4 Tests, 182 runs (Av. 22.75) and 4 catches.

MOONEY, FRANCIS LEONARD HUGH

New Zealand (born 1921) - A wicket-keeper and a right-handed stroke-maker batsman. He played for Wellington. Test Record - 14 Tests, 343 runs (Av. 17.15), and 30 dismissals (22 ct, 8 st).

MORE, KIRAN SHANKAR

India (born 1962) - A wicket-keeper and a right-handed batsman. He played for Boroda. Test Record - 24 Tests, 576 runs (Av.21.33) and 59 dismissals (44 ct.,15 st.)

MORGAN, ROSS WINSTON
New Zealand (born 1941) - A sound right-handed batsman and also useful off-spin change-bowler. He played for Auckland. Test Record - 20 Tests, 734 runs (Av. 22.24), 5 wickets (Av. 121.80) and 12 catches.

MORKEL, DENYS PAUL BECK
South Africa (1906-1980) - A right-handed batsman and a right-arm medium-fast bowler. He played for Western Province. Test Record - 16 Tests, 663 runs (Av. 24.55), 18 wickets (Av. 45.61) and 13 catches.

MORLEY, FREDERICK
England (1850-1884) - A left-arm medium-fast bowler. He played for Nottinghamshire. Test Record - 4 Tests, 6 runs (Av. 1.50), 16 wickets (Av. 18.50) and 4 catches.

MORONEY, JOHN
Australia (born 1917) - A right-handed opening batsman. He played for New South Wales. Test Record - 7 Tests, 383 runs (Av. 34.81) including 2 centuries.

MORRIS, ARTHUR ROBERT
Australia (born 1922) - He was a left-handed attacking opening batsman. He played for New South wales. Test Record - 46 Tests, 3,533 runs (Av. 46.48) including 12 centuries, 2 wickets (Av. 25.00) and 15 catches.

MORRISON, JOHN FRANCIS MACLEAN
New Zealand (born 1947) - A right-handed batsman a left-arm spin change-bowler. He played for Central Districts. Test Record - 17 Tests, 656 runs (Av. 22.62) including 1 century, 2 wickets (Av. 35.50) and 9 catches.

MOTZ, RICHARD CHARLES
New Zealand (born 1940) - A right-handed fast bowler and a late-order batsman. He played for Canterbury. Test Record - 32 Tests, 612 runs (Av. 11.54), 100 wickets (Av. 31.48) and 9 catches.

MUDASSAR NAZAR
Pakistan (born 1956) - A right-handed opening batsman and a useful medium-pace bowler. He played for Lahore, Punjab, Pakistan Universities. Test Record - 76 Tests,4,114 runs (Av.38.09) including 10 centuries, 66 wickets (Av. 38.36) and 48 catches.

MUDDIAH, VENATAPPA MUSANDRA
India (born 1929) - A right-handed batsman and right-arm off-break bowler. He played for Services. Test Record - 2 Tests, 11 runs (Av. 5.50) and 3 wickets (Av. 44.66).

MURDOCH, WILLIAM LLOYD
Australia (1855-1911) - A good wicket-keeper and a right-handed batsman. He played for New South Wales and Sussex. Test Record - (Australia - 18) - 896 runs (Av. 32.00) including 2 centuries and 14 dismissals (13 ct, 1 st). (*England* - 1) - 12 runs (Av. 12.00) and 1 dismissal (1 st).

MURRAY, BRUCE ALEXANDER GRENFELL
New Zealand (born 1940) - A right-handed opening batsman. He played for Wellington. Test Record - 13 Tests, 598 runs (Av. 23.92) and 21 catches.

MURRAY, DAVID ANTHONY
West Indies (born 1950) - A right-handed batsman and a useful wicket-keeper. He played for Barbados. Test Record - 19 Tests, 601 runs (Av. 21.46), and 62 dismissals (57 ct, 5 st).

MURRAY, DERYCK LANCE
West Indies (born 1943) - A useful batsman and a good wicket-keeper. He played for Trinidad, Cambridge University, Nottinghamshire and Warwickshire. Test Record - 62 Tests, 1,993 runs (Av. 22.90) and 189 dismissals (181ct, 8st).

MUSHTAQ ALI
India (born 1914) - A right-handed batsman and left-arm slow spin bowler. He played for Holkar. Test Record - 11 Tests, 612 runs (Av. 32.31) including 2 centuries, 3 wickets (Av. 67.33) and 7 catches.

MUSHTAQ MOHAMMAD

Pakistan (born 1943) - A stocky right-handed batsman. He played for Pakistan International Airlines and Karachi. Test Record - 57 Tests, 3,643 runs (Av. 39.17) including 10 centuries, 79 wickets (Av. 29.24) and 42 catches.

NADKARNI, RAGHUNATH GANGARAM

India (born 1932) - A left-handed batsman and a left-arm slow spin bowler. He played for Maharashtra and Bombay. Test Record - 41 Tests, 1,414 runs (Av. 25.70) including 1 century, 88 wickets (Av. 29.07) and 22 catches.

NAIK, SUDHIR SAKHARAM

India (born 1946) - A right-handed batsman. He played for Bombay. Test Record - 3 Tests, 141 runs (Av. 23.50).

NIAZ AHMAD

Pakistan (born 1945) - A competent right-arm medium-fast bowler and late-order batsman. He played for East Pakistan. Test Record - 2 Tests, 17 runs, 3 wickets (Av. 31.33) and 1 catch.

NAVLE, JANARDHAN GNANOBA

India (1902-1979) - A right-handed batsman and a useful wicket-keeper. He played for Gwalior. Test Record - 2 Tests, 42 runs (Av. 10.50) and 1 catch.

NAYAK, SUVENDRA VITHAL

India (born 1954) - A stroke-playing right-handed batsman and a medium-pace swing bowler. He played for Bombay. Test Record - 2 Tests, 19 runs (Av. 9.50) and 1 catch.

NAYUDU, COTTARI SUBBANNA

India (born 1914) - A right-handed batsman and a right-arm leg-break and googly bowler. He played for Central India and Madhya Pradesh. Test Record - 11 Tests, 147 runs (Av. 9.18), 2 wickets (Av. 179.50) and 3 catches.

NAYUDU, COL. COTTARI KANKAIYA

India (1895-1967) - A right-handed batsman and a right-arm off-break bowler. He played for Madras, Holkar and United Provinces.
Test Record - 7 Tests, 350 runs (Av. 25.00), 9 wickets (Av. 42.88) and 4 catches.

NAZAR MOHAMMAD

Pakistan (1921) - A right-handed opening batsman and a close fielder. He played for Northern India, Karachi and Sind. Test Record - 5 Tests, 277 runs (Av. 39.57) including 1 century and 7 catches.

NICHOLS, MORRIS STANLEY

England (1900-1961) - A right-arm bowler and a left-handed batsman. He played for Essex. Test Record - 14 Tests, 355 runs (Av. 29.58), 41 wickets (Av. 28.09) and 11 catches.

NICHOLSON, FRANK

South Africa (1909-1982) - An opening batsman and a wicket-keeper. He played for Griqualand West. Test Record - 4 Tests, 76 runs (Av. 10.85) and 3 dismissals (3ct).

NISSAR, MAHOMED

India (1910-1963) - A right-handed batsman and a right-arm medium-fast bowler. He played for Southern Punjab. Test Record - 6 Tests, 55 runs (Av. 6.87), 25 wickets (Av. 28.28) and 2 catches.

NOBLE, MONTAGUE ALFRED

Australia (1873-1940) - A right-handed batsman. He played for New South Wales. Test Record - 42 Tests, 1,997 runs (Av. 30.25) including 1 century, 121 wickets (Av. 25.00) and 26 catches.

NOURSE, ARTHUR DULEY

South Africa (1910-1981) - A right-handed batsman. He played for Natal. Test Record - 34 Tests, 2,960 runs (Av. 53.81) including 9 centuries and 12 catches.

NOURSE, ARTHUR WILLIAM

South Africa (1878-1948) - A left-handed batsman.

He played for Natal, Transvaal and Western Province.Test Record - 45 Tests, 2,234 runs (Av. 29.78) including 1 century, 41 wickets (Av. 37.87) and 43 catches.

NUNES, ROBERT KARL
West Indies (1894-1958) - A fine left-handed opening batsman. He played for Jamaica. Test Record - 4 Tests, 245 runs (Av. 30.62) and 2 catches.

NUPEN, EIULF PETER
South Africa (1902-1977) - A right-arm medium-fast bowler.He played for Transvaal. Test Record - 17 Tests, 348 runs (Av. 14.50), 50 wickets (Av. 35.76) and 9 catches.

NURSE, SEYMOUR MC DONALD
West Indies (born 1933) - A right-handed stroke-playing batsman and off-spin bowler.He played for Barbados. Test Record - 29 Tests, 2,523 runs (Av. 47.60) including 6 centuries and 21 catches.

NYALCHAND, SHAH
India (born 1919) - A left-handed batsman and a left-arm slow spin bowler. He played for Kathiawar. Test Record - 1 Tests, 7 runs.(Av.3.50) and 3 wickets.

O'BRIEN, LEO PATRICK JOSEPH
Australia (born 1907) - A left-handed opening batsman. He played for Victoria. Test Record - 5 Tests, 211 runs (Av. 26.37) and 3 catches.

O'BRIEN, SIR TIMOTHY CAREW BART
England (1861-1948) - A dashing right-handed batsman. He played for Oxford University and Middlesex. Test Record - 5 Tests, 59 runs (Av. 7.37) and 4 catches.

O'CONNOR, JACK
England (1897-1977) - A right-handed batsman and a good fine hooker. He played for Essex and Buckinghamshire. Test Record - 4 Tests, 153 runs (Av. 21.85) and 2 catches.

O'CONNOR, JOHN DENIS ALPHONSUS
Australia (1875-1941) - A right-arm fattish medium pace bowler. He played for New South Wales and South Australia. Test Record - 4 Tests, 86 runs (Av. 12.28), 13 wickets (26.15) and 3 catches.

O'KEEFFE, KERRY JAMES
Australia (born 1949) - A right-arm leg-break bowler and right-handed batsman. He played for New South Wales and Somerset. Test Reocrd - 24 Tests, 644 runs (Av. 25.76), 53 wickets (38.07) and 15 catches.

O'LINN, SYDNEY
South Africa (born 1927) - A left-handed batsman and strong wicket keeper. He played for Western Province and Kent. Test Record - 7 Tests, 297 runs (Av. 27.00) and 4 catches.

O'NEILL, NORMAN CLIFFORD
Australia (born 1937) - A right-handed stroke-maker batsman and a useful leg-spin bowler. He played for New South Wales. Test Record - 42 Tests, 2,779 runs (Av. 45.55) including 6 centuries, 17 wickets (Av. 39.23) and 21 catches.

O'REILLEY, WILLIAM JOSEPH
Australia (born 1905) - A left-handed batsman and also a leg-break bowler. He played for New South Wales. Test Record - 27 Tests, 410 runs (Av. 12.81), 144 wickets (Av. 22.59) and 7 catches.

OLD, CHRISTOPHER MIDDLETON
England (born 1948) - A left-handed batsman and also a right-arm,fast-medium pace bowler. He played for Yorkishre, Northern Transvaal and Warwickshire. Test Record - 46 Tests, 845 runs (Av. 14.82), 143 wickets (Av. 28.11) and 22 catches.

OLDFIELD, WILLIAM ALBERT STANLEY
Australia (1894-1976) -An artisic wicket-keeper and right-handed batsman. He played for New South Wales. Test Record - 54 Tests, 1,427 runs (Av. 22.65) and 130 dismissals (78 ct, 52 st).

PAGE, MILFORD LAURENSON

New Zealand (born 1902) - A right-handed batsman, a useful slow change-bowler. He played for Canterbury. Test Record - 14 Tests, 492 runs (Av. 24.60) including 1 century, 5 wickets (Av. 46.20) and 6 catches.

PAIRAUDEAU, BRUCE HAMILTON

West Indies (born 1931) - A right-handed opening batsman. He played for British Guiana and Northern Districts. Test Record - 13 Tests, 454 runs (Av. 21.61) including 1 century and 6 catches.

PALIA, PHIROZ EDULJI

India (born 1910-1981) - A left-handed batsman and left-arm slow spin bowler. Test Record - 2 Tests, 29 runs (Av. 9.66).

PALMER, GEORGE EUGENE

Australia (1860-1910) - A right-arm medium-pace spin bowler. He played for Victoria and Tasmania. Test Record - 17 Tests, 296 runs (Av. 14.09), 78 wickets (Av. 21.51) and 13 catches.

PARFITT, PETER HOWARD

England (born 1936) - A left-handed high class batsman, a useful off-spinner and a superb fielder. He played for Norfolk and Middlesex. Test Record - 37 Tests, 1,882 runs (Av. 40.91) including 7 centuries, 12 wickets (Av. 47.83) and 42 catches.

PARKER, JOHN MORTON

New Zealand (born 1951) - A right-handed batsman. He played for Northern Districts and Worcestershire. Test Record - 36 Tests, 1,498 runs (Av. 24.55) including 3 centuries and 30 catches.

PARKIN, CECIL HARRY

England (1886-1943) - A good off-spin bowler. He played for Durham, Yorkshire and Lancashire. Test Record - 10 Tests, 160 runs (Av. 12.30), 32 wickets (Av. 35.25) and 3 catches

PARKS, JAMES MICHAEL

England (born 1931) - A brilliant right-handed stroke-maker batsman and a good wicket-keeper. He played for Sussex and Somerset. Test Record - 46 Tests, 1,962 runs (Av. 32.16) including 2 centuries, and 114 dismissals (103ct, 11st).

PARRY, DEREK RICALDO

West Indies (born 1954) - A right-arm off-spin bowler and a useful right-handed batsman. He played for Leeward Islands and Cambridgeshire. Test Record - 12 Tests, 381 runs (Av. 22.41), 23 wickets (Av. 40.69) and 4 catches.

PASCOE, LEONARD STEPHEN

Australia (born 1950) - A very determined right-arm fast-medium bowler and a good outfielder. He played for New South Wales. Test Record - 14 Tests, 106 runs (Av. 10.60), 64 wickets (Av. 26.06) and 2 catches.

PATAUDI, NAWAB OF IFTIQAR ALI KHAN

England (1910-1952) - A right-handed batsman. He played for Oxford University, Worcestershire and Southern Punjab. Test Record - (England - 3) - 144 runs (Av. 28.80) including 1 century. (India -3) - 55 runs (Av. 11.00).

PATAUDI, NAWAB OF MANSUR ALI KHAN JUNIOR

India (born 1941) - A right-handed batsman and right-arm off-spin bowler. He played for Sussex and Hyderabad. Test Record - 46 Tests, 2,793 runs (Av. 34.91) including 6 centuries and 27 catches.

PATEL, BRIJESH PARSURAM

India (born 1952) - A right-handed batsman. He played for Karnataka. Test Record - 21 Tests, 972 runs (Av. 29.45) including 1 century and 17 catches.

PATEL, JASUBHAI MOTIBHAI

India (born 1924) - A right-handed batsman and right-arm off-break bowler. He played for Gujarat. Test Record - 7 Tests, 25 runs (Av. 2.77), 29 wickets (Av. 21.96) and 2 catches.

PATIL, SANDEEP MADHUSUDAN
India (born 1956) - A right-handed batsman and right-arm medium-pace bowler. Test Record - 29 Tests, 1,558 runs (Av. 36.93) including 4 centuries, 9 wickets (Av. 26.66) and 12 catches.

PATTERSON, BALFOUR PATRICK
West Indies (born 1961) - A right-arm fast-medium opening bowler. He plays for Jamaica and Tasmania. Test Record - 17 Tests, 88 runs (Av. 8.80), 59 wickets (Av. 29.81) and 2 catches.

PAYNTER, EDWARD
England (1901-1979) - A left-handed batsman. He played for Lancashire. Test Record - 20 Tests, 1,540 runs (Av. 59.23) including 4 centuries, and 7 catches.

PEARSE, CHARLES ORMEROD CATO
South Africa (1884-1953) - A useful batsman and a change bowler. He played for Natal. Test Record - 3 Tests, 55 runs (Av. 9.16), 3 wickets (Av. 35.33) and 1 catch.

PEEL, ROBERT
England (1857-1941) - A left-arm spin bowler. He played for Yorkshire. Test Record - 20 Tests, 427 runs (Av. 14.72), 102 wickets (Av. 16.81) and 17 catches.

PELLEW, CLARENCE EVERARD
Australia (1893-1981) - He was a good batsman. He played for South Australia. Test Reocrd - 10 Tests, 484 runs (Av. 37.23) including 2 centuries and 4 catches.

PETRIE, ERIC CHARLTON
New Zealand (born 1927) - A neat wicket-keeper. He played for Auckland and Northern Districts. Test Record - 14 Tests, 258 runs (Av. 12.90), and 25 dismissals (25 ct).

PHADKAR, DATTARAY GAJARAN
India (1925-1985) - A right-handed batsman and a right-arm medium-fast bowler. He played for Bombay and Railways. Test Record - 31 Tests, 1,229 runs (32.34) including 2 centuries, 62 wickets (Av. 36.85) and 21 catches.

PHILLIPS, WAYNE BENTLEY
Australia (born 1958) - A left-handed opening batsman. He played for South Australia. Test Record - 27 Tests, 1,485 runs (Av. 32.28) including 2 centuries and 52 catches.

PHILPOTT, PETER IAN
Australia (born 1934) - A right-arm leg-break bowler and a very useful batsman. He played for New South Wales. Test Record - 8 Tests, 93 runs (Av. 10.33), 26 wickets (Av. 38.46) and 5 catches.

POCOCK, PATRICK LAN
England (born 1946) - A right-arm off-spinner bowler. He played for Surrey and Northern Transvaal. Test Record - 25 Tests, 206 runs (Av. 6.24), 67 wickets (Av. 44.41) and 15 catches.

POLLARD, RICHARD
England (1912-1985) - A right-arm fast-medium paced bowler. He played for Lancashire. Test Record - 4 Tests, 13 runs (Av. 13.00), 15 wickets (Av. 25.20) and 3 catches.

POLLARD, VICTOR
New Zealand (born 1945) - A right-handed attacking batsman, and a useful off-spin bowler and a brilliant fielder. He played for Central Districts and Canterbury. Test Record - 32 Tests, 1,266 runs (Av. 24.34) including 2 centuries and 40 wickets (Av. 46.32) and 19 catches.

POLLOCK, PETER MACLEAN
South Africa (born 1941) - A fast-medium bowler and right-handed batsman. He played for Eastern Province. Test Record - 28 Tests, 607 runs (Av. 21.67), 116 wickets (Av. 24.18) and 9 catches.

POLLOCK; ROBERT GRAEME

South Africa (born 1944) - A left-handed hard hitting batsman and off-spin bowler. He played for Eastern Province and Transvaal. Test Record - 23 Tests, 2,256 runs (Av. 60.97) including 7 centuries, 4 wickets (Av. 51.00) and 17 catches.

PONSFORD, WILLIAM HAROLD

Australia (born 1900) - An opening right-handed batsman. He played for Victoria. Test Record - 29 Tests, 2,122 runs (Av. 48.22) including 7 centuries and 21 catches.

POOLE, CYRIL JOHN

England (born 1932) - A left-handed attacking stroke-maker batsman. He played for Nottinghamshire. Test Record - 3 Tests, 161 runs (Av. 40.25) and 1 catch.

POORE, BRIGADIER GENERAL ROBERT

South Africa (1866-1938) - He was a good batsman. He played for Hampshire and Natal. Test Record - 3 Tests, 76 runs (Av. 12.66) and 3 catches.

POORE, MATT BERESFORD

New Zealand (born 1930) - A right-handed batsman and a useful off-spin change-bowler. He played for Canterbury. Test Record - 14 Tests, 354 runs (Av. 15.43), 9 wickets (Av. 40.77) and 1 catch.

PRASANNA, ERAPALLY ANANTHARAO SHRINIVASA

India (born 1940) - A right-handed batsman and a right-arm off-break bowler. He played for Mysore. Test Record - 49 Tests, 735 runs (Av. 11.48), 189 wickets (Av. 30.39) and 18 catches.

PRICE, JOHN SIDNEY ERNEST

England (born 1937) - A right-arm medium-fast bowler. He played for Middlesex. Test Record - 15 Tests, 66 runs (Av. 7.33), 40 wickets (Av. 35.02) and 7 catches.

PRIDEAUX, ROGER MALCOLM

England (born 1939) - A right-handed opening batsman. He played for Cambridge University, Kent, Northamptonshire and Orange Free State. Test Record - 3 Tests, 102 runs (Av. 20.40).

PRINGLE, DEREK RAYMOND

England (born 1958) - A hard-hitting right-handed batsman and a right-arm medium-fast bowler. He played for Cambridge University and Essex. Test Record - 14 Tests, 413 runs (Av. 18.77), 29 wickets (38.89) and 7 catches.

PROCTER, MICHAEL JOHN

South Africa (born 1946) - A left-arm fast bowler. He played for Natal, Western Province, Rhodesia and Gloucestershire. Test Record - 7 Tests, 226 runs (Av. 25.11), 41 wickets (Av. 15.02) and 4 catches.

PULLAR, GEOFFREY

England (born 1935) - A tall, left-handed batsman. He played for Lancashire and Gloucestershire. Test Record - 28 Tests, 1,974 runs (Av. 43.86) including 4 centuries, and 2 catches.

PUNA, NAROTAM

New Zealand (born 1929) - A right-arm off-spin bowler and a useful batsman. He played for Northern Districts. Test Record - 3 Tests, 31 runs (Av. 15.50), 4 wickets (Av. 60.00) and 1 catch.

PUNJABI, PANANMAL HOTCHAND

India (born 1921) - A right-handed opening batsman. He played for Gujarat. Test Record - 5 Tests, 164 runs (Av. 16.40) and 5 catches.

QAIFE, WILLIAM

England (1872-1951) - A right-handed batsman and slow leg-break bowler. He played for Sussex and Warwickshire. Test Record - 7 Tests, 228 runs (Av. 19.00), and 4 catches.

QASIM ALI OMAR

Pakistan (born 1957) - A right-handed batsman. He

played for Karachi and Muslim Commercial Bank. Test Record - 23 Tests, 1,431 runs (Av. 39.75) including 3 centuries and 15 catches.

RABONE, GEOFFREY OSBOURNE
New Zealand (born 1921) - He was a right-handed batsman and off-spin bowler. He played for Wellington and Auckland.Test Record - 12 Tests, 562 runs (Av. 31.22) including 1 century, 16 wickets (Av. 39.68) and 5 catches.

RACKMANN, CARL GRAY
Australia (born 1960) - A tall, right-hand fast bowler. He plays for Queensland. Test Record - 5 Tests, 16 runs (Av. 3.20), 23 wickets (Av. 23.43) and 2 catches.

RADFORD, NEAL VICTOR
England (born 1957) - A right-arm medium-fast bowler, a good right-handed batsman. He played for Lancashire and Transvaal.
Test Record - 2 Tests, 13 runs (Av. 6.50) and 3 wickets (Av. 73.00).

RADLEY, CLIVE THORNTON
England (born 1944) - He was a right-handed batsman. He played for Middlesex. Test Record - 8 Tests, 481 runs (Av. 48.10) including 2 centuries and 4 catches.

RAJPUT, LALCHAND SITARAM
India (born 1961) - A right-handed opening batsman. He plays for Bombay. Test Record - 2 Tests, 105 runs (Av. 26.25) and 1 catch.

RAMADHIN, SONNY
West Indies (born 1930) - A right-arm off-break and leg-break bowler. Test Record - 43 Tests, 361 runs (Av. 8.20), 158 wickets (Av. 28.98) and 9 catches.

RAMASWAMI, COTA
India (born 1896) - A left-handed batsman.He played for Madras. Test Record - 2 Tests, 170 runs (Av. 56.66).

RAMCHAND, GULABRAI SIPAHAHIMALANI
India (born 1927) - A right-handed batsman and a right-arm medium-fast bowler. He played for Sind and Bombay. Test Record - 33 Tests, 1,180 runs (Av. 24.58) including 2 centuries, 41 wickets (Av. 46.34) and 20 catches.

RAMEEZ RAJA
Pakistan (born 1962) - A balanced and gifted right-handed batsman. He plays for Lahore. Test Record -25 Tests,1156 runs (Av. 30.42) including 2 centuries and 16 catches.

RANASINGHE, ANURA NANDANA
Sri Lanka (born 1956) - A right-handed batsman and medium-pace left-arm seamer. He played for Bloomfield. Test Record - 2 Tests, 88 runs (Av. 22.00), 1 wicket (Av. 69.00)

RANATUNGA, ARJUNA
Sri Lanka (born 1963) - A right-arm medium-pace bowler, and right-handed hard-hitting batsman. He played for Sinhalese. Test Record - 24 Tests, 1,537 runs (Av. 37.48) including 2 centuries,11 wickets (Av. 55.81) 11 catches.

RANDALL, DEREK WILLIAM
England (born 1951) - A right-handed batsman. He played for Nottinghamshire. Test Record - 47 Tests, 2,470 runs (Av. 33.37) including 7 centuries and 31 catches.

RANGACHARI, COMMANDUR
India (born 1916) - A right-handed batsman and right-arm medium-fast bowler. He played for Madras. Test Record - 4 Tests, 8 runs (Av. 2.66) and 9 wickets (Av. 54.77).

RANGNEKAR, KHANDERAO MORESHWAR
India (1917-1984) - A left-handed batsman. He played for Bombay, Holkar and Madhya Pradesh. Test Record - 3 Tests, 33 runs (Av. 5.50) and 1 catch.

RANJANE, VASANT BABURAO
India (born 1937) - A right-handed batsman and a right-arm medium-fast bowler. He played for Maharashtra and Railways. Test Record - 7 Tests, 40 runs (Av. 6.66), 19 wickets (Av. 34.15) and 1 catch.

RATNAYAKE, RUMESH JOSEPH
Sri Lanka (born 1964) - A right-arm medium-fast bowler and a right-handed batsman. He plays for Nondescripts. Test Record - 14 Tests, 272 runs (Av. 14.31), 41 wickets (Av. 36.87) and 5 catches.

RATNAYEKE, JOSEPH RAVINDRAN
SriLanka (born 1960)- A tall right-arm medium-fast bowler and a left-handed batsman. He played for Nondescripts. Test Record - 20 Tests, 676 runs (Av.23.00),55 wickets (Av.33.27) and 1 catch.

READ, JOHN MAURICE
England (1859-1929)- A right-handed batsman and a useful medium-fast change bowler. He played for Surrey. Test Record - 17 Tests, 463 runs (Av.17.14) and 8 catches.

READ, WALTER WILLIAM
England (1855-1907) - A right-handed batsman. He played for Surrey. Test Record - 18 Tests, 720 runs (Av.27.69)including 1 century and 16 catches.

REDPATH, IAN RITCHIE
Australia (born 1941)- A right-handed batsman and a brilliant fielder close to the wicket. He played for Victoria. Test Record - 66 Tests, 4,737 runs (Av.43.45) including 8 centuries and 83 catches.

REDDY, BHARAT A.
India (born 1954) - A right-handed batsman and a wicket-keeper. He played for Madras. Test Record - 4 Tests, 38 runs (Av. 9.50) and 11 dismissals (9ct, 2st).

REID, BRUCE ANTHONY
Australia (born 1963) - A left-arm fast bowler, six foot eight inches tall. He plays for Western Australia. Test Record-18 Tests, 75 runs (Av.6.25), 62 wickets (Av.29.61) and 2 catches.

REID, JOHN FULTON
New Zealand (born 1958) - A right-handed batsman. He played for Auckland. Test Record - 19 Tests, 1,296 runs (Av. 46.28) including 6 centuries and 9 catches.

REID, JOHN RICHARD
New Zealand (born 1928) - A very strong, sturdy built, a natural forcing right-handed batsman and also outstanding medium-fast bowler. He played for Wellington and Otago. Test Record - 58 Tests, 3,248 runs (Av. 33.28) including 6 centuries, 85 wickets (Av. 33.41), 43 catches and 1 stumpings.

RELF, ALBET EDWARD
England (1874-1937) - A right-arm medium-pace bowler. He played for Norfolk, Sussex and Auckland. Test Record - 13 Tests, 416 runs (Av. 23.11), 25 wickets (Av. 24.96) and 14 catches.

RENNEBERG, DAVID ALEXANDER
Australia (born- 1942) - A right-arm medium-fast bowler. He played for New South Wales. Test Record - 8 Tests, 22 runs (Av. 3.66), 23 wickets (Av. 36.08) and 2 catches.

RHODES, WILFRED
England (1877-1973) - He was a left-arm bowler, a right-handed opening batsman. He played for Yorkshire. Test Record - 58 Tests, 2,325 runs (Av. 30.19) including 2 centuries, 127 wickets (Av. 26.69) and 60 catches.

RICHARDS, ISAAC VIVIAN ALEXANDER
West Indies (born 1952) - An orthodox right-handed batsman and also a capable off-spinner. He played for Leeward Islands, Somerset and Queensland. Test Record - 108 Tests, 7,849 runs (Av.51.98) including 24 centuries, 32 wickets (Av.56.56) and 112 catches.

RICHARDSON, ARTHUR JOHN

Australia (1888-1973) - A right-handed opening batsman and medium-pace off-break bowler. He played for South Australia and Western Australia. Test Record - 9 Tests, 409 runs (Av. 31.00) including 1 century, 12 wickets (Av. 43.41) and 1 catch.

RICHARDSON, PETER EDWARD

England (born 1931) - A left-handed opening batsman and also a useful change bowler. He played for Worcestershire and Kent. Test Record - 34 Tests, 2,061 runs (Av. 37.47) including 5 centuries, 3 wickets (Av. 16.00) and 6 catches.

RICHARDSON, RICHARD BENJAMIN

West Indies (born 1962) - A right-handed batsman. He played for Leeward Islands. Test Record - 45 Tests, 3,320 runs (Av. 48.11) including 10 centuries and 57 catches.

RICHARDSON, THOMAS

England (1870-1912) - A right-arm off-break bowler. He played for Surrey and Somerset. Test Record - 14 Tests, 177 runs (Av. 11.06), 88 wickets (Av. 25.22) and 5 catches.

RITCHIE, GREGORY MICHAEL

Australia (born 1960) - A right-handed batsman with flair. He played for Queensland and Buckinghamshire. Test Record - 23 Tests, 1,374 runs (Av. 35.23) including 3 centuries and 10 catches.

RIXON, STEPHEN JOHN

Australia (born 1954) - A neat and lively wicket-keeper and a useful right-handed batsman. He played for New South Wales. Test Record - 13 Tests, 394 runs (Av. 18.76) and 47 dismissals (42 ct, 5 st).

RIZWAN-UZ-ZAMAN

Pakistan (born 1962) - A right-handed opening batsman. He played for Pakistan International Airlines and Karachi. Test Record - 11 Tests, 345 runs (Av 19.16), 4 wickets (Av. 11.50) and 4 catches.

ROACH, CLIFFORD ARCHIBALD

West Indies (born 1904) - A right-handed opening batsman. He played for Trinidad. Test Record - 16 Tests, 952 runs (Av. 30.70) including 2 centuries, 2 wickets (Av. 51.50) and 5 catches.

ROBERTS, ALBERT WILLIAM

New Zealand (1909-1978) - A right-arm medium-pace bowler. He played for Canterbury and Otago. Test Record - 5 Tests, 248 runs (Av. 27.55), 7 wickets (Av. 29.85) and 4 catches.

ROBERTS, ANDERSON MONTGOMERY EVERTON

West Indies (born 1951) - A right-arm medium-fast bowler, useful right-handed bowler. He played for New South Wales, Leicestershire and Hampshire. Test Record - 47 Tests, 762 runs (Av. 14.94), 202 wickets (Av. 25.61) and 9 catches.

ROBINS, ROBERT WALTER VIVIAN

England (1906-1968) - A right-arm leg-break and googly bowler. He played for Cambridge University and Middlesex. Test Record - 19 Tests, 612 runs (Av. 26.60) including 1 century, 64 wickets (Av. 27.46) and 12 catches.

ROBINSON, RICHARD DARYL

Australia (born 1948) - An attacking right-handed batsman and useful wicket-keeper. He played for Victoria. Test Record - 3 Tests, 100 runs (Av. 16.66) and 4 catches.

ROBINSON, ROBERT TIMOTHY

England (born 1958) - A right-handed batsman and an excellent fielder. He plays for Nottinghamshire. Test Record - 16 Tests, 1,052 runs (Av. 42.08) including 3 centuries, and 6 catches.

RODRIGUEZ, WILLIAM VINCETE

West Indies (born 1934) - A right-handed batsman and a useful leg-break bowler. He played for Trinidad. Test Record - 5 Tests, 96 runs (Av. 13.71), 7 wickets (Av. 53.42) and 3 catches.

ROOPE, GRAHAM RICHARD JAMES
England (born 1946) - A right-handed middle-order batsman. He played for Berkshire, Surrey and Griqualand West. Test Record - 21 Tests, 860 runs (Av. 30.71) and 35 catches.

ROOT, CHARLES FREDERICK
England (1890-1954) - A right-arm leg-break bowler and a master of spin. He was a hard-hitting batsman. He played for Derbyshire and Worcestershire. Test Record - 3 Tests, Did not bat, 8 wickets (Av. 24.25) and 1 catch.

RORKE, GORDON FREDERICK
Australia (born 1938) - A right-arm medium-fast bowler. He played for New South Wales. Test Record - 4 Tests, 9 runs (Av. 4.50), 10 wickets (Av. 20.30) and 1 catch.

ROSE, BRIAN CHARLES
England (born 1950) - A left-handed batsman. He played for Somerset. Test Record - 9 Tests, 358 runs (Av. 25.57) and 4 catches.

ROWAN, ERIC ALFRED BURCHELL
South Africa (born 1909) - A right-handed batsman. He played for Transvaal. Test Record - 26 Tests, 1,965 runs (Av. 43.66) including 3 centuries and 14 catches.

ROWE, GEORGE ALEXANDER
South Africa (1874-1959) - A left-arm slow bowler. He played for Western Province. Test Record - 5 Tests, 26 runs (Av. 4.33), 15 wickets (Av. 30.40) and 4 catches.

ROWE, LAWRENCE GEORGE
West Indies (born 1949) - A right-handed opening batsman . He played for Jamaica and Derbyshire. Test Record - 30 Tests, 2,047 runs (Av. 43.55) including 7 centuries and 17 catches.

ROY, AMBAR
India (born 1945) - A left-handed batsman. He played for Bengal. Test Record - 4 Tests, 91 runs (Av. 13.00).

ROY, PANKAJ
India (born 1928) - A right-handed opening batsman and right-arm medium-pace bowler. He played for Bengal. Test Record - 43 Tests, 2,442 runs (Av. 32.56) including 5 centuries and 16 catches.

ROY, PRONOB PANKAJ
India (born 1957) - A right-handed opening batsman. He played for Bengal. Test Record - 2 Tests, 71 runs (Av. 33.50) and 1 catch.

RUMSEY, FREDERICK EDWARD
England (born 1935) - A left-arm medium-fast bowler. He played for Worcestershire, Somerset and Derbyshire. Test Record - 5 Tests, 30 runs (Av. 15.00) and 17 wickets (Av. 27.11).

RUTHERFORD, KENNETH ROBERT
New Zealand (born 1965) - A right-handed batsman and a fine fielder. He played for Otago. Test Record - 16 Tests, 368 runs (Av. 15.33), 1 wicket (Av. 65.00) and 9 catches.

RYDER, JOHN
Australia (1889-1977) - An attacking right-handed batsman and a medium-fast change-bowler. Test Record - 20 Tests, 1,394 runs (Av. 51.62) including 3 centuries, 17 wickets (Av. 43.70) and 17 catches.

SADIQ MOHAMMAD
Pakistan (born 1945) - A left-handed opening batsman and useful leg-spin bowler. He played for Karachi, United Bank and Tasmania. Test Record - 41 Tests, 2,579 runs (Av. 35.81) including 5 centuries and 28 catches.

SAEED AHMED
Pakistan (born 1937) - A stroke-making right-handed batsman and a useful slow to medium off-break bowler. He played for International Airlines. Test Record - 41 Tests, 2,991 runs (Av. 40.42) including 5 centuries, 22 wickets (Av. 36.45) and 13 catches.

SAGGERS, RONALD ARTHUR
Australia (born 1917) - An accomplished second-string wicket-keeper and an attractive batsman. He played for New South Wales. Test Record - 6 Tests, 30 runs (Av. 10.00) and 24 dismissals (16ct, 8st).

SALAH-UD-DIN
Pakistan (born 1947) - A right-handed batsman, a useful slow off-break bowler and a good close fielder. He played for Karachi. Test Record - 5 Tests, 117 runs (Av. 19.50), 7 wickets (Av. 26.71) and 3 catches.

SALEEM ALTAF
Pakistan (born 1944) - A right-arm medium-fast bowler, using both in and out-swingers, and an uninhibited batsman. He played for Pakistan International Airlines. Test Record - 21 Tests, 276 runs (Av. 14.52), 46 wickets (Av. 37.17) and 3 catches.

SALEEM JAFFAR
Pakistan (born 1962) - A left-arm medium-fast bowler. Test Record - 9 Tests, 22 runs (Av.3.66), 24 wickets (Av.34.70) and 1 catch.

SALEEM MALIK
Pakistan (born 1963) - A natural right-handed batsman. He plays for Lahore and Habib Bank. Test Record - 52 Tests, 2,352 runs (Av. 39.20) including 6 centuries, 5 wickets (Av.19.80) and 42 catches.

SALEEM YOUSUF
Pakistan (born 1959) - An agile wicket-keeper and skilful hard-hitting right-handed batsman. He played for Sind, Karachi, Industrial Development Bank of Pakistan and Allied Bank. Test Record - 24 Tests, 838 runs. (Av.31.03) and 77 dismissals (66ct,11st).

SANDHAM, ANDREW
England (1890-1982) - He was a right-handed opening batsman. He played for Surrey. Test Record - 14 Tests, 879 runs (Av. 38.21) including 2 centuries and 4 catches.

SANDHU, BALWINDER SINGH HARBANS SINGH
India (born 1956) - A left-arm opening medium-fast bowler and a right-handed tail-end batsman. He played for Bombay. Test Record - 8 Tests, 214 runs (Av. 30.57), 10 wickets (Av. 55.70) and 1 catch.

SARDESAI, DILIP NARAYAN
India (born 1940) - A right-handed batsman and a right-arm off-spin bowler. He played for Bombay. Test Record - 30 Tests, 2,001 runs (Av. 39.23) including 5 centuries and 4 catches.

SARFRAZ NAWAZ
Pakistan (born 1948) - A medium-fast bowler. He played for Lahore, United Bank and Northamptonshire. Test Record - 55 Tests, 1,045 runs (Av. 17.71), 177 wickets (Av. 32.75) and 26 catches.

SARWATE, CHANDRASEKHAR TRIMBAK
India (born 1920) - A right-handed batsman and a right-arm leg-break googly bowler. He played for Central Provinces and Berar.Test Record - 9 Tests, 208 runs (Av. 13.00) and 3 wickets (Av. 124.66).

SAUNDERS, JOHN VICTOR
Australia (1876-1927) - A left-arm medium-pace bowler. He played for Victoria and Wellington. Test Record - 14 Tests, 39 runs (Av. 2.29), 79 wickets (Av. 22.74) and 5 catches.

SCHWARZ, REGINALD OSCAR
South Africa (1875-1918) - A googly bowler and a useful batsman. He played for Oxfordshire and Transvaal. Test Record - 20 Tests, 374 runs (Av. 13.85), 55 wickets (Av. 25.76) and 18 catches.

SCOTTON, WILLIAM HENRY
England (1856-1893) - He was a left-handed batsman and a good close fielder. He played for Nottinghamshire. Test Record - 15 Tests, 510 runs (Av. 22.17) and 4 catches.

SERJEANT, CRAIG STANTON
Australia (born 1951) - A right-handed batsman, a powerful hitter of the ball. He played for Western Australia. Test Record - 12 Tests, 522 runs (Av. 23.72) including 1 century and 13 catches.

SHARMA, CHETAN JAGATRAM
India (born 1966) - A five-foot-eight-inch right-arm medium-fast bowler. A right-handed batsman and also a fine fielder. He plays for Haryana. Test Record - 23 Tests,396 runs (Av. 22.00), 61 wickets (Av. 35.45) and 7 catches.

SHARMA, GOPAL
India (born 1960) - A slightly built off-spin bowler with nice flight and good control and also a right-handed late-order batsman. He plays for Uttar Pradesh. Test Record - 4 Tests, 11 runs (Av. 5.50), 9 wickets (Av.39.22) and 1 catch.

SHARPE, PHILIP JOHN
England (born 1936) - A stocky right-handed batsman and also a good silp fielder. He played for Yorkshire and Derbyshire. Test Record - 12 Tests, 786 runs (Av. 46.23) including 1 century, and 17 catches.

SHASTRI, RAVISHANKAR JAYADRITHA
India (born 1962) - A right-handed batsman and right-arm spin bowler. He plays for Bombay. Test Record - 65 Tests, 2,872 runs (Av.34.60) including 8 centuries,139 wickets (Av.38.75) and 30 catches.

SHEAHAN, ANDREW PAUL
Australia (born 1946) - A right-handed batsman and a brilliant fielder. He played for Victoria. Test Record - 31 Tests, 1,594 runs (Av. 33.91) including 2 centuries and 17 catches.

SHINDE, SADASHIV GARPATRAO
India (1923-1955) - A right-handed batsman and a right-arm leg-break bowler. He played for Baroda and Bombay. Test Record - 7 Tests, 85 runs (Av. 14.16) and 12 wickets (Av. 59.75).

SHREWSBURY, ARTHUR
England (1856-1903) - A right-hadned batsman and a fine fielder. He played for Nottinghamshire. Test Record - 23 Tests, 1,277 runs (Av. 35.47) including 3 centuries and 29 catches.

SHRIMPTON, MICHAEL JOHN FROUD
New Zealand (born 1940) - A right-handed batsman and an occasional leg-break bowler. He played for Hawke's Bay, Central Districts and Northern Districts. Test Record - 10 Tests, 265 runs (Av. 13.94), 5 wickets (Av. 31.60) and 2 catches.

SHUJA-UD-DIN
Pakistan (born 1930) - A right-handed batsman and a useful slow left-arm bowler of great stamina. He played for Services and Northern India. Test Record - 19 Tests, 395 runs (Av. 15.19), 20 wickets (Av. 40.05) and 8 catches.

SHUTTLEWORTH, KENNETH
England (born 1944) - A very fine fast bowler and also a fine fielder. He played for Lancashire and Leicestershire. Test Record - 5 Tests, 46 runs (Av. 7.66), 12 wickets (Av. 35.58) and 1 catch.

SIKANDER BAKHT
Pakistan (born 1957) - A medium-fast bowler and a right-handed batsman. He played for United Bank, Public Works Department, Pakistan International Airlines. Test Record - 26 Tests, 146 runs (Av. 6.34), 67 wickets (Av. 35.98) and 7 catches.

SIMPSON, REGINALD THOMAS
England (born 1920) - A right-handed batsman . He played for Sind and Nottinghamshire. Test Record - 27 Tests, 1,401 runs (Av. 33.35) including 4 centuries, 2 wickets (Av. 11.00) and 5 catches.

SIMPSON, ROBERT BADDELEY
Australia (born 1936) - A right-handed batsman, a good leg-spin and googly bowler. He played for New South Wales and Western Australia. Test Record - 62 Tests, 4,869 runs (Av. 46.81) including

10 centuries, 71 wickets (Av. 42.26) and 110 catches.

SINCLAIR, BARRY WHITLEY

New Zealand (born 1936) - A right-handed batsman. He played for Wellington. Test Record - 21 Tests, 1,148 runs (Av. 29.43) including 3 centuries, 2 wickets (Av. 16.00) and 8 catches.

SINCLAIR, JAMES HUGH

South Africa (1876-1913) - A right-hadned hard-hitting batsman and also a medium-fast bowler. He played for Transvaal. Test Record - 25 Tests, 1,069 runs (Av. 23.23) including 3 centuries, 63 wickets (Av. 31.58) and 9 catches.

SINCOCK, DAVID JOHN

Australia (born 1942) - A left-arm googly bowler. He played for South Australia. Test Record - 3 Tests, 80 runs (Av. 26.66), 8 wickets (Av. 51.25) and 2 catches.

SMITH, ERNEST JAMES

England (1886-1979) - A right-handed opening batsman. He played for Warwickshire. Test Record - 11 Tests, 113 runs (Av. 8.69) and 20 dismissals (17ct, 3st).

SMITH, FREDERICK W.

South Africa - Details not known. A middle-order batsman. He played for Transvaal. Test Record - 3 Tests, 45 runs (Av. 9.00) and 2 catches.

SMITH, IAN DAVID STOCKLEY

New Zealand (born 1957) - A right-handed batsman and a useful wicket-keeper. He played for Central Districts. Test Record - 33 Tests, 808 runs (Av. 22.44) including 1 century and 98 dismissals (92ct, 6st).

SMITH, MICHAEL JOHN KNIGHT

England (born 1933) - A right-handed batsman. He played for Oxford University and Warwickshire.Test Record - 50 Tests, 2,278 runs (Av. 31.63) including 3 centuries and 53 catches.

SMITH, O'NEIL GORDON

West Indies (1933-1959) - An off-break bowler and a right-handed batsman. He played for Jamaica. Test Record - 26 Tests, 1,331 runs (Av. 31.69) including 4 centuries, 48 wickets (Av. 33.85) and 9 catches.

SMITH, STEPHEN BARRY

Australia (born 1961) - A right-handed opening batsman and a fine fielder. He played for New South Wales. Test Record - 3 Tests, 41 runs (Av. 8.20) and 1 catch.

SNEDDEN, MARTIN COLIN

New Zealand (born 1958) - A right-arm medium-fast bowler and useful left-handed batsman. He played for Auckland. Test Record - 11 Tests, 147 runs (Av. 14.70), 24 wickets (Av. 38.75) and 2 catches.

SNOOKE, SIBLEY JOHN

South Africa (1881-1966) - A right-handed stroke batsman. He played for Border. Test Record - 26 Tests, 1,008 runs (Av. 22.40) including 1 century, 35 wickets (Av. 20.05), and 24 catches.

SNOW, JOHN AUGUSTINE

England (born 1941) - A right-arm medium-fast bowler and a right-handed batsman. He played for Sussex and Warwickshire. Test Record - 49 Tests, 772 runs (Av. 13.54), 202 wickets (Av. 26.66) and 16 catches.

SOBERS, SIR GARFIELD ST AUBRUN

West Indies (born 1936) - A left-handed batsman. He was one of the greatest batsmen and left-arm medium-fast over-the-wicket bowler.He played for Barbados, South Australia and Nottinghamshire. Test Record - 93 Tests, 8,032 runs (Av. 57.78) including 26 centuries, 235 wickets (Av. 34.03) and 109 catches.

SOHONI, SRIRANGA WASUDEO

India (born 1918) - A right-handed batsman and a right-arm medium-fast bowler. He played for Maharashtra, Baroda and Bombay. Test Record - 4 Tests, 83 runs (Av. 16.60), 2 wickets (Av. 101.00) and 2 catches.

SOLKAR, EKNATH DHONDU

India (born 1948) - A left-handed batsman and a left-arm medium-pace and slow spin bowler. He played for Bombay and Sussex. Test Record - 27 Tests, 1,068 runs (Av. 25.42) including 1 century, 18 wickets (Av. 59.44) and 53 catches.

SOLOMON, JOSEPH STANISLAUS

West Indies (born 1930) - A right-handed batsman, a useful medium-pace leg-break change bowler. He played for British Guiana. Test Record - 27 Tests, 1,326 runs (Av. 34.00) including 1 century, 4 wickets (Av. 67.00) and 13 catches.

SPOFFORTH, FREDERICK ROBERT

Australia (1853-1926) - A famous medium-fast bowler. He played for New South Wales, Victoria and Derbyshire. Test Record - 18 Tests, 217 runs (Av. 9.43), 94 wickets (Av. 18.41) and 11 catches.

SPOONER, REGINALD HERBERT

England (1880-1961) - A useful right-handed batsman. He played for Lancashire. Test Record - 10 Tests, 481 runs (Av. 32.06) including 1 century and 4 catches.

SRIKANTH, KRISHNAMACHARI

India (born 1959) - A smiling cavalier of a right-handed batsman also a useful right-arm bowler. He plays for Tamil Nadu. Test Record - 35 Tests, 1,830 runs (Av.33.88) including 2 centuries and 32 catches.

ST HILL, EDWIN LLOYD

West Indies (1904-1957) - He was a right-arm medium-pace bowler and also a useful batsman. He played for Trinidad. Test Record - 2 Tests, 18 runs (Av. 4.50) and 3 wickets (Av. 73.66).

STACKPOLE, KEITH RAYMOND

Australia (born 1940) - A right-handed opening batsman and a useful leg-break bowler. He played for Victoria. Test Record - 43 Tests, 2,807 runs (Av. 37.42) including 7 centuries, 15 wickets (Av. 66.73) and 47 catches.

STANYFORTH, LT-COL.RONALD THOMAS

England (1892-1964) - A useful wicket-keeper. He played for Yorkshire. Test Record - 4 Tests, 13 runs (Av. 2.60) and 9 dismissals (7 ct, 2 st).

STATHAM, JOHN BRIAN

England (born 1930) - A right-arm great medium-fast bowler and a left-handed batsman. He played for Lancashire. Test Record - 70 Tests, 675 runs (Av. 11.44), 252 wickets (Av. 24.82) and 28 catches.

STAYERS, SVEN CONRAD

West Indies (born 1937) - A good right-handed batsman and a medium-fast bowler. He played for British Guiana. Test Record - 4 Tests, 58 runs (Av. 19.33) and 9 wickets (Av. 40.44).

STEEL, ALLAN GIBSON

England 1858-1914) - A right-arm slow bowler and right-handed batsman. He played for Cambridge University and Lancashire. Test Record - 13 Tests, 600 runs (Av. 35.29) including 2 centuries, 29 wickets (Av. 20.86) and 5 catches.

STEELE, DAVID STANLEY

England (born 1941) - A right-handed batsman, a slow left-arm bowler. He played for Staffordshire and Northamptonshire. Test Record - 8 Tests, 673 runs (Av. 42.06) including 1 century, 2 wickets (Av. 19.50) and 7 catches.

STODDART, ANDREW ERNEST

England (1863-1915) - He was a right-handed batsman. He played for Middlesex. Test Record - 16 Tests, 996 runs (Av. 35.57) including 2 centuries, 2 wickets (Av. 47.00) and 6 catches.

STOLLMEYER, JEFFREY BAXTER

West Indies (1921-1989) - A right-handed opening batsman, a useful leg-break bowler. He played for Trinidad. Test Record - 32 Tests, 2,159 runs (Av. 42.33) including 4 centuries, 13 wickets (Av. 39.00) and 20 catches.

SUBBA, ROW RAMAN

England (born 1932) - A left-handed batsman and also a good close fielder. He played for Cambridge University, Surrey and Northamptonshire. Test Record - 13 Tests, 984 runs (Av. 46.85) including 3 centuries and 5 catches.

SUBRAMANYAM, VENKATRAMAN

India (born 1936) - A right-handed batsman and a right-arm leg-break and googly bowler. He played for Mysore. Test Record - 9 Tests, 263 runs (Av. 18.78), 3 wickets (67.00) and 9 catches.

SURENDRANATH, R.

India (born 1937) - A right-handed and a right-arm medium-fast bowler. He played for Services. Test Record - 11 Tests, 136 runs (Av. 10.46), 26 wickets (Av. 40.50) and 4 catches.

SURTI, RUSI FRAMROZ

India (born 1936) - A left-handed and left-arm medium-pace and slow-spin bowler.He played for Gujarat, Rajasthan and Queensland. Test Record - 26 Tests, 1,263 runs (Av. 28.70), 42 wickets (Av. 46.71) and 26 catches.

SUTCLIFFE, BERT

New Zealand (born 1923) - A left-handed opening batsman and left-arm slow bowler . He played for Auckland, Otago and Northern Districts. Test Record - 42 Tests, 2,727 runs (Av. 40.10) including 5 centuries, 4 wickets (Av. 86.00) and 20 catches.

SUTCLIFFE, HERBERT

England (1894-1978) - He was an opening batsman. He played for Yorkshire. Test Record - 54 Tests, 4,555 runs (Av. 60.73) including 16 centuries, and 23 catches.

TABER, HEDLEY BRIAN

Australia (born 1940) - A very slow bowler and also a wicket-keeper. He played for New South Wales. Test Record - 16 Tests, 353 runs (Av. 16.04) and 60 dismissals (56ct, 4st).

TAHIR NAQQASH

Pakistan (born 1959) - A right-handed middle-order batsman and also a right-arm medium-fast bowler. He played for Punjab, Lahore and Muslim Commerical Bank. Test Record - 15 Tests, 300 runs (Av. 21.42), 34 wickets (Av. 41.11) and 3 catches.

TAMHANE, NARENDRA SHANKER

India (born 1931) - A right-handed batsman and a wicket-keeper. He played for Bombay. Test Record - 21 Tests, 225 runs (Av. 10.22) and 51 dismissals (35ct, 16st).

TATE, MAURICE WILLIAM

England (1895-1956) - A right-handed batsman and also a right-arm slow off-break bowler. He played for Sussex. Test Record - 39 Tests, 1,198 runs (Av. 25.48) including 1 century, 155 wickets (Av. 26.13) and 11 catches.

TATTERSALL, ROY

England (born 1922) - A right-arm off-break spin bowler. He played for Lancashire. Test Record - 16 Tests, 50 runs (Av. 5.00), 58 wickets (Av. 26.08) and 8 catches.

TAUSEEF AHMED

Pakistan (born 1960) - A right-arm off-spin bowler. He played for Public Works Department and United Bank. Test Record - 28 Tests,242 runs (Av. 17.28), 87 wickets (Av. 29.58) and 8 catches.

TAVARE, CHRISTOPHER JAMES

England (born 1954) - A right-handed batsman, a right-arm bowler. He played for Oxford University. Test Record - 30 Tests, 1,753 (Av.33.07) runs including 2 centuries and 20 catches.

TAYFIELD, HUGH JOSEPH

South Africa (born 1928) - A right-arm off-spin bowler and a useful batsman. He played for Natal, Rhodesia and Transvaal. Test Record - 37 Tests, 862 runs (Av. 16.90), 170 wickets (Av. 25.91) and 26 catches.

TAYLOR, BRUCE RICHARD

New Zealand (born 1943) - A left-handed batsman and a right-arm medium-fast bowler. He played for Canterbury and Wellington. Test Record - 30 Tests, 898 runs (Av. 20.40) including 2 centuries, 111 wickets (Av. 26.60) and 10 catches.

TAYLOR, HERBERT WILFERD

South Africa (1889-1973) - A right-handed opening batsman and a useful change bowler. He played for Natal, Transvaal and Western Province. Test Record - 42 Tests, 2,936 runs (Av. 40.77) including 7 centuries, 5 wickets (Av. 31.20) and 19 catches.

TAYLOR, ROBERT WILLIAM

England (born 1941) - A capable orthodox batsman and also a useful wicket-keeper. He played for Derbyshire and Staffordshire. Test Record -57 Tests, 1,156 runs (Av. 16.28) and 174 dismissals(167ct,7st.)

TITMUS, FREDERICK JOHN

England (born 1932) - An off-spin bowler and a useful batsman. Test Record - 53 Tests, 1,449 runs (Av. 22,29), 153 wickets (Av. 32.22) and 35 catches.

TOLCHARD, ROGER WILLIAM

England (born 1946) - A good wicket-keeper and a useful batsman. He played for Devon and Leicestershire. Test Record - 4 Tests, 129 runs (Av. 25.80) and 5 catches.

TOOHEY, PETER MICHAEL

Australia (born 1954) - A small right-handed middle-order batsman. He played for New South Wales. Test Record - 15 Tests, 893 runs (Av. 31.87) including 1 century and 9 catches.

TROTT, GEORGE HENRY STEPHENS

Australia (1866-1917) - A right-handed batsman and a right-arm leg-spin bowler. He played for Victoria. Test Record - 24 Tests, 921 runs (Av. 21.92) including 1 century, 29 wickets (Av. 35.13) and 21 catches.

TROUP, GARY BERTRAM

New Zealand (born 1952) - A left-arm medium-fast bowler. He played for Auckland. Test Record - 15 Tests, 55 runs (Av. 4.58), 39 wickets (Av. 37.28) and 2 catches.

TRUEMAN, FREDERICK SEWARDS

England (born 1931) - A right-handed batsman, a useful right-arm bowler and a brilliant natural fielder. He played for Yorkshire. Test Record - 67 Tests, 981 runs (Av. 13.81), 307 wickets (Av. 21.57) and 64 catches.

TRUMBLE, HUGH

Australia (1867-1938) - A right-arm medium-pace off-spin bowler. He played for Victoria. Test Record - 32 Tests, 851 runs (Av. 19.78), 141 wickets (Av. 21.78) and 45 catches.

TRUMPER, VICTOR THOMAS

Australia (1877-1915) - A right-handed attacking batsman. He played for New South Wales. Test Record - 48 Tests, 3,163 runs (Av. 39.04) including 8 centuries, 8 wickets (Av. 37.62) and 31 catches.

TURNER, CHARLES THOMAS BIASS

Australia (1862-1944) - A medium-fast bowler. He played for New South Wales. Test Record - 17 Tests, 323 runs (Av. 11.53), 101 wickets (Av. 16.53) and 8 catches.

TURNER, GLENN MAITLAND

New Zealand (born 1947) - A right-handed stroke-maker batsman. He played for Otago and Worcestershire. Test Record - 41 Tests, 2,991 runs (Av. 44.64) including 7 centuries and 42 catches.

TYLDESLEY, JOHN THOMAS
England (1873-1930) - An attacking right-handed batsman on all wickets. He played for Lancashire. Test Record - 31 Tests, 1,661 runs (Av. 30.75) including 4 centuries and 16 catches.

TYSON, FRANK HOLMES
England (born 1930) - A right-arm medium-fast bowler. He played for Northamptonshire. Test Record - 17 Tests, 230 runs (Av. 10.95), 76 wickets (Av. 18.56) and 4 catches.

ULYETT, GEORGE
England (1851-1898) - He was one of the best fast bowlers and a reliable fielder. He played for Yorkshire. Test Record - 25 Tests, 949 runs (Av. 24.33) including 1 century, 50 wickets (Av. 20.40) and 18 catches.

UMRIGAR, PAHLAN RATANJI
India (born 1926) - A right-handed batsman and a right-arm medium-pace and off-break bowler. He played for Bombay and Gujarat. Test Record - 59 Tests, 3,631 runs (Av. 42.22) including 12 centuries, 35 wickets (Av. 42.08) and 33 catches.

UNDERWOOD, DEREK LESLIE
England (born 1945) - A left-arm spin bowler and also a right-handed batsman. He played for Kent. Test Record - 86 Tests, 937 runs (Av. 11.56), 297 wickets (Av. 25.83) and 44 catches.

VALENTINE, ALFRED LEWIS
West Indies (born 1930) - He was left-arm slow-medium bowler. He played for Jamaica. Test Record - 36 Tests, 141 runs (Av. 4.70), 139 wickets (Av. 30.32) and 13 catches.

VALENTINE, BRYAN HERBERT
England (1908-1983) - A right-handed batsman. He played for Cambridge University and Kent. Test Record - 7 Tests, 454 runs (Av.64.85) including 2 centuries and 2 catches.

VERITY, HEDLEY
England (1905-1943) - He was the best left-arm spin bowler and also a lower-order batsman. He played for Yorkshire. Test Record - 40 Tests, 669 runs (Av. 20.90), 144 wickets (Av. 24.37) and 30 catches.

VENGSARKAR, DILIP BALWANT
India (born 1956)- A right-handed batsman and right-arm bowler. He plays for Bombay. Test Record - 98 Tests, 6,256 runs (Av.46.00) including 17 centuries.

VENKATRAGHAVAN, SRINIVASRAGHAVAN
India (born 1946)- Right-handed batsman and right-arm off-break bowler. He played for Tamil Nadu. Test Record - 57 Tests, 748 runs (Av.11.68), 156 wickets (Av.36.11) and 43 catches.

VERIVERS, THOMAS ROBERT
Australia (born 1937) - A right-arm off-break bowler. He played for Queensland. Test Record - 21 Tests, 813 runs (Av. 31.26), 33 wickets (Av. 41.66) and 7 catches.

VILJOEN, KENNETH GEORGE
South Africa (1910-1974) - A right-handed batsman and a brilliant fielder. He played for Orange Free State and Transvaal. Test Record - 27 Tests, 1,365 runs (Av. 28.43) including 2 centuries and 5 catches.

VINCENT, CYRIL LEVERTON
South Africa (1902-1968) - A left-arm spin bowler and a competent batsman. He played for Transvaal. Test Record - 25 Tests,526 runs (Av.20.23),84 wickets (Av.31.32) and 27 catches.

VISWANATH, GUNDAPPA RANGANATH
India (born 1949) - A right-handed batsman and a right-arm leg-break bowler. He played for Karnataka. Test Record - 91 Tests, 6,080 runs (Av. 41.93) including 14 centuries, 1 wicket (Av. 46.00) and 63 catches.

VISWANATH, SADANAND

India (born 1962) - A wicket-keeper and useful right-handed batsman. He played for Karnataka. Test Record - 3 Tests, 31 runs (Av. 6.20) and 11 catches.

VIVIAN, GRAHAM ELLERY

New Zealand (born 1946) - A left-handed stroke-playing batsman and a leg-spin and leg-break bowler. He played for Auckland. Test Record - 5 Tests, 110 runs (Av. 18.33), and 3 catches.

VIZIANAGRAM, MAHARAJAH SIR VIAJAYA

India (1905-1965) - A right-handed batsman. He played for United Province. Test Record - 3 Tests, 33 runs (Av. 8.25) and 1 catch.

VOCE, WILLIAM

England (1909-1984) - A left-arm slow, medium-fast over the wicket bowler. He played for Nottinghamshire. Test Record - 27 Tests, 308 runs (Av. 13.39), 98 wickets (Av. 27.88) and 15 catches.

VOGLER, ALBERT EDWARD ERNEST

South Africa (1876-1946) - A right-arm leg-break and googly bowler and also a right-handed batsman. He played for Natal. Test Record - 15 Tests, 340 runs (Av. 17.00), 64 wickets (Av. 22.73) and 20 catches.

WADDINGTON, ABRAHAM

England (1893-1959) - A left-arm medium-fast bowler and a tail-end batsman. He played for Yorkshire. Test Record - 2 Tests, 16 runs (Av. 4.00) and 1 catch.

WADEKAR, AJIT LAXMAN

India (born 1941) - A left-handed batsman and left-arm slow spin bowler. He played for Bombay. Test Record - 37 Tests, 2,113 runs (Av. 31.07) including 1 century and 46 catches.

WADSWORTH, KENNETH JOHN

New Zealand (1946-1976) - A right-handed batsman and a useful wicket-keeper. He played for Central Districts and Canterbury. Test Record - 33 Tests, 1,010 runs (Av. 21.48) and 96 dismissals (92ct, 4st).

WAINWRIGHT, EDWARD

England (1865-1919) - A right-handed batsman and an off-break bowler. He played for Yorkshire. Test Record - 5 Tests, 132 runs (Av. 14.66) and 2 catches.

WAITE, JOHN HENRY BICKFORD

South Africa (born 1930) - A right-handed batsman and a useful wicket-keeper. He played for Transvaal. Test Record - 50 Tests, 2,405 runs (Av. 30.44) including 4 centuries and 141 dismissals (124ct, 17st).

WAITE, MARVYN GEORGE

Australia (1911-1985) - An honest type of batsman and medium-pace bowler. He played for South Australia. Test Record - 2 Tests, 11 runs (Av. 3.66), and 1 catch.

WALCOTT, CLYDE LEOPOLD

West Indies (born 1926) - A very useful medium-fast change-bowler, a right-handed batsman. He played for Barbados and British Guiana. Test Record - 44 Tests, 3,798 runs (Av. 56.68) including 15 centuries, 11 wickets (Av. 37.09) and 64 dismissals (53ct, 11st).

WALKER, MAXWELL HENRY NORMAN

Australia (born 1948) - A right-arm medium-pace bowler and a willing and determined batsman. He played for Victoria. Test Record - 34 Tests, 586 runs (Av. 19.53), 138 wickets (Av. 27.47) and 12 catches.

WALKER, PETER MICHAEL

England (born 1936) - A hard-hitting right-handed batsman. He played for Glamorgan and Western Province. Test Record - 3 Tests, 128 runs (Av. 32.00), and 5 catches.

WALLACE, WALTER MERVYN

New Zealand (born 1916) - A right-handed attacking batsman. He played for Auckland. Test Record - 13 Tests, 439 runs (Av. 20.90) and 5 catches.

WALL, THOMAS WELBOURNE
Australia (1904-981) - A right-arm medium-fast bowler. He played for South Australia. Test Record - 18 Tests, 121 runs (Av. 6.36), 56 wickets (Av. 35.89) and 11 catches.

WALSH, COURTNEY ANDREW
West Indies (born 1962) - A right-arm medium-fast bowler. He played for Jamaica and Gloucestershire. Test Record - 34 Tests, 277 runs (Av. 10.25), 122 wickets (Av. 24.24) and 4 catches.

WALTERS, KEVIN DOUGLAS
Australia (born 1945) - An all-rounder. He was a useful batsman and also a useful medium-pace swing bowler. He played for New South Wales. Test Record - 74 Tests, 5,357 runs (Av. 48.26) including 15 centuries, 49 wickets (Av. 29.08) and 43 catches.

WAQAR HUSSAN
Pakistan (born 1932) - An attractive right-handed batsman and a fine fielder. He played for Services and Karachi, Test Record - 21 Tests, 1,071 runs (Av. 31.50) including 1 century and 10 catches.

WARD, THOMAS ALFRED
South Africa (1887-1936) - A wicket-keeper and a useful batsman. He played for Transvaal. Test Record - 23 Tests, 459 runs (Av. 13.90) and 32 dismissals (19ct, 13st).

WARDLE, JOHN HENRY
England (1923-1985) - A left-arm orthodox and googly bowler. He played for Yorkshire and Cambridgshire. Test Record - 28 Tests, 653 runs (Av. 19.78), 102 wickets (Av. 20.39) and 12 catches.

WARNER, SIR PELHAM FRANCIS
England (1873-1963) - A right-handed batsman. He played for Oxford University and Middlesex. Test Record - 15 Tests, 622 runs (Av. 23.92) including 1 century and 3 catches.

WASHBROOK, CYRIL
England (born 1914) - A right-handed batsman. He played for Lancashire. Test Record - 37 Tests, 2,569 runs (Av. 42.81) including 6 centuries, and 12 catches.

WASIM AKRAM
Pakistan (born 1966) - A left-arm medium-fast bowler. He plays for Lahore and PACO. Test Record - 20 Tests, 284 runs (Av. 14.94), 63 wickets (Av. 26.61) and 7 catches.

WASIM BARI
Pakistan (born 1948) - An outstanding natural wicket-keeper and also a late middle-order, right-handed batsman. He played for Pakistan International Airlines and Sind. Test Record - 81 Tests, 1,366 runs (Av. 15.88) and 228 dismissals (201ct, 27st).

WASIM HASAN RAJA
Pakistan (born 1952) - A left-handed batsman and a right-arm leg-break top-spin bowler. He played for Lahore and Combined Universities. Test Record - 57 Tests, 2,821 runs (Av. 36.16) including 4 centuries, 51 wickets (Av. 35.80) and 20 catches.

WATSON, WILLIAM
England (born 1920) - A natural left-handed batsman. He played for Yorkshire and Leicestershire. Test Record - 23 Tests, 879 runs (Av. 25.85) including 2 centuries, and 8 catches.

WAZIR ALI SYED
India (1903-1950) - A right-handed batsman and a right-arm medium-fast bowler. He played for Southern Punjab. Test Record - 7 Tests, 237 runs (Av. 16.92) and 1 catch.

WAZIR MOHAMMAD
Pakistan (born 1929) - A right-handed middle-order batsman. He played for Bahawalpur and Karachi.Test Record - 20 Tests, 801 runs (Av. 27.62) including 2 centuries and 5 catches.

WEEKES, EVERTON DE COURCRY

West Indies (born 1925) - A brilliant stroke-maker batsman. He played for Barbados. In his first class career he made, 12,010 runs including 36 centuries, 125 catches and 1 stumping. Test Record - 48 Tests, 4,455 runs (Av. 58.61) including 15 centuries and 49 catches.

WEEKES, KENNETH HUNNELL

West Indies (born 1912) - A stylish and fast-scoring left-handed batsman and also a good reserve wicket-keeper. He played for Jamaica. In his first class career he made, 1,731 runs including 3 centuries. Test Record - 2 Tests, 173 runs (Av. 57.66) including 1 century.

WEIR, GORDON LINDSAY

New Zealand (born 1908) - A right-handed batsman and a right-arm medium-pace change-bowler. He played for Auckland. In his first class career he made, 5,022 runs including 10 centuries and took 107 wickets. Test Record - 11 Tests, 416 runs (Av. 29.71), 7 wickets (Av. 29.85) and 3 catches.

WELLARD, ARTHUR WILLIAM

England (1902-1980) - A right-arm medium-fast bowler and a useful batsman. He played for Somerset. In his first class career he made, 12,515 runs including 2 centuries, took 1,614 wickets and 375 catches. Test Record - 2 Tests, 47 runs (Av. 11.75), 7 wickets (Av. 33.85) and 2 catches.

WELLHAM, DIRK MACDONALD

Australia (born 1959) - A compact right-handed batsman. He played for New South Wales. In his first class career he made, 4,833 runs including 11 centuries. Test Record - 5 Tests, 239 runs (Av. 26.55) including 1 century, and 2 catches.

WESSELS, KEPLER CHRISTOFFEL

Australia (born 1957) - A left-handed opening batsman and a useful bowler. He played for Orange Free State and Sussex. Test Record - 24 Tests, 1,761 runs (Av. 42.95) including 4 centuries and 18 catches.

WHITE, GORDON CHARLES

South Africa (1882-1918) - A right-handed batsman and a leg-break and googly bowler. He played for Transvaal. Test Record - 17 Tests, 872 runs (Av. 30.06) including 2 centuries, 9 wickets (Av. 33.44) and 10 catches.

WHITE, JOHN CORNISH

England (1891-1961) - A left-arm bowler. He played for Somerset. Test Record - 15 Tests, 239 runs (Av. 18.38), 49 wickets (Av. 32.26) and 423 catches.

WHITTY, WILLIAM JAMES

Australia (1886-1974) - A left-arm medium-fast bowler. He played for New South Wales and South Australia. Test Record - 14 Tests, 161 runs (Av. 13.41), 65 wickets (Av. 21.12) and 4 catches.

WILLEY, PETER

England (born 1949) - A right-handed middle-order batsman and also a right-arm medium-pace off-spin bowler. He played for Northamptonshire and Eastern Province. Test Record - 26 Tests, 1,184 runs (Av. 26.90) including 2 centuries, 7 wickets (Av. 65.14) and 3 catches.

WILLIS, ROBERT GEORGE DYLAN

England (born 1949) - A right-arm medium-fast bowler. He played for Surrey, Warwickshire and Northern Transvaal.Test Record - 90 Tests, 840 runs (Av. 11.50), 325 wickets (Av. 25.20) and 39 catches.

WOOD, BARRY

England (born 1942) - A correct and patient opening batsman, a fine gully fielder and also a useful slow-medium bowler. He played for Yorkshire and Eastern Province. Test Record - 12 Tests, 454 runs (Av. 21.61), and 6 catches.

WOOD, GRAEME MALCOM

Australia (born 1956) - A neat left-handed opening batsman. He played for Western Province. Test Record - 59 Tests, 3,374 runs (Av. 31.83) including 9 centuries and 41 catches.

WOODFULLL, WILLIAM MADLON

Australia (1897-1965) - A right-handed opening batsman. He played for Victoria. Test Record - 35 Tests, 2,300 runs (Av. 46.00) including 7 centuries and 7 catches.

WOOLLEY, FRANK EDWARD

England (1887-1978) - A great all-rounder. He was a left-handed batsman and also a left-arm slow bowler. He played for Kent. Test Record - 64 Tests, 3,283 runs (Av. 36.07) including 5 centuries, 83 wickets (Av. 33.91) and 64 catches.

WOOLMER, ROBERT ANDREW

England (born 1948) - A graceful right-handed batsman and a useful medium-fast bowler. He played for Kent, Natal and Western Province. Test Record - 19 Tests, 1,059 runs (Av. 33.09) including 3 centuries, 4 wickets (Av. 74.75) and 10 catches.

WRIGHT, DOUGLAS VIVIAN PARSON

England (born 1914) - A leg-spin bowler, a useful tail-end batsman and also a good fielder. He played for Kent. Test Record - 34 Tests, 289 runs (Av. 11.11), 108 wickets (Av. 39.11) and 10 catches.

WRIGHT, JOHN GEOFFREY

New Zealand (born 1954) - A left-handed opening batsman and also a fine fielder. He played for Northern Districts and Derbyshire. Test Record - 63 Tests, 3,635 runs (Av. 33.34) including 7 centuries and 28 catches.

WRIGHT, KEVIN JOHN

Australia (born 1956) - A wicket-keeper and a right-handed batsman. He played for Western Province and South Australia. Test Record - 10 Tests, 219 runs (Av. 16.84) and 35 dismissals (31ct, 4st).

WYATT, ROBERT ELLIOTT STOREY

England (born 1901) - A right-handed batsman a useful medium-pace swing bowler. He played for Warwickshire and Worcestershire. Test Record - 40 Tests, 1,839 runs (Av. 31.70) including 2 centuries, 18 wickets (Av. 35.66) and 16 catches.

YADAV, NANDIAL SHIVLAL

India (born 1957) - A right-handed batsman and a right-arm off-break bowler. He played for Hyderabad. Test Record - 35 Tests, 403 runs (Av. 14.39), 102 wickets (Av. 35.09) and 10 catches.

YAJURVINDRA SINGH JASWANTSINGH

India (born 1952) - A right-handed batsman and a right-arm medium-pace and off-break bowler. He played for Maharashtra and Saurashtra. Test Record - 3 Tests, 94 runs (Av. 18.80), and 10 catches.

YALLOP, GRAHAM NEIL

Australia (born 1952) - A determined, vigourous and orthodox left-handed batsman, who hit the ball very hard. He played for Victoria. Test Record - 39 Tests, 2,756 runs (Av. 41.13) including 8 centuries and 23 catches.

YARDLE, BRUCE

Australia (born 1947) - An all-rounder. He was a hard-hitting right-handed batsman and and off-spin bowler. He played for Western Province. Test Record - 33 Tests, 978 runs (Av. 19.56), 126 wickets (Av. 31.63) and 31 catches.

YARDLEY, NORMAN WALTER DRANSFIELD

England (born 1915) - A right-handed batsman and a right-arm medium-pace bowler. He played for Cambridge University and Yorkshire. Test Record - 20 Test, 812 runs (Av. 25.37),21 wickets (Av. 33.46) and 14 catches.

YASHPAL SHARMA

India (born 1954) - A right-handed batsman. He played for Punjab and Haryana. Test Record - 37 Tests, 1,606 runs (Av. 33.45) including 2 centuries, 1 wickets (Av. 17.00) and 16 catches.

YOGRAJ SINGH BHAGSINGH BHUNEDEL

India (born 1958) - A right-handed batsman and

a right-arm medium-fast bowler. He played for Haryana and Punjab. Test Record - 1 Test, 10 runs (Av.5.00) and 1 wicket.

YUILE, BRYAN WILLIAM

New Zealand (born 1941) - A left-arm slow-medium bowler and also a right-handed middle-order batsman. He played for Manawatu and Central Districts. Test Record - 17 Tests, 481 runs (Av. 17.81), 34 wickets (Av. 35.67) and 12 catches.

ZAHEER ABBAS

Pakistan (born 1947) - A stylish and prolific right-handed middle-order batsman. He captained the Pakistani side for the first three Tests in 1983-84 in Australia. He played for Karachi and Gloucestershire. Test Record - 78 Tests, 5,062 runs (Av. 44.79) including 12 centuries, 3 wickets (Av. 44.00) and 34 catches.

ZAKIR KHAN

Pakistan (born 1963) - A tall and well-built right-arm seam bowler, with an aggressive streak. The bouncer is constant. He plays for Agricultural Development Bank. Test Record - 1 Test, 13 runs and 1 wicket.

ZOEHRER, TIMOTHLY JOSEPH

Australia (born 1961) - A talented wicket-keeper. He played for Western Australia. Test Record - 10 Tests, 246 runs (Av. 20.50) and 19 dismissals (18ct,1st).

ZULCH, JOHN WILLIAM

South Africa (1886-1924) - A right-handed opening batsman with a wide range of strokes and sound defence, a very good fielder and a useful change-bowler. He played for Transvaal. Test Record - 16 Tests, 985 runs (Av. 32.83) including 2 centuries and 4 catches.

ZULFIQAR AHMED

Pakistan (born 1926) - A right-arm off-break bowler and also a reliable late-order batsman. He played for Bahawalpur and Pakistan International Airlines. Test Record - 9 Tests, 200 runs (Av. 33.33), 20 wickets (18.30) and 5 catches.

CRICKET CUP & TROPHY

CHALLENGE CUP

Decided by the MCC on a knock-out basis between county clubs at Lord's in January, 1873. Only one match was played in this competition in June 1873 when Kent beat Sussex by 52 runs, at Lords.

COOCH-BEHAR TROPHY

WINNERS

1945-46	Sind
1946-47	Sind
1947-48	Not played
1948-49	Saurashtra
1949-50	Bombay
1950-51	Final not played
1951-52	National Academy
1952-53	West Zone
1953-54	West Zone
1954-55	West Zone
1955-56	West Zone
1956-57	West Zone
1957-58	West Zone
1958-59	West Zone
1959-60	West Zone
1960-61	South Zone
1961-62	Not held
1962-63	West Zone
1963-64	West Zone
1964-65	North Zone
1965-66	West Zone
1966-67	West Zone
1967-68	North Zone
1968-69	East Zone
1969-70	South Zone
1970-71	Not held
1971-72	East Zone
1972-73	South Zone
1973-74	East Zone
1974-75	South Zone

1975-76	West Zone
1976-77	West Zone
1977-78	North Zone
1978-79	North Zone
1979-80	North Zone
	West Zone (jt.)
1980-81	Not held
1981-82	North Zone
1982-83	Central Zone
1983-84	West Zone
1984-85	East Zone
1985-86	North Zone
1986-87	West Zone
1987-88	South Zone
1988-89	North Zone

COUNTY CHAMPIONSHIP

Winners

1864	Surrey
1865	Nottinghamshire
1866	Middlesex
1867	Yorkshire
1868	Nottinghamshire
1869	Nottinghamshire
	Yorkshire
1870	Yorkshire
1871	Nottinghamshire
1872	Nottinghamshire
1873	Gloucestershire
	Nottinghamshire
1874	Gloucestershire
1875	Nottinghamshire
1876	Gloucestershire
1877	Gloucestershire
1878	Undecided
1879	Nottinghamshire
	Lancashire
1880	Nottinghamshire
1881	Lancashire
1882	Nottinghamshire
	Lancashire
1883	Nottinghamshire
1884	Nottinghamshire
1885	Nottinghamshire
1886	Nottinghamshire
1887	Surrey
1888	Surrey
1889	Surrey
	Lancashire
	Nottinghamshire
1890	Surrey
1891	Surrey
1892	Surrey
1893	Yorkshire
1894	Surrey
1895	Surrey
1896	Yorkshire
1897	Lancashire
1898	Yorkshire
1899	Surrey
1900	Yorkshire
1901	Yorkshire
1902	Yorkshire
1903	Middlesex
1904	Lancashire
1905	Yorkshire
1906	Kent
1907	Nottinghamshire
1908	Yorkshire
1909	kent
1910	Kent
1911	Warwickshire
1912	Yorkshire
1913	Kent
1914	Surrey
1915	Not held
1916	Not held
1917	Not held
	1918 Not held
1919	Yorkshire
1920	Middlesex
1921	Middlesex
1922	Yorkshire
1923	Yorkshire
1924	Yorkshire
1925	Yorkshire
1926	Lancashire
1927	Lancashire

1928 Lancashire
1929 Nottinghamshire
1930 Lancashire
1931 Yorkshire
1932 Yorkshire
1933 Yorkshire
1934 Lancashire
1935 Yorkshire
1936 Derbyshire
1937 Yorkshire
1938 Yorkshire
1939 Yorkshire
1940 Not held
1941 Not held
1942 Not held
1943 Not held
1944 Not held
1945 Not held
1946 Yorkshire
1947 Middlesex
1948 Glamorgan
1949 Middlesex
Yorkshire
1950 Lancashire
Surrey
1951 Warwickshire
1952 Surrey
1953 Surrey
1954 Surrey
1955 Surrey
1956 Surrey
1957 Surrey
1958 Surrey
1959 Yorkshire
1960 Yorkshire
1961 Hampshire
1962 Yorkshire
1963 Yorkshire
1964 Worcestershire
1965 Worcestershire
1966 Yorkshire
1967 Yorkshire
1968 Yorkshire
1969 Glamorgan
1970 Kent
1971 Surrey
1972 Warwickshire
1973 Hampshire
1974 Worcestershire
1975 Leicestershire
1976 Middlesex
1977 Middlesex
Kent
1978 Kent
1979 Essex
1980 Middlesex
1981 Nottinghamshire
1982 Middlesex
1983 Essex
1984 Essex
1985 Middlesex
1986 Essex
1987 Nottinghamshire
1988 Worcestershire
1989 Worcestershire

CURRIE CUP WINNERS (SOUTH AFRICA)

Winners

1889-90 Transvaal
1890-91 Griqualand West
1891-92 Not held
1892-93 Western Province
1893-94 Western Province
1894-95 Transvaal
1895-96 Not held
1896-97 Western Province
1897-98 Western Province
1898-99 Not held
1899-00 Not held
1900-01 Not held
1901-02 Not held
1902-03 Transvaal
1903-04 Transvaal
1904-05 Transvaal
1905-06 Not held
1906-07 Transvaal
1907-08 Not held
1908-09 Western Province

1909-10	Not held
1910-11	Natal
1911-12	Not held
1912-13	Natal
1913-14	Not held
1914-15	Not held
1915-16	Not held
1916-17	Not held
1918-18	Not held
1918-19	Not held
1919-20	Not held
1920-21	Western Province
1921-22	Transvaal/Natal/W.Prov.(Tied)
1922-23	Not held
1923-24	Transvaal
1924-25	Not held
1925-26	Transvaal
1926-27	Transvaal
1927-28	Not held
1928-29	Not held
1929-30	Transvaal
1930-31	Not held
1931-32	Western Province
1932-33	Not held
1933-34	Natal
1934-35	Transvaal
1935-36	Not held
1936-37	Natal
1937-38	Natal/Transvaal (Tied)
1938-39	Not held
1939-40	Not held
1940-41	Not held
1941-42	Not held
1942-43	Not held
1943-44	Not held
1944-45	Not held
1945-46	Not held
1946-47	Natal
1947-48	Natal
1948-49	Not held
1949-50	Not held
1950-51	Transvaal
1951-52	Natal
1952-53	Western Province
1953-54	Not held
1954-55	Natal
1955-56	Western Province
1956-57	Not held
1957-58	Not held
1958-59	Transvaal
1959-60	Natal
1960-61	Natal
1961-62	Not held
1962-63	Natal
1963-64	Natal
1964-65	Not held
1965-66	Natal/Transvaal (Tied)
1966-67	Natal
1967-68	Natal
1968-69	Transvaal
1969-70	Transvaal/W.Province (Tied)
1970-71	Transvaal
1971-72	Transvaal
1972-73	Not held
1973-74	Natal
1974-75	Western Province
1975-76	Natal
1976-77	Natal
1977-78	Western Province
1978-79	Transvaal
1979-80	Transvaal
1980-81	Natal
1981-82	Western Province
1982-83	Transvaal
1983-84	Transvaal
1984-85	Transvaal
1985-86	Western Province
1986-87	Transvaal
1987-88	Transvaal
1988-89	Eastern Province

DEODHAR TROPHY TOURNAMENT

Instituted in 1973-74. It is the limited- overs competition in India.

The winners have been as follows:

Year	Venue	Winner—Runner-up
1973-74	Bombay	South-West
1974-75	Hyderabad	South-West

1975-76	Madras	West-South
1976-77	Calcutta	Central-South
1977-78	Pune	North-West
1978-79	Delhi	South-North
1979-80	Delhi	West-North
1980-81	Madras	South-West
1981-82	Chandigarh	South-Central
1982-83	Cuttack	West-North
1983-84	Sholapur	West-North
1984-85	Vijawadada	West-North
1985-86	Madras & Hyderabad	West-North
1986-87	Delhi	North-West
1987-88	Faridabad	North-West
1988-89	Kanpur	North-South

DULEEP TROPHY CHAMPIONSHIP

Year	**Winner**	**Venue**
1961-62	West Zone	Bombay
1962-63	West Zone	Calcutta
1963-64	West Zone-South Zone (jt. Winners)	Delhi
1964-65	West Zone	Bombay
1965-66	South Zone	Madras
1966-67	South Zone	Bombay
1967-68	South Zone	Bombay
1968-69	West Zone	Hyderabad
1969-70	West Zone	Ahmedabad
1970-71	South Zone	Bombay
1971-72	Central Zone	Bangalore
1972-73	West Zone	Bombay
1973-74	North Zone	Bombay
1974-75	South Zone	Hyderabad
1975-76	South Zone	Madras
1976-77	West Zone	Baroda
1977-78	West Zone	Bombay
1978-79	North Zone	Delhi
1979-80	North Zone	Bombay
1980-81	West Zone	Calcutta
1981-82	West Zone	Bombay
1982-83	North Zone	Bombay
1983-84	North Zone	Cuttack
1984-85	South Zone	Delhi
1985-86	West Zone	Bangalore
1986-87	South Zone	Bombay
1987-88	North Zone	Bhilai
1988-89	North Zone-West Zone	Delhi

GILLETTE CUP (SOUTH AFRICA)

Limited overs competition in South Africa.

Winners

1969-70	Western Province
1970-71	Western Province
1971-72	Eastern Province
1972-73	Western Province
1973-74	Transvaal
1974-75	Natal
1975-76	Eastern Province
1976-77	Natal

After this Gillette Cup competition was replaced by Datsun Shield.

Datsun Shield

1977-78	Rhodesia
1978-79	Transvaal
1979-80	Transvaal
1980-81	Transvaal
1981-82	Western Province
1982-83	Transvaal
1983-84	Transvaal
1984-85	Transvaal

GILLETTE CUP (WEST INDIES)

Sponsored by Gillette for the first two seasons. The competition is played on a zonal basis with three teams in each zone. Cup Final Results

Gillette Cup (Winner)

1975-76	Barbados
1976-77	Barbados

After this Gillette Cup competition was replaced by Geddes Grant/Harrison Line Trophy.

Winners

1977-78	Jamaica
1978-79	Trinidad
1979-80	Guyana
1980-81	Trinidad
1981-82	Leeward Islands

1982-83	Guyana
1983-84	Jamaica
1984-85	Guyana
1985-86	Guyana
1986-87	Jamaica
1987-88	Barbados

GILLETTE CUP (ENGLAND)

This competition was held from 1963 to 1980 and then was replaced by Nat West Bank Trophy.

Winners

1963	Sussex
1964	Sussex
1965	Yorkshire
1966	Warwickshire
1967	Kent
1968	Warwickshire
1969	Yorkshire
1970	Lancashire
1971	Lancashire
1972	Lancashire
1973	Gloucestershire
1974	Kent
1975	Lancashire
1976	Northamptonshire
1977	Middlesex
1978	Sussex
1979	Somerset
1980	Middlesex

After this Gillette Cup competition was replaced by Nat West Bank Trophy.

Winners

1981	Derbyshire
1982	Surrey
1983	Somerset
1984	Middlesex
1985	Essex
1986	Sussex
1987	Nottinghamshire
1988	Middlesex

GOPALAN TROPHY

Winners

1952-53	Ceylon won by 95 runs (Madras)
1953-54	Ceylon won by an innings and 108 runs (Colombo)
1954-55	Not held
1955-56	Ceylon won by an innings and 14 runs (Madras)
1956-57	Ceylon won by 5 wickets (Colombo)
1957-58	Madras won by 2 wickets (Madras)
1958-59	Drawn (Colombo)
1959-60	Madras won by 8 wickets (Madras)
1960-61	Ceylon won by 169 runs (Colombo)
1961-62	Ceylon won by an innings and 66 runs (Madras)
1963-64	Ceylon won by 6 wickets (Colombo)
1964-65	Not held
1965-66	Madras won by first innings lead (Colombo)
1966-67	Madras won by first innings lead (Madras)
1967-68	Ceylon won by 105 runs (Colombo)
1968-69	Ceylon won by first innings lead (Madras)
1969-70	Ceylon won by first innings lead (Colombo)
1970-71	Tamil Nadu won by first innings lead (Madras)
1971-72	Tamil Nadu won by one innings and 9 runs (Colombo)
1972-73	Tamil Nadu won by 3 runs (Madras)
1973-74	Sri Lanka won by first innings lead (Colombo)
1974-75	Tamil Nadu won by an innings and 73 runs (Salem)
1975-76	Sri Lanka won by 22 runs (Colombo)
1976-77	Sri Lanka won by first innings lead (Madras)
1977-78	Not held
1978-79	Not held
1979-80	Not held
1980-81	Sri Lanka won by first innings lead (Salem)
1982-83	Sri Lanka won by first innings lead (colombo)

Since 1983-84 this Trophy has not been held.

ICC TROPHY

This competion has been staged three times, each time in England. Only associate members of ICC take part in this competition.

The results of the finals were:

1979	Sri Lanka beat Canada
1982	Zimbabwe beat Bermuda
1986	Zimbabwe beat Holland

IRANI CUP MATCH

The Irani Cup Match, associated with the name of the late Mr. Z.R. Irani. The match is played on annual basis between last season's Ranji Trophy champion team and Rest of India.

Year	*Venue*	*Winners—Runners-Up*
1959-60	New Delhi	Bombay-Rest of India
1960-61	No Match	
1961-62	No Match	
1962-63	Bombay	Bombay-Rest of India
1963-64	Anantapur	Bombay-Rest of India
1964-65	Not held and match shifted to start of the season.	
1965-66	Madras	Bombay and Rest of India. (Joint winners as first innings was not completed).
1966-67	Calcutta	Rest of India-Bombay
1967-68	Bombay	Bombay-Rest of India
1968-69	Bombay	Rest of India-Bombay
1969-70	Poona	Bombay-Rest of India
1970-71	Calcutta	Bombay-Rest of India
1971-72	Bombay	Rest of India-Bombay
1972-73	Poona	Bombay-Rest of India
1973-74	Bangalore	Rest of India-Bombay
1974-75	Ahmedabad	Karnataka-Rest of India
1975-76	Nagpur	Bombay-Rest of India
1976-77	Delhi	Bombay-Rest of India
1977-78	Bombay	Rest or India-Bombay
1978-79	Bangalore	Rest of India-Karnataka
1979-80	Jullundur	No Match.
1980-81	Delhi	Delhi-Rest of India
1981-82	Indore	Bombay-Rest of India
1982-83	New Delhi	Rest of India-Delhi
1983-84	Rajkot	Karnataka-Rest of India
1984-85	New Delhi	Rest of India-Bombay
1985-86	Nagpur	Bombay-Rest of India
1986-87	Jodhpur	Rest of India-Delhi
1987-88	Hyderabad	Hyderabad-Rest of India
1988-89	Madras	Tamil Nadu-Rest of India

MCDONALD'S CUP

Competion between the six first-class states.

Winners

1969-70	New Zealand
1970-71	Western Australia
1971-72	Victoria
1972-73	New Zealand
1973-74	Western Australia
1974-75	New Zealand
1975-76	Queensland
1976-77	Western Australia
1977-78	Western Australia
1978-79	Tasmania
1979-80	Victoria
1980-81	Queensland
1981-82	Queensland
1982-83	Western Australia
1983-84	South Australia
1984-85	New South Wales
1985-86	Western Australia
1986-87	South Australia
1987-88	New South Wales

NAT WEST BANK TROPHY AND GILLETTE CUP

Winners

1963	SUSSEX beat Worcestershire by 14 runs.
1964	SUSSEX beat Worcestershire by eight wickets.
1965	Yorkshire beat Surrey by 175 runs.
1966	WARWICKSHIRE beat Worcestershire by five wickets.
1967	KENT beat Somerset by 32 runs.
1968	WARWICKSHIRE beat Sussex by four wickets.
1969	YORKSHIRE beat Derbyshire by 69 runs.
1970	LANCASHIRE beat Sussex by six wickets.
1971	LANCASHIRE beat Kent by 24 runs.

1972 LANCASHIRE beat Warwickshire by four wickets.

1973 GLOUCESTERSHIRE beat Sussex by 40 runs.

1974 KENT beat Lancashire by four wickets.

1975 LANCASHIRE beat Middlesex by seven wickets.

1976 NORTHAMPTONSHIRE beat Lancashire by four wickets.

1977 MIDDLESEX beat Glamorgan by five wickets.

1978 SUSSEX beat Somerest by five wickets.

1979 SOMEREST beat Northamptonshire by 45 runs.

1980 MIDDLESEX beat Surrey by seven wickets.

1981 DERBYSHIRE beat Northamptonshire by losing fewer wickets with the scores level.

1982 SURREY beat Warwickshire by nine wickets.

1983 SOMERSET beat Kent by 24 runs.

1984 MIDDLESEX beat Kent by four wickets.

1985 ESSEX beat Nottinghamshire by 1 run.

1986 SUUSEX beat Lancashire by seven wickets.

1987 NOTTINGHAMSHIRE beat Northamptonshire by three wickets.

1988 MIDDLESEX beat Worcestershire by three wickets.

1989 WARWICKSHIRE beat Middlesex.

NISSAN SHIELD

The major limited-overs competition in South Africa is played between the leading sides on a knock-out system with 55 overs.

Winners

1969-70	Western Province
1970-71	Western Province
1971-72	Eastern Province
1972-73	Western Province
1973-74	Transvaal
1974-75	Natal
1975-76	Eastern Province
1976-77	Natal
1977-78	Rhodesia
1978-79	Transvaal
1979-80	Transvaal
1980-81	Transvaal
1981-82	Western Province
1982-83	Transvaal
1983-84	Transvaal
1984-85	Transvaal
1985-86	Transvaal
1986-87	Natal
1987-88	Eastern Province

PLUNKET SHIELD

This was recognized first class cricket tournament in New Zealand.

The competition was reorganized on a league system for the 1921-22 season. The Plunket Shield was replaced by the Shell Trophy after the 1974-75 season.

PLUNKET SHIELD AND SHELL TROPHY *WINNERS*

1921-22	Auckland
1922-23	Canterbury
1923-24	Wellington
1924-25	Otago
1925-26	Wellington
1926-27	Auckland
1927-28	Wellington
1928-29	Not held
1929-30	Wellington
1930-31	Canterbury
1931-32	Wellington
1932-33	Otago
1933-34	Auckland
1934-35	Canterbury
1935-36	Wellington
1936-37	Auckland
1937-38	Auckland
1938-39	Auckland
1939-40	Auckland
1940-45	No competition
1945-46	Canterbury
1946-47	Auckland
1947-48	Otago

1948-49	Canterbury
1949-50	Wellington
1950-51	Otago
1951-52	Canterbury
1952-53	Otago
1953-54	Central Districts
1954-55	Wellington
1955-56	Canterbury
1956-57	Wellington
1957-58	Otago
1958-59	Auckland
1959-60	Canterbury
1960-61	Wellington
1961-62	Wellington
1962-63	Northern Districts
1963-64	Auckland
1964-65	Canterbury
1965-66	Wellington
1966-67	Central Districts
1967-68	Central Districts
1968-69	Auckland
1969-70	Otago
1970-71	Central Districts
1971-72	Otago
1972-73	Wellington
1973-74	Wellington
1974-75	Otago
1975-76	Canterbury
1976-77	Otago
1977-78	Auckland
1978-79	Otago
1979-80	Northern Districts
1980-81	Auckland
1981-82	Wellington
1982-83	Wellington
1983-84	Canterbury
1984-85	Wellington
1985-86	Otago
1986-87	Central Districts
1987-88	Otago

PRUDENTIAL WORLD CUP

The most ambitious of all sponsored one-day cricket competitions has been Prudential's support of the World Cup. Admittedly, it has to date taken place on only four occasions, in 1975, 1979, 1983 and 1987 yet it has been such an unqualified success that there can be little doubt that it is certain to be a permanent fixture every four years.

WINNERS OF PRUDENTIAL WORLD CUP

1975	WEST INDIES
1979	WEST INDIES
1983	INDIA
1987	AUSTRALIA

QUAID-E-AZAM TROPHY

Pakistan's principal first-class competition, which was instituted in 1953-54.

Winners

1953-54	Bahawalpur
1954-55	Karachi
1956-57	Punjab
1957-58	Bahawalpur
1958-59	Karachi
1959-60	Karachi
1961-62	Karachi Blues
1962-63	Karachi
1963-64	Karachi Blues
1964-65	Karachi Blues
1966-67	Karachi
1968-69	Lahore
1969-70	PIA
1970-71	Karachi Blues
1972-73	Railways
1973-74	Railways
1974-75	Punjab
1975-76	National Bank
1976-77	United Bank
1977-78	Habib Bank
1978-79	National Bank
1979-80	PIA
1980-81	United Bank
1981-82	National Bank
1982-83	United Bank
1983-84	National Bank
1984-85	United Bank
1985-86	Karachi

1986-87	National Bank
1987-88	PIA
1988-89	Agricultural Development Bank of Pakistan

RANJI TROPHY

The Board arranged fixtures for the competition for 1934-35 between all the Cricket Associations then affiliated to the Board. The Trophy was organised by dividing India into four zones: North, South, East and West. Each zonal competition was by knock-out with the zonal winners then meeting in two semi-finals and a final. Now the format is changed.There are five zones.Two teams qualify from each to play in the knockout round.

Winners

1934-35	Bombay
1935-36	Bombay
1936-37	Nawanagar
1937-38	Hyderbad
1938-39	Bengal
1939-40	Maharashtra
1940-41	Maharashtra
1941-42	Bombay
1942-43	Baroda
1943-44	Western India
1944-45	Bombay
1945-46	Holkar
1946-47	Bombay
1947-48	Holkar
1948-49	Bombay
1949-50	Baroda
1950-51	Holkar
1951-52	Bombay
1952-53	Holkar
1953-54	Bombay
1954-55	Madras
1955-56	Bombay
1956-57	Bombay
1957-58	Baroda
1958-59	Bombay
1959-60	Bombay
1960-61	Bombay
1961-62	Bombay
1962-63	Bombay
1963-64	Bombay
1964-65	Bombay
1965-66	Bombay
1966-67	Bombay
1967-68	Bombay
1968-69	Bombay
1969-70	Bombay
1970-71	Bombay
1971-72	Bombay
1972-73	Bombay
1973-74	Karnataka
1974-75	Bombay
1975-76	Bombay
1976-77	Bombay
1977-78	Karnataka
1978-79	Delhi
1979-80	Delhi
1980-81	Bombay
1981-82	Delhi
1982-83	Karnataka
1983-84	Bombay
1984-85	Bombay
1985-86	Delhi
1986-87	Hyderabad
1987-88	Tamil Nadu
1988-89	Delhi

REFUGE ASSURANCE SUNDAY LEAGUE

Refuge Assurance took over the sponsorship of the John Player Sunday League in the 1987 season. The League was instituted in 1969 and the title winners are as follow:

Winners

1969	Lancashire
1970	Lancashire
1971	Worcestershire
1972	Kent
1973	Kent
1974	Leicestershire
1975	Hampshire
1976	Kent
1977	Leicestershire
1978	Hampshire

1979	Somerset
1980	Warwickshire
1981	Essex
1982	Sussex
1983	Yorkshire
1984	Essex
1985	Essex
1986	Hampshire
1987	Worcestershire
1988	Worcestershire
1989	Lancashire

SHEFFIELD SHIELD

The trophy for which six States of Australia now compete in a home-and-away series of four-day games each season. The trophy was commissioned after the Earl of Sheffield who had donated $150 for the promotion of cricket in Australia. The competition began between New South Wales, Victoria and South Australia in the 1892-93 season. Queensland was admitted in 1926-27, Western Australia in 1947-48 and Tasmaina in 1977-78.

Winners

1892-93	Victoria
1893-94	South Australia
1894-95	Victoria
1895-96	New South Wales
1896-97	New South Wales
1897-98	Victoria
1898-99	Victoria
1899-00	New South Wales
1900-01	Victoria
1901-02	New South Wales
1902-03	New South Wales
1903-04	New South Wales
1904-05	New South Wales
1905-06	New South Wales
1906-07	New South Wales
1907-08	Victoria
1908-09	New South Wales
1909-10	South Australia
1910-11	New South Wales
1911-12	New South Wales
1912-13	South Australia
1913-14	New South Wales
1914-15	Victoria
1915-19	No competition
1919-20	New South Wales
1920-21	New South Wales
1921-22	Victoria
1922-23	New South Wales
1923-24	Victoria
1924-25	Victoria
1925-26	New South Wales
1926-27	South Australia
1927-28	Victoria
1928-29	New South Wales
1929-30	Victoria
1930-31	Victoria
1931-32	New South Wales
1932-33	New South Wales
1933-34	Victoria
1934-35	Victoria
1935-36	South Australia
1936-37	Victoria
1937-38	New South Wales
1938-39	South Australia
1939-40	New South Wales
1940-46	No Competition
1946-47	Victoria
1947-48	Western Australia
1948-49	New South Wales
1949-50	New South Wales
1950-51	Victoria
1951-52	New South Wales
1952-53	South Australia
1953-54	New South Wales
1954-55	New South Wales
1955-56	New South Wales
1956-57	New South Wales
1957-58	New South Wales
1958-59	New South Wales
1959-60	New South Wales
1960-61	New South Wales
1961-62	New South Wales
1962-63	Victoria
1963-64	South Australia
1964-65	New South Wales

1965-66	New South Wales
1966-67	Victoria
1967-68	Western Australia
1968-69	South Australia
1969-70	Victoria
1970-71	South Australia
1971-72	Western Australia
1972-73	Western Australia
1973-74	Victoria
1974-75	Western Australia
1975-76	South Australia
1976-77	Western Australia
1977-78	Western Australia
1978-79	Victoria
1979-80	Victoria
1980-81	Western Australia
1981-82	South Australia
1982-83	New South Wales
1983-84	Western Australia
1984-85	New South Wales
1985-86	New South Wales
1986-87	Western Australia
1987-88	Western Australia
1988-89	Western Australia

SHELL SHIELD AND RED STRIPE CUP

The Shell Shield for Caribbeam Regional Cricket Tournament was instituted in 1965-66 under the sponsorship of Shell.

The Shell Shield was replaced by the Red Stripe Cup after the 1986-87 season.

Winners

1965-66	Barbados
1966-67	Barbados
1967-68	No Competition
1968-69	Jamaica
1969-70	Trinidad
1970-71	Trinidad
1971-72	Barbados
1972-73	Guyana
1973-74	Barbados
1974-75	No Competition
1975-76	Trinidad, Barbados
1976-77	Barbados
1977-78	Barbados
1978-79	Barbados
1979-80	Barbados
1980-81	Combined Islands
1981-82	Barbados
1982-83	Guyana
1983-84	Barbados
1984-85	Trinidad & Tobago
1985-86	Barbados
1986-87	Guyana
1987-88	Jamaica
1988-89	Jamaica

SHELL TROPHY

New Zealand's major first-class competition.

Winners

1975-76	Canterbury
1976-77	Otago
1977-78	Auckland
1978-79	Otago
1979-80	Northern Districts
1980-81	Auckland
1981-82	Wellington
1982-83	Wellington
1983-84	Canterbury
1984-85	Wellington
1985-86	Otago
1986-87	Central Districts
1987-88	Otago
1988-89	Auckland

BHARAT RATNA AND THE PADMA VIBHUSHAN WINNERS

1-K.Nayudu	1956
2-Vijayanand of Vizianagar	1958
3-Himatlal Mankad	1973
4-Manohar Gavaskar	1980
5-Deodhar	1990
6-M.Amarnath	1990
7-Kapil Dev	1990

ARJUNA AWARDS WINNERS

1961	Shri Saleem Durani
1964	Nawab of Pataudi
1965	Shri Vijay Manjrekar
1966	Shri Chandrakant G. Borde
1967	Shri Ajit Wadekar
1968	Shri E.A.S. Prasanna
1969	Shri Bishen Singh Bedi
1970	Shri D.N. Sardesai
1971	Shri S. Venkataraghavan
1972	Shri Eknath Dhondu Solkar
1975	Shri Sunil Gavaskar
1976	Km. Shanta Rangaswamy
1977-78	Shri G.R. Vishwanath
1979-80	Shri Kapil Dev Nikhanj
1980-81	Shri C.P.S.Chauhan
	Shri Syed M.H. Kirmani
1981	Shri Dilip Vengsarkar
1982	Shri Mohinder Amarnath
1983	Km. Diana Edulji
1984	Shri Ravi Shastri
1985	Km. Shubhangi Dattatraya Kulkarni
1986	Mohd. Azharuddin

PADMA SHRI WINNERS

1- Jasu Patel
2- Vijay Hazare
3- J.J. Contractor
4- P.R.Umrigar
5- S. Mushtaq Ali
6- M.J. Gopalan
7- D.B. Deodhar
8- Mansur Ali Khan Pataudi
9- C.G. Borde
10- B.S. Bedi
11- E.A.S. Prasanna
12- G.R.Vishwanath
13- Ajit Wadekar
14- B.S. Chandrashekhar
15- Farokh Engineer
16- Pankaj Roy
17- Kapil Dev
18- Syed Kirmani
19- Swarup Krishan Reu
20- D.B. Vengsarkar
21- Mohammed Azharuddin

DARTS

It is not illegal for teetotalers to play Darts, but the game as we know it grew in the bar. The suggestion has been made that our contemporary clock-spoke dart-board divided by thin wires into twenty triangular sections of equal size, higher numbers sandwiched between low ones, is the descendant of beer barrel bottoms, the line being traced through the old wooden board marked with concentric circles. Very likely. A dart in the narrow wired outer circle of our present board counts double the points scored by a plain throw into the section, and a throw into a narrow wired circle halfway between the uttering and the bull's-eye counts treble the number. The bull's eye consists of two small concentric circles counting 25 and 50 points respectively. The board is placed so that the centre is 5 ft. 8 in. from the ground and the throwing line is drawn 9 ft. from the board.

In the normal darts game the player who throws closest to the bull has first turn, a turn consisting of three darts thrown in succession. In doubles, players of opposing sides throw in order and alternately. The method of scoring is by subtraction from the target total 301 in singles, 501 in doubles. A side must score a 'double' that is, lodge a dart in the outer ring before beginning to score and must also finish on a double or a bull's eye, achieving the exact target score. If a player scores more or one less than the target his turn is over, and his score during it is not counted.

RULES OF THE GAME

1. To reach a pre-agreed score quicker than your opponent. The winner is the person who gets their score down to nil first, providing the last score is achieved by means of scoring a double.
2. A toss of coin decides which player goes first. If a match consists of more than one game, the 1st throw alternates after each game.
3. In a game of 501 the players go straight off, and start scoring immediately without a double. The total obtained with 3 darts is noted and deducted from 501. The second player has his 3 throws and so on until either player gets down to a score requiring one of the doubles available on the board (the bull counts as double 25). Once a player has reached his score by completing the game on a double, the game is over, irrespective of who played first.
4. A game is controlled by a referee who

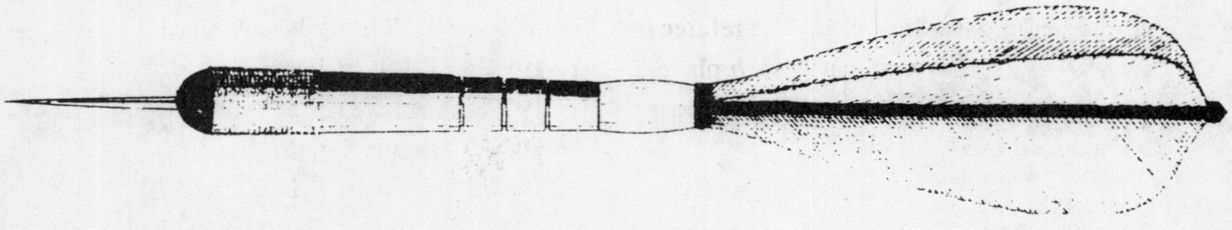

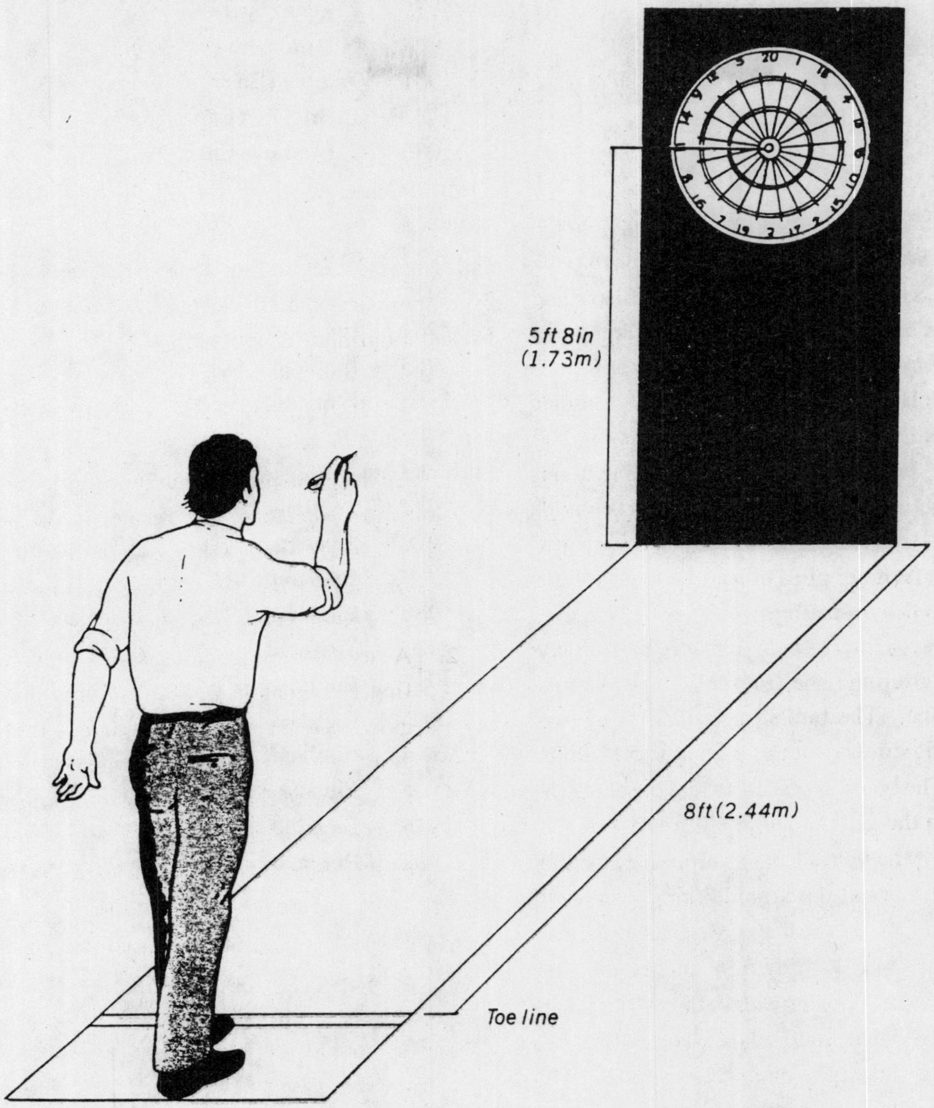

calls out a player's score after the completion of his throw. He also tells the player the score required if it is possible for him to complete the game in 3 darts. The referee is assisted by a scorer who marks each players score after every 3 darts, and also indicates his reduced total.

CUP & TROPHIES

World Professional Championship

First held in 1978 in Stoke-on-Trent.

1978	L.Rees (Wal)
1979	J.Lowe (Eng)
1980	E.Bristow (Eng)
1981	E.Bristow (Eng)
1982	J.Wilson (Sco)
1983	K.Deller (Eng)

1984	E.Bristow (Eng)
1985	E.Bristow (Eng)
1986	E.Bristow (Eng)
1987	J.Lowe (Eng)

World Masters

First held at the West Centre Hotel, London, in 1974. Sponsored by Winmau.

1974	C.Inglis (Eng)
1975	A.Evans (Wal)
1976	J.Lowe (Eng)
1977	E.Bristow (Eng)
1978	R.Davies (Wal)
1979	E.Bristow (Eng)
1980	J.Lowe (Eng)
1981	E.Bristow (Eng)
1982	D.Whitcombe (Eng)
1983	E.Bristow (Eng)
1984	E.Bristow (Eng)
1985	D.Whitcombe (Eng)
1986	B.Anderson (Eng)

World Cup

Individual

First held in 1977 at the Wembley Conference Centre, London.

1977	L.Rees (Wal)
1979	N.Virachkul (USA)
1981	J.Lowe (Eng)
1983	E.Bristow (Eng)
1985	E.Bristow (Eng)

Team

1977	Wales
1979	England
1981	England
1983	England
1985	England

Nations Cup

1977	Scotland
1978	Sweden
1979	England
1980	England
1981	Scotland
1982	England
1983	England
1984	England
1985	Finland
1986	England
1987	England

DIVING

Competitive diving developed in Europe during the late nineteenth century, being much influenced by slightly earlier advances in gymnastics. Diving was first included in the Olympic programme in 1904, when there were "plain" and "variety" events for men only. Women's diving was first included in the Olympics of 1912. Safety standards have improved greatly during the present century, both in the design of diving boards and in dive specifications. Diving is governed by the same international governing body as swimming-the Federation Internationale de Natation Amateur (FINA), founded in 1908.

Performed from a springboard of 3 metres (9' 10") above the water. divers take part in an elimination series of dives which reduces the field to 12.

The 12 finalists have another 11 dives -5 compulsory and 6 voluntary-for men, and another 10 (5 compulsory, 5 voluntary) for women.

Performed from a rigid platform of 10 metres (32'10") above the water, scoring is the same as for springboard, but the 12 finalists have 10 dives (4 compulsory, 6 voluntary) for men, and 8 dives (4 compulsory, 4 voluntary) for women.

Dives : There are no fewer than 83 dives officially registered by the sport's governing body, FINA - forward, backward, reverse, inward, twisting, handstand dives performed with pikes, tucks,somersaults and other combinations. Look out for the spectacular 3 (½) forward somersault, the forward 1(½) somersault with 3 twists, and in all probability the inverted bellyflop with 1(½) gallons of swallowed chlorine.

Scoring : There are seven judges. They mark each dive from nil for a complete failure up to a 10-point maximum for perfection. The highest and lowest marks are discarded and the remaining five added together and multiplied by the tariff which was the degree of difficulty for the dive. If, for instance, a swimmer goes for a forward 3 (½) somersault, which has a tariff of 3.5, and scores 7.2, 7.4, 6.9, 6.7, 7.0, 7.2 and 7.3, the highest and lowest (7.4 and 6.7) would be discarded, the rest added up (35.6) and multiplied by 3.5 to give a total of 124.6.

No dives are ever repeated by a contestant, and the less splash you make the better the judges will mark.

The depth of water under the diving platforms is 5 metres (16'5").

RULES OF THE GAME

Rule 1:

All diving competitions organized at international level are subject to these rules.

Rule 2:

The springboards, the platforms and all diving installations shall be in accordance with these rules and shall be examined and approved by a delegate of FINA before the competition begins.

Rule 3:

All diving installations shall be available for use by entered competitors;

(1) Not earlier than eight days before the competition.

(2) During a contest day when no contest is in progress.

(3) Seating positions shall be provided for all competitors, team and technical officials from which they may properly observe the

Diving Platform

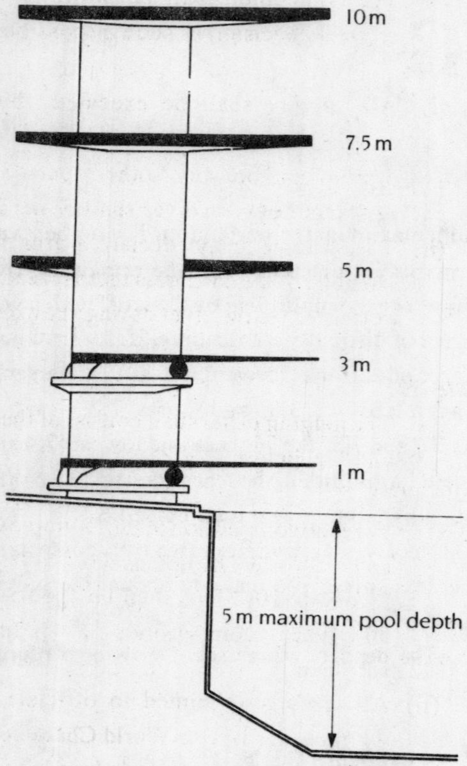

diving competitions from the side.

Rule 4:

The order of starting shall be decided by lot in both preliminary and final competitions.

Rule 5:

The draw shall be made in public; and the place and time of the draw shall be stated in the announcements of the competitions.

Rule 6:

(i) Where the total number of dives to be executed in one diving competition is excessive, the competition shall be divided into several groups of dives, so that the number of dives to be executed in any one group shall be not more than 210.

(ii) The dives in each group shall be executed by all the competitors consecutively; and by the different groups shall be executed in separate sessions.

(iii) The results of all the dives shall be collected to find the placings.

(iv) The referee may postpone a portion of a contest because of adverse weather or unforeseen circumstances.

(v) Points scored during that portion of a competition, through the latest full round of dives, completed prior to a declaration of postponement, shall be carried forward into the remaining portion of the competition whenever it is held.

Rule 7:

(i) Before each dive, the referee or the official announcer shall announce in the language of the host country, the name of the competitor and the dive which he is about to execute.

(ii) The number of the dive to be performed, and the manner of execution thereof, shall be displayed on an indication board visible to both divers and judges, and shall take precedence over the verbal announcement of the dive.

Rule 8:

(i) Each competitor shall be given sufficient time for the preparation and execution of the dive.

(ii) The dive to be executed shall not be announced before the diver has assumed his position on the board or platform.

Rule 9:

(i) The dive shall be executed after a signal given by the referee, preferably by a whistle.

(ii) Where the competitor executes his dive before the signal is given, the referee shall decide whether the dive shall be repeated or not.

Rule 10:

Only such dives as are mentioned in the tables may be executed.

Rule 11:

(i) Each competitor shall deliver to the diving secretary, not less than 24 hours before the commencement of each competition, on an official form and written in ink or typewritten four copies of a complete statement of the dives selected.

(ii) This list of dives shall be presented in English or French.

(iii) On that form shall be stated:

(a) the group, the number, and the denomination of each dive according to FINA diving tables:

(b) the manner of the take-off (running or standing) for platform contest only:

(c) the execution of dive; that is

(A) straight

(B) with pike

(C) with tuck

(D) free

(d) height of the board or platform.

Rule 12:

(i) Required dives and voluntary dives with limit shall not be repeated as voluntary dives without limit.

(ii) All dives of the same number shall be considered to be the same dive.

Rule 13:

(i) The list of dives shall be signed by the competitor and the dives shall be executed in the order listed on the diving form.

(ii) Where the closing date has passed, no change shall be permitted in the dives to be performed, or in the order of execution of the dives.

(iii) Each competitor is fully responsible for the accuracy of the statement in the list.

Rule 14:

Unless the list is presented within the required time, a competitor shall not be admitted to the competition.

Rule 15:

(i) The referee shall inspect the list and where the statement in the list is not according to the rules, the referee, before the beginning of the competition, shall decide how the statement can be corrected, or whether the competitor shall be excluded from the competition.

(ii) The competitor shall be informed of the referee's decision as soon as possible.

Rule 16:

(i) All dives shall be executed by the competitors themselves without any assistance from any other person, but asistance between dives shall be permitted.

(ii) The referee may declare a dive to be irregular if he considers that assistance has been given to the diver during the execution of the dive.

Rule 17:

The judging panel shall consist of the refree and the judges.

Rule 18:

(i) For each competition of the Olympic Games and World Championships, 7 judges recognized by FINA shall be appointed; for all other competitions 5 judges are sufficient.

(ii) All judges appointed to officiate at the Olympic Games or World Championships must have functioned as judges in at least 4 open competitions of National or International level during the preceding calender year.

(iii) In Olympic Games and World Championships the panel of judges for a final contest shall consist of judges whose nationalities are different to those of any of the contestants in the final, if such judges are available.

(iv) The referee may propose the removal of any judge, whose judgement he regards is unsatisfactory; and may propose another judge to replace him, subject to the approval of the appointed jury of appeal for that competition.

(v) Such a change in judges shall take place only at the end of a session or when a group of dives have been performed by each competitor.

Forward somersault—tuck position.

Forward somersault—pike position.

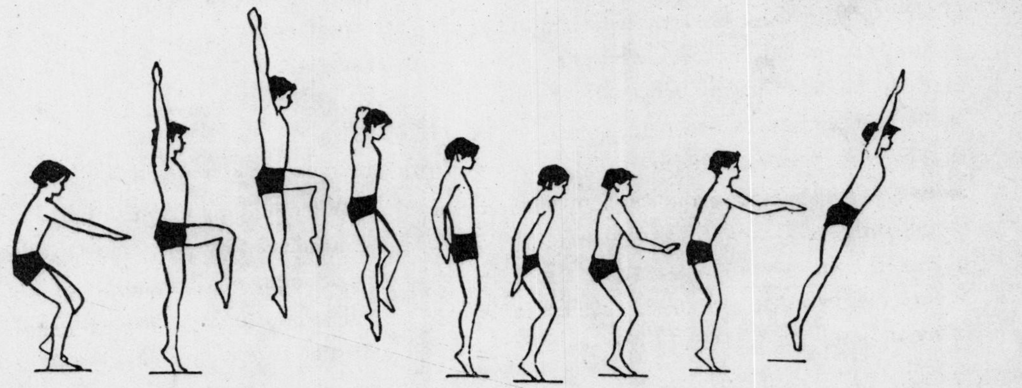

(vi) For Olympic Games and World Championships the scoring shall be shown by an electrical machine which displays the judges' awards simultaneously.

Rule 19:

(i) The referee shall manage the competition, and shall ensure that the rules are observed.

(ii) The referee may delegate an assistant to observe the performance on a platform.

Rule 20:

The records of the constest shall be kept by two independent secretarial groups.

Rule 21:

(i) The judges shall be placed separately, by the referee and preferably on each side of the diving board, if practicable; but where this is not practicable, they shall be placed together on one side.

(ii) Once placed, a judge shall not change his position, except at the direction of the referee, and that too in exceptional circumstances.

(iii) The position of each judge shall be identified by a distinctive number.

Rule 22:

After each dive, on a signal given by the referee, each of the judges, without communicating with one another, shall immediately and simultaneously, and in a distinct manner indicate the marks awarded by him.

Rule 23:

(i) The judge's awards shall be dictated one by one, in the same consecutive order to the first secretarial group, who shall place them on their score sheet and cancel the highest and lowest awards.

(ii) The second secretarial group shall enter on their score sheet the awards as shown by the judges.

(iii) Where two or more awards that are to be cancelled are equal, either of them can be cancelled.

Rule 24:

(i) The secretaries shall independently state the total of the remaining awards and multiply it by the degree of difficulty to determine the score for the dive.

(ii) In contests where there are 7 judges, the score shall be divided by 5 and then multiplied by 3 in order to establish a comparable score obtained in contests where there are 5 judges.

(iii) In order to facilitate the scoring computations a calculator or chart may be used.

Rule 25:

The final result shall be obtained from the list of results as shown in the main minutes book at the end of the contest.

Rule 26:

At the end of the contest, the referee shall supervise the score sheets and the list of results in co-ordination with the two secretarial groups, and shall confirm the final result by singing the main minutes.

Rule 27:

(i) The winner of the contest is the competitor who obtained the greatest number of points.

(ii) When two or more divers score the same number of points, a tie shall be declared for that particular place.

Rule 28:

Points or half points shall be awarded from 0 to 10 on opinion of the judges according to the following table:

Completely failed	0 points
Unsatisfactory	½ - 2 points
Deficient	2(½) - 4 (½) points
Satisfactory	5-6 points
Good	8(½) - 10 points

Rule 29:

(i) When judging a dive, a judge must not be influenced by any factor other than the technique and exceution of the diver.The dive is to be considered, accomplished without regard to the approach to the starting position or the difficulty of the dive.

(ii) The points to be considered are:
The run steps. The take-off. The technique and grace of the dive during the passage through the air. The entry into the water.

Rule 30:

(i) Where the referee is certain that a diver has performed a dive of a number other than announced, the referee shall declare it a failed dive.

(ii) Dives of the same number shall be considered to be the same dive.

(iii) Where a dive is performed clearly in a position other than that announced, the dive shall be considered to be unsatisfactory. The highest award for such a dive is 2 points.

(iv) Where it is quite clear that the dive has been performed in another position, the referee shall repeat the announcement, and declare the maximum award of 2 points.

(v) Where dive is performed partially in a position other than that announced, the judges shall award up to a maximum of 4(½) points.

(vi) The referee may have a spoiled dive repeated, if, in his opinion, the execution of the dive was influenced by exceptional circumstances.

(vii) The request for such a repetition must be made immediately.

(viii) Where a repetition of a dive is granted, the first dive shall stand cancelled.

(ix) Where a judge considers that a dive of a different number has been performed he may award 0 point not withstanding that the referee has not declared it to be a failed dive.

Rule 31:

(i) Where a dive is incorrectly announced, the diver, or his representative, shall have it rectified at once before its execution.

(ii) If the incorrectly announced dive is executed by the diver, the referee may cancel it and have the correct dive announced and performed immediately.

Rule 32 :

A diver who refuses the execution of a dive shall receive 0 point.

Rule 33 :

(i) Where a judge is unable to continue to function after a competition has started, he shall be replaced by another judge.

(ii) Where a judge, by reason of illness or other unforeseen circumstances, has made no award for a particular dive, the average of the awards of the other judges shall be adopted as his award; and it shall be calculated to the nearest half-point.

Rule 34 :

Dives shall be executed and judged on the following principles:

(i) The starting position shall be free and unaffected.

(ii) The starting position in standing dives shall be assumed when the competitor stands on the front end of the board or platform.

(iii) The body shall be straight, head erect, with the arms straight on the sides or above the head.

(iv) The arm swing commences when the arms leave the starting position.

(v) Where the correct starting position is not assumed, each judge shall deduct 1 to 3 points from his award, according to circumstances.

(vi) The starting position of a running dive shall be assumed when the competitor is ready to take the first step of the run.

(vii) Forward take-off dives from the springboard may be performed either standing or running at the option of the diver.

(viii) A prior declaration of the manner of take-off from the springboard is not required.

(ix) The judges shall award points for a standing dive, bearing in mind the height and standard of execution which might be expected from a running dive.

(x) During the competiton, a diver may not bounce on the springboard, until the score of the previous diver has been announced.

(xi) The run shall be smooth, straight, and without hesitation.

(xii) In a running dive, from either the springboard or the platform, the diver shall take at least four steps in all, including the hurdle.

(xiii) Where a diver takes less than four steps, the referee shall deduct two points from the award of each judge.

(xiv) The take-off shall be bold, reasonably high and confident.

(xv) In running dives, the take-off from the springboard must be from both the feet simultaneously, or the referee shall declare it a failed dive; but from platform, the take-off can be from one foot.

(xvi) When executing a standing dive, tne diver must not bounce on the board before the take-off otherwise the referee shall declare it a failed dive.

(xvii) If in the course of executing a running dive, the diver stops his run before the end of the board, or makes more than one jump on the same spot before the final take-off, the referee shall declare it a failed dive.

(xviii) Where a diver, preparing for a backward take-off, lifts his feet slightly off the board, that shall not be considered to be a bounce, but deduct from his award according to his individual opinion.

(xix) Where, in any dive, the diver touches the end of the board, or dives to the side of the direct line of flight, indicating that he was too close to the board for proper execution, no matter how well the dive may have been executed, each judge shall exercise his own wisdom regarding the deduction to be made.

(xx) A diver who loses his balance and makes a second attempt shall receive 2 points less than what he would have obtained in the first attempt.

(xxi) The deductions, under clauses, 13 and 20, shall not be made by the judges, but from the award of each judge.

(xxii) Where the second attempt to obtain a balance is unsuccessful, and the feet return to the platform, the referee shall declare it a failed dive.

Rule 35:

(i) During the passage through the air, the body can be carried straight (A) with pike (B), with tuck (C), or free position (D).

(ii) In the straight position, the body shall not be bent, either at the knees or at the hips, the feet however must be together and the toes pointed.

(iii) In the pike position, the body shall be bent at the hips, but the legs must be kept straight at the knees, the feet shall be together and the toes pointed.

(iv) The whole body must be bunched, with the knees together, the hands on the lower legs and the toes pointed.

(v) In the free position, the body position is optoinal but the legs shall be together and the toes pointed

(vi) If a diver opens his knees in the tuck, the judges shall deduct one to two points.

(vii) The diving illustrations serve as guides only and the position of the arms is at the choice of the diver.

(viii) In all flying somersault dives, a straight position shall be clearly shown for approximately half a somersault; and that position shall be assumed from the take-off except in dive No. 11, Table B, in which the straight position shall be shown after one somersault has been completed.

(ix) Where a twist is greater or less than that announced, by 90 degrees or more the referee shall declare it a failed dive.

(x) The pike dives, with twist, shall not be started until there has been a marked pike position.

(xi) In somersault dives with twist, the twist may be performed at any time during the dive at the option of the diver.

(xii) All head first entries shall be executed with the arms stretched beyond the head in line with the body, with the hands close together.

(xiii) Where the arms are not in the correct position on entry into water, each judge shall deduct 1-3 points from his award according to the circumstances.

Rule 36:

(i) The height of the springboards and each platform above the water level may vary by plus 0.05m from the heights prescribed in the rules.

(ii) In the area of full water depth, the bottom of the pool may rise up to 2%. In the diving pool, the depth of the water shall not be less than 1.8m at any point.

(iii) In pools for the Olympic Games and the World Championships the dimensions shall be the prescribed dimensions set out in these rules.

(iv) In outdoor pools, springboards and platforms are recommended to face north in the Northern hemisphere and south in the Southern hemisphere.

(v) The minimum illumination at a level of 1 metre above the water surface shall be 500 lux.

(vi) The water temperature in a diving pool shall not be less than 26 degree Centigrade.

(vii) The springboards shall be placed on either one or both the sides of the platforms.

(viii) It is preferable that a platform should not be constructed directly under any other platform.

(ix) It is recommended that the seats to be provided for the judges should be at a height of 1.5 to 2.0m above the water level depending on the circumstances.

CUP & TROPHIES

World Championships (Men)

Springboard Diving

1973	P.Boggs (USA)
1975	P.Boggs (USA)
1978	P.Boggs (USA)
1982	G.Louganis (USA)
1986	G.Louganis (USA)

Highboard Diving

1973	K.Dibiasi (Ita)
1975	K.Dibiasi (Ita)
1978	G.Louganis (USA)
1982	G.Louganis (USA)
1986	G.Louganis (USA)

Women

Highboard Diving

1973	U.Knape (Swe)
1975	J.Ely (USA)
1978	I.Kalinina (USSR)
1982	W.Wyland (USA)
1986	Chen Lin (Chn)

Springboard Diving

1973	C.Kohler (GDR)
1975	I.Kalinina (USSR)
1978	I.Kalinina (USSR)
1982	M.Meyer (USA)
1986	Gao Min (Chn)

FENCING

One of the original sports held in 1896, when the first Olympic champion was Emile Gravelotte (FRA) in the foil. It is the only sport in which professionals have openly competed in the Games, as special events for fencing masters were held in 1896 and 1900. At the latter Games they even competed against the other competitors so that Albert Ayat (Fra) beat his pupil Ramon Fonst (Cub) in the epee.

Fencing has been included in each of the modern Olympic Games, and Olympic Championships are recognised as World Championships in Olympic years. World Championships are held annually, and have had official status since 1936, but followed European Championships which were first held in 1921. Women's events were first held in 1929.

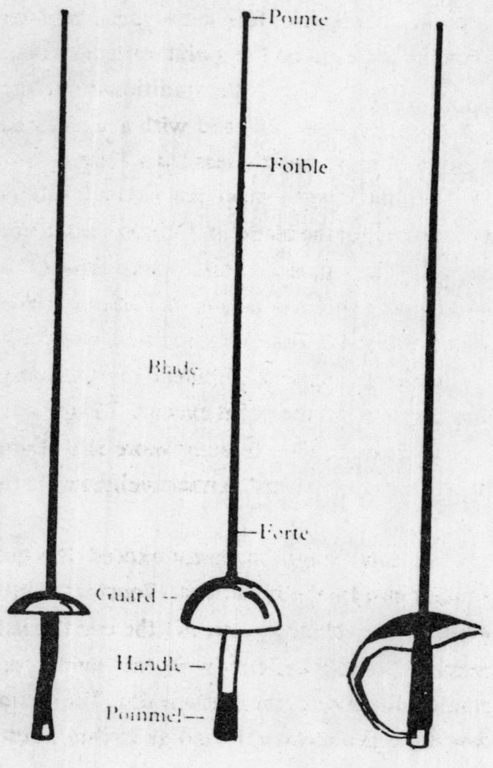

Foil *Épée* *Sabre*

The sabre is a weapon of cut and thrust. In other words, hits can be scored by striking with the edge as well with the point. For this purpose the whole of the front edge, as well as the third of the back edge, nearest the point, are used. The valid target is also altered to include everything above the hips.

The sabre is held firmly between the thumb and index finger, the handle lying across the second phalanges of the other fingers. It is not, as in foil and epee, held in the hollow of the hand, but is brought to bear against the heel of the hand by the little finger. The weapon is carried in the fingers, rather than gripped, as any tendency to grip tightly will contact the hand and cause it to tire quickly. The manipulation is obtained, mainly, by the thumb, index finger and little finger.

The area within which fencers may move is restricted. This area is called the Piste. The piste is 2 metres (6ft. 7 in.) wide. The foil piste is 14 metres (46 ft.) and is suitable for all three weapons but at epee and sabre each fencer is allowed to retire once the length of the piste and is then put on guard at the warning line 2 metres (6ft. 7in.) from the rear limit. The Piste is divided by lines drawn across its breath.

A Jury is made up of a President and four Judges. The President has complete control over the fencers, judges, and spectators. His duties are to award hits according to the Rules of the weapon being fought, and to see that order is maintained

Correct shoulder and hip position on the lunge

RULES OF THE GAME

Weapons (general rules): All weapons are subject to official scrutiny and it is the responsibility of each competitor to ensure that his own weapons conform to precise regulations, some of which are described here. No weapon must be constructed in such a way that it might normally injure either the user or his opponent.

All weapons-foil,epee, and sabre- (a) have a hilt, (b) a guard and (c) a flexible steel blade, (d) with a button, at its tip. For foil and epee,(e) a martingale, a strap holding the sword to the hand- is compulsory if the weapon is not otherwise secured by an attachment of the body wire.

(1) ***Foil*** : This is a light sword that was developed for fencing practice in the eighteenth century. It must weigh less than 500g.

The total length must not exceed 110cm (90cm maximum for the blade and 20cm for the hilt and guard). The guard must pass through a cylindrical gauge 12cm in diameter.Blade flexibility must be within the range 5.9-9.5cm if the blade is fixed horizontally 70cm from the tip of the button and a 200g weight is suspended 3cm from the button tip. The point must either be covered, or fitted with an electric point . In electric foil a hit must register only when the pressure on the point exceeds 500g.

(2) ***Epee*** : This is the traditional dueling sword, heavier than the foil and with a wider and deeper guard. It must weigh less than 770g.

The total length must not exceed 110cm (90cm maximum for the blade and 20cm for the hilt and guard). The guard must pass through a cylindrical gauge with a diameter of 13.5cm. Blade flexibility must be 4.5-7cm (measurement as a foil).

In electric epee a hit must register only when the pressure on the point exceeds 750g.

(3) ***Saber*** : The fencing sabre is a light version of the cavalry sword. It must weigh less than 500g.

The total length must not exceed 105 cm (88cm maximum for the blade and 17cm for the hilt and guard). If the blade is curved, the curve must be continuous, with a deflection of less than 4cm. and not in the direction of the cutting edge. The guard must pass through a rectangular gauge 15 into 14 cm in section.

Blade flexibility must be 7-12cm if the blade is fixed horizontally 70cm from the tip of the

blade and a 200g weight is suspended 1cm from the tip.

CUP & TROPHIES

Gold In Olympics

Fencing has been included in each of the modern Olympic Games, and Olympic Championships are recognised as World Championships in Olympic years.

Foil (Individual)

1896 Emile Gravelotte (Fra) 4 wins
1900 Emile Coste (Fra) 6 wins
1904 Ramon Fonst (Cub) 3 wins
1906 Georges Dillon-Kavanagh (Fra) data not available
1912 Nado Nadi (Ita) 7 wins
1920 Nedo Nadi (Ita) 10 wins
1924 Roger Ducrett (Fra) 6 wins
1928 Lucien Gaudin (Fra) 9 wins
1932 Gustavo Marzi (Ita) 9 wins
1936 Giulio Gaudini (Ita) 9 wins
1948 Jean Buhan (FRA) 8 wins
1952 Christian d'Oriola (Fra) 8 wins
1956 Christian d'Oriola (Fra) 6 wins
1960 Viktor Zhdanovich (USSR) 7 wins
1964 Egon Franke (Pol) 3 wins
1968 Ion Drimba (Rom) 4 wins
1972 Witold Woyda (Pol) 3 wins
1976 Fabio Dal Zotto (Ita) 4 wins
1980 Vladimir Smirnov (USSR) 5 wins
1984 Mauro Numa (Ita)
1988 Stefano Cerioni (Ita)

Foil (Team)

1904 Cuba
1920 Italy
1924 France
1928 Italy
1932 France
1936 Italy
1948 France
1952 France
1956 Italy
1960 USSR
1964 USSR
1968 France
1972 Poland
1976 FRG
1980 France
1984 Italy
1988 USSR

Epee (Individual)

1900	Ramon Fonst	(Cub)
1904	Ramon Fonst	(Cub) 3 wins
1906	Georges de la Falaise	(Fra) data not available
1908	Gaston Alibert	(Fra) 5 wins
1912	Paul Anspach	(Bel) 6 wins
1920	Armand Massard	(Fra) 9 wins
1924	Charles Delporte	(Bel) 8 wins
1928	Lucien Gaudin	(Fra) 8 wins
1932	Giancarlo Cornaggia-Medici	(Ita) 8 wins
1936	France Riccardi	(Ita) 5 wins
1948	Luigi Cantone	(Ita) 7 wins
1952	Edoardo Mangiarotti	(Ita) 5 wins
1956	Carlo Pavesi	(Ita) 5 wins
1960	Giuseppe Delfino	(Ita) 5 wins
1964	Grigoriy Kiss	(USSR) 2 wins
1968	Gyozo Kulcsar	(Hun) 4 wins
1972	Csaba Fenyvesi	(Hun) 4 wins
1976	Alexander Pusch	(FRG) 3 wins
1980	Johan Harmenberg	(Swe) 4 wins
1984	Phillippe Boisse	(FRA)
1988	Arnd Schmitt	(W.Ger)

Epee (Team)

1896	France
1908	France
1912	Belgium
1920	Italy
1924	France
1928	Italy
1932	France
1936	Italy
1948	France
1952	Italy
1956	Italy
1960	Italy
1964	Hungary
1968	Hungary
1972	Hungary
1976	Sweden
1980	France
1984	FRG
1988	France

Sabre (Individual)

1896	Jean Georgiadis	(Ger) 4 wins
1900	Georges de la Falaise	(Fra) data not available
1904	Manuel Diaz	(Cub) 4 wins
1906	Jean Georgiadis	(Ger)d.n.a.
1908	Jeono Fuchs	(Hun) 6 wins
1912	Jeono Fuchs	(Hun) 6 wins
1920	Nedo Nadi	(Ita) 11 wins
1924	Sandor Posta	(Hun) 5 wins
1928	Odon Tersztyanszky	(Hun) 9 wins
1932	Gyorgy Piller	(Hun) 8 wins
1936	Endre Kabos	(Hun) 7 wins
1948	Aladar Gerevich	(Hun) 7 wins
1952	Pal Kovacs	(Hun) 8 wins
1956	Rudolf Karpati	(Hun) 6 wins
1960	Rudolf Karpati	(Hun) 5 wins
1964	Tibor Pezsa	(Hun) 2 wins
1968	Jerzy Pawlowski	(Pol) 4 wins
1972	Viktor Sidiak	(USSR) 4 wins
1976	Viktor Sidiak	(USSR) 5 wins
1980	Viktor Sidiak	(USSR) 5 wins
1984	Jean Francois L.	(Fra)
1988	Jean Francois L.	(Fra)

Sabre (Team)

1906	Germany
1908	Hungary
1912	Hungary
1920	Italy
1924	Italy
1928	Hungary
1932	Hungary
1936	Hungary
1948	Hungary
1952	Hungary
1956	Hungary
1960	Hungary
1964	USSR
1968	USSR
1972	Italy
1976	USSR
1980	USSR
1984	Italy
1988	Hungary

Women's Foil (Individual)

1924 Ellen Osiier (Den) 5 wins
1928 Helene Mayer (Ger) 7 wins
1932 Ellen Preis (Aut) 9 wins
1936 Ilona Elek (Hun) 6 wins
1948 Ilona Elek (Hun) 6 wins
1952 Irene Camber (Ita) 5 wins
1956 Gillian Sheen (UK) 6 wins
1960 Heidi Schmid (Ger) 6 wins
1964 Ildiko Ujlaki-Rejto (Hun) 2 wins
1968 Elena Novikova (USSR) 4 wins
1972 Antonella Regno-Lonzi (Ita) 4 wins
1976 Ildiko Schwarczenberger (Hun) 4 wins
1980 Pascale Trinquet (Fra) 4 wins
1984 Jujie Luan (Chn)
1988 Anja Fichtel (W.Ger)

Women's Foil (Team)

1960	USSR
1964	Hungary
1968	USSR
1972	USSR
1976	USSR
1980	France
1984	FRG
1988	W.Ger

GOLF

It is not quite clear just where and when golf originated, although many accept the claim that it was invented by the Scots. It is known that, as early as 1440, golf was enjoying some popularity in the British Isles. Nor is the beginning of golf in this country or even in North America very clear. There were organizations known as golf clubs in the eighteenth century, but there is no proof that the actual game of golf was played at these clubs. It is a fact that a three-holed golf course was built in Montreal, Canada somewhere in the late 1850's.

The real story of the game in the United States begins in the 1880's. A golf club was formed in Foxburg, Pennsylvania in 1885, when Joseph Fox of Philadelphia brought back the game from a trip to Scotland. A few years later John G. Reed, a Scotsman living in Yonkers, New York, introduced the game in Yonkers on February 22, 1888. Since then it has developed and today it is one of the most popular recreational sports in the India.

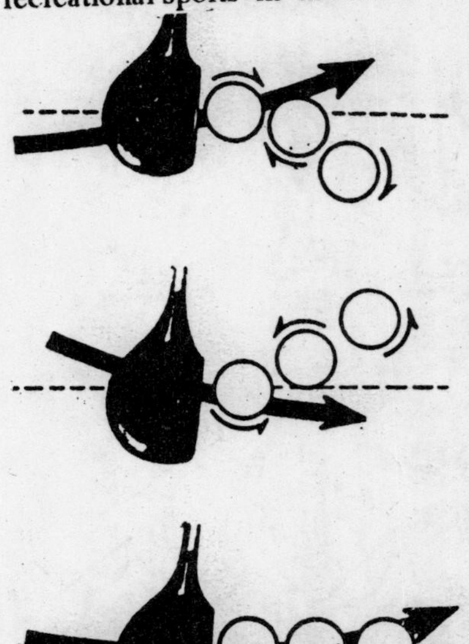

RULES OF THE GAME

In 1896, after representations from competitors in the Amateur Championship, the Royal and Ancient Golf Club established a committee to deal with all aspects of the rules of golf. The committee still exists and is composed of twelve members of the Royal and Ancient and eight other members representing golf bodies in the British Isles and overseas. The committee has a close contact with the United States Golf Association which has its own code of rules. Fundamentally, golf competitions all over the world are played according to the rules laid down by the Royal and Ancient Rules of Golf Committee.

ETIQUETTE

Etiquette is just as important as the rules themselves. It really amounts to showing consideration for other players, and certainly no one wants to play with an ill-mannered golfer. Here are some vital rules of etiquette for conduct on the golf course.

1. Always replace and press back divots from the fairway.
2. Always repair pitch marks on the green.
3. Always smooth out foot marks in a sand bunker.
4. Never talk or move when another player is making his shot, and never stand immediately behind him.
5. When attending the flag stick keep perfectly still, and do not sand immediately beside the hole.
6. Be careful never to tread on the line of an opponent's putt.

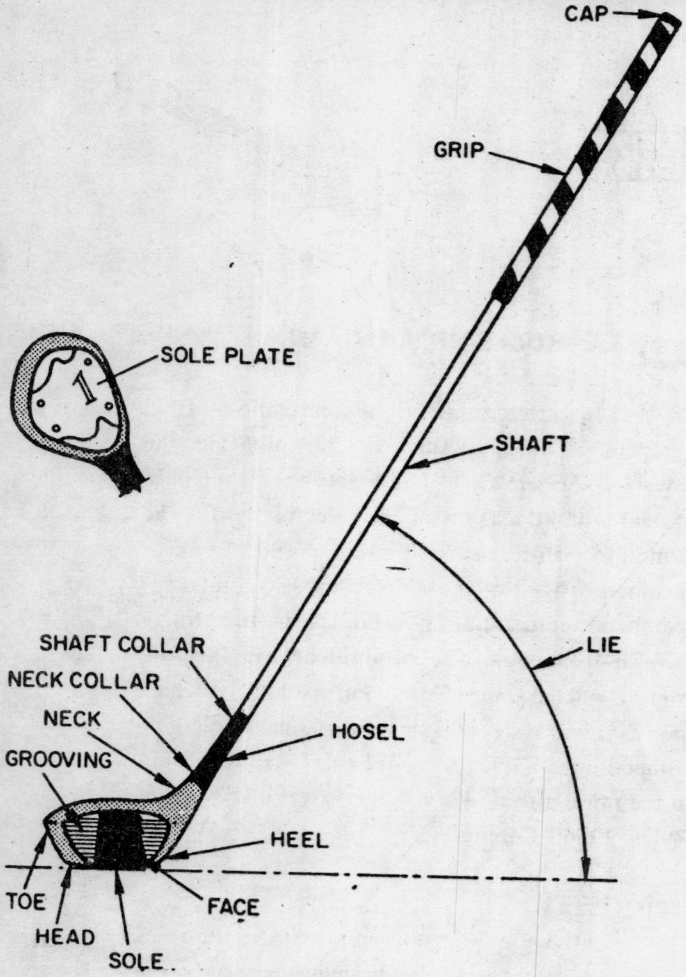

WOOD CLUB

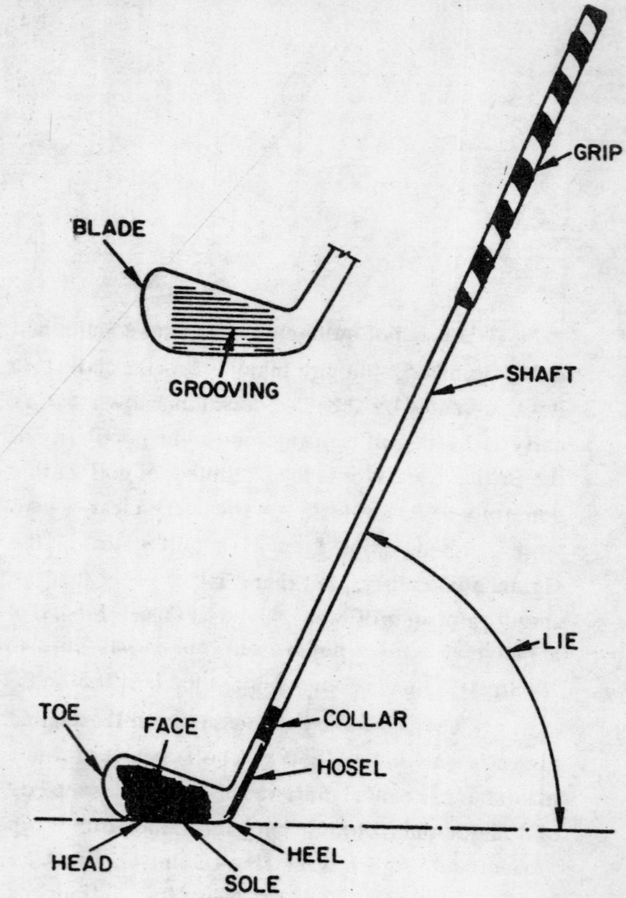

IRON CLUB

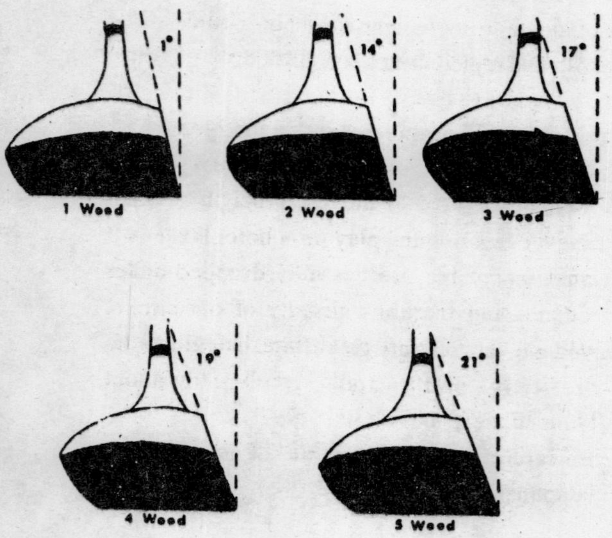

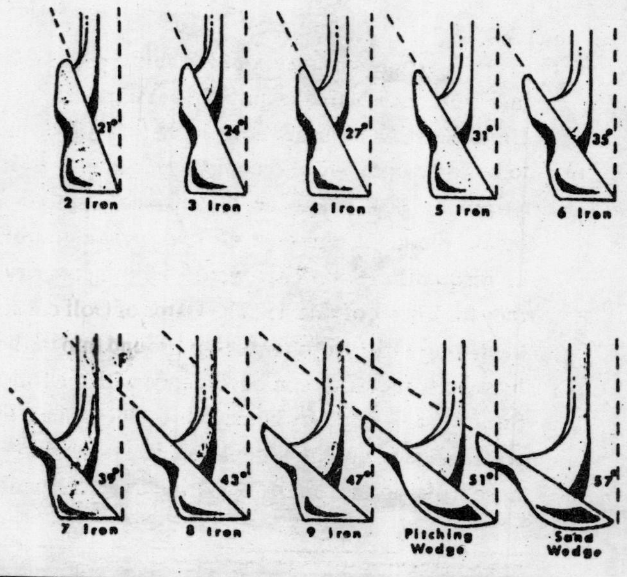

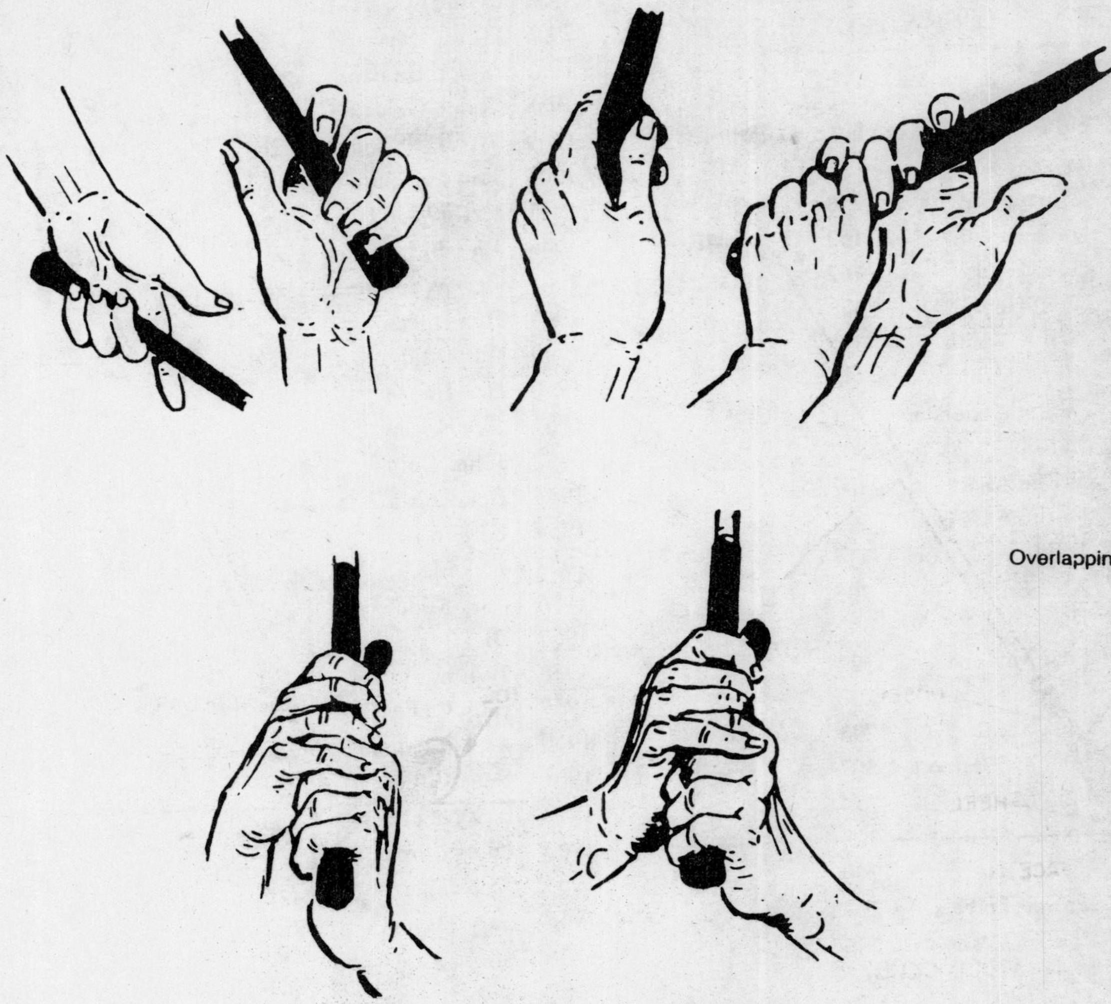

Overlapping grip.

After a revision of the rules, which came into force in Britain in April 1984 (1st January in the United States), there are now thirty-four - there used to be forty-one - with accompanying notes and it is surprising how often the professionals ignore or break them, at the cost of two penalty strokes or disqualification. That would be unnecessary if they took head of rule 1: 'The Game of Golf consists in playing a ball from the teeing ground into the hole by successive strokes in accordance with the Rules.' Simply said, and yet human differences lead to a wide range of interpretations and disputes, which all have to be sorted out by the twin governing bodies, the Royal and Ancient and the USGA.

Two of the most important basic rules of golf are:

1. The ball must be played where it lies and must not be touched or moved, other than when playing a shot, during the play of a hole. If the ball is declared unplayable, or it has to be dropped under some other ruling, there is a penalty of one stroke. However, on the putting green, the ball may be marked, lifted, cleaned and replaced without penalty.

2. In either a water hazard or sand bunker, the club must not be grounded.

CUP & TROPHIES

US Open

First held in 1895. Stroke play over 72 holes.

Winners

1895	Horace Rawlins	173
1896	James Foulis	152
1897	Joe Lloyd	162
1898	Fred`Herd	328
1899	Willie Smith	315
1900	Harry Vardon	313
1901	Willie Anderson	331
1902	Laurie Aucht.	307
1903	Willie Anderson	307
1904	Willie Anderson	303
1905	Willie Anderson	314
1906	Alex Smith	295
1907	Alex Ross	302
1908	Fred McLeod	322
1909	George Sargent	290
1910	Alex Smith	298
1911	John McDermott	307
1912	John McDermott	294
1913	Francis Ouimet	304
1914	Walter Hagen	290
1915	Jerome Travers	297
1916	Charles Evans, Jr	286
1919	Walter Hagen	301
1920	Edward Ray	295
1921	Jim Barnes	289
1922	Gene Sarazen	288
1923	Robert T. Jones, Jr	296
1924	Cyril Walker	297
1925	Willie Macfarlane	291
1926	Robert T. Jones,Jr	293
1927	Tommy Armour	301
1928	Johnny Farrell	294
1929	Robert T.Jones,Jr	294
1930	Robert T. Jones,Jr	287
1931	Billy Burke	292
1932	Gene Sarazen	286
1933	John Goodman	287
1934	Olin Dutra	293
1935	Sam Parks, Jr	299
1936	Tony Manero	282
1937	Ralph Guldahl	281
1938	Ralph Guldahl	284
1939	Byron Nelson	284
1940	Lawson Little	287
1941	Craig Wood	284
1946	Lloyd Mangrum	284
1947	Lew Worsham	282
1948	Ben Hogan	276
1949	Cary Middlecoff	286
1950	Ben Hogan	287
1951	Ben Hogan	287
1952	Julius Boros	281
1953	Ben Hogan	283
1954	Ed Furgol	284
1955	Jack Fleck	287
1956	Cary Middlecoff	281
1957	Dick Mayer	282
1958	Tommy Bolt	283
1959	Billy Casper	282
1960	Arnold Palmer	280
1961	Gene Littler	281
1962	Jack Nicklaus	283
1963	Julius Boros	293
1964	Ken Venturi	278
1965	Gary Player	282
1966	Billy Casper	278
1967	Jack Nicklaus	275
1968	Lee Trevino	275
1969	Orville Moody	281
1970	Tony Jacklin	281
1971	Lee Trevino	275
1972	Jack Nicklaus	290
1973	Johnny Miller	279
1974	Hale Irwin	287
1975	Lou Graham	287
1976	Jerry Pate	277
1977	Hubert Green	278
1978	Hale Irwin	285
1979	Hale Irwin	284
1980	Jack Nicklaus	272
1981	David Graham	273
1982	Tom Watson	282

1983	Larry Nelson	280
1984	Fazzy Zoeller	276
1985	Andy North	279
1986	Ray Floyd	279
1987	Scott Simpson	277
1988	Curtis Strange	278

British Open

The first championship was held at Prestwick in 1860. In 1892 the competition was extended from 36 to 72 holes.

Winners

1860	Willie Park, Sr	174
1861	Tom Morris, Sr	163
1862	Tom Morris,Sr	163
1863	Willie Park, Sr	168
1864	Tom Morris, Sr	167
1865	Andrew Strath	162
1866	Willie Park, Sr	167
1867	Tom Morris, Sr	170
1868	Tom Morris, Jr	170
1869	Tom Morris,Jr	154
1870	Tom Morris, Jr	149
1871	Not held	
1872	Tom Morris, Jr	166
1873	Tom Kidd	179
1874	Mungo Park	159
1875	Willie Park, Sr	166
1876	Robert Martin	176
1877	Jamie Anderson	160
1878	Jamie Anderson	157
1879	Jamie Anderson	170
1880	Robert Ferguson	162
1881	Robert Ferguson	170
1882	Robert Ferguson	171
1883	Willie Fernie	159
1884	Jack Simpson	160
1885	Bob Martin	171
1886	David Brown	157
1887	Willie Park, Jr	161
1888	Jack Burns	171
1889	Willie Park, Jr	155
1890	John Ball	164
1891	Hugh Kirkaldy	169
1892	Harold Hilton	305
1893	William Auchterlonie	322
1894	John Taylor	326
1895	John Taylor	322
1896	Harry Vardon	316
1897	Harry Hilton	314
1898	Harry Vardon	307
1899	Harry Vardon	310
1900	John Taylor	309
1901	James Braid	309
1902	Alexander Herd	307
1903	Harry Vardon	300
1904	Jack White	296
1905	James Braid	318
1906	James Braid	300
1907	Arnaud Massy	312
1908	James Braid	291
1909	John Taylor	295
1910	James Braid	299
1911	Harry Vardon	303
1912	Edward Ted Ray	295
1913	John Taylor	304
1914	Harry Vardon	306
1915	Not held	
1916	Not held	
1917	Not held	
1918	Not held	
1919	Not held	
1920	George Duncan	303
1921	Jock Hutchinson	296
1922	Walter Hagen (USA)	300
1923	Arthur Havers	295
1924	Walter Hagen (USA)	301
1925	James Barnes (USA)	300
1926	Robert T. Jones,Jr	291
1927	Robert T. Jones, Jr	285
1928	Walter Hagen (USA)	292
1929	Walter Hagen (USA)	292
1930	Robert T. Jones,Jr	291
1931	Tommy Armour (USA)	296
1932	Gene Sarazen (USA)	283
1933	Denny Shute (USA)	292
1934	Henry Cotton	283
1935	Alfred Perry	283

1936 Alfred Padgham 287
1937 Henry Cotton 283
1938 Reg Whitcombe 295
1939 Richard Burton 290
1940 Not held
1941 Not held
1942 Not held
1943 Not held
1944 Not held
1945 Not held
1946 Sam Snead (USA) 290
1947 Fred Daly 293
1948 Henry Cotton 284
1949 Bobby Locke(S.Afr) 283
1950 Bobby Locke (S.Afr) 279
1951 Max Faulkner 285
1952 Bobby Locke (S.Afr) 287
1953 Ben Hogan (USA) 282
1954 Peter Thomson (Aus) 283
1955 Peter Thomson (Aus) 281
1956 Peter Thomson (Aus) 286
1957 Bobby Locke (S.Afr) 279
1958 Peter Thomson (Aus) 278
1959 Gary Player (S.Afr) 284
1960 Kel Nagle (Aus) 278
1961 Arnold Palmer (USA) 284
1962 Arnold Palmer (USA) 276
1963 Bob Charles (NZ) 277
1964 Tony Lema (USA) 279
1965 Peter Thomson (Aus) 285
1966 Jack Nicklaus (USA) 282
1967 Robert de Vicenzo 278
1968 Gary Player (S.Afr) 299
1969 Tony Jackline 280
1970 Jack Nicklaus (USA) 283
1971 Lee Trevino (USA) 278
1972 Lee Trevino (USA) 278
1973 Tom Weiskopf (USA) 276
1974 Gary Player (S.Afr) 282
1975 Tom Watson (USA) 279
1976 Johnny Miller (USA) 279
1977 Tom Watson (USA) 268
1978 Jack Nicklaus (USA) 281
1979 Severiano Ballesteros (Spain) 282
1980 Tom Watson (USA) 271
1981 Bill Rogers (USA) 276
1982 Tom Watson (USA) 284
1983 Tom Watson (USA) 275
1984 Severiano Ballesteros (Spain) 276
1985 Sandy Lyle (UK) 282
1986 Greg Norman (Aus) 280
1987 Nick Faldo (UK) 279
1988 Severiano Ballesteros (Spain) 273

US Masters

Played each year at the Augusta National Gulf Course, Augusta, Georgia, Instituted in 1934. Stroke play over 72 holes.

Winners

1934 Harton Smith 284
1935 Gene Sarazen 282
1936 Horton Smith 285
1937 Byron Nelson 283
1938 Henry Picard 285
1939 Ralph Guldahl 279
1940 Jimmy Demaret 280
1941 Craig Wood 280
1942 Byron Nelson 280
1943 Not held
1944 Not held
1945 Not held
1946 Herman Keiser 282
1947 Jimmy Demaret 283
1948 Claude Harmon 279
1949 Sam Snead 282
1950 Jimmy Demaret 283
1951 Ben Hogan 280
1952 Sam Snead 286
1953 Ben Hogan 274
1954 Sam Snead 289
1955 Cary Middlecoff 279
1956 Jack Burke 289
1957 Doug Ford 283
1958 Arnold Palmer 284
1959 Art Wall 284

1960	Arnold Palmer	282
1961	Gary Player	280
1962	Arnold Palmer	280
1963	Jack Nicklaus	271
1964	Arnold Palmer	276
1965	Jack Nicklaus	271
1966	Jack Nicklaus	288
1967	Gay Brewer	280
1968	Bob Goalby	277
1969	George Archer	281
1970	Billy Casper	279
1971	Charles Coody	279
1972	Jack Nicklaus	286
1973	Tommy Aaron	283
1974	Gary Player	278
1975	Jack Nicklaus	276
1976	Ray Floyd	271
1977	Tom Watson	276
1978	Gary Player	277
1979	Fuzzy Zoeller	280
1980	Severiano Ballesteros	275
1981	Tom Watson	280
1982	Craig Stadlerr	284
1983	Severiano Ballesteros	280
1984	Jack Nicklaus	279
1985	Larry Mize	285
1986	Jack Nicklaus	279
1987	Larry Mize	285
1988	Sandy Lyle	281

US PGA Championship

First played in 1916. From then until 1957 it was a knock-out match play tournament, but since 1958 has been decided over 36 holes of stroke play.

Winners

1916	James Barnes
1917	Not held
1918	Not held
1919	Jmes Barnes
1920	Jock Hutchison
1921	Walter Hagen
1922	Gene Sarazen
1923	Gene Sarazen
1924	Walter Hagen
1925	Walter Hagen
1926	Walter Hagen
1927	Walter Hagen
1928	Leo Diegel
1929	Leo Diegel
1930	Tommy Armour
1931	Tom Creavy
1932	Tom Creavy
1933	Gene Sarazen
1934	Paul Runyan
1935	Johnny Revolta
1936	Denny Shute
1937	Denny Shute
1938	Paul Runyan
1939	Henry Picard
1940	Byron Nelson
1941	Vic Ghezzi
1942	Sam Snead
1943	Not held
1944	Bob Hamilton
1945	Byron Nelson
1946	Ben Hogan
1947	Jim Ferrier
1948	Ben Hogan
1949	Sam Snead
1950	Chandler Harper
1951	Sam Snead
1952	Jim Turnesa
1953	Walter Burkemo
1954	Chick Harbert
1955	Doug Ford
1956	Jack Burke
1957	Lionel Hebert
1958	Dow Finsterwald
1959	Bob Rosburg
1960	Jay Hebert
1961	Jerry Barber
1962	Gary Player
1963	Jack Nicklaus
1964	Bob Nichols
1965	Dave Marr
1966	Al Geiberger
1967	Don January
1968	Julius Boros

1969	Ray Floyd
1970	Dave Stockton
1971	Jack Nicklaus
1972	Gary Player
1973	Jack Nicklaus
1974	Lee Trevino
1975	Jack Nicklaus
1976	Dave Stockton
1977	Lanny Wadkins
1978	John Mahaffey
1979	David Graham
1980	Jack Nicklaus
1981	Larry Nelson
1982	Ray Floyd
1983	Hal Sutton
1984	Lee Trevino
1985	Hubert Green
1986	Bob Tway
1987	Larry Nelson
1988	Jeff Sluman

US Women's Open

Winners

1947	Betty Jameson	295
1948	Mildred Zaharias	300
1949	Louise Suggs	291
1950	Mildred Zaharias	291
1951	Betsy Rawls	293
1952	Louise Suggs	284
1953	Betsy Rawls	302
1954	Mildred Zaharias	291
1955	Fay Crocker	299
1956	Kathy Corelius	302
1957	Betsy Rawls	299
1958	Mickey Wright	290
1959	Mickey Wright	287
1960	Betsy Rawls	292
1961	Mickey Wright	293
1962	Murle Lindstrom	301
1963	Mary Mills	289
1964	Mickey Wright	290
1965	Carol Mann	290
1966	Sandra Spuzich	297
1967	Catherine Lacoste	294
1968	Sue Berning	289
1969	Donna Caponi	294
1970	Donna Caponi	287
1971	JoAnne Carner	288
1972	Sue Maxwell Berning	290
1973	Sue Maxwell Berning	290
1974	Sandra Haynie	295
1975	Sandra Palmer	295
1976	JoAnne Carner	292
1977	Hollis Stacy	298
1978	Hollis Stacy	289
1979	Jerilyn Britz	284
1980	Amy Alcott	280
1981	Pat Bradley	279
1982	Janet Alex	283
1983	Jan Stephenson	290
1984	Hollis Stacy	290
1985	Kathy Baker	280
1986	Jane Geddes	287
1987	Laura Davies	285
1988	Liselotte Neumann	277

US Amateur

Winners

1895	Charles Macdonald
1896	H.J. Whigham
1897	H.J.Whigham
1898	Findlay Douglas
1899	H.M.Harriman
1900	Walter Travis
1901	Walter Travis
1902	Louis James
1903	Walter Travis
1904	Chandler Egan
1905	Chandler Egan
1906	Eben Byers
1907	Jerome Travers
1908	Jerome Travers
1909	Robert Gardner
1910	William Fownes, Jr
1911	Harold Hilton
1912	Jerome Travers
1913	Jerome Travers
1914	Francis Ouimet

1915 Robert Gardner
1916 Charles Evans, Jr
1917 Not held
1918 Not held
1919 Davidson Herron
1920 Charles Evans, Jr
1921 Jesse Gullford
1922 Jesse Gullford
1923 Max Marston
1924 Robert T.Jones,Jr
1925 Robert T.Jones,Jr
1926 George Von Elm
1927 Robert T. Jones, Jr
1928 Robert T. Jones, Jr
1929 Harrison Johnston
1930 Robert T.Jones, Jr
1931 Francis Ouimet
1932 Ross Somerville
1933 George Dunlap, Jr
1934 Lawson Little
1935 Lawson Little
1936 John Fisher
1937 John Goodman
1938 William Turnesa
1939 Marvin Ward
1940 Richard Chapman
1941 Marvin Ward
1942 Not held
1943 Not held
1944 Not held
1945 Not held
1946 Stanley Bishop
1947 Robert Riegel
1948 William Turnesa
1949 Charles Coe
1950 Sam Urzertta
1951 Billy Maxwell
1952 Jack Westland
1953 Gene Littler
1954 Arnold Palmer
1955 Harvie Ward
1956 Harvie Ward
1957 Hillman Robbins
1958 Charles Coe
1959 Jack Nicklaus
1960 Deane Beman
1961 Jack Nicklaus
1962 Labron Harris
1963 Deane Beman
1964 Bill Campbell
1965 Bob Murphy
1966 Gary Cowan
1967 Bob Dickson
1968 Bruce Fleisher
1969 Steve Melnyk
1970 Lanny Wadkins
1971 Gary Cowan
1972 Marvin Giles
1973 Craig Stadler
1974 Jerry Pate
1975 Fred Ridley
1976 Bill Sander
1977 John Fought
1978 John Cook
1979 Mark O'Meara
1980 Hal Sutton
1981 Nathaniel Crosby
1982 Jay Sigel
1983 Jay Sigel
1984 Scott Vertplank
1985 Sam Randolph
1986 Stewart Alexander
1987 Billy Mayfair
1988 Eric Meeks

ARJUNA AWARD WINNERS

1961 P.G.Sethi
1963 A.S. Malik
1967 A.K. Pitamber
1972 Anjani N. Desai
1973 Vikramjit Singh
1975 S.K. Jamshed
1977-78 Sita Rawlley
1982 Lakshman Singh
1987 Nonita Lall

GYMNASTICS

Gymnastics concerns a system of physical exercises either for recreation or for promoting health and body-building. Today it is a popular sport. In earlier times gymnastics was an essential part of the training of army recruits and highly beneficial results were obtained. It has also been used as means for the improvement of the physique of children.

Gymnastics is a sport in which individuals or teams compete by performing routines-either compulsory, optional, or both-in the following four events: floor exercise, balance beam, side horse vault, and uneven parallel bars. These four events are the one included in competition throughout the world. In the United States two other events are included in many gymnastic competitions. The definition therefore, might be modified to read "six events" with "tumbling" and "trampoline" being added to the four international events.

GIRLS GYMNASTICS

Balance Beam

Balance and rhythm, rather than a number of difficult stunts, are what judges look for in this event. The gymnast should include turns, jumps and running steps in her routine, making sure that she uses the whole length of the beam, and that the difficult elements are logically distributed throughout her routine.

Judges also seek variety in the rhythm of a routine on the balance beam. A slow exercise, with careful stops before each element of difficulty, makes a routine too easy. Even if many difficult stunts are performed, a lack of rhythm, due to too many stops before each difficulty, lowers the score. The gymnast should try to vary her rhythm, making sure that the exercise as a whole appears lively, uninterrupted, and natural to her.

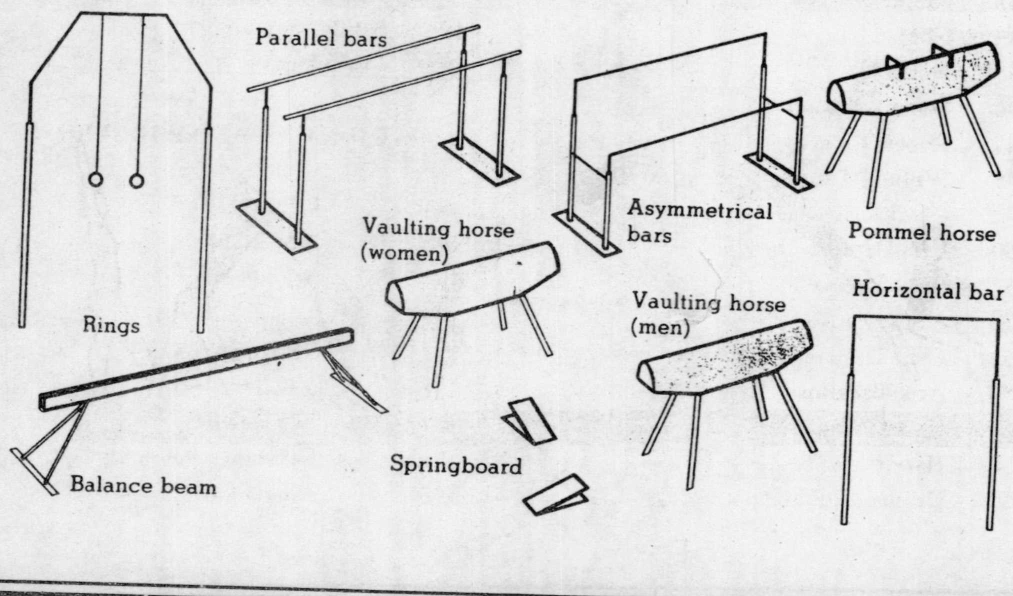

Arabesque Handstand

Forward roll mount

Back walkover

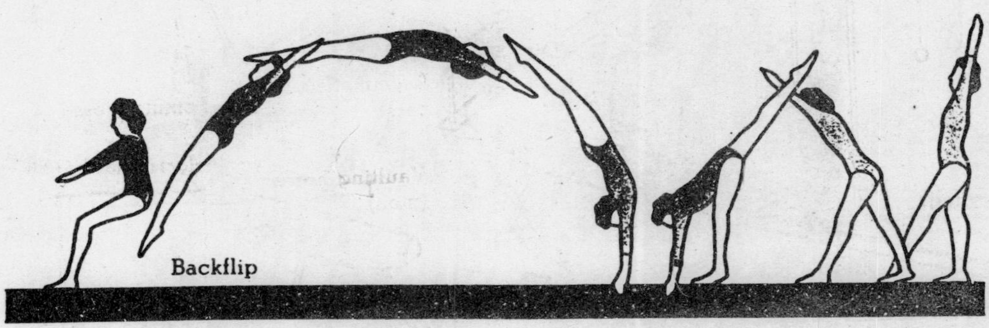

Backflip

Walkover

Front handspring

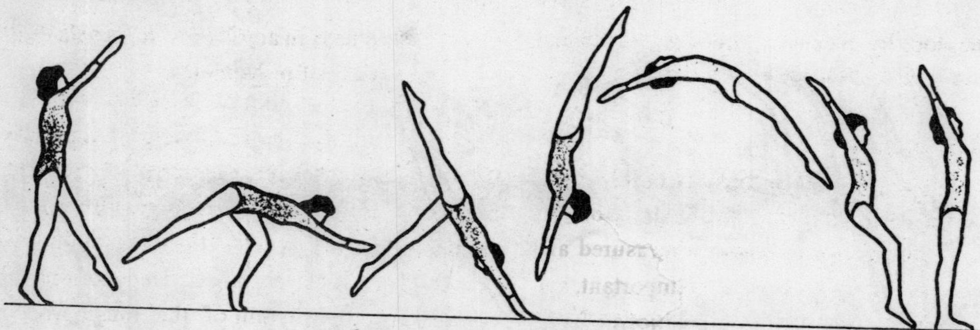

Front somersault

Leaps

If a performer falls from the apparatus in this exercise, she is allowed to remain on the floor only 10 seconds. She may then continue with a penalty. If, however, she takes longer to begin again, the exercise will be considered finished at the time of her fall.

Height of the beam (upper ridge) 100 to 120 cm.

Length 500 cm.

Cross-secion of the beam 10 cm., swelling in the centre to 13 cm.

Thickness of beam, from upper to lower ridge, 16 cm.

The beam is solidly attached on a stand which permits some adjustments in the height. The stand rests on the floor by means of three feet with rubber bottoms to prevent skidding.

Asymmetric Bars

In this event, as on the balance beam, a large quantity of difficult elements is not desirable, as they hinder the performance of a measured and assured exercise. Here, movement is important, and should be almost continuous. Static positions may be only momentary and should be avoided whenever possible. A maximum of two stops during an exercise is allowed, but only if the stops are in balance, and are in a brief moment of concentration before a difficult element.

If the gymnast falls during her performance, she will be allowed to continue before 30 seconds have passed. If she does not continue after 30 seconds, however, the exercise will be considered finished.

Height of upper bar 230 cm.

Height of lower bar 150 cm.

Length of bars 240 cm. each

Diameters of bar, oval form 42 and 48 mm.

When the bars are at their proper height, they must show the same tension; a test load of 135 kg. must produce a sag of 60 to 70 mm. After release, the bar must come back to the horizontal position.

The width between the two bars must be adjustable and may interfere with the efficiency of the apparatus when in use.

The uprights (vertical supports) of the bars must be adjustable in height, 3 x 5 cm.

The bars must not have crosspieces running in the same direction as the hand-bars.

Floor Exercise

This event allows the performer much freedom, and she should use as many 7 varied sequences as she can. As judging is based on the excellence and control of performance in relation to the difficulty of the movements attempted, more points will be scored by choosing a complicated routine and perfecting it than by sticking to elementary stunts. Special attention should be paid to the following:

sureness in acrobatics, turns and balancing
variety of movements
general posture of the body
coordination, consisting of lightness and suppleness relaxation

Music is frequently an accompaniment to floor exercise, and the gymnast thus has another way to personalize her performance. Her motions should complement the rhythm of the music, becoming livelier or more restful as the music directs. Her performance should never be dull.

The following list should be carefully considered before organizing a routine:

1. In executing the exercise, a gymnast must cover the entire floor area.
2. No more than two stops, and preferably only one, are allowed in the exercise.
3. There must be no repetition of parts.
4. Do not engage in rest positions: time is precious, and you should perform as many different movements as possible, without seeming rushed.
5. Parts of no aesthetic or athletic value should be eliminated.

Area of floor : 12 x 12 metres, distinctly marked on the ground by white lines. A padded area is recommended. If the area of performance is elevated, it must be at least 14 x 14 metres large, with the designated area clearly marked.

Vaulting Horse

Judging in this event is somewhat different than in others: here, the gymnast may perform twice,

Single-leg circle

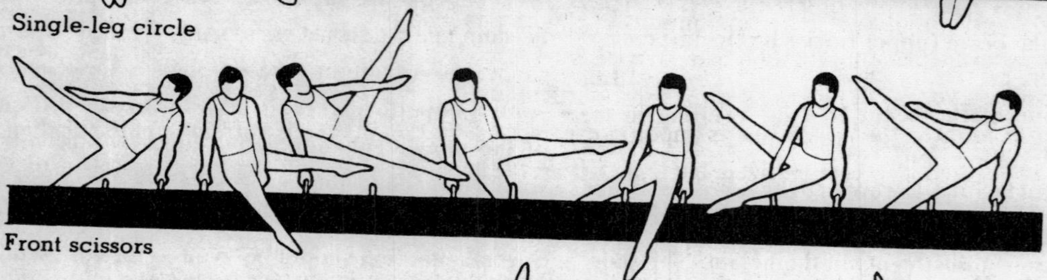

Front scissors

Back scissors

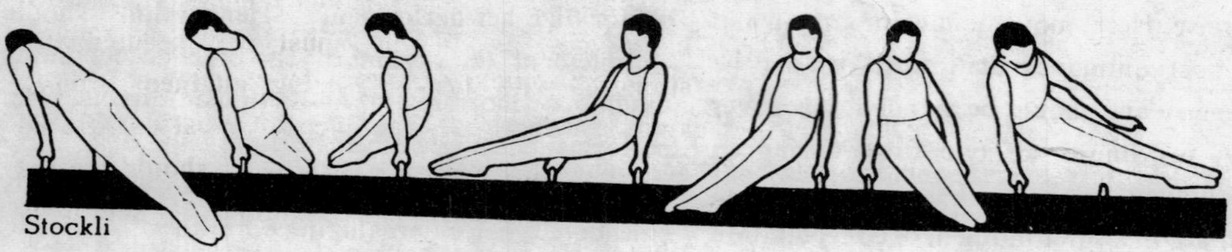

Stockli

the higher score counting in her total and the lower one being disregarded. The difficulty of the vault can be determined by referring to the Table of Vaults (prepared by the A.A.U.). If the vault selected is not listed on this table, a complete description should be sent to the President of the Technical Committee, and a duplicate to the Secretary, a month in advance of the competition.

The landing on the floor is just as important as the vault itself; one step is authorized, but it must be taken in the direction of descent. It cannot be provoked by an obvious unbalance.

Height 110 to 135 cm., from floor to top of horse.

Length 160 cm.

There must be special device for fixing the apparatus to the ground.

A minimum distance of 20 meters, including a springboard, must be provided for the run up.

MEN GYMNASTICS

Floor Exercises

The men's floor exercise event requires that the routine be done within a specified time period of 50 to 70 seconds. The gymnast must cover the entire 40 x 40 foot area with a predominance of complex tumbling skills. These tumbling skills must be accompanied by transitional movements including balance, flexibility and strength elements that need to be executed with rhythm and harmony. There are no hard and fast requirements as to the type or sequence of movements that a gymnast must execute, but the entire routine must be aesthetically appealing. It is recommended that the gymnast build the entire routine in difficulty and finish with a strong tumbling pass, leaving a positive impression at the conclusion.

Pommel Horse

The pommel horse exercise must be composed of clean swings without stops, in which the gymnast's legs must never come into contact with the horse. Double leg circle movements must be predominant in the exercise, but forward and backward scissors must also be shown, of which at least one must be executed twice in succession. All three parts of the horse must be used and to use each part completely both hands must come into contact with that part.

Rings

The rings exercise offers a unique challenge to the gymnast, because of the instability of the apparatus. The rings are the only piece of apparatus which is not firmly anchored so as to provide the gymnast with a firm surface to work on.

The rings exercise must contain movements varying between swings, strength parts and held parts, without any unwanted swing of the rings themselves being evident. This unrequired swing would be noticeable during the held parts and is not the movement of rings required to perform certain movements. The exercise must contain at least two handstands, one of which must be executed with strength, with the other being attained from a swing. Furthermore, the exercise must contain an additional held strength part which should be of at least 'B' difficulty. The duration of all held parts must be two seconds.

Long Horse Vault

This is the most unusual event in gymnastics competition. In vaulting, the gymnast runs to the horse and vaults over it, using a variety of body positions to do so. The difficulty of the vault is determined by the complexity of the vault during the flight phases, i.e., from the board to the horse, and from the horse to the landing. The vault is judged in terms of height, distance, and execution, as well as the control demonstrated in the landing.

Parallel Bars

The parallel bars offer the gymnast an infinite variety of movements and combinations. The parallel bars exercise must consist of swinging, flight and held parts, and may also contain a certain measure of strength. The swinging and flight parts

The Stulze

The Felgen or undersomersault

Front somersault dismount

should be predominant. The exercise should also contain at least one movement of grade B difficulty under or over the bars, where both hands are released simultaneously. Also, there may not be more than three 'pronounced' stops and all the held parts must be of two seconds duration.

Due to the nature of the apparatus, special attention must be given to the development of the swing and support strength.

Horizontal bar

The horizontal bar is the most basic and the most attractive piece of apparatus for the beginner gymnast. This is because it does not require specialist techniques or highly developed strength in order to master the basic skills.

The horizontal bar exercise must be made up exclusively of swinging elements, consisting of long swinging movements and movements where the body is brought close to the bar. The exercise must also contain a movement in dorsal hang or eagle grasp, plus at least one movement where the gymnast releases the bar with both hands simultaneously.

RULES OF THE GAME

Competitors :- Teams in Competition consist of six gymnasts.

Officials :- In men's competitions there are four judges and a head judge.

In women's competitions there are four judges, and a head judge (two in Competition 3) who is aided by a Scientific Technical Collaborator (STC) and assistants.

Dress (Men):- Men must wear a shirt (jersey) in all events. In the events performed on the pommel horse, rings, parallel bars, or horizontal_bar, men must wear long white pants and footwear (gym shoes and/or socks). The same clothing may be worn for the floor exercise and vault, or else short pants with or without footwear. In Competition 1 the members of a team must wear uniform clothing of the same colour, but an individual's choice of long or short pants for the floor exercise and vault is unaffected.

Dress (Women):- Women wear leotards (with a national emblem in international competitions), the precise cut of which may be varied to suit a particular event provided the general appearance remains essentially unchanged. Securely fastened bandages are allowed, but padding is prohibited. The wearing of gymnastic slippers and socks is optional. In competition 1 the members of a team must wear identical leotards.

Scoring:- Each competitor's performance on each apparatus is marked on the scale 0-10.

Each judge, including the head judge, assesses the gymnast's performance in strict accordance with the standards and points of reference laid down by the FIG. Deductions of whole, half, and one-tenth points may be made.

In some events there is a starting score, with a possible bonus for risk, originality, and virtuosity, which together make up the maximum possible of 10.

Basically gymnasts are penalized for general faults, such as lack of assurance, rhythm, or suppleness, or for faults specific to the apparatus or exercise.

Exercises and movements are officially defined and graded in terms of difficulty into three categories-A,B and C (being the most difficult). In the optional exercises, a competitor must include a specified number of A,B and C elements (also called parts) in order to score the highest possible marks for diffiuclty.

Bonus points can be earned by the demonstration of risk and originality in the B and C parts selected.

Order of Events:-Competitors perform the various events in the order given in the table, although because all types of apparatus are in use simultaneously, different competitors begin at different points on the list.

Adjustment of Scores:- Of the scores awarded by the four judges, the highest and lowest are disregarded and the average is taken of the two

Dislocation catch

remaining. If the difference between these two remaining scores exceeds a certain margin (also in women's competitions if their average differs from the head judge's score by such a margin) then the following action is taken. In men's competitions the head judge tries to reduce the difference by discussion with the judges concerned. In women's competitions all four judges are consulted. If this does not produce a remedy then the "base score" is calculated. This is done by adding the average of the two middle judges' scores to the head judge's score (or to the average of both head judges' scores in women's Competition 3) and dividing the resulting figure by two.

Olympics :- Gymnastics have been included in each Olympic Games since 1896. Since the 1948 Games the events have been:

Men :-Floor exercises, side horse, rings, long horse vault, parallel bars, horizontal bar.

Women :-Horse vault, asymmetrical bars, balance beam, floor exercises.

CUP & TROPHIES

Gold In Olympics (Men)

Team

1904	USA	374.43 pts
1906	Norway	19.00 pts
1908	Sweden	438.00 pts
1912	Italy	265.75 pts
1920	Italy	359.85 pts
1924	Italy	839.05 pts
1928	Switzerland	1718.62 pts
1932	Italy	541.850pts
1936	Germany	657.430pts
1948	Finland	1358.30 pts
1952	USSR	575.40 pts
1956	USSR	568.25 pts

1960	Japan	575.20 pts
1964	Japan	577.95 pts
1968	Japan	575.90 pts
1972	Japan	571.25 pts
1976	Japan	576.85 pts
1980	USSR	589.60 pts
1984	USA	591.40 pts
1988	USSR	data not available

Individual Combined Exercises

1900	Gustave Sandras (Fra)	302.00 pts
1904	Julius Lenhart (Aut)	69.80 pts
1906	Pierre Paysse (Fra)	97.00 pts
1908	Alberto Braglia (Ita)	317.00 pts
1912	Alberto Braglia (Ita)	135.00 pts
1920	Giorgio Zampori (Ita)	88.35 pts
1924	Leon Stukelj (Yug)	110.340 pts
1928	Georges Miez (Sui)	247.50 pts
1932	Romeo Neri (Ita)	140.625 pts
1936	Alfred Schwarzmann (Ger)	113.100 pts
1948	Veikko Huhtanen (Fin)	229.7 pts
1952	Viktor Chukarin (USSR)	115.70 pts
1956	Viktor Chukarin (USSR)	114.25 pts
1960	Boris Shakhlin (USSR)	115.95 pts
1964	Yukio Endo (Jpn)	115.95 pts
1968	Sawao Kato (Jpn)	115.90 pts
1972	Sawao Kato (Jpn)	114.650 pts
1976	Nikolai Andrianov (USSR)	116.650 pts
1980	Aleksandr Ditiatin (USSR)	118.650 pts
1984	Koji Gushiken (Jpn)	118.700 pts
1988	Vladimir Artemov (USSR)	d. n. a.

Floor Exercise

1932	Istvan Pelle (Hun)	9.60
1936	Georges Miez (Sui)	18.666
1948	Ferenc Pataki (Hun)	38.7
1952	William Thoresson (Swe)	19.25
1956	Valentin Muratov (USSR)	19.20
1960	Nobuyuki Aihara (Jpn)	19.450
1964	Franco Menichelli (Ita)	19.45
1968	Sawao Kato (Jpn)	19.475
1972	Nikolai Andrianov (USSR)	19.175
1976	Nikolai Andrianov (USSR)	19.450
1980	Roland Bruckner (GDR)	19.750
1984	Li Ning (Chn)	19.925
1988	Sergey Kharkov (USSR)	d. n. a.

Parallel Bars

1896	Alfred Flatow (Ger)	d.n.a.
1904	George Eyser (USA)	44.00
1924	August Guttinger (Sui)	21.63
1928	Ladislav Vacha (Tch)	18.83
1932	Romeo Neri (Ita)	18.97
1936	Kornad Frey (Ger)	19.067
1948	Michael Reusch (Sui)	39.5
1952	Hans Eugster (Sui)	19.65
1956	Viktor Chukarin (USSR)	19.20
1960	Boris Shakhlin (USSR)	19.400
1964	Yukio Endo (Jpn)	19.675
1968	Akinori Nakayama (Jpn)	19.475
1972	Sawao Kato (Jpn)	19.475
1976	Sawao Kato (Jpn)	19.675
1980	Aleksandr Tkachev (USSR)	19.775
1984	Bart Conner (USA)	19.950
1988	Vladimir Artemov (USSR)	data not available

Pommel Horse

1896	Jules Zutter (Sui)	d.n.a.
1904	Anton Heida (USA)	42
1924	Josef wilhelm (Sui)	21.23
1928	Hermann Hanggi (Sui)	19.75
1932	Istvan Pelle (Hun)	19.07
1936	Konrad Frey (Ger)	19.333
1948	Paavo Aaltonen (Fin)	38.7
	Veikko Huhtanen (Fin)	38.7
	Heikki Savolainen (Fin)	38.7
1952	Viktor Chukarin (USSR)	19.50
1956	Boris Shakhlin (USSR)	19.25
1960	Eugen Ekman (Fin)	19.375
	Boris Shaklin (URS)	19.375
1964	Miroslav Carar (Yug)	19.525
1968	Miroslav Carar (Yug)	19.325
1972	Viktor Klimenko (URS)	19.125
1976	Zoltan Magyar (Hun)	19.700
1980	Zoltan Magyar (Hun)	19.925
1984	Li Ning (Chn)	19.950
1988	Lyubomir Geraskov (Bulgaria)	d. n. a.
	Zsolt Borkai (Hungary)	d. n. a.
	Dmitri Bilozertchev (USSR)	d. n. a.

Rings

1896	Ioannis Mitropoulos (Ger)	d. n. a.
1904	Herman Glass (USA)	45.00
1924	Franco Martino (Ita)	21.553
1928	Leon Skutelj (Yuj)	19.25
1932	George Gulack (USA)	18.97
1936	Alois Hudec (Tch)	19.433
1948	Karl Frei (Sui)	39.60
1952	Grant Shaginyan (USSR)	19.75
1956	Albert Azaryan (USSR)	19.35
1960	Albert Azaryan (USSR)	19.725
1964	Takuji Hayata (Jpn)	19.475
1968	Akinori Nakayama (Jpn)	19.450
1972	Akinori Nakayama (Jpn)	19.350
1976	Nikolai Andrianov (USSR)	19.650
1980	Aleksandr Ditiatin (USSR)	19.875
1984	Koji Gushiken (Jpn)	19.850
1988	Holger Behrendt (E.Ger)	d. n. a.
	Dmitri Bilozertchev (USSR)	d. n. a.

Horizontal Bar

1896	Hermann Weingartner (Ger)	d. n. a.
1904	Anton Heida (USA)	40
	Edward Henning (USA)	40
1924	Leon Strukelj (Yuj)	19.730
1928	Georges Miez (Sui)	19.17
1932	Dallas Bixler (USA)	18.33
1936	Aleksanteri Saarvala (Fin)	19.367
1948	Josef Stalder (Sui)	39.7
1952	Jack Gunthard (Sui)	19.55
1956	Takashi Ono (Jpn)	19.60
1960	Takashi Ono (Jpn)	19.60
1964	Boris Shakhlin (USSR)	19.625
1968	Mikhail Voronin (USSR)	19.550
	Akinori Nakayama (Jpn)	19.550
1972	Mitsuo Tsukahara (Jpn)	19.725
1976	Mitsuo TSUkahara (Jpn)	19.675
1980	Stoyan Deltchev (Bul)	19.825
1984	Shinje Morisue (Jpn)	20.00
1988	Vladimir Artemov (USSR)	d. n. a.
	Valeri Lyukhin (USSR)	d. n. a.

Horse Vault

1896	Carl Schuhmann (Ger)	d. n. a.
1904	Anton Heida (USA)	36.00
	George Eyser (USA)	36.00
1924	Frank Kriz (USA)	9.98
1928	Eugen Mack (Sui)	9.58
1932	Savino Guglielmetti (Ita)	18.03
1936	Alfred Schwarzmann (Ger)	19.200
1948	Paavo Aaltonen (Fin)	39.10
1952	Viktor Chukarin (USSR)	19.20
1956	Helmuth Bantz (Ger)	18.85
	Valentin Muratov (USSR)	18.85
1960	Takashi Ono (Jpn)	19.350
	Borish Shakhlin (USSR)	19.350
1964	Haruhiro Yamashita (Jpn)	19.600
1968	Mikhail Voronin (USSR)	19.000
1972	Klaus Koste (GDR)	18.850
1976	Nikolai Andrianov (USSR)	19.450
1980	Nikolai Andrianov (USSR)	19.825
1984	Yun Lou (Chn)	19.950
1988	Lou Yun (Chn)	d. n. a.

WOMEN

Team

1928	Netherlands	316.75 pts
1936	Germany	506.50 pts
1948	Czechoslovakia	445.45 pts
1952	USSR	527.03 pts
1956	USSR	444.80 pts
1960	USSR	382.32 pts
1964	USSR	380.89 pts
1968	USSR	382.85 pts
1972	USSR	380.50 pts
1976	USSR	390.35 pts
1980	USSR	394.90 pts
1984	Romania	392.20 pts
1988	USSR	d. n. a.

Individual Combined Exercise

1952	Maria Gorokhovskaya (USSR)	76.78
1956	Larissa Lathynina (USSR)	74.933
1960	Larissa Latynina (USSR)	77.564
1964	Vera Caslavska (Tch)	77.564
1968	Vera Caslavska (Tch)	78.25
1972	Ludmila Tourischeva (USSR)	77.025

1976	Nadia Comaneci (Rom)	79.275
1980	Elena Davydova (USSR)	79.150
1984	Mary Lou Retton (USA)	79.175
1988	Elena Shushunova (USSR)	d. n. a.

Asymmetrical Bars

1952	Margit Korondi (Hun)	19.40
1956	Agnes Keleti (Hun)	18.966
1960	Polina Astakhova (USSR)	19.616
1964	Polina Astakhova (USSR)	19.332
1968	Vera Caslavska (Tch)	19.650
1972	Karin Janz (GDR)	19.675
1976	Nadia Comaneci (Rom)	20.000
1980	Maxi Gnauck (GDR)	19.875
1984	Ma Yanhong (Chn)	19.950
1988	Daniela Silivas (Rom)	d.n.a.

Balance Beàm

1952	Nina Bocharova (USSR)	19.22
1956	Agnes Keleti (Hun)	18.80
1960	Eva Bosakova (Tch)	19.283
1964	Vera Caslavska (Tch)	19.449
1968	Natalya Kuchinskaya (USSR)	19.650
1972	Olga Korbut (USSR)	19.575
1976	Nadia Comaneci (Rom)	19.950
1980	Nadia Comaneci (Rom)	19.800
1984	Simona Pauca (Rom)	19.800
	Ecaterina Szabo (Rom)	19.800
1988	Daniela Silivas (Rom)	d. n. a.

Floor Exercises

1952	Agnes Keleti (Hun)	19.36
1956	Larissa Latynina (USSR)	18.733
	Agnes Keleti (Hun)	18.733
1960	Larissa Latynina (USSR)	19.583
1964	Larissa Latynina (USSR)	19.599
1968	Larissa Petrik (USSR)	19.675
	Vera Caslavska (Tch)	19.675
1972	Olga Korbut (USSR)	19.575
1976	Nelli Kim (USSR)	19.850
1980	Nelli Kim (USSR)	19.875
	Nadia Comaneci (Rom)	19.875
1984	Ecaterina Szabo (Rom)	19.975
1988	Daniela Silivas (Rom)	d. n. a.

Horse Vault

1952	Yekaterina Kalinchuk (USSR)	19.20
1956	Larissa Latynina (USR)	18.833
1960	Margarita Nikolayeva (USSR)	19.316
1964	Vera Caslavska (Tch)	19.483
1968	Vera Caslavska (Tch)	19.775
1972	Karin Janz (GDR)	19.525
1976	Nelli Kim (USSR)	19.800
1980	Natalya Shaposhnikova (USSR)	19.725
1984	Ecaterina Szabo (Rom)	19.875
1988	Svetlana Boginskaya (USSR)	d. n. a.

ARJUNA AWARD WINNERS

1961	Shyam Lal
1975	Montu Debnath
1985	Sunita Sharma

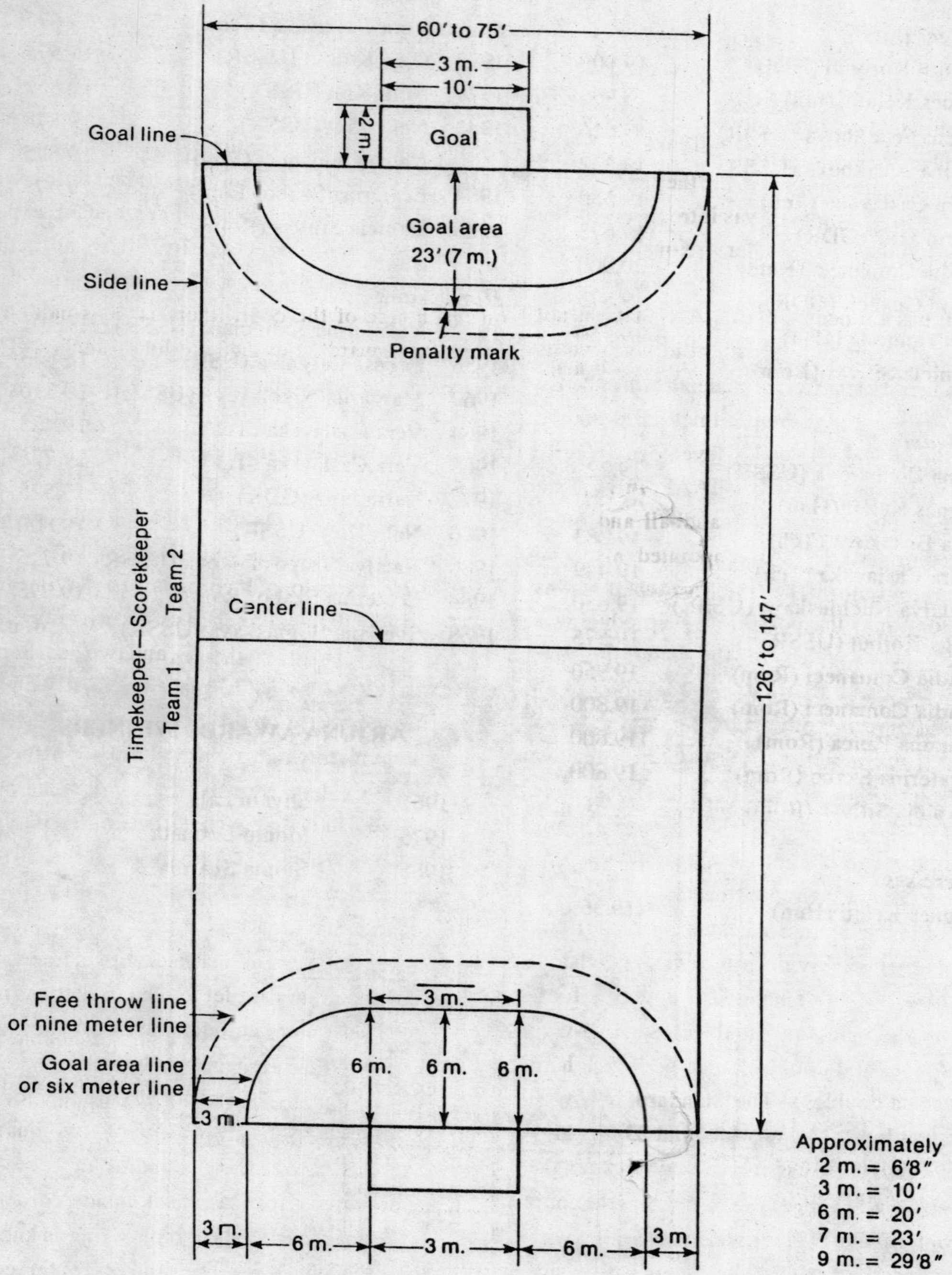
60′ to 75′
3 m.
10′
2 m.
Goal
Goal line
Goal area
23′ (7 m.)
Side line
Penalty mark
Timekeeper—Scorekeeper
Team 1
Team 2
Center line
126′ to 147′
Free throw line
or nine meter line
Goal area line
or six meter line
3 m.
6 m.
6 m.
6 m.
3 m.
3 m.
6 m.
3 m.
6 m.
3 m.
Approximately
2 m. = 6′8″
3 m. = 10′
6 m. = 20′
7 m. = 23′
9 m. = 29′8″

HANDBALL

The game of Handball that we know today originated in Germany at the end of the nineteenth century, when it was introduced to the world by a gymnastics master, Konard Koch. However, the development of the game since its introduction has not been smooth. At first it was not recognized as a separate sport. It did not have its own governing body and it came under the jurisdiction of the International Amateur Athletic Federation.

From 1904, handball developed steadily under the watchful eye of the IAAF. In 1862, to keep pace with the progress of handball and other developing sports, the IAAF appointed a special committee, representing the countries where it was played, to look into the possibility of producing a standardized set of rules for the game. In 1928, eleven handball playing nations met in Amesterdam on the occasion of the Olympic Games and as a result of this meeting, the International Amateur Handball Federation was formed. In 1931, just three years after attaining separate entity, handball was included in the programme of the game by the International Olympic Committee. This game was first included in the Olympics held in Berlin in 1936.

Handball is divided into many division: four-wall soft ball (both singles and doubles), four-wall hard ball (singles and doubles), and one-wall hard ball (singles and doubles), and one-wall hard ball (singles and doubles). The standard four-wall court in 46 feet long, 23 feet wide, and 23 feet high with a back wall 10 feet high. Half-way between the front and back walls a line is drawn across the court 5 feet in front of the center line, and parallel with it is another line, the service line. There is a service box in which the partner of the server stands while the service is being made. There is an area in the service zone 18 inches from and parallel to the side wall. The one wall court is 34 by 20 feet with a wall 16 feet high. The side line should extend 3 feet past the back line. Sixteen feet back from the wall, a line is drawn across the court; nine feet back of this line, on each side of the court, there is a small line extending inward from the side line 4 inches. This designates the serving area.

RULES OF THE GAME

1. The full sized court is a rectangle, the sidelines being 40 metres long. The goal lines being 20 metres long. It consists of a playing area divided into two halves by a centre line parallel to the goal lines, and two goal areas.
2. Each goal must be placed centrally on its respective goal line. Each goal consists of two metre high posts, vertically placed 3 metres between their facing sides and equidistant from the corners of the playing court. These goal posts must be firmly attached to the ground and joined by a horizontal crossbar.
3. The goal area is marked with a line three metres long parallel to and 6 metres from the goal line, equidistant from the side lines. (Measurements include the thickness of all lines). The ends of this line are joined to the goal line by means of two quarter circles each having a radius of 6 metres measured from the back inside corner of the goal posts. This complete line is known as the goal area line and its outer edge defines the goal area.

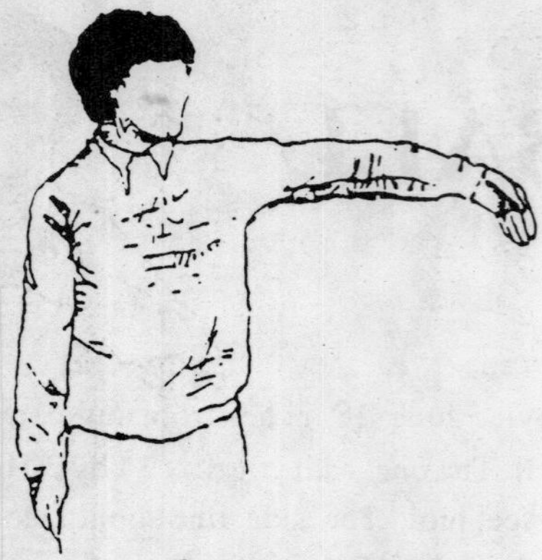

Goal throw

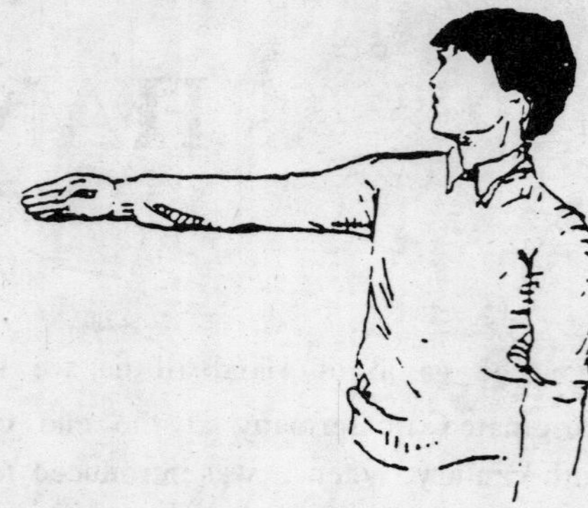

Free throw—direction

Referee throw

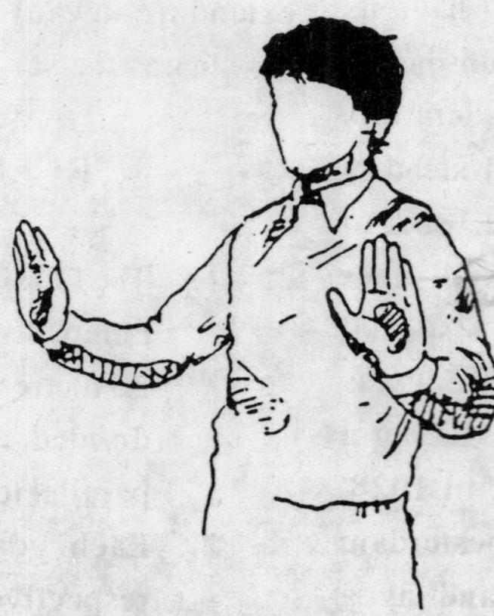

Keep the distance of 3 meters

Warning (yellow)
Disqualification (red)

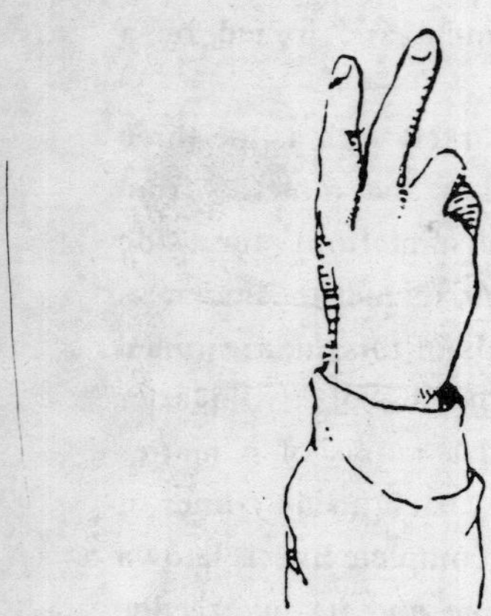

Suspension (2 minutes)

Exclusion

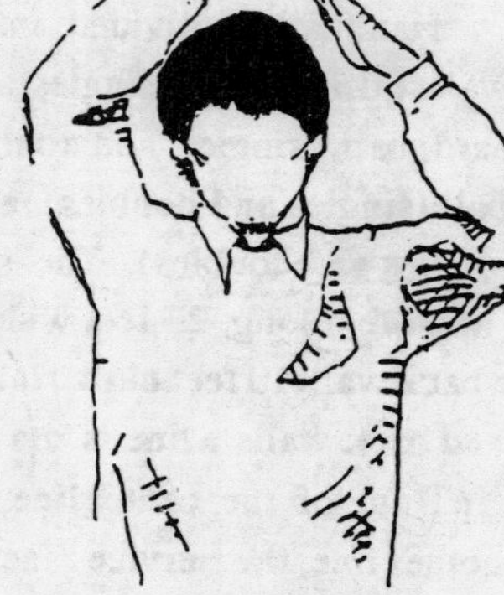

Time out

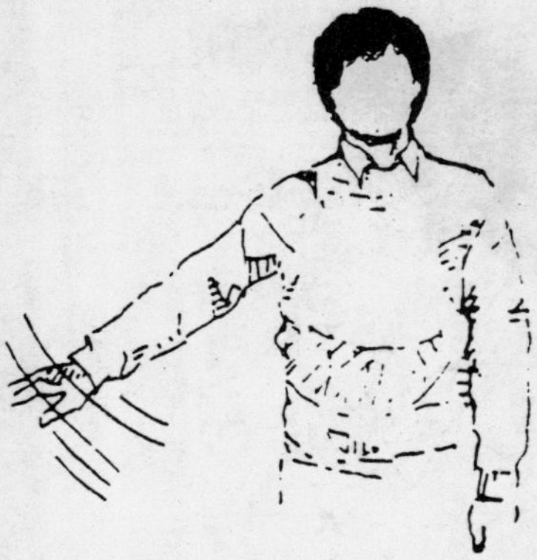

Entering the goal area

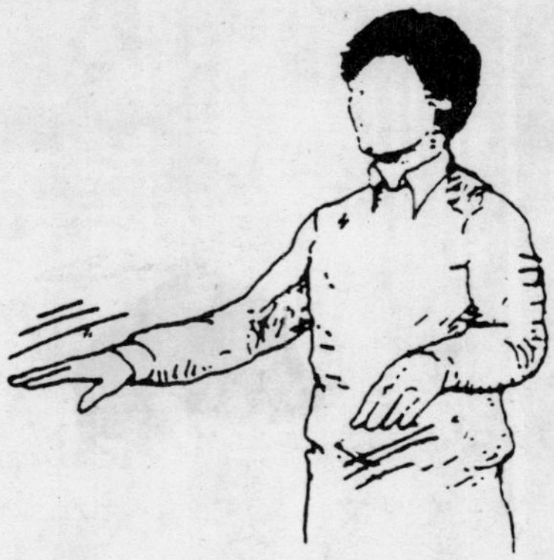

Illegal catching, bouncing, or fumbling

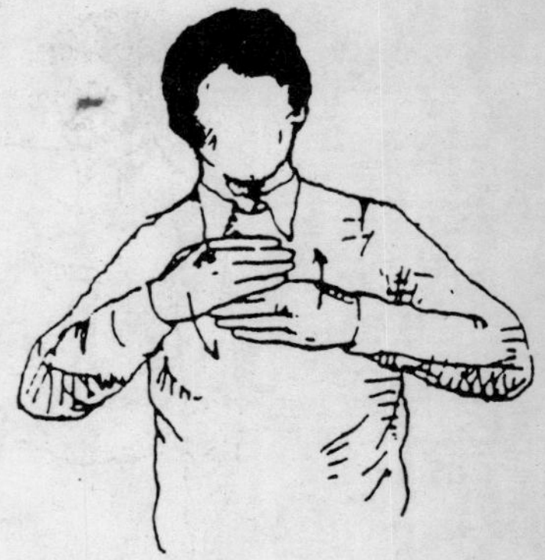

Too many steps or holding the ball too long

Time wasting

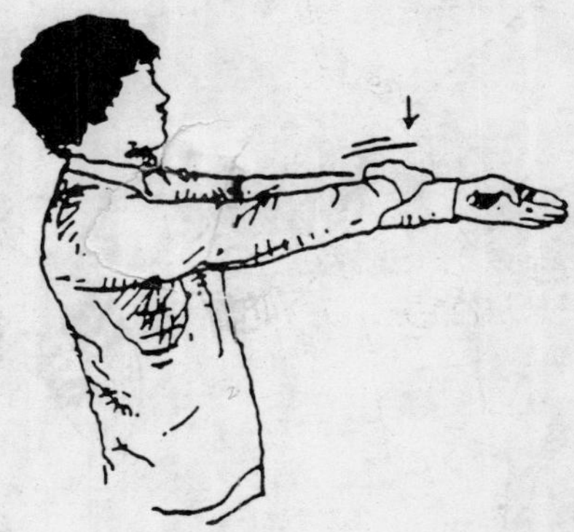

Stroke on the arm

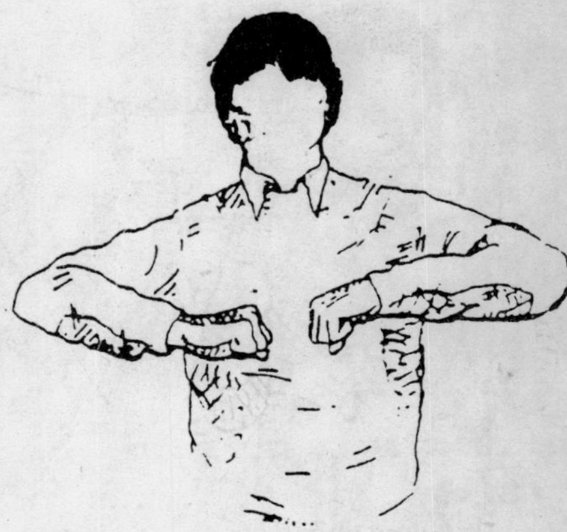

Holding

Pushing, running into, jumping into

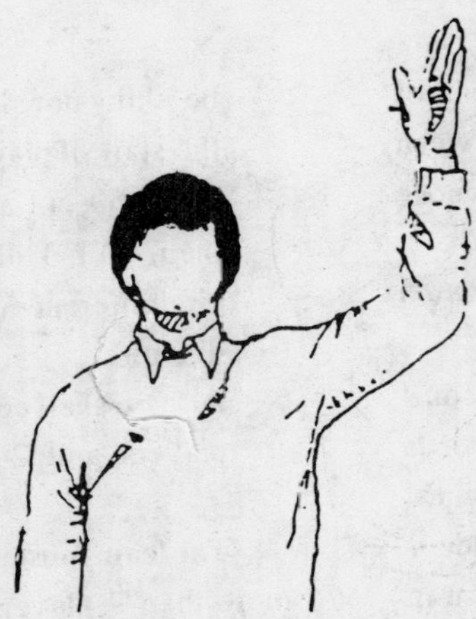

Goal

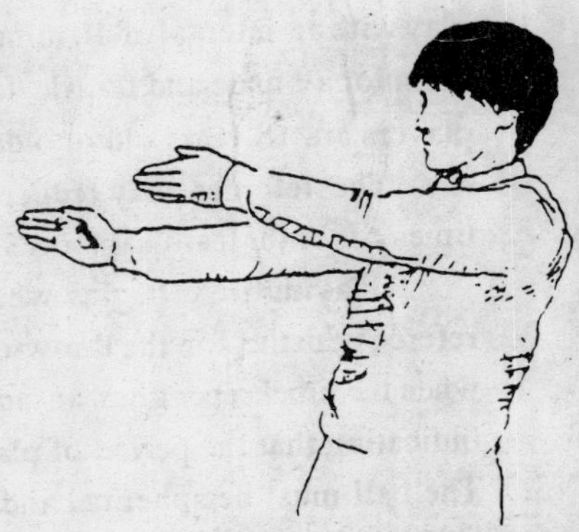

Throw in

4. There shall be two 30 minute periods of play with an interval of 10 minutes between them for all male and female teams whose players are 18 years old or older.

   The referees may reduce the interval times if both team captains agree.

   Playing time begins when the court referee whistles for the throw-off and ends when the timekeeper gives an audible signal indicating that the period of play is ended.

5. The ball must be spherical and uniform in colour constructed of a solid casing of leather or synthetic material. The surface must not be shiny nor slippery. The ball measured at the start of play, must have a circumference of 58-60 cm and weight 425-475 gm for men. For ladies the ball must have a circumference of 54-56 cm and weight 325-400 gm.

6. A team shall consist of 12 players (10 court players and 2 goalkeepers).

The team must use a goalkeeper at all times. Not more than 7 players, i.e. 6 court players, and goalkeeper, may be present on the court at any time. The remaining players are substitutes.

A goalkeeper must never replace a court player. However, a court player may replace a goalkeeper.

The scorekeeper must be informed if a goalkeeper is to be replaced by a court player.

Only the goalkeeper is allowed to enter the goal area (cf 6:3). The goal area, which includes the goal-area line is regarded as entered when a court player touches the ground therein with any part of the body.

CUP & TROPHIES

Professional Singles

1951	Walter Plekan
1952	Vic Hershkowitz
1953	Bob Brady
1954	VicHershkowitz
1955	Jim Jacobs
1956	Jim Jacobs
1957	Jim Jacobs
1958	John Sloan
1959	John Sloan
1960	Jim Jacobs
1961	John Sloan
1962	Oscar Obert
1963	Oscar Obert
1964	Jim Jacobs
1965	Jim Jacobs
1966	Paul Haber
1967	Paul Haber
1968	Simon (Stuffy) Singer
1969	Paul Haber
1970	Paul Haber
1971	Paul Haber
1972	Fred Lewis
1973	Terry Mack
1974	Fred Lewis
1975	Fred Lewis
1976	Fred Lewis
1977	Naty Alvarado
1978	Fred Lewis
1979	Naty Alvarado
1980	Naty Alvarado
1981	Fred Lewis
1982	Naty Alvarado
1983	Naty Alvardo
1984	Naty Alvardo
1985	Naty Alvardo

Four -Wall Doubles

1951	Frank Coyle and Bill Baier
1952	Frank Coyler and Bill Baier
1953	Sam Haber and Harry Dreyfuss
1954	Sam Haber and Ken Schneider
1955	Sam Haber and Ken Schneider
1956	Sam Haber and Ken Schneiber
1957	Phil Collins and John Sloan
1958	Phil Collins and John Sloan
1959	Phil Collins and John Sloan
1960	Jim Jacobs and Dick Weisman
1961	John Sloan and Vic Hershkowitz
1962	Jim Jacobs and Marty Decatur
1963	Jim Jacobs and Marty Decatur
1964	John Sloan and Phil Ebert
1965	Jim Jacobs and Marty Decatur
1966	Pete Tyson and Bob Lindsay
1967	Jim Jacobs and Marty Decatur
1968	Jim Jacobs and Marty Decatur
1969	Lou Kramberg and Lou Russo
1970	Carl Obert and Ruddy Obert
1971	Ray Neveau and Simie Fein
1972	Dent Fusselman and Al Drews
1973	Ray Neveau and Simie Fein
1974	Ray Neveau and Simie Fein
1975	Steve Lott and Marty Decatur
1976	Dan O'Connor and Gary Rohrer
1977	Matt Kelley and Skip McDowell
1978	Marty Decatur and Simon (Stuffy) Singer
1979	Marty Decatur and Simon (Stuffy) Singer
1980	Skip McDowell and Marry Robertson
1981	Jack Roberts and Tom Kopatich
1982	Vern Roberts and Naty Alvarado
1983	Vern Roberts and Naty Alvarado
1984	Vern Roberts and Naty Alvarado
1985	Vern Roberts and Naty Alvarado

Gold In Olympics

First held in the Olympic Games in 1936, the sport for men was re introduced in 1972, and is now held indoor.

Men

1936	Germany
1972	Yugoslavia
1976	USSR
1980	GDR
1984	Yugoslavia
1988	USSR

Women

1976	USSR
1980	USSR
1984	Yugoslavia
1988	S.Korea

THE ENCYCLOPAEDIA OF SPORTS & GAMES

THE ENCYCLOPAEDIA OF SPORTS & GAMES

(In Two Volumes)

Volume 2

Edited by
YOGRAJ THANI

Compiled by
LOKESH THANI

The Encyclopaedia of Sports and Games

ISBN: 81-212-0407-0 Set
ISBN: 81-212-0411-9 (Vol. 2)

Reprinted in 2013 in India by
Gyan Publishing House
23, Main Ansari Road, Daryaganj,
New Delhi - 110002
Phone : 23282060, 23261060
Fax : (011) 23285914
E-mail : books@gyanbooks.com
Website: gyanbooks.com

Printed at: G. Print Process, Delhi

FOREWORD

The history of Indian sports in encyclopaedic form by Mr. Lokesh is yet another landmark in the ever growing field of Indian sports literature. It comes on the heels of his *Encyclopaedia of Cricket* which was well received.

Mr. Lokesh has codified 41 sports disciplines in well defind pattern listing each game's history, skills, rules, cup and trophies and award winners in that order. A final chapter on terminology is added to explain to the reader the nuances of sports language.

The disciplines had been listed in alphabetical order beginning with the game of American Football and covers even non-conventional Indian games such as Kabaddi and Kho-kho. The range also extends to baseball, billiards, carrom, motor racing and riding.

The inclusion, in brief of rules of each game should make the anthology a really useful publication for particularly the young reader who is ever in search of information and knowledge.

Mr. Lokesh draws most of its inspiration from Mr. Yog Raj Thani who has been dominating the Indian sports journalism scene for more than three decades now. He has established quite a place for himself in Indian language sports journalism and his column/stories today publish in more than 30 publications all over India. He is also a well-known personality over the radio and his inimitable style of writing has no peers.

The latest anthology should go well with the Indian sports reading public and I am happy to lend my name to this work of great industry and imagination.

Gopesh Mehra

CONTENTS

HOCKEY

The hit

There is every reason to believe that hockey is of Greek origin, although the only evidences of that fact today are the figures of "Hockey players" in old Greek friezes.Some writers prefer to consider "hurley," an old Irish game, the first reference to which is found in the will of the Irish king Cathair Mor in 148 A.D., as the forerunner of hockey. An early Scotch game known as "shinty" was in all probability the direct ancestor of the modern game. In London the same game was known as "hackie," while in Wales during the same period, the game of "bandy" bore a close resemblance to the ancestor of hockey.

The game of hockey as now played may be considered to have originated in the year 1883,the first attempt to establish the game under a definite code of rules being successfully under taken by the Wimbledon Club in that year. The game had of-course existed in various forms for a very long time, but how long no one can well say, as there do not appear to be any records preserved. In Ireland it was long known as Hurly, and in Scotland as Shinty. In England,it was played a good deal round London in the 17th century, but seems to have died out for some years before the Wimbledon Club was formed in 1883. Since that date it has prospered and developed to such an extent both in the number of clubs all over that country and in the skill displayed in the game, that players of twelve or fourteen years ago, who have given up their interest in the game, would scarcely recognise it now. Combination was then a thing unknown.The side consisted, it is true, of the same number of players, viz.,eleven, but of these eight were forwards, two so-called half-backs, and a goalkeeper. The disproportion between attack and defence seems absurd, but the game then consisted almost entirely of scrimmages between the two sets of forwards varied by ocasional individual dribbling which the half-backs generally proved equal to checking. As the idea of combination developed, the number of backs was increased, making the proportions more equal.First a third half-back was introduced.After that one of these three was placed behind the other two as a back.Next the forwards were reduced to six, the half-backs again numbering three, and finally a second back was added,making the number of attack and defence pratically equal,for forwards numbering five, with three half-backs two backs and a goalkeeper.This arrangement of the side did not become general until the season of 1889-90, so it will be seen that the changes mentioned were only gradually introduced, but they have undoubtedly conduced to the improvement and development of the game.

The Hockey Association was formed in 1886 and from that date has been the recognised authority for the control of the game. In the north of England the game was not taken up until the year 1887, and for some years it was confined to Manchester and Liverpool and the neighbourhood.

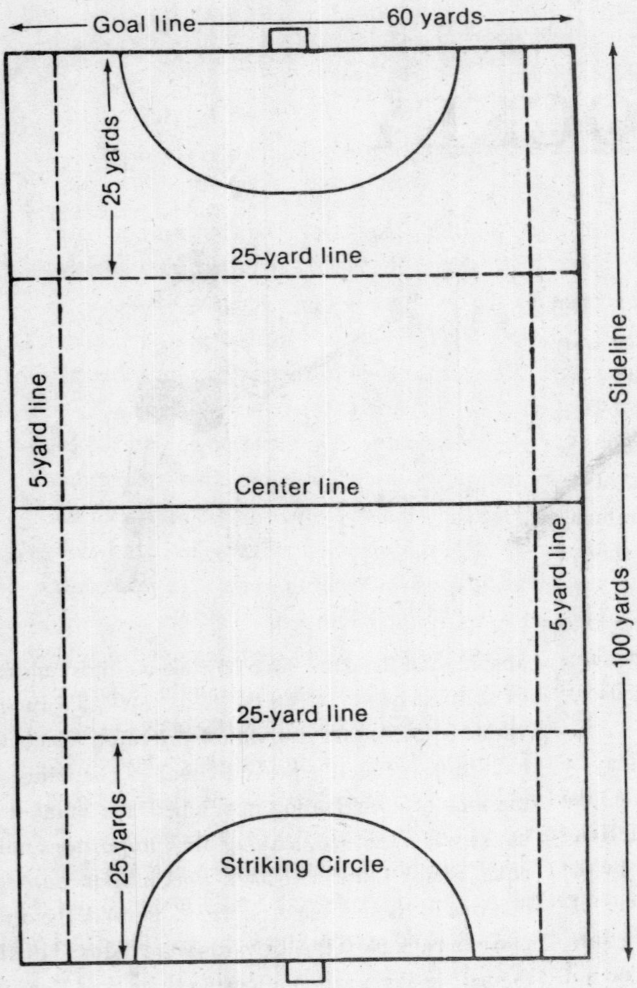

The playing field

At the present time, however,it is spreading fast in Yorkshire and the other Northern counties. The Northern Counties Hockey Association was formed in the winter of 1889-90,but has always been under the control of Hockey Association. Most of the countries in which the game is played have their own associations,which are affiliated to the Hockey Association,but they exist for little more than the arrangement and control of inter-county matches. and the details connected with them. Ireland has taken up the game in the last few years,as well as Wales and international matches first took place in the season 1894-95,Ireland playing England and Wales.These matches have now become regular fixtures. Wales has not yet encountered England as the game has not yet made enough progress in the principality. The oldest clubs in the South of England are Wimbledon, Molesey, Surbiton, Teddington and Ealing, and in the North and Western(Eccles),Didsbury, Bowdon, and Kersal.

Early in the nineteenth century the regulation concerning the playing of the game of hockey began to appear in standardized form.To quote from the Rev. A.E.Bevan,an English writer of that period,"Hockey was played twenty a side, with an Indian rubber ball,about the size of cricket ball, but cut in angles allaround, so that it should not bounce equally.Our weapons were light oak sticks, often Weighed with lead to give greater driving power as a goal might be scored from anywhere in the field,the half circle not being in existence. There was no limit, to the best of my recollection, to the field of play,except as far as the goal line was concerened.Should a player come in on the wrong side (i.e.,the left side)as you were dribbling down, you were at liberty to hit him across the shins,and if one of your own players was following up closely, instead of shouldering the ball he could apply kindly but hurtful attentions in the same way."

Over five thousand years ago, the Persians are known to have played from horsebacks, a game like Polo.Whether this was the forerunner of Hockey or in itself a development from a game like Hockey, we are only left to conjecture. The popular belief, however, is that when the elders on horsebacks ran about enjoying themselves, the little ones imitated . But as they could neither get one nor climb a horse, nor could negotiate the long sticks in play over the earth, the use of short sticks suited them.

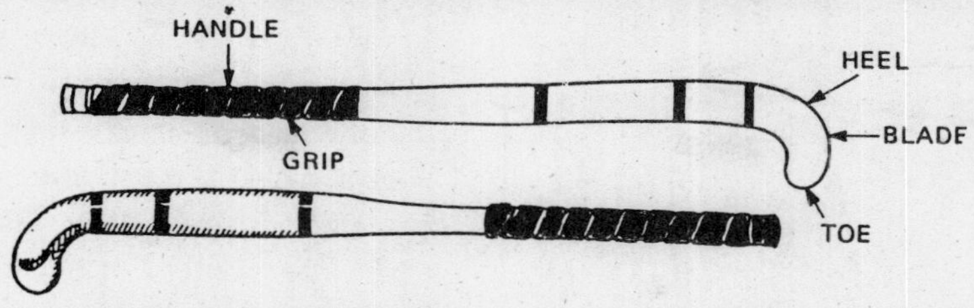

Perhaps they hit at pebbles when they could not get balls made of wood used by the elders.The next stage was the manufacture of a Hockey stick with it head sawn from ash wood.It was momentarily popular and returned the advantage to the dribbler. The next step-that of splitting the wood straight along the grain and bending it to shape by heat and moisture followed swiftly as did the introduction of the sprung cane handle.

The Manufacture of a Stick : Probably very few players are acquainted with the manufacture of hockey sticks and to those who can spare the time and visit one of the big makers, it is an education to see the various processes necessary before a stick is completed.It will be of interest to many to know about this, and the following is a brief description.

Raw Material : The blade is made of prime quality English ash, and the handle of the best Sarawak or Rattan cane, with finest strip Para rubber.

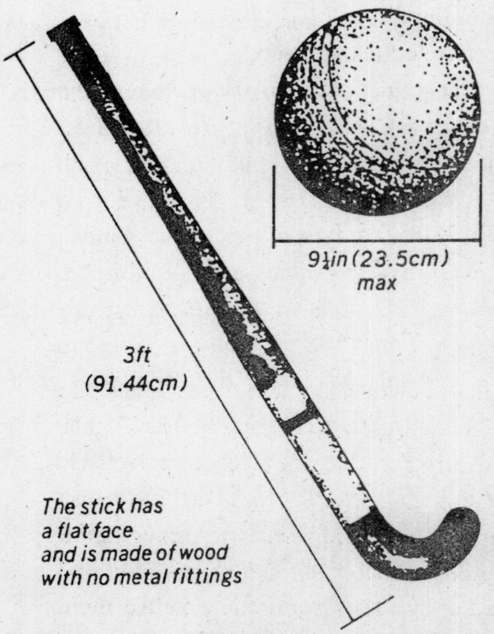

Bending the Ash : The first process is to bend the ash to the shape required, and for this purpose the ash is cut into lengths 4ft.6in.by 3 (½)in.by 2(¼) in. These are placed in a tube under steam pressure for a short time, after which they are bent on a block made to the required shape.

A considerable amount of power is used for this operation, cross chains being attached to either end of the ash length, which is drawn round the block by a double-handled winch.The bend now resembles a horseshoe,and to keep it in position a strut of wood is fixed across it.

After a few days the block is removed and the bend is stored away for nine or ten months to season off and is then ready to be used for hockey sticks.

During the bending process the compression is so great that there is a shortening of six inches on the inside of the bend.It is therefore, quite easy to understand why hockey sticks should not be allowed to get too wet, as the tendency is very great for the ash to get back to its normal straight condition. Heat will also have the same effect. Most manufacturers are not in favour of oiling sticks like cricket bats, as they say it opens up the grain, thereby causing them to split and break.

Selecting the Head : Each bend, when fully sasoned, should, under ordinary circumstances, make four heads. First of all it is divided in two by saw across the top, then through the centre of the remaining portions lengthwise, thus producing the four heads.

Special experts mark up the numerous shapes and grades, as the grain must not be allowed to run off near the striking portion of the stick. The width of the grain, whether wide or narrow, does not always denote the quality.The most important point to consider is the density of the fibre, and it requires years of experience before one is able to select a

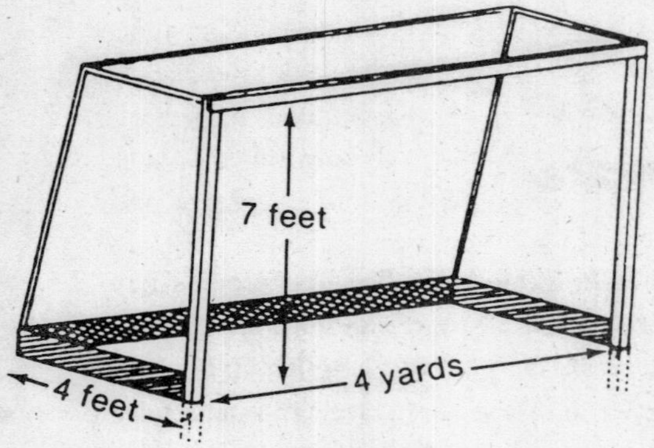

The goal

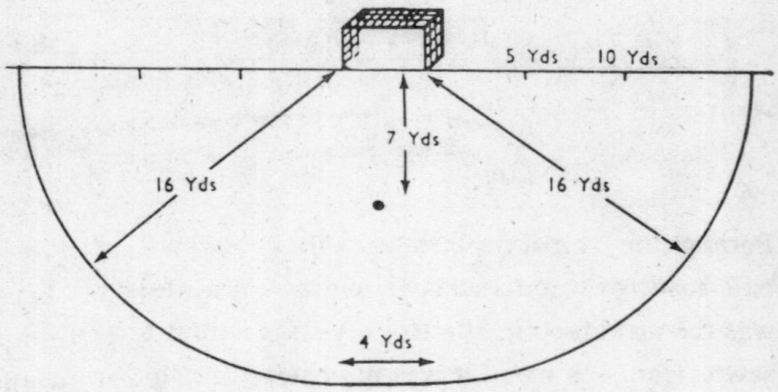

The striking circle

really good piece of ash that can be relied upon to stand the strain of present-day hockey-especially as the modern stick is much thinner and lighter than was used some years ago.

The Handle : The construction of the handle is also extremely interesting. The cane arrives in England in bundles 16ft.18ft. long, each bundle weighing about 3/4cwt.

It is selected and cut into various lengths; each piece is planed on two sides, three pieces then being glued together under pressure for about twelve hours, when they are again plainedon two sides,forming a flat jointed combination of cane 2(¼)in. by 1/2 in.Again three of these are glued together after inserting two strips of rubber,and this forms a solid block of nine square pieces of varying lengths,one end being turned to make the knob of the handle and the other cut to a wedge shape to fit the splice of hockey head.

Assembling and Finishing : The selected head, having been marked to the required pattern,is roughly sawn into shape, and the splice cut out by band saw, ready for the cane handle to be inserted.It is most essential that the splicing together of the head and handle be absolutely perfect,and the joining must be practically air-tight before glueing, as all the playing strain is taken at this point.

Once this is done, machine work on the stick is completed and the stick is finished off by hand by skilled workmen.

It is really amazing to see the way they take the rough-cut hockey stick, and with various tools, such as the draw-knife,rasp,stock-scraper, hand-scraper,special planes, etc.,turn out the finished article. The last worker is the handle binder, who must find it very tiring for the eyes, with binding and finishing about 25 or more sticks an hour.

Footgear, Pads,etc : In hockey, where one has to turn and stop exceptionally quickly, the question of being correctly shod is of the utmost importance. Players of all grades, from the novice to the International,do not pay half enough attention to this very important point.At all the well known sports dealers, special hockey boots of a very light weight with proper protection for the ankles can be obtained, and it is always advisable to have these, as the ordinary boot, converted, does not give adequate protection to the toe or ankle.

The chief point for players to remember is to see each week before playing that the studs or bars on the boots are in good condition and of sufficient length. Whilst on this point, the question arises as to what is the best type of bar or stud.Some players prefer bars in place of studs, and one of the best ideas in that respect is to have the bars on the sole in the shape of a Z and two parallel bars across the heel. A pair of light pads inside the stockings is always advisable, not for stopping the ball intentionally with the legs, but to save the shins from getting badly bruised or cut by the ball or stick.

The general principles of Association Football and Hockey as regards positions,marking, etc.,are the same, except that in place of the foot a stick is used in hockey,and for this reason anyone who has played in a certain position in Association Football, is quite likely to do well in the same position on the Hockey field.

Otherwise,in deciding upon a position one is desirous of taking up,there are one or two rather important points to consider.In Hockey forwards and half-backs require to be very speedy, but at back great speed is not quite so essential, and so, in commencing the game, it is advisable to bear this in mind.

CONDITIONS OF PLAY

The game is played on a ground 100 yards long and 60 yards wide.

The width may vary from 50 to 60 yards, but it has been found that the full width allowed conduces to the best game. The goals are 12ft. wide and 7ft.high and should always be fitted with goal nets, which prevent any disputes as to whether a shot has gone between or outside the posts. Fifteen yards in front of the goal, a line parallel to the goal-line is marked,also 12ft. long, and from each extremity of this line, taking each goal post as a centre,is described a segment of a circle terminating at the goal-line.This constitutes what is, roughly speaking, semicircle in front of the goal,and the attacking side cannot score a goal unless the ball was last hit by one of them inside this line. The object of this is to prevent a goal being scored by indiscriminate hitting from any part of the field. The game is started by what is called a bully in the centrre of the ground.The centre forward on each side strikes with his stick, first the ground, then his opponent's stick thrice, after which proceeding the ball is in play.When the ball is driven over the goal-line by one of the attacking side, a bully takes place 25 yards from the goal-line in a direct line from where the ball passed over it. When a defending player hits the ball over his own goalline,or the ball glances off him or his stick and goes behind the line, the penalty is a corner hit. This is a free hit

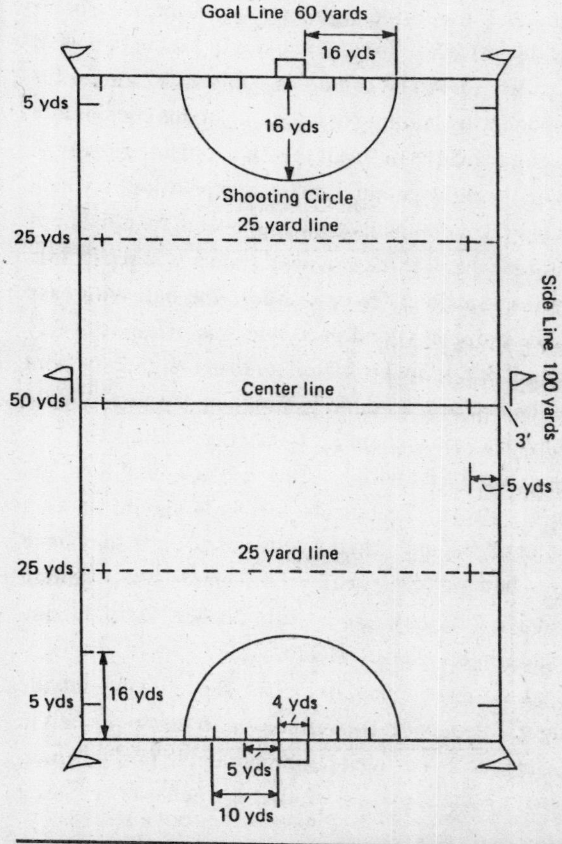

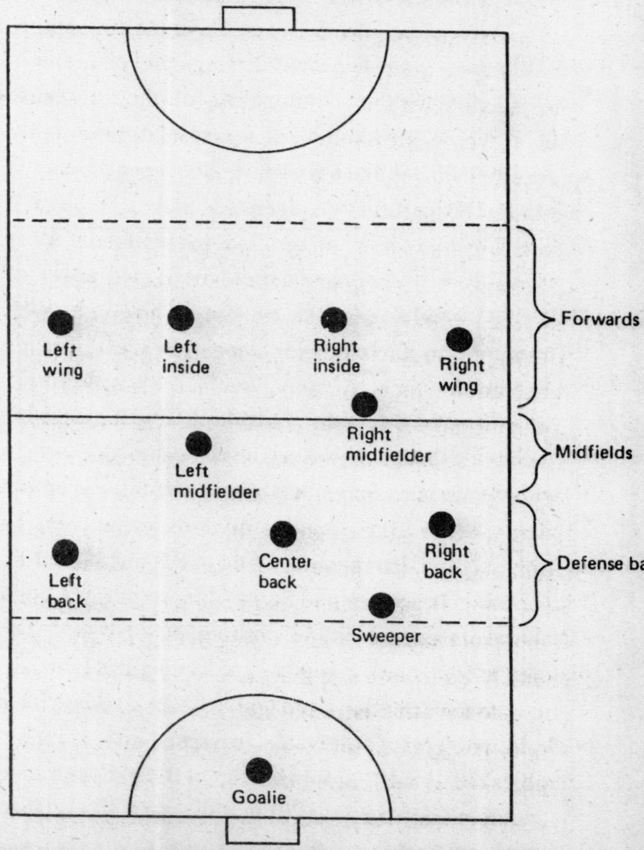

by the attacking side from the corner flag,usually hit by the outside forward or a half-back, whilst the other forwards range round the circle line. The defending side must stand with feet and sticks behind the goal-line until the ball is hit, when they may run out. The attacking side cannot score a goal from a corner hit, unless the ball has been first stopped dead on the ground, or been touched by one of the defending side. A penalty bully is given for deliberately unfair play by the defending side in their own circle. It consists of a bully between the offender and any one player of the attacking side. The rest of the defending side must stand behind their goal-line, and the rest of the attacking side may range round the circle, but neither side may enter the circle or play the ball until it has been hit outside the circle again by one of the players taking part in the bully.

THE PLAYERS

Of the five forwards the most important is of course, the centre forward. He is the connecting link between the two sets of wing players, and is responsible for the combination of the front rank as a whole. He should be a fast and thoroughly unselfish player and a first-rate shot at goal. He must always be careful to keep his place, or he will interfere with his wings. His passes to the other forwards in two kinds, the short pass to either of the inside wing players, or the long pass well forward to the outside men. He must use his discretion which to imply, but he is always safer in passing out hard to the outside man when near his own goal. On the other hand he should not do so when approaching his opponents' circle, the only exception being when the inside forwards cannot get an opening and the outside men are left unguarded. In shooting at goal he should be able to put in a good shot from a pass, without waiting to stop it first. The shot will go harder, and the goalkeeper has less time to note the direction from which the ball comes. This rule will apply to all the forwards, and countless goals are lost by stopping the ball first, and then trying to shoot. By that time it is more likely than not,the backs will have deprived the forward of the ball.These flying shots may not always be accurate, but more opportunities are gained for scoring and some of the shots are sure to be successful.The inside wing players should be considered as partners of the outside men, and are responsible for their getting proper opportunities. Nothing is prettier than a combined run of two wing players passing and re-passing to each other. The inside men should always try to pass well forward to the outsides so as to allow the latter, who should always be fast men, to get well into their stride before taking the ball. They should try and draw the opposing half-back away from the outside men before passing, and if they are successful in this, the way is cleared for a good run down the ground. Inside forwards should not pass out too much near their opponents' circle,unless both, they and the centre are unable to get an opening for a shot. When a ball is thrown in from touch they have to try to get possession of it, and should generally pass it back to the outside man. This is a comparatively easy task for inside right,but by no means so for inside left,who cannot reach out to hit the ball as it is rolled in. All he can do as a rule is to hamper his opponent by hooking or knocking up his stick before he can reach the ball. Of the two outside forwards, he on the right has much the easier position in which to play. Unless the half-back opposed to him keeps out near the line, he can nearly always slip past him on the outside. He can middle the ball with ease while going at a good pace, which is an impossibility for outside left,who has either to get slightly in front of the ball as it is running, and then try and middle it, with a good chance of missing it altogether, or else stop it first with his foot or stick, and then get in his stroke.The outside forwards should make a point of passing into the centre as soon as they have got beyond the twenty-five yard line, though outside left may go a little further than outside right,for his passes always come more at right angles to the side line than those from outside right.The outside forwards have to throw the ball in from touch, and must remember not to throw in hard nearer their own goal, but when near their

Flick Push Scoop (reversed stick) Drive

opponents' to get the ball into the centre if possible. All the forwards should make a point of taking passes with their sticks, and not waste time by stopping the ball with their hands or feet before hitting it.Individual play is quite useless,and no team with selfish forwards can expect to meet with much success.

Half-backs are perhaps the most important element in the team.Three good halves certainly go further towards making a good team than any other three players. Both backs and forwards are dependent on them. A good set of forward will lose half their opportunities with weak half-backs behind them. Half-back is without doubt the position in the field that entails the hardest work, and, of the three, centre half has the most to do. Their duty is to support their forwards when they have the ball, and to break up the passing of the opposing forwards, and when they have done this, to feed their own forwards. They must assist the backs by falling back at once directly they have themselves failed to stop a run, taking care not to get in their way. They must never deprive a back of the ball when he is in a position to get in a good hit, as he is much better able to clear his lines than a half-back rushing towards his own goal. Centre half is perhaps the most difficult position of the three. He has practically to look after all the three inside forwards,whilst the wing half at the most two forwards to mark and should devote his chief attention to the outside forward. In feeding the forwards, the centre half has much more scope, as he is in a position to pass to any of the five, and must be able to see at a glance which of them is in the most favourable position to start an effective run.

GOALKEEPER

The goalkeeper should stand about 2 feet in front of the cage, slightly to the left of the center.The stick should be carried in any position below the shoulder.Many goalkeeper prefer to carry

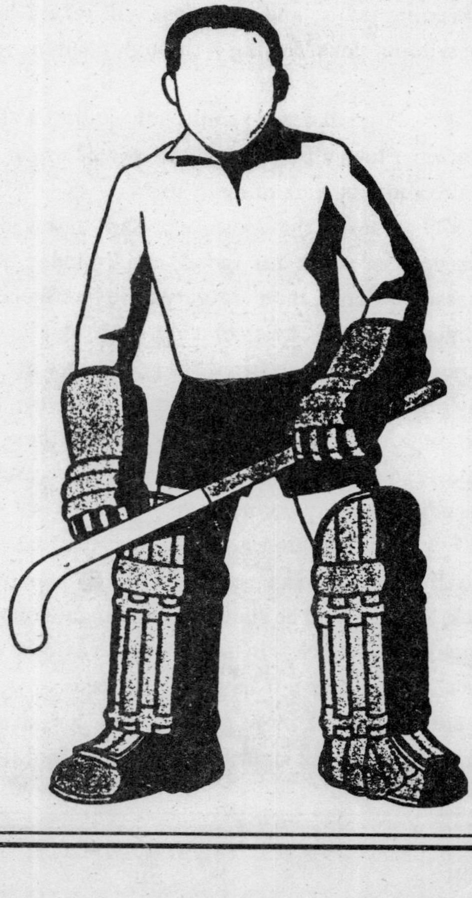

the stick in the right hand,holding it about halfway down the handle.

The knees should be in a short side stride position.The trunk should be inclined slightly forward. *Application of force* - The ball should be stopped full on the pads with the knees together and slightly bent. The goalkeeper should meet the ball in that position.

Goalkeeping is neither such a bad job nor such a dangerous one as the average person is inclined to think.When you take up the position, you are fully aware before hand of the responsibilities and of the knocks which may come your way, and accordingly are prepared for them by well padding yourself and having the proper equipment in the way of boots,gloves,etc.

Your opponents object is to get the ball past you,and you,in turn,are there to stop it by any means as possible in accordance with the Rules- *i.e.*,by hand, stick, body,or foot.Naturally,the feet play the most important part, for a goalkeeper is allowed to kick the ball anywhere in the circle, and so the first point is to see that you have proper goalkeeping boots, and pads that will take a hard drive without your feeling it through them on your shins.

A goalkeeper should not require a stick any heavier than a forward or half-say 22 ozs.at the outside, and less, according to size.

One of the most important assets of a goalkeeper is pluck and good eye.Provided he is possessed of these, there is very little likelihood of his getting badly hurt, or even hurt at all, and although cases have occurred of a goalkeeper getting badly injured, they are very few and far between.It is very important that a goalkeeper should have an uninterrupted view of the ball. especially in cases of corners and penalty corners.

The position a goalkeeper must take up naturally depends to a large extent, upon the point of attack, and as a rule he should be about foot outside the goal. If the attack is in the centre it is safe for him to be slightly on the left-hand side of the goal, as he can not only cover more ground, but his natural defence is with the right hand and right foot.If the attack is coming from the wing and the shot is likely to come from one of the outside players, cut off the angle so that it is impossible for the forward to shot into the net between you and the nearer goal-post.Learn to rely on your feet as far as possible for stopping a shot, and if you have time to hit the ball clear with the stick, do so in preference to kicking.

It is here that the goalkeeper has to use great judgment in deciding whether by running out he can get to the ball first,and having once decided, he must not hesitate under any circumstances.Very often he calls to his backs to advice them,so that he and they shall not hamper one another, and in such case the back will probably fall back to protect the goal in case of accident.

A slow dribbling shot is one that is very often missed, as goalkeepers are tempted to take a hit at it without stopping the ball first and unless the ground is perfectly true it is liable to bounce at the critical moment.

Follow Through - The goalkeeper should lean forward into the clearing kick or drive which follows the stop.There should be a follow through of the kicking leg in the direction of the kick.The foot should be kept close to the ground to prevent a lofted ball.The ball should be met with the side of the big toe in a clearing kick.

Goalkeeper often cary the stick in the right hand in order to be able to reach out farther to deflect a shot.

Coaching Suggestions:

Adjust the position in the cage depending upon the angle of approach of the ball.

Clear to the side with a kick or a drive after stopping the ball.

Use the stick to clear only if the ball has first been stopped. The safest clear is parallel to and close to the goal line. Practice with a stick.

If necessary to kick on the fly the inside of the instep or the top of the instep should be used.

Use the stick for deflecting balls which cannot be stopped with the feet.

Use the hand for stopping high balls.When

clearing a ball on the fly push the foot into it rather than kicking at it.

When hard pressed use any legal means of stopping the ball. Clear the ball quickly.

RULES OF THE GAME

Captain

(a) In the beginning captains of both the teams toss for the choice of ends or doing pass. The winner of the toss can select one of the two-pass or end.

(b) He will work as umpire in his absence.

(c) If necessary, the captains shall change their respective goal keepers and will inform the umpire about this change.

Field of Play

The Hockey playground is rectangular. It is 100 yards long and 60 yards wide. The longer lines are called the side lines and the shorter ones goal lines. The goal lines shall be 3" wide throughout.

The Centre line shall be marked in its length and 25 yards lines shall be marked as a broken line. To assist in the control of push-in, across the centre line respectively 25 yards line, parallel to and five yards from a side line a mark two yards in length will be provided. Inside playfield, on each side line and parallel to the goal line 16 yards from its inner edge shall be indicated. This mark will not exceed 12" in length. For hits of penalty corner, the field shall be marked by the goal lines on both sides of the goal at 5 yards and 10 yards from the nearer goal post. The field of play shall be marked by the goal lines and the side lines, 5 yards on either side of the corner flags. This is for corner hits. At a distance of 7 yards in front of the centre of each goal a spot shall be marked, which will not be more than 6" in diameter.

Flag posts shall be placed on each corner of the field at a distance of one yard at least from the centre line.

Goal Post

(a) At the center of each goal line, there shall be a goal,consisting of two perpendicular posts 4 yards apart.These are joined together by a horizontal crow bar, seven feet from the ground (from inside).The front part of the goal post shall touch the outer edge of the goal line. Goal post shall not extend the cross bars and cross bars shall also not extend goal posts.The goal posts and cross bars will be 2" wide and 3" deep nets will be firmly attached behind the goal posts.

(b) Inside the goal posts, a black board of 4 yards in length and not more than 8" in height shall be placed.These boards on each side shall make an angle of 90 degree at the goal line. These boards should be made of wood.

(c) In order to support the boards, no wooden flats shall be placed inside them.

***Shooting Circle*:** A 4 yards long and 3 inches wide line shall be drawn in front of each goal, which is parallel to and 16 yards from the goal line. This line having the inner front corner of the goal posts as centre,will reach each way to meet the goal lines by quarter circles. The space enclosed by these lines shall be called the shooting circle.

***The Ball*:** The ball shall be made of white leather or of any other leather painted with white material. Its size is similar to that of cricket ball.Its circumference shall be between 131/16" and 37/4".The weight of hockey ball shall not exceed 23/4 ounces to 1½ ounces.

***Hockey (Stick)*:** A stick shall have a flat face on the left side alone. Its end should not be made of metal or attached with any metal.Its weight should not exceed 28 ounces. Its size is such as may pass through a ring having a diameter of 2 inches. Each player of the team shall wear the dress approved by its Association or club.Every player shall wear foot-wear which are not dangerous to any

Back Pass **:** It is given at the start of the play, from the centre of field. This is also given at the re-start of the game after a goal is scored.

The winner of the toss if there is a goal, that player and after half time the player of the opponent team will do back pass. The player doing the back pass may place his foot on the centre line or on the other side.

Conduct of the Game :

1. A player shall not play the ball with the opposite side of his stick;only flat side should be used. No player can interfere with the game without having his own stick.
2. Either at the beginning or at the end of a stroke, a stick may go over the shoulder but neither the ball be dangerous nor any other danger may arise.
3. Hitting wildly to an opponent which may prove dangerous, is forbidden.
4. A player shall not stop or deflect the ball on the ground or in the air with any part of his body even hand, to his or his team's advantage.
5. A player shall not use the foot or leg to support the stick in order to check the rival player.
6. Except with the stick, the ball cannot be picked up, kicked, thrown, carried or propelled in any manner or direction.
7. Hitting, hooking, holding, striking at or intervening with a rival's stick is not favoured.
8. A player shall not obstruct the game by running between an opponent and the ball or intercept himself or with his stick as an obstacle.
9. A player may kick or stop the ball with any part of his body if the ball is in the circle of goal keeper. If the ball is lodged in the pads of a goal-keeper or in the clothing of any player the game will be stopped. The umpire shall re-start it by a bully on the spot where this accident occurs. This bully cannot be done within five yards of the goal line. If the ball strikes an umpire the game shall continue.
10. Rough or dangerous play, any type of misconduct or time wasting shall not be allowed.

Penalty :

1. A free hit shall be awarded to the opposing team if infringement has taken place outside the shooting circle. But if in the opinion of the umpire the player of any defending team has committed this offence within 25 yards, he shall be awarded a penalty corner.
2. If the offence is done inside the circle by an attacker, a free hit shall be awarded to the defending team. A penalty corner or a penalty stroke shall be given.
3. If two opponents commit an offence at the same time,inside and outside the circle, the umpire shall order for a bully to be played at the breach spot.
4. For rough play or misconduct, the umpire can:

   (a) Warn the offending player.

   (b) Suspend him temporarily.

   (c) Suspend him from playing the game further.

   It is done with the help of coloured cards.

Note :-- A player temporarily suspended shall remain standing behind the net of his goal,until the umpire calls him back.

Goal -When a ball has passed completely and according to the rules over the goal lines, between the goal posts and under the cross bars, a goal is scored. At that time the ball should be within the circle, having been hit by the stick of an attacker. The team that scores greater number of goals shall be the winner.

If the goal keeper plays foul at the time of penalty stroke,it is not necessary for the ball to cross the goal line.

Off-side

(a) A player of the same team as the striker, or pusher-in, is in an off-side position if, at any moment when the ball is hit or pushed-in, he be nearer to this opponnts' goal-line than the ball is, unless he is in his own half of the field or there are at least two opponents nearer to their own goal-line than he is.

For the purpose of this Rule, a player of either team shall be deemed to be on the field of play even though he be outside the side-line or behind the goal-line.

(b) A player who is in an off-side position shall not play or attempt to play the ball or gain any advantage for his team or influence the play of an oponent.

Free Hits

1. Free hit is normally taken from the place of offence. If an offence is committed by an attacker within the circle, a free hit shall be taken from any side within the circle.
2. While taking free hit, the ball shall remain stationary. Any type of hit can be used for it but the ball must not rise above knee height. Scoop-stroke will not be allowed.
3. A free hit shall be taken from the breach place, provided that a free hit is given to the defending team within 16 yards of the inner edge of their goal-line.
4. When a free hit is taken, no player other than the striker shall be within five yards of the circle.

   It is not essential for the player of the host team to be at a distance of five yards.
5. If the striker misses to hit the ball, he can re-take the hit.
6. The striker after taking free hit, shall not play ball, until it has been touched or played by another player of either team.

Penalty

(a) Opposing team shall be awarded one free hit.

(b) Inside the shooting circle-The opposing team shall be awarded a free-hit from a distance of 16 yards.

The attacking team shall be awarded a penalty corner or penalty stroke against the defending team.

Push-in :

(i) When a ball passes completely across the side-line it is given a push-in or hit from the same spot. The ball shall be pushed in or hit by a player of the opposing team to the player who last touched it.

(ii) When push-in is being taken, no player of either team shall stand within 5 yards. If this rule is not observed the umpire can ask for the second push-in.

(iii) After a push-in, a player shall not play or touch that ball until it has been touched or played by another player of either team.

Penalty :

(i) If a player while taking a push-in commits any offence, the opposing team shall be given a push-in.

(ii) Push-in shall be taken, in case of breach by some other player. But for constant breach a free hit may be awarded to the attacking team.

Ball Outside the Playfield :

(i) When the ball is sent by one of the teams over the goal-line and the goal is not scored or it is sent indeliberately over the goal line by one of the defending teams, from more than a distance of 25 yards from the goal line, the same shall be re-started by a hit by the defending team. A free hit shall be awarded from a distance of 16 yards.

(ii) The opponent team shall be awarded a penalty corner, if the ball unintentionally, has gone out of the goal-line by 25 yards, and the goal is not scored.

(iii) A penalty corner shall be awarded to the attacking team provided the ball is unintentionally hit over the goal-line.

With effect from Sept.1982, during Penalty corner, the ball is not allowed to be checked by hand, after push. This rule has been approved by International Hockey Federation (I.H.F.). According to Olympian Gurbaksh Singh it is more suitable for traditional style hockey than International style hockey.

(iv) The opposing team shall be awarded a penalty corner, if in the opinion of umpire, a player of a defending team has sent the ball intentionally within 25 yards of the line.

Corner :

The attacking team will be given free hit in a circle of 5 yards from the flag post at the corner of goal line or side line.

While taking Penalty Corner if before doing pushing the ball the players of the defending team begin running, the referee will ask to push the ball again.

While taking Penalty Corner, a player will pushing the ball from a point inside the circle on the

Penalty stroke

goal line, then the player standing on the edge of D will play with hockey and the third will hit the ball. The penalty corner will be regarded as goal but the goal should not be higher than the plank of the goal or there should not be under cut. The goal should cross the line.

Penalty Stroke :

(i) The penalty stroke is given to the attacking team when foul is intentionally committed by the defending team in the circle. At the time of corner hit, the players of both the teams may stand where they like. According to new rules if the team checking the attack commits any foul-whether intentionally or unintentionally, a penalty stroke is given against it.

Penalty stroke is a hit to a player of offending team in front of goal-line from 7 yards. It is faced by the goal keeper of the defending team. But the rules related to goal keeper shall be completely applied on him.

(ii) At the time of penalty stroke, all the players of both the teams shall stand outside the rear line of 25 yards.

(iii) The offending player first of all stands near the ball at the whistling of umpire and puts one step forward at the time of the stroke after the blowing of the whistle.

(iv) He touches the ball only once. After this he will go neither to the ball nor to the goal-keeper.He will hit penalty stroke at the whistle of the umpire.

(v) The goal-keeper will stand on goal-line.He shall not change his place until the ball is hit.

(vi) The goal-keeper shall not touch a ball above shoulders with any part of his stick.Facilities given to the goal-keeper shall be given to his substitute, but he shall not be awarded dress and other equipment during penalty stroke. He or she can wear pads, gloves and other material which the goal-keeper can

use.

(vii) A ball can rise to any height by penalty stroke.

(viii) If the goal-keeper is compelled to move a little by the striker or the striker faints the stroke shall be re-taken.

(ix) As a result of the penalty stroke:

(a) If the ball completely crosses the goal post, under the crosss bars and goal lines, a goal is scored.

(b) If goal keeper commits any breach and hinders the score. It is also considered a scored goal.

(c) If the goal keeper catches the ball or it lodges in his pad it is called'stopped'.

(d) A penalty stroke ends if the game becomes stationary in the circle or passes over it.

(e) The play is re-started with a free hit even if the goal is scored or not.The defending team shall be given a free hit from 16 yards of goal line.

(f) Duration between the penalty stroke and the re-start of the play will be added in the same half.

Penalty:

1. In case of breach of rule by the attacking player, the game shall be re-started by the

defending team with a free hit from 16 yards.

2. If the goal keeper breaks this rule the umpire shall ask for second stroke.

Accidents :

(a) If an umpire or a player is incapacitated by some accident the game shall be temporarily stopped by the umpire. The time for stopping the game shall be noted if a goal is scored before the game is stopped. It shall be allowed, if in the referee's opinion it would have been scored before the accident.

(b) The umpire shall re-start the game without any loss of time.The play will re-start by bully from the spot chosen by the umpire.

The taking of position by the players in the ground- There are eleven players in each team of Hockey with 5 extra.Five of them are forward,3 half back,2 full back and one goal-keeper.

CUP & TROPHIES

Gold In Olympics

Winners of the men's hockey title at the Olympic Games-first included in 1908:

Men

1908 England
1920 England
1928 India
1932 India
1936 India
1948 India
1952 India
1956 India
1960 Pakistan
1964 India
1968 Pakistan
1972 FRG
1976 New Zealand
1980 India
1984 Pakistan
1988 UK

Women

1980 Zimbabwe
1984 Netherlands
1988 Australia

World Cup

The first men's World Cup was held in 1971.

Men

1971 Pakistan
1973 Holland
1975 India
1978 Pakistan
1982 Pakistan
1986 Australia

Women

1974 Holland
1976 West Germany
1978 Holland
1981 West Germany
1983 Holland
1986 Holland

PADMA SHRI AWARDS WINNERS

1- Balbir Singh
2- Digvijay Singh Babu,
3- Charanjit Singh,
4- Kishan Lal, 5- Prithipal Singh,
6- Shankar Laxman,
7- Leslie Claudius,
8- V. Hhaskaran, 9- Eliza Nelson,
10- Mohammed Shahid,
11- Jhaman Lal Sharma
12- Selma D'Silva

ARJUNA AWARD WINNERS

1961 Prithipal Singh
Ann Sharma
1963 Charanjit Singh
1964 S. Laxman
1965 Udham Singh
Elvera Britto

1966	V.J. Peter	1975	B.P. Govinda
	Sunita Puri		Rupa Saini
	Gurbaksh Singh	1977-78	Harcharan Singh
1967	Harbinder Singh		Lorraine Luna Fernandes
	Jagit Singh	1979-80	Vasudevan Bhaskaran
	Mohinder Lal		Rekha B. Mundphan
1968	Balbir Singh	1980-81	Mohammed Shahid
1970	Ajit Pal Singh		Eliza Nelson
1971	P. Krishnamurthy	1981	Versha Soni
1972	Michael Kindo	1983	Zafar Iqbal
1973	M. P. Ganesh	1984	Rajbir Kaur
	Otilia Mascarenhas	1985	Somaiya Maney Panda Muthanna
1974	Ashok Kumar		Prem Maya Sonir
	Ajinder Kaur	1986	Joaquim Martin Carvalho
		1988	M.P. Singh

ICE HOCKEY

Around 1740, explorers along the St. Lawrence Valley in Canada discovered Indians playing hockey in the air, or 'lacrosse' as we now know it. The Indians called it 'baggataway', and rumour has it that each time a brave was clobbered, he would yell 'Ho eee' which is equivalent to our present day 'Ouch'. Some say the word hockey came from this exclamation. Baggataway was played on dry dusty plains in summer and on frozen lakes and ponds in winter. The game on ice was later called 'bandy'.

The first professional league was set up in 1909, and the National Hockey League was formed in 1917-18.

In Britain in the late 20s and 30s ice hockey was considered more of a hobby than a sport to be taken seriously. It was not until the Empire Pool was built at Wembley in 1934, with the formation of the National League in the same year, that things began to happen. Drawing players from the Wembley Lions, Wembley Canadians, Earl's Court Rangers, Streatham, Richmond Hawks and the Brighton Tigers, the British Olympic ice hockey team was able to walk away from the 1936 Winter Olympics in Garmisch, Germany, clutching the much-cherished gold medal.

The game consists of twelve skaters using long flat-heeled sticks to hit a draught-like vulcanised rubber puck into opposing goals, and begins with a 'face-off', two players, one from each team, facing one another with the full blades of their sticks on the ice. The referee drops the puck between them and the fun begins.

A goal can be scored directly by the stick of an attacker, or indirectly if an attacker hits the puck with his stick and it flies off another attacker's body into goal. The puck must always be kept in motion; and although players may handle the puck for three seconds they must not pick it from the ice. Kicking the puck is allowed but a goal cannot be scored direct from a kick. Players must not carry their sticks above shoulder level. Body checking (a defender in his own half checking an opponent, from a standstill, with chest, back or hip) is allowed, but charging and cross-checking (swinging your butt-end at an opponent) are forbidden. The six members of a team on the ice may be changed at any time during a game so long as no one other than the twelve stipulated members of that team take part. This means that six reserves are always sitting on the player's bench beside the rink.

The most unusual rule in ice hockey is the one about 'icing the puck'. If any player shoots the

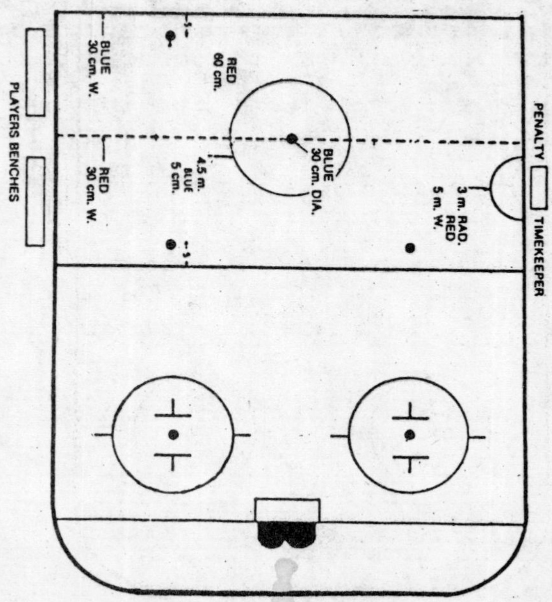

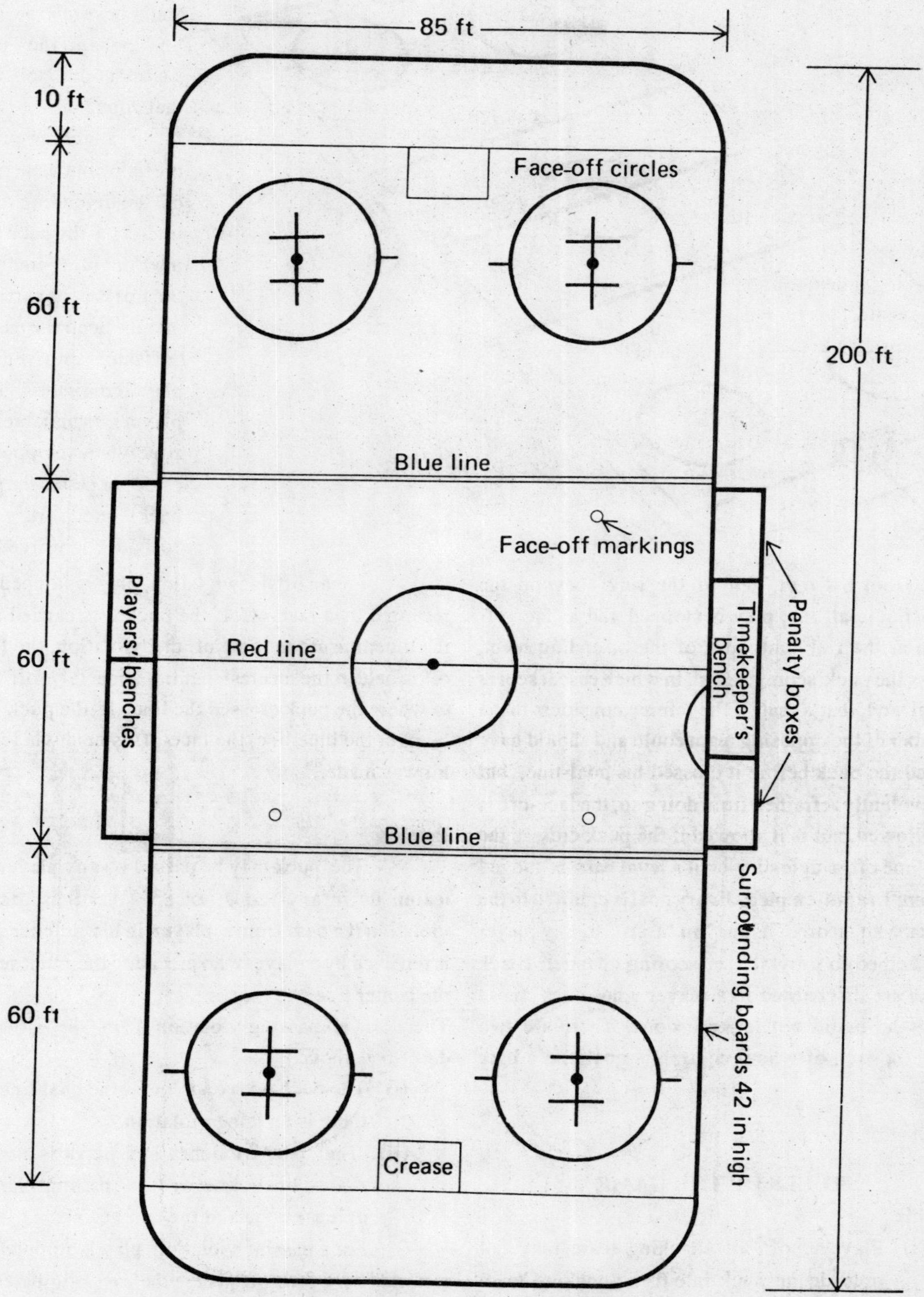
85 ft
10 ft
60 ft
60 ft
60 ft
200 ft
Face-off circles
Blue line
Face-off markings
Players' benches
Red line
Timekeeper's bench
Penalty boxes
Blue line
Surrounding boards 42 in high
Crease

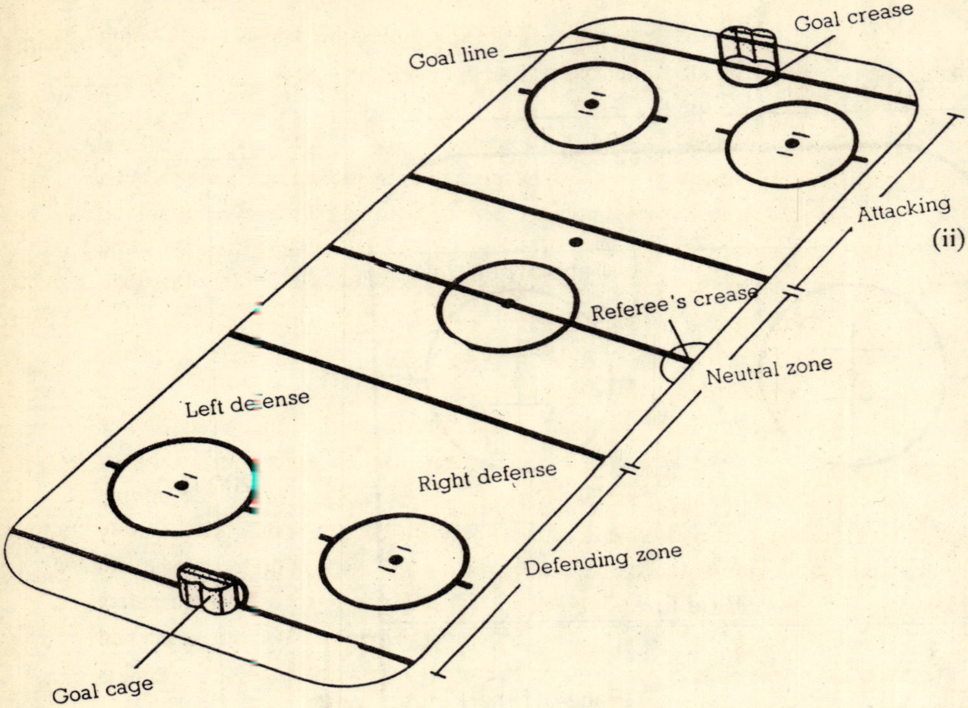

puck from his own half of the rink beyond the opposing goal line, play is stopped and a face-off taken at the rink-end spot of the offending team, unless the puck scores a goal, in which case it scores a goal and that's that. If the referee considers that a member of the opposing team could and should have played the puck before it crossed his goal-line, but malevolently refrained from doing so, the face-off is not allowed, nor is it allowed if the puck crosses the goal-line off a defender or if a legal pass is judged to have been attempted. Every goal is credited to the player who scores it, and an 'assist' to any player who helped to provide the scoring change. Black marks are discredited to a player who does those things he ought not to have done. There are two referees, each of whom controls a goal and a blue line.

RULES OF THE GAME

Offside

(i) Players of an attacking team may not precede the puck into their attacking zone; an attacker is deemed offside only if both his skates are completely within the attacking zone and beyond the blue line when the puck passes completely into that zone.

(ii) If an attacking player is offside but a member of the defending team intercepts the puck at or near the blue line and then passes or carries it into the neutral zone, the "offside" is waived and play continues. If a player is in his attacking zone when an opponent carries or passes the puck back into it, the "offside" is waived.

For an offside violation, play is stopped and restarted by a face-off. If the puck was carried over the blue line at the time of the violation, the face-off is held at the nearest neutral zone face-off spot to where the puck crossed the line. If the puck was hit over the blue line, the face-off is held where the hit was made.

Passing

The puck may be passed by any player to a teammate in any zone, except that it is passing violation if a pass from a player in his defence zone is received by a player who precedes the puck across the center line.

There is no passing violation if, in the situation described above:

(i) The puck goes on to cross the goal line and there is an icing violation.

(ii) The puck touches any player's person, skates, or stick between the passing player's defense zone and the center line.

For a passing violation, play is stopped and restarted by a face-off where the pass originated, or at the nearest face-off spot.

Puck in motion

The puck must be kept in motion at all times.

A team in its own defence area may carry the puck behind its own goal once; otherwise it must advance the puck toward its opponents' goal unless it is prevented from doing so by its opponents' actions. For a first infringement, a warning is given to the team captain, and a face-off is held at either face-off spot adjacent to the goal of the offending team. For a second infringement in the same period by a member of the same team, a minor penalty is imposed on the second offender.

Only if his team has fewer players on the ice than the opposing team, may a player beyond his defence zone pass or carry the puck back into that zone with the purpose of delaying the game. For an infringement, a face-off is held at the nearest end face-off spot in the offending team's defence zone.

Any player who holds, freezes, or plays the puck with his stick, skates, or body along the boards in such a way that a stoppage is caused, is given a minor bench penalty, unless he was actually being checked by an opponent.

Kicking the puck

The puck may be kicked in all zones, but a goal may not be scored from a kick by an attacking player. However, if an attacker kicks the puck and it is deflected into the goal by a defender other than the goalkeeper, the goal is allowed.

Handling the puck

A player may push the puck along the ice with his hand, or may use his open hand to stop or "bat" a puck in the air. However, if the referee considers that a player used such actions deliberately to direct the puck to a teammate, a face-off is held at the appropriate face-off spot. Also, if the puck enters the goal after being batted by an attacking player and deflected off any player or goalkeeper, the goal is disallowed.

A minor penalty is incurred if:

(i) A goalkeeper holds the puck in his hand(s)

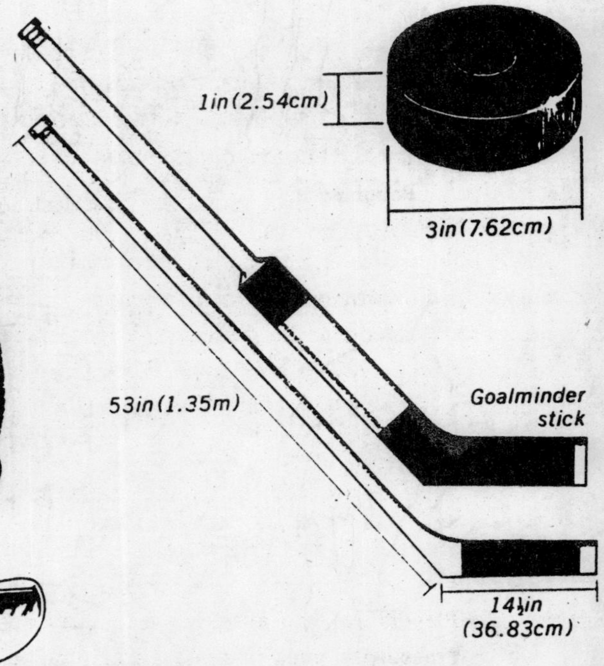

Interference

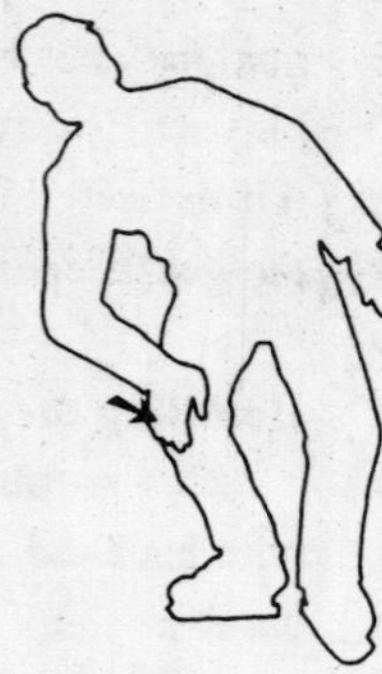

Kneeing

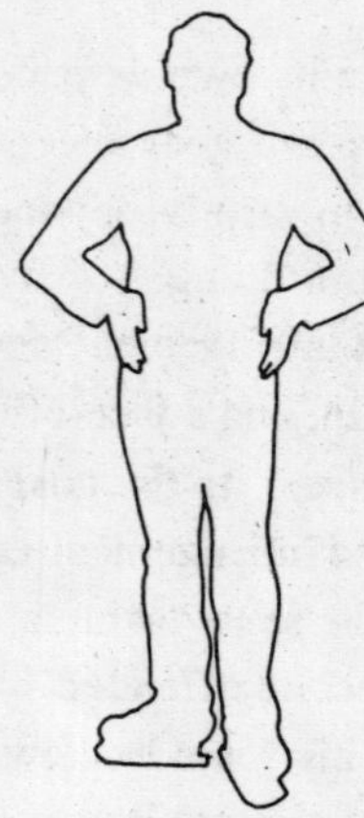

Misconduct

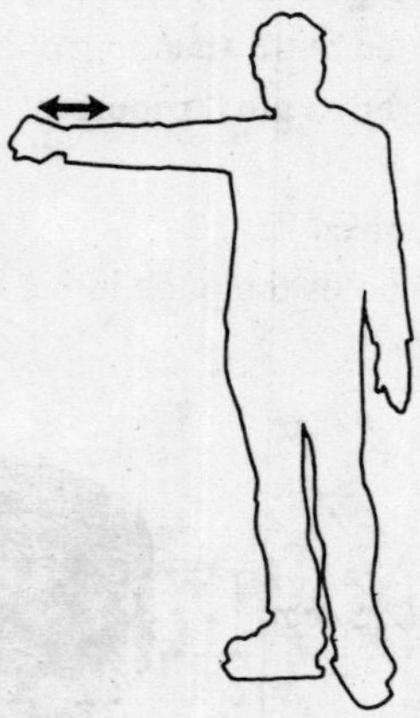

Roughing

Slashing

Spearing

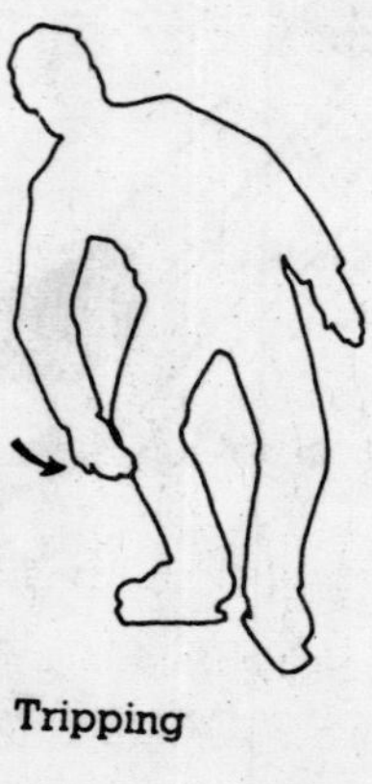

Tripping

Unsportsmanlike Conduct

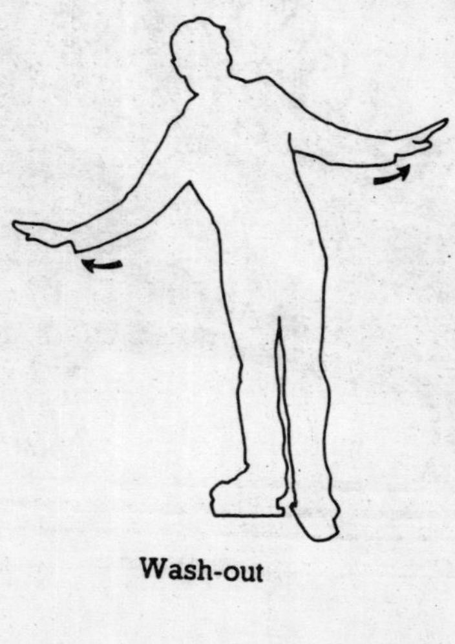

Wash-out

The Referee's Signals

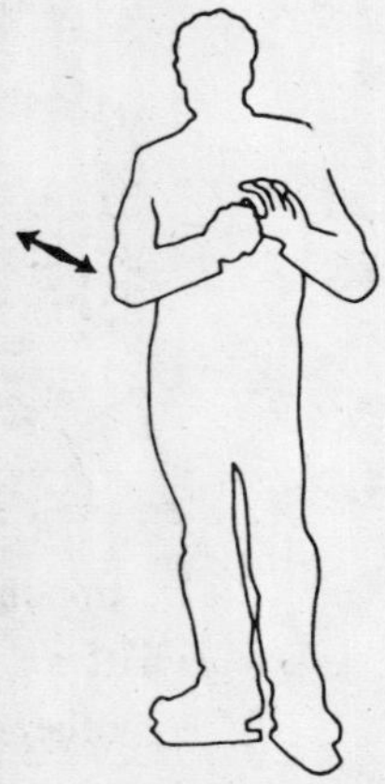

Boarding

Charging

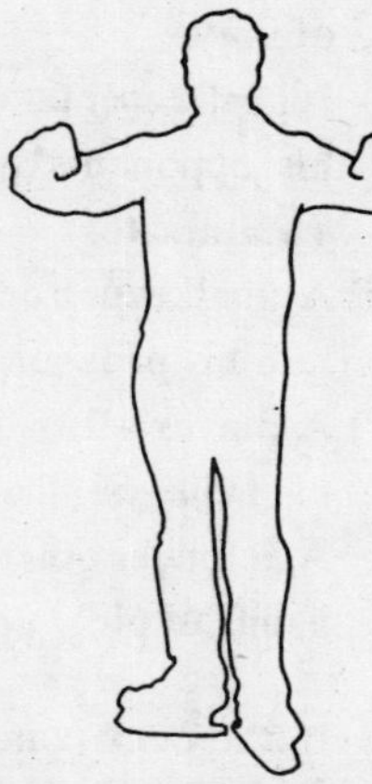

Crosschecking

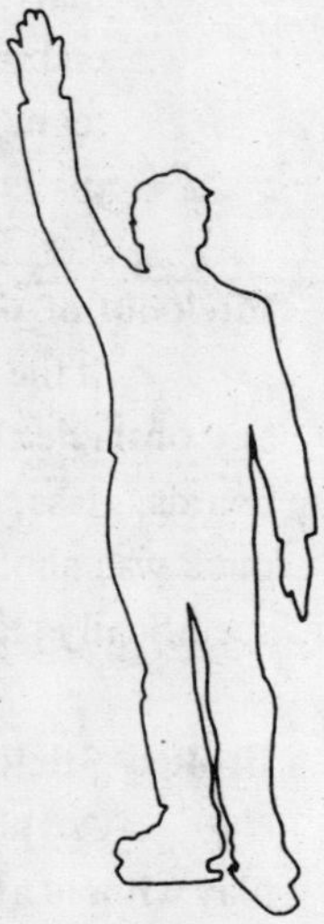

Delayed Penalty
(slow whistle)

Elbowing

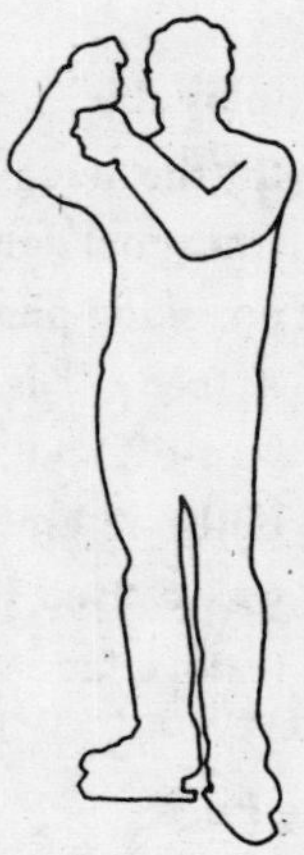

Highsticking

Holding

Hooking

Icing (folded arms)

for more than three seconds, or in any way that the referee considers causes a stoppage of play.

(ii) A goalkeeper throws the puck forward toward his opponents' goal and it is first played by a teammate.

(iii) A goalkeeper deliberagely drops the puck into his pads or onto the goal net.

(iv) A player other than the goalkeeper closes his hand on the puck.

(v) A defender other than a goalkeeper uses his hands to pick up the puck from the ice.

If the puck comes to rest on the top of the boards, it is considered still in play and may be played legally with the hand or stick.

Puck Unplayable

If the puck is unplayable through being lodged in the goal netting or frozen against the goal between opposing players:

(i) A face-off is held at the nearest end zone face-off spot; or

(ii) If the referee considers that the stoppage was caused by a player of the attacking team, a face-off is held in the neutral zone.

Icing the Puck

The puck is "iced" if a player hits or deflects the puck from behind the center line to beyond his opponents' goal line, and the puck is then first touched by a defender other than the goalkeeper. Icing is not called and play continues:

(i) If the attacking team has fewer players on the ice than its opponents;

(ii) If the puck entered the goal (in which case the goal is allowed);

(iii) If an onside player of the team that hit the puck is the first to touch it;

(iv) If the puck goes beyond the goal line directly from a face-off;

(v) If before reaching the goal line, the puck passes through any part of the goal crease;

(vi) If before beaching the goal line, the puck touches the person, skates, or stick of an

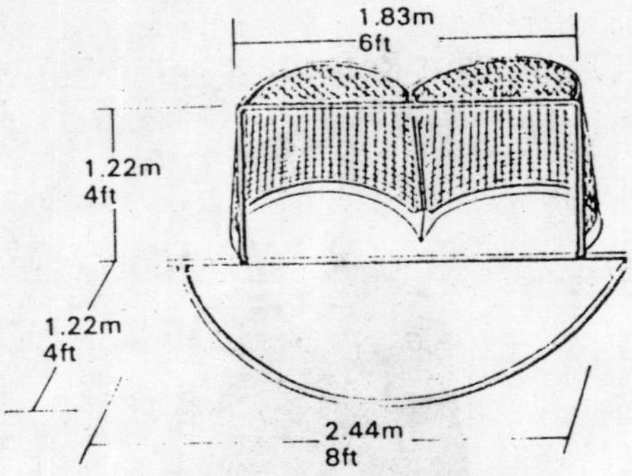

opponent other than the goalkeeper;

(vii) If an official considers that an opponent other than the goalkeeper could have played the puck but did not do so (except that the referee will order a face-off at the end zone face-off spot nearest the offending team's goal if he considers that failure to play the puck was deliberate).

Puck out of Bounds

If the puck leaves the playing area or strikes any obstacle above the playing surface other than the boards, glass, or wire, a face-off is held where the puck was shot or deflected, except when the rules specifically state otherwise.

Broken Stick

A player other than the goalkeeper may play without a stick, or with a broken stick if he drops the broken portion. He must not receive a stick thrown onto the ice for him; he must collect a new stick from his team bench.

A goalkeeper may continue to play with a broken stick until a stoppage of play, or until a teammate legally hands him a replacement. He must not receive a stick thrown onto the ice, nor may he go to his team bench to obtain a new stick during a stoppage of play.

Interference by Spectators

If a player is being interfered by a spectator, play is stopped and restarted by a face-off where the puck was last played at the time of the stoppage; if the team of the player being interfered with is in possession of the puck, the stoppage is delayed until the end of that play.

CUP & TROPHIES

Olympic Games

Winners

1920 Canada
1924 Canada
1928 Canada
1932 Canada
1936 Great Britain
1948 Canada
1952 Canada
1956 USSR
1960 USA
1964 USSR
1968 USSR
1972 USSR
1976 USSR
1980 USA
1984 USSR
1988 USSR

World Championships

First held in conjunction with the Olympics, and amateur only until 1976, but now held annually.

Winners

1920 Canada
1924 Canada
1928 Canada
1930 Canada
1931 Canada
1933 USA
1934 Canada
1935 Canada
1936 UK
1937 Canada
1938 Canada
1939 Canada
1947 Czechoslovakia
1948 Canada
1949 Czechoslovakia
1950 Canada
1951 Canada
1952 Canada
1953 Sweden
1954 USSR
1955 Canada
1956 USSR
1957 Sweden
1958 Canada
1959 Canada
1960 USA
1961 Canada
1962 Sweden
1963 USSR
1964 USSR
1965 USSR
1966 USSR
1967 USSR
1968 USSR
1969 USSR
1970 USSR
1971 USSR
1972 Czechoslovakia
1973 USSR
1974 USSR
1975 USSR
1976 Czechoslovakia
1977 Czechoslovakia
1978 USSR
1979 USSR
1980 USA
1981 USSR
1982 USSR
1983 USSR
1984 USSR
1985 Czechoslovakia
1986 USSR
1987 Sweden

JUDO

Judo is truly a sport of the 1970s. It is exciting to watch, deeply rewarding for the competitor and absorbing for the instructor. Young people all over the world are taking up judo and finding it a sport which fits the modern idiom. Hard work is needed for success in judo- but nothing worth having was ever acquired easily.

Judo is an ideal activity for just about everyone. It is not only a fighting sport which, therefore, instills intiative and self-confidence but is also a really first class exercise. It comes as a surprise to many people to find that there are very few injuries - far fewer than those occur in the average football team.

SKILLS OF THE GAME

The object of a judo competition is to throw one's opponent cleanly, hold him immobile on his back for 30 seconds, forcing him to submit through the pressure of an armlock or stranglehold, or more usual in top-class competitions- to gain a decision given by two judges and a referee. Only one point 'an ippon' is needed to decide a contest, because the theory is that in early times a single clean throw, a strangle hold, or a hold-down could disable a person. The two judges sit at two diagonally opposite corners of the mat, and the referee conducts the contest from the mat itself.

The fighters approach one another, and after a caremonial bow they take hold of each other by the jacket. They are permitted to grab at the legs or hold the belt to assist with throws. Newaza (groundwork) is resorted to when the competitors fight on the ground. Some competitors specialize in this aspect of the sport and lure their opponents onto the ground and use their strength there.

When practising, judo experts attempt to be more free than in contests. Randori forms the basis of training, but techniques are improved with frequent practice of movements or parts of movements. Weight training and running are part of the training of more ambitious competitors.

Because judo throws are violent, a system of breakfalls has been evolved which allows the expert to soften his own fall. He relaxes and hits the mat with an outstretched arm to prevent any serious damage.

RULES OF THE GAME

***Article 1.* Competition Area**

The competition area be of a minimum of 14 m x 14 m and a maximum of 16 m x 16 m and shall be covered by tatami or a similarly acceptable material.

The competition area shall be divided into two zones. The demarcation between these two zones shall be called the danger area and shall be indicated by a coloured area, generally red, approximately 1 metre wide forming part of or attached to the mat, parallel to the four sides of the competition area.

The area within and including the coloured area shall be called the contest area and shall be always of a minimum of 9 m x 9 m or a maximum of 10 m x 10 m. The area metres 50 cm wide.

***Article 2.* Costume**

The contestants shall wear judogi (judo costume) and generally, as directed, shall also wear a red or white tape or ribbon tied over the regulation belt.

The judogi (judo costume) to be worn by the

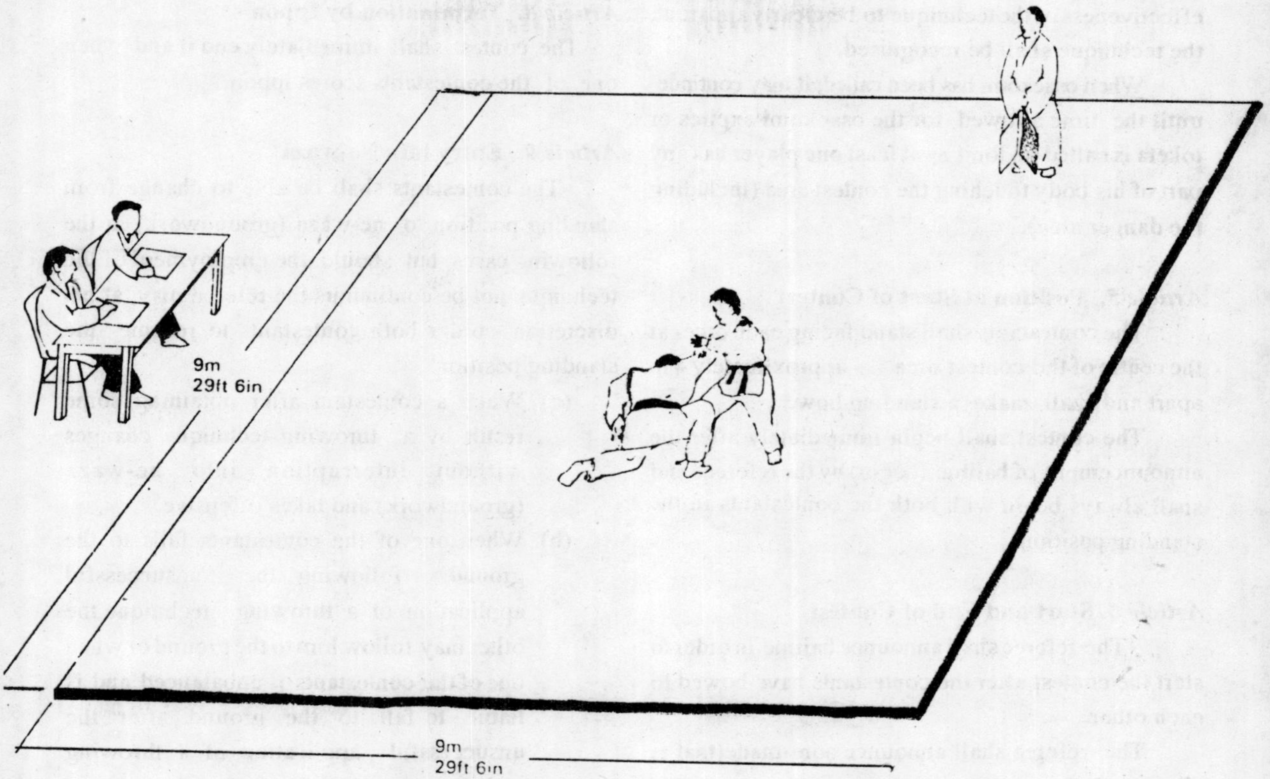

contestants shall comply with the following conditions:

(a) The jacket shall be long enough to cover the hips and be tied at the waist by the belt.

(b) The sleeves shall be loose and long enough to cover more than half of the forearm (there should be an opening of between 3 and 5 cm between the cuff and the largest part of the forearm).

(c) The trousers shall be loose and long enough to cover more than half of the lower leg (there should be an opening of between 5 and 8 cm between the bottom of the trousers and the largest part of the calf).

(d) The belt shall be tied with a square knot tight enough to prevent the jacket from being too loose and long enough to go twice round the body and leave about 15 cm protruding from each side to the knot when tied.

***Article 3.* Personal Requirements**

The contestants shall keep their nails cut short and shall not wear any metallic articles which may possibly injure or endanger the opponent.

***Article 4.* Location**

The contest shall be fought in the contest area. However, any technique applied when one or both of the contestants is outside the contest area shall not be recognised. That is to say that if one contestant shall have even one of his feet outside the contest area while standing or more than half of his body outside the contest area whilst doing sutemi-waza (sacrifice throws) or ne-weza (groundwork) he shall be considered as being outside the contest area.

However, where one contestant throws his opponent outside the contest area but himself stays within the contest area long enough for the effectiveness of the technique to be clearly apparent, the technique shall be recognised.

When osaekomi has been called, it may continue until the time allowed for the osaekomi expires or toketa is called-so long as at least one player has any part of his body touching the contest area (including the danger area).

Article 5. **Position at Start of Contest**

The contestants shall stand facing each other at the centre of the contest area approximately 4 m apart and shall make a standing bow.

The contest shall begin immediately after the announcement of hajime (begin) by the refereee and shall always begin with both the contestants in the standing position.

Article 6. **Start and End of Contest**

The referee shall announce hajime in order to start the contest after the contestants have bowed to each other.

The referee shall announce sore-made(that is all) to end the contest.

At the end of the contest the contestants shall return to the places in which they after the referee has indicated the result of the contest.

Article 7. Result

The result of a contest shall be judged only on the basis of nage-waza (throwing techniques) and katame-waza (grappling techniques).

Article 8. **Termination by Ippon**

The contest shall immediately end if and when one of the contestants scores ippon.

Article 9. **Entry into Ne-waza**

The contestants shall be able to change from standing position to ne-waza (groundwork) in the following cases, but should the employment of the technique not be continuous the referee may, at his discretion, order both contestants to resume the standing position.

(a) When a contestant after obtaining some result by a throwing technique changes without interruption into ne-waza (groundwork) and takes offensive.

(b) When one of the contestants falls to the ground, following the unsuccessful application of a throwing technique,the other may follow him to the ground or when one of the contestants is unbalanced and is liable to fall to the ground after the unsuccessful application of a throwing technique the other may take advantage of his opponent's unbalanced position to take him to the ground.

(c) When one contestant obtains some considerable effect by applying a shimewaza (strangle) or kansetsu-waza (a lock) in the standing position and then changes without

interruption to ne-waza (groundwork).

(d) When one contestant takes his opponent down into ne-waza (groundwork) by the particularly skillful application of movement which although resembling a throwing technique does not fully qualify as such.

(e) In any other case where one contestant may fall down or be about to fall down not covered by the preceding sub-sections of the article the other contestant may take advantage of his opponent's position to go into ne-waza (groundwork).

***Article 10.* Duration**

The duration of the contest shall be arranged in advance and shall be not less than 3 minutes and not more than 20 minutes. This arranged time may however be extended in certain special cases.

***Article 11.* Time Signal**

The end of the time allotted for the contest shall be indicated to the referee by the ringing of a bell or other similar audible method.

***Article 12.* Technique Coinciding with Time Signal**

Any throwing technique which is applied simultaneously with the bell (or other method of indicating the end of the time allotted) shall be recognised and when an osaekomi holding is similarly announced simultaneously with the signal bell, etc., the time allotted for the contest shall be extended until either ippon is scored or the referee announces toketa (hold broken).

***Article 13.* Sono-mama**

In any case where the referee wishes to stop the contest (e.g.in order to adjust the dress of the players, or to address either of them without causing a change in their position), he will call 'sono-mama'. To recommence the contest, he will call 'yoshi'.

The time between the announcement of sono mama (do not move) and yoshi (carry on) shall be excluded from the specified time for the duration of the contest.

***Article 14.* Responsibility**

All actions and decisions taken in accordance with the majority of three rules as in Article 26 by the referee and judges shall be final and without appeal.

***Article 15.* Officials**

In general,the contest shall be conducted by one referee and two judges. However, in certain circumstances it may be permissible to have one referee and judge or even just one referee.

***Article 16.* Position and Function of Referee**

The referee shall stay generally within the contest area and has the sole responsibility for conducting the contest and administering the Judgement.

Article 17. **Position and Function of Judges**

The judges shall assist the referee and shall be positioned opposite each other at two corners outside the contest area.

Article 18. **Ippon**

The referee shall announce ippon (full point) when in his opinion a throwing or grappling technique applied by a contestant merits the score of ippon and indicate the winner by raising his hands towards him after returning both contestants to the places in which they began the contest.

Article 19. **Waza-ari (almost ippon)**

The referee shall announce waza-ari (almost ippon) when in his opinion the technique applied by a contestant merits the score of waza-ari (almost ippon).

Should one contestant gain a second waza-ari (almost ippon) the referee shall announce instead waza-ari awasete ippon (two waza-aris score ippon) stop the contest and indicate the winner by raising his hands towards him after returning both contestants to the places in which they started the contest.

Article 20. **Yuko (almost waza-ari)**

The referee shall announce 'yuko' (almost waza-ari) when in his opinion the technique applied by the contestant merits the score of yoko.

Should either contestant score two or further yukos, then the referee shall announce them as they are scored but shall not stop the contest for that reason.

Regardless of how many yukos are announced, no amount will be considered as being equal to a waza-ari. The total number announced will be recorded and used in arriving at the decision whenever a contest is not won by ippon.

Article 21. **Koka (almost yuko)**

The referee shall announce 'koka' (almost yuko) when in his opinion the technique applied by the contestant merits the score of koka (almost yuko).

Should either contestant score two or further kokas, then the referee shall announce them as they are scored but shall not stop the contest for that reason.

Regardless of how many kokas are announced, no amount will be considered as being equal to a yuko or waza-ari. The total number announced will be recorded and used in arriving at the decision whenever a contest is not won by ippon.

Article 22. **Sogo-Gachi (compound win)**

The referee shall stop the contest and following the usual procedure indicate the winner after announcing sogo-gachi (compound win) in the following cases.

Where on contestant has gained a waza-ari and his opponent whose opponent has already received a penalty of keikoku (warning) is subsequently himself awarded a waza-ari .

Article 23. Osaekomi

The referee shall announce osaekomi (holding) when in his opinion one contestant is successfully holding the other by a holding technique. The referee shall immediately announce toketa (hold broken) at any time after the announcement of osaekomi when he considers the hold to be broken.

***Article 24.* Judges, Unsolicited Opinion**

Any judge shall indicate by making the appropriate signal whenever he holds a different opinion about an announcement made by the referee. When both judges indicate the same opinion, the judge closest to the referee shall immediately approach him requesting that he stops the contest and rectifies the decision. If the second judge does not hold the same opinion as the first judge, he shall make no signal and the decision of the referee shall prevail.

***Article 25.* Hantei (Request for Decision)**

The referee shall announce sore-made (that is all), stop the contest and return both contestants to their original starting places should the time allotted for the contest expire without there having been a score of ippon. Should the recorded scores indicate an advantage for either contestant on the following scale-one waza-ari wins over any number of yukos or kokas and when no waza-ari has been scored, one or more yukos wins over any number of kokas [see Article 36 (d)] - the referee having confirmed which contestant has won, will so indicate by raising his hand towards the winner.

Should the recorded scores either indicate no scores or be exactly the same under each of the headings (waza-ari, yuko, koka), then the referee shall call 'hantei' while raising a hand high in the air. The judges shall in response to this signal, raise either the white or red sign (flag) above their heads in order to indicate which contestant they consider merits the decision. To indicate hiki-wake (draw) the judges shall raise the red and white signs (or flags) simultaneously.

***Article 26.* Declaration of Decision**

The referee shall add his own opinion to that indicated by the two judges and shall declare hiki-wake (draw) or yusei-gachi (superiority) according to the majority decision of all three.

Should the opinion of the two judges differ the referee shall make the decision.

When there is only one judge the referee shall take into consideration the opinion of the judge before announcing either yusei-gachi or hiki-wake .

***Article 27.* Application of Matte (Wait)**

The referee shall announce matte (wait) in order to stop the contest temporarily in the following cases and to recommence the contest shall announce hajimi .

Should the referee call jukan (time) or sono-

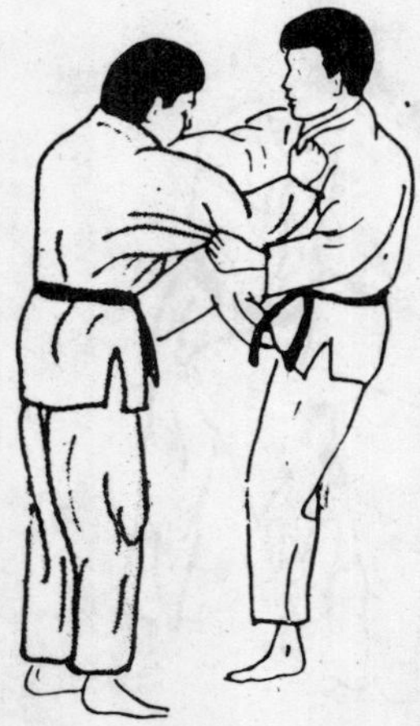

mama the time between this announcement and the subsequent recommencement of the contest by the call of either hajime or yoshi shall not count as being part of the time allotted for the contest or the osaekomi .

(a) When one or both of the contestants go outside or are about to go outside the contest area.

(b) When one or both of the contestants perform or are about to perform one of the prohibited acts.

(c) When one or both of the contestants are injured or taken ill.

(d) When it is necessary for one or both of the contestants to adjust their costume.

(e) When during ne-waza (groundwork) there is no apparent progress and the contestants lie still in a position such as ashi-garami (entangled legs).

(f) When in any other case that the referee deems it necessary to do so.

***Article 28.* Decision After Prohibited Act**

Whenever a contest has been decided by hansoku (prohibited act), fusen (default), kiken (withdrawal), injury or accident the referee shall indicate to the contestants the winner of the contest, or if the decision is hiki-wake (draw) the referee shall so announce the result.

***Article 29.* Penalties**

The referee shall declare shido (note), chui(caution), keikoku (warning) or hansokumake (disqualification) according to the gravity of any infringement of the regulations. In general a simple repetition of an infringement in one of the above mentioned categories shall merit a penalty of the next highest category.

If chui (caution) is announced to one contestant the other shall be regarded as having scored yuko, . Similarly, if keikoku (warning) is awarded to one contestant the other shall be considered as having been awarded waza-ari .

Should the referee award chui he shall temporarily stop the contest, return the contestants to the standing position in which they started the contest, and announce chui whilst raising his hands towards the contestant who committed the prohibited act.

Should the referee award keikoku he shall temporarily stop the contest, return the contestants to the standing position in which they started the contest and after making them adopt the correct sitting position shall announce keikoku whilst raising his hand towards the contestant who committed the prohibited act.

However, if the referee has called osaekomi and it is the contestant being held down who commits the offence meriting a keikoku, then the referee shall call sono-mama, announce the keikoku

in the osaekomi position and then recommence the contest by calling yoshi.

***Article 30.* Assessment of Ippon**

The decision of ippon shall be given in the following cases:

(a) Nage-waza (throwing techniques)

(1) When the contestant applying a technique or countering his opponent's attacking technique throws his opponent largely on his back with considerable force or impetus.

(2) When a contestant skillfully lifts his opponent who is lying with his back on the mat up to about the height of his own shoulders.

(b) Katame-waza (grappling techniques)

(1) When one contestant says maitta (I give up) or taps his or his opponent's body or the mat with his hand or foot twice or more.

(2) When one contestant holds the other, who is unable to get away, for 30 seconds, after the announcement of osaekomi (holding).

(3) Where the effect of a technique of shime-waza (strangle) or kansetsu-waza (lock) is sufficiently apparent.

***Article 31.* Assessment of Waza-ari**

The decision of waza-ari shall be given in the following cases:

(a) Nage-waza

When a contstant applying a throwing technique is not completely successful and does not quite merit the score of ippon.

(b) Osaekomi-waza

When one contestant is holding another as in Article 30 (b) (2) for 25 seconds or more but less than 30 seconds.

***Article 32.* Assessment of Yuko**

The decision of yuko shall be given in the following cases:

(a) Naga-waza

When a contestant applying throwing techniques is only partially successful, for example is lacking more than is required to score waza-ari, of one of the three elements of: largely on the back, force or impetus, and does not quite merit the score of waza-ari.

(b) Osaekomi-waza

When one contestant is holding another, as in Article 30 (b) (2), for 20 seconds or more, but less than 25 seconds.

***Article 33.* Assessment of Koka**

The decision of koka shall be given in the following cases:

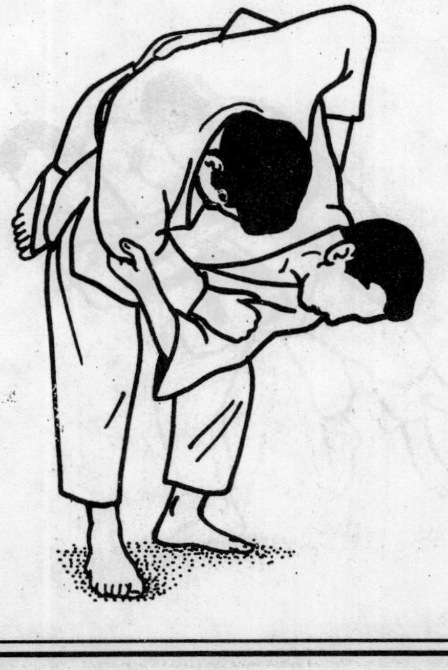

(a) Naga-waza

When a contestant makes a throwing technique which is not successful, but with some force or impetus puts his opponent on to his side, thigh (s), stomach or buttocks and does not quite merit the score of yuko.

(b) Osaekomi-waza

When one contestant is holding another for 10 seconds or more but less than 20 seconds.

***Article 34.* Assessment of Yusei-gachi**

The decision if yusei-gachi (superiority win) shall generally be given in the following cases:

(a) Where there has been a score of waza-ari or penalty of keikoku

(b) Where there has been a score of yuko or chui .

(c) Where there has been a score of koka (almost yuko) or shido (note).

(d) Where all scores as recorded in Article 25 are equal for both contestants, the yusei-gachi shall be given to the contestant who has the least severe penalty recorded against him.

(e) Where there is a recognisable difference in the attitude during the contest or in the skill and effectiveness of technique.

***Article 35.* Assessment of Hiki-wake**

The decision of hiki-wake (draw) shall be given when there is no positive score and where it is impossible to judge the superiority of either contestant in accordance with Article 34 above within the time allotted for the contest.

***Article 36.* Assessment of Hansoku-make**

The decision of hansoku-make (disqualification) should be given.

(a) Where one contestant has had the penalty of keikoku awarded against him and then receives a further penalty.

(b) Where any act on the part of one contestant gravely.

***Article 37.* Default and Withdrawal**

The decision of fusen-gachi (win by default) shall be given to any contestant whose opponent does not appear for his contest.

The decision of kiken-gachi (win by withdrawal) shall be given to any contestant whose opponent withdraws from the competition during the contest.

***Article 38.* Injury, Illness or Accident**

In every case where a competition is stopped because of injury to either or both of the contestants, the referee and judges may permit a maximum time of

five minutes to the injured player (s) for recuperation.

The decision of kachi (win), make (loss), hiki-wake (draw) where one contestant is unable to continue because of injury, illness or accident during the contest shall be given by the referee after consultation with the judges according to the following clauses:

INJURY

Where the cause of the injury is attributed to the injured contestant he shall lose the contest.

Where the cause of the injury is attributed to the uninjured contestant the uninjured contestant shall lose the contest.

Where it is impossible to attribute the cause of injury to either contestant the decision of hiki-wake (draw) may be given.

***Article 39.* Situations Not Covered by the Rules**

Where any situation arises which is not covered by these rules it shall be dealt with and a decision given by the referee after consultation with the judges.

CUP & TROPHIES

Gold In Olympics

Judo was first included in the Olympic Games at Tokyo in 1964, but was not included in 1968.

Open Category, No Weight Limit

1964 Antonius Geesink (Hol)
1968 Not held
1972 Wilhelm Ruska (Hol)
1976 Haruki Uemura (Jap)
1980 Dietmar Lorenz (GDR)
1984 Yasuhiro Yamashita (Jpn)

Over 95 kg

1980 Angelo Parisi (Fra)
1984 Hitoshi Saito (Jpn)
1988 Hitoshi Saito (Jpn)

Up to 95 kg

1980 Robert Van de Walle (Bel)
1984 Hyoung-Zoo Ha (Kor)
1988 Aurelio Miguel (Bra)

Up to 86 kg

1980 Jurg Rothlisberger (Sui)
1984 Pet er Seisenbacher (Aut)
1988 Peter Seisenbacher (Aut)

Up to 78 kg

1980 Shota Khabaleri (USSR)

1984	Frank Wieneke (FRG)
1988	Waldemar Legien (Pol)

Up to 71 kg

1980	Ezio Gamba (Ita)
1984	Byeong-Keun Ahn (Kor)
1988	Marc Alexandre (Fra)

Up to 65 kg

1980	Nikolai Solodukhin (USSR)
1984	Yoshiyuki Matsuoka (Jpn)
1988	Lee Kyung-keun (S.Kor)

Up to 60 kg

1980	Thierry Rey (Fra)
1984	Shinji Hosokawa (Jpn)
1988	Kim Jae-yup (S.Kor)

Previous Winners

(Categories changed in 1980)

Over 93 kg

1964	Isao Inokuma (Jpn)
1972	Wilhelm Ruska (Hol)
1976	Sergey Novikov (USSR)

80 kg to 93 kg

1972	Shota Chochoshvili (USSR)
1976	Kazuhiro Ninomiya (Jpn)

70 kg to 80 kg

1964	Isao Okano (Jpn)
1972	Shinobu Sekine (Jpn)
1976	Isamu Sonoda (Jpn)

63 kg to 70 kg

1964	Takehide Nakatani (Jap)
1972	Toyokazu Nomura (Jap
1976	Vladimir Nevzorov (USSR)

Up to 63 kg

1972	Takao Kawaguchi (Jap)
1976	Hector Rodriguez (Cub)

World Championships

World championships were first held in 1956 and are now held biennially, though they were cancelled in 1977.

Open

1956	S.Natsui (Jap)
1958	K.Sone (Jap)
1961	A.Geesink (Hol)
1965	I.Inokuma (Jap)
1967	M.Matsunaga (Jap)
1969	M.Shinomaki (Jap)
1971	M.Shinomaki (Jap)
1973	K.Ninomiya (Jap)
1975	H.Uemura (Jap)
1981	Y.Yamashita (Jap)
1983	A.Parisi (Fra)
1985	Y.Masaki (Jap)

Over 95 kg

1965	A.Geesink (Hol)
1967	W.Ruska (Hol)
1969	S.Suma (Jap)
1971	W.Ruska (Hol)
1973	C.Tagaki (Jap)
1975	S.Endo (Jap)
1979	Y.Yamashita (Jap)
1981	Y.Yamashita (Jap)
1983	Y.Yamashita (Jap)
1985	Y.C.Cho (S.Korea)

Under 95 kg

1967	N.Sato (Jap)
1969	F.Sasahara (Jap)
1971	F.Sasahara (Jap)
1973	N. Sato (Jap)
1975	J.L.Rouge (Fra)
1979	T.Khubuluri (USSR)
1981	T.Khubuluri (USSR)
1983	V.Divisenko (USSR)
1985	H.Sugai (Jap)

Under 86 kg

1965	I.Okano (Jap)
1967	E. Maruki (Jap)

1969 I.Sonoda (Jap)
1971 S.Fujii (Jap)
1973 S.Fujii (Jap)
1975 S.Fujii (Jap)
1979 D.Ultsch (GDR)
1981 B.Tchoullouyan (Fra)
1983 D.Ultsch (GDR)
1985 P.Seisenbacher (Aut)

Under 78 kg

1967 H.Minatoya (Jap)
1969 H.Minatoya (Jap)
1971 H.Minatoya (Jap)
1973 K.Nomura (Jap)
1975 V.Nevzorov (USSR)
1979 S.Fujii (Jap)
1981 N.Adams (UK)
1983 N.Hikage (Jap)
1985 N.Hikage (Jap)

Under 71 kg

1965 H.Matsuda (Jap)
1967 T.Shigeokoa (Jap)
1969 Y.Sonoda (Jap)
1971 T.Kawaguchi (Jap)
1973 Y.Minamo (Jap)
1975 Y.Minamo (Jap)
1979 K.Katsuki (Jap)
1981 Chong Hak Park (S.Korea)
1983 H.Nakanichi (Jap)
1985 A.Byeong-Keun (S.Korea)

Under 65 kg

1979 N.Soludukhin (USSR)
1981 K.Kashiwazaki (Jap)
1983 N.Soludukhin (USSR)
1985 Y.Sokolov (USSR)

Under 60 kg

1965 H.Minatoya (Jap)
1967 T.Shigeoka (Jap)
1969 Y.Sonoda (Jap)
1971 T.Kawaguchi (Jap)
1973 Y.Minamo (Jap)
1975 Y.Minamo (Jap)
1979 T.Ray (Fra)
1981 Y.Moriwaki (Jap)
1983 K.Tleseri (USSR)
1985 S.Hosokawa (Jap)

KABADDI

This is basically an outdoor game of Indian origin. It requires no special equipment to play and is thus an inexpensive game. Players should have courage, stamina and presence of mind to play this game. The players should have stamina to be able to utter a word without breathing which is possible with strong lungs. This game combines the qualities of Wrestling and Rugby. Due to its inexpensiveness the game of Kabaddi is gaining popularity outside India also. It was known by various names. For example, as Chedugudu or Hu-Tu-Tu in Southern parts of India. Hadudu (Men), Chu Kit-Kit (Women) in Eastern India and Kabaddi in Northern India.

The playground of Kabaddi shall be level and soft. It shall be preferably made of earth, manure or saw dust. For men, ground shall be of 12(½) metres x 10 metres. Middle line shall divide it into two halves. Each half shall measure 10 metres x 6(¼) metres. For women and juniors the measurement shall be 11 metres x 8 metres. There shall be a strip of 1 metre wide on each side of the play field, which is called lobby. In each half, at a distance of 3 metres on the centre line and parallel to it, lines of the full width of ground shall be drawn. These are baulk lines. The mid line marked distinctly is drawn which divides the playground into two courts. The width of mid line and other lines shall be 5 cm or 2".

Outside the side line and towards the end line 4 metres space is left empty. The sitting block shall be 2 metres from the end line. The sitting block for men shall be 2m. x 8m. and for women and juniors shall be 2m. x 6m.

SKILLS OF THE GAME

(i) The side that wins the toss shall have the choice of the court or the raid. In the second half the court shall be changed and the side which had not sent their raider first shall send their raider first. The game in the second half shall continue with the same number of players as it was at the end of the first half.

(ii) A player shall be out if any part of his body touches the ground outside the boundary but during the struggle a player shall not be out if any part of his body touches directly the ground or a player who is inside the boundary.

(iii) If any player goes out of the boundary during the course of play he shall be out. The umpire or referee shall declare such player out by shouting his number. No whistle shall be blown as the raid may continue.

If an anti or anties who have gone out of bounds (as per rules) hold a raider, the raider shall be declared not out. The anti or anties who have gone out of bounds will only be declared out.

(iv) When the struggle begins, the playfield includes the lobbies. After the struggle is over, the players involved in the struggle may use the lobbies to enter their respective courts.

(v) A raider shall keep the cant with kabaddi as the word for sounding. If he is not keeping the cant he shall be ordered back and warned by the umpire or referee and the opponents be given a chance to raid.

(vi) A raider must start his cant before he touches the opponents' court. If he starts the cant late, he shall be ordered back and warned by the umpire or referee, and the opponent be given chance to raid. In case of late starting of the cant the opponent or opponents shall not be declared out even if the raider has touched the anti or anties.

(vii)If the raider, even after a warning, is purposely violating rules 5 and 6, the umpire or referee shall declare his turn over and award one point to the opponentss but he shall not be declared out.

(viii) After a raider has reached his court or is out in the opponents' court, the opponents shall send their raider within 5 seconds. Thus alternately each side shall send their raider until the end of play.

(ix) If a raider, who is caught by the anties, escapes from their attempt to hold him and reaches his court safely he shall not be pursued.

But if a raider merely touches the anti or anties and reaches back to his court safely he may be pursued.

(x) Not more than one raider shall enter the opponents' court at a time. If more than one raider do so, the umpire shall order all of them to go back to their court and declare their turn of raiding over and shall declare those anties touched by those raiders as not out.

(xi) When a side sends more than one raider at a time a warning shall be given by the umpire or referee and if in spite of the warning, it continues to do so, the umpire or referee shall declare all the raiders out except the first one.

(xii)If a raider, while in the opponents' court, loses his cant he shall be out.

(xiii) When a raider is held, the anties shall not try deliberately to stifle his cant by shutting his mouth. If such incident occures, the umpire or referee shall declare the raider not out.

(xiv) No anti shall wilfully push the raider out of the boundary by any part of his anti's body, nor any raider shall wilfully push or pull an anti or anties out of the boundary. If the raider is pushed outside the boundary or the anti is pushed or pulled outside the boundary, the umpire or referee shall declare the raider or the anti, as the case may be, as not out, and the anti or the raider who pushes or pulls the opponents outside the boundary shall be declared out.

(xv) As long as a rider has not reached his court, none of the anties shall touch the ground of the raider's court, beyond the midline with any part of his body. If he does so, he shall

SCORE SHEET

TOURNAMENT

Toss.................. ....Choice of the winner team....................................First point....................
Date..............*Time*....................*Place*....................*Ground*....................*Round*....................*Scored by*....................
Team..*Vs. Team*..
Time out..............*No. of Substitute*....................*No. of Substitute*....................................*Time out*....................

No.		No.	
1.		1.	
2.		2.	
3.		3.	
4.		4.	
5.		5.	
6.		6.	
7.		7.	
8.		8.	
9.		9.	
10.		10.	
11.		11.	
12.		12.	

MEN

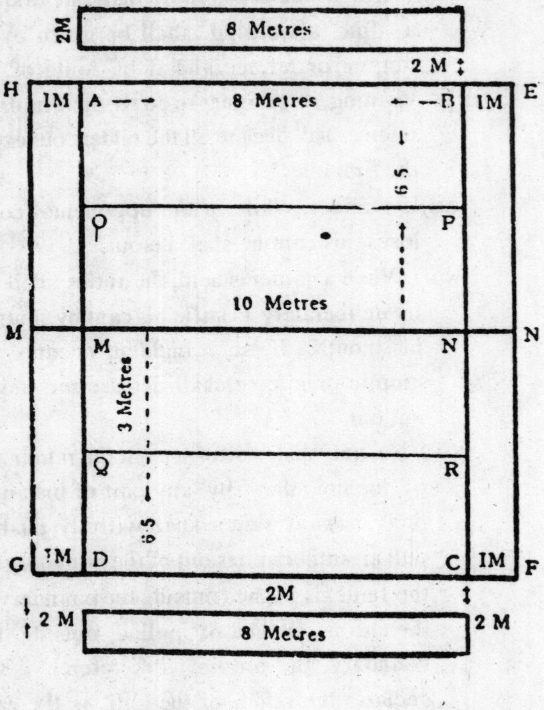

WOMEN AND JUNIORS

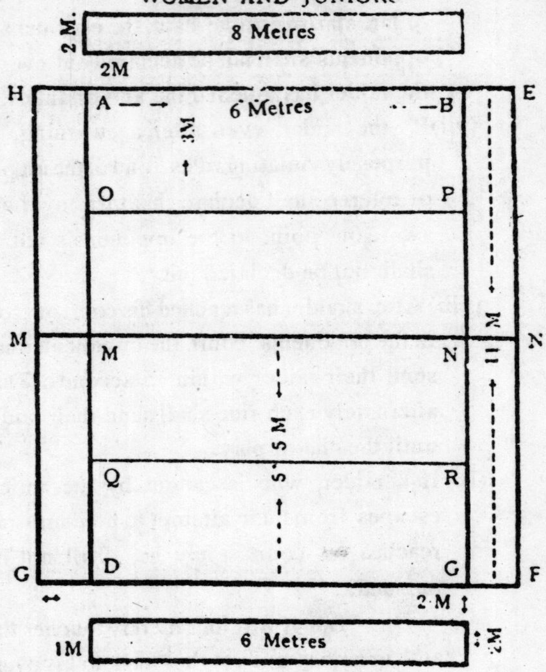

be out.

(xvi) If an anti or anties who are out, having violated rule 15, holds a raider or have violated the said rule while holding or helping to hold the raider, the raider shall be declared not out and the anti or anties who touch the raider's court shall be declared out.

(xvii) If a raider goes out of turn, the umpire or referee shall order him to go back and warn him, If in the opinion of the umpire or referee, such entry is being made persistently, he may award one point to the opponents (such point should be declared at least after giving one warning to the offenders).

(xviii) When a team manages to put out or the entire opponent team is out and no one of the opponents is entitled to be revived, they shall score a "lona" and two points shall be awarded in addition to the points scored by putting out individual players. The play continues and all the players of both sides enter their respective courts within ten seconds otherwise the umpire or referee shall award one point for every five seconds. Thus the game continues till the end of the play.

(xix) If a raider is warned against any dangerous play or is in any way instructed by one of his own side, the umpire or referee shall award one point to the opponent.

(xx) A raider or an anti is not to be held by any part of his body deliberately other than his limb on trunk. The one who violates the rule first shall be declared out. The umpire or referee shall declare such raider not out.

(xxi) When only one or two players of a team are left during the game and the captain of the team declares them out in order to bring in the full team, the opponents shall score as many points as there were players just before declaring, as well as two points for lona.

RULES OF THE GAME

1. Each side shall have 12 players. Seven players shall take the ground at one time.
2. The duration of a match for men shall be 2 halves of 20 minutes each. For women and juniors there will be 2 halves of the duration of 15 minutes each. There shall be an interval of 5 minutes between both the halves.
3. One point shall be secured by each side for each opponent who is out. The side that gets a lona shall score 5 points extra for the same.
4. The side that scores the highest number of points when the play ends shall be a winning team.
5. (a) In case of a tie, two extra durations of 5 minutes each shall be played. The game shall continue in the extra periods with the same number of players as were there at the end of second half.

(b) If the tie occurs at the end of 50 minute game, the team that scores the first point shall be the winning one.

Lona - When all players of a team are out the opposing team gets a score of 2.We call it Lona.

6. If a match is not completed due to some reason it shall be replayed.
7. Time out shall be called by the captain in case of an injury to a player. But the time-out shall not be more than two minutes, and the player hit can be changed. Before starting the second two players can be changed. The game can be started by one or two or minimum number of players. At the time of starting the game those referee must be informed. If the injury is serious, he may be substituted by another player. By the end of the first game, only two players can be substituted.
8. A match may be started in case five players are less in one team,but :-

(i) When all the players of one side are out, absentees shall include them and lonas scored against the side.

(ii) When the absentees come, they shall enter the play after getting the permission of the referee.

(iii) Substitutes in the place of absent players may be taken at any time, but when they are taken in this way no change of players may be allowed afterwards until the end of the match.

(iv) When a match is re-played, the players need not be the same for the second time.

(v) Doping is not allowed. Raids must be closely paired. The players shall be properly numbered at their back and front. The length of the numbers should be at least four inches. The minimum dress of player must be banian, shorts, with jangia or loin-cloth inside. Use of oil or any other substance on the body is not allowed. A player shall not be allowed to use any metallic thing.

9. During the play except the captain or leader, no player can instruct.The captain or leader alone can speak to his players in his own half.

CUP & TROPHIES

Gold in Asian Games

1990	India

ARJUN AWARD WINNERS

1972	Sadanand Mahadeo Shetty
1973	Bhola Nath Guin
1978-79	Shakuntala Pandharinath Khatavkar
1980-81	Shantaram Jadhav
1981	Monika Nath
1983	Maya Kashinath

KHO-KHO

Kho-Kho is primarily an Indian game. No authentic records are available to trace the origin of this game, but traditionally this game has had been played since long. The game is quite simple and inexpensive. It neither requires a big play-ground nor any expensive playing equipment. Due to inexpensive' nature and its simplicity the game is quite popular particularly among the school children. This game is widely played in the State of Haryana and Maharashtra.

The Kho-Kho field is rectangular and measures 34 metres by 16 metres.

M and N are two rectangles. One side of the rectangle is 16 metres (breadth of the playfield) and the other side is 4.8 metres.

At X and Y there shall be two wooden poles.

XY is a central lane 24.4 m long and 30 cm wide. There are eight small squares of 30 cm by 30 cm on the lane (G). The centre of each square is at a distance of 2.7 m from the centre of its adjacent square.

There are eight crosslanes which lie across the small squares and each of which is 16 metres in length and 30 cm in breadth, at right angles to the central lane and divided equally into two parts of 7.85 m each by the central lane (AB).

End Lines :- The lines AB and CD measuring 16 metres in length and running parallel to each other at a distance of 31 metres are known as end lines.

Side Lines :- The lines AD and BC measuring 31 metres in length and running parallel to each other at a distance of 16 metres, are known as side lines.

Posts :- Two string wodden posts shall be fixed at X and Y. They shall be 120 cm above and perpendicular to the ground and their circumference shall be uniform from 30 to 40 cm. Top of the posts shall be flat and free sharp edges. The posts shall not toper but smooth all over.

Central-lane :- The rectangle 24.4 m long and 30 cm broad between the posts X and Y dividing the playfield into two halves, is known as the centre-lane.

Cross-lane :- Each of the rectangles 16m long and 30cm broad, intersecting the central-lane at right angles at regular intervals and itself being divided into two halves, is known as a cross lane. There are eight cross lanes.

Square :- Each of the rectangles 30cm x 30 cm which is formed by the intersection of the central-lane and the crosslane is known as a square. There are eight squares, the centre of each being at a distance of 270 cms from the centre of its adjacent square.

The Line of the Post : -The line which goes through the centre of the post up to the sidelines and is at a distance of 260 cms from the nearest cross lane running parallel to it is known as the line of the post or the post line .

The Rectangle :- The field outside the line of the post is known as the rectangle. One side of the rectangle is 16 metres (Break of play field) and the other side is 330 cms.

The Limits :- The limits of the Kho-Kho field, admeasuring 31 metres x 16 metres are formed by meeting the end lines and the side lines at A,B,C,D.

Chaser :- The players sitting in the squares are known as chasers. An active chaser is a player who pursues the players of the opposite side (runner) with a view to tag and touch them.

Runners :- The players of the side other than

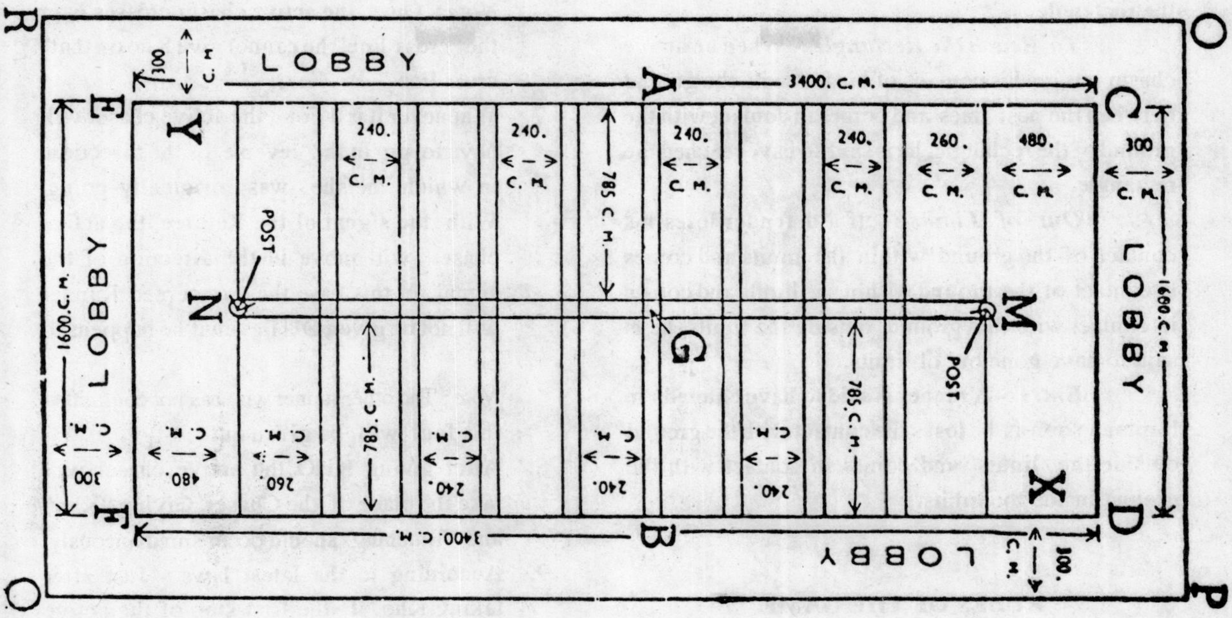

the chasers side are knwon as runners.

To give Kho :- To give kho perfectly, an active chaser should utter the word 'Kho' loudly and distinctly as soon as he/she touches the sitting chaser by hand from behind a sitting chaser.

Foul :- If a sitting or an 'active chaser violates or commits the breach of any rule, it is known as foul. A foul is to be declared by a continuous "short" whistle until the foul is corrected.

To Take a Direction :- To go from one post to another post is known as taking a direction.

To Turn the Face :- When an active chaser while going in a particular direction, turns his/her shoulderline (The imaginary line joining his/her shoulders) through more than a right angle to the direction, he or she is said to have turned the face and commits a foul.

To Recede :- When an active chaser, while going in a particular direction, goes in the opposite direction he/she is said to have receded. And he commits a foul.

To Leave the Post Line :- When an active chaser lets go his/her hold or touch of a post or goes beyond and leaves the rectangle, his action is known as leaving the post-line.

Foot Out :- When both the feet of a runner are touching the ground outside the limits, he/she is said to have placed his/her feet out. And he/she is out.

Lona :- When all the runners are out, a lona is said to be scored against the runners by the chasers.

Lobby :- There shall be a lobby surrounding the limits at a distance of three metres.

Width of the Line :- Width of each line should be between 2.5 cm and 3 cm. The dimension of the ground will be inclusive of the width of the line.

Defenders :- The runners who are inside the limits of their turn of running are knwon as defenders.

To Leave the Rectangle :- When an active chaser lets go his contact of his feet with the rectangle and comes in contact with the ground between the post lines, he is said to have left the rectangle.

To Reach the Rectangle :- When an active chaser lets go his contact of his feet with the ground between the post lines and comes in contact with the ground of the rectangle, he is said to have reached the rectangle.

Out of Limits :- If a defender loses his contact of the ground within the limits and comes in contact of the ground within the limits and comes in contact with the ground outside the limits, he is said to have gone out of limits.

Entry :- A runner is said to have entered the limits as soon as he loses the contact with the ground outside the limits and comes in contact with the ground inside the limits.

RULES OF THE GAME

1. The play ground will be marked according to the figure.
2. To be a 'Runner' or a 'Chaser' will be decided through a toss.
3. All chasers, except one, will sit in their squares such that no two face each other. The Ninth (active chaser) will stand in the Rectangle near some pole lane.
4. No part of the active chaser's body will touch the Central lane. He cannot cross the central lane through the posts.
   Note : It will not be a foul, if after getting a Kho first step of the active chaser touches the Central lane.
5. Kho should be given to a sitting chaser in loud and clear voice. The sitting chaser cannot stand without getting a Kho; nor he will try to touch by stretching his arms or legs.
6. If an active chaser comes out of the centre lane of the square in which a passive chaser is sitting and if he leaves the hold of the passive chaser, the active chaser will not give him a Kho.
   Note : Once the active chaser crosses over the "cross line" he cannot give Kho on that" cross line."
7. Whenever it is a Foul, the active chaser will have to go in the reverse of the direction, in which he/she was originally going. With the signal of the Referee, the active chaser will move in the direction of the signal. In this case the concerned Runner will not be given OUT even if he happens to be.
   Note : The other runner who has not committed this foul will be given out.
8. After giving KHO the active chaser will take the place of the Chaser. Giving "Kho" and "Touching" should occur simultaneously.
9. According to the latest laws - Just after taking Kho, if the first step of the active chaser touches centre lane then its not foul if he, crosses Centre lane, it will be a foul.
   Note: So long the foot of the player touches the cross lane, he will not be treated out of the lane.
10. Direction. After taking a direction an active chaser can re-strike in the cross lane and this will not be treated as a foul.
11. According to the rule No.9 and 10,active chaser will take only one direction.
12. After taking direction towards opposite, he will go upto the Post line in that direction till he does not say a KHO. Active chaser will not go to the other side of the centre lane till he does not go round the post.
13. If an active chaser leaves a post he will go towards the next post, while remaining in the central lane of the Post left.
    Note : The active chaser will not cross the central lane. Either he will give KHO or will go round the post.
14. Active chaser will always face towards his new direction. He cannot change direction.

15. Chaser will sit such that they do not obstruct the runners. If a runner is out due to some obstruction, he will not be declared as out.
16. Rules about taking direction and receding do not apply in rectangles.

    Note : For touching a player, a chaser can move around in the rectangle. This is not foul.
17. During an inning, active chaser can go out of the limits but there he is to observe the rules regarding taking directions and receding.
18. A defender runner shall not touch a sitting chaser. If he does so, he shall be warned once. If he repeats the same he shall be declared out.
19. A runner is declared out if his both feet are out of the limits.
20. Active chaser shall not violate any of the rules from 4 to 14. It shall be a foul, if any rule is violated. If a defender is out as a result of such a foul the defender shall not be declared out.
21. A defender (Runner) shall be declared out, if he is touched by an active chaser without violating any rule.
22. If an active chaser violates any of the rules from 8 to 14, the umpire shall compel him to take correct direction.

ARJUN AWARD WINNERS

1970	Sudhir Baskarrao Parab
1971	Achala Suberao Devre
1973	Bhavana Hasmukhalal Parikh
1974	Nilima Chandrakant Sarolkar
1975	Sheerang Janardan Inamdar
	Usha Vasant Nagarkar
1976	S. Dharwadka
1981	Hemant Mohan Takalkar
	Sushma Sarolkar
1983	Veena Narayan Parab
1984	S. Prakash
1985	Surekha Bhagwan Kulkarni

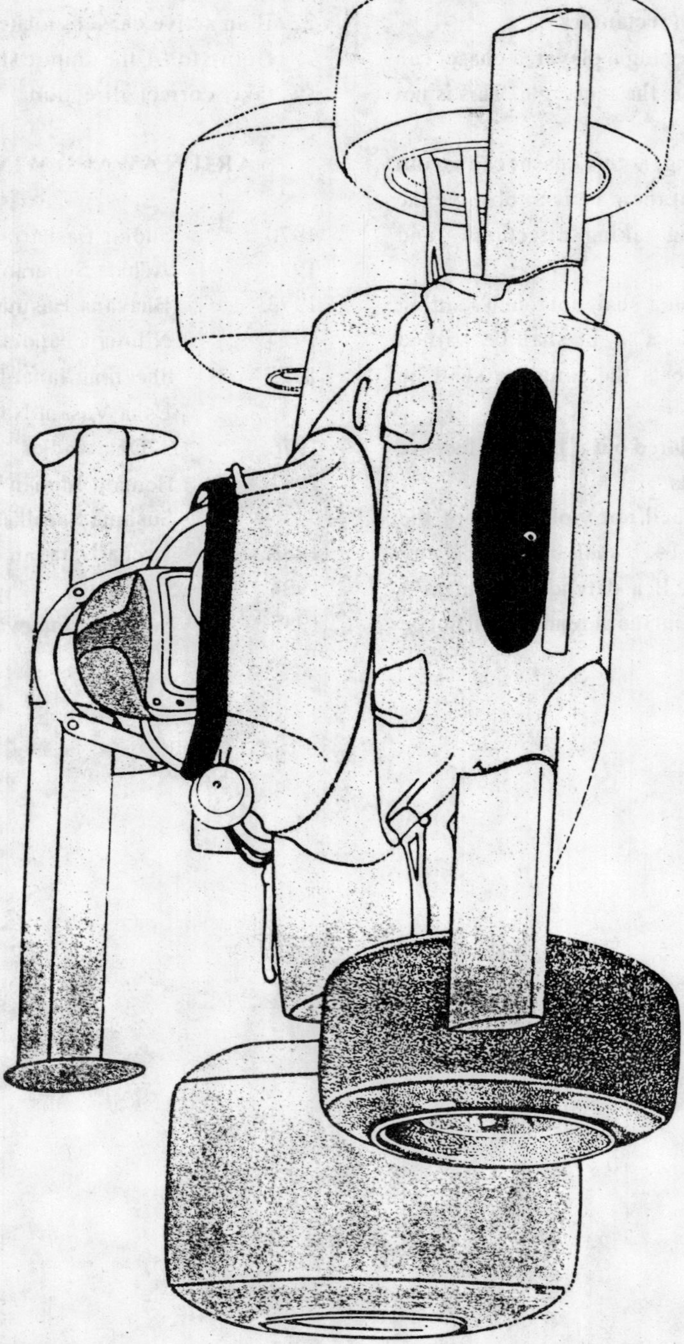

MOTOR RACING

Motor Racing is the staging of a competition of speed capabilities between two or more mechanically-propelled land vehicles over an accepted point-to-point course or closed circuit, the competitors running either together or being timed separately over the course. It is a dangerous sport,the driver's skill being expended on controlling a light-weight projectile capable of speeds in the region of 200 m/h.(322 km/h) and in taking it round the bends on a road course as fast as possible, balancing power available at the driving wheels with the grip afforded by the tyres. Modern racing tyres are of special rubber mixes which give a tenacious grip up to a sudden break-away point, so that a car is apt to go out of control and slide off the road at very high speed. The machines used, vary greatly in the technical construction and races are held under a wide diversity of rules and formulae; in most cases the skill of the driver in extracting maximum performance from his car has to be weighed against the efficiency, in terms of acceleration, speed, reliability, cornering power and other factors of the machine he is occupying.

Road racing is the highest form of the sport, but track racing, over courses in which the corners and turns were banked as on a railway, enabling the cars to negotiate them at speed without much skidding, was popular prior to the Second World War. The Indianapolis 500, the most famous American race, is run over an oval with slightly blanked corners, calling for a special driving technique.

TYPES OF MOTOR RACES

In addition to races of from a few miles to 24 hours' duration, the various categories of racing cars take part in hill-climb and speed trial contests, running one at a time, or sometimes in pairs over a straight course, and in all divisions of the sport various championships are recognized, International Motor Racing. The Federation International de l' Automobile (FIA), which governs the sport, sets rules for the main types of motor race,changing those for the top rank. Formula one,as it considers expedient, both to encourage technical advancement and to ensure control over the safety of the drivers. The first true motor race took place in France in 1895 and for some years public roads served as courses. Following accidents which involved spectators as well as drivers, present-day racing, with the one exception of Sicily's Targa Florio, takes place over private closed circuits, in which the cars cover on a time or distance basis, lap after lap. Races can be run on a scratch or handicap basis, and heat-by-heat and relay contests are not unknown. The makers of the racing cars score points towards a manufacturers' championship and various other championships are recognized each season.

The considerable cost of building cars for Grand Prix races, as the top contests are designated, was originally found by rich amateur sportsmen and by the motor manufacturers who supported racing. But in recent years outside sponsorship by such industrial concerns as perfume makers,cigarette companies, and food manufacturers has become necessary.

Grand Prix Car

The modern road racing or Grand Prix car is very scantily constructed , the rear-placed engine often forming a major part of the structure, and the driver, safeguarded by elaborate protective clothing, space-type crash helmet, and goggles or visor,lies

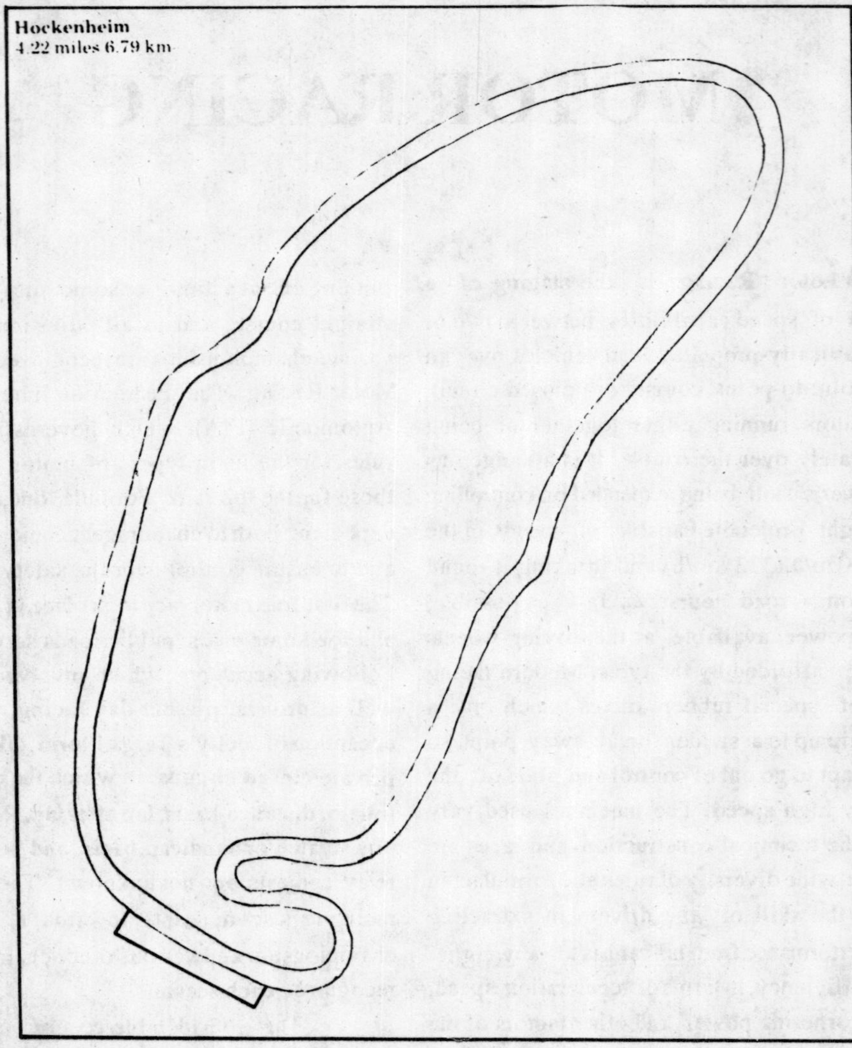

almost on his back in the cockpit,steering with a very small steering wheel, to reduce air drag to a minimum. Great skill is required to corner such fast,light cars at maximum speed,engine power being used to promote deliberate skids, which develop into four-wheel drifting or sliding - the fastest way through the faster bends.

In longer sports/racing-cars have to stop for replenishment of fuel and oil and possibly to be fitted with new tyres, and the driver may be changed for another who is sharing the car. These stops are made at special 'pits'.

The technique of racing car construction is bound up with extracting the maximum of power from a given engine which, under prevailing rules, burns ordinary petrol. In earlier years special racing fuels were permissible and engines were sometimes supercharged,by a mechanical pump, driven from the engine, which forced the petrol/air gas mixture into the cylinders under pressure, thus enabling greater power to be developed from a given capacity of cylinder. More recently attention has been paid to getting the power developed effectively on to the road; very wide tyres on the driving wheels sophisticated suspension systems, tyres made from chemical-rubber mixes to ensure good adhesion on wet or dry tracks,and aerofoils to force the wheels of the car on to the road being means to this end.

RULES OF THE GAME

International races are subdivided into various categories. Some are for pure racing vehicles, others are confined to cars which carry some road equipment, lamps, all-enveloping body work,etc., and are known as sports or sports/racing cars. Such cars can maintain speed at night and some of their races continue through the hours of darkness. Pure racing cars are normally single-seaters, carrying only the driver, a safety requirement introduced in the 1920s, before which mechanics were carried. The top class of single-seater is an expensive piece of machinery and lesser versions of racing car, which can be built and raced far a smaller expenditure, are also recognized.

Racing Car Formulae

The main racing car formulae recognized officially are:

Formula One which admits the following cars:

Validity from 1 January 1965 to 31 December 1972.

Engines with reciprocating pistons:

(a) engine cylinder capacity without supercharging, inferior to 3,000 cc.;

(b) engine cylinder capacity with super-charging, inferior or equal to 1,500 cc., minimum weight without ballast 530 kg.

As from 1st January 1972, the following prescriptions come into force for the prescriptions come into force for the Formula Two: Validity, 1st January 1972 to 31st December 1975. Non - supercharged reciprocating piston engines: Engine cylinder capacity inferior or equal to 2,000 cc.

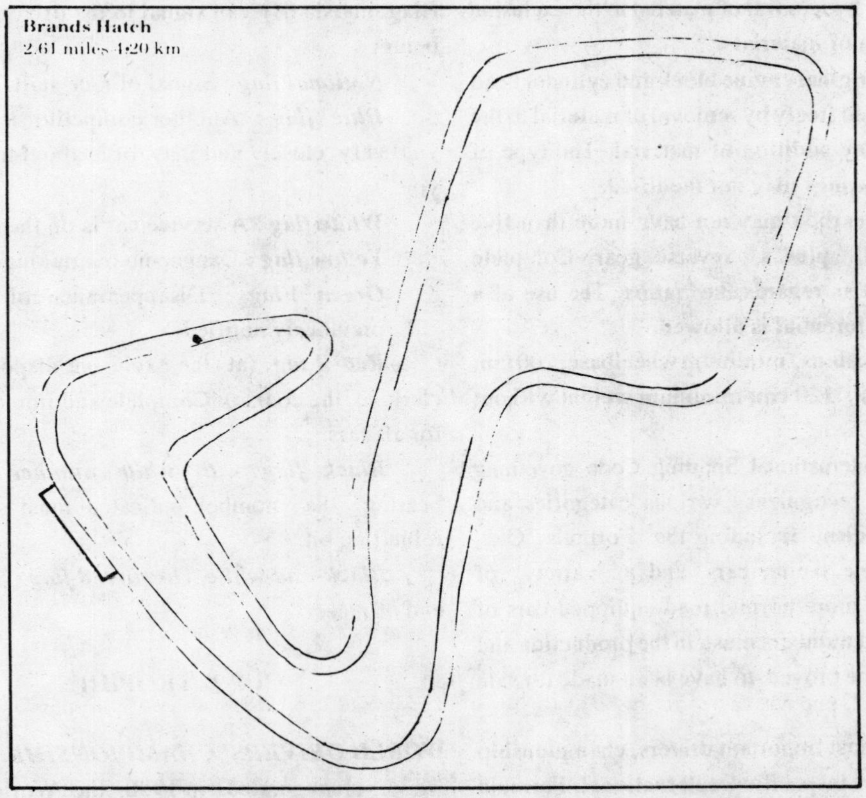

Minimum weight without ballast: cars equipped with a four cylinder engine, 450 kg; cars equipped with a six- cylinder engine, 475 kg; cars equipped with more than six cylinders, 500 kg. The engine must be derived from an engine equipping a model of car for which the F.I.A. has ascertained a series production of atleast 1,000 units.

Formula three cars, by which is implied to following: validity as from 1st January 1971 to 31st December 1974.

Reciprocating piston engines only, maximum cylinder capacity 1600 cc. The maximum cylinder capacity may be obtained by increasing or reducing either the bore or stroke or both dimensions.

Maximum number of cylinders, four. The engine block and cylinder head castings, machining completed, must be those of a series production car manufactured in at least 5,000 ;units in 12 consecutive months of a model recognized by the F.I.A. The original engine block and cylinder head may be modified freely by removal of material to the exclusion of any addition of material.

The original engine block and cylinder head may be modified freely by removal of material to the exclusion of any addition of material. The type of crank-shaft bearings may not modified.

The gearbox may not have more than five forward speed, plus a reverse gear. Complete freedom is left as regards the ratios. The use of a limited slip differential is allowed.

Dimensions, minimum wheelbase, 200 cm; minimum track, 120 cm; minimum weight without ballast, 440 kg.

The. International Sporting Code governing motor racing recognizes various categories and groups of vehicles, including the Formula One, Two, and Three racing cars, and a variety of prototype and more normal road-equipped cars of which specified numbers must, in the production and sports classes, be proved to have been made for sale of customers.

The most important drivers, championship is that raced for inspecified international Formula One races, under a points system. The eligible races include the Grand Prix in Austria, Beligium, Canada, France, Germany, Great Britain, Italy, Mexico, Monaco, Netherlands, South Africa, Spain, and the U.S.A. Apart from the driver's world championship, the F.I.A. recognizes graded drivers. Since 1968, the list of F.I.A. graded drivers includes:

(1) World Champion drivers of the five previous years.

(2) Drivers who, in one and the same year, have been classified at least twice among the first six in a race of the world championship for drivers, while taking into account the championship of the two previous years.

Cars are usually started from a numbered grid, positions thereon being in accordance with practice times, the fastest driver starting from the best position on the front row. Races electrically timed in many instances, to three places of decimals, in kilometres per hour. An International system of flag signals is in force, by which officials (flag marshalls) can signal to the drivers, the code being:

National flag : Signal of race start.

Blue flag : Another competitor is following you very closely and may, or is about to, overtake you.

White flag : A service car is on the circuit.

Yellow flag : Danger-no overtaking.

Green Flag : Disappearance of a danger previously notified.

Red Flag (at the exclusive disposal of the clerk of the course): Complete and immediate stop for all cars.

Black flag with white number : The car bearing the number indicated must stop at its refuelling pit.

Black-and-white, chequered flag : Signal of end of race.

CUP & TROPHIES

WORLD DRIVERS' CHAMPIONSHIP

Inaugurated in 1950, the World Drivers'

Championship is made up of specified Formula One Grand Prix races each season.

Winners

1972 E.Fittipaldi (Bra)
1973 J.Stewart (UK)
1974 E.Fittipaldi (Bra)
1975 N.Lauda (Aut)
1976 J.Hunt (UK)
1977 N.Lauda (Aut)
1978 M.Andretti (USA)
1979 J.Hunt (UK)
1980 A.Jones (Aus)
1981 N.Piquet (Bra)
1982 K.Rosberg (Fin)
1983 N.Lauda (Aut)
1984 N.Lauda (Aut)
1985 A.Prost (Fra)
1986 A.Prost (Fra)

BELGIAN GRAND PRIX

Winners

1950 J.M.Fangio (Arg)
1951 G.Farina (Ita)
1952 A.Ascari (Ita)
1953 A.Ascari (Ita)
1954 J.M.Fangio (Arg)
1955 J.M.Fangio (Arg)
1956 P.Collins (UK)
1957 Not held
1958 T.Brooks (UK)
1959 Not held
1960 J.Brabham (Aus)
1961 P.Hill (USA)
1962 J.Clark (UK)
1963 J.Clark (UK)
1964 J.Clark (UK)
1965 J.Clark (UK)
1966 J.Surtees (UK)
1967 D.Gurney (USA)
1968 B.Mclaren (NZ)
1969 Not held
1970 P.Rodriguez (Mex)
1971 Not held
1972 E.Fittipaldi (Bra)
1973 J.Stewart (UK)
1974 E.Eittipaldi (Bra)
1975 N.Lauda (Aut)
1976 N.Lauda (Aut)
1977 G.Nilsson (Swe)
1978 M.Andretti (USA)
1979 J.Scheckter (S.Af)
1980 D.Pironi (Fra)
1981 C.Reutemann (Arg)
1982 J.Watson (UK)
1983 A.Prost (Fra)
1984 M.Albereto (Ita)
1985 A.Senna (Bra)
1986 N.Mansell (UK)
1987 A. Prost (Fra)

BRAZILIAN GRAND PRIX

Winners

1973 E.Fittipaldi (Bra)
1974 E.Fittipaldi (Bra)
1975 C.Reutemann (Bra)
1976 N.Lauda (Aut)
1977 C.Reutemann (Arg)
1978 C.Reutemann (Arg)
1979 J.Laffite (Fra)
1980 R.Arnoux (Fra)
1981 C.Reutemann (Arg)
1982 A.Prost (Fra)
1983 N.Piquet (Bra)
1984 A.Prost (Fra)
1985 A.Prost (Fra)
1986 N.Piquet (Bra)
1987 A. Prost (Fra)

BRITISH GRAND PRIX

First run as the RAC Grand Prix at Brooklands in 1926, and later as the Donhington Grand Prix in 1937 and 1938. The name British Grand Prix was first used in 1949.

Winners

1950 G.Farina (Ita)
1951 J.F.Gonzalez (Arg)
1952 A.Ascari (Ita)
1953 A.Ascari (Ita)

1954 J.F.Gonzalez (Arg)
1955 S.Moss (UK)
1956 J.M. Fangio (Arg
1957 T.Books/s. Moss (UK)
1958 P.Collins (UK)
1959 J.Brabham (Aus)
1960 J.Brabham (Aus)
1961 Trips (Frg)
1962 J.Clark (UK)
1963 J.Clark (UK)
1964 J.Clark (UK)
1965 J.Clark (UK)
1966 J.Brabham (Aus)
1967 J.Clark (UK)
1968 J.Siffert (Swi)
1969 J.Stewart (UK)
1970 J.Rindt (Aut)
1971 J.Stewart (UK)
1972 E.Fittipaldi (Bra)
1973 P.Revson (USA)
1974 J.Scheckter (S.Af.)
1975 E.Fittipaldi (Bra)
1976 N.Lauda (Aut)
1977 J.Hunt (UK)
1978 C.Reutemann (Arg)
1979 C.Regazzoni (Swi)
1980 A.Jones (Aus)
1981 J.Watson (UK)
1982 N.Lauda (Aut)
1983 A.Prost (Fra)
1984 N.Lauda (Aut)
1985 A.Prost (Fra)
1986 N.Mansell (UK)

DETROIT GRAND PRIX

Winners

1982 J.Watson (UK)
1983 M.Alboreto (Ita)
1984 N.Piquet (Bra)
1985 K.Rosberg (Fin)
1986 A.Senna (Bra)
1987 A.Senna (Bra)

GERMAN GRAND PRIX

Winners

1951 A.Ascari (Ita)
1952 A.Ascari (Ita)
1953 G.Farina (Ita)
1954 J.M.Fangio (Arg)
1955 Not Held
1956 J.M.Fangio (Arg)
1957 J.M.Fangio (Arg)
1958 T.Brooks (UK)
1959 T.Brooks (UK)
1960 Not held
1961 S.Moss (UK)
1962 G.Hill (UK)
1963 J.Surtees (UK)
1964 J.Surtees (UK)
1965 J.Clark (UK)
1966 J.Brabham (Aus)
1967 D.Hulme (NZ)
1968 J.Stewart (UK)
1969 J.Ickx (Bel)
1970 J.Rindt (Aut)
1971 J.Stewart (UK)
1972 J.Ickx (Bel)
1973 J.Stewart (UK)
1974 C.Regazzoni (Swi)
1975 C.Reutemann (Arg)
1976 J.Hunt (UK)
1977 N.Lauda (Aut)
1978 M.Andretti (USA)
1979 A.Jones (Aus)
1980 J.Laffite (Fra)
1981 N.Piquet (Bra)
1982 P.Tambay (Fra)
1983 R.Arnoux (Fra)
1984 A.Prost (Fra)
1985 M.Alberto (Ita)
1986 N. Piquet (Bra)

MONACO GRAND PRIX

Winners

1950 J.M.Fangio (Arg)
1951 Not held
1952 Not held

1953	Not held
1954	Not held
1955	M.Trintignant (Fra)
1956	S.Moss (UK)
1957	J.M Fangio (Arg)
1958	M.Trintignant (Fra)
1959	J.Brabham (Aus)
1960	S.Moss (UK)
1961	S.Moss (UK)
1962	B. McLaren (NZ)
1963	G.Hill (UK)
1964	G.Hill (UK)
1965	G.Hill (UK)
1966	J.Stewart (UK)
1967	D.Hulme (NZ)
1968	G.Hill (UK)
1969	G.Hill (UK)
1970	J.Rindt (Aut)
1971	J.Stewart (UK)
1972	J.P. Beltoise (Fra)
1973	J.Stewart (UK)
1974	R.Peterson (UK)
1975	N.Lauda (Aut)
1976	N.Lauda (Aut)
1977	J.Scheckter (S.Af.)
1978	P.Depziller (Fra)
1979	J.Scheckter (S.Af.)
1980	C.Reutemann (Arg)
1981	G.Villeneuve (Can)
1982	R.Patrese (Ita)
1983	K.Rosberg (Fin)
1984	A.Prost (Fra)
1985	A.Prost (Fra)
1986	A.Prost (Fra)
1987	A. Senna (Bra)

SAN MARINO GRAND PRIX

Winners

1981	N.Piquet (Bra)
1982	D.Pironi (Fra)
1983	P.Tambay (Fra)
1984	A.Prost (Fra)
1985	E.de Angelis (Ita)
1986	A.Prost (Fra)
1987	N.Mansell (UK)

INDIAN POLIS 500

America's most famous motor race was first held in 1911.Anthony (A.J.)Foyt is the only man to have won on four occasions.

Winners

1911	R.Harroun
1912	J.Dawson
1913	J.Goux
1914	R.Thomas
1915	R.DePalma
1916	D.Resta
1917-18	Not held
1919	H.Wilcox
1020	G.Chevrolet
1921	T.Milton
1922	J.Murphy
1923	T.Milton
1924	L.Corum/J.Boyer
1925	P.DePaolo
1926	F.Lockhart
1927	G.Souders
1928	L.Meyer
1929	R.Keech
1930	B.Arnold
1931	L.Schneider
1932	F.Frame
1933	L.Meyer
1934	B.Commings
1935	K.Petillo
1936	L.Meyer
1937	W.Shaw
1938	F.Roberts
1939	W.Shaw
1940	W.Shaw
1941	F.Davis/M.Rose
1942-45	Not held
1946	G.Robson
1947	M.Rose
1948	M.Rose
1949	B.Holland

1950	J.Parsons
1951	L.Wallard
1952	T.Ruttmann
1953	W.Vukovich
1954	W.Vukovich
1955	B.Sweikert
1956	P.Flaherty
1957	S.Hanks
1958	J.Bryan
1959	R.Ward
1960	J.Rathmann
1961	A.J.Foyt,Jnr.
1962	R.Ward
1963	P.Jones
1964	A.J.Foyt,Jnr
1965	J.Clark (UK)
1966	G.Hill (UK)
1967	A.J.Foyt,Jnr
1968	B.Unser
1969	M.Andretti
1970	A.Unser
1971	A.Unser
1972	M.Donohue
1973	G.Johncock
1974	J.Rutherford
1975	B.Unser
1976	J.Rutherford
1977	A.J.Foyt,Jnr
1978	A.Unser
1979	R.Mears
1980	J.Rutherford
1981	B.Unser
1982	G.Johncock
1983	T.Sneva
1984	R.Mears
1985	D.Sullivan
1986	B.Rahal
1987	A.Unser

LE MANS

The world's most important race for sports cars was first held in 1923. The most wins by one man is four by Olivier Gendebien (Bel) and Jackie Ickx (Bel).

Winners

1923	A.Lagache/R.Lenord
1924	J.Duff/F. Clement
1925	H.de Ciyrcells/A.Rossignol
1926	R.Bloch/A.Rossignol
1927	J.Benjafield/S.Davis
1928	W.Barnato/B.Rubin
1929	W.Barnato/H.Birkin
1930	W.Barnato/G.Kidston
1931	E.Howe/H.Birkin
1932	R.Sommer/L.Chinetti
1933	R.Sommer/T.Nuvolari
1934	L. Chinetti/P.Etancelin
1935	J.Hindmarsh/L.Fontes
1936	Not held
1937	J-P. Wimille/R.Benoist
1938	E. Chaboud/J.Tremoulet
1939	J-P Wimille/P.Veyron
1940	Not held
1941	Not held
1942	Not held
1943	Not held
1944	Not held
1945	Not held
1946	Not held
1947	Not held
1948	Not held
1949	L.Chinetti/P.Whitehead
1950	L. Rosier/J-L. Rosier
1951	P.Walker/P.Whitehead
1952	H.Lang/K.Riess
1953	T.Rolt/D.Hamilton
1954	F.Gonzalez/M.Trintignant
1955	M.Hawthorn/N.Sanderson
1956	R.Flockhart/N.Sanderson
1957	R.Flockhart/I.Bueb
1958	O.Gendebien/P.Hill
1959	C.Shelby/R.Salvadori
1960	O.Gendebien/P.Hill
1961	O.Gendebien/P.Hill
1962	O.Gendebien/P.Hill
1963	L.Scarfiotti/L. Bandini
1964	J.Guichet/N.Vaccarella

1965	J.Rindit/M.Gregory
1966	C. Amon/B.Mclaren
1967	D.Gurney/A.J.Foyt,Jnr.
1968	P.Rodriguez/L.Bianchi
1969	J.Ickx/J.Oliver
1970	H.Herrmann/R.Attwood
1971	H.Marko/G.van Lennep
1972	H.Pescarolo/G.Hill
1973	H.Pescarolo/G.Larrousse
1974	H.Pescarolo/G.Larrousse
1975	J.Ickx/D.Bell
1976	J.Ickx/G.van Lennep
1977	J.Ickx/J. Barth/H.Haywood
1978	J-P Jaussaud/D.Pironi
1979	K.Ludwig/Whittington D. Whittington
1980	J-P. Jaussaud/J.rondeau
1981	J.Ickx/D.Bell
1982	J.Ickx/D.Bell
1983	V.Schuppan/H.Haywood/A.Holbert
1984	K.Ludwig/H.Pescarolo
1985	K.Ludwig/P.Barillo/John Winter'
1986	H-J. Stuck/D.Bell/A. Holbert
1987	H.J. Stuck/D.Bell/A. Holbert

NET BALL

Netball is played between two teams of seven players - three of which are forwards or attackers and named Wing Attack, Goal Attack and Goal Shooter; one is the player positioned in the middle called the Centre; and three are backs or defenders and are named Wing Defence, Goal Defence and Goal Keeper. The aim of the game is to score goals. A goal is scored when the ball is thrown over and through a ring on the top of the goal post from within the attacking teams's shooting circle. To start the game or restart it after a goal the ball is thrown off by the Centre from the centre circle and then passed from player to player until it can be caught in the goal circle by one of the two goal-scoring players who then throws for goal.

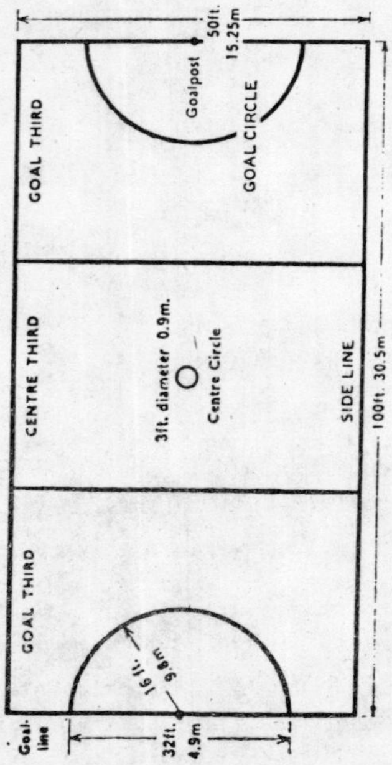

SKILLS OF THE GAME

Each team consists of seven players: goal keeper, goal defence, wing defence, centre, wing attack, goal attack, and goal shooter. Players are restricted to certain areas of the court, and should a player go out of bounds she is ruled offside and a free pass is given to the opposing team.

Matches are of 15 minute quarters, with 3 minutes intervals after the first and third quarters and a 10 minute break at half-time. Teams change ends after each quarter. In certain circumstances, a game may consist of two 20-minute halves.

Play starts and restarts after a goal or an interval with a centre pass taken alternately by opposing centres. The centre pass must be caught or touched by another player in or landing in the centre third, and each player must then pass the ball within a maximum three seconds. Footwork rules are most precise, limiting the player in possession to movement with one foot only while pivoting on the other foot although the pivotal foot may be lifted as long as the ball is released before it lands again. The ball must not be passed over a complete third without being touched by another player, and must not be deliberately kicked, rolled or punched. Players must avoid bodily contact, and must not obstruct play by being closer than 3 feet to the player with the ball.

The game is controlled by two umpires, each looking after half the court and one whole side-line. There are no clothing restrictions, except on footwear: spiked shoes are prohibited.

First-class netball requires exceptional muscle control in twisting and jumping, and stopping dead to avoid offside, illegal foot movements, or

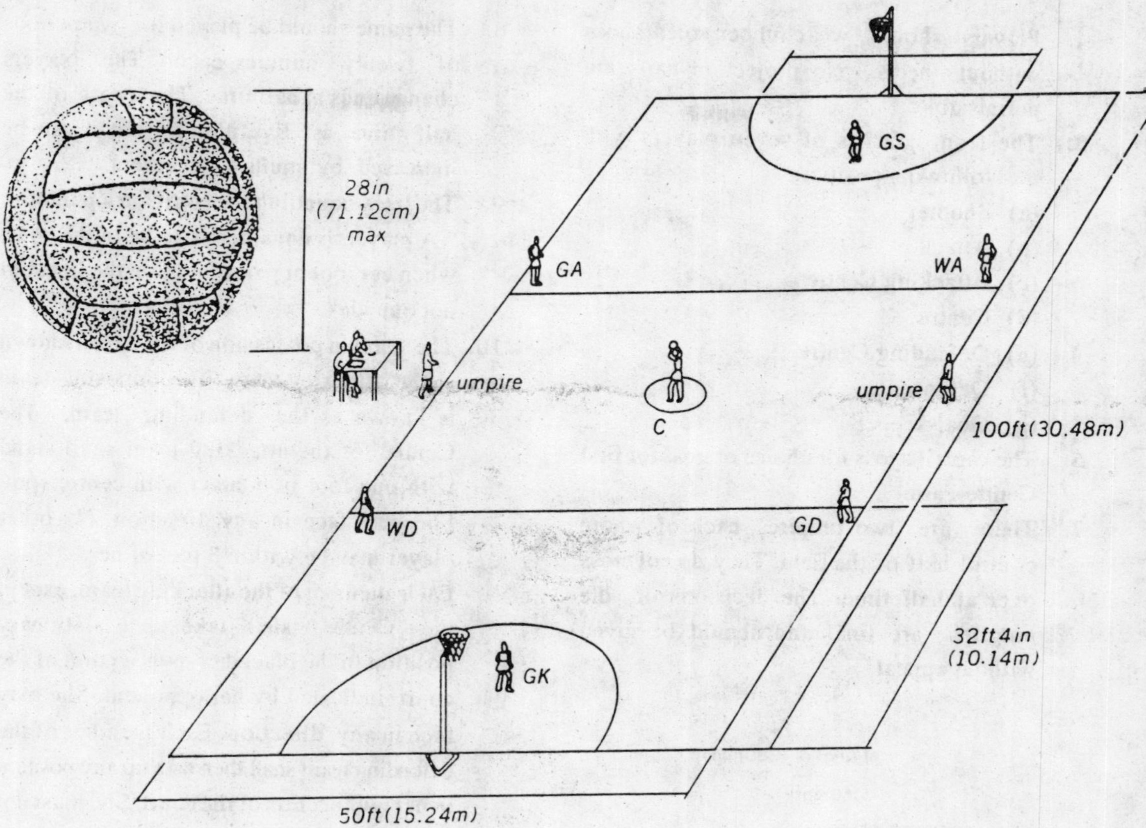

bumping. With scoring the object, speed and accuracy of passing are essential, and for the two concerned with shooting, accurate aim and judgement are additionally vital.

RULES OF THE GAME

1. Length, 100ft. (30.48m). Width, 50ft. (15.24m).

   The two long lines are called side lines: the two short lines goal lines. Court is divided down side lines by two transverse lines into three equal thirds, named centre third and goal thirds.

   A semi-circle in each goal third; centre, middle of goal line; radius, 16 ft.(4.88m). Circle drawn in the middle of the centre Third. diameter 3ft. (914 mm).

   The court, thirds and circles are marked clearly with lines. Lines must not be more than two inches wide. They should be painted with a hard wearing paint or, if temporary, with whitewash or distemper, or by laying adhesive tape.

2. A goalpost 10 ft.(3.05m) high is placed at the mid point of each goal line, neither in front nor behind the line.

   The ring has a diameter of 15in. (380mm). The material of which the ring is constructed is now laid down; it shall be tubular steel and shall be 5/8in. (15mm) in diameter, and fitted with a net open at both ends.

3. The ball used is a Netball or size 5 Association Football, and measures between 27 in. (690mm) and 28 in. (710 mm) in circumference and weight between 14 oz. (400g) and 16 oz. (450 g)

4. Players should wear rubber soled shoes without heels. No projection nails are permissible.
5. The team consists of seven players with the following position:-
   (a) Shooter
   (b) Attack
   (c) Attacking Centre
   (d) Centre
   (e) Defending Centre
   (f) Defence
   (g) Goal-keeper
6. The captains toss for choice of goal for first Centre Pass.
7. There are two umpires, each of whom control half of the field. They do not cross over at half time. The decisions of the umpires are final and should be given without appeal.

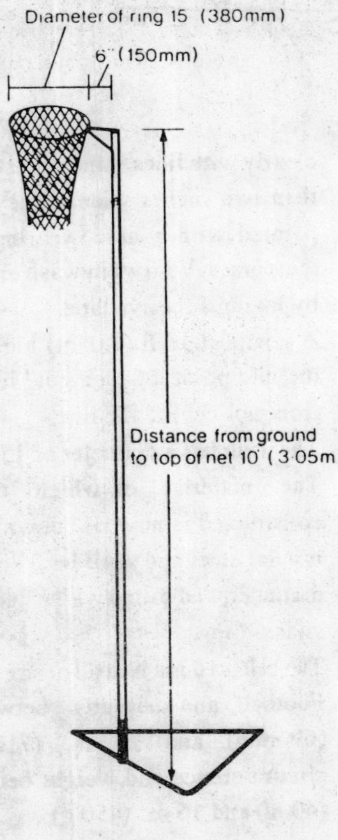

8. The game should be played for two periods of twenty minutes each. The players change ends at half time. The length of the half time is five minutes but it can be increased by mutual agreement.
9. The lines bounding the court are a part of it. " A player is considered to be in the court when her foot or part of it is on the line, but not outside".
10. The team in possession of the ball is known as the attacking team. The opposing team is known as the defending team. The Centre of the attacking team shall stand with one foot in contact with centre spot. She may face in any direction. No other player may be within 3 feet of her.
    Each member of the attacking team, except the Centre, shall take up a stationary position in the place her own section of the court indicated by her opponent. She may face in any direction. Each member of the defending team shall then take up any position in her own section of the court. She must not touch her opponent and must be stationary.
11. Play shall be started by a centre pass which should be taken alternately by the two teams after each goal and after half time. Immediately the whistle sounds, all players are free to move except the Centre holding the ball which she must pass ;within three seconds.
12. The player in the defending team (i.e., Goal-keeper and Defence) shall be offside if they enter the attacking court,but they may play in their own court and in the centre court. Players in the centre court (i.e.,Centre, Attacking Centre and Defending Centre) shall be off-side if they enter either circle. If a player is on the line bounding the off-side territory, she is not off-side.
    A free pass to the possible side is taken from the place where the infringement occurred,by a player allowed in that area.
13. To be in possession of the ball a player must

have control of it or have hold of it with one or both hands.

(a) She may throw it with one or both hands to another player.

(b) Bounce it with one or both hands to another player.

14. A goal (other than one resulting from a free shot) is scored when the ball is thrown or batted over and completely passes through the ring into the net, by Shooter or Attacker, from any point within the shooting circle, including the line bounding the circle.

15. A player shall not hold the ball for more than three seconds in the following events :-

(a) While it is in play

(b) while taking a shot or free shot at goal

(c) while taking a free pass

(d) after she has taken her stand for the throw in

(e) after the whistle for the centre pass.

Penalty for above offences will be as follows:-

(i) Free pass to the opposite side for offences (a),(b) and (c)

(ii) Throw into the opposite side for offence (d)

(iii) Centre pass to the opposite side for offence (e)

16. A substitute is allowed when a player is hurt or ill with the condition that once the substitute has played, the injured or sick player cannot return.

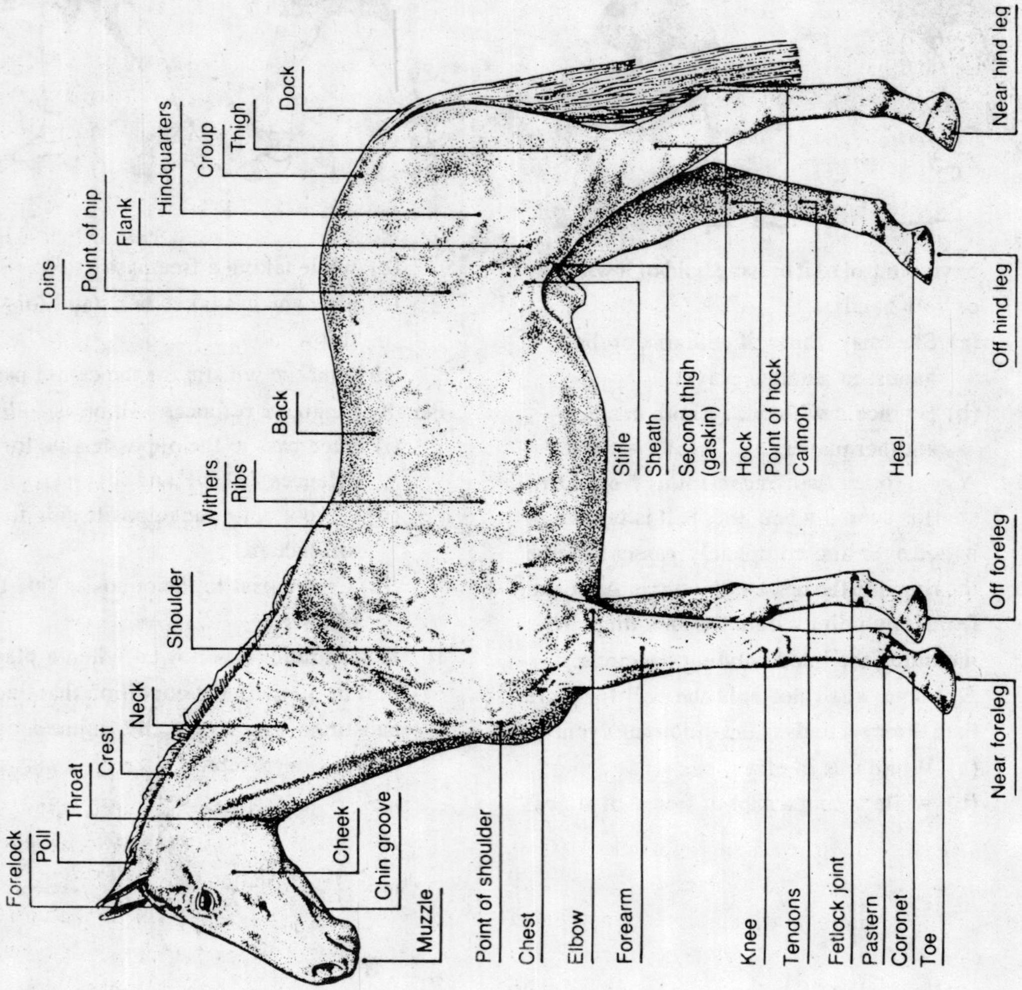
Forelock
Poll
Throat
Crest
Neck
Shoulder
Withers
Ribs
Back
Loins
Point of hip
Flank
Hindquarters
Croup
Thigh
Dock
Cheek
Chin groove
Muzzle
Point of shoulder
Chest
Elbow
Forearm
Knee
Tendons
Fetlock joint
Pastern
Coronet
Toe
Stifle
Sheath
Second thigh
(gaskin)
Hock
Point of hock
Cannon
Heel
Near foreleg
Off foreleg
Off hind leg
Near hind leg

RIDING

The explosion of interest in riding that has taken place in the last forty years may seem astonishing alongside the rapid progress of mechanization, but on reflection the reasons for it are easy enough to understand. The attractive nature of the horse and his versatility have appealed to man for longer, probably, than history relates. For centuries the horse was principal means of transport but now the emphasis has moved from utility to pleasure.

One of the greatest attractions of riding is that it can be enjoyed at every level, according to skill and experience. More and more people of all ages and backgrounds are discovering this pastime and deriving unlimited pleasure from it, either as active participants or interested spectators. This development owes a great deal to the guidance and encouragement of dedicated organizations such as the Pony Club and riding clubs which have sprung up all over the world.

Many people still think you have to be rich and live in the country to be able to ride. It's simply no longer the case. An estimated two million children and adults ride regularly in Britain, and the numbers are growing. Many of these people, particularly newcomers to the sport, do not own their own horses. They use the services of the many excellent riding schools which are often situated near towns and cities. If, after while, you decide you want to ride your own horse, you can go ahead with some experience, knowing the likely pitfalls and costs.

We have to remember first of all that the horse, and more especially the pony, which is closer to Nature, is not really at home in a stable or in the life he has to lead serving man's needs and commands. It is not natural for him to be covered with rugs, or to sleep under a roof, or to eat at regular intervals, or to gallop violently after a fox, or to 'fly through the air with the greatest of ease' in the show ring, or to beat long-distance records, or carry heavy weights on his back-although, when we come to examine his anatomy, it will really seem that he was made with that purpose in view. The point is, however, that, if the horse is left alone to live its own life in a wild state, it will do none of these things. It is not the least bit interested in jumping for its own sake, nor in beating records, and its first reaction to a weight on its back is often quite lively. The things we do to the horse in its domesticated life, in the management of its food and so on, are more or less the opposite of what it would do on its own, and are designed to balance and compensate for the things it has lost.

RULES OF THE GAME

In addition to the specific regulations for the various equestrian sports included in this section (dressage, showjumping and three-day event) there are a number of general rules applicable to horses and riders taking part at international level in all sports under the jurisdiction of the FEI.

Horses must be registered with a National Federation, which keeps a record of any change of ownership as well as other information.

Horses are in one of three categories - Competition, International Competition, or International Champion horses - according to the major competitions in which they have competed or been placed. A horse that has reached a higher category cannot then return to a lower one.

Some events are restricted to Competition

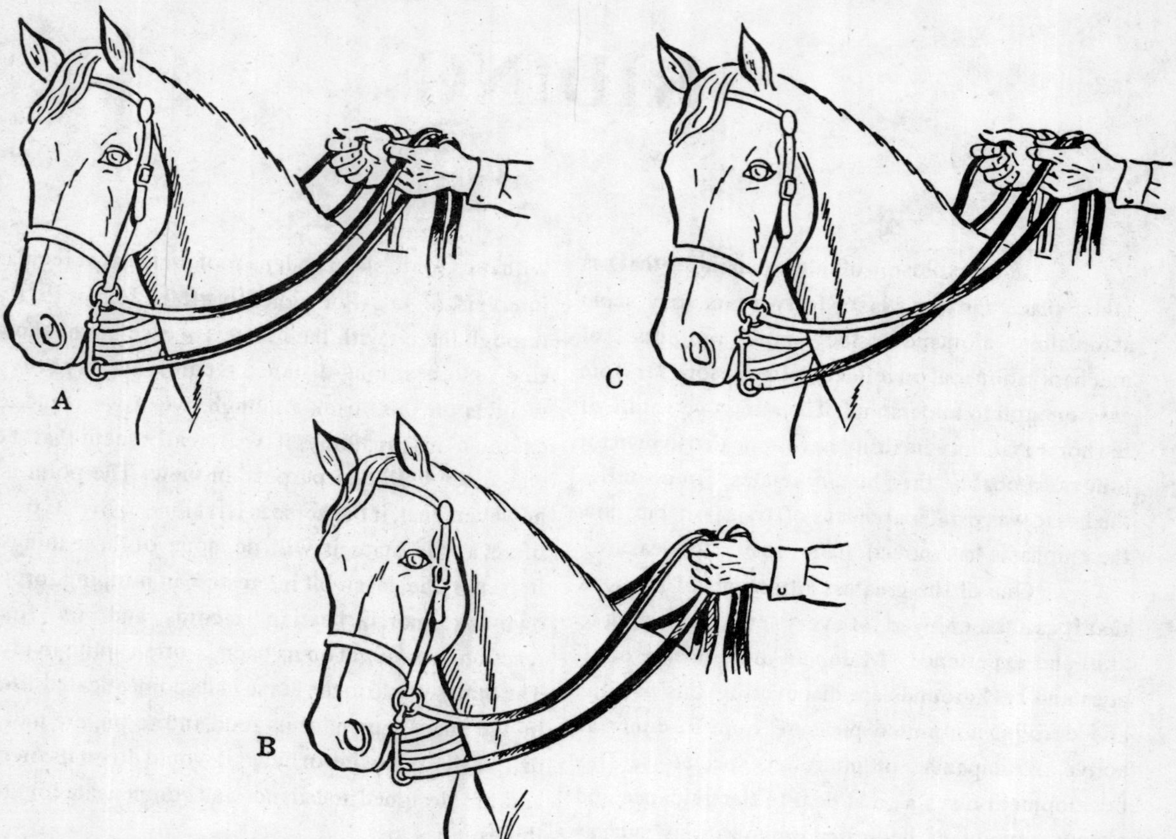

A. Correct method of holding reins of a Weymouth or Pelham bridle
B. Correct method of using reins of a Weymouth or Pelham bridle for efficient use in training.
C. Incorrect and inefficient method of using reins of Weymouth or Pelham bridle with one hand.
the purpose for which two bits are intended. Such method defeats

horses, or to Competition and International Competition horses. Championships, Official International Competitions, and Regional and Olympic Games are open to all categories of horses.

In Olympic Games, horses must have rider of the same nationality as the owner.

Riders in international competitions must be officially entered by their National Federation, and must be in possession of either an amateur or a professional license from that National Federation, according to their status.

Only amateurs may take part in Championship and Official International competitions for dressage and three-day event, and in dressage, show jumping, and three-day event competitions at Olympic Games. National teams for Official International jumping competitions and Championships may include professionals.

All juniors under 18 are classified as amateurs. Riders in Senior competitions should be over 18 years of age.

There are separate competitions for Juniors, aged 14 to 18, and for Young Riders aged 16 to 21. Riders under 18 may not take part in both Junior and Young Riders' events in the same discipline in the same year. Riders aged from 18 to 21 may not

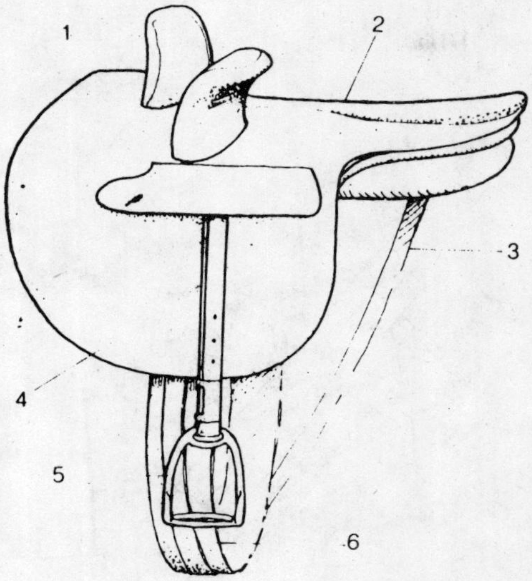

1 Pommels; 2 Seat; 3 Balance strap;
4 Stirrup leather; 5 Stirrup iron; 6 Girth

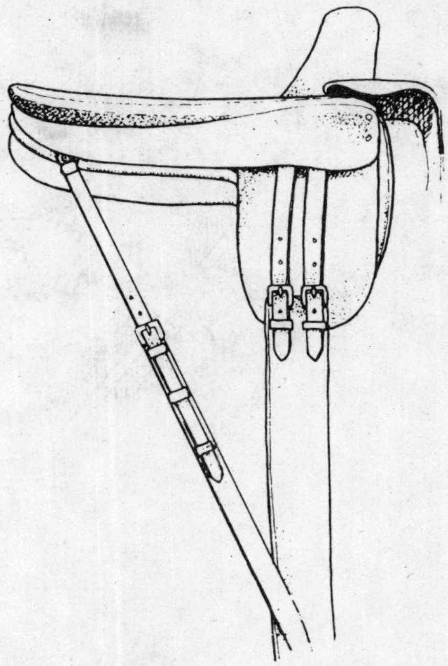

The side-saddle from the off side, showing the balance strap in position.

The rider's position at halt.

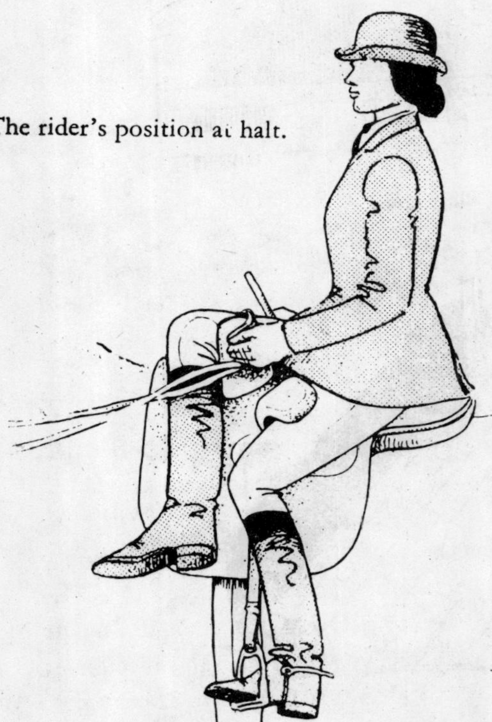

take part in both Young Riders' and Senior events in the same year in the same discipline.

RULES OF THREE-DAY EVENT

The three-day event consists of three distinct equestrian competitions-

(1) dressage
(2) endurance and
(3) show jumping

The different competitions are held on consecutive days,and each competitor must ride the same horse throughout. The event is designed to test the harmonious development,speed,endurance, obedience, and jumping ability of the horse, and requires excellent understanding between horse and rider.

Event Categories - Major international three-day events are categorized as follows (a)At a CCI (Concours Complet International) there may be an individual and a team classification,but

Water jump

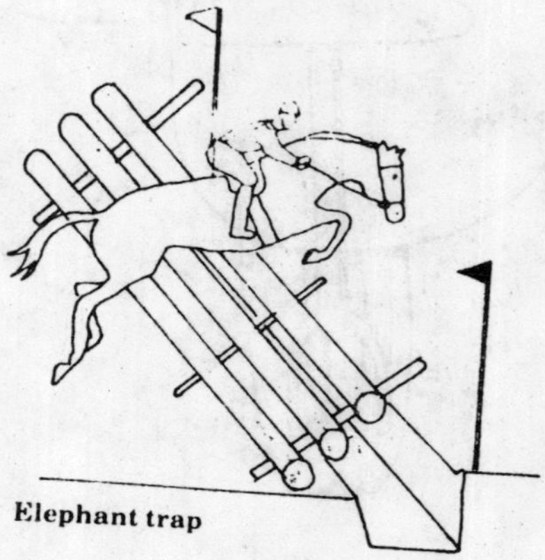

Elephant trap

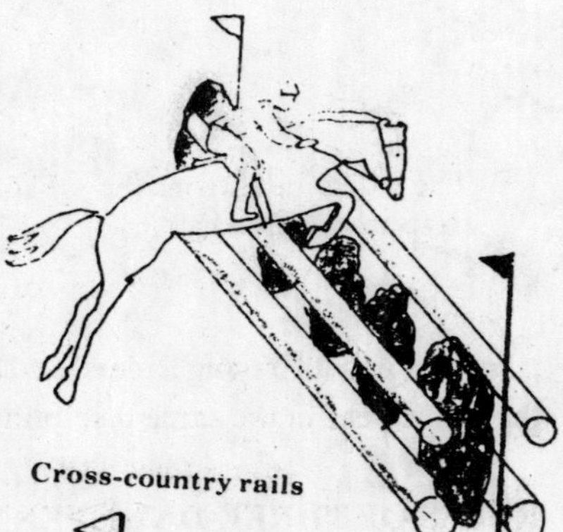

Cross-country rails

Plain fence

Lane crossing

event's three competitions is as close as possible to the ratio: dressage 3: endurance 12: jumping 1. A multiplying factor is used to adjust the relative influence of the dressage:the factor to be used ,which must be between 0.5 and 1.5, is flexible by the technical delegate (at CCIOs) or the ground jury (at CCIs) after an inspection of the endurance course and before the start of the dressage competition.

Horses must conform with general rules for equestrian events, and must be at least six years old. At CCIOs horses must be ridden by competitors of the same nationality as their owners.

A competitor must ride the same horse in all three stages of the event. If competitors are allowed to enter more than one horse, the horse nominated for the team classification must always be ridden first.

Horses are inspected for fitness before the dressage competition,between phases C and D of the endurance competition, and before the jumping competition. Any horse that is found to be unfit at an inspection is eliminated without right of appeal.

Riders may compete as an individual or as a member of a team. A team usually consists of four members, but only the best three results are considered for the final classification. If a team of three is allowed to enter, all three competitors must compete the event and all three results are counted.

Officials : A ground jury of three members judges the dressage and show jumping, and

only the individual classification is recognized by the FEI. An FEI technical delegate may be appointed. (b) At a CICO (Concours Complet Internatinal Officiel) there must be official FEI individual and team classifications. Each nation may enter only one team, and there must be at least three teams competing. An FEI technical delegate must be appointed to approve the course and conditions.

(All the laws described here as relating to CCIOs also refer to Olympic events.)

Competition Ratio : Courses and conditions are arranged so that the relative influence of the

supervises all arrangements for the judging and timing of the endurance competition. The ground jury and a veterinary official check that horses are fit to participate. At CCOs without an FEI technical delegate, the ground jury is also responsible for approving the endurance course.

Dress requirements are different for the three competitions.

For the dressage competition, civilians must wear hunting dress or a riding club uniform, white shirt and tie,white or fawn breeches, a hunting cap or top hat, gloves and black boots. Service members must wear service uniform with regulation headgear. Normal blunt spurs are compulsory for all competitors.

For the endurance competition, lightweight clothing is considered appropriate. Protective headgear secured by a chinstrap is compulsory, as are boots.

For the jumping competition, dress for civilians and service members is as for the dressage except that top hats are not worn, and spurs are optional.

Saddlery for the dressage competition, a double bridle or a snaffle, and an English saddle are compulsory. Martingales, blinkers, bandages, and any kind of gadgets (such as bearing, side, running, or balancing reins) are all forbidden.For the endurance and jumping competitions,saddlery is optional except that blinkers and hoods are forbidden. Only running unrestricted martingales are permitted. Any rein must be attached to the bit or bits but gags and hackamores are allowed.

Whips may not be weighed and must not

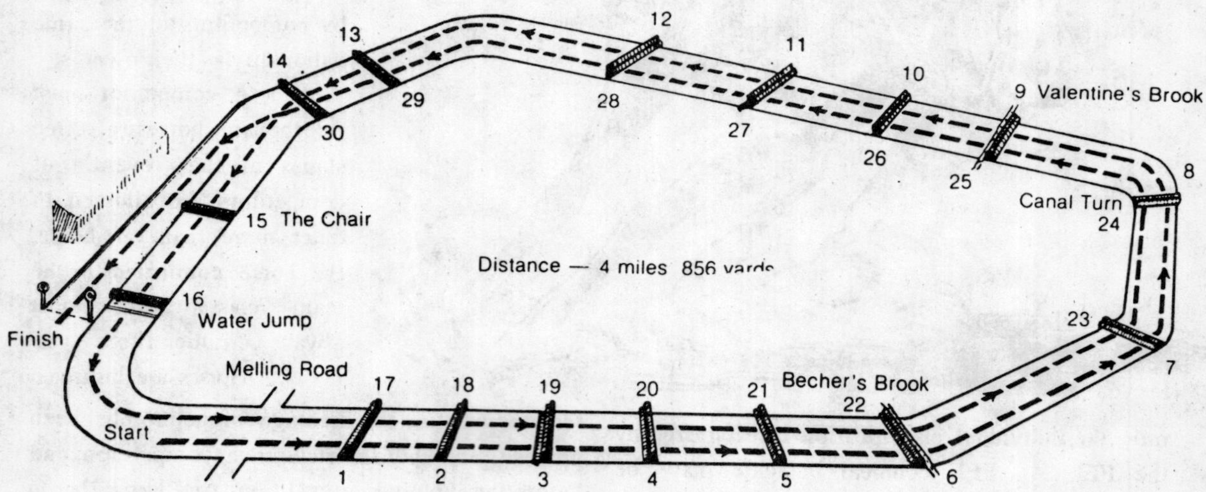

The Grand National Course at Liverpool (Aintree) as it is today.

Height of fences

No. 1 & 17 - 4 ft 6in. fence
No. 2 & 18 - 4 ft 7 in. fence
No. 3 & 19 - Open ditch - ditch 6 ft, fence 5 ft
No. 4 & 20 - 4 ft 10 in. fence
No. 5 & 21 - 5 ft fence
No. 6 & 22 - 'Bechers Brook' - 4 ft 10 in. fence, 5 ft 6in. brook with drop
No. 7 & 23 - 4 ft fence at angle
No. 8 & 24 - 5 ft fence
No. 9 & 25 - 'Valentine's Brook' - 5 ft fence, 5 ft 6in. brook
No. 10 & 26 - 5 ft fence
No. 11 & 27 - Open ditch - 6 ft ditch, 5 ft fence
No. 12 & 28 - 5 ft fence followed by 5 ft 6 in. ditch
No. 13 & 29 - 4 ft 7 in. fence
No. 14 & 30 - 4 ft 6 in. fence
No. 15 - 'The Chair' - Open ditch - 6 ft; fence - 5 ft 2 in.
No. 16 - 'The Water Jump' - 12 ft 6 in. (width) × 2 ft 6 in. (depth)

exceed 75cm in length.

Weight : There is no minimum weight for the dressage competition. For the endurance and show jumping competitions, a minimum weight of 75 kg must be carried.

Riders are weighed at the start and finish of the endurance competition and at the end of the jumping . If necessary riders are weighed with saddlery and equipment carried by the horse the bridle may be included only in finish weights. Whips must not be weighed.Failure to be weighed in front of the offical steward or dismounting before he gives the order results in elimination, as does failure to reach the minimum weight.

Schooling during the three days preceding the dressage competition and for the entire duration of the event, a horse may be schooled only by its normal competitor or by a team member or individual competitor from the same country. A groom is also permitted to school a horse but not when mounted.

Starting Order : The order of starting is determined by a draw. Starting order within a team is decided by the team captain.

Starting order is the same for all three competitions, except that where there is no team classification the organizing committee may order that competitors start in the jumping competition in the reverse order of their classification after the endurance competition.

Elimination from one competition means elimination from the entire event.

Scoring and Result : Scoring of all three competition is in penalty marks. Event classifications are obtained by adding together the penalty marks from each competition. The individual winner is the competitor with fewest penalty marks. In the case of a tie, the winner is the competitor with the best cross-country result. If there is still a tie, the best steeplechase result decides. In the final resort, a tie is broken in favor of the competitor whose cross-country time was closest to the optimum time.

The winning team is the team with fewest penalty marks after adding together the penalties incurred by its three best-placed riders. In the case of a tie, the event is won by the team whose third competitor had the best result.

CUP & TROPHIES

Gold In Olympics

Grand Prix (Jumping)

1900 Aime Haegeman (Bel), Benton II
1912 Jean Carious (Fra) 186 pts, Mignon
1920 Tommaso Lequio (Ita) 2 faults, Trebecco
1924 Alphonse Gemuseus (Sui) 6 faults, Lucette
1928 Frantisek Venture (Tch)no faults, Eliot
1932 Takeichi Nishi (Jpn) 8pts, Uranus
1936 Kurt Hasse (Ger) 4 faults, Tora
1948 Humberto Mariles Cortes (Mex) 6.25 faults
1952 Pierre Jonqueres d'Inzeo (Ita) 12 faults, Posillipo
1956 Hans Gunter Winkler (Ger) 4 faults, Halla
1960 Raimondo d'Inzeo (Ita) 12 faults, Posillipo
1964 Pierre Jonqueres d'Oriola (Fra) 9 faults, Lutteur
1968 William Steinkraus (USA) 4 faults, Snowbound
1972 Graziano Mancinelli (Ita) 8 faults, Ambassador
1976 Alwin Schockemohle (FRG) no faults, Warwick Rex
1980 Jen Kowalczyk (Pol) 8 faults), Artemor
1984 Joe Fargis (UUA) 4 faults, Touch of Class
1988 Pierre Durand (Fra)

Grand Prix (Jumping) Team

1912	Sweden 545 pts
1920	Sweden 14 faults
1924	Sweden 42.25 pts
1928	Spain 4 faults
1932	Not held
1936	Germany 44 faults
1948	Mexico 34.25 faults
1952	UK 40.75 faults
1956	Germany 40 faults
1960	Germany 46.50 faults
1964	Germany 68.50 faults
1968	Canada 102.75 faults
1972	FRG 32 faults
1976	France 40 faults

1980 USSR 16 faults
1984 USA 12 faults
1988 Germany

Grand Prix (Dressage)

1912 Carl Bonde (Swe) 15pts, Emperor
1920 Janne Lundblad (Swe)27.237 pts, Uno
1924 Ernst Linder (Swe) 276.4 pts, Piccolo-mini
1928 Carl von Langen (Ger) 237.42pts, Draufaganger
1932 Xavier Lesage (Fra) 1031.25pts, Taine
1936 Heinz Pollay (Ger) 1760 pts, Krones
1948 Hans Moser (Sui) 492.5 pts, Kummer
1952 Henri St Cyr (Swe) 561 pts, Master Rufus
1956 Henri St Cyr (Swe) 860 pts, Juli
1960 Sergey Filatov (USSR) 2144 pts, Absent
1964 Henri Chammartin (Sui) 1504 pts, Woermann
1968 Ivan Kizimov (USSR) 1572 pts, Ikhov
1972 Liselott Linsehoff (FRG) 1229 pts, Piaff
1976 Chistine Stuckelberger (Sui) 1486 pts, Granat
1980 Elisabeth Theurer (Aut) 1370 pts, Mon Cherie
1984 Reiner Klimke (FRG) 1504 pts, Ahlerich
1988 Nicole Uphoff (W.Ger)

Grand Prix (Dressage) Team

1928 Germany 669.72 pts
1932 France 2818.75 pts
1936 Germany 5074 pts
1948 France 1269 pts
1952 Sweden 1597.5 pts
1956 Sweden 2475 pts
1960 Not held
1964 Germany 2558 pts
1968 FRG 2699 pts
1972 USSR 5095 pts
1976 FRG 5155 pts
1980 USSR 4383 pts
1984 FRG 4955 pts
1988 Germany

Three-day Event

1912 Axel Nordlander (Swe) 46.59pts, Lady Artist
1920 Helmer Morner (Swe) 1775 pts, Germania
1924 Adolph van der Voort van Zijp (Hol)1976 pts Silver Piece
1928 Charles Pahud de Mortanges (Hol) 1969.82 pts, Marcroix
1932 Charles Pahud de Mortanges (Hol) 1813.83pts, Marcroix
1936 Ludwig Stubbendorff (Ger) 37.7 faults, Nurmi
1948 Bernard Chevallier (Fra) + 4pts, Aiglonne
1952 Hans von Blixen-Finecke (Swe) 28.33 faults, Jubal
1956 Petrus Kastenman (Swe) 66.53 faults, Iluster
1960 Lawrence Morgan (Aus)+ 7.15 pts, Salad Days
1964 Mauro Checcoli (Ita) 64.40 pts, Surbean
1968 Jean-Jacques Guyon (Fra) 38.86 pts, Pitou
1972 Richard Meade (UK) 57.73 pts, Laurieston
1976 Edmound Coffin (USA) 114.99 pts, Bally-Cor
1980 Federico Roman (Ita) 108.60 pts, Rossinan
1984 Mark Todd (NZL) 51.60 pts, Charisma
1988 Mark Todd (NZL), Charisma

Three Day Event Team

1912 Sweden 139.06 pts
1920 Sweden 5057.5 pts
1924 Netherlands 5297.5 pts
1928 Netherlands 5865.68 pts
1932 USA 5038.08 pts
1936 Germany 676.75 pts
1948 United States 161.50 faults
1952 Sweden 221.49 pts
1956 UK 355.48 pts
1960 Australia 128.18 pts
1964 Italy 85.80 pts
1968 UK 175.95 pts
1972 UK 95.53 pts
1976 USA 441.00 pts
1980 USSR 457.00 pts
1984 USA 186.00 pts
1988 W.Germany d.n.a.

WORLD CHAMPIONSHIPS

Show Jumping (Men)

1953 F.Goyoago (Spa)
1954 H.G.Winkler (Frg)
1955 H.G.Winkler (Frg)
1956 R.d'Inzeo (Ita)
1960 P.d'Inzeo (Ita)

1966	P.d'Oriola (Fra)
1970	D.Broome (UK)
1974	H.Steenken (Frg)
1978	G.Wiltfang (Frg)
1982	N.Koof (Frg)
1986	G.Greenhough (Can)

Women

1965	M.Coakes (UK)
1970	J.Lefebvre (Fra)
1974	J.Lefebvre-Tissot (Fra)

Team

1978	Great Britain
1982	France
1986	United States

Three-day Event

Individual

1966	C.Moratorio (Arg)
1970	M.Gordon-Watson (UK)
1974	B.Davidson (USA)
1978	B.Davidson (USA)
1982	L.Green (UK)
1986	V.Leng (UK)

Team

1966	Ireland
1970	Great Britain
1974	United States
1978	Canada
1982	Great Britain
1986	Great Britain

Dressage

Individual

1966	J.Neckarmann (FRG)
1970	E.Petouchkova (USSR)
1974	R.Klimke (FRG)
1978	C.Stuckelberger (Swi)
1982	R.Klimke (FRG)
1986	A.Jensen (FRG)

Team

1966	West Germany
1970	USSR
1974	West Germany
1978	West Germany
1982	West Germany
1986	West Germany

EUROPEAN SHOW JUMPING CHAMPIONSHIPS

Men

1957	H.G.Winkler (FRG)
1958	F.Thiedemann (FRG)
1959	P.d'Inzeo (Ita)
1961	D.Broome (UK)
1962	C.D.Barker (UK)
1963	G.Mancinelli (Ita)
1965	H.Schridde (FRG)
1966	N.Pessoa (Bra)
1967	D.Broome (UK)
1969	D.Broome (UK)
1971	H.Steenken (FRG)
1973	P.McMahon (UK)
1975	A.Schockemohle (FRG)
1977	J.Heins (Hol)
1979	G.Wiltfang (FRG)
1981	P.Schockemohle (FRG)
1983	P.Schockemohle (FRG)
1985	P.Schockemohle (FRG)

BADMINTON HORSE TRIALS

1949	J.Shedden (UK)
1950	Capt. J.A.Collings (UK)
1951	Capt. H.Schwarzenbach (Swi)
1952	Capt. M.A.Darley (UK)
1953	Maj. L.Rook (UK)
1954	M.Hough (UK)
1955	Maj.F.W.C.Weldon (UK)
1956	Majj. F.W.C.Weldon (UK)
1957	S.Willcox (UK)
1958	S.Willcox (UK)
1959	S.Waddington-Willcox (UK)
1960	W.Roycroft (Aus)
1961	L.Morgan (Aus)
1962	A.Drummond-Hay (UK)

1963	S.Fleet (UK)
1964	Capt.J.R.Templer (UK)
1965	Maj.E.A.Boylan (Ire)
1966	Not held
1967	C.Ross-Taylor (UK)
1968	J.Bullen (UK)
1969	R.Walker (UK)
1970	R.Made (UK)
1971	Lt M.Phillips (UK)
1972	Lt.M.Phillips (UK)
1973	L.Prior-Palmer (UK)
1974	Capt.M.Phillips (UK)
1975	Cancelled after dressage
1976	L.Prior-Palmer (UK)
1977	L.Prior-Palmer (UK)
1978	J.Holderness-Roddam (UK)
1979	L.Prior-Palmer (UK)
1980	M.Todd (NZ)
1981	Capt.M.Phillips (UK)
1982	R.Meade (UK)
1983	L.Green (UK)
1984	L.Green (UK)
1985	V.Holgate (UK)
1986	I.Stark (UK)
1987	Not held

ARJUN AWARD WINNERS

1973	Dafadar Khan Mohammad Khan
1976	H.S. Sodhi
1982	Rapinder Singh Brar
	Raghubir Singh
1984	Ghulam Mohd. Khan
1987	Jitendarjit Singh Ahluwalia

ROWING

In ancient times, rowing was the chief means of propelling vessels of war. With the increase in size of vessels, oars were replaced by sails. The first English regatta took place on the Thames in 1775. Rowing is now confined almost entirely to small boats. Rowing is the propulsion of a boat by means of oars in a succession of strokes. In rowing, the oarsman seated on thwart, faces the stern and pulls the oar handle towards his body. The sport has two forms, rowing and sculling, though for convenience both come under the generic title of rowing. The main distinction is that the rower has one oar whereas the sculler has two sculls. Rowing events are for coxed and coxless pairs, coxed and coxless fours and eights which by necessity, are coxed. Sculling events are the single, double and quadruple sculls. In Olympic, World Championships and the other international regattas, events are contested in lanes over standard FISA distances of 2000m for men, 1500m for junior men (under 18) and 1000m for women. Heats are usually held, with a repechage system operating to produce the required finalists. Other forms of rowing that have achieved popularity are head of the river races, bumps and coastal rowing.

The Rowing Terminology:

The first thing to master when learning to row is the terminology of boat,oar and gear as well as the various words of command and other phrases that will be used by the coach and cox. Both the terminology of the equipment and the commands used in the boat are there for a specific purpose; to enable exact instructions to be given succinctly, not to fool the oarsman or to impress the layman with esoteric words. A command of these special words and terms is essential.

The boat is usually wooden, about 60 ft. long in the case of an eight, and only 2 ft. wide at its greatest beam. The forward end is the bow and the rear the stern and to the latter is attached the rudder on older boats. To provide the necessary keel area to prevent the boat skidding on corners there is a small fin mounted underneath the boat just to the rear of the cox's seat; on newer boats the rudder is frequently hinged on the rear edge of this fin.

The crew compartment of the boat is naturally open,but the boat is kept buoyant by covered areas at bow and stern,known as canvasses. The seat nearest the bow is called bow, the next one down towards the stern's' and so on until you reach the eighth seat,known as stroke. Just to the sternward of stroke sits the cox.(On smaller boats there are obviously fewer numbers between bow and stroke and sometimes no cox.)

Round the crew compartment runs a raised coaming, known as the breakwater in front of bow, and saxboard the rest of the way round. Through the saxboard are bolted the riggeıs, the outriggers that carry the rowlock or swivel, a rotatable device through which goes the other. After the oar has been dropped into the swivel, the latter's top is closed by the gate to prevent the oar jumping out. The whole swivel/gate combination is often called just the gate and can be adjusted backwards and forwards, as well as up and down, to alter the gearing of the oar and the height at which its work is transmitted to the boat via the rigger.

Each oarsman sits on a sliding seat, which moves on a wheeled trolley up and down a pair of parallel runners between 28 and 32 in. long. There is a front stop and back stop to prevent the seat coming off the runners at either end. The sliding seat is

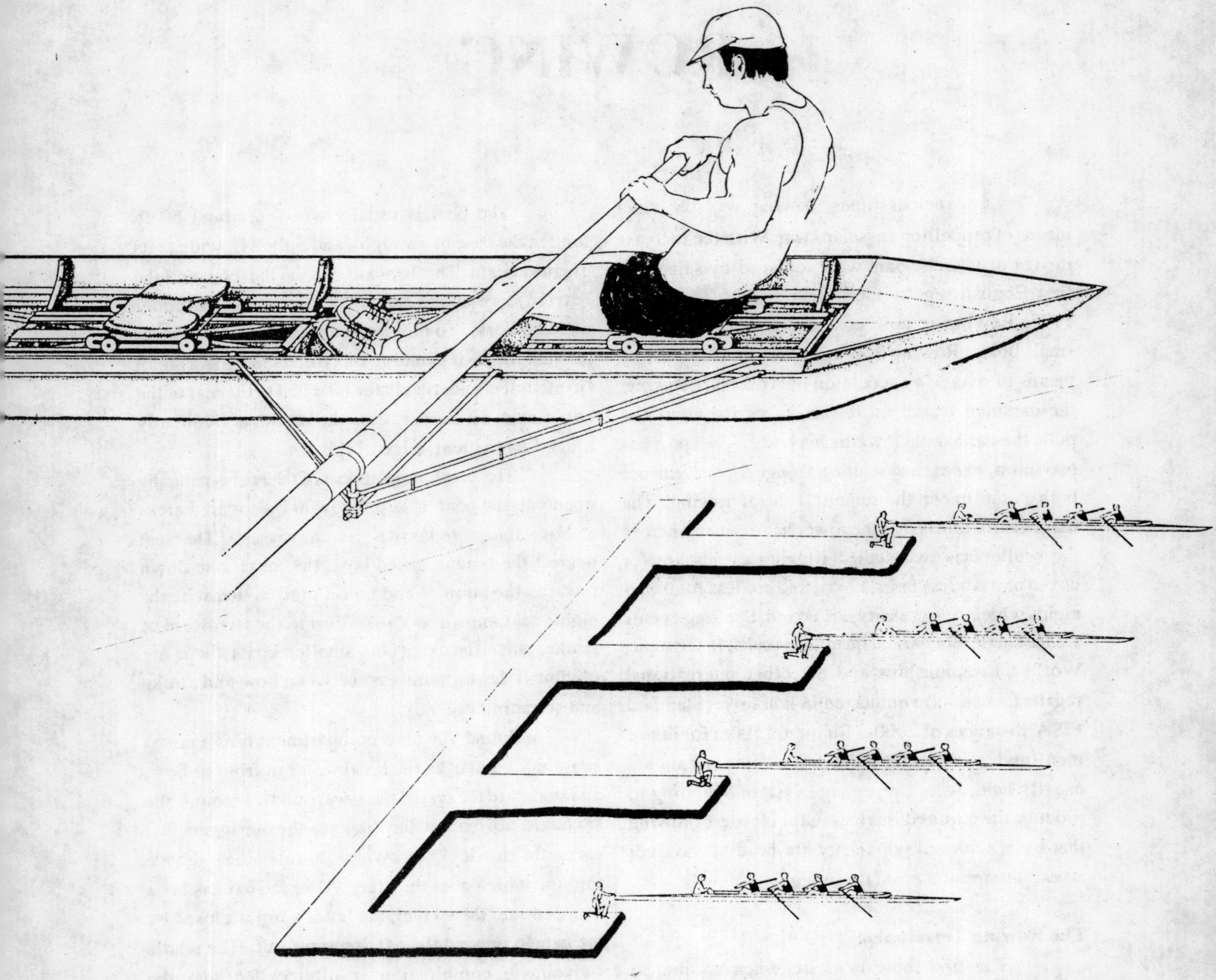

necessary to allow each oarsman to use his legs to full effect by pushing away from the front position. The portion of the runners that extends towards the rear of the boat, past a line drawn perpendicularly through the long axis of the boat and the hole pin of the gate, is described as 'forward of the work',and boats which have 4 in so prejecting and described as having their seats 'going 4 in through the work'.

While the oarsman can travel up and down the runners on his seat,his position in the boat is fixed by his feet,which rest in clogs on the stretcher, a wooden frame attached as its base to the internal keel of the boat and at top on each side to the lower edges of the saxboard.This stretcher is adjustable so that each oarsman may set the position of his feet at which fully bent legs allow the seat almost to touch the frontstop of the runners.

All the crew with the exception of the cox face the stern with their oars arranged alternately to bowside or strokeside.Bow usually sits with his oar out to his left, with the oars of numbers 3,5 and 7 on the same side. These four man are thus normally the bowside oarsmen, on the other side are 2,4,6 and stroke himself.

This leaves the oar itself, which is usually about 12 ft.3 in. long, and made of wood. The inboard end, the handle which the oarsman holds, is unvarnished and shaved down to provide a good handfold. Where the oar goes through the gate there is leather or plastic sheath round the oar to prevent it getting worn and a button or collar round the oar to prevent it slipping down through the gate. Outboard of the gate is the shaft or loom of the oar and finally the blade itself, which can be of various shapes and areas depending on factors such as the weight of the crew, the length of the race and other considerations. The gearing of the oar(or blade as it is commonly called) obviously depends on the position of the button (which is usually about 3 ft.9 in. from the inboard end of the handle) and the overall length of the oar.

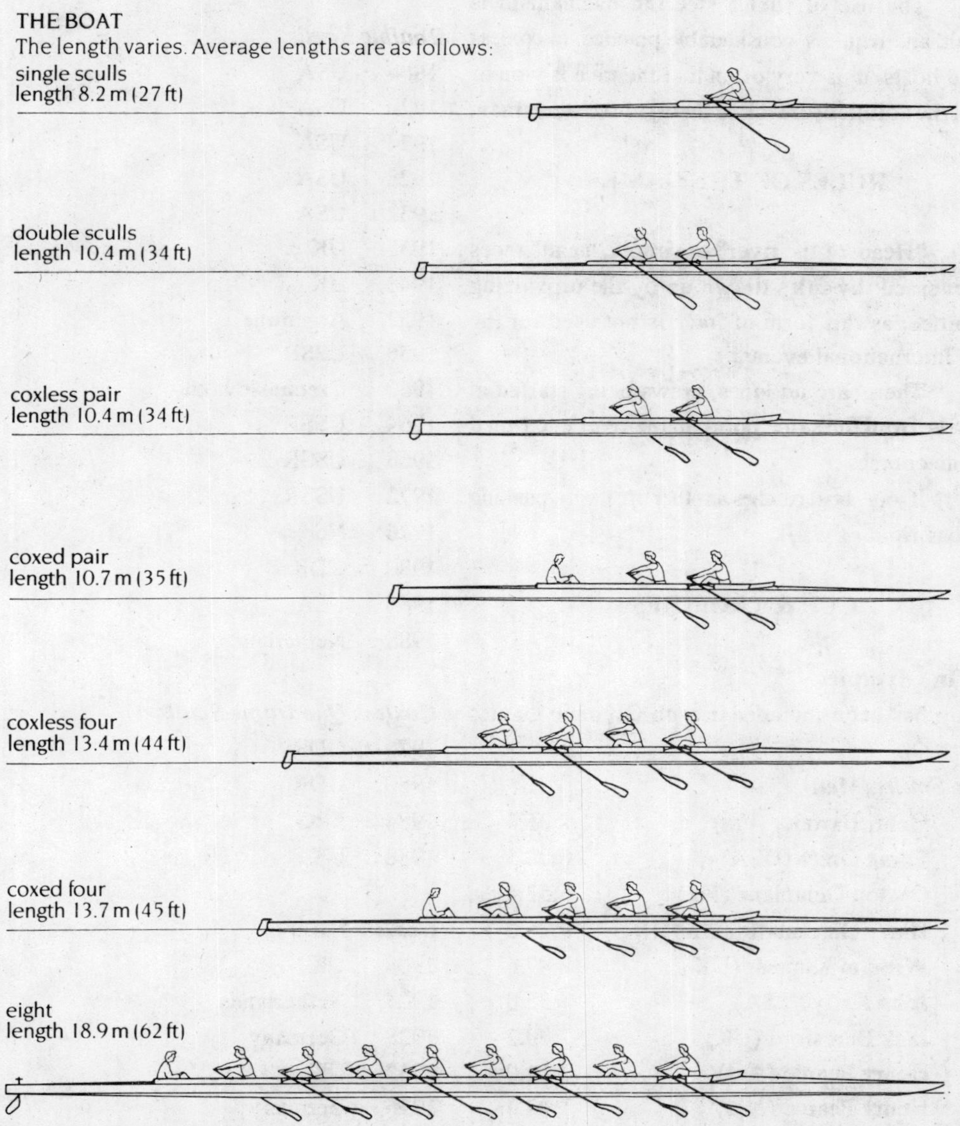

When do you steer with your feet?

Oared boats are steered in one of two ways. If coxed, the rudder is moved by strings or wires operated directly by the cox itself; if coxless, a special stretcher is provided for one of the crew. This has one clog hinged near the heel so that the wearer may move its toe to the left or right. To the toe are connected wires that run via a series of pulleys to the rudder, the wires being crossed once so that when the steerer wishes the boat to go to his right he merely moves his foot to the right and the wires move the rudder in the correct direction.

The use of such a steering mechanism is difficult, and requires considerable practice. In coxless steered boats it is very often that the race is won or lost on the abilities (or lack of them) of the steersman.

RULES OF THE GAME

"Head of the river" or simply "head" races are governed by rules drawn up by the organizing committee, as this form of race is not used for the major international events.

There are no lanes, crews being started at intervals from the same point on the river and timed over the course.

If one boat catches another up, the overtaking boat has right of way.

CUP & TROPHIES

Gold In Olympics

Rowing has been included in each Olympic Games since 1900.

Single Sculls (Men)

1900	Henri Barrelet (Fra)	7:35.6
1904	Frank Greer (USA)	10:08.5
1906	Gaston Delaplane (Fra)	5:53.4
1908	Harry Blackstaffe (UK)	9:26.0
1912	William Kinnear (UK)	7:47.6
1920	John Kelly (USA)	7:35.0
1924	Jack Beresford (UK)	7:49.2
1928	Henry Pearce (Aus)	7:11.0
1932	Henry Pearce (Aus)	7:44.4
1936	Gustav Schafer (Ger)	8:21.5
1948	Mervyn Wood (Aus)	7:24.4
1952	Yuriy TYukalov (USSR)	8:12.8
1956	Vyacheslav Ivanov (USSR)	8:02.5
1960	Vyacheslav Ivanov (USSR)	7:13.96
1964	Vyacheslav Ivanov (USSR)	8:22.51
1968	Henri Jan Wienese (Hol)	7:47.80
1972	Yuriy Malishev (USSR)	7:10.12
1976	Pertti Karppinen (Fin)	7:29.03
1980	Pertti Karppinen (Fin)	7:09.61
1984	Pertti Karppinen (Fin)	7:00.24
1988	Thomas Lange (E.Ger)	6:49.86

Double Sculls

1904	USA	10:03.2
1920	USA	7:09.0
1924	USA	7:45.0
1928	USA	6:61.4
1932	USA	7:17.4
1936	UK	7:20.8
1948	UK	6:51.3
1952	Argentina	7:32.2
1956	USSR	7:24.0
1960	Czechoslovakia	6:47.50
1964	USSR	7:10.66
1968	USSR	6:51.82
1972	USSR	7:01.77
1976	Norway	7:13.20
1980	GDR	6:24.33
1984	USA	6:36.87
1988	Netherlands	6:21.13

Coxless Quadruple Sculls

1976	GDR	6:18.65
1980	GDR	5:49.81
1984	FRG	5:57.55
1988	UK	6:36.84

Coxless Pairs

1908	UK	9:41.0
1924	Netherlands	8:19.4
1928	Germany	7:06.4
1932	UK	8:00.0
1936	Germany	8:16.1

1948	UK	7:21.1
1952	USA	8:20.7
1956	USA	7:55.4
1960	USSR	7:02.1
1964	Canada	7:32.94
1968	GDR	7:26.56
1972	GDR	6:53.16
1976	GDR	7:23.31
1980	GDR	6:48.01
1984	Romania	6:45.39
1988	Italy	6:58.79

Coxed Pairs

1900	Netherlands	7:34.2
1904	Italy	14:23.0
1906	Italy	7:32.4
1920	Italy	7:56.0
1924	Switzerland	8:39.0
1928	Switzerland	7:42.6
1932	USA	8:25.8
1936	Germany	--
1948	Denmark	8:00.5
1952	France	8:28.6
1956	USA	8:26.1
1960	Germany	7:29.14
1964	USA	8:21.23
1968	Italy	8:04.81
1972	GDR	7:17.25
1976	GDR	7:58.99
1980	GDR	7:02.54
1984	Italy	7:05.99
1988	Not held	

Coxless Fours

1904	USA	9:53.8
1908	UK	8:34.0
1924	UK	7:08.6
1928	UK	6:36.0
1932	UK	6:58.2
1936	Germany	7:01.8
1948	Italy	6:39.0
1952	Yugoslavia	7:16.0
1956	Canada	7:08.8
1960	USA	6:26.26
1964	Denmark	6:59.30
1968	GDR	6:39.18
1972	GDR	6:24.27
1976	GDR	6:37.42
1980	GDR	6:08.17
1984	New Zealand	6:03.48
1988	E. Germany	6:03.11

Coxed Fours

1900	Germany	5:59.0
	France	7:11.0
1906	Italy	8:13.0
1912	Germany	6:59.4
1920	Switzerland	6:54.0
1924	Switzerland	7:18.4
1928	Italy	6:47.8
1932	Germany	7:19.0
1936	Germany	7:16.2
1948	USA	6:50.30
1952	Czechoslovakia	7:33.4
1956	Italy	7:19.4
1960	Germany	6:39.12
1964	Germany	7:00.44
1968	New Zealand	6:45.62
1972	FRG	6:31.85
1976	USSR	6:40.22
1980	GDR	6:14.51
1984	UK	6:20.28
1988	E. Germany	6:10.74

Eights

1900	USA	6:09.8
1904	USA	7:50.0
1908	UK	7:52.0
1912	UK	6:15.0
1920	USA	6:02.6
1924	USA	6:33.4
1928	USA	6:03.2
1932	USA	6:37.6
1936	USA	6:25.4
1948	USA	5:56.7
1952	USA	6:25.9
1956	USA	6:35.2
1960	Germany	5:57.18

1964	USA	6:18.23
1968	FRG	6:07.0
1972	New Zealand	6:08.94
1976	GDR	5:58.29
1980	GDR	5:49.05
1984	Canada	5:41.32
1988	W. Germany	5:46.05

World Championships (Men)

World Championships weie first held in 1962 at Lucerne and have subsequently been held in 1966,1970,1974,1975,1977,1978,1979, 1981, 1982, 1983, 1985 and 1986. Women'sWorld Championships were first held in 1974.

Single Sculls

1962	V.Ivanov (USSR)
1966	D.Spero (USA)
1970	A.Demiddi (Arg)
1974	W.Honig (GDR)
1975	P.M.Kolbe (FRG)
1977	J.Dreifke (GDR)
1978	P.M.Kolbe (FRG)
1979	P.Karppinen (Fin)
1981	P.M.Kolbe (FRG)
1982	R.Reiche (GDR)
1983	P.M.Kolbe (FRG)
1985	P.Karppinen (Fin)
1986	P.M.Kolbe (FRG)

Double Sculls

1962	France
1966	Switzerland
1970	Denmark
1974	East Germany
1975	Norway
1977	Great Britain
1978	Norway
1979	Norway
1981	East Germany
1982	Norway
1983	East Germany
1985	East Germany
1986	Italy

Coxless Pairs

1962	West Germany
1966	East Germany
1970	West Germany
1974	East Germany
1975	East Germany
1977	USSR
1978	East Germany
1979	East Germany
1981	USSR
1982	Norway
1983	East Germany
1985	USSR
1986	USSR

Coxed Pairs

1962	West Germany
1966	Holland
1970	Romania
1974	USSR
1975	East Germany
1977	Bulgaria
1978	East Germany
1979	East Germany
1981	Italy
1982	Italy
1983	East Germany
1985	Italy
1986	Great Britain

Coxed Fours

1962	West Germany
1966	East Germany
1970	West Germany
1974	East Germany
1975	USSR
1977	East Germany
1978	East Germany
1979	East Germany
1981	East Germany
1982	East Germany
1983	New Zealand
1985	USSR
1986	East Germany

Coxless Fours

1962	West Germany
1966	East Germany
1970	East Germany
1974	East Germany
1975	East Germany
1977	East Germany
1978	USSR
1979	East Germany
1981	USSR
1982	Switzerland
1983	West Germany
1985	West Germany
1986	United States

Quadruple Sculls

1974	East Germany
1978	East Germany
1979	East Germany
1981	East Germany
1982	East Germany
1983	West Germany
1985	Canada
1986	USSR

Eights

1962	West Germany
1966	West Germany
1970	East Germany
1974	United States
1975	East Germany
1977	East Germany
1978	East Germany
1979	East Germany
1981	USSR
1982	New Zealand
1983	New Zealand
1985	USSR
1986	Australia

Women

Single Sculls

1974	C.Scheiblich (GDR)
1975	C.Scheiblich (GDR)
1977	C.Scheiblich (GDR)
1978	C.Scheiblich-Hahn (GDR)
1979	S.Toma (Rom)
1981	S.Toma (Rom)
1982	I.Fetisova (USSR)
1983	J.Hampe (GDR)
1985	C.Linse (GDR)
1986	J.Hampe (GDR)

Double Sculls

1974	USSR
1975	USSR
1977	East Germany
1978	Bulgaria
1979	East Germany
1981	USSR
1982	USSR
1983	East Germany
1985	East Germany
1986	East Germany

Coxless Pairs

1974	Romania
1975	East Germany
1977	East Germany
1978	East Germany
1979	East Germany
1981	East Germany
1982	East Germany
1983	East Germany
1985	Romania
1986	Romania

Quadruple Sculls

1974	East Germany
1975	East Germany
1977	East Germany
1978	Bulgaria
1979	East Germany
1981	USSR
1982	USSR
1983	USSR
1985	East Germany
1986	East Germany

Coxed Fours

1974	East Germany
1975	East Germany
1977	East Germany
1978	East Germany
1979	USSR
1981	USSR
1982	USSR
1983	East Germany
1985	East Germany
1986	Romania

Eights

1974	East Germany
1975	East Germany
1977	East Germany
1978	USSR
1979	USSR
1981	USSR
1982	USSR
1983	USSR
1985	USSR
1986	USSR

ARJUN AWARD WINNERS

1983	Pravin Kumar Oberoy
1984	Mohd. Amin Naik

SHOOTING

The origin of target shooting dates back to the fourteenth century. The firearms used that time were crude having wooden barrels. Shooting competitions with sophisticated weapons in various parts of the world have been heldsincethe middle of the eighteenth century. The International Shooting Union (ISU) was formed in 1907. ISU conducts World Championships every four years.

An Olympic sport since the first modern Games in 1896, and theWorld Championshipssince 1897, target rifle shooting is today practiced under UIT rules at a 10-zone target over 11yd for air rifles, 55 yd for small-bore rifles, and 328yd for full-bore rifles. Shooting is three-positional, except in the case of air rifles and the small-bore English match. Away from international competition, however, the sport is enjoyed under the rules of individual national governing bodies, whose classes frequently derive from historical motives for the growth of rifle shooting. For example, in Britain, which had lagged behind Europe in the adoptionof the rifled gun, full-bore shooting developed under the auspices of the British NRA, formed in 1860 to fulfill a semi-military function: `.... the encouragement of Volunteer Rifle Corps and the promotion of rifle shooting ...', and in small bore under the auspices of the NSRA. Britain's empire followed the example of the motherland, and the close ties between the shooters of the British Commonwealth are epitomized by the attendance at the annual Imperial Prize Meeting at Bisley in

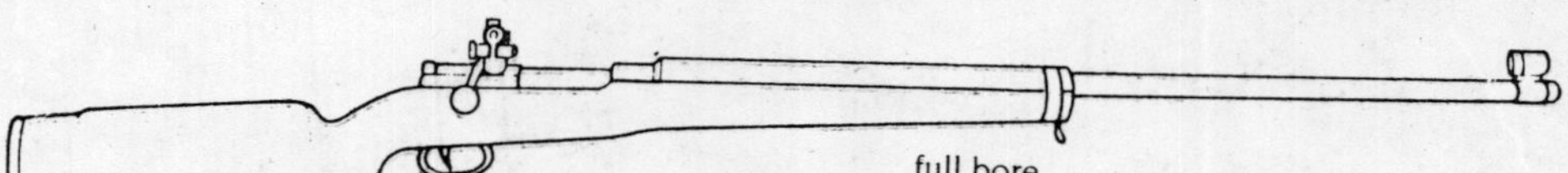

full bore

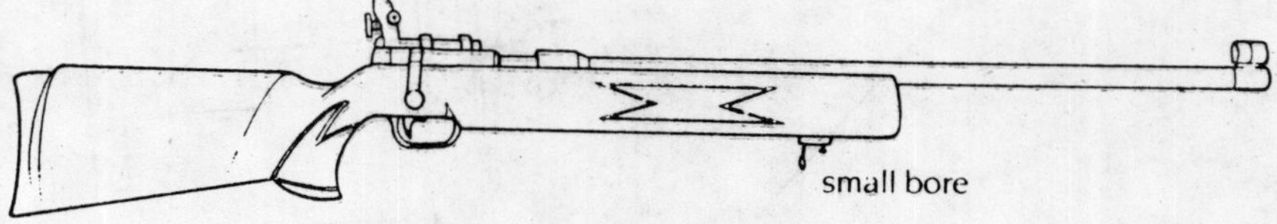

small bore

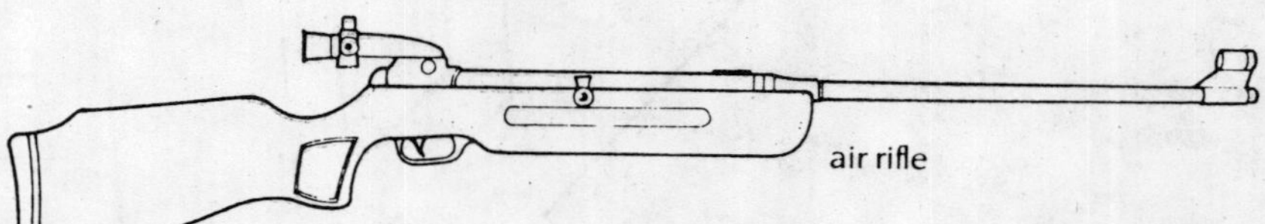

air rifle

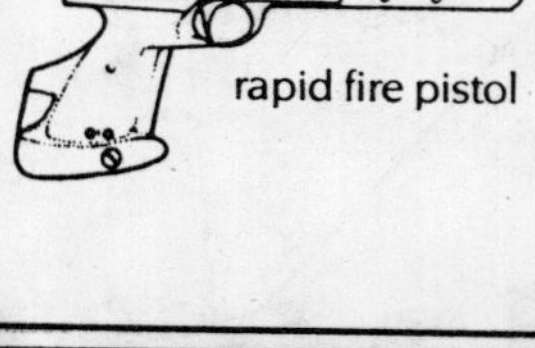

rapid fire pistol

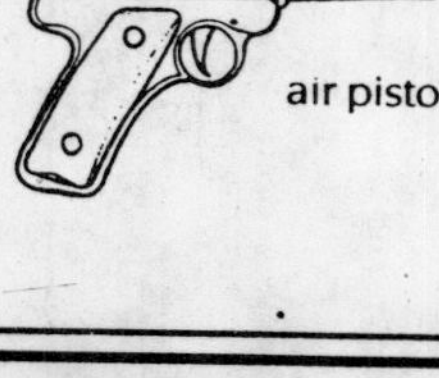

air pistol

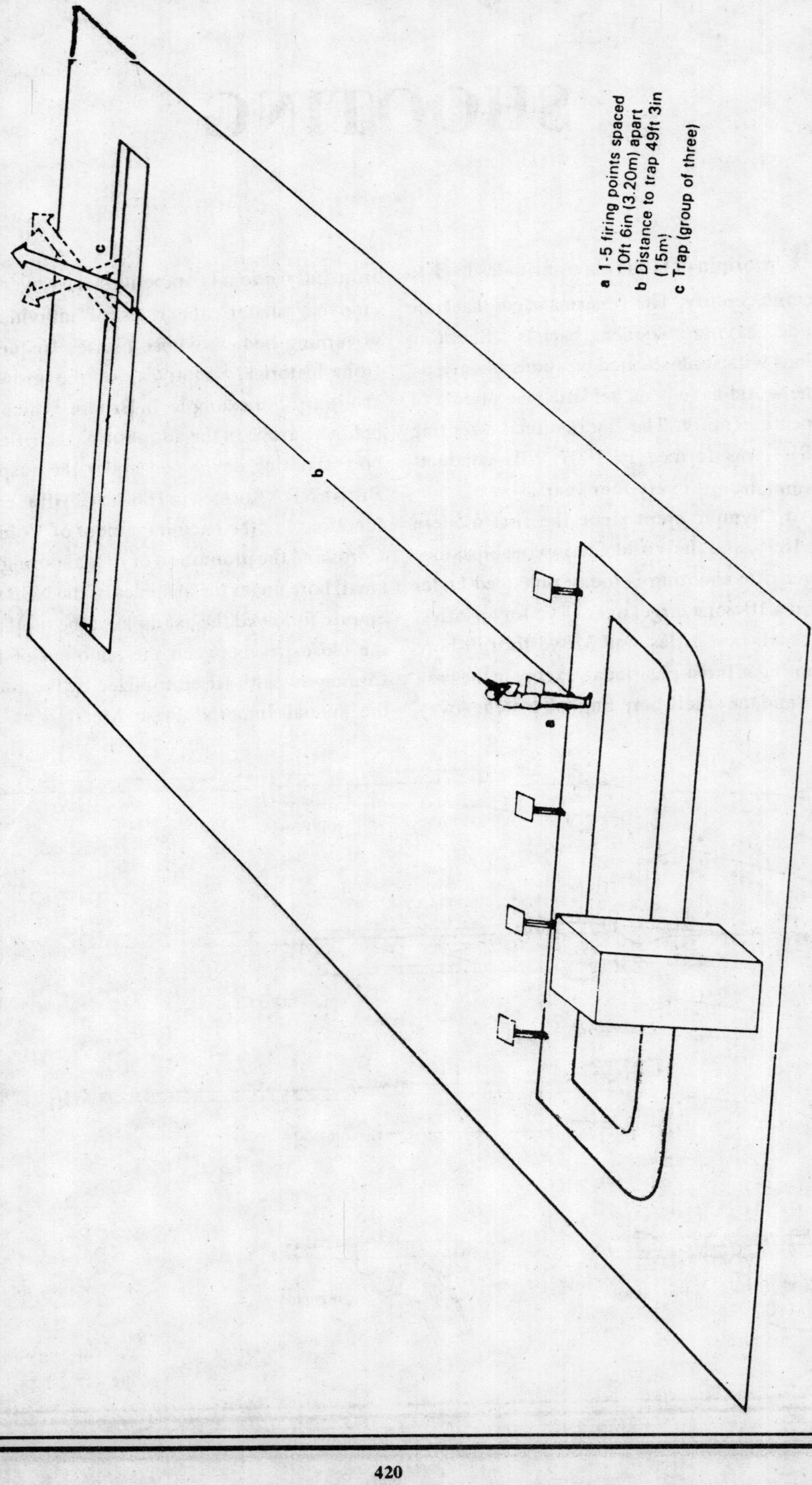
a 1-5 firing points spaced 10ft 6in (3.20m) apart
b Distance to trap 49ft 3in (15m)
c Trap (group of three)

Surrey.

There are ten different categories, varying from air pistol to rifle and for each category there are individual and pairs events.

In competitive shooting the following fireams are used:

(1) Pistol
(2) Rifle
(3) Shot gun

1- PISTOL SHOOTING

(i) Rapid-Fire Pistol

The competitor may use any type of pistol with a .22 calibre (abore of 5.6 mm). Sixty shots are fired over two days in four groups of 15 shots each. There are five targets at a range of 25 metres. The targets pop up one after another. One shot is made at each target each time. First time around the marksman has 8 seconds for his attempt; in the second series the time comes down to 6 seconds; and in the final series a mere4 seconds are allowed (that really is rapid firing). The maximum score is 600.

(ii) FreePistol

The weapon is similar to the rapid-fire pistol, i.e. 22 calibre, but the design of the pistol may be different.

Competitors fire at one target - the traditional bullseye with surrounding rings. Points' values range from 10 for the bull to 1 for the outer ring. Competitors have a maximum time of 2(½) hours to fire 60 shots at the target, which is 50 metres away. The bull is 5 cm in diameter and the maximum score is 600, i.e. 60 bulls.

(iii) Centre-Fire Pistol

This is an event for pistols of unlimited calibre. The marksmen fire at both fixed and turning targets at 25 metres. The turning target appears for 3 seconds in every 10. Sixty shots are fired, 30 at each target, and the maximum score is again 600.

(iv) Air Pistol

The target is set at 10 metres and 60 shots are fired, for a maximum600. The pistols work on a compressed-air basis.

2 - RIFLE SHOOTING

(i) Small-Bore Rifle Prone

The rifles have a maximum calibre of 5.6 mm. The marksman is in the prone position. A `bullseye' type of target is used, and 60 shots in all are fired at a range of 50 metres, giving a maximum score of 600. The time limit is 2 hours.

(ii) Small-Bore Rifle _ Three Positions

The rifles used are as above, and the target is similar, but the marksman fires from three positions - prone, kneeling on one knee, and standing. Forty shots are fired from each position. The target bullseye is just about the size of an English 1 p coin. As with other events there is 10 points for a bull, giving a possible maximum of 1200.

(iii) Full-Bore Rifle

This is the `heavy' of the armaments used in shooting. It is a large-calibre rifle (7.62 mm). Targets are set at 300, 500, 600, 900 and 1000 yards. In the first series competitors fire 7 shots each at 300, 500 and 600 yards; in the second series they fire 10 shots each at 300, 500 and 600 yards; and in the third series they fire 15 shots each at 900 and 1000 yards. That's 81 shots in all, scoring 5 for a bull, for a maximum of 405.

(iv) Air Rifle

A similar event to Air Pistol. The target is set at 10 metres and 60 shots are fired.

3- SHOTGUNS

(i) Olympic Trench

This is one of the clay-pigeon shooting disciplines. The targets are clay discs, released from a trap 15 metres away from the competitor. The marksman loads two catridges and on the command `Pull' the

Kneeling position

disc is released into the air. If the marksman misses with his first shot he is allowed to use the second cartridge (giving it both barrels!) 200 targets are released and a marksman scores 1 per hit for a maximum of 200. A hit is when the target visibly breaks in the air. If the target is released before the marksman's instruction (or too late) it does not count.

(ii) Skeet

This is the other event where clay pigeons are used. Here, the competitor must move to different stations (there are eight in all) from which to fire.

The targets are exactly the same as for Olympic Trench, but this time two are released and marksman must hit both of them, so reactions have to be lightning-quick. 200 discs are released, leaving the trap at around 90 mph. The maximum score is again 200.

LAW OF THE GAME

Safety

The potential dangers of firearms are obvious, but are eliminated by strict rules so effectively that shooting is in fact far less dangerous than many other sports. The most basic of these rules, applicable to all the events that follow, is that no person may load his firearm except on the firing line and when given the order to do so by the referee. At the end of firing, or on being given the order "cease fire," the breech is opened, inspected, and kept open.

Inspection of firearms, equipment, and clothing may be undertaken by referees and juries at any time, in order to ensure compliance with UIT rules. Firearms must be inspected before each competition. In prone and three-position rifles events the firer's clothing is minutely regulated because of the possibility of gaining unfair advantage from excessive padding or from restrictive and thus supportive garments. It is the competitor's duty to submit any doubtful item for approval. To curb misplaced ingenuity, there is a catch-all rule that forbids any device that is contrary to the spirit of the rules although not expressly forbidden by them.

Competitors

In the Olympic Games only two individual competitors are permitted from each nation in each event.

In World Championships four individual competitors may be entered by each nation. Their individual scores are added together to produce the team result.

Contingencies

There are special rules in each event, designed to cover every possible contingency, which may be summarized as follows.

Ties in deliberate fire events may be "broken" or resolved by "counting out"; this involves the comparison of scores, shot by shot, in a predetermined sequence (usually working back from the last shot) until a difference is found. In rapid fire and skeet and trap events a "shoot-off" is staged.

A shot hole gauge is used to decide the value of a shot close to the line between two scoring areas. It consists of a plug with a flange 5.6mm in diameter (for the events described in this book), and is necessary because the bullet hole invariably closes slightly after the bullet has passed through. If the flange touches any part of the line, the higher value is awarded.

If a firearm malfunctions through no fault of the firer a reshoot is usually allowed.

Infringements of rules may result in a warning, in the deduction of points, or in disqualification.

Protests by the firer or a team official at any alleged irregularity in match conditions must be made immediately to the range officer or jury, and will be dealt with at once. Protests regarding scores must be made within one hour of their entry on the main scoreboard. Further appeals to the jury of appeal may require a monetary deposit.

GOLD IN OLYMPICS

Free Pistol (50 metres)

1896	Summer Paine (USA)	442
1900	Karl Roderer (Sui)	503
1906	Georgios Orghanidis (Ger)	---
1912	Alfred Lane (USA)	499
1920	Karl Frederick (USA)	---
1936	Torsten Ullmann (Swe)	559
1948	Edwin Vazpuez Cam (Per)	545
1952	Huelet Benner (USA)	553
1956	Pentti Linnosvuo (Fin)	556
1960	Aleksey Gushchin (USSR)	560
1964	Vaino Markkanen (Fin)	560
1968	Grigory Kossykh (USSR)	562
1972	Ragnar Skanakar (Swe)	567
1976	Uwe Poteck (GDR)	573
1980	Aleksandr Melentyev (USSR)	581
1984	Haifeng Xu (Chn)	566
1988	Sorin Babii (Rom)	---

Rapid-Fire Pistol

1896	Jean Phrangoudis (Ger)	344
1900	Maurice Larrouy (Fra)	58
1906	Maurice Lecoq (Fra)	250
1908	Paul van Asbroeck (Bel)	490
1912	Alfred Lane (USA)	287
1920	Guilherme Paraense (Bra)	274
1924	Paul Bailey (USA)	18
1932	Renzo Morigi (Ita)	36
1936	Cornelius van Oyen (Ger)	36

1948	Karoly Takacs (Hun)	580
1952	Karoly Takacs (Hun)	579
1956	Stefan Petrescu (Rom)	587
1960	William McMillan (USA)	587
1964	Pentti Linnosvuo (Fin)	592
1968	Jozef Zapedzki (Pol)	593
1972	Jozef Zapedzki (Pol)	593
1976	Norbert Klaar (GDR)	597
1980	Corneliu lon (Rom)	596
1984	Takeo Kamachi (Jpn)	595
1988	Afanasi Kouzmin (USSR)	---

Small-Bore Rifle (Prone)

1908	A.A.Carnell (UK)	387
1912	Frederick Hird (USA)	194
1920	Lawrence Nuesslein (USA)	391
1924	Pierre Coquelin de Lisle (Fra)	398
1932	Bertil Ronnmark (Swe)	294
1936	Willy Rogeberg (Nor)	300
1948	Arthur Cook (USA)	599
1952	Josif Sarbu (Rom)	400
1956	Gerald Ouellette (Can)	600
1960	Peter Kohnke (Ger)	590
1964	Laszlo Hammeri (Hun)	597
1968	Jan Kurka (Tch)	598
1972	Ho Jun Li (PRK)	599
1976	Karlheinz Smieszek (FRG)	599
1980	Karoly Varga (Hun)	599
1984	Edward Etzel (USA)	599
1988	Miroslav Varga (Czech)	600

Small-Bore Rifle-Three Positions (Prone, Kneeling, Standing)

1952	Erling Kongshaug (Nor)	1164
1956	Anatoliy Bogdanov (USSR)	1172
1960	Viktor Shamburkin (USSR)	1149
1964	Lones Wigger (USA)	1164
1968	Berned Klingner (FRG)	1157
1972	John Writer (USA)	1166
1976	Lanny Bassham (USA)	1162
1980	Viktor Vlasov (USSR)	1173
1984	Malcolm Cooper (UK)	1173
1988	Malcolm Cooper (UK)	

Running Game Target

1900	Louis Debray (Fra)	20
1972	Lakov Zhelezniak (USSR)	569
1976	Aleksandr Gazov (USSR)	579
1980	Igor Soklov (USSR)	589
1984	Yuwei Li (Chn)	587
1988	Tor Heiestad (Norway)	---

Olympic Trap Shooting

1900	Roger de Barbarin (Fra)	17
1906	Garald Merlin (UK)	24
	Sidney Merlin (UK)	15
1908	Walter Ewing (Can)	72
1912	James Graham (USA)	96
1920	Mark Arie (USA)	95
1924	Gyula Halasy (Hun)	98
1952	George Genereux (Can)	192
1956	Galliano Rossini (Ita)	195
1960	Ion Dumitrescu (Rom)	192
1964	Ennio Mattarelli (Ita)	198
1968	Robert Braithwaite (UK)	198
1972	Angelo Scalzone (Ita)	199
1976	Don Haldeman (USA)	190
1980	Luciano Giovanetti (Ita)	198
1984	Luciano Giovanetti (Ita)	192

Skeet Shooting

1968	Evgeny Petrov (USSR)	198
1972	Konrad Wirnhier (FRG)	195
1976	Josef Panacek (Tch)	198
1980	Hans Kield Rasmussen (Den)	196
1984	Matthew Dryke (USA)	198

Air Rifle

1984	Philippe Herberle (Fra)	589
1988	Goran Maksimovic (Yugo)	---

Discontinued Events

Free Rifle (3 positioons)

1896	Georgios Orphanidis (Ger)	1583
1906	Gudbrand Skatteboe (Nor)	977
1908	Albert Helgerud (Nor)	909
1912	Paul Colas (Fra)	987
1920	Morris Fisher (USA)	997

1924	Morris Fisher (USA)	1095
1948	Emil Grunig (Sui)	1120
1952	Anatoliy Bogdanov (USSR)	1123
1956	Vasiliy Borissov (USSR)	1138
1960	Hubert Hammerer (Aut)	1129
1964	Gary Anderson (USA)	1153
1968	Gary Anderson (USA)	1157
1972	Lones Wigger (USA)	1155

Shooting Women (Introduced in 1984)

Sport Pistol

1984	Linda Thom (Can)	585

Air Rifle

1984	Pat Spurgin (USA)	393
1988	Irina Chilova (USSR)	---

ARJUN AWARD WINNERS

1961	H.H. Maharaja Sri Karni Singh of Bikaner
1968	Princess Rajyashree Kumari of Bikaner
1969	Kumari Bhuvaneshwari Kumari
1971	Maharao Bhim Singh of Kota
1972	Udyan Chinubhai
1978-79	Randhir Singh
1981	Sharad P. Chauhan
1983	Mohinder Lal
1985	Ashok J. Pandit
	Soma Dutta
1986	Bhagirath Samai

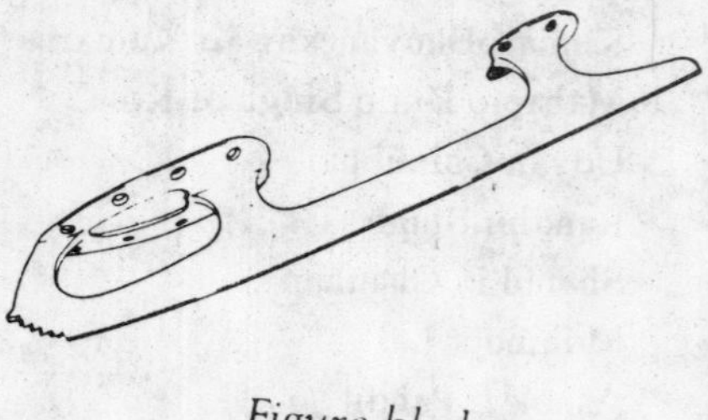

Figure blade

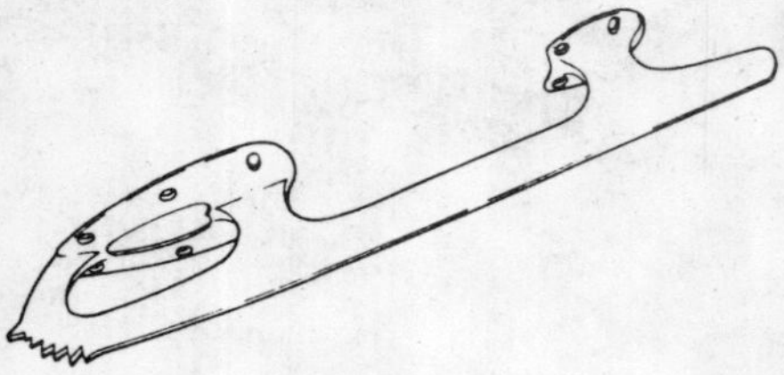

Free skating blade.

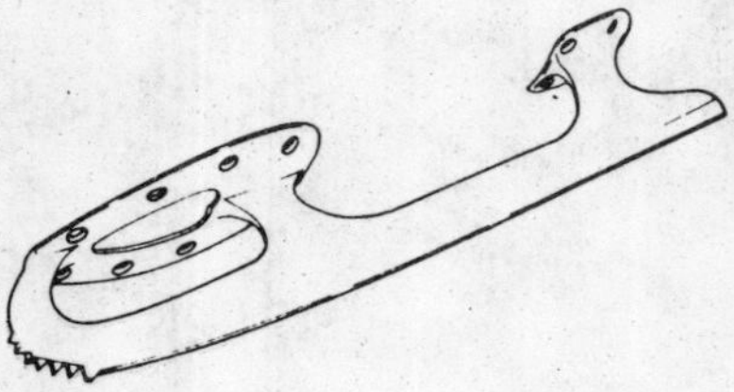

Dance blade

SKATING

Ice skating is a sport that involves travelling over ice using skates. The skater's weight is borne by the narrow blade of the skate. This causes enormous pressure on the surface of the ice below, a thin layer of which then melts and the ice becomes smooth enough to enable the skater to glide easily over it. The melted ice acts like oil, reducing friction. As soon as the skate has passed over a section of ice, the melted snow immediately freezes again. The art of moving over a frozen surface on the blades of skates, ice skating is thought to have been practiced for almost 2000 years. However, it was only in the nineteenth century that it became an organized, competitive sport. As such, it today takes three individual forms: figure skating for solo and pair skaters, ice dancing, and speed skating. Of these, the last is held on closed, outdoor tracks, while figure and dance skating, which call for much precision from their exponents, are performed on artificial indoor rings so that competitors are not disturbed by the vagaries of the elements. All three are included in the Winter Olympic Games, dancing gaining admittance to the Olympic arena as recently as 1976. In addition each has its own World Championships: figure skating since 1896 (men), 1906 (women), and 1908 (pairs); dancing since 1952; and speed skating since 1893 (men) ad 1936 (women).

RULES OF THE GAME

Of the 41 compulsory figures officially recognized by the International Skating Union, the following are perhaps the best known.

The eight, a figure resembling the numberal'8' composed of two adjacent circles executed in any of several prescribed ways. The loop, a two lobed figure in which each lobe is skated on the same

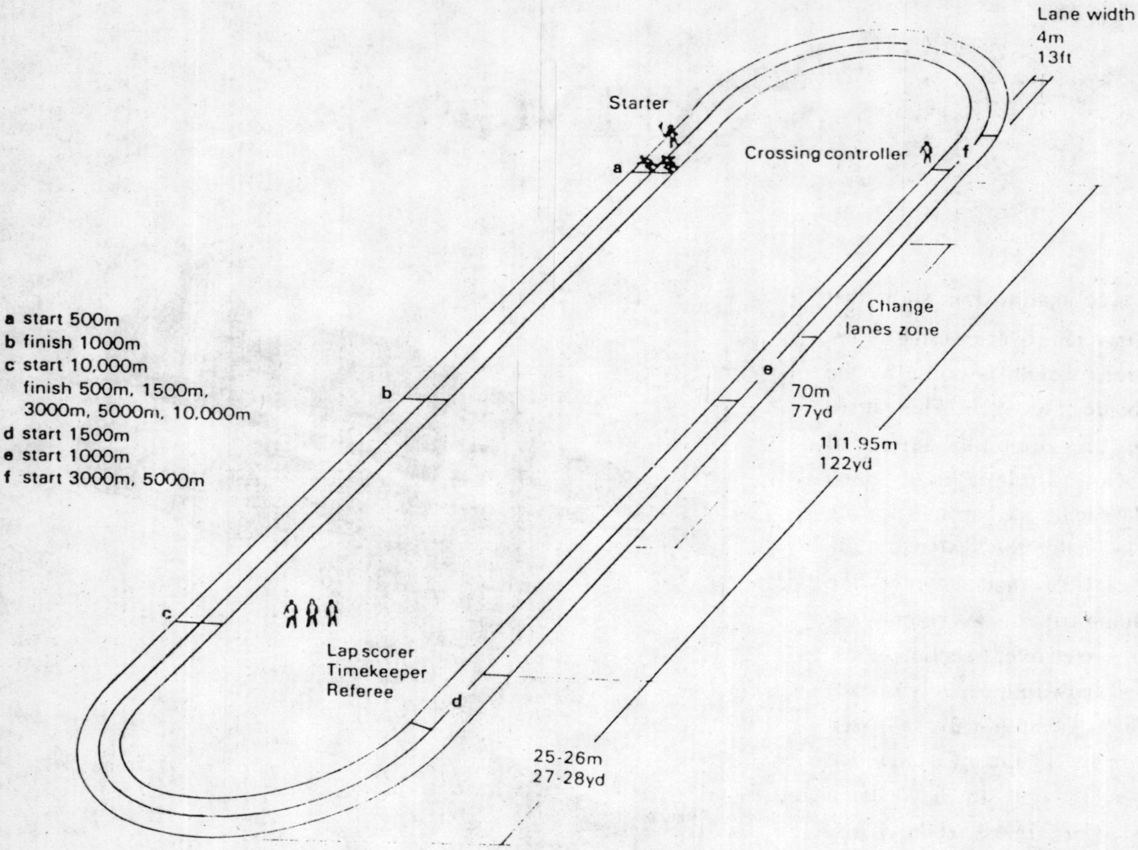

foot and on the same continuous edge, with a small loop at the top and inside each of the circles.

The three, a two lobed figure,so named because the turn involved at the extreme end of each circle leaves a tracing ice resembling the numeral '3'.

The rocker, a three lobed figure involving turns in which the skater rotates sufficiently to come out of the turn on the same edge but in a different direction.

Each of the compulsory figures may be executed on either foot or on a combination of both, on the inside or the outside edge of the blade and forwards or backwards. Points up to maximum of 6 are awarded for each figure and these marks are subsequently multiplied by a factor of between 1 and 6 according to the recognized standard of the figure.

Free Skating is the climax of the competition: the most spectacular part and that most readily appreciated by the spectators. In this, the precise edges and turns learned in figures are combined to create intricate footwork embellished with jumps and spins, and spaced between spirals and linking steps.

Spirals are sustained one foot glides, in either backward or forward direction, performed holding the body in various positions, simulating moving statues. While some depict feminine grace, others imply masculine strength. Holding the position unwaveringly is the hallmark of a good spiral, and the ability to control it either forward or backward, provides a sound basis for a free style repertoire. A spread eagle is a two footed glide in which the feet are positioned in line with each other, heels together and toes pointing outwards. Two turns frequently used are the bracket, a half turn from one edge to the opposite edge of the same skate, with the body turning inside the circle; and the counter, a half turn maintaining the same edge of the skate.

The art of jumping depends on the strength of spring as well as the timing of take off. The tree jump comprises a half turn in mid air, taking of from the forward outside edge of one skate and landing on the back outside edge of the other. The loop jump, requiring a full revolution in the air, is important as the basis of several more advanced jumps.The take off is from a back outside edge, landing on the same edge of the same foot.

The flip jumps a toe jump, taking off from the back outside edge of the skating blade, assisted by the toe point of the non skating blade of the free foot,rotating in mid air before landing on the back outside edge of the original non skating blade.

The lutz in which the skater takes off from a back outside edge, helped by the toe point of the free foot, rotating clockwise ;in mid air before landing on the back outside edge of the original free foot

The salchow in which the skater takes off from a back inside edge, rotating in mid air before landing on the back outside edge of the opposite foot.

The split jump, a tol jump in which the skater takes off from a back inside edge, assisted by the toe point of the free foot, half turning in mid air while swinging the legs up into a horizontal position, closing them before landing on the forward inside edge of the original free foot and the toe point of the original skating foot.

The single, flat foot spring is performed on the flat of the skate, with balance centred over the ball of the foot. A single toe spin is similary performed, except that the weight is on the point of the toe.

The sit spin starts as a standing spin, the skater immediately afterwards sinking on his skating knee to a sitting posture, with the free leg extended in front. The camel spin is a one foot spin executed on the flat of the skate blade, holding the body and the non skating leg in a horizontal position paralle to the ice, with the back arched.

In the layback spin, another one foot spin, the body is bent backwards, spinning parallel to the ice. More advanced are change foot spins, which, when sufficiently well executed, lead to jumping from one spin to another.

Probably the most impressive of all spins in the cross foot spin, performed on the flat of both skate blades, with the legs in crossed position, toes together and heels apart. This is often used to conclude a performance because of its dramatic effect of speedy rotation. This is often used to conclude a performance because of its dramatic effect of speedy rotation.

An advanced free style repertoire is enhanced by the combining jumps and spins and so special spins such as the flying sit spin and the flying camel a jump variation of the camel spin have been evolved. The performer is in no way restricted in what heattemptsor in what sequence, but tries to incorporate as many difficult movements as are possible within the time allotted, in order to gain the highest possible marks.

Technical merit and artistic impression are assessed separately. The judges have to take into account the variation of contents, degree of difficulty and manner of performance, taking into consideration such questions as: was speed gathered without visible effort: did the skater make intelligent use of the entire ice area; and did his performance give the feeling of being planned and skated to the music, rather than of being a set show where the music is only incidental. Scoring is again graded up to a maximum of 6 and the totals multiplied by a factor to ensure an aggregate parity with the marks awarded for figures.

Ambitious figure skaters and pair skaters improve their technical standards by taking graduated proficiency tests, simple at first,progressively winning bronze, silver, and gold medals, with intermediate certificates between. The highest, test a skater has passed determines the class of competition

he or she is qualified to enter.

Ice Dancing, a relatively modern off-shoot of ice figure skating, is despite its name a sport in its own right, with movements based largely on those learned in figures.

There is a great difference between ice dancing and pair skating. In ice dancing, for example, lifts are not permissible and free dancing, more specific in its requirements, ideally consists of a non repetitive performance of novel movements and variations of known ice dances, or parts thereof combined into a programme of original design and arrangement.

Certain free skating movements which are in keeping with the character of the dances are allowed, but feats of strength and skating skill which do not form part of the dance sequence, but which to quote the rule book, are inserted to show physical prowess, are counted against the competitors using them. Free skating movements, such as some spins brief arabesques or pivots, and separations to accomplish changes of position, are suitable for ice dancing lonely when used with the following limitations

(a) separations of partners must not exceed the time necessary to change position

(b) arabesques of pivots must not exceed in

duration the longer movements of the compulsory dances;

(c) spins must not exceed one and a half revolutions;

(d) the maintenance of any position should not be prolonged. The rule makers are constantly watchful to curb the infiltration of irrelevant movements more suitable to pair skating.

Rules of Ice Dancing

Following are a few of the turns and sequences commonly used in ice dancing:

The chasse,a sequence in which the free foot during the period of becoming the skating foot does not pass the original skating foot but is placed on the ice beside the skating foot with the new free foot coming off the ice slightly ahead of beside the new skating foot.

The choctaw, a turn from forward to backward, or vice versa, from one foot to the other on blade edges of different character, i.e. outside to inside or inside to outside.

The mohawk, a half turn from forward to backward, or vice versa, from one foot to the other on blade edges of the same character, i.e. outside to outside or inside to inside.

The twizzle, a rotation through a complete revolution performed so rapidly that it takes place almost on one spot.

The most popular ice dance is the graceful European waltz; it was the earliest standardized ice dance, and is the easiest ;to learn, though by no means easy to perform really well. The initial hazard seems to be the tendency to hurry, as a result of anticipating the beat. Smooth, clean turns should be essayed, with three turned between the partner's feet. All ice dances progress in a counter clockwise direction round the rink. Synchronization with the music is naturally more important, and participation at public rink sessions has a social appeal. Since 1950, in Britain atleast one person in every five who sets out to learn to skate has done so primarily with the ambition to take part in ice dancing.

As in ordinary dancing, provided the learner

Triple axel

Single lutz

Double toe loop

Triple salchow

possesses the basic essentials of a sense of rhythm and an ear for the beat, few lessons are required to enable enjoyable participation, as distinct from polished performance. If possible, as in ballroom dancing, it is advisable to learn with a reasonably experienced`partner. The instructions for executing all the steps of every ice dance are fully set out and illustrated by diagrams in a standard booklet approved by the International Skating Union. Graduated proficiency tests, for which certificates and medals are awarded, are organized in many countries on a national basis, with dances suitably graded into levels of difficulty.

CUP & TROPHIES

Championship competitions are in two parts, compulsory dances and free style each carrying half of the total marks assessed by a panel of judges as in figure skating. For the compulsory section, three specific dances are drawn from the international schedule. Each couple also skates a original set dance to a specific rhythm. The judges award one set of marks for each of the first three compulsory dances and two sets of marks for the set pattern dance and for the free dancing. In the latter,they separately assess technical merit and artistic impression.

World Championship

World figure skating championships were first held in 1896 for men, and 1906 for women. Pairs skating titles have been decided since 1908 and ice dancing since 1952.

Olympic Championships

Figure skating was first included in the Olympic Games in 1908, and has been included at each celebration since 1920.

Figure Skating (Men)

1908	Nikolai Panin (USSR)	219.00 pts
1908	Ulrich Salchow (Swe)	1886.50 pts
1920	Gillis Grafstrom (Swe)	2838.50 pts

1924	Gillis Grafstrom (Swe)	2575.25 pts
1928	Gillis Grafstrom (Swe)	2698.25 pts
1932	Karl Schafer (Aut)	2602.00 pts
1936	Karl Schafer (Aut)	2959.00 pts
1948	Richard Button (USA)	1720.60 pts
1952	Richard Button (USA)	1730.30 pts
1956	Hayes Alan Jenkins (USA)	1497.95 pts
1960	David Jenkins (USA)	1440.20 pts
1968	Manfred Schnelldorfer (Ger)	1916.90 pts
1972	Wolfgang Schwarz (Aut)	1894.10 pts
1976	Ondrej Nepela (Tch)	2739.10 pts
1980	John Curry (UK)	192.74 pts
1984	Scott Hamilton (USA)	---
1988	Brian Boitano (USA)	---

Figure Skating (Women)

1908	Madge Syers (UK)	1262.5 pts
1920	Magda Julin-Mauroy (Swe)	913.50 pts
1924	Herma Planck-Szabo (Aut)	2094.25 pts
1928	Sonja Henie (Nor)	2452.25 pts
1932	Sonja Henie (Nor)	2302.25 pts
1936	Sonja Henie (Nor)	2971.40 pts
1948	Barbara Scott (Can)	1467.70 pts
1952	Jeanette Altwegg (UK)	1455.80 pts
1956	Tenley Albright (USA)	1866.39 pts
1960	Carol Heiss (USA)	1490.10 pts
1964	Sjoukje Dijkstra (Hol)	2018.50 pts
1968	Peggy Fleming (USA)	1970.50 pts
1972	Beatrix Schuba (Aut)	2751.50 pts
1976	Dorothy Hamill (USA)	193.80 pts
1980	Anett Potzsch (GDR)	189.00 pts
1984	Katarina Witt (GDR)	---
1988	Katarina Witt (GDR)	---

Pairs

1908	Germany	56.00 pts
1920	Finland	80.75 pts
1924	Austria	74.50 pts
1928	France	100.50 pts
1932	France	76.70 pts
1936	Germany	103.30 pts
1948	Belgium	123.50 pts.
1952	Germany	102.60 pts
1956	Austria	101.80 pts
1960	Canada	80.40 pts
1964	Soviet Union	104.40 pts
1968	Soviet Union	315.20 pts
1972	Soviet Union	420.40 pts
1976	Soviet Union	140.54 pts
1980	Soviet Union	147.26 pts
1984	Soviet Union	---
1988	Soviet Union	---

SPEED SKATING (MEN)

500 Metres

1924	Charles Jewtraw (USA)	44.0
1928	Clas Thunberg (Fin)	43.4
	Bernt Evensen (Nor)	43.4
1932	John Shea (USA)	43.4
1936	Ivar Ballangrud (Nor)	43.4
1948	Finn Helgesen (Nor)	43.1
1952	Kenneth Henry (USA)	43.2
1956	Yevgeniy Grischin (USSR)	40.2
1960	Yevgeniy Grischin (USSR)	40.2
1964	Richard McDermott (USA)	40.1
1968	Erhard Keller (FRG)	40.3
1972	Yevgeniv Kulikov (USSR)	39.17
1980	Eric Heiden (USA)	38.03
1984	Sergey Fokitchev (USSR)	38.19
1988	Jens-Uwe Mey (FRG)	36.45

1000 Metres

1976	Peter Mueller (USA)	1:19.32
1980	Eric Heiden (USA)	1:15.18
1984	Gaetan Boucher (Can)	1:15.80
1988	Nikolai Gouliaev (USSR)	1:13.03

1500 Metres

1924	Clas Thunberg (Fin)	2:20.8
1928	Clas Thunberg (Fin)	2:21.1
1932	John Shea (USA)	2:57.5
1936	Charles Mathiesen (Nor)	2:19.2
1948	Sverre Farstad (Nor)	2:17.6
1952	Hjalmar Andersen (Nor)	2:20.4
1956	Yevgeniy Grischin (USSR)	2:08.6
	Yuriy Michailov (USSR)	2:08.6
1960	Roald Aas (Nor)	2:10.4
	Yevgeniy Grischin (USSR)	2:10.4

1964	Ants Antson (USSR)	2:10.3
1968	Cornelis Verkerk (Hol)	2:03.4
1972	Ard Schenk (Hol)	2:02.96
1980	Eric Heiden (USA)	1:55.44
1984	Gaetan Boucher (Can)	1:58.36
1988	Andre Hoffman (FRG)	1:52.06

5000 Metres

1924	Clas Thunberg (Fin)	8:39.0
1928	Ivar Ballangrud (Nor)	8:50.5
1932	Irvin Jaffee (USA)	9:40.8
1936	Ivar Ballangrud (Nor)	8:19.6
1948	Reidar Liaklev (Nor)	8:29.4
1952	Hjalmar Andersen (Nor)	8:10.6
1956	Boris Schilkov (USSR)	7:48.7
1960	Yiktor Kositschkin (USSR)	7:51.3
1964	Knut Johannesen (Nor)	7:38.4
1968	Anton Maier (Nor)	7:22.4
1972	Ard Schenk (Hol)	7:23.6
1980	Eric Heiden (USA)	7:02.29
1984	Tomas Gustafson (Swe)	7:12.28
1988	Tomas Gustafson (Swe)	6:44.63

10,000 Metres

1924	Julius Skutnabb (Fin)	18:04.8
1928	Irvin Jaffee (USA)	19:13.6
1932	Ivar Ballangrud (Nor)	17:24.3
1936	Ake Seyffarth (Swe)	17:26.3
1948	Hjalmar Andersen (Nor)	16:45.8
1952	Sigvard Ericsson (Swe)	16:35.9
1956	Knut Johannesen (Nor)	15:46.6
1960	Jonny Nilsson (Swe)	15:50.1
1964	Johnny Hoglin (Swe)	15:23.6
1968	Ard Schenk (Hol)	15:01.35
1972	Piet Kleine (Hol)	14:50.59
1980	Eric Heiden (USA)	14:28.13
1984	Igor Malkov (USSR)	14:39.90
1988	Tomas Gustafson (Swe)	13:48.20

500 Metres (Women)

1960	Helga Haase (Ger)	45.9
1964	Lydia Skoblikova (USSR)	45.0
1968	Ludmila Titova (USSR)	46.1
1972	Anne Henning (USA)	43.33
1976	Sheila Young (USA)	42.76
1980	Karin Enke (GDR)	41.78
1984	Christa Rothenburger (GDR)	41.02
1988	Bonnie Blair (USA)	39.10

1000 Metres

1960	Klara Guseva (USSR)	1:34.1
1964	Lydia Skoblikova (USSR)	1:33.2
1968	Carolina Geijssen (Hol)	1:32.6
1972	Monika Pflug (FRG)	1:31.40
1976	Tatyana Averina (USSR)	1:28.43
1980	Natalya Petruseva (USSR)	1:24.10
1984	Karin Enke (GDR)	1:21.61
1988	Christa Rothenburger (FRG)	1:17.65

1500 Metres

1960	Lydia Skoblikova (USSR)	2:25.2
1964	Lydia Skoblikova (USSR)	2:22.6
1968	Kaija Mustonen (Fin)	2:22.4
1972	Dianne Holum (USA)	2:20.85
1976	Galina Stepanskaya (USSR)	2:16.58
1980	Annie Borckink (Hol)	2:10.95
1984	Karin Enke (GDR)	2:03.42
1988	Yvonne Van Gennip (Neth)	2:00.64

3000 Metres

1960	Lydia Skoblikova (USSR)	5:14.3
1964	Lydia Skoblikova (USSR)	5:14.9
1968	Johanna Schut (Hol)	4:56.2
1972	Christina Baas-Kaiser (Hol)	4:52.14
1976	Tatyana Averina (USSR)	4:45.19
1980	Bjorg Eva Jensen (Nor)	4:32.13
1984	Andrea Schoene (GDR)	4:24.79
1988	Yvonne Van Gennip (Neth)	4:11.94

5000 Metres

1988	Yvonne Van Gennip (Neth)	7:14.13

SKIING

There is evidence that skiing may be at least 5,000 years old. Skiing, which was primarily a means of travel in snow-bound countries, has now become one of the most popular winter sports throughout the world and in those portions of the United States where snow is plentiful. It is believed that as early as 1850 there was ski racing and jumping competition in Norway. It is known that in the United States skis were used during the gold rush to the Pacific Coast in the 1850's. There was also a famous mail carrier, John A. Thompson, who in 1849 carried the United States mail from Placeville, California to Carson City, Nevada and returned on skis. The first ski club in the United States was formed at Berlin, New Hampshire in January, 1872. On February 21, 1904, officials from various ski clubs organized a national body and conducted a national ski tournament. The third Winter Olympics, held at Lake Placid, New York, in 1932 did a great deal to popularize skiing in this country.

The various phases of skiing as a sport include jumping, downhill, slaom, and cross-country.

Walking and gliding.

The side step.

Downhill schussing.

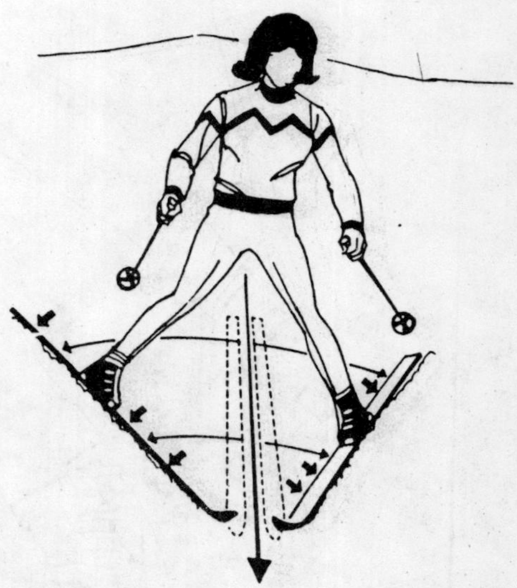

Snowplow braking technique.

Traversing.

Stem turn.

Parallel turn.

SKILLS OF THE GAME

The essence of successful skiing-at recreational or competitive level-is in a correct distribution of weight on one ski or the other, the proper movements of the body to move the skis in any particular direction and knowledge of the use of the edges of the skis in side-stepping uphill or side-slipping downhill.

The basic Alpine skiing technique is based largely on the stem turn, in which the heel of one ski (or both) is pushed outwards to change the direction of movement.

The more advanced christiana is a medium-to-fast swing turn. Mastery of this technique give a skier a high degree of control and after this the more sophisticated techniques can be learnt. Skiing skill improves rapidly with the use of the ski edges.

Nordic or cross-country skiing involves different techniques, more suited to less undulating terrain. It is becoming increasingly popular in countries better known for Alpine skiing. The basic equipment is different: cross-country skis are longer and narrower, and the bindings allow more heel movement. The Nordic technique, which is more like walking-though more energy-sapping-is based on a long, rhythmic stride, a pronounced arm swing, and use of the longer poles to give added propulsion.

RULE OF THE GAME

The most important F.I.S. rules governing courses are:-Length: For seniors (minimum age at 1 January in a competition year 18 for a woman and 20 for a man), men 10,15 and 50 km. (6.2,9.3, and 31 miles); women 5 and 10 km. (3.1 and 6.2 miles). Relay races: men 3.10 km. or 4.10 km; women 3.5km. Altitude : Not to exceed 1,650 m. (5,362 ft.) at Winter Olympic Games and World Championships.

Vertical Change :Up to 1965,F.I.S. regulations specified the maximum total difference in elevation between the lowest and highest point on a course, but the 1965 congress in Mamaia, Romania, adopted standards for total elevation gain (the sum of all elevation differences around a course) because it gave a more realistic picture of the course's difficulty. In the women's kilometers the gain should be 150 to 200 m. (492-656 ft.); the 10 kilometers 250 to 350 m. (820-1,148 ft.); the men's 10 kilometers (300 to 450m.) (984-1,476 ft.); the 15 kilometers 450 to 500 m. (1,476-1,640 ft.) the 30 kilometres 750 to 1,000 m.(2,460-3,281 ft.); and the 50 kilometres 1,200 to 1,500 m. (3,937-4,921 ft.).

Laps : At Winter Olympics and World Championships no course or part of a course may be run more than twice to comprise the required distance. At other international events, a course or part of it may be run several times.

Marking: The course must be clearly marked with marks of a single colour. Signs given in course distance should be set up at least every fifth kilometre along the whole course and every kilometre for the last 10 km.

Start and finish must be at the same place and at the same altitude. Incoming and outgoing tracks must be separated so that there is no confusion.

Feeding Stations : On 20 to 30 km. courses there must be at least one feedingstation. Warm beverages and food are permitted; wine and spirits are prohibited.

The basic stride is a kick-off from one foot and a gliding step with the other. Kick-offs and glides are alternated between one foot and the other to give a smooth and rhythmical stride. The ski is waxed so that the action is much like a brush on a wet floor and the ski will glide as long as it is in motion. Once it stops it will stick until it is picked up slightly and pushed on with a kicking motion. Known in Norwegian as fraspark, the pole in each hand is planted alternately as the leg on the opposite side starts its kick. This is the basic step, to which there are variants. The diagonal stride is similar to that of ice skating, where-by the forward force is gained with a push forward off a slightly angled, edged ski, so that progress is maintained in a series of opened Vs.

Ski jumping

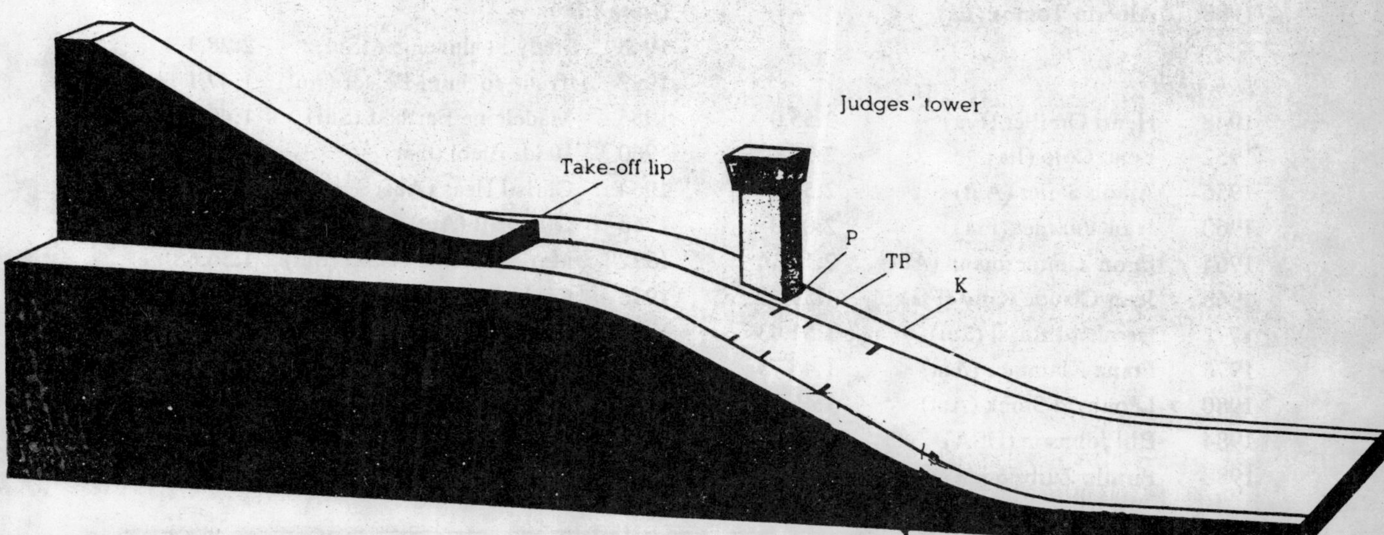

CUP & TROPHIES

Gold In Olympics

Alpine skiing has been included in the winter Olympic Games since 1948.

Men

Slalom (Men)

1948	Edi Reinalter (Sui)	2:10.3
1952	Othmar Schneider (Aut)	2:00.0
1956	Anton Sailer (Aut)	3:14.7
1960	Ernest Hinterseer (Aut)	2:08.9
1964	Josef Stiegler (Aut)	2:21.13
1968	Jean-Claude Killy (Fra)	1:39.73
1972	Francisco Fernandez (Esp)	1:49.27
1976	Piero Gros (Ita)	2:03.29
1980	Ingemar Stenmark (Swe)	1:44.26
1984	Phil Mahre (USA)	1:39.21
1988	Alberto Tomba (Ita)	---

Giant Slalom

1952	Stein Eriksen (Nor)	2:25.0
1956	Anton Sailer (Aut)	3:00.1
1960	Roger Staub (Sui)	1:48.3
1964	Francois Boulieu (Fra)	1:46.71
1968	Jean-Claude Killy (Fra)	3:29.28
1972	Gustavo Thoeni (Ita)	3:09.62
1976	Heini Hemmi (Sui)	3:26.97
1980	Ingemar Stenmark (Swe)	2:45.74
1984	Max Julen (Sui)	2:41.18
1988	Alberto Tomba (Ita)	---

Downhill

1948	Henri Oreiller (Fra)	2:55.0
1952	Zeno Colo (Ita)	2:30.8
1956	Anton Sailer (Aut)	2:52.2
1960	Jean Vuarnet (Fra)	2:06.0
1964	Egon Zimmermann (Aut)	2:18.16
1968	Jean-Claude Killy (Fra)	1:59.85
1972	Bernhard Russi (Sui)	1:51.43
1976	Franz Klammer (Aut)	1:45.73
1980	Leonhard Stock (Aut)	1:45.50
1984	Bill Johnson (USA)	1:45.59
1988	Pirmin Zurbriggen (Switz)	---

Alpine Combination (Downhill and Slalom)

1936	Franz Pfnur (Ger)	99.25 pts
1948	Henri Oreiller (Fra)	3.27 pts

Women

Slalom

1948	Gretchen Fraser (USA)	1:57.2
1952	Andrea Mead-Lawrence (USA)	2:10.6
1956	Renee Colliard (Sui)	1:52.3
1960	Anne Heggtveit (Can)	1:49.6
1964	Christine Goitschel (Fra)	1:29.86
1968	Marielle Goitschel (Fra)	1:25.86
1972	Barbara Cochran (USA)	1:31.24
1976	Rosi Mittermaier (FRG)	1:30.54
1980	Henni Wenzel (Lie)	1:25.09
1984	Paoletta Magoni (Ita)	1:36.47
1988	Vreni Schneider (Switz)	---

Giant Slalom

1952	Andrea Mead-Lawrence (USA)	2:06.8
1956	Ossi Reichert (Ger)	1:56.5
1960	Yvonne Rueggu (Sui)	1:39.9
1964	Marielle Goitschel (Fra)	1:52.24
1968	Nancy Greene (Can)	1:51.97
1972	Marie-Therese Nadig (Sui)	1:29.90
1976	Kathy Kreiner (Can)	1:29.13
1980	Hanni Wenzel (Lie)	2:41.66
1984	Debbie Armstrong (USA)	2:20.98
1988	Sigrid Wolf (Austria)	---

Downhill

1948	Hedy Schlunegger (Sui)	2:28.3
1952	Trude Jochum-Beiser (Aut)	1:47.1
1956	Madeleine Barthod (Sui)	1:40.7
1960	Heidi Biebl (Ger)	1:37.6
1964	Christl Haas (Aut)	1:55.39
1968	Olga Pall (Aut)	1:40.87
1972	Marie-Therese Nadig (Sui)	1:36.68
1976	Rosi Mittermaier (FRG)	1:46.16
1980	Annemarie Moser-Proll (Aut)	1:37.52
1984	Michela Figini (Sui)	1:13.36
1988	Marina Kiehl (FRG)	---

Alpine Combination (Downhill and Slalom)

1936	Christel Cranz (Ger)	97.06 pts
1948	Trude Beiser (Aut)	6.58 pts

Alpine World Cup

Men

1967	J.Killy (Fra)
1968	J.Killy (Fra)
1969	K.Schranz (Aut)
1970	K.Schranz (Aut)
1971	G.Thoeni (Ita)
1972	G.Thoeni (Ita)
1973	G.Thoeni (Ita)
1974	P.Gros (Ita)
1975	G. Thoeni (Ita)
1976	I.Stenmark (Swe)
1977	I.Stenmark (Swe)
1978	I.Stenmark (Swe)
1979	P.Luescher (Swi)
1980	A.Wenzel (Lie)
1981	P.Mahre (USA)
1982	P.Mahre (USA)
1983	P.Mahre (USA)
1984	P.Zubriggen (Swi)
1985	M.Girardelli (Lux)
1986	M.Girardelli (Lux)
1987	P.Zurbriggen (Swi)

Women

1967	N.Greene (Can)
1968	N.Greene (Can)
1969	G.Gabl (Aut)
1970	M.Jacot (Fra)
1971	A.Proll (Aut)
1972	A.Proll (Aut)
1973	A.Proll (Aut)
1974	A.Proll (Aut)
1975	A.Moser-Proll (Aut)
1976	R.Mittermaier (Ger)
1977	L.M. Morerod (Swi)
1978	H.Wenzel (Lie)
1979	A. Moser-Proll (Aut)
1980	H.Wenzel (Lie)
1981	M.T.Nadig (Swi)
1982	E.Hess (Swi)
1983	T.McKinney (USA)
1984	E.Hess (Swi)
1985	M.Gigini (Swi)
1986	M.Walliser (Swi)
1987	M.Walliser (Swi)

Alpine World Championships

Men

1932	O.Furrer (Swi)
1933	A.Seelos (Aut)
1934	D.Zogg (Swi)
1935	A.Seelos (Aut)
1936	R.Rominger (Swi)
1937	E.Allais (Fra)
1938	E.Allais (Fra)
1939	J.Jennewein (Ger)
1940	Not held
1941	Not held
1942	Not held
1943	Not held
1944	Not held
1945	Not held
1946	Not held
1947	Not held
1948	Not held
1949	Not held
1950	Not held
1951	Not held
1952	Not held
1953	Not held
1954	S.Eriksen (Nor)
1956	T.Sailer (Aut)
1958	T.Sailer (Aut)
1960	G. Perillat (Fra)
1962	K.Schranz (Aut)
1964	L.Leitner (Ger)
1966	J.C.Killy (Fra)
1968	J.C.Killy (Fra)
1970	W.Kidd (USA)
1972	G.Thoeni (Ita)
1974	F.Klammer (Aut)
1976	G.Thoeni (Ita)
1978	A.Wenzel (Lie)

1980 W.Kidd (USA)
1982 M.Vion (Fra)
1985 P.Zurbriggen (Swi)
1987 M.Garardelli (Lux)

Women

1932 R.Streiff (Swi)
1933 I.Wersin-Lantschner (Aut)
1934 C.Cranz (Ger)
1935 C.Cranz (Ger)
1936 E.Pinching (UK)
1937 C.Cranz (Ger)
1938 C.Cranz (Ger)
1939 C.Cranz (Ger)
1940 Not held
1941 Not held
1942 Not held
1943 Not held
1944 Not held
1945 Not held
1946 Not held
1947 Not held
1948 Not held
1949 Not held
1950 Not held
1951 Not held
1952 Not held
1953 Not held
1954 I.Schopfer (Swi)
1956 M.Berthod (Swi)
1958 F.Danzer (Swi)
1960 A.Heggtveit (Can)
1962 M.Goitschel (Fra)
1964 M.Goitschel (Fra)
1966 M.Goitschel (Fra)
1968 N.Greene (Can)
1970 M.Jacot (Fra)
1972 A.Proll (Aut)
1974 F.Serrat (Fra)
1976 R.Mittermaier (FRG)
1978 A.Moser-Proll (Aut)
1980 M.Jacot (Fra)
1982 E.Hess (Swi)
1985 E.Hess (Swi)
1987 E.Hess (Swi)

SNOOKER

The game of Snooker (or Snooker's Pool) is played on an English Billiard Table, and may be played by two or more persons, either as sides or individually. It is a game of winning hazards: cannons are ignored. The winner is the player or side making the highest score.

Snooker is an indoor game played by 2 players, as individuals, or 4 players, as doubles.

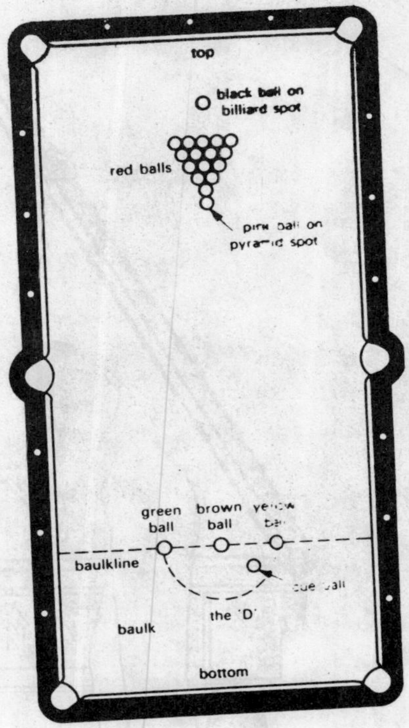

TECHNICAL TERMS AND SKILLS

(a) The white ball is referred to as the cue-ball; the yellow, green, brown, blue, pink and black, as the pool balls, or colours, the red (or pyramid) balls as reds.

(b) Any ball which is forced off the table becomes out of play, but with the exception of a red ball, which is immediately replaced upon its allotted spot.

(c) A player is said to be on a ball when such ball may be lawfully struck by the cue-ball under these Rules. He is on a pool ball nominated under Rules 5 and 10.

(d) A player is said to be snookered with regard to any ball when a direct stroke in a straight line of the cue-ball to any point of such ball is obstructed by any ball which is not on. If a player is in hand after a foul, he cannot be snookered with regard to any ball that is on, if he can get a direct stroke in a straight line from some part of the 'D'. When the ball on is snookered by more than one ball, the effective snookering ball is the cue-ball.

(e)The cue-ball is said to be angled when the corner of the cushion prevents a stroke being made, in a straight line, directly on any part of any ball that may be lawfully struck.

(f) A Nominated Ball is the object-ball which the striker declares he undertakes to strike with the first impact of the cue-ball.

(g) Fifteen reds in the form of a traingle, the ball at the apex standing as near to the pink ball as possible, without touching it; the base being parallel with and nearest to the top cushion. BLACK on the BILLIARD SPOT; PINK on the PYRAMID SPOT; BLUE on the CENTRE SPOT; BROWN on the MIDDLE of the baulk-line; GREEN on the LEFT-HAND and YELLOW on the RIGHT-HAND corner of the 'D'.

(h) Snooker consists of 22 balls as follows : 1 white ball, known as the cue-ball, plus 15 reds and 6 colours, known as the object balls.

The scoring values of the balls are:

- red - 1
- yellow - 2
- green - 3
- brown - 4
- blue - 5
- pink - 6
- black - 7

Each ball has a diameter of 2(1/16)in.(5.2cm) with a tolerance of +0.05mm to -0.08mm. They shall be of equal weight with a tolerance of 3g per set.

Snooker is played on a standard English Billiard table which has a playing area, within the cushion faces, of 11ft 8(½) in (3.56m) x 5 ft 10in (1.78m). The height of the table from the floor to the top of the cushion rail is between 2ft 9(½)in (85.2cm) and 2ft 10(½) in (87.2cm). The bed of the table is made of slate and covered in a stretched cloth. The cloth is marked with 6 spots, each of which is the home of one of the coloured balls. The area between the yellow, green and brown spots, and the end cushion nearest them is known as the baulk area. The cushions are vulcanized rubber. The cushion at the baulk end of the table is known as the bottom cushion. There are 2 pockets at either end of this cushion. The cushion at the opposite end of the table is known as the top cushion and the 2 pockets at the end of it are the top pockets. There are also 2 pockets at the middle of the table.

Only the referee is allowed to clean a ball on the table. He should do so at a player's request.

It is the striker's responsibility to see that the balls are correctly spotted before playing his stroke.

If the referee considers that a player is taking an abnormal amount of time over his stroke, with the intention of upsetting his opponent, the referee should warn him that he runs the risk of being disqualified if he pursues these tactics.

A player should not be penalised if, when using the rest, the rest head falls off and touches a ball.

Unless a foul stroke is awarded by the referee, or claimed by the non-striker, before the next stroke is made, it is condoned.

If the striker plays with the balls improperly spotted, he scores all points made until the foul is awarded by the referee, or claimed by the non-striker.

The referee should not give any indication that a player is about to make a foul stroke.

If the striker makes a miss, the referee can order him to re-play the stroke penalising him the requisite forfeit for each miss, but he scores all points in any subsequent stroke.

When snookered after a foul stroke, a player must nominate the ball he intends to play.

If at the opening stroke of a game the striker fails to hit a red, the next player plays from where the cue-ball has come to rest.

7. A player must be able to strike both sides of the ball on free of obstruction from any ball or balls not on. It virtually means the diameter of a ball on either side of the ball on.

If a player is coloured blind, the referee should tell him the colour of a ball if requested.

A referee must declare when a player has a free ball without appeal from a player.

As from 1 December 1973, players will not be required to nominate their colour when taking a free ball unless there is doubt over which ball the player is attempting.

Stance, grip, and the basic techniques of screw, stun and side are exactly the same in snooker as in billiards, although a snooker break a sequence of scoring shots-is compiled through potting alone. Billiards breaks are compiled through a combination of potting, in-offs and cannons. To compile a snooker break calls for a combination of potting ability, positional play involving manoeuvring the cue ball in such a way that following pots are as easy as possible, and a clear enough brain to plot these chess-like sequences.

One snooker shot rarely needed in billiards is the swerve, which may be used to get out of a snooker, but only if there is some distance between the cue ball, the intervening ball, and the ball 'on'. A player imparts swerve by raising his bridge (the hand he rests the cue on), lifting the butt of the cue, and striking the cue-ball a short, sharp stroke on th side to which he requires to swerve it.

Technique with the spider rest is a valuable snooker requisite, as this instrument, which is rarely needed in billiards, is often employed in snooker, where the cue-ball is likely to finish up in an inaccessible position. It is used when another ball is behind and so close to the cue-ball that the player cannot strike the cue-ball where he wants to, even with an elevated bridge. He must be careful to avoid touching any balls with the spider either when placing it near the cue ball or when removing it from the table.

THE RULES OF SNOOKER

The Balls :- The set of balls should be twenty-two in number, consisting of fifteen reds, one black, one pink, one blue, one brown, one green, one yellow and a white ball, which is called the cue-ball. In the game on the B. & S.C.C. 6ft. Standard Table the set of balls shall be seventeen in number, consisting of ten reds, one black, one pink, one blue, one brown, one green, one yellow and a white ball, which is called the cue-ball.

Playing order is determined by drawing lots or by some other convenient method such as "stringing". In stringing, players simultaneously play one ball each from the baulk line with the object of making it rebound off the top cushion and come to rest as near as, possible to bottom cushion.

Order of play :- Within a pair or team must remain the same throughout a frame. Turns alternate between sides.

Start of play :- All the object balls-reds and colours-must be set up in their corrrect position:

(i) The 15 reds are set up in the form of a triangle, its base parallel with and nearest to the top cushion, and the ball at its apex as near as possible to, but not touching, the pink ball positioned on the pyramid spot;

(ii) The yellow is positioned on the right-hand corner of the "D" (looking down the table from the baulk end);

(iii) The green is positioned on the left-hand corner of the "D".

(iv) The brown is positioned on the baulk spot;

(v) The blue is positioned on the centre spot;

(vi) The pink is positioned on the pyramid spot;

(vii)The black is positioned on the billiard spot;

(viii) The cue ball may be put into play from anywhere within, or on the lines of, the "D".

It is a player's responsibility to ensure that the balls are correctly positioned before he makes any stroke.

Players take turns in attempting to complete the frame by poketing all the objects ball in the correct sequence. A player's turn continues as long as he scores with every stroke (consecutive scoring strokes in any turn are called a "break"). Once a player fails to score with any stroke his turn comes to an end and his opponent takes up play from whatever point in the frame has already been reached.

In the opening stages of a frame (as long as any reds remain on the table), a player must begin his turn by attempting to pocket a red. If he succeeds, the red is left in the pocket and one point is scored. All other balls are left as they lie after his stroke, and the player now nominates any colour of his choice. If he succeeds in pocketing the nominated ball with his next stroke, he scores the value of that ball.

Stroke :- A stroke begins when a player touches a ball with his cue, and ends when all the balls have come to rest. For a stroke to be fair:

(i) Only the white cue ball may be struck with the cue;

(ii) The cue ball must be struck with the tip of the cue;

(iii) The cue ball must be struck and not pushed (it is a push stroke if the cue remains in contact with the cue ball after it begins its forward motion, or after the cue ball makes contact with an object ball);

(iv) The cue ball must not be struck more than once in the same stroke, either before or after contact with another ball;

(v) The cue ball may be struck directly at the object ball aimed at, or it may contact the object ball after bouncing off one or more cushions;

(vi) No ball must be forced off the table;

(vii) At the moment that the cue ball is struck, one of the player's feet must be touching the floor.

"On" ball :- The ball that is next due to be pocketed is termed the "on" ball. If asked to do so by the referee, a player must always state which ball he is "on". A player's cue ball must always strike the "on" ball before it strikes any other ball. A player must always try his best to strike the "on" ball; intentional misses are prohibited.

Snookers :- A player is snookered when a ball he must not play obstructs a straight line between the cue ball and the ball that is "on". He must attempt his shot and will be penalized for missing the "on" ball or for hitting another ball first.

If a player is due to play a red but is snookered with regard to all reds following an opponent's foul stroke, he may nominate any other ball. This ball then counts as a red, except that it must be respotted it pocketed.

If an opponent's foul stroke snookers a player with regard to a coloured ball that is "on", he may nominate any other ball. This ball then counts as the "on" ball, except that if it is legally pocketed it is respotted and the player continues his break on the ball that he was "on" but for the snooker. If a result of playing the nominated ball the player pockets the "on" ball, he scores that ball and continues his break. If a player pockets both the nominated ball and the "on" ball with the same stroke, the nominated ball is respotted. Only the "on" ball is scored, and the player continues his break.

Respotting balls :- Illegally pocketed coloured balls and coloured balls that are legally pocketed while there are reds still on the table must normally be respotted in their starting positions.

If its own spot is covered, a ball should be respotted on the first available spot in descending order of value, starting with the black spot.

If spots are covered, any ball but the black and pink is placed as near as possible to its own spot, in a position between that spot and the nearest part of the top cushion, and without touching any other ball. The black and pink balls are replaced as close to their own spots as possible, on the centreline of the table, toward the top cushion, and without touching any other ball. Only if all positions toward the top cushion are occupied, should the black or pink ball be respotted below its own spot in the direction of the bottom cushion.

CUP & TROPHIES

World Professional Championship

The championship was held annually from 1927 to 1940 and 1946 to 1957, when the winners were:

1927	J.Davis (Eng)
1928	J.Davis (Eng)
1929	J.Davis (Eng)
1930	J.Davis (Eng)
1931	J.Davis (Eng)
1932	J.Davis (Eng)
1933	J.Davis (Eng)
1934	J.Davis (Eng)
1935	J.Davis (Eng)
1936	J.Davis (Eng)
1937	J.Davis (Eng)
1938	J.Davis (Eng)
1939	J.Davis (Eng)
1940	J.Davis (Eng)
1941	Not held
1942	Not held
1943	Not held
1944	Not held
1945	Not held

1946	J.Davis (Eng)
1947	W.Donaldson (Sco)
1948	F.Davis (Eng)
1949	F.Davis (Eng)
1950	W.Donaldson (Sco)
1951	F.Davis (Eng)
1952	H.Lindrum (Aus)
1953	Not held
1954	Not held
1955	Not held
1956	Not held
1957	Not held
1958	Not held
1959	Not held
1960	Not held
1961	Not held
1962	Not held
1963	Not held

The championship was resumed in 1964 on a challenge basis after the Professional Billiard Players' Association and the Billiards Association and Control Council had reconciled their differences. The championship reverted to an open tournament in 1969.

1964	J.Pulman (Eng)
1965	J.Pulman (Eng)
1966	J.Pulman (Eng)
1967	J.Pulman (Eng)
1968	J.Pulman (Eng)
1969	J.Spencer (Eng)
1970	R.Reardon (Wal)
1971	J.Spencer (Eng)
1972	A.Higgins (NI)
1973	R.Reardon (Wal)
1974	R.Reardon (Wal)
1975	R.Reardon (Wal)
1976	R.Reardon (Wal)
1977	J.Spencer (Eng)
1978	R.Reardon (Wal)
1979	T.Griffiths (Wal)
1980	C.Thorburn (Can)
1981	S.Davis (Eng)
1982	A.Higgins (NI)
1983	S.Davis (Eng)
1984	S.Davis (Eng)
1985	Dennis Taylor (NI)
1986	J.Johnson (Eng)
1987	S.Davis (Eng)

Benson & Hedges Masters

1975	J.Spencer (Eng)
1976	R.Reardon (Wal)
1977	D.Mountjoy (Wal)
1978	A.Higgins (NI)
1979	P.Mans (S.Af)
1980	T.Griffiths (Wal)
1981	A.Higgins (NI)
1982	S.Davis (Eng)
1983	C.Thorburn (Can)
1984	J.White (Eng)
1985	C.Thorburn (Can)
1986	C.Thorburn (Can)
1987	D.Taylor (NI)

World Rankings

1976	R.Reardon (Wal)
1977	R.Reardon (Wal)
1978	R.Reardon (Wal)
1979	R.Reardon (Wal)
1980	R.Reardon (Wal)
1981	C.Thorburn (Can)
1982	R.Reardon (Wal)
1983	S.Davis (Eng)
1984	S.Davis (Eng)
1985	S.Davis (Eng)
1986	S.Davis (Eng)
1987	S.Davis (Eng)

SOCCER

It is impossible to say exactly when football began, because its origins are lost, literally, in the mists of time. Some say men (and women)first began kicking 'an object' around as far back as the twelfth century. Perhaps they did, but it took a long time for the game to become organized.

The first real stirrings were in the middle of last century, when boys at established English public schools and at universities such as Cambridge, began to play a form of soccer which at least bore some resemblance to our modern game.It is surprising that a game thought of mainly as a working man's pastime should have originated in the very bastions of the so-called privileged classes.

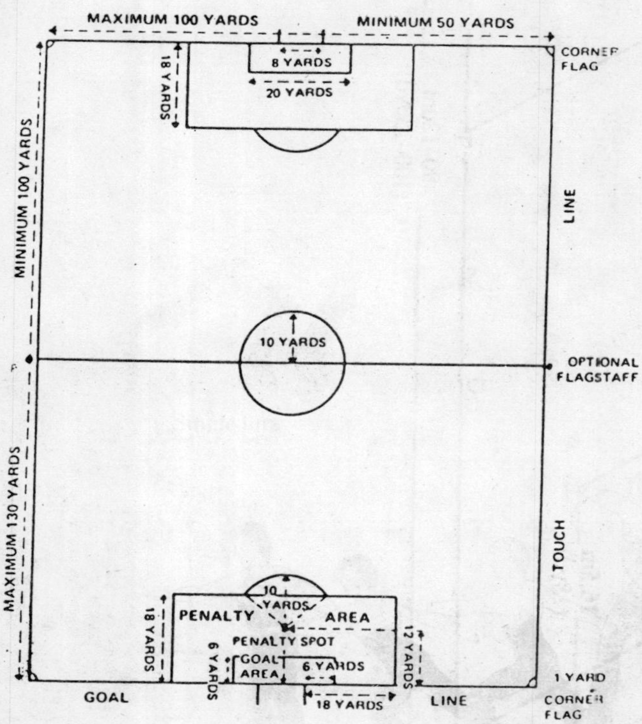

However, such was the popularity of football that it was not long before it appealed to a wider audience. The oldest Football League club was founded in 1862-26 years before the formation of the League itself-Notts County,which came into existence three years before their arch-rivals Nottingham Forest.

The following year, 1863,saw the formation of the Football Association-in a public house in central London. This was the world's first organized attempt at controlling the game at national level and it was from the new body's little that Association football, or soccer, got its name.

Many people north of the border believe that Scotland, not England, gave football to the world. With due respect to the Scots, who have contributed so much to the game, this is not so. The first Scottish club, the famous and once powerful Queen's Park, did not appear on the field until 1867, and the Scottish Football Association waited until 1873 for its inception.

FITNESS AND KIT

Fitness:

Stamina, strength and speed are influential factors at any level of football and fit players will gain more enjoyment from the game.The professional has to be fit if he is to survive the rigours of a long season. On the other hand,those who are not being paid, who are simply playing for pleasure must decide what level of fitness they are aiming for.

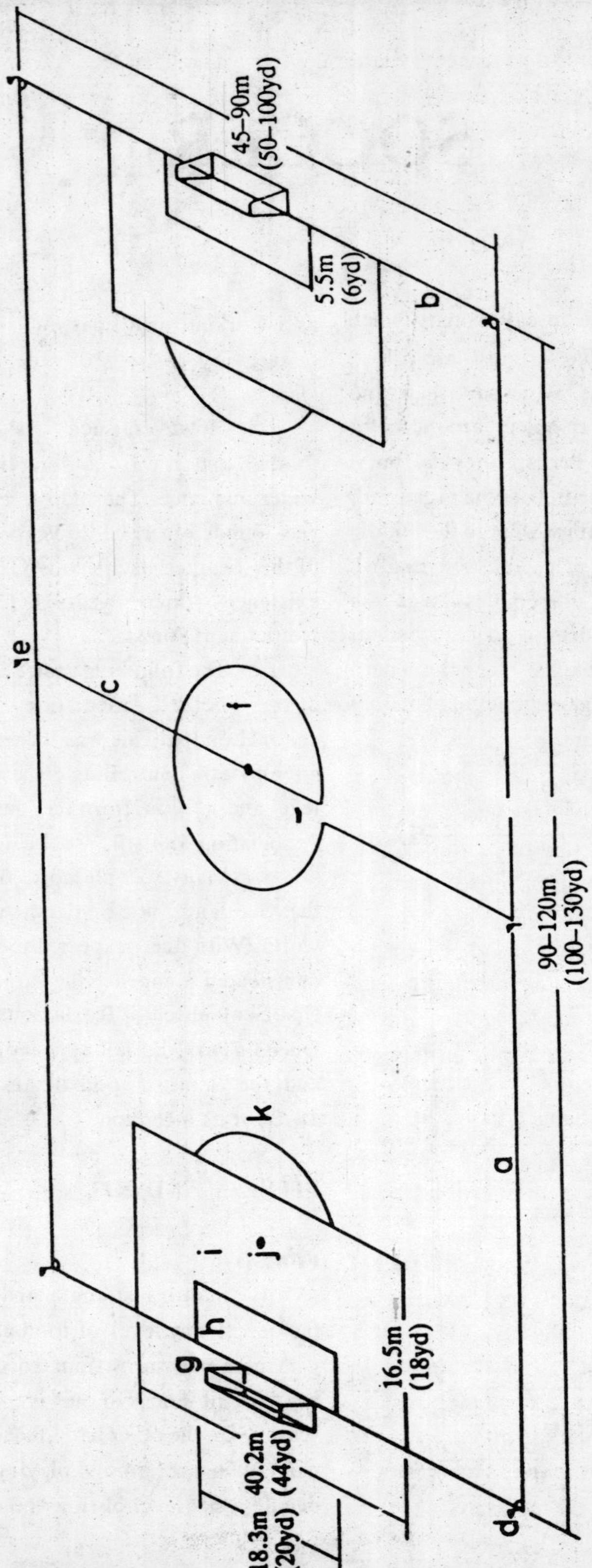
45–90m
(50–100yd)
5.5m
(6yd)
90–120m
(100–130yd)
16.5m
(18yd)
40.2m
(44yd)
18.3m
(20yd)
a
b
c
d
e
f
g
h
i
j
k

The aim is to develop the efficiency of the heart and lungs so that the blood and oxygen supply to the working muscles is increased.This helps muscles to function and reduces fatigue.Training consists of rhythmical exercise, skipping movements and running. Use other movements that are related to soccer. Stop, start running, change of pace and direction, jumping, kicking and dribbling.

Every coach will have his own ideas of how to get his team into condition and each will know the differences in the individuals under his care. However, I think that a few general ideas on the achievement of fitness for soccer should be included at this stage. All will not appeal, but the coach may use those that interest him and develop them. Remember that fitness, in this context, is really the ability to keep up a high level of play throughout the game.

1. Hard training should be hard. Investigations have shown that there is little or no carryover effect from training until a player has gotten his heart rate;to do that requires effort. In training, don't allow shortcuts. It may hurt; it will be worth it.
2. Begin training, if possible, for a lengthy period before the season commencees, but make this training gradual in intensity and severity.
3. All sessions, should be aimed to improve the players' speed, stamina, and agility. At the same time it is good to introduce a spirit of competition, for it keeps the players up to the mark and helps them to estimate their own improvement.
4. Always start a session in a mild fashion. Let the players run freely and exercise to prepare their bodies for greater efforts. If a man does not warm up and attempts to do something of a strenuous nature straightaway, he is very likely to strain a muscle. Players can warm up using soccer balls; one each or one between two is excellent.
5. Make the whole session, including the part just mentioned, as varied as possible; use your surroundings, whether they include a track, a hill, or sand, for example.
6. Sprinting is the essence of the game, so all training schedules must include it. Sprints of 10,20, or 30 yards can be introduced through relays, for speed off the mark is fundamental for every player.
7. Interval-type sprint training will not only increase speed but also build up the stamina of a player. Have players sprint 50 yards, jog back to the start, and sprint 50 again. Aim to build up the number of sprints to perhaps ten or a down, from an initial four or five.
8. Players need exercises to develop the whole body. I remember one college player with a fine pair of legs who could not see the need for upper body development; alas, he never became much good at the game, for he lacked the necessary overall strength and stamina.
9. Don't be afraid of weight-training. It is a vital part of the preparation programmes for most sports, and provided that a player is advised as to the correct schedule, it will do a great deal for the physical buildup of any player.
10. Circuit training is a fine way to develop endurance. It consists in a player moving around a number of stations (eight suggested) as quickly as possible against the stopwatch, doing a specified number of exercises at each one. They can be simple or difficult, according to the facilities and equipment available, and include sit-ups, press-ups, forearm and biceps curl (with weights), 5-yard sprinting with turn, etc. A coach can make up his own circuit according to what he feels are the particular needs of his players. As progress is made, time may be reduced, the number of repetitions increased, or the rest period

between circuits shortened. There are the three variables for consideration.

11. An occasional long run in the country is a good variation to be introduced. Don't make it one long grind, but rather let the players run as to how they feel-jogging, striding, or sprinting, more or less as the moód moves them. This is based on the Hungarian Fartlek training, which certainly assists in building up the endurance of athletes.
12. Five or six-a-side games are excellent for stamina. The players have a great deal of ground to cover, and they should make every effort to keep moving during the game.
13. Any game is good for fitness; players should be encouraged to participate in other activities they enjoy which will have carryover value to soccer.

Kits:

Boots were made of thick leather which stretches above the ankle and had solid toe-caps.Professional players use to buy a size below their real sizè and squeeze them on to their feet, then stand in a hot bath to allow the leather to expand. This way they were able to mould the boot to suit the size of their feet. But it could be an uncomfortable process and it took a long time to wear boots in properly.The professional player has three types of boot: the studded boot with screw-in studs which can be changed to suit conditions and is used mainly on dry grass pitches, the moulded rubber boot for hard grounds, and the boot with a pimpled sole suitable for use on artifical pitches or training grounds.Today's boot is low-cut around the ankle and has a soft toe-cap.There is a greater chance of injury but players prefer the lightness and comfort.They believe they can 'feel' the ball better.

Players who go on the field without shinpads are taking an unnecessary risk.Fortunately,most players recognise the need for protection, and up to seventy-five percent of League players now wear a type of pad which also incorporates an ankle protector.

Most players wear underpants or swimming trunks under their shorts rather than traditional jock-strap.Shirts and shorts have changed over the years, mainly in design, but the basic format remain. A player should not wear anything which may cause injury to another player. He may wear spectacles at his own risk and at the discretion of the referee.

SAFEGUARDS IN TEACHING SOCCER

Common Types of Injuries

They include:

1. Sprained ankles or knees due to slipping.
2. Sprained toes caused by kicking with inadequate protection to the foot or by lack of skill in kicking.
3. Face and body injuries caused by being hit with kicked ball. This includes bloody nose, black eyes, body bruises and similar injuries.
4. Charley horse, muscle strain and the like caused by lack warm-up periods.

Prevention of Injuries

Teacher activities to prevent injuries should include:

1. Selection of proper playing equipments.
2. Provision for care of field.
3. Check costume and personal equipments.
4. Thorough knowledge of skills.

KICKING

Kicking technique cannot be practised effectively until the players have gone through the exercises in the previous sections. Kicking and trapping are above all a question of feel for the ball.This explains why all technically gifted players have a good kicking technique even though they have undergone no special training for it. Having a feel for the ball also makes it a lot easier to develop the player's weak leg, something which must be done,because in modern football players have neither the time nor the space to transfer the ball to their strong leg.

Kicking practice can take a varied form, with the trainer determining distance and intensity. In practising kicking techniques you automatically practise trapping. As kicking technique also forms part of the sections on receiving and coming away with the ball, getting past an opponent, making one-two combinations, shooting and heading, every player will acquire a good kicking technique without any trouble.

Kicking with the Inside of the Foot

Starting Position :- The right leg should be raised diagonally outward and backward.
The right knee should be slightly bent.
The toe should be pointed toward the ground.
The weight should be supported on the left leg.
The eyes should be on the ball.
The ball should be in front of the player.
The arms should be free at the sides.

Application of Force:- The right leg should be swung diagonally across the body to meet the ball with the inside of the foot.
The knee should be straightened at contact.

Follow Through :- There should be a short follow through of the leg in the direction of the kick. The length of the follow through is limited by contact of body parts.
The trunk should lean slightly to the right.

Uses :- Used for a diagonally forward pass or shot.(The right foot should be used for a pass to the left, and the left foot for a pass to the right.)
Used as the beginning of a dodge.
Used for place kicks which include free kicks, penalty kicks, kick offs and defense kicks.

Kicking with the Outside of the Foot

Starting Position:- The left leg should be raised diagonally forward toward the right.
The knee should be bent.
The toe should be pointed toward the ground.
The arms should be free at the sides.
The ball should be in front of and outside of the left foot.
The body weight should be supported on the right foot.
The eyes should be on the ball.

Application or Force:- The leg should be swung sharply toward the left.
The outside of the foot should meet the ball just below the center.

Follow Through :- There should be a slight follow through of the left leg in the direction of the kick.
The body should lean slightly to the right to aid in balance.

Uses :- Used as a short pass diagonally ahead.
Used as a shot at goal.

Used as a place kick.
Used as the beginning of a dodge.

Kicking with the Top of the Instep

Starting Position :- The right leg should be swung back with the knee bent.
The toe should be pointed toward the ground.
The body weight should be supported on the left leg.
The arms should be free at the sides or balance.
The eyes should be on the ball.
The ball should be in front of the player and slightly toward the right foot.

Application of Force :- The entire leg, with the knee slightly bent, should be swung forward to meet the ball below the center.
The top of the instep should come in contact with the ball.
Additional force can be added if the kick is preceded with a step or two.

Follow Through :- If a horizontal kick is desired the knee should remain bent and the leg should follow through in the direction of the kick.
If a raised kick is desired the knee should be straightened at the moment of contact with the ball, and the follow through should be high.
The trunk should be bent forward to maintain balance.

Uses :- Used for a long pass in the direction in which the player is facing.
Used for a long shot at goal.
Used for place kicks of any sort.

Kicking with the Heel

Starting Position :- The right leg should be raised forward with the knee slightly bent.
The heel should be toward the ground.
The body weight should be supported on the left leg.
The arms should be free at the sides.
The ball should be 4 to 8 inches behind the right foot.

Application of Force :- The right leg should be swung backward so that the heel meets the ball below the center.
The knee should be straightened just before contact with the ball.

Follow Through :- There should be a slight follow through in the direction of the kick.
The knee should bend on the follow through.
The trunk should incline slightly forward to aid in maintaining balance.

Uses :- Used to pass the ball backward.
Used to save the ball from going out-of-bounds.

Kicking with the Toe

Starting Position :- The right leg should be swung straight back.
The knee should be slightly bent.
The arms should be free at the sides for balance.
The body weight should be supported on the left leg.
The eyes should be on the ball.
The ball should be directly in front of the right foot.

Application of Force :- The right leg shou7ld be swung forcibly forward.
The knee should be straightened at the moment of contact with the ball.
The ankle should be flexed from the starting position so that the toe is pointing straight ahead at the moment of contact with the ball.

Follow Through :- The leg should follow through in an upward direction.
The force of this kick should lift the player onto her toes or even off the ground.
The trunk should be bent forward from the waist to aid in maintaining balance.

Uses :- Used for place kicks, especially for penalty kicks and free kicks near the player's own goal.
Used for volleying the ball.
Used for meeting the ball at the top of a high bounce.

TRAPPING

Trapping with the Inside of the Lower Leg

Starting Position :- The right leg, with the knee bent and the foot in contact with the ground, should form a 45 degree angle with the ground.
The weight should be on the left foot which should be obliquely ahead of the right.
The left knee should be bent.
The trunk should be inclined forward.
The arms should be free at the sides.
The player should be in line with the ball.

Application of Force: - The ball should be caught in the pocket formed by the inside of the leg and the ground.

Follow Through :- There should be no follow through.

Uses :- Used to stop a fast moving ball coming toward the player. Used to stop a ball moving toward the player from the side.

Trapping with the Inside of Both Legs

Starting Position :- The feet should be in a narrow side stride position, the toes pointing slightly outward.

The knees should be bent forward and inward.

The trunk should be inclined forward.

The weight should be evenly distributed on the inner part of both feet.

The body should be directly in line with the oncoming ball.

The arms should be free at the sides.

Application of Force :- As the ball rolls to the player the knees should bend deeply until the ball is trapped between the inside of both legs and the ground.

Uses :- Used to stop a fast moving ground ball.

Used to stop a ball as it starts to rise from the ground.

Trapping with the Front of Both Legs

Starting Position :- The player should be directly in line with the oncoming ball.

The feet should be together, toes pointing forward.

Both knees should be bent, heels off the ground.

The trunk should be inclined forward.

The weight should be carried evenly on the balls of the feet.

The eyes should be on the ball.

The arms should be free at the sides.

Application of Force :- As the ball rolls toward the player the knees should be deeply bent until the ball is caught in the pocket formed by the front of the legs and the ground.

CONTROLLING THE BALL

Feet Control : -To control the ball effectively, the part of the body to be used must relax slightly when contact is made with the ball in order to take the pace out of the ball, bring it under control and stop it rebounding.

Points to Watch:

1. Use the instep to cushion the ball's impact, withdrawing the foot to control the ball successfully.
2. Ensure the foot is correctly angled horizontally to make contact through the centre before withdrawal takes place.

3. Balance is important. The upper part of the body should be slightly bent over the ball.

Thigh Control :- Since a player may on occasions need to control a high ball before it reaches the ground, especially if he is being hotly challenged, the thigh may sometimes be used.

Points to Watch:

1. At all times get the body in the line of flight of the ball.
2. Ensure the thigh is placed at the correct angle to control the ball effectively.
3. Cushion the ball upon impact before withdrawing the leg to control it.
4. The body should be well balanced,the arms being used as stabilizers.

Chest Control :- Chest control is useful when a player hasn't time to step backwards and control the ball with his foot.

Points to Watch :

1. Watch the flight of the ball through the air and decide early what part of the chest is going to be used to control it.
2. Position the body in the path of the ball.Bend the knees slightly when contact is made, and lower the chest to form a platform.
3. When the ball strikes the body, the body should relax to produce a cushioning effect before withdrawing to allow the ball to reach the ground.
4. Notice the angle of the chest in relation to the ball.

PASSING

Having examined how important the techniques of control, pass and support to maintaining possession of the ball, we should now bring them together and relate the topic of passing to the match situation.So far we have explored them as individual aspects and looking at basic ideas to improve the understanding and practical ability at technique level. However players of all ages and abilities must be exposed to completely realistic situations. Unless players grow up with the problems presented by opponents, they will not become tremendous ball players, but disastrous footballers. Opposed practices, to encourage skill, and unopposed practices are equally necessary for players at all levels, but there is no point in presenting inexperienced players with a physical challenge from an opponent until he can perform the technique efficiently.

One of the prime objectives in developing talent is to impart confidence to the player.Practices should be set up to allow players plenty of time(space) to undertake the required skill. Players who are confronted by an over competitive

situation will never improve and before any practice is set up a great deal of consideration should be given to the number of players being used in relation to the area selected. Small-sided opposed practices using only a few players can quickly expose the problems confronted in matches.

If we use an area of approximately 10 metres square and set three players to retain possession against a challenger the fundamentals are quickly realised. Players off the ball must work hard to provide a good angle for the pass to be made.Even in basic forms of passing, supporting players will hide behind the challenger, making safe passing difficult. They must be educated to show for the ball in the best possible position to receive it. Often a movement of a metre or two can make the difference between a possible pass and a probable pass. The margin of error should be made as wide as possible to allow for an inaccurate pass or for the defender to read the direction of the ball. This exercise requires players to work hard at supporting one another. A constant change of position always working to find the best angle and at the same time keeping as far away from the passer as possible will give the best chance of stringing passes together.If the distance between the two players is too restricted the receiver will be closed down very quickly and the sequence will be jeopardised. Supporting at a slightly greater distance will enable the receiver to have enough space to control the ball before selecting the next pass. Control is an important factor and as the area is fairly tight, the first touch of the ball must be relaxed to allow the ball to be retained close enough to guarantee possession.

This routine will also provide an insight and a learning platform in the timing of a pass.Opposing players should be committed to the player in possession before the pass is played. If the ball is played too early, or too softly, the challenging player will have a chance to adjust his position to make things difficult for the receiver. Equally,if the ball is played too soon the receiving player may not have had a chance to move into position.If the pass is delayed too long the challenger will be able to deny passing possibilities completely. As players gain more experience a feeling for releasing the ball at the correct moment will be developed.

DRIBBLING

Dribbling is the art of carrying the ball on one's own, under control, in order to beat an opponent. To do this succesfully it is essential to have the ability not only to keep the ball close to one's feet but also to swerve and body feint in order to send the opponent the wrong way. It is a move that can look good and can at times be very effective but is often overdone and proves to be a waste of time. Given the right situation, players are able to beat their opponents but the true artist will work towards moving the ball on to his teammates as quickly as possible.

The man to beware of is the one who tries to beat one,two, or three men from the opposition, when he could serve his side much better by a quick pass to colleague. In dribbling,the ball is moved forward by the use of the inside and outside of the foot, while keeping the ball as close to the body as possible, and with the body leaning over the ball and the eyes focusing on it. Change of pace and change of direction are two important skills for a good dribbler to develop. The essence of dribbling really, is to get the opponent off balance and then to move past him.

Again it must be said that good teamwork can often be ruined by just one player who tries to do too much on his own. Good passing is always more effective and certainly produces greater understanding among the players.

Dribbling with the Inside of the Foot

Starting Position :- The leg should be rotated outward so that the inside of the foot is in position to meet the ball.

Both feet should be used in dribbling and the ball should be touched every two or three steps.

The ball should be 10 to 12 inches in front of the

dribbler.

The arms should be free at the sides.

The eyes should be on the ball most of the time, but the dribbler should look up occasionally.

Application of Force :- The ball should be tapped lightly below its center.

The inside of the foot should come in contact with the ball.

Follow Through :- The body weight should follow through onto the foot which last tapped the ball or with a hop onto the other foot.

Use :- Used to maintain possession of the ball and to carry it while running.

Dribbling with the Outside of the Foot

Starting Position :- The foot should be rotated inward so that the outside of the foot is in position to meet the ball.

The ball should be 10 to 12 inches ahead of the dribbler.

The toe of the foot contacting the ball should be pointed diagonally toward the ground.

The arms should be free at the sides.

The eyes should be on the ball.

Application of Force :- Running normally, the foot should be turned inward to meet the ball with the outside of the instep.

Follow Through :- The body weight should follow through onto the foot which last contacted the ball or with a hop on the other foot.

Uses :- Used to carry the ball while running. Especially usable when combined with use of the inside of the foot for dribbling in a circular direction. Dribbling with the inside of one foot and the outside of the other foot makes it possible to turn more quickly. Used as the beginning of a dodge.

Dribbling with the Toe

Starting Position :- The feet should point in the direction in which the player is progressing.

The ball should be 10 to 12 inches in front of the dribbler.

The arms should be free at the sides.

The eyes should be on the ball at the moment of contacting it.

Application of Force :- The foot should contact the ball every two or three steps.

The toe should be directed slightly under the ball in order to impart the backspin necessary to keep the ball close to the dribbler.

Follow Through :- The body weight should follow through onto the foot which last contacted the ball or with a hop onto the other foot.

Use :- Used to carry the ball while running. This method of dribbling is difficult and should be taught to advanced players only.

VOLLEYING THE BALL

Volleying With The Knee

Starting Position :- The body should be in line with the descending ball.

The weight of the body should be supported on one foot.

The other leg should be raised forward, the knee slightly bent.

The trunk should be inclined slightly forward, unless the ball is dropping perpendicularly, in which case it should be inclined backward.

The arms should be free at the sides for balance.

The eyes should be on the ball.

Application of Force :- As the ball drops, the knee should be raised to meet it.

Follow Through :- There should be a slight follow through of the leg in the direction of the volley.

Use :- Used to play a descending ball. Correctly speaking, the volley should be used only on a ball which has not touched the ground, but this type of the play can also be used on a ball which bounces high.

Volleying With The Foot

Starting Position :- The weight should be carried on the left foot.

The right leg should be extended backward, in line with the oncoming ball.

The right knee should be slightly bent and the toe should be pointed toward the ground.

The trunk should be inclined slightly forward.

The arms should be free at the sides.

The eyes should be on the ball.

Application of Force :- As the ball comes within reach of the player the right leg should be swung forward to meet it.

The top of the instep should contact the ball.

Follow Through :- The right leg should follow through in the direction of the kick.

If the kick is hard the body should rise on the toe of the left foot.

The trunk should incline forward from the hips.

In this volley the inside or the outside of the foot may also be used.

The mechanics are essentially the same as those for kicking.

Use :- Used to play a descending ball.

Volleying With The Shoulder

Starting Position :- The weight should be on both feet.

The arms should be free or folded across the chest.

Application of Force :- As the ball comes toward the player the entire body should be extended toward the ball.

Follow Through :- The entire body should follow through with a jump in the direction of the volley.

Use :- Used to play a descending ball which is too low to head and too high for a knee a foot volley.

HEADING

This is the art of passing, scoring, clearing, or controlling the ball by use of the head.When he does this skillfully, a player will find that he can send the ball both accurately and powerfully without any discomfort to himself. Perhaps the two men on a team who should be particularly capable in this way are the center half, who has to deal with all the high balls coming into his penalty area, and the center forward, who often jumps against the opposing center half. With skill in heading, he can deflect the ball to his colleagues, or may often be able to score goals himself.

A hard head is not a prerequisite for this skill;confidence and good neck muscles are. Very often in a game, a player will find that he is jumping in the air to head the ball, and by the correct use of his neck muscles he will be able to propel the ball in the direction he wants. The forehead, just below the hairline,is used for heading the ball in a forward direction, and the area just above and forward of the temples to move it to the left or right. The secret is in meeting the ball with the head, not allowing it to hit you, and never using the top of the head in the action; this would be painful, and accuracy would be impossible.

As a player improves with this skill,he will find that he uses more and more trunk movement, particularly when he is leaping for a ball and endeavouring to send it a considerable distance. Remember, always keep your eyes on the ball, and,just as important ,keep them open during the action. One other important point to remember: You will often find that you are jumping against an

complete extension as the ball is touched.
The ball should be met with the part of the head just above the forehead.
A forward arm swing as the player leaves the ground will add height to the jump.

Follow Through :- The body should follow on upward in the direction of the jump.

Use :- Used to play a ball descending from a height or bouncing height.

opponent, both of you trying to head the ball. In this circumstance, you must not charge the opposition that would be a foul. You must simply go for the ball, and in trying to outjump your man, meet the ball at your peak.

Body Machines

Starting Position :- The feet should be in a slight stride psoition, forward preferably.
The arms should be free at the sides.
The body should be inclined slightly forward.
The eyes should be on the ball.

Application of Force :- A jump into the air should precede contact with the ball. This adds force and gives additional height.
The neck muscles should be firm and the body in

TACKLING

Perhaps this skill should be among the first to be taught, so as to differentiate early between tackling in soccer and tackling in football.

Tackling in soccer is the method used to take the ball away with the feet from a member of the opposition. This is the one time in the game when physical contact is permitted, but even so, a player must be making a positive attempt to play the ball.

Most tackles are made slightly from the side, with a defensive player-the one not in possession of the ball- going in towards his opposite to stop his progress by playing the ball, or blocking it with his feet, or taking it away from him in the one movement. He must tackle his man with one foot only: two-footed tackling is a foul and will be duly penalized. He must watch man and ball closely, and try to make his move when the opponent is slightly off balance or has allowed the ball to move just a little too far ahead of him. Sometimes, however, he must tackle when the opponent has the ball in perfect position. He must use his body weight in the act and not merely stick out a leg (this is the most common cause of ankle and knee injuries) so that if he comes into bodily contact, it will be shoulder-to-shoulder.

Sliding tackle is one made at an atttacker from his rear; having raced alongside the attacker, the tackler literally slides in a semi-sitting position on his free leg and thigh,hooking the ball with the tackling foot, and endeavouring to take it on the instep. Very often this tackle will bring an opponent to the ground,but if the tackler has played the ball, he will not be penalized.Split-second timing is vital here, for otherwise the tackler will be left on the ground with the attacker yards away, in possession.

FRONT TACKLE

Starting Position :- The tackler should be directly in front of the oncoming opponent.

The feet should be in a slight forward stride position.

The knees should be easy.

The weight should be evenly divided on both feet.

The trunk should be inclined forward.

The arms should be free at the sides.

The eyes should be on the ball.

Application of Force :- One foot should be placed on the ball.

The knee of the near leg should bend.

The weight should be shifted to the rear foot.

The tackler should reach forward as far as possible to contact the ball.

Follow Through :- There should be no follow through.

Uses :- Used as a head-on tackle against a player dribbling the ball.

Used to block the ball as a player starts to kick.

SIDE TACKLE

The side tackle is similar to the circular tackle in hockey, but since there is no obstruction in soccer it may be done from either side. The tackler should run parallel with his opponent and attempt the tackle in one of the following ways:

1. By getting ahead of his opponent and dribbling around in front of his, using a combination of dribble with the inside of the foot and dribble with the outside of the foot.
2. By tapping the ball to the opponent's side, using the outside of the nearer foot.

Use :- Used to tackle a player while running parallel with him.

HOOK TACKLE

Starting Position :- The tackler should face the oncoming opponent, should be ahead of him and

Block Tackle

Side Block Tackle

slightly to one side.
The feet should be in a side stride position.
The knees should be easy.
The weight should be evenly divided on both feet.
The trunk should be inclined slightly forward.
The arms should be free at the sides.
The eyes should be on the ball.

Application of Force:- The leg near the opponent should be extended sideways with the inside of the foot toward the ground.
The weight should be transferred to the stationary foot.
The knee of the stationary leg should bend deeply.
The trunk should bend to the stationary leg.
The moving leg, after contact with the ball, should pull toward the tackler.

Follow Through :- There should be no follow through.

Uses :- Used to tackle a player when slightly to one side. Used only to hook the ball away from an opponent.

SPLIT TACKLE

Starting Position :- The tackler should be in front of or to the side of his opponent.
The feet should be apart in an easy stride position, the weight evenly divided.
The knees should be relaxed.
The trunk should be inclined slightly forward.
The arms should be free at the sides.
The eyes should be on the ball.

Application of Force :- The tackler should drop on one knee while extending the other leg in the direction of the ball.
The toe should be toward the ball and the knee should be straight.
The weight should be on the bent knee.
The tackler should lean away from the ball.

Follow Through :- There should be no follow through.

Use :- Used to tackle a player when the ball cannot be reached by any other method.

DUTIES OF TEAM MEMBERS

GOALKEEPER

The goalkeeper is the specialist in the team.His position demands that he should be able to handle the ball with the expertise of a slip fielder, and that he should have the agility of a gymnast and the composure of a ballet dancer. He is responsible for stopping opponents from scoring and, by skilful kicking and throwing,he can also be instrumental in starting an attack.'Safety first' is the golden rule, since guarding the goal is his number one priority.

The goalkeeper is the last line of defense, and also the man who can start an attack, the man who must by his every action give confidence to his teammates. In one sense, he controls the defense, particularly when the play is near his own goal. He must have strength, agility,and dareness. He must be extremely skilled in catching and throwing a ball, and must be able both to jump and to dive to catch or punch away a ball. He must be able to kick accurately and strongly from the ground and with a punt. He, as much as anyone, must have an ability to read or anticipate the play. The best goalkeeper is the one who seldom appears to have to made an incredible dive or leap, who positions himself so that the ball comes to him and by positioning, makes an angle for scoring very difficult for an attacker.

Sometimes, however, he will have to dive at the feet of an opponent who is in possession of the ball. This requires both courage and perfect timing: At the second of clutching the ball,he turns his back into his opponent's feet.He must have a perfect understanding with his other defenders, must know their methods, and must call for the ball and expect to receive it. He will realize that as often as possible he will have his body behind the ball when he is catching it. If he then makes an error it will not be fatal, resulting in a goal.He will know that moving out from his goal line in a particular direction will lessen the angle of shot for an attacker. He should be confident and bold, but not flashy. All

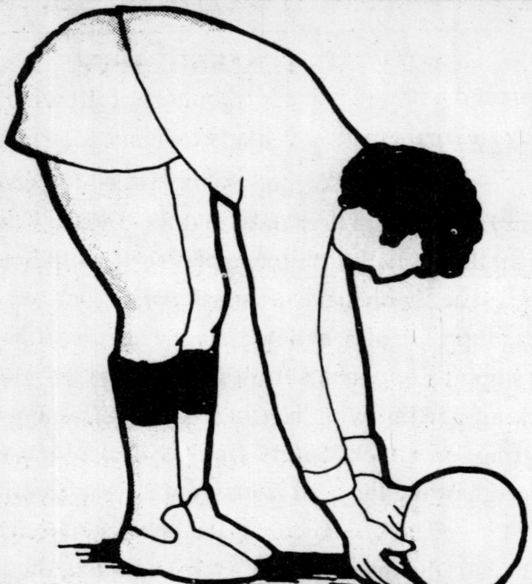

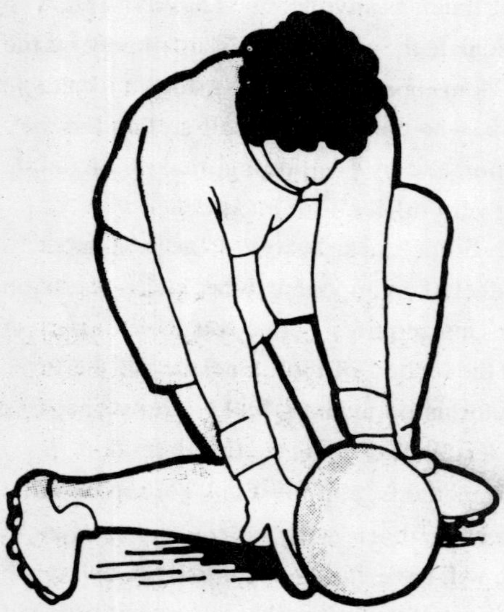

of his work should be done with a minimum of show. One final word: All of his clearances should be made to his wings;if he makes an error or his own man is immediately dispossessed, the danger is not so imminent if his clearance has been straight up the field.

FULLBACKS

These men are primarily defenders, but they must be all-round players, with strength in the tackle, clever anticipation,speed on the turn, the ability to use both feet equally well and skill in the use of the head. When the full back is not directly concerened with the play, he should be following it closely and reading what is likely to happen: he must work in formation with his co-defenders.When committing himself to a tackle, he should be 99 percent certain that he will be successful. If not, he will be completely out of position and will leave a gap in the defense of his team.

The fullback will know the set position he should take up for corner kicks and free kicks.A fullback should never be afraid to join in an attack when the chance presents itself.When it does, it is important that his fellow back fall slightly farther back to cover for him; a plan for what to do in such a situation is essential. Fullbacks and the center half are usually more than adequate in their heading ability, and they therefore should occasionally go upfield when their side is awarded a corner. Their height and ability can often be a menace to an opposing defense.

FORWARD

The forwards are named as follows: right wing, right inner, center forward,left inner, and left wing or left outer forward. These five players cover the entire field literally, and the distance which they travel up and down .

Center Forward : The center forward is the general of the forward line. He must be able to direct the play to the advantage of his team and must be able to keep it well distributed, using both sides equally. The center forward must quickly see openings and be able to accept half chances, for most that come his way will be like that. He will have nuisance value, always troubling the opponent by his movement. Moreover,he will have a fine understanding with his fellow forwards, knowing how he can help them and vice versa.He will move back when his team is defending, in the hope of receiving a clearance pass.

Wing Forwards : The prime requisite of a wing is ability to control the ball while travelling at top speed. He must also have dribbling ability, for very often he will find himself hemmed into the touchling by the fullback and his only way out is to attempt to reach his man.He must be able to pass,center or cross the ball accurately. He must be able to shoot hard with both feet, because one of the attacking moves of a wingman is to cut inside his opposing fullback and shoot at the goal.The wing forward will be good at kicking a dead ball, for he is the man to take the corner kicks.

Inner Forward : Like the wing halfbackss, the two inner forwards (right and left) are the workers of the team, but they must attack slightly more than the halfbacks do. Each will cover the area behind his own center forward, working with the ball by chasing, tackling passing and creating openings for their teammates and when scoring opportunity arises they must be able to take it.

They must know when to stop a pass and when to let it go on through to another player, remembering that every pass which crosses their territory is not meant for them. Frequently, especially when on the defensive the inners play well back of the rest of the forward line.

Half Back : The halfbacks have the most grueling positions on the team. They must be ready to back up their own forward line, and quick to shift to a defense position.

Center Halfback : The center halfback marks the most dangerous player on the opposite forward line, namely the center forward. He must be a speedy, heady player, and the leader of the half back line.The center halfback must be a sound kicker, and like the other members of his defense,he must be able to use the ball and not merely clear it wildly away. He must have a complete understanding with his goalkeeper and his fellow fullbacks; he will often find himself covering his other men. He must have full comprehension of the offside law, and know when to try to apply a play to foil an opponent's attack. In short, he must be the pillar of any defensive system.

RULES OF THE GAME

Law I - *The Field of Play*

The Field of Play and appurtenances shall be as shown in the following plan:

(1) *Dimensions* : The field of play shall be rectangular, its length being not more than 130 yards nor less than 100 yards and its breadth not more than 100 yards nor less than 50 yards.(In International Matches the length shall be not more than 120 yards nor less than 110 yards and the breadth not more than 80 yards nor less than 70 yards.)The length shall in all cases exceed the breadth.

(2) *Marking :* The field of play shall be marked with distinctive lines, not more than 5 inches in width, not by a V-shaped cut, in accordance with the plan, the longer boundary lines being called the touch-lines.A flag on a post not less than 5 feet high and having a non-pointed top, shall be placed at each corner; a similar flag-post may be placed opposite the half-way line of play shall be indicated by a suitable mark and a circle

with a 10-yard radius shall be marked round it.

(3) *The Goal-Area:* At each end of the field of play two lines shall be drawn at right angles to the goal-line,6 yards from each goal-post.These shall extend into the field of play for a distance of 6 yards and shall be joined by a line drawn parallel with the goal-line. Each of the spaces enclosed by these lines and the goal-line shall be called a goal area.

(4) *The Penalty-Area :* At each end of the field of play two lines shall be drawn at right angles to the goal-lines,18 yards from each goal-post.These shall extend into the field of play for a distance of 18 yards and shall be joined by a line drawn parallel with the goal-line.Each of the spaces enclosed by these lines and the goal-line shall be called a penalty-area.A suitable mark shall be made within each penalty-area,12 yards from the mid-point of the goal-line,measured

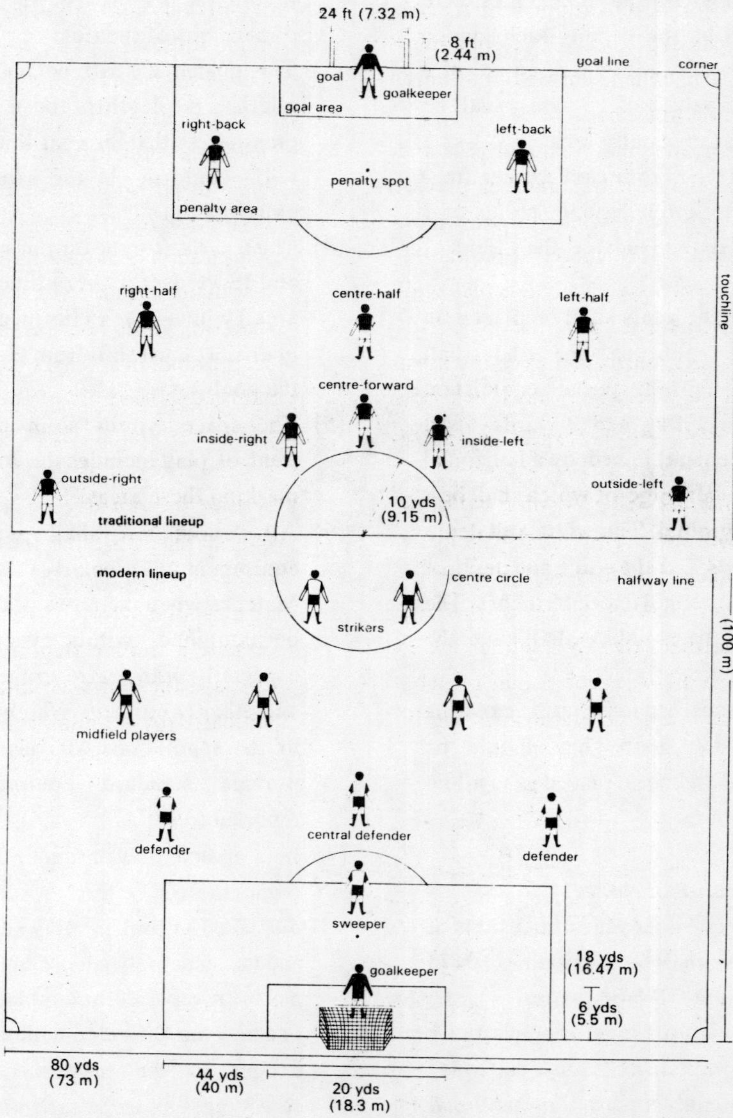

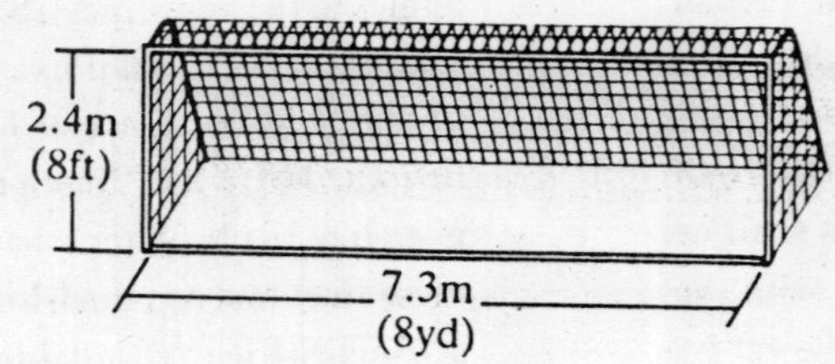

alohg an undrawn line at right angles there to.These shall be the penalty-kick marks. From each penalty-kick mark an arc of a circle,having a radius of 10 yards, shall be drawn outside the penalty-area.

(5) *The Corner-Area* : From each corner flag-post a quarter circle,having radius of 1 yard,shall be drawn indside the field of play.

(6) *The Goals* : The goals shall be placed on the centre of each goal-line and shall consist of two upright posts, equidistant from the corner-flag and 8 yards apart (inside measurement),joined by a horizontal crossbar the lower edge of which shall be 8 feet from the ground. The width and depth of the goal-posts and the width and depth of the crossbars shall not exceed 5 inches. The goal-posts and the crossbars shall have the same width.

Nets may be attached to the posts, crossbars and ground behind the goals.They should be appropriately supported and be so placed as to allow the goalkeeper ample room.

Decisions of the International Board

(1) In International Matches the dimensions of the field of play shall be:maximum 110x75 metres: minimum 100x64 metres.

(2) National Associations must adhere strictly to these dimensions.Each National Association organising an International Match must advise the visiting Association, before the match, of the place and the dimensions of the field of play.

(3) The goal-line shall be marked the same width as the depth of the goal-post and the crossbar, so that the goal-line and goal-post will conform to the same interior and exterior edges.

(4) The 6 yards (for the outline of the goal area) and 18 yards (for the outline of the penalty-area) which have to be measurd along the goal-line, must start from the inner sides of the goal-posts.

(5) The space within the inside areas of the field of play includes the width of the lines marking these areas.

(6) All Associations shall provide standard equipment, particularly in International Matches when the Laws of the Game must be complied within every respect and especially with regard to the size of the ball and other equipment which must conform to the regulations.All cases of failure to provide standard equipment must be reported to FIFA.

(7) In a match played under the rules of a competition,if the crossbar becomes displaced or broken, play shall be stopped and the match abandoned unless the crossbar has been repaired and replaced in position or a new one provided without such being a danger to the players.A rope is not considered to be a satisfactory substitute for a crossbar.

In a Friendly match, by mutual consent, play may be resumed without the crossbar, provided it has been removed and no longer consitutes a danger to the players. In these circumstances, a rope may be used as a substitue for a crossbar. If a rope is not used and the ball crosses the goal-line at a point which in the opinion of the Referee is below where the crossbar should have been, he shall award a goal.

The game shall be restarted by the Referee dropping the ball at the place where it was when play was stopped, unless it was within the goal-area at that time, in which case it shall be dropped on that part of the goal-area line which runs parallel to the goal-line, at the point nearest to where the ball was when play was stopped.

(8) National Associations may specify such maximum and minimum dimensions for the crossbars and goal-posts, within the limits laid down in Law 1, as they consider appropriate.

(9) Goal posts and crossbars must be made of wood, metal or other approved material as decided from time to time by the International FA Board. They may be square, rectangular, round, half-round or elliptical in shape. Goal-posts and crossbars made of other materials and in other shapes are not permitted.

(10) Curtain-raisers to International Matches should only be played following agreement on the day of the match, and taking into account the condition of the field of play, between representatives of the two Associations and the Referee (of the International Match).

(11) National Associations, particularly in International Matches, should

- restrict the number of photographers around the field of play.

- have a line (photographers' lone) marked behind the goal-lines at least 2 metres from the corner-flag going through a point situated at leat 3.5 metres behind the intersection of the goal-line with the line marking the goal-area to a point situated at least six metres behind the goal-posts,

- prohibit photographers from passing over these lines,

-forbid the use of artificial lighting in the form of flashlights.

Law II - ***The Ball***

The ball shall be spherical; the outer casing shall be of lather or other approved materials. No material shall be used in its construction which might prove dangerous to the players.

The circumference of the ball shall not be more than 28 inches and not less than 27 inches. The weight of the ball at the start of the game shall not be more than 16 ounces not less than 14 ounces. The pressure shall be equal to 0.6-1.1 atmosphere, (=600-1100gr/cm2) at sea level. The ball shall not be changed during the game unless authorised by the Referee.

Law III- ***Number of Players***

(1) A match shall be played by two teams, each consisting of not more than eleven players, one of whom shall be the goalkeeper.

(2) Substitutes may be used in any match played under the rules of an official competition at FIFA, Confederation or National Association level.

(3) Substitutes may be used in any other match, provided that the two teams concerned reach agreement on a maximum number, not exceeding five, and that the terms of such agreement are intimated to the Referee, before the match. If the Referee is not informed, or if the teams fail to reach agreement, no more than two substitutes shall be permitted. In all cases the substitutes must be chosen from not more than five players whose names shall be given to the Referee prior to the commencement of the match.

(4) Any of the other players may change places with the goalkeeper, provided that the Referee is informed before the change is made, and provided also, that the change is made during a stoppage in the game.

(5) When a goalkeeper or any other player is to be replaced by a substitute, the following conditions shall be observed:

(a) The Referee shall be informed of the proposed substitution, before it is made.

(b)The substitute shall not enter the field of play until the player he is replacing has left, and then only after having received a signal from the Referee.

(c) He shall enter the field during a stoppage in the game, and at the half-way line.

(d) A player who has been replaced shall not take any further part in the game.

(e) A substitute shall be subject to the authority and jurisdiction of the Referee whether called upon to play or not.

(f) The substitution is completed when the substitute enters the field of play, from which moment he becomes a player and the player whom he is replacing ceases to be a player.

Punishment

(a) Play shall not be stopped for an infringement of paragraph 4. The players concerned shall be cautioned immediately after the ball goes out of play.

(b) If a substitute enters the field of play without the authority of the Referee, play shall be stopped. The substitute shall be cautioned or sent off according to the circumstances. The game shall be restarted by the Referee dropping the ball at the place where it was when play was stopped, unless it was within the goal-area at that time, in which case it shall be dropped on that part of the goal-area line which runs parallel to the goal-line, at the point nearest to where the ball was when play was stopped.

(c) For any other infringement of this Law, the player concerned shall be cautioned, and if the game is stopped by the Referee, to administer the caution, it shall be restarted by an indirect free-kick, to be taken by a player of the opposing team from the place where the ball was, when play was stopped, subject to the over-riding conditions imposed in Law XIII.

Law IV - *Players' Equipment*

A player shall not wear anything which is dangerous to another player. Footwear (boots or shoes) must conform to the following standard:

(a) Bars shall be made of leather or rubber and shall be transverse and flat, not less than half an inch in width and shall extend the total width of the sole and be rounded at the corners.

(b) Studs which are independently mounted on the sole and are replaceable shall be made of leather, rubber, aluminium, plastic or similar material and shall be solid. With the exception of that part of the stud forming the base, which shall not protrude from the sole more than one quarter of an inch, studs shall be round in plan and not less than half an inch in diameter. Where studs are tapered,the minimum diameter of any section of the study must not be less than half an inch. Where metal seating for the screw type is used, this seating must be embedded in the sole of the footwear and any attachment screw shall be part of the stud. Other than the metal seating for the screw type of stud, no metal plates even though covered with leather or rubber shall be worn, neither studs which are threaded to allow them to be screwed on to a base screw that is fixed by nails or otherwise to the soles of footwear, nor studs which, apart from the base, have any form of protruding edge rim or relief marking or ornament should be allowed.

(c) Studs which are moulded as an integral part of the sole and are not replaceable shall be made of rubber,plastic polyurethene or similar soft materials. Provided that there are no fewer than ten studs on the sole, they shall have a minimum diameter of three eighths of an inch(10mm).Additional supporting material to stabilise studs of soft materials, and ridges which shall not protrude more than 5mm from the sole and moulded to strengthen it, shall be permitted provided that they are in no way dangerous to other players. In all other respects they shall conform to the general requirements of this Law.

(d) Combined bars and studs may be worn, provided the whole conforms to the general requirements of this Law.Neither bars nor studs on the soles or heels shall project more than three-quarters of an inch.If nails are used they shall be driven in flush with the surface.

The goalkeeper shall wear colours which distinguish him from the other players and from the Referee.

Punishment

For any infringement of this Law,the player at fault shall be sent offf the field of play to adjust his equipment and he shall not return without first reporting to the Referee, who shall satisfy himself that the player's equipment is in order;the player shall only re-enter the game at a moment when the ball ceased to be in play.

Law V - *Referees*

A Referee shall be appointed to officiate in each game. His authority and the exercise of the powers granted to him by the Laws of the Game commence as soon as he enters the field of play.

His power of penalising shall extend to offences committed when play has been temporarily suspended, or when the ball is out of play. His decision on points of fact connected with the play shall be final, so far as the result of the game is concerned. He shall:

(a) Enforce the Laws.

(b) Refrain from penalising in case where he is satisfied that, by doing so, he would be giving an advantage to the offending team.

(c) Keep a record of the game, act as timekeeper and allow the game for full or agreed time, adding there to all time lost through accident or other cause.

(d) Have discretionary power to stop the game for any infringement of the Laws and to suspend or terminate the game whenever, by reason of the elements, interference by spectators, or other cause, he deems such stoppage necessary. In such a case he shall submit a detailed report to the competent authority, within the stipulated time, and in accordance with the provisions set up by the National Association under whose jurisdiction the match was played. Reports will be deemed to be made when received in the ordinary course of post.

(e) From the time he enters the field of play, caution any player guilty of misconduct or ungentlemanly behaviour and if he persists, suspend him from further participation in the game. In such cses the Referee shall send the name of the offender to the competent authority, within the stipulated time and in accordance with the provisions set up by the National Association under whose jurisdiction the match was played. Reports will be deemed to be made when received in the ordinary course of post.

(f) Allow no person other than the players and Linesmen to enter the field of play without his permission.

(g) Stop the game if, in his opinion, a player has been seriously injured; have the player removed as soon as possible from the field

Direct Free-Kick
The hand and arm clearly indicate the direction.

Corner-Kick

Caution or Expulsion
With the card system in operation, the card shall be shown in the manner illustrated. The player's identity *must* be recorded at the time

Penalty-Kick
The referee clearly indicates the penalty-mark, but there is no need to run towards it

Goal-Kick

SIGNALS BY THE LINESMEN

Off-side
Flag held upright to indicate Off-side

Off-side
When the referee stops play, linesman indicates position on far side of the field

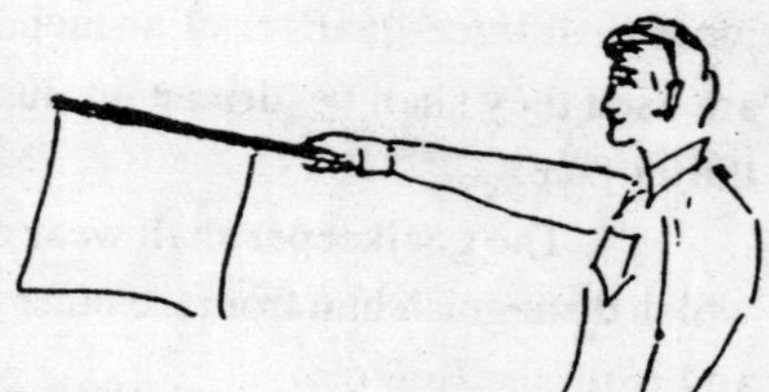

Off-side
Position near the centre of the field

Off-side
Position on near side of the field

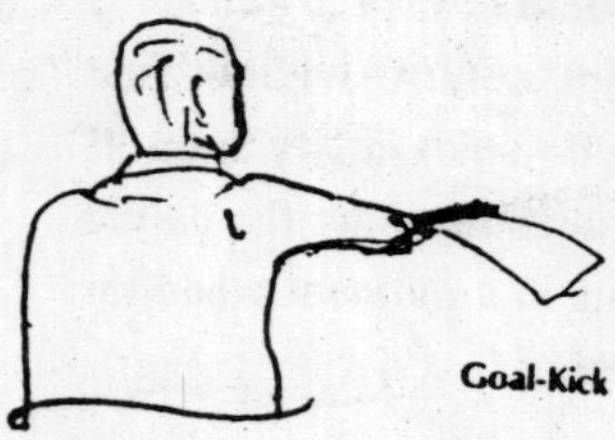

Goal-Kick

of play, and immediately resume the game. If a player is slightly injured, the game shall not be stopped until the ball has ceased to be in play. A player who is able to go to the touch-or goal-line for attention of any kind, shall not be treated on the field of play.

(h) Send off the field of play, any player who, in his opinion, is guilty of violent conduct, serious foul play, or the use of foul or abusive language.

(i) Signal for recommencement of the game after all stoppages.

(j) Decide that the ball provided for a match meets with the requirements of Law II.

Law VI - ***Linesmen***

Two Linesmen shall be appointed, whose duty (subject to the decision of the Referee) shall be to indicate when the ball is out of play, which side is entitled to the cornerkick, goal-kick or throw-in, and when a substitution is desired. They shall also assist the Referee to control the game in accordance with the Laws. In the event of undue interference or improper conduct by a Linesman,the Referee shall dispense with his services and arrange for a substitute to be appointed. (The matter shall be reported by the Referee to the competent authority.)The Linesmen should be equipped with flags by the Club on whose ground the match is played.

Law VII - ***Duration of the Game***

The duration of the game shall be two equal periods of 45 minutes, unless otherwise mutually agreed upon, subject to the following:

(a) Allowance shall be made in either period for all time lost through substitution,the transport from the field of injured players,time-wasting or other cause, the amount of which shall be a matter for the discretion of the Referee.

(b) Time shall be extended to permit a penalty-kick being taken at or after the expiration of the normal period in either hallf.

At half-time the interval shall not exceed five minutes except by consent of the Referee.

Law VIII - ***The Start of Play***

(a) At the beginning of the game, choice of ends and the kick-off shall be decided by the toss of a coin. The team winning the toss shall have the option of choice of ends or the kick-off.The Referee having given a signal,the game shall be started by a player taking a place-kick(i.e.a kick at the ball while it is stationary on the ground in the centre of the field of play) into his opponents'half of the field of play. Every player shall be in his own half of the field and every player of the opposing team of the kicker shall remain not less than 10 yards from the ball until it is kicked-off;it shall not be deemed in play until it has travelled the distance of its own circumference.The kicker shall not play the ball a second time until it has been touched or played by another player.

(b) After a goal is scored ,the game shall be restarted in like manner by a player of the team losing the goal.

(c) After half-time:when restarting after half-time, ends shall be changed and the kick-off shall be taken by a player of the opposite team to that of the player who started the game.

Law IX - ***Ball In and Out of Play***

The ball is out of play:

(a) When it has wholly crossed the goal-line or touch-line, whether on the ground or in the air.

(b) When the game has been stopped by the Referee.

The ball is in play at all other times from the start of the match to the finish including:

(a) If it rebounds from a goal-post, crossbar or corner flag-post into the field of play.

(b) If it rebounds off touching either the Referee

or Linesmen when they are in the field of play.

(c) In the event of a supposed infringement of the Laws, until a decision is given.

Law X - ***Mehtod of Scoring***

Except as otherwise provided by these Laws, a goal is scored when the whole of the ball has passed over the goal-line, between the goal-posts and under the crossbar, provided it has not been thrown, carried or intentionally propelled by hand or arm,by a player of the attacking side, except in the case of a goalkeeper who is within his own penalty-area.

The team scoring the greater number of goals during a game shall be the winner; if no goals, or an equal number of goals are scored, the game shall be termed a draw.

Law XI - ***Off-Side***

(1) A player is in an off-side position if he is nearer to his opponents' goal-line than the ball, unless
(a) he is in his own half of the field of play,or
(b) there are at least two of his opponents nearer their own goal-line than he is.

(2) A player shall only be declared off-side and penalised for being in an off-side position, if,at the moment the ball touches, or is played by, one of his team, he is, in the opinion of the Referee
(a) interfering with play or with an opponent, or
(b) seeking to gain an advantage by being in that position.

(3) A player shall not be declared off-side by the Referee
(a) merely because of his being in an off-side position, or
(b) if he receives the ball, direct, from a goal-kick, a corner-kick, a throw-in, or when it has been dropped by the Referee.

(4) If a player is declared off-side, the Referee shall award an indirect free-kick, which shall be taken by a player of the opposing team from the place where the infringement occurred, unless the offence is committed by a player in his opponents goal-area, in which case, the free-kick shall be taken from a point anywhere within that half of the goal-area in which the offence occurred.

Law XII - ***Fouls and Misconduct***

A player who intentionally commits any of the following offences:

(a) kicks or attempts to kick an opponent;
(b) trips an opponent, *i.e.* throwing or attempting to throw him by the use of the legs or by stopping in front of or behind him;
(c) jumps at an opponent;
(d) charges an opponent in a violent or dangerous manner;
(e) charges an opponent from behind unless the latter be obstructing;
(f) strikes or attempts to strike an opponent;
(g) holds an opponent;
(h) pushes an opponent;
(i) handles the ball,i.e. carries, strikes or propels tha ball with his hand or arm. (This does not apply to the goalkeeper with in his own penalty-area.) shall be penalised by the award of a direct free-kick to be taken by the opposing side from the place where the offence occurred,

Should a player of the defending side intentionally commit one of the above nine offences within the penalty-area he shall be penalised by a penalty-kick.

A penalty-kick can be awarded irrespective of the position of the ball,if in play, at the time an offence within the penalty-area is committed.

A player committing any of the five following offences:

(1) Playing in manner considered by the Referee to be dangerous,e.g.,attempting to kick the ball while held by the goalkeeper:

(2) Charging fairly,i.e.,with the shoulder,when

the ball is not within playing distance of the players concerned and they are definitely not trying to play it;

(3) When not playing the ball, intentionally obstructing an opponent, i.e., running between the opponent and the ball, or interposing the body so as to form an obstacle to an opponent;

(4) Charging the goalkeeper except when he

(a) is holding the ball;

(b) is obstructing an opponent;

(c) has passed outside his goal-area.

(5) When playing as goalkeeper and within his own penalty-area,

(a) From the moment he takes control of the ball with his hands, he takes more than four steps in any direction whilst holding, bouncing or throwing the ball in the air and catching it again, without releasing it into play, or, having released the ball into play before, during or after the four steps, he touches it again with his hands, before it has been touched or played by another player of the same team outside of the penalty-area, or by a player of the opposing team either inside or outside of the penalty-area, or

(b) indulges in tactics which, in the opinion of the Referee, are designed merely to hold up the game and thus waste time and so give an unfair advantage to his own team, shall be penalised by the award of an indirect free-kick to be taken by the opposing side from the place where the infringement occurred, subject to the overriding conditions imposed in Law XIII.

A player shall be cautioned if:

(j) he enters or re-enters the field of play to join or rejoin his team after the game has commenced, or leaves the field of play during the progress of the game (except through accident) without, in either case, first having received a signal from the Referee showing him that he may do so. If the Referee stops the game to administer the caution the game shall be restarted by an indirect free-kick taken by a player of the opposing team from the place where the ball was when the Referee stopped the game, subject to the over-riding conditions imposed in Law XIII. If, however, the offending player has committed a more serious offence, he shall be penalised according to that section of the Law he infringed:

(k) he persistently infringes the Laws of the Game;

(l) he shows, by word or action, dissent from any decision given by the Referee;

(m) he is guilty of ungentlemanly conduct.

For any of these last three offences, in addition to the caution, an indirect free-kick shall also be awarded to the opposing side from the place where the offence occurred unless a more serious infringement of the Laws of the Game was committed, subject to the over-riding conditions imposed in Law XIII.

A player shall be sent off the field of play if, in the opinion of the Referee,

(n) he is guilty of violent conduct or serious foul play;

(o) he uses foul or abusive language;

(p) he persists in misconduct after having received a caution.

If play be stopped by reason of a player being ordered from the field for an offence without a separate breach of the Law having been committed, the game shall be resumed by an indirect free-kick awarded to the opposing side from the place where the infringement occurred, subject to the over-riding conditions imposed in Law XIII.

Law XIII - *Free-Kick*

Free-kicks shall be classified under two headings: 'Direct' (from which a goal can be scored direct against the offending side), and 'Indirect' (from which a goal cannot be scored unless the ball has been played or touched by a player other than the kicker before passing through the goal).

When a player is taking a direct or an indirect free-kick inside his own penalty area,all of the opposing players shall be at least 10 yards from the ball and shall remain outside the penalty-area until the ball has been kicked out of the area.The ball shall be in play immediately it has travelled the distance of its own circumference and is beyond the penalty-area.The goalkeeper shall not receive the ball into his hands, in order that he may thereafter kick it into play. If the ball is not kicked direct into play, beyond the penalty-area, the kick shall be retaken.

When a player is taking a direct or an indirect free-kick outside his own penalty area, all of the opposing players shall be at least 10 yards from the ball,until it is in play,unless they are standing on their own goal-line, between the goal-posts.The ball shall be in play when it has travelled the distance of its own circumference.

If a player of the opposing side encroaches into the penalty-area,or within 10 yards of the ball, as the case may be, before a free-kick is taken, the Referee shall delay the taking of the kick, until the Law is complied with.

The ball must be stationary when a free-kick is taken, and the kicker shall not play the ball a second time, until it has been touched or played by another player.

Notwithstanding any other reference in these Laws to the point from which a free-kick is to be taken:

(1) Any free-kick awarded to the defending team, within its own goal-area,may be taken from any point within that half of the goal-area in which the free-kick has been awarded.

(2) Any indirect free-kick awarded to the attacking team within its opponents' goal-area shall be taken from that part of the goal-area line which runs parallel to the goal-line, at the point nearest to where the offence was committed.

Punishment

If the kicker, after taking the free-kick, plays the ball a second time before it has been touched or played by another player, an indirect free-kick shall be taken by a player of the opposing team from the spot where the infringement occurred, unless the offence is committed by a player in his opponents'goal-area,in which case the free-kick shall be taken from a point any-where within that half of the goal-area in which the offence occurred.

Law XIV - *Penalty-Kick*

A penalty-kick shall be taken from the penalty-mark and,when it is being taken,all players with the exception of the player taking the kick,properly identified, and the opposing goalkeeper, shall be within the field of play but outside the penalty-area,and at least 10 yards from the penalty-mark.The opposing goalkeeper must stand (without moving his feet) on his own goal-line,between the goal-posts,until the ball is kicked. The player taking the kick must kick the ball forward;he shall not play the ball a second time until it has been touched or played by another player.The ball shall be deemed in play directly when it is kicked, when it has travelled the distance of its circumference.A goal may be scored directly from a penaly-kick. When a penalty-kick is being taken during the normal course of play, or when time has been extended at half-time or full-time to allow a penalty-kick to be taken or retaken, a goal shall not be nullified if, before passing between the posts and under the cross-bar, the ball touches either or both of the goal-posts, or the cross bar, or the goalkeeper,or any combinations of these agencies, providing that no other infringement has occurred.

Punishment

For any infringement of this Law:

(a) by the defending team, the kick shall be retaken if a goal has not resulted;

(b) by the attacking team other than by the player taking the kick, if a goal is scored it shall be disallowed and the kick retaken.

(c) by the player taking the penalty-kick,

committed after the ball is in play, a player of the opposing team shall take an indirect free-kick from the spot where the infringement occurred, subject to the over-riding conditions imposed in Law XIII.

Law XV *-Throw-In*

When the whole of the ball passes over a touch-line,either on the ground or in the air, it shall be thrown in from the point where it crossed the line, in any direction,by a player of the team opposite to that of the player who last touched it. The thrower at the moment of delivering the ball must face the field of play and part of each foot shall be either on the touch-line or on the ground outside the touch-line.The thrower shall use both hands and shall deliver the ball from behind and over his head. The ball shall be in play immediately it enters the field of play, but the thrower shall not again play the ball until it has been touched or played by another player.A goal shall not be scored direct from a throw-in.

Punishment

(1) If the ball is improperly thrown in, the throw-in shall be taken by a player of the opposing team.

(2) If the thrower plays the ball a second time before it has been touched or played by another player, an indirect free-kick shall be taken by a player of the opposing team from the place where the infringement occurred, subject to the over-riding conditions imposed in Law XIII.

Law XVI - *Goal-Kick*

When the whole of the ball passes over the goal-line excluding that portion between the goal-posts,either in the air or on the ground, having last been played by one of the attacking team, it shall be kicked direct into play beyond the penalty-area from a point within that half of the goal-area nearest to where it crossed the line, by a player of the defending team. A goalkeeper shall not receive the ball into his hands from a goal-kick in order that he may thereafter kick it into play. If the ball is not kicked beyond the penalty-area,i.e.,direct into play, the kick shall be retaken.The kicker shall not play the ball a second time until it has touched-or been played by-another player.A goal shall not be scored direct from such a kick. Players of the team opposing that of the player taking the goal-kick shall remain outside the penalty-area until the ball has been kicked out of the penalty-area.

Punishment

If a player taking a goal-kick plays the ball a second time after it has passed beyond the penalty-area, but before it has touched or been played by another player, an indirect free-kick shall be awarded to the opposing team,to be taken from the place where the infringement occurred, subject to the the over-riding conditions imposed in Law XIII.

Law XVII - *Corner-Kick*

When the whole of the ball passes over the goal-line,excluding that portion between the goal-posts,either in the air or on the ground,having last been played by one of the defending team,a member of the attacking team shall take a corner-kick, *i.e.*,the whole of the ball shall be placed within the quarter circle at the nearest corner flagpost,which must not be moved, and it shall be kicked from that position.A goal may be scored direct from such a kick.Players of the team opposing that of the player taking the corner-kick shall not apporoach within 10 yards of the ball until it is in play,i.e.,it has travelled the distance of its own circumference,nor shall the kicker play the ball a second time until it has been touched or played by another player.

Punishment

(1) If the player who takes the kick plays the ball a second time before it has been touched or played by another player, the Referee shall award an indirect free-kick to the opposing team,to be taken from the place where the infringement occurred , subject to the over-riding conditions imposed in Law XIII.

(2) For any other infringement the kick shall be retaken.

CUP & TROPHIES

World Cup Winners

	Winners	Venue
1930	Uruguay	Uruguay
1934	Italy	Italy
1938	Italy	France
1950	Uruguay	Brazil
1954	W.Germany	Switzerland
1958	Brazil	Sweden
1962	Brazil	Chile
1966	England	England
1970	Brazil	Mexico
1974	W.Germany	W.Germany
1978	Argentina	Argentina
1982	Italy	Spain
1986	Argentina	Mexico
1990	W.Germany	Italy

Gold In Olympics

	Winners	Runners-Up
1896	Denmark	Greece
1900	UK	France
1904	Canada	USA
1908	UK	Denmark
1912	UK	Denmark
1916	Not held	
1920	Belgium	Spain
1924	Uruguay	Switzerland
1928	Uruguay	Argentina
1932	Not held	
1936	Italy	Austria
1940	Not held	
1944	Not held	
1948	Sweden	Yugoslavia
1952	Hungary	Yugoslavia
1956	USSR	Yugoslavia
1960	Yugoslavia	Denmark
1964	Hungary	Czechoslovakia
1968	Hungary	Bulgaria
1972	Poland	Hungary
1976	East Germany	Poland
1980	Czechoslovakia	East Germany
1984	France	Brazil
1988	USSR	Brazil

South American Championship

	Winners
1916	Uruguay
1917	Uruguay
1919	Brazil
1920	Uruguay
1921	Argentina
1922	Brazil
1923	Uruguay
1924	Uruguay
1925	Argentina
1926	Uruguay
1927	Argentina
1929	Argentina
1935	Uruguay
1937	Argentina
1939	Peru
1941	Argentina
1942	Uruguay
1945	Argentina
1946	Argentina
1947	Argentina
1949	Brazil
1953	Paraguay
1955	Argentina
1956	Uruguay
1957	Argentina
1959	Argentina
1961	Uruguay
1963	Bolivia
1967	Uruguay
1975	Peru
1979	Paraguay
1983	Uruguay
1987	Uruguay
1989	Brazil

South American Cup

Winners (Clbus)

1960	Penarol (Uruguay)
1961	Penarol (Uruguay)
1962	Santos (Brazil)
1963	Santos (Brazil)
1964	Independiente (Argentina)
1965	Independiente (Argentina)
1966	Penarol (Uruguay)
1967	Racing Club (Argentina)
1968	Estudiantes (Argentina)
1969	Estudiantes (Argentina)
1970	Estudiantes (Argentina)
1971	Nacional (Uruguay)
1972	Independiente (Argentina)
1973	Independiente (Argentina)
1974	Independiente (Argentina)
1975	Independiente (Argentina)
1976	Cruzeiro (Brazil)
1977	Boca Juniors (Argentina)
1978	Boca Juniors (Argentina)
1979	Olimpia (Paraguay)
1980	Nacional (Uruguay)
1981	Flamengo (Brazil)
1982	Penarol (Uruguay)
1983	Gremio Porto Alegre (Brazil)
1984	Independiente (Argentina)
1985	Argentinos Juniors (Argentina)
1986	River Plate (Argentina)
1987	Penarol (Uruguay)
1988	Nacional (Uruguay)
1989	Nacional (Colombia)

World Club Championship

Played annually up to 1974 between the winners of the European Cup and the winners of the South American Champions Cup.

Winners

1960	Real Madrid
1961	Penarol
1962	Santos
1963	Santos
1964	Inter-Milan
1965	Inter-Milan
1966	Penarol
1967	Racing Club
1968	Estudiantes
1969	AC Milan
1970	Feyenoord
1971	Nacional
1972	Ajax
1973	Independiente
1974	Atletico Madrid
1975	Not held
1976	Not held
1977	Not held
1978	Not held
1979	Not held
1980	Nacional
1981	Flamengo
1982	Penarol
1983	Gremio Porto Alegre
1984	Independiente
1985	Juventas
1986	River Plate
1987	FC Porto
1988	Nacional
1989	AC Milan

FA Cup Finals

Winners

1872	Wanderers
1873	Wanderers
1874	Oxford University
1875	Royal Engineers
1876	Wanderers
1877	Wanderers
1878	Wanderers
1879	Old Etonians
1880	Clapham Rovers
1881	Old Carthusians
1882	Old Etonians
1883	Blackburn Olympic
1884	Blackburn Rovers
1885	Blackburn Rovers
1886	Blackburn Rovers
1887	Aston Villa
1888	West Bromwich A.

1889	Preston N. End
1890	Blackburn Rovers
1891	Blackburn Rovers
1892	West Bromwich A.
1893	Wolverhampton W.
1894	Notts County
1895	Aston Villa
1896	The Wednesday
1897	Aston Villa
1898	Nottingham Forest
1899	Sheffield United
1900	Bury
1901	Tottenham Hotspur
1902	Sheffield United
1903	Bury
1904	Manchester City
1905	Aston Villa
1906	Everton
1907	The Wednesday
1908	Wolverhampton W.
1909	Manchester United
1910	Newcastle United
1911	Bradford City
1912	Barnsley
1913	Aston Villa
1914	Burnley
1915	Sheffield United
1916	Not held
1917	Not held
1918	Not held
1919	Not held
1920	Aston Villa
1921	Tottenham Hotspur
1922	Huddersfield Town
1923	Bolton Wanderers
1924	Newcastle United
1925	Sheffield United
1926	Bolton Wanderers
1927	Cardiff City
1928	Blackburn Rovers
1929	Bolton Wanderers
1930	Arsenal
1931	West Bromwich A.
1932	Newcastle United
1933	Everton
1934	Manchester City
1935	Sheffield Wed
1936	Arsenal
1937	Sunderland
1938	Preston N. End
1939	Portsmouth
1940	Not held
1941	Not held
1942	Not held
1943	Not held
1944	Not held
1945	Not held
1946	Derby County
1947	Charlton Athletic
1948	Manchester United
1949	Wolverhampton W.
1950	Arsenal
1951	Newcastle United
1952	Newcastle United
1953	Blackpool
1954	West Bromwich A.
1955	Newcastle United
1956	Manchester City
1957	Aston Villa
1958	Bolton Wanderers
1959	Nottingham Forest
1960	Wolverhampton W.
1961	Tottenham Hotspur
1962	Tottenham Hotspur
1963	Manchester United
1964	Westham United
1965	Liverpool
1966	Everton
1967	Tottenham Hotspur
1968	West Bromwich A.
1969	Manchester City
1970	Chelsea
1971	Arsenal
1972	Leeds United
1973	Sunderland
1974	Liverpool
1975	Westham United
1976	Southampton

1977	Manchester United
1978	Ipswich Town
1979	Arsenal
1980	Westham United
1981	Tottenham Hotspur
1982	Tottenham Hotspur
1983	Manchester United
1984	Everton
1985	Manchester United
1986	Liverpool
1987	Coventry C.
1988	Wimbledon
1989	Liverpool
1990	Manchester United

FA Charity Shield

Winners

1908	Manchester U.
1909	Newcastle U.
1910	Bighton & Hove A.
1911	Manchester U.
1912	Blackburn Rovers
1913	Professionals
1914	Not held
1915	Not held
1916	Not held
1917	Not held
1918	Not held
1919	Not held
1920	West Bromwich A.
1921	Tottenham H.
1922	Huddersfield T.
1923	Professionals
1924	Professionals
1925	Amateurs
1926	Amateurs
1927	Cardiff City
1928	Everton
1929	Professionals
1930	Arsenal
1931	Arsenal
1932	Everton
1933	Arsenal
1934	Arsenal
1935	Sheffield Wed
1936	Sunderland
1937	Manchester City
1938	Arsenal
1939	Not held
1940	Not held
1941	Not held
1942	Not held
1943	Not held
1944	Not held
1945	Not held
1946	Not held
1947	Not held
1948	Arsenal
1949	Portsmouth
1950	World Cup XI
1951	Tottenham H.
1952	Manchester U.
1953	Arsenal
1954	Wolverhampton W.
1955	Chelsea
1956	Manchester U.
1957	Manchester U.
1958	Bolton W.
1959	Wolverhampton W.
1960	Burnley
1961	Tottenham H.
1962	Tottenham H.
1963	Everton
1964	Liverpool
1965	Manchester U.
1966	Liverpool
1967	Manchester U.
1968	Manchester City
1969	Leeds United
1970	Everton
1971	Leicester City
1972	Manchester City
1973	Burnley
1974	Liverpool
1975	Derby County
1976	Liver pool
1977	Liverpool
1978	Nottingham Forest

1979	Liverpool
1980	Liverpool
1981	Aston Villa
1982	Liverpool
1983	Manchester U.
1984	Everton
1985	Everton
1986	Everton
1987	Everton
1988	Liverpool
1989	Liverpool

SCOTTISH LEAGUE

Winners

1893	Celtic
1894	Hearts
1895	Celtic
1896	Hearts
1897	Celtic
1898	Rangers
1899	Rangers
1900	Rangers
1901	Rangers
1902	Hibernian
1903	Third Lanark
1904	Celtic
1905	Celtic
1906	Celtic
1907	Celtic
1908	Celtic
1909	Celtic
1910	Rangers
1911	Rangers
1912	Rangers
1913	Celtic
1914	Celtic
1915	Celtic
1916	Celtic
1917	Rangers
1918	Celtic
1919	Rangers
1920	Rangers
1921	Celtic
1922	Rangers
1923	Rangers
1924	Rangers
1925	Celtic
1926	Rangers
1927	Rangers
1928	Rangers
1929	Rangers
1930	Rangers
1931	Motherwell
1932	Rangers
1933	Rangers
1934	Rangers
1935	Celtic
1936	Rangers
1937	Celtic
1938	Rangers
1939	Not held
1940	Not held
1941	Not held
1942	Not held
1943	Not held
1944	Not held
1945	Not held
1946	Rangers
1947	Hibernian
1948	Rangers
1949	Rangers
1950	Hibernian
1951	Hibernian
1952	Rangers
1953	Celtic
1954	Aberdeen
1955	Rangers
1956	Rangers
1957	Hearts
1958	Rangers
1959	Hearts
1960	Rangers
1961	Dundee
1962	Rangers
1963	Rangers
1964	Kilmarnock
1965	Celtic
1966	Celtic

1967 Celtic
1968 Celtic
1969 Celtic
1970 Celtic
1971 Celtic
1972 Celtic
1973 Celtic
1974 Rangers
1975 Rangers
1976 Celtic
1977 Rangers
1978 Celtic
1979 Aberdeen
1980 Celtic
1981 Celtic
1982 Dundee U.
1983 Aberdeen
1984 Aberdeen
1985 Celtic
1986 Rangers
1987 Celtic
1988 Rangers
1989 Rangers

SCOTTISH FA CUP

Winners

1874 Queen's Park
1875 Queen's Park
1876 Queen's Park
1877 Vale of leven
1878 Vale of leven
1879 Vale of leven
1880 Queen's Park
1881 Queen's Park
1882 Queen's Park
1883 Dumbarton
1884 Queen's Park
1885 Renton
1886 Queen's Park
1887 Hibernian
1888 Renton
1889 Third Lanark
1890 Queen's Park
1891 Hearts
1892 Celtic
1893 Queen's Park
1894 Rangers
1895 St. Bernards
1896 Hearts
1897 Rangers
1898 Rangers
1899 Celtic
1900 Celtic
1901 Hearts
1902 Hibernian
1903 Rangers
1904 Celtic
1905 Third Lanark
1906 Hearts
1907 Celtic
1908 Celtic
1909 Not held
1910 Dundee
1911 Celtic
1912 Celtic
1913 Falkirk
1914 Not held
1915 Not held
1916 Not held
1917 Not held
1918 Not held
1919 Not held
1920 Kil marnock
1921 Partick th
1922 Morton
1923 Celtic
1924 Airdrieonians
1925 Celtic
1926 St. Mirren
1927 Celtic
1928 Rangers
1929 Kilmarnock
1930 Rangers
1931 Celtic
1932 Rangers
1933 Celtic
1934 Rangers
1935 Rangers

1936	Rangers
1937	Celtic
1938	East Fife
1939	Clyde
1940	Not held
1941	Not held
1942	Not held
1943	Not held
1944	Not held
1945	Not held
1946	Not held
1947	Aberdeen
1948	Rangers
1949	Rangers
1950	Rangers
1951	Celtic
1952	Motherwell
1953	Rangers
1954	Celtic
1955	Clyde
1956	Hearts
1957	Falkirk
1958	Clyde
1959	St. Mirren
1960	Rangers
1961	Dunfermline Ath
1962	Rangers
1963	Rangers
1964	Rangers
1965	Celtic
1966	Rangers
1967	Celtic
1968	Dunfermline Ath
1969	Celtic
1970	Aberdeen
1971	Celtic
1972	Celtic
1973	Rangers
1974	Celtic
1975	Celtic
1976	Rangers
1977	Celtic
1978	Rangers
1979	Rangers
1980	Celtic
1981	Rangers
1982	Aberdeen
1983	Aberdeen
1984	Aberdeen
1985	Celtic
1986	Aberdeen
1987	St. Mireen
1988	Celtic
1989	Celtic

SCOTTISH LEAGUE CUP

Winners

1945-46	Aberdeen
1946-47	Rangers
1947-48	East Fife
1948-49	Rangers
1949-50	East Fife
1950-51	Motherwell
1951-52	Dundee
1952-53	Dundee
1953-54	East Fife
1954-55	Hearts
1955-56	Aberdeen
1956-57	Celtic
1957-58	Celtic
1958-59	Hearts
1959-60	Hearts
1960-61	Rangers
1961-62	Rangers
1962-63	Hearts
1963-64	Rangers
1964-65	Rangers
1965-66	Celtic
1966-67	Celtic
1967-68	Celtic
1968-69	Celtic
1969-70	Celtic
1970-71	Rangers
1971-72	Partick Thistle
1972-73	Hibernian
1973-74	Dundee
1974-75	Celtic

1975-76 Rangers
1976-77 Aberdeen
1977-78 Rangers
1978-79 Rangers
1979-80 Aberdeen
1980-81 Dundee
1981-82 Rangers
1982-83 Celtic
1983-84 Rangers
1984-85 Rangers
1985-86 Aberdeen
1986-87 Rangers
1987-88 Rangers
1988-89 Aberdeen

EUROPEAN SUPER CUP

Winnners

1972 Ajax
1973 Ajax
1974 Not held
1975 Dynamo Kiev
1976 Anderlecht
1977 Liverpool
1978 Anderlecht
1979 Nottingham Forest
1980 Nottingham Forest
1981 Not contested
1982 Aston Villa
1983 SV Hamburg
1984 Juventas
1985 Not held
1986 Steaua Bucharest
1987 FC Porto
1988 Mechelen
1989 Barcelona

UEFA CUP

Winners

1972 Tottenham Hotspur
1973 Liverpool
1974 Feyenoord
1975 Borussia Moenchengladbash
1976 Liverpool
1977 Juventas
1978 PSV Eindhoven
1979 Borussia Moenchengladbach
1980 Borussia Moenchengladbach
1981 Ipwich T.
1982 IFK Gothenburg
1983 RSC Anderlecht
1984 Tottenham H.
1985 Real Madrid
1986 Real Madrid
1987 IFK Gothenburg
1988 Bayer Leverkusen
1989 Napoli

EUROPEAN

Winners

1956 Real Madrid
1957 Real Madrid
1958 Real Madrid
1959 Real Madrid
1960 Real Madrid
1961 SL Benfica
1962 SL Benfica
1963 AC Milan
1964 Inter Milan
1965 Inter Milan
1966 Real Madrid
1967 Celtic
1968 Manchester U.
1969 AC Milan
1970 Fyenoord
1971 Ajax Amsterdam
1972 Ajax Amsterdam
1973 Ajax Amsterdam
1974 Bayern Munich
1975 Bayern Munich
1976 Bayern Munich
1977 Liverpool
1978 Liverpool
1979 Nottingham F
1980 Nottingham F
1981 Liverpool

1982 Aston Villa
1983 SV Hamburg
1984 Liverpool
1985 Juventus
1986 Steaua Bucharest
1987 FC Porto
1988 PSV Eindhoven
1989 AC Milan

EUROPEAN CUP

Winners

1961 Fiorentina
1962 Atletico Madrid
1963 Tottenham Hotspur
1964 Sporting Lisbon
1965 Westham U.
1966 Borussia Dortmund
1967 Bayern Munich
1968 AC Milan
1969 Slovan Bratislava
1970 Manchester C
1971 Chelsea
1972 Rangers
1973 AC Milan
1974 FC Magdeburg
1975 Dynamo Kiev
1976 RSC Anderlecht
1977 SV Hamburg
1978 RSC Anderlecht
1979 Barcelona
1980 Valencia
1981 Dynamo Tbilisi
1982 Barcelona
1983 Aberdeen
1984 Juventas
1985 Everton
1986 Dynamo Kiev
1987 Ajax Amsterdam
1988 Mechelen
1989 Barcelona

PADMA SHRI AWARDS

1. Gostha Behari Pal
2. Sailen Manna
3. Chuni Goswami
4. P.K.Banerji

ARJUNA AWARD WINNERS

Football

1961 P.K. Banerjee
1962 T. Balaram
1963 Subimal (Chuni) Goswami
1964 Jarnail Singh
1965 Arun Lal Ghosh
1966 Yousuf Khan
1967 Peter Thangaraj
1969 Inder Singh
1970 Syed Naeemuddin
1971 Chandeshwar Parshad Singh
1973 Magan Singh Rajvi
1978-79 Gurdev Singh
1979-80 Prasun Banerjee
1980-81 Mohammed Habib
1981 Sudhir Karmakar
1983 Shanti Mullick

SOFTBALL

Softball game is played between two teams. One team plays, the other team fields. The object of the game is to secure runs. The batsman attempts to hit the ball into the fair field of the play. Having done so, he circles the three bases to return to the home base. A run is scored, provided the batsman-runner is not tagged with the ball while circling the bases. The outfield area has three players stationed in each of the areas of the out field.

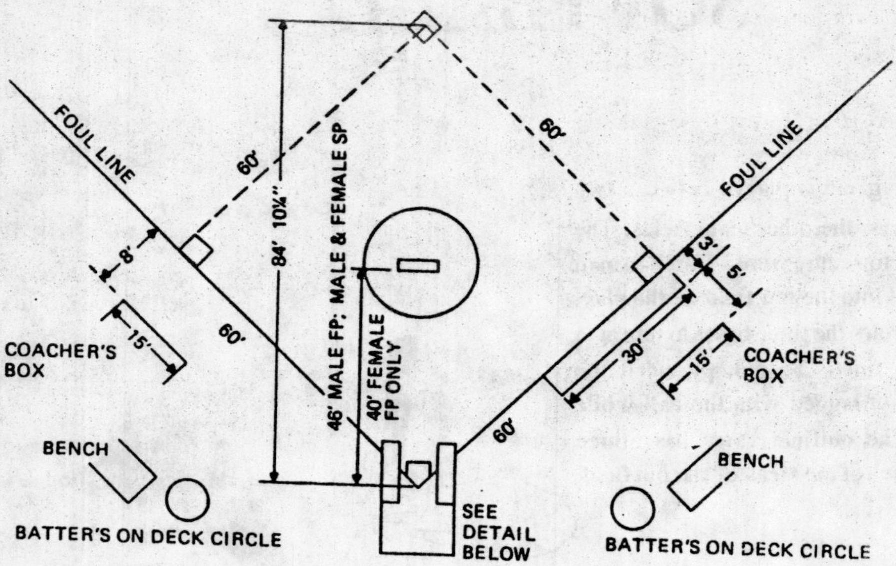

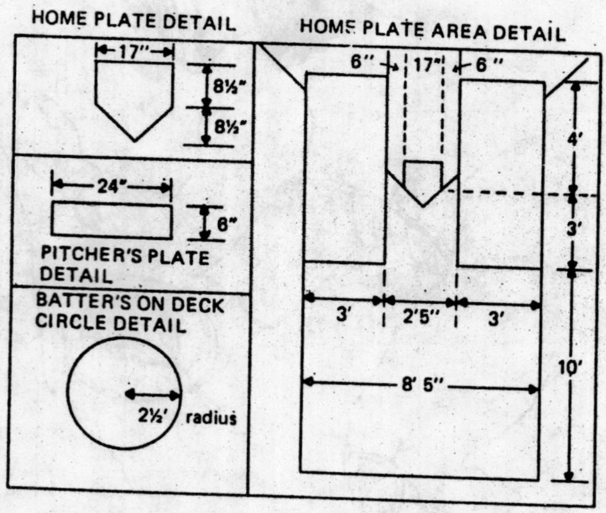

Distances	Fast Pitch	Slow Pitch
Bases		
Male	60 feet	65 feet
Female	60 feet	60 feet
Pitching		
Male	46 feet	46 feet
Female	40 feet	46 feet
Fences		
Male	225 feet	275 feet
Female	200 feet	250 feet

(i) left field (ii) centre field (iii) right field.

If a batter without being out, comes back to the home base running after touching the second and third base he is awarded a run. After this, the other members of his team do the same turn by turn. After the three players are out the batters play the game.

The basic skills in Softball are pitching, catching, throwing, batting, and base running. While batting the ball is kept in front of the body and both the feet are placed long on the ground. The ball must be kept to the pitcher plate for one second minimum at the beginning of wind up or back swing. The arm should spin parallel to the line in the direction of ball. The batter should catch the bat by head and keep it on the back of the right shoulder, keep the arm away from the body and elbows high to the level of shoulders. While hitting the ball, the batter should spin the bat forward and bring it back to its original position after the hit.

RULES OF THE GAME

1. The playing field, the area within which the ball may be legally played or fielded should have a clear area within a radius of 200 feet from the home plate between the foul lines. Between the home plate and the backstop there should be an area of 25 feet in width.
2. The official diamond shall have 60-base-lines with a pitching distance of 46 feet.

   For women and girls the official pitching distance shall be 35 feet.
3. To determine the position of the home plate, draw line in the direction it is desired to lay

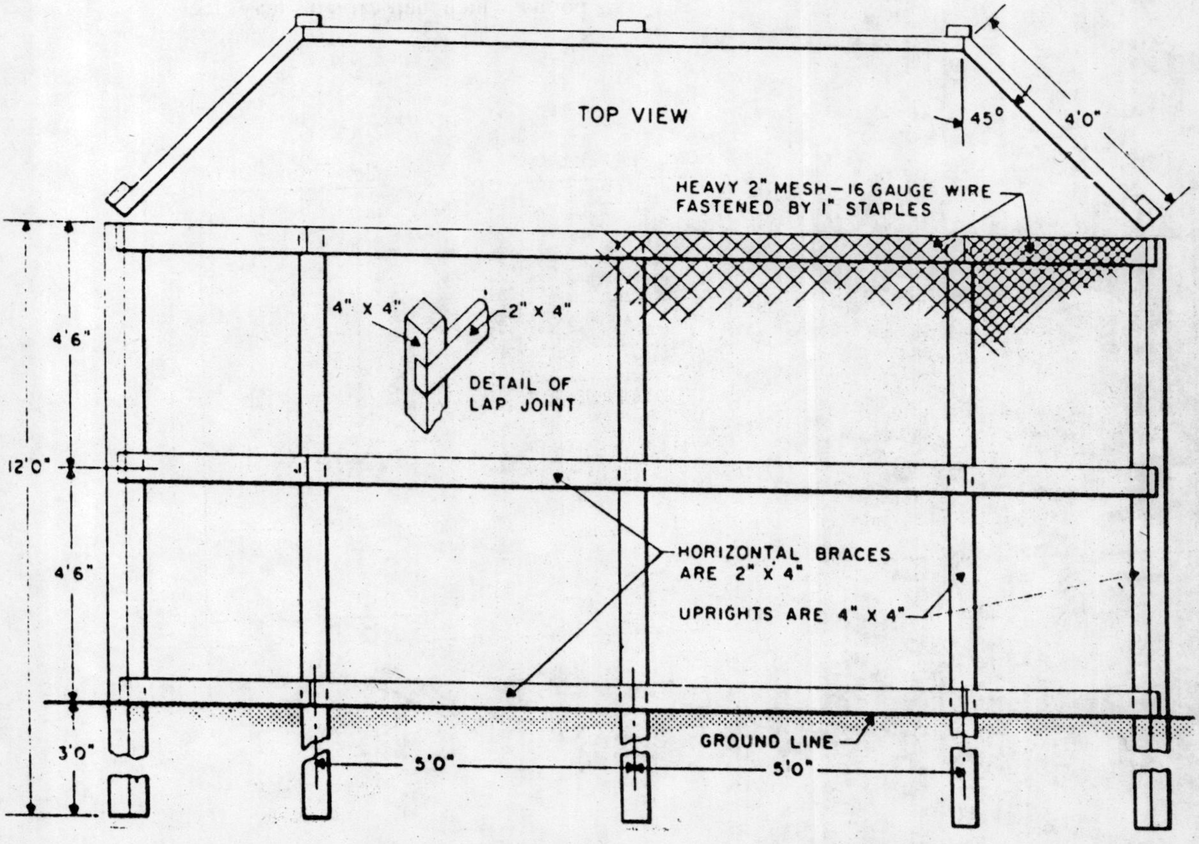

the diamond. Drive a stake at the corner of the home plate nearest the catcher. Fasten a cord to this stake and tie knots, or otherwise mark the cord, at 46 feet, 60 feet, 84 feet 10 (¼) inches and at 120 feet.

4. To check the diamond, place the home plate end or the cord at the first base stake and the 120 foot marker at third base. The 60 foot marker should now check at home plate and second base.
5. The bat should be rounded, made of hard wood,and should be of only one piece, not more than 34 inches in length and not more than 2 (½) inches in diameter at its largest part.
6. The official soft-ball shall be a regular, smooth-seam concealed stitch of flat surfaced ball of any type. It should be machine-wrapped or hand compressed with fine quality twisted yarn covered with latex or rubber cement.

   The finished ball should not be less than 11 (7/8) inches nor more than 12 (1/8) inches in circumference and should weigh not less than 6 ounces nor more than 6 (3/4) ounces.
7. A team shall consist of nine players whose position shall be as follows:-
   (a) Catcher
   (b) Pitcher
   (c) First Baseman
   (d) Second Baseman
   (e) Third Baseman
   (f) Shortstop
   (g) Left Fielder
   (h) Centre Fielder
   (i) Right Fielder

Players of the field may be stationed at any points which their captains may elect.

SQUASH

Squash is an easy game to play badly - it is a difficult game to play well.

Any two people, with a reasonable amount of ball sense, can walk onto a court for exercise and satisfaction from the experience. The game currently is one of the world's fastest growing sports, having earned this popularity because of a number of factors. Unlike a game such as tennis where the ball must go over the net for the game to continue, the squash ball rebounds off the wall for the opponent to return.

RULES OF THE GAME

1. The match shall consist of the best of 3 or 5 games at the option of the organisers of the competition. Each game is of 9 points, in that the player who scores 9 points wins the game except that, on the score being called 8 all for the first time, the receiver shall choose, before the next service is delivered to continue that game either to 9 points (known as "no set")or to 10 points (known as "set two"), in which latter case the player who scores 2 more points wins the game. The receiver shall in either case clearly indicate his choice to the marker, referee and his opponent.
2. Points can be scored only by the server. When the server wins a stroke, he scores a point; when the receiver wins a stroke, he becomes the server.
3. After a good service has been delivered the players return the ball alternately until one fails to make a good return. The ball otherwise ceases to be in play in accordance with the rules, or on a call by the marker or referee.
4. A let is an undecided stroke, and the service or rally in respect of which a let is allowed shall not count and the server shall serve again from the same box. A let shall not cancel a previous fault.
5. A match is normally controlled by a referee, assisted by a marker. One person may be appointed to carry out the functions of both referee and marker. When a decision has been made by the referee, he shall announce it to the players and the marker shall repeat it with the subsequent score.

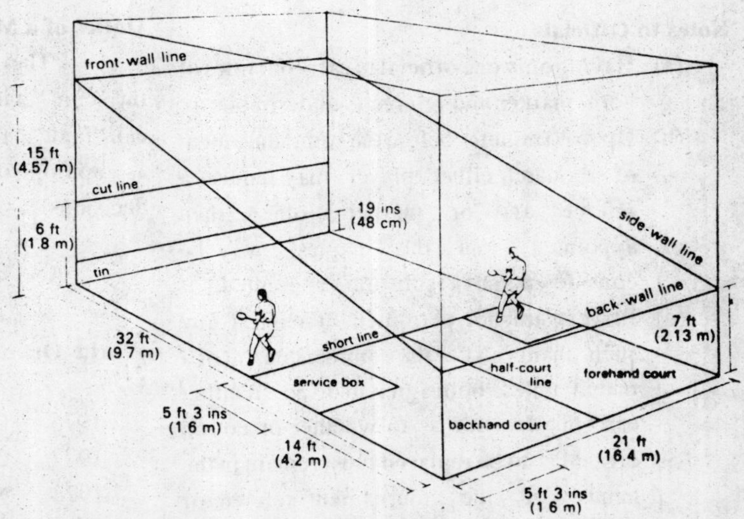

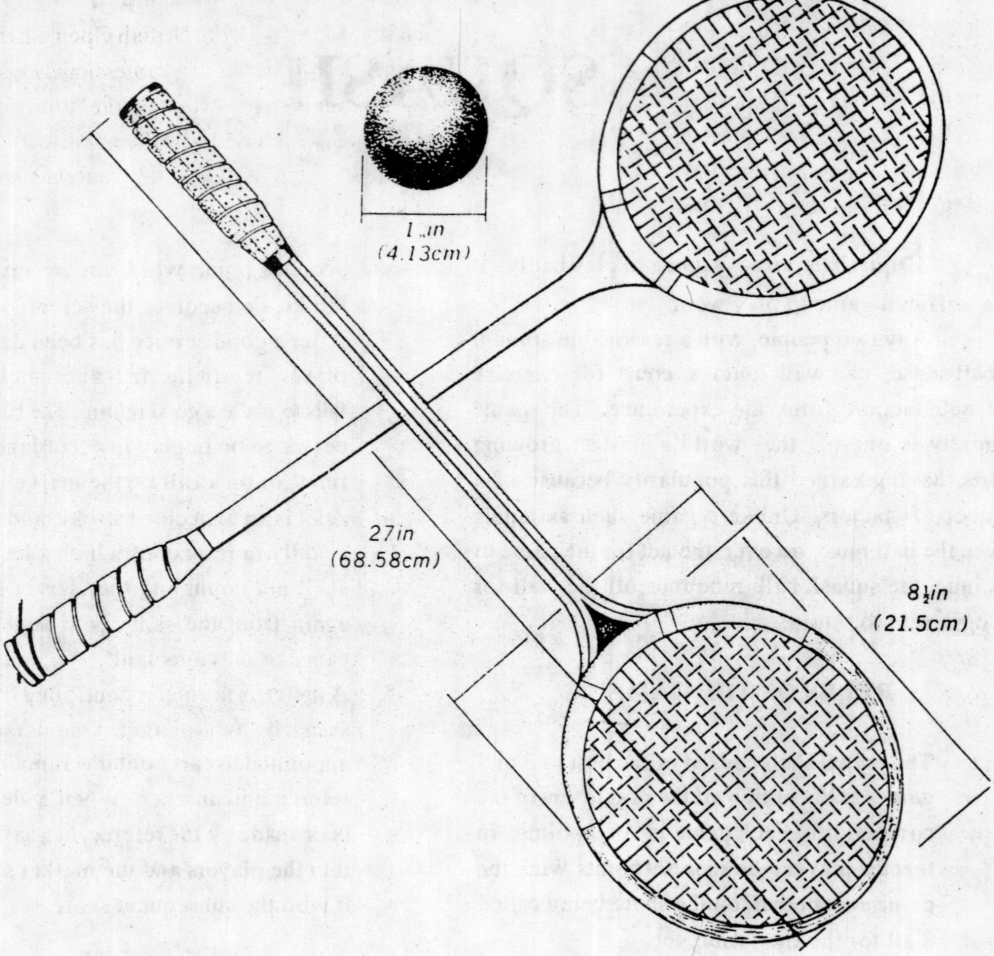

Notes to Officials

(a) Having only one official to carry out roles of both marker and referee is undesirable.

(b) Up to 30 minutes before the commencement of a match either player may request a referee and /or marker other than appointed, and this request may be considered and a substitute appointed.

(c) Players are not permitted to request any such changes after the commencement of a match, unless both agree to do so. In either case the decision as to whether or not an official is to be replaced must remain in the hands of the tournament referee or adjudicator where applicable.

Duties of a Marker

The marker calls the play followed by the score, with the server's score first. He shall call "fault", "foot-fault", "out", "not up", or "down" as appropriate, and shall repeat the referee's decisions.

CUP & TROPHIES

World Open Championship

Men

1976	G.Hunt (Aus)
1977	G.Hunt (Aus)
1978	Not held
1979	G.Hunt (Aus)

1980	G.Hunt (Aus)
1981	Jahangir Khan (Pak)
1982	Jahangir Khan (Pak)
1983	Jahangir Khan (Pak)
1984	Jahangir Khan (Pak)
1985	Jahangir Khan (Pak)
1986	R.Norman (NZ)

Women

1976	M.McKay (Aus)
1979	H.McKay (Aus)
1981	R.Thorne (Aus)
1983	V.Cardwell (Aus)
1985	S.Devoy (NZ)

World Amateur Championship

First held in 1967, it is contested every two years. Individual and team winners.

Individual

1967	G.Hunt (Aus)
1969	G.Hunt (Aus)
1971	G.Hunt (Aus)
1973	C.Nancarrow (Aus)
1975	K.Shawcross (Aus)
1977	M.Ahmed (Pak)
1979	Jahangir Khan (Pak)
1981	S.Bowditch (Aus)
1983	Jahangir Khan (Pak)
1985	Jahangir Khan (Pak)

Team

1967	Australia
1969	Australia
1971	Australia
1973	Australia
1975	Great Britain
1977	Pakistan
1979	Great Britain
1981	Pakistan
1983	Pakistan
1985	Pakistan

British Open Championship

First played in 1930, the British Open Championship in which both amateurs and professionals may compete was for years regarded as the unofficial world championship. Until 1947 the event was held on a challenge system with two-leg matches between the holder and his challenger.

1930	D.Butcher (UK)
1931	D.Butcher (UK)
1932	Abdel Fattah Amr Bey (Egy)
1933	—
1934	Abdel Fattah Amr Bey (Egy)
1935	Abdel Fattah Amr Bey (Egy)
1936	Abdel Fattah Amr Bey (Egy)
1937	Abdel Fattah Amr Bey (Egy)
1938	J.Dear (UK)
1939	—
1940	Not held
1941	Not held
1942	Not held
1943	Not held
1944	Not held
1945	Not held
1946	Mahmoud el Karim (Egy)
1947	Mahmoud el Karim (Egy)
1948	Mahmoud el Karim (Egy)
1949	Mahmoud el Karim (Egy)
1950	Hashim Khan (Pak)
1951	Hashim Khan (Pak)
1952	Hashim Khan (Pak)
1953	Hashim Khan (Pak)
1954	Hashim Khan (Pak)
1955	Hashim Khan (Pak)
1956	Roshan Khan (Pak)
1957	Hashim Khan (Pak)
1958	Azam Khan (Pak)
1959	Azam Khan (Pak)
1960	Azam Khan (Pak)
1961	Azam Khan (Pak)
1962	Mohibullah Khan (Pak)
1963	Abou Taleb (Egy)
1964	Abou Taleb (Egy)
1965	Abou Taleb (Egy)
1966	Abou Taleb (Egy)

1967 J.Barrington (UK)
1968 J.Barrington (UK)
1969 G.Hunt (Aus)
1970 J.Barrington (UK)
1971 J.Barrington (UK)
1972 J.Barrington (UK)
1973 J.Barrington (UK)
1974 G. Hunt (Aus)
1975 Qamar Zaman (Pak)
1976 G. Hunt (Aus)
1977 G. Hunt (Aus)
1978 G. Hunt (Aus)
1979 G. Hunt (Aus)
1980 G. Hunt (Aus)
1981 G. Hunt (Aus)
1982 Jahangir Khan (Pak)
1983 Jahangir Khan (Pak)
1984 Jahangir Khan (Pak)
1985 Jahangir Khan (Pak)
1986 Jahangir Khan (Pak)

Women

1922 J.Cave (UK)
S.Huntsman (UK)
1923 N.Cave (UK)
1924 J.Cave (UK)
1925 C.Fenwick (UK)
1926 C.Fenwick (UK)
1927 Not held
1928 J.Cave (UK)
1929 N.Cave (UK)
1930 N.Cave (UK)
1931 C.Fenwick (UK)
1932 S.Noel (UK)
1933 S.Noel (UK)
1934 S.Noel (UK)
1934 M.Lumb (UK)
1935 M. Lumb (UK)
1936 M. Lumb (UK)
1937 M. Lumb (UK)
1938 M. Lumb (UK)
1939 M. Lumb (UK)
1940 Not held
1941 Not held
1942 Not held
1943 Not held
1944 Not held
1945 Not held
1946 Not held
1947 J.Curry (UK)
1948 J.Curry (UK)
1949 J.Curry (UK)
1950 J.Morgan (UK)
1951 J.Morgan (UK)
1952 J.Morgan (UK)
1953 J.Morgan (UK)
1954 J.Morgan (UK)
1955 J.Morgan (UK)
1956 J.Morgan (UK)
1957 J.Morgan (UK)
1958 J.Morgan (UK)
1959 J.Morgan (UK)
1960 S.Macintosh (UK)
1961 F.Marshall (UK)
1962 H.McKay (Aus)
1963 H.McKay (Aus)
1964 H.McKay (Aus)
1965 H.McKay (Aus)
1966 H.McKay (Aus)
1967 H.McKay (Aus)
1968 H.McKay (Aus)
1969 H.McKay (Aus)
1970 H.McKay (Aus)
1971 H.McKay (Aus)
1972 H.McKay (Aus)
1973 H.McKay (Aus)
1974 H.McKay (Aus)
1975 H.McKay (Aus)
1976 H.McKay (Aus)
1977 H.McKay (Aus)
1978 S.Newman-King (Aus)
1979 B.Wall (Aus)
1980 V.Hoffman (Aus)
1981 V.Hoffman (Aus)
1982 V.Hoffman-Cardwell (Aus)
1983 V.Hoffman-Cardwell (Aus)

1984	S.Devoy (NZ)
1985	S.Devoy (NZ)
1986	S.Devoy (NZ)

ARJUNA AWARD WINNERS

1961	K.S.Jain
1969	Anil Nayar
1979-80	Raj Kumar Manchanda
1982	Bhuvaneshwari Kumari

SWIMMING

In Japan, swimming continued to be widespread. In 36 B.C. competitions took place, and in A. D. 1603 an Imperial edict made swimming a compulsory part of the school curriculum. But although swimming continued to be an important part of Japanese school life, the isolation of the country inhibited the spread of ideas and competitive swimming in its modern context really began, inevitably, in mid 19th-century in Britain.

Men such as George Pulton, George Pewters, Samuel Hounslow, and Horold Kenworthy (who beat American Indians of the Ojibway tribe in races at the Holborn Baths in London in 1844) were all renowned at that time. Nobody thought about amateurism and professionalism then, when money was to be made out of competing. Side bets and money prizes, and payments for exhibitions of trick and ornamental swimming- the forerunners of the modern synchronized swimming-were common.

An embryonic swimming organization-the National Swimming Association - was formed in London in 1837, but the oldest acknowledged national body was formed in 1869. On January 7 that year, at the German Gymnasium in London, the Associated Metropolitan Swimming Clubs was formed, later known as the Amateur Swimming Association, the governing body of swimming in England. The first acts of the AMSC were to define an 'amateur' and establish rules of competition. As a result, the first amateur swimming champion in history is recognized as Tom Moris, who won the mile championship, then swum in the River Thames, in 1869. Other national associations followed. The American Athletic Union (AAU) was founded in 1878, the German Federation in 1896, and the French in 1899, The New Zealand ASA 1890.

Here is a grand sport that will give you hours of enjoyment and exercise, and, if you become proficient as a life-saver, may enable you some day to be of very great service to others.

Practise walking about in the water, jumping up and down, kneeling on the bottom of the bath if the water is shallow enough, and so on. Next, try putting your face into the water. It is a good plan to practise this at home in the wash basin, and, once your face is under the water, open your eyes so that you can see the plug at the bottom. You will soon be just as happy with your face in or out of the water, and your eyes open all the time. The most important thing of all however, is to learn to breathe in the water, and this should be done before you try to swim.

Now you are ready to start swimming, and you will find it very useful if you have a friend to learn with you, so that you can help one another. FIRST you must learn the actual strokes, and here again it is very helpful to practise them on land before you try them in the water.

The arm movements you can do standing up, preferably in front of a mirror, so that you can see if you are doing them correctly. For the leg movements, it is best to lie face downwards on the bed with your legs over the edge, or to balance yourself across a chair or padded stool. When you have tried the arm and leg movements separately, try both together.

When you have practised the stroke thoroughly at home and can do it without hesitation, try it in the water. Practise the legs alone, while holding on to the bath rail with your hands. Then practise the arms alone, getting your friend to hold

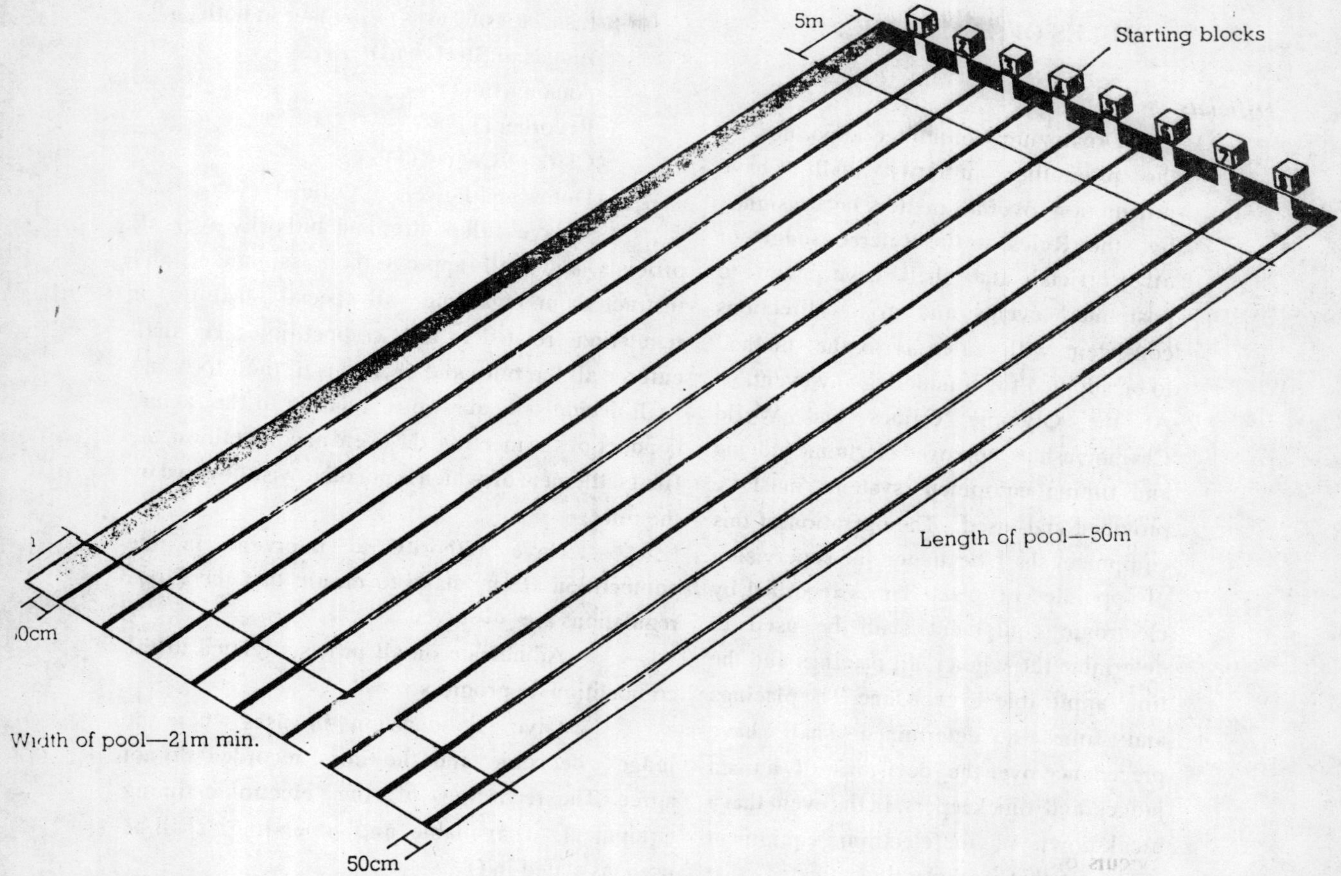

you up at the waist, practise the "Ready" position by itself. We call this the glide. Stand with your back to the side of the bath, lean forward with your shoulders under the water, press the sole of one foot against the side. As you give yourself a push off with this foot, shoot your arms forward, with your head between your arms and your face in the water (and don't forget to keep your eyes open). Your body should lie quite horizontal and fully stretched out, and you will find yourself gliding gently along. To begin with, get your friend to stand 5 or 6 paces away, ready to help you to get upright again when you have finished your glide. This is done by throwing your head backward and bending your knees up learn to stand upright without help, and then you are ready to try the complete swimming stroke.

Your confidence in the water will be immensely increased when you can dive. There is nothing difficult about it and you can teach yourself to dive as soon as you can swim.

Sit on the steps with your arms stretched straight above your head, and your thumbs touching, bend over until your hands are pointing downwards, tuck your head well forward between your arms with your ears in front of your arms, and then lean gently forward until you overbalance, and fall in head first.

When you can do this from the top step, try at from the side of the bath. Next, stand on the side with your arms and head held as before, bend your knees, and lean forward over the water. Then, with a little spring, straighten your knees, so that you go in head foremost. Once in the water, turn your hands up to bring you to the surface.

RULES OF THE GAME

Officials

1.1 The Organizing Committee appointed by the promoting authority shall have jurisdiction over all matters not assigned by the Rules to the Referee, Judges or other officials and shall have power to postpone events and give directions consistent with rules as to the method to be adopted for conducting any event.

1.2 At the Olympic Games and World Championships approved electronic judging and timing equipment systems must be provided and used. The operation of this equipment shall be under the supervision of appointed officials. Times recorded by electronic equipment shall be used to determine the winner, all placings and the time applicable to each lane. The placings and times so determined shall have precedence over the decisions of human judges and timekeepers. In the event that a break-down of the electronic equipment occurs or that it is clearly indicated that there has been a failure of the equipment, or that a swimmer has failed to activate the equipment, the decisions of the human judges and recordings of the human timekeepers shall be officials.

1.3 The governing body is required to appoint, subject to the approval of the FINA Bureau or the respective Regional or International Authorities, the following officials for the control of all competitions at Olympic Games, World Championships, Regional Games and important International fixtures;

A minimum of :

Referee (1)
Starter (1)
Chief Timekeeper (3 per lane)
Chief Judge (1)
Finishing Judges (3 per lane)
Inspector of Turns (1 per lane at both ends)
Judges of Strokes (2)
Announcer (1)
Recorder (1)
Clerk of Course (1)

1.4 Duties and Powers of Officials

Have full control and authority over all officials and shall approve their assignments and instruct them regarding all special features or regulations related to the competition. He shall enforce all the rules and decisions of the FINA and shall decide all questions relating to the actual conduct of the meeting, the event or competition, the final settlement of which is not otherwise covered by the rules.

Have authority to intervene in the competition at any stage to ensure that the FINA regulations are observed.

Adjudicate on all protests related to the competition in progress.

Give a decision in cases where the judges decision and the times recorded do not agree. The recordings of the electronic timing equipment, if available and operating shall be used as stated in (1.2).

Ensure that all necessary officials for the conduct of the event or competition are at their respective posts. He may appoint substitutes for any who are absent, incapable of acting or found to be inefficient. He may appoint additional officials if considered necessary. He shall assign the judges of strokes.

The Start

2.1 The start in Freestyle, Breaststroke and Butterfly races shall be with a dive.

On the signal from the Referee the competitor shall step onto the back surface of the starting block and remain there. On the preparatory command from the starter "take your marks" (which must be in the English language at the Olympic Games and at World Championships) they shall immediately take up a starting position at

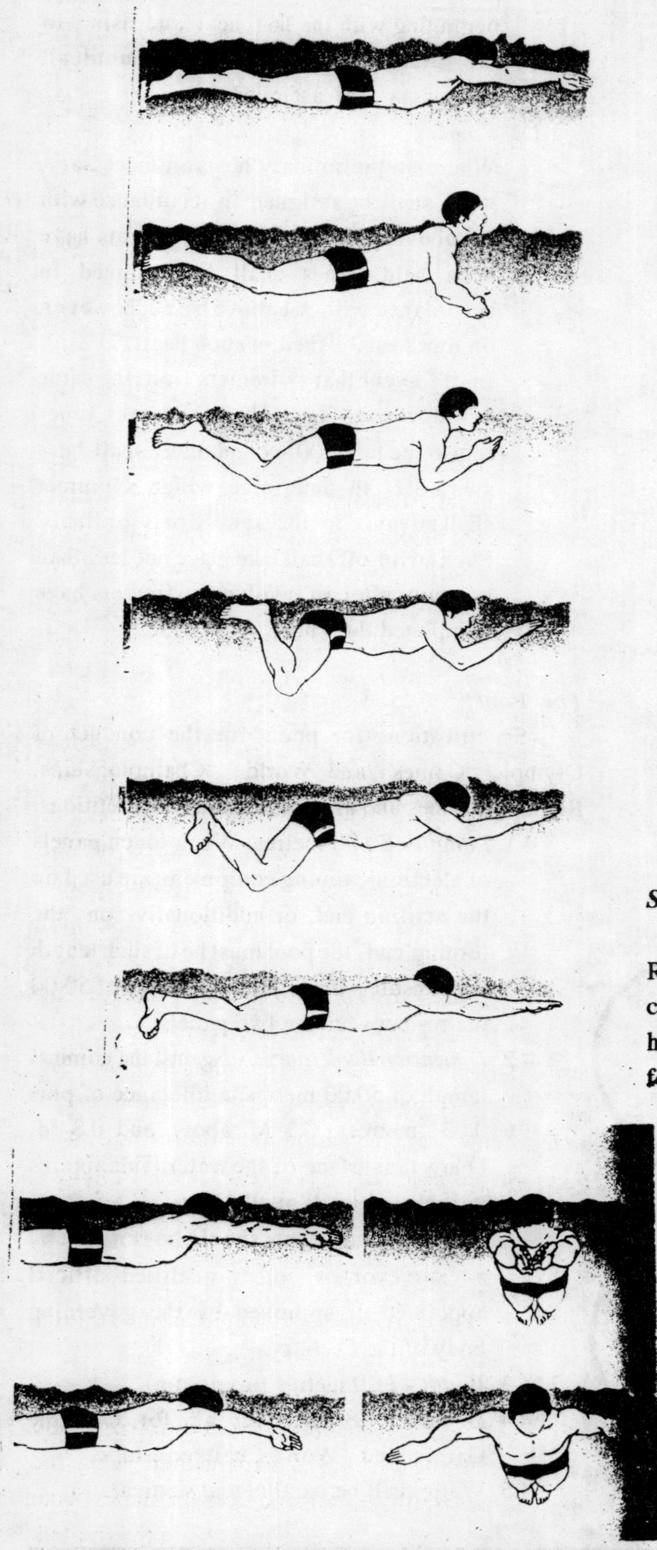

the front of the starting block. When all competitors are stationary, the starter shall give the starting signal (shot, whistle, or command).

2.2. The start in Backstroke swimming shall be as stated in SW8. (Backstroke and Medley relay races).

2.3 The starter shall call back the competitors at the first or second false start and remind them of not strarting before the starting signal. After the second false start any swimmer starting before the starting signal has been given shall be disqualified. If the starting signal sounds before the disqualification is declared, the race shall continue and the swimmer or swimmers shall be disqualified upon completion of the race. If the disqualification is declared before the starting signal, the gun shall not be fired but the remaining competitors shall be called back, reminded by the starter of the penalties, and shall start again.

2.4 If a swimmer has been disqualified under 1.4.10 for misconduct on the start, it shall not be counted as a false start..

Seeding of Heats and Finals

In the Olympic Games, World Championships, Regional Games, and all open international competitions, the starting stations for all events heats, semi-finals and finals shall be by seeding as follows:

3.1 Trial Heat

The best competitive times of all entrants shall be submitted on entry forms, and listed in order of times by the meet committee. Contestants who do not submit times shall be considered the slowest and shall be placed at the end of the list. If there is more than one such entry, their placing shall be determined by draw. The fastest swimmer or team, shall be placed in the last heat, the next fastest in the next to the last heat and so on, following which

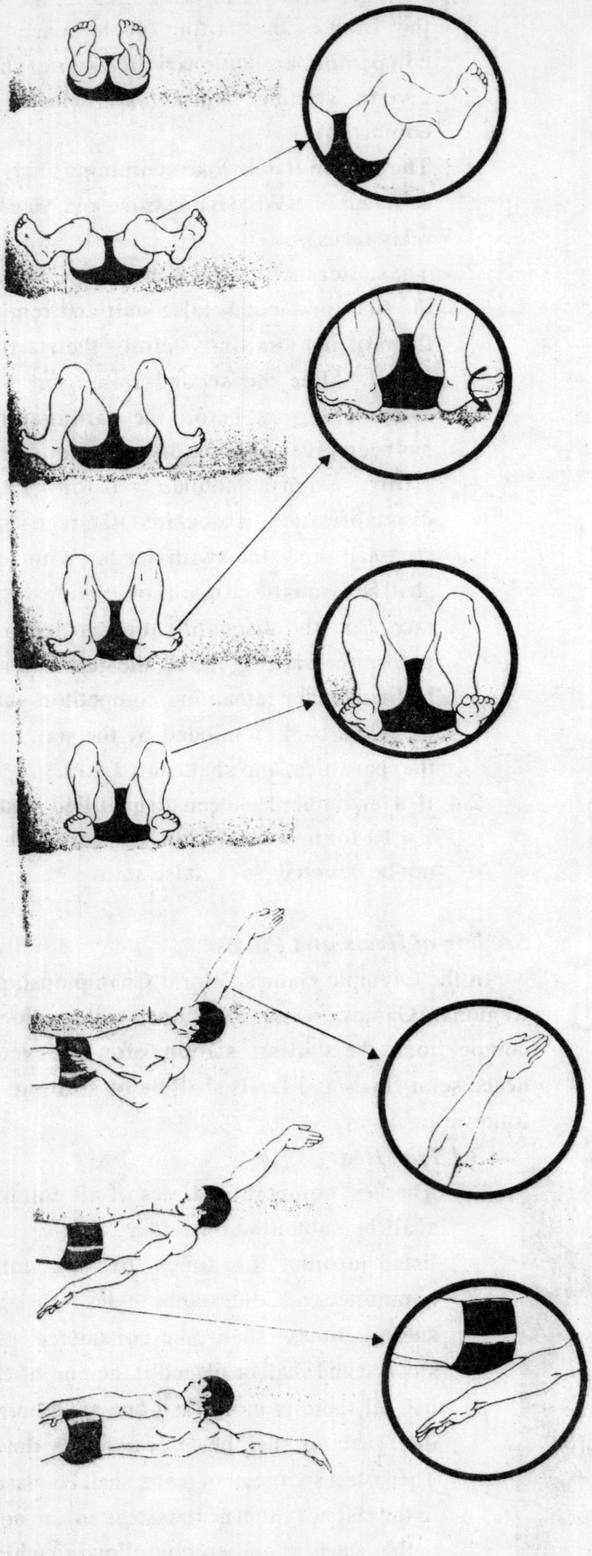

the second swimmer in each heat will be assigned in the same ascending order, beginning with the last heat and rising to the first heat, and thereafter until all swimmers are assigned.

3.2 Final

Where no preliminary heats are necessary, lanes shall be assigned in accordance with 3.1 above. Where preliminary heats have been held, lanes shall be assigned in accordance with 3.1 above based, however, on times established in such heats.

In the event that swimmers from the same or different heats have equal times registered to 1/100 second, there shall be a swim-off to determine which swimmer shall advance to the semi-finals or finals. Such swim-off shall take place not less than one hour after all involved swimmers have completed their heat.

The Pool

Specifications for pools for the conduct of Olympic Games and World Championships, Regional Games and all international competitions.

4.1 *Length* - 50.00 metres. When touch panels of electronic timing equipment are used on the starting end, or additionally on the turning end, the pool must be of such length that ensures the required distance of 50.00 metres between the two panels.

4.2 *Dimensional tolerances* - Against the nominal length of 50.00 metres, a tolerance of plus 0.03 metres; 0.3 M. above and 0.8 M. below the surface of the water. This applies to both end walls at all points.

These measurements should be certified by a surveyor or other qualified official appointed or approved by the governing body of the Country.

4.3 *Width* - 21.0 metres (minimum).

4.4 *Depth* - 1.8 M. over all for Olympic Games and World Championships.

4.5 Walls shall be parallel and vertical.

4.6 *Number of Lanes* -8.

4.7 *Width of Lanes* -2.5 M. each, with 2 spaces each of 50cm: (0.5 M.) width outside of lanes 1 and 8. There must be a lane rope separating these spaces from lanes 1 and 8 respectively.

4.8 *Lane Ropes* - shall extend the full length of the course, secured at each end wall to anchor brackets recessed into the end walls. Each lane rope will consist of floats placed end to end having a minimum diameter of 5cm.to a maximum of 11cm. The colour of the floats extending for a distance of 5.0M. from each end of the pool shall be distinct from the rest of the floats.

4.9 *Starting Platforms* - The height of the platform above the water surface may be from 0.5M. to 0.7.5M.

The surface area - minimum 0.5M.x 0.5M. Surface to be covered with non slip material.

Maximum slope - not more than 10 degrees.

Handgrips for backstroke starts - must be placed with in 0.3M. to 0.6M. above the wter surface horizontally and vertically. They must be parallel to the surface of the end wall and must not protrude beyond the end wall.

Numbering - Each starting block must be distinctly numbered on all 4 sides, clearly visible to the judges, No. 1. being on the right hand side when facing down the course (pool).

4.10 *BackstrokeTurn Indicators* -Flagged ropes suspended across the pool 1.8 M. above the water surface from fixed supports or stands, shall be set 5.0M. from each end wall.

4.11 *False Start Rope* - shall be suspended across the pool from fixed standards placed 15.0M. in front of the starting end. It shall be attached to the standards by a quick release mechanism.

4.12 *Water Temperature* - 24 Centigrade. Minimum.

+ 7 Fahrenheit. Minimum.

Level - During competition the water in the pool must be kept at a constant level, with no appreciable movement.

4.13 *Lighting* - Light intensity over starting platforms and turning ends must not be less than 100 foot candles.

4.14 Lane Markings shall be of a dark contrasting colour, placed on the floor of the pool in the centre of each lane.

Width - Min. 0.20 M.: Max. 0.30M.

Length - 46.0M.

Each lane line shall end 2.0M. from the end walls of the pool with a distinctive cross line 1.0M. long and of the same width as the lane line.

4.15 Distance separating swimming pool from diving well-minimum 5.0M.

The Race

5.1 Obstructing another competitor by swimming across or otherwise interfering shall disqualify the offender and should the foul be intentional the Referee shall report the matter to the Association promoting the race, and to the Asociation of the swimmer so offending.

5.2 Should a foul endanger the chance of success of a competitor the referee shall have power to allow him to compete in the next round, or should the foul occur in a final, he may order it to be reswum.

5.3 In all events, a swimmer when turning shall make physical contact with the end of the bath or course. The turn must be made from the wall, and it is not permitted to take a stride or a step from the bottom of the bath. The finish line shall be the unobstructed, clearly definable vertical face of the wall, which shall have no handrails or similar structures.

5.4 Standing on the bottom during a race shall not disqualify a competitor, but he shall not walk.

5.5 A competitor swimming over the course alone shall cover the whole distance to qualify.

5.6 In relay races, the team of a competitor whose feet have lost touch with the starting block before his preceding partner touches the wall shall be disqualified, unless the competitor in default returns to the original starting point at the wall but it shall not be necessary to return to the starting platform.

5.7 No competitor shall be permitted to use or wear any device that may aid his speed, buoyancy or endurance during a competition (such as webbed gloves, flippers, fins, etc.) Goggles may be worn.

5.8 A swimmer must end the race in the same lane as that in which he started. A breastroke swimmer will not be disqualified if he submerges below the surface for not more than 1 stroke, for the purpose of returning to his proper lane.

5.9 Any swimmer entered in a race, who enters the water in which an event is being conducted, before all swimmers there in have completed the race, shall be disqualified from his next scheduled competition in the meet.

5.10 Any relay team member and his relay team shall be disqualified from a race if a team member, other than the swimmer designated to swim that length, enters the water when the race is being conducted, before all competitors of all teams have finished the race.

CUP & TROPHIES

Gold In Olympics

Swimming events have been held at each Olympic Games since 1896, when three men's events were included - 100, 500 and 1200 metres freestyle. Women's events were first included in 1912.

Men

100 Metres Freestyle

1896	Alfred Hajos (Hun)	1:22.2
1904	Zoltan Halmay (Hun)	1:02.8
1906	Charles Daniels (USA)	1:13.4
1908	Charles Daniels (USA)	1:05.6
1912	Duke Kahanamokuy (USA)	1:03.4
1920	Duke Kahanamoku (USA)	1:01.4
1924	Johnny Weissmuller (USA)	59.0
1928	Johnny Weissmuller (USA)	58.6
1932	Yasuji Miyazaki (Jpn)	58.2
1936	Ferenc Csik (Hun)	57.6
1948	Walter Ris (USA)	57.3
1952	Clarke Scholes (USA)	57.4
1956	Jon Henricks (Aus)	55.4
1960	John Devitt (Aus)	55.2
1964	Don Schollander (USA)	53.4
1968	Mike Wenden (Aus)	52.2
1972	Mark Spitz (USA)	51.22
1976	Jim Montgomery (USA)	49.99
1980	Jorg Woithe (GDR)	50.40
1984	Ambrose Gaines (USA)	49.80
1988	Matt Biondi (USA)	48.63

200 Metres Freestyle

1900	Frederick Lane (Aus)	2:25.2
1904	Charles Daniels (USA)	2:44.2
1968	Mike Wenden (Aus)	1:55.2
1972	Mark Spitz (USA)	1:52.78
1976	Bruce Furniss (USA)	1:50.29
1980	Sergey Koplakov (USSR)	1:49.81
1984	Michael Gross (FRG)	1:47.44
1988	Duncan Armstrong (Aus)	1:47.25

400 Metres Freestyle

1896	Paul Neumann (Aut)	8:12.6
1904	Charles DAniels (USA)	6:16.2
1906	Otto Scheff (Aut)	6:23.8
1908	Henry Taylor (UK)	5:36.8
1912	George Hodgson (Can)	5:24.4
1920	Norman Ross (USA)	5:26.8
1924	Johnny Weissmuller (USA)	5:04.2
1928	Alberto Zorilla (Arg)	5:01.6
1932	Buster Crabbe (USA)	4:48.4

1936	Jack Medica (USA)	4:44.5
1948	William Smith (USA)	4:41.0
1952	Jean Boiteux (Fra)	4:30.7
1956	Murray Rose (Aus)	4:27.3
1960	Murray Rose (Aus)	4:18.3
1964	Don Schollander (USA)	4:12.2
1968	Mike Burton (USA)	4:09.0
1972	Brad Cooper (Aus)	4:00.27
1976	Brian Goodell (USA)	3:51.93
1980	Vladimir Salnikov (URS)	3:51.31
1984	George DiCarlo (USA)	3:51.23
1988	Uwe Dassler (GDR)	3:46.95

1500 Metres Freestyle

1896	Alfred Hajos	18:22.2
1900	John Jarvis (UK)	13:40.2
1904	Emil Rausch (Ger)	27:18.2
1906	Henry Taylor (UK)	28:28.0
1908	Henry Taylor (UK)	22:48.4
1912	George Hodgson (Can)	22:00.0
1920	Norman Ross (USA)	22:23.2
1924	Andrew Charlton (Aus)	20:06.6
1928	Arne Borg (Swe)	19:51.8
1932	Kusuo Kitamura (Jpn)	19:12.4
1936	Noboru Terada (Jpn)	19:13.7
1948	James McLane (USA)	19:18.5
1952	Ford Konno (USA)	18:30.0
1956	Murray Rose (Aus)	17:58.9
1960	John Konrads (Aus)	17:19.6
1964	Bob Windle (Aus)	17:01.7
1968	Mike Burton (USA)	16:38.9
1972	Mike Burton (USA)	15:52.58
1976	Brian Goodell (USA)	15:02.40
1980	Vladimir Salnikov (USSR)	14:58.27
1984	Michael O' Brien (USA)	15:05.20
1988	Vladimir Salnikov (USSR)	15:00.40

100 Metres Backstroke

1904	Walter Brack (Ger)	1:16.8
1908	Arno Bieberstein (Ger)	1:24.6
1912	Harry Hebner (USA)	1:21.2
1920	Warren Kealoha (USA)	1:15.2
1924	Warren Kealoha (USA)	1:13.2
1928	George Kojac (USA)	1:08.2
1932	Masaji Kiyokawa (Jpn)	1:08.6
1936	Adolf Kiefer (USA)	1:05.9
1948	Allen Stack (USA)	1:06.4
1952	Yoshinobu Oyakawa (USA)	1:05.4
1956	David Theile (Aus)	1:02.2
1960	David Theile (Aus)	1:01.9
1968	Roland Matthes (GDR)	58.7
1972	Roland Matthes (GDR)	56.58
1976	John Naber (USA)	55.49
1980	Bengt Baron (Swe)	56.53
1984	Richard Carey (USA)	55.79
1988	Daichi Suzuki (Jap)	55.05

200 Metres Backstroke

1900	Ernst Hoppenberg (Ger)	2:47.0
1964	Jed Graef (USA)	2:10.3
1968	Roland Matthes (GDR)	2:09.6
1972	Roland Matthes (GDR)	2:02.82
1976	John Naber (USA)	1:59.19
1980	Sandor Wladar (Hun)	2:01.93
1984	Richard Carvey (USA)	2:00.23
1988	Igor Polianski (USSR)	1:59.37

100 Metres Breaststroke

1968	Don McKenzie (USA)	1:07.7
1972	Nobutaka Taguchi (Jpn)	1:04.94
1976	John Hencken (USA)	1:03.11
1980	Duncan Goodhew (UK)	1:03.34
1984	Steve Lundquist (USA)	1:01.65
1988	Adrian Moorhouse (UK)	1:02.04

200 Metres Breaststroke

1908	Frederick Holman (UK)	3:09.2
1912	Walter Bathe (Ger)	3:01.8
1920	Haken Malmroth (Swe)	3:04.4
1924	Robert Skelton (USA)	2:56.5
1928	Yoshiyuki Tsuruta (Jpn)	2:48.8
1932	Yoshiyuki Tsuruta (Jpn)	2:45.4
1936	Tetsuo Hamuro (Jpn)	2:42.5
1948	Joseph Verdeur (USA)	2:39.3
1952	John Davies (Aus)	2:34.4
1956	Masaru Furukawa (Jpn)	2:34.7
1960	William Mulliken (USA)	2:37.4
1964	Ian O'Brien (Aus)	2:27.8

1968	Felipe Munoz (Mex)	2:28.7
1972	John Hencken (USA)	2:21.55
1976	David Wilkie (UK)	2:15.11
1980	Robertas Shulpa (USSR)	2:15.85
1984	Victor Davis (Can)	2:13.34
1988	Jozsef Szabo (Hungary)	2:13.52

100 Metres Butterfly

1968	Doug Russell (USA)	55.9
1972	Mark Spitz (USA)	54.27
1976	Matt Vogel (USA)	54.35
1980	Par Arvidsson (Swe)	54.92
1984	Michael Gross (FRG)	53.08
1988	Anthony Nesty (Surinam)	53.00

200 Metres Butterfly

1956	William Yorzyk (USA)	2:19.3
1960	Mike Troy (USA)	2:12.8
1964	Kevin Berry (Aus)	2:06.6
1968	Carl Robie (USA)	2:08.7
1972	Mark Spitz (USA)	2:00.70
1976	Mike Bruner (USA)	1:59.23
1980	Sergey Fesenko (USSR)	1:59.76
1984	Jon Sieben (Aus)	1:57.04
1988	Michael Gross (FRG)	1:56.94

200 Metres Individual Medley

1968	Charles Hickcox (USA)	2:12.0
1972	Glunnar Larsson (Swe)	2:07.17
1984	Alex Baumann (Can)	2:01.42
1988	TamasDarnyi (Hun)	2:00.17

400 Metres Individual Medley

1964	Richard Roth (USA)	4:45.4
1968	Charles Hickcox (USA)	4:48.4
1972	Gunnar Larsson (Swe)	4:31.98
1976	Rod Strachan (USA)	4:23.68
1980	Aleksandr Sidorenko (USSR)	4:22.89
1984	Alex Baumann (Can)	4:17.41
1988	Tamas Darnyi (Hun)	4:14.75

4 x 100 Metres Freestyle Relay

1964	USA	3:33.2
1968	USA	3:31.7
1972	USA	3:26.42
1984	USA	3:19.03
1988	USA	3:16.53

4 x 200 Metres Freestyle Relay

1906	Hungary	16:52.4
1908	UK	10:55.6
1912	Australia	10:11.6
1920	USA	10:04.4
1924	USA	9:53.4
1928	USA	9:36.2
1932	Japan	8:58.4
1936	Japan	8:51.5
1948	USA	8:46.0
1952	USA	8:31.1
1956	Australia	8:23.6
1960	USA	8:10.2
1964	USA	7:52.1
1968	USA	7:52.3
1972	USA	7:35.78
1976	USA	7:23.22
1980	USSR	7:23.50
1984	USA	7:16.59
1988	USA	7:12.51

4 x 100 Metres Medley Relay

1960	USA	4:05.4
1964	USA	3:58.4
1968	USA	3:54.9
1972	USA	3:48.16
1976	USA	3:42.22
1980	Australia	3:45.70
1984	USA	3:39.30
1988	USA	3:36.93

Women

100 Metres Freestyle

1912	Fanny Durack (Aus)	1: 22.2
1920	Ethelda Bleibtrey (USA)	1:13.6
1924	Ethel Lackie (USA)	1:12.4
1928	Albina Osipowich (USA)	1:06.8
1932	Helena Madison (USA)	1:06.8
1936	Henrika Mastenbroek (Hol)	1:05.9
1948	Greta Andersen (Den)	1:06.3

1952	Katalin Szoke (Hun)	1:06.8
1956	Dawn Fraser (Aus)	1:02.0
1960	Dawn Fraser (Aus)	1:01.2
1964	Dawn Fraser (Aus)	59.5
1968	Jan Henne (USA)	1:00.0
1972	Sandra Neilson (USA)	58.59
1976	Kornelia Ender (GDR)	55.65
1980	Barbara Krause (GDR)	54.79
1984	Carrie Steinseifer (USA)	55.92
	Nancy Hogshead (USA)	55.92
1988	Kristin Otto (GDR)	54.93

200 Metres Freestyle

1968	Debbie Meyer (USA)	2:10.5
1972	Shane Gould (Aus)	2:03.56
1976	Kornelia Ender (GDR)	1:59.26
1980	Barbara Krause (GDR)	1:58.33
1984	Mary Wayte (USA)	1:59.23
1988	Heike Friedrich (GDR)	1:57.65

400 Metres Freestyle

1920	Ethelda Bleibtrey (USA)	4:34.0
1924	Martha Norelius (USA)	6:02.2
1928	Martha Norelius (USA)	5:42.8
1932	Helena Madison (USA)	5:28.5
1936	Henrika Mastenbroek (Hol)	5:26.4
1948	Ann Curtis (USA)	5:17.8
1952	Valeria Gyenge (Hun)	5:12.1
1956	Lorraine Crapp (Aus)	4:54.6
1960	Chris von Saltza (USA)	4:50.6
1964	Virginia Duenkel (USA)	4:43.3
1968	Debbie Meyer (USA)	4:31.8
1972	Shane Gould (Aus)	4:19.04
1976	Petra Thuemer (GDR)	4:09.89
1980	Ines Diers (GDR)	4:08.76
1984	Tiffany Cohen (USA)	4:07.10
1988	Janet Evans (USA)	4:03.85

800 Metres Freestyle

1968	Debbie Meyer (USA)	9:24.0
1972	Keena Rothhammer (USA)	8:53.68
1976	Petra Thuemer (GDR)	8:37.14
1980	Michelle Ford (Aus)	8:28.90
1984	Tiffany Cohen (USA)	8:24.95
1988	Janet Evans (USA)	8:20.20

100 Metres Backstroke

1924	Sybil Bauer (USA)	1:23.2
1928	Marie Braun (Hol)	1:22.0
1932	Eleanor Holm (USA)	1:19.4
1936	Dina Senff (Hol)	1:18.9
1948	Karen Harup (Den)	1:14.4
1952	Joan Harrison (Saf)	1:14.3
1956	Judy Grinham (UK)	1:12.9
1960	Lynn Burke (USA)	1:09.3
1964	Cathy Ferguson (USA)	1:07.7
1968	Kaye Hall (USA)	1:06.2
1972	Melissa Belote (USA)	1:05.78
1976	Ulrike Richter (GDR)	1:01.83
1980	Rica Reinisch (GDR)	1:00.86
1984	Theresa Andrews (USA)	1:02.55
1988	Kristin Otto (GDR)	1:00.89

200 Metres Backstroke

1968	Lillian Watson (USA)	2:24.8
1972	Melissa Belote (USA)	2:19.19
1976	Ulrike Richter (GDR)	2:13.43
1980	Rica Reinisch (GDR)	2:11.77
1984	Jolanda De Rover (Hol)	2:12.38
1988	Krisztina Egerzegi (Hun)	2:09.29

100 Metres Breaststroke

1968	Djurdjica Bjedov (Yug)	1:15.8
1972	Catherine Carr (USA)	1:13.58
1976	Hannelore Anke (GDR)	1:11.16
1980	Ute Geweniger (GDR)	1:10.22
1984	Petra Van Staveren (Hol)	1:09.88
1988	Tania Dangalakova (Bul)	1:07.95

200 Metres Breaststroke

1924	Lucy Morton (UK)	3:33.2
1928	Hilde Schrader (Ger)	3:12.6
1932	Claire Dennis (Aus)	3:06.33
1936	Hidedo Maehata (Jap)	3:03.6
1948	Petronella van Vliet (Hol)	2:57.2
1952	Eva Szekely (Hun)	2:51.7
1956	Ursula Hoppe (Ger)	2:53.1
1960	Anita Lonsbrough (UK)	2:53.1
1964	Galina Prozumenshchikova (USSR)	2:46.4

1968	Sharon Wichman (USA)	2:44.4
1972	Beverley Whitfield (Aus)	2:41.71
1976	Marina Kosheveya (USSR)	2:33.35
1980	Lina Kachushite (USSR)	2:59.54
1984	Anne Ottenbrite (Can)	2:30.38
1988	Silke Hoerner (GDR)	2:26.71

100 Metres Butterfly

1956	Shelley Mann (USA)	1:11.0
1960	Carolyn Schuler (USA)	1:09.5
1964	Sharon Stouder (USA)	1:04.7
1968	Lynette McClements (Aus)	1:05.5
1972	Mayumi Aoki (Jpn)	1:03.34
1976	Kornelia Ender (GDR)	1:00.13
1980	Caren Metschuck (GDR)	1:00.42
1984	Mary Meagher (USA)	59.26
1988	Kristin Otto (GDR)	59.00

200 Metres Butterfly

1968	Ada Kok (Hol)	2:24.7
1972	Karen Moe (USA)	2:15.57
1976	Andrea Pollack (GDR)	2:11.41
1980	Ines Geissler (GDR)	2:10.44
1984	Mary Meagher (USA)	2:06.90
1988	Kathleen Nord (GDR)	2:09.51

200 Metres Individual Medley

1968	Claudia Kolb (USA)	2:24.7
1972	Shane Gould (Aus)	2:23.7
1984	Tracy Caulkins (USA)	2:12.64
1988	Daniela Hunger (GDR)	2:12.59

400 Metres Individual Medley

1964	Donna De Varona (USA)	5:18.7
1968	Claudia Kolb (USA)	5:08.5
1972	Gail Neall (Aus)	5:02.97
1976	Ulrike Tauber (GDR)	4:42.77
1980	Petra Schneider (GDR)	4:36.29
1984	Tracy Caulkins (USA)	4:39.24
1988	Janet Evans (USA)	4:37.76

4 x 100 Metres Freestyle Relay

1912	UK	5:52.8
1920	USA	5:11.6
1924	USA	4:58.8
1928	USA	4:47.6
1932	USA	4:38.0
1936	Netherlands	4:36.0
1948	USA	4:29.2
1952	Hungary	4:24.4
1956	Australia	4:17.1
1960	USA	4:08.9
1964	USA	4:03.8
1968	USA	4:02.5
1972	USA	3:55.19
1976	USA	3:44.82
1980	GDR	3:42.71
1984	USA	3:43.43
1988	GDR	3:40.63

4 x 100 Metres Medley Relay

1960	USA	4:41.1
1964	USA	4:33.9
1968	USA	4:28.3
1972	USA	4:20.75
1976	GDR	4:07.95
1980	GDR	4:06.67
1984	USA	4:08.34
1988	GDR	4:03.74

World Championships

Men

100m Freestyle

1973	J.Montgomery (USA)
1975	A.Coan (USA)
1978	D.McCagg (USA)
1982	J.Woithe (GDR)
1986	M.Biondi (USA)

200m Freestyle

1973	J.Montgomery (USA)
1975	T.Shaw (USA)
1978	W.Forrester (USA)
1982	M.Gross (FRG)
1986	M.Gross (FRG)

400m Freestyle

1973	R.DeMont (USA)

1975 T.Shaw (USA)
1978 V.Salnikov (USSR)
1982 V.Salnikov (USSR)
1986 R.Henkel (FRG)

1500m Freestyle
1973 S.Holland (Aus)
1975 T.Shaw (USA)
1978 V.Salnikov (USSR)
1982 V.Salnikov (USSR)
1986 R.Henkel (FRG)

100m Backstroke
1973 R. Matthes (GDR)
1975 R.Matthes (GDR)
1978 R. Jackson (USA)
1982 D. Richter (GDR)
1986 I. Poliansky (USSR)

200m Backstroke
1973 R.Matthes (GDR)
1975 Z.Verraszto (Hun)
1978 J.Vassallo (USA)
1982 R.Carey (USA)
1986 I. Poliansky (USSR)

100m Breaststroke
1973 J.Hencken (USA)
1975 D.Wilkie (UK)
1978 W.Kusch (GDR)
1982 S.Lundquist (USA)
1986 J.Szabo (Hun)

200m Breaststroke
1973 D.Wilkie (UK)
1975 D.Wilkie (UK)
1978 N.Nevid (USA)
1982 V.Davis (Can)
1986 J.Szabo (Hun)

100m Butterfly
1973 B.Robertson (Can)
1975 G.Jagenburg (USA)
1978 J.Bottom (USA)
1982 M.Gribble (USA)
1986 P.Morales (USA)

200m Butterfly
1973 R.Backhaus (USA)
1975 W.Forrester (USA)
1978 M.Bruner (USA)
1982 M.Gross (FRG)
1986 M.Gross (FRG)

200m Individual Medley
1973 G.Larsson (Swe)
1975 A.Hargitary (Hun)
1978 G.Smith (Can)
1982 A.Sidorenko (USSR)
1986 T.Darnyi (Hun)

400m Individual Medley
1973 A.Hargitay (Hun)
1975 A.Hargitay (Hun)
1978 J.Vassallo (USA)
1982 R.Prado (Bra)
1986 T.Darnyi (Hun)

4 x 100m Freestyle Relay
1973 United States
1975 United States
1978 United States
1982 United States
1986 United States

4 x 200m Freestyle Relay
1973 United States
1975 West Germany
1978 United States
1982 United States
1986 East Germany

4 x 100m Medley Relay
1973 United States
1975 United States
1978 United States
1982 United States
1986 United States

Women

100m Freestyle

1973 E.Ender (GDR)
1975 E.Ender (GDR)
1978 B.Krause (GDR)
1982 B.Meineke (GDR)
1986 K.Otto (GDR)

200m Freestyle

1973 K.Rothhammer (USA)
1975 S.Babashoff (USA)
1978 C.Woodhead (USA)
1982 A.Verstappen (Hol)
1986 H.Friedrich (GDR)

400m Freestyle

1973 H.Greenwood (USA)
1975 S.Babashoff (USA)
1978 T.Wickham (Aus)
1982 C.Schmidt (GDR)
1986 H.Friedrich (GDR)

800m Freestyle

1973 N.Calligaris (Ita)
1975 J.Turrall (Aus)
1978 T.Wickham (Aus)
1982 K.Linehan (USA)
1986 A.Strauss (GDR)

100m Backstroke

1973 U.Richter (GDR)
1975 U.Richter (GDR)
1978 L.Jezek (USA)
1982 O.Kristin (GDR)
1986 B.Mitchell (USA)

200m Backstroke

1973 M.Belote (USA)
1975 B.Treiber (GDR)
1978 L.Lezek (USA)
1982 C.Sirch (GDR)
1986 C.Sirch (GDR)

100m Braststroke

1973 R.Vogel (GDR)
1975 H. Anke (GDR)
1978 J.Bogdanova (USSR)
1982 U.Geweniger (GDR)
1986 O.Gerasch (GDR)

200m Breaststroke

1973 R.Vogel (GDR)
1975 H.Anke (GDR)
1978 L.Kachushite (USSR)
1982 S.Varganova (USSR)
1986 S.Hoerner (GDR)

100m Butterfly

1973 K.Ender (GDR)
1975 K.Ender (GDR)
1978 M-J.Pennington (USA)
1982 M.Meagher (USA)
1986 K.Gresler (GDR)

200m Butterfly

1973 R.Kother (GDR)
1975 R.Kother (GDR)
1978 T.Caulkins (USA)
1982 I.Geissler (GDR)
1986 M.Meagher (USA)

200m Individual Medley

1973 A.Hubner (GDR)
1975 K.Heddy (USA)
1978 T.Caulkins (USA)
1982 P.Schneider (GDR)
1986 K.Otto (GDR)

400m Individual Medley

1973 G.Wengner (GDR)
1975 U.Tauber (GDR)
1978 T.Caulkins (USA)
1982 P.Schneider (GDR)
1986 K.Nord (GDR)

4 x 100m Freestyle Relay

1973 East Germany

1975	East Germany
1978	United States
1982	East Germany
1986	East Germany

4 x 200m Freestyle Relay

1986	East Germany

4 x 100m Medley Relay

1973	East Germany
1975	East Germany
1978	United States
1982	East Germany
1986	East Germany

WORLD RECORDS

Freestyle

50 metres	22.23	M.Biondi (USA)
100 metres	48.74	M.Biondi (USA)
200 metres	1:47.44	M.Gross (FRG)
400 metres	3:47.80	M.Gross (FRG)
1500 metres	14:54.76	V.Salnikov (USSR)

Backstroke

100 metres	55.19	R.Carey (USA)
200 metres	1:58.14	I.Poliansky (USSR)

Breastroke

100 metres	1:01.65	S.Lundquist (USA)
200 metres	2:13.34	V.Davis (Can)

Butterfly

100 metres	52.84	P.Morales (USA)
200 metres	1:56.24	M.Gross (FRG)

Medley

200 metres	2:01.42	A.Baumann (Can)
400 metres	4:17.41	A.Baumann (Can)

Relay

4 x 100 Free	3:17.08	United States
4 x 100 Free	7:15.69	United States
4 x 100 Medley	3:38.28	United States

Women

Freestyle

50 metres	25.08	T.Costache (Rom)
100 metres	54.73	K.Otto (GDR)
200 metres	1:57.55	H.Friedrich (GDR)
400 metres	4:06.28	H.Friedrich (GDR)
800 metres	8:24.62	T.Wickham (Aus)

Backstroke

100 metres	1:00.59	I.Kleber (GDR)
200 metres	2:08.50	B.Mitchell (USA)

Breaststroke

100 metres	1:08.11	S.Gerasch (GDR)
200 metres	2:27.40	S.Hoerner (GDR)

Butterfly

100 metres	57.93	M. Meagher (USA)
200 metres	2:05.96	M. Meagher (USA)

Medley

200 metres	2:01.42	A. Baumann (Can)
400 metres	4:36.10	P. Schneider (GDR)

Relay

4 x 100 Free	3:17.08	East Germany
4 x 100 Free	7:15.69	East Germany
4 x 100 Medley	3:38.28	East Germany

NATIONAL RECORDS (INDIA)

Men

50m Freestyle	Khazan Singh	24.61	1988
100m Freestyle	Khazan Singh	54.67	1988
200m Freestyle	Khazan Singh	2:00.10	1988
400m Freestyle	Reza Shirazi	4:20.61	1985
1500m Frestyle	Khazan Singh	17:35.78	1986
100m Backstroke	Wilson Cherian	59.84	1986
200m Backstroke	Gaurav Kapoor	1:02.42	1988
100m Breaststroke	S.Radhakrishnan	1:10.40	1985
200m Breaststroke	S.Radhakrishnan	2:34.04	1986
100m Butterfly	Khazan Singh	56.84	1985
200m Butterfly	Khazan Singh	2:01.11	1986
200m I. medley	Khazan Singh	2:17.14	1988

400m I. medley	Khazan Singh	4:54.49	1988
4 x100 m Freestyle	Railways	3:49.08	1988
4 x 200 m Freestyle	Railways	8:25.73	1986
4 x 100m M. relay	Railways	4:11.51	1987

Women

100m Freestyle	Anita Sood	1:01.05	1984
200m Freestyle	Anita Sood	2:11.82	1984
400m Freestyle	Anita Sood	4:40.70	1982
800m Freestyle	Anita Sood	9:32.04	1984
100m Backstroke	Persis Madan	1:10.79	1982
200m Backstroke	Persis Madan	2:33.82	1982
100m Breaststroke	Sarita Kinare	2:33.82	1982
200m Breaststroke	Geeta Ahmed	2:54.06	1982
100m Butterfly	Bula Choudhary	1:05.27	1986
200m Butterfly	Bula Choudhary	2:19.60	1986
200m I. medley	Persis Madan	2:32.50	1982
400m I. medley	Persis Madan	5:26.97	1982
4 x100m Freestyle	Maharashtra	4:25.60	1983
4 x 100m M. relay	Maharashtra	4:55.05	1984

BHARAT RATNA AND THE PADMA VIBHUSHAN

Mihir Sen 1967

PADMA SHRI AWARDS

Mihir Sen

Arti Gupts

Taranath Shenoy

ARJUNA AWARD WINNERS

1961	Bajrangi Prasad
1966	Rima Datta
1967	Arun Shaw
1969	Baidyanath Nath
1971	Bhanwar Singh
1973	Dhanvir (Tingoo) Khatau
1974	Avinash B. Sarang (Long Distance)
	Manjari Bhargava (Diving)
1975	M.S. Rana
	Smita Desai
1982	Persis Madan
1983	Anita Sood
1984	Khajan Singh
1985	Taranath N. Shenoy

TABLE TENNIS

Many youngsters today are taught the modern style of table tennis that involves the loop.This is a shot imparting exaggerated topspin, with the ball rotating forwards with the trajectory the word suggests-a loop.But in many ways this can lead to more harm than good if it is done too soon. It is important to develop as wide a range of strokes as possible, for there are plenty of loopers around and it is always likely that you will come up against somebody who has a better loop than you. And if you have nothing else, you've had it.

Apart from that it makes more sense to build up basic strokes first and go on later to the loop, which is not always easy for everybody.The trouble is when players are young they often see a star and try to copy him and that's it. The loop is flashy shot and exciting to see, so people naturally want to try it. It is not perhaps till later that they go to a table tennis camp and find that they have developed faults. And by then it may be too late to correct them.

One other word of warning. Beginners should concentrate on building up fluent and consistent strokes.If you have a good wrist you should use it because you can do a lot more shots that way, but make sure that you can control it.

Choosing Rackets :

It is difficult to generalize about racquets because there are so many varieties.Basically,there are threee different type of rackets .

(i) Defensive (slow)

(ii) Allround (medium)

(iii) Offensive(fast)

But, each racquet has many variations and combinations. There are three different factors to be considered in the make-up of your racket:

1. Type of wood
2. Type of sponge
3. Type of rubber

***Type of wood* :**

The blade of racquet can be made from 1-,3-,5-,or7- plywood,but the 5-ply blade is the one most commonly used.Usually, there are three type of wood which can be used in varying combinations to give different effects when playing strokes.

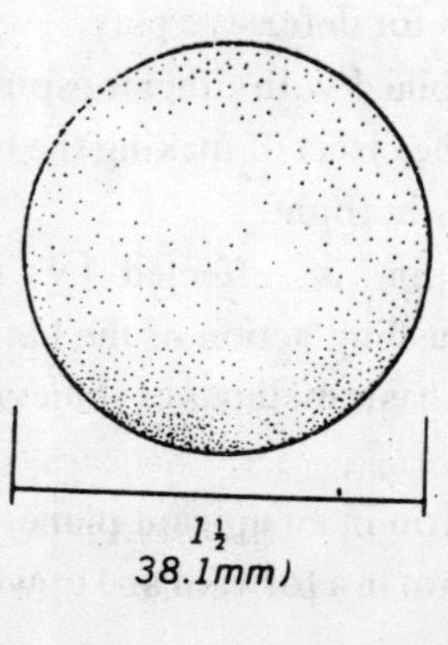

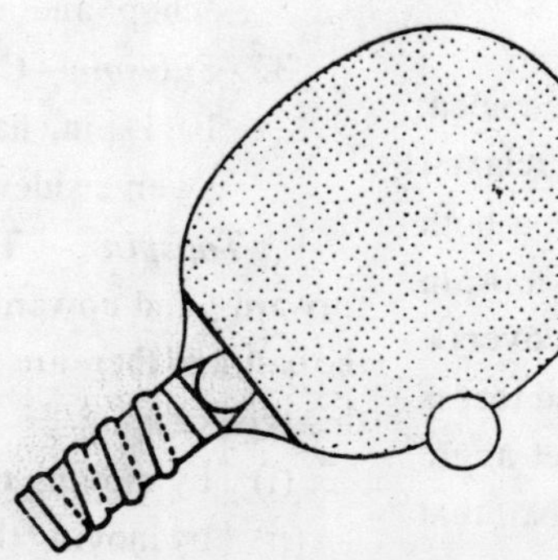

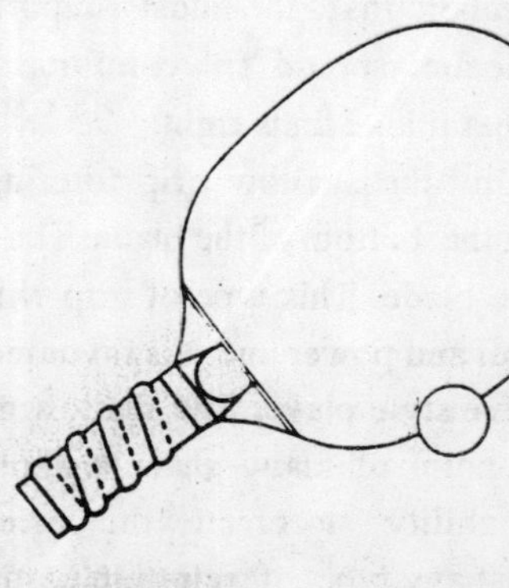

The back of the bat is exempted from the covering rules

Type of Sponge .

The sponge is attached to the rubber. The thickness of the spong is an influencing factor over the amount of control, spin and speed that can be applied to a stroke. If the spong is soft and is on a defensive blade, this will make the racket slow. If the sponge is hard and on an offensive blade, this will tend to make the racquet fast and also produce excessive spin, which could be difficult for some players to control.

Type of Rubber :

There are many different types of rubber that could be attached to the sponge, with the pimples either in or out. Each would have different effect on the ball.

The playing surface is smooth with the pimples on the inside. This playing surface is the most commonly used in today's game. With this type of surface the player can produce maximum spin and speed as there is no restriction on the smooth surface.

With the pimple out gives a lesser degree of topspin, but gives the player good control and also tends to keep the ball low.

You must also consider the covering on the blade of the racquets and this usually causes quite a problem to the beginner.

THE GRIP

There are two basic styles of grip: the shakehand and the penhold. There are, however, many variations to these grips so you must consider carefully and choose a grip which will suit you and your style of game. Whichever grip you use, remember that the most important thing is that the racquet should fit comfortably in the hand and that it also feels right.

In the shallow grip forefinger is extended along the bottom of the blade. The thumb is relaxed on the blade. This type of grip will give you both control and power and it is favoured by the topspin or drive style player.The shallow grip also covers a weak point of many shakehand players, and that is the ability to create the correct racquet angle against any type of return,in particular, a ball that is played just over the net.

Shakehand deep grip is favoured by the backspin player. The player has firm control over the racquet, as he will in the main, be receiving fast,or spinning returns away from the table. The movements of the backspin player when playing his strokes are not as fast as his topspin or drive counterparts.

The penholder grip holds the bat rather like chopsticks and means one side of the bat is used all the time. It is used mostly by Eastern players, especially the Chinese. There is continual argument as to whether the penholder or the Western shakehands grip is superior. For some time it was thought that, because the penholder did not have to be turned round for forehand and backhand in the quick rallies, and because it enabled a great deal of flexibility to be used in the wrist, it was superior.Usually the Chinese serve very well with the penholder because they can get a variety of spins with the same action. They then attack on the third or fifth ball of the rally, and by playing as quickly as possible, hit a lot of balls on the forehand anyway so the backhand isn't exposed much.It is true that the Chinese have a mixture of penholder and Western-grip players now-to defend you really need to have a Western grip.

SPIN

Most people realize that any spherical object can be made to spin and a table tennis ball is no exception. The majority of shots in table tennis employ spin of one kind or another in varying degrees of rotation. The three types of spin are:

1. *Topspin* – Used mainly as an attacking stroke.
2. *Backspin* – Often reffered to as 'underspin'or 'chop' and used for defensive play.
3. *Sidespin* – Combined with either topspin or backspin, has the effect of making the ball swerve sideways in flight.

Topspin :- Topspin is effected by the forward and upward'brushing'action of the bat on the ball, and there are two basic methods of achieving this type of spin:

(i) by moving the arm in an upward plane.

(ii) by moving the arm in a forward and upward direction.

In both cases the effect is to make the ball rotate in a forward direction, the effects of which are as follows:

The ball in flight will fend to dip suddenly and on landing will 'kick off' at a low angle and consequently on contact with the receiver's racket will tend to shoot up sharply.

Backspin :- As the name suggests,the object here is to make the forward-moving ball rotate backwards, toward the striker, and this is achieved by moving the racket in a downward direction and 'cutting ' the ball with an openangled racket.The ball with backspin imported tends to soar in flight and on landing, the breaking effect of the backspin induces the ball to spin back toward the net, particularly so after contact with the receiver's bat.

Sidespin :- Sidespin is usually accompanied by either topspin or backspin, but the general effect of sidespin is to make the ball swerve in flight and deflect sideways on contact with the table surface.

Sidespin is achieved by drawing the racket around the ball and the application of either an upward or downward action will determine the additional topspin or backspin effect.

The degree and speed of the spin imparted can and should be varied by altering the angle of the racket, the contact position on the ball and the emphasis of the arm and body movement.

As a general rule, the slighter the contact between racket and ball,the greater will be the spin imparted, and conversely, heavier or fuller contact will produce less spin.There are so many spin variations that it is quite impossible to detail every one, but it is nevertheless important to practise and experiment with spin so that eventually you will become aware of your own limitations in using spin tactically and effectively.

SERVICES

Just as it is necessary to be an individual in your style and technique, it is equally important to create an individual style of service. Many players regard service as a means of introducing the ball into play-this is wrong.The service is your first chance of winning a point. If you do not win the point on service, then you must attack the ball at the first opportune moment.

History of Service :— Before 1950 when everybody played with pimpled bats (no sponge) the long sweeping service was favoured to drive the opponent away from the table. With the advent of sponge, maximum spin was the order of the day since most players did not understand the mechanics of spin. By the 1960s, everybody had adapted to this new concept and returned service easily with a 'cushioned touch' against the spin or else'knocked the spin off' by attacking the ball. Other players received the ball late, allowing the spin to die.

As a result a tighter service was needed and by 1970 most players could serve well with spin, while keeping the ball short. In table tennis a short ball is defined as one which will bounce twice on the other side of the table,thus restricting the opponent's backswing and hence his choice of return.

This was highlighted in 1979 when England's Desmond Douglas played Dragutin Surbek of Yugoslavia in the European League. Desmond served the whole of his quota of services short to prevent the loop attack. He achieved this but his tactics never changed throughout the whole match and so Des eventually lost.

Disguise has always been important in service and the 1977 World Championships in England marked the advent of the combination racket. This racket has two sides of rubber giving very different levels of spin and gave the Chinese players a great advantage. They 'twiddled' the bat for service, first with the fast,spinny rubber then played the same service with the anti-spin rubber.

A good service in the 1980s utilizes all the various historical developments and spin, speed, placement, variation and deception are all part of the server's repertoire.

Top players serve just short of the middle area in order that the second bounce lands just before, just after or on the baseline. This is often called the 'half-long' service since the receiver cannot tell whether the service is long enough to loop. This makes him indecisive and forces many weak returns.

Of course good players now have a wide armoury of services,many of which have an identical backswing for maximum deception and minimum predictability.

The service is an individual skill which requires copying and developing ingenuity and above all, practice.

Return of Service:

If the service is tactically the most important stroke then the return must be a close second. A variety of returns is required to meet the ever expanding range service.

There are four standard returns. The secret is to ensure your preparation (backswing) which is similar for all of these so you don't give away any cluses.

Return 1: A short touch-push return is effective against a short serve. This prevents the server from following up with a long stroke. This return of service is well demonstrated by the Swede ULF Bengtsson, who is the 1984 European Champion.

Return 2: A more aggressive return from a short service is the flick. A good backhand or forehand flick can put the server on his heels.

Return 3: All types of long service should be attacked with speed and topspin (for choppers too!) and this should be instinctive.

Return 4 : This is an interesting ball which arose in the 1984 European Championships. The receiver would push (chop) the service very long and very fast with plenty of backspin,inviting the server to loop. Most players accepted this invitation whereupon the receiver would then loop-the-loop very early, brushing the very top of the ball. This sent it back very fast with topspin,catching the opponent cold on his loop's follow-through.

This is a risky tactic that was used mainly aginst the better services, but as the SAS motto goes, 'Who dares wins'.

Third, Fourth and Fifth Ball Attack:

The service is the first ball of the rally and the return is the second.To continue the rally you must then deal with the third ball, *i.e.* the server's follow-up stroke.

Most players serve to enable a forehand loop or smash to follow. This is impossible if the return is short and low and easiest when the ball is returned long and slow. Such players therefore try to avoid serving either long or very short,concentrating mainly on the half-long service. This encourages a longer return without great speed.The server can then cover most of table with a forehand loop or smash as his third ball attack.

Fourth Ball :

It follows that the ball is usually long by this stage, so that the receiver can loop the fourth ball. If the third ball is weak it is certainly best to loop or drive this ball, but if the third ball is strong then the best tactic is to block or chop. A sensible blocked or chopped fourth ball is often the switch, buying a little time to settle into the rally.

Fifth Ball Attack :

In top-class table tennis, nearly half the points are decided by the fifth ball, which is increasingly becoming the point winner. If the server cannot win the point directly from service or third ball, he normally tries to place his third ball well enough to force a weak chop or block.

Statistics show that if the server hasn't won the point after the fifth ball he is the underdon for the remainder of the rally.

LAWS OF THE GAME

1. **The Table** - The table shall be in surface rectangular,2.74m in length and 1.525m in width; it shall be supported so that its upper surface, termed the 'playing surface', shall lie in a horizontal plane 760 mm above the floor. It shall be made of any material and shall yield a uniform bounce of not less than 220 mm and not more than 250 mm when a standard ball is dropped from a height of

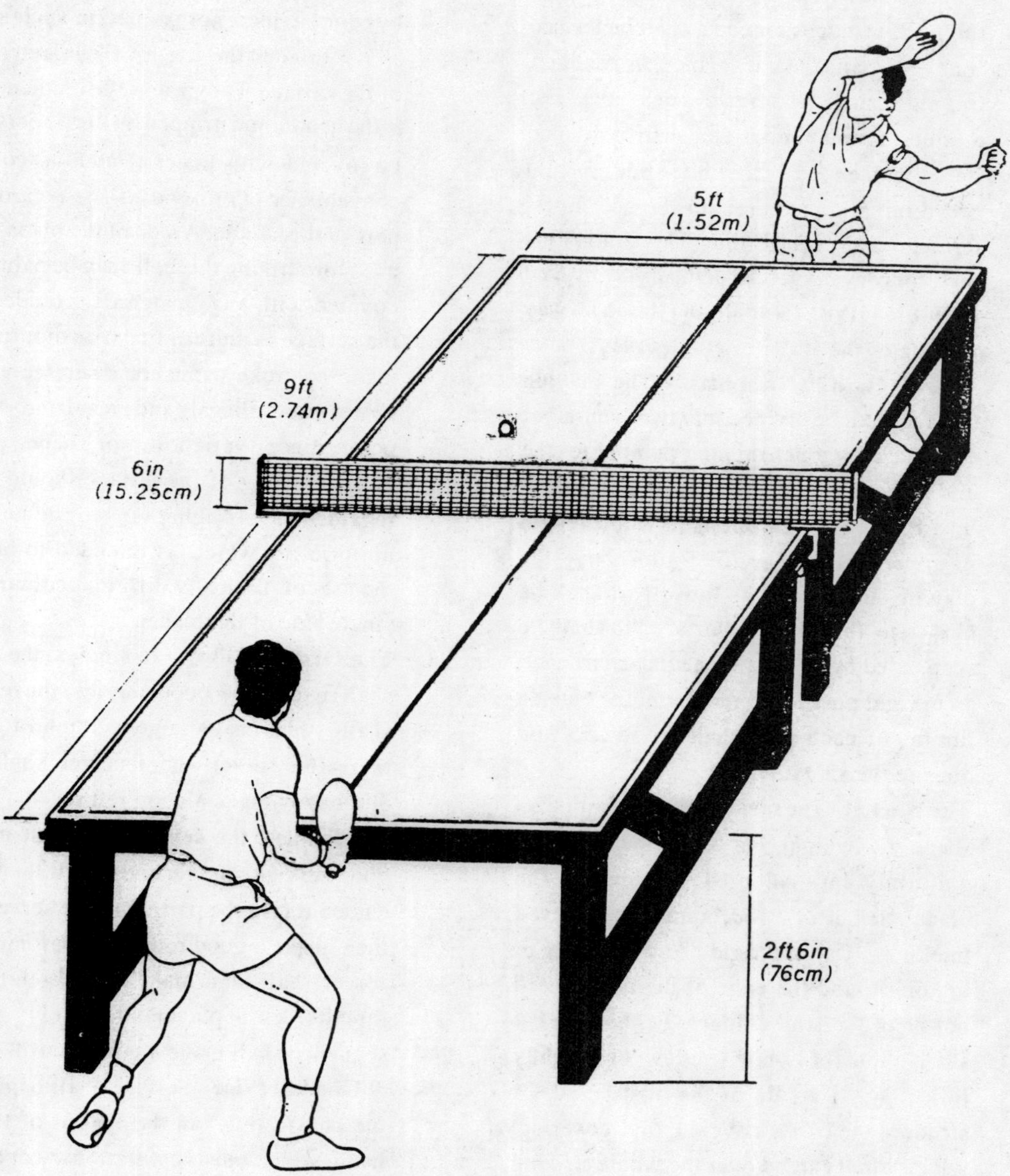
5ft
(1.52m)
9ft
(2.74m)
6in
(15.25cm)
2ft 6in
(76cm)

305 mm above its surface. The playing surface shall be dark-coloured, preferably dark green, and matt, with a white line 20mm board along each edge. The lines at the 1.525m edges, or ends, shall be termed 'end lines', and the lines at the 2.74m edges, or sides,shall be termed'sides lines'.For doubles, the playing surface shall be divided into halves by a white line 3 mm broad,running parallel to the side lines, termed the 'centre line'.The centre line may, for convenience, be permanently marked in full length on the table and this in no way invalidates the table for singles play.

2. **The Net and its Supports** - The playing surface shall be divided into two 'courts' of equal size by a net running parallel to the end lines. The net,with its suspension, shall be 1.83 m in length; along its whole length its upper part shall be 152.5 mm above the playing surface and its lower part shall be close to the playing surface. It shall be suspended by a cord attached at each end to an upright post 152.5 mm high; the outside limits of each post shall be 152.55 mm outside the side line.

3. **The Racket** - The racket may be of any size, shape or weight, but each side shall be uniformly dark-coloured and matt. The blade shall be of wood, continuous, of even thickness, flat and rigid. Any trimming or binding round the edge of the blade need not be of the same colour as neither side but shall not be white, yellow or brightly reflecting. If a side of the blade used for striking the ball is covered, this covering, which shall extend over the whole striking surface, shall be either ordinary pimpled rubber, with pimples outwards, having a total thickness including adhesive of not more than 2 mm, or' sandwich' rubber, consisting of a layer of cellular rubber surfaced by ordinary pimpled rubber,with pimples inwards or outwards, having a total thickness including adhesive of not more than 4 mm.If a side of the blade used for striking the ball is not covered the wood shall be dark-coloured, either naturally or by being stained, not painted,in such a way as not to alter the frictional characteristics of the surface. The part of the blade nearest to the handle and gripped by the fingers may be covered with material such as cork for convenience of grip and is to be regarded as part of the handle. A side of the blade never used for striking the ball may be painted or covered with any material provided that the surface is uniformly dark-coloured and matt; a stroke with such a surface would, however,be illegal and result in a lost point.Minor variations of shade, due to wear or ageing of the surface,should not be regarded as infringing the requirement for uniformity, which is intended to prevent the use of basically different colours on a single side of the blade.

4. **The Order of Play** - In singles, the server shall first make a good service, the receiver shall then make a good return and thereafter server and receiver shall each alternately make a good return.

   In doubles, the server shall first make a good service, the receiver shall then make a good return,the partner of the server shall then make a good return,the partner of the server shall then make a good return, and threafter each player alternately in that sequence shall make a good return.

5. **A Good Service** - Service shall begin with the ball resting on the palm of the free hand, which must be stationary,open and flat, with the fingers together and the thumb free. The free hand,while in contact with the ball in service, shall at all times be above the level of the playing surface.

   The server shall then project the ball upwards within 45 degree of the vertical, by hand only and without imparting spin, so that the ball is visible at all times to the umpire and so that it visibly leaves the palm.

As the ball is then visibly descending from the height of its trajectory it shall be struck so that it first touches the server's court and then, passing directly over or around the net, touches the receiver's court.

In doubles, the ball shall touch first the server's right half-court or the centre-line on his side of the net and then,passing over or around the net,touch the receiver's right half-court or the centre line on his side of the net.

At the moment of the impact of the racket on the ball in service, the ball shall be behind the end-line of the server's court or an imaginary extension thereof.

Strict observance of the prescribed method of service may be waived where the umpire is notified, before play begins, that compliance is prevented by physical disability.

6. **A Good Return** - The ball having been served or returned in play shall be struck so that it pass directly over or around the net and touch directly the opponent's court,provided that if the ball, having been served or returned in play,return with its own impetus over or around the net it may be struck while still in play so that it touch directly the opponent's court. If the ball, in passing over or around the net, touch it or its supports it shall be considered to have passed directly.

7. **In Play** - The ball is in play from the moment it is projected from the hand in service until:

(a) It has touched one court twice consecutively.

(b) It has, except in service,touched each court alternately without having been struck with the racket intermediately.

(c) It has been struck by a player more than once consecutively.

(d) It has touched a player or anything he wears or carries, except his racket or his hand below the wrist.

(e) It has been volleyed.

(f) It has touched any object other than the net,supports,or those referred to above.

(g) It has, in a doubles service, touched the left half-court of the server or of the receiver.

(h) It has,in doubles, been struck by a player out of proper sequence,except as provided in Law 15.

(i) It has, under the Expedite System, been returned by thirteen successive good returns of the receiving player or pair.

8. **A Let** - The rally is a let:

(a) If the ball served, in passing over or around the net,touch it or its supports, provided the service be otherwise good or be volleyed by the receiver,or his partner.

(b) If a service be delivered when the receiver or his partner is not ready,provided always that a player may not be deemed to be unready if he or his partner attempt to strike at the ball.

(c) If, owing to an accident not within his control,a player fail to make a good service or a good return.

(d) If it be interrupted for correction of a mistake in playing order or ends.

(e) If it be interrupted for application of the Expedite System.

9. **A Point** - Except as provided in Law 8, a player shall lose a point:

(a) If he fails to make a good service.

(b) If, a good service or a good return having been made by his opponent,he fail to make a good return.

(c) If he, or his racket or anything that he wears or carries, touch the net or its supports while the ball is in play.

(d) If he, or his racket, or anything that he wears or carrie, move the playing surface while the ball is in play.

(e) If his free hand touch the playing surface while the ball is in play.

(f) If, before the ball in play shall have passed over the end lines or side lines not yet having touched the playing surface on his side of the net since being struck by his opponent, it come in contact with him or anything he wears or carries.

(g) If he volley the ball.

(h) If, in doubles, he strike the ball out of proper sequence, except as provided in Law 13.

(i) If, under the Expedite System, his service and the twelve following strokes of the serving player or pair be returned by good returns of the receiving player or pair.

10. **A Game** - A game shall be won by the player or pair first scoring 21 points,unless both players or pairs shall have scored 20 points, when the winner of the game shall be the player or pair first scoring 2 points more than the opposing player or pair.

11. **The Choice of Ends and Service** - The choice of ends and the right to serve or receive first in a match shall be decided by toss. The winner of the toss may choose the right to serve or receive first and the loser shall then have the choice of ends and vice versa; the winner of the toss may, if he prefer it, require the loser to make first choice.

In doubles, the pair who have the right to serve the first five services in any game shall decide which partner shall do so. In the first game of a match the opposing pair shall then decide similarly which shall be the first receiver. In subsequent games the serving pair shall choose their first server and the first receiver will then be established automatically to correspond with the first server as provided in Law 12.

12. **The Change of Ends and Service** - The player or pair who started at one end in a game shall start at the other in the immediately subsequent game, and so on until the end of the match. In the last possible game of the match the players or pairs shall change ends when first either player or pair reaches the score 10.

In singles, after five points, the receiver shall become the server and the server the reciver, and so on until the end of the game or the score 20-20, or until the introduction of the Expedite System.

In doubles, the first five services shall be delivered by the selected partner of the pair who delivered by the selected partner of the pair who have the right to do so and shall be received by the appropriate partner of the opposing pair. The second five services shall be delivered by the receiver of the first five services and received by the partner of the first server. The third five services shall be delivered by the partner of the first server and receiver by the partner of the first receiver. The fourth five services shall be delivered by the partner of the first receiver and received by the first server. The fifth five services shall be delivered as the first five and so on in sequence until the end of the game or the score 20-20, or until the introduction of the Expedite System. From the score 20-20, or if the game is being played under the Expedite System, the sequence of serving and receiving shall be the same but each player shall deliver only one service in turn until the end of the game. The player or pair who served first in a game shall receive first in the immediately subsequent game, and so on until the end of the match. In the last possible game of a doubles match, the receiving pair shall alter its order of receiving when first either pair reaches the score 10.

In each game of a doubles match the initial order of receiving shall be opposite to that in the preceding game.

13. Out of Order of Serving, Receiving and Ends

(i) If the players have not changed ends when they should have done so, play shall be interrupted by the umpire as soon as the error is discovered and shall resume with the players at the ends at which they should be at the score that has been reached, according to the sequence established at the beginning of the match.

(ii) If a player serves or receives out of turn, play shall be interrupted as soon as the error is discovered and shall resume with those players servinng and receiving who should be server and receiver respectively at the score that has been reached, according to the sequence established at the beginning of the match, and, in doubles, to the order of serving chosen by the pair having the right to serve first in the game during which the error is discovered.

(iii) In any circumstances, all points scored before the discovery of an error shall be reckoned.

CUP & TROPHIES

Swaything Cup

The Men's World Team Championship. First held in 1927 and from then until 1957, with the exception of the war years, it was contested annually; since then it has been held biennially.

Winners

1927	Hungary
1928	Hungary
1929	Hungary
1930	Hungary
1931	Hungary
1932	Czechoslovakia
1933	Hungary
1934	Hungary
1935	Hungary
1936	Austria
1937	United States
1938	Hungary
1939	Czechoslovakia
1940	Not held
1941	Not held
1942	Not held
1943	Not held
1944	Not held
1945	Not held
1946	Not held
1947	Czechoslovakia
1948	Czechoslovakia
1949	Hungary
1950	Czechoslovakia
1951	Czechoslovakia
1952	Hungary
1953	England
1954	Japan
1955	Japan
1956	Japan
1957	Japan
1959	Japan
1961	China
1963	China
1965	China
1967	Japan
1969	Japan
1971	China
1973	Sweden
1975	China
1977	China
1979	Hungary
1981	China
1983	China
1985	China
1987	China

Corbillon Cup

The women's equivalent of the Swaything Cup. First held in the 1934 season, and like the Swaything Cup was contested annually until 1957 and biennially since then.

Winners

1934	Germany
1935	Czechoslovakia

1936	Czechoslovakia
1937	United States
1938	Czechoslovakia
1939	Germany
1940	Not held
1941	Not held
1942	Not held
1943	Not held
1944	Not held
1945	Not held
1946	Not held
1947	England
1948	England
1949	United States
1950	Romania
1951	Romania
1952	Japan
1953	Romania
1954	Japan
1955	Romania
1956	Romania
1957	Japan
1958	Japan
1961	Japan
1963	Japan
1965	China
1967	Japan
1969	USSR
1971	Japan
1973	South Korea
1975	China
1977	China
1979	China
1981	China
1983	China
1985	China
1987	China

World Championships

Men

1927	R.Jacobi (Hun)
1928	Z.Mechlovits (Hun)
1929	F.Perry (UK)
1930	V.Barna (Hun)
1931	M.Szabados (Hun)
1932	V.Barna (Hun)
1933	V.Barna (Hun)
1934	V.Barna (Hun)
1935	V.Barna (Hun)
1936	S.Kolar (Tch)
1937	R.Bergmann (Aut)
1938	B.Vana (Tch)
1939	R.Bergmann (Aut)
1940	Not held
1941	Not held
1942	Not held
1943	Not held
1944	Not held
1945	Not held
1946	Not held
1947	B.Vana (Tch)
1948	R.Bergmann (Eng)
1949	J.Leach (Eng)
1950	R.Bergmann (Eng)
1951	J.Leach (Eng)
1952	H.Satoh (Jap)
1953	F.Sindo (Hun)
1954	I.Ogimura (Jap)
1955	T.Tanaka (Jap)
1956	I.Ogimura (Jap)
1957	T.Tanaka (Jap)
1959	J.Kuo-tuan (Chn)
1961	C.Tse-tuan (Chn)
1963	C.Tse-tuan (Chn)
1965	N.Hasegawa (Jap)
1967	N.Hasegawa (Jap)
1969	S.Ito (Jap)
1971	S.Bengtsson (Swe)
1973	H.En-Ting (Chn)
1975	I.Jonyer (Hun)
1977	M.Kohno (Jap)
1979	S.Ono (Jap)
1981	G.Yue-Hua (Chn)
1983	G.Yue-Hua (Chn)
1985	J.Jialiang (Chn)
1987	J.Jialiang (Chn)

Women

1927	M.Mednyanszky (Hun)
1928	M.Mednyanszky (Hun)
1929	M.Mednyanszky (Hun)
1930	M.Mednyanszky (Hun)
1931	M.Mednyanszky (Hun)
1932	A.Sipos (Hun)
1933	A.Sipos (Hun)
1934	M.Kettnerova (Tch)
1935	M.Kettnerova (Tch)
1936	R.Aarons (USA)
1937	
1938	T.Pritzi (Aut)
1939	V.Depetrisova (Tch)
1940	Not held
1941	Not held
1942	Not held
1943	Not held
1944	Not held
1945	Not held
1946	Not held
1947	G.Farkas (Hun)
1948	G.Farkas (Hun)
1949	G.Farkas (Hun)
1950	A.Rozeanu (Rom)
1951	A.Rozeanu (Rom)
1952	A.Rozeanu (Rom)
1953	A.Rozeanu (Rom)
1954	A.Rozeanu (Rom)
1955	A.Rozeanu (Rom)
1956	T.Okawa (Jap)
1957	F.Eguchi (Jap)
1959	K.Matsuzaki (Jap)
1961	C.Chung-hui (Chn)
1963	K.Matsuzaki (Jap)
1965	N.Fukazu (Jap)
1967	S.Morisawa (Jap)
1969	T.Kowada (Jap)
1971	L.Hui-Ching (Chn)
1973	Hu Yu-Lan (Chn)
1975	P.Yung-Sun (N.Korea)
1977	P.Yung-Sun (N.Korea)
1979	K.HsinAi (Chn)
1981	T.Ling (Chn)
1983	C.Yan-Hua (Chn)
1985	C.Yan-Hua (Chn)
1987	H.Zhili (Chn)

Men's Doubles

1927	R.Jacobi	D.Pesci (Hun)
1928	A.Liebster	R.Thum (Aut)
1929	V.Barna	M.Szabados (Hun)
1930	V.Barna	M.Szabados (Hun)
1931	V.Barna	M.Szabados (Hun)
1932	V.Barna	M.Szabados (Hun)
1933	V.Barna	S.Glancz (Hun)
1934	V.Barna	M.Szabados (Hun)
1935	V.Barna	M.Szabados (Hun)
1936	R.G.Blattner	J.H.McClure (USA)
1937	R.G.Blattner	J.H.McClure (USA)
1938	S.Schiff	J.H.McClure (USA)
1939	V.Barna (Hun)	R.Bergmann (Aut)
1940	Not held	
1941	Not held	
1942	Not held	
1943	Not held	
1944	Not held	
1945	Not held	
1946	Not held	
1947	B.Vana	A.Slar (Tch)
1948	B.Vana	L.Stipek (Tch)
1949	F.Tokar	I.Andreadis (Tch)
1950	F.Sido	F.Soos (Hun)
1951	B.Vana	I.Andreadis (Tch)
1952	N.Fujii	T.Hayashi (Jap)
1953	J.Koczian	F.Sido (Hun)
1954	V.Harangozo	Z.Dolinar (Yug)
1955	I.Andreadis	L.Stipek (Tch)
1956	I.Ogimura	Y.Tomita (Jap)
1957	L.Andreadis	L.Stipek (Tch)
1959	I.Ogimura	T.Murakami (Jap)
1961	N.Hoshino	K.Kimura (Jap)
1963	C.Shih-Lin	W.Chih-Liang (Chn)
1965	C.Tsa-Tung	H.Yin-Sheng (Chn)
1967	H.Alser	K.Johansson (Swe)
1969	H.Alser	K.Johansson (Swe)
1971	I.Jonyer	T.Klampar (Hun)
1973	S.Bengtsson	K.Johansson (Swe)

1975	G.Gergely	I.Jonyer (Hun)
1977	Chen-Shih Li	L.Ko Liang (Chn)
1979	D.Surbek	A.Stipancic (Yug)
1981	C.Zhen-Hua	L.Zhen-Shi (Chn)
1983	D.Surbek	Z.Kalinic (Yug)
1985	M.Appelgren	U.Carlsson (Swe)
1987	C.Longcan	W.Quingguang (Chn)

Women's Doubles

1927	M.Mednyanszky(Hun)	F.Flamm (Aut)
1928	E.Metzger	E.Ruester (Ger)
1929	M.Mednyanszky	A. Sipos (Hun)
1930	M.Mednyanszky	A.Sipos (Hun)
1931	M.Mednyanszky	A.Sipos (Hun)
1932	M.Mednyanszky	A.Sipos (Hun)
1933	M.Mednyanszky	A.Sipos (Hun)
1934	M.Mednyanszky	A.Sipos (Hun)
1935	M.Mednyanszky	A.Sipos (Hun)
1936	M.Kettnerova	M.Smidova (Tch)
1937	V.Depetrisova	V.Votrubcova (Tch)
1938	V.Depetrisova	V.Votrubcova (Tch)
1939	T.Pritzi	H.Bussmann (Aut)
1940	Not held	
1941	Not held	
1942	Not held	
1943	Not held	
1944	Not held	
1945	Not held	
1946	Not held	
1947	G.Farkas (Hun)	T.Pritzi (Aut)
1948	V.Thomas	M.Franks (Eng)
1949	G.Farkas (Hun)	E.Elliot (Sco)
1950	D.Beregi (Eng)	H.Elliot (Sco)
1951	D.Rowe	R.Rowe (Eng)
1952	S.Narahara	T.Nishimura (Jap)
1953	A.Rozeanu (Rom)	G.Farkas (Hun)
1954	D.Rowe	R.Rowe (Eng)
1955	A.Rozeanu	E.Zeller (Rom)
1956	A.Rozeanu	F.Zeller (Rom)
1957	L.Mosoczy	A.Simon (Hun)
1959	T.Namba	K.Yamaizumi (Jap)
1961	M.Alexandru	G.Pitica (Rom)
1963	K.Matsuzaki	M.Seki (Jap)
1965	C.Min-Chih	L.Hui-Ching (Chn)
1967	S.Morisawa	S.Hirota (Jap)
1969	S.Grinberg	Z.Rudnova (USSR)
1971	L.Hui-Ching	C.Min-Chih (Chn)
1973	M.Alexandru (Rom)	M.Hamada (Jap)
1975	M.Alexandru (Rom)	S.Takashima (Jap)
1977	Y.Ok Pak (N.Korea)	Y.Yang (Chn)
1979	Z.Li	Z.Deijing (Chn)
1981	C.Yan-Hua	Z.Deijing (Chn)
1983	S.Jianping	D.Lili (Chn)
1985	D.Lili	G.Lijuan (Chn)
1987	Y.Young-Ja	H.Jung-Hua (S.Korea)

Mixed Doubles

1927	M.Mednyanszky	Z.Mechlovits (Hun)
1928	M.Mednyanszky	Z.Mechlovits (Hun)
1929	A.Sipos	I.Kelen (Hun)
1930	M.Mednyanszky	M.Szabados (Hun)
1931	M.Mednyanszky	M.Szabados (Hun)
1932	A.Sipos	V.Barna (Hun)
1933	M.Mednyanszky	I.Kelen (HUn)
1934	M.Mednyanszky	M.Szabados (Hun)
1935	A.Sipos	V.Barna (Hun)
1936	G.Kleinova	M.Hamr (Tch)
1937	V.Votrubcova	B.Vana (Tch)
1938	W.Woodhead (Eng)	L.Bellak (Hun)
1939	V.Votrubcova	B.Vana (Tch)
1940	Not held	
1941	Not held	
1942	Not held	
1943	Not held	
1944	Not held	
1945	Not held	
1946	Not held	
1947	G.Farkas	F.Soos (Hun)
1948	T.Thall	R.Miles (USA)
1949	G.Farkas	S.Sido (Hun)
1950	G.Farkas	S.Sido (Hun)
1951	A.Rozeanu (Rom)	B.Vana (Tch)
1952	A.Rozeanu (Rom)	F.Sido (Hun)
1953	A.Rozeanu (Rom)	F.Sido (Hun)
1954	G.Farkas (Hun)	I.Andeadis (Tch)
1955	E.Koczian	K.Szepesi (Hun)
1956	L.Neuberger	E.Klein (USA)
1957	F.Eguchi	I.Ogimura (Jap)

1959	F.Eguchi	I.Ogimura (Jap)
1961	K.Matsuzaki	I.Ogimura (Jap)
1963	K.Itoh	K.Kimura (Jap)
1965	M.Seki	K.Kimura (Jap)
1967	N.Yamanaka	N.Hasegawa (Jap)
1969	Y.Konno	N.Hasegawa (Jap)
1971	L.Hui-Ching	C.Shih-Lin (Chn)
1973	Li Li	L.Ko-Liang (Chn)
1975	A.Ferdman	S.Gomozkov (USSR)
1977	C.Bergeret	J.Secretin (Fra)
1979	K.Hsin-Ali	L.Ko-Liang (Chn)
1981	H.Junquin	X.Saike (Chn)
1983	N.Xialin	G.Yue-Hua (Chn)
1985	Cao Yan	Cai Zhenhua (Chn)
1987	H.Jun	G.Lijuan (Chn)

ARJUNA AWARD WINNERS

1961	J.C. Vohra
1965	Goutam R. Deewan
1966	Usha Sundararaj
1967	Farouk R. Khodaiji
1969	Mir Kasim Ali
1970	Gudalore Jagannath
1971	Kaity Farrokh Khodaiji
1973	Niraj Ramakrishna Bajaj
1976	Salokhe Shailaja
1979-80	Indu Puri
1980-81	Manjit Dua
1982	V. Chandrasekhar
1985	Kamlesh N. Mehta

TENNIS

For the tennis-player imbued with the antiquarian spirit, the early history of this ancient, beautiful, and complicated game - the charm of which is indeed largely due to its complication - has much fascination. It was played in France in some form or other so far back as the thirteenth century. In the following century it was introduced into many French towns, and buildings were adapted, or constructed, for the purposes of the game. These were called tripots and we hear of the erection early in the fifteenth century of a tripot in Paris in the Rue Grenier Saint Lazare, called Le Petit Temple, in which one Margot, a woman, used to play about 1427, with such skill that she could hold her own with all but the best players of the opposite sex. The game in which she was so proficient is spoken of as "hand-ball," and there is other evidence to show that, up to the beginning of the sixteenth century, the hand had not been entirely superseded by the racket, as the weapon with which the ball was struck.

Of the professional tennis-players, who, in modern times, have attained the highest distinction in the tennis-courts at home and abroad, the name of J.Edmond Barre, the great French player, stands pre-eminent. J.M.Heathcote, an accomplished writer on tennis and perhaps the greatest of all amateur players of the game, has placed on record his opinion of Barre as being "the finest all-round player the world ever produced or is likely to produce". Barre, who died in 1873, appears, indeed, to have been much superior to any of his contemporaries and to have enjoyed a special reputation as a match-player of extraordinary staying power and a remarkable giver of odds. Another great French player is Charles Delahaye, nicknamed "Biboche", who, in his prime, was inferior only to Barre. He has long since been on the retired list; and the leading professional players in Paris, at the present time, are Ferdin and and G. Lesueur, known as "Le Biscon".

SKILLS OF THE GAME

The most important point in tennis is to keep the eyes on the ball and watch the ball upto its point of contact with the racket. This will reduce the

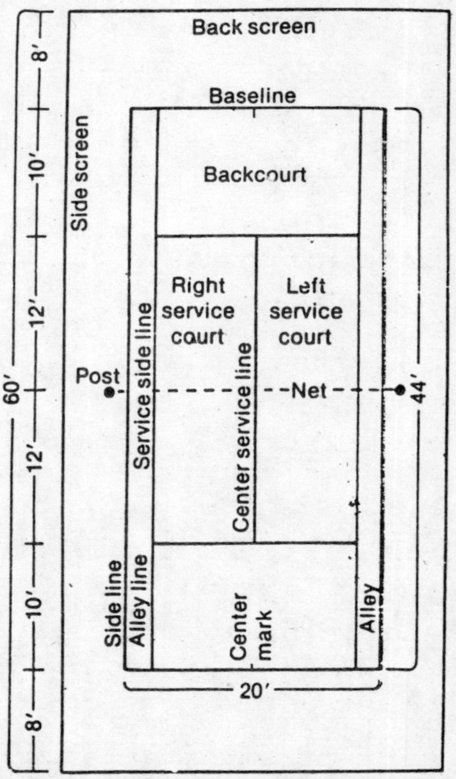

percentage of slipshod shots. Try to practice some shots before the match is actually played. Take a good long warm up on the court and go through repertoire of shots before the start of play.

Grips

The importance of a proper grip cannot be stressed enough. There may be adjustments made in a player's swing, but a proper grip will last a player for a lifetime.

Special names have been given to the forehand grips, based upon the position of the palm against the racket handle.

The backhand grip advocated in this chapter is the Eastern backhand grip. This is attained by putting the palm on the top of the racket, the knuckle of the index finger rides the top right ridge and the thumb can be placed either behind the racket or underneath. This grip position provides the most stability and requires the least amount of wrist adjustment in order to provide a vertical racket head at impact.

Forehand Drive

The player should hold the racket at the ready, with his arms slightly bent, but relaxed, in front of him, steadying the racket with his left hand, so that his right hand can get a grip on it quite easily (forehand Eastern grip). The knees should be bent slightly. Watch the ball. Both hands should be close to the body. This is known as the position of readiness. The upper part of the body should start to twist.

Back Hand Drive

Readiness position as in the forehand drive. The body starts to twist, left shoulder backwards. The racket is lightly rested on the left hand.

Forehand Drive

The Overhead Smash

As the player runs towards the ball, he begins his swing. He takes the racket back with his left hand so that it points diagonally up and backwards and lies close to the body- start of the curve. At this stage, the right wrist moves slightly to the left.

Service

The action of serving corresponds with that of throwing a ball and in teaching, professional coaches encourage pupils to 'throw your racket at the ball'. The first service of a game is made from the right-hand side of the court.

Theoretically, a person 6 feet 3 inches or more tall can, when reaching to full height with a racket, serve a ball that travels in a straight line to the spot where it bounces just within the service line. Players less tall must allow for the ball to dip in flight, either by reducing speed or by applying a spin which uses wind resistance to enforce the necessary dip.

Volley

Such strokes are called volleys and because they are usually made from positions near to the net, they are essentially aggressive; there is no time for a full swing but the volleyer is positioned dangerously so he must try to end the rally immediately. This usually involves a shortened movement which is likened by coaches to everday actions by the words 'punch your volleys'.

Smash

The smash is the answer to the lob. If the lob is not played high enough, the ball can be smashed. Smashing demands a good eye, exact timing, agility and a strong wrist.

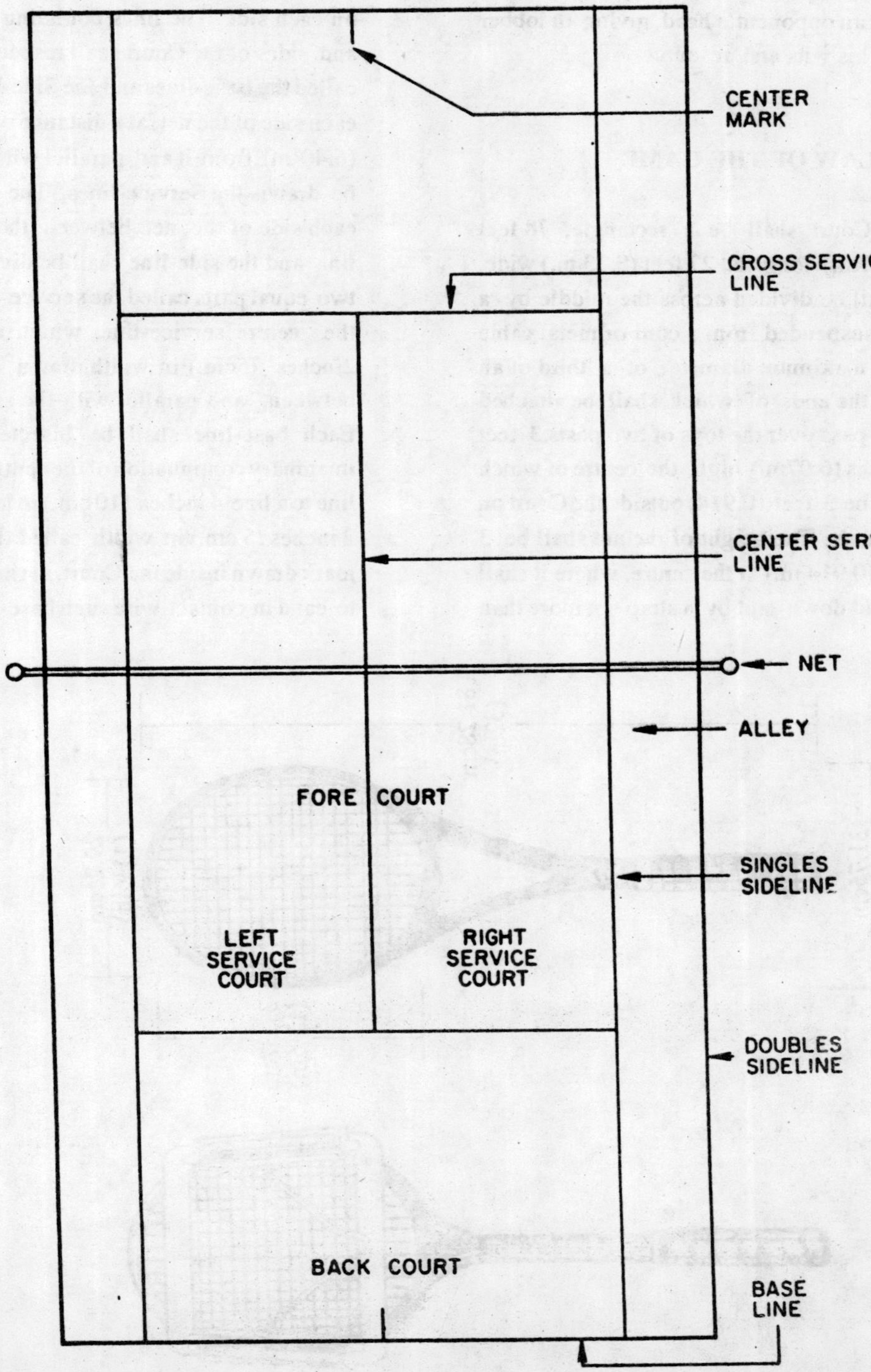
CENTER
MARK
CROSS SERVICE
LINE
CENTER SERVICE
LINE
NET
ALLEY
FORE COURT
SINGLES
SIDELINE
LEFT
SERVICE
COURT
RIGHT
SERVICE
COURT
DOUBLES
SIDELINE
BACK COURT
BASE
LINE

Lob

The simplest and most effective shot in tennis is basically a drive with a lifted follow through up and under the ball. In this way the ball is hoisted over an opponent's head, giving th lobber time to gather his wits and resources.

LAW OF THE GAME

1. The Court shall be a rectangle, 78 feet (23.77m.) long and 27 feet (8.23 m.) wide. It shall be divided across the middle by a net, suspended from a cord or metal cable of a maximum diameter of a third of an inch, the ends of which shall be attached to,or pass over the tops of two posts,3 feet 6inches (6.07m.) high, the centre of which shall be 3 feet (0.914) outside the Court on each side. The height of the net shall be 3 feet (0.914 m.) at the centre, where it shall be held down taut by a strap not more than 2inches (5 cm.) wide. There shall be a band covering the cord or metal cable and the top of the net for not less than 2inches (5 cm.) nor more than 2- ½ inches (6.40 m.) in depth on each side. The lines bounding the ends and sides of the Court shall respectively be called the Base-lines and the Side-lines. On each side of the net, at a distance of 21 feet (6.40 m) from it and parallel with it, shall be drawn the Service-lines. The space on each side of the net between the service-line and the side-line shall be divided into two equal parts called the service-courts by the centre service-line, which must be 2inches (5cm.) in width,drawn half-way between, and parallel with the side-lines. Each base-line shall be bisected by an imaginary continuation of the centre service line to a line 4 inches (10 cm.) in length and 2 inches (5 cm.) in width called the centre mark drawn inside the Court, at right angles to eand in contact with such base-lines. All

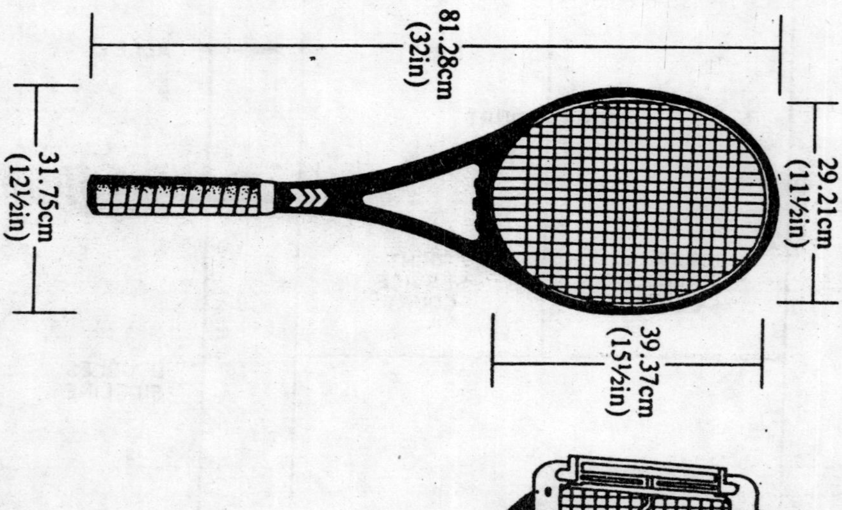

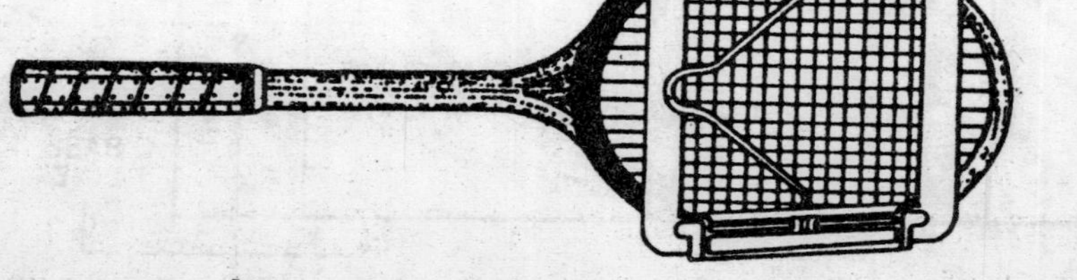

other lines shall be not less than 1 inch (2.5 cm.) and not more than 2 inches (5 cm.) in width, except the base-line, which may be 4 inches (10 cm.) in width and all the measurements shall be made to the outside of the line.

NOTE - 1. In the case of International Lawn Tennis Championship (Davis Cup) or other Official Championships of the International Federation, there shall be a space behind each base-line of not less than 21 feet (6.40 m), and at the sides of not less than 12 feet. (3.66 m.)

2. The permanent fixtures of the Court shall include not only the net, posts, cord or metal cable, strap and band, but also, where there are any chairs around the Court, and their occupants, all other fixtures around and above the Court, and the Umpire, Foot-fault Judge and Linesman when in their respective places.

NOTE - For the purpose of this Rule the word "Umpire" comprehends the Umpire and all those persons designated to assist him in the conduct of a match.

3. The ball shall have uniform outer surface. If there are any seams they shall be stitchless. The ball shall be more than two and a half inches and less than two and five-eights inches in diameter and more than two ounces and less than two and one-sixteenth ounces in weight. The ball shall have a bound of more than 53 inches (153 cm.) and not less than 58 inches (147 cm.) when dropped 100 inches (254 cm.) upon a concrete base, and a deformation of more than 265 of an inch and less than 290 of an inch (.74 cm.) when subjected to a pressure of 18 lb. applied to each end of any diameter. All the tests for bound, size and deformation shall be made in accordance with the Regulations in the official Rule Book.

4. The players shall stand on the opposite sides of the net; the player who first delivers the ball shall be called the Server, and the other the Receiver.

5. The choice of the sides and the right to be Server or Receiver in the first game shall be decided by toss. The player winning the toss may choose or request his opponent to choose :-

(a) the right to be Server or Receiver, in which case the other player shall choose the side;

(b) the side, in which case the other player shall choose the right to be Server or Receiver.

6. The service shall be delivered in the following manner. Immediately before commencing to serve, the Server shall stand with both feet at rest behind (i.e. further from the net than) the base-line and within the imaginary continuations of the centre-mark and side-line. The Server then shall project the ball in hand into the air in any direction and before it hits and ground, strike it with his racket and the delivery shall be deemed to have been completed at the moment of the impact of the racket and the ball. A player with the use of only one arm may utilize his racket for the projection.

7. The Server shall throughout the delivery of the service :-

(a) not change his position by walking or running

(b) not touch, with either foot, any area other than that behind the base-line within the imaginary extension of the centre mark and sideline.

NOTE - The following interpretation of Rule 7 was approved by the International Federation on 9th July. 1958 :-

7. (a) The Server shall not, by slight movements of the feet which do not materially affect the location originally taken up by him, be deemed "to change his position by walking or running"

(b) The word "foot" means the extremity of the leg below the ankle.

8. (a) In delivering the service, the Server shall stand alternately behind the right hand left Courts, beginning from the right in every game. If service from a wrong half of the court occurs and is undetected, all play resulting from such wrong service or services shall stand, but the inaccuracy of station shall be corrected immediately atter it is discovered.

(b) The ball served shall pass over the net and hit the ground within the Service Court which is diagonally opposite, or upon any line bounding such Court, before the Receiver returns it.

9. The service is a fault :

(a) if the Server commits any breach of Rules 6,7,or 8;

(b) if he mises the ball in attempting to strike it;

(c) if the ball served touches a permanent fixture (other than the net, strap or band) before it hits the ground.

10. After a fault (if it be the first fault) the Server shall serve again from behind the same half of the Court. The wrong half, when in accordance with Rule 8, the Server shall be entitled to one service only from behind the other half A fault may not be claimed after the next service has been delivered.

11. The Server shall not serve until the Receiver is ready. If the latter attempts to return the service, he shall be deemed ready. If however, the Receiver signifies that he is not ready, he may not claim a fault because the ball does not hit the ground within the limits fixed for the service.

12. In all cases where a let has to be called under the rules, or to provide for an interruption to play, it shall have the following interpretations :-

(a) When called solely in respect of a service, that one service only shall be replayed.

(b) When called under any other circumstances, the point shall be replayed.

13. The service is a let :-

(a) if the ball served touches the net, strap or band, and is otherwise good or after touching the net, strap or band, touches the Receiver or anything which he wears or carries before hitting the ground.

(b) if a service or a fault be delivered when the Receiver is not ready (see Rule 11.) In case of a let, that particular servic shall not count, and the Server shall serve again, but a service let does not annul a previous fault.

14. At the end of the first game the Receiver shall become Server, and Receiver the Server; and so on alternately in all the subsequent games of a match. If a player serves out of turn, the player who ought to have served shall serve as soon as the mistake is discovered, but all the points scored before such discovery shall be reckoned. If a game shall have been completed before such discovery, the order or service remains as altered. A fault served before such discovery shall not be reckoned.
15. A ball is in play from the moment at which it is delivered in service. Unless a fault or a let be called it remains in play until the point is decided.
16. The Server wins the point :-

    (a) if the ball served, not being a let under Rule 13, touches the Receiver or anything which he wears or carries, before it hits the ground;

    (b) if the Receiver otherwise loses the point as provided by Rule 18.
17. The Receiver win the point

    (a) if the Server serves two consecutive faults ;

    (b) if the Server otherwise loses the point as provided by rule 18.
18. A player loses the point if :-

    (a) he fails, before the ball in play has hit the ground twice consecutively, to return it directly over the net [except as provided in Rule 22 (a) or (c)] ; or

    (b) he returns the ball in play so that it hits the ground , a permanent fixture, or other object, outside any of the lines which beyond his opponent's Court [except as provided in Rule 22 (a) and (c)] ; or

    (c) he volleys the ball and fail to make a good return even when standing outside the Court;or

    (d) he touches or strikes the ball in play with his racket more than once in making a stroke ; or

    (e) He or his racket (in his hand or otherwise) or anything which he wears or carries touches the net, posts, cord or metal cable, strap or band, or the ground within his opponent's Court at any time while the ball is in play; or

    (f) he volleys the ball before it has passed the net;or

    (g) the ball in play touches in or anything that he wears or carries, except his racket in his hand or hands; or

    (h) he throws his racket and hits the ball.
19. If a player commits any act either deliberately or involuntarily which, in the opinion of the umpire, hinders the opponent in making a stroke, the Umpire shall in the first case award the point to the opponent, and in the second case order the point to be replayed.
20. A ball falling on a line is regarded a falling in the Court bounded by that line.
21. If the ball in play touches a permanent fixture (other than the net, posts, cord or metal cable, strap or hand) after it has hit the ground, the player who struck it wins the point; if before it hits the ground his opponent wins the point.
22. It is a good return :-

    (a) if the ball touches the net, posts, cord or metal cable, strap or band, provided that it passes over any of them and hits the ground within the court; or

    (b) if the ball, served or returned, hits the ground within the proper Court and rebounds or be blown back over the net, and the player whose turn it is to strike reach over the net and play the ball, provided that neither he nor any part of his clothes or racket touch the net, posts, cord or metal cable, strap or band or the ground within his opponent's Court, and that the stroke be otherwise good; or

(c) if the ball be returned outside the post, either above or below the level of the top of the net, even though it touches the post, provided that it hits the ground within the proper Court;or

(d) if a player's racket passes over the net after he has returned the ball, provided the ball passes the net before being played and be properly returned; or

(e) if a player succeeded in returning the ball, served or in play, which strikes a ball laying in the Court.

NOTE TO RULE 22- In a singles match, if for the sake of convenience a doubles Court be equipped with singles posts for the purpose of a singles game, then the doubles posts and those portions of the net, cord or metal cable and band outside such singles posts or parts of the net of a singles game. A return that passes under the net cord between the singles and adjacent doubles post without touching either net cord, net or doubles post and falls within the area of play, is a good return.

23. In case a player is hindered in making a stroke by anything not within his control, except a permanent fixture of the Court, or

except as provided for in Rule 19, the point shall be replayed.

24. If a player wins his first point, the score is called 15 for that player ; on winning his second point, the score is called 30 for that player; on winning his third point, the score is called 40 for that player, and the fourth point won by a player is scored game for that player except as below:-

If both the players have won three points, the score is called deuce; and the next point won by a player is scored advantage for that player. If the same player wins the next, he wins the game; if the other player wins the next point the score is again called deuce; and so on, until a player wins the two points immediately following the score at deuce, when the game is scored for that player.

25. A player (or players) who first wins six games win a set; except that the must win by a margin of two games over his opponent, and, where necessary, a set shall be extended until this margin be achieved.

26. The players shall change sides at the end of the first, third and every subsequent alternate game of each set and at the end of each set unless the total number of games in such set be even, in which case the change is not made until the end of the first game of the next set.

27. The maximum number of sets in a match shall be 5, or , where women take part, 3.

28. Except where otherwise stated, every reference in these Rules to the masculine includes the feminine gender.

29. Modified form of Law 29 according to International Lawn Tennis Federation, on 7th July 1971.

In matches where an Umpire is appointed, his decision shall be final; but where a Referee is appointed, an appeal shall lie to him from the decision of an Umpire on a question of law and in all such cases the decision of the Referee shall be final except that in Davis Cup matches the decision of a linesman can be changed by the Referee, or by the Umpire with the consent of the Referee.

The Referee, in his discretion, may at any time, postpone a match on account of darkness or the condition of the ground or the weather. In any case of postponement the previous score and previous occupancy of Courts shall hold good, unless the Referee and the players unanimously agree otherwise.

30. Play shall be continuous form the first service till the match be concluded; provided that after the third set, or when women take part the second set, either player is entitled to a rest, which shall not exceed 10 minutes, or in countries situated between Latitude 15 degrees North and Latitude 15 degrees South, 45 minutes, and provided further that when necessitated by circumstances not within the control of the players, the Umpire may suspend play for such a period as he may consider necessary. If play be suspended and be not resumed until a later day the rest may be taken only after the third set (or when women take part, the second set) of play on such later day, completion of an unfinished set being counted as one set. These provisions shall be strictly construed , and play shall never be suspended, delayed or interfered with for the purpose of enabling a player to recover his strength or his wind, or to receive instruction or advice. The Umpire shall be the sole judge of such suspension, delay or interference, and after giving due warning he may disqualify the offender.

CUP & TROPHIES

Wimbledon Tournament Winners

The most celebrated of the world's major

championships, the Wimbledon championships were first played in 1877.

Men's Singles

1919	Gerald Patterson	Aus
1920	Bill Tilden	USA
1921	Bill Tilden	USA
1922	Gerald Patterson	Aus
1923	William Johnston	USA
1924	Jean Borotra	Fra
1925	Rene Lacoste	Fra
1926	Jean Borotra	Fra
1927	Henri Cochet	Fra
1928	Rene Lacoste	Fra
1929	Henri Cochet	Fra
1930	Bill Tilden	USA
1931	Sidney Wood	USA
1932	Ellsworth Vines	USA
1933	Jack Crawford	Aus
1934	Fred Perry	UK
1935	Fred Perry	UK
1936	Fred Perry	UK
1937	Donald Budge	USA
1938	Donald Budge	USA
1939	Bobby Riggs	US
1940	Not held	
1941	Not held	
1942	Not held	
1943	Not held	
1944	Not held	
1945	Not held	
1946	Yvon Petra	Fra
1947	Jack Kramer	USA
1948	Bob Falkenburg	USA
1949	Ted Schroeder	USA
1950	Budge Patty	USA
1951	Dick Savitt	USA
1952	Frank Sedgman	Aus
1953	Vic Seixas	USA
1954	Jaroslav Drobny	Cze
1955	Tony Trabert	USA
1956	Lew Hoad	Aus
1957	Lew Hoad	Aus
1958	Ashley Cooper	Aus
1960	Neale Fraser	Aus
1961	Rod Laver	Aus
1962	Rod Laver	Aus
1963	Chuck McKinley	USA
1964	Roy Laver	Aus
1965	Roy Emerson	Aus
1966	Manuel Santana	Spa
1967	John Newcombe	Aus
1968	Rod Laver	Aus
1969	Rod Laver	Aus
1970	John Newcombe	Aus
1971	John Newcombe	Aus
1972	Stan Smith	USA
1973	Jan Kodes	Cze
1974	Jimmy Connors	USA
1975	Arthur Ashe	USA
1976	Bjorn Borg	Swe
1977	Bjorn Borg	Swe
1978	Bjorn Borg	Swe
1979	Bjorn Borg	Swe
1980	Bjorn Borg	Swe
1981	John McEnroe	USA
1982	Jimmy Connors	USA
1983	John McEnroe	USA
1984	John Mcenroe	USA
1985	Boris Becker	W.Ger
1986	Boris Becker	W.Ger
1987	Pat Cash	Aus
1988	Stefan Edberg	Swe
1989	Boris Becker	W.Ger
1990	Stefan Edberg	Swe

Women's Singles

1919	Suzanne Lenglen	Fra
1920	Suzanne Lenglen	Fra
1921	Suzanne Lenglen	Fra
1922	Suzanne Lenglen	Fra
1923	Suzanne Lenglen	Fra
1924	Suzanne McKane	UK
1925	Suzanne Lenglen	Fra
1926	Kathleen Godfree	UK
1927	Helen Wills	USA
1928	Helen Wills	USA
1929	Helen Wills	USA
1930	Helen Wills Moody	USA

1931	Cilly Aussem	Ger
1932	Helen Wills Moody	USA
1933	Helen Wills Moody	USA
1934	Dorothy Round	UK
1935	Helen Wills Moody	USA
1936	Helen Jacobs	USA
1937	Dorothy Round	UK
1938	Helen Wills Moody	USA
1939	Alice Marble	USA
1940	Not held	
1941	Not held	
1942	Not held	
1943	Not held	
1944	Not held	
1945	Not held	
1946	Pauline Betz	USA
1947	Margaret Osborne	USA
1948	Louise Brough	USA
1949	Louise Brough	USA
1950	Louise Brough	USA
1951	Doris Hart	USA
1952	Maureen Connolly	USA
1953	Maureen Connolly	USA
1954	Maureen Connolly	USA
1955	Louise Brough	USA
1956	Shirley Fry	USA
1957	Althea Gibson	USA
1958	Althea Gibson	USA
1959	Maria Bueno	Bra
1960	Maria Bueno	Bra
1961	Angela Mortimer	UK
1962	Karen Susman	USA
1963	Margaret Smith	Aus
1964	Maria Bueno	UK
1965	Margaret Smith	Aus
1966	Billie Jean King	USA
1967	Billie Jean King	USA
1968	Billie Jean King	USA
1969	Ann Jones	UK
1970	Margaret Smith Court	Aus
1971	Evonne Goolagong	Aus
1972	Billie Jean King	USA
1973	Billie Jean King	USA
1974	Christine Evert	USA
1975	Billie Jean King	USA
1976	Christine Evert	USA
1977	Virginia Wade	UK
1978	Martina Navratilova	Cze
1979	Martina Navratilova	Cze
1980	Evonne Goolagong Cawley	Aus
1981	Christine Evert Lloyd	USA
1982	Martina Navratilova	USA
1983	Martina Navratilova	USA
1984	Martina Navratilova	USA
1985	Martina Navratilova	USA
1986	Martina Navratilova	USA
1987	Martina Navratilova	USA
1988	Steffi Graf	W.Ger.

Men's Doubles

1965	John Newcombe,Tony Roche	Aus
1966	Ken Fletcher, John Newcombe	Aus
1967	Bob Hewitt, Frew McMillan	S.Af
1968	John Newcombe, Tony Roche	Aus
1969	John Newcombe, Tony Roche	Aus
1970	John Newcombe, Tony Roche	Aus
1971	Roy Emerson,Rod Laver	Aus
1972	Bob Hewitt,Frew McMillan	S.Af
1973	Jimmy Connors (US),Ilie Nastase	Rom
1974	John Newcombe, Tony Roche	Aus
1975	Vitas Gerulaitis,Sandy Mayer	USA
1976	Brian Gottfried (US)Raul Ramirez	Mex
1977	Ross Case, Geoff Masters	Aus
1978	Bob Hewitt, Frew McMillan	S.Af
1979	Peter Fleming, John McEnroe	USA
1980	Peter McNamara, Paul McNamee	Aus
1981	Peter Fleming, John McEnroe	USA
1982	Peter McNamara, Paul McNamee	Aus
1983	Peter Fleming, John McEnroe	USA
1984	Peter Fleming, John McEnroe	USA
1985	Heinz Gunthardt (Switz) Bela Taroczi (Hungary)	
1986	Mats Wilander (Swe) AHND Joakim Nystram (Swe)	
1987	Ken Flach, Robert Seguro	USA
1988	Ken Flach, Robert Seguro	USA

Women's Doubles

1965 Maria Bueno (Bra), Billie Jean Moffitt(USA)
1966 Maria Bueno (Bra), Nancy Richey (USA)
1967 Rosemary Casals, Billie Jean King (USA)
1968 Rosemary Casals, Billie Jean King (USA)
1970 Rosemary Casals, Billie Jean King (USA)
1971 Rosemary Casals, Billie Jean King (USA)
1972 Billie Jean King (USA), Betty Stove (HOL)
1973 Rosemary Casals, Billie Jean King (USA)
1974 Evonne Goolagong (Aus), Peggy Michel (USA)
1975 Ann Kiyomura (USA), Kazuko Sawamatsu (Japan)
1976 Christine Evert (USA), Martina Navratilova (Cze)
1977 Helen Cawley (Aus) , Jonne Russell (USA)
1978 Kerr Reid, Wendy Turnbull (Aus)
1979 Billie Jean King (USA), Martina Navratilova (Cze)
1980 Kathy Jordan, Anne Smith (USA)
1981 Martina Navratilova (Cze), Pam Shriver (USA)
1982 Martina Navratilova (USA), Pam Shriver (USA)
1983 Martina Navratilova (USA), Pam Shriver (USA)
1984 Martina Navratilova (USA), Pam Shriver (USA)
1985 Kathy Jordan (USA), Liz Smylie (Aus)
1986 Martina Navratilova (USA), Pam Shriver (USA)
1987 Claudia Kohde-Kilsch (W.Ger), Helena Sukova (Czech)
1988 Steffi Graf (W.Ger), Gabriella Sabatini (Arg)

USA Open Tournament

Men's Singles

1919	W.M.Johnston	USA
1920	Bill Tiden	USA
1921	Bill Tiden	USA
1922	Bill Tiden	USA
1923	Bill Tiden	USA
1924	Bill Tiden	USA
1925	Bill Tiden	USA
1926	Rene Lacoste	FRA
1927	Rene Lacoste	FRA
1928	Henri Cochet	FRA
1929	Bill Tiden	USA
1930	John Doeg	USA
1931	H.Ellsworth Vines	USA
1932	H.Ellsworth Vines	USA
1933	Fred Perry	UK
1934	Fred Perry	UK
1935	Wilmer Allison	USA
1936	Fred Perry	UK
1937	Don Budge	USA
1938	Don Budge	USA
1939	Robert Riggs	USA
1940	Don McNeil	USA
1941	Robert Riggs	USA
1942	F.R.Schroeder Jr.	USA
1943	Joseph Hunt	USA
1944	Frank Parker	USA
1945	Frank Parker	USA
1946	Jack Kramer	USA
1947	Jack Kramer	USA
1948	Pancho Gonzales	USA
1949	Pancho Gonzales	USA
1950	Arthur Larsen	USA
1951	Frank SEdgman	AUS
1952	Frank Sedgman	AUS
1953	Tony trabert	USA
1954	E.Victor Seixas Jr	USA
1955	Tony Trabert	USA
1956	Ken Rosewall	AUS
1957	Malcolm Anderson	AUS
1958	Ashley Cooper	AUS
1960	Neale A.Fraser	AUS
1961	Neale A. Fraser	AUS
1962	Rod Laver	AUS
1963	Rafael Osuna	MEX
1964	Roy Emerson	AUS
1965	Manuel Santana	SPA
1966	Fred Stolle	AUS
1967	John Newcombe	AUS
1968	Arthur Ashe	USA
1969	Rod Laver	AUS
1970	Ken Rosewall	AUS
1971	Stan Smith	USA
1972	Ilie Nastase	ROM

1973	John Newcombe	AUS
1974	Jimmy Connors	USA
1975	Manuel Orantes	SPA
1976	Jimmy Connors	USA
1977	Guillermo Vilas	ARG
1978	Jimmy Connors	USA
1979	John McEnroe	USA
1980	John McEnroe	USA
1981	John McEnroe	USA
1982	Jimmy Connors	USA
1983	Jimmy Connors	USA
1984	John McEnroe	USA
1985	Ivan Lendl	CZ
1986	Ivan Lendl	CZ
1987	Ivan Lendl	CZ
1988	Mats Wilander	SWE

Women's Singles

1919	Wightman	USA
1920	Mallory	USA
1921	M.Mallory	USA
1922	M.Mallory	USA
1923	Wills	USA
1924	Wills	USA
1925	Wills	USA
1926	Mallory	USA
1927	Wills	USA
1928	Wills	USA
1929	Wills	USA
1930	Nuthall	UK
1931	Moody	USA
1932	Helen Jacobs	USA
1933	Helen Jacobs	USA
1934	Helen Jacobs	USA
1935	Helen Jacobs	USA
1936	Alice Marble	USA
1937	Anita Lizana	CHI
1938	Alice Marble	USA
1939	Alice Marble	USA
1940	Alice Marble	USA
1941	Mrs Sarah P. Cooke	USA
1942	Pauline Betz	USA
1943	Pauline Betz	USA
1944	Pauline Betz	USA
1945	Sarah P. Cooke	USA
1946	Pauline Betz	USA
1947	A. Louise Brough	USA
1948	Mrs. Margaret O. duPont	USA
1949	Mrs. Margaret O. duPont	USA
1950	Mrs. Margaret O. duPont	USA
1951	Maureen Connolly	USA
1952	Maureen Connolly	USA
1953	Maureen Connolly	USA
1954	Doris Hart	USA
1955	Doris Hart	USA
1956	Shirley J. Fry	USA
1957	Althea Gibson	USA
1958	Althea Gibson	USA
1959	Maria Bueno	BRA
1960	Darlene Hard	USA
1961	Darlene Hard	USA
1962	Margaret Smith	AUS
1963	Maria Bueno	BRA
1964	Maria Bueno	BRA
1965	Margaret Smith	USA
1966	Maria Bueno	BRA
1967	Billie Jean King	USA
1968	Virginia Wade	UK
1969	Margaret Smith Court	AUS
1970	Margaret Smith Court	AUS
1971	Billie Jean King	USA
1972	Billie Jean King	USA
1973	Margaret Smith Court	AUS
1974	Billie Jean King	USA
1975	Chris Evert	USA
1976	Chris Evert	USA
1977	Chris Evert	USA
1978	Chris Evert	USA
1979	Tracy Austin	USA
1980	Chris Evert Lloyd	USA
1981	Tracy Austin	USA
1982	Chris Evert Lloyd	USA
1983	Martina Navratilova	USA
1984	Martina Navratilova	USA
1985	Hana Mandikova	CZ
1986	Martina Navratilova	USA
1987	Martina Navratilova	USA
1988	Steffi Graf	W.GER

Men's Doubles

1919	N.E.Brookes - G.L. Patterson	AUS
1920	W.M. Johnston - C.J. Griffin	USA
1921	Bill Tilden - Vincent Richards	USA
1922	Bill Tilden - Vincent Richards	USA
1923	Bill Tilden - Brian Norton	SA
1924	Howard Kinsey - Robert Kinsey	USA
1925	R.Norris Williams - Vincent Richards	USA
1926	R.Norris Williams - Vincent Richards	USA
1927	Bill Tilden - Francis Hunter	USA
1928	George Lott - John Hennessey	USA
1929	George Lott - John Doeg	USA
1930	George Lott - John Doeg	USA
1931	Wilmer Allison - John Van Ryn	USA
1932	H. Ellsworth Vinces - Keith Gledhill	USA
1933	George Lott - Lestr Stoefen	USA
1934	George Lott - Lestr Stoefen	USA
1935	Wilmer Allison - John Van Ryn	USA
1936	Don Budge - C. Gene Mako	USA
1937	Baron G. von Carmm - Henner Henkel	GER
1938	Don Budge - C. Gene Mako	USA
1939	Adrian Quist - John Bromwich	AUS
1940	Jack Kramer - Frederick Schroeder Jr.	USA
1941	Jack Kramer - Frederick Schroeder	USA
1942	Gardner Mulloy - William Talbert	USA
1943	Jack Kramer - Frank Parker	USA
1944	Don McNeill - Robert Falkenburg	USA
1945	Gardner Mulloy - William Talbert	USA
1946	Gardner Mulloy - William Talbert	USA
1947	Jack Kramer - Frederick Schroeder Jr.	USA
1948	Gardner Mulloy - William Talbert	USA
1949	John Bromwich - William Sidwell	AUS
1950	John Bromwich - Frank Sedgman	AUS
1951	Frank Sedgman - Kenneth McGregor	AUS
1952	Mervyn Rose - E. Victor Seixas Jr.	USA
1953	Rex Hartwig - Mervyn Rose	AUS
1954	E. Victor Seixas Jr - Tony Trabert	USA
1955	Kosel Kamo - Atsushi Miyagi	JPN
1956	Lewis Hoad - Ken Rosewall	AUS
1957	Ashley Cooper -Neale Fraser	AUS
1958	Hamilton Richardson - Alejandro Olmedo	USA
1959	Neale A. Fraser - Roy Emerson	AUS
1960	Neale A. Fraser - Roy Emerson	AUS
1961	Dennis Ralston - Chuck McKingley	USA
1962	Rafael Osuna - Antonio Palafox	MEX
1963	Dennis Ralston - Chuck McKinley	USA
1964	Dennis Ralston - Chuck McKinley	USA
1965	Roy Emerson - Fred Stolle	AUS
1966	Roy Emerson - Fred Stolle	AUS
1967	John Newcombe - Tony Roche	AUS
1968	Robert Lutz - Stan Smith	USA
1969	K.R.Rosewall & F.S.Stolle	AUS
1970	Pierre Barthes - Nicki Pilic	YUG
1971	John Newcombe - Roger Taylor	UK
1972	Chiff Darysdale - Roger Taylor	UK
1973	John Newcombe - Owen Davidson	AUS
1974	Bob Lutz - Stan Smith	USA
1975	Jimmy Connors - Ilie Nastase	ROM
1976	Marty Riessen - Tom Okker	USA
1977	Bob Hewitt - Frew McMillan	SA
1978	Stan Smith - Bob Lutz	USA
1979	John McEnroe - Peter Fleming	USA
1980	Stan Smith - Bob Lutz	USA
1981	John McEnroe - Peter Fleming	USA
1982	Kevin Curren - Steve Denton	USA
1983	John McEnroe - Peter Fleming	USA
1984	John Fitzgerald - Tomas Smid	CZ
1985	Ken Flach - Robert Seguro	USA
1986	Andres Gomez - Slobodan Zivolnovic	YUG
1987	Stefan Edberg - Anders Jarryd	SWE
1988	Sergio Csal - Emilio Sanchez	SPA

Women's Doubles

1919	E.E.Goss - M.Zinderstein	USA
1920	E.E.Goss - M.Zinderstein	USA
1921	M.K. Browne - L.Williams	USA
1922	M.Jessup (nee Zinderstein) - H.N.Wills	USA
1923	P.Covell (nee Howkins) - K.Mckane	UK
1924	H.V.Wightman (nee Howkins) - K.McKane	UK
1925	M.K.Browne - H.N.Wills	USA
1926	E.E.Goss - E.Ryan	USA
1927	K.Godfree (neeMcKane) - E.H.Harvey	UK
1928	H. V. Wightman (nee Hotchkiss) & H.N.Wills	USA
1929	P.Michel (nee Saunders) & P.H.Watson	UK
1930	B.Nuthall (UK) - S.Palfrey	USA

1931 B.Nuthall - E.Whittingstall (nee Bennett) UK
1932 H.H.Jacobs - B.Nuthall UK
1933 F.James - B.Nuthall UK
1934 H.H.Jacobs - S.Palfrey USA
1935 H.H.Jacobs - S.Fabyan (nee Gladman) USA
1936 Mrs. M.G. Van Ryn - Carolin Babcock USA
1937 Mrs. Sarah P. Fabyan - Alice Marble USA
1938 Alice Marble - Mrs. Sarah P. Fabyan USA
1939 Alice Marble - Mrs. Sarah P. Fabyan USA
1940 Alice Marble - Mrs. Sarah P. Fabyan USA
1941 Mrs. S.P. Cooke - Margaret Osborne USA
1942 A.Louise Brough - Margaret Oborne USA
1943 A. Louise Brough - Margaret Oborne USA
1944 A. Louise Brough - Margaret Oborne USA
1945 A. Louise Brough - Margaret Oborne USA
1946 A. Louise Brough - Margaret Oborne USA
1947 A. Louise Brough - Margaret Oborne USA
1948 A. Louise Brough - Mrs. M.O. duPont USA
1949 A. Louise Brough - Mrs. M.O. duPont USA
1950 A. Louise Brough - Mrs. M.O. duPont USA
1951 Doris Hart - Shirley Fry USA
1952 Doris Hart - Shirley Fry USA
1953 Doris Hart - Shirley Fry USA
1954 Doris Hart - Shirley Fry USA
1955 A. Louise Brough - Mrs. M.O. duPont USA
1956 A. Louise Brough - Mrs. M.O. duPont USA
1957 A. Louise Brough - Mrs. M.O. duPont USA
1958 Darlene Hard - Jeanne Arth USA
1959 Darlene Hard - Jeanne Arth USA
1960 Darlene Hard (USA) - Maria Bueno (BRA)
1961 Darlene Hard (USA) - Lesley Turner (AUS)
1962 Maria Bueno (BRA)- Darlene Hard (USA)
1963 Margaret Smith - Robyn Ebbern AUS
1964 Billie Jean Moffitt - Karen Susman USA
1966 M.E.Bueno (BRA) - Nancy Richey (USA)
1967 Rosemary Casals - Bilie Jean King USA
1968 M.E.Bueno (BRA) - M.Court (AUS)
1969 Francoise Durr (FRA) - Darlene Hard (USA)
1970 M.S.Court - Judy Tegart Dalton AUS
1971 Rosemary Casals (USA) - Judy Tegart Dalton (AUS)
1972 Francoise Durr (FRA) - Betty Stove (NETH)
1973 Margaret S. Court (AUS) - Virginia Wade (UK)
1974 Billie Jean King - Rosemary Casals USA
1975 Margaret Court (AUS) - Virginia Wade (UK)
1976 Linky Boshoff - Ilana Kloss SA
1977 Betty Stove (NETH) - Martina Navratilova (CZ)
1978 Martina Navratilova (CZ) - Billie Jean King (USA)
1979 Betty Stove (NETH) - Wendy Turnbull (AUS)
1980 Martina Navratilova (CZ) - Billie Jean King (USA)
1981 Kathy Jordan - Anne Smith USA
1982 Rosemary Casals (USA) - Wendy Turnbull (AUS)
1983 Martina Navratilova - Pam Shriver USA
1984 Martina Navratilova - Pam Shriver USA
1985 Claudia Kohde-Kilsch (W.GER) Helena Sukova (CZ)
1986 Martina Navratilova - Pam Shriver USA
1987 Martina Navratilova - Pam Shriver USA
1988 Gigi Fernandez (P.RICO) - Robin White (USA)

Davis Cup

Men's International Team Championship

Year	*Winner*	*Runner-Up*	*Venue*
1919	Australasia	British Isles	Sydney
1920	United States	Australasia	Auckland
1921	United States	Japan	New York
1922	United States	Australia	New York
1923	United States	Australia	New York
1924	United States	Australia	Philadelphia
1925	United States	France	Philadelphia
1926	United States	France	Philadelphia
1927	France	United States	Philadelphia
1928	France	United States	Paris
1929	France	United States	Paris
1930	France	United States	Paris
1931	France	Great Britain	Paris
1932	France	United States	Paris
1933	Great Britain	France	Paris
1934	Great Britain	UnitedStates	Wimbledon
1935	Great Britain	UnitedStates	Wimbledon
1936	Great Britain	Australia	Wimbledon
1937	UnitedStates	Great Britain	Wimbledon
1938	UnitedStates	Australia	Philadelphia

1939	Australia	United States	Philadelphia
1940	Not held		
1941	Not held		
1942	Not held		
1943	Not held		
1944	Not held		
1945	Not held		
1946	UnitedStates	Australia	Melbourne
1947	UnitedStates	Australia	New York
1948	UnitedStates	Australia	New York
1949	UnitedStates	Australia	New York
1950	Australia	UnitedStates	New York
1951	Australia	UnitedStates	Sydney
1952	Australia	UnitedStates	Adelaide
1953	Australia	UnitedStates	Melbourne
1954	UnitedStates	Australia	Sydney
1955	Australia	UnitedStates	New York
1956	Australia	UnitedStates	Adelaide
1957	Australia	UnitedStates	Melbourne
1958	UnitedStates	Australia	Brisbane
1959	Australia	UnitedStates	New York
1960	Australia	Italy	Sydney
1961	Australia	Italy	Mlbourne
1962	Australia	Mexico	Brisbane
1963	UnitedStates	Australia	Adelaide
1964	Australia	UnitedStates	Cleveland
1965	Australia	Spain	Sydney
1966	Australia	India	Melbourne
1967	Australia	Spain	Brisbane
1968	UnitedStates	Australia	Adelaide
1969	UnitedStates	Romania	Cleveland
1970	UnitedStates	W. Germny	Cleveland
1971	UnitedStates	Romania	Charlotte
1972	UnitedStates	Romania	Bucharest
1973	Australia	UnitedStates	Cleveland
1974	South Africa	India	(WALKOVER)
1975	Sweden	Czechoslovakia	Stockholm
1976	Italy	Chile	Santiago
1977	Australia	Italy	Sydney
1978	UnitedStates	Great Britain	Palm Springs
1979	UnitedStates	Italy	San Francisco
1980	Czechoslovakia	Italy	Prague
1981	UnitedStates	Argentina	Cincinnati
1982	UnitedStates	France	Grenoble
1983	Australia	Sweden	Melbourne
1984	Sweden	United States	Gothenburg
1985	Sweden	W. Germany	Munich
1986	Australia	Sweden	Melbourne
1987	Sweden	India	Gothenburg

Wightman Cup

International Match between United States and Great Britain

Women

1923	United States	NewYork
1924	GreatBritain	Wimbledon
1925	GreatBritain	NewYork
1926	UnitedStates	Wimbledon
1927	UnitedStates	NewYork
1928	GreatBritain	Wimbledon
1929	UnitedStates	NewYork
1930	GreatBritain	Wimbledon
1931	UnitedStates	NewYork
1932	UnitedStates	Wimbledon
1933	UnitedStates	NewYork
1934	UnitedStates	Wimbledon
1935	UnitedStates	NewYork
1936	UnitedStates	Wimbledon
1937	UnitedStates	NewYork
1938	UnitedStates	Wimbledon
1939	UnitedStates	NewYork
1940	Not held	
1941	Not held	
1942	Not held	
1943	Not held	
1944	Not held	
1945	Not held	
1946	UnitedStates	Wimbledon
1947	UnitedStates	NewYork
1948	UnitedStates	Wimbledon
1949	UnitedStates	Philadelphia
1950	UnitedStates	Wimbledon
1951	UnitedStates	Boston
1952	UnitedStates	Wimbledon
1953	UnitedStates	Rye
1954	UnitedStates	Wimbledon
1955	UnitedStates	Rye
1956	UnitedStates	Wimbledon

1957	UnitedStates	Sewickley
1958	GreatBritain	Wimbledon
1959	UnitedStates	Sewickley
1960	GreatBritain	Wimbledon
1961	UnitedStates	Chicago
1962	UnitedStates	Wimbledon
1963	UnitedStates	Clevland
1964	UnitedStates	Wimbledon
1965	UnitedStates	Clevland
1966	UnitedStates	Wimbledon
1967	UnitedStates	Clevland
1968	GreatBritain	Wimbledon
1969	UnitedStates	Cleveland
1970	UnitedStates	Wimbledon
1971	UnitedStates	Cleveland
1972	UnitedStates	Wimbledon
1973	UnitedStates	Boston
1974	GreatBritain	Deeside
1975	GreatBritain	Cleveland
1976	UnitedStates	London
1977	UnitedStates	Oakland
1978	GreatBritain	London
1979	UnitedStates	West Palm Beach
1980	UnitedStates	London
1981	UnitedStates	Chicago
1982	UnitedStates	London
1983	UnitedStates	Williamsburg
1984	UnitedStates	London
1985	UnitedStates	Williamsburg
1986	UnitedStates	London
1987	UnitedStates	Williamsburg

French Championships

Men's Singles

1925	R. Lacoste	FRA
1926	H. Cochet	FRA
1927	R.Lacoste	FRA
1928	H. Cochet	FRA
1929	R.Lacoste	FRA
1930	H.Cochet	FRA
1931	J.Borotra	FRA
1932	H. Cochet	FRA
1933	J.H.Crawford	AUS
1934	G. von Cramm	GER
1935	F.J.Perry	UK
1936	G. von Cramm	GER
1937	H. Henkel	GER
1938	J. D. Budge	USA
1939	W. D. McNeill	USA
1940	Not held	
1941	Not held	
1942	Not held	
1943	Not held	
1944	Not held	
1945	Not held	
1946	M.Barnard	FRA
1947	J.Asboth	HUN
1948	F.A.Parker	USA
1949	F.A.Parker	USA
1950	J.E.Patty	USA
1951	J.Drobny	EG
1952	J.Drobny	EG
1953	K.R.Rosewall	AUS
1954	M.A. Trabert	USA
1955	M.A. Trabert	USA
1956	L.A.Hoad	AUS
1957	S.Davidson	SWE
1958	M.G.Rose	AUS
1959	N.Pietrangeli	ITA
1960	N. Pietrangeli	ITA
1961	M.Santana	SPA
1962	R.G.Laver	AUS
1963	R.S.Emerson	AUS
1964	M.Santana	SPA
1965	F.S.Stolle	AUS
1966	A.D.Roche	AUS
1967	R.S.Emerson	AUS
1968	K.R.Rosewall	AUS
1969	R.G.Laver	AUS
1970	J.Kodes	CZ
1971	J.Kodes	CZ
1972	A.Gimeno	SPA
1973	I.Nastase	ROM
1974	B.Borg	SWE
1975	B.Borg	SWE
1976	A.Panatta	ITA
1977	G.Vilas	ARG
1978	B.Borg	SWE

1979	B.Borg	SWE
1980	B.Borg	SWE
1981	B.Borg	SWE
1982	M.Wilander	SWE
1983	Y.Noah	FRA
1984	I.Lendl	CZ
1985	M.Wilander	SWE
1986	I.Lendl	CZ
1987	I.Lendl	CZ
1988	M.Wilander	SWE

Women's Singles

1925	S. Lenglen	FRA
1926	S.Lenglen	FRA
1927	K.Bouman	NETH
1928	H.N.Wills	USA
1929	H.N.Wills	USA
1930	H.N.Moody	USA
1931	C.Aussem	GER
1932	H.N.Moody	USA
1933	M.C.Scriven	UK
1934	M.C.Scriven	UK
1935	H.Sperling	DEN
1936	H.Sperling	DEN
1937	H.Sperling	DEN
1938	S.Mathieu	FRA
1939	S.Mathieu	FRA
1940	Not held	
1941	Not held	
1942	Not held	
1943	Not held	
1944	Not held	
1945	Not held	
1946	M.E.Osborne	USA
1947	P.C.Todd	USA
1948	N.Landry	FRA
1949	M.E.du Pont	USA
1950	D.J.Hart	USA
1951	S.J.Fry	USA
1952	D.J.Hart	USA
1953	M.C.Connolly	USA
1954	M.C.Connolly	USA
1955	A.Mortimer	UK
1956	A.Gibson	USA
1957	S.J.Bloomer	UK
1958	S.Kormoczy	HUN
1959	C.C.Truman	UK
1960	D.R.Hard	USA
1961	A.S.Haydon	UK
1962	M.Smith	AUS
1963	L.R.Turner	AUS
1964	M.Smith	AUS
1965	L.R.Turner	AUS
1966	A.S.Jones	UK
1967	F.Durr	FRA
1968	N.Richey	USA
1969	M.Court	AUS
1970	M.Court	AUS
1971	E.F.Goolagong	AUS
1972	B.J.King	USA
1973	M.Court	AUS
1974	C.M.Evert	USA
1975	CM.Evert	USA
1976	S.Barker	UK
1977	M.Jansovec	YUG
1978	V.Ruzici	ROM
1979	C.Lloyd	USA
1980	C.Lloyd	USA
1981	H.Mandlikova	CZ
1982	M.Navratilova	USA
1983	C.Lloyd	USA
1984	M.Navratilova	USA
1985	C.Lloyd	USA
1986	C.Lloyd	USA
1987	S.Graf	W.GER
1988	S.Graf	W.GER

Australian Championships

Men's Singles

1919	A.R.F.Kingscote	UK
1920	P.O'Hara Wood	AUS
1921	R.H.Gemmell	AUS
1922	J.O.Anderson	AUS
1923	P.O'Hara Wood	AUS
1924	J.O. Anderson	AUS
1925	J.O.Anderson	AUS
1926	J.B.Hawkes	AUS
1927	G.L.Patterson	AUS

1928	J.Borotra	FRA
1929	J.C.Gregory	UK
1930	E.F.Moon	AUS
1931	J.H.Crawford	AUS
1932	J.H. Crawford	AUS
1933	J.H. Crawford	AUS
1934	F.J.Perry	UK
1935	J.H.Crawford	AUS
1936	A.K.Quist	AUS
1937	V.B.McGrath	AUS
1938	J.D.Budge	USA
1939	J.E.Bromwich	AUS
1940	A.K.Quist	AUS
1941	Not held	
1942	Not held	
1943	Not held	
1944	Not held	
1945	Not held	
1946	J.E.Bromwich	AUS
1947	D.Pails	AUS
1948	A.K. Quist	AUS
1949	F.A.Sedgman	AUS
1950	F.A.Sedgman	AUS
1951	R.Savitt	USA
1952	K.McGregor	AUS
1953	K.R.Rosewall	AUS
1954	M.G.Rose	AUS
1955	K.R.Rosewall	AUS
1956	L.A.Hoad	AUS
1957	A.J.Cooper	AUS
1958	A.J.Cooper	AUS
1959	A.Olmedo	USA
1960	R.G.Laver	AUS
1961	R.S.Emerson	AUS
1962	R.G.Laver	AUS
1963	R.S.Emerson	AUS
1964	R.S.Emerson	AUS
1965	R.S.Emerson	AUS
1966	R.S.Emerson	AUS
1967	R.S.Emerson	AUS
1968	W.W.Bowrey	AUS
1969	R.G.Laver	AUS
1970	A.R.Ashe	USA
1971	K.R.Rosewall	AUS
1972	K.R.Rosewall	AUS
1973	J.D.Newcombe	AUS
1974	J.S.Connors	USA
1975	J.D.Newcombe	AUS
1976	M.R.Edmondson	AUS
1977	R.Tanner	USA
1978	G.Vilas	ARG
1979	G.Vilas	ARG
1980	B.Teacher	USA
1981	J.C.Kriek	SA
1982	J.C.Kriek	SA
1983	M.Wilander	SWE
1984	M.Wilander	SWE
1985	S.Edberg	SWE
1986	Not held	
1987	S.Edberg	SWE
1988	M.Wilander	SWE

Women's Singles

1922	M.Molesworth	AUS
1923	M.Molesworth	AUS
1924	S.Lance	AUS
1925	D.Akhurst	AUS
1926	D.Akhurst	AUS
1927	E.F.Boyd	AUS
1928	D.Akhurst	AUS
1929	D.Akhurst	AUS
1930	D.Akhurst	AUS
1931	C.Buttsworth	AUS
1932	C.Buttsworth	AUS
1933	J.Hartigan	AUS
1934	J.Hartigan	AUS
1935	D.E.Round	UK
1936	J.Hartigan	AUS
1937	N.Wynne	AUS
1938	D.M.Bundy	USA
1939	E.Westacott	AUS
1940	N.Bolton	AUS
1941	Not held	
1942	Not held	
1943	Not held	
1944	Not held	
1945	Not held	
1946	N.Bolton	AUS

1947	N.Bolton	AUS
1948	N.Bolton	AUS
1949	D.J.Hatt	USA
1950	A.L.Brough	USA
1951	N.Bolton	AUS
1952	T.Long	AUS
1953	M.C.Connolly	USA
1954	T.Long	AUS
1955	B.Penrose	AUS
1956	M.Carter	AUS
1957	S.J.Fry	USA
1958	A.Mortimer	UK
1959	M.Reitano	AUS
1960	M.Smith	AUS
1961	M.Smith	AUS
1962	M.Smith	AUS
1963	M.Smith	AUS
1964	M.Smith	AUS
1965	M.Smith	AUS
1966	M.Smith	AUS
1967	N.Richey	USA
1968	B.J.King	USA
1969	M.Court	AUS
1970	M.Court	AUS
1971	M.Court	AUS
1972	S.V.Wade	UK
1973	M.Court	AUS
1974	E.F.Goolagong	AUS
1975	E.F.Goolagong	AUS
1976	E.F.Cawley	AUS
1977	K.Reid	AUS
1978	C.O'Neil	AUS
1979	B.K.Jordan	USA
1980	H.Mandlikova	CZ
1981	M.Navratilova	USA
1982	C.Lloyd	USA
1983	M.Navratilova	USA
1984	C.Lloyd	USA
1985	M.Navratilova	USA
1986	Not held	
1987	H.Mandlikova	CZ
1988	S.Graf	W.GER

BHARAT RATNA AND THE PADMA VIBHUSHAN

Ramanathan Krishnan	1967
Raj Kumar Khanna	1975

PADMA SHRI AWARDS

Ramanathan Krishnan
Ghaus Mohammed Khan
Raj Kumar Khanna
Vijay Amritraj

ARJUNA AWARDS WINNERS

1961	R. Krishnan
1963	Naresh Kumar
1966	Jaideep Mukherjee
1967	Premjit Lall
1974	Vijay Amritraj
1978-79	Nirupama Mankad
1980-81	Ramesh Krishnan
1985	Anand Amritraj

VOLLEYBALL

Volleyball was originated by William G.Morgan at the Holyoke, Massachusetts, Young Men's Christian Association in 1895. In his search to find a sport requiring sufficient activity to be interesting, yet not as strenuous as basketball. Morgan devised the game of volleyball.

The original rules permitted a player to carry the ball by bouncing it, provided that it was not caught. Within a few years this rule was eliminated, and few changes have been made since.

With the impetus given to the game through Y.M.C.A. promotion, the growth in popularity was rapid.

Around 1915, the game became offensive and more scientific. Since its origin, the rotation of team at change of service has been a special feature of the game.

The game is played with six players on each side. The officials consists of a referee, an umpire, a scorer and two linesmen. The game is started with the server hitting the ball with his hand and tossing the ball in air, so as to cross the net. The service is done by a player in right back position. The other team is required to send the ball back by volleying (the name of the game is derived from the fact that only volleying is permitted in this game). The ball may be relayed a maximum - three times before it is sent to the opponent's court. Touching the ball simultaneously more than once by the same player is not allowed. If the team doing service is not able to make a good return, "side out" is given, and the next service is done by the opponent's team.

The Court : The playing surface shall be 18 m long by 9 m wide including outer edge of lines.

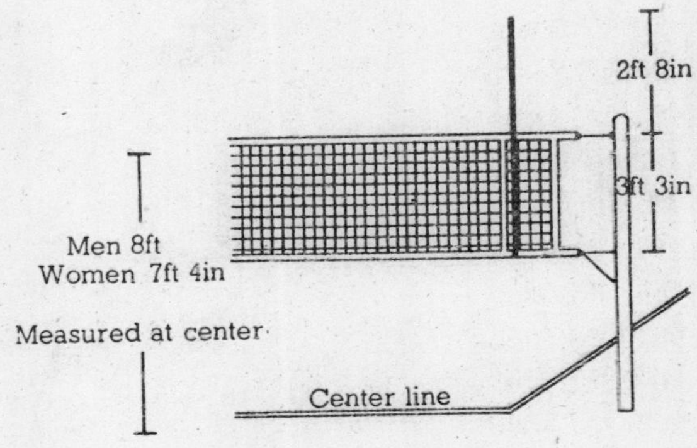

The clearance above the court shall be 7 m or more and free from obstruction. The courts shall be banded by lines 5 cm wide which shall be at least 2 m from all walls or obstructions. A line 5 cm wide shall be darwn across the centre of the playing surface separating the two courts. In each court a line (Attack Line) shall be drawn across the court, 3 m from and parallel to the centre line.

Two lines 15 cm by 5 cm and 3 m apart shall be drawn at the back of the end line so as to permit service from any-where between them and the end line. The service area shall be a minimum of 2 m in depth. The surface of the playing area may be either ash, earth, grass or wood.

Net: The net shall be 1 m deep and 9.50 m. long. The mesh shall be 10 cm with a double thickness of 5 cm wide canvas or line shall be stitched across the top. A flexible cable stretches the upper edge of the net and passes inside the band of canvas. Flexible antennae 1 m 80 cm long shall extend 80 cm above the net. They are set 20 cm outside the markers. Each antenna shall be 10 mm in diameter fibreglass with contrasting colour sections 10 cm long. They indicate when a ball is completely outside the markers.

Height of Net : The height of the net at the centre shall be 2.43 m for men and 2.24 m for women. The height for juniors and children is left to the discretion of national associations. The two ends of the net shall be of the same height from the ground and it must not be more than 2 cm above regulation height at the ends.

Markers : A movable band of white material 5 cm in width shall be placed at the extremities of the net, perpendicular to and directly above, the side and centre lines.

Bracing the Net : In top class play a referee's platform is essential. This can take the same form as that used in lawn tennis only 1 m higher. It is essential that the net be taut, for the ball may often rebound from it and still remain playable.

Ball : The ball shall be spherical, made either of a supple leather case, laceless, inside which is a rubber bladder, or it can be rubber cased, for harder wear at practice sessions. Circumference:65 -67 cm., Weight : 260-280 g.

Number : The number of players shall be six, whatever the circumstances. A team with less than six players automatically forfeits the game. Substitution is allowed and this is dealt with under a separate rule.

Equipment : Members of the team must appear on the court dressed alike. The players shall wear a vest or shirt shorts and rubber or leather shoes (without heel). It is forbidden to wear headgear or any other article which can cause injury to other players. All players shall wear, on their back, numbers 15 cm high and on their chest 10 cm high.

Rights and Duties of Players

(a) Every player must know the rules and strictly follow them.

(b) During the game,a player can only address the referee through the captain of his team.

(c) Conduct of players, substitutes and coaches. The following offences shall be punished:

  (i) persistently addressing the officials on their decisions.

  (ii) making unpleasant remark to officials.

  (iii) committing unpleasant acts or actions tending to influence their decisions.

  (iv) making unpleasant act or personal remarks on opponents.

  (v) deliberate coaching during the game from any one outside the court except during 'Time Out'.

(d) Sanctions.

  (i) for a slight fault; a single warning.

  (ii) for a serious fault; a personal warning recorded on the score sheet.This automatically entails the loss of a point or change of service. In case of repetition of the offence the referee may disqualify the player for the set or match.

Position of Players : At the time the ball is served the players of the two teams must be placed in their own court in two lines of three players; these lines may be broken ones.The players nearest the net are the front line players, the others three forming the back line.

As soon as the ball is served each player may cover any section of his own court. Until the end of the set the 'rotation'order must be observed. Before the beginning of each set this rotation order may be changed on condition that the change is denoted on the score sheet.

Scoring

The Set : A game is won when one team leads by two points with a minimum of 15 points. If the score reaches 14-14 it is necessary to play to reach one of the following scores; 16-14,17-15,18-16,19-17,etc.

Match : A match is played in two or three winning sets, *i.e.* ,'best of three' or 'best of five'games by decision of the organising committee or, in its absence, by agreement of the two parties. All international matches are played to 'best of five'sets.

Points : The serving team wins a point when:

1. the ball touches the ground inside the opponents court;
2. opponents have played the ball more than three times consecutively;
3. opponents have held or pushed the ball;
4. the ball has touched an opponent under the belt;
5. an opponent touches the ball two consecutive times;
6. an opponent has touched the net;
7. an opponent has reached over the net to play the ball except to block or to hinder an opponent;
8. an opponent reaches under the net and touches the ball or any opposing player when the ball is in play on that side;
9. an opponent has completely crossed the centre line;
10. at the moment of service the opposing them has committed a fault of position, e.g., on winning service has not rotated one position clockwise;
11. a returned ball has crossed or touched the net outside the antennae determining the width of court;
12. a returned ball goes out of court,passes under the net, touches an object outside the court, is returned by a player aiding himself with any object as a point of support;
13. an opposing back line player in the attack area has incorrectly returned the ball;
14. an opponent has received a personal warning;
15. after a warning from the referee if the opponents have received from their manager, coaches or players, deliberate coaching during the game;
16. opponents delay the game in a persistent manner;
17. opponents illegally replace a player;
18. opponents prolong the interruption of the game for more than half a minute.

Game Interruptions :

1. Legal interruptions of the game are the time-outs and the substitutions. They are only granted by the referees when the ball is dead at the request of either the coach or the game captain.
2. A maximum of two time-outs(T) and 6 substitutions per team per set are permitted.
3. An interruption will be granted only upon request by the game captain or the coach through use of the respective offcial signal (manual or electric)

   An interruption for substitution shall last only the time necessary to register the change and allow the entry and exit of the players.

   Each time-out has a time limit of 30 seconds. The team requesting the time-out has the right to shorten its time limit and the game should be resumed immediately.

   A time-out will be charged to the team that prolongs an interruption after the referee's signal to resume the game.
4. One or two time-outs may be followed or preceded by a substitution, requested by either team, during the same interruption with no need to resume the game.

   The same team is not allowed to request two consecutive game interruptions for substitution unless the game has been resumed. But 2 or more players may be substituted at the same time.
5. In the event a serious accident occurs while the ball is in play, the referee must stop the game and direct a play-over.

   If a player is injured and cannot continue to play, he must be legally substituted.

   If the legal substitution is not possible, the first referee shall authorize an exceptionally illegal substitution for the injured player.

   If no substitution is possible the first referee give 3 minutes to the injured player.

   If the injured player does not recover within 3 minutes the team is declared incomplete.

SKILLS OF THE GAME

The ball may be played back on either the first, second, or third touch, but it is the basis of modern tactics to use all three touches to build up a strong attack. The normal pattern is to use the first touch to get the ball up close to the net, then play it high above and close to the net so that for the third touch a player can run in and jump up to smash the ball down into the opposition court.

The opposing team try to intercept the smash by suing one, two, or three players jumping up together and reaching over the net to block the path of the smash or force the ball back into the attackers' court. If the blockers do not cut out the smash, the rest of the team try to control it and build up their own attack.

If the serving team win the rally, they score a point, but if the receiving team win it they gain the right to serve. A team winning the right to serve rotate one place round so that during a game the players have to play in all positions. The first team to 15 points by a margin of 2 points wins the set. Ordinary club matches are the best of three sets, and championship and international games are the best of five set.

Underhand Pass:- Many a time the ball changes direction suddenly and falls too close to the net making the execution of upperhand difficult. In such a situation the underhand pass (with one or both the hands) should be employed.

The standing position in this is the same as in upperhand pass. Both the arms work simultaneously and should be joined together, with fingers of one hand kept over the other and gripped with the help of the thumbs. This position is very important otherwise arms may not remain intact. The hands should normally remain below the waist-level and the upper part of the body should be inclined forward. The main aim of this pass is to raise the ball upwards.

Upperhand Service:- The player should stand with his face towards the net with the leg nearer the hitting hand placed backward. The ball should be tossed up perpendicularly and upto head level.

Simultaneously, the body weight should shift from the front to the back leg. Then the hitting hand should take a forward swing, hitting the ball with the palms towards the back line of the opponent's court.

Smash:- Without smash, the game of volleyball would be totally incomplete. It is the final and decisive form of attack. Without this skill no team can attain any standard of proficiency in this game. There are many types of smashes in the game but the straight smash is basic.

The straight smash is that when a player smashes the ball in the direction corresponding to the direction of his approach. The following points must be borne in mind for proper execution of this stroke.

The Hit:- Ball must be hit with the outstretched arms at the highest point of jump when the ball is half-a-metre in front. When the ball is near the net, the hit should be more towards the top side of the ball. When it is a little away, the hit should be towards its back and when the ball is still more away from the net the hit will be more towards the bottom side

Approach : — The approach should be straight and not zigzag and the smasher's speed during the approach must be steadily increased upto the end. The distance for a good approach should generally be 3 to 4 steps and the angle should be 45 degree to 60 degree.

Jump:- In volleyball a smasher has to take many types of jumps according to the position of the ball. Therefore, he should practice different kinds of jumps. Some of those are:

(i) high jump from the spot with both legs;
(ii) jump after one step;
(iii) some exercise with longer step;
(iv) jump against an object like the wall or basketball board;
(v) jump after 2,3,4 steps.

Take off:- There are two types of take off: one-leg take off; and two-leg take off.

In one-leg take off it is generally the leg towards the net which takes part in giving the player jump flight. In two-leg take off the legs are bent at knees at an angle of 90 degrees to 110 degrees, but the hip joint should not go below the knee.

CUP & TROPHIES

GOLD IN OLYMPICS

Men

1964	USSR
1968	USSR
1972	Japan
1976	Poland

1980	USSR
1984	USA
1988	USA

Women

1964	Japan
1968	USSR
1972	USSR
1976	Japan
1980	USSR
1984	China
1988	USSR

WORLD CHAMPIONSHIPS

Men

1949	USSR
1952	USSR
1956	Czechoslovakia
1960	USSR
1962	USSR
1966	Czechoslovakia
1970	East Germany
1974	Poland
1978	USSR
1982	USSR
1986	United States

Women

1952	USSR
1956	USSR
1960	USSR
1962	Japan
1966	Japan
1970	USSR
1974	Japan
1978	Cuba
1982	China
1986	United States

WATER POLO

Water polo was invented in England in the decade between 1860 and 1870, the main object being to relieve the boredom of spectators having to watch incessant swimming races. In spite of the facts that there were only three players on each side, that no goalkeepers were appointed and that goals were scored by placing a rubber bladder on rafts 60 yards apart, interest was aroused, and in 1870 the London Swimming Association appointed a Committee to draw up rules for Water Soccer.

The first recorded international match was between England and Scotland and took place in 1880, but it was not until the last decade of the nineteenth century that countries like Germany, France, Belgium and Hungary took up the game. Now it is played in every continent, and most countries have international teams which meet in competition at appropriate performance levels.

RULES OF THE GAME

(1) The uniform distance between the respective goal lines is 30 m. The uniform width of the field of play is 20 m. The depth of water must nowhere be less than 1.80 m. For matches played by women, the maximum measurements are 25 x 17 m.

Distinctive marks must be provided on both sides of the field of play to denote the goal line, lines 2 m and 4 m from that line, and half distance between the goal lines. These markings must be clearly visible throughout the game. As uniform colours the following are recommended for these markings: goal line and half distance line white, 2 m from goal line red, 4 m from goal line yellow. A red or any other visible coloured sign shall be placed on the goal line, 2 m from the corner of the field of play on the side of the goal judge (or on the side opposite the timekeeper if there are no goal judges).The boundary of the field of play at both ends is 0.30 m behind the goal line. Sufficient space must be provided to enable the referees to have free way from end to end of the field of play. Space must also be provided at the goal lines for the goal judges.

(2) The goal posts and crossbar must be of wood, metal or synthetic (plastic), with rectangular sections of 0.075 m, square with the goal line and painted white. The goal posts must be fixed, rigid and perpendicular at each end of the playing space, equal distances from the sides and at least 0.30 m in front of the ends of the field of play or of any obstruction. Any standing or resting place for the goal-keeper, other than the floor of the bath, is not permitted. The inner sides of the goal posts must be 3 m apart.

The underside of the crossbar must be 0.90 m above water suface when the water is 1.50 m or more in depth, and 0.40m from the bottom of the bath when the depth of the water is less than 1.50 m. Limp nets must be attached to the goal fixtures to enclose the entire goal space, securely fastened to the goal posts and crossbar and allowing not less than 0.30 m clear sace behind the goal line everywhere within the goal area.

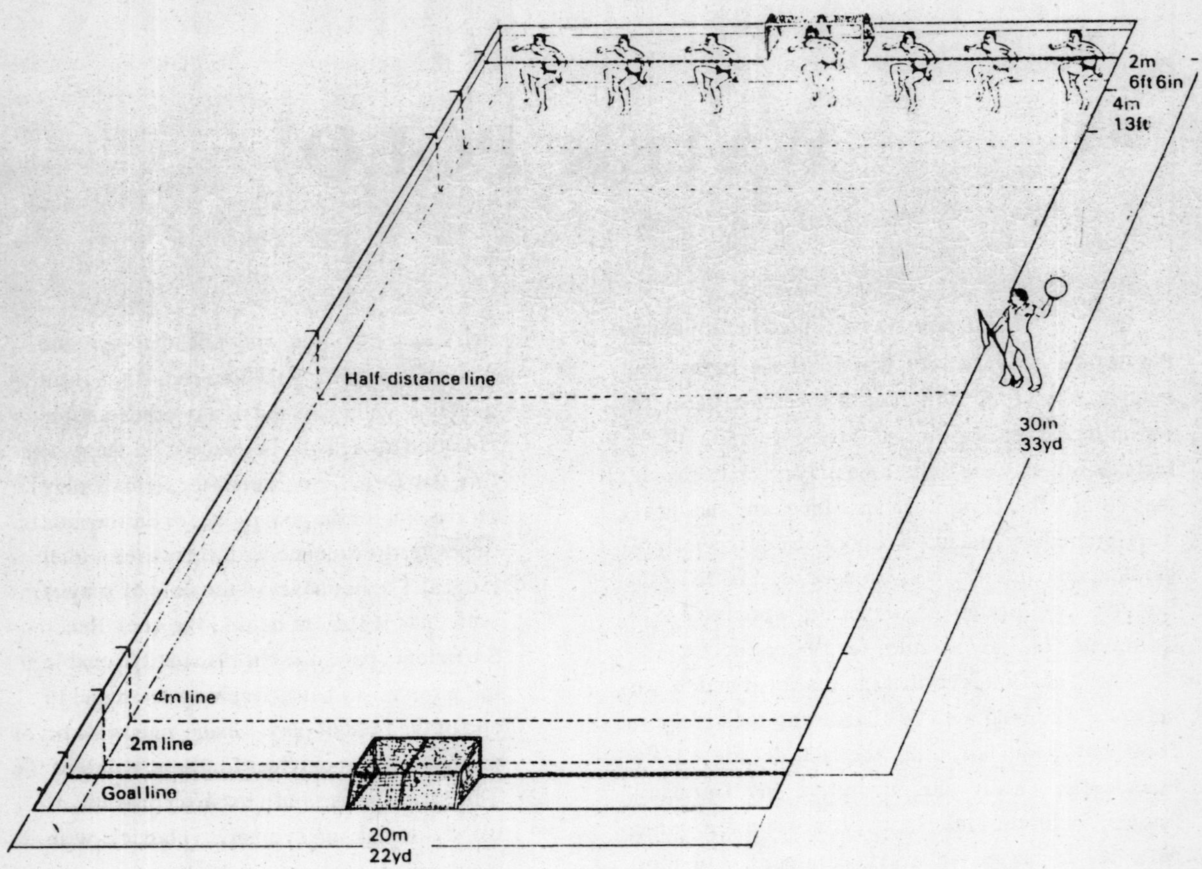

(3) The ball must be round and fully inflated and with an air chamber with a self-closing valve. The pressure in the ball shall be 13-14 Ib atmospheres. The circumfernce must not be less than 0.68 m nor more than 0.71 m. It must be waterproof, without external strappings and without a covering of grease or similar substance. The weight of the ball must not be less than 400 nor more than 450 g.

(4) The referee must be provided with a stick 70 cm long, fitted with a white flag on one end and blue flag on the other, each flag to be 35 x 20 cm. Each goal judge must be provided with a red flag and a white flag, each 35 x 20 cm, mounted on seperate sticks 50 cm long. One of the secretaries must be provided with a white flag and a blue one, to signal re-entrance of excluded players and the other with a red flag with which to signal third personal faults. These flags shall also be of the dimensions prescribed above.

(5) One team must wear dark blue and the other white caps except goalkeepers, who must wear red caps. Caps must be tied with tapes under the chin. If a player loses his cap it must be replaced at the next stoppage of the game. For Olympic Games and World Championships, caps must be fitted with malleable ear protectors and it is recommended that they be used for all other competitions. The malleable ear protectors of the goalkeepers must be of the same colour as that of the team's field players' caps. Caps must be numbered on both sides, numbers being 0.10 m in height.

The goalkeper shall wear cap No.1 and the other caps shall be numbered 2 to 13. A substitute goalkeeper shall wear the goalkeeper's cap. No player is allowed to change his cap number without a referee's permission.

(6) Each team shall consist of 7 players, one of whom will be the goalkeeper and wear the goalkeeper's cap and no more than 6 reserves who may be used as substitutes. Prior to taking part in a match, the players must discard all articles likely to cause injury. The referee shall satisfy himself that the players observe this condition. A player failing to comply must be dismissed from the game. Players must wear trunks with separate drawers or slips underneath. When a player is dismissed from the game in accordance with this paragraph a reserve player may immediately take his place.

Players shall not be allowed to have grease,oil or any similar composition on the body. If the referee ascertains before starting the game that such substance has been used he must order the offending substance to be removed immediately. Should this offence be detected after the game has started, the player concerned must be ordered out from the water for the whole game and a substitute may enter immediately within 2 m from the corner of the field of play at his own goal line at the point nearest the goal-judge (or on the side opposite the time-keeper if there are no goal judges). The Captains must be playing members and be responsible for the good conduct and discipline fo their respective teams. Prior to the commencement of the game the Captains must, in the presence of the referee, toss for choice of ends or colours. The winner have the choice of ends or colours.

(7) For Olympic Games and World Championships, the officials shall consist of two referees, two goal-judges, time-keepers and secretaries. For all other competitions there must be at least a secretary, a time-keeper and either two referees, or one referee, and two goal-judges. However, it is recommended that two referees be used for all competitions. Each time-keeper and secretary may have assistants as needed.

(8) The referees are in absolute control of the game. Their authority over the players is effective during the whole of the time that they and the players are within the precincts of the bath. Each must be provided with a shrill whistle with which to start and re-start the game and to declare goals, goal throws, corner throws (whether signalled by the goal-judge or not) and infringements of the rules.

All decisions of the referees on questions of fact are final and their interpretation of the rules must be obeyed during the game.

If the game has to be stopped, the referee must report his actions to the competent authority.

(9) The time-keepers must be fully acquainted with the Rules and each must be provided with a Water-Polo Stop-Watch and a shrill whistle.

(10) The duration of the game shall be four periods of 7 minutes each, actual play. The teams shall change ends before commencing a new period. There shall be a 2-minute interval between periods. Time starts when a player touches the ball at the start of any period of the game. At all signals for stoppages the recording watch must be stopped until play is resumed.

(11) At the commencement of each period of play, the players must take up positions on their respective goal lines about 1 m apart and at least 1 m from either goal post. More than two players are not allowed between

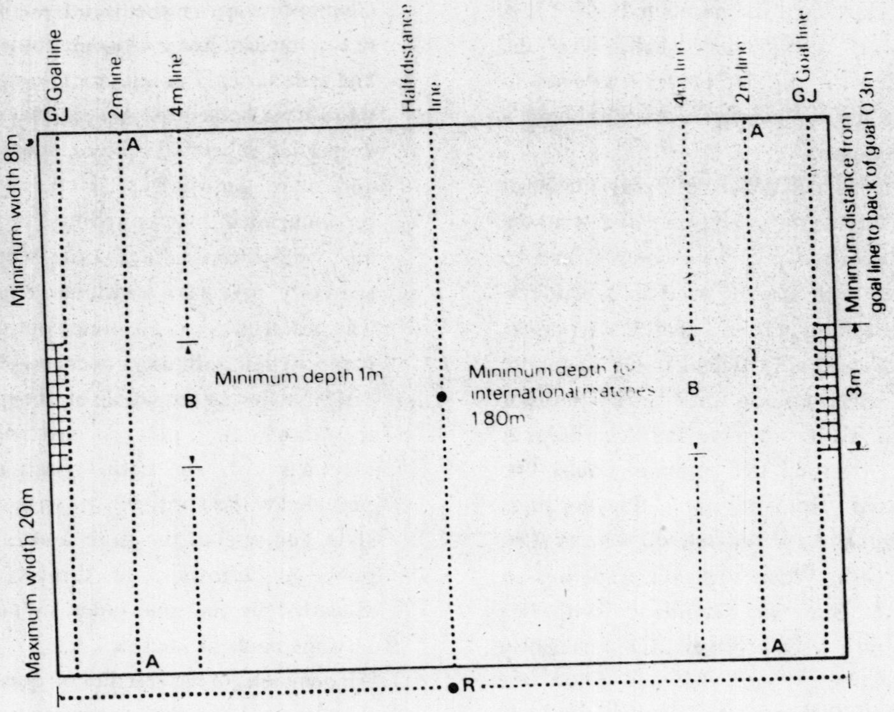

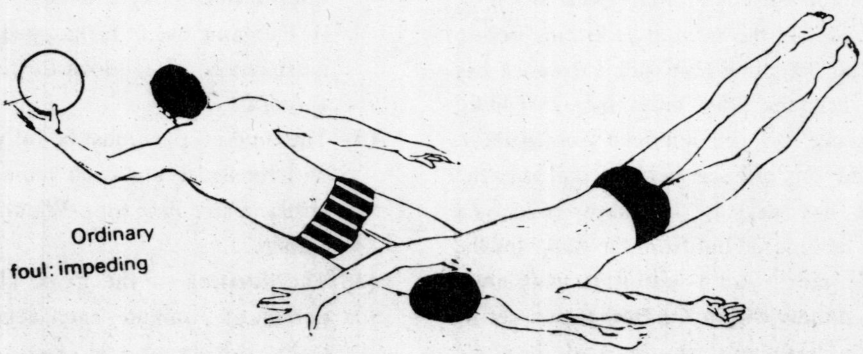

Ordinary foul: impeding

the goal posts. When he has ascertained that the teams are ready, the referee shall give the starting signal by a blast on his whistle and immediately afterwards release or throw the ball into the centre of the field of play.

(12) A goal is scored by the ball passing fully over the goal line between the goal posts and subject to the following conditions: A goal may be scored by any part of the body, except the clenched fist, provided that at the start or re-start of the game the ball has been played by two or more players. The team to which they belong or the place in the field of play from where the goal is scored is immaterial.

Any attempt by the goalkeeper to stop the ball before it has been played in this way does not constitute "playing" and should the ball cross the goal line or hit the goal post or goalkeeper, the goalkeeper must be awarded a goal throw. Dribbling the ball through the goal posts is permissible.

(13) Should a player send the ball out of the field of play at either side, a free throw is awarded to the opposing team, to be taken from nearest to the place where the ball left the field of play.

Should the ball go out of the field of play between the goal line and the 2 m line the free throw must be taken from the 2 m mark on the side where the ball went out.

(14) Should there be level scores at full time in any game for which a definite result is required, any continuation into extra time must be after 5 minutes interval. There shall then be played two periods of 3 minutes each actual play, with an interval of 1 minute for changing ends.

This system of extra time shall be continued until a decision has been reached. A player who has been ordered from the water by the referee - but not for the rest of the game - shall resume with his team for extra time only when his penalty time has expired or a goal has been scored.

CUP & TROPHIES

GOLD IN OLYMPICS

First contested in 1900 although the teams in 1900 and 1904 were club rather than national teams.

1900	UK
1904	USA
1908	UK
1912	UK
1920	UK
1924	France
1928	Germany
1932	Hungary
1936	Hungary
1948	Italy
1952	Hungary
1956	Hungary
1960	Italy
1964	Hungary
1968	Yugoslavia
1972	USSR
1976	Hungary
1980	USSR
1984	Yugoslavia
1988	Yugoslavia

WORLD CHAMPIONSHIPS

1973	Hungary
1975	USSR
1978	Italy
1982	USSR
1986	Yugoslavia

WEIGHT LIFTING

Lifting of weights is very ancient sport. There are evidences to support the theory that organised competitions in lifting stones were being held in 15th century. In 1490, a weightlifter by the name Duke Christopher lifted a stone weighing 400 pounds. Stonelifting even now is a popular sport in some parts of France and Spain.

Modern weightlifting is a very well organised sport. The first ever International Competition was held in England in the year 1891. Weightlifting was introduced in Olympics in the year 1896. In earlier weightlifting competitions, various types of lifts were permitted, but by the year 1936, the following three lifts were standardised:

(a) The two hands clean and press;

(b) The two hands clean and jerk; and

(c) The two hands snatch.

The two hands clean and press was discontinued after 1972, because the lift was considered very difficult to judge.

Equipment

The bar is 2.13 metres (7') long and 2.8 cm (1.1") thick. The weights are attached to the ends of the bar, and must be the same at each end for balance. The smallest weights are 1.25 kg (2.76 lbs) and the heaviest 9.2 kg (45 lbs).

Lifters use either low-or high topped shoes. In many cases these are specially made to give maximum support to ankles and Anchiles tendons.

Back Support. A maximum width of 12 cm (4.7") is permitted, and it is usually in the form of a leather belt.

Bandages are used on wrists and knees for additional support. Chalking of hands is allowed, to counteract perspiration and give extra grip.

Most weightlifters wouldn't be seen dead at a major event without their baby powder. They have the movement of the bar over the skin. Who wants to see these muscular chaps with chaps.

Classiffication of Man's lifters

Weightlifting competition is divided into ten weight classes listed below:

1. Flyweight	up to 52kg	114.5 lbs
2. Bantamweight	up to 56kg	123.5 lbs
3. Featherweight	up to 60kg	132.25 lbs
4. Lightweight	up to 67.5kg	148.75 lbs
5. Middleweight	up to 75kg	165.25 lbs
6. Light heavy weight	up to 82.5kg	182.00 lbs
7. Middle heavyweight	up to 90kg	198.5 lbs
8. 100 kg.	up to 100kg	220.5 lbs
9. Heavyweight	up to 110kg	242.5 lbs
10. Super heavyweight	over 110kg	242.5 lbs

Classiffication of Women's lifters

Classification of women's weight lifters shall be made according to their body weight as par table below:

44 kg, 48 kg, 52 kg, 56 kg, 60 kg, 67.5 kg, 75 kg, 82.5 kg, 82.5 kg,

RULES OF THE GAME

1. The technique known as "hooking" is permitted. It consists of covering the last joint of the thumb with the other fingers of the same hand at the movement of gripping.
2. In all lifts, pulling from the hang is forbidden.
3. In all lifts, touching the bar against the legs below the knees shall not render the lift" No lift."
4. In all lifts the refree must count as "No Lift" any unfinished attempt in which the bar has arrived at the height of the knees.
5. In all lifts, if the bar touches the thighs with a visible stop, it shall render the attempt " No lift". But, if during the pull the bar grazes or slides along the thighs without stopping, it shall not render the lift"No lift".
6. The use of grease, oil, water or any lubricant of any kind on the thighs to facitatate the sliding of the bar is forbidden. The competitor is only allowed to use chalk. If the Jury find the use of any of the above material except chalk, they will order the competitor to wipe it off. The Jury will decide if during the wiping off the clock will go on or not.
7. In all lifts, touching the ground with any part of the body other than the feet shall render the attempt "No lift."
8. Any clean jerk in which the bar is placed on the chest before the turining over of the elbows shall render the attempt "No lift."
9. In fany clean touching the thighs or knees with the elbows or upper arms shall render the attempt "No lift."
10. In the Jerk any apparent effort from the shoulders, if the lift is not completed, must be counted as "No lift" This includes lowering the body or bending the knees.
11. After the referee's signal to replace the bar, the lifter must lower the bar and not let it drop either deliberately or accidently. The lifter must retain both hands on the barbell until it is replaced on the platform. If he releases his grip with one or both hands before the barbell is replaced on the platform, this shall be considered dropping the bar which shall render the attempt "No lift". There is no case for giving a lifter a warning the first time that he drops the barbell.
12. If a competitor cannot fully stretch his arms resulting from anatomical deformation of his elbow, he must report to the three Referees, as well as the Jury before the beginning of the competition.

CUP & TROPHIES

WORLD WEIGHTLIFTING RECORDS

Body weight class lifts kg Name and country date

52kg

Snatch 120 264(1/2) Sevdalin Marinov (Bulgaria)1988

Jerk 153 337(1/4) He Zhouyqiang (China) 1987

Total 270 595(1/4) Sevdalin Marinov (Bulgaria)1988

56kg

Snatch 134 295(1/4) He Yingqiang (China) 1988

Jerk 171 377 Neno Terziiski (Bulgaria) 1987

Total 300 661(1/4) Neun Shalamanov (Bulgaria)1984

60kg

Snatch 152.5 336 Naim Suleimanoglou (Turkey) 1988

Jerk 190 418(3/4) Naim Suleimanoglou(Turkey)1988

Total 342.5 755 Naim Suleimanoglou (Turkey) 1988

67.5kg

Snatch 158.5 349(1/4) Israel Militossyan (USSR)1988

Jerk 200.5 442 Mikhail Petrov (Bulgaria) 1987

Total 335 782(1/2) Mikhail Petrov(Bulgaria)1987

75kg

Snatch 170 374(3/4) Angel Guenchev (Bulgaria) 1987

Jerk 215(1/2)475 Aleksandr Varbanov (Bulgaria)1988

Total 382.5 843 (1/4) Aleksandr Varbavov (Bulgaria) 1988

82.5kg

Snatch 183 403(1/4) Asen Zlatev (Bulgaria) 1986

Jerk 225 496 Asen Zlatev (Bulgaria) 1986

Total 405 892(1/2) Yurik Vardanyan (USSR) 1984

90kg

Snatch 195.5 431 Blagoi Blagoyev (Bulgaria) 1983

Jerk 235 518 Anatoliy Khrapatiy (USSR) 1988

Total 422.5 931(1/4) Viktor Solodov (USSR) 1984

100kg

Snatch 200.5 442 Nicu Vlad (Romania) 1986

Jerk 242.5 532(1/4) Aleksandr Popov (USSR) 1988

Total 440 970 Yuriy Zakharevich (USSR) 1988

110kg

Snatch 210 462(3/4) Yuriy Zakharevich (USSR) 1988

Jerk 250.5 552(1/4) Yuriy Zakharevich (USSR)1988

Total 455 1003 Yuriy Zakharevich (USSR) 1988

Over110kg

Snatch 216 476 Antonio Krastev (Bulgaria) 1987

Jerk 265.5 585(1/4) Leonid Taranenko (USSR)1987

Total 472.5 1041(1/2) Aleksandr Kurlovich (USSR) 1987

NATIONAL RECORDS (INDIA)

Men

52kg

Snatch	102.5	G.Muthuswamy	1986
Jerk	132.5	G.Muthuswamy	1985
Total	230	G.Muthuswamy	1985

56kg

Snatch	110	M.Kumaran	1986
Jerk	140	P.Rangaswamy	1989
Total	245	M.Kumaran	1987

60kg

Snatch	120	M.T.Selvan	1982
Jerk	148.5	Pravesh Chander	1989
Total	262.5	M.T.Selvan	1982

67.5kg

Snatch	130	Paramjit Sharma	1989
Jerk	160	J.M.Sapra	1985
Total	290	Paramjit Sharma	1989

75kg

Snatch	140	K.D.Mondal	1989
Jerk	180	K.D.Mondal	1989
Total	315	K.D.Mondal	1989

82.5kg

Snatch	140.5	P.R.Hegde	1987
Jerk	183	Hernek Singh	1989
Total	315	P.R.Hegde	1987

90kg

Snatch	150.5	Mehar Chand	1986
Jerk	190	Mehar Chand	1986
Total	340	Mehar Chand	1986

100kg

Snatch	150	Mehrar Singh	1987
Jerk	191	Mehrar Singh	1987
Total	341	Mehrar Singh	1987

110kg

Snatch	150.5	A.K.Joshi	1987
Jerk	200	Tara Singh	1986
Total	340	Tara Singh	1986

110kg

Snatch	150	Ernest Berry	1986
Jerk	191.5	N.K.Daroga	1987
Total	335	N.K.Daroga	1987

WORLD POWERLIFTING RECORDS (WEIGHT IN POUNDS)

***MEN* (Squat)**

52kg	535.7	Hideaki Inaba (Jap)	1986
56kg	529.1	Hideaki Inaba (Jap)	1987
60kg	650.4	Joe Breadley (US)	1980
67.5kg	661.4	Jesse Jackson (US)	1987
75kg	722.1	Roberts Wahl (US)	1980
82.5kg	836.6	Mike Bridges	1982
90kg	826.7	Fred Hatfield (US)	1980
100kg	903.0	Ed Coan	1988
110kg	867.5	Dan Wohelber (US)	1981
125kg	909.4	Dave Waddington (US)	1981
125+kg	981.1	Dwayne Fely (US)	1982

Bench Press

52kg	322.9	Joe Cunha (US)	1982
56kg	352.0	Hiro Isagawa (Jap)	1988
60kg	396.8	Joe Bradley	1980
67.5kg	440.9	Kristhoffer Huylecki (Swe)	1985
75kg	479.5	James Rouse (US)	1980
82.5kg	529.1	Mike Bridges	1981
90kg	562.1	Mike MacDonald(US)	1980
100kg	576.5	Mike MacDonald (US)	1977
110kg	595.2	Jeff Magruder (US)	1982
125kg	614.0	Tom Hardman (US)	1982
125+kg	661.4	Bill Kazmaier (US)	1981

Deadlift

52kg	523.6	Hideaki Inaba	1987
56kg	638.2	Lamar Gant(US)	1982
60kg	683.0	Lamar Gant	1988
67.5kg	690.0	Daniel Austin(US)	1987
75kg	733.1	Johan Inzer(US)	1987
82.5kg	788.1	Veli KUmpuniemi(Fin)	1980
90kg	823.4	Eddie Coppin(Belg)	1987
100kg	832.2	James Cash(US)	1982
110kg	870.8	John Kuc(US)	1980
125kg	854.4	Lars Noren(Swe)	1987
125+kg	892.9	Lars Noren	1987

Total

52kg	1;273.1	Hideaki Inaba	1986
56kg	1,377.9	Lamar Gant	1982
60kg	1,559.7	Joe Bradley	1982
67.5kg	1,653.0	Daniel Austin	1988
75kg	1,873.9	Rick Gaugler(US)	1982
82.5kg	2,105.4	Mike Bridges	1982
90kg	2,066.8	Mike Bridges	1980
100kg	2,203.0	Ed Coan	1988
110kg	2,204.6	John Kuc	1980
125kg	2,215.6	Ernie Hackett(US)	1982
125+kg	2,425.8	Bill Kazmaier	1981

Women

(Squat)

44kg	314	Delcy Palk(US)	1988
48kg	325	Majik JOnes(US)	1984
52kg	380	Sissy Dolman(Hol)	1984
56kg	421	Vicki Steenrod(US)	1984
60kg	442	Ruthi Shafer(US)	1983
67.5kg	509	Ruthi Shafer(US)	1984
75kg	473.3	Terri Byland(US)	1987
82.5kg	507	Junita Trujillo(US)	1986
90kg	556	Loraine Costanzo(US)	1988
90+kg	546	Jan Todd (US)	1983

Bench Press

44kg	165	Terri Hoyt	1982
48kg	182	Michelle Evis(US)	1981
52kg	209	Mary Ryan(US)	1984
56kg	253	Mary Jeffrey	1988
60kg	232	Vicki Steenrod	1985
67.5kg	233.7	Heidi Wittesch(Aus)	1986
75kg	309	Bev Francis(Aus)	1981
82.5kg	331	Bev Francis	1981
90kg	296	Lorraine Costanzo	1988
90+kg	297	Myrtle Augee(GB)	1988

Deadlift

44kg	364	Nancy Belliveau(US)	1985
48kg	402	Majik Jones	1984
52kg	434	Diana Rowell(US)	1984
56kg	441	Diana Rowell	1984
60kg	470	Ruthi Shafer	1983
67.5kg	539	Ruthi Shafer	1984
75kg	468	Marie Geldhof(Belg)	1988
82.5kg	501	Vicki Gagne(US)	1981

90kg	501	Lorraine Costnzo	1988
90+kg	507	Wanda Sander(US)	1983

Total

44kg	777	M.F.Vassart(Bel)	1985
48kg	860	Majik Jones	1984
52kg	942	Diana Rowell	1984
56kg	1,069	Mary Jeffrey	1988
60kg	1,108	Vicki Steenrod	1985
67.5kg	1,246	Ruthi Shafer	1984
75kg	1,212	Bev Francis	1981
82.5kg	1,273	Bev Francis	1983
90kg	1,339	Lorraine Costanzo	1988
90+kg	1,251	Gail Mulhall	1982

GOLD IN OLYMPICS

Flyweight

Up to 52kg

1972	Zygmunt Smalcerz (Pol)	337.5kg
1976	Aleksandr Voronin (USSR)	242.5kg
1980	Kanybek Osmonoliev (USSR)	245.00kg
1984	Zeng Guoqiang (Chn)	235.00kg
1988	Sevdalin Marinov (Bul)	

Bantamweight

Up to 56kg

1948	Joseph de Pietro (USA)	307.5kg
1952	Ivan Udodov (USSR)	315.0kg
1956	Charles Vinci (USA)	342.5 kg
1960	Charles Vinci (USA)	345.0kg
1964	Aleksey Vakhonin (USSR)	357.5 kg
1968	Mohammad Nassiri (Irn)	367.5 kg
1972	Imre Foldi (Hun)	377.5 kg
1976	Norair Nurikyan (Bul)	262.5 kg
1980	Daniel Nunez (Cub)	275.0 kg
1984	Wu Shude (Chn)	267.5 kg
1988	Oksen Mirzoyan (USSR)	

Featherweight

Up to 60kg

1920	Frans de Haes (Bel)	220.0kg
1924	Pierino Gabetti (Ita)	402.5kg
1928	Franz Andrysek (Aut)	287.5kg
1932	Raymond Suvigny (Fra)	287.5kg
1936	Anthony Terlazzo (USA)	312.5kg
1948	Mahmoud Fayad (Egy)	332.5kg
1952	Rafael Chimishkyan (USSR)	337.5kg
1956	Isaac Berger (USA)	352.5kg
1960	Yevggeniy Minayev (USSR)	372.5kg
1964	Yoshinobu Miyake (Jpn)	397.5kg
1968	Yoshinobu Miyake (Jpn)	392.5kg
1972	Norair Nurikyan (Bul)	402.5kg
1976	Nikolai Kolesnikov (USSR)	285.0kg
1980	Viktor Mazin (USSR)	290.0kg
1984	Chen Weiqiang (Chn)	282.5kg
1988	Naim Suleimanoglou (Tur)	

Lightweight

Up to 67.5kg

1920	Alfred Neuland (Est)	257.5kg
1924	Edmond Decottignies (Fra)	440.0kg
1928	Kurt Helbig (Ger)	322.5kg
	Hans Haas (Aut)	322.5kg
1932	Rene Duverger (Fra)	325.0kg
1936	Anwar Moh md. Mesbah (Egy)	342.5kg
	Robert Fein (Aut)	342.5kg
1948	Ibrahim Shams (Egy)	360.0kg
1952	Tommy Kono (USA)	362.5kg
1956	Igor Rybak (USSR)	380.0kg
1960	Viktor Bushuyev (USSR)	397.5kg
1964	Waldemar Baszanowski (Pol)	432.5kg
1968	Waldemar Baszanowski (Pol)	437.5kg
1972	Mukharbi Kirzhinov (USSR)	460.0kg
1976	Pyotr Korol (USSR)	305.0kg
1980	Yanko Rusev (Bul)	342.5kg
1984	Yao Jingyuan (Chn)	320.0kg
1988	Joachim Kunz (E.Ger)	

Middleweight

Up to 75kg

1920	Henri Gance (Fra)	245.0kg
1924	Carlo Galimberti (Ita)	492.5kg
1928	Roger Francois (Fra)	335.0kg
1932	Rudolf Ismayr (Ger)	345.0kg
1936	Khadr El Thouni (Egy)	387.5kg
1948	Frank Spellman (USA)	390.0kg
1952	Peter George (USA)	400.0 kg
1956	Fyodor ogdanovski (USSR)	420.0kg

1960	Aleksandr Kurinov (USSR)	437.5kg
1964	Hans Zdrazila (Tch)	445.0kg
1968	Viktor Kurentsov (USSR)	475.0kg
1972	Yordan Bikov (Bul)	485.0kg
1976	Yordan Bikov (Bul)	335.0kg
1980	Asen Zlatev (Bul)	360.0kg
1984	Kari-Heinz Radschinsky (FRG)	340.0 kg
1988	Borislav Gudikov (Bul)	

Light-Heavyweight

Up to 82.5kg

1920	Ernest Cadine (Fra)	290.0kg
1924	Charles Rigoulot (Fra)	502.5kg
1928	Said Nosseir (Egy)	355.0kg
1932	Louis Hostin (Fra)	372.5kg
1936	Louis Hostin (Fra)	372.5kg
1948	Stanley Stanczyk (USA)	417.5kg
1952	Trofim Lomakin (USSR)	417.5kg
1956	Tommy Kono (USA)	447.5kg
1960	Ireneusz Palinski (Pol)	442.5kg
1964	Rudolf Pulkfelder (USSR)	475.0kg
1968	Boris Slitsky (USSR)	485.0kg
1972	Leif Jenssen (Nor)	507.5kg
1976	Valerity Shary (USSR)	365.0kg
1980	Yurik Vardanyan (USSR)	400.0kg
1984	Petre Becheru (Rom)	355.0kg
1988	Israil Arsamakov (USSR)	

Middle-Heavyweight

Up to 90kg

1952	Norbert Schemansky (USA)	445.0kg
1956	Arkadiy Vorobyev (USSR)	462.5kg
1960	Arkadiy Vorobyev (USSR)	472.5kg
1964	Vladimir Golovanov (USSR)	487.5kg
1968	Kaarlo Kangasniemi (Fin)	517.5kg
1972	Andon Nikolov (Bul)	525.0kg
1976	David Rigert (USSR)	382.5kg
1980	Peter Baczako (Hun)	377.5kg
1984	Nicu Vlad (Rom)	392.5kg
1988	Anatoliy Khrapatiy (USSR)	

Up to 100kg

1980	Ota Zaremba (Tch)	395.0kg
1984	Rolf Milser (FRG)	385.0kg
1988	Pavel Kouzyetsov (USSR)	

Heavy weight

Up to 110kg

1920	Filippo Bottino (Ita)	270.0kg
1924	Giuseppe Tonani (Ita)	517.5kg
1928	Josef Strassberger (Ger)	372.5kg
1932	Jaroslav Skobla (Tch)	380.0kg
1936	Josef Manger (Aut)	410.0kg
1948	John Davis (USA)	452.5kg
1952	John Davis (USA)	460.0kg
1956	Paul Anderson (USA)	500.0kg
1960	Yuriy Vlasov (USSR)	537.5kg
1964	Leonid Zhabotinsky (USSR)	572.5kg
1968	Leonid Zhabotinsky (USSR)	572.5kg
1972	Jan Talts (USSR)	580.0kg
1976	Yuriy Zaitsev (USSR)	385.0kg
1980	Leonid Taranenko (USSR)	422.5kg
1984	Norberto Oberburger (Ita)	390.0kg
1988	Yuri Zakharevich (USSR)	

Supter-Heavy weight

Over 110kg

1972	Vasiliy Alexeyev (USSR)	640.0kg
1976	Vasiliy Alexeyev (USSR)	440.0kg
1980	Sultan Rakhmanov (USSR)	440.0kg
1984	Dinko Lukin (Aus)	412.5kg
1988	Aleksandr Kurlovich (USSR)	

ARJUNA AWARD WINNERS

1961	A.N.Ghosh
1962	L.K. Dass
1963	Kamineni Eswara Rao
1965	Balbir Singh Bhatia
1966	Mohan Lal Ghosh
1967	Savarimuthu John Gabriel
1970	Arun Kumar Das
1971	Shyam Lal Salwan
1972	Anil Kumar Mandal
1974	S. Vellaiswamy
1975	Dalbir Singh
1976	K. Balamuruganandam

1977-78	Muniswamy Tamil Selvan	1983	Vispy K. Daroga
1978-79	E. Karunakaran	1985	Mehar Chand Bhasker
1981	Bijaya Kumar Satpathy	1986	Jag Mohan Sapra
1982	Tara Singh	1987	G. Devan

WRESTLING

Wrestling is as old as the human race and dates back to primitive man's earliest beginnings. Of course, modern wrestling is very far removed from the caves - whether in professional form catering for live and television audiences or in the amateur Olympic contests on the lines of Graeco-Roman style.

Wrestling is a hand-to hand contest between two opponents in which each attempts to control the other by placing him on his back, with both shoulders touching the mat for a given number of seconds. The techniques used in wrestling have been passed down from ancient times.

The wrestler with a superior knowledge of takedowns has tremendous advantage. This chapter demonstrates various takedowns and shows the rewards of knowing these techniques and rules.

The wrestling area shall be covered with a mat of 9 metres diameter and 10 cm. thick. All round the mat a free space of width 1.2 metres to 1.5 metres is provided. A red band 1 metre wide (with inner diameter = 8 metres and outer diameter = 9 metres) is provided along the periphery of the mat. The red zone is the zone of passivity. No ropes shall be used around the fighting area.

The contestants must wear either red or blue one piece dress. Swimming costume is not permitted. The shoes should not have any metallic parts. The matallic parts of the laces shall be removed. Each contestant shall be weighed nude on all the days of the competition. He shall also be medically examined. Also in case of injury or accident during the contest, if the doctor feels that the wrestler is not in a position to continue the fight, he may stop the fight. The maximum time out for injury shall not exceeed 5 minutes.

The wrestling competition is arranged in various categories and the participants can contest in a particular category depending upon their weight as follows:

Light flyweight	48kg and under	105.0lbs
Flyweight	52kg and under	114.5lbs
Bantamweight	57kg and under	125.5lbs
Featherweight	62kg and under	136.75lbs
Lightweight	68 kg and under	150 .0lbs
Welterweight	74kg and under	163.0lbs
Middleweight	80kg and under	180.75lbs
Light-heavyweight	90kg and under	198.5lbs
Middle-heavyweight	100kg and under	220.5lbs
Heavyweight	Over 100kg	220.5 lbs

Similar to boxing, except that competition is not on knock-out basis. Two pools of wrestlers are formed in each weight and each competitor meets the others in his pool. However, any wrestler who loses two bouts is eliminated.

The winners of each pool meet to decide gold and silver, the runners-up meet for bronze or sympathy from team-mates.

Three officials control a bout-mat chairman,referee and judge. The mat chairman is in overall control and his decision in the event of a dispute is final.

The referee wears a red band on one arm and a blue band on the other and signals the number of points awarded at any given time with the appropriate arm for the wrestler concerned.

The judge is there for confirmation and is overall scorer.

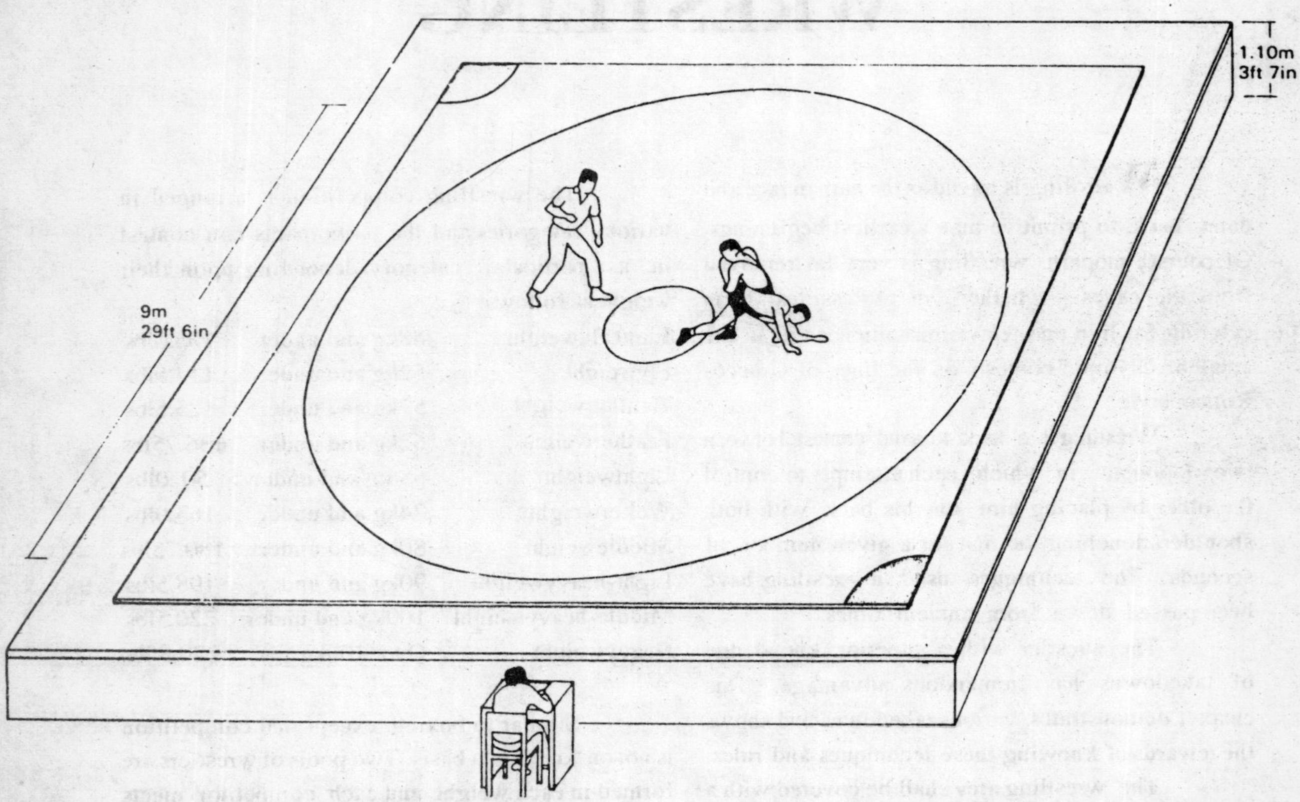

RULES OF WRESTLING

Dress

Competitors shall appear before the public in a one-piece singlet and under this they shall wear a truss or a suspender-belt.

The singlet shall be tight-fitting and shall cover the body from the middle of the thighs upward; it shall not be cut away by more than two palm-widths around the neck and arms.

The use of light knee-guards shall be permitted.

Nothing whatsoever may be added to this dress, save in the event of a stoppage of the bout on account of injury or for any other reason, when the wrestlers may cover themselves with a warm garment.

The use of shoes with heels or with nailed soles shall be forbidden; contestants shall likewise be fordidden to cover their bodies with greasy or sticky products and they shall not be in a prespiring condition.

No bandages shall be allowed on the wrists, arms or ankles, save in the case of injury and on the doctor's prescription.

The wearing of rings, bracelets, buckles-type shoes and all objects liable to injure an opponent shall likewise be forbidden.

Each competitor shall be freshly shaven at the time of the weighing-in.

Each competitor shall be provided with a handkerchief.

Each competitor shall be given two anklets with a width of 10 centimetres and of the colour attributed to him(red or green). Competitors shall be forbidden to wear shoes, socks and laces coloured green or red or with a colour close to green or red.

The Mat

A mat having a diameter of 9 metres surrounded by a border of the same thickness and with a width from 1.20 to 1.50m., is obligatory in all international competitions.

On the inside of the circle of 9 m. in diameter and running all along its circumference, a 1 metre wide band of red colour is traced, this being an integral part of the wrestling surface.

Referee

In all international competitons , the officials for each bout shall consist of one mat chairman, one referee and one judge.
The changing of a judge during a bout shall be forbidden.

In order to avoid all partiality, compatriots of the competitors may not be a judge; the same shall apply in the case of the referee.

The referee shall be responsible for the evolution of the bout, which he shall control in conformity with the rules. The bout shall start, be interrupted and end when he blows his whistle. He alone shall be authorised, after consulting the judges, to give cautions. He alone shall order the wrestlers to return to the mat should they have left it, or order the bout to be continued in the standing position or on the ground, with the respective opponents in the on-top or underneath positions, this with the approval of the majority of the judge.

The referee and the judge shall be dressed in white and they shall wear the badges of their countries.

The judge and referee shall assume all the duties, prerogatives and responsibilities provided for in the rules for international wrestling competitions, by the interpreatations included in this appendix, by the regulations of the Technical Committee and by the regulations for the organisation of competitions.

Danger Position

The wrestler shall be considered in the "danger position" when the line of his back (or the line of his shoulders), vertically or in parallel with the mat, forms an angle of less than 90 degree with the said mat and when he resists, with the upper part of his body,to avoid a "fall."

The wrestler can resist with his head, elbows and shoulder, and also by an "instantaneous fall" position.

The following shall be considered "danger positions."

(a) when the defending wrestler assumes the bridge position to keep from being pinned;
(b) when the defending wrestler, his back toward the mat, supports himself on one or both elbows in order to avoid having his shoulders forced to the mat, or when he is blocked in this position on both hands.
(c) when the wrestler has one shoulder in contact with the mat and at the same time exceeds the 90 degree vertical line with the other shoulder (acute angle);
(d) when the wrestler finds himself in the "instantaneous fall" position,i.e., when he is on both shoulders for less than fast 1-2 count.

Freestyle

Greco-Roman

In the event that the referee notes the "danger position,"he then scores two or four points-depending on the type of move used - by raising his arm and extending the proper number of fingers on his hand.

The Fall

It is considered to a fall (TOUCHE) when the defensive wrestler is held by his opponent with his two shoulders or base of his scapulate against the mat for a sufficient time to allow the referee to count ONE, or to pronounce mentally the word "TOMBEY" (fall) and strike the mat with his hand.

In order for a fall to be recognized at the edge of the mat, it is sufficient for the shoulders of the contestant to touch the mat at the moment of falling (as is stated above), but his head must remain within the limits of the mat. That is, head must not touch out of bounds.

The fall established by the referee will be valid if the judge indicates his agreement, for if, in the requisite consultation of the judge by the referee, there is a difference of opinion, the final decision must be given by the mat chiarman.

Consequently, to be established and acknowledged, the fall must be clearly maintained, i.e., the two shoulders of the wrestler in question must be simultaneously touching the mat during the short period of time specified in the first paragraph of this Article, even in the cause of a standing rear body-lock and lift. In any case, the referee will strike the mat only after he has obtained the confirmation of the judge, or failing that, of the mat chairman and then he would blow his whistle.

Technical Superiority

In addition to cases of a fall, withdrawal and disqualification, the bout must be terminated before time elapses when there is a difference of 12 points between the wrestlers (includes points scored for fleeing from the mat and illegal holds). The bout, however, will not be stopped to declare a winner by technical superiority until completion of the action, including attacks and counterattacks. The judge or the mat chairman signals the referee when the 12-point difference is effective. After consultation of the officials, the referee will declare the winner, when permission is given by the mat chairman.

Flight Against Passivity

Passivity Procedures: Basically there are four steps involved in the application of penalizing passive wrestling. The referee, however, may issue verbal encouragement throughout the match, without having to give a caution.

1. Signalling by the referee or judge that a werstler is passive. The bout is not interrupted. This indication will be noted with a circle on the bout sheet by the judge and the mat chairman. The referee must use words and must clearly pronounce, showing the wrestler at fault; the word defining the nature of the fault, for example;

   red: action
   blue: contact
   red: open

   The referee gives the caution by stretching to the side his arm wearing the colour of the passive wrestler (red or blue) without interrupting the bout. The referee does not seek the approval of the judge and mat chairman, nor does he look at them. He only addresses the wrestlers on the mat.

2. If the same wrestler continues to be passive, the referee again stretches to the side his arm wearing the colour corresponding to the passive wrestler. After a few seconds he should consult the mat chairman (not the judge) by looking at him, before deciding whether he should interrupt the bout. The mat chairman may also interrupt the bout. In case the referee overlooks passivity, the judge and the mat chairman must signal it.

Passivity (Stalling)

Passive considerations detrimental to Total Wrestling (Partial List)

(a) not using proper holds

not attacking forcefully
preventing the opponent from attacking
intentionally fleeing the mat
prolonged two hands on one
pushing the opponent into zone or off the mat.

(b) Particulars to ground wrestling:
lying flat on the stomach with no counter attack
crossing one's ankles with the legs straight
gripping the opponent's leg with two legs while lying flat on the stomach

(c) Stalling the fleeing on the mat shall be handled as follows:

1. referee blows his whistle to stop the bout when a wrestler goes off the mat.
2. in case of obvious avoidance of combat the faulty wrestler receives an immediate caution upon confirmation of two or more officials.
3. on the second and third avoidance of combat, either standing or on the mat, a caution likewise shall be given with confirmation.
4. any further avoidance of combat shall then be penalized by disqualification. The mat chairman is empowered, after the second caution is given, to interrupt the bout to briefly inform the wrestler and coach of the dangers of a third caution.
5. loss of two points and enforcement of the passivity criteria should occur when the fleeing wrestler goes off the mat into a danger position.

Scoring

The judge shall mark the wrestlers' points on their scoring forms as follows:

1 point: (a) to a wrestler who brings down his opponent and holds him on the ground by getting on top;

(b) to a wrestler who reverses his opponent and holds him down;

(c) to a wrestler who applies a correct hold and does not cause his opponent to touch the mat with either his shoulder or head during the execution of the hold.

A caution shall count as one point to the opponent.

2 points: (a) to a wrestler who applies a correct hold and places his opponent momentarily in danger (less than five seconds);

(b) to a wrestler whose opponent is in an instantaneous fall, accidental fall, or rolling fall.

3 points: (a) to a wrestler who keeps his opponent in danger (the shoulders forming an angle of less than 90 degree with the mat) for five seconds.

A series of rolling falls and bridges for five seconds, continuously, will count for three points. In this case, the referee shall count the seconds.

The judge shall mark down the points as and when they are awarded in each period.

When the difference between the two opponents is less.

4 points: for a perfect technical throw.

A Win on Points

Should there be no fall within the nine minutes laid down for the duration of the bouts in both styles, the judge shall hand in his scoring form to the mat chairman and he shall name the winner or decide that the bout has been drawn.

CUP & TROPHIES

GOLD IN OLYMPICS (FREESTYLE)

Free-Style-Light Flyweight

1904	Robert Curry (USA)
1972	Roman Dmitriev (USSR)
1976	Khassan Issaev (Bul)
1980	Claudio Pollio (Ita)
1984	Robert Weaver (USA)
1988	Takashi Kobayashi (Jpn)

Free-Style-Flyweight

1904	George Mehnert (USA)
1948	Lennart Viitala (Fin)
1952	Hasan Gemici (Tur)
1856	Mirian Tsalkalamanidze (USSR)
1960	Ahmed Bilek (Tur)
1964	Yoshikatsu Yoshida (Jpn)
1968	Shigeo Nakata (Jpn)
1972	Kiyomi Kato (Jpn)

1976 Yuji Takada (Jpn)
1980 Anatoliy Beloglazov (USSR)
1984 Saban Trstena (Yug)
1988 Mitsuru Sato (Jpn)

Free-Style-Bantamweight

1904 Isidor Niflot (USA)
1908 George Mehnert (USA)
1924 Kustaa Pihlajamaki (Fin)
1928 Kaarlo Makinen (Fin)
1932 Robert Pearce (USA)
1936 Odon Zombori (Hun)
1948 Nasuk Akar (Tur)
1952 Shohachi Ishii (Jpn)
1956 Mustafa Dagistanli (Tur)
1960 Terrence McCann (USA)
1964 Yojiro Uetake (Jpn)
1968 Yojiro Uetake (Jpn)
1972 Hideaki Yanagide (Jpn)
1976 Vladimir Yumin (USSR)
1980 Sergey Beloglazov (USSR)
1984 Hideyaki Tomiyama (Jpn)
1988 Sergey Beloglazov (USSR)

Free-Style - Featherweight

1904 Benjamin Bradshaw (USA)
1908 George Dole (USA)
1924 Robin Reed (USA)
1928 Allie Morrison (USA)
1932 Hermanni Pihlajamaki (Fin)
1936 Kustaa Pihlajamaki (Fin)
1948 Gazanfer Bilge (Tur)
1952 Bayram Sit (Tur)
1956 Shozo Sasahara (Jpn)
1960 Mustafa Dagistanli (Tur)
1964 Osamu Watanabe (Jpn)
1968 Masaaki Kaneko (Jpn)
1972 Zagalav Abdulbekov (USSR)
1976 Jung-Mo Yang (Kor)
1980 Magomedgasan Abushev (USSR)
1984 Randy Lewis (USA)
1988 John Smith (USA)

Free-Style - Lightweight

1904 Otto Roehm (USA)
1908 George de Relwyskow (UK)
1920 Kalle Anttila (Fin)
1924 Russell Vis (USA)
1928 Osvald Kapp (Est)
1932 Charies Pacome (Fra)
1936 Karoly Karpati (Hun)
1948 Celal Atik (Tur)
1952 Olle Anderberg (Swe)
1956 Emamali Habibi (Ira)
1960 Shelby Wilson (USA)
1964 Enyu Valtschev (Bul)
1968 Abdollah Movahed Ardabili (Irn)
1972 Dan Gable (USA)
1976 Pavel Pinigin (USSR)
1980 Saipulla Absaidov (USSR)
1984 In-Tak You (Kor)
1988 Arsen Fadzayev (USSR)

Free-Style - Welterweight

1904 Charles Erickson (USA)
1924 Hermann Gehri (Sui)
1928 Arvo Haavisto (Fin)
1932 Jack van Bebber (USA)
1936 Frank Lewis (USA)
1948 Yasar Dogu (Tur)
1952 William Smith (USA)
1956 Mitsuo Ikeda (Jpn)
1960 Douglas Blubaugh (USA)
1964 Ismail Ogan (Tur)
1968 Mahmut Atalay (Tur)
1972 Wayne Wells (USA)
1976 Jiichiro Date (Jpn)
1980 Valentin Raitchev (Bul)
1984 David Schultz (USA)
1988 Kenneth Monday (USA)

Freestyle - Middleweight

1908 Stanley Bacon (UK)
1924 Eino Leino (Fin)
1928 Fritz Hagmann (Sui)
1932 Ivar Johansson (Swe)

1936 Emile Poilve (Fra)
1948 Glen Brand (USA)
1952 David Tsimakuridze (USSR)
1956 Nikola Stantschev (Bul)
1960 Hasan Gungor (Tur)
1964 Prodan Gardschev (Bul)
1968 Boris Gurevitch (USSR)
1972 Levan Tediashvili (USSR)
1976 John Peterson (USA)
1980 Ismail Abilov (Bul)
1984 Mark Schultz (USA)
1988 Han Myang-woo (S.Kor)

Free-Style- Light-Heavyweight

1920 Anders Larsson (Swe)
1924 John Spellman (USA)
1928 Thure Sjostedt (Swe)
1932 Peter Mehringer (USA)
1936 Kunt Fridell (Swe)
1948 Henry Wittenberg (USA)
1952 Wiking Palm (Swe)
1956 Gholam Reza Tahkti (Ira)
1960 Ismet Atli (Tur)
1964 Aleksandr Medved (USSR)
1968 Ahmed Ayik (Tur)
1972 Ben Peterson (USA)
1976 Levan Tediashvili (USSSR)
1980 Sansar Oganesyan (USSR)
1984 Ed Banach (USA)
1988 Makharbek Khadartsev (USSR)

Free-Style - Heavyweight

1904 Bernhuff Hasen (USA)
1908 George O'Kelly (UK)
1920 Robert Roth (Sui)
1924 Harry Steele (USA)
1928 Johan Richthoff (Swe)
1932 Johan Richthoff (Swe)
1936 Kristian Palusalu (Est)
1948 Gyula Bobis (Hun)
1952 Arsen Mekokishvili (USSR)
1956 Hamit Kaplan (Tur)
1960 Wilfried Dietrich (Ger)
1964 Aleksandr Ivanitsky (USSR)
1968 Aleksandr Ivanitsky (USSR)
1972 Ivan Yargin (USSR)
1976 Ivan Yargin (USSR)
1980 Ilya Mate (Yug)
1984 Lou Banach (USA)
1988 Vasile Puscasu (Rom)

Free-Style - Super-Heavyweight

1972 Aleksandr Medved (USSR)
1976 Soslan Andiev (USSR)
1980 Soslan Andiev (USSR)
1984 Bruce Baumgartner (USA)
1988 David Gobedzhichvili (USSR)

GRECO-ROMAN

Greco-Roman- Light-Flyweight

1972 Gheorghe Berceanu (Rom)
1976 Aleksey Shumakov (USSR)
1980 Zaksylik Ushkempirov (USSR)
1984 Vincenzo Maenza (Ita)
1988 Vincenzo Maenza (Ita)

Greco-Roman - Flyweight

1948 Pietro Lombardi (Ita)
1952 Boris Gurevich (USSR)
1956 Nikolai Solovyov (USSR)
1960 Dumitru Pirvulescu (Rom)
1964 Tsutomu Hanahara (Jpn)
1968 Petar Kirov (Bul)
1972 Petar Kirov (Bul)
1976 Vitaliy Konstantinov (USSR)
1980 Vakhtang Blagidze (USSR)
1984 Atsuji Miyahara (Jpn)
1988 John Ronningen (Nor)

Greco-Roman - Bantamweight

1924 Eduard Putsep (Est)
1928 Kurt Leucht (Ger)
1932 Jakob Brendel (Ger)
1936 Marton Lorincz (Hun)
1948 Kurt Pettersen (Swe)
1952 Imre Hodos (Hun)
1956 Konstantin Vyrupayev (USSR)
1960 Oieg Karavayev (USSR)

1964 Masamitsu Ichiguchi (Jpn)
1968 Janos Varga (Hun)
1972 Rustem Kazakov (USSR)
1976 Pertti Ukkola (Fin)
1980 Shamil Serikov (USSR)
1984 Pasquale Passarelli (FRG)
1988 Andras Sike (Hun)

Greco-Roman - Featherweight

1912 Kaarlo Koskelo (Fin)
1920 Oskari Friman (Fin)
1924 Kalle Antila (Fin)
1928 Voldemar Vali (Est)
1932 Giovanni Gozzi (Ita)
1936 Yasar Krkan (Tur)
1948 Mehmet Oktav (Tur)
1952 Yakov Punkin (USSR)
1956 Rauno Makinen (Fin)
1960 Muzahir Sille (Tur)
1964 Imre Polyak (Hun)
1968 Roman Rurua (USSR)
1972 Gheorghi Markov (Bul)
1976 Kazimierz Lipien (Pol)
1980 Stilianos Migiakis (Ger)
1984 Weon-Kee Kim (Kor)
1988 Kamandar Madzhidov (USSR)

Greco-Roman - Lightweight

1906 Rudolf Watzl (Aut)
1908 Enrico Porro (Ita)
1912 Eemil Ware (Fin)
1920 Eemil Ware (Fin)
1924 Oskari Friman (Fin)
1928 Lajos Keresztes (Hun)
1932 Erik Malmberg (Swe)
1936 Lauri Koskela (Fin)
1948 Gustaf Freij (SWe)
1952 Shazam Safin (USSR)
1956 Kyosti Lehtonen (Fin)
1960 Avtandil Koridze (USSR)
1964 Kazim Ayvaz (Tur)
1968 Munji Mumemura (Jpn)
1972 Shamil Khisamutdinov (USSR)
1976 Suren Nalbandyan (USSR)
1980 Stefan Rusu (Rom)
1984 Vlado Lisjak (Yug)
1988 Levon Dzhulfalakyan (USSR)

Greco-Roman - Welterweight

1932 Ivar Johansson (Swe)
1936 Rudolf Svedberg (Swe)
1948 Gosta Andersson (Swe)
1952 Miklos Szilvasi (Hun)
1956 Mithat Bayrak (Tur)
1960 Mithat Bayrak (Tur)
1964 Anatoliy Kolesov (USSR)
1968 Rudolf Vesper (GDR)
1972 Vitezslav Macha (Tch)
1976 Anatoliy Bytkov (USSR)
1980 Ferenc Kocsis (Hun)
1984 Jonko Salomaki (Fin)
1988 Kim Young-nam (S.Kor)

Greco - Roman - Middleweight

1906 Verner Weckman (Fin)
1908 Frithiof Martensson (Swe)
1912 Clase Johansson (Swe)
1920 Carl Westergren (Swe)
1924 Eduard Westerlund (Fin)
1928 Vaino Kokkinen (Fin)
1932 Vaino Kokkinen (Fin)
1936 Ivar Johansson (Swe)
1948 Axel Gronberg (Swe)
1952 Axel Gronberg (Swe)
1956 Givi Kartoziya (USSR)
1960 Dimiter Dobrev (Bul)
1964 Branislav Simic (Yug)
1968 Lothar Metz (GDR)
1972 Csaba Hegedus (Hun)
1976 Momir Petkovic (Yug)
1980 Gennadiy Korban (USSR)
1984 Ion Draica (Rom)
1988 Mikhail Mamiashvili (USSR)

Greco-Roman - Light-Heavyweight

1920 Claes Johansson (Swe)
1924 Carl Westergren (Swe)
1928 Ibrahim Moustafa (Egy)

1932 Rudolf Svensson (Swe)
1936 Axel Cadier (Swe)
1948 Karl-Erik Nilssson (Swe)
1952 Kaelpo Grondahl (Fin)
1956 Valentin Nikolayev (USSR)
1960 Tevfik Kis (Tur)
1964 Boyan Radev (Bul)
1968 Boyan Radev (Bul)
1972 Valeriy Rezantsev (USSR)
1976 Valeriy Rezantsev (USSR)
1980 Norbert Nottny (Hun)
1984 Steven Fraser (USA)
1988 Atanas Komchev (Bul)

Greco-Roman - Heavyweight

1896 Carl Schuhmann (Ger)
1906 Soren Jensen (Den)
1908 Richard Weisz (Hun)
1912 Yrjo Saarela (Fin)
1920 Adolf Lindfors (Fin)
1924 Henri Deglane (Fra)
1928 Rudolf Svensson (Swe)
1932 Carl Westergren (Swe)
1936 Kristjan Palusalu (Est)
1948 Ahmed Kirecci (Tur)
1952 Johannes Kotkas (USSR)
1956 Anatoliy Parfenov (USSR)
1960 Ivan Bogdan (USSR)
1964 Istvan Kozma (Hun)
1968 Istvan Kozma (Hun)
1972 Nicolae Martinescu (Rom)
1976 Nikolai Bolboshin (USSR)
1980 Gheorghi Railkov (Bul)
1984 Vasile Andrei (Rom)
1988 Andrzej Wronski (Pol)

Greco-Roman- Super Heavyweight

1972 Anatoliy Roschin (USSR)
1976 Aleksandr Kolchinsky (USSR)
1980 Aleksandr Kolchinsky (USSR)
1984 Jeffrey Blatnick (USA)
1988 Aleksandr Kolchinsky (USSR)

PADMA SHRI AWARDS

1- Chandgi Ram
2- Guru Hanuman
3- Sat Pal Singh
4- Kartar Singh

ARJUNA AWARD WINNERS

1961 Udey Chand
1962 Malwa
1963 G. Andalkar
1964 Bishamber Singh
1966 Bhim Singh
1967 Mukhtiar Singh
1969 Chandgi Ram (Indian Style)
1970 Sudesh Kumar
1972 Prem Nath
1973 Jagroop Singh
1974 Satpal
1978-79 Rajinder Singh
1980-81 Jagminder Singh
1982 Kartar Singh
1985 Mahabir Singh
1987 Subhash

YACHTING

In modern scientific terms, because a sailing yacht is neither completely immersed in the sea nor entirely borne in the air but operates along the turbulent margin between the two elements it is by definition an interface vehicle. In another sense, too, it is also an interface vehicle. Its design is neither entirely art nor yet entirely science and again, in design terms, it falls in the turbulent margin between them.

In the global sense-viewed that is as a whole-the process of the evolution of the modern yacht from the rough working boat of antiquity to its present-day form takes place against a background familiar in many other spheres of human activity from medicine to astronomy.

The first recorded yacht race took place in England in 1661, between King Charles Ii and his brother, the Duke of York. The yachts were attended by the royal barge and kitchen-boat, and the King won the wager of 100 Pounds Organized regattas and small boat sailing races are first recorded in the late nineteenth century; earlier yacht races had been private matches, arranged between the owners of large sea-going yachts. Inshore yacht racing has been included in the Olympic program since the first games of the modern series. The international governing body, the International Yacht Racing Union IYRU was founded in 1907.

SOME HISTORIC PRFORMANCES

The times in the following table are not record-breaking performances. They are included here to show how even over a period of one hundred years, 'round trip' speeds in terms of speed/length ratios have not altered appreciably.

YEAR	YACHT	ROUTE	DISTANCE (nm)	TIME (days)
1866	Henrietta	Sandy Hook-Needles	3100	13
1870	Cambria	Danut Rock-Sandy	2900	23
1887	Coronet	New York-Ireland	2900	15
1905	Atlantic	Sandy Hook-Lizard	3000	12
1928	Nina	New York-Santander	3300	24
1931	Dorade	Newport-Plymouth	2800	17
1935	Stormy	Newport-Bergen	3100	19

PARTS OF THE BOAT

1. Forestay (attached to the bow by a shackle)
2. Mast
3. Shroud (made of wire)
4. Jib tack strap
5. Adjustable rigging screws (or lanyard)
6. Chainplate (secure point for rigging)
7. Foredeck
8. Goose0neck (see inset diagram)
9. Boom
10. Kicking strap (to hold boom down)
11. Side deck
12. Thwart (a seat across the boat)
13. Centre board case
14. Toestraps (as support when 'sitting out')
15. Bottom boards
16. Jamb cleat (to trap jib sheet)
17. Fairlead (a ring to alter direction of jib sheet)
18. Mast step
19. Mainsail clew outhaul (rope to 'stretch' sail aft)
20. Mainsheet blocks (which you know on land as pulleys)
21. Mainsheet (to pull in or let out mainsail and boom)

22. After-deck (the back end is called the 'after-end')
23. Tiller (for turning the rudder)
24. Tiller extension (used when 'sitting out')
25. Transom (or stern, as opposed to the bow of the boat)
26. Rudder stock
27. Rudder pintles and gudgeons (the rudder is removable)
28. Drain hole (sometimes flaps, but both to let water out)
29. Rudder blade (which is 'liftable')

RULES OF THE GAME

Yacht racing rules are few but mandatory, and infringement results in immediate disqualification. All disputes are settled by protest before the Race Committee, for yacht racing is the one sport without referee or umpire.

The rules are framed to avoid collision between boats and to encourage fair sailing, with encouragement to the attacking boat but allowing the boat ahead to defend her position. Some rules apply at all times, others on specific occasions. A yacht is racing under rules from the five-minutes signal before the start until she has finished.

The Start

There are two warning signals for the start, one 10 minutes before, when the class flag is hoisted and the other 5 minutes before, when the international code flag P (for Blue Peter) is hoisted with the class flag. Shots are fired to bring the competitors attention to these flag signals. At the start both flags are dropped and there is another shot. If any boat is over the line, a second shot is fired and the class flag held at half-mast until the boat or all boats have recrossed the line and started correctly. A yacht that has corssed the line before the starting gun and has to go back has no right of way whatsoever when going back. If there has to be a complete restart it is signalled by the hoisting of the First Substitute of the international code and the firing of three shots. A yacht is considered to have started when any part of her crosses the line in the direction of the first mark after the start.

When Yachts are on the Same Track

A windward yacht shall keep clear of a leeward yacht;

A yacht clear astern shall keep clear of one clear ahead;

A yacht that establishes an overlap to leeward from clear astern shall allow the windward yacht to keep clear and must not sail above her proper course;

A yacht clear ahead or to leeward may luff to try to prevent a winward yacht overtaking until the helmsman in the windward boat is forward of the mainmast of the leeward yacht which must then return to its proper course;

An overlap exists only when the boats are within two lengths of each other;

A yacht must not sail below her proper course when she is within three lengths of a leeward yacht or a yacht clear astern that is steering a path to leeward.

When Changing Track

A yacht tacking or gybing shall keep clear of all others;

A yacht shall not tack to get right of way unless it does so in sufficient time to allow others to keep clear.

When Rounding Marks

The yacht inside has right of way over all those outside her;

An inside overlap must be established before the leading boat is within two lengths of the mark.

At one time a yacht that touched a mark had to retire immediately, but now most sailing instructions allow the correction of this mistake by a complete re-rounding of the mark. In such circumstances the yacht has no right of way whatsoever.

Those Rules That Always Apply

A yacht that makes no attempt to avoid a collision resulting in serious damage, even if she has right of way, may be disqualified;

A yacht with right of way shall not alter course to prevent another yacht from keeping clear;

A yacht with right of way must hail before making an alternation of course that may not be foreseen by another yacht;

A port-tack yacht shall keep clear of a starboard-tack yacht.

CUP & TROPHIES

AMERICA'S CUP

The America's Cup is an international challenge trophy, named after the schooner America, the winner of a race around the Isle of Wight in 1851. All the winning yachts listed here have come from the USA.

Winners

1870	Magic
1871	Columbia
1871	Sappho
1876	Madeleine
1881	Mischief
1885	Puritan
1886	Mayflower
1887	Volunteer
1893	Vigilant
1895	Defender
1899	Columbia
1901	Columbia
1903	Reliance
1920	Resolutest
1930	Enterprise
1934	Rainbow
1937	Ranger
1958	Columbia
1962	Weatherly
1964	Constellation
1967	Intrepid
1970	Intrepid
1974	Courageous
1977	Courageous
1980	Freedom
1983	Australia II
1987	Stars & Stripes

OLYMPIC GAMES

The types of boat specified for Olympic competition have varied considerably over the years since 1900 when yachting was first included in the Olympic Games.

Soling Class

1972	United States
1976	Denmark
1980	Denmark
1984	United States
1988	East Germany

Flying Dutchman Class

1956	P.Mander/J.Cropp (NZ)
1960	P.Lunde, jnr / B.Bergvall (Nor)
1964	H.Pedersen / E.Wells (NZ)
1968	R.Pattisson/I.Macdonald Smith (UK)
1972	R.Pattisson / C.Davies (UK)
1976	J.Diesch/E.Diesch (FRG)
1980	A.Abascal/M.Noguer (Spa)
1984	J.McKee/C.Buchan (USA)
1988	Jorgen Bojsen -Moller/Christian Gronborg (Den)

International Star Class

1932	G.Gray/A.Libano,jnr (USA)
1936	P.Bischoff/H-J.Weise (Ger)
1948	H.Smart'P.Smart (USA)
1952	A.Straulino /N.Rode (Ita)
1960	T.Pinegin/F.Shutkov (USSR)
1964	D.Knowles /C.Cooke (Bah)
1968	L.North/P.Barrett (USA)
1972	D.Forbes /J.Anderson (Aus)
1976	Not held
1980	V.Mankin/A.Muzychenko (USSR)
1984	W.Buchan/S.Erickson (USA)
1988	Michael McIntyre/Bryn Vaile (UK)

Finn Class

1920	F.Hin/J.Hin (Hol)
1920	F. A.Richards/T.Hedburg (UK)
1924	L.Huybrechts (Bel)
1928	S.Thorell (Swe)

1932 J.Lebrun (Fra)
1936 D.Kagchelland (Hol)
1948 P.Elvstrom (Den)
1952 P.Elvstrom (Den)
1956 P.Elvstrom (Den)
1960 P.Elvstrom (Den)
1964 W.Kuhweide (Ger)
1968 V.Mankin (USSR)
1972 S.Maury (Fra)
1976 J. Schumann (GDR)
1980 E.Rechardt (Fin)
1984 R.Coults (NZ)
1988 Jose Luis Doreste (Spa)

International 470 Class

1976 F.Hubner/H.Bode (FRG)
1980 M.Soares/E.Penido (Bra)
1984 L.Doreste/R.Molina (Spa)
1988 Thierry Peponnet/Luc Pillot (Fra)

International Tornado Class

1976 R.White/J.Osborn (UK)
1980 A.Welter/L.Bjorkstrom (Bra)
1984 R.Sellers/C.Timms (NZ)
1988 Jean - Yves Le Deroff / Nicolas Henard (Fra)

GLOSSARY

A

A.A.U.:- (Athletics) Amateur Athletic Union.

AAHPER:- (Gymnastics) American Association for Health, Physical Education and Recreation.

ABUTMENT:- (Motorcycling) A stop to limit wheel lock, or, on the end of a control cable, to locate the outer covering.

ACE:- (Golf) A hole in one.
(Handball) A service which completely eludes the receiver.
(Tennis) A ball served and untouched by the opponent's racket.

ACEY DEUCY:- (Equestrian) Having the right stirrup than the left so that the jockey can more easily equalize his weight on the turms.

ACCELERATION:- (Athletics) Increasing speed of body motion.

A.C.U.:- (Motorcycling) Auto Cycle Union, which controls most types of motorcycle sport in Britain.

AD:- (Tennis) An abbreviated form of the word "Advantage".

ADDRESS:- (Golf) The position taken by a player in preparing to start a stroke.

ADDRESSING THE TARGET:- (Archery) Standing ready to shoot with a proper shooting.

ADVANCE:- (Fencing) A step taken toward an opponent while remaining on-guard.

ADVANCE LUNGE:- (Fencing) An attack that combines an advance and a lunge.

ADVANCING:- (Field hockey) A foul that results when a player advances the ball with any part of the body instead of the stick and that is penalized by awarding a free hit to the opposing team.

AERIAL:- (Gymnastics) A type of somersault used in tumbling with a one-foot takeoff back arched, and a one-foot landing. It may be executed forward or sideward.

AGE-GROUP SWIMMING:- (Swimming) Development system in which children compete against others of the same age from ages 9 to 17.

AGGRESSIVE HIGH SERVE:- (Badminton) One falling vertically near singles back line (useful tactic sometimes in doubles).

ALBION ROUND:- (Archery) A target round in women's competition in which each competitor shoots 36 arrows at a distance of yards, 36 at 60 yards and 36 at 50 yards.

ALLEY:- (Badminton) The 1(1/2) foot wide extension on both sides of the court used in doubles play.
(Field Hockey) Area of the field between the sideline and the five yard or alley line.
(Tennis) The 4(1/2)ft. strip on either side of the singles court, used to enlarge the court for doubles.

ALLEY-OOP SHOT:- (Basketball) A shot made by a player who leaps high in the air near the basket to catch a lob pass and immediately drops or throws the ball in the basket before landing.

ALL THE WAY:- (Football) For a touchdown. (Went all the way on a perfectly executed sweep).

ALL-ROUND:- (Women Gymnastics) An event in which the winner is determined by totalling the scores received in the following four events: balance beam, floor exercise, side horse vaulting, and uneven parallel bars.

ALL-ROUNDER:- (Cricket) Phrase used mainly to describe a player who is capable at both batting and bowling; lately also applied to one who is outstanding at batting and wicketkeeping. The term 'genuine all-rounder' is used to describe one assessed as being so good at each of his departments that he could gain selection in a team for either.

ALPINE SKIING:- (Skiing) Downhill and slalom skiing as opposed to cross-country or Nordic skiing.

ALTERING DECISIONS:- (Cricket) An umpire may change his decision for any number of reasons, e.g. he may wish to reverse a dismissal, change a singalled four to a six, or change a call of legbyes to runs.

The captain of the fielding side also may seek the permission of the umpire to withdraw an appeal by a member of the fielding side, giving the umpire a chance to alter his decision.

Further, an umpire may alter a decision of his own volition, provided he does so promptly.

ALTERNATE CAPTAIN:- (Ice Hockey) A designated player who performs the duties of team captain when the captain is not on the ice.

AMATEUR ATHLETIC ASSOCIATION:- (Athletics) The A.A.A.was founded at Oxford on April 24th,1880, when the representatives of the Chiel clubs met and formed a federation.It is the governing body in all athletic matters and every athletic meeting must be held under its rules.

AMERICAN HOP:- (Athletics) A method of getting the body into position for throwing the javelin.

AMERICAN FOOTBALL :- A football game resembling rugby that is played with an oval football between teams of 11 players each and that features running, forward passing, and kicking of the ball.

AMPLITUDE:- (Gymanastics) Fullest extent to which a movement can be performed. Used as a standard of judging.

ANCHOR POINT:- (Archery) Specific location on the archer's face to which the index finger comes while holding and aiming.

ANGLE BLOCK:- (Football) A block made from the side and intended to drive the defender sideways; a block made at an angle on an opponent who is not lined up directly opposite the blocker.

ANGLE OF DELIVERY:- (Athletics) Angle to the ground at which an implement is released.

ANALYSIS:- (Cricket) Relates to the figures in a bowler's performance, in terms of overs bowled, maiden overs, runs conceded and wickets taken for a given period. The figure are usually shown this way: 15-3-44-2.

ANATOMICAL SADDLE:- (Cycling) Saddle, probably plastic, designed to provide padding to match the shape of the pelvis; different designs are available for men and women.

ANCHOR:- (Athletics) The final or fourth leg of a relay.

ANGLING LINE:- (Football) A defensive line which charges at an angle.

APPEAL PLAY:- (Softball) A play upon which an umpire cannot make a decision until requested by a player or a coach.

APPROACH:- (Athletics) The run and/or adjustments made by the athlete prior to the actual competitive effort.

APPROACH SHOT:- (Golf) A shot made from the fairway to the putting green.
(Tennis) A shot hit inside the baseline while approaching the net.

APPLE:- (Bowling) The ball.

APRON:- (Golf) The area immediately surrounding the green.

AQUATICS:- Water sports including swimming, diving, surfing, skin diving, boating, and sailing.

ARABESQUE:- (Gymanstics) A pose calling for balance common to dance and gymanastics. The gymnast stands on one leg with the other stretched back. One arm is extended upwards and the other arm side-ways.

ARCH:- (Gymnastics) A position in which the body is curved, like an arc of a circle, with the hips forward and the upper trunk and legs extended backward.

ARCHERY GOLF:- (Archery) An adaptation of the game of golf to the sport of archery. Players shoot for the holes, and score according to the number of shots required to hit the target.

AREA BLOCKING:- (Football) Blocking any opponent in a particular area or zone instead of a designated player (also called zone blocking).

ARM:- (Cricket) Word loosely applied to a player's strength and accuracy when throwing the ball in from the outfield.

ARM BALL:- (Cricket) A delivery by a finger-spin bowler that seems to be going to spin in the regulation manner, but in act bends the other way through the air. So called because it swings in the direction of the bowling arm coming through its downswing.

ARM GUARD:- (Archery) A piece of leather or plastic that is worn on the inside of the forearm to protect the arm from the bowstring.

ARM THROWER:- (Baseball) A player who fails to coordinate the arm and stride.

ARMLOCK:- (Judo) A hold in which the opponent's arm is stretched out and held in that position with pressure applied to the back of the elbow.

AROUND THE HORN:- (Baseball) A double play, third to second to first.

ARROW PLATE:- (Archery) A protective piece of hard material set into the bow where the arrow crosses it.

ARROW REST:- (Archer) A small projection at the top of the bow handle where the arrow rests.

ASIAN GAMES:- An amateur sports competition identical to the Olympic Games that is held every 4 years in the interval between Olympics among nations of Asia.

ASHES:- (Cricket) A small urn containing the ashes of a bail presented to the Hon. Ivo Bligh by certain ladies of Melbourne when he took the MCC team to Australia following Australia's first victory over England in England in 1882. No doubt, the ladies' gesture was prompted by the mock obituary that appeared in 1882 in the London newspaper The Sporting Times, lamenting the death of English cricket and saying that 'the body will be cremated and the Ashes taken to Australia'. The urn is on display in the Museum at Lord's cricket ground in London. It has become traditional for Test series between Australia and England to be played for the Ashes, but the urn doesn't leave its resting place even when Australia has been victor.

ASHIWAZA:- (Judo) Technique of foot throws.

ASSIST:- (Ice Hockey) Individual point-scoring

credit to the player who makes the final pass to the goal scorer.

ASTROTURF:- (Hockey) A trademark used for a synthetic surface that is used in place of grass.

ATTACK:- (Cricket) The bowling battery at a captain's disposal. The word also refers to aggression in batting or field placings. i.e., an attacking batsman or attacking field placing (men set in close-in catching positions).
(Fencing) The initial forward movement of the weapon with an extended arm to threaten the opponent's valid target.

ATTITUDE:- (Gymnastics) A leg position in which the leg is raised forward or backward with the knee bent and turned outward.

AUSTRALIAN CRAWL:- (Swimming) Early crawl stroke; first to involve alternate vertical leg-kicks.

AVERAGE:- (Cricket) The figure reached when computing a batsman's performance in terms of runs scored per completed innings played or a bowler's performance in terms of runs conceded per wicket taken, in each case achieved by dividing the former by the latter. Usually, considered to be important yardsticks in measuring a player's achievements over a season or his career.

AWAY-SWINGER:- (Cricket) A delivery by a pace bowler that swings from the line of the stumps away towards the slips.

B

BACK:- (Archery) The side of the bow away from the shooter.

BACKBOARD:- (Basketball) The vertical surface behind the basket from which ball will bounce when shot is missed.

BACK FLIP:- (Gymnastics) A back handspring.

BACK-CHECK:- (Hockey) To skate back forward one's goal while closely defending against the offensive rushes of an opposing player.

BACK COURT :- (Basketball) The divison of the court between end line and division line which the offensive team must leave before ten seconds.
(Tennis) The area between the service line and the baseline.

BACKCOURTMAN:- (Basketball) A guard on a basket-ball team.

BACKFIELD IN MOTION:- (Football) One offensive back moving forward or more than one offensive back moving in any direction before the ball is snapped. (Illegal).

BACKFOOT:- (Cricket) In batting, in response to a short-pitched delivery, when the batsman uses his back foot to retreht close to the stumps in an effort to handle a rising ball. Usually deployed defensively, but can also be employed to play attacking back-foot strokes, i.e. the back-foot drives, the cuts, the pull and hook and the leg glide off the hip. In bowling, the foot planted down by the stumps at the begining of the delivery stride.

BACKHAND:- (Badminton) Any stroke made on the side of the body opposite the racket side.
(Tennis) Strokes hit on the left side of a right-handed player.

BACKPADDLE:- (Cycling) To paddle in a canoe in a backward direction.

BACKPLAY:- (Cricket) Playing the ball by drawing the bat backwards.

BACKSPIN:- (Tennis) Spin acquired on a ball dropping from a vertical position, which forces the ball to bounce back toward the hitter.

BACKSTROKE:- (Swimming) A swimming stroke executed on the back.

BACK STROKE:- (Cricket) A stroke played with the weight on the back foot usually off a short-pitched ball.

BACKSWING:- (Tennis) The beginning of all ground strokes and service motion requiring a backswing to gather energy for the forward swing.

BACK UP:- (Batting) The batsman at the nonstriker's end leaving his ground after the bowler has released the ball in readiness to take a run. (Fielding) The second-chance defensive movement in which a fieldsman runs into a position from where he can cover an ill-directed throw- usually in a direct line with the thrower and the target stumps-or a misfield by a teammate.

BACK WALL SHOT:- (Handball) A shot made from a rebound off the back wall.

BACKWARD:- (Cricket) Description given to field placings behind the line square of the wicket from the batsman, e.g. backward point and backward square leg. (Gymnastics) A direction of movement in which the back of the head and back lead the movement (there are a few exceptions).

BAD BALL OR PITCH:- (Baseball) A pitch outside the strike zone.

BAILS:- (Cricket) The two small pieces of turned wood or moulded plastic that sit atop the three stumps to complete a wicket.

BAG,BIG:- (Boxing) A long, suspended, padded bag used for striking practice and power of punch, both at long and short range.

BAG, PLATFORM :- (Boxing) A small,leather bag hanging from an overhead platform and used for obtaining rhythm in punching.

BAG,SWINGING:- (Boxing) A bag mounted on a flexible spring stand. It is used for hitting and avoiding a dodging object, to perfect aim and the judging of distance and for counter-punching.

BALE:- (Skiing) A metal device that presses the sole of the boot over three pins, thus securing the boot to the ski.

BALL:- (Cricket) The projectile used by the bowler to set play in motion. Usually made of a leather casing with a bound cork interior, but in the case of lower grades or cricket and for practice purposes can be made of cork alone, cork coated with plastic, or solely synthetic materials.

BALLHAWK:- (Baseball) An outfielder who covers ground.

BALL-HEEL-BALL:- (Athletics) Method in which distance runners touch the foot to ground while running.

BALK:- (Baseball) An illegal action of the pitcher which permits base runners to advance one base.

BANANA BALL:- (Golf) A slice.

BANGBOARD:- (Basketball)The glass, metal, or wood surface above and to the sides of the basket, used for carrom shots taken from an angle, particularly lay-ups.

BARANI:- (Gymnastics) A version of the aerial cartwheel or beam dismount performed without hands touching floor or beam.

BARMAID:- (Bowling) Same as sleeper.

BARONI:- (Gymnastics) A name given to a special type of half-twisting front somersault with the body in a pike position.

BASELINE:- (Basketball) The endline. (Tennis) The end line of a tennis court, located 39 ft. from the net.

BASE OPEN:- (Baseball) First base unoccupied

with second or second and third occupied.

BASKET:- (Basketball) The net suspended from the backboard; also a goal from the field which counts two points.
(Skiing) Circular portion, usually made of plastic, near the bottom end of the ski pole that prevents the pole from sinking too deeply into the snow.

BASKET BALL:- Ball used which must not weigh less than 20 ounces nor more than 22 when inflated.

BAT:- (Cricket) The implement used by the batsman to defend or attack against the ball projected at his stumps by the bowler. The blade is made of willow and the handle, spliced in at the top, of cane strips layered with rubber, bound by twine, and covered with a rubber grip. The shape of the bat has undergone many changes over the years, and changes still are being rung by batmakers in an attempt to produce an eye-catching and more marketable product. Now-a-days, bats are adorned by coloured decals in an attempt to make them readily indentifiable from the boundary and on television.

BATON:- (Athletics) The stick that is passed by a relay team.

BAT OUT:- (Bowling) Same as strike out.

BATSMAN'S PARADISE:- (Cricket) A pitch that clearly favours the batsman.

BATTERY:- (Softball) The pitcher and the catcher.

BATTING:- (Cricket) Making use of the bat in defending or attacking after the ball has been delivered by the bowler.

BATTING AVERAGE:- (Softball) The number of hits divided by the times at bat.

BATTING CREASE:- (Cricket) Also known as the popping crease;the line marked 48 inches forward of the stumps that defines the batsman's safe ground in the terms of whether he can be stumped or run out. This line is also used to determine whether a bowler has transgressed in bowling a no-ball.

BALLOONING:- The act or sport of ribbing in a balloon.

BARBELL:- (Weight lifting) A bar with adjustable weighted discs attached to each end that is used for exercise and in weight lifting.

BAR BILLIARDS:-(Billiards) A form of billiards in which some pockets are guarded by obstacles and in which an automatic device prevents the use of the balls after a certain time.

BARRAGE:- (Fencing) Fencing a fight-off.

BASELINE:- (Baseball) Any of the lines marking the area within which a baseball player must keep when running between bases.
(Tennis) The back line at each end of a court in various games.

BATTERY:- (Baseball) The pitcher and catcher of a baseball team.

BATTING:- (Cricket) 1. The act of one who bats. 2. The use of or ability with a bat.

BATTLEDORE AND SHUTTLECOCK:- (Badminton) An ancient oriental children's game that evolved into badminton.

BEAMER:- (Cricket) A fast full pitch which endangers the batsman's head, usually bowled accidentally. It is universally deplored because it is diffcult to sight and may cause serious injury.

BEARING AWAY:- (Yachting) Altering course away from the wind until the yacht begins to gybe. Also known as falling off the wind.

BEAT ATTACK:- (Fencing) A sharp blow given to the opponent's blade to create an opening for an attack.

BEAT BOARD:- (Gymnastics) A short inclined

board used for mounting the balance beam and uneven parallel bars.

BEATING:- (Sailing) Sailing as close into the wind as possible. Also known as close-hauled.

BED OF TRAMPOLINE:- (Gymnastics) A term used to refer to the woven nylon or canvas surface of the trampoline on which the performer bounces.

BED POSTS:- (Bowling) The 7-10 split.

BELL:- (Boxing) This is rung at the start of a contest, to end each round or to silence the spectators before an announcement is made from the ring. Sometimes a gong or a whistle is used instead. The bell is solely for the use of the timekeeper.

BELLY:- (Yatching) The part of a soil that swells out when filled with wind.

BELLY BOARD:- A short surfboard on which one lines rather than stands.

BELOW THE BELT:- (Boxing) The body from the top of the hips downward. Any punch here is a foul.

BENEFIT:- An entertainment game, or social event to raise funds for a person or cause.

BERMUDAN RIG:- (Yatching) A rig for a yacht carrying a high, tapering sail.

BEST BALL TOURNAMENT:- (Golf) Competition in which the better score of a partnership on each hole is used as the team score.

BETTER-BALL:- (Golf) A golf match in which one player competes against the best individual score of two or more players for each hole.

BICYCLE POLO:- A game resembling polo played on bicycle instead of horses.

BIG BALL:- (Bowling) An effective hook.

BIG EARS:- (Bowling) The 4-6-7-10 split.

BIG FILL:- (Bowling) Anything over eight on a spare.

BIG FIVE :- (Bowling) Three pins on one side and two on the other, as the 4-7 on left and 6-9-10 on right.

BIG FOUR:- (Bowling) The 4-6-7-10 split.

BILL:- (Yatching) The end of an anchor fluks or of a sailed yatch.

BIRD:- (Badminton) Another name for the shuttlecock.

BIRDIE:- (Golf) The score of one under par on a hole.

BISHOP:- (Chess) Either of two pieces of each colour in a set of chessmen having the power to move diagonally across any number of consecutive unoccupied squares.

BLANK:- (Baseball) To prevent scoring.

BLIND PASS:- (Athletics) A relay pass with the outgoing man looking forward.

BLOCK:- (Baseball) To stand in the path of the ball.
(Boxing) To use the arms, elbows, hands and wrists to minimize the effects of a blow and cause the opponent to waste his punches and energy.
(Badminton) A stroke whereby the racket is placed in front of the shuttle almost as if trying to catch it. Very little motion is used.
(Volleyball) Defensive play by players (or a player) in the forward positions who place their hands and arms above the net so that a spiked ball rebounds into the opponents' court or back to their own.

BLOCKED BALL:- (Baseball) A batted or thrown ball touched, stopped, or handled by a person not engaged in the game.

BLOCK HOLE:- (Cricket) The hole made by the batsman just behind the popping crease to mark the guard given him by the umpire.

BLOCKING:- (Rugby Football) A player on the offensive team using body or forearm to prevent a defender reaching the ballcarrier.

BLOCKING OUT :- (Basketball) Method of getting between the opponent and the basket in order to secure a rebound.

BLOOPER:- (Softball) A batted fly ball that goes just over the head of the infielders and just in front of the outfielders.

BLOW UP:- (Athletics) To run out of energy in any sporting event and thereafter perform mediocrely.

BLUE:- (Shooting) To colour gun barrels.

BOARD:- (Squash) The expression denoting a band, the top edge of which is 17 inches from the floor across the lower part of the front wall, above which the ball must be returned before the stroke is good.

BOARD-CHECKING:- (Ice Hockey) Deliberately pushing a player onto the barrier boards.

BOBBING AND WEAVING:- (Boxing) Ducking and dodging intended blows. Some fighters weave into an attack, they crouch slightly and move the shoulders as they advance, usually in an effort to get to close range.

BOBBLE:- (Baseball) To mishandle the ball-make an error.

BODY-CHECKING:- (Ice Hockey) Throwing oneself in front of an opponent to block his progress.

BODYLINE:- (Cricket) Term stemming from the tactics adopted by England's fast bowler during the 1932-33 tour of Australia: a barrage of short-pitched balls aimed at the body with a packed leg-side field devised to blunt the effectiveness of the great Australian batsman Don Bradman. The batsman has four choices in handling such a persistent attack: take evasive action, be hit by the ball,pop up a catch to the close-in-fieldsman on the leg side, or try the hook shot and risk being caught in the deep on the leg side.

BOLSA:- (Bowling) A light or thin hit.

BOGEY:- (Golf) A score of one over par on a hole (United States rules). In countries playing the British rules, a bogey is the score an average golfer should make on a hole; on easier holes, par and bogey might be the same score.

BOSIE:- (Cricket) In Australia a googly is called a 'bosie' after its inventor in the early 20th century, BJT Bosenquet. See GOOGLY.

BOTTOM:- (Athletics) Basic conditioning or basic stamina.

BOTTOM BRACKET:- (Cycling) The axle on which the chainset and pedal cranks are mounted, sited at the bottom of the seat tube.

BOTTOM POSITION:- (Wrestling) A four point stance assumed at the start of a period or when the referee signals a restart. A position of disadvantage.

BOUNCE PASS:- (Basketball) A pass which bounces once while going from sender to receiver.

BOUNCER:- (Cricket) The bouncer, or bumper, is a fast short-pitched ball which lifts to the upper part of a batsman's body or above. Much legislation has been directed over the years at restricting short bowling by fast bowlers as being dangerous.

BOUNDARY:- The limits of the match-enclosure.

BOUNDARY LINES:- (Basketball) Lines surrounding playing area.

BOUT:- (Fencing) A competition between two fencers.

BOW ARM:- (Archery) The arm that holds the bow; this would be the left arm for a right-handed person.

BOW SIGHT:- (Archery) A device attached to the bow through which the archer sights when aiming.

BOW WEIGHT:- (Archery) Designates the amount of effort (in pounds) needed to pull a bowstring for a specific distance (usually 28 inches).

BOWL:- (Cricket) To deliver the ball in a manner deemed fair by the umpires.

BOWLED:- (Cricket) If the ball, bowled by the bowler, strikes, the wicket, the batsman is bowled and the wicket is also said to be bowled.

BOWLER:- (Cricket) The player who delivers the ball to set play in motion. The style of bowling varies from player to player and fits no rigid pattern other than those decribed in the laws. In the earliest days of the game, however, it was the fashion to deliver the ball with an underarm action. In 1835, the laws were changed to allow roundarm bowling and then, in 1864, the current style of overarm was permitted for the first time.

BOWLING, CREASE:- (Cricket) The line that runs through the stumps square to the wicket or pitch, extending four feet either side of the stumps and bounderd by the 'return crease'.

BOX;- (Bowling) Synonym for frame.
(Athletics) The container in which pole vaulters plant the tips of their poles before taking off.

BOX AND ONE:- (Basketball) A defense in which one player is playing man to man and the other four players are playing zone in the lane area.

BOXING :- Modern boxing developed from the bare-knuckle prize-fights that look place in Britain during the 18th and 19th centuries. Contests are now decided by points, by the referee deciding that a boxer is outclassed.

BOXING OUT:- (Basketball) Keeping an opposing player behind you so he cannot rebound the ball.

BOYLE'S LAW:- (Underwater Diving) Law formulated by Robert Boyle governing relation between pressure and volume of a gas.

BREAK:- (Cricket) A change of direction taken by the ball after touching the ground.
(Bowling) Failure to make a strike or spare in frame.
(Athletics) Leaving the starting blocks before the gun sounds.
(Gymnastics) A point in an exercise at which a gymnast makes a mistake or has an unintentional pause.
(Boxing) A command by the referee for the men to end a prolonged clinch; it is universally used by referees. It is an offence to 'hit on the break'.
(Tennis) Relates to the act of winning a game in which the opponent serves.

BREAKDOWN:- (Wrestling) A manoeuvre in which the wrestler in the position of advantage forces the opponent flat to the mat.

BREAST STROKE:- (Swimming) A swimming stroke executed on the front by extending the arms in front of the head while drawing the kness forwards and outwards and then sweeping the arms back with palms out while kicking outwards and backwards.

BRIDGE:- (Cards) Any various card games for usually four players in two partnership that bid for the right to name a trump suit, score points for tricks made in excess of six, and play with the hand of declarer's partner exposed and played by declarer.
(Wrestling) Supporting one's weight on the feet and head, with the back arched, thus keeping the shoulders away from the mat.

BROKEN FIELD RUNNING:- (Rugby Football) Seen on punt and kick-off returns where the ball-carrier often has to dodge his way past defenders without the help of blocking from his team-mates.

BRONZE MEDAL:- A medal of bronze awarded to one who comes third in any or several competitions.

BUCKET PLAYER:- (Basketball) An offensive player who stands with his toward his basket, usually the tallest man.

BUMP BALL:- (Cricket) A ball hit hard into the ground but which leaps up and may give the appearance of being a catch.

BUGGY-WHIP ARM:- (Baseball) A loose arm.

BULLY:- (Field Hockey) A procedure for starting or restarting play in a hockey match in which two opposing players face each and alternatively strike the ground and the opponent's stick three times before attempting to gain possession of the ball.

BUMP PASS:- (Tennis) The forearm pass made on low balls.

BURGEE:- (Sailing) Small flag flown at the masthead, used to indicate the club (if triangular) or when the dinghy is racing (if square, when strictly speaking it is not a burgee but a flag).

BUTT:- (Boxing) To place the head beneath an opponent's chin and jerk upwards: a foul.

BUTTERFLY:- (Swimming) A swimming stroke executed on the front by moving both arms together forward out of the water and then pulling them back through the water whille kicking the legs up and down together.

BYES:- (Cricket) This term refers to runs scored when the ball passes the striker without either being hit or touching part of his person, whether or not a stroke has been offered.

In the instance of byes being runs off a wide or a noball, the scorer record them as wides or no-balls, not as byes.

C

C & B:- (Cricket) Caught & Bowled.

CABRIOLE:- (Gymnastics) A jump from one foot, raising the legs and bringing them together in the air (either forward, sideward, or backward) to a landing on the takeoff leg.

CADDIE:- (Golf) To serve as a caddie.

CADGE:- (Hockey & Football) A goal structure enclosed with netting.

CAGER:- (Basketball) A basketball player.

CAGOULE:- A usually calf-length hooded pullover parka worn especially for hiking in rain. It may be designed to allow the bottom to be buttoned up out of the way in fair weather.

CALISTHENICS:- (Athletics) Simple exercises done to warm up and prepare the body for activity.

CALL:- (Cricket) Used in three senses. The batsman better placed to see may 'call' his partner for a run. When several fielders converge under a high catch, the captain, to prevent confusion. 'calls' the name of the player to take it. An umpire 'calls' a no-ball, a bowler in this sense is 'called'.

CALL ONE'S SHOTS:- (Billiards) To specify the object ball that one intends to pocket and the pocket as required in certain games (as straight pool).

CAMEL SPIN:- (Gymnastics) A spin or turn in a front-scale position.

CAMPO:- A boccie court.

CAMPSITE:- A place suitable for the site of a camp.

CANT:- (Archery) The act of holding the bow tilted

or slightly turned while shooting.

CANVAS:- (Boxing) The canvas-covered mat which forms the floor of the ring.

CANVASBACK:- (Boxing) A boxer who is easily or often knocked out.

CAP:- (Cricket) Peaked headgear worn by a cricketer, usually in the colours and bearing the badge of the team for which he is playing.

CARRY:- (Badminton) An illegal shot where the shuttle does not rebound immediately off the racket at point of contact.

CARRY ONE'S BAT:- (Of a cricket batsman) To end the innings or the period of play without being out.

CARRYING THE BALL:- (Tennis) The ball must be clearly batted. If it rests momentarily in the player's hands, it is considered illegal.

CAR-TOP:- To transport a small boat on top of a car.

CARTOPPER:- A small boat that may be transported on top of a car.

CAST:- (Archery) The distance a bow can shoot an arrow.
(Gymnastics) A term used to describe movements in which the body is first piked and then extended upward and away from the point of grasp in either a forward or a backward direction.

CAST OFF:- (Boating) To untie a line or knot; to untie a boat from a mooring.

CATCH:- (Cricket) 1. To hold the ball, when hit, before it touches the ground.
2. The holding of the ball, so struck.
3. A man is described as a good or bad "catch" who generally holds or fails to hold such a ball.

CATCH-AS-CATCH-CAN:- (Wrestling) Another name for freestyle wrestling, but an expression falling out of use.

CAUGHT BEHIND:- (Cricket) To be caught by the wicket-keeper.

CAURSE RATING:- (Golf) The comparative difficulty of a specific course. Usually computed by a committee of a local association in order to have uniform handicapping for all courses within a district.

CC:- (Bowling) A 200 game.

CLEANUP HITTER:- (Softball) The number four batter in the batting order, a position usually occupied by the team's heaviest hitter.

CEILING SHOT: (Handball) A shot striking the ceiling first, then the front wall.

CENTER:- (Basketball) The player who jumps at mid-court to start each quarter of play.

CENTRE CIRCLE:- (Basketball) The mid-court area where two centers jumps for ball possession.

CENTER OF GRAVITY:- (Athletics) Point on which body can be balanced.

CENTERMAN:- (Ice Hockey) A center.

CENTER MARK:- (Tennis) A short line that extends inward from the midpoint of the baseline and that marks the edge of the area in which a player stands when serving.

CENTER SERVICE LINE:- (Tennis) The line perpendicular to the net which divides the two service courts.

CENTER STRAP:- (Tennis) A strap placed at the center of the net and anchored to the court to facilitate a constant three foot height for the net at the center.

CENTER STRIP:- (Tennis) Same as the center service line which divides the two service courts into halves.

CENTURY:- (Cricket) The scoring of hundred runs.

CENTURY (DOBULE):- (Cricket) The making of two "centuries" in the same match.

CHANCE:- (Cricket) An opportunity given by the batsman to the fieldsmen to get him out.

CHANGE-BOWLER:- (Cricket) A bowler who is only invited to bowl when presumably better men have failed.

CHANGE ENDS:- (Cricket) To bowl from one wicket, having previously bowled from the other.

CHANNELS:- (Football) Term used to describe areas of play on either side of the pitch.

CHARGING:- (Basketball) Personal contact against the body of an opponent by a player with the ball.

CHASSE:- (Gymnastics) A dance step in which a slide on one foot is followed closely and in a gallop-like rhythm by a slide on the other.

CHEEKY SINGLE:- (Cricket) When batsman run very smartly between the wicket to complete a run that appeared to be risky.

CHEESE CAKES:- (Bowling) Lanes on which strikes are easy to get.

CHENE TURN:- (Gymnastics) A three-step turn pivoting a half turn on each of the first two steps.

CHERRY:- (Cricket)The new ball, bright red and shiny like a cherry.
(Bowling) A ball that chops off the front pin of a spare and leaves standing the pin behind and/or to right or left.

CHEST GUARD:- (Cricket) Recently developed piece of batsman's equipment worn over the chest to protect him, should he be hit by a fast ball.

CHEST PASS:- (Basketball) A two-handed pass delivered with a snap of the wrist from chest level to the receiver's chest level.

CHECK OFF:- (Football) To change the play at the line of scrimmage by calling an audible.

CHECKED-SMASH:- (Badminton) Fast action is checked abruptly before impact, deceptively becoming softly pushed steep drop shot.

CHECK REIN:- (Equestrian) A rein that goes over a horse's head and serves to hold his head up or back.

CHESS:- The chessboard in made up of 64 equal squares in colour alternatively light and dark. ("white" and "black" squares respectively).
The chess board is placed batween the players in such a way that the squares in the corner to the right of each player is white.
The eight rows of squares running from one player to the other are called "files".
The eight rows of squares running at right angles to the files are called "ranks".
The rows of squares of the same colour touching at comers are called "diagonals".

CHECK SIDE:- (Billiards) British term for draw.

CHEEKPIECE:- (Shooting) A part of the stock of some firearms against which a shooter may rest his cheek while aiming and firing.

CHICKEN COOP:- (Equestrian) An obstacle for show jumping which resembles a snapped roof.

CHICKEN-FIGHT:- (Football) To repeatedly block a defensive lineman from an upright position on a pass play.

CHINAMAN:- (Cricket) A ball bowled by a left-arm spin bowler which is an off-break to a right-handed batsman.

CHIP:- (Football) A pass made by a stabbing action of the kicking foot to achieve a sharp trajectory.
(Tennis) Refers to the short chopping motion of the racket against the back and bottom side of the ball.

CHOP:- (Cricket) A batsman coming down sharply in a chopping action on a ball outside the off stump,in an effort to run it down behind point; usually between gully and the slips with a pace bowler in operation, or wide of the slip with a spinner.
(Tennis) Used in the same manner as "Chip" by many. Refers to the placement of backspin on the ball with a short high to low forward swing.

CHRISTMAS TREE:- (Bowling) The 3-7-10 for night-hander; the 2-7-10 for left-hander.

CHUCKER:- (Cricket) A bowler who has been deemed by the umpire to have thrown the ball while attempting to make a legitimate delivery.

CHUI:- (Judo) Warning for an infringement.

CINCINNATI:- (Bowling) The 8-10 split.

CIRCLE:- (Athletics) Competitive area for the shot, discus and hammer.
(Gymnastics) A movement in which the body (or sometimes a part of the body, such as the legs) travels completely around a point of support.

CIRCLE EIGHT:- (Skating) A school figure which requires the skater to skate a full circle on one skate in one direction and then a full circle in another direction on the other skate so that the 2 circles form a figure eight.

CIRCLE PASS:- (Football) A pass thrown to a receiver running a cirlce pattern.

CLEAN:- (Weight Lifting) The act of cleaning a weight, an exercise in which a weight is cleaned.

CLEAN BOWLED:- (Cricket) To be bowled by a ball which hits the wickets without previously touching the bat or person.

CLEAN GAME:- (Bowling) Complete game with no open frames.

CLEAR:- (Badminton) A high shot (or lob) which falls close to the back line.

CLEARANCE:- (Athletics) Distance or area between the body and an object (usually a cross bar.)

CLEAT:- (Sailing) Fitting to which a rope may be secured.

CLINCH:- (Boxing) To go into a hold, usually after a mishit from one or both fighters. The object of a clinch is to trap the opponent's arms so that he cannot use them. Prolonged holding or clinching and ignoring an instruction from the referee to break may result in disqualification.

CLIP:- (Cricket) To firmly strike the ball off the toes into the onside.

CLIPPING:- (Rugby Football) Bringing down an opponent, who is not carrying the ball, by throwing the body across the back of his legs. It is illegal, and brings a 15-yards penalty.

CLONK:- (Badminton) Backhand attacking net shot, short rebound action, no follow-through.

CLOSE:- (Cricket) To declare the innings closed with batsmen still intact. Also the end of a day's play, the close of play.

CLOSED POSITION:- (Athletics) A powerful throwing position for shot and discus men in which the right shoulder and hip are back.

CLOSURE:- (Cricket) The captain of the batting side may declare his innings closed at any time during the match.
If a side doesn't have a big enough lead to enforce the follow-on (See FOLLOW-ON), this law allows a captain to forfeit his second innings.

CLOTHESLINE:- (Bowling) Same as left- and right-hand picket fence.

CLOUT SHOOTING:- (Archery) A sype of shooting that uses a target 48 ft in diameter, laid on the ground at distance of 180 yards for men and 140 or 120 yards for women. Usually 36 arrows (6 ends with 6 arrows) are shot per round.

CLEAN-AND-JERK:- (Weight Lifting) To lift a usually specified amount of weight in the clean and jerk.

CLUB PLAYER:- (Tennis) A tennis player who regularly plays at a club rather than on a professional tour.

CLUB SPORT:- (Athletics) An inter collegiate sport that is not a part of the regular school athletic programme and that is not funded by the school but is run wholly by the student participants.

COCK FEATHER:- (Archery) Now called the "index feather." The feather that is set at a right angle to the arrow nock; differently colored than other two feathers.

CODY:- (Gymnastics) A name given to a backward somersault on the trampoline executed from a front drop landing.

COLTS:- (Cricket) Young and untrained cricketers.

COMMITTING A DEFENDER:- (Football) Ensuring that an opponent is brought into play by moving towards him.

COMPULSORY EXERCISE:- (Gymnastics) The term used to refer to a competitive gymnastics exercise that every competitor must perform.

CONDITIONS:- (Cricket) The terms agreed upon by both teams before a game and by both participating countires before a touring party arrives to play a Test Series.

CONTINUITY:- (Gymnastics) A term used to refer to the smoothness or flowing quality of a routine or series. A series is said to possess continuity if it is not interrupted by undesirable pauses, stops, or extra movements.

CONTROL:- (Softball) The ability of a pitcher to throw the ball to a desired area when pitching.
(Wrestling) One wrestler is positioned in such a way that his opponent is immobilized or restrained.

CO-ORDINATION:- (Athletics) Well adjusted and efficient muscle movements.

CONDITIONED PLAY:- (Football) A training exercise where a condition is imposed.

CONTAIN:- (Cricket) To hold an opponent in check; to prevent an opponent from scoring, advancing, or mounting a successful attack.

CONSOLATION RACE:- (Athletics) A race at the close of an athletic meeting, for which all may enter without extra fee who have competed in previous events but have failed to win a prize.

CORNER:- (Field Hockey) A play following certain infringements of the rules; the formation used in such a play.

CORNER KICK OR CORNER:- (Football) A free kick awarded to the attacking team from the corner area when a defender drives the ball beyond his own goal line.

CORNER PLAYERS:- (Basketball) Tall players who are responsible for the rebounding and shooting phases of the team's operation. They make up the sides of the offensive set-up.

CORNER SHOT :- (Squash) A shot in racketball or squash racket that is aimed at a front corner of the court so as to hit the side wall and then low on the front wall and drop to the floor.

CORNER THROW:- (Team Handball) When the ball is played over his own goal line by a defending player (except the golkeeper), on either side of the goal, the game is restarted by means of a throw from the corner of the court by one o the attacking players. The player must place one foot on the corner and throw the ball in, using either hand.

CORNISH:- (Wrestling) A form of wrestling in jackets practised in the West of England.

CORPS-A-CORPS:- (Fencing) Physical contact between two fencers at close quarters.

COUNTER:- (Wrestling) A block or a movement which prevents the execution of a manoeuvre by the opponent.

COUNTER PARRY:- (Fencing) A circular parry that deflects an attacking blade into a line opposite to that of a simple parry.

COURT:- (Basketball) The playing area.

COURT PLAYER:- (Team Handball) Member of the handball team actually playing on the court, except the goalie.

COVER-DRIVE:- (Cricket) An Attacking stroke off the front or back foot looking to hit the ball through the covers region.

COVER-POINT:- (Cricket) A fieldsman on the off-side, somewhat in front of the batsman.

COVERING:- (Field Hockey) Defensive anticipatory position much nearer the defending goal than the play at that given time. As opposed to marking.

COVERS:- (Cricket) The materials used to protect the pitch or wicket and its immediate surrounding from the ravages of the weather.

COW SHOT:- (Cricket) See. AGRICULTURAL SHOT.

CRADLE:- (Cricket) The implement shaped roughly like a large cradle used in fielding practice to offer players at both ends the chance to develop their skills in catching. When the ball is thrown on to the cradle, it comes off at unexpected angles to the group at the other end.
(Wrestling) A pin hold executed by pulling the opponent's head and leg together and holding his shoulders to the mat.

CREATING SPACE:- (Football)Increasing the distance from opponents.

CREEPER:- (Bowling) Same as powder puff.

CREEPING:- (Archery) Letting the drawing hand move forward at the release.

CREST:- (Archery) The archer's indentifying marks shown just below the fletchings on the arrow.

CROSS:- (Football) To play the ball from a wide position into a more central position.
(Boxing) The breaking of an agreement by one of the two boxers making it. Usually the agreement is to arrange the result of their contest in advance.
(Gymnastics) A position in which the breadth axis of the performer is perpendicular to the long axis of the apparatus.

CROSS ALLEY:- To aim to the left from extreme right-hand corner of approach, or to the right from extreme left-hand corner.

CROSS BAT:- (Cricket) When the batsman plays across the line of a ball with the bat not perpendicular.

CORSS BODY:- (Wrestling) A means of breaking the opponent down and controlling him until a pin can be applied; it is executed by grapevining one of his legs, stretching across his back,and holding his opposite arm just above the elbow.

CROSS-COURT:- (Badminton) A shot in which the bird crosses the net in a diagonal direction.
(Tennis) A shot hit diagonally from one corner of the court over the net into the opposite corner of the court.

CROSS OVER:- (Football) Two attacking players moving in different directions pass each other.

CROSSCOURT SHOT:- (Squash)A shot hit to the front wall so as to land in the other side of the court.

CROSS FACE:- (Wrestling) A manoeuvre used either as a counter or as an offensive breakdown by reaching across the side of the opponent's face and grasping his opposite arm just above the elbow.

CROTCH BALL OR CROTCH SHOT:- (Handball) A shot that hits a crotch.

CROTCH:- (Handball) The juncture of any two playing surfaces, as between the floor and any wall.

CROTCH SHOT:- (Handball) A ball that strikes the front wall and floor simultaneously. Not good.

CROTECHED:- (Of a billiard ball) Lying within a crotch.

CROUCH-DEFENCE:- (Badminton) Standing nearer to net straight-on, racket up in front of face ready to defend either side.

CROW HOPPER:- (Bowling) A clawlike, loose grip on ball.

CRUMBLE:- (Cricket) When a pitch surface starts to break up, usually late in the game and often favouring the spin bowler, because it can offer his deliveries more grip or bite.

CUE:- (Badminton) Signal given of player's next shot by shuttle position in court and in relation to body stance and movement.

CURLER:- Someone who plays curling.

CUT:- (Gymnastics) A movement in which one or both legs swing between the hand or hands and a piece of requipment. In a cut-on the performer starts on the floor and ends on the equipment. In a cut-off the performer dismounts during the cut.

CUT OFF THE ANGLE:- (Tennis) To move forward quickly against an opponent's cross-court shot, allowing the player to hit the ball near the center of the court rather than near the sidelines.

CUT THROAT:- (Handball) A three-man game in which the service plays against the other two players, with each player keeping an individual score. Not played in official competition.

CUTOVER:- (Fencing) A disengagement attack in which the blade is lifted over the defender's foil. Also called a coupe.

CUT-OFF:- (Softball) A throw from the outfield that is intercepted by an infielder for the purpose of throwing out a runner other than the intended runner.

CUSHION:- (Football) To control the ball by withdrawing the surface in contact with the ball.

CUMBERLAND-AND-WESTMORELAND:- (Wrestling) Form of wrestling in which competitors start with their arms clasped behind each other's backs and maintain their grip throughout a bout.

CUSP:- (Skating) the point in a turn (as a three turn or bracket) at which a skater changes from one edge to the other on the same foot.

CUT:- (Cricket) In pace bowling, when the ball deviates on pitch because the bowler has imparted varyingspins on it. More readily available on the softer wicket surface in England than in other parts of the cricketing world. In batting, the range of scoring strokes aimed from point to just wide of the wicket-keeper and played with a cross-bat motion to short-pitched deliveries outside the off stump. The 'square cut' is aimed at the point region, the 'back cut' fine of the gully, and the 'late cut' is played very late and with a chopping motion to angle the ball just wide of a single slip or the wicketkeeper.

(Basketball) A quick offensive move by a player trying to get free for a pass.

CUT-DOWN:- (Athletics) The dropping of the lead

leg in hurdle clearance.

CUT LINE:- (Squash) A line set out upon the front wall, the top edge of which is 6.6 feet above the floor, and extending the full width of the court.

CUTMAN:- (Boxing) A second who specializes in stopping the bleeding of cuts.

CUTTER:- (Bowling) A sharp-breaking hook that cuts down the pins.
(Basketball) The player diving for the basket anticipating a pass from a teammate.

CUTTHROAT:- An informal game (as of handball or billiards) in which each of 3 people plays for himself against the other 2.

CUT-UP (THE WICKET):- (Cricket) To spoil the turf where the ball is likely to pitch, by running over it.

CUTTERS:- (Cricket) Deliveries that deviate off the pitch because a pace bowler has made them spin.

CYCLING:- The road racing bicycle is a light vehicle, having no mudguards. It has lighter wheels with narrow rims and plentiful of spokes. It has slimmer and tubular tyres. It has double clutch and ten gears.
The gearing depends on the racer's height, weight and power. The bicycle is capable of travelling 4.7 to 7.93 m for each turn of the pedal depending on the gears used.
The track racing cycle has neither brakes nor gears and is thus lighter than the road racer. Its frame is lower and crankshaft higher to avoid touching the ground when turning. It travels 7 to 8m for each turn of pedal. The rear wheel clutch is missing but one fixed sprocket is provided.

D

'D':- The arc marked outside the penalty- area.

DAISY-CUTTER:- (Cricket)The same as "sneak" or "grub." A ball pitched close to the bowler's foot, which runs along the ground without bouncing.

DAN:- (Judo) Degree.

DANGER AREA:- (Cricket) This area of the pitch is four feet forward of the popping crease and extends one foot either side of the line from centre stump to centre stump into which bowlers must not run after delivering the ball and fieldsman and batsman must not run in the course of their activities. Also see Unfair Play for the umpire's procedure should any player violate the area.

DAVIS CUP:- (Tennis) An international team contest for men's national tennis teams; also the trophy itself.

DEAD APPLE OR BALL:- (Bowling) Ball which fades when it hits pins; ineffective ball.

DEAD BALL:- (Cricket)The ball is "dead" when it is out of play.

DEAD-BALL LINE:- (Soccer) A line at either end of a rugby field parallel to and 5.5 - 2.3 metres (about 6-25 yeards beyond the goal line).

DEAL:- (Cards) The act or right of distributing cards to players in a card game.

DEADWOOD :- (Bowling) Pins that have been knocked over by the ball and are lying on the alley or in pit.

DECATHLON:- (Athletics) A men's athletic contest in which each competitor competes in 10 events, the 100m, 400m, and 1500m runs, the 110m high hurdles, and the javelin, discus, shot put, pole vault, high jumps, and long jump.

DECEIVE:- (Fencing) To offensively avoid contact by a defender's blade.

DECLARE:- 1. To announce (e.g. a trump suit) in a card game.
2. A captain or team to decide to end one's side's innings in cricket before all the batsman are out.
Also to close an innings.

DECOY RUN:- (Football) A run to take a defender out of position with the aim of creating space for a colleague.

DEEP:- (Tennis) A shot that bounces near the baseline on ground strokes and near the service line on serves.

DEFAULT;- (Tennis) A player who fails to play his scheduled match in a tournament and thus forfeits his position.

DEFENCE:- (Cricket) The action of a batsman offering a stroke with no thought to scoring runs. Also in captaincy, setting a field and directing an attack aimed not at taking wickets, but at saving runs.

DEFENSE HIT:- (Field Hockey) Term used to denote play when the ball goes over the goal line under certain circumstances. The ball is placed 16 yards from the end line opposite the spot where it left the field.

DEFENSIVE TEAM:- (Basketball) The team not in possession of the ball.

DELAY GAME:- (Basketball) Slowing the game up by a deliberate offense that does allow lay-ups or sometimes any good percentage shot within from 6 to 12 feet of the basket (used to alter the tempo against a team that likes to run hard).

DELIVERY:- (Cricket) A ball bowled.

DENIAL DEFENSE:- (Basketball) Aggressive individual defense where the defensive player works hard to keep the offensive player from receiving a pass.

DERAILLEUR:- (Cycling) Gearing mechanism in which the chain is 'derailled' onto chainwheels of varying sizes to effect changes in gear. Derailleurs are used for both front and rear changers.

DEUCE:- (Tennis) Scoring term used when the game score is 40-40.

DIG:- (Volleyball) A shot played just before the ball would have hit the ground.

DIME STORE:- (Bowling) The 1-2-10 split.

DINK:- (Tennis) A ball normally hit very softly and relatively high to ensure its safe landing.
(Volleyball) A soft shot off the fingertips used when faking a spike.

DINNER:- Refers to the break between innings in a day-night game when, in fact, the players can have meal if they wish.

DIRECTOR:- (Fencing) The official in charge of a jury. In EUROPE the director is called the president.

DISCUS:- (Athletics) A solid disc weighing 2 Kg for men and 1 Kg for women, 22cm across for men and 18 cm for women that is thicker in the centre than at the perimeter and is thrown for distance in an athletic field event; also this event.

DISENGAGEMENT:- (Fencing) An attack in which the blade passes under the defender's foil.

DISHING:- (Cycling) Offsetting the hub of the rear wheel to allow correct alignment of the block.

DISGUISE:- (Football) Concealing your intentions by pretending to do one thing and then doing something else.

DISLOCATE:- (Gymnastics) A movement in which the body, while suspended from a fixed point by the hands, makes a complete circle or revolution, rotating around the sholulder joint, in a backward direction.

DISMOUNT:- (Gymnastics) The last movement in an asymmetric bars or beam exercise, when the gymnast jumps down from the apparatus.

DIVE CENTRE:- (Underwater Diving) Commercial base for sport diving usually arranging dives and dive boats and having a dive shop and lecture room.

DIVE LEADER:- (Underwater diving) Person in charge of another, or small group, underwater.

DIVE SHOT:- (Team Handball) A means of trying to score a goal by launching the entire body into the air toward the goal in an attempt to gain more distance.

DIVING:- The competitive sport of executing prescribed gymnastic manoeuvres during a plunge into water from a board.

DIVISION LINE:- (Basketball) To center line on the court dividing the area in half.

DIVOT:- (Golf) Sod cut with the clubhead when executing or attempting to execute a shot.

DODGE:- (Field Hockey) Play used to evade an opponent while maintaining control of the ball.

DOGLEG:- (Golf) A golf hole having an angled fairway.
(Bowling) The 1-2-10 leave.

DOJO:- (Judo) Judo Practice hall.

DOLPHIN KICK:- (Swimming) Leg action- vertical symmetrical movements - used in butterfly stroke.

DONKEY-DROP:- (Cricket) A delivery from a slow bowler that loops very high in the air.

DOUBLE:- Two strikes in sucession.

DOUBLE-CROSS:- (Boxing) The breaking of an agreement by both people making it. There is a boxing joke that whereas an illiterate boxer may sign with a cross, a manager uses a double-cross.

DOUBLE FOUL:- (Volleyball) Infraction of rules by both teams during the same play.

DOUBLE FAULT:- Two consecutive serivce faults. resulting in the loss of a point (e.g. in tennis) or of the service (*e.g.* in squash).
(Basketball) When two opponents commit personal fouls against each other at the same time.

DOUBLE HIT:- (Badminton) An illegal shot where in the shuttle is hit twice in succession on the same stroke.

DOUBLE-LEG TAKEDOWN:- (Wrestling) A takedown performed by gaining control of both of the opponent's legs.

DOUBLE PINOCHLE:- (Bowling) The 4-6-7-10 split.

DOUBLE PINOCHLE WITH THE ACE OF SPADES:- (Bowling) The 4-6-7-10 split plus the 9-pin.

DOUBLE PLAY:- (Softball) Two consecutive put-outs occuring between the time the ball leaves the pitcher's hand and its return to the pitcher.

DOUBLE-TEAM:- (Basketball) To put two defensive men on one offensive player.

DOUBLE TOUCH:- (Fencing) A situation in which both fencers had equal right of way and both landed touches. No point is awarded.

DOUBLE WICKET:- (Cricket) The game as usually played.

DOUBLE WOOD:- (Bowling) One pin directly behind another; the 2-8 and the 3-9 leaves.

DOUBLES:- (Tennis) A game between two pairs of players.

DOUBLES LINE:- (Tennis) The outside sideline on a court-used in doubles only.

DOUBTFUL TOUCH:- (Fencing) This is the decision whenever the polling of the jury does not produce a majority opinion. No point is awarded.

DOWN:- (Rugby Football) Action is broken up into individual plays called downs. A down starts with the snap of the ball through the centre's legs, and continues until the ball next becomes dead-e.g.because the ball-carrier has been tackled, or because a toudown has been scored. The average down lasts only about 15 seconds.

DOWN-THE-LINE:- (Tennis) A shot hit near a sideline which travels close to, and parallel to, the same line from which the shot was initially hit.

DOWN TUBE:- (Cycling) The tube of the frame extending from the head tube to the bottom bracket.

DRAW:- 1. To require (a specified depth) to float in.
2. To take (cards) from a stack or from the dealer.
3. To bend (a bow) by pullng back the string.
4. To strike (a ball) so as to impact a backward spin.
5. To leave (a contest) undecided, specify because of an equality in scores; also to have equal scores in.
6. To leave (a contest) undecided; specify to leave (a cricket match) unresolved through lack of time.
7. To drive game out of a sail to swell out in a wind .. to come out even in a contest.
8. (Archery) The act of pulling the bow string back into the anchor position.

DRIBBLE:- (Football) An attacker taking the ball past one or more opponents.
(Basketball) The act by an offensive player of bouncing the ball to the floor.
(Field Hockey) Series of short strokes used to take the ball down the field while maintaining constant control of it.

DRINKS:- The break in play, usually about midway through a session, when drinks are brought onto the ground for the refreshment of the players. On very hot days, the captains and umpires may agree to two drinks breaks during one session.

DRIVE:- 1. To cause to move in desired direction.
2. To search (a district) for game.
3. To propel (an object of play) swiftly (drove the ball towards goal).
4. To hit (a golf ball) from the tee esp with a driver.
5. To play a drive in cricket at (a ball) or at the bowling of (a bowler) to drive an object of play (e.g. a golf ball).
6. (Badminton) A hard-driven stroke which just clears the net and does not rise high enough for an opponent to smash.
7. (Field Hockey) Hard stroke with a back swing. May be done to right, left, or straight ahead.
8. (Tennis) An offensive shot hit with extra force.

DRIVE-IN:- (Basketball) To travel at top speed toward the basket in an effort to score.

DRIVE LEG:- (Athletics) The leg exerting the force during stride.

DRIVE SERVE:- (Badminton) The flight of a serve similar to a drive. Used mostly in doubles from the right court to a right-handed player.

DRIVE SHOT:- (Handball) A power shot against the front wall which rebounds fast, low, and in a straight line.

DROP:- 1. Of a card to become played by reason of the obligation to follow suit.
2. Of a ball to roll into a hole or basket.
3. To move with a favouring wind or current or blow 2 to cause (a high card) to fall 3 to

toss or roll (a ball) into a hole or basket 4 to score (a goal) with a drop kick 5 to drop a catch offered by (a batsman).
4. (Badminton) A shot which barely clears the net and immediately drops sharply.

DROP ONE SHORT:- (Cricket) In fast bowling, to fire in a short-pitched delivery.

DROP SHOT:- A delicately hit ball or shuttlecock (e.g. tennis, badminton, or squash) that drop quickly after crossing the net or dies after hitting a wall.

DROP VOLLEY:- (Tennis) A volley hit in such a manner as to drop just over the net with little or no forward bounce.

DUCK:- (Boxing) To bend quickly esp. to avoid a blow.
(Cricket) A score of nought. Originating from 'duck's egg', an expression dating back to the 1860s.

DUNK SHOT :- (Basketball) To throw a basketball into the basket from above the rim.

DUTCH 200 :- (Bowling) A 200 game made by alternate strikes and spares.

DUTCHMAN :- Same as Dutch 200.

E

EAGLE:- (Golf) A score for a hole played in two strokes under par.

EASTERN STYLE:- (Athletics) A once popular method of high jumping.

EDGE:- 1. To incline (a ski) sideways so that one edge cuts into the snow.

EIGHT-TEN:- (Bowling) The 8-10 split.
2. To hit (a ball or the bowling of a bowler) in cricket with the edge of the bat, especially so as to give a catch.

END:- (Archery) A specified number of arrows shot at one time or from one position before retrieval of arrows.

END LINES:- Boundary lines at either end of the court.

ENDURANCE:- (Athletics) Strength and ability to perform work over a long period.

ENGAGEMENT:- (Fencing) A held contact of blades when neither fencer is attacking.

EPEE:- (Fencing) One of the three competitive weapons. Only the electrical version is used in meets. The bell is large and the entire body is valid target. There is no right of way.

ERROR:- (Softball) A misplay or mistake by the defensive team that results in prolonging the turn at bat of the batter or the time on base of the baserunner.
(Tennis) A mistake made by a player during competition.

ESCAPE:- (Wrestling) Coming from a position of disadvantage to a neutral position.

EVENT:- 1. Any of the contests in a sporting programme or tournament.
(Equestrian) Of a horse or rider to take part in an equestrian event, to enter (a horse or rider) in an equestrian event.

EXTRAS:- (Cricket) Those runs not scored by the batsman, that is byes, leg-byes, wides, and no-balls. Called 'sundries' in Australia.

EXTRA TIME:- A period of time added on to the end of match in certain competitions to resolve a draw.

F

FACE:- (Archery) The part of the bow facing the shooter.

FACE HOLD:- (Wrestling) An illegal hold in which the mouth, nose, or eyes are covered.

FACE OF RACKET:- (Tennis) The hitting surface of the racket.

FACE OFF:- To take part in a face-off. (The opposing centers face-off after a goal.)
(Ice Hockey) Method of starting or restarting play, when the referee drops the puck on the ice between two opposing players.

FACE PLATE:- (Diving) The glass or plastic front of a skin diver's face mask.

FAIRWAY:- (Golf) The course between the teeing ground and the putting green, exclusive of hazards.

FAITH, HOPE AND CHARITY:- Same as Christmas tree.

FAKE:- Any body movement to deceive an opponent.

FALL:- (Wrestling) Another name for a pin, when a competitor has both his shoulders pressed to the floor.

FALL NELSON:- (Wrestling) A means of turning the opponent to his back by prying an arm upward, using his head as a fulcrum.

FAST BREAK:- A type of offense used, usually starting from defensive team's basket.

FAST MEDIUM:- (Cricket) A pace bowler whose speed of delivery ranks somewhere between medium-paced and fast.

FAST POOL:- (Swimming) Swimming bath with qualities tending to minimize wavemaking.

FAT:- (Golf) The broad part of a putting green away from the hole.

FAULT:- (Squash) A service that strikes the front wall between the tin and the cut line; or lands short of the short line; or lands in the server's court.
(Badminton) Any infraction of the rules, either on the serve or after the shuttle has been put in play, the penalty for which is loss of serve or point.
(Handball) An illegally served ball.
(Tennis) A serve which lands out of bounds or is not hit properly.

FEATHERWEIGHT:- (Boxing) A boxer or weight lifter who competes in the featherweight division.

FEED:- To pass a ball or puck to a teammate who is in position or who has an opportunity to score.

FEEDER:- A player who feeds a teammate.

FEINT:- To deceive an opponent by making a feint.
(Basketball) As in Fake, any body movement to deceive the opponent.
(Fencing) Any movement of the blade or body that will obtain a parry or other reaction from an opponent.

FELL RACE:- (Athletics) A single event in fell running.

FENCE POSTS:- (Bowling) Same as bed posts.

FENCING MEASURE:- (Fencing) The distance that fencers normally maintain between each other for most effective swordplay.

FENCING POSITION:- (Fencing) The position in which a fencer stands on guard covering a particular line of attack.

FIELD:- The ground on which the game is played. Also refers to the placement of fieldsmen. For positions in the field.
(Athletics) Area of participation, as contrasted with the running track.

FIELD GOAL:- (Bowling) Sending ball between the pins of a split and hitting neither of them.
(Basketball) A basket scored from the floor.

FIELDSMAN:- (Cricket) In the fielding or bowling side, all but the bowler and wicket-keeper. Also called "fielder."

FIELD ARROW:- (Archery) An arrow intended for field archery use and normally having a constant-diameter shaft, a field point, and large feathers.

FIELD EVENT:- (Athletics) An event other than a race including the high jump, pole, vault, long jump,triple jump, shot put, discus throw, javelin throw, hammer throw, and weight throw.

FIELD GENERAL:- (Football) A football quarterback.

FIELDING:- (Field Hockey) Controlling an approaching ball before it is passed or played.

FILL :- (Bowling) The number of pins knocked down following a spare.

FILL A FRAME:- (Bowling) To get a strike or spare in a given frame.

FINGER HOLD:- (Wrestling) An illegal hold that involves any bending of the opponent's thumb or fingers except when grasping the opponent's hand in an attempt to break a hold.

FINGER TAB:- (Archery) A leather flap worn on the drawing hand to protect the fingers and provide a smooth release of the bow string.

FIRE OUT:- (Football) Of an offensive lineman to move off the ball quickly and forcefully at the snap.

FIREPOWER:- The scoring action or potential of a team.

FIRING LINE:- (Shooting) A line which is a specified distance in front of targets and behind which competitors must ramain in shooting.

FIRST AND TEN:- (Rugby Football) The beginning of a series of downs: first down and 10 yards to gain. A gain of 4 yards on a first down will bring up a second-and six' situation.

FIT-IN-SHOT :- (Bowling) Any spare requiring exact placement of the ball between two pins to make the shot.

FIXED WHEEL:- (Cycling) Removal of the freewheel mechanism such that the pedals and wheels turn together.

FLAG:- (Golf) Banner on top of the flagstick identifying the cup.

FLANK:- (Gymnastics) A term used to describe a movement, stunt, or position in which the side of the body is toward the apparatus.

FLANK CIRCLE:- (Gymnastics) A double leg circle performed on the pommel horse while the performer faces continuously in one direction.

FLANK VAULT:- (Gymnastics) A vault sideways over a vaulting horse in which the gymnast goes over the horse with his legs out to one side and pushes off with one hand.

FLANKER BACK:- (Rugby Football) A back positioned wide to act as a pass receiver.

FLARE:- (Football) A short pass thrown to a back who is running toward the sideline at or behind the line of scrimmage.

FLAT:- (Athletics) Level ground.

FLAT BOW:- (Archery) A bow made with the sam thickness throughout its length-compare LONGBOW.

FLAT FOOTED:- (Athletics) Landing on heel and ball of foot simultaneously.

FLAT KILL:- (Handball) A kill shot made to rebound very low off the front wall.

FLAT SHOT:- (Tennis) A ball hit in such a manner as not to rotate when travelling through the air.

FLAT APPLE OR BALL:- (Bowling) Same as dead apple or ball.

FLATS:- (Athletics) Track shoes without spikes.

FLECHE:- (Fencing) An attack in which the rear foot crosses in front of the leading foot. It is often followed by a short run because of the momentum developed. Potentially dangerous, this attack is not recommended for beginners.

FLETCHINGS:- (Archery) The feathers of the arrow, which give guidance to its flight.

FLIC-FLAC:- (Gymnastics) A back handspring.

FLICK:- (Field Hockey) A wrist stroke having no back swing. Ball rises slightly. Stick is brought around the ball during execution. Good for close shooting or passing to a marked player.

FLICK SERVE:- (Badminton) A fast low serve made with a flick of the wrist at the moment of contact. It is commonly used for deception in order to pass an opponent who is playing close to the net.

FLIGHT THROUGH:- (Basketball) To stay with the player being guarded despite his use of a pick or screen, by forcing one's way through between the player and his picker or screener.

FLIGHT SHOOTING:- (Archery) Shooting an arrow the farthest possible distance.

FLIP:- (Gymnastics) A common term for somersault.

FLOATER:- (Bowling) A ball that goes where the lane lets it go.

FLOOR:- (Boxing) To knock down an opponent.

FLOOR HOCKEY:- A version of Ice Hockey played by children on a floor without the use of skates.

FLUTTER KICK:- (Swimming) A kick used in the crawl and backstroke in which the legs are alternately moved past each other.

FLY KILL:- (Handball) A kill shot made by hitting the ball before it bounces.

FLYAWAY:- (Athletics) Act of leaving the pole at the height of a vault.

FOLLOW-ON:- (Cricket) This term describes the option of a side in a four innings match to require the opposition to follow its innings after trailing on the first innings by 200 runs in a match of five days, 150 runs in a three- or four-day match, 100 runs in a two-day match, and seventy-five runs in a one-day match.

FOLLOW SHOT:- (Billiards) A shot in which the cue ball is made to continue forward after striking an object ball.

FORWARD PASS:- (Rugby Football) One forward pass is allowed during each play. It is usually thrown by the quarterback, using a regular one-handed throwing motion. In a well-thrown pass the ball travels pointed and forward, spinning in flight. Accurate passes of up to 60 yards can be thrown. The pass must be caught before it hits the ground. The down is lost on an incomplete forward pass, i.e. when it is not held.

FOOT FAULT:- (Badminton) Illegal position or movement of the feet by either the server or receiver.

(Tennis) Illegal foot movement before service that is penalized by the loss of that particular serve. Common foot faults are: stepping on or ahead of the baseline before the ball has been contacted: and running along the baseline before serving.

FOOT SWEEP:- (Judo) A throw in which the defender grabs the attacker by the lapels as the attacker is stepping forward and sweeps his front foot out from under him just as he is shifting his weight to it.

FOOZLE:- (Golf) A bungling stroke.

FORCE OUT:- (Softball) An out as a result of a defensive player with the ball tagging a runner or the base to which the baserunner must go because the batter became a baserunner.

FORCING SHOT:- (Tennis) A shot that forces an opponent to be on the defensive or out of position for a subsequent shot.

FOREARM PASS:- (Volleyball) A pass made off the forearms. Used to play served balls, hard-driven spikes, or any low ball.

FORECADDIE:- (Golf) A caddie stationed down the fairway to point out where the ball lands.

FORECOURT:- (Tennis) The area between the net and the service line.

FOREHAND:- (Badminton) Any stroke made on the racket on side of the body.
(Tennis) The stroke hit on the right side of a right-handed player.

FORKS:- (Cycling) The extensions of the headset, on which the front wheel is mounted.

FORMATION:- (Football) An alignment of players on offence or defence at the beginning of each play (also called set).

FORWARD:- (Basketball) A player's position; the player in that position.

FORWARD:- (Gymnastics) A direction of movement in which the face or chest leads the movement.

FORWARD STROKE:- (Cricket) A stroke played with the weight on the front foot, the left foot in the case of a right-handed batsman.

FOUL:- (Basketball) A rule infraction which results in the fouled player's being awarded one or two free throws at his basket. Each successful foul throw is attempted.
(Athletics) A competitive effort wasted due to an infracton of a rule.
(Field Hockey) Infringement of rules. Penalty may be a free hit short corner, or penalty stroke.
(Football) An act against the laws of the game. An infringement or attempted infringement of these laws. The referee can award a direct or indirect free kick when a foul occurs, while also having the power to take disciplinary action if he sees fit. He can caution players or eject them.

FOUL THROW:- (Atletics) A throw that is counted as a trial but is not measured because the competitor fouled.

FOUNDATION:- (Bowling) A strike in the ninth frame.

FOUR - SIX:- (Bowling) The 4-6 split.

FOUR-TIMER:- (Bowling) Four strikes in a row.

FRAME:- (Tennis) The rim of the racket head plus the handle of the racket.

FREE:- (Swimming) Short for freestyle.

FREE BALL:- (Volleyball) A return of a ball by the opponent that my easily be handed.

FREE HIT:- (Field Hockey) A play following certain infringements of rules. Taken by a player on the team fouled against.

FREESTYLE:- (Wrestling) The most popular type of wrestling, and one of the three styles recognized by the FILA.
(Swimming) Common term for front crawl stroke.

FREE THROW:- (Basketball) A foul shot from the foul line with no hindrance by the defensive team.
(Free Throw) A throw awarded to the opposing team when the other team is in violation of certain rules of the game.

FREE THROW AREA:- (Basketball) The free throw lane sometimes including also the free throw circle.

FREE-THROW LINE :- (Team Handball) The broken line parallel to the goal-area line at an extra distance of 10 feet; from this line free throws awarded near the goal area are taken.

FOOTBALL:- The pitch is rectangular in shape, its length varying between 110 and 120 yards and width between 70 yards. The outer lines shall be 5 lines thick. The longer lines are called touch lines and shorter lines are called goal lines. The line which divides the court in two equal parts is called halfway line. A circle with 10 yards radius is marked in the centre of the field. The goal shall be 20 yards long and 6 yards wide. The penalty area shall be marked around the goal area.

FREE THROW CIRCLE:- (Basketball) Either of the 2 restraining circles that are bisected by the free throw lines.

FROG HEAD BALANCE:- (Gymnastics) A position identical to the frog balance but with the head touching the mat for additional support.

FRONT:- (Gymnastics) Terms used to describe a movement, stunt, or position in which the front of the body is facing the apparatus.

FRONT COURT:- (Basketball) The area of the court between the offensive team's division line and the basket.

FRONT CROSS:- (Athletics) Finnish method of getting the body into position for javelin throwing.

FRONT FOOT:- (Cricket) In bowling, the foot closest to the batsman in the delivery stride; in batting, the foot closest to the bowler when taking stance.

FRONT RUNNER:- (Athletics) One who can run well leading and setting pace.

FULL-AND-BY :- (Sailing) Sailing close hauled but with sails full, the course being altered as the wind direction changes.

FULL NELSON:- (Wrestling) A hold allowed in senior amateur wrestling in which a wrestler places both arms beneath his opponent's armpits and clasps his hands behind his opponent's neck.

FULL TOSS OR FULL PITCH:- (Cricket) A ball which reaches the batsman without touching the ground.

FUMBLE:- (Rugby Football) When the ball-carrier drops the ball or has it fairly knocked out of his hands.

FUNGO BAT:- (Softball) A lightweight bat used in hitting balls to fielders during practice.

FURL:- To roll or fold a sail and tie it to a boom.

FURLONG:- (Equestrian) One eighth of a mile.

G

GAME:- (Tennis) A player has won a game by winning four points before his opponent and holding a minimum two-point lead.

GAME AND MATCH BALL:- (Squash) The state of the game when the server requires one point to win is said to be game ball.

GAME POINT:- (Tennis, Table Tennis & Badminton) A situation in which one player will win the game by winning the next point; also the point won.

GATHER:- (Athletics) Composure for additional greater effort, as in the broad jump take-off.

GETTING THE COUNT:- (Bowling) Same as steal.

GETTING THE WOOD:- (Bowling) Knocking down a good score.

GIVE-AND-GO:- (Basketball) A manoeuvre in which the offensive player makes a short pass to a teammate, and then cuts in toward the basket for a return pass.

GIVE THE BALL AIR:- (Cricket) Refers to the spinner tossing a delivery well up in the air.

GLANCE:- (Cricket) In batting, to deflect the ball off the angled face of the bat away behind square leg.

GLASS JAW:- (Boxing) Mocking epithet for a boxer who cannot withstand a blow to the chin or suffers repeatedly from punches to the jaw; a man who can be put down by a jaw punch or is repeatedly staggered by one. Usually attributed to a man who has been knocked out a number of times.

GLIMA:- (Wrestling) A form of harness wrestling popular in Iceland.

GO TO THE ROUTE:- (Bowling) Same as strike out.

GOAL:- 1. The terminal point of a race.
2. An area or object towards which players in various games attempt to advance a ball or puck and push through or into which the ball or puck must go in order to score points.
3. The act or action of scoring a goal; also the resulting score.

GOAL AREA:- A rectangular area 20 yards (about 18m) wide and 6 yards (about 5.5m) deep in front of both goals.

GOAL POSTS:- (Bowling) Same as bed posts.

GOALIE:- A goalkeeper.

GOALKEEPER:- A player who defends the goal in any of various games (e.g. football, hockey, or lacrosse).

GOALKEEPING:- The act of guarding a goal.

GOAL KICK:- (Football) A freekick awarded to a defensive player, especially the goalkeeper, when the ball is sent over the goal line by an opposing player.

GOAL LINE:- A line at either end and running the width of a playing area on which a goal or goal post is situated.

GOALMINDER:- A goalkeeper.

GOALMOUTH:- The area of a playing field directly in front of the goal (e.g. in soccer or hockey).

GOALSIDE:- (Football) A position between the ball and the goal you are defending.

GOLDEN GATE:- (Bowling) The 4-6-7-10 or big four split.

GOLF:- The golf course may be 6,000 yards to 7,000 yards long. Eighteen holes are provided at different locations, the spacing between each hole varying from 150 yards to 600 yards.
Wherever threre are space limitations, a nine-hole course is provided. In such courses the game is played in two circuits. Each hole is sometimes provided with two different starting points, the object being that the player encounters different hazards in the second round. Each hole has a diameter of 4(1/2) inches and a minimum depth of 4 inches. Each hole is marked by a flag.
The diameter of the golf ball varies between 1-5/8 inches and 1-3/4 inches, its maximum weight being 1.62 ounces.

GOALPOST:- Two vertical posts that with or without a crossbat constitute the goal in various games (e.g. football and hockey).

GOLD MEDAL:- A medal of gold awarded to one who comes first in any of several competitions.

GOOGLY:- (Cricket) A ball bowled by a right-hand leg-break bowelr with what is apparently a leg-break action but which is in fact an off-break. In the case of a left-arm bowler, the googly will be a leg-break bowled with an off-break action. Also called in both cases the 'wrong'un'.

GRIP OF RACKET:- (Tennis) That portion of the racket which is grasped in the player's hand.

GRAB:- (Bowling) Same as dive.

GRAECO-ROMAN:- (Wrestling) A mixture of the ancient styles of Greece and Rome. Now an official FILA style, it is similar to freestyle except that the use of the legs and holding below the waist are forbidden.

GRAND PRIX:- (Often cap G & P) 1. A long-distance vehicle race usually over a road course; specifically one of a series of international formula car races.
2. A major competition in show jumping.
3. A eries of major tennis tournaments.

GRAND SLAM:- (Bridge) The winning of all the tricks in one hand of a card game.
(Tennis) The winning of the Australian, French, All-England, and US tennis championship in the same year. The winning of the USPGA, British Open, US Masters, and US Open golf championship in the same year.
(Softball) The batter hits a home run with the bases loaded.

GRASHOPPER:- (Bowling) A good working ball which splashes the pins.

GRAVEYARDS:- (Bowling) The toughest pair of alleys in a bowling center.

GREEN PITCH:- (Cricket) A well-grassed pitch with some moisture in it, likely to favour the faster bowlers, especially early in the day before it has dried out

GRIDIRON:- (Rugby Football) Another name for the football field, the transverse marking give it a gridiron appearance.

GRIP:- (Athletics) Hand hold on an implement.

GROOVE:- (Bowling) An apparent depression that carries the ball into the pocket.

GROUND STROKE:- (Tennis) Any ball hit after it has bounced.

GUARD:- (Cricket) The postition in line from stumps to stumps at which the batsman desires to take his stance. When he wants to acquaint himself with the position, usually on his arrival at the crease, the batsman asks the umpire to pinpoint it, requesting either 'middle' or 'centre', 'leg' or `middle' and leg' (halfway between the two), and then holding his bat upright while the umpire gives him the desired line from his position over the stumps at the nonstriker's end.
(Basketball) A player's position; the player in that position; also the act of defending against an offensive opponent.

GUY:- (Sailing) Line used to control spinnaker boom.

GYAKU:- (Judo) Reverse-applied to locks, holds, etc.

GYBE:- (Sailing) To alter course by turning the stern through the direction from which the wind is blowing.

H

HACKER:- (Tennis) A poor player.

HACKING:- (Basketball) A personal foul that results when a player strikes an opponent's arm with his hand.

HAIRPIN NET SHOT:- (Badminton) A shot hit near the net after the shuttle has dropped quite low. The shuttle will rise almost straight up, barely clearing the net, and drop sharply.

HALF-COURT LINE:- (Squash) A line set out upon the floor, parallel to the side walls, dividing the back half of the court into two equal parts.

HALF-SMASH:- (Badminton) Hit at about half to three quarter pace, often with an angled racket face (sliced).

HALF STRIKE:- (Bowling) A setup in which the 2-,4 -,5-,7-, and 9- pins are left standing.

HALF VOLLEY:- (Cricket) A delivery that is pitched full enough for the batsman playing forward to strike it just after in has landed. An ideal delivery to be firmly driven. (Tennis) A ball hit only inches away from the court's surface after the ball has bounced.

HALF VOLLEY KICK:- (Football) A kick of the ball just as it rebounds from the ground.

HALF MILE:- (Athletics) A middle distance race one and half mile in length.

HALF MILER:- (Athletics) An athlete who competes in the half mile.

HALVE:- (Golf) To play a hole or a round in match play in the same number of stroke as one's opponent.

HAMMER THROWER:- (Athletics) An athlete who competes in the hammer throw.

HANDBALL:- This game resembles football but is played with rest of the body except feet. It is played on a marked indoor court 40m X 2m. The ball for this game is 55-60 cm in diameter. Each team consists of 12 members and at a time 5 to 7 players of a team play on the field. There is a 2m high goal at either end of the pitch. The goal is scored when the ball crosses the goal line between the posts and under the crossbar.

HANDICAPPING:- The act or practice of trying to predict a winner especially on the basis of published data.

HANDLE:- (Archery) The grip at the midsection of the bow.

HANDLE THE BALL:- (Cricket) To touch the ball in play with the hands except at the specific request of the fielding side and thereby cause oneself to be out.

HANDOUT:- (Badminton) Term used in doubles to show that one player has lost service. (Handball) Retiring the server who fails to serve legally or when the serving team fails to return a ball that is in play.

HAND-OFF:- (Basketball) Handing the ball from one player to another.

HANG:- (Gymnastics) A position in which the center of gravity, and usually the entire body, is below the point of support. The point of support is usually the hands but is sometimes the knees, feet, elbows, or arms.

HANK:- (Sailing) A fitting that is used to attach a sail to a stay.

HARD WAY:- (Bowling) Same as dutch 200.

HARNESS HORSE:- (Equestrian) A standard bred that is run in harness racing.

HARNESS RACE:- (Equestrian) A single race in harness racing.

HARRIER:- A runner on a cross-country team.

HAR-TRU:- (Tennis) A trademark used for a composition surface for tennis courts.

HASH MARK:- (Football) One of the sections of an inbounds line marked on the ground where it crosses a yard line.

HAT-TRICK:- (Cricket) The taking of three wickets in successive balls by a bowler. The balls may be split by an intervening over bowled from the other end or indeed by on interval between two innings as long as the innings are in the same match.

HAZARD SIDE:- (Court tennis) The side of the court on which the receiver stands to receive the serve.
(Golf) Any bunker, water hazard, or

lateral water hazard.

HEAD COACH:- The principal coach of a staff who has overall control of the team and its strategy.

HEAD WIND:- (Athletics) Wind blowing against the runner's course.

HEADHUNTING:- The play or actions of a headhunter.

HEAD LEVER:- (Wrestling) A means of breaking the opponent to the mat by exerting pressure with the head on his arm at the armpit, at the same time pulling backward on the corresponding wrist.

HEADPIN :- The 1-pin.

HEADSET:- (Cycling) The assembly where the forks and handlebars turn within the head tube.

HEEL CUP:- (Athletics) A usually soft plastic cup that fits around the heel inside the shoe to protect the heel from becoming bruised as it hits the ground on takeoffs in jumping events.

HEEL KICK:- (Football) A kick made by kicking the ball backward with the heel.

HELD BALL:- (Basketball) A situation in which two opponents are in firm possession of the ball.

HELMET . DIVING:- (Underwater diving) Traditional form of commercial diving in which the diver wears a metal helmet attached to a suit. Air is pumped down to him.

HELMSMAN:- (Sailing) Person who operates the helm.

HEN FEATHERS:- (Archery) The two feathers that are not set at right angles to the arrow nock.

HIGH BOARD:- (Bowling) The condition existing when a board contracts or expands a trifle due to atmospheric conditions, changing course of ball.

HIGH 10 AND 30 :- (Bowling) Western term for high game and high three-game total.

HIGH HURDLE:- (Athletics):- A 42-inch high hurdle (39 inches high in high school competition) that is used in the high hurdles.

HIGH-STICKING:- (Ice Hockey) Illegal carrying of the stick above shoulder level.

HINDER:- (Handball) Accidental interference or obstruction of the flight of the ball during play. Point will be played again.

HINDER POINT:- (Handball) A point or the serve won because one's opponent has committed an avoidable hinder.

HIP CIRCLE:- (Gymnastics) A circle around a bar in which the gymnast hold her hips close to the bar.

HIP PADS:- Part of the equipment worn to prevent injury.

HIT:- (Softball) A ball hit in such a way that the batter or preceding baserunners are not retired by good defensive play.

HITCH KICK:- (Gymnastics) A forward and upward swing or kick of one leg with a leap off the other leg, followed by a scissoring of the legs in the air so that the landing is on the kicking leg.

HIT WICKET:- (Cricket) When a batsman breaks his wicket with any part of his equipment or person in the act of receiving or playing at the ball or taking off for his first run, he must be given out on appeal.

HOCKEY:- The pitch shall be 100 yards long and 60 yards wide. The 100 yard line are called side lines and the shorter sides are called goal lines. Flags are placed at each corner and also at a distance of 1 yard from side lines, the spacing of these flags being 25 yards. The goal area is 12' wide and 7" high with vertical posts on sides and horizontal post at top. The goal board 1' 6"high is placed at bottom, while the top area is covered with net. The area comprising a rectangle and two semicircle around the goal is called "striking circle

HOLD:- (Bowling) The fastness of a lane.
(Archery) Steadily holding the arrow at full draw before release.

HOLDING LANE :- (Bowling) Fast lane.

HOLDING THE WHISTLE:- (Field Hockey) Term used when the umpire allows play to continue after a foul when, in her opinion, this is more advantageous to the team fouled against than stopping play and awarding a penalty.

HOLD SERVE:- (Tennis) To win your own serve. If you lose your own serve, your serve has been "broken".

HOLE:- (Golf) Small cup sunk into the green, into which the golf ball is hit. The hole is 4(1/4) inches in diameter and at least 4 inches deep.

HOME COURT ADVANTAGE:- (Basketball) The advantage a team feels it has in playing before a home crowd.

HOME LANE :- (Bowling) Lanes on which bowlers get more strikes than on others; also home lane of a travelling team.

HONOR:- (Golf) The side which is entitled to play first from the teeing ground is said to have the honor. This is usually determined by a coin flip on the first tee. Once play begins, the player having the lowest score on the previous hole is said to have the honor thereafter.

HOOK:- (Cricket) A stroke played to a short-pitched delivery going down the leg side from a fast bowler when the batsman swips at the ball with a cross-batted action and tries to hit it away be given out.
(Golf) A ball in flight that curves from right to left (for a right-handed golfer).

HOOKING:- (Ice Hockey) Illegally using the blade of a stick to hook an opponent from behind.

HOOK LANE:- (Bowling) Slow lane.

HOOK PASS:- (Basketball) A pass made in the manner of a hook shot by swinging the arm through an arc while jumping.

HOOK SHOT:- (Basketball) A shot attempted while the player's back or side is toward the basket; thrown over the player's head.

HOP:- (Gymnastics) A spring into the air with a takeoff from one foot and a landing on the same foot.

HOT CORNER:- (Softball) The third base area.

HOW'S THAT:- (Cricket) The traditional form of appeal to the umpire when a bowler or a fieldsman considers the batsman should be given out.

HUB GEAR:- (Cycling) Type of gear (usually offering three or four gears) incorporating a 'sun-and-planet' system within the hub of the rear wheel.

HULL:- The body of a boat from the keel to the deck exclusive of the cabin, mast, spars, and rigging.

HULL SPEED:- The theoretical maximum speed of a boat based on its hull design.

HURDLE:- (Gymnastics) The last step in a run before a two-foot takeoff for a vault or mount on the bars or beam.

I

I.C.A.A.A.A.:- (Athletics) Intercollegiate Association of Amateur Athletes of America.

ICE DANCING:- An ice skating event for male-female pairs derived from figure skating but with movements based on dance sequences.

ICE HOCKEY:- A game played on an ice ring by two teams of six players on skates whose object is to drive a puck into the opponent's goal with a hockey stick.

ICE PICK:- A hand tool ending in a spike for chipping ice.

ICE RACING:- The racing of motor cycles with spiked tyres on ice in a way similer to speedway.

ICE SKATE:- A shoe with a metal runner attached for ice-skating.

ICE SKATING:- The sport of skating on ice, including figure skating, ice dancing, and pairs skating.

I.F.W.H.A.:- International Federation of Women's Hockey Association; the world governing body of women's hockey.

I.H.F.:- (Handball) International Handball Federation; the world governing body of team handball.

I.I.H.F.:- (Ice hockey) International Ice Hockey Federation; the world governing body of amateur ice hockey.

IN:- (Cricket) The time from when a player has begun his innings until it is ended.

IN THE DARK:- (Bowling) Same as sleeper.

IN THERE DARK:- (Bowling) Ball was a good pocket hit.

INDIVIDUAL MEDLEY:- (Swimming) Race consisting of equal legs of butterfly, backstroke, breaststroke and another different stroke (front crawl).

INNING:- (Bowling) Each bowler's turn.
(Badminton) The time during which a player or team holds service.

INFIELD:- (Cricket) Fieldsman placed beyond the inner catching positions, but usually no more than 30 to 40 metres from the bat e.g. point, covers, mid-wicket.

INFIELD FLY:- (Softball) A fair fly ball that can be caught by an infilder with runners on first and second, or first, second, and third before two are out. The batter is declared out by the umpire.

INFIGHTING:- (Boxing) Fighting close together so as to use short-arm punches, hooks or uppercuts to the body and head. Both hands must be free, it being an offence to hold with one hand and hit with the other. When there is a deadlock between the men, the order comes to break.
(Fencing) Close combat that is permitted so long as there is no body contact or other violations such as use of the left hand or turning the back.

INSIDE:- (Basketball) The area close to the basket, usually the lane, called inside because when the ball or man is there, the defense has been penetrated.

INTERVAL TRAINING:- (Swimming) Method of training, not exclusive to swimming, which involves performing a certain number of repeat swims with a set rest interval.

INSTINCTIVE SHOOTING:- (Archery) Aiming and shooting instinctively, rather than using a bow sight or point-of-aim method.

IN-SWINGER:- (Cricket) A stroke made with weight on the back foot, off a short rising ball which is hit on the leg-side.

INTENTIONAL FOUL:- (Basketball) A deliberate personal foul.

INTERCOLLEGIATE:- (Athletics) Competition between institutions at the college level.

INTERSCHOLASTIC:- (Athletics) Competition between institutions on the secondary level.

INVITATION:- (Fencing) Any deliberate exposure of target that is intended to draw an opponent's attack.

I.O.C.:- International Olympic Committee.

IPPON:- (Judo) One point.

I.S.H.R.F:- International Squash Rackets Federation; the world governing body of squash rackets.

I.T.F.:- International Tennis Federation; the world governing body of table tennis.

I.T.T.F.:- International Table Tennis Federation; the world governing body of table tennis.

I.Y.R.U.:- International Yacht Racing Union; the world governing body of yachting.

J

JACK MANDERS:- (Bowling) The ball goes through middle of 7-10 split.

JACKPOT:- 1. A large pot (e.g. in poker) formed by the accumulation of skates from previous play.
2. A combination on a fruit machine that wins a top prize or all the coins in the machine.
3. The amount of jackpot won.

JAVELIN:- (Athletics) A slender usually metal shaft at least 2.6 metres (about 8(1/2 feet) long that is thrown for distance in an athletic field event; also this event.

JIB:- (Sailing) Small sail set ahead of the mast.

JIGOTAI:- (Judo) Defensive posture.

JOGGING:- (Athletics) Easy running at a very slow pace.

JOKER:- A playing card added to a pack as a wild card or as the highest-ranking card.

JUDGE:- (Gymnastic) Four judges, supervised by a superior or master judge, mark gymnasts on each piece of apparatus in major competitions.

JUDO:- A martial art developed from ju-jitsu that emphasizes the use of quick movement and leverage to throw an opponent.

JUDOKA:- (Judo) Person who practises judo.

JUMP:- (Gymnastics) A spring into the air with a takeoff from both feet.

JUMP BALL:- (Basketball) A method of putting the ball into play by tossing it up between two opponents in one of the three circles.

JUNIOR LIGHTWEIGHT:- A professional boxer who weighs not more than 59 kilograms (9 stone 4 pounds).

JUNIOR MIDDLEWEIGHT:- A professional boxer who weighs not more than 69.9 kilograms (11 stone).

JUNIOR WELTERWEIGHT:- A professional boxer who weighs not more than 63.5 kilograms (10 stone).

JU-NO-KATA:- (Judo) Demonstration of judo principles in slow motion.

JUMP BALL:- (Basketball) A ball, tossed in the air by an official, to be batted by two opposing jumpers.

JUMP PASS:- (Basketball) A pass attempted while

the feet are in the air.

JUMP SHOT:- (Basketball) A shot attempted while the feet are off the court.

JUMP-SMASH:- (Badminton) Body in the air to reach shuttle earlier by a one-footed leap to either side or two-footed straight up.

JURY:- (Fencing) Made up of the director and the four judges.

K

KAESHIWAZA:- (Judo) Counter-attack techniques.

KATA:- (Judo) A series of pre-arranged movements. Now performed as a training method and for demonstrations.

KATSU:- (Judo) A method of resuscitation.

KEEP:- To act as wicketkeeper or goalkeeper.

KEEPER:- 1. A gamekeeper.
2. A goalkeeper.
3. A wicketkeeper.
4. Any of various devices (e.g. a stitched loop on a strap) for keeping something in position.

KEGELER-KEGELER:- (Bowling) Synonym for bowler, from German kegel (Indian club).

KEYSTONE SACK:- (Softball) The second base area.

KHO-KHO:- The Kho-Kho field is rectangular and measures 34 metres by 16 metres. X and Y are two rectangles. One side of the rectangle is 16 metres (breadth of the playfield) and the other side is 4.8 metres. At M and N there shall be two wooden poles. M N is central lane 24.4 metres long and 30 cm. wide. There are eight small squares 30 cm. by 30 cm. on the lane (G). The centre of each square is at a distance of 2.7 meters from the centre of its adjacent square.

KICK:- To strike out with the foot or feet.
(Football) To make a kick in football.
(Swimming) To use the legs in swimming; specially to practise using the legs alone. To make a spurt in a race, 2 to score by kicking a ball.
(Athletics) Leg first leg over a hurdle.

KICKER:- (Athletics) Runner who depends upon kick to win.

KICKING BOARD:- (Swimming) Training aid to support the upper body when swimming, using the legs alone.

KICK OFF:- (Bowling) Effective delivery of a good ball.

KIDNEY PUNCH:- (Boxing) A blow to the area of the kidneys: a foul.

KILL:- (Requetball) To hit (a ball) so hard in a racket game that a return is impossible.
(Handball) A ball directed to the front wall in such a way that it rebounds so close to the floor that it is impossible to retun.
(Volleyball) A spike that cannot be returned.

KILLING THE BOUNCE:- (Gymnastics) A term used when the bounce on the trampoline is suddenly stopped so that the feet remain in contact with the bed. It is accomplished by flexing the knees rapidly as the feet contact the bed.

KINDLING WOOD:- (Bowling) Light pins.

KING:- (Chess) The principal piece of each colour in a set of chessman having the power to move ordinarily one square in any direction and to capture opposing men but being obliged never to enter or remain in check.
(Cards) A playing card that is marked with a stylized figure of a king and ranks usually below the ace.

KIP:- (Gymnastics) A movement from a hang to a support in which the body pikes and then rapidly extends.

KNEE GUARD:- (Basketball) Equipment which protects the player's knees from injury.

KNOCKDOWN:- (Boxing) The movement in a boxing match when one boxer has been knocked down.

KNOCKOUT:- (Boxing) The termination of a boxing match when one boxer has been knocked unconscious or has been knocked down and is unable to rise and resume boxing within a specified time.
2. A blow that knocks out an opponent.

KOSHIWAZA:- (Judo) Techniqes of hip -throws.

KRESGE:- (Bowling) The 5-7 split.

KYU:- (Judo) Pupil degree.

L

"L":- (Gymnastics) A position in which the legs are forward in a horizontal plane so that they form a right angle with the trunk. The correct term is a half lever.

LANCASHIRE STYLE:- (Wrestling) An ancestor of freestyle wrestling which was popular in Lancashire.

LATE CUT:- (Cricket) A stroke played late to a shortish ball outside the off-stump with the weight on the back foot which is thrust over towards the slips. The bat comes down on the ball which should be hit through the slips. A stroke less frequently played in the modern game.

LATE TEN :- (Bowling) A strike in which 10-pin is the last to be knocked down.

LAWN TENNIS:- The court shall be rectangular in shape, 78' long and 27' wide. The outer 78' lines and 27' lines are called side line and base lines respectively.
The lines parallel to base lines and at a distance of 18' from base lines are called service lines. Two double matches the size of court being 78' X 36'.
The ball shall be spherical, smooth without any stickers on outer surface. the dismeter of the ball shall vary between 2-1/2" and 2-5/8" and its weight shall be between 2 ounces and 2-1/6" ounces.

LAYERING:- (Skiing) Wearing loose layers of clothes over undergarments so that the skier may easily add on for extra warmth or remove excess if too warm.

LAYOUT:- (Gymnastics) A straight and extended position of the body in vaulting, swinging or somersaulting.
(Athletics) Extension of the body with no flexion.

LADDER:- A Flight of stairs on board a boat.

LADY PARAMOUT:- (Archery) The woman who presides over a woman tournament. In Britain the term is used for a lady who sponsors an archery tournament.

LANDING HILL:- (Skiing) The hill on which competitors land in ski jumping competition.

LANGLAUF:- (Skiing) Cross-country skiing.

LANGLURER:- (Skiing) A cross-country skier.

LAY-UP:- (Basketball) A shot made from near the basket at the top of a jump usually by playing ball off the backboard. (also called lay-in).

LAY-UP:- (Golf) To hit a shot (as a fairway shot or approach shot) so that it stops short of a normal distance in order to avoid the risk of the ball's going into a hazard.

LEAD-LEG:- (Athletics) The first leg, or kicking leg, in jumpers.

LEAD-OFF:- (Athletics) The first man to run on a

relay team.

LEAP:- (Gymnastics) A spring into the air, taking off from one foot and landing on the other.

LEFT-HAND BUCKET:- (Bowling) The 2-4-5-8 leave.

LEG:- (Athletics) A section of a relay.

LILY:- (Bowling) The impossible 5-7-10 split.

LEG BREAK:- (Cricket) A ball which turns from the leg-side to the off and is most frequently associated with a right-arm bowler who turns the wrist over in delivery. However, the term 'leg-break' is also used for the orthodox ball of the left-arm spin bowler.

LEG-CUTTER:- (Cricket) Bowled by a bowler of medium-pace and above who cuts his fingers across the seam of the ball and achieves a faster if less sharp version of the leg-break.

LEG-SIDE:- (Cricket) The side of the playing area behind the batsman as he takes his stance at the crease.

LEE:- The side of a boat away from the wind.

LEGAL:- Permitted by the rules of a games or competition.

LENGTH:- (Cricket) A good length ball is one off which the batsman finds it difficult to score because it is neither short enough to cut, hook or play off the back foot not full enough to drive.
(Squash) The ball that strikes the back wall nick on the second bounce.

LET:- (Squash) In general terms, the recommencement of the rally with the same server. The rules on let are quite lengthy and players are advised to obtain a copy of these rules.
(Badminton) The stopping of play due to some type of outside interference. The point is replayed.

LET BALL:- (Tennis) Any point which is played over because of some kind of interference.

LET SERVE:- (Tennis) A serve which touches the net tape and falls into the proper square and is played over.

LEVER:- (Gymnastics) A position in which the body is held horizontal to the floor. If the legs only are horizontal, the position is called a half lever.

LIE:- (Golf) The position of the ball on the playing ground. Also refers to the angle of the clubhead.

LIFE SAVING:- (Swimming) Swimming techniques for saving people from drowning.

LIGHT FLYWEIGHT:- (Boxing) A boxer who competes in the light flyweight division.

LIMBS:- (Archery) Upper and lower parts of the bow; divided by the handle.

LINE:- (Fencing) A target area; may be referred to as high or low, inside or outside. It is also the term used to define a defender's position when the arm is fully extended and the point is threatening, that is, in line.

LINEMAN:- (Football) 1. Any of the offensive or defensive players who play on the line-es

LINE OF ENGAGEMENT:- (Fencing) The position of the sword with respect to a particular line of attack during engagement.

LINESMAN:- (Tennis) A match official who calls balls "in" or "out".

LINKSMAN:- (Golf) A golfer.

LOAF :- (Bowling) To put improper hook action on the ball so it fails to come up to objective.

LOB":- (Tennis) A ball hit sufficiently high to pass over the outstretched arm position of the net player.

LOBE:- (Skating) A circle of a school figure.

LOB SERVE:- A lob hit underhand on the serve (as in badminton, handball, or squash).

LOB VOLLEY:- (Tennis) A shot hit high into the air from a volleying position.

LOFTING IRON:- (Golf) An old name for a number 8 iron.

LONG CORNER:- (Field Hockey) The play awarded to the attack after the ball goes over the end line unintentionally, off the stick of a defender. The ball is placed five yards from the corner.

LONG COURSE:- (Swimming) Baths 50 metres of 55 yards long.

LONG-DISTANCE SWIMMING:- (Swimming) Openwater swimming in lakes, rivers, and the sea; races range from 1 mile to 40 miles.

LONG HOP:- (Cricket) A short ball allowing the batsman time to cut or hook.

LOST BALL:- (Cricket) A ball hit away which cannot be recovered.

LOOP DRIVE:- (Table Tennis) A shot made with a lot of topspin and just enough forward movement to enable it to clear to net so that the ball will rebound very low and when hitting the opponent's paddle will bounce straight up.

LOOPER :- (Bowling) Hook ball which describes a wide arc; an "out and in" ball.

LOOSE IMPEDIMENTS:- (Golf) Natural objects not fixed or growing and not adhering to the ball, and including stones not solidly embedded, leaves, twigs, branches, and the like, dung, worms, and insects, and casts or heaps made by them.

LOVE GAME:- (Tennis) A game in which the losing player scores no points.

LOUIE:- (Bowling) In some localities, synonym for headpin.

LOVE:- (Badminton) The term used to indicate zero in scoring.

LOW HURDLE:- (Athletics) A 30-inch-high hurdle used in the low hurdles.

LOW LINE:- (Fencing) That part of the target that is below the defender's hand level in the on guard stance.

LUNGE:- (Fencing) A means of delivering a touch by moving the leading foot substantially forward while the rear foot remains stationary.
(Field Hockey) Stroke used in attempting to take the ball from an opponent on the player's left. May be used for a pass or follow-up shot when a long reach is necessary.
(Gymnastics) A standing position in which the legs are apart with one knee bent and the other straight. This term also refers to the "movement" from a vertical standing position to the position described.

M

MAIDEN:- (Cricket) An over off which no runs are scored. If it also includes the taking of a wicket, it is a 'wicket maiden'.

MAINSAIL:- (Sailing) The largest working sail.

MAKE IT FIT :- (Bowling) Trying to make the 4-5, 9-10 or similar splits where both sides of ball must contact pins.

MAPLES :- (Bowling) The pins.

MAN-FOR-MAN MARKING:- (Football) Marking one opponent exclusively.

MAN-TO-MAN OFFENSE:- Any offense designed for use against a man-to-man defense.

MAN-TO-MAN DEFENSE:- (Basketball) The most popular and widely used type of defense. Each defensive player stays with his assigned opponent.

MARATHON (MEN):- (Athletics)The origins of the Marathon are as romantic as the modern history of the event itself. Popular legend holds that it commemorates an Athenian soldier named Pheidippedes who ran from Marathon to Athens with news of victory over the invading Persians and then dropped dead in 490BC.

MARK:- (Football) To take up a position to deny the opponent the ball or tackle him. (Bowling) A strike or space.

MARKER:- 1. An object used to indicate or record position.
2. One who marks (an opponent).
3. A scorer and referee in certain games (e.g. squash).

MARKING:- (Field Hockey) The act or process of staying close to an opposing player.

MARKS:- (Athletics) An athlete's starting point and points of check during approach.

MARTIAL ART:- Any of the Oriental arts of combat (e.g. judo,karate, and kendo) widely practised as sports.

MASSE:- (Billiards) A shot in billiards or snooker made by hitting the cue ball vertically or nearly vertically on the side to drive it around one ball in order to strike another.

MATCH:- (Fencing) A contest between two teams in any weapon. A series of bouts between the fencers of two different teams.
(Tennis) To win a match is to win the contest between two or four opponents.

MATCH PLAY:- (Golf) Competition in which the winner is decided by the number of holes won.

MATCH POINT:- (Tennis) A situation in which one player will win the match by winning the next point; also the point won.
(Badminton) The point which, if won by the server, makes that person the winner of the match.

MEDLEY:- (Athletics) Relay where members run different distances.

MEDLEY RELAY:- (Swimming) 4-man relay of equal legs of backstroke, breaststroke, butterfly and another different stroke (front crawl).

MEET:-(Fencing)A full tournament between teams or individuals. A series of matches, bouts, or pools of bouts.

METER:- (Athletics) 39.37 inches.

MIDFIELD:- (Football) 1. The middle portion of a field; especially the portion of a playing field that is midway between the goals.
2. The player in a team that normally play in midfield.

MIDDLE-ORDER:- (Cricket) The batting positions numbered five six and seven between the top-order and the tail.

MIDCOURT:- (Tennis) The area in front or in back of the service line of the playing court.

MID-OFF:- (Cricket) A fieldsman on the off-side, in front of the batsman.

MID-ON:- (Cricket) A fieldsman on the on-side, in front of the batsman.

MID-WICKET:- (Cricket) Another name for mid-on or mid-off.

MILLING:- (Boxing) Boxing ,fighting or exchanging blows. Milling on the retreat: Backing off and drawing an advancing opponent on to your own punches so that they have a double effect. Although attack is considered the best form of defence, a retreating boxer can wear a rival down and then set up an attack of his own.

MINIATURE GOAL:- (Golf) A golf game played

with a putter on a miniture course having tunnels, bridges, sharp corners and obstacles.

MIXED:- Made up of both man and woman.

MIXED DOUBLE:- (Tennis) A tennis pair of a man and a woman; also play a match between two such pairs.

MOMENTUM:- (Athletics) Force possessed by an athlete in motion.

MONOCOQUE:- Of a method of car construction using a shell frame and no chassis.

MONOPOSTO:- Of a racing car having only one seat.

MOTHER-IN-LAW:- (Bowling) The 7-pin.

MOUNT:- (Gymnastics) A stunt used by the performer to get on the apparatus. In a competitive exercise it is the first stunt or shot series of stunts in a balance-beam or uneven-bar routine. The first series in floor exercise is sometimes referred to as a mount.

MOUNTAINEERING:- The pastime or technique of climbing mountains and rock faces.

MOUNTING BLOCK:- (Equestrian) A block, platform with steps or convenient stone from which a rider many mount his horse.

MOUTH:- (Equestrian):- A horse's response to pressure on the bit.

MULE EARS :- (Bowling) Same as bed posts.

MULLIGAN OR SHAPIRO:- (Golf) Permitting a second hit of a badly played ball-usually on a tee shot

N

NAP HAND:- A favourable chance that invites the taking of risks.

N.C.A.:- (Athletics) National Federation of State High School Athletic Associations.

NEAR FALL:- (Wrestling) A position in which the offensive wrestler maintains his opponent in a controlled pinning situation.

NECKTIE TACKLE:- (Rugby Football) A high tackle, around the neck. Its opposite is the shoestring tackle.

NETBALL:- A game usually for women played between two sides of seven players each who score goals by tossing an inflated ball through a horizontal ring raised on post at each end of a hard court.

NET BALL:- (Tennis) A ball which hits the net and falls back on the same side as the hitter.

NET-FLICK:- (Badminton) Quick underarm clear met high at net flying flat to back court.

NET MAN:- (Tennis) The player who has gained position at the net and is prepared to volley.

NEUTRAL CORNER:- (Boxing) The corners of a ring unoccupied by the boxers and their seconds. A referee usually goes to one of them to add up his score card.

NEUTRAL POSITION:- (Wrestling) Both wrestlers face each other on their feet or knees with neither maintaining control.

NEWAZA:- (Judo) Groundwork.

NEW BALL:- (Cricket) As suggested, a ball that is brand new or in the very early stages of its use in a game, but more relevant in terms of the taking of a second or third new ball in a long innings. Over the years of competitive cricket, the time when a new ball could be taken has varied significantly. At one stage it even related to the number of runs scored by the batting side. It now relates to overs bowled, and the minimum figure for a first-class game is 75 six-ball overs.

NICK:- (Squash) The corner where the floor meets the wall.

NIGHT WATCHMAN:- (Cricket) A lower-order batsman sent in prematurely when a wicket falls a few minutes before the close of play to avoid risking one of the better batsman.

NINE:- (Golf) The first or last nine holes of an 18-hole golf course.

NOCK:- (Archery) The groove in the end of the arrow in which the string is placed.

NOCKING POINT:- (Archery) The point on the string at which the arrow is placed.

NOD:- (Boxing) To deceive an opponent by moving the head slightly to imply one type of punch is coming and then delivering another.

NO MAN'S LAND:- (Tennis) A general area within the baseline and proper net position area where, when the player is caught, he must volley or hit ground strokes near his feet.

NONSWIMMER:- (Swimming) One who is unable to swim.

NORDIC SKIING:- (Skiing) Cross-country-skiing and ski jumping.

NOSE HIT :- (Bowling) To hit a pin dead center.

NOTCH:- (Archery) The grooves of the upper and lower tips of the limbs into which the bow string is fitted.

NOT OUT:- (Cricket) To be undismissed during or after an innings. Also the umpire's negative response to appeal from the fielding side.

NOT-UP:- (Squash) The expression used to denote that a ball has not been served or returned above the board in accordance with the rules.

O

OBSTRUCTION:- (Field Hockey) A foul made by placing the body or any part of it between the opponent and the ball so as to intrfere with the opponent's effort to play or reach the ball.
(Golf) An artificial object erected, placed, or left on a course and not an integral part of the course.

OFFENSIVE TEAM:- (Basketball) The team in possession of the ball.

OFF-BREAK:- (Cricket) A ball which turns from off to leg after pitching. Bowled by a right-arm bowler, the ball is gripped between the first and second fingers with the seam usually at right angles between them. The top joint of the first finger is on the seam and the hand turns clockwise as the ball is delivered.

OFF-CUTER:- (Cricket) As with the leg-cutter, the bowler cuts his fingers down the side of the ball (the other side) and hopes to produce a fast off-break.

OFF-DRIVE:- (Cricket) A drive off the front foot of the wicket on the on-side usually between midwicket and the bowler.

OFFENSIVE LOB:- (Tennis) A ball hit just above the racket reach of an opposing net player.

OFFICIALS:- (Basketball) The referee, umpire, scorer and timer.

OFFSIDE:- (Field Hockey) A foul committed by a player receiving the ball while in an illegal position.
(Rugby Football) A player who advances beyond the line of scrimmage before the ball is snapped is offside. The penalty is 5 yards.

(Ice Hockey) Offside occurs when an attacking player precedes the puck into the attacking zone or when the puck travels untouched over more than one line. The position of a player is taken from his skate, and not from the stick.

OLD ENGLISH BACKSTROKE:- (Swimming) Early technique of swimming on the back using a kind of inverted breaststroke.

OLMPIAD:- The period of 4 years between Olympic Games.

OLYMPIAN:- A participant in the Olympic Games.

ONE-HANDED:- Effected by the use of only one hand.

ONE TOUCH:- (Football) Passing the ball first time (without controlling it first.)

ONE -TWO :- (Football) A quick exchange of passes between two players.
(Fencing) An attack made up ot two disengagements.

ON-GUARD:- (Fencing) The position assumed by a fencer when ready to fence.

ON DECK:- (Softball) The player in line to follow batter at the plate. The place for waiting is the " On-deck Circle."

OPEN FACE RACKET:- (Tennis) A racket whose face is moving under the ball. A wide open racket face is parallel to the court surface.

OPEN GLOVE PUNCH:- (Boxing) Hitting with the inside of the glove or slapping with the open glove: a foul.

OUT:- (Squash) The ball is out when it touches the front, sides, or back of the court above the area prepared for play or passes over any cross bars or other part of the roof of the court. The lines delineating such area, the lighting equipment, and the roof are out.

OUT AND IN BALL:- (Bowling) Same as curve ball.

OUTLET PASS:- (Basketball) A term used to designate a direct pass from a rebounder to a teammate, with the main objective being the start of a fast break.

OUT-OF-BOUNDS:- (Basketball) The area beyond end lines and sidelines. The ball is out of play in this area.

OUTPLAY:- To defeat or play better than in a game.

OUTPLAYER:- The side or player in a court or get game without the strike.

OUTSWINGER:- (Cricket) A ball which swings from leg to off in the air, that is, away from the right-handed batsman.

OVER:- (Cricket) A series of six ball delivered alternately from either end.

OVERHAND PASS:- (Volleyball) A pass made by contacting the ball above the head with the finger pads.

OVERHEAD:- (Badminton) A motion used to strike the shuttle when it is above the head.
(Tennis) A shot hit from a position higher than the player's head.

OVERHEAD SMASH:- (Tennis) A shot hit from a position higher than the player's head and hit extremely hard.

OVERBOW:- (Archery) Using too strong a bow that is too powerful to pull a bowstring to proper distance.

OVERDRAW:- (Archery) Drawing the bow so that the pile of the arrow is inside the bow.

OVERHITTING:- (Tennis) A player who tends to put too much force into each shot.

OVER THE WICKET:- (Cricket) Indicates that the hand with which the bowler, whether right-arm or left-arm, is bowling is the one nearer the bowler's wicket.

OVERTHROW:- (Cricket) The extra run or runs scored when a throw at the stumps runs away.

(Softball) A thrown ball bat goes into foul territory beyond the boundary lines of the playing field in an attempt to retire a runner who has not reached or is off a base.

OVERSTRICK:- A card trick won in excess of the number bid.

P

PACE:- (Athletics) The rate of covering ground while running.

(Tennis) The speed of the ball.

PACEMAKER:- One who sets a fast pace or leads (in the early stages of) a race.

PADDLE TENNIS:- A game similar to tennis played on a half-sized court with sponge balls and wooden paddles.

PALMING:- (Boxing) To rub an opponent's face upwards with the palm of the hand when in a clinch: a foul.

PAR:- (Golf) The standard score for a hole.

PARK:– An enclosed arena or stadium used especially for ball games.

PARLOUR GAMES:- A game suitable for playing indoors.

PARRY:- (Boxing) To push away an aimed blow or misdirect a punch, either by turning a delivery out of its intended course by hitting at the glove or arm, or coming inside the offensive arm and turning it away from its target.

(Fencing) A deflection of an attacking blade. It is simple if it moves directly to the blade and counter if it describes a circle.

PART OF THE BUILDING:- (Bowling) Expression used when 7- or 10-pin stands on a good hit.

PASE:- A movement of the cape by a matabor that draws the ball.

PASS:- (Basketball) To throw the ball from one player to another; the act of so throwing it.

PASSAGE:- A slow elected trot in dressage with movements of suspension between the paces.

PASSER:- (Athletics) The relay runner who "hands off" the baton.

PASSED BALL:- (Softball) A legally delivered pitch that should have been held or controlled by the catcher, which allows a baserunner to advance. A dropped third strike that permits the batter to reach first base in Fast Pitch is an error, not a passed ball.

PASSING:- (Athletics) Not taking one's jump or vault as it comes up.

PASSING SHOT:- (Tennis) A stroke in tennis drives the ball to one side and beyond the reach of an opponent who is at or coming towards the net.

(Handball) A placement driven out of opponent's reach on either side.

PASSING ZONE:- (Athletics) A 20-yard zone in which a pass must be made during a relay.

PAVILION:- A building on a sport ground that contains changing usually also containing seats from which spectators, esp. members of the home club, can watch matches.

PENALTY GOAL:- (Football) A goal scored from a penalty kick.

PENALTY SHOT:- (Field Hockey) An unhindered shot at the goal in hockey awarded to an individual for certain violations by an opponent.

(Ice Hockey) A clear shot at goal, awarded if an attacking player is tripped or pulled down when he is in a scoring position in front of the goal. Only the goalkeeper is allowed to defend, and no goal can be scored from a rebound.

A shot at the goal awarded to a team for certain violations by an opponent in any of several games.

PERIOD:- Any of the divisions of the playing time of a game.

PERSONAL FOUL:- (Basketball) A player foul which involves contact with an opponent while the ball is alive or after the ball is in possession of a player for a throw-in.

PERSONAL SURVIVAL:- (Swimming) Techniques of keeping alive in open water using clothes, etc. as flotation aids.

PETTICOAT:- (Archery) That part of the target face outside the white ring.

PHRASE:- (Fencing) Any unbroken series of offensive and defensive exchanges.

PICK:- (Bowling) To knock down some pins while leaving others when shooting a spare. (Basketball) A special type of screen where a player stands so the defensive player slides to make contact, freeing an offensive teammate for a shot or drive.

PIKE:- (Gymnastics) A position when the gymnast folds or bends her body at the hips, keeping her legs straight.

PICK-UP:- To cover an offensive player who is momentarily not guarded.

PILE (POINT):- (Archery) The pointed metal tip of the arrow.

PIN:- (Wrestling) Holding an opponent's shoulders on the mat: it automatically ends a contest in both freestyle and Graeco-Roman.

PIN BINDING:- (Skiing) A type of toe binding that has three pins that are projected into the sole of the boot, securing the boot to the ski.

PINCH:- (Archery) To squeeze the nock of the arrow.

PINCHING THE BALL:- (Bowling) Gripping ball too hard and causing an unnatural delivery.

PITCHER:- (Baseball) One who pitches; the player who pitches in a game of baseball.

PIVOT:- (Basketball) To turn the body and move one foot while keeping the other foot stationary.

PIVOT PUNCH:- (Boxing) A backwards swing whereby an opponent is hit by the back knuckles: a foul.

PLACED:- (Equestrian) Having finished in a leading place, especially second or third place, in a competition, especially a horse race.

PLACEMENT:- (Tennis) A shot hit inbounds and untouched by the opponent.

PLATOONING:- (Rugby Football) The practice of using two different teams for offensive and defensive play.

PLAY:- (Cricket) The call given by the umpire to indicate that the game should begin. Also, the active part of the game is known as 'play'.

PLAYBOOK:- (Rugby Football) Each player has a book containing detailed instruction of his roles within the team's rehearsed plays.

PLAYER:- One who plays a game.

PLAYING CARD:- Any of a set of 52 thin rectangular pieces of cardboard or plastic marked on one side to show its rank and suit and used in playing any of numerous games.

PLAY OFF:- To decide the winner of (a competition or match) or break (a tie) by a play-off.

PLUCKING:- (Archery) Jerking the drawing hand literally away from the face on the release, which will cause arrow flights to the left.

PLUNGING:- (Swimming) Event to determine who can get farthest simply by diving-not using arms or legs and lasting a maximum of 60 seconds.

POACH:- (Tennis) To cross over into your partner's territory.

POINT:- (Volleyball) A point is scored when the receiving team fails to return the ball legally to the opponent's court.

POINT-BLANK RANGE:- (Archery) The only distance from the target at which the point of aim is right on the bull's-eye.

POINT-OF-AIM:- (Archery) A method of aiming in which the pile of the arrow is aligned with the target.

POLE PLANT:- (Skiing) Action in which the poles are put into the snow at a particular place and during a particular time.

POLO:- A game of oriental origin played by teams of usually four players on horseback using mallets with long flexible handles to drive a wooden ball into the oppoents' goal; also any of serveal games in which horses are replaced by vehicles.

POOL:- (Fencing) A group of fencers who will meet one another in round-robin competition.

POSTING UP:- (Basketball) A player cutting to the three-second lane area, pausing, and anticipating a pass.

POWDER PUFF:- (Bowling) A slow ball that fails to carry.

POWER PLAY:- (Ice Hockey) Sustained attack by one team, particularly when the opposition is numerically below strength.

POWER SERVE:- (Volleyball) A fast serve hit with an overhand action.

POWERHOUSE:- (Bowling) A strike ball that carries all ten pins into the pit.

PRIZE:- Something awarded to outstanding competitors in a sports event.

PROOF:- The means of testing a gun to ensure its safety.

PUDDLE:- The turbulence left by an oat at the end of a stroke.
(Bowling) A gutter ball.

PUFF BALL:- (Bowling) Same as powder puff.

PUGILISM:- (Boxing) Fighting with the fists.

PULL:- (Cricket) A shot played by a batsman moving across his wicket to a short ball, perhaps on the line of the off-stump or outside, to the area of midwicket.

PULL-SHOT:- (Golf) To hit a ball straight, but to the left of the target (for a right-handed golfer).

PULLED MUSCLE:- (Athletics) The pulling apart of muscle fiber.

PULLING:- (Swimming) Swimming with the arms only.
(Boxing) Dragging a rival forward into a punch: foul.

PULL-UP:- (Athletics) Raising, by pulling, of the body in pole vaulting.

PUMPKIN:- (Bowling) Same as dead apple.

PURGE VALVE:- (Underwater Diving) Portion at front of second stage of demand valve that can be pressed to get extra air or to expel water from the mouthpiece.

PUSHER:- (Athletics) A chamois toe sock.

PUSH-IN:- (Field Hockey) Method of putting the ball into play after it has gone over the sideline.

PUCH-PASS:- (Field Hockey) A quick wrist stroke having no back swing. The ball does not rise. When the strike is executed the stick faces the direction of the pass in contact with the ball. Accurate and easy to receive.

PUSH-OFF:- (Athletics) Pushing up and away from the vaulting pole at the top of the vault.

PUSH-SHOT:- (Golf) To hit a ball straight, but to

the right of the target (for a right-handed golfer).

PUT-OUT:- (Softball) An out credited to the fielder who last handles the ball on a play that retires the batter or a baserunner.

PUTTER:- (Golf) A golf club used in putting.

PUT UP:- To start (games) from cover.

Q

QSAEKOMIWAZA:- (Judo) Holding techniques.

QUAD:- Short for quadruple sculls.

QUADRANGULAR MEET:- A meet (as in track and field, swimming, or wrestling) in which 4 teams compete together but which is scored as if each team were competing against each of the other teams simultaneously.

QUADRUPLE SCULLS:- (Rowing) Competition for 4 man sculls.

QUALIFIER:- A competitior who qualifies for the final stages of a competition.

QUALIFYING:- The process of determining which competitors will be in a contest or in the final stage of competition on the basis of preliminary heats or time trials.

QUARRY:- The object of a hunt; a game animal or bird hunted hawks or falcons.

QUARTERBACK:- 1. To play the position of quarterback.
2. To direct the offensive play of a team.

QUARTERBACK DRAW:- (Football) An offensive play in which the quarterback drops back as if to pass and then breaks quickly forward past the pass rushes.

QUARTERBACKING:- The play of a team's quarterback or quarterbacks.

QUARTERBACK SNEAK:- (Football) An offensive play in which the quarterback runs directly forward with the ball immediately after receiving the snap (also called sneak).

QUARTERFINALS:- The round of an elimination tournament which precedes the semifinal round and in which 8 contests remain to be played.

QUARTERING:- (Of a wind) Blowing toward something at an oblique angle; coming over a boat's quarter.

QUARTER-MILE:- (Athletics) An athlete who competes in the quarter mile race.

QUICK COUNT:- (Football) A shortening of the signals called by a quarterback at the line of scrimmage that is intended to catch the defensive team by surprise.

QUICK KICK:- (Football) A punt attempted on first, second, or third down from a passing or running formation that is intended to take the opposing team by surprise and ultimately to gain better field position.

QUICK-PITCH:- (Of a baseball pitcher) To make a quick pitch.

QUINTET:- (Basketball) A basketball team.

QUIVER:- (Archery) A receptacle for carrying or holding arrows.

QUOIT:- A metal, plastic, or rope ring used in the game of quoits.

R

RABBIT BALL:- The present-day baseball is sometimes considered to be a rabbit ball in comparison with the ball used in the era before World War II.

RABBIT EARS:- An extreme sensitivity to criticism.

RABBIT PUNCH:- (Boxing) A hit on the back of the neck: a foul.

RACE:- A contest of speed in which the participants compete directly against one another.

RACE COMMITTEE:- (Yacht Racing) A committee usually from the yacht club sponsoring a race that is responsible for conducting the race and ruling on all aspects of the race and on all protests.

RACECOURSE:- A course used for racing.

RACEDRIVER:- Someone who frequently attends races (as horse races or dog races).

RACEGOER:- Someone who drives a racing car.

RACEHORSE:- (Basketball) Being a style of basketball characterized by a lot of running and fast breaks with little use of set plays and. minimal attention to defence.

RACER:- 1. Someone who races.
2. A vehicle used for racing.

RACERS EDGE:- (Auto racing) The maximum speed at which a driver can negotiate a turn and maintain control of his car.

RACETRACK:- (Equestrian) A closed course on which races are run-often used for courses for horse racing or auto racing all distinguished from running track.

RACE-WALK:- (Athletics) To compete in a competitive walk.

RACE WALKER:- Someone who competes in racewalks.

RACE-WALKING:- (Athletics) The competitive walk; competing in a walk.

RACERWAY:- A course for racing and especially a racetrack for harness racing.

RACING:- The sport or profession of engaging in or holding race.

RACING COMMISSION:- The controlling body of horse racing in each state.

RACING DIVE:- A flat shallow dive from the starting platform for the beginning of a race or a leg of a relay race to be swum in the crawl, breaststroke, or butterfly.

RACING SOUND:- (Of a racehorse) Considered able to race though not necessarily fit or in good health.

RACK:-(Billiards) To arrange the balls in a rack for a break shot.

RACKET FACE:- (Tennis) The hitting surface of the racket.

RACKET GAME:- Any of numerous games (as tennis, badminton, or squash racquets) in which a ball or shuttlecock is driven over a net or against a wall with a racket.

RACKET HEAD:- (Tennis) Top portion of the racket frame which houses the strings.

RAG:- (Hockey)To maintin possession of the puck or ball in ice hockey.

RAIL:- A fence bounding the edge of a racetrack (as for horse racing or dog racing).

RAIL OR RAILROAD:- (Bowling) Synonym for split.

RAILBIRD:- A racing enthusiast who sits on or near the track rail to watch a race or workout.

RAIL LUGGER:-(Eqeustrain)A horse that usually

runs close to the inside rail in a race.

RAIN CHECK:- A ticket stub that is good for admission to another contest (as a baseball game) when the scheduled one is rained out.

RAIN OUT:- To rain to such an extent that a particular game is postponed.

RAINOUT:- (Baseball) A game suspended or postponned because of rain.

RAISE:- (Curling) To hit another stone and knock it closer to the tee.

RAISE TWO FLAGS:- (Football) Australian rules to kick a goal.

RAKE:- (Sailing) The fore-and-aft inclination of a mast.
(Bowling) Same as cutter.

RALLY:- (Badminton) An exchange of shots either in practice or during a match.
(Handball) Continuous play of the ball by opponents.
(Tennis) The act of hitting balls back and forth across the net. A rally includes all shots other than the serve.

RALLYING:- A person who organizes and conducts a rally and who is responsible for selecting the route to be taken and publishing the instructions.

RANDOLPH:- (Trampolining) A stunt performed on the trampoline which consists of a one and a half forward somersault with 2 full twists of the body.

RANDORI:- (Judo) Free play or sparring between 2 players.

RAPID FIRE:- (Shooting) Rifle competition in which each competitor is required to fire 10 rounds a minute.

RAPPEL:- To make a rappel; to descend a cliffy by means of a rappel (also rope down).

RAPPEL POINT:- (Mountain climbing) The point to which a rappel rope is secured at the top of a cluff.

RASPBERRY:- A Bronx cheer.

RAT TAIL:- (Skating) A short scratch mark made on the ice by a figure skating blade as the skater pushes off from one foot to glide backward on the other foot.

RAZORHEAD:- (Archery) A hunting arrow equipped with a razorhead.

RBI:- (Baseball) A run batted in.

REACH:- (Sailing) A course that is approximately at right angles to the wind.

REACH:- To sail on a reach.

REACH BASE:- (Baseball) To be successful in getting to first base (reached base on a throwing error).

REACTION TIME:- (Athletics) Latent time between stimulus and first stride.

READ THE GREEN:- (Golf) To analyze the slope of a putting green to determine how much and in what direction a put will break.

READ:- To correctly anticipate the action (as the defensive coverage or offensive blocking) of an opponent by observing the opponent's position or movement.

REAPING THROW:- (Judo) A method of throwing one's opponent from a standing position by sweeping a leg into the opponent leg to upset his balance.

REARGUARD:- (Ice Hockey) An ice hockey defenseman.

REBOUND:- (Basketball) A ball which bounces from the backboard or basket rim.

RECALL:- The act of calling back the competitors just after the start of a race (as by repeating the starting signal) because of a false start.

RECEIVE:- To catch or gain possession of a kickoff or punt.

RECEIVER:- The player in a court game who receives the serve compare server. (Athletics) The man receiving the baton in a relay pass.

RECEIVING BARN:- (Equestrian) A barn at a racetrack in which horses that have been stabled at another track and shipped in for a race are held prior to the race.

RECEIVING LINE:- (Racquetball) An imaginary line 5 feet behind which the receiver must stand until the ball is served.

RECEIVING ZONE:- (Handball) The floor area of the court between the short line and the rear of the court in which a player receives the serve.

RECORD:- An attested top performace or prominent achievement.

RECOVER:- To make a recovery.

RECURVED BOW:- An archery bow is constructed so that the tips of the limbs curve toward the back when the bow is unstrung.

RECOVERY:- (Swimming) The non-propulsive phase of a stroke, when the limb is moved forward to begin the propulsive action.

RED CARD:- (Football) A red card shown by the referee (as in international football) to indicate that a player is being sent off.

RED-DOGGER:- (Football) A linebreaker or defensive back who blitzes.

RED FLAG:- (Motor Racing) To stop a race by signalling with a red flag.

REDOUBLEMENT:- (Fencing) Any attack made by the opponent parties. The original attack but does not follow immediately with a riposte.

REDSHIRT:- A college athelete who remains out of intercollegiate competition for a year while attending school in order to recover from an injury or in order to extend his eligibility for an additional year and in the meantime gain experience practicing but not playing with the team.

REDSHIRT:- To keeping a player out of varsity competition by making him a redshirt.

REEBOUNDER:- (Basketball) A player skilled at rebounding.

REEF:- (Sailing) A part of a sail that is reefed.

REEF BREAK:- (Surfing) Waves that begin to break over an underwater reef.

REEF POINT OR REEFING POINT:- (Sailing) One of a number of short ropes or strips of material usually sewn in a row to a sail by means of which that sail is secured to the mast when reefed (also called stop).

REEOUND:- To gain possession of a rebound.

REEVE:- (Boating) To pass the end of a line through the hole or opening in a fitting (such as a block).

REF:- Short for referee.

REF:- To serve as a referee.

RE-FACE:- (Ice Hockey) To face the puck again after calling a violation in the previous face-off.

REFEREE:- (Badminton) An official whose duties are identical to those of a tennis referee.

REFEREE'S:- A semicircle with a radius of 10 feet marked on the surface of an ice hockey rink or a box lacrosse box directly in front of the penalty timekeeper in which one is permitted while the referee is in discussion with the penalty timekeeper (as when handing out penalties).

REFEREE'S POSITION:- (Wrestling) Starting

position for the opening of the second or third periods and for all restarts not from a neutral position. Wrestlers assume a top man and bottom man position as directed by the referee.

REFEREE'S THROW:- (Team handball) A method or restarting play after an unusual interruption or after both teams commit an action simultaneously in which the referee rolls the ball along the ground or bounces the ball in the air with both teams seeking to gain possession.

REFLEX:- (Athletics) Automatic and involuntary muscle reaction.

REFLEXED BOW:- (Archery) A bow whose limbs spring toward the back when it is unstrung.

REFUSAL:- (Equestrian) The act or an instance of a horse's refusing to make a jumps in show jumping or steeplechase competition.

REGATTA:- A rowing speedboat, or sailing race of series of races. In rowing, a regatta is distinguished by the fact that a number of boats start together and cover the course in adjacent lanes.

REGISTERED PLAYER:- (Tennis) A player permitted by a governing body to keep all prize money won in an open tournament but still be eligible to compete in amateur competition.

REIN OR REINS:- The lines connected to a bit in a horse's mouth by which the horse is controlled.

RELAT OR RELAY RACE:- A race (as in swimming or track and field) between teams that consists usually of 4 stage (legs) with only a single team member competing at a tie and a different team member competting on each legs.

RELEASE:- To move from one's normal position in order to assume another position or to perform a second assignment.

REMATCH:- A second match between the same 2 competitors and especially a boxing match that gives a defeated champion a chance to win back the title.

REMISE:- (Fencing) An immediate continuation of an attack that has been parried. A touch by remise can be allowed only if the riposte misses or is delayed.

RENEWED ATTACK:- (Fencing) Any of the 3 attack of redoublement, remise, and reprise.

REPECHAGE:- A second chance heat in cycling or rowing in which losers of the first round of competition are matched against each other for another chance to qualify for the final heat.

REPETITON TRAINING:- (Swimming) Form of training in which swimmer tries to reproduce pre-set times. eg 16 times 100 metres all under 64 seconds.

REPETITIVE DIVE:- (Scuba Diving) A second dive performed within 12 hours of a previous dive.

REPRISE:- (Fencing) A second attack made after returning momentarily to the on guard position.

RESERVE:- A substitute player.

RESTRAINING CIRCLES:- (Basketball) Three circles of six-foot radius, one located in the center of the court and one located at each of the free throw lines.

RESTRAINING LINE:- Any of the numerous real or imaginary lines on a playing field or court (as in football, rugby, soccer or lacrosse) behind which certain players must remain until the ball is in the play (as in a face-off or free kick).

REST STEP:- (Hiking) a method of conserving energy while maintaining a steady climbing pace pausing momentarily as each leg is advanced but before the weight is shifted to it.

RETIRE:- To put out an opposing batter, batsman, or side in baseball or cricket.

RETREAT:- (Fencing) To move back from an opponent by first stepping back with the rear foot and then bringing the front back to the same distance.

RETURN:- 1. To hit a ball or shuttlecock back to the front wall or back over the net in a court game.
2. (Football) To advance the ball after receving a kickoff or punt or after intercepting a pass.

RETURN TO GUARD:- (Fencing) To return to the on guard position after making a lunge.

REVERSAL:- (Wrestling) A manoeuver in which a wrestler goes from a position of disadvantage to a position of advantage and for which he is awarded 2 points.

REVERSE:- (Football) An offensive play in which a back moving laterally in one direction gives the ball to a teammate moving in the opposite direction.
(Athletics) The follow through after a put or throw.

REVERSE CORNER:- (Squash) A crosscorner shot in squash racquet.

REVERSE CRADLE:- (Wrestling) A cradle hold taken by a wrestler on an opponent who is behind him by looping one arm under the opponent's leg and getting a headlock and then joining hands.

REVERSE CURL:- (Weight training) A curl performed with the palms turned down rather than up.

REVERSE LAY-UP:- (Basketball) A lay up shot made after crossing underneath the basket to the far side.

REVERSED POINT:- The point of a fishhook that is set to the right of the line of the shank when viewed from above with the point up.

REVERSE DUNK:- (Basketball) A dunk shot made by approaching the basket backwards or by driving underneath the basket and dunking the ball back over the head or over the shoulder.

REVERSE ENGLISH:- (Billiards) English which causes a ball to spin in the opposite direction to that in which it is travelling so that when it strikes a cushion or another ball it tends to stop or come back or rebound at much less of an angle than it would if it had no English; draw.

REVERSE STICK:- (Field hockey) The stick turned around and held with the toe pointing towards the player so that it may be swung from left to right to hit a ball with the flat part, which is the only part with which the ball may be legally played.

REVOCERY LEG:- (Athletics) The non-driving leg during runner's stride.

RHUBARB:- (Baseball) A heated dispute on the field during a baseball game.

RHYTHM:- (Athletics) Uniform well-coordinated running action.

RIB:- A metal ridge running the length of a shotgun barrel to assist in sighting.

RIDDEN OUT:- (Equestrian) Winning a race under moderate urging so as to maintain a comfortable lead.

RIDE:- 1. Wrestling: The maintaining of control over an opponent while one has a position of advantage.
2. To maintain control over one's opponent on the mat.

RIDE THE BENCH:- (Of a player in a team game) To spend most of one's time on the bench as a substitute rather than playing as a regular.

RIDE TO HOUNDS:- (Equestrian) To ride a horse following foxhounds; to engage in foxhunting.

RIDELING OR RIDGLING:- (Equestrian) A particularly castrated horse.

RIFLE:- A shoulder weapon that has a stock and a long barrel with spiral grooves on the inside and that is designed to shoot a bullet.

RIFLESCOPE:- (Shooting) A telescopic sight used on a rifle barrel.

RIGGER:- (Rowing) Short for outrigger.

RIGHT-HANDER:- A player who is right-handed and especially one who throws right-handed as distinguished from batting right-handed.

RIGHT OF WAY:- (Fencing) A fundamental rule in foil and sabre that determines which fencer had priority in a phrase.

RIGHTY:- A player who is right-handed.

RIM:- (Basketball) The circular frame of the basket from which the net is suspended. See GOAL. (Golf) The edge of the cup.

RIMFIRE :- (Of a cartridge) Having the primer in a rim surrounding the base.

RING:- (Boxing) The circle of ropes used in the earliest days of bare-knuckle fighting. It was held by the spectators, who in moments of excitement would close in around the fighters. Eventually, to avoid interference, stakes were driven into the ground to form a square in which the contestants could fight but it retained the name of ring, which is still used.

RINGS:- (Gymnastics) A pair of metal or wooden rings 236 millimeters (approximately 9(1/4) inches) in diameter suspended 500 millimeters (191/2 inches) apart and 2500 milliters (aproximately 8 feet) high that are used in gymnastic competition.

RINGSIDER:- (Boxing) Some who watches a boxing match from ringside.

RINGSIDE:- (Boxing) Located at or near the side of a ring. (the ringside officials).

RIPOSTE:- (Fencing) The return action that follows a successful parry.

ROACH:- (Sailing) The outward curve in the leech of a sail.

ROAD:- Being or relating to a game or a series of games played on an opponent's home field, court, or rink. (a 10-day roadtrip) (seventh consecutive road loss).

ROADRUNNER:- (Racquetball) A player who specializes in making defensive shots.

ROADWORK:- A part of an athlete's (as a boxer's) training and conditioning programme which consists of long-distance running usually along public road before normal traffic hours.

ROAN:- A horse with a black, red, gray, or browncoat muted with an admixture of white hairs.

ROB THE CRADLE:- (Bowling) To make only one of the pins of a bady split.

ROCK:- A curling stone.

ROCK CLIMBING:- The aspect of mountain climbing which involves climbing up rock cliffs by means of available footholds as distinguished from climbing on ice or hiking up a trail. Rock climbing normally involves the use of such techniques as bridging, laybacking, and jumming and often such artificial aids as chockstones, pitons and bolts.

ROD:- Short for fishing rod.

RODE:- Short for anchor rode.

ROLL BACK DODGE:- (Lacrosse) A dodge made by stopping in front of the opponent turning away from him as in a pivot dodge, and then as he reacts returning to the original position and continuing around him.

ROLL BAR:- (Auto Racing) A heavy bar of usually tubular steel that is built into a racing car and that extends above the driver's head to protect him in the event his car overturns.

ROLL BLOCK:- (Football) A cut block in football.

ROLLER SKATER:- Someone who roller-skates.

ROLL-IN:- (Field Hockey) A method of putting the ball in play after it has gone out of bounds across a sideline in which a member of the non-offending team rolls the ball back across the line to a teammate.

ROLLING START:- (Auto Racing) A start of a race in which the competitors are moving towards the starting line usually at less than racing speeds as the starting signal is given; flying start.

ROLL-OFF:- (Bowling) A play-off match.

ROLLOUT:- (Football) A play in which the quarterback rolls to his left or right after receiving the snap but before handing off or passing.

ROOKIE:- A first-year player in professional sports.

ROOSTERTAIL:- An arching spray of water thrown up behind a racing hydroplane.

ROPE:- (Boxing) Any of the 3 or 4 strands of rope surrounding a ring. The ropes are between one and 2 inches thick and are covered with a soft material. When 3 ropes are used on a ring, they are placed at heights of 2, 3 and 4 feet from the ring floor (40, 80 and 130 centimeter in international amateur boxing). When 4 ropes are used, they are at heights of 18, 30 42 and 54 inches.

ROSTER:- The members of a team; a list of these member.

ROTATE:- (Of a defensive player or the defensive backs in football) To move in a circular pattern to cover a weakness in the formation or to protect against a particular type of offensive play.

ROTATION:- (Football) A movement by the defensive backs and sometimes by the linebackers in a somewhat circular direction with one or more players moving into an area to protect against a particular offensive play or to fill a gap in the defensive coverage and with other players shifting towards the area vacated so that no area is left totally unprotected. (Volleyball) Shifting of the players clockwise, when gaining the ball from the opponents.

ROUGH:- (Golf) An area of rough ground usually having tall grass that borders the fairway.

ROUND:- (Archery) The term used to indicate shooting a designated number of arrows at a designated distance or distances.

ROUND THE HEAD SHOT:- (Badminton) Hit from high backhand side with overhead forehand, footwork and hitting action.

ROUND THE WICKET:- (Cricket) Indicates that the hand with which the bowler, whether right-arm or left-arm, is off-stump or outside, to the area of mid-wicket.

ROUNDBALL:- (Basketball) The game of basketball.

ROUNDER:- (Boxing) A match lasting a specified number of rounds. (won a dull 10-rounder).

ROUNDHOUSE KICK:- (Karate) A kick started with the leg held out at the side of the body and snapped forward in a relatively horizontal area while pivoting on the other foot.

ROUND ROBIN:- A tournament in which every contestant meets every other contestant in turn with the overall won-lost records determining final standings.

ROUND-THE-HEAD SHOT:- (Badminton) An overhead shot in which contact with the shuttlecock is made above the left shoulder of a right-handed player or above the right shoulder of a left-handed player.

ROUND THE HOUSES:- (Motor Sports) British term for racing on a road course set up on city streets.

ROUT:- To defect decisively.

ROUT:- A one sided contest; decisive defeat.

ROUTE:- (Football) 1. A pass pattern.(Horse racing) 2. A race one mile in length or longer.

ROUTINE:- (Gymnastics) A series of movements and stunts performed as a unit on an apparatus or in floor exercises.

ROVERBACK:- (Football) A defensive player whose duties are a combination of those of a linebacker and a cornerback.

ROVING:- (Archery) Archery game played outdoors in which natural targets (stumps, trees, bushes, ets.) are selected for competition.

ROW :- To propel a boat as a member of a crew by pulling a single oar with both hands.

ROWING:- The sport of racing long narrow shells propelled by oars. As a sport, rowing encompasses both rowing and sculling competition. A shell is a long narrow, extremely lightweight boat designed exclusively for racing.

ROWING TANK:- (Rowing) A large tank of water containing a mock-up of a shell in which an oarsman or sculler can practice his stroke and work on technique.

RUCKSACK:- A large backpack that typically has 2 or more outside pockets and that is designed to be worn without a packframe.

RUDDER:- A flat piece of wood or metal that is attached to the stern of a boat and extends into the water or that is attached to the rear of a keel to offer resistance to the water when it is turned to one side or the other forcing the bow of the boat to turn in the same direction.

RUDDERPOST:- The vertical frame on which a rudder pivots.

RUGGER:- 1. The game of rugby.
2. A rugby player.

RULE OFF:- (Equestrian) To bar an individual from racing or from entering the tracks controlled by a particular racing authority.

RUN A COUP:- (Billiards) To scratch the cue ball into a pocket after missing the object ball in English billiards.

RUN AND GUN:- (Basketball) To employ a fast freewheeling style of play without emphasis on set plays or defense.

RUN-AROUND SHOT:- (Handball) Ball that strikes one side wall, the rear wall, and other side wall.

RUNAWAY:- A one-sided or overwhelming victory.

RUN AWAY AND HIDE:- (Of a competitor in a race of contest) To take such a commanding lead that the opposition is unable to catch up.

RUNBACK:- (Football) A run made to advance the ball after catching a kick or punt or after intercepting a forward pass.

RUN BACK:- (Football) To return the ball after a free kick, punt, or intercepted pass.

RUN FREE:- To sail before the wind; sail on a run.

RUNLESS:- (Baseball) Without having scored a run (held them runless for 7 innings).

RUNNING GAME:- (Football) Offence based on use or running rather than passing plays.

RUNNING HIGH JUMP:- (Athletics) A high jump in which each competitor is permitted to run up to the takeoff point.

RUNNING LANE:- (Bowling) Slow lane.

RUNNING LONG JUMP OR RUNNING BROAD

JUMP:- (Athletics) A long jump in which each competitor is permitted to run up to the takeoff point. The term is used to distinguish the popular event from a less common variation in which competitors jump from a standing position.

RUNNING SQYEEZE:- (Softball) A play where the runner on third base starts for home with the pitch because the knows he batter is going to bunt the ball.

RUNNING TIME:- (Basketball) Not letting the clock stop for fouls or violations. Usually used in a recreational situation.

RUNNING TRACK:- (Athletics) A track used for foot races in track and field competition.

RUNWAY :- (Bowling) Approach.

RUSHER:- A player who rushes.

RUSH LINE:- (Football) The defensive line.

RUSH THE NET:- (Tennis) To charge to the net immediately after making a stroke in order to be close to the net in position to volley the opponent's return.

S

SABRE (SABER):- (Fencing) One of the three competitive weapons. The cutting edge is used more often than the point, and the target area is all parts of the body above the hip level, including the head and arms.

SACRIFICE BUNT:- (Softball) A play where the batter bunts the ball to advance a baserunner and is thrown out at first base or would have been if the ball was played properly.

SACRIFICE FLY:- (Softball) A fly ball that is caught and after which a baserunner crosses home plate to score a run.

SAFETY:- (Basketball) An offensive player who remains farther out than the defense as a shot goes up so that he will have good defensive position following a change of possession.

SAFETY SQUEEZE:- (Softball) A play where the baserunner on third base starts for home after the batter bunts the ball.

SAILING:- 1. The technical skills of managing a ship or boat.
2. The sport of handling a sailing boat.
3. A departure from a port, especially a scheduled passenger vessel.

SALLE D'ARMES:- (Fencing) French term for fencing school or club.

SALT WATER:- (Swimming) Some swimming baths are filled with salt water. This is more buoyant than fresh water but is also denser and there is thus little advantage to be gained from it.

SALUTE:- (Fencing) A universal gesture used before practice or a bout. A simple version is the raising of the weapon to vertical position, bell at face level.

SAMBO:- (Wrestling) Russian form of jacket wrestling similar to judo. Accepted by the FILA as their third official style.

SANBON:- (Judo) A score of three points in judo or karate.

SAND YACHTING:- (Yachting) The sport of racing sand yachts.

SANDWICH GAME:- (Bowling) Same as dutch 200.

SCHLEIFER (Bowling) Thin hit strike, similar to spiller type where pins seem to fall one by one.

SCISSORING:- (Basketball) Occurs when a defensive player "pick-up" his opponent after being temporarily screened from play.

SCISSORS STYLE:- (Athletics) Style involving a scissors-like action of the legs.

SCOOP:- (Field Hockey) Stroke without back swing in which the ball is lifted slightly with the toe of the stick. Can be used as a dodge.

SCORE:- (Cricket) The state of the game, in terms of runs made and wickets lost, e.g. five wickets down for 242. Also, the amount of runs made by an individual in an innings.

SCORE BOARD:- (Cricket) A structure prominently placed outside the boundary but wihtin the ground confines upon which score is displayed prominently enough to be readable by those out in the middle.

SCORE LINE:- The result or sports match.

SCORER:- An official who records the score during a game or contest.

SCORESHEET:- A sheet of paper for recording the scores of a game.

SCRATCH:- (Athletics) To remove an athlete from competition.

SCREEN:- (Football) To shield the ball to prevent an opponent reaching it.
(Basketball) A legal block set up by an offensive team to shake a player loose from his guard.
(Handball) A hinder due to an obstruction of vision by opponent.

SCREW-KICK:- (Swimming) Colloqualism for an irregularity of the breaststroke kick.

SCOOP:- (Field Hockey) Stroke without back swing in which the ball is lifted slightly with the toe of the stick. Can be used as dodge.

SCOTCH FOURSOME:- (Golf) A competitive round in which two partners play the same ball,taking alternate shots.

SENESI:- (Judo) Teacher.

SELL:- To 'sell' yourself means committing yourself to go for the ball when the odds favour the opponent.

SELLING-PLATER:- A horse that runs in selling races.

SERIES:- A number of matches played between two teams.

SERVER:- The player who serves.
(Handball) Person (or persons, in doubles) in the "hand-in" position and eligible to serve.

SERVICE BOX, OR BOX:- (Squash) A delineated area in each half court from within hand-in serves.
(Handball) Area within the service zone bounded by the side wall and a parallel line 18 inches away; denotes where server's partner must stand in doubles when serve is being made.

SERVICE COURT:- (Handball) The area in which the ball must land when returning from the front wall on the serve.

SERVICE LINE:- (Tennis)The end line of the service courts running parallel to the net.

SERVICE ZONE:- (Handball) The area where the serve must stand when serving the ball. Located between the service line and the short line, usually 5 feet wide, and extending across the court.

SERVING:- (Archery) The thread wrapped around the bowstring at the nocking point.

SET:- (Tennis) The first player to win six games with a minimum two game lead has won a set.
(Volleyball) The placement of the ball near the net to facilitate spiking.

SET PLAY:- A rehearsed series of movements planned by a team.

SET POINT:- (Tennis) A situation in which one player will in the set by winning the next point; also the point won.

SET SHOT:- (Basketball) A shot taken without leaving the feet.

SETTER:- (Volleyball) Person assigned to set the ball.

SETTING:- (Badminton) Choosing how many more points to play when certain tie scores are reached.

SETTING AN EDGE:- (Skiing) A technique used to prevent a skier from slipping by angling the edge of the ski into the hillside.

SHADOW BOXING:- (Boxing) Solitary training by a boxer to sharpen up his movements and punches. In the ring by himself he fights an imaginary opponent, concentrating on footwork and speed, varying his actions both for attack and defence.

SHAFT:- (Archery) The long, body part of the arrow.

SHIAI:- (Judo) Contest.

SHIFT:- (Athletics) Moving the vaulting pole from the carry position into the vaulting box.

SHIHAN:- (Judo) Master.

SHINE:- (Cricket) The smooth polished surface of the ball when new is zealously preserved by the faster bowlers especially because it may help the ball to swing.

SHIN SPLINTS:- (Athletics) Sore shin bone muscles.

SHOOT:- (Handball) To attempt kill shots.

SHOOTER:- A person who fires a missile-discharging device .

SHORT CORNER:- (Field Hockey) The play awarded to the attack for a fould by the defense inside the circle or when the defense intentionally hits the ball over the end line. The ball is placed 10 yards from the goal post. Also called penalty corner.

SHORT COURSE:- (Swimming) Any bath length under 50 metres: usually refers to 25-yard or 25-metre courses.

SHORT LINE:- (Squash) A line set out upon the floor, parallel to and 22 feet from the front wall, and extending the full width of the court.
(Handball) A line on the floor parallel to front wall and equidistant fron front and back wall. Serve must carry over this line on its return from the front wall.

SHORT PIN:- (Bowling) A pin, rolling on lane, that fails to hit a standing pin.

SHORT RUN:- (Cricket) If one of the batsman fails to ground his bat over the popping crease while they are running two or more runs, the umpire signals 'one short'

SHOT PUT :- (Athletics) Iron or brass spheres 8, 12 or 16 pounds in weight that are used for competition.

SHORT SERVE:- (Badminton) A serve that scarcely clears the net and lands barely inside the opponents' front service line. This serve is used primarily in doubles.

SHUT- OUT:- (Ice Hockey) Goalkeeper's achievement of not conceding a goal throughout a match or period.

SHUTTLE:- (Athletics) A relay where the legs are run back and forth.

SHUTTLECOCK:- (Badminton) The feathered, plastic, or nylon "bird" which is batted back and forth in badminton.

SIDE-OUT:- (Badminton) When the individual (in singles) or team (in doubles) loses serve and becomes the receiver.

SIDE OUT:- (Volleyball) Side is out when the

serving team fails to win a point or plays the ball illegally.

SIDESPIN:- (Tennis) A ball hit and rotating on a horizontal plane.

SIDE STEP:- (Skiing) A technique used to climb a hill on skis. The skis are parallel to each other as the skier steps up along the length of the ski.

SIGNAL:- (Baseball) Movements of the hands to convey strategy to players.

SINGNALS IN DOUBLES :– (Tennis) Signalling your partner that you are going to poach at the net.

SILVER MEDAL:- A medal of silver awarded to one who comes second in any of several competitions.

SIN BIN:- (Ice Hockey) Colloquial term for the penalty box in which a term of suspension is served.

SINGLES LINE:- (Tennis) The first sideline closer to the center mark and running the entire length of the court.

SINKER:- (Baseball) A fast ball which goes down - released with inward wrist roll.

SITTER:- An easy shot at goal.

SKATER:- One who skates.

SKATING:- The act, art, or sport or glibing on skates.

SKIFF:- (Sailing) A light or sailing boat.

SKIPPER:- To act as captain of.

SLAM:- (Wrestling) A technique illegal in amateur wrestling in which a wrestler lifts his opponent above his head and then slams him to the mat.

SLEEPER :- (Bowling) Hidden or obscured pin.

SLICE:- (Golf) A ball in flight that curves from left to right (for a right-handed person). (Tennis) Motion of the racket head going around the side of the ball and producing a horizontal spin on the ball; also called a slice.

SLIDER:- (Baseball) A modified curve- slid out of the hand, not spun.

SLIDING TACKLE:- (Football) Tackle from the side, along the ground.

SLOW BALL:- (Baseball) A half-speed slow ball or curve.

SLOW POOL:- (Swimming) Bath in which waves build up and inhibit speed.

SLTE:- (Underwater diving) Diver's writing slate, often backed with a decompression table.

SMALL BALL:- A ball that has to hit pins almost perfectly for strikes.

SMASH:- A hard overhand stroke. (Badminton) The hard overhead stroke hit downward with great velocity and angle. It is the principal attacking stroke in badminton.

SNAKE EYES:- (Bowling) Same as bed posts.

SNAP:- (Rugby Football) The action of the centre in passing the ball back to the quarter-back which starts a play from scrimmage.

SNOW PLOW:- (Skiing) A technique used ot slow the skier down while going downhill by spreading the tails and keeping the ski tips close together.

SPAR:- (Boxing) To box in a friendly contest. Sparring partner A person who boxes in a make-believe contest in the gymnasium, when either punches are 'pulled' or large sparring gloves are used to minimise hitting power.

SPARK PLUG:- (Baseball) A player with a fiery temperament - full to pep.

SPEARHEAD:- (Swimming) The arrangement of comperitors in a swimming race so that the faster competitors are in the centre of the course.

SPEEDWAY:- (Racing) The sport of racing motorcyles usu belonging to professional teams on closed cinder or dirt tracks.

SPILLER :- (Bowling) Strike from a thin hit where pins seem to melt away.

SPIKE :- (Volleyball) A ball hit with a strong downward force into the opponent's court.

SPIKER:- (Volleyball) Person assigned to spike the ball.

SPINE:- (Archery) The characteristic rigidity and flexibility of an arrow.

SPIT BALL:- (Baseball) A pitch delivered with spit on the first two fingers (now barred).

SPLASH:- (Bowling) Strike where pins are knocked off almost instantaneously.

SPLASH SPILLER:- (Bowling) A strike made by a thin hit.

SPORT:- Physical activity engaged in for pleasure.

SPORTIVE:- Relating to sports.

SPORTSMANSHIP:- Conduct becoming of a sportsman.

SPOTTER:- (Rugby Football) A coach placed high up the stadium where he has a bird's eye view of the game, and can sometimes see developments not apparent from ground level. He is in telephone contact with the head coach on the bench.

SPREAD:- (Football) A goalkeeper 'spreads' himself to block the view of goal of an attacking player by use of his arms and body.

SPRING:- (Athletics) Bounce or lightness of foot.

SQUARE CUT:- (Cricket) Played to a short ball outside the off-stump. The batsman thrusts his back foot across and is down on the ball, with wrists active, aiming square on the off-side.

SQUEEZING :- (Bowling) Same as pinching the ball.

STADIUM:- A sport ground surrounded by a large usually unroofed building with tiers of seats for spectators.

STAG:- (Gymnastics) A leap or pose with one leg bent and the other held straight back.

STANCE:- (Athletics) Particular starting position of an athlete.

STANDARDS:- (Athletics) Upright objects used to hold cross-bars during jumping or vaulting contests.

STAND ON YOUR EAR:- (Baseball) To be off balance.

STAND OUT:- To steer away from shore.

STAND UP:- (Cricket) Of a wicket keeper to take up a fielding position immediately behind the stumps.
(Wrestling) An escape executed by standing up from a bottom man position.

STARBOARD:- (Sailing) Right-hand side looking forward.

STARBOARD TACK:- (Sailing) When the boat is sailing with its starboard side to windward.

STEAL:- (Bowling) To get more pins than deserved on a hit.

STEEPLECHASE:- (Athletics) A race involving a water jump and hurdles.

STEERSMAN:- One who steers; a helmsman.

STEM:- (Cycling) The device that links the handlebars to the headset assembly.

STEP:- (Skiing) A type of ski bottom design found on waxless skis.

STEP IN THE BUCKET:- (Baseball) Pull away from the plate.

STICK HANDLING:- (Ice Hockey) Retaining possession of the puck while in motion. The equivalent of dribbling in soccer, it is achieved by flicking the puck alternately with each side of the blade. Among the well-known players with a rare ability to control the puck, were Bobby Hull, of the Chicago Black Hawks, and Howie Morenz.

STICK SIDE:- (Field Hockey) The player's right side. So called because the stick meets the ball on that side of the body.

STICKS:- (Field Hockey) Raising the stick above the shoulder at either the beginning or end of a stroke. It is a foul.

STIFF LANE:- (Bowling) Fast lane.

STOCK CAR RACING:- The racing of adeped or especially built cars around small cinder circuits.

STOKER:- (Cycling) The cyclist who supplies the power in the back seat of a tandem.

STOOP:- (Gymnastics) When the gymnast leans forward or stoops as she vaults over the horse.

STOP:- (Squash) Expression used by the referee to stop play.

STRAIGHT-ARM:- (Rugby Football) Equivalent to a rugby hand-off; can be used only by the ball-carrier.

STRAIGHTAWAY:- (Athletics) Straight area of the track from one curve to the next.

STRAIGHT-AWAY HITTER:- (Baseball) A player who hits the ball where it is pitched.

STRADDLE:- (Athletics) A method of high jumping by straddling the bar, face down.

STRIDE:- (Athletics) The distance covered by a leg cycle while running.

STRIDING FOOT:- (Baseball) The stepping foot for throwing or batting.

STRIKE OUT:- (Bowling) Rolling three consecutive strikes in the tenth frame.

STRIKER:- A player in any of several games who strikes; especially a soccer player who main duty is to score goals.

STRIKING CIRCLE:- (Field Hockey) The goal-shooting area; the curved line that encloses it.

STRIP:- (Fencing) The fencing area. It may be of any material and is marked with the boundary and warning lines. In electric foil and epee fencing, a copper strip is used in order to ground out touches made on the floor.

SUCKER PUNCH:- (Boxing) Any blow that should have been avoided: often a chance blow against a confident opponent that comes when least expected. Sensational endings to many contests have been caused by sucker punches.

SUMO:- (Wrestling) Traditional Japanese form of wrestling fought out with tremendous ceremony by huge men weighing in excess of 25 stone.

SUPBORT:- To bid in bridge so as to show suport for.

SUPLAY:- (Wrestling) Illegal takedown whereby the wrestler picks up his opponent around the waist and falls backward in an attampt to put the opponent's shoulders to the mat.

SUTEMIWAZA:- (Judo) Sacrifice throws.

SWEEP:- (Cricket) A stroke played at a ball on or outside the leg-stump with the front leg thrust forward and the bat coming down round it until after impact the bat is parallel to the ground.

SWEEPER:- (Bowling) Same as cutter.

SWIMMING:- The length of the pool shall be 50 metres. Additional 1 cm length shall be provided where removable electronic system for recording time is provided. The width of the pool shall be 21 meters. Along the width, the pool shall be 21 meters. Along the width, the pool shall be divided in eight lanes (by providing ropes running parallel to the long sides) of 2.5 meters width each. A free space of 0.5 meters shall be left on each side in exterior lanes, i.e. lanes 1 and 8.

The height of starting blocks shall vary between 50 cm and 75cm. These block's shall have nominal slope (not exceeding 10 degress) and shall be provided with top material having high friction value, so as to avoid sliping while taking a start.

The water in the pool shall not have temperature below 24 degress centigrade.

100m FREESTYLE (MEN): Sprinters from the United States, Australia and East Germany have done most of the breaking in swimming's blue riband event, the 100m freestyle.

SWING:- (Athletics) Pendulum action of the body or a part of the body.

SWITCH:- (Basketball) To change individual defensive assignments.

(Wrestling) A reversal executed by bottom man by applying leverage near the opponent's shoulder and sitting out to side.

SWITCH HITTE:- (Softball) A batter who bats both right-and left-handed.

SYNCHRONIZED SWIMMING:- (Swimming) A competitive form of 'water ballet', for women only in format, competitions are similar to ice skating.

T

TAB:- Short for finger tab.

TABLE TENNIS:- Table tennis is an indoor game and is played on table top with the help of a racquet and a ball.

The table shall be 9' long 5' wide and 2' 6" high. The table is usually of wood, but the specifications permit the use of any material which will give a bounce of 8 (3/4") to the ball, when it is dropped vertically from a height of 12". The boundary lines of the table shall be 3/4" thick, and the certral line shall be 1/8" thick. These lines shall be of white colour. The lines along the length are called side lines and lines along the width are called end lines.

The weight of the ball shall be between 37 grams and 39 grams and its circumference shall vary between 4(1/2) and 4-3/4".

TACHIZAWA:- (Judo) Throwing techniques.

TACKLE:- (Football)A challenge to win the ball by use of the feet.

(Archery) Archery equipment referred to as a whole.

TACKLE BACK:- (Field hockey) To tackle a player who has himself just gained possession of the ball on a tackle.

TACKLE ELIGIBLE PLAY:- (Football) An offensive play in which one of the tackles becomes eligible to receive a pass by being the outermost player on one side of an unbalanced line.

TACKLER:- A player who makes a tackle.

TACKLING:- The action, manner, or quality of making tackles.

TAIL:- (Skiing) The back or end portion of a ski.
(Cricket) Late-order batsmen and generally not very good ones.

TAKE A DIVE:- (Boxing) To cause an opposing batsman to be out.

TAKE CROQUET:- (Croquet) To croquet a ball.

TAKEDOWN:- (Wrestling) The act or an instance of gaining control over an opponent and forcing him to the mat. A takedown is worth 2 points.

TAKE GAS:- (Of a surfer) To loss control and wipe out.

TAKE GUARD:- (Cricket) To assume a defensive position with the bat in front of the wicket.

TAKE OFF:- To make a takeoff.
(Athletics) Act of leaving ground as in hurdles.

TAKE-OF BOARD:- (Athletics) A rectangular board set into the ground at the end of the long jump and triple jump runways that assists the jumper in his takeoff.

TAKE-OFF FOOT:- (Athletics) The foot in which a take off is made.

TAKE-OFF MARK:- (Athletics) Spot at which athlete leaves the ground.

TAKEOVER:- (Athletics) The exchange on the baton in relay race.

TAKE OVER:- (Football) To gain possession of the ball on a turnover. (took over on downs).

TAKE THE CHARGE:- (Basketball) To allow an offensive player to collide with you in hope of getting a foul called on him.

TAKE THE COUNT:- (Boxing) To fail to rise before a count of 10 is reached and thereby lose by a knockout; to be counted out.

TALLY:- A score or point in a competition.

TANDEM:- (Bowling) Same as double wood.

TANK JOB:- The act or an instance of deliberately losing a contest.

TANK SUIT:- (Swimming) A lightweight tight-fitting swim suit worn in competition as distinguished from one worn for casual bathing (as at a beach).

TAP:- (Badminton) Forehand attacking net-shot, short action with no follow-through.
(Bowling) Pin left standing on an apparently perfect hit, either the 7-8- or the 10-pin.

TAPE:- (Tennis) The band of cloth or plastic running across the top of the net.

TAPE-IN:- (Basketball) A field goal made by tapping a rebound into the basket.
(Golf) A putt made from very close to the cup.

TARGET ARCHERY:- (Archery) Competition in which archers shoot at a standard target at a fixed distance.

TARGET ARROW:- (Archery) An arrow used for target shooting that normally has an equal-diamater shaft, a relatively small fetching, and a target point.

TARGET DIVING:- (Diving) The sport of diving for accuracy from a high platform or tower (as 80 feet high) into a target (as a paper circle or a ring of balloons) on the water.

TARGET FACE:- (Archery) The painted front of target, usually replaceable.

TARGET POINT:- (Archery) An arrow pile that tapers conically to a point and that is used in competitive shooting.

TARTAN:- A trademark used for a synthetic surface used in place of cinder or dirt for running tracks and racetracks.

TARTAN TURF:- A trademark used for a synthetic surface used in place of grass especially on baseball and football fields.

TEAMMATE:- Someone who plays on the same

team as another.

TEAMPURSUIT :- (Cycling) A pursuit race between 2 or more teams.

TEAM TENNIS:- Tennis played between teams with a match consisting of 5 sets: men's singles, women's single's, men's doubles, women's doubles and mixed doubles. Each set is won by the side winning 6 games; a game is won by the side first getting 4 points. The winning team is the one winning most of the games during the match.

TEEING GROUND:- (Golf) The area from which a ball is driven at the beginning of play on a hole; tee.

TELEGRAPH:- To inadvertently reveal one's intention to do something (as to make a shot or pass or throw a punch) usually by some recognizable preliminary pattern of movement.

TELEGRAPHING THE PLAY:- (Tennis) To indicate the direction of one's intended target before actually hitting the ball.

TELEPHONE POLES:- (Bowling) Same as bed posts.

TENDINITIS:- Inflammation of a tendon that occurs most often in the elbow or shoulder (as of quarterback or pitcher) or in the knee (as of a runner or basketball player). Also apelled tendonitis.

TENNIS:- A singles or doubles game played usually outdoors on a rectangular court in which players using rackets hit a pressurized ball back and forth over a low net with the object of making a stroke that will land within the court boudaries but that the opponent cannot return. Players play on opposite sides of a net and are not permitted to 'interfrere with the movements of their opponents.

TENNIS GRIP:- (Tennis) A grip normally used in holding a tennis racket and especially the Eastern grip.

TENNIST:- (Tennis) A tennis player.

TENPINS:- A bowling game in which a large heavy ball with finger holes is rolled at tenpins.

TAXAS LEAGUER:- (Softball) Same as a Blooper.

THIN HIT:- (Bowling) When the ball hits the headpin lightly.

THREE-BASE HIT:- (Baseball) A triple in baseball.

THREE-DAY EVENT:- (Equestrian) Equestrian competition held over 3 consecutive days that includes dressage competition on the first day, cross-country and endurance tiding on the second, and stadium show jumping on the third day.

THREE FOOT LINES:- (Baseball) The lines marking the last half of the distance to first base.

THREE-SECOND RULE:- (Basketball) A rule prohibiting an offensive player from remaining in the free throw land for more than 3 consecutive seconds while his team is in possession of the ball in its frontcourt.

THREE-SECOND VIOLATION:- (Basketball) A violation of the three-second rule.

THREE-TWO-ZONE:- (Basketball) A type of zone defense with three gaurds stationed between the foul line and the division line, two gaurds playing between the foul line and the end line.

THROTTLE:-(Motor Sports) A control that regulates the flow of fuel to an engine.

THROUGH-BALL:- (Football) A pass through the opposing defence, usually up the middle, for a player to run on to in space.

THROUGH THE GREEN:- (Golf) The area of a course in which play is permitted excluding the teeing ground, hazards and the putting green of the hole being played; the fairway and rough.

THROW:- (Badminton) An illegal shot in which

the shuttle is carried or thrown by the racket.

THROWAWAY:- (Swimming) A freestyle turn in which the swimmer pushes himself round by hand, or by holding a rail or scum trough to do it.

THROW-ON:- (Handball) The method of putting the ball in play at the start of the game and after a goal is scored. The throw is made from the center of the court.

THROW-OUT:- (Handball) The means the goalkeeper takes of throwing the ball onto the court after he has obtained possession of the ball in his goal area. Defensive players may place themselves at the goal-area line.

THROW-OFF:- (Handball) The means the goalkeeper takes of throwing the ball onto the court after he has obtained possession of the ball in his goal area.

THROW ROCKS:- (Bowling) To throw a lot of good strike balls.

THROWER:- (Athletics) Some-one who throws something and especially someone who is a participant in a throwing event in track and field.

THROWER-IN:- (Basketball) The player who inbounds the ball.

THROWING EVENT:- (Athletics) Any of the field event in which an object is thrown, hurled, or put for distance including the shot put and the javelin, discus, hammer, and weight throws. Events in which a ball is thrown for distance (as a baseball throw) are also included when they are part of the competition.

THRUST:- (Athletics) Force exerted upon an implement by the athlete.

THWARTSHIPS:- (Sailing) Across the boat.

TIMER:- (Basketball) One in charge of keeping the time of the game.

TIMING:- (Athletics) Coordination between various body movements.

THIN:- (Squash) A strip of resonant material covering the lower part of the front wall between the board and the floor.

TIP:- (Basketball) To bottom the ball with the finger tips to a teammate or toward the basket.
(Skiing) The front end or leading point of a ski.

TOE BOARD:- (Athletics) A restraining board for certain field events, such as the shot put and broad jump.

TOP POSITION:- (Wrestling) Wrestler is above and behind the bottom wrestler, with one arm encircling the waist and another placed on the elbow of the near arm. A position of advantage.

TOPSPIN:- (Tennis) The clockwise rotation of the ball at a 90 degree angle.

TOUCH:- (Tennis) The ability to make delicate soft shots from several positions on the court.

TRACK:- (Skiing) The trail that is left by skis as the skier moves through snow. These may be machine made.

TRAJECTORY:- (Archery) The path of the arrow in flight.

TRAP:- (Basketball) To double-team a ball handler, usually along a sideline, so he cannot dribble free.
(Golf) A hazard, technically known as a bunker.

TRAVERSE:- (Skiing) Movement back and forth across the face of a hill; the technique may be done uphill or downhill.

TRUDGEN:- (Swimming) Early ancestor of the crawl stroke: breaststroke legs action with alternate arm recovery over the water.

TRUE WIND:- (Sailing)The wind which is actually blowing and which is felt only by a